FROST
AT
MIDNIGHT

Caroline Sullivan, Senior Editor

THE NATIONAL LIBRARY OF POETRY

Frost at Midnight

Copyright ©1996 by The National Library of Poetry
as a compilation.

Rights to individual poems reside with the artists themselves.
This collection of poetry contains works submitted to the Publisher by individual authors who confirm that the work is their original creation. Based upon the authors' confirmations and to the Publisher's actual knowledge, these poems were written by the listed poets. The National Library of Poetry does not guarantee or assume responsibility for verifying the authorship of each work.

The views expressed within certain poems contained in this anthology do not necessarily reflect the views of the editors or staff of The National Library of Poetry.

All rights reserved under International and Pan-American copyright conventions. No part of this book may be reproduced, stored in a retrieval system or transmitted in any form, electronic, mechanical, or by other means, without written permission of the publisher. Address all inquiries to Jeffrey Franz, Publisher, One Poetry Plaza, Owings Mills, MD 21117.

Library of Congress
Cataloging in Publication Data

ISBN 1-57553-159-3

Proudly manufactured in the United States of America by
Watermark Press
One Poetry Plaza
Owings Mills, MD 21117

Editor's Note

Whether it is joy or trepidation, the first frost undoubtedly evokes a mix of emotions at the thought of another winter season's approach. One may feel awe at the sight of millions of tiny ice crystals glittering on the grass and sparkling in the morning light; or conversely, one may dread that early morning rasping scrape of ice off the windshield. Winter signals for some a period of hibernation or winter sports, yet for others simply a period to tolerate until spring's arrival once again. Regardless of how one views frost, it does mark the changing of the seasons – a metamorphosis which inspires wonder at the miracles of nature.

Each of the seasons is exalted in the closing lines of Samuel Taylor Coleridge's "Frost at Midnight":

> *Therefore all seasons shall be sweet to thee,*
> *Whether the summer clothe the general earth*
> *With greenness, or the redbreast sit and sing*
> *Betwixt the tufts of snow on the bare branch*
> *Of mossy apple-tree, while the nigh thatch*
> *Smokes in the sun-thaw; whether the eave-drops fall*
> *Heard only in the trances of the blast,*
> *Or if the secret ministry of frost*
> *Shall hang them up in silent icicles,*
> *Quietly shining to the quiet Moon.*

And just as Coleridge draws upon the beauty of various aspects of nature to create a cohesive admiration of the changing seasons, so do you, the poets, create this anthology, a cohesive volume representing modern society through your panoply of thoughts and experiences.

As you peruse *Frost at Midnight,* you will find poems that range from broad-sweeping nature poems that launch you into the poet's surroundings to introspective pieces that plunge you into the abstruse depths of a poet's soul. There are so many exceptional works published here that the already daunting task of narrowing the poems to only 70 prize-winners became even more formidable. And while all the works presented here merit praise, some are deserving of special recognition.

In John Harris's "Picture Postcard Meditations," the reader is surrounded by an imaginative painting skillfully expounded in poetic language:

> *The mist enshrouds the distant dome;*
> *The near hill slopes t'ward palm fringed cone; and here,*
> *Where, in a gentler tone, the river leaves its weight of loam,*
> *Two little men now cease to roam, and travel home.*

What makes this poem particularly worth reading is the internal rhymes and end rhymes artistically draped in flowing language.

Another poem worth consideration for its expertly crafted language and innovative ideas is "Sonnet To A Psychopath" by Norman Ellis. This poem is interesting in that the persona challenges the thinking of a psychopath:

> *The mask you wear belies the barren soul,*
> *Evoking trust, securing aid to ply*
> *The plans and checkered patterns of your role,*
> *and leave aghast the bonded friends to sigh.*

And in addressing the psychopath, the persona attempts to understand him:

> *How soon the gleam that shimmers in your eyes*
> *Betrays the hope to plumb a deeper vein,*
> *The charm and grace and wit in quick surprise*
> *Upstage the heartless player's sad domain.*

In the closing couplet, the persona comes no closer to understanding, but accepts the fact that he will never fully appreciate why this person has no desire to become a part of society: "How strange to know and not know indeed / A mortal blind to life's primeval need." It is interesting to note that only in the thirteenth line – "How strange to know and not know indeed" – does the poet stray from the iambic pentameter customarily representative of the sonnet. In this way, the text reflects the persona's uncertainty at comprehending the psychopath's character.

Unlike the above poem where the persona is addressing another character, Bryan VanDyke's "Forsaken Baker" is an introspective piece in which the persona dissects an aspect of his own personality, in this case, his guilt. He begins the poem by describing the regenerative nature of guilt: "I'm making the guilt again / preparing it like some unholy grandmother's recipe." This experience is torturous, as the guilt is made "in a wooden churn with holes and rust / and a splintering rod that pokes my hands with slivers."

VanDyke acknowledges that in order for one to feel guilt, one must first possess some sort of moral code by which he lives that creates a sense of "responsibility"; and then he must do something wrong, immoral, "illicit":

> *"Pour the oozy soup of responsibility*
> *that makes everything stick together*
> *add a dash of illicit pleasures for flavoring."*
> . . . .
> *"Pour the white-hot mass into a cauldron*
> *for the final ingredient."*

This final ingredient is the persona's soul.

> *The heat melds it all into a giant needy bubble*
> *begging and ready at last*
> *to accept my soul*
> *for a coating of candy-apple hell.*

VanDyke cleverly plays with words in that this candy-apple coating on the soul is not only the soul's "guilt" but the soul's "gilt," and like gilding, the coating is a "yellowing liquid foam."

Throughout the work, it almost appears that the persona receives masochistic pleasure from making and immersing himself in the guilt when he speaks of "illicit pleasures," the stench's "tendril of desire," or "candy-apple hell." The guilt is tinged with enjoyment.

Another well-crafted introspective work, and the one which the panel of judges awarded our Grand Prize, is Francesca Aragon Azevedo's "My Nearness." This soul-delving piece takes the reader into the persona's painstaking journey of self-discovery, but as the title implies, the persona gets "near" but never quite arrives.

In the first stanza, footprints are introduced as a metaphor for the persona's past selves – the parts of her that once were but are no longer. It is as if these pasts are insignificant, and the sun's presence which dries the footprints – referred to here as "tentacles" – is a menacing agent that further disintegrates the preceding selves.

> *My footprints wear no skin*
> *wear nothing weigh nothing*
> *are visible on granule lid of earth,*
> *spread out are dried*
> *by the nearness of the sun's tentacles.*

The second stanza describes the persona as turning back to see what she was, and in doing so prevents herself from moving forward toward her goal:

> *I turn back to find one, then another;*
> *the innumerable traces of myself*
> *that have no relative shadows*
> *Each print halts my nearness*

In the third stanza, the persona again refers to the sun as the destroyer of her previous lives, as the pieces "crumble / from the tentacles' touch" and are "driven into hungry sunlight." The brightness of the sun affords the persona a flash of clarity that suggests to her perhaps her previous selves do not have much significance. What she has done in the past is only significant if it prevents her from moving toward the future.

In the closing stanzas of the work, the persona is surrounded by night: "Naked bits of life dash in brilliance / through swatches of evening." The same bits of life which are destroyed by the sun during the illumination of day now "dash in brilliance" in the comfort of the night. During the day, "each print halts my nearness," while in the evening, "the night crowds my closeness." Her retrospection is halted during the day, yet at night the bits of life crowd her closeness; i.e., in the comfort of evening, the bits bring her closer to her self-discovery and ultimately toward the end of her search:

> *I listen to the swish of wings*
> *that with sleep will close the night*

There are many fine poems published here that, like the prize-winning works, are unique, fresh, skillfully crafted verse overflowing with feelings and insight. I truly wish I had the space to provide individual critiques for each of them. I congratulate all of you featured here and hope you enjoy reading *Frost at Midnight*.

Frost at Midnight is a culmination of the efforts of many individuals. Editors, assistant editors, customer service representatives, typesetters, graphic artists, layout artists, mail room and shipping personnel, and office administrators have all brought their respective talents to bear on this project. I am grateful for the contributions of these fine people.

Caroline Sullivan, Senior Editor

Cover Art: Tracy Hetzel

Grand Prize

Francesca Aragon Azevedo / Napa, CA

Second Prize

Jennifer Allen / Portland, ME
Robert Birch / Media, PA
Roger G. Cortes / Ferndale, NY
John Crosby / Portland, OR
Carole Dombroski / Seattle, WA

Norman Ellis / Cadiz, KY
John S. Harris / Anaheim Hills, CA
Reshmi Hebbar / Orlando, FL
Hillary G. Moon / Lake Orion, MI
Bryan VanDyke / Evanston, IL

Third Prize

Emily Ackman / Cambridge, MA
Keith V. Andi / Castleton, NY
Dustin Arellano / Casper, WY
David R. Bowman / Steamboat Springs, CO
James C. Bruggeman / Belle Fourche, SD
Michael R. Burns / Atlanta, GA
Kathryn C. Chancey / Pasadena, TX
Roberta A. Contreras / Santee, CA
Mario C. Davis / Evanston, IL
Julia L. Dickson / Sacramento, CA
Scott Dilworth / Novi, MI
William S. Dvorak / Rialto, CA
Colleen Ewing / Lafayette, IN
Melissah J. Falavolito / Pittsburgh, PA
Caroline Gabrielli / Manhasset, NY
Michael Gibson / Brea, CA
Simon Gordon / Chamblee, GA
James G. Gostlin / Coldwater, MI
Jane M. Haner / Morrhead, IA
Kayembe Henderson / Wheaton, IL
Sabrina Henry / La Porte, TX
Aja Horwitz / Teaneck, NJ
Melissa Hudler / Beaumont, TX
George Klenk / Fontana, CA
Wilfrid R. Koponen / Albuquerque, NM
E. Kevin Kreps / Whitmore Lake, MI
Cody N. Larson / Ashland, OR
Marilyn Lerch / Washington, DC
Kenneth Lieberman / Albany, NY
Anthony J. Loftsgaarden / Prior Lake, MN

Josh Lund / Ventura, CA
Anthony Mastroianni / Barrington, IL
Julie McHale / Brookfield, WI
Julia McIlverey / Ridgewood, NJ
Anthony Meixner / Arcata, CA
John A. Melson / Simpsonville, SC
Carol Monticue / Monessen, PA
Pat Morrison / Ashland, OR
Wendy M. Mossman / Flushing, MI
Seamus O'Toole / Elmira, NY
Vickie Y. Ogunlade / Atlanta, GA
Mark F. Owens / Dallas, GA
Cile Pace / Denver, CO
Kirsten Parker / Chicago, IL
Patrick G. Pettis / Scotia, NY
Greg Przwara / Madison, WI
Bonnie Rogers / Vallejo, CA
Jeane Ross / Carmichael, CA
Dena R. Seibert / Terre Haute, IN
Diana Seymour / Washington, DC
C. V. Compton Shaw / Dallas, TX
Richard G. Smith / Ogden, UT
Nathan E. Steury / Marathon, FL
Percy Totheroh / Phoenix, AZ
Tory True / Pocatello, ID
Olive West / Long Beach, CA
Randal M. Weston / Connersville, IN
Dave Willis / Clive, IA
Karen S. Wolven / Phoenix, AZ

Grand Prize Winner

My Nearness

*My footprints wear no skin
wear nothing weigh nothing
are visible on granule lid of earth,
spread out are dried
by the nearness of the sun's tentacles*

*I turn back to find one, then another;
the innumerable traces of myself
that have no relative shadows
Each print halts my nearness*

*I watch them crumble
from the tentacles' touch
Pieces are driven into hungry sunlight,
acquainting in the air*

*Naked bits of life dash in brilliance
through swatches of evening
I look through night windows
The night crowds my closeness*

*I listen to the swish of wings
that with sleep will close the night*

Francesca Aragon Azevedo

Second Day Of Spring

I hear the blue bird singing up in the weeping willow
Where his house swings in a gentle breeze,
That my Kenny made for me
Right this second a bluebird came,
And flew at the window as I sat in amazement
Right in front of me —
Sitting quiet, gathering my thought's
Thinking on what to write next
It seems a moth was inside the window pane
And this is what the bluebird sought in vane,
Right in front of me
He looked real sweet struggling for his footing on the sash
You see I've ran out of seed, I hate to say,
The birds I've given my banana bread
There's nearly a foot of snow lying on the ground,
And more is now falling, It would be fine with me
If this wasn't the second day of spring!
What would you say if I told you
Now he's back perched on the pergola
Looking for that moth I killed
Susan R. Layne

Absolute Love

Absolute love is the deepest form of human adoration.
It is more than the meeting of hearts and the meshing of flesh.
It is the bonding of Souls that makes the circle of love
complete.

The coming together of two souls that are meant to be; forms a
bond of eternal oneness.
It is a love that springs from the beginning of time and will go
till the end of eternity.

Many who Live and Love, never know the truest Love.
However, there are a special few who are lucky enough to live to
Love, as we so intensely do.

Absolute Love is the combining of heart, body, and soul.
It is a feeling of freshness; like everyday is a new day with
anticipation of things to come.
It is a feeling of agelessness; like something that has been
around and a comfort forever.

Absolute Love is You and Me,
For we exemplify the emblem of Love Everlasting.
Emma M. Cook

The Lottery

A knot of anxiety me as I sit and hear the tragedies
  of another life, another time.

But the time is now.

As children die, their last breath stolen too soon,
Cries and helpless screams echo from those not prepared to say
  goodbye.

Across the sea, hate of incompassionate brothers
  flood the street with innocent blood.

Bodies, like rag dolls, tossed and forgotten,
  Their souls searching for beauty.

And here I sit, surrounded by plenty,
  and wonder how I was so fortunate
  to have opportunity and freedom
  in the lottery of birth.
Diane Joyce Mehagian

Winter In Peace Mongolian Plateau In My Recollection

When winter comes, the plateau
puts on a white mantle;
sheep in a flock wearing one garment over another
all fall into a doze;
grasses vying with each other for green
under the seize of snow,
throb with spring.
A concerto of wind whispering in the sky
sings the lullaby to its best.
Mongolia, the ancient plateau, where Genghis Khan
once galloped his horse like a gust of wind
and at sunset blood of soldiers assuaged the land's thirst.
Peace reigns once more in winter;
the grassland is covered all over by snow, gently and quietly,
as long as the white guardian in heaven takes charge.
Seiko Y. Tu

Dreams Of Peace

A child lays wondering at night,
Do grown-ups know the difference
Between wrong and right?
In a world of bombs, terrorists, and war,
She often wonders what the future has in store.
In her mind she finds a playground of love and peace,
But still she wonders will the war ever cease?
When she mourns the death of a close friend,
Her precious heart the mother tries to mend.
But the war has caused her great pain,
And still many a day the soldiers slain.
Feelings of people, they try to hide,
Make them think more and more of suicide.
But still she wonders at night,
Do grown-ups know the difference
Between wrong and right?
Ellie M. Wright

Never Thought

My nights were filled with lonely endless searching,
but now I have to praise;
a princess came into my life
and brought sunshine to my days.
She filled my life with riches and treasure
beyond my wildest dreams.
The flowers of spring bloom no beauties that compare to her
of which I've ever seen.
To search for another would be in vain
for there is no need.
Like two oaks standing tall that have grown and matured
from a solitary seed.
My love for her shall never die;
just grow stronger every day.
I never thought love could be this way.
Jay Smith

Dear Mom

Dear mom
Have I ever told you how much you mean to me.
If not you will found out how much I love you in this
poem.
You are the wind beneath my wings.
I am that one lost sheep you set out to look for.
You have given me the power, strength, and energy to live
my life.
But all I need is you in my life for me to live my life as
a strong black woman.
Thank you for your care and respect.
I love you mom.
Nyasha Williams

Thoughts Of Reflection

Let me do right in this world of wrong
God give me courage and help me be strong
In this world of hate, where babes carry guns
Where corruption reigns and poison runs
Where justice is gone and evil flows free
Where Powers of Darkness now close upon me
Help me to turn wrong into right,
War into peace, blindness to sight.

It is the less taken path that I want to follow
I shall walk forward always, today and tomorrow
Striving to do right in this world of wrong,
To stay on the path that seems so long,
To be blind to the temptations that evil brings,
And to hear the sweet song that an angel sings.
God grant me the courage you love to give
And because of you, I will love to live.
Lisa M. Buettner

Truth's Voice

Echoing deep within the heart of the endless wind, a voice calls to me from nothingness, and then flows
back into obscurity again. Beneath the mid-day sun, I sit, wholly absorbed, as one. Drifting clouds beckon to me, with promises to make me eternally free.
A full and healthy treeline dances in the distance. Millions of supple branches and leaves interpret
blissfully, the sacred answer to all life's encompassing mystery. The moment is real. The truth will heal.
With my ear to fertile earth, I can hear the sound of eternal rebirth.
The look of purity shines in the instinctual eyes of brilliant crimson cardinals, and subdued gray doves, gliding effortlessly by.
The night creeps in upon the threshold of a fading day.
You and I sit entranced by the suns fading pastel rays.
The words you whisper softly in my ear, I have heard before, echoing silently, and manifesting infinitely
beyond times' door.
Christopher Marana Schofill

Oversized Are Despised

On a program called 20/20,
I heard something that wasn't funny.
Certain children are despised,
Because they happen to be oversized.
Among their peers they just don't rate,
Simply because they're overweight.
Some five year olds were interviewed.
I thought their answers were quite rude.
They said they'd rather be stupid than fat.
I wonder what you think about that?
They said they'd prefer a missing arm.
This should give us cause for alarm.
Must we all be put in a blender?
Must we all be tall and slender?
It seems only attractive people receive recognition.
I'm glad God's love is without condition.
Renee Y. Doyen

Thanks To You

I felt like a little bird who was so scared.
You nurtured and you cared.

I felt like a little bird perched on the nest.
You encourage me to take the test.

Now. I felt like a little bird soaring to the blue.

Thanks to you.
K. Borba

Conductor

The stick glides effortlessly through the air
And etches its shapes with the utmost care.
Directed by a disembodied hand with relative ease
Instruments follow while it dots i's and crosses t's.
The baton languidly floats through space thick with suspense
The audience shifts uncomfortably as the situation begins to tense.
Trombones bellow and tubas release a low growl
While a single flute goes on the prowl.
The conductor tightly grips his wand
While clarinets and drums begin to bond.
Urgency builds as the stick waves in frenzied motions.
Similar to the unrestrained fury exhibited by the ocean.
The conductor begins to thrust and parry
Like the sword fighter cornering its quarry.
The jabs punctuated by the timpani
Mimic the fencer fighting within me.
Laura Naomi Leeb

Born Out Of Time

I was born late.
When I came in the world my parents knew I would never be great.
My father ran away.
My mother struggled to make it every day.
She worked her fingers to the bone
I ended up all alone
They moved me from place to place
Each time I put on a different face.
I finally grew up.
I never had any luck.
I made a bad choice
because I wanted people to hear my voice
I had too many scars
I ended up behind bars.
My life was pure hell
My soul people tried to sell
Nothing was ever right
I had to fight for my life.
Born out of time
Will I ever get what's mine?
Sophia Signal

Rest Easy

Rest easy, my sweet one, my dear
With my arms holding you tight
There is nothing for you to fear
For I will be with you all this night

But should your dreams be troubled
Wake and tell me what they meant to you
For while your joy shared is doubled,
Your sorrows shared are cut in two.

Rest easy, my love, my dear one
Sleep long and deep by my side
Don't fear the fruition of what has begun
Nor the washing out of evening's tide.

Let the morning bring what it may
For we cannot halt Time's Sun above
And though we must part our separate ways
Know that you go always bearing my love.
Robin Siddique

Reality

As he sat on the boat
that did not quite float,
he thought of having wings with golden glare
to coast up on Spring's whirling air.
He thought of fins that flashed
to swim in streams and splash,
and of the tails that move so free that
would not fail when in a tree.
He thought of the world as one big pearl
and of pollution and its dissolutions.
He knows what is going on
and .... that it is very wrong.
He is a child of sense,
the savior of ourselves.
Fritz Finley

It Helps — Always

I love you, you are sweet
That is not always a statement complete.
In living and doing what is best
Sometimes it is hard to get it off your chest.
We usually make it for we all try
To see matters so they can comply.
But life is hard, but look on right side
We perform better as we look on bright side.
Think positive - I've been told
Helps us succeed in reaching our goal.
When we get there make it shine
There is always, always plenty of time.
Somebody always need help,
Assist, encourage to do by self.
There comes a day we are glad we shared,
Because of sadness and tears we've been spared.
Elizabeth Stroburg

Life's Illusions

Sometimes life brings us moments of perfection;
Experiences so wonderful that it brings us hope.
Life challenges our illusions.

Nights are filled with grace and days with wonder;
We realize how great our dreams are,
How fulfilling illusions can be.

Hope, dreams and illusions are all part of life;
They bring us joy in times of despair,
Remembrances that quicken our pulse.

Times may be tough and life may be hard;
Life has a way of bringing us hope.
The hope that we have always dreamed of.
Ryan S. Griffin

Why?

Why is it that with our supreme brains
And our masterful intelligence
We bring upon us this gloomy dark rain?
The rain of death from human negligence.

Why is it that we humans are so proud
Of our wonderful technology?
It spreads like a blanket of death, like a cloud.
Grossly strange is this human psychology.

Our technology may kill us and,
Only when we are gone, can nature recover.
She can't be fooled by a mortal hand.
Yes, our end is near, it is almost over.

Soon, our busy world will become still.
I wonder, is this suicide God's will?
Sam Grammer

Kindness

Kindness is universal,
It is something that never dies;
Yet we often fail to use it,
Never knowing quite the reason why.

We plead that we're too busy,
Too wrapped up in daily life.
We can't spare the time to show concern,
So instead we choose to live in strife.

Each in our own sterile bubble,
That love can never touch.
So we can then save ourselves,
By saying we really didn't care that much.

How sad it truly must be,
To live in a world all alone.
Never knowing what we missed,
If only we had known.

Don't let this be your epitaph,
"He died alone and blue,
If only he had thought to share,
The beauty that he knew."
Minerva De La Pena

Cats

If Jelical cats are black and white,
And Vampire cats are glowing with fright,
Then what are Alley cats?
    If many cats just love to drink milk,
And other cats' fur are smooth as silk,
Then what about Alleys cats?
    Then all of the cats go meow, meow, meow,
And eat some cat food with fish or sow,
But is junk with Alley cats?
    Alley cats are all colors each way,
And their fur is messy and eat junk each day,
Then what about Persian cats?
    Persian cats are silky and smooth,
They're white and gray and eat fancy cat food,
Then what about other cats?
    I know about cats you can really say,
I can go on and on each day,
But that is because I'm a cat!
    Meow,
    Meow!
Jennifer Zuckerman

Untitled

Life moves by me in a glance,
In a bug tapping on the window,
and I sit, silently.
The sororities with their big hair and short skirts,
Like overgrown cheerleaders,
prance by me in utter contempt.
And the fraternity men brawl and drink
and slap the asses of the before mentioned,
and I sit, silently.
Like a dumb car on the Ferris wheel.
Never swaying or rocking, just still
with the spinning of the whole thing.
And their contentedness with bars and one night stands
and vanity, holds me like a paperweight,
I sit upon these lines.
They puff on their dainty cigarettes,
and I take a drag of mine
and slip back into the shadow
of nonexistence.
Dawn Scherbarth

My Last Breath

Someday my journey will come to an end.
As I breathe my last breath, my soul will ascend.

Up into heaven to a gate opened wide,
the saints will all greet me, as I enter inside.

I'll be guided by mansions prepared by God's hand,
down streets of gold, in that glorious land.

Then they'll lead me down to give thanks by the sea,
I'll see all of my loved ones waiting for me.

"Welcome Home" they'll be shouting, oh, wait till you see,
all the wonders in heaven, oh, how happy are we.

There's no more fear, no more suffering, no more pain, no more tears,
And never again will you be aged by the years.

There's no sin here in heaven, it's been all left behind,
endless love from the master is all you will find.

Then I'll turn from my loved ones to the steps of his throne,
all the names of his angels engraved in each stone.

The choirs of heaven will be singing for me,
as I climb ever nearer, my saviour to see.

Then I'll fall on my knees, in his presence I'll be,
for on my knees before Jesus, is reward enough for me.
  Will Davis

Wild Ponies

Wild ponies, soft as silk
With white skin as a glass of milk
They dance around like a ballerina
Light as a feather, quiet as a rat
Hurray for wild ponies, and that's that.

They dance through the night.
Glowing like a bright light.
And they look so right
It's a beautiful sight.

Listen to the beat of the playing drums
It sounds like wild ponies getting on down
All the wild ponies run wild
Side by side, they gallop astride
So hurray for wild ponies, and that's that!
  Sarah Khan

A Wedding Prayer

As we cherish these moments today
always keep them dear to our hearts.
For it is your unconditional love for all
that we shall want to live by and never part.

Throughout the days to come
the good times we will surely treasure.
What we do naturally now out of love for each other
in time God, remind us, these deeds should not be measured.

When troubled times come and confuse our minds
please God, bless us through our prayer.
For our commitment was bonded with you
because of the love we share.

Some of our friends and family will be far from us
in our hearts we know they care and wish us well.
God, let us all be good examples
for someday there will be children to tell.

Our life together will be an adventure
we must forgive, sacrifice, listen, and understand.
God, you do this for us and so much more
and it is in your name that we pray, amen.
  Sandy Ruhter

A Mother's Love

One more year has come and gone.
The sad fact is that life goes on.
But I will always have to say,
That part of me died too that day.

Sometimes I try but I can't recall,
Your voice or your laugh—nothing at all.
It's times like this that I just close my eyes,
And you're there, and I hear you as I fantasize.

I try to remember the times that we had.
They were special, whether good times or bad.
Moments taken for granted when you were here.
Moments cherished now, and held very dear.

I can hear you now, I can smell your sweet breath.
My love for you grows even as you sleep in death.
It's only in my dreams that you move and you play,
But I can still hear you clearly as you say:
"Mama, I love you, so dry your tears."
"Mama, come hug me, I want you near."
"Hang on a while and we'll be together."
"Just a little bit more and we'll have forever...."
  Jean Erardi

Run Away

I wish day after day
that I could just simply run away
but I know, in this place I must stay.
The voice in my head tells me I do wrong,
I try to ignore them but I'm not that strong.
People, they yell at me to,
can't they see all the things I go through.
Time does not exist, yet still it goes by.
I am, but I try not to act shy.
This anger of mine I tried to keep inside,
but at least I really really tried.
My good half 1 day I'll find
till that day I hope many people don't mind
that I get a little out of control
but one day they'll all behold
the real me——runaway.
  Jillian Kaufmann

Thy Will

I can not foresee the future, nor at times understand the past
but I must believe, I must have faith
Thy will be done.

I work, I struggle, then pray
sometimes the answer is yes, sometimes the answer is no
Thy will be done.

Fate nor destiny, rather my plan with His
but in the end, neck and knee must bow
Thy will be done.

Through tears of sadness or joy
be still my heart and know, his love leads the way
Thy will be done.
  Wendy L. Callahan

No Escape

In my mind, all I can see
are waves from the ocean devouring me.
Pulling, twisting, entangling my soul,
my once beating heart now an empty hole.
Further and further I'm being tugged down,
nowhere to run, only to drown.
No escaping the thoughts that are consuming my life,
no retreating from that which has caused so much strife.
My only hope now is that I can be strong,
to find happiness again so that I can go on.
  Lori L. Schick

Mary And Martha

Mary who loves the Master, cares above all.
Willing to listen to His voice, she hears His call.
Knowing time with Him is limited
She gives of herself freely.

Martha, too, loves Him as did Mary
She, wishes to listen and to tarry
But household cares she did carry.
And for this she was rebuked.

In this life, we care for mundane things.
But need to have the better part.
Take up His cause within our heart.
Let worldly cares depart.

Choose ye this day - Martha or Mary.
    Ruth N. Scofield

The Reality Of A Lie

Unleash the power of imagination-let the soul speak;
Let it sing;
Let it dance;
Let it live.

Poetry-the language of the soul.
It pours out of my heart, like a waterfall of blood;
  Flowing through my veins, in my immortal body of youth.

The power of my soul rages out,
In the beauty of a poetic dream.

Reality-what is the point?
  Has it ever been made?

Live free-become what you want.
Go insane-become one with your mind.
Die-become one with your soul.

I live a dream that I dreamt in a lie.
I am the one-who will never die.

Living the lie of reality.
Kill the poetic beauty of life.
    Debby Hathaway

Lime Lake

Lime Lake is a place,
Not so far away.
Where the vision you see,
You think is nothing but a fantasy.
Where morning dew caresses the grass..
And another fisherman catches a bass.
When the sun rises, and you see its reflection
On the water,
You wonder to yourself, "How could anything
Be better?"

When the moon and stars come out to play,
You wonder, "How long will they
Stay?"
While the crickets are singing, and the trees
Are swaying,
You consciously remember that it is time to
Go away,
And all you need to know is that,
Lime Lake is a place,
Not so far away.
    Kimberly M. Kowalski

"If I Were A Cat"

I woke up this morning before my clock rang
I woke up this morning before the birds sang
I heard all my friends running up and down the street
I heard all the girls double dutching with their feet
Shouting aloud in a holler as one
I could not wait to go out and join in the fun
But I have this cold that's kept me inside
I caught this cold when I took my bike out to ride
That cold and brisk day I did not wear my hat
That cold and brisk day I wish were a cat
I'd run outside without a stitch of cloth or shoe
I'd run so fast until I felt brand new
I may even chase my next door neighbor's bird
I may even find this wish to be absurd
But I know if I were a cat, I'd have 9 lives to go
And I'd ride my bike in the rain and in the snow
And if I truly had a chance to be a cat you see
I'd be the smartest kind and help all humanity.
    John Bellon Jr.

Grandma

I have so much I want to say,
But don't know where to start.
My pen cannot express today
The sadness in my heart.

The joy, the pain, the memories,
And now so many tears
As I look back, dear Grandma,
On those most special years.

You taught me things not found in books
About kindness, love, and sharing.
And through it all, I have learned
Your greatest gift was caring.

I have a void here in my heart
That God and time will heal.
And I have precious memories
That even death can't steal.

I know that you're not really gone.
We'll be together again.
I love you, dear Grandma,
My most special, precious friend.
    Barbara S. Landuyt

Lonely Girl

Lonely girl sitting on the street,
please tell me why do you weep.
Is it because you got kicked out of your home?
Is it because you ran away all alone?
Lonely girl sitting on the street,
please tell me why do you cross your feet.
Is it because you're cold? Is it because your shoes are old?
Lonely girl sitting on the street,
can I please come and have a seat.
Do you wish me to go away? Do you wish me to hold you and stay?
Lonely girl there's a tear in your eye,
please tell me why do you cry.
Is it because you haven't heard a caring voiced in a while?
Is it because there's no more acid in your vile?
Lonely girl your soul is burnt,
there is a way you don't have to hurt.
Close your eyes and set your head on your knees,
there is a part of you no one see's.
Lonely girl is sleeping now, no more hurting, no more frown.
    Breanna Sall

The Divine Cycle

Once, I saw a wild rose dying in the last glimmerings of light
from the setting sun...
She was proud, and beautiful still, yet, much the same as
the Day's time was now spent and it had
abdicated to the Night,
So too had her time passed, and she was forced to
at last let loose her hold
on the Beauty of Life.
I remarked to the trees around me, as I was alone in the wood,
on the sadness of seeing such an
enchanting beauty end.
Why must she pass? I would let her stay forever, if I could.
And they answered, in the whisper of
the early autumn wind...
Beauty such as hers forever gives.
You see? She has just now laid the seed...
She lives.
   Bill Harmon III

"No Solace In The Dark"

Listen ye to this wisdom that I do impart
   O' ye victims of a broken heart
Do not traverse on this trail on which I have embarked
   For you see there is no Solace awaiting ye in the dark
Study thee well the wisdom of this remark
   Before ye cast yourself in this lightless part
Seek thee the light and its wondrous healing art
   I implore thee do not follow this voyager of the broken heart
For within its woeful shadows agony is most abundantly fraught
   Be thee careful or gloom will enter and devour your wounded heart
For you like I will find no Solace awaiting you alone in the dark
   James L. Tashoty

Love Is...

Love looks like two people kissing.

Love tastes like a fresh baked cookie
right out of the oven.

Love smells like a sweet red rose freshly picked.

Love feels like a soft hand on your
shoulder when you're feeling down.

Love is the color of bright red, the color of a heart.

Love is the best feeling you could ever feel.
   John Billings

Here We Stand

Here we stand on the battlefield of a war we have not won.
We have lost the lives of millions, and saved not even one.
Today we stand here hopeless nothing to live for.
We have lost the lives of family, fighting this great war.
For all the lives we lost, and not one saved, is it worth it
   anymore?
Today we stand here wishing it was tomorrow, because we
   might just find a cure, for this war we now call AIDS.
How can so few letters take so many lives?
One day we must stand on this battlefield, and win this great
   war, not for glory, not for strength, but for the dying to
   be no more.
   Amy Pascalide

Visions

To have seen what is there, but is not,
To see what's not there, but is
To have seen what was lost, but has been found,
To have seen what was found but is now lost.

In your heart you can see what
isn't there, and find what you have lost.
You can see love through they eyes, but
Only can love be felt through the heart.
Only when they come together shall you
Know that you have found
Your one and only true Love.
A love that shall last forever.
We will overcome any problem together.

Together hand in hand
   Ralph Ferrucci

Passages

He sat on the stoop with the bugs he'd collected
A man with a strange new dilemma
From behind him, dressed in Oshkosh, he thought he heard -
"Where'd you get those Grandpa?"

He turned and found not the five year old boy
With whom he'd shared backyard issues at random
But a great grandson held decidedly close
In the arms of a confident young man

Unable to speak he was drawn toward the two
Past the bench they'd built together
Dreams and hopes and plans, all at once
Eclipsed by the force of nature...

...When from around the corner a painting appeared
Then a hand and a little red sweater
The smile that showed next drenched his heart in relief
From the daydream that beset him that September

Into open arms a young boy ran and there proceeded a joyful dance
And tears to which the boy was oblivious
Ran three in a row down his back, as he said,
"I went to school today Gramps".
   Jo Anne McCartney

Children Of The Flowers

Many flowers have I in my garden today
Each year the grow in many ways
Each blossoms in a different way
Each have their good days

With the flowers I must stay
Each good seed I will watch them lay
My knowledge to them I must feed
I am their source and they follow my seed

More and more each day they grow
Not knowing enough which way they'll go
Each year a different bloom
Each will carry their own little tune.

Which way will their lives go
Will they learn from what I know
Will it be that they are strong
Have I led their lives wrong

My children are my garden of flowers
I pray their lives are not sour
To teach them right I plead
And to help them plant their own seed.
   Sue Vanover

Light And Dark

The day-light is falling, the night is hurrying
in. Just how life ends and death begins. This
is a poem about fear and terror as it grips you
in the dark hours of the night! People go on
about the day as if night will never come. The
light of the day seems to protect. The darkness
of the night seems to bring death. The cold hands
of fear wrap around my neck. As night comes
my last breathe escapes me. Please let the
day come, before someone else drifts away.
Let my feelings flow thru the pen. Let the
grief, sadness, pain, death, and the horror
of the beasts leave my eyes and mind forever.
Amanda Thorpe

Myself

I'm alone again, all by myself.
There's words around me, yet I don't hear.
There's music in my mind, but I hear no rhythm.

I feel myself floating away-never wanting to
Come back to reality. A trip I take alone,
Fearful, yet somewhat content, I think of yesterday.

I count the days as they go by.
They seem short, but they are so long.

When I enter my world everything's just a dream-
No problems, no fears and promises to myself that
May someday be fulfilled.

A world of peace, a world of love. Wishing everyone
Could enter— Becoming a family within a perfect
Paradise.
Michelle D. Lavallee

Time

Where did the years go?
Does anyone know?
Can anyone say, of the nights and days,
where they have flown?
We just know they're gone.

We once were so young...
Were we ever that young
with a future to spend? It's hard to say when
time spun away.
Now, it's today!!!

Frost stings the air,
and touches our hair.
Our children are grown..what's more, they're gone
to nests of their own.
Time marches on!!!!

Life still has joys..
but the girls and boys
of that long ago time, are hard to find.
Where did the years go?
Does anyone know???
Juanita Tabor Utley

Untitled

Our vows said until death do us part.
I never guessed my promised would shadow
us so soon.
Ten years we shout!
Ten years we weep.
A lifetime isn't enough.
Ten years is a moment!
God, let there be an after life
Melissa Slapak

Stop The Violence

Let's stop the stealing shooting and killing,
Pull together and stop this illing.
Another young life taken away,
You've heard the saying crime does not pay.
I see a young kid on the street, it makes me wonder.
How long will it be before he's six feet under?
Out on the street selling dope.
Trying to find a way to cope.
Another young kid that's been misled,
He'll end up in jail or somewhere dead.
Instead of sitting back praying it never happens to you,
Why don't you help? Do whatever you can do.
Let's all pull together and do our part,
Talking to your own kid is a very good start.
The violence must stop here today,
Do your part. What more can I say?
Leval Jones

My Victorian Doll

Soft unblinking hazel eyes
so thoughtful above the embrace
of cold taut pearls on a delicate throat
and a dainty web of lace
veiling romantic shoulders
and a bodice ever still
never to rise and fall with breath
of her passions or her will.
Such falsely blushing cheeks!....
like rosebuds in upswept hair
are kissed by dark and wispy tendrils,
not a lover who might dare
to press the bounds of etiquette
stealing many a secret caress
from a smooth white hand poised at her side
in the folds of a peach-colored dress.
The tender little figure
stands as an endearing reminder of
past times when simple gentle charm
was the embodiment of love.
Marie M. Priest

"Best Friend"

I was issued my M-16 rifle today
Don't sell, throw, or give it away
It's your ticket in, and your ticket out
Take care of this sweetie she's now your spouse

Keep her clean, and oiled well
She'll make sure you don't go to hell
Everywhere you go take her along
Before you sleep make sure she's not gone

Talk nicely to this beauty, be extra sweet
This way if you use her your sure she'll repeat
Don't over do her on rock, and roll
You'll wear her out or melt her hole

This lady's with you through thick and thin
She'll rest on your shoulder, rest on your chin
If you're lucky enough to make it back
Your lovely lady will go back on the rack

Don't you worry she'll be just fine
There's a good looking G.I. waiting in line
You might think bad, think she's a whore
She's really not guy's, just a lady of war
"Pleiku" Vietnam 70-71

In The Deep Of Space

A cyborg spider
clicks across the vast
plastinium wasteland
of the wall:
a windup arachnid
seeking automaton flies
to wind up in its
spun-steel web:
cries from its scuttling or zooming
titanium prey unheeded:
for the spider intends to play
before its mechanical mandibles
munch another set of gossamer glassine wings;
or bloated nomex thorax.
Artificial arachnids:
essential to the exploitation
of the grand expanse of space:
no human did foresee
the spontaneous generation of an
endless pestiferous race
of plastinium parasites.
    Gary M. Ryan

Barnum's Parade

"It takes the ragged boys to fight" said George
to a girl, proud of his soldiers' courage
in defeating the redcoats near Bridgeport
where the slain were put to rest with much import.
For peaceful decades undisturbed they lay
when P.T. Barnum's circus came to stay,
and wrangled a deal for the land to steal,
for gold and a promise the bodies he'll
move across town to a more holy ground.
The graves were undug, rotten coffins found
and stacked without markers on wagon beds.
At night, down Main Street a parade of dread
as the coffins burst open and out fell
the ragged boy's unknown bones thrown pell-mell
onto the blue, gas lighted cobblestones.
    John J. Koller

I Had A Dream

  The star was you.
  The grass was green and the sky was blue.
  You were sitting under the bows
of an old oak tree.
  With a tear in your eye you called out to me.
  I ran threw a field of yellow flowers
then over a riverbed of cold grey stones.
  I sat down beside you and it felt like coming home.
  We laughed and we talked for what seemed like most of the day.
  Then you reached out your hand,
touched my cheek, and asked me to stay.
  This brought me so much joy down to the very marrow of my bones.
  I then picked you up over my shoulder and carried you back over
the cold grey stones.
  When we reached the field of flowers we laid down in the grass
and made love for what must have been hours.
  And while nestled in each others arms we fell asleep under a
canopy of twinkle, twinkle little stars.
  When I awoke reality set in.
  I was alone once again, and I had just had a dream.
    William J. Behrens

The Disillusionment Of Love Sonnet

The world doth cry of that desire, his fire.
The flames that reign throughout his brain, insane!
This things began without a drop of pain,
Instead it grew from lowest joy, desire.
His tongue was numb, ears numb, she was his sire.
He could not see; He could not thin, insane!
He could but taste the sweet perfume, disdain!
His love was more than this world entire.

How could he be so blind, not to see deceit.
At last the shade was cast, now he could see.
Perfume not sweet, disdain now brings conceit.
Her coquetry did not trick me, nor he.
The song of joy is sung, no flames, no heat.
The fool now laughs, the clown now cries, funny.
    Omar Rashid

Isabeau's Lament

"How can this be," asked the moon of the morrow.
"Art thou of flesh or of spirit?"
In truth? Of sorrow.
"Listen," he said, "'tis the wolf I hear cry!"
(I knew then that soon would come my time to fly.)
"Please don't fade," I cried, "the night is still young!"
"But I must," he replied, "for here comes the sun..."

Doth then he fade? Yes! The moon 'tis almost away
when devoured by fire before birth of the day.
His red 'tis the blood of my passion and pain,
knows my death which will come if the black wolf be slain...

W'In the chasm of half-lives in which we exist,
'tis ponderous; I gaze toward the hills framed in mist.
Aquila's Lucifer drove a stake through my heart
cursing us to be together while eternally apart-

Bursting outside! The wind whips cold
where only the shadows attempt to be bold-
Enraptured desolation stings my ears from afar
beyond the hills and the woods, beyond port cutlas bar-
the howl of the wolf...is the cry of Navarre.
    Ariana Schrader

The Maiden

Walking through the fields of fire aglow with sweet delight
Your balmy breath twists phantom trails which swiftly blaze alight.
The trees bow down to touch your hair like serpents in the breeze
All filled with rampant, mad desire; this jewel cannot be seized.

And though these wanton harpies dare to clutch the dreamer's web,
The monstrous creatures' razor claws retract as oceans ebb.
The passion pure ignites the sky: A fusillade of pain
Which scatters all these broken beasts who thought they might detain
This gentle fawn of perfect cast all fashioned by the sun
In hues of vibrant halcyon her spirit has been spun.

And here I stand across from her, in aspect like a star,
Which fills me with resplendent hope: So near and yet so far.
I shield my eyes in bitter fear that soon I will be blind,
But then I come to realize I've left my sight behind.
I draw her close against my heart and hunger for the heat
Which sinks beneath my lizard skin and makes me feel complete.

Her eyes become a world of light and I, a pebble, drawn
So swiftly down the maelstrom which, beneath me, madly yawns.
I draw a breath or two in hopes the ocean's not too deep
But then I know this is my tomb and seekers should not weep.
    Craig A. Knight

Explanations Of Malice

There is a scale that weighs malice and questions its
strength.

There is a rainstorm that soaks the grains of sand
in a desert and is sucked dry of its sustenance.

There is a hand that shakes another while its counterpart
wipes the blood off a knife.

There are perverted snickers as noxious as the green bile
from a freshly slaughtered calf.

Rainstorms, hands, snickers - for these, malice is a playground,
where the children disregard the swings.

There is a smile of delight on the face of
malice as the aroma of decaying flesh is sensed.

There are revelations, of which malice is the mother, and
the child is obedient.

There are explanations of malice that prolong its existence, but:

There is a scale that weighs malice and questions its
strength - and malice is conquerable.

Martha Kehagias

Dust In The Wind

Something is wrong but I don't know what,
It's like knowing I'm bleeding but not finding a cut.

I'm lost in sadness and feelings of despair,
This causes me vulnerability so open and bare.

I want to be rescued and taken away,
I don't like the feeling of being astray.

If only it were as easy as 1, 2, 3,
And I could start over just being ME.

But who am I, and where am I going?
Is there anyone out there who's "so-knowing"?

Maybe there are no answers to be found in the end.
And the theory of Recovery is just dust in the wind.

In my heart I can't accept this as true,
But my feeling of Serenity is long over due.

Koressa Gregory

Flowers Or Loves

A flower is like love,
it needs special things to survive.
It requires care and rain and
without these, it does not grow.
Care is the food that nurtures the flower,
without care, the weeds grow high
which chokes the life from the flower.
Rain allows for further growth,
with little rain, the flower dries up.
Whereas too much rain, causes it
to drown and die.
Sometimes, it is hard to give a right
amount of care and rain to flowers.
That is why in life, we go through many
Flowers - or loves.

Robert Otto Davis

I Remember

I Remember laughing with you
I Remember the day you left me
I Remember visiting you
I Remember going to your wedding
I Remember being alone
I Remember skiing with you on an icy, sun shining day
   And I will always remember you telling me you love Me

Kelly Winter

In Search For God

I climbed the highest mountain in search of God
I stared in the heavens and he was not there.
I climbed a mountain and looked in a eagle nest.
I walked in the meadow, and I just stared.
I dove in the ocean, and he was not there.
I stared in the waters and looked behind a reef.
And start to disbelief.
I stared in the mist of dawn, he was no where around.
I walked for hours, and stop near a pond,
and looked in the water, and behold I seen the face of God.

Nicholas Garcia

Just Pray

Before I lay down at night I put my knees on
the floor then pray, I thank the Lord Jesus for anointing
me with the Holy Spirit, then ask him to prepare my
coming day. When the Lord wakes me up in the
morning, I don't start brushing my teeth or combing
the hair on my head. I put my knees on the floor then
pray as soon as I get out of bed. People may ask me,
why do you live in such a way? With a smile on
my face and with the Lord's grace I say, "Put
the lord first," now you won't need to fear the
grave. Instead you will have gained life that
comes with an abundance of love. You, your brothers
Your sister will rejoice proclaiming the Christ,
Jesus the Lord who is above. On that coming
day when the Lord's trumpet sounds I'll be
lifted up to heaven, on earth I will not be
found. So to all my Brothers and Sisters I
would like to say I hope the message of
this Poem, Puts you on your knees each
Night and Day. Just Pray.

Stanley L. Turner

Why?

As I look into the clear night sky,
I can only wonder why?
Why are we here?
It's not just to party and drink beer.
I decided that life isn't supposed to go waste.
So without haste
I stood there—and I said a prayer.

As I began to pray
everything around me began to sing,
and I heard Him say
the answer is not far away.
It is in your heart
and if you let me in, it will be a great start.

As I let God in
and he washed away all my sin,
I no longer wondered why we are here.
I have no more fear.
He is with me,
and to Him—faithful—I will always be.

Kevin Ketchum

Untitled

I found direction from my feet and kicked
leaves; no longer with tearful screaming, but
vomit in a plastic bag and on one
hand pretending the wall is you, still here
in my bed - a message flashing again
on the machine, from another; I won't
play the 'Fairytale' lasting three minutes
and two seconds only, supposing all
starts and ends when meant to, always stagnant
direction from my mind - gone unnoticed.

Amy Kalil

Life's Misgiving

It's all so new and quite unique
But, yet, I know not why,
I have the will and want to speak
As time starts passing by.

I hear the song, I learn it's tune
With hopes to reach up high,
A wise man said "don't reach too soon"
Or time will pass you by.

With outstretched hands I climb the peak
And visions all so nigh,
Alas my hands are growing weak
As time keeps passing by.

Can I now be so distraught
To think I'm but a lie,
For in my haste I never thought
That time could pass me by.

Now tired and low, and painfully spent
I tremble with a sigh,
I see now what the wise man meant
As time just passed me by.
   Paul Cuculic

To Johnine Francesca Waters-Brown "With Love"

From the sparkle in your eyes,
exuded are the hopes and dreams of a chosen child—
whose price is far above rubies, whose virtues
are all the same, whose beauty is far reaching,
beyond the scope of human intellect.

The dreaminess of your eyes, mellow
skin, reveal the depth and purity
of your character. Clothed with
dignity and strength...you speak
with wisdom and faithful instruction.

For many men can tell tales of
beautiful women, but it is I who can
speak truthfully of a noble woman,
whose inspiring beauty, reverence for God,
love and inner peace are far above the
price of anything in life.
   Allen J. Brown

The Chain

When you are a grown-up person
And read these lines that I write,
I want you to believe what I'm saying
And feel a twinge of delight.

   How your Grandmother went to the doctor
   And heard with her very own ears
   Your strong heart beating in cadence
   Which suddenly moved her to tears.

Now I know what is "Grand" about Grandma.
It's knowing that when I am gone
There's a part of me still on earth, living
And I will live on, ever on.

   When your mother was born, I was happy.
   I was one with Our Mother Eve.
   And my Mother was very excited.
   She said why, but now I believe.

We are all waiting here, anxious to meet you.
The celebration will be very great.
May you come to us already knowing
How much you are loved — don't be late!
   Merilyn E. Alexander

A Question Of When

The stage is complete and finally set-
old loves in the past without a regret.
Preparation for new beginnings are made,
the dues for wrong choices you've already paid.

The heart has been tested and made it through
tears are all dried, finally less blue.
Protected emotions are free once again,
they're vibrant, eager, it's time to begin.

You're actually ready - time to move on...
the scars are all healed, the darkness all gone.
With eyes open wide - you look straight ahead.
Proud and secure by the life that you've led.

Time waits for none - not even for you,
be willing, be open, accept something new.
True love is not instant, it may take awhile,
where will you find it? A new face, an old smile.

Eyes that speak words, a kiss on the cheek,
the real things in life are all that you seek.
You're anxious to find it - get past where you've been.
All that's left now ~ is a Question of When?
   Carolyn J. Hechler

The Picker

From within a red haze I move mechanically,
   a mighty blazing teardrop slips languid across heaven
      like a bleeding eggshell
         cracking, creaking in the hollow of my back pushed curvidly
            into the dome of blue, mixed into clouds like they were painted
         first.
A crimson tide waves to me, beckoning me onward
   to its lush ripe rotting crop
      on all sides, the dirt grips my feet and squishes
         between and my straddle one trail of green
            reaching far, the path of life and later death.
I have been here before and before and before
   I shuffle forward, bending to the sun as the plants
      beneath me breath in cool gasps of time and wind upon you
         leaves rustling out the throbbing harmonic song
            of the picker treading beneath a pillow of smothering air.
   Dena R. Seibert

History's Youth

The old man I see before me,
Like years of history flash before my eyes,
The many wrinkles and lines on his face.
Foretell the major events that he has lived
To see and remember.
Look into his eyes,
They speak a thousand words,
There underlies the prevailing truth.
First young and fragile like the newborn babe,
Then free and spirited as the wind itself.
As time has aged the youth through history,
It has made him a little bolder
And a little wiser.
His youth through time has set him to depart,
And become history...
   Stacey Lemay

Inspiration

Inspiration, like a light rain,
falls softly on anyone standing outside
vulnerable to it,
but only the person who stands
there long enough will get his imagination
whet by it,
and only the person who opens
his mind to it
will feel the trickle of ideas
flowing across his forehead.
Maybe it's true that a genius
doesn't know enough to
get out of the rain,
but if he did,
he wouldn't be struck by an
inspiration.
Alicia M. Clark

My Soul

Don't deny my soul of you
Can't you see my love is true
Your eyes are blind you cannot see
Who to love, her or me

My mind is clear and soul is pure
So you love her more.... Are you sure
Well if you do then I will go on
But if you don't then I have won

I've won your heart and I'll cherish your soul
You've made me free, you've made me whole
I'll never return to yesterday
I'll never hide or run away

I'll never leave your love behind
You'll never know your soul is mine
I'll never run and hide my fears
I will not restrain those endless tears....
Amy Cerella

"One's Life"

One's life is like the sunset
Rosy at the close of day
One's worries are once more combated
And silently tucked away.

One's life is like the dewdrops
They sparkle in God's morning light
Their gleam disappears in the toil of the day
And comes forth in the cool of the night.

One's life is like an aged tree
With numerous rings running round
But what would we take for one of those rings
Nothing - they're ours to keep when found.

One's life is like a soaring bird
Whose wings are clipped and it falls
When the God-given power is taken
It is ready to heed God's call.

One's life here on earth is a glorious thing
Full from morn 'til the close of day
But the reward which comes from our work on earth
Is the Home at the end of the way.
Starling Pauline Neff

For Joe

Bring some firewood my love I do say -

Understand, comprehend, relate -
   then if you must, go away.

It's not whether dark or light,
   former thieving or a hated lily white.

The heart and soul are all that matter.

The spoken and felt differences merely
   cause a clatter.

What exists within your heart without me -
   emptiness or relief?

Be honest please tell me. We'll either
   begin again or adjust to the grief.
Alison Garnica

The Hunt

The blood hounds howl,
That blood-curdling howl,
And the hunter raises the barrel of his rifle
And fires.
The deer bounds gracefully,
Covering ten feet in a single leap,
And, stumbling slightly,
Disappears into the thorny thicket.
The hunter curses,
Swears,
Turns and stamps away,
with the dogs behind.
While in the thicket,
The deer lies motionless,
Its breath stilled,
Eyes open, yet glazed and unseeing,
Fiery crimson
Covering
Its
Breast.
Briana Karp

"I Am"

I am just a precious girl who loves ice - skating.
I wonder if I will ever be an Olympic Skater.
I hear the music as I skate.
I see the people practice hard for competitions.
I want to try to be first all the time.
I am just a precious girl who loves ice - skating.
I pretend to be an Olympic Skater when I practice.
I feel the cool breeze pass my face.
I touch the ice with my shiny blades.
I worry if I don't win first place.
I am just a precious girl who loves ice - skating.
I understand if I won second or third, but not first.
I say to myself try harder and practice if I don't win first.
I always try my best each time.
I hope to be an Olympic Skater.
I am just a precious girl who loves ice - skating.
Roshni Rathi

Kindness Counts

All over the world kindness counts,
   so don't have your doubts.
You can be kind,
   if you think with your mind.
It doesn't matter what race,
   even though we all have a different face.
Remember, we are all the same on the inside,
   and that should not be denied.
Heather Oister

Am I Even There?

No one knows me, sees me
Am I even there?
The hands that try to touch
Are reaching but just not enough
I push away so you can't see
What is really inside of me
The tears are here, so far below
Search and you will find
The scars I have came very slow
not only in my heart, but in my mind
No one knows me, sees me
Am I even there?
Love is not true, only a shadow
Step from the sun, the light will be done
Darkness surrounds, I'm the only one
Heart beating, one sound at a time
Listen carefully you will hear
Silence, now I am there
No one knows me, sees me
Am I even there

Susan Mendence

Loneliness

It's like a jail cell with one sole occupant,
Stuck with her own company and thoughts.
Knowing no one will happen by,
No light will shine for her.
No love will make itself known to her,
No warmth from another presence will pervade her silence.
She is alone with only herself to be with.
She will wait and wish for someone to come,
Dawn after a lifetime of night,
And take her solitary vigil away.
Only to know, deep down inside,
That she will wait and wish for the rest of her life.
Loneliness.

Tanisha Campbell

Alone With Nature

There is a place, in this land of ours,
Where you can be yourself, beneath the stars.
Of all the world, it's a place to be,
alone with nature, now that's for me.

It may be the mountains, that reach so high,
or it may be the eagle, that lives in the sky.
Wonders of the world, they're there to see,
alone with nature, now that's for me.

You may have your city, and smoke filled streets,
buildings an machines, and man-made feats,
It will bother you nought, to bend your knee,
alone with nature, now that's for me.

Second to heaven, an the peace it can bring,
to body and soul, it's a beautiful thing.
God's great world and he charges no fee,
alone with nature, now that's for me.

Jim L. Hibner

Mice

Mice are so small and lovable you see
Everybody hates them except me
I do not see why
They are so cute and cuddly

They have big funny ears in the shape of a "C"
And a chubby little body as fat as a tree
They have big curly tails as long as can be
They have long curly whiskers that curve like a "Z"

I don't understand why they are so hated
To me a perfect "10" they are rated

Deanna Nicole Gardner

Change

There is a time of change,
A time for holding back or letting go.
It's as natural as the autumn passing,
making room for the winter and snow.

Our change came calmly, silently,
and caught me unaware.
That the snow is gently falling now,
Where,
Only yesterday the falling golden leaves
of autumn,
were all that was lying there.

Minarose R. Owens

For One Lonely Moment

For one lonely moment
I saw the world through tortured eyes.
I saw the destiny of mankind.

For one lonely moment,
I spoke through sorrowful lips.
I preached of things to come.

And yet in that lonely moment,
I allowed Faith to seize my heart.
I saw the birth of Hope
And lived with Peace and Harmony.
I saw Goodness and Charity with the hearts of man.
I tasted Piety and smelled Utopia.
I saw all we dream of but never achieve.

Yes, for one lonely moment, I walked from Beginning to End.
Alpha and Omega of Life itself.

Sheley Thompson

180/90

Retrospect is not an anecdote for what ails you.
It is a reminder that maturity doesn't mean you have to be your age
or act "old."
Dispense and embrace advice (laughter)!
When you find what you need-suddenly
it dawns on you that life and how you play it
is more important than the destination.
Journey-miraculously. Journey heartily yet peacefully.
Wasted so much time wearing my martyr badge.
See it floating with my dreams.
Let me fly with the smiling angels and
leave the kleenexed-ones alone.
Surprise-this is easier than diuretics,
aggravation, holding on too tightly, anti-inflammatory
anything, biofeedback, mantras and
    Reactions versus actions.
180/90 is something extra-unnecessary!

Madlyn Steinhart

Healer

I plead with you to stay.
You smile a sad smile and reply nay.
This causes my heart to shatter.
And the shards to scatter.
For now I shun the light of the golden orb.
I no longer wish my soul to absorb,
The days unhealthy light.
For now I treat it as if it were a blight.
Upon heavens golden door.
Now I spend my time researching ancient lore.
For I have withdrawn from life's grand scheme.
I now associate with the moons pale beam.
But you could commence my healing.
If only you could show me a little feeling.

James Nilolis Miller

Lost Love!

A love I found a love then lost,
I think and wonder was it worth
 the cost?

To have you once then to lose
 you so fast,
Like a forgotten dream lost in the
 past.

Don't ever forget what we once had,
How could something so good suddenly
 turn so bad?

Our love was great once wild and free,
I was made for you and you for me.

Our love like a storm left us with a roar,
Making us wonder would there ever be
 more?
Bridget Farfel

Emergence

The fading of light
 against a blackened sheet
The coming of night
 against a hard-spent day
Scaly, slivers of branches
Slide past a sensual horizon
 Silky form arising from my soil
Scarred tissue
Triumphant
 Emergence of yet another forbidden dawn.
Malini Nangia

Untitled

My mind has the rhythm of a glass eye
It sees only darkness when the mood blankets my brain
Intent on remaining in a veiled logic
of seeing only inward
Inward is not the solution
Inward is the problem.
The glass has the image of being ever-present
The eye holds steady on its own truth
A truth none perceive other than the beholder
Determined to remain
Unchanged
by a speck of light
a slice of tomorrow
a knowingness of beyond
And when I write...
I know.
Adrienne Meltzer

Sonnet 10

A ghost of you appears within my room,
And sits upon my bed and looks at me;
And from the ghost I smell your sweet perfume,
As it begins to safely talk to me.

Its deep set eyes gaze sadly into mine,
It whispers, "Please forgive me but I had
To leave you, sweetest love, for it was time;
But please don't cry and please do not be sad."

Those placid words, once spoken, dry my tears
A ghostly hand is placed upon my own;
The spirit says, "Be brave, and have no fear
And know, my love, you'll never be alone."

All life will end, 'tis but a common thing;
Still, endless joy a loving spirit brings.
Sarah Carlough

Time

Time is the measurement
Of distance between events.
It is the wings on which
The mind flies to happenings
Not yet in its consciousness.
It is the unexplored regions,
Waiting for the first footstep.
It is the realm of thought
Yearning for the first syllable.
It is the Almighty
Molding together, shaping
The myriad pieces into a definable whole.
It is the future, present, past.
It is the Lord,
The Author of Time,
In His wondrous power and might.
It is eternity,
Where it exists no more.
Helen T. Thomas

Grandfather

Right now my dear grandfather
You must be feeling blue
And since you shared a poem with me
I must share one with you.

To let you know how much I care
How much you mean to me
You are the greatest man I know
My hero you'll always be.

Through the years we may not have been as close
As a grandfather and granddaughter should
But I wanted you to know how I feel and to tell you all I could

At this point in your life, you must be very strong.
You have to know any pain you feel, will not last very long
Every night I get down on my knees and for you I say a prayer
I hope you realize how much I love you and that I'll always be there

So please be strong and brave and true
You'll pull through - I know you can
Just know I love you my dear grandfather
You are one heck of a man!
Tera Ann Barnes

It's Not Hard To Remember...

It's not hard to remember,
 some of your favorite hard rock songs.
It's not hard to remember,
 even some of your favorite foods.
It's not hard to remember,
 the simple color of your hair.
It's not hard to remember,
 the warm, sweet shape of your thin, oval face.
It's not hard to remember,
 some of our small, unimportant, yet open
 conversations.
It's not hard to remember,
 the comforting warmth of your heart.
It's not hard to remember,
 the Love we had (and still have) for each other.
It's not hard to remember,
 to remember you every day.
Katie Scott

The Element Called Water

You step into the flowing stream—the blood
Of Adam—once. And it is tinged with you,
By what you are, by what you choose to add
To mankind's river. Always new, the flood
Extends to you its water, though no clue
Will tell how old it is; or mad
With tears; tomorrow's rain; the sweat of lad
Who picnicked with our Lord; or all who drew
Sweet water from a desert well. The rain,
The mist, is drawn to cloud, and from the blue
Springs up another life when you are mud.
Through past millenniums, and then again
Through all millennia to come, the vein
Is opened once for you — a stream of tears — or Good.

Alfhild Wallen

Dreams And Schemes

Dreams and schemes, so it seems, dissolve
To reality, some to plurality.

Frustrations abound all around, when dreams
Dissipate and float away.

If we're short, we'd wish for tall,
If poor, need I say more.

When we're rich, believe or not, we'd
Wish at times to be of
Ordinary lot.

Try to accept your inherited spot,
A "Higher Power" is calling
The shots.

However never, never, cease, to "Dream"
And attain your "Very Best", for
After all is said and done,
This "Life on Earth"
Is but a test.

Barbara Ann Beaven Buhl

Moral Injustice

This world is a hard place to live in at the time of conflict and
　mayhem
We can not trust our own people
So why do we believe what our side says?
To be betrayed by our own people, the country hurts
Will they be punished or just slapped on the wrist?
Life is precious and sometimes we take it for granted
The innocent are scarred and there is nothing we can do about it now
The land cries for its dead and injured
They are absorbed into the land where their killers were born
Our fore fathers are crying at the sight of this hate
We will all but destroy ourselves and not have to worry about another
　country doing the job for us
We wept but that does not help
We mourn but that does not help
Justice is all we ask for
Will it prevail or just be washed aside by the system?

Sharon Franklin

Twilight

The day sets into night as gracefully as a gull flies over the sea in
　search of new worlds,
The moon is lord of the sky and the stars are his followers,
Across the ocean you see a star falling as dew from a petal,
My mind is set free as I concentrate on the wonders of the Creator.

I dream of what lies beyond the ocean and my eyes grow weary,
As if a song has been sung and there is a stillness upon the earth,
I forget all the sorrows of the land and meditate on the beauty of
　the sea.

Robyn Ayn Hendrickson

Grandma's Love

Our Mama wasn't around much when we were very small.
Aunts and Uncles took us in, but Grandma was best of all.
We know she really loved us, she'd let us snuggle so close at night.
Grandma's love to this very day is the reason we turned out right
I remember once we were hungry, as Mama left our bags by the door
Grandma dug in her closet, found money and we went to the store.
Yall got to have some milk she said, and some cereal too.
She was holding a two dollar bill in her hand and a silver dollar too.
Although we didn't know it that was money was very old,
But she said she couldn't take it with her when she's dead and cold.
She'll be 95 this year, she gets around the best she can,
Every time I think of love, I think of Grandma's hands.
I think of things she's told me that's helped me in this life.
Do your part pay your way, make some man a good wife.
I wish I could make them special, her last few years on earth.
For if love was measured in riches, Fort Knox wouldn't hold
　her worth!

Nancy Kay Keaton

A Shattered Mind

Tear stained windows crash to the floor
I've been given love but I beg for more
And now pieces of sanity fly everywhere
I look for someone to cling to but no one's there

I scream out in terror for my life
As I feel the stinging crack of you shoving the knife
You slash through my emotions and through my name
I never knew I could cause such shame

The pain causes me to go blind
When I let you sneak up on me from behind
Now my frustrations lie all spilled out
In a puddle around me-never talked it out

And those eyes you loved will blink no more
You left them staring wide as I fell to the floor
Cradle my body drenched with sticky blood
Feel my heart breaking as you knew it would

Beg for forgiveness; you'll still go to hell
At least ten years in a prison cell
Because you can't just silently commit a crime
Without leaving behind a shattered mind

Tracy Jackowiak

His House

When dusk starts to settle and all is so still
I sit by my window and gaze from its sill
I think of the past and the troubles I've known
And I thank dear God for the kindness He's shown

For it always seems that when things look the worst
When I'm tired and weary and think I've been cursed
From out of the darkness comes a ray of light
A gleam of hope, a voice in the night

And I think to myself, things aren't quite so bad
I really should be happy, rather than sad
For God is with me, I'm not alone
This world is His house, I'm in His home

My thoughts then turn to the setting sun
To the fields and meadows where small brooks run
It's truly beautiful, this sunset of ours
Bringing its cool nights and bright shining stars

And I can't help thinking, how wonderful it is
To be able to live in this house of His

C. B. Merrill

Follow Me

Follow me as my mind fades to black.
Walk within my footsteps as the earth
crumbles beneath my feet.
Listen to the words that I alone am able to hear.
Taste my fear as it rises in my throat.
Breathe my breath as it is lost to the darkness.
Think my thoughts and let them poison your soul.

Follow me as my mind fades to black.
Hold my hand as it encircles your heart.
Suffer my pain as I have yours.
Look closely at the specter
that is my world.

It is not what you see.
Jennifer Heinze

A Mother's Legacy

Filled with her spirit we are near her in time.
Yet she is alone with heights.

Blessed with her features we have grown to hear her call.
In astonishment we've watched her flight.

Now we too soar, but watch to glimpse our mother, to replicate her.
The air crosses our wings, we need her no longer.

We see her and love her.
Marcus Bloom

These Children

Stop what you're doing, and look around
Children are dying... parents can't be found

Alone in the gutters, on the streets at night
No one to care for them... to chase away their fright

Tears on their cheeks, Hearts full of sadness
Dirt on their faces... minds full of madness

"Why Am I Here? What Did I Do Wrong!
They think to themselves.... as they try to be strong

Their hopeful eyes - steer up to the moon
They pray to God, "May I have shelter soon"

Shivering in the cold, snow falls from the sky
Their cold little hearts, may soon alone die.

"Please someone help us!" They say in their minds
"I'm right here waiting..... for you to find."

So stop what you're doing, and look around
These children are dying! They must soon be found.
Maria Brestan

Soul Truth

And sometimes you want to go back,
to the beauty and intelligence,
you once knew before.
A time not in essence with this lifetime,
because the culture's currents do not flow in the same era,
as the customs are of a different plane.
And perhaps you may come to realize
that the driving path of this persuasion,
although foreign,
is heart-close and home-within.
And the phenomenon is fascinatingly deep,
bringing into view
the combination of physical and metaphysical
as the only two truths
that ultimately hearten you.
Sandra P. Holton

The Time Has Come

The time has come to look around me
To see the person I have become to be
Let's be honest and say what you're feeling
Then the process within will begin the healing
Look at me and you think things has been so easy
Things that you want, things that you've accomplished-
never have been what they seem
Have faith in your feelings, never stray from what you mean
In time of dark and time of light let your heart be so bright
It is not easy to start over again
Have faith it's not as hard as it seems
Believe in yourself, believe what you're feeling
Not everyone will know what you mean
The greatest fear is within yourself
What you can not see, what you can not feel is indeed the mystery
Always have an open mind within that mind you will always find
The strength and ability to conquer yourself
Letting the world know you've found yourself
It doesn't matter what others may think
Only you will taste the victory drink
Willieetta M. Smith

Untitled

Why do soldiers fight the war;
No matter how much they have to snore;
And the officers get to stay in if they are a little bit sore
Why do our soldier friends feet freeze;
And end up lying dead on their knees;
While our officers sit inside and eat cheese?
Why do some soldiers get mass graves;
And others if they're lucky become slaves;
While officers grieve and complain about rationed maize?
The generals sit on their horses;
And yell in rough voices;
While soldiers are put on shell watch;
And dream someday owning a fine watch;
Is it only because officers outrank;
that they don't have to sleep in the dank;
And while soldiers live and die in the mud;
Officers sip fine tea, and lie beneath a fine oak tree;
And dream of never ending war;
Just as long as they don't have to fight it.
Eric Gehrie

The Cockatiel Among Sparrows and Wrens

I looked among the trees today,
At the place where the pathway bends,
To see the songbirds as they hop and play,
The sparrows and the wrens.

Among them was a new little fellow,
Standing out from the feathers brown,
He donned a coat of white, grey and yellow,
A cockatiel freshly shed of his down.

My first thought was to get a cage,
And surely he would fly in,
But he looked so happy taking center stage,
His freedom he deserved to win.

The songbirds didn't treat him with difference,
As he chirped and sang along.
His color to them was not a hindrance,
He displayed the same needs, same size, same song!

I took note as I dressed and planned for the day,
Of the cockatiel among sparrows and wrens.
I'll look for others in need and say,
"Come join me and we'll be friends."
Ronda Gregorius

Quicksand

Walking through the desert
No one around no one to hold
No one to love alone with my thoughts
Of a world with romance and everlasting friendships
What's that in the distance?
An oasis? An answer to my most private dreams?
Lost in unreal friendships
Lust without love, love without commitment
Flying high with the eagles falling as low as gravity goes
Failing to open my eyes to the truth
The oasis was just a mirage
Instead I had wandered into a pit of quicksand
Up to my neck with no way out
An inch deeper with each lie and deceit
Will I ever overcome the thirsty quicksand
Or will it swallow me up and leave nothing?
No thoughts, no dreams, nothing.
Waiting for its next victim like a cobra hunting for prey
Promising security and trust
And then swallowing you whole.

Alison Glass

Drums

They say the drums are silent,
lost in the distant past.
The beats of hearts in unison,
for beliefs that would not last.

They say our customs were savage,
the Ghost Dance had to halt!
When we broke the shackles,
they said it was our fault.

To stand together as we do now,
amidst the fire light.
Is proof enough we are the ones,
to carry on the fight!

So brothers and sisters if you are told,
the drums are in the past.
Stand proud and let them know.
In your hearts the beat will last!

Gary C. Crippen

Rooftops

High upon a rooftop
the perfect place to be
with many splendid sounds
and countless sights to see
grassy hills and airplanes
the children skipping by
holding strings to kites
hat dance across the sky
cotton candy clouds
wrap mountains capped with snow
and winds that carry flowers
from gardens far below
and orchestra of blue birds
their concert in the trees
brings buzzing from the hives
or harmonizing bees
golden fields and church bells
the horns from passing cars
when after satin sunsets
to gaze upon the stars
high upon a roof top upon a throne of kings
embraced by Gods creation
and all His living things

Donald Sean Ritter

Wonderment Wedding

A church with a bride walking down the aisle
People standing with smiles
A man stands waiting for her and a stuck out child
She walks what seems like miles
A face she sees within her mind
And wishes it was real
She wonders where that person is
And why they're not in teal
Questions filling up her mind without an end in sight
The pictured face is missing here because she's filled with fright
Will the man be there to guide her home
In the dark of night

Kathleen Doyle

Temples

Starting not with stone but bone,
To build a temple known as home.
To comprehend is only the beginning,
Now glorify the One who is giving.

God Almighty, The Great Creator,
Give [praise] to Him now and later;
He is the One who gives this gift,
[Praise] the Lord's Almighty fist.

Listen and hear the word He sends,
Eternal life is without end!
He gave His Son to die for our sins,
He is the One we must confide in.

Today, tomorrow, foreverafter;
His light it shines! Rejoice with laughter!
Forget your sorrow, forget your guilt,
God forgives the temples He built.

William R. Wallace

My Lord To Thee

My God and Savior, Lord to thee
I lay my life down, at your feet
Have mercy Lord, meet my needs
My God and Savior, I trust in thee

Ever faithful, strong and true
Lord Jesus, I believe in you
You're my companion my closest friend
You'll be with me until the end

Struggles and troubles can't wear me down
Jesus will help me stand
From the battlefield to his throne
The blood of Jesus cleans all

My God and Savior, Lord to thee
I lay my life down, at your feet
Have mercy Lord, meet my needs
My God and Savior, I trust in thee

Dawn Lashley

Spots

I hate spots,
I hate them alots.

Still,
everywhere I go I see them.

I wish these spots would leave me alone,
if they did, I would gladly free them.

'Cause for them it must be equally bad,
floating in front of my eyes.

Getting so wet that they might get a cold,
every time I get sad and I cries.

Sky Randall

My Little One

I woke up this morning and went into your room
It was late enough that I knew you'd be up soon

Watching you sleep filled my heart with such joy
Because there in your crib was my first baby boy

Your big wondering eyes that look up at me
Help open up the world for me to see

With cute little smiles and your curious ways
You make me laugh every single day

I'm so glad I have time to give lots of hugs
And even to play with you right down on the rug

You've made my life richer beyond compare
To all of the treasures on earth everywhere

Your life is so precious to me little one
A true gift from God, such a special son

Sweet little baby with eyes so blue
Hope you'll always know how much mommy loves you

Angela Cummings

The Real Game

Their field is a moderate cleavage,
in the breast of a tenement called home.
Freckled with paper, and boards, and rocks,
encased in high walls of stone.

I watched as the players entered with gear,
to start setting the stage for their game.
The wind entered with them, then echoed back out,
seeming to cheer them by name.

Clothes that were strung on lines overhead,
waved in rhythmic applause.
Tension grew as game time drew near,
and in unison they pondered their cause.

First base - is the stone against the wall,
Second, is the hub from the Ford.
Third, is chalked on the opposite wall,
Home, is a splintery board.

The sun peeks over the eastern roofs,
making shadow dances across the west wall.
The stage is set, and the players ready,
out comes the cry, "play ball".

Ken Hartlage

To Risk

To get out on the court is to risk making
mistakes
To play tough is to risk pains and aches
To have courage is to risk the faith in
yourself and your team
To play before the crowd is to risk shame
To work the hardest you ever have
is to risk everything.

But the team who risks nothing, does
nothing, has nothing, and is nothing.

You may avoid suffering or a foul or two,
but to not take risks is to not go for the
steal, to not drive and to not score.

Without taking these risks the team
will achieve nothing.

After all when you're not striving to
improve, what's the point?!

Jill Christensen

Time

Thoughts to think and songs to write,
Time to spend yet most in spite.
Dreams to do it all but then
Something blocks the path again.
The voice of reason shouts from the back,
"Listen up, Mac!
You know what you want, you know where it is.
Fight for it friend, lest it becomes his;
His who knows the want and where,
And his who even knew how to get there.
Give it all up, there is no shame;
Work hard as you can, risk everything for fame.
Then he who knew how may even be beat
Because you worked so hard and rose to the feat."

Van Tompkins

The Water's Edge

As I stand on the banks of the creek, where I played as a child,
I remember the days when I was happy to just be wild.

The days rolled by, the months went fast,
it seems like yesterday that all those
years have passed.

I think back now at how time flew,
at how the ocean and sky were such a pretty blue.
Now those colors don't seem so clear.

The years have come and gone with nothing more to show
than those happy memories
of so long ago.

I am a grown man now, and as I stand at the water's edge once again
I want so badly for the sky to be the same color blue
and for the water to be as clear as it is in
my mind's eye, but I guess there comes
a time when we must all let go.

John Meleski

She Appeared

She appeared to me in a dream
It was the only place a woman like her could live
I couldn't get her out of my mind, or maybe she was part of my soul

On the beach, she appeared to me
But how
Was she a reflection off the sea
No, because I touched her golden hair
In the forest, she appeared to me
But how
Was it a disfigured bush to look like her
No, because she touched my hand
She appeared to me in the sky
But how
Was it a cloud molded to look like her
No, because our tender lips met
And then she was gone forever.

Randy Ray Cunningham

Friend

"Jesus is my very best friend." I talk to him
each day, "as we walk along, together we
talk we sing we pray, as we go on our way!"
I walk with him over hills and dales, and
through Valleys as well. I love him more
and more each day, as we go on our merry way,
he never seems to tire of me. He just says
let's pray.

Helen L. Lehman

For My One True Love

Meeting her was not expected.
It was out of the blue.
Falling in love with her was like magic.
It was a dream come true.
Nobody touched my heart the way she does.
Nobody loved me the way she loves.
I may be crazy about her, there's nothing to hide.
But she'd understand if she saw how my heart cried.
When I look into her eyes, I see the sun
Shining through me with her fashion.
When I hold her body, I feel her soul
Warming me with her passion.
The feelings I have for her are so strong and so real;
And I know that they'll never go away.
For we have a special romance;
And in each other's heart we'll always stay.
I sincerely care for my one true love.
The beauty in her I'll always see.
And I thank the heavens up above
Because she took a chance with me.
Ralph J. DeGroat, Jr.

Untitled

What lies ahead?
Will you be lying on your death bed?
Leaving behind broken hearts,
where did it all start?
Crossing those tracks,
wishing you could go back.
To late, you made a big mistake.
Now I feel sorrow, cause you
will never see tomorrow.
Cross those tracks you may never turn back.
This was your time, will tomorrow be mine?
Will I remember where it all lead?
Of, course I will your dead.
Stephanie Crabtree

Religion

Picture a man, a young man,
trying to find his place in the world.
He is rich, but money doesn't fill his heart.
He is handsome, but looks leave him empty.
He is educated, but not in the ways of God.
Religion isn't a place to go on Sunday; it's not a club to belong to.
It gives you a sense of inner peace, a feeling that can
only come from your soul.
You may be right, you may be wrong, but you must believe.
A religious man believes everything is for the best;
in this he finds inner peace.
Is everything for the best, is anything?
It matters not;
for he is indeed happy, just believing.
This young man shall find happiness.
He shall live a full life.
After-life or not, his hope for a better life shall lead him
to attain one.
Robin Moskowitz

Untitled

Spirits young and clean,
Would be people imagined but never seen,
Denied life and all its grace,
These shall be the ones that
Bring tears to God's face.
Dennis L. Grandinetti

Visions Of White

A myriad of wonders
   appear before my eyes,
A multitude of mysteries
   traverse the azure skies,
A castle wall, a dragon's breath,
   a knight vying for his Lady fair,
A rocket ship, a lion's roar,
   an eagle dueling a grizzly bear,
A closing fist, a windmill turns,
   a single rose given lovingly,
A warrior's lance, a unicorn,
   a pirate ship on a golden sea,
These visions float on billowed sails,
   an ever altering array,
While I recline beneath this tree
   and watch the clouds slowly drift away.
Michelle Richardson

That Is Life

Maybe I won't
ever be able to drive a car
never to lose weight
or wear contact lenses
might get epilepsy
when I'm fifty years old
never get a job
men keep staring at me
I'll never get a ten
never learn algebra
or budget my money
won't be able to smell
or taste as long as I live
and I'll never write as neat as it should be
which can't be beat
as they say there is
no way to undo some things
I will have to accept what life brings
this poem is sad
I'm glad it is finished...
Nancy Arocho

The Magic Of Spring

Did you ever sit beside the sea,
On a starry night in June?
Listen to the roar of the breakers,
And smell the salty sweet perfume?

Did you ever watch the sea gulls,
Swirling gracefully through the air?
Diving for a bit of food,
Then up again in a flair?

Did you ever sit alone,
In a deep dark forest of pine?
Silently watching the woods folk,
Building their nest in time?

Have you ever walked down a country road,
And listen to a robin sing?
Or strolled through a field of clover,
In the early days of Spring?

If you have lived these experiences,
Then you are very rich indeed.
Not in gold or silver,
But God's blessing to receive.
Martin V. Bennett

Tranquility

Snowflakes gently dancing from a lovely wintry sky
Daring to kiss the earth below and on her softly lie,
Mounding up like whip cream on boughs of evergreen
Unfolding a picture of beauty, an equal I've never seen.

The night seems wondrously special
The moon smiles through the trees.
The night wind lies in rest
Allowing snowflakes to twirl and fall free.

The brightness of the falling snow
Entwined in the moon's soft glow
Embraces the night
With an almost mystic light.

And I am absorbed in this breathless display,
While my anxious soul gives way
To cherished tranquility.
And my mind finds renewal for another day.
Betty Carr Ross

Through Eyes Of A Child

What shall we do, now that we're here?
When I grow up, it would all become clear

As years toiled on and hope faded away
Skies that were blue had all turned to grey
It was there in my darkest and deepest despair
That my faint soul attempted to whisper a prayer
Peace came upon me, I cannot explain
I found my refuge when I called out His name

Through eyes of a child, we can understand
The wondrous creation, was done by His hand
It's this precious faith in Him we will find
A love so complete and true peace of mind
His child He died for, so thankful I see
Each drop of blood He shed was for me
Theresa Meyer

For The Love Of Tori

You could be my everything,
    Like a heavenly dream come true.
If God could only make you feel
    Just half the way that I do.

Through life's trials and tribulations,
    For you I would always be there.
Would that God should touch your heart
    And tell you just how much I care.

I can only imagine in my dreams
    Just what your love could be.
The answer that only He in heaven
    Could grant on earth to me.

Often I kneel and pray at night
    To the merciful God above.
But, alas, I am just a prisoner
    Of this one-sided love.

Though you'll never be my lover,
    And I was just your friend;
God knows how much I need you,
    But your love He'll never send.
Michael W. Klobnak

For Barbara

You don't know it, but...
I never really leave you behind
When I leave the house to go to work
Or travel to the store for a carton of milk.

I tuck the warmth of you under my sweater
And fold the sound of you into my mind
I roll up your smile and hide it behind my eyelids
So every time I blink, I laugh with you.

I paint the touch of you...
On every spot that might be vulnerable
And just before I walk into the world
I raise the parasol of your love over me.

Safe...Until I am home once more!
Robert E. Smith

Dear Lord

I would like to know
Do you have my son's soul?
Has he passed through those pearly gates,
Or is He roaming in other unknown places
he was young, when he left home to join
The army too learn and play war games.
Two years nearly passed, before he
Would finish and go to school, to become
A state trooper, to uphold societies rules.
Unfortunately, while my son slept,
A jealous, mad man passed with a grudge,
he dropped a match, that caused a fire,
Which took four life's, in a flash forever,
on February. 12 1994, My heart sunk when
   an army office knocked at
     the door, for I knew
       at once my son was gone
         forever.
Kathleen F. Williams

Graced By Your Presence

All that are living prosper in your revelation.
You, the shining sun, are the vitality of all creation.

You break through the darkness with a brilliance of light.
Overpowering the blackness of the calm, cool night.

Spilling orange, lavender and pink in breath-taking array.
Marking the commencement of a brand new day.

The clouds soak in the luminescence of your majestic beams.
Slowly creeping by as if mesmerized by the scene.

You awaken the birds;they sing in harmonic bliss.
So energized by your undying graciousness.

The trees slightly sway in complete felicity.
Waving to the heavens with grace and dignity.

The sunflower turn to face you, standing straight and tall.
They spread their leaves and worship the splendor of it all.

The grass seems to salute you in a welcoming gesture.
Stretching toward you with gratitude and pleasure.

All that are living know of your essence.
All that are living are graced by your presence.
Jane M. Haner

Unsewn Tapestry

Misty renaissance memories of you;
full almond fragrance, textured love dew,
warm tingle, intrigue;
Captured. Time passes.

Together, savoring time;
embellished and embraced by the soft petal of
a violet flower. Time slips.

The scent of musty cedar, thru my grey wood,
splintered attic, fondles faded, antique photographs.
Snapshots revisiting a palace-like park, a colorful
Victorian theater, an intoxicating foreign city.
Time lingers

Irreplaceable you, unreachable you,
non-embraceable you, you unsewn tapestry,
You-Phobia-You, forever you.
So beautiful you;
Released.

Time passes, time slips, time lingers.
Memories fade.

Susan A. Martin

Ode To Bonnie

I swanie, dear Bonnie, what a sister to me.
We laughed and giggled in that old maple tree.

As we grew up together, we played many games.
Dancing to the radio, rolling down hills,
then catching fireflies when the dark finally came.

Bicycling, sleighing, then driving the car;
Keeping in touch as we got older, whether near or far.

Your life was so full, so busy you stayed.
"Let's do this, let's do that, so I can still hear you say.

Out for a walk one night, you were taken so fast.
He was sixteen and drunk with his foot on the gas.

Oh Bonnie, I swanie, are you at peace at last?
Wish you were still with us, not part of the past.

You won't be forgotten for we all loved you so.
I think you can see us. You're smiling, I know.

Linda A. Dickerson

Volcano

O.J. we can't get you out of our minds - we all thought you
were ever so fine - "little lost child" - you've run your last mile
with your special smile. He hurts deep in his soul so much so,
he stabbed Nicole - such jealous rage - Now a bird in a cage
His fans cheered him on, still others cried on the phone - He seemed
to have it all - when he played ball - he was to many an icon
Transformed to a man on the run - They were in each other
blood now their names are but mud - O.J. couldn't get the
attention he wanted from the one person he loved. Now he has
the attention of the nation, - while Nicole rests above. Our
hearts are saddened while we try to understand the madding cry
The whole situation doesn't make much sense as we wave goodbye
Goodbye to the O.J. we once knew-who's in his cell all alone and blue
He seem to have it all - when he played ball. He was to many an icon.
Transformed to a man on the run. Their hearts beat as one while
they were having fun - Lord only knows where O.J. goes now that
his world has come crumbling down on a tabloid that shows
all his friends and foes, The end of a journey now only God knows

Susan Richardson

"My Unforgotten Love"

Love as I did that first tender caress,
True love that filled me with happiness,
I dare not think of my broken heart,
Of how we loved and had to part,
My sorrow is great but yet so small,
Because losing you has been worst of all,
I'll remember my dear, and always be true,
To the star that I left in the sky of blue!
You left this earthly realm, you're no longer here with me,
Those fifty-four years of marriage, are now
A loving memory,
It was heaven here on earth with you,
In my heart you will remain,
Someday there will be two stars together
In God's heaven of blue again!

Jo Vinsand

Marianne At Eighty

I have an old friend
Whose name I won't share
Take her out-like to lunch-
I no longer dare.

She's blind and she's deaf
and she walks with a cane.
Getting her out of a car
can be quiet a pain...

She's old and I love her,
though she likes to get ripped-
Heaven help us both
if she ever slipped.

It's not her infirmity that hampers
It's not because she has to wear Pampers.
It's not that she can't tell her corn from her 'taters
It's just simply this-
she gooses the waiters!

Cheryl Bluestein

"Round About Aways"

Round about aways the passing of winter, glacial and
brilliant, with snow capped hills abounding,
Recalling each evening Sun's passing turn
some with others, I recollect, friends;
Once and round about aways a springtime's aerial
create calling, of doves, a naming call of mourning
Of gulls, a laughing call round about aways the
noontime hours, chickadees- the children playing
in summer, when life is a peak of sensations:
A first kiss, warm rain, an angel's passing
Round about aways of autumn, when the trees
shine bright and the misty rights, a thousand
cool evenings with the fire and the greater
gathering of all people;
Round about aways the everyday, never plain,
and fastly fading toward memory.

Charles Tamboer

Diana Luna

Why moon? Thy pale countenance upon the ethereal night
Sparkling stars arrest their wondering plight?
A lady transfixed upon a gentleman's orb
Gentle earth's majestic reflection with verdant words!
Mystery enthralling reason confusing beauty
Pharaohs wonder at your power and might
While language unknown transfixes intelligent life
Plato's reason nor Buddha's serenity alter your continuous flight
Hover above in a sea of dark light and roam until eternity ends
What life without your shadow means?
If only humanity could bring a consummation that eternity could end!

C. V. Compton Shaw

Innocence Lost

My pulse is low and my heartbeat's weak;
I haven't expired, but lost my desire.
And was mistakenly labeled a freak.
It all began without any plan to speak of;
I set out run 'til I met with the sun,
and never succeeded, now I've nothing to dream of.
There's something to say for innocence;
I'm not sure what for my doors been shut,
by a world of suppression and indifference.
So who survives in this world of lies?
I know today, I learned it the hard way,
though I'm too weak for a second try.
When they attempt to put out your fire;
oh, an extinguishing cost, for innocence lost,
relight it with a burning desire.
Joe Brath

Your Mask

I can not see you;
The you! That I should be able to see.
You wear this mask.
A mask you say is you, but it is not.
This mask is a cover-up,
It hides all your emotions.
When you are truly sad, it shows your false happiness.
When you are full of rage it shows a deceptive calm.
Please take off your mask.
For I am your friend.
I will not hurt you.
You can tell me anything.
You can do nothing wrong.
You need not a mask.
The mask changes you, you do not act yourself.
You act the way others wish you to act.
The mask is your crutch,
It's your way of avoiding things.
Please take off your mask!
For I am a friend, who is always here for you!
Tanya Lane

Gray Matter

When did the world become so gray
As the way we see it now today?
Why was it that we said so-long
To a difference twixt right and wrong?
The birth of Darwin, it seems to me,
Was the birth of virtual morality.
Neither scientific nor biblical truth
Had but one single shred of rock solid proof.
No prefect answer could be found,
So man created common ground.
For some reason we thought we were bright
To make everything half-wrong, half-right
If everything is half-right and half-wrong
Maybe we've always been right all along.
There's nothing wrong with murder or rape,
Robbery, war and all forms of hate.
What the heck, if nothing we do can be wrong,
Then maybe we've always been "gods" all along.
You New Age people say you use your own eyes.
Well, your way of life came from a compromise.
Joshua M. Du Brock

Flight Of Fancy

I walk lonely in Eden sometimes...
Our live's paradise through crystal tears.
Amongst the beauty,
I look to the gate where I'd like to wander alone,
And look into the mirrored waters of my own soul.

Though in love with my heart's captor,
I long to touch the latch
And dance from under the shadow of its immensity
Without the heavy shawl of my guilt.

Yet, still today, I sit and stare at the world
Through a glass panel prison
An insignificant little bird in a great golden cage
That nonetheless
Foolishly yearns to fly...
Helen L. Mellott

This Thing Called "Love"

A whirlwind of emotions.
It has dragged you down,
It will lift you up.
A heart-warming source of happiness...
Something that will leave you exposed and vulnerable...
Totally naked
Sheepish grins that make others wonder,
Smoldering heat of over-due kisses,
Reassurance through looks of love.
A brush of the knee that can send you flying...
A day full of dreams, and a night of longing.
Unselfish acts of unconditional love...
Fears of rejection hanging in the midst.
Cruel words that bring shattered images.
The beauty of a smile, the eyes baring your soul.
Lost identities and false faces.
The burdens you carry,
Endless hours of confusion and heartbreak.
Lusting for something you cannot understand,
Leaving you breathless, and asking for more...
Sarah Sharich

Challenge

Somewhere in the future dim
A light of hope shines on,
In dreams we see the ray of light
And waken to meet the dawn.

We wonder now, we must find our own way,
Though the darkness unending be;
Our hopes seem to fail us, our strength drained away,
We seek a way to flee.

Yet stop! Ye called apart, and seek the truth to know
Of life and death, while yet the life blood flow.

Know that our God will lead the way
Though dark and rough it seem,
He'll guide and love through endless day,
With wondrous heavenly beam.

So march on through life, as true soldiers of light,
With shoes of Christ's Gospel be shod.
Strive on to that city, where there is no night,
And look into the face of thy God.
Amma C. Flickinger

"The End Of Words"

Heaven assumes smooth white shoulders continuously hit by rain
while church bells chime in the distance - a gloomy nostalgia
the scent of rose falls all around us
mingling with the rain and our glances
Your smile twists and fades - cerulean in its purity
Diving in and out of consciousness
your soul hovers just above mine on the bleeding horizon
the result is blinding
thrashing nightmares
I'm staggering stumbling
trying to find the truth
Lips are sealed with jagged threads
Lies hang like stars
As the ominous air of a storm at dawn floats by
Chilly frost of a new season cuts my throat
Brutal in its cruel seduction
Falling down stairs that mutate into faces and grasping hands
I'd scream but something took my voice away
Strange associations that smear and play on glass
like the firefly's phosphorescence—glowing

Brigitte Whisler

The Game

You're Dangerous,
   and Mysterious...
Maybe that's why I care so much.
You are a Master at Your Game.
I am just the pawn.
You choose my destination...
   Heaven or Hell?
The only Winner is you.
And me, I walk away with endless memories and
   a broken heart.
I am helpless in Your Game.
Is it a game of Love?
No, that game has Two winners.
What game are you playing?
When do I fall?
It's too late...
I've already fallen for you.
   Your turn.

Laura Anne Rodriguez

Ain't A Lookin' Back

As I was brandin' steers
My wife of just three years
Lit out with all her gear

Who cares...I ain't a lookin' back

While I was in town
A cryin' in my brew
My house got blown away
By Hurricane Andrew

Who Cares...I ain't a lookin' back

Well, the insurance company
Said they weren't gonna pay me
And as I was seein' red
They up and paid the mortgage company instead

Who cares...I ain't a lookin' back

Now I'm headin' down the road
Passed all those acres I just mowed
...Damn— I just ran over a toad!!

Well who cares
I ain't a lookin' back

Rodney K. Harsh

Gratitude Born At Gettysburg

I in my cloak of flesh and bone
roam these fields but not alone.
Wafting along on a breeze are borne
lonely sounds—ghostly and forlorn.

How many here in agony cried?
Midst pain and suffering they slowly died.
Years have passed, yet still there remains
scars of battle in this hallowed domain.

Out of the meeting of this human flood,
the soul of a nation is bathed in blood.
The gift of freedom for all has begun
at the cost of a nation's valiant sons.

Think, you all who fleetingly gather here,
what price the rights you hold so dear
was paid by those whose memories are lost.
It staggers the mind this human cost.

Down with bondage of the human heart!
May freedom for all now truly start.

Marvin Lee Mortensen

My Inspiration

You were my true inspiration and encouragement.
You never laughed at my exotic ideas.
When I was happy, you shared my joy.
When I was upset, you comforted me.

You became someone very close and special to me.
You brought me laughter, never pain.
I could always rely on you,
Whenever I was in trouble, whenever I needed a friend.

You taught me how to look at the world
With different eyes, to be positive with life,
And not hate it.
Your warm smile would make my day just right.

Now through our past three years together our time must part,
And you must start a new life.
You'll be deeply missed by all who know and love you,
Especially me.

I'll always remember you:
My laughter, my joy, my courage,
My strength, my innocence,
My friend, my Ayala.

Shauna Stebner

Help Me!

Help me please
I know you understand
Hold me in your arms
Guide me with your hands
Be there for me whenever I'm in need
I recognize you, for with you I am freed.
Speak your gentle comforting thoughts
Look into my eyes
Look on into my heart
I know we are strangers yet we are so close
Out of all that I know, you I trust the most
Help me please
Can you not see I'm going down
Pick me back up for with you I am found
When you are not near, loneliness is my fear
Take away the pain, drain away the tears
yes I do love you
You are my closest friend
For you I would do anything
For you I'd come to an end!

Daniele Tella

"Why Must It Be So"

Oh! Why must it be so—
I'm here, alone, without you.
And, why did you leave me
For someone new?
Can't you recall all our past times
All the dreams we had, had in our minds,
Oh! Why must it be so, since—, then?

Oh! Why must it be so
Since your love has gone
And, how could you forget
A love—, so strong
For can't it be me, that you miss
Forgetting, that affectionate kiss
Oh why can't it be so—Once Again.

Dante J. Sarro

"Soulmate"

I am here, oh, I am here,
Where the sea meets the sky, as the wind whips by,
As the birds fly high, as the clouds sail nigh,
  Be one with me!

Open your heart, that you may see,
that you may feel, that you may be.
Hear my song, know my feelings,
  Be one with me!

Oh, come to where, the earth meets sea,
And sea meets sky, and sun meets both.
Away from cares, far from stress,
  Be one with me!

Cling to me, as I to you,
As grass to sand, as sky to sea.
Oh, take my love, under my sky,
Hear my lament, a cry for you,
  Be one with me!

Marie Cronin (nee Ruth Sampson)

The Love I Once Had

I once had a love, unlike any other.
He always looked past the bad, and only for the good.
It seemed to be the "Perfect" love, but was it really truly love?
He told me he loved me, and I loved him too.
But deep down inside his heart, he was loving another.
Never speaking of any feelings or pain, making promises to me.
Were the promises true? Were they really meant for me?
Yes I do believe he had love for me, but he had a greater love for
another. I wish him all the love and happiness, but a heart in pain
can only give so much. Will the pain, emptiness, and shallowness
ever end? Will the missing piece of my heart ever be filled? Can a
person ever really be "Whole"? The confused and hurting feelings
seem neverending. Will it ever really end? It seems to me that no
matter how hard people try, everything seems so easy to lose,
thrown away at the drop of a dime. What happens to the promises,
were they meant for me or another? Another lesson to be learned,
will "True Love" ever really come?

Renee Peetz

The Feeling Of Alone

Where sunlight through the windows sprays
And dust upon the wall does play
As silence in the corner sleeps
Through the door no shadow sweeps
As silence in the corners sleeps
No crimes for which one must confess
Colors jump in cracking walls
In sunset as a darkness falls
And other life is long since gone
This is the feeling of Alone...

Amanda Anne Woodard

"The Family"

Loving voices raise in good cheer, as we
sit at the table to partake our meal, a meal
so prepared with love from Mama's Hands.
She puts a cup of Love in every
recipe; she works endless hours in search of
knowing when her family sits to eat; she's
fed each and everyone with Love.
Her Hands grow tired as she dries the
last dish and puts it back in its place; then
her apron hung on her chair to wait until
her next Meal of Love to be made; all for
her family.

Jo Tschappat

The Songs Of Moonlight

Moonlight caresses the ground and trees that lay before me.
It comes through the trees like dew drops from a leaf, smoothly and
  almost rhythmic.
I hear the songs of moonlight.
A lark perhaps, crickets with their noise that fits so perfectly.
My pony awakens my trance with a soft whinny, and we continue
  upon the road.

But wait! What is that sound? I surely did hear it, my pony too.
Is it a wild beast waiting for our embracement of going further?
Surely it can't, there are no wild beasts. But yet I did hear it.
The breeze then whispered in my face to go on.

I had to, I couldn't show my face again where I had been.
They might think that we were scared.
Nudging my pony, we continued tensely past the group of shrubs
  and into the clearing.
Then I saw a fawn drinking from the stream.
It was surely more beautiful than the moonlight going through the
  trees.

Gina Marie Buss

Heart's Of Eternity

Even though we're miles and miles apart,
I'll always hold you deep in my heart.

If I was there to show you I care,
It would always and forever be fair.

When I dream of you a twinkle appears
in my eye. It gives me the wisdom and
strength to want a try.

With you and me together my love, we
will always be whole, so there will always
be True Love forged in our souls.

Always remember this till the end, I
want to always and forever be your man
and Best Friend.

But then again my love, there will
never be no end for you and me will
always be together for all eternity...

Vern Davison

Greg

Through the crowd I feel
your eyes,
And my world has never seemed so bright.
Through the crowd I see
your smile,
and the dark has turned to light.
Now I've heard you speak,
and your voice, oh so soft
made this hard heart weak.
Thank you
for touching my soul.

Jo Ramirez

"Where Have All The Flowers Gone?"

The GIs die, two score eleven years have passed.
(In 1916 gray- and blue-clad beards dispersed;
Huzzas rang, dimming, mythic tales rehearsed
By GAR and UDC held fast.)

The "last just war"—its heroes shrunk to tiers
Of Joe-sized merchandise—
Evokes no piety, begs no sighs.
As obits fill page 2,2000 nears.

(Napoleon's army, legend-fired, left wives,
Memorials, proud eclat, and horseback mimes.
As Highlanders cursed Hanoverian crimes
They kept alive the "45's.")

Our age of peace, unquiet, breeds no dread
Of hist'ry happ'ning. Boomers' flags stay furled.
And Generation X ignores the world.
No notice for the passing, piping for the dead.

Old soldiers seldom die, they weigh too light
In laundered uniforms: ODs fade.
(Ten millions drift to five.) The "Now decade"
Expires, foreswearing in its slight.
Harold W. Mann

Beyond The Point.... No Return

My feet stepped out sure of my path
through drifting fog upon a hill;
abruptly then my feet stood still.

Then through the mist I heard a sound
a bell of warning turned me around.

Across the hill of mossy green
through shrouds of fog cannot be seen.

Divine the hand that made me stop
upon the hill, the edge, the top.

And to this day the mist has come
all through the years I know not from.

But guided by His unseen hand
like a beacon across the land.

Today I know I'll never stray
because He's there to show the way.

Beyond the point lies the abyss again
so I'll hold His hand and walk close to Him.
Vilet R. Weaver

Life's River

A river is like life's changing streams
It's filled with chances, choices, and dreams
It branches off and divides its path
It steadily flows and swiftly laughs
You can't change the direction of its flow
Or calm its waters when rough storms blow
But choose the path you wish to take
And if it's right you'll find the lake
But if this path you unwisely choose
Just start again you cannot loose
If you keep trying until the end
The race of rivers you will win
But if you give up and ride with pace
You'll never meet this challenge you face
And the waters you ride will swiftly flow
And take you nowhere on the path you go
So fight to win and try try again
Don't ever give up on life's journey my friend.
Angela W. Davis

Winter

Winter is:
  A time when Jesus was born
  A time of getting and giving presents
  A time to cook food for a family dinner
  A time for Christmas vacation
  A time to get days off from school
  A time to celebrate a New Year
  A time to share love
  A time for a little or a lot of snow
  A time for a hot chocolate
  A time for fun
  A time for family birthdays
Winter is supposed to be cold but with all the love, it's warm!
Jason Trenchard

A Brief and Flawed Forever

The light ash of a shortened wick dimly floats above liquid wax
Their palling flames my only light fading quietly into the night
Across the darkened walls and ceiling each piece of light dances
with torment each shadow embracing the idle bleak of night
The chill of loneliness caresses the swollen red from my eyes
The wrinkles of an empty yellow and plaid shirt lay sulking on my lap
Wilted desires lay limp with rejection
Old Spice lingering faintly within the fabric of an unstarched collar
a thinned teasing reminder of seclusion
A starting craving for warmth trembles at my bare and numbed breast
Draping the hollowed shirt across the broadness of my shoulders
each twisted fiber conforms to my body's every throb
My fingers wrap tightly over the crushed cuff of white knuckles
gripping fiercely around the cold silver medallion that lies heavy
upon my chest dry eyes weakened by a salty lather of tears close at
moistened edges as the frail gentile touch of my own caring hands
cup the ache of my moving shoulders my body, guided by a song
that trails intimately within my soul, follows each beat to my knees
as its tone softens slowing closer to its varied end the biting orange
of the last ember breaks away and enfolding with the night... dies
Melissah J. Falavolito

Love Is...

Love is red,   Love is true,
Love is warm,   Love is real,
Love is affection,   Love is trust,
Love is pure,   Love is special
Love is natural,   Love is fulfilling,
Love is unexpecting;   Love is from the heart;

Love is caring,   Love is blind,
Love is sharing,   Love is faithful,
Love is commitment, Love is forgiving,
Love is compassion, Love is compromise,
Love is sensitive,   Love is beautiful,
Love is emotional;   Love is forever.
Sebastian V. Pandolfo Jr

Untitled

In the quiet of a warm afternoon breeze
Feeling sultry an unexplained calm
Reliving moments tucked away
Allowing the special memories to escape from the heart

The magnitude of such feelings
Overpower by very being
Silent tears speaking my soul
Comparing only to beauty of a magical sunset

Haunting memories bring me alive
To breath is only secondary
To be truly happy with tears can only happen once
To be lucky enough to feel will last a lifetime
Linda Hafford

In Springdale Cemetery

They laid my tiny, tiny son in a beautiful, small, white casket.
And they buried him at the foot of Grandma's grave.
His soul was oh so very young and yet so very, very brave.

At first the song birds sang to him; they sang from the beautiful
trees all around. And the soft, green grass was a warm sweet
blanket where small purple flowers abound.

For many years he shared nature's beautiful joy.
This tiny, tiny baby boy.

Then something changes all of this.
Something around him was amiss.

The birds no longer sang from the beautiful trees around.
Because the trees had all died and fell to the ground.

No one came to clear the land of the fallen trees. So the
blanket of green grass turned brown and was covered with limbs
and leaves.

Oh please let's bring back some love and some joy to this
tiny, tiny baby boy.
And let's do whatever needs to be done. And make this part of
Heaven beautiful again for everyone.
Virginia M. Raistrick

Dying Hopes

Misrepresented in the land of the free.
My country always ignoring me.
I have always loved you red, white, and blue.
I wish that I could not see right through you.
The pursuit of happiness a forgotten game.
Today, hate, greed, and vengeance seem the same.
Top officials that create mistrust and fear.
Our people blind, stand by and cheer.
Millions of mice in a really small cage.
Sitting on top of a mountain of rage.
Raining cats and dogs is such a small tale.
In light of catastrophe about to prevail.
In one final plea to the land of the free.
Where oh where is my liberty?
Billy Seiver

The Sands Of Time

How the sands of time...
Slipped thru our fingers
As we walked down yesteryear.

Never knowing in our youth
We would someday return to learn....
The crushing blow..of the sands of time.

We walked down that pathway...years ago.
Young mother and child
Gleefully laughing...with family and friends
out for the day.

Some played in the pool
Some fished by the shore.
They played ball.
And some just sat and ate.

Each summer, we all went down that pathway
or years ago.
Some days dragged and some days flew.

Just like .....the sands of time
That slipped thru our fingers,
As we walked down yesteryear.
Patricia Bulauski

My Little Brother

My little brother is such a brat.
His cheeks are chunky and really fat.
He sleeps in a crib.
He has to use a bib.
He can barely talk.
He just learned how to walk.
He is really funky.
He has short hair.
And is as mean as a bear.
That's all I have to say about my little bro.
I guess it's time for me to go.
Sam Summers

The Hug

I hugged you this morning.
Your head lay on my breast, trusting, safe.
Holding you close, you drifted into sleep
Hearing my heart beat just for you.

Soon you'll wake and burst into your world,
Arms flailing, legs churning, senses reeling;
Watching, listening, touching, tasting your fists.
You're six weeks old.

I hugged you this morning.
Your head lay on my breast.
You clung, then pulled away and lingered
Taking my hand for a squeeze
Reluctant to leave the haven of mother.

Soon you'll leave and burst into your world,
Body failing, mind reeling, emotions churning,
Observing, reasoning, feeling, tasting your own ideas.
You're twelve years old.
Judith Berens

Dear Katlyn

This poem is for Katlyn, My only niece
A poem filled with love, a poem filled with peace.
I've watched you grow from a sweet little baby
And now I can't watch you grow into quite a young lady.
We fought each other over silly stuff
That's when I realized you'll be pretty tough.
But underneath that tough disguise
Is a young lady that laughs and cries.
With so much to say I don't know where to start
But what I tell you comes straight from my heart.
I've let you and me down in more than one way
So I'm making you a promise on this very day
I'm changing my ways, I promise, you'll see
The person I'm now, is a whole different me.
Though I won't be there for the next few years
Anything that happens remember I have ears.
I may be up here and you're down yonder
But people say, Absence makes the heart grow fonder.
So, I'm sorry for what I've put myself through
Please remember I'll always love you.
Mark A. Appler

The Answer

How do you describe a miracle?
Is it a chance occurrence or
a predetermined act of fate?

How do you described an angel?
Is it a soft heavenly body or
a person filled with warmth and beauty so innate?

The answer to all of these is quite simple.
You are my miracle, my angel, my love.
You are the answer to all above.
Ostap M. Mohyla

My Sister-Sheila

We haven't always been the best of friends.
There were times I thought the fighting would never end.

We'd kick and scream, fight and yell
and more often than not, I'd run and tell.

Mom would say "fight your own battle".
My sister would call me "a little tattle".

Though things have changed since we've grown-up.
Now that she's older, she's not so tough.

Now we're the best of friends.
Just like Mom always said.

It's funny how things change with time.
Kind of like an aging wine.

Something that was once acid and tart.
Now I cherish with all my heart.

She's my older sister, my best friend.
A relationship I hope, that never ends.

Traci J. Delaney

A Cloud Gliding Through The Breeze

A cloud gliding through the breeze.
Covering the blue sky with pure whiteness.
Peaceful designs that it makes.
Not much symmetry because it is different in all ways.

I have different attitudes.
Fright with thunder and lightning.
Beauty with sunshine and colors.
I bring rain and life.
In a child's mind I'll be what they want me to be.
Usually they prefer cotton candy.
I see happiness, glitter, and joy.
But I also see sadness, gloom, and poverty.
I am all the way up here.
And you are all the way down there.
For I can not help.
Oh! But I wish I can.
When you are sad and depressed, I am always there to remind you that there is a brighter side to every situation.
I am proud of who I am.
A cloud with a silver lining.

Shyam Tanguturi

Untitled

Life is but a fleeting glimpse
of someone you think you recognize;
a shaft of sun upon a pond, that
dances with the dragonfly.

When one is young, and sings with love,
the heart aligns with the stars above;
full of vision and future plans
of moonlit evenings and island sands.

When one is old and knows of life,
the gentle heart, softly scarred with strife,
can only sigh a weary breath,
can only ask what more is left?

When first we land upon this shore,
we have ourselves and nothing more;
when last we leave this earthly plane
only the dust of our lives remain.

Each speck of dust that trails our soul,
each golden moment that filled our bowl,
is all we own and all we leave
to comfort those we've loved, bereaved.

D. R. Heuman

Sisters

They're there when you need them
My goodness they can relate to you
When you're ready to cry or don't
Understand men or anything
Older sisters are there to guide you
Through the problem.
You can relate because you might
have the same blood.
Don't let your sisters go
You will need them in your life
Even when you think she won't trust you, she will.
Little sisters are great because
Then they look up to you and
You can guide them, remember
The older sisters must and will guide the way.

Melissa Hayden

Untitled

Along the way of all passing days
some led astray and others will never come
down again.
And others lost at their own cost
pushed and tossed into life's lost failure's and
different bin.
And others stoned, by themselves were thrown,
out of the throne of the world they temporarily
reigned.
And I am crazed and amazed
as I gaze at this world that I love has
permanently gone insane.
But will it heal, this world unreal,
or will it still be ever so down hill
from here.
My generation's determination
to end all indications that the powers holding
us down are near.

Brooks Bevil

Friendship Often Ends Too Soon

A harsh grave, an early end
 a lost friend.
I miss you, why did you have to go?
 When they told me that my best friend had died,
I felt alone but never cried.
 Where you died there's still a stain,
as in agony you had lane.
 People don't notice and life goes on,
but not for everyone who needed to survive.
 So now I feel like I'm going to cry one last time,
Good-bye my friend,
 For I shall miss you always.

Megan Dell

"Reasonings"

Without God   ... Comes doubt
With doubt   ... Comes uncertainty
With uncertainty ... Comes fear
With fear   ... Comes anger
With anger   ... Comes war
With war   ... Comes destruction.

But

With God   ... Comes faith
With faith   ... Comes acceptance
With acceptance ... Comes love
With love   ... Comes peace
With peace   ... Comes worship
With worship   ... Comes eternal life.

Jennifer T. Babin

A Special Prayer

I said a prayer for you last night
I prayed to my father above
I asked him to protect and strengthen you
by showering you with his love

I asked him to hold your hand
for I knew I couldn't be there
"stay by her side, comfort her Lord"
Please show her that we do care!!!

Things don't always happen as we plan
It's not always easy to understand
It's always important to keep the faith
you sometimes feel defeated, don't worry, just pray

All of God's children are certainly blessed
stumbling blocks we encounter, are parts of his test
No matter how long or lonely the road
"Prayer" is the instrument that calms the soul
Stacy Law

I See, But I Don't See

I see, but I don't see
The things all around me.
I see an elderly man crossing the street.
What I don't see is the pain in his feet.

I see, but I don't see
The things all around me.
I see a basketball player dunking a ball.
What I don't see is last night's drunken fall.

I see, but I don't see
The things all around me.
I see a baseball player on a Major League strike.
What I don't see are the bruises on his little tyke.

I see, but I don't see
The things all around me.
I see the world as a wonderful place.
What I don't see is love on each face.
Nick Crossman

A Mother's Love

I've been molded to believe, through and through-that a Mother's
love should be treasured and true.
A mother's love should care not how far it has to go, nor what it
has to do but only about how it can protect you.
The object being never to leave you sad and blue.

A mother's love is a soft caress, no other able to take the place
of her special touch.
Always happy to give-no matter how little-no matter how much.
Never fear the fall, for a mother's love is your crutch.

A mother's love should never push-nor should it shove.
A child should never bear the bruises of a mother's boxing glove.
Never to put the child below, but always one step above
for what else have we got, if not a mother's love?
Susan J. Dilley

Last Rites And Genocide (Near Misses)

Promises make our bellies feel pink,
and smiles turn into earth.
The hair on our necks jumps quick,
like a priest,
piously striving for first.

Fear and memories squeeze through the skin,
while something sticks in our hearts.
The last great race caused the trip
of our feet,
trying to get where we aren't.
Michael R. Burns

Quest For Peace

It's an obscured world.

Is there a place in time
Where war and peace collide?
When will this madness end?
If we keep the madness in our minds,
This madness will bring the seasons of destruction.
I will not be a slave of your mindless beliefs.
Stop the bloodshed.

The sands of time are running low.
Open your eyes.
Stop living in lies.
We can't like this anymore
Seal the planets fate.
Stop the hate.
One as one in this precious land
Let's stand together hand in hand.
Dauzed Melgarejo Jr.

Wasted Beauty

A warm gentle breeze
robins in the trees

Sea shells in the sand
a squirrel eating from my hand

The sound of the ocean
a deer standing without motion

A flower in bloom
the stars and the moon

Children playing in the park
the sounds of crickets after dark

The green grass below
a firefly's blinking glow

The blue skies above
coo's of a morning dove

Illusion of a Dream
Or so it might seem

No, these are realities
that will soon be fatalities

Because these are some things we take for granted
on this cold and heartless planet
Francine L. Yenner

The Breath Of Spring

Winter snow slowly melts away.
A Robin sings I'm back to stay.
Something's in the air.
Must be the breath of spring.

Early sun rising on the hill.
His smiling face wakes Daffodils.
Something's in the air.
Must be the breath of spring.

Among blossoms again the world is blessed.
With chirping sounds from a new nest.
Some things in the air.
Must be the breath of spring.

From Den there are suckling sounds
With soft whimpers beneath the ground.
Something's in the air.
Must be the breath of spring.
Joe Bisko

Blind

My soul searches for you as I cry for you.
The days seem endless as my love for you.
For only I can see the fires of hell, as
My soul soars through the passages of time.
I fear no evil, for I am an unending spirit
that has no barrier of time. Reach within
me, for my heart, for once you have it
there will be no doubts. The mind is
imaginary with its place and time, for what
I feel for you will never change, for it is
unending, a love that you will never know,
if you are blind.

Pamela Tackman

Untitled

At home,
The children run smiling.
They don't know what's happening over there.
Others, older than children and younger than men,
March instead of run.
Their faces are so changed from the times
Of the smiling children.
No one knows what they have seen, in hot,
Buttoned up shirts with stripes and colored bars.
At home,
Men and women talk and laugh.
They don't know what's happening over there.
The old boys and young men
Talk haltingly,
And never know when to laugh.
The fighting goes on all around them.
As they slowly march, life rushes by
In a flurry next to those
At home.

Meghan Magill

Beauty To The Beholder

As I pass through life,
My mind encounters things of beauty.

Like the fresh dew lacing the trees,
And as the sun shines, butterflies floating on air.

The clouds passing by in their arrays of imagination,
The wind slightly waving the fields of harvest.

The smell of fresh cut grass,
The flowers dancing with colors supreme.

These things God has given all to enjoy
while cascading through life's daily bidding.

Candace O. Taylor

Unreflected Souls

Shadows in a mirror, come to play a game.
Whisper to me softly, come and take my hand.
Want to take me with them, to a place beyond.
Lost and can't remember, find my way back home.
Don't you see me in here, I am not a name.
If you close your eyes now, believe that I am true.
Come with me I'll show you, least you doubt no more.
Once I was a being, heart that beat within.
Now I'm but reflections, of who I may have been.
Mine is not a fable, not a story nor.
Will I ever be, an unreflected soul?
Once that I cross over, time will be no more.
If you see my Mommy, tell her I'm a girl.

Cathy Oiterong

Sleep My Baby Sleep

Sleep, my brown eyed baby, sleep,
Even though for you I weep.
You are at peace and finally at rest,
If I only knew, to you I'd have been the very best.
It's too late now you're gone from me,
No matter what I do or say you will never again be.
So sleep, my baby, sleep,
Your love and memories I will always keep.
You'll always have a place in my heart,
Until I also depart.
Then I will never again have to weep,
So sleep, my baby, sleep.

Carol Maxwell

The Future

The future is ten minutes, the future is ten years, the future
Is tomorrow, the future comes for years.

When you think of the future you think of our kids, our kids
Are the future, they make good from what bad we did.

So clean up the streets, recycle the paper, and respect the
Earth for the upcoming birth.

Angela C. Pauline

"Wouldn't It Be Great"

Wouldn't it be great to be lifted up and taken
far away. Taken to a place where there is an open
field that goes beyond what our eyes can behold.

>We could run as fast as we want.
>We could laugh until we roll in the grass.
>We could play lots of games.
>We could watch the waters of the ocean rush to shore.
>We could watch the sun rise and set.
>We could feel the gentle breeze as it touch our faces
> and the morning dew as it wet our heads.
>We could hear the birds singing as they begin their day.

We could rejoice and say, "this is the day that the Lord
has made; we are rejoicing and are glad in it.

Wouldn't it be great?

C. Lorraine Butler

Mood

I seem to be in a somber mood
that doesn't match this sunny day,
this mild fall day
with a gentle breeze
that blows the fallen crispy leaves.
These days are a gift
before the coming cold.
But my mind isn't here for it.

I need to find a peaceful place
inside this mind that wants to race
a quietness, an easiness, a trustingness
that I don't need to do anything
or plan to do anything,
just being really here, always
and on this gentle sunny day
with the breeze on my face
and the warmth in my bones,
that is enough.

Margaret Dubay Mikus

The Sea

The sea creeps silently in,
Then in its final moment,
It roars for all the world to hear,
No one notices.

Its icy fingers reach out to grasp the shore,
Rejected,
It slips silently back,
Beginning its long journey once more.

So too am I like the sea,
I come softly,
No one notices.

To let my presence be known,
I cry out,
No one hears.

I reach out to grasp reality,
Rejected,
I silently go back into my own world.

Waiting, waiting for someone to reach out,
Someone to care,
Someone to take me from my sea of loneliness.
   Mary Ann White

The Lord's Seraphim

Nocturnal masses of flesh are strewn across the landing, down stairs and in the foyer. Glistening spittle dried on these lamb's lips, the bomb went off in everyone's head and left them ignorant to the dry, live world, I passed angry thoughts and ducked out of reach so they didn't get in my hair; they were looming of lightings and columns. Playful lust casted its shroud into bedrooms, leaving violet shines of sweat and smell over canopies. I fell in a hole in the carpet and looked to see that the fear had caught me. "Don't fight" said the man swinging in my head. "Stand into its wirey face, let him rape your femininity, rapture a wet human body", "steal his awe, power and strengths, then let him rot and fester in his own excrements", I fell down, to orgasmic and trembly I fought to walk. My glassy eyes were fixed upon my candidate for hate, my evil came out of its pungent shell. I gashed him with fiery nails, licked blood from his neck, hardening him as he fell in a crimson tide. I stood and spat on a weak man. I got what I came for, I ran to the glass balcony door and beyond it. I fell from mountains, castle of the souls, glass engraving tokens of love on my calm skin. Escaping my human body before death, I then watched my white coffin hit waves so hard it was split. My powder blue legs folded up as white strong wings flew my solid soul to my heavens, a bird of beast, a messenger of God.
   Suzzie Paramito

A Thought Of An American Woman

A tear rolled down her cheek,
Her heart cried, "Why do we fight for these people?"
She cried for the women of this far away land.
How cruel are these people.
Fighting for a people with hearts of ice,
How cruel are these people.
A mother begs to feed her child.
Where is father now?
How cruel are these people.
Cheers in the square,
Another woman is stoned to death,
How cruel are these people.
Shadows in the streets,
Forbidden to show their face,
How cruel are these people.
She cries for the women of this land,
They'll never know real freedom,
How cruel are these people.
A tear rolls down her cheek.
   Pocho

Untitled

My life is as calm as a still pool
Content with myself I am no one's fool.
Unaware I saw not it coming
There you stood so young and charming
You take my hand my poor heart flutters
A wave appears upon the surface of my water
Is this right? Are you the one?
My anxious spirit ponders on
Fear like none ever known before
Quivers within, Do I have control?
I feel as thought I am falling
I keep hearing your voice calling
Running forward I know not where
I feel only tenderness when you are there
A mist is rising sweet and cool
But what has happened to my pool?
Calm has gone. Love has come.
I answered your call
Now my life resembles a beautiful waterfall.
   Stephanie Dawn

Nature's Hostage

It is dawn again, the tide is rushing in
Catapulting the waves upon earth's rocky walls,
I sit here and ponder what could be my crushing sin,
No answers are apparent, my heart falls.

High noon illuminates the full sun's light
Producing diamonds dancing on white capped waves,
I feel there should be hope somewhere in my fight,
Yet my sole seems lost in deep dark caves.

Dusk brings the bounding race of the day's last tide
Causing the same endless painful pounding,
I see the unlearned repetitions of my life's ride,
Maybe there is some redemption is my sounding.

Night arrives with a soothing grace radiated by the moon's lore,
The waves slow, simply tickling and teasing their counterpart,
Death has stolen him through it's impassible door,
My perpetual relentless dawns are the only place to start.
   Sally Ruff-Martin

Why The Violence

 I don't know why
people want others to die
why violence is becoming more and more
or why there is a such thing called war
why we have knives, bombs, cannons, and guns
or why people kill their husbands, wives, daughters, and sons

 I don't know why
when people see violence, they only sigh
why when you ask who opposes it, you hear me, me, me
but violence is what you still see
many oppose, few try to stop it
it's getting worse little by little; bit by bit

 I don't know why
love, peace, and happiness people deny
why more don't try to make violence cease
or why we don't live in a world of peace
why violence instead of love becomes more and more
or why we don't live in a place without war
   Joseph Mancuso

Mediocrity

If I'd the nerve to punch his nose
When first he started to impose
His threat of mediocrity
On what I called my being free
Then maybe once or maybe twice
He might have thought it somewhat nice
To live the life that I choose to
Still he could do what he must do

But... then again, to strike a blow
Is something that I surely know
Would never get my point across
At twice the work and twice the cost.

And so I watched him in his ways
And found about them much to praise
I set about to make a plan
To be somewhat a different man.

Although it seemed to work for him my future seemed to me so dim
I gave up on my guiding light and wandered out into the night.

And though I fall and stumble much I still retain the magic touch
Of getting by and being free and shunning mediocrity.

Roger G. Cortes

He Is There

I see Him in the flowers that grow
  to brighten life's rough way.
I see Him in the children He's loaned
  us for this day.

I see Him in the mountains tall
  that reach to touch the sky.
  Seeing Him in everything brings gladness
  to my life, if I but open my eyes and see.

I hear Him in the wind that blows, the
  rain that falls, the creek that flows.
I hear Him when the thunder rolls and
  lightning glows.
I know I can hear Him in everything if I but listen.

I touch Him when the gentle breeze brings quiet
  joy to my heart.
I touch Him when I touch the hand of a little
  trusting child.
I can reach out and touch Him, if I but only believe,
  He's here and there and everywhere, if I would only reach.

Hazel T. Hill

Dad, We Love You

There was a person in our lives
whom we loved with our hearts and minds
he was awake when we slept
to take care of us when we rest

Then one day he fell sick
on the bed he lay deep in sleep
Oh! Mother we failed to keep
when it was time for him to leave

Though it's many years since that fateful day
it appears it occurred yesterday
many a day may come to pass
but the grief in us will ever last

You are always there in our hearts
and in the memories of the days past
we love you more than we ever did
as a part of us you shall ever live.

Sudhakar Rajamannar

Winter World

Winter is a glorious time;
There is brilliance all around-
Icicles gleaming from the eaves
While snow glistens on the
ground.
Yes, winter brightens up our lives
With its overcoat of white. It's
fun to walk in snow by day. And gaze
out at it by night.

The winter world is like a movie
With scenes forever changing; Where
once snow made specific views, Now the
snow is rearranging. We know that
soon all this will end, Into
spring we'll soon reenter; But out thoughts
and hopes carry on
To next year's would of
winter.

Barbara Turner

Sweet Love

  Heaven put us together, me and you!
For a future of happiness. Strong and true.
A bond of love from two to one.
  Before there was darkness,
and now there's sun.
  Twinkles of gleam stars of light.
Our love so full shining bright.
Forever a future from above.
  For me and you this bond,
our most precious
  Sweet Love!

James Etue

Out Cast

I stand in a field full of people
yet, I stand alone.
Everyone's talking and playing with joy
yet, I stand alone.
Staring and being as quiet as the oxygen in the air
I can move and I can talk
yet, when I try, nothing happens,
everyone here and everyone there
but, I still stand alone.
When all leave and have gone for the day
I stand alone.
No way to go, yet, no where to go
I guess I do what I always have
so, I stand alone.

Aaron Davis

Ode To A Friend

I remember you well my friend,
Your gentle smile and twinkling eyes.
Even when your life came to an abrupt end,
I know you're above in the Heavenly skies.

The talks we had and the laughs we shared
Only you knew me so very well,
For you were the only one who cared
And the secrets we had, I still won't tell.

Many things have happened over the years
I still need to feel your warm embrace.
And my eyes still fill with lonely tears
But I know in Heaven you've found grace.

You'll always be my best and closest friend
For there is no one else like you.
So until the day my life comes to an end,
I'll treasure our memories, like new.

Christy H. Kinsey

Class

I have nothing to say,
so I wont say it.
Words, sentences, thoughts,
where did they go?
Rushing through my head like, like
speeding cars.

But to me, it's rush hour.

I see myself behind the wheel,
doing ninety.
Ever so smoothly, I lean over
whispering petits fours nothings into her ear.
But what am I saying,
I can't hear myself,
it's all happening so fast, so loud
my mind races

Stop.
Red light.

Let the Others go ahead.
I'll just sit back and think
of something to say.
Jonathan Beninson

Friendships

Someone to talk to when you are down,
Someone you hoped would always be around.

Someday that friend will go away,
taking hopes that you will stay,
good friends forever,
that might be the way.

Then someday you will come across,
that friend you thought you lost.

You see what time can do,
to that friend you thought you knew.

That friend doesn't act the same,
you might think the whole relationship was just a game.

On that day you come across,
that friend you thought you lost.

Just think of all the wonderful times you had together,
and vanish the thought that your life was ruined forever.
Jennifer Fabianski

"Halloween"

Halloweens a holiday that's really keen,
But it gives me chills and invades my dreams.
There's witches running around with brooms-
And goblins ready to fly over the moon!
Black-cats hunch-backed are ready to pounce-
While skeletons invade every house.
It's enough to make anyone scream,
But I still love it when it's Halloween!
There's cookies, candy, fruits and things
And every child knows when it's Halloween.
Dressed as ghost and ghouls and by all means,
Begging tricks and treats are the spookiest I've seen.
There's Halloween party's and apple dunkin-
And look what happens to a silly ol' pumpkin,
Cut big eyes and then a ghastly smile,
A ol' jack-o-lantern makes me jump a mile!
So when autumn comes and night winds scream,
With haunting sounds of bats and things,
Don't be scared that it's all not a dream-
Just be happy that it's Halloween!
Darold Deaton Fry

Untitled

I feel sometimes like a bird in a cage
black mesh all around - as cold as steel
unable to spread my wings as I wish to do.
Not living a life - like it's fully real.

My mind is free to roam as I wish
Museums, the arts, beautiful seas
but my body is encaged - it cannot move
even my spirit is wanting release.

Shall I remain in this cage and
cease to grow?
With body old - wrinkled and gray
No, I'll spread my wings and break this cage,
Escaping these bars to soar away.
Marie Packard

The Darkest Of Creatures

Ruby red like a garnet ring,
lush like an apple on a weighted limb,
through the thinnest veil of a trailing cloud,
there's a top and bottom to the rising sun.

Mauve sucks chocolate from the passing cloud
while the bottom half of a fading moon
settles slowly on the other dawn
like a passing sweep of an eagle's wing.

The fading done, an amber ring,
lush like a peach on a brighter limb,
bursts in flame like a blazing log
spitting lemon in the strongest eye,

and even the raven, dipping his beak,
with a swarthy swashing of fanned out wings,
proves to the world with his fashion of play
that the darkest of creatures have something to say.
James Clark Batts

The Eyes Mind

The eyes sees it all be it big or be it small
The eye sees the colors so vivid and clear
The eye sees far and the eye sees near
The eye sees Tragic
And the eye sees fear
The eye sees all that can been seen
But most important
The eye can see the joy and happiness the
Mind can perceive

And the mind is the recorder of all the eye
Has seen
And what the mind has stored will forever
Be in the eyes mind
Davis Raver

Amanda

Almost felt like thee ultimate dream
The most unbelievable night of my life
Ending with that terrible word: Good-bye
I wish she was still here
Think about her every second and every blink of an eye
The glorious night we had will always be remembered
The word the night ended with will also: Good-bye
After that night I didn't have to sleep
I already had my dream
Next morning I felt something through my heart
As I thought about her and the last; Good-bye
Scott Gacki

My Thoughts

As I was washing the dishes the other day
These thoughts came to me as I started to pray

I was thanking God for the love and care he gave
to me the day before
As to the out patient operating room I had to go

The Lord loves and looks after me every day and night
And he never lets me out of his sight

He only asks that I love him with all of my heart
I should always thank him and tell him I love him
before the day starts

I thought to myself do I really live each day as I should
But does anyone of us try as hard as we could

We take life and every day so much for granted
We don't stop and thank him for the beautiful
things he has planted

How much time do we spend reading and studying our Bible
each day
How often do we stop doing our chores and start to pray

Lord I just ask that you keep blessing me each day
And for the rest of my life close to you I'll try to stay

Mildred Dillon

World Without End

One day the world must change and all the madness shall
come to an end.

For there will be no suffering nor pain and all our hatred
and love will blend.

For our love for one another will cease as with the world
filled with beasts.

There will be no more breaths taken for we shall all be
shaken.

God will take us one day and none of us will have a say.

It will be one way or the other Satan or another.

Katherine Ford

The Beast

Stalking the jungle, swift and eager,
Moving with grace, a glimpse of grandeur.
Threatening the very being of innocence,
Merciless to the plight of sad ignorance.

The sleek, smooth power overwhelms,
Animal instinct perfectly performs.
Posing, in a ready position,
Awaiting the prey, the object of abduction.

Choosing a target to fulfill her hunger,
She lunges quickly, the kill to be sure.
Savagely sinking her claws within,
Devouring the helpless, with need or sin.

The task completed, she quaintly moves along,
Satisfied for now, perhaps till dawn.
Conquering the quest, her lust for flesh,
She leaves the soul to wither and perish...

Again the night, loins burning,
Again the crave, a renewed yearning.
She sits upon the bar stool, ready to feast,
Transforming into man's lonely ecstasy... The beast.

Ted Trejo

I See

I see a house standing on a cloud, I wish one day
I can reach up and touch one.
I see silent doves and white unicorns flying
grace fully through the deep blue sky.
I see the sky touching the ocean as far as thee
eye can see.
I see me one sweet day with wings when I become
an angel.
I see myself in a past life wishing on a bright
shooting star, wishing that one day I will be able
to reach up into the night sky and hold the hands
of God.

Heather L. Carpenter

"Lost Love"

There is a man, I Love so much
it's deep with all my heart
But for some reasons that were beyond
our control; we were made to part.
As I sit here now, and look
Back in time of how I thought it would be;
I had stars in my eyes and a thorn
in my pride can't help wonder why your
not with me?
I hope that Life will treat you
well, and I know you will Go Far;
And if By chance you think of me,
in my heart is where you are!
Someday I will get over you,
But never will I forget.
Because your memories are in my
mind, along with my regret!

Stacey L. Bruce

Captivity

A spider's web is threaded across my way.
Raising my hand to tear it down...
I see the spider alerted, and guarding her prey.
A large brown beetle is hanging bound.
Renewing its struggle as I touch the web...
it is hope filled, anticipating freedom now.
Its captivity is made instead...
a bit more secure by her gossamer thread.

Marion Nelson

Senseless Tragedy

Impoverished in an unknown world, a world one cannot see
perceptibility is not a choice
and virginity cannot be.

A rhyme misspelled without a cause, or trashed for its unworthy
grace
rooted with the mourning botan
whose realm will never be traced.

Lament the souls of the dying few, whose worldly song was such:
"I once was found but now I'm lost..."
their sadness is far too much.

A weapon disclosed in sorrow, inside a mind so dim,
though not in talent or comprehension,
but with where their hearts have been.

To try so hard and live so somber, is not a lifelong dream
so long as selfism exists inside
their souls are personally redeemed.

An internal duel of broken dreams, with a slice, a pull, or a pill
a do-it-yourself to happiness
their souls remain here still.

Leigha Marie Ward

A Mother's Memories

Once again it's Mother's Day
So many tears I've wiped away
From little faces when they were hurt or sad
Or couldn't have their way and they got mad
The tender touch from a little child
Makes everything seen worthwhile
From a broken wagon to a headless doll
God gave me the know-how to fix them all
Then came the time to put the toys away
Because the children were too big to play
A car is the next thing on their mind
They want to drive it all the time
Their girlfriends and boyfriends they brought to our home
because they had no desire to roam
Then comes the prom and other things
And then it's time for wedding rings
With a tear in your eye you give them away
On their happy wedding day
Then you realize it's not the end
Because they will always be your friend.
Nancy Nissen

My Sisters And Me

Black Woman filled with grace
Black Woman a smile upon her face
Black Woman eager and strong
Black Woman knows where she belongs.

Black Woman sophisticated and unique
Black Woman from her head to her feet
Black Woman confident and in control
Black Woman knows how to play the role.

Black Woman filled with wisdom as old
Black Woman faith fills her soul
Black Woman tears are sometimes poured
Black Woman knows help comes from her Lord.

Black Woman never sips of tea
Black Woman drinks black brewed coffee
Black Woman knows what it takes
Black Woman no need to imitate.

Black Woman, Daughter of Pearl, Mother of Gold
Black Woman this is what I've been told
Black Woman, Princess of Spirit, Queen of Destiny
Behold, Black Woman, My Sisters and Me.
Sandra I. Williams

Old Sailor's Prayer

Blow gentle breeze be kind to me today withhold your glee to bring a harsh wind my sails are old and would easily tare before your gale. My decks are bleached by age and warped by seas that through the years have sprayed my bough and washed my decks a salty white. I can handle the gentle running swells while swinging on my anchor the rise and fall of the tides disturb me little though my chain is brittle and thin from clinging barnacles. The phantom crew which awake with each reveille and go to rest at taps no longer maintain the watch for long ago the boatswain's pipe was silenced. So gentle breeze blow softly I do not wish to heave or pitch today let the strains of your music that whistle through my guys and stays and around my mast be forever gentle oh soft wind be kind to me today.
William W. Gaines

"My Sweet Child"

Where have you gone, my sweet child?
Into the shadows, you are lost.
My heart is searching for you in the night.
You are gone into the dark, cold frost.
My mind is searching for you in your dreams.
You are the victim of her thoughtless crime.
Why can't I find you, my sweet child?
Are you lost in the spaces of time?
My body is searching for you, on these drug-littered streets,
But I cannot feel your tender, soft skin.
Your silky blond hair brushes against my face,
And I awaken from my dreams again.
I touch my face, I feel you there.
I touch my heart, you are there too.
I touch my body, you are inside.
And, I touch my mind, I've found you.
We are one in the same, my sweet child.
She chased you away long ago.
But now that I've found you, inside of me,
Have no worries, I'll never let go...
Shannon Mayfield

Oklahoma City Bombing

I am a young child. A child who is stuck in all the debris.
Debris covering all my friends. Friends who are dead for no reason.
Reasonable people just don't kill innocent children.
Children who were once alive, now dead.

Me, I wish I could join my friends
So I will not suffer any longer
Longer and longer the wait seems to be.
Being frightened is the worst feeling of all.

All is quiet around this building.

Building a staircase to Heaven soon,
if no one finds me.

Me, I am slowly fading, fading,
gone.

I am a young child.
Suzanne Scott

You And I In A Clear Blue Sky

You and I in a clear blue sky,
White cotton clouds dance with joy, Gentle noonday breeze
disturbed not our thoughts,
golden sun touches our inner warmth, Birds enchanting sweet song
fill the heart.

You and I in a fading sky,
Clouds gray tremble in discontent, resentment flairs in restless breeze,
Fearful sun hides in cool dark, Birds fearful chatter pierce the heart.

You and I in a darkened sky,
Colliding clouds fury no longer contained, Angry lightning's sharp
words pierce,
Violent thunder replies rumble rage, Frigid air hardens hostile heart.

You and I in a blackened sky,
Black cloud's anger overtake with vengeance, Howling winds sting
with tempers green,
Wild rains pelt bitterness, frightened bird cower in fear.

You and I in a gray-pink sky,
Gentle white clouds soothe black anger, Howling winds calm in
still air,
Crimson sun reaches to embrace, Weeping birds' tears turn silent thoughts.

You and I in a clear blue sky,
Cloud's feather white tickle laughter, Joyous sun rays spread
peaceful happiness,
Bird's sweet song fills rejoicing heart, Radiant rainbow's treasure
reflects friendship forever.
Ruth Douthett

"Two Little Girls"

Both as lovely as a flower.
Both as sweet as can be.
Straight and true as an ivory tower,
Flowing and pure as a sunset at sea.

Two hearts, tow great minds,
Two arms, two legs, one body so pure.
Love and respect, the ties that binds,
There needs together so great and sure.

A sister named abigail,
And a sister named brittany.
No need for hearts to wail,
Our love for each is for eternity.

Now you know we are twins,
Not the same you usually know.
Our love and kindness always wins,
Were together as the four winds blow.

The Lord made us
as we are today,
His reason is not ours to question.
Just his Godly rules to obey,
To be close again in the glory of heaven.

William R. Noland

Link Me

Link me, please, to the trees.
   Link me to a quiet breeze.
Link me to the mountain streams.
   Link me to your Springtime dreams.
Link me to the meadow's flowers.
   Link me to gentle showers.
Link me to daises, in a row.
   Link me to a rainbow's glow.
Link me to the Summertime.
   Link me to a nursery rhyme.
Link me to the Autumn's call.
   Link me to the mountains tall.
Link me to a snowflakes's sound
   Link me to the snow on the ground.
Link me to life's simple things.
   Link me not to diamond rings.
Link me to the mountain air.
   Link me to thee, with love, not despair

Nancy Ellen

Midnight Hunt

The light glistened in my eye,
from the moon, while I ran through the rye.
Peaceful to the extreme that I could.
I didn't elude you, you saw where I stood.

I ran and pleaded you let me alone,
you still raised your gun aiming to own.
I ran from the weeds, my legs did strain,
but I couldn't run away from your persistent aim.

My knees hit the ground, I was left at your wait.
I thought of my life and its ending fate.
Because of lost time, escape was not enough.
I saw you rise checking my bluff.

You stood in the foliage with your hand on the trigger.
But you released the finger your conscience was bigger.
Was it compassion, or my antlers too small?
Will your poaching continue, or your blood lust fall?

But no matter of this, do what you will.
Just let it be known, it's me you won't kill.
I ran from you as fast as I could,
to live another day, the sky as my hood.

Jeremy Johnson

"Spiral Time"

Slowly fading 'way, the sunlit day-
Skyline bright, clouds pink, red, and white.

Darkness near, chill wind in the air-
Goodnight Sun, rise Eve, Day is done.

Twilight speaks, grey shadows bleak-
Venus rise, shine vivid in eyes.

Moonlight bright, all through the night-
Starlight too, gleaming midnight blue.

Day will come with new dawning Sun-
Then more night, a spiral time flight.

Course so real, time is but a wheel-
Round and round, no ending, no bounds.

Laurie Graham

Not A Sparrow Falls

I saw you fall along the way, when no other eyes beheld you.
Your wounds were deep and so severe, I wondered what could I do.
I knew you must be broken when I saw you take the fall, but the wounds you had were not fresh wounds, they had been there for awhile.

As I looked I saw a scar the engravement in it read discouragement, it was so deep and running blood from a friend it said was sent. Then there was another even worse than the one before, it said I don't love you anymore. Many more I did see, but then I saw the part, I knew that I could never fix, it was a broken heart.
Then I saw to my surprise two tender loving hands in them was a healing balm not made by any man. They picked you up and oh so gentle was the touch. The bleeding wounds the broken heart for them was not too much. I then saw you rise his hands they held you up, they seemed to know you needed them and then they held a cup. It was so full of love and spilling over with compassion. You could drink until you were filled from it, you were not rationed. Right there before my eyes I beheld a mighty wonder, an Angelic wing came down and there you were placed under. Never more to despair of life's slings and arrows, for there you'll find shelter and peace among the fallen sparrows.

Sandra Weaver

Don't Be Afraid

We'll never know if tomorrow will come
so we must do our best until the day is done.
Say what you mean and mean what you say
Cause we don't know if we have one more day.
Don't be afraid to show how you feel
Especially if your feelings are real.
Who's to say you can tell him tomorrow?
Tell him today so you'll both know.
Live for the moment and not for the day
And hopefully things will go your way.
Hold on tight and enjoy the ride
Enjoy each day; take it all in stride.
Take the good with the bad
the right with the wrong
The nice with the nasty
the dance with the song.
Hold on to your dreams and make them come true
And never be afraid to show the real you.

Rebekka Corey

Footsteps

Fading footsteps,
water marks on the floor,
how do I say what you are?
When you go to your inner sanctum
To explore the past,
you notice the footsteps fading fast.
Near a crack in the floor,
near a crack in the past,
how do you explain what you were?
How can you complain about what you aren't?
I take my life one footstep at a time,
and whether the things of my life stay or go,
they will always be mine.
    John T. McDowell

"Time Undefined"

Given the fall and the flaw of the aeons
Seeing the passage of dust, eroding the land and
Weathering the soil

Lines of age coarsen the sides of the mounts and
faces of those who would not otherwise show
The features of turmoil

Wisdom is unerring, a profound abstraction, and yet
May rend he particles which build upon selves to
Define the light of the halo

With renewed vigor and hope springs thus
The sound of vision, and the vision of music
Reaching the final crescendo

The magic of life, newfound and august
And death, the bold nether twin to be nevermore feared
Hold the intrepid in thrall

Unearthing the verity: New life waxes and wanes eternal
Neither originating nor concluding
It exists, and that is all
    Suzanne Bonney

Untitled

Any day I doubt you
Any day I fear
Everyday without you
is everyday I wish you were here

When my feeling makes no sense
and my confidence begins to fade
it breaks down all of my defense
and I question the trust that we have made

When I look in a mirror
and I'm running out of things to do
Somewhere in the distance I can hear
Someone calling me a fool
but when the leg I stand on is my last
and I question what I believe
any fear, any doubt, or negative feeling that I have
crumbles like an autumn leaf
because no matter how hard negativity tries
to draw my eyes from the truth
there is always a sudden end to its demise
by one simple thing: my faith in you.
    Mark Allen

A Net To Catch My Silver Tears

I'm building a net of silver thread to
catch my tears in mourning for the dead.

I cry for the mothers who've lost their sons,
who left for battle with hope and guns.

I cry for the men of the blue and the gray
who will never see another day.

I pray that no man has died in vain,
but I cry for those who are caused hurt and pain.

I cry for the day that I will see
when my boy does not come back to me.

I cry for all my angers and fears
so I build a net to catch my tears.
    Erin Rainey

Natures Vision

   The beauty of sunsets
the wind in the pines,
the pride of the Rockies
and the tall growing vines.
   The bed of red roses
is like the carpet of green grass,
and the sweet golden sun which is the color of brass.
   Nature provides such lovely things,
such as the space for an eagle to spread out its wings.
   The earth that we walk upon,
brings all living creatures life and energy to keep walking on.
   These wonderful things makes me want to keep on wishin'
that I could live in natures vision.
    Felicia Sewolt

The Names Upon "The Wall"

There is a place in Washington, located on the Mall,
Where Americans pay honor to the Names upon "The Wall."

It's not a place of glory, a monument straight and tall.
Earth's pulled apart, to reveal her heart,
etched with each Name upon "The Wall."

A wound that tore this nation, divided one and all,
Is bound together by our love for the Names upon "The Wall."

Those who come here understand the price was paid by all,
The families, friends, and lovers of the Names upon "The Wall."

So when the winds of war do blow, and other nations call,
Make decisions based upon the wisdom of the Names upon "The Wall."

People of America - understand and listen all,
Each of you is accountable to the Names upon "The Wall."

Flowers and flags, pictures and poems—symbols are they all,
Of a nation's love and indebtedness to the Names upon "The Wall."

And when our days on earth are o'er, and we hear the distant call,
We will be united with the Names upon "The Wall."

So teach your children, every one, so that they can recall,
The sacrifice of, and reason for, each Name upon "The Wall."

God watches over this place, and those who come to see "The Wall."
Guardian angels walk among us; they're the Names upon "The Wall."
    Catherine Mooney

Winds Of Yesterday's Tomorrow

Rose petals fall in the depth of the shadows
When it comes time for dusk to end.
Skies will fill with black tinge as midnight approaches.
Leaves dance with the sense of death around them.
Winds create the music of change
As a new day comes near.
Branches move gracefully to the voice of
The unknown whispers.
Captured souls will try to escape from the
Lonely hands of emptiness.
Fires die from the suffering of too much
Pain that people inflict.
Each energy will be renewed for a new beginning.
Mist rises from grounds that have a resurfaced past.
Silent beats of drums are heard in distant memories.
Cries of sorrow, tears of sadness, and the
Pain of love are now owned and cherished by the
Winds of Yesterday's Tomorrow.
Jennifer Lee Zsido

When Will It End?

It's hard to think with a head full of pain.
They have nailed me to the oak cross.
And when I walk it drags behind me.
I am the Electric Messiah
The descendant locked away.
In this dark room,
In this dark century
Is it any wonder the world sickens and dies?
I don't know how many times I have to say this,
I am sane, I am perfectly and completely sane
We are the acid scarred victims of history of evil
And hypocrisy
Exalt criminals to office, Vietnam, El Salvador,
Chile with lovely Missiles roaring,
Bombs of the rich and the poor and the pious.
And they burned the children,
And tortured the women,
Forever and ever amen
Heather Willcox

Butterflies

When I was very young, no more than seven springs,
I used to capture butterflies
And hold their trembling wings within my tiny hand.
And then I'd let them fly again.
I did not understand the why of it,
But sensed in growing,
I had no right to halt their going.

Now being older, closer to winter than to spring.
I found a butterfly in you,
And for a moment, just as then
I did not want to let you go.
You charmed me so.

But I am wise as any child and know I have no right
To stop or slow your flight.
The strings I use to bind all things are even looser now,
So when I say "You're free," I know you'll go,
But even so, I will have other springs
And always the sweet remembrance
Of having touched
Your velvet wings.
Julie McHale

Ashes

Self doubt widens the cracks.
Like a ravenous flame, it licks at the heart of me.
It laughs as the fibers of my being blister, then boil,
    and finally disintegrate.
I am a pile of ashes again, and here comes the wind...

It takes ever so long to gather me up,
to make something that looks like a woman in charge of her life.
I'm so tired of sweeping the pieces together,
of losing some and finding some, and never knowing
when it will all come apart again,
or if there will ever be enough glue.

You can see light through porcelain, but sometimes it shatters,
especially when dropped from great heights.
Sometimes you just can't repair it.
Sometimes there's just a fine dust and a faint sadness remaining.
Sometimes lovely things just don't exist anymore...

All I want is the soft comfort of my knowing.
All I want is the mercy of living honestly.
All I want is the sweet peace of loving myself for that.
I can almost remember what it was like before the dust,
    and the wind, and the rain.
Dear God, lift me up... carry me Home again.
Teryl Moyer Carpenter

Loveburn

I saw him again,
And I know he saw me.
The distance between us,
Causes me too much pain.
We never really said good-bye.
He'll always be with me... In the
Shadows of my mind.
When Cupid shot his arrow,
In my heart it was buried deep.
And when the time came to rip it out,
It really made me bleed.
My heart has since been hardened;
So, my love is not a free.
The time that I spent thinking about him,
That he can't give back to me.
When I see him next, I'll be more careful,
Not to hang on to the past.
I just don't want this pain to last.
Cassandra Riedl

Incomprehensibilities

Beneath the window
the street's
hot humid air
presses her face
in whispers of song.

   There's a beat
   like engines rev
   Trees sway in the breeze
   a promise and a kiss.

   Tonight, though, lock your door inside your heart
   for passions warm in the rain of a summer so tender.

   And she asks why?

She breathes because she presses her lips to the glass

For the darkness is like that
in mornings of youth.

Pavement is hot
the stone soft
against cold muscles
of flesh, life and-
incomprehensibilities.
D. J. Saint Amant

Marq

A little boy with lots to do.
He's always in a hurry too.
Running, jumping, flying high.
Skipping, hopping, asking why.
Questions, questions every day
"What does that mean? What's that say?"
Doesn't like a lot of squeezin'
Loves a joke and lots of teasin'.
He's enough to wear me out!
What is this boy all about?
I will tell you what I know
He may have wild oats to sow.
But deep down in his heart he cares.
He has lots of love to share.
One more thing I'll say to you,
From my heart, I love him too.
  Sue Neilsen

The Angels Among Us

In this world there
are angels among us,
They walk with us through all our hard times,
and make sure we make it through them.
They show us the light,
When we are in complete darkness.
They hold our hands and tell us everything will be ok,
When were positive it won't.
When we are all in denial,
They are the ones who tell us the truth.
If ever we need someone,
They will always be there.
These angles that are among us
Are our true friends.
  Heather Arnett

'Til We Live Again

Once upon a time I met a pretty girl
A Princess I thought, as emotions began to swirl

The beauty she offered filled my every need
And with her as my goal, I hoped to succeed

Her hair was gorgeous, with eyes to match
Being the perfect young lady, for me to catch

We feel in love as our time was going by
And from that moment, she's been the "Apple of my Eye"

It was years later, when she went on without me
Creating an emptiness, that may always be

Since she's the only woman I've ever loved so
My heart's with her always, forever in tow

If good fortune exists, we'll meet again
Fulfilling those dreams we'd let begin

And make it last thru life's hardships and fun
Completing our circle that's not yet done

Every day's been the same, since I still care
I miss her every moment, with so much to share

Until I hold her again, my life'll stand still
Growing old alone, 'Till The Day She Will.
  W. Richard Berry

My Fight For Life

Now that the cancer is gone, and I am free once more
I have decided not to walk thru death's door
I will leave this place called life when the time is right
Be it during the day or late at night
My family and friends have helped me through
With lots of time not knowing what to do
Thank you those who worried so I am not going to die I told you so
It's time for me to live again to pull my life around this bend
As each day goes by I am learning to walk a straighter mile
And have even found how to greet pain and sadness with a smile
I have learned what is real and what is make believe
I think I am learning to be more tolerant with others and myself
And that one cannot really give until one gives of himself
I am learning to appreciate the days that hurry by
To be content and realize that there is no one as rich as I.
To those who need it take his hand
And God will guide you through this savage land.
  Angelo J. Digregorio

A Shakespearean Sonnet

Two lovers kept at a distance so great
Bore forbidden love for one another
For they inherited such adored hate
For the families belonging to each other
Still, two kept sacred trysts by night
By day the families brutally fought
And since love, heaven-sent was blind to there sight,
Reasons to stop warlike-acts were not sought
In faith, the date of nuptials was set
In hopes of ending the feud of the past.
But that set date was of their debt
Debt of their lives to the devil's repast
For love as theirs could not be shared by all
Since love was naught in such a senseless brawl.
  Marie Cheng

Writing Poetry

I'm making love again
And I'm writing poetry
There was always a new connection
Between the two activities

There about 5 billion poems I could write
I never wrote a poem directly about unsanity
although I've been there.
But I think I'm going to stop writing poetry now
Because wherever I write a poem
I think of making love desperately
And I want it was too much
(And for this seems it's unavailable)
To radiate a poetry
  Bonnie Totherow

In The Masters Hands

As I watched the ruler of the canvas of life,
creating a masterpiece was his goal.
His brush strokes were with great confidence,
so as to bring a calm to my soul.
His look of power shown from above,
Yes, the look on his face told a story of love.
"Too much too soon will ruin the work I am doing."
As I looked at the work, I said to him,
"When shall it be done, for I've waited so long."
"Are you not willing to accept the look of incompletion,
patience, I am creating a beautiful song."
  George E. Lane Jr.

The Idea Of Medicine
David Nalen 1958-1995
The night swells fitfully and far
From factory smoke and diesel roar and city shapes
One lantern's belljar light illuminates
The pond the water lilies water snakes

Which slither past and on and through the grass
Then disappear braid by bone by curve
Against the black and fierce the long
Hiss of tongues that fling and flick and swerve

Is all we hear and we forget what we
Believe the near embrace of this disease
That coils and chokes is quick to shut
Like ice like lightning the asp and frieze

Around this night that wrap the world in code
Honeyed webs of light the moon the pond
The black black swan all covered in
Asleep now in a time near and beyond
John Crosby

Being Human
At the dawn of life
we emerge into this world like lost creatures,
not knowing in which direction to turn
among our turbulent surroundings.

We are given a conscience,
a mind, a voice,
intelligence, and natural instincts,
yet we feel lost.

We have four things to which we must cling;
faith, hope,
determination, and love.
Without these we are truly lost.

So have faith in thy God and thy self,
forever have hope, for without hope there is nothing,
be determined that you shall find what you seek,
and give forth your love,
for love and you will be loved in return.
John Campbell

Wall Within
Silken fingers, unlined hands,
search for themselves in the wall without:
names in stone, etched in granite,
signs without meaning like an autograph.

Stand aside, listen to them prattle,
hear them argue, the best and the brightest.
Watch them rub, let them polish,
until all that remains are the shadows within.

Touch the wall as they steal away,
feel the tremor of the life within.
Hide the shadows in the folds of your hands;
gather the names in the womb of your mind.

Say the secret words when all is quiet;
say goodbye, say "see you in the world."
And as you leave blow a silent kiss
to the forgotten flowers in the garbage heap.

Shuffle along, don't look back,
hands in your pockets, in your starburst of time.
Shuffle along in the falling light,
gripping the shadows in the wall within.
James Ezra Griffin

Spring
When Winter has ended, Spring brings in a fresh, new, blossom of life to the ever-changing world. Flowers of soft pastel colors burst out of the tarnished soil as if they are trying to gasp for breath after the cold, hard Winter. The trees blossom with what seems to be cheerful, lush green leaves that look as if they have been waiting for the right moment to burst out and show their beauty. The wild animals slowly come out of their hidden hibernation homes under the brush of the meadow. The warm, sweet-tasting rain sweetly falls from the never ending sky. Now nature is rejoicing that the white winter is over and has brought in the new, green, Spring flowing with the colors of life and happiness. For now it is truly Spring.
Leigh McCallen

Barnus P.J. Wilkerson The III
Puppy, puppy running through the trees.
Why are you so full of fleas?

Who gave you this tick-infested coat
and congenital mange around your throat?

Who brought you to this lowly state?
Was it your fate?

You are a pedigree.
I can see.

Do you need someone to give you care
so you won't become bare?

Puppy, puppy running through the trees
this time without mange, ticks, or fleas.
Caroline Mays

The Miracle Of Giving
Give, and you will get a heap
If you sow, you're going to reap
But remember when you sow
Thorns, as well as roses grow.

Don't sow a thorn and expect a rose
That's against the Master's plan
But plant, instead, good deeds that grows
And glows, and make the man.

Give your best, and sift the rest,
Always sow the seed of Love;
As sure as East is far from West,
A guaranteed Harvest from above.

There's joy in giving, like sowing seeds
Like painting the fields with green
But greater joy blooms with the deeds
When roses set the scene.
Henry Jackson

Dreamer
I sat in the sun for hours today,
Watched the breezes blow the clouds away,
The flowers open one by one
And not a speck of work was done.

I sat in the sun for hours today,
And thought of you so far away.
It was so quiet and the sun so warm
The few hours spent should do no harm.

But while I was letting time slip away
One could hear other people say,
She is like a cricket in the sun
Dreams and leaves all her work undone.
Enid C. McNeff

Friendship

A friendship is a cherished relationship that
is one of a kind

One that comes from a mutual understanding
between us mortals, that is very hard to find.

An heartfelt passion to help and to forgive,
A wanting for each other to be healthy and to live.

A relationship of deep feelings,
Where material things or wealth have no meaning.

And when life draws to an end,
There by your side will be your friend.

One friend to another
Ralph L. Cote

Changes

This is life how we made it, people dying oh so fast
People wondering what's causing this chaos
And, how long will these days last
No morals, no respects, and not a care in their head
Spitting in your face as you lay dying on your death bed
Why did they forget about us, we were left to grow up on our own
Caring and loving are feelings that are no longer shown
Not having a Father, Mother's always hard at work
Face's always bearing misery no time for a friendly smirk
So I will continue trying to change life day by day
Wondering when it will once again be safe
For children to go outside and play
Timmy Wolfe

Truth Turns

Broken hearts, broken lives
stillborns pained to respire
creeping shadows-earthworms dwelling

*She was not supposed to be there
opening to me as an emerging horizon*

Labored, corrupted form
slumped into empty rooms
trimmed with stillness-pathetic blue

*Splendor flowing rushing up my spine
prickly rousing fabric tingling my soul*

Patchy makeshift confidence
recycled rekindled dreams
coma silent jolted - folly waking fully

*All eyes turn as she envelopes my life
grave knowledge veiled in deeper understanding*

No trace remaining
of the sinking sorrow
behold the spinning truth-turn the wheel

*My tears moisten the scattered earth
as she rides the potter's tool*
Philip Domenico

The Heart Of A Mother

The heart of a mother is loving and kind
A more precious gift, I couldn't find

A mother who knows when I'm sad or blue
Some have only one, God gave me two

You're always there to lend a hand
More ways than one, you understand

Blest am I more than others
Happy and proud to call you, "Mother"
Martha Skellenger

"The Unfailing Light"

Lord, my soul moves as in strange waters.
Opposing waves of life disturb its assurity,
Tis seen as an overladen ship
Rocked about a troubled journey,
Though commanded, yet found wavering
As rising waters hide its true identity,
Believed to be lost and forsaken
On a lone course to its final destiny.

Man overboard, cries out my soul,
Drifting in waters of life's uncertainty,
Make steady this vessel oh Lord,
Waves of fear overwhelm me on a stormy sea,
Suddenly, out of this troubled vessel
A christ light shines that all heaven can see,
And God knows the light for I hear his voice,
Fear not, be still, Jesus sails the course with thee.
Michael R. Figel

Poverty

What smell doesn't leave?
What smell is of young children who cannot walk?
What smell is of sour milk because the refrigerator doesn't work?
What smell is of rotting garbage?
Poverty, that is the smell.

She needs help, there is no one here to help her.
She won't stay long, just to unfreeze her feet that's all.
You won't help because she is dirty.
She used to be just like you,
she had a job, she was clean.
This is poverty.

She wants to have a future.
She can't have one because she has no money.
Her kids are crying, they are cold.
You don't care, you are warm.
She's smart, she could cure AIDS, yet you still don't care
She tries to stay clean, yet the water is dirty.
Why? Because she is outside now.
You laugh, you stare, you don't care, no you are clean.
This is poverty.
Annoria Friend

Your Love

Your love for me I cannot tell
Even though you caught me when I fell
I dream about you everyday
I wish it would turn out my way

You act like you love me
It's so plain to see
But I'm not sure
If you love is for me

Every single day I pray
That I could be with you everyday
I don't ever want us to be apart
Because if we were it would break my heart

But I don't know how to tell you
I want you to stay
I want to be with you
Each and everyday
Jennifer Bulmer

The Father

As he nears the clearing, he pauses smiling to himself.
He knows he will be home soon.
The eagle greets him as he passes through the meadow.

"My brother, good to see you home!"
The wolf nods, and scanning the tree line,
he looks for a small sign.
A waving leaf or rustling bush.

His eyes settle on a slight movement in the distance.
What could this be?
The two pups, thinking they are hidden, quiver with excitement!

As their father pretends to not see them,
they can no longer hold back the element of surprise!
Leaping together, they head straight for the mighty gray wolf.

Piling on top of him, all three wrestle in the snow.
Peace and joy fill the gray wolf's heart,
traveling with his pups to their den.
    Lea Brown

A Parent's Final Dream

As I lay here waiting for the Lord I asked "Why Lord have you not come for me?"
And I here nothing.
Then I hear a whisper and I say "Lord is that you?"
And I hear no answer.
Time and time goes on and I'm still suffering and waiting and I see a shadow-
"Lord I say is that you?" Yes, I am here with you.
"Why haven't you taken me Lord?"
And the Lord answered, "Because you still have one more lesson to teach your children,
because that is what parents are for.
I asked myself "What else can I teach my children?"
I have taught them how to laugh, how to cry and many other things."
And then I realized the only thing I can teach them is how to die;
with strength and with dignity,
then I felt the Lord touch my lips and I knew I had taught my final lesson.
    JoAnn Lopez

Spare The Tree

It has been said with certainty
That only God can grow a tree.
Man does not seem to understand
That trees are part of God's great plan.

Through the ages trees have provided
Many things required for man's survival.
They've given man wood to keep him warm —
And for shelters to protect him from harm.

Trees have supplied food for man and beast
And haven't seemed diminished in the least.
And even though it was not their duty,
They have delighted man with their beauty.

Let's hope man will display due respect
And before downing a tree he will reflect.
That it has taken years for the tree to grow.
Is it really necessary for it to go?

If it is possible, please spare the tree;
Don't chop it down unless it's a necessity.
Let's let God know that we do understand
That trees are a great gift from God to man!
    Mary F. Green

Field Of My Soul

As I walk through the field of my soul
Winter reigns
The walls around my heart are dark and cold
Like the mountains around the field of my soul
The bare trees whisper haunted thoughts
And I am cold

A man is walking through the field of my soul
His eyes melt the ice I thought could not break
A blood-stained hand reaches out and picks me up
While his tears flood over me

As I walk through the field of my soul
Summer reigns
The buds of my heart blossom and grow
Like the trees around the field of my soul
I sing a love song with the birds
Of a man who made me clean

And I walk with You
    Rachelle Lantis

Moon Walk

Moon walks the night sky.
She shimmers on the distant part of lake
That loves to bask in radiant beams of light.

The queen of sky, distant among the stars,
She hides among the clouds.
Her glory fades away.
Then veiled in mist, obscured,
She reappears and climbs yet
higher still.
    Audrey Williams

A Voice That Speaks Of Freedom

Dedicated to my mother
Oh!, Loud is his voice,
Just meant to be heard,
Standing by Martin (King), the two can compare
Jesse (Jackson) moves on, day-in and night-out
Expressing for freedom,
Loud with a shout
Requesting our rights, to be discrimination free,
Let the brother preach on,
Words are the key!
Liberate the people
teach everyone, to sanction what's right,
Continue to strive, continue to fight,
For the struggle for freedom (All people)
is what's written and right
Jesse's just one man,
who's taken this flight
    Virginia V. King (Sissy)

Flowers Discrimination

Lilies are dillies and Columbine's fine,
But who gives a hoot for the bitterroot?

Laurel is floral and a Zinnia can win ya,
But nobody's crying for the Dandelion.

Everyone knows a Cherokee Rose,
There's sonnet to the Texas Bluebonnet

But hardly a soul would put much stock,
In an Easter corsage of Hollyhock!
    Neil B. Satterfield

My Last Plea

I'm a small frightened child with nowhere to go
My mother doesn't love me for this I do know

I live a nightmare every moment that I'm awake
Because of the spirits that my mother has drank

She calls me to her side, then just pushes me away
And never does she listen to anything I do say

Sometimes she yells and slaps me all around
I sob all night long, can't she hear my small sound

What can I do I love her so very much
I know she drinks, because it's a crutch

Why don't she just see what her life is like
I would do more but I'm just a small tike

They say if she don't stop she soon will die
Then at night no one will hear my soft cry

I want to help her why can't she just see
All she can say to me is "just let me be"

I'll miss her when she's gone, I'll be alone
Maybe she'll be happy when she reaches Gods throne

Patricia A. Zamboni

Untitled

Kind hearted and—
Ever faithful that's what you are to us.
Never disagree to someone good ideas.
Can always be ready to help one—
Another. Your enthusiasm and—
Respected guidance inspired us.
On whatever God words you preach.
The logical and hope is with you and—
You always have—
Needful hands to touch us.

Letty F. Mendoza

Come With Me Into The Fields

Come with me into the fields
Together we will play
Come with me into the fields
To spend another day
Come with me into the fields
While the days are long and warm
Come with me into the fields
Where life can do no harm
Let us sit very still and
Listen for a Robin's song
Let us find our other friends and
Let them come along.
Friendships of childhood sometimes
Fade away to fast
Friendships as we grow older
Are the ones we make last.
When the Robin's song is silent and
The grass no longer grows and childhood is just a dream.,
Once more, come with me into the fields.
For life is not what it seems.

Emily Hornak

Considered Obstructions

If death is an enemy, then what would that make life?
It cannot be that of a friend, after all, friends of enemies are enemies themselves,
But it can't be an enemy either, can it?
Being afraid of death is thought to be normal... It's not.
Being afraid of death means you are afraid of life.
Being afraid of life means you're already dead.

Alexander Palmer

Special Friends

Friendship is something you can not buy
It has to be earned with respect and caring.
It can last, as long as you want it or can be broken into pieces.
It is sharing your most precious and private thoughts,
understanding without judging, accepting and giving
of yourself in your everyday living.
Speaking the truth without deception,
Being tactful when giving advice.
There can be no exceptions.
In time of need and sorrow
Friendship is solid and clear,
When all others forsake you
True friendship is always near.
So cherish it with all your heart.
Never let it die of pettiness or doubt.
Enjoy it as long as you are living
And you never have to be without
Friendship

Erika Beck

Untitled

Come to me and say I'm yours-
Say that you're mine, too.
And together we'll climb the highest mount
To touch the sky of blue.

Hold me in your tight embrace-
Whisper your secrets to me.
And we'll find an ivory gondola
To sail the shining sea.

Place your ring upon my hand-
Tell me that you do.
And we'll stroll the beach on a starry night
Beneath a harvest moon.

Kiss me softly and speak my name
When home to me you return.
And hand-in-hand we'll wander the wood
Surrounded by tree and fern.

And when we grow gray and crippled with age,
Whisper you love me so.
And we'll throw off our burdens, forget all our pain,
And go dancing in the snow.

Maggie Trollinger

What Is Silver?

Silver's a breeze on a misty day,
That whispers the tales of the crystals.
Silver's the shawl of winter's dismay,
That chills the very flakes of snow.
Silver's the crown,
That sits on Frost's head.
Silver's smooth as velvet
And hums the tune of winter.
Filtered moonlight,
Streaming into a cave is silver.
A silver crayon,
Held by a child.
Scribbles a cloud here and there.
Silver is cold but comforting,
It's a friend,
Deep down,
That listens.

Clara Schuhmacher

A Letter For Moms

For all the jokes and loving care,
I hope this day we can share.
You cook, clean, and sew,
Without you I just wouldn't know
Acrobats and lion tamers too,
are nothing compared to you!
You're courageous and experienced, so much I can't say,
You're like a flower that just won't wilt or fade away!
So, as I close this letter today,
I hope it brightens your day!
Erin Gildon

Our School

In this town we have St. Anne's School.
We hope everyone lives by the golden rule.
St. Anne's has kids of many ages.
Let us help them turn the pages.
We have Father Thom to do the preaching,
And Sister Rose Ellen to help with the teaching,
Plus other sisters and teachers at school,
And many parents, who help, isn't that cool.
So let us watch the kids eyes glow with gleam,
And maybe your efforts will be more than a dream.
Your potential at St.Anne's is great,
Now let's get started, and don't be late.
Let us take a good look,
And I think It's time to open that book.
So if you have that big test,
Don't forget to study, and do your best.
It's the end of the day, time to shout,
Probably, because classes just let out.
Dan Micsak

Eggnog And Fudge

Eggnog and fudge are a wonderful pair,
If anyone thinks different I really don't care.
They put me on a sugar high,
So much that I feel I could fly.
It is a good thing Christmas comes only once a year,
Because eggnog and fudge my Mother does fear.
Eggnog and fudge I dare you to try,
Then next Christmas you'll turn down your pie.
Once you try eggnog and fudge they'll be your favorite meal,
But until you try it you'll think, no big deal.
Eggnog and fudge what a wonderful sight,
Then, you too dream about them on Christmas night.
Peter W. Van Druten

A Selfish Decree

As I stand here, eyes wide, arms outstretched, holding my breath
looking out at you looking in to me, I wonder why I do this,
why I so wish to please you when you will not be pleased.

I want to exhale, let my breath rush forth with all the fortitude
and might I can muster, for I declare to the world that I shall
only please myself.

Do not dare to compare me to others that have come before;
I am only myself at my very best - I deny responsibility for
me at my worst; and yet, even at my very worst it is still
a grave and vintage me that must stare into the mirror.

To those who deem it necessary to deter me, I say from the
heavens, or shout it from the dankest, darkest depths of hell
that I shall remain true to all that I am, good or bad, and
let those that wish to get the best of me be damned.
Nancy Wernert

Desensitized

Freakishly large,
It lies imprisoned in the circus car.

"Come look at the Great Unnatural Angst!"

And they do come and look.
Then they move on with their lives.

And all along it whispers to me,
"You're a sideshow fear.
Come get inside your fear."

So I go into the cage,
And put it on,
This costume I step into.

I hover there,
Ungrounded.

"I'm a sideshow fear."
I stay inside my fear.

Then once more they come to look,
And again they move on with their lives.

"And all this time,"
I said to myself,
"I thought that I scared them."
Wade Everett Neff

The Steps Of My Life

Through the emptiness of yesterday
I stand in the present
Viewing the brightness that tomorrow brings.
To my right are stairways
Leading outward to nothing.
Then there is my left
Without steps there is no view.
Below me there is an endless hole
Going to hell.
Above me is beyond my reach.
The images of death surrounds me
As my life
Is within me and not around me.
Behold the beauty
I HAVE FOUND;
Bill Monroe Smith

Through The Callous Years

As I look through callous years,
to recollect those painful tears,
with heedful eyes I watch for thee,
my weary heart I must set free.

Enduring streams of water run,
warm and frigid our time must flow,
in its delusion I see my sorrow,
relinquished memories that long tomorrow.

Nostalgic souls our hands demise,
sterile dreams our hearts will find,
insecurities secure my light,
as wings of eagles guide my flight.

My soul and mind now intertwine,
my body folds, my skin unwinds;
wrestling, struggling, in my delight,
what consequences my heart will find.

The cries I gave and you returned,
obscure a promise that was unheard.
The life that fills in me a rush,
Shadows ours and what is left of us.
Linda M. Roman

Colors Of The Sky

Colors of the sky, How beautiful you are, you speak to us from way up high. Colors instead of words, what an amazing way, instead of words, your colors has something to say.

Come blue, come gray, your rainbow of shades, will the sun shine, or will it rain today? And when bright colors of light begin to change, even the color of black darkness has something to say. Come milky-way, come dipper, come venus, come stars, colors of the sky, how wonderful you are.

The colors of the sun rise, the colors of the sunset, if you have never seen these colors, you have seen nothing yet.

So if you are sad, lonesome or cheerful too, look to the sky and see what the colors say to you.
Joyce Williams

Our Cameo

These are treasures kept apart
cradled securely in our hearts,
etched for ageless time to be
our Theresa, like a cameo in memory.

There is no small face to wash at night,
no questions or troubles for us to put right,
the playthings have been put up to keep.
No pink and white softness lying asleep.

No bruises and bumps for us to caress...
where is the assortment of four-legged pets...
with poise and assurance and delightful grace
a tall, sweet young lady has taken that place.

We have taught you the good things of life
of love and forgiveness and goodness and right.
What we've given to you is now yours to give.
Pluck the fruits, dear one, you are so eager to live

We cannot imagine where time has flown
There is only stillness.....
 Our last child has grown.

Mom and Dad
Delores A. Lintel

Laundromat Lovelorn

The almond-eyed girl and the sun blond boy
whispered their argument.

He stood with legs spread, vulnerable....
She, cross-legged, stood still.

He followed limply through sort, and soap, and push coins into slots.
She slipped slowly into silence.

Her breath with no sounds, spun his mind and dried his lips.
Still no response.......

He waited, watching her mechanical movements....
unloading the washer, loading the dryer.

The clink and the drop of the dime, mirrored his sinking heart.
The whir of the motor echoed the throbbing in his ears.

When the cycle was finished, she folded the clothes.
He felt the futility of forcing her feelings.

He folded his heart, placed it on top of the pile.
And threw in the towel.
A. J. Halsey

Dear Jeffrey

I feel the sun that warms his heart
He is a Picasso, a work of art.
I love to see his handsome face
His smile, I would never erase.
His voice, so warm and tender
My one and only, I'll love him forever.
He has a genuine personality
He's a dream, no-reality.
A silhouette of dark and light
He holds me as we say goodnight.
He's someone that means the world to me
He's my heart, my soul, my life - he's my Jeffrey.
Karen P. Murphy

Contentment

Way up North where the icicles hang,
The sun woke up as the winter birds sang.
And snug in a shack in the way back woods,
A woman yawned and a tall man stood.

She made breakfast as he pumped water,
She heard a bump, he heard a splatter.
He turned to watch as she wiped up,
She listened stern as he worked the pump.

He knew she loved him, she the same,
And neither one spoke the other ones name.
They worked together side along,
She silently, he singing songs.

Dark in the eve' as the sun sank low,
He trudged in through the deepening snow.
In through the door with a contented sigh,
Happy to see that crisp cherry pie.

Together they snuggled in the great big bed,
His arm around her, his chest near her head.
They closed their eyes as the last bird peeped,
All in those woods were fast asleep.
Holly Margaret Knell

Mind In Fear

Darkness in fear and dread, the night with sounds she be.
Fear of what cannot be seen stirs the mind beyond belief.
A tree branch upon her shoulder, brush, and within she
trembles more, her mind, the thing that deserts her most,
down to its very core.
Fear not she struggles to say, but a dread comes over her.
She feels the branch and thoughts of hell come unto her.
An owl, in tree above, hoots its cry and panic again
grips her mind.
Her legs, run they try, are held fast because of strain.
Tear to eyes do come and wets her face with warm embrace.
Her love is but a grasp away if she would not turn away.
Shaken, her mind and body be, she trembles in dark of night.
She prays for this to pass and safely home to be.
A hand grasps with tender love, her mate at side be he.
Anthony J. Germano

"The Two Sides Of Beauty"

There is beauty; beauty on the surface and beauty within.
The beauty on the surface is only what we see,
but the beauty within radiates abroad.
Beauty on the surface is a porcelain face,
so beautifully made, yet so easily cracks.
The beauty within is a rubberband; simple, but yet so flexible,
allowing it to reach abroad.
Greater is the beauty within; than the beauty on the surface.
The beauty within lasts forever, but the beauty on the surface is
swept down the streams of life; by time, never to return again.
Beauty on the surface, or beauty within?
Stacy LaShun Menafee

"Tina"

I sat alone looking at negatives, of pictures that were taken.
Alone with the memories of your leaving so long ago.

The times I would see you, I'd tremble inside.
I didn't know how to touch you.
I didn't know what to say.

She took the pictures, she took you.
Alone am I with the negatives and memories.

I'd hug you good-bye, with none in return.
I'd look hopefully in your eyes, looking for a sign you cared.
Years of waiting, years of trying.
One day you hugged me back, one day daddy's girl said
I love you too.

She took the pictures, she took you.
Alone am I with negatives and memories.

She took the pictures, she took you.
Alone am I with negatives and memories and you.
Robert Bailiff

No Marker For Your Grave

I saw the angels in my dream.
They smiled when they brought you to me.
An unexpected gift from God to share.
For me to love and nourish and care.
I felt your presence though I could not see.
You laid in the warmth becoming a part of me.
I wondered about you, who would you be?
Then realized it didn't matter so much to me.
My heart so full of love and joy.
I wanted a girl, but would be happy with a boy.

I saw the angels in my dream
The tears they shed as they took you away.
I prayed for them to let you stay.
They promised to return another day.
My heart now sad that you are gone.
Your stay with me not very long.
Now only emptiness inside of me.
A part of me you will always be.
Silently I mourn your death, close my eyes and try to rest.
And I wonder; was it really for the best?
Shelly A. Black

Dreams

When I am asleep and having my dreams.
I see so many wonderful things.
But when I awake. I can't
  quite explain.
The places I've been
  The things that I've seen.
I wish I could show you
  my favorite dream.
And how I can fly without any strings
At first it is hard to get off the ground.
But people are watching
  and I can't give up now.
I try and I try and I try once again.
And to many surprise
  I am up in the wind
They said it couldn't happen
  they didn't believe.
But I know all along what they could not see.
If your wishes were dreams than maybe we could see.
If only we dreamed then wishes could be.
Sandi Conomikes

Survival

The passion of splendor is all that I feel,
I close my eyes,
How could this be real?
My desire pleads for your every touch,
Yearning and aching, I want you so much.

The darkness captures us, making us blind,
Our love is so powerful,
Our souls become entwined.
There is no cure for the pain of delight,
The climax of sheer ecstasy,
Gets us through another night.

Ripping and tearing at the depths of my soul,
Your body devours mine,
A hunger out of control.
You make my body feel alive,
My longing to taste you,
You help me survive.

Even if this is all it can be,
Locked in our pleasure,
I will always be free.
Stacie Lianne Cook

Storm

I fear the storm is more ardent than even God can bellow his alarm
Roots of the giant sequoias, jerking and snapping as they hug the earth like a gigantic blanket

The orchestrated assault as a conductor on his podium
Clouds clapping like the drums of an eminent marching band

The whistling wind akin to the wolf howling in the cryptic, mystifying night
Bending and twisting trees as masts of great ships in the fiery, bright lightning

Rains pouring down as single sheets of polished glass
Making it impossible to see the dancing lights along the mud drenched harbor

Fingers of the ominous storm hurling bricks and debris afar in the weightless air
Sirens distantly wailing like a newborn's cry for its mothers milk

The storm surge rising several feet as if leaping over the final hurdle
Catastrophic destruction without warning from darkened pits of the unknown

All God's creatures scurrying about in a frenzied, fright-filled ire
the storm weakens as fast as its whirling, spinning, ruination

Skies clear as crystal blue diamonds in the pure white sand
Years ahead, will anyone remember, the storm that cast its deadly bone chilling breath across the shore
I think not
Robert R. Brewer

To Grandma

I've seen it in her clear blue eyes.
A glimmer of hope, can't be disguised.
She comes in dreams when life's hard to bear.
To share a hug, and let me know she's there.
A cool breeze touches my face.
A hint of violets out of time and place.
It's a comfort to know that she's nearby.
At times I see her at the edge of my eye.
You see, Grandma died this summer past.
I wish I'd known that day was her last.
I used to miss her, but now I know.
That she's in my heart, and in my soul.
And on this day I send to her
A warm hug and a kiss from her Granddaughter.
Kathy L. Busbee

A Glimpse Ahead

I walk furiously in no direction at all
Looking for a mere slit in this balloon world
An opening, a portal to the other side
Where hard coldness slaps reality in your face
And everything must become steady again.
Giant leaps must be made and big shoes filled
These footsteps are made by me and me alone
Because only I know where I should be
Looking for the other side, in no direction at all.
Resonated walls make it tough to breath
Because only through stained glass can I see.
Rage, fright, fury, spite
Wicked things fly through the night
Wicked things fly through the night
Scared to stay and scared to go flowers in my world sometimes grow
But in which direction nobodies know. Forty lashes to himself
Bottled breath of fine wisdom and emotion
To be had by nobody but himself
Nobody knows in which direction at all.
Derek Kulikauskas

Remembrances Of A Watery Past

There is a certain
    sensual knowledge within all
      living beings,
    a knowledge of the past when
water was the Universal element and envy,
    when rain sank into embracing flesh
      and all life,
    even the great, silent albatross
was cradled in its mother's arms
            and grew
            and sang
              such
              sweet
              songs
         as we now only hear when the moon
       is full and draws the tide
       closer to our coveted
       existence on the
    cold,
  dry
 land.
Barbara G. Seaman

A Stage Of Nothingness

As darkness covers the sky,
Our bodies are in a blank world,
Floating in our mind's vivid imagination.
Short life-like pictures flash in our dreams,
Creating images of fear or happiness.
Although most dreams send messages,
Messages that can change people's existence forever.
Some dreams haunt and enchant,
Influencing people to change their lives.
All of this is possible in a blank stage of nothingness.
Anish Dhadwal

Grades

Colors, Ranges, Shades of gray,
similarities, differences...
- it's better this way -
with different thoughts and dreams
- desires and fears -
expressed on paper
- with laughter or tears -
and Forced to be judged, evaluated, and changed...
because of a standard instead of free range.
Rebecca Hall

"Oh" That Mother Of Mine

From kissing a scrape, to throwing a ball
seemed no matter how high or low she would always hear my call.
When I tried my best to do something it never was to her small.

From getting us off to school,
or making grand applause at our talent shows.
At Christmas time and throughout the year
her homemade gifts couldn't be more cherished
but blessed with tears.

The memories we have made together
will in fact stand times test.
She was not only my mother, but as friend she was the best.
There is no stronger love than that of a mother for the child she
bore was actually part of her.

The Lord deemed it time for her eternal rest
we never know when it's time to be eternally blessed.
When I see her in heaven I will surely be able to attest.
"Oh" yes that's that mother of mine!
Bruce Seuser

A New Song

The snow lays cold upon the ground
The trees stand silent as I look around;
The birds have all ceased to nest
It seems all nature needs a rest.
Then just around the corner comes a breath of spring
And wakes the budding trees to hide the birds that sing.
Winter is a passing time in the life of man
When nothing ever seems to go according to our plan;
When we begin to wonder is there now no spring?
Or is there any reason for me to ever sing.
Then I must take his promise and trust Him day by day
that through the lonely winter he still leads the way;
When again the winter fades away to spring
Life renews afresh and birds come back to sing.
It brings again the summer with life's very best
Then I can clearly see through the winter
I was blessed.
Delores Hansen

Untitled

He remembers the star-filled night
as if it were yesterday.
The way she looked, the way she smelled.
Her eyes, how they sparkled in the moonlight,
and her lips,
these divine lips in which he kissed
A kiss they have both been yearning for.
A kiss between two friends
who desperately wanted to be more.
Who wanted to show each other
how they really felt
and how much they really cared.
But in actuality
they know what that kiss really meant
and that was, Good-bye!
Chris Marinello

Life

Life is hard-help.
Life is short-have fun.
Life is stressful-relieve it.
Life is not fair-deal with it.
Life is confusing-figure it out.
Life is fun-enjoy it while it lasts.
Life is mind boggling-try to understand it.
Amy Saenz

The Test Of Truth

It's called the twist of fate
Hang on to love before it's too late
Don't let hurt and anger cause love to slip away
Hang on, forgive and start a new day
Silence in the halls, yelling and crying
is the only sound heard
(Missing line it was cut)
Begin a new spark of love, let it start

The test of truth for me and you
The test of courage to make wrong turn right
The test of faith in what we believe
The test of enduring to make love last
Let our friendship help, let's talk before we
face the test of truth for me and you

When push comes to shove
Let's save our love
The heart, the mind, let's become one again
We haven't tried love since I don't know when
Let our friendship come first, so we can talk
Before we need the test of truth

Colleen Pruitt Stanhouse

"Dear Mother"

Once I saw it all so clearly,
now how could it be so dark.
I spent my life searching for tomorrow,
to learn the betrayal never ends eternally.
Signs of positivity create in my head
just to be broken by the wickedness of humanity.
I visualized a perfect picture
Never will it come true thinking it would be okay
Never thought it would be you to take my hope away from me,
and replace it with vulgar thoughts.
Deprived of life
Never to have a future
Never to have laughter
How could you make my existence so immoral
Here I go another prolonged day of misery no one can help me now
You shattered my mind with your ugly thoughts
Now I'm forever stricken with your words
You have polluted my mind and soul
But still I undertake every possible
alternative to reconstruct my vitality

Terri Wilcox

Untitled

Yellowed leaves fall sadly to the ground
From trees that stood so proudly in the Spring
When gentle rains reduced their thirst
And pushed their new born growth from earth.

Floods wash away what some possess
Man and beast feel nature's fury.
All manner of violence seems to erupt
Throughout our land that flies Old Glory.

Who knows the reason for all our travails?
Does the Almighty wish to make us aware
That we fail to thank Him for past successes,
But let greed cloud our eyes to how we've been blessed.

It's time we forget to rant and rave
Demanding more than we can repay
To this land that gives us blessings abound
More plentiful than many a nation around —

Marion K. Wilson

A Victim Of Alzheimer's

Good morning, dear!!
What would you like to have for breakfast?
I heard no reply.
I asked again but still no reply,
Then all of a sudden I realized
I didn't hear what I thought I had said,
I tried to speak again but no words would come.
I thought, oh no, I've got Alzheimer's
I won't be able to say, "I love you,"
or put my arms around you.
Please stay close and talk to me.
As I will need your help, as you will see.
Dear, Don't feel sorry for me.
For I have had such a fulfilling life
With Christ and you by my side.
Please, keep talking to me and loving me.
For that is all I will ever need.

Irma A. Flesner

"Two Special Daughters"

I have two special Daughters pretty as can be,
Wake up every morning wishing them to see.
Sadly they're not there, but they're always in my heart,
I've always loved them dearly from the very start.
Oh how I miss them I really miss them so,
When ever they're around me I don't want them to go.
Two special daughters they make me very proud,
Whenever I think of them I'm always on a cloud,
They make me very happy just being who they are,
I truly wish them happiness even from a far.
I remember when they were born their wrinkled little faces,
I dreamed of us together in all kinds of pretty places.
Two special daughters their hearts are pure and kind,
I thank our Lord for making them he really makes them shine.
So when they read this and catch a happy grin,
Let them know I'll love them forever and ever...amen.

Rodney D. Wilson

Darkness Of The Night

The darkness of the night spreads its way vigorously
over the face of the sky,
In its own forceful grasp it races deeply into the heart of space,
The moon struck world is full of beauty in its nascent nature,
Fragrances of dusk ponders its self deeply into the
millions of memories before it,
As the moon, stars and space unit spontaneously as far
and distance as their bodies,
Moon spears strike the land and sea as all the stars look and gleam,
The distant sparkles of light call out their dreams of
the future and past as they seem,
Telling tells of comets' graceful paths leading them far and vast,
Knowing of worlds that have begun or passed and the
life cycle that seems to last.

Donald L. Savage

The Dawn of Night

Night lasts as long as day
and in thy time
When crickets sing their sorrow song
and children are tucked away in their beds
and owls hoot and search for prey
All I do is think of day
Thy time when everything is visible
and shadows don't creep along my walls
and screech owls no longer make my spine cringe
and I can do the things I love
Until night dawns again.

Michelle Decker

"There Shines The Sun"

So much time has passed, but that fatal shot still can be heard
echoing through my mind.
The random act of violence that robbed me of your presence, replayed,
over and again, at least a thousand times.
We routinely set out that morning to watch the arising sun.
No signs foretold the danger, that hadn't yet begun.
A stranger came across our path, asking if we knew the way.
While we were still telling him, he robbed us and ran away.
You tried to stop him and make things right.
You ran so fast. You flew into the night.
I'll never forget that moment, or the scars of that dreadful day.
When I held you in my arms, after a lone shot in the dark went astray.
I held you close to my heart and as I began to pray.
You whispered sweetly, the last words I ever heard you say.
They say that they found me face down on my knees,
incessantly crying a single word, "Please!"
When the dreaded news came that you were gone with the sun,
I knew in my heart that the poison had only begun.
Walking along the paths of my dreams, where once we use to run.
I see you here beside me and in your face, there shines the sun.

Melissa Bauknight

"I Choose Me"

My love, is he? Or is it my contentment that let it be.
My heart drives to be near him, but my mind steers me from him.
Can it be as is, or must I see what could be?
Will society accept as I, or will the negativity rule my fate?
should I be the norm of society or will I stay the odd?
"I choose me."

Stephanie A. Williams

Bedtime

Moon rise
short of dusk,
Waters rise
with no tide in sight,
Winds changing,
the trees, the land.
Something terrible is coming this way again.
See the moon
amber and orange,
an illuminating glow.
See the water
neon and glowing,
for the sea of tears is overflowing.
Taste your tears for the first time tonight,
see your fears as you hold your pillow tight.
See the darkness turn into light,
good morning son, how was dreamland
last night?

Shawn A. Snider

My Life

Look the way my life is.
Why all the trouble be?
I'm just a teenager trying to do,
all the things I want to be.
Whenever you wake up,
you won't know what the day will be like.
But as you start to settle down
you realize you just started your hike.
All things I try to do,
why must they all be so hard?
But if I want to like the life I'll have,
I have to pick up the right card.
If life were so easy,
as everyone says we have it,
How come I don't understand,
not even a little bit?

Kelly Schultz

My Guardian Angel

A friend that I can turn to, a shelter from the storm,
When I am cold or frightened, in his arms I'm safe and warm.
He is my guardian angel on whose love I can depend,
And I know if I should lose him, my world would surely end.

All through my life he's been there whenever there was need.
He is so good and wonderful, so kind in thought and deed.
He's just what God intended for an imperfect child like me,
He is God's perfect man and father, I know he has to be.

I can't find the words to tell him, just what he means to me.
Words like that, the kind I need, just haven't come to be.
He means much more than I can say, you just can't measure worth
Especially when it involves the sweetest man on earth.

I thank God for His kindness in what He's done for me
Giving me the very best of men to guide my family.
I love him with all my heart, and please know that it's true
The finest Dad in all the world, my father dear, is You!!!

Gail Keller

Winter Day Of February

Snowflakes dance, and fall today,
   Around my tiny poplar tree,
In their own self silent way,
   Winter wins the battle for now;
     Till spring takes over the slender tree's boughs.
Till it turns those buds to bright green leaves,
   And takes away our warm flannel sleeves.

The tranquil peace, of this winter day,
   The dormant life, the meadow hay,
Will hear the call, the birds will sing,
The now quiet earth will seem to ring;
   With such new life, a precious thing.

February weakens, her days to end,
   With March on her heels, those strong playful winds,
Children and kites, in the wide open spaces,
   Girls in dresses, trimmed with laces.
I like winter, with its look of rest,
   And short lived rays from sunshine's breast.
But about this time, one longs for spring,
   When once again, a thrill it brings.

Tony Lee Skiles

Winters Gone By

Whirls of wind spinning around
Stirring up dust shaking the ground.
Leaves of crimson in a field of gold
Each has its own story, a story to behold.

Creased with time wrinkled with age
He looked deep into the eyes of a sage.
Capturing his spirit, a childish glow
Reading the story his eyes surely told.

Caught in the wind of winters gone by
Branches of an oak that reach for the sky.
Cold of winter the smell of spring
Listen to the wind as it starts to sing.

The flutter of wings as the wind settles down
His spirit awoke in a sleepy little town;
The chill of winter never to return,
He sits with a sage, from the sage he will learn.

Michael A. Yaverski

I Believe In Santa Claus

2am...Sitting at a diner counter
he pulls down the fake white beard under his chin...
scratches his face...orders a coffee.
He drags the red and white hat down the side of his head...
drops it on the stool next to him.
He fingers through the pack until he finds a dry one...
lights it...takes a long drag...tries to exhale his troubles.
The rent, the bills...constantly poking at the back of his head...
...so often he doesn't feel them anymore, but knows they're there.
I feel his pain, his emptiness, how he suppresses his hopelessness,
so he can relax for a moment into the peaceful numbness.
Nothing is sometimes better than something,
especially when the something sucks.
I like his simple nature, his humility.
I admire his courage...I feel his fatigue
and his inner struggle...that dies a little each day.
I like how he gathers it all up and shoves it in a dresser drawer
and gives you a big smile when you come up to him.
You give him a handshake and pat him on the back...
knowing your comfort requires his poverty.

Kenneth R. Conover Jr.

In Eternity

What is it called when Eternity is on your mind
string out from the beginning till the end of time
twisting struggling as a misguided vine
with the grapes so wise, delicate and refine
through a forest so dark and trees so thick
callings of the wild and a distant mechanic like tick
of the recoiling chambers that are loading thoughts
ready to shoot the idea dead until it rots?

What is it when Eternity is in your soul
filling you with life yet it seems empty and whole
as riding a cosmic stream into a mysterious black hole
or sliding down your makers galactica pole
into the waters of communing constellations
a sabbath of the immortal's sacred incantations
where eternity gains a perspective in the mind it hosts
and configures its destination after leaving a body a ghost?

John S. Clark

Armadillo Woman

She waddles through life just trying to survive.
Some people say, "She is so ugly, she's cute."

Some say it is what is inside that counts.
When trouble or fear strike
She rolls into an impregnable ball of steel—
until the truck runs her over and makes her a pancake!

The outer layer is hard and tough.
Calloused from years of pain
Inside is soft and ticklish - no one is allowed in
this special once violated space.

When trouble strikes she tries to fight but
finds it easier to roll into a ball and exit life.
The friends of this armadillo maiden try to coax her out
but fear and distrust win and she stays put.

She knows taking chances and trusting can lead to death
and sadness — so there she sits in her leather ball.
Warning! Intruders Will Be Bitten!!

Pamela S. Burris

Untitled

My Self is confined so that finger and
toes may be lifted,
And voice raised from beneath the weight
of flesh and bone.
But for a minute a day, my body relieves
my keeper of her duty;
Yes, as my body lies still on a carpet of
clover,
My Self is free -
Radiating through the wind,
Speaking only when caught on the branches
of an oak,
Bruising the earth as dappled patches of
light -
Self sings her song of freedom;
A ballad that she alone my hear;
Not of body, nor of mind,
But of being,
I will allow my Self to sing.

Julie Vergados

While Waiting For Him...I'm Finding Me

Alone once again, this is not the way it should be.
How long will this go on...with me, being just me?

"One," "Single," and "Alone," are three words I thought I'd never be.
"Two," "Together," and "With someone," sounds much better to me.

I'm reading and learning the characteristics to look for when
   finding a mate.
Books can tell you what to find, but don't guarantee your getting a
   date.

I know the luck I'm having thus far, and with that luck...
I'd probably run my "Prince Charming" over with my very own car!

Finding out who I am and knowing what I have to give,
Gives me purpose, hope and reason to go on and continue to grow and
   live.

As for rainbows, they appear only after the storm and rain.
And when he comes into my life, nothing will ever be the same.

The more I'm able to find the true me,
The closer I am getting to not being with just me.

Stacey L. Dando

Better Days Will Come Down The Road

Gray skies mean sorrow
But there's always tomorrow
Even when your whole world is looking down
Life takes the good along with the bad
It doesn't matter how many chances you've had

You've got to hold on and you've got to be strong
Better days will come down the road
If you're not daring and you're not bold
You'll find that your heart turns to stone
Keep your head up and don't get fed up
Even when life deals you a bad hand

You've got to hold on and you've got to be strong
Better days will come down the road
When it seems like life is just making you old
And the pain gets too strong to withhold
You've got to walk on and sing life's song
Better days will come down the road

Jacklyn Lizotte

Someday

His eyes were sad and filled
with tears as he stood over the mound,
Covered with a sea of flowers, whose
petals the rain did pound.
The cold damp grass beneath his
feet with sadness seemed to part,
As he gazed upon the earth
that held the sweet love of his heart.
For one short year he held her dear, but
fate stepped in and took her from his life.
The one that he held near and dear
his lovely sweet young wife.
As he sadly turned and walked
away, he heard a soft voice say,
it's not the end my dearest one
we'll meet again some day!

Ruby F. Roosa

From Deep Pools, To High Branches

There was a sad remembrance on the hill,
   Below, ran a river.
On the hill grew an oak tree,
   Below, ran a river.

The river was full of itself;
   In it the trout swam
The river was bathed in oxygen.
   The speckled trout ate the insects.

A fisherman stood in the middle of the stream
   He cast dry-flies to the trout
A swarm of mayflies filled the sky
   They made rings as they landed on the water

Someday, I will return to the river.
   I will swim in the icy water.
Someday, is a long time from now;
   I will let the trout grow large.

And does it mean anything to you?
   The river is out of your reach
You are the oak tree's child
   The river is out of your way

Joe Sands

The Trial

You gave so many trials to all of us,
A will to understand them
Wisdom to see them through
Lord I know it's you who brought comfort and rest.
This is when I know I have been blest.

Some seem to have many,
Others seem to never have any.
The strength and knowledge of holding you dear,
Make all my problems a way to see clear.

You've brought to me deep wealth of faith;
For this is what my trials are for
To believe in you only opens the door.
For this day I will be happy in my Saviour.

When I've spent all day feeling your love,
Holding your psalms in my heart,
I can open my eyes and look above
Knowing I can sleep well in the protection of God's love.

Rose Ann Hall

"The Long Road"

I left the house to roam past town,
To find a road with trees all around.
Walking the dusty road, with no end in sight,
Oh, what I'd give to have my friends tonight.

We could talk and laugh and even play,
The dusty road wouldn't be so long today.
I'd tell them my secrets and all my fears.
Until the end of the road came near.

On this dismal, barren, country drive,
I'm trying much too hard; I'm wanting to strive.
I'm thinking much about the good ol' times,
When I had a home, and friends of mine.

Now there's darkness building in the sky,
The road is much too long to sit and cry.
I have to keep going until the end,
When I finally find my forgotten friends.

This endless road is lonelier than my heart,
I only wish we weren't so far apart.
Instead of all my dreams of endless light,
I got a dusty road and endless night.

Jacqueline Rae Harris

She Sits Alone

Why does she sits alone?
She's in deep depression and has no expression
She always has tears and fears
Fears of being and living
There is somewhere to turn, but she runs.
She has no home or job
She feels helpless and worthless
She bums the street and wants something to eat
The winter has now come
She is shivering from the rapid wind
There is no shelter to be found, so she sleeps on a bench
She's scared more than ever
She wishes he parents were there, they
would ease her pain.
She's thinking about all the dreams she had
gone down the drain.
She's thinking about suicide, what does she have to gain
She jumps in a river, it's to late to save her
She's no longer in poverty she's in a place
Where there is peace and happiness.

Tanesha Stewart

Dance Child

Crouched in back the child
Small enough to hide
Her legs beneath her body, tucked tight
Under starched white pinafore pressed
For grandma's inspection, it's Sunday and
She peeks above the vinyl seat
Of her father's rusty Fairmont.

Far from father's white knuckles, clenched
Locked in the ridges of the wheel which
Moves without thought - Far from mother's
Heavy eyelids and wrinkled blouse,
Feigning sleep, the child dances
With the pine cones quickly
Passing by.

Drifting into sleep, the child
Small enough to tuck her legs tight
Dreams of moon stones in circles
Underneath whispering pine cones
Underneath waving branches
Where she dances alone, happy.

Karen Frazier

Different, No Different

We say all men are brothers, each different from the others!
All innocent at birth... existing, who knows why on earth?
Fighting to make a living, while moral majority is giving,
us a hard time for standing up to their crime,
of creating social classes, so they can show their asses!
And being so damned greedy they overlook the needy,
by cutting social spending in favor of sending, billions
of dollars to defenses, it boggles all my senses!
So brothers die of starvation, while they protect our nation,
of oil well and corporation.
Government of procrastinators, thriving off dictators.
This country is just a whore, if the term applied to war,
in which our brother have died, while our leaders lied!
To turn us against our brothers, really,
no different from all the others!!!!!!

Robert F. Hicks

April 20

On April 20 you still be set free. To
pursue your dreams, what ever they maybe.
May you find that special someone who
will love you even thou, there may be times
when you'll say "honey I gotta go."
That special someone who understands that
there will be times, when you remember to call
it's almost 12 - midnight.
So my friend as you prepare to spread
your wings and fly.
Although having money is oh so very nice,
don't work to hard or life will pass you by.
So as I close this note to you, all though
our times together were few and far apart.
You will always have a special place
deep within my heart.

Marcella E. Montoya

Puppies

They wiggle and giggle, they bunt and grunt,
Sometimes they retrieve, and sometimes they hunt.
But God didn't give us a pretty white dove,
He gave us a puppy, to treasure and love.

E. Fiorenza

Flying For Freedom

Sitting in class looking out the window
Wanting to be free and fly with the eagles
spreading my wings and flapping
away.....
Wondering will my fear and rage still be
every-day
Looking back while flying high wondering if
The poacher is trying to shoot me out of the sky
cause things are rough and they
may feel in danger
Cause I'm a rare bird from an unknown
Place that people run from when I fly from
place to place
not willing to stay and see what
I am about
So I fly for freedom to stay with
my kind and fly
side by side
A bird that's flying for freedom just like
I!!!!

Tiffany M. Marquis

The Grey Veil

The grey veil came to visit today
An unwelcome visitor, indeed
Whenever it visits, all will be black and muted,
Thoughts confused, thinking slow.
Life is like a slow motion film
Pulsating pain in the head and eyes that don't focus.
Sleep is a welcome relief to get away
From this unwelcome, insidious intruder of life.
Finally, you wake up, emerge at the end of the tunnel,
The bright sunlight warming you.
You are ready to think, laugh, play again
Until the visitor makes his presence known - again.

Virginia Ann Green

My Dogs

It's only for my dogs that I survive
If I had hogs, I'd probably take a dive.
They really are wonderful to keep me going
Sometimes they upset me to the point of blowing.

We've got Precious, who does no wrong
She's never been vicious, but soon will be gone.
She is a saint, good as can be
Never got spanked, for my fault, you see.

Then there's Tuffy, who's really a pain
Always in trouble and usually a strain.
He is the smallest, who acts like the biggest
Wants to be tallest, definitely the wickedest.

Then came Lucky, who's really a brat
She's good at heart, but sometimes a rat.
When she gets bored she's really trying
Because of her nose, she's constantly prying.

My dogs are playful and act like kids
They should be grateful in showbiz.
They're puppies at heart, they're really fun
They're sharp as a dart while on the run.

Celinda Crouch

Life, A River, And A Rose

Life isn't a rose, it is a river.
Many people see a dainty flower with
its beauty and grace.
I see a calm, flowing blue-green, with its
sedimentary floating by.
I see the bridge that people stop over
to wonder.
I see the calm, I foresee the rocks, I see
the foam.
Alas, the tempest. It rages deep within!
Hold tight my dear, to your rough inflatable dinghy
and teddy-bear.
The walls creep wearily inward and narrow
as life falls short.
Behold, don't fret; it gets wider.
Crystal clear goes the H2O.
The water, essence of the river,
doesn't have a scent, or prickly thorns
Because life isn't a rose, it is a river.

Steven Dewain Boyd

Why Is The Sky Blue And Gray

Why is the sky blue and gray
Is it that the sun is too bright
Or is it that the stars are too bright at night
Or is it that the people are too loud
Or is it that the clouds are too close together
Why is the sky blue and gray

Megan Nichols

"From Me To You"

In dreams we dream of friends like you,
But seldom do our dreams come true.
I find within your smiling faces
Friends so warm and true.
You fill my heart with happiness
Just to be with you.
And there is nothing I want more
Throughout the days to be
Than just to go on being your friend
And know that you're with me.
I'll carry you within my heart.
Please carry me with you.
For it's precious to have friends like thee.
God bless and keep you,
Just for me.
Alma Boose

We Are Sacred

To living in this enduring, world I see.
I cherish these words, I write to me.
Of this sacred time, involved in our souls and minds.
To help this world be brighter.
In these felt emotions true.
Dedicated to what is faith to me.
Set apart by my own feelings true.
Of this protected place I know.
Where angels share and I can go.
Far away from corruption and sin.
From the sights my heart has been shown,
And the pain this body has felt.
Hearing earths own violence groan.
This nourishment now, so bitter sweet in taste.
What I've been given I will not waste.
In the pain that life bares,
so the joy that life shares, is so much sweeter.
That come from my hands and heart, this very moment.
I write to me, to share you see,
in this truly sacred time, in rhyme set free to heaven.
Bonnie Broesel

As I Lay in My Bed

As I lay in my bed
I hold her picture in my head
I can see her next to me
How I wish she could be
In my arms so I can hold her tight
And show my love for her through the night
I can feel her kiss
I can feel her touch
I can feel her soft skin that
I love so much
If I close my eyes she'll be in my sight
and it will help me dream of her tonight
One day soon, I'll hold her again
But until that day finally when
She's in my arms and I hold her near
I can only dream of my sweet dear
I'll kiss her in my mind
I'll hold her in my heart
I hope someday we're together
and never torn apart.
Michael DaForno

Raging Beauty

Heaven explodes with frenzied eye,
As earth below is surely victim.
One is not to wonder why,
As weather falls in vigor rhythm.

Abundant flakes knit a blanket of white,
Its beauty speaks no word.
Ever so silent is the dead of night,
Tranquility is heard.

Elegantly clinging, suspended in air,
Striking visions of perfection.
Branches and twigs with canopy quite fair,
Is purely sight for direction.

The fluff of snow, the charm it brings,
Its cleansing so enhancing.
The joy above to those who sing,
Is natures way of dancing.
Paul L. Bergeron

Planetary Plight

Man's strain at gain,
Keeping the beast tamed;
His over bearance at who's to be blamed,
He just keeps the feast of the heavens entertained.

All around the planet,
Degradation is ravaged,
Salvation sometimes seems savage.

Remaining souls are reluctant to connect.
As a whole the world itself don't protect.
Guiding forces tend to defect,
Confiding sources aren't always correct.

The guiding forces among the wise are unique literary.
Few sources surmise discreet itinerary.
Courses in disguise may oblige some similarity.
Few recognize the parity.
Anthony F. Messina

The Opposite Sex Of Man

Man's greatest achievements
May begin with a whim
While his greatest struggles
Can be just within him

What drives him on and gives him courage
To accomplish the impossible with ease
At the same time makes him feel
Like a coward and brings him to his knees

What ignites the flame inside him
And fills him with desire
Who warms his aching heart
And sets him all on fire

Of all the forces on earth
The one he can never control
The force that from birth
Provides him with an everlasting goal

Who else is there to help him
Whenever they possibly can
The answer of course is a woman
The opposite sex of man.
Arnold Paul Shindler

The Worm And The Cockroach

The worm and the cockroach were both feeling quite lame
So the worm and the cockroach played a good game
They wanted to see which bug had the mostest
And become the champion; the grossest of grossest!
When they could not out gross each other, they had to save face
And see who would be the first to win the great gross out race
Calling all the other bugs to serve and act as judges
And requesting the caterpillar to sweep up all the smudges
They gathered up some children lots of girls and boys
And cleverly disguised themselves as simple, plastic toys
Once the kiddies got up the nerve to play out their childish plan
The buggies would then come to life - that's when the fun began!
They wiggled and they squirmed, they did; those naughty, little
  buggies
Boy, they sent those small one's screaming home to mommy for some
  huggies
All at once, the judges cheered, with oh so joyful glee
"The race was such a marvelous thing!" said the friendly, little flea
"But wait! But wait! Who won? Who won?" Both worm and
  cockroach cry
"Well, both of you, of course, my dears," said Ladybug,
  "For it ended in a tie!"
  Lisa M. Johns

Reddening

It is the blatant absence of touch
When my heart cries for feeling.
It is my work to go unrewarded, my task.
I have begun to call it my life.

I grew to this mad form from an angry boyhood in bright color.
I dressed as a devil to dull the blue clouds,
Danced with the green men to scarlet my soul,
And twirled from the raw cold of any given choice
   To the red flame of real love.

   (That was you, Alexander.
   And if there is a trace of auburn in your hair
   I am all the better for it.)

I have not been so lost in color since that girl.

I speak of that incident in the hot summer
As if it were as light as a feather.
But I felt so trapped by the young woman's beauty
I forgot to dream of beautiful men.

I was so young once.
  W. Louis Gum

A Glance At October

Sunlit ferns, rocking in the gentle breeze
brush lightly against an old cedar stump.
Autumn leaves walk slowly over cooling pavements;
no longer warmed by the sun of summer.
Landscapes peppered with fallen pinecones,
sprawled over pine-needle blanketed lawns.

Golden/red leaves anchored to mother trees
reluctant to loosen their ties and return to native land.
Brown laced plants parched beneath summer's sun
capture fleeting leaves journeying to their earth destination.

Autumn wind, invisible aid to nature's transition;
sometimes whispering, silently controlling
and at all times master of shifting and redesigning.
Artfully clever, uniquely programed, you rearrange to delight
our senses and bring nature to new horizons.
  Sidne Fuller

Being Black

Someone asked me, what it means to be black
And why it seems we as a race, want to be at bottom of the stack;
Being black means having to put your pride aside, and ignore the
negative talk;
Because you're judged not only by the way you dress, but by the way
you walk.
They say crime, killings, drugs, and playing sports are all we can do;
At the rate we're going we're proving them to be true.
I know there are good things blacks can do,
Because there are doctors, lawyers and teachers, too.
They have tried to say we played no part in making this country great;
But we all know that's a lie, just study the tapes.
If only we would study black history and see the part we played;
And learn how so many blacks helped paved the way.
They say there is no future, but this is not because I'm black;
So what it means to be black in this land of the free is to be
positive and walk with dignity.
  Sharlitta Novella Myrick

Thoughts Of A Bachelor

Was it or was it not to be
that I was rendered so very lonely?
Could it be (m)y fortun(e) fate
my mi(n)dless motions did d epr i cia(t) e?
I'm v a lueless to those who c(all) and
wander wearil(y) through infinite (i)nfinite   in fin ite halls.

though no fault
and b(l)ameless none

I'm stttillll in youth
and a(l)most

gone
  Cheryl L. Butkus

The Music Box

She danced, while he watched,
Day after day and night after night.
Lost in this unexplained trance.
Mist and Fog surrounds her
As she continues to dance,
"El Baile Del Fantazma". (The ghost dance)
He urges her on.
He told her he'd love her forever...
...If she dance just as long.
The world was nothing to her.
She could not see past the mist that came from his eyes,
or hear past the music that moved her feet.
And it went on.
Until one day the music stopped.
she had grown old dancing.
He grew old watching.
They both as pale as the moonlight
Standing like statues for eternity
The day the music in the box died
  Elidia Espinosa-Sabral

One Will Stand

There is one, I promise it's so,
There may not be several but there is one,
The rest will go as the wind will blow,
They will do as the others do,
They will do what is wrong to make themselves look better,
and they will set by as others do wrong around them.
Maybe they are scared, or maybe they just don't care,
but as sure as the sun will set one will stand.
He will stand because it is right and for no other reason,
Thank the Lord, One Will Stand
  Chad S. Arthur

"Christmas Dream"

Looking back on Christmas past
and the memories of childhood dreams.
Waiting up to catch a glimpse of Santa,
Leaving milk and cookies under the tree,
then getting up early to see what goodies he had left for me.
Soon came the time when the mystery was revealed,
You, Mom, were Santa all along.

   Now Christmas is here once more,
   and many things have changed.
   It is my turn to be Santa now,
   to make my own child's dreams come true.

I look at my son, and I know now
how much you loved me then, and yes,
how much you still do.

   Although time and miles have come between us, and
   at times we may have disagreed
   the bond between us will never be broken,
   For I am a part of You, as He is a part of Me.

Christmas future is yet unseen, but one thing I do know,
You will always be a part of my own Christmas dream.

Kendra L. Piotrowski

For Our Son

Today is a special day for me,
Today God took you and set you free.

He took away all of the pain you endured,
He made you whole and sweet and pure.

God made all of your suffering disappear,
Now you are seeing bright and clear.

You went with him where you belong,
The angels were singing their own sweet song.

We miss you son, more than you will ever know,
As the years go by, our love will continue to grow.

Please think of us once in awhile,
Knowing we miss your beautiful smile.

Remember us son with love in your heart,
Know that we were never meant to part.

God gave you his ultimate test,
As we all know, he only takes the best!

C. I. Margretta

Separated But In Love

We've been separated for a long, long time
But now I realize true love is never blind
We've tried hard to make up
But we must forget the past
If our love my baby is ever going to last

So just hold me in your arms and
Make sweet passionate love to me
Tell me there is no other and here is
Where you belong and want to be
Love me forever, love me like you never loved before
All that I ask is you give me your heart
I'll give you my heart
And love me forever more.

Just hold me in your arms and
Make sweet passionate love to me
Tell me there is no other and here is
Where you belong and want to be
Love me forever, love me like you know
You really want to all that I ask is you give me your
Heart and tell me baby I love you

Garna O'Neal

Stephen Kent Fridley

Stephen the summer of "85" is when it all had begun.
That is when I knew you were the only one.
Enticing feelings blew us into a brand new flight.
Perfectly lifting our love to a greater height.
Happy lifelong friends and lovers is what it is all about.
Every day I love you more without a doubt.
Naturally loving you with a true feeling in my heart.

Kent our lives together just had to start.
Even when things fall apart and seem to be at their worst.
Now remember our love and friendship will always come first.
Timeless memories of love is what we share.

Fridley what we have together is so very rare.
Reminiscing time together makes me feel like we possess the earth.
It is intended that only you and I will know what it is worth.
Delighted and captivated by all your charm.
Longing to spend each and every moment of the day in your arms.
Exquisite is the word that really defines you.
Yearning to make it last and forever after true.

Colleen E. Fridley

Formica

There is a dent in the metal that frames the counter,
it runs almost a foot in front of my stool,
oil has blackened in this crease to form an arrow
that points to the napkin holder.

There is a pattern of brown, like a fan,
beneath the thinness of the worn yellow,
and a ring that I have left,
of strong coffee on the formica.

I run my thumb around the thick white
rim of my warm cup
then drop my nail to perfect
the dirt arrow.

I keep my eyes down and my ears open,
I came to be alone and listen,
to hear stories of people I would never know.

How could I have known that you were missing,
and why did I have to hear,
sitting here alone,
that you've been found.

Carol Waldmann

A Substance Without Form

Born of a child and death of a memory, are we
to ignore that the winds told us about today?!
   My soul moves; cautiously creating a substance
without form.
   A sacred potential, a shadow of loss, water
from stone, an unfolding fear. Hope renewed by trust,
she awaits the verdict.
   A memory filtered, pain that is being born in a
burning desire on this alter long forgotten.
   I scoff at the sorcerer, knowing the life.
   I mock the arrogant, knowing their failure.
   I protect you, seeing your weakness.
   With violence, I avenge the insult of the enemy.
   Time enabling we embrace the future.
   With honesty we preserve it.
   With trust we build it.
   If the midnight breath you take was your last would
you be so certain to say it could have been love?!

Tammy Lynn Damron

"Happy Anniversary, Love"

Happy anniversary, Love
We've made it through a year!
Each and every single day,
Our love becomes more dear.

Through all the ups and all the downs,
You've always got a smile.
No matter what I say or do.
You always go the extra mile.

There's no greater love that we can share
Than the arrival of our son.
Nothing matters more in life,
When all is said and done.

I hope I have another century
To show thanks for all you do,
And to prove how much I care,
And how, truly, I love you!

Carolyn Downs

Arlington Cemetery

To pass them every day
lined up like keys on a piano
the weathered almost black ones
from the civil war
with moss and unreadable names
the white ones so new, so fresh
like gaping teeth in need of braces
but twenty even thirty years old already
(how can that be
with the wounds still so fresh)
and he asks us to forgive him
in his book how dare he
even look upon these vertical bodies
that can never lie down and rest
even in eternity
it isn't his brother
it isn't his son it isn't his father
who stands at attention
forever and ever
amen

Carol Van Lehel

I Spy

My, my, I spy.
Some people never change, they can't.
They don't know how.
They are so impressed with themselves.
I'm refined you know.
I know all the best people.
I live in the best place in the world.
I hurt inside but no one can tell.
I ring a bell and all the people jump.
I do hope I won't end up like all the others.
Wandering around,
Gone off into space,
Only left with a critical face
Which has no base and no case.
Just a place of refinement.
Where is it?
Where am I?
Gone, never to say I love you.
Goodbye.

Ann Stott

Session #24

Men are such wankers. Just ask any woman
who's been the object of a fantasy.

There isn't a man alive who hasn't wrought
Penelope from the girl next door
or Helen from an ordinary woman.

It's too pathetic. I don't know
whether to laugh or cry.

We often say Penelope when we think we want Helen.
But I'm here to tell you all men are the same
in not knowing behind every gross fantasy
of this or that woman stands undaunted
neither Penelope nor Helen but Aphrodite.

Our stupidity is two-fold. Aphrodite unrecognized
confirms our ignorance of having had her
the moment we first drew breath.

We are ignorant of ourselves and of our origins.
We remain as we were in the Garden.
Adam and Eve knew nothing about desire; neither do we.

Our myths do not spring from desire;
they aspire to it in peregrine undulations of anguish.

Peter Gallo

You

Like the last flower of the season
Like the last line of a painfully sweet song
Like the lull and silence of a fading dusk
Like the silent sorrow of a falling dew
Oft I see you on your lonely track
Lost in solitude and never turning back
Once, ages ago, you flowered in my silence
Like a heavenly song lost but suddenly remembered
Like a wandering bird, a solitary bard
Like the mountain snows of November
The first flakes in the chill of the morn
Heralding a silent eternity
Then the eternity died, the spell of silence too
Like the mountain fog in summer beam
Like the vernal down by a mountain stream
Like the wordless agony of a lucid thought
I found you melting never to be caught

Alex Paikada

Beginning To End

We started out as friends, and lovers we soon became;
Living with each other in happiness, thinking marriage had more to bring.

But instead of bringing us closer together, it drove us further apart;
Breaking up our friendship, and tearing up my heart.

No longer husband and wife, but just man and woman again;
The life vows taken with each other, had soon came to an end.

We still keep in touch, yet at the same time we're distant.
It's funny how you gain love so fast only to lose it in an instant.

But when the decision was made, I knew it meant losing you.
This was hard for both of us, but it was something we had to do.

There is no need for bitterness my dear, I guess our love didn't
  pass the test.
Maybe it was too hard for us, or we just didn't give it our best.

Living happily ever after together, that's what we hoped to do.
But it didn't end like in the storybook, our fairytale didn't come true.

Tiffany Reid

Life

Sometimes I kind of lose perception,
Of what life is all about.
It's like nothing comes along,
And then everything crashes in on you.

Love and heartache is a part of life,
And everybody knows both of those.
Sometimes you just have to go with the flow,
And let things fall where they may.

Sometimes life does get tough,
And you don't know if you want to go on.
But suicide is not the solution,
It's just taking the easy way out.

I've tried to keep my perspective on life,
But no one can predict everything.
I've figured out that life is a game,
And that you can only win if you're alive.

I guess what I'm trying to say is,
That when life does crash in on you.
Just let the good things in life,
Carry you through the tough times.
   Roy L. Weber

My Baby Brother

From the day you were born
and I looked into your eyes
  I knew something special
had come into our lives
From then on till now and even so
I made myself a promise
to never let you go
you are my baby brother
There is no one that can compare
cause when I chore you give me air
and when I'm down, you lift me up
For days that seem bad, you bring me luck
you have became the light for my days
I know this because you have my way
For when I'm down nd can do nothing but cry
you are the one who stops the tears from my eyes.
All I need to do, is think of one like no other
and that one, my dear is my
  Baby Brother
   Sharice Hughes

"Two Thumbs Up"

  The sense of feeling good emanates an aura,-of the appearance of inward tranquility.

  At that time the look is more expressive,-and can be considered more reliable than words can tell.

  It may be construed, as if it would be like speaking a language, which is understood by all.

  May I reiterate that the language itself is to be interpreted by the appearance as the overall message is uttered.

  We are all designed with this in mind....

  By the one...the Creator to manifest a looked for endeavor for the good of Mother Earth's humanity.

  Good habits, attitude, and at times being bigger than life,-point to the most rewarding, generating energy to the most positive, unquestioned endeavor.

  Looking into the eastern sky,-the colorful rainbow is slowly forming to vividly see.

  With that to think of,-since it is the Celestial promise of the age,...it is thumbs up all the way!
   Weston W. Rudel

How Shall We Use Our Gifts?

God, in His divine wisdom, has generously scattered
A varied assortment of talents among us all.
It is our turn to initiate our use of them.
Thinking, feeling, adjusting, planning—
These thought-problems control our actions.
We hide our talents or use them and they increase.

Eyes to see sand-polished gems, blooming flowers,
Art works and even words formed on another's lips;
Ears to pick up sounds of bird calls, rustling leaves,
Music variations, and important instructions;
Nose to catch the scent of dinner cooking,
And perhaps exotic fragrances of a beloved;
Skin to feel the warmth of sun, gusts of wind,
And distinctions in the texture of fine cloth;
Taste buds to savor sweetness of fruit, tartness,
Plants, and succulent meat roasting over flames;
Bones for strength, grasping, running, touching.

More awareness than enough to share with others:
How wonderful and numerous are our tools!
The lifetime question is: How shall we use them?
   Mildred Watts

Her Protector

Let her go fowl demon!
Back to the hellish depths you go.
Nothing on earth can keep me
From protecting the lady that I love so.

The demons that haunt her mind
Though I cannot control.
She is so very heavily burdened
With an emptiness in her soul.

There are things in this world
That we are needed for.
When the fragile ones call out to us
We answer, caring more.

The reality is the demons
That all of us must confront at times.
Some fare better than others.
Some need the protector whose spirit shines.

I am her protector.
   Kevin Sproles

Coming Of Age

Faster and faster,
  As your mind starts to reel.
Everything's different-
  Don't trust what you feel!
You can't stop the arrival;
  It's been coming all your life.
And there's no time to decide
  Between what's wrong and what's right.
Emotions alter,
  Images change.
How can it be different
  When it's still the same?
The tides of sound roll
  Your tenure's almost up.
You know so many people-
  But there's no one you can trust!
In your book of life,
  You're just turning the page.
Not realizing yet,
  It's your coming of age.
   Katie Hallahan

"Summertime Storm"

The freshly fallen snow covers her grave,
And the wind slowly drifts through the trees.
The summertime storm is over,
But it will always haunt me.

My baby died in the summertime storm,
She died without a warning.
And I still cry when I think of her,
And now my heart is yearning.

All of the times I held her.
When she was crying in despair.
Now I cry and open my arms,
But she's no longer there.

My baby left me all alone,
In a world cold and dark.
Left me with no one to hold,
Her fate has torn us apart.

Now I watch as the snow falls,
And a tear runs down my cheek,
Forever my love, I'll miss you,
Until I no longer have to seek.

Scott Malley

How Long?

Victims of a generation with
Souls dying fast in our hands;
We plead aloud for repentance,
"God please heal our troubled land."

Constant prayers of insincerity,
With rebellious blood in our veins;
Now it seems so clear to me,
Why His love must flow untamed.

In a time when diseases are rampant,
True families are nearly obsolete;
Millions are facing famine,
The prophecies are soon to be completed.

How much farther is His love willing to reach?
How long until the Father's wrath is unleashed?

Jennifer A. Faulkner

The Fallen Angel

An angel with a beautiful soul
Gave her heart and lost control
An angel in a devil's disguise
Kissed her soft and told no lies
Took my spirit, set me free
Earthbound love for you and me
The fire burned and held us together
The wind letting us soar forever
A devil in mind but an angel at heart
You let yourself get torn apart
You took my love and held it like a child
Ignoring your pain all the while
I took your love and pushed it to the limit
But never gave it all I could give it
I often cried for my angel in disguise
Feeling all the pain in his eyes
His wings grew weak, he stayed on the ground
And cried a little when no one was around
One day he jumped and tried to fly
But fell to Earth and burned and died

Amanda Harlin

Today

He peered through the window
up into the powder blue sky
And he caught himself,
wondering why
on such a beautiful day as Today,
the world revolved with nothing meaningful to say
about the inequities, dissolution and despair
that has turned happy people
into something rare,
but the sun still shines,
the rain still falls,
the air is breathed
the water still flows
the birds chirp and sing
the telephone rings
a baby is born
we smile and laugh
and the world just turns

Frank Sheehan

I Oft' Times Dream

I oft' times dream of days gone by,
   The laughs we shared,
The times we cried.

I oft' times did dream,
   To take the track,
But knew in my heart,
   There would be no going back.

I oft' times dream,
   Of the things that could be,
The precisely how much you mean to me.

I oft' times dream
   How you stood by me,
To see the hard times through,
   Giving love and understanding,
To start the task anew.

The dreams have long since left me,
   As we face new day's sky of blue,
The dreams have long since left me,
   All because of you.....

   My dreams have finally come true.....

Dana Lynch

Heaven Sent

To be Heaven Sent,
   Takes a Christ like love.
   A love that will show, when looked upon,
   A willingness to help,
   A helping hand without pay,
   A kindness that is true and pure,
   A smile that will cheer, the saddest of people,
   A countenance full of joy,
For this is Heaven Sent.
   I know a lady that is Heaven Sent,
   Because, she has all of this and more,
   Sky blue eyes, long dark brown hair,
   A countenance of pure joy,
   A smile that is bright and full of cheer,
   A kindness beyond kind,
   A pure love for all,
   A helping hand to everyone,
   And most of all, A Great Love For Christ.
For my Lady, is,
   Heaven Sent.

Anthony Mathison

A Mind's Journey

Fear is the only way to describe the feeling that night
As the night before, and the night before
I felt an eerie chill in the air,
A damp smell, a cold wind swept under my bare feet,
I was uncertain where I was or where I was going,
I had the sensation I was being watched
As if eyes were starting from every corner,
Where am I? Where am I trying to get to?
I seem to be walking down a narrow path,
With these feelings all around me,
When I sensed I've reached the end of this strange journey,
There is a bright glowing light in front of me,
A warm comforting feeling came over my body,
I reached out my hand to touch it,
Suddenly I'm surrounded by more familiar things,
Lying in my bed starring at the ceiling,
I think to myself, maybe tomorrow I'll get there

Karen A. Paradiso

French Flowers

French flowers are watered by small merry girls,
With innocent looks and strawberry curls.
  Their petals are covered with tiny drops,
By a five year old child with a lace on her socks.
  She holds two beautiful daisies in her dainty pale hand,
While the other one clinches to a watering can.
  Even the roses can't match her perfection,
As she stands in the sun with her creamy complexion.
  She matches the garden in an indigo dress,
Carnation cheeks and gentleness.
  The buttons and bow on that coat of hers,
Are as white as a doves delicate feathers.
  Begonias and daffodils, they never will wilt,
When this little one gives the can a tilt.
  This will go on for many more years,
As long as the earth, has these precious dears.

Elissa Lawrence and Kimberly Clarke

Pleasures Sin

The smell of roses on the morning wind,
Bringing thought of life's sweet sin.
Thought of day and done by night,
All in secrecy and passionate delight.
Fulfilling more than the earthly pleasure...
The pleasures of the soul can not be measured.
Next the morn of the roses.
Sin is done, but never over.
One last kiss before the dawn,
Bliss and laughter merge as one.
Then on the comets tail she rides.
Magic trails their every stride.
Her body comprised by soul and fire,
By God's hands and mans' desire.
Ride now, ride now, on the wind;
Disappear with the passionate sin.

Aaron Carricato

"Happy Feet"

My dog and I go walking through the woods.
His happy feet are prancing all the way.
We see the squirrel, the rabbit and the deer
And many scenes of nature on display.
Excitement reigns in every step he takes.
Increasing more as through the woods he goes.
I cannot see the half with naked eye
The many things that he sees with his nose;
And when I'm home I often reminisce
And think of all the many things I saw.
Then happy feet flash by the inward eye
And prove that watching him was best of all.

Robert E. Faust

God's Golden Grace

My golden years began
The day that I met you.
I didn't know the treasure
I'd have my whole life through!
My Father knew my heart's desire
He knew you would feed that burning fire!
Well, the fire's not out, it rages on,
Transcending the times when this life is gone!
My love for you will always be,
Forever and ever, just you wait and see.
The gold that glitters in the morning sun,
Is just as pure, when the day's most done.
Maybe even more precious in the twilight hour,
While enjoying God's grace, His love and His power!
Our time spent together.....God's riches untold,
These fifty years.....God's grace made in gold.

Tommy Alexander

The Earth Weeps

The Earth weeps as the trees are cut down and the grass is ripped up.
The birds scream in terror and sadness as their homes are destroyed.
The wind whips and snaps angrily at us with nothing to slow it down.
We choke for with fewer trees and plants, there is less oxygen to breathe.
The people cry from the dirt blown in their eyes and stinging their skin.
The environment yells its vow of revenge as it is polluted.
And the Earth weeps as it is torn apart for the sake of "progress".

Crystal K. Stearns

Untitled

His hand whispered slickly across his now-sweaty forehead.
His turn was coming up, he could almost feel the hiss
of fire-snapping tombs, screaming ash from
soot-choked pillars.
The blast from another loaded body stung his skin.
An eternal step forward (shuffleshuffle)
with an agonizingly dead whoosh of a forgotten human.
He hoped that the murmur of helicopters would echo
the freedom long-sought by many, but
that slowly diminished with his halting footsteps onward toward
the kiln. One tread out of line,
and quick!-like a shot-
a gun clicked to the head and a hollow barrel was purring doom.
But he would risk it (maybe). He would fight,
(for a few precious seconds, anyway)
anything to not feel that dirty heat
of the many scorched before him.

Hillary G. Moon

Guardian Angel

Guardian angel watching over me,
your physical being I no longer see.

I close my eyes and open my heart,
you're in my dreams we're never apart.

Your life on earth came to an end,
but your spirit lives on whispering in the wind.

Guardian angel I want you to know,
I love you so much and I miss you so.

I hope I can one day be as strong as you,
giving to others as you always would do.

You earned your wings a long time ago,
now it's your turn to fly and away you go.

Fly high guardian angel but not too far,
I need you to guide me like the bright northern star.

Kathryn A. Finnegan

I Am

I am an Indian
who speaks a language you can not understand.

I am a well known Englishman
who plays in a well known band.

I am an African God overhead
who takes care of all you can see.

I am an Asian story teller
who ate with the queen and drank some tea.

I am an ordinary kid from New Jersey
who likes to sit and dream.

I am me, the only one, a one of a kind,
a leader who leads the team.
   Sarah Anne Vizzini

To Sarah

Hath thou more dauntless grace than butterflies
Aflit air's ball on wispy wings of gold,
More tenderness than with which babe shouldst lie
Within Eve Mother's ever passioned hold.
Berth thou a maiden's skin ten-thousand more
Which hath birthed mendicant even vain rank;
Ability none less doth thou ador':
A mere buffoon hath sageful monarch sank.
So hath thee inner beauty none canst serve,
Mass strength to shed eclipse from somber womb;
How cometh term, thou, shouldst I, in false, deserve
None other than Nature's heaven assume.
O, such a universe you've brought to me...
A long beloved friend you've come to be.
   Jacob Callcut

Untitled

It is summer and the wind
Blows my hair.

The smell of flowers fills the air.

In my garden I plant seeds,
when they grow I'll pick the weeds.

The hot sun heats my neck.
soon I'll be sipping lemonade on my deck.
Now it's night and the day is done.

Man I wish I'd had some fun!
   John Gran

Knowing Her Unknown

Five thousand stories up she sits alone,
Reflecting on her life she feels deprived,
for comfort and for help she grabs the phone,
She wants to call that emptiness inside.

Clutching the phone she sits and waits in fear,
Her hungry eyes they prey for something real,
Her inner voice pleading hopes someone's near,
She knows not what she calls but hopes she'll heal.

There comes no answer from the telephone,
The tele line is dead no life thrives there,
For this device is made of meatless bone,
It cannot help because it does not care.

Although no one answers her telephone,
She knows herself inside of her unknown.
   Danielle Licht

Halted Ascent

And so I have risen
Foolish man has opened the door to glorious reign.
Lord of darkness, given,
Power over all that is worthless, those who are useless.
Master tell me,
Why am I here,
Why have I,
   Forsaken you so?
Continued lies, my intention
Is over all that is
Honor among thieves, non existent
Exist then in my own damnation.
My ascent halts
I see all that my power is over, enlightened,
To my perverted thoughts.
My realization commence, I have no power at all.

Master tell me
Can you forgive
For I have
Failed myself.
   Shawn Parks

To Be A Mother

To be a mother, the love is for real
It's something that no one else can make you feel
To hold your child so close to your heart
There's nothing that could ever tear you two apart
To comb their hair or change a diaper
There's nothing that could make a mother happier
To hear her child giggle and coo
There's nothing you would rather listen to
To watch them grow-up every day
And see them learn things in their own way
Learning new words and saying them loud
When you hear them you feel so proud
As time passes by and they get older
They start to rebel and their attitudes get bolder
Especially in their teens, they try to be adults
That's when every thing that happens is your fault
That's when you think of how you miss
That sweet little baby that you loved to kiss.
   Stephanie Campbell

Pain

Twisted thoughts do wrack my brain.
Why do I wonder or feel such pain?
When will it go, why does it stay?
I do not know, please go away!
Pain is too real, it is too deep.
It burdens my mind so I cannot sleep.
I toss and turn the night away.
My heart does burn, as the pain does stay.
I curse, I cuss, I damn these thoughts.
Why do I fuss when pain cant be fought?
It wins my time just like a game.
When will it lose, will I ever be the same?
Annoying like tiny drops of rain.
Thoughts with spikes, thoughts of pain.
Sorrow bleeds as my heart breaks.
Pain it feeds, my mind does ache.
Sweet thoughts where are you?
Please do show.
Pleasant thoughts, sweet memories?
I'd love to know...
   Kiana Hernandez

The Secret

Among the greatest greenest grass,
There lies a secret never told.
A flower bed that shall ever last,
And this shall tell you what it holds.
Tall and long Morning glories,
Shine upon the world so bright.
And in the wind they whisper,
of the strongest stories ever told.
The darkest black,
The brightest yellow,
is what makes up the tall sunflower.
They're feed to the bees.
Then at four o'clock,
The blossoms shall bloom,
And the four o'clocks shall sing their tune.
Now may this garden ever last,
For now the secret has been told,
Of what this garden has to hold.
And let God shed glory,
on all these living works of art.

Allison Kretz

Life

I walk this world blind,
tripping over everything in my way,
and all in my mind falls into a grind,
self destruction is all I'd say.

How do you turn away from this pain,
this suffering,
there's nothing left to lose and nothing left to gain,
the life is without sovereignty.

What is going to stay,
what's to become of the problems of life,
or will they all melt away,
where's the end to this strife.

Aaron J. Kurpiewski

Last Wish

Be sure when I go that everyone will know just how important they were to me.

When you're walking around trying to sort things out. Never let there be any doubt.

The love I feel for my children, grandchildren, and great-grandchildren, is all the same. No one got less and no one got more. So don't try to keep score.

In the end the most important part to me was that you all were there to show your love and how much you cared.

And I will take with me my beautiful thoughts and memories of you, my family. And know in my heart that through you and all your children a part of me, now and forever lives on.

Tamra Breitenfeldt

To Die?

Hi my name is Bob. I have no life. I have a girlfriend and she's really pretty. I can't talk to her very well though. I'm grounded for a week. Did I mention I have no life. I hate my parents. What's it like to die. To sleep as hamlet said. I can't find time for the things I enjoy anymore. I don't have the time. I get up to go to school track go home and talk on the phone. I have no life. What's it like to die. I want to know but I don't want to have to show myself. That makes no sense. I mean I don't want to have to kill myself. If I just die I don't think I'd care. Everyone will get over it soon enough...they'll forget, eventually. Even if I'm not here to help them through it. They'll get over it. Eventually...I'm not worth it anyway....no one cares; or they shouldn't... I don't...
what's it like to die.

Robert W. Marshall

Memories Of The Unknown

In the mystifying and somber corners of the brain,
Lies a cryptic boundary of the forgotten truth.
Its meaning and vivacious messages,
   are to be solved only by one's own sleuth.

As I begin my journey's end and trek into
   an eccentric voyage;
I must always protect the remaining memories I have,
   in a well-restrained and secret storage.

High and low I searched;
   every twist and turn led me no where.
Looking beyond in the continuing distances,
   I've realized that the truth wasn't out there.

As I traveled far and away from authenticity,
   I was suddenly awakened by a radiant sun stream.
Although my journey has been put on hold,
   I am certain to remember that unforgettable dream.

John Acquaviva

The Strangers

Under the lone flame's passionate eyes
king of the deep, clear blue skies,
three strangers search for treasure rocks,
it is them who the sea gently mocks.
The tallest one a dark-haired male
hair blowing in the forceful gale,
the other two both females
mysterious mermaids without tails.
They look high, look low amongst the wonders
the sea left behind,
not satisfied till they like what they find.
The seals all hide for there are strangers at bay,
no more in the sun do they innocently lay.
The strangers go back, the treasure sought is won,
under the eyes of the pure golden sun.

Emily Eslami

The Joy Of Love

Between dresses and gowns and flowers and prayers.
Your day is arriving, anxiety scares.
But seeing you both, so loving and free, and happy and peaceful, how great it will be.

To love someone more that you thought you could, when the vows are exchanged it will feel so good.

Some envy your love, some envy your joy,
some envy the two of you for not being coy.

You say "I Love You" before you hang up the phone.
And kiss each other before being alone.

You make it so easy, the love that you share as the day becomes closer you both will dare, to show off your love between family and friends, in hopes that it lasts and never ends.

Tina Villas

Crash

A child stolen from his bed,
Everyone presumes him dead.
Guilt lies upon his mother's head,
To what cruel fate had he been led?
For so long the hunt goes on,
No clue from dusk til dawn,
No one believes he's gone,
'Till they find something on the lawn,
Curled up and frozen cold his body lies
Unprotected from the merciless skies,
A banshee couldn't match his mother's cries,
But screams will not make the dead rise

Jenn Staub

My Mother

I looked at my mother standing
there. Holding back the tears as she
rubbed his hair. Saying good-bye to
yet another brother. Gone to heaven or
hell. One place or the other.
As she stood there looking out into
space, wondering why this thing bad
taken place. My cheeks began to fill
with tears, seeing my mother facing her fears.
I thought how thankful I was to
have my mother. I couldn't see
being raised by any other.
Lord, I thank you for, your kindness
and love. The only hand that
comes from above.
Please Lord, give my mother the
strength for today. I know you're the only way...

Deborah Fiddell

Surfer's Rendezvous

It's unbelievable how good the surf was today!
Small 2-3 footers smoked along the reef.
The low afternoon tide registering in the negatives.
Rain and fog handing off duties back and forth.
Yet here I was in the midst of it all
Enjoying wave after wave without a crowd;
My longboard finding its way into several pockets,
Screaming down the line to carve off the top.
It's all in a day's play,
This daily rendezvous with the ocean.
Birds chant a continual hymn.
Waves pound endlessly in a rhythm
That calls me back again, and again.
Is there such a thing as blessed bondage?

Tom Neth

"In The Future"

Shall we be again as we are?
Will our future world be the same?
Perhaps our footprints around the Earth
will be gone with the strength of time.
Nobody will have your name and my name
Only the wind will know where they are
And our words through the time
will be like snow above in the sky,
and at any place of that new world
you will be shining as a star
and the Moon will be your secret guardian,
witness of all what happened once a time,
and the cold winter of any day
will freeze your body and my face.
But we will not worry, as we will be back
perhaps as a stone, perhaps as a fire,
and the World will give birth to a new era
where I will be a rolling stone,
but never a sword.

Cesar J. Moreda

Untitled

God made many people black and
many people white. His choice, not ours.
We should respect this. Color, race or creed
are not important. What is important is
what man has in his head and his heart.
We should not touch another person except
in love of friendship. We should be kind to
each other we are all God's children.

Marian L. Harnett

Political Big Party

Grand ballroom the largest in town!
Red, white and blue balloons everywhere.
Pretty girls, and handsome guys greeting everyone.
Enchanting smiles, twinkling eyes, exquisitely attired guests
arrive in shiny limousines.
Everyone "looking good" long flowing gowns, expensive tuxedos,
Including too tight cummerbunds, high heeled shoes and
"crying out loud feet hurting" guests.
Plenty free liquor and good food, "it don't get no better
than this" guests!
New and used lies, endless speeches, feigns laughter and
tears abound,
The final hoax, the real classic joke, we will vote for
these clowns!

Annette M. Branche

Teardrop

A teardrop of love upon a heart,
Signals the end as lovers soon part.
A teardrop of love upon a smile,
Tells the story of parting for awhile.
A teardrop of love upon a soul,
Serves as hopes, or many a role.
A teardrop of love upon a life,
Presents itself as the blade of a knife.
A teardrop of love becomes a belief,
And helps to heal a lover's grief.
A teardrop of love forming a lake,
A place to gaze and hope whenever awake.
A teardrop of love, soon going away,
Replaced by a love that will always stay.

Galyn M. Thompson

"My Mothers Hands"

She never had time for taking a nap
nor for sitting quickly, hands in her lap
Until; she was old and worn & gray;
But still her hands moved in their restless way.

She'd rock back and forth in her old rocking chair
moving her hands, I remember her there.
Constantly moving, her dear sweet hands
as if she were working. One understands.

Her hands were then so soft and sweet
But moving, even while she was asleep
Her hands were restless until the day
My dear old mother had passed away

We stood and looked upon her face
Where shadows of sorrow had left their trace;
We knew her reward for doing his will,
and at last my mother's hands were still.

Irma M. Nava

Affected?

The sidewalk ice is smooth below my gait.
I tread with utmost caution, to ensure
A safe and fruitful day without ill fate.
The sun lies high above, its smile demure.
Behind the flurry white and cold is sky
Of summer past, a heaven blue in tint.
Through the beauty of the day, cars still fly
En masse, and of their goal I see no hint.
Inside the school the heaters puff away;
Within its walls are those of ruddy face.
I shed my gloves and much to my dismay,
My numb fingers seem molded firm in place.
Forsooth, the winter cannot hold me down;
The day excites but a grim little frown.

Markus Nystrom

Sea Of Whiskey

And I've lapped the loon, on the sea of whiskey.

There is nothing I wanted more than to claw night
slain on your back
And defer to time whose perfection reincarnates stale flesh to
    wined dreadnaught.

Here, where all I can think about is how I've lapped the loon,
    on the sea of whiskey.

Fallen drunk... rose ahead to the beat of a wisp. Rhythmless help
while stale life dates a lively death. Sacrificed spurred creativity
heeds toward grand nothingness.

And still the loon, lapped, shared... on the sea of whiskey

The sacred junction marks the realization of morality to mortality.
Lost pleasure meanders through weeping willows and birch sash.
The art of disintegration matches that of the latter (appreciation
worth seconds), As I assist my self destruction and in turn, wither
my brigade!

And the loon I've lapped might not have been apt,
If attention wasn't drawn from the poor to the scorned.
Mere, frail boy. Diminished amongst silenced witnesses; engulfed
by dark embarrassment of bodily reliance on substance alliance.

And the lapped loon peers aching disparity.
Eyes on lost me. Subtly unconscious to addiction
When the loon's tears rage... unto the sea of whiskey.
A. J. Fiorella

Sunflowers

Sunflowers aren't too bright or too big.
To me, they seem like green slender bodies,
With brown faces wearing yellow wigs.
And leafy hands that move like busybodies.

When the sun rises in the east.
They tilt toward the sun for a sunshine feast.
As the sun sets in the west.
They nod to sleep knowing they've impressed.

When their shoulder droops and their beauty fades,
And they approach their final hour.
They tenderly drop their precious seeds.
To reproduce next summer's sunflowers.

Their wigs blown off, and their bodies bent.
Their sweet, short life, I don't regret
Although the sunflowers lives are at an end.
Their seeds will soon bring me happiness again.
Cecilia Yuen

Patriotism

Patriotism, do you know what it means?
The red, white, and blue is the banner for our teams.
The Army, the Air force, the Navy, and Marines.
They uphold it with honor and respect, as it gleams.
But they alone can't do it all, they need each of us to wave it
as we stand proud and tall.

Freedom and liberty are words we don't hear often anymore,
it's certainly not something we can buy at a store.
We can't put a price on the cost of these,
but we can be thankful as we fall on our knees.
Thankful to our service personnel and veterans, and thankful to God,
that war is not being waged on American sod.

The 4th of July should be a glorious day, when we celebrate our
nation's birthday.
Picnics and fireworks we can all enjoy, but only when safety measures
we employ.
It's a day when we should show everyone world wide,
that we honor our country,
and will defend our liberty and freedom with pride.

God Bless America
Ellen M. Fisher

"My Little Boy's Pockets:"

My little boy's pockets, what do they hold?
Dozens of treasures, more precious than gold;
An old rusty knife with a very dull blade;
A piece of green glass, looking like jade.

   A key badly bent that won't fit any lock,
   An intricate part of an old broken clock
   Marbles, some gum, and bits of string too,
   An old bottle cap with a beautiful hue.

The foot of a rabbit, a "lucky sea shell,"
Some bark of a tree and a little Xmas red bell.
A little lead soldier, some thick rubber bands,
And stamp and two coins from far distant lands

   Part of a map to his treasures, all tattered and torn
   A whistle of tin all battered, bent and worn,
   A frog or small snake he has captured himself
   And six shiny pennies, to add to his wealth.

A hand full of marbles to challenge his friends
The days are so short and the night has no need.
With all of these treasures, he's as rich as three kings;
My little boy's pockets are filled with, such wonderful things!
Charlotte Childers

Prey Be Polite

An owl sat beneath a summer's night moon
   As a frog croaked a gravelly tune:
"I'm an old bull frog and I rest on this log
   "Where I shall sing to my lady fair:
"We live in the swamp where it's terribly damp
   "And our skin doesn't have any hair."
The owl looked about and gave out a hoot:
   "You've a croaky old voice and that I salute,
"But your costume's unclean, so warty and green,
   "That your garb you ought to forswear,
"Along with your queen, if you know what I mean,
   "'Cause just one of you's worse than a pair."
The frog flicked out his tongue as a dragonfly clung
   To a blade where some swamp grass had sprung,
Then gave out a belch that surely did squelch
   The owl's thought to make further remark;
He just flew from that limb, glided over the rim
   And swooped down with a silence quite stark,
Hauled the frog to his nest where he put him to rest,
   And grilled grenouilles for a visiting shark.
James McTighe

On The Occasion Of Cutting Down My Apple Tree

I tried my best to save you!
We argued and I was loyal to you.
I fought a valiant battle to save you;
But, you see, I lost the war.

Each year you gave me joy when, on Mother's Day,
You transformed into an enormous ball of popcorn.
I felt this performance was for me alone,
And I was honored.

Your flowers were so abundant
That admirers would stop to pay homage.
Yet, as much as I loved you,
I couldn't protect you from the others.

I cannot imagine your age!
As your gnarled branches became hollow,
And little wild creatures nested within your shell,
Rendering you hollower still,
They felt you had become a danger,
Yet I refused to believe them.

But now I stand before you, unable to contain my sorrow,
And I apologize.
Mary De Longis

My Memory of Little Allan

There's a little boy in Tennessee
Who means the whole world to me.
  It broke my heart to see him go
  because I wanted the chance to watch him grow.

There are many things of which I will not part
Those are the memories close to my heart.
  He has touched my life beyond measure
  Time spent with him was such a pleasure.

His toys are packed and stored away
Until his arms can hold them again someday
  I no longer live in the house that he knew
  I no longer dwell in the rooms where he grew.

When I drive by the playground where he used to play
My mind recollects many a day
  When he'd swing on the swings and play on the slide
  And dig in the sand with his pail at his side.

He never wanted to leave that fun filled park
Some days we didn't leave until it got dark.
  My Grandson means the world to me
  Here in my heart he will always be.

Darlene D. Laurie

It's Already Been

    Standing strong with my spiritual awareness.
Clenching violently for any shred of sanity.
Fearful of loosing any hopes for love. Searching
desperately for the path, that I've gone as try.
Putting anything in my body, trying to ease the
pain. Isolating my memory, and all emotions
stored away. Trying to fight the hatred, that grows
more and more each day. A hatred that burns
so deep, blackening out all the warmth,
while love waits shivering in the dark. Freedom
rests, behind a locked door, searching for that
fallen key, somewhere on the darkened floor.
    Waiting for a sign, from a father, I can not
find. Traveling far, searching wide, for the boy I
left behind, still he cry's, for the love, he can not
find. Rejected by happiness, grieving inside,
wondering how he wants to die. Giving up, for
he fears he's to weak inside. He left his
home, all of his emotions, seamed to have died.
Forced to live on, he try's to rebuild what's already been destroyed.

Glen Kleinheksel

A Poem Of Faith

Oh God I pray to thee, to hear
the prayers that come from me.

Some of them may be selfish
request, yet I know "THY WILL
BE DONE" is always best.

You see dear Lord I am very ill,
my faith causes me to depend upon thy will.

I believe you will not permit
more than I can bear.
So wrap me in thy loving care.

Lord do not leave me all alone,
and when its time please call me home.

I confess to thee, dear Lord, of
all my sins, and I ask in Jesus'
name my soul to cleanse.

I look not Lord for glory or fame,
I pray this prayer in Jesus" name.
I pray too, Lord, that all who
suffer shall be blessed, and when
this life is over their souls shall rest... Amen.

Charles W. McLeod

Mind's Garden

There in the dirt, where all things begin, life's lessons run long
and deep-rooted in the mind—

Grandpa's corn: Dig the hole medium-deep to provide
the young seed a strong foundation.

A golden, six-foot, snow-topped Oak tree with trembling hands
provided a foundation that always helped his corn grow strong in
spirit and soul, ———" Anything, you can do anything"

Mama's "chile": Trench a shallow circle all around to ensure water
and nourishment always.

Such nourishment from the forever care giver alowed that "chile" to
in turn nourish all passers-by when served in a "molcajete" with her
authentic tortillas and beans, ——"Sit, stay a while"

Dad's tomatoes: Tie the young plant around a vertical stick to
help it grow straight and tall, all the while being very careful not
to hurt the plant's fragility.

Hands together, gently he points his plants and his children to God.
The provider beams with pride as he looks at his prize tomatoes
round the family dinner table,
——"Let us bow our heads and pray for God's blessing"

There in the dirt, where all things begin, life's lessons run long
and deep-rooted in the mind.

Pearl R. Perez

Story Of The Fieldmouse

When they strode onto the field,
Their guns were gleamin' bright.
With faces hoping, looking, wanting,
Brave men who fought, 'gainst evil wrought.

They stood their lines, they held their stay,
Against the flying horrors.
But one by one, they struck them down,
Their screams a mingled chorus.

Their bodies lay, against the dirt,
Their hands outstretched in need.
Their faces sad, their clothes in rags,
No mouths with which to plead.

As days went by, their bodies rotted,
Hearts become the earth.
Their skeletons lay there, hungry, empty,
No longer did they hurt.

Brave men who fought, 'gainst evil wrought,
Sacrificial, in its way.
But no one cries, or says goodbye,
It's just the price they have to pay.

Adam Steel

Full Open Throttle

Roaring thunder, chrome steel and wheel,
Full length chap, spur on heel.
Open road in wind past sage,
Broad smile, true heart, turned page.

Black glove, buckled boot, strong conviction,
Long hair curled, loving contradiction.
Friend of all, family tie,
Charming glint in brown eye.

Fringed leather, red wing, gold letter,
Worn by new angel — free, untethered.
Hard long day, love of child,
Spirit strong, brave but mild.

Freedom ride on eagle wing,
Heaven's music spoke will sing.
Engine heated, oil over rod,
Devil cheated, true with God.

Jim Rainguet

The Cycle Of Salvation

Spring.
Budding in the wisdom of God,
the tree exercises faith
in the unforseen weather of hope.
Summer.
Greenery,
dancing in knowledge of the redemption,
enjoys the truths of freedom,
as it lives in the moment.
Autumn.
Brilliant flaunting colors,
enmeshed in self righteousness,
take pride in their beauty,
forgetting their creator.
Winter.
Stripped of all treasures and glory,
earth's structure is scorned and chastised.
In humility,
the tree bares it naked soul
and pleads for forgiveness.

Gabrielle Allen

Poem For The Children

How can someone do this to our country?
To blow up our friends, or people we love.
It must be hard to live with it.
The people who did it must have felt great hatred
for people they did not even know.
The people who did this must have got
pleasure out of killing people.

To the person who did this, I wonder...
Did you do it of your own free will,
or did someone pay you?

All you will remember is...
the bomb and
the deaths.

We have to remember.
losing our loved ones...
and the people we knew,
most of all...

the children...

Cameron P. Apple

From Me Two You

It's time I told you what I meant. Love? Yes
it's gone to that extent.

Your love a warm breeze always so gentle.
Touching aspects of my being spiritual,
physical and mental.

The personification of beauty it's you I seek.
Your essence signifies love so profound, so unique.

Your inner beauty reflects a positive vibe. An
inner glow of warmth I can't describe.

A cloak of elegance beyond compare. Your love,
your life! I hope to share.

Embodied with peace from true feelings it's
inspired. It's your selfless acts of love I
always admired.

Eternity's captive my love for you stands all
time. As it reaches its zenith, the beauty of its prime.

I pledge my love, my heart for all infinity.
With love, respect and trust the one true trinity.

Garry C. Brown

A Love Not Forgotten

Remembering the good times is often hard to do,
because of all the bad times we had to struggle through.

I remember your warmth, your gentle kiss and
touch, and how you'd look at me and say,
"I love you so very much."

Your strength and concern, your love and comforting
voice, made me want to be with you, no matter
what the choice.

You'll never find comfort and devotion like mine
how faithful I was for "5" years of our time.

I wish I was dreaming, told everything's okay,
what a lesson I learned, how differently I'd live today.

A dream is a wish your heart makes, one day my
dream came true. I'm grateful for the memories
and the chance at loving you.

I'll always love you, and never forget - 3/10/89 -
on the day that we met.

The years they were hard, but we made it this far -
July 94' when my heart got its scar.

Robyn Lash

A Message To My Daughter

When you were small and held my hand,
Way back then I didn't understand

How I'd feel to be your mother
Or what we'd mean to one another.

When you were small and you'd cry and pout
I didn't know what it was all about.

I didn't know that as you grew,
And time went by, that I'd grow too.

And in those years when we drew apart
And you pulled against me and hurt my heart.

I didn't know that was growing too.
And it bound us closer, me and you.

And when I look, now, I can see
A part of you in every part of me.

You won't feel, yet, quite like a mother
Or what you'll mean to one another,

But when your daughter holds your hand
You, too, one day will understand.

Betsy Montoya

Stevie Ray

Although I never got to meet you we had
some really great times together. Your music
inspired me more than words can say. You
had the talent that will go a long way. It helped
others that is in the same path today.
You will always be a great memory as will
your music is of today. I will always miss
you Stevie Ray Vaughan. You will always
have more than just my love. You will always
be remembered forever by everyone today.
Some people make the world special just
be being in it. Stevie Ray made the world
a special place.

Samantha Brady

The Handsome Stranger

The most lovely where all were beautiful....How should I forget
thee........Are thou the chosen one? At length your presence left
my lady compelled to inquire about thee., having possibly seen thou
in my dreams and that thou appeared delighted with my lady's
notice. At length your statuesque seemed of a novel gentleman
glowing of supreme
chacator, your loveliness indeed exquisite. Thou's presence indeed
spellbinding; my lady's senses became heightened, my lady's
heart began to race, her blood stir....as intimacy arose.
Thoroughly
astonished I was possessed with a passion.

My lady wishes to bestow herself unto thee., To visit thou's
chambers
or sanctuary. I behold thee, presenting a gobletful of wine to thou
lips....to brighten thou's wits while my lady reads, and
you listen to one of your favorite romances as we carelessly take no
note of time. Come, let us drink and sweetly converse. An excellent

jest and a well contrived pleasantry if I do say so myself.

Hoping to have much in unison, I shall unburden my soul....as we
blissfully travel together passed the second star to the right and
straight on till morning's first light of day.

For only passion and time will completely tell the tale!

The Hopeless romantic.
Pam H. Moreland

Red Night

A red night is knocking to my window sorrow
A red night is whispering fear
A red night is here
forever talking of your dreams,
anguish
A red night, my ichor.

A red night may enter to my alcove
   clapping, sobbing, claiming
for the path to be open, for the heart to be broken, for the
child to be buried, for the parents to be forgotten, for the
light to be crushed, for a prayer to be splattered.

A red night hangs on my tree, usually
within seven days, turning it in hardbound anthologies
of sorrow.
   WHY?

Red night, train me hard and treat me like you're really
unborn, a name to be created, a shadow to be
transplanted, a heart to be aflame, a poem to be thread,

Red night, love me.
Maria Zielina

Reunited

Someday thou wish thee wed,
To surmise bears pain - a dream.
Don't believe though I foreseen?
A ghastly doubt from you I dread.
When the warmth of the sun comes along again,
And our last footprints have sunk in sand.
You will envision a love, an utter recall,
Within moments you shall appall.
But this shall not happen for I'll be damned.
I shall call for you to reach out your hand.
My angel don't fear I shall come,
Together reunited as one.
Michael James Caputi

Jessica

We all dream.
Dreams are noble
And should be followed
We can make it happen
We have that choice

You studied and worked
Used all your capabilities
You were brave.

Still writing in print
Just learning fractions
Your average child
With a world record
In your eyes.

The people who lead you
Didn't realize
That sometimes the best time
Isn't now.

They denied you that choice.

You gave it your best shot
But you will never have the chance to try again.
Mary Dillon

Hello Darlin

As my body lies next to the warmth of you
I feel your tender, wonderful touch
and listen for the words spoken so much
They could be special if only you'd see
That they were spoken only for me
Hello Darlin is what I hear
But are you ever really sincere.

I shall never change my mind about you
But oh how I wish you would be true
I'll miss you my Darlin if you should go
So please stay with me, so I will know
the warmth of your love that I need so

Get closer now so our bodies touch
and turn our love into wonderful lust
We feel the heat as our bodies entwine
Slowly and passionately we become one
Rising and meeting, over and over
Completing our love and passion forever
Sharon Voorhis

Our Earth

Towering mountains reach for the sky,
storms so violent, birds dare not fly.
Rivers run swollen, so deep and so fast,
fires scorch trees, winds come as blasts.
Some of us stare, some of us moan,
but this is our earth, this is our home.

This blue green orb, moving through space,
is home to many, not only our human race.
The animals and plants, who we all know so well,
our companions today, tomorrow we kill.
But the earth keeps track, and she knows the score,
for the earth is alive, and ready to roar.

From deep within, molten rocks still flow,
our earth is still changing, continuing to grow.
When the upper-crust breaks, people yell "quakes,"
When the rivers flood, they wallow.
When the hurricanes blow, the sailors all know,
how easily the great seas can swallow.

As time goes on, soon we'll all be gone,
but the earth, of course will live on.
Peter T. Brightwell

Open Your Eyes... A Villanelle

Open your eyes and you will agree;
Sadness remains and people ask why
There are things in this world that just shouldn't be.

A begging man who cannot see,
Poor children abandoned and left to cry;
Open your eyes and you will agree.

A girl supporting her fatherless baby,
Seeing bright toys which she cannot buy;
There are things in this world that just shouldn't be.

A man jailed in innocence, longing to be free
From the injustice of another man's lie;
Open your eyes and you will agree.

Street-living families who can't pay the fee,
Kids who spend money just getting high;
There are things in this world that just shouldn't be.

This sadness can be changed into hope that maybe
We can make a difference if we try.
Open your eyes and you will agree
There are things in this world that just shouldn't be.

Catherine Cuccia

Who Wants My Vote

Who wants my vote?
Please tell me who wants my vote.

Every election is the same: Scrambling, struggling, jockeying, criticizing-each other.
Appeasing, cajoling, promising, serenading-me;
What? No sincerity, hope, prosperity, resolve, character?
Who wants my vote?

The representative of my morality? My heritage? My finances?
Please tell me who wants my vote?

No one?
What if no one wants my vote?
Does it still count as much?
If it is cast and nothing is caught, did it make a sound?
Who gets my vote?

Distinguished or honest or pragmatic or ignoble, humble or resilient,
or experienced or earnest?
Infidelity or wimp, innate or impractical, stubborn and a buffoon.
Court me, whine me, spend the most time and rubles on me, but if I don't know who gets my vote, you won't either.

Brian Rossman

Wings Of A Dream

Adrift, adrift towards slumber of night
Enfold me under white wings of flight.
An origin of pleasure, no reality
Just angelic peace and tranquility.
Life and Love that seldom satisfy me
Can saturate my soul with such ecstasy.

Accepting no warning if evil since birth
Adrift my soul feels no fear of this Earth.
Into the silence of the night I fly
Beneath the arch of the vast clear sky.
Where the white clouds gather and rest
From crest to violet crest.

On the face of rain covered fields I flew
Embrace me, tease me with a rainbows hue.
The sun is rising as the nightingale sings
Behold what soon the morning brings.
Adrift, adrift on the wings of moonbeams
Awakened, I merely have known but a dream!

Charlotte Hovis

A Child Within

Sometimes I wonder what it would feel like to be a child within.
Waiting for sunshine and for my life to begin.
Wondering if my parents really wanted me to be conceived
Then I heard my mother's voice and felt just so relieved.
Her voice is always gentle and I feel my father's touch
Knowing they will love me, for I love them very much.
Then once I'm finally born, I want my mother to hold me tight
Never letting me go, just loving me with all of her might.

Tracey Bonidie

Friendship

A Wedding Toast for Amy and Gerard - July 15, 1995
Whether across the street or miles away,
Some "Friendship" thoughts on your special day......

Friendships are life's greatest pleasure.
Surely, one's Most Valued Treasure.

Honesty - to rule your thought.
Happiness - to guide your heart.

Love to give. No hesitation.
Sound advice. No limitation.

Fears to hold to share, to hide.
Tears to flow from all your pride.

Due respect one to another.
Sharing, caring not to hover.

Friendships are used to learn and teach...
So keep these rules within your reach.

May your life together-as-one be filled with joy and happiness!!
Prosit!!
NA ZDROWIE!!

John "Deco" Decolati, Best Man

Mother To Son — Sons And Mothers

First I say —
That being a Mother is tough...

Bring a Mother-in-law to my Son,
is tougher...

And I know too,
When sons marry, they must leave behind
The shelter — of their Moms.

Those she is either trial or tribute—
To the Man he has become—

And — outside the wall that must surround
his life

We — now Mothers-in-law — stand
like beggars — peering over...

Chickki Salmon

On Nearing The End

Last fall I lived to see the autumn breeze
Dance with leaves of red and yellow in the trees
And knew perhaps when fields were white with snow
The call might come and I would have to go.

But April's here and still my heart beats on.
The blooms of tulips rule where snow is gone.
They'll bloom again when spring is back next year
For other eyes to watch as they appear.

Perhaps their colors may be mine to share
From paradise - or else the blossoms there
Will be so grand no grief will interfere
To make my spirit wish it were still here.

Lorene C. Nelken

An Enlightened Youth

Ah! That it would be so!
That I should love this house,
But this town has grown too old for me,
My room has grown too cold for me.

Ah! That I should leave forever!
I've grown too old for this,
And my room is as a child's —
Pink with linen sheets.

Ah! How I long to grow up!
How I wish never to return!
Oh! How many years from now
My ghost shall come and say:

"In this house I played once,
I was young and alive once,
Ah! How I wasted my youth
On thinking that to be old is to be free!"

"And I shall stand in this room
Far colder, and far older than it,
A child will be on the bed
Young and alive soon old and dead!"
Cara M. Nasello

The Moment

How quietly and gently did you come
Into my heart and mind with peace and love
The moon could not your steps reflect,
  nor yet the sun
Tho' with your entrance time below, above
  were one

None else but we, as spirits in a time

Together we were lifted up on high

So pure and clear our treasurers
  thine and mine
To glimpse. all else is nought
  we give to find

You came to give this moment finely spun

In gold and purple, knowing how my soul

Would swell with one embrace
  then you were gone
To show the way, Oh thank you
  precious one.
Carolyn Mendenhall-Lynch

Our Life

They met at a health club, amongst the free weights,
After a bit, they went on a few dates.
They parted as close friends, and still always talked...
Yet deep in their hearts feelings remained locked.

They saw others as the years passed, ...
If nothing else, their friendship did last.
There never seemed a time when both were unattached,
Little did they know; they were wrongly matched.

Until one year ago, on New Years Eve,
Feelings poured out; it was fate we believe!
Now the couple is rarely seen apart, ...

NEVER underestimate the Power
  of
    the
      HEART
JoAnn J. Perloski

"'Twas The Day Before Christmas"

'Twas the day before Christmas and all through the bakery
every creature was stirring and something good making.

The cookies and pies were all nestled snug on the shelves.
While we bakers all were quiet proud of ourselves.

I in my apron and Deb in her vest
were gazing to see what needed baked next.

When out on the floor there arose such a clatter
we ran to the front to see what was the matter.

When what to our wondering eyes should appear
but a hoard of 800 shopping carts guests were trying to steer.

They were grabbing the cookies, the pies and the cakes
and shouting for more, "we simply can't wait!"

They reached for the bread and cinnamon rolls, too.
They bought every muffin and donut as they passed through.

The bakery was empty with not a package in sight
and Deb turned and shouted as she jumped into flight.

More Donuts! More Muffins! More bread and cream pies!
More bagels, more pretzels, more cakes and more pies.

Now laying her hand aside of her head and wishing she was still home in her bed.

We heard her exclaim! As she ran through the bakery and ducked out
  of sight.
"It's overtime for everyone this Christmas Eve Night.!"
Judy Fultz

Geopolitical Variation

Self fertilization kills specie:
genetics limited to singularity disappear

into dust and emerge as waste molecules
between air and egg; geopolitics creeps

into greed: species spontaneously
metastasize, and those immune to

eccentricity wither by righteous
unilateral design, spurning adaptation,

disinclined to survive tragedy,
the rigid, crippled, cannot crawl

under the geopolitical fence to cross
breed on sunless granite plates.
Cile Pace

Thanksgiving to God

I thank my God for all He has given;
Each day the night, and the "Son" that has risen.
I thank Him for this cycle of life;
For the son, the daughter, the husband, the wife.

I thank my God for His blessings to me;
For spiritual healing, for my "green tree."
I thank Him for love, deep in my soul,
From the beginning, and now, and when I grow old.

I thank my God with tears, unashamed;
Singing His song, honoring His name.
And in the end, a place to rest,
And pray with those who loved me best.
Charlene M. Sypien

Like Him

I'll tell you what I'd like to be;
To be a part of every tree
The drops of dew on all the grass
To ride the wind as it goes past
The snow on every mountaintop
The drop of pearl in each raindrop
In every kind and gentle smile
To have no hate, to speak no guile
In streams of tears that wet each cheek
To beat with hearts so brave, yet meek
I cannot be for I'm too small
But I've a friend who's over all
He sees the sparrows when they fall
He calls the winds and they obey
He sends the night and brings the day
I cannot be what I'd like to be
But I've a promise from my friend to me
That someday I will be like he
Beyond this time, beyond this place
On wings of love by boundless grace
I shall behold his wondrous face for I shall be like him
And I shall see him as he is!
   Barbara A. Dixon

In Loving Memory

I still remember you,
always will.
You will never be
far from my mind.
The way you made people
smile or the way
you helped with other's troubles
You never complained,
always content with the happiness of your children.
Lived life for the joy of being in it, bringing amusement
wherever you went.

But that has all changed, you are no longer with us.
Passed on to something much better
Hopefully you can see how everybody has missed you so,
your memory has been burned into our heart.
We will never forget.
   David Emerson Johnson

My Soul Yearns

My soul yearns for the day that my dreams are fulfilled.
My soul yearns for God to make all of my dreams for real.
My eyes cry the tears of heartache, waiting for that day.
My eyes cry often because this world seems to take my dreams away.
My heart cries out because it seems to feel a loss.
My heart cry out because to take a chance there's a cost.
Taking a chance on being happy taking a chance on being hurt.
One day feeling high as a cloud, one day feeling low as dirt.
Never really going through the sunshine, but always seem to find the
   rain.
Hoping for that special treasure, but trying to cope with my pain.
Something in my heart tells me to keep on waiting for that day.
Something in my soul makes me feel that everything will be okay.
I have no choice but to hold on to what I hope for.
Without my hopes and dreams, my life would be no more.
I have to be strong and make it through the days
because I've been told that trouble don't last always.
   Tommikco T. Brown

Rhythms Of Life

Summer of change intense and hot
   Sun spoken dreams that I forgot.
As others bask in warmth and fun,
   I see the life that I've begun.
On the path of life I take a new walk
   But the birds still sing and the flowers talk.
Spring and her light were mine for a time
   But autumn will send new chapters of rhyme.
September leaves of splendor play and
   Shuffle dance to skies of gray.
Each bold hue of yellow and red color
   facets of life which soon are dead.
Lonely winter cries cold with rain
   But rhythmic tears fall not in vain.
They wash away a saddened past—
   They splatter dreams that couldn't last.
The snowfall dance of wisdom's song
   Paints the path I walk along.
Because seasons are pages in the book
   Of time, they set smiles and tears to rhyme.
   Debra Van Ness

It's Just Me

   Look at the outside, not within, and you will have
lost before you begin.
   If you had just taken the time to peal off my layers,
you would have answered one of my prayers.
   You could be wrong by what you think you see, you know
we might have been friends, you and me.
   We could have worked things out, we just needed to
talk and share.
   But because you saw only the outside. I'm not there.
   Donna Templemire

Dear Margaret — Our 58th Anniversary
(2/22/38 - 2/22/96)

To Us

Come! Take my hand as we stroll down the memory mile,
And at our secret rendezvous, we will linger a little while
Softly reflecting the moments of the past
Happily noting our love did really last
The tears, the joys and thoughts, yet to come
The laughter and the pleasure, oh, it was so much fun!
Holding hands with you, so dearest to my heart
Sharing our love, that was with us from the start.
And now, returning from years that used to be
To the gracious twilight years for you and me!
   Nunzio Cerniglia

Ashes To The Sea

The one true love of my life, now you are gone,
how in this world am I supposed to carry on.

With the very special bond between me and thee,
one that I believe will last through eternity.

Your memory, lovingly etched in my heart
mind and soul, will help me to do my best,
until it is my turn to lay at rest.

We may not lay in the ground side by side,
but will be together with each turning tide.

As I will have my ashes scattered to the sea,
and as ocean always touches land,
I always will be touching thee.
   Mary Trout

What Do You Do?

What do you do,
When the wide world goes dark
and the sun goes out,
When even the tallest trees cry
and all the flowers pout?

What do you do,
When the moon stops smiling
and the stars stop winking,
When the blue ocean fades gray
and your ship starts sinking?

What do you do,
When the Earth falls to a sad silent
and the music ceases,
When the grand gold disappears
and your rainbow shatters to pieces?

What do you do,
When the wish isn't worth the penny you threw,
When life is an endless maze
What do you do?
ENDURE
Tina M. Sand

Looking To The Rainbow

Looking to the rainbow
The light of God's love glows.
The many colors - brilliant and fair
Reassures His mercy's always there.

Red represents Jesus' blood that flowed
Orange for the warmth of a firelight's glow
Yellow for the sun's warmth and light
Green represents continued growth and life
Blue for the never-ending sky
Indigo for the deep blue seas
And violet represents God's royalty

The colors together number seven
All created by God in His heaven.
Yes, looking to the rainbow
God's loving grace surely shows.
Wendy M. Eckert

My Grandpa

Many's the hour as a child I spent
With my Grandpa, a kindly old gent.
We would walk for miles down country lanes
In summer sunshine and early spring rains.

Some afternoons we would stroll for a while
Along an old footpath and sit on the stile.
He'd light up his pipe and puff smoke rings high
And shout out a welcome to folks who passed by.

They would all know him and shout back,
"Everything's fine,"
For everyone loved him, that old Grandpa of mind.
Now I look back to the days that have gone,
There is the field gate that we both sat upon.

And the old country lanes that we walked early morn.
And I thank you, Dear God, from the day I was born.
For you gave me a person, who was sweetly divine,
A beautiful person, that Grandpa of mine.
Peter Rouch

Pearl

My freshwater pearl in an ocean despair,
Broken waves dash high against the shore,
I too am alone
A broken wing floating through the winds of time.
My eyes are gray;
My heart is torn.
I am only a memory, gone forever, never to return,
Never to float on a sparkling river that still runs free.
I am only a haunting voice, echoing down a distant canyon,
Illuminated only by the night moon.
Julie Trahan

One Man's Life

The beginning...birth
A son, brother, pampered...amused
Childhood exploring, rebellious ...abused
Teenager
   sports, drugs, runaway ...confused
Adult
   society member, lonely, unmotivated ...bruised
Marriage
   husband, provider, expectations ...amused
Military
   war, separation, scared ...misused
Birth
   father, family, overwhelmed ...enthused
Divorce
   angry, drinking, spiteful ...refused
Death
   a gun, a note, suicide .. excused
After death
   a memory, sadness the end...
LesLee J. Fornof

Burning Song

   Burning Song, within the breath of my soul. Your love is brighter than the morning star, giving light to all! Reasons, for being on this earth's core.

   Burning Song, within the breath of my soul. Days have gone into years, as darkness is falling into rest, We know seeing all glory, in the twinkle of your eye, shining brighter than all the stars in the sky. As one light unto all.

   Burning Song; within the breath of my soul. Your tears are as precious as rain's morning dew.
As all is prepared for the warm rays to come, shining forth the earth's beauty. No comparison to your love!

   Burning Song! Within the breath of my soul. Releasing all truth, within the freeing of a darkened soul, once forgotten. Sacrificing all for love. Fulfilling the eternal heavens as we return together forever. (AMEN)
Paul L. Henson, Jr.

Life

Life is lived, as life is taught.
No life starts, with its own thought.

Our plans are made, from what we learn.
Our minds made up, in silent turn.

Close your eyes, and picture when.
Your parents told you, now and then.

We become what they project.
Their plans for life, we protect.

So simple as it all may seem.
We live first, in our parents' dreams.
James Callaway

Ready Or Not

Ready or not it was then time to rise.
All those who yielded were counted as wise.
Passion for sleeping meant missing the mark.
Too many slumbered from dawn through the dark.
Useless was effort to quicken their pace.
Regrets revealed they were out of the race.
Erase this long nightmare many did cry.
Dying they'd missed flying high in the sky.
Courage couldn't conquer fountains of tears.
Appraising the future only bred fears.
The trump had sounded removing all hope.
Coming disasters would cause them to grope.
Henceforth the slothful would realize the cost.
Ignoring the truth had rendered them lost.
Now all the faithful were soaring above.
God had them sheltered in fathomless love.
Always watchful and prayerful were they.
While working they squandered no time with play.
Alarms had rung out warning everyone.
You can ascend by following the Son.
Beverly Jean Smith

The Black Of My Mind

Life continues day by day
Moving forth in such a pitiful way,
Motivation decreases as I go
Feeling down, self-worth at a low,
  My friend, for you,
  Anything I would do,
  My love for you so dear,
  But you're not here,
The killer killed again
Something no one else could mend,
My heart gray and filled with fear
And the pain doesn't fade through all these tears,
My memory is all that is left
You're someone that I can't forget,
  Please live through me,
  And see what I see,
  There's so much I didn't show you.
Lori Quantrille

Lovers Fruit Basket

I choose to love you as a desired fruit "to preserve
you" that you may keep your freshness.
I choose to help you shine, from the love that I'll
give you.
I choose to handle you wisely, to prevent any bruises.
I choose to wipe you down slowly, to maintain the softness
of you skin.
I choose not to peel, before I bite, that I may enjoy
your true flavor.
I choose to get to the core of things, so that new seeds
may spring forth.
Be to me like, the fruit of this basket. So that I can
fill you with variety, dress you daily. Be here for you
no matter what the reason, change with you for every
season.
Janice Grannum

Sunset

The sunset was a pad of melting butter,
glittering, glowing in the golden western sky.
Twas all shades of the rainbow,
was setting o'er the ocean like a dolphin diving into the sea.
It seemed to take an eternity to melt past the horizon.
The sun walked down, down, out of sight.
Mary Counts

The Real You Lost?

You play different roles for different folks, your old friends and
  the new, you play different roles for family and for strangers too.

You may try hard at playing a carefree happy "nut."
  But if you are not careful, you'll end up in a rut.

That rut then if not changed wears into a deep groove,
  The groove becomes a trench from which you cannot move.

Your soul, your heart, your mind, screams out for you to save,
  That deep dark trench from becoming an even deeper grave.

Life becomes a challenge as from role to role you're tossed,
  But if you do not know yourself, the real you is truly lost!
Madeline S. Roman

The Worthy Patron Elect

In the East, sits the Worthy Patron Elect,
his head held high, his body erect.
The Worthy Matron, beside him stands,
looking like a saint.
She turns to call on him,
and he looks as though he will faint!

His face takes on a sickly grin,
sweat begins dripping off his chin.
His knees begin to tremble,
his hands begin to shake.
Inaudibly he says "Oh Lord, I've
made a terrible mistake."

He knows he cannot leave the platform now,
so he executes a feeble bow.
He reaches for his notes,
which he knows, will leave the crowd in stitches.
He finds, to his dismay,
he's left them in his other britches!
Donald E. Henderson

Child's Safety

Wanting to be held like a child
whose dreams have gone wild
Paying the price for 'safety'
after all nothing in life is ever free

Consumed by lust
uncontrollably falling fast
trying to recall decent ideas from the past

So hold me like your scared child
That I might rest my swollen eyes for just a little while
Entering a world of unpredictable dreams
where things are always what they seem...
Victoria A. Elliott

The Smells At My Father's Grave

  My father was a farmer
Some days stern from his childhood pain
Sometimes stronger from his will and gain.
  I remember that he'd pray for a farmer's
good yield, as I go down a country road
and smell wheat and hay in the fields.
  The cherry blossoms he'd bring in
for my mother, put a smile on her face
as they smelled so sweet in the morning haze.
  When I go to his grave though not often
enough, I smell those smells at my
father's grave.
  A tribute to my father
I love you and miss you dearly.
Christine P. Sheetz

Faith

Heart sighs whispering softly,
Unknown rhythms beating melody.
Gently focus on the specter,
Rays of thought gliding in wonder.
Tremors of hope falsely accusing.
Shaken within perseverance surging.

Questioning all that drives one on,
Lifting spirits of dreams bygone.
Never doubting in ultimate fate,
Resolving oneself in languorous wait.
The will of One Greater alone cries out,
Steady belief in His hands held out.

Prayers unanswered beg to question,
Herein lies the only solution.
Love unconditional so purely felt,
Hands of fate securely dealt.
Unquestioned faith in the path set down,
Holy love within arms held bound.
   Tony H. Haverda

Pages Of Time

If memories were money, I'd be a millionaire.
God has really filled my life with tender loving care.

He gave me parents who were poor, but loving, kind and true.
With seven hungry children, there were many things to do.

Hunting mushrooms, picking berries, planting gardens, canning cherries.
We all worked when we were able, just to kept food on the table.

"Children, now you stay together" Mother said in days of yore.
Daddy with his arm around her, waving out the kitchen door.

Looking backward through my life, there's nothing left to gain.
Our children with their children, we're like an endless chain.
   Rowena L. Bacon

Day Dreams

Today I walked down Willow Creek
   crossed that old wooden bridge
the way I did so many times
   when I was just a kid.

I walked down to the swimming hole
   in the shade of the big oak tree
and took a swing on the old bag swing
   that brother made for me.

I walked along a meadow,
   and smelled the new mown hay
and heard the cry of a red tail hawk
   searching for its prey.

I set down to rest on a hickory stump
   and watched two squirrels at play
and I had to smile as I thought to myself
   you've had a busy day.

It's strange the way one's mind goes back
   when you day dream all alone.
Just sitting here in this old wheelchair
   on the porch of the old rest home.
   Mitchell Langford

Winter

In the winter snow falls, children play
   and animals hibernate everyday
Sometimes you just want to curl up in bed
   and watch the fire that is o so red
Or, you can wake up to a snowy day, enjoy your hot coco,
   and then set out to play.
   Jenna Spates

Rebel Heart

Brought to this life by chance.
Born in an era of old despair.
What was it to have not a care?

A loner by choice.
Always haunted by that inner voice.
With only a restless rebel heart for company.

Though he had a family, wife, and children dear.
The path he followed was his own, and clear.
The quest to seek - for one such as he.
A mortal, yet kindred soul.
A brother.

Reaching mid-life, his age two-score and four.
He met his brother, come from a far distant shore.
Borne not of one blood, yet brothers true.
Of one heart, and one mind, these two, were two of a kind.

Words weren't necessary, of that, there was no need.
What, and when one thought, the other would heed.
In more important ways they brothers be.
Two rebel hearts, two kindred souls.
Brothers throughout eternity.
   Amanda Jeffers Cooler

"I Feel"

It's when I lay the kiss you gave, sent exuberant waves, is what I crave.
It's the hair that stands upon the arm it makes me write such lonely
poems it wakes me in the break of dawn I swore never because I've
been scorn to let this take me in scares me deep my heart I lend.
But the kiss and the warm felt touches within my heart so much
my eyes they search in the windows to see if your search back and
look at me like an extra layer upon the skin touches thy heart so
deep within.

The walk, the talk not perfect at all but yet the jokes and
laughter calls calls upon but barely feels that kiss, the touch, it
softly kills
It's not a kill, that does the harm it's chilling kill that feels
the morn.
Cause in the morn it's you that lies upon the thing that hate despise,
won't speak of hate no room for it, can't split thy heart it eternal
but the kiss, the touch, the after blast hopes and prays it this
that last so I write for eyes to see the song, the dance, makes sense
to me I am the poet that bring no harm just the kiss, the touch, you
feel in the morn and for this I write such lovely poems for a woman
who's been so deeply scorned
   Roxanne Jones

Life Is Never As It Seems

My life is warm and wonderful.
I am living a beautiful dream.
My husband is very special and
He treats me like a queen.

But demons stalk this lonely earth,
Satan's evil destroyers of dreams.
One comes to me on a cold, dark night.
Life is never as it seems.

The demons calls on me work.
This rapist steals my soul.
What a tragedy struck that night!
My life is a deep, dark hole.

Not satisfied with just my soul,
He shout and tried to kill.
God plucks his bullets from the air.
My bullets leave him dead still.

It has been a long time now.
The demon still haunts my dreams,
But my soul is slowly returning,
For remembering, life is never as it seems.
   Sylvia Hauser

Roses

I saw you once picking the roses,
You moved with grace, picking the best,
Picking the best among the roses,
And place them nicely on your chest.

Your posture, head, your way of being,
The way you move, you blink your eyes,
The glance of your eyes, your grace of being,
Spread charm, and made the roses nice.

All this belongs to me forever,
Your eyes, your grace, your smile, o heaven!
All this belongs to me, because.........

I saw you once picking the flowers,
You moved with grace, picking the best,
Picking the best among the roses,
And place them nicely on your chest.
Wadim Kurjanowicz

Big Foot

Not frequently seen; he has many sobriquets
Huge and execrable, some have claimed him to be
Enigmatical and hermitical seem to be his ways
As he moves and saunters somewhat stoically

Some have serious doubts and do not believe
That such an eerie creature even exists
Still, others ignore what they can't conceive
But his validity certainly attracts much gist

Of his particular origin, no one really knows
Although, to be some unknown primate, he appears
With more study and research, biologists may disclose
This legend's identity and rid us of our fears

If big foot truly lurks around our forests and farms,
It is obviously evident that he means us no harm.
Randal M. Weston

Man

The children smile as she watches.
Her eyes light up.
Joy that will last forever.

I see her sit there calm and happy.
How unique.
A mystery to me.

A beautiful sight.
If you dare observe.

An unborn mother.
Yet ready for the day.

So intense, but worth every minute.

I do not know this feeling and can not relate.
For I am only
Man.
Lee Kolinsky

Hawks

Smooth and sleek as they soar the sky,
Looking for prey as the time rolls by.

And swooping down for the catch of the day,
The hawk brings back its greatest prey.

Back to the nest were their ready to eat,
On the tasty bits of gray mouse meat.

And back to the nest where they turn in for the night,
Until the time comes for another big flight.
Tyler Grant

Seasons Of The Heart

The very first time I met you
I knew I could never forget you
And when our friendship had its start,
There was spring-time in my heart.

Soon our friendship grew
Until at last we knew
That love was now a part
Of the summer in our hearts.

Saying "I do" was the best thing we had done
Our love grew even stronger when we became one
Now we feel lost when we are apart
We're aware of the autumn of life in our hearts.

As we approach the winter of our life
We have come to realize, as husband and wife
Dealing with joy, pain, and sorrow - whatever
We will abide if we do it together...
   (With God by our side)
    I Love you
Darlene M. Hughes

The Realm Where Roams His Spirit

The realm where roams his spirit
Is a realm he never may leave by foot.
Far and wide has he traveled,
But his spirit, sad and gloomy, forever
   with him remains.
Long ago in his days of youth,
When his world was sheltered and small,
And he brooded in the quiet of his chambers,
He dreamed of quitting that place of drear,
Quitting that small world of odious
   familiarity,
Thinking that if only he left, then all
   would be well for him.
Truly a change of scenery diverts the mind,
   but the distraction is transient.
Always his spirit remains in this realm,
   hidden in the shadows of his soul.
To ignore it, he is forced to roam the world
   without rest, without comfort in travel or in stillness.
Nathan Daniel

The Littlest Teachers

In a world where problems are great
And solutions are few,
Look to the little ones-
For they have the answers.

Watch for their smiles,
Their determined little faces,
And the life giving laughter-
For they only know of happiness.

Pay attention to their eyes
Teemed with miracles,
Only looking at good happenings-
For they don't know of adversity.

For once, don't allow them to be the followers.
Follow in their footsteps,
Live life through the eyes of a child-
For they are the littlest teachers.
Laura J. Day

From: Mommy....in Heaven

My loves, I can't be with you, to watch you learn and grow,
For I've gone to be with Jesus,
And these things I want you to know.

That I love you and I miss you, and I pray that you
Will see....
That when I was there with you,
You meant the world to me.

Please take care of grandma and grandpa, they love you like I
Do...and I know they will be comforted,
By seeing "me" in "you".

Guys, I want you to be happy, and walk with Jesus each day,
For he'll comfort and protect you,
In a very special way.

In heaven I have a mansion, it's here for me and you...
With fields of flowers and crystal clear lakes,
One day it will be yours too.

Good-bye is never easy, so I'll see you again someday....
I look forward to our meeting,
And on streets of gold we'll play.

Kelly Renee Akers

Heaven's Peril

I see her as I saw her first, so long ago,
as delicate and fair as Irish lace -
I saw and loved at once but could not speak.
She passed, but oh, how beautiful her face.

I think what wondrous things God gives to us in life,
and promises of what will still unfold.
This world has love, the sky, the stars, and her -
to come there's peace and happiness untold.

And when I've died and purged my sins in hellish flames,
is my reward to join the Seraphim?
There is no greater happiness we're told,
than be at His right side adoring Him.

But wait! We're told that heaven's all we'd ever want,
and those we loved so much, again we'll see.
Yet doctrine says we'll live in Godliness
to love just Him for all eternity.

I pray for Him to understand - I just want her.
But it rejecting Him, would my hell be
that she might chose to spend forever with
someone she may have loved much more, not me?

John J. Nolan

"My Love"

  You are forever gone, yet not forgotten.
To hear your name makes me sigh, and then I just
begin to cry. I say to myself, why Lord, why?
  Your joyful ways, those playful days, reminds me
of the sunshine rays, for when you were near, you
made the darkness in my clouds disappear.
  To hear you laugh, to see you smile, made it worth
walking the extra mile.
  Your soft skin, your silly grin, you could light
up a room, and a heart within.
  Your soft lips, set my soul on fire,
you are the one I truly desire.
  Your warm eyes, your beating heart,
makes it so hard to be apart.
  Your gentle caress, your lovingness,
all were the meaning of my happiness,
and for you my love, I seal this with a kiss,
for you are the one I desperately miss!
  My love you are forever gone, yet,
truly not forgotten.

Sheila A. Ball

October Oak

Majestic, proud, and lofty, all-
The tree stands mute in autumn's haze.
The nip of frost has warned of fall
And advent of the winter's days.

What secrets must its visage hold
Throughout the century as it stood?
A home for squirrels, and shade for those
Who wandered through the scented wood.

But time can't wait. We don't ask why,
And all must change in nature's plan.
As for the tree, it too must die,
But slowly, as an aging man.

This gorgeous oak, its copper leaves
Against the azure blue of sky,
Must pass its way, and one who grieves
Will know he loved it, and he'll know why.

Keith Marvin

Myself

The correlation of two minds intertwining together
coming up with a distinctly correct hypothesis
may be impressive. However,
an extreme introvert reluctant to share a part of
him or herself caused by an overpowering abusive
childhood carrying on into the future of this person's
subconscious fetal mind causing severe depression
and maliciousness converting into violence,
suddenly engaged by an intense self realism and
change of thinking habits by such a person
systematically causing a total reproduction of the mind
converting the person into an extrovert
in his or her life.
Now that's impressive.

Evan F. Amrhein

"Wallpaper-Flowers (The Diary)"

Wallpaper-flowers repeat our old familiar conversations in the hall.
Cold evenings by the firelight, is that your reflection on the wall?
If you still need me, you've paid me with an arrow and a stone.
Each day, they say you might be found...or lost and wandering alone.

I fixed the screen-door; now the porch will need a coat of paint.
The courtyard garden fills my eyes: your roses by the peaceful saint.

Oh Heaven! heal me like the sparrow; I need to be someone who flies.
Time handed me a bargain-box of pretty all-occasion lies.

Here in the attic, things are gold in sun-streams flecked with dust.

Lace gown, dress-uniform, oh we were splendid then, so full of trust.
You said forever, signed your name and gave yourself to me.
It's funny how one keeps the vows; and one tears up the guarantee!

In winter's darkness, a new detective brought a light that's free.
In May you're found in old Madrid and you're sailing home to me!
I've gone to England. He wouldn't leave till I agreed to go along;
And searching through old castles we might hear a new love song.

Please keep the house, dear; by the way, my diary's in the hall.
On quiet, lonely mornings, walk near the flowers on the wall.
Twelve years they've known us very well; they have so much to tell.
They wait for you...I promise you...they've seen and heard it all.

Rebecca Evans-Howe

Full Circle

Baby Boomers beware!
The seeds of discontent so fashionable once
Have spread beyond the wildest calculations.

Long to wear the flowers, sing the songs, dance the dance
Of anti-Establishment days.
Peace is love
Love is peace...
Drones ever the refrain.
The protest rages on
But alas—

The greatest irony apparent-we have become the Establishment!
And the psychoanalysts are getting fatter still,
The peace but a facade
Of vanished values
And paradise lost.

Cherylyn S. Porter

Florescent Lighting

The cool cruel bars
emit a dismaying
array of decay

Their pale hue
will continue to undo

Grip the white lines of your confinement
(no shadows to hide in)

Vast corpulent radiance
persuade to evade and stand remade
run to the sun it's time for your fun.

Jonlee D. Hardy

Fear

I fear I will never again see the color purple.
Or feel warm bath water against my skin on a cold winter night
I fear I will never again see the color blue.
Or feel a cool summer rain against my skin
I fear I will never again see the color green.
Of feel my daughters hugs and kisses at bedtime
I fear I will never again see the color red.
Or feel my cheeks getting flush during a passionate kiss.
I fear I will never again see the color pink.
Or feel a newborn baby's skin against my skin.
I fear I will never again see the color orange.
Or feel goosebumps running up and down my arms.
I fear I will never again see the color yellow.
Or feel the sun rays warming my face.

I fear death will take my rainbow and feelings from me.
Now I am weak, and the colors are fading.
But in you I see a rainbow of life and hope.

Kathryn Johnson

A Glimpse In The Past

As secretive as life may be
I treasure the secrets between you and me
an undying love shared amidst
that very night with an everlasting kiss

To this present day I keep inside, locked deep
  in my soul, in an attempt to hide
running from my thoughts, my feelings my fears
  the secret I've kept these many years

All in all the secret was safe until that day when it escaped
nothing said, nor nothing I could do, could apologize for the
  secrets that came between me and you
for now and forever the secret was gone; to forget the past
  and let the memories live on.

Gregory Bailey

Untitled

Bleed me, for I've been stricken with poisonous emotions,
and still yet this love tears at my heart like winds at sea,
my love for you is not optional!
Thus doubt has surely surfaced a spliced seam of a broken heart,
and security is never certain within,
And this love shall never regress to the elementary ways
of the unguided,
Her love, shall once again ease my sufferings with her gentle breath
I know I shall not pass this way again,
For the burning bliss of neglect has prompted my unfounded
emotions of love and tenderness,
And I shall not label, nor be labeled,
For I'm just a happy traveler in the midst of rapture,
So I stand out among the weak and the sick
and pronounce my forgivings and my repentance
to mankind, For I've cheated the value of love,
that none can imitate.

Tony Pattillo

The Bonnet

A simpler time it must have been; when women were
  porcelain and men were men.
Chivalry abounded, a social plague, a glint of ankle, God
  forbid of leg.
Days of leisure, as told through the pages of an aging sage's
  restless tongue.

"A recall," it began, "a day, a time, when times were hard on
  me and mine.
Plowed and labored a hundred days for love and life and pay;
of valiant efforts; of suppers; to survive."

"Our women bore children 'midst the high cotton, nursed, cursed
  quietly, and continued as if gotten
Behind in the pillage, looked toward the village
Head shaded by a bonnet now mine."

Said grinning as if knowing, arms outstretched and
  showing
Faded, folded cloth to my eyes.
"So's you'll know when I die, the stories that lie
In the sonnet of the bonnet;
  Now mine."

Mitzi B. Hutchinson

"Paradise Downtown"

  Hearts as soft as granite,
Eyes as warm as steel
  Walking the tightrope between love and hate,
Finding out dreams just aren't real.
  Marching in time to the funeral dirge
For the bride who's all dressed in black.
  She waits at the altar,
But her hopes will soon falter
  and fade...
The groom's not coming back.
  Faces etched from cold, hard stone
Carved into my mind.
  Day and night is spent trying
to forget them,
  But I can't seem to leave them behind.
Love is a word that is foreign to me,
  I heard it once long, long ago
  The bride learns to cry
As her soul learns to die
  This cruel joke named Fate taught her so.

Okeyna Loving Perry

My Communion

I took a look at the world today,
   And what did I see?
An ocean of broken hearts, And life's torn asunder.
I thought to myself, how can this be,
   When God has provided everything we need?
I prayed a silent prayer with tears welling in my eyes,
"Father what is the answer, and then he replied",
"My child look not at the world, but look to me".
"I have in store many blessings for thee".
Poverty comes to those who are wild,
but you will succeed, for your my child.
Lessons learned while walking this earth,
Not only adds to your spiritual girth, but enables others to
understand, God's plans while he was a man. Mysteries of life are
given to those whose hearts are bent to heavenly things,
They know what obedience brings.
Eyes are being opened around you daily,
Satan is being exposed.
Those who follow me closely will not fall.
Listen, learn, walk tall.
   Betty Watson Norman

Back To The Good Old Days

Oh, I want to go back to the good old days, when life was a bit less hectic,
And we measured things by the foot and yard, not by this stuff called metric!

When moms watched from the kitchen door for kids to come home from school;
And along with their daily lessons they were taught the Golden Rule

"Spare the rod and spoil the child," back then was put to use,
Now, if you dare to spank a child, it's considered child abuse.

Kids didn't sit in front of TV, waiting to be entertained
Nor depend on store bought toys, instead, they used their brain.

They swam in the creek or river, acting like silly fools;
That kind of fun and adventure's not found in today's backyard pools.

a picnic in the countryside was a happy treat for all.
Now this fun has been replaced with shopping in air-cooled malls.

The coffee pot was always hot, on the back of the old cook stove,
And nobody really cared about the kind of car they drove.

With no automatic dryers, clothes dried in the sun and air.
A sheet of fabric softener with that aroma cannot compare.

No, I'd not enjoy reading by the light of a kerosene lamp;
But what a pleasure it would be to mail a letter with a three-cent stamp!

True, cutting wood and stoking fires wasn't an easy chore,
But there are times when I really yearn to go back to the days of yore
   Evelyn Brightwell

The End Of The Day

When the sun goes down at the end of the day,
the sky is filled with the colors of sunset.
As twilight comes to a close, it is covered
by a mantle of darkness—the night.
The people give a sigh of relief.
The work is done for this day.

Homeward bound for their supper, they
open the door and smell the food of the fare.
With a kiss for the wife and a smile for
the kids, they are soon seated to ask the
blessing and give thanks to God for everything.

After supper with dishes done, the evening is
filled with a variety of activity, needed or fun.
Then on to bed for the rest needed for
another day.
   John A. Novak

Do You?

Have you ever taken time out and thought about the life you're living?
Were you ever generous in your giving?

Do you do good works to be noticed by man
or are you doing it for Jesus and thinking of the Promise Land?

Do you go to church to hear the word
or are you one of those gossiping birds?

Do you know how to worship the Lord?
Do you carry His powerful sword?
Are you deceitful and full of the devil lies?

If you're wrong, Are you bold enough to apologize?

Do you love with a genuine heart or do you enjoy tearing people apart?
Do you read the bible, do you pray or are you fooled to let the
devil have his wicked way?

Do you go to the churches with religion or those that teach the
word and have a Godly vision.

Are you a real Christian or a sinner.

Do you know how to confess and be a winner.
My God is merciful you see and the time is now for you to be free.

Search yourself because the time is now.
Do you wish to be caught up or more you going to be bound?
   Jacqueline Galloway

They're Singing The Saddest Songs

They're singing the saddest songs today
Since you said goodbye and went away
It seems the message they reveal
Tells me exactly how I feel

They're singing the saddest songs it seems
Since you left and shattered all our dreams
Those happy songs they used to sing
It seems no longer are the thing

I wonder why you said goodbye
My heart hurts so I want to cry
Forgive me darling if ever I hurt you
'Cause loving you is all I want to do

They're singing the saddest songs of all
And their words bring tears that start to fall
When you return and bring me cheer
Those sad sad songs will disappear
   Louis J. Pourciau Jr.

Contemplative

I should like to think that love is a beautiful thing,
Like starlight and moonlight,
Like misty mornings and fog floating between rooftops
And treetops,
Like the voice of rain,
Like jazz and the light shed by soft white light bulbs,
Like the slim smooth curve of a woman's thigh
And the husky warm scent of young men,
Like the shape of a sonnet
And the
chAo
sof pr!ose...,
Like the hem of God's robe and a sense of divinity in quiet hours,
Like driving too fast to music too loud,
Like secluded snowy Sundays,
Like a heart at peace when it's alone.
   Erica N. Waibel Sphar

The One Who Loves

Long ago, on a lonely street,
A little girl plods on bare feet.
Although she is poor, she walks with a shining face,
For she thinks of God's mercy, tender love, and grace.
Yet a single tear rolls down her cheek,
For she had earned but a penny this week.
She longs for some bread from the bakery,
But cannot have any for lack of money.
Oh, but wouldn't she give anything for some bread,
To fill the mouth so seldom fed.
Later, down this same lonely street,
With the girl's small hands gently warming her feet,
A young mother thinks about inhumanity.
She wishes she could help her daughter,
For she hates to see her child suffer,
And everything, to her own life, would she offer,
But since there is no other choice,
Every night she prays in a small voice,
Asking God to watch the child she loves,
For her only hope is in the One above.

Jennifer Yoo

Dreams

I rarely ever see you, maybe twice each day
Wishing we were together, when you seem so far away
Cherishing each moment I've spent with you, near or far
With these moments I build my dream, I try to catch a falling star
Dreams of moonlit walks on a beach, just you and I
Hand in hand with you, so happy I could cry
Dreams of dancing, of holding you close to me
I am yours forever with no wish to be free
Alas, we are but friends and nothing more
Between us an eternal ocean, a distance no bird could soar
Though I wish we could be together until the end of time
I would rather see you happy in someone else's arms than miserable
  in mine
Dreams of seeing you happy, an angel glowing bright
I watch a falling star streak across the night.

Scott Francis Wellman

A Quiet Place

Sweet breath of life, gentle wind of God,
Guide me softly as I walk on this earth.
Full my eyes with the wondrous beauty of life.
Let them sparkle and shine with joyful glee.
Let my wings take flight and let happiness
  find a quiet place within me.

Let me know life's most precious treasures;
A child at play, sunshine upon my face,
Laughter, a kind word, a loving embrace,
Memories of a happy past, deep faith.
Fill my cup with love and let happiness
  find a quiet place within me.

Let me be peaceful and full of grace.
Give me mother's milk, the magic potion,
A warm and soothing, loving lotion. Save me
From common discontent. Keep me on my path
Loving bent, God sent, and let happiness
  find a quiet place within me.

Beverly J. Sweeney

Hunted

A young deer screeches
and has but one care
as his mother's flesh fills the cool air

He sees the hunter
with knife and gun, walking away from the battle he won

The hunter turns 'round, lifting his rifle
The fawn stands silent, not moving a trifle

The hunter strolls back
to where the doe is dead
The deer hears noises, deep down in his head

And as the last cold rays of the moon has faded
the fawn knows men are the champions
  of the game

They created

Richard Hobson

Under The Stars

Under the stars there I lay.
The stars are such a pretty sight.
I wish I could be an astronaut tonight.
I would fly high to the moon.
Instead of sitting here in my room.
As I fly high to the moon,
I reach for the stars, and
realize it is no use. As I look out my room again.
All I see is daytime instead of night.
My favorite place is gone and in its
place is dawn.

Kristine Gilliland

Sherwood Forest

In a world where there is no definite end and no definite beginning,
I get lost in the woods of my own imagination.
Others try to enter my Sherwood Forest,
But my ghosts keep them out.

A child's toy sits in the corner of the room,
spinning and glowing by the power of it own will.
It is the memory of my child who will never see the light
outside of my cursed womb.

Gates crash down to keep everyone in.
Trampling, torturing souls, psychotically insane from their own
  actions.
They will die while fighting to live.
Soon they will enter my forest and be my ghosts.

The vulture eye illuminates the room in a pale blue hue.
Though it seems dead, it lives in everyone who passes by.
It envelopes those who's curiosity
Will soon kill them in their sleep.

Katherine M. Hein

Images Of The Nightingale

Hear the soft melody of the Nightingale,
Healing sound wafting
On nightfall's tremorous breeze.
The song precipitates images that assail
Spirit's drifting
Yearning for healing squeeze.

Nightingale forebears a myriad
Of feelings mirroring
The images' caring suggestion.
A triad
Of sight, sound, and touch remembering
The healing care and repatriation.

Ronald D. Rudy

The Truth

Twas a long time ago, on a midwinters day
When something was shown to my eyes.
And as hard as it is, I regret to say,
That the truth had been hidden in lies.
My fellow man, sleeping in the streets
Who is just as much human as I,
Is forced to travel by use of his feet
And he sleeps in the cold of the night.
He's under a bridge, I'm snug in my home
With everything that I know is mine.
In his only coat, he will die alone
Hungry and cold at age nine.
So now I ask: How hard is it for us to help each other?
Much to hard for most of us to care for one another.

Margarito Montoya

"Poetry Is A Cry Wrenched From The Soul"

So claimed Miss Eareckson in English IOI.
My seldom cries have been more inner prayers
Wrenched out in moments of great fear,
As: Father, keep her from her own undoing!
Father, it is my constant deepest wish this
Friendship never cease.
Father, you can bring them through these earthquakes whole.
Father, may this man be mine?
Enable me to see when, and how and surely, vividly, where?
I know not how to do; but certainly, assuredly you do.
So show me, tell me, nudge me, open my eyes and mind.
May I, please, foresee some usefulness in this day to do?

And thank you, Lord, for this blessed, non-cluttered
Graceful quiet here
In which to be, and breathe, and think, and joy.

Betty Chadbourne du Bois

Love Is

Love is a precious gem,
as precious as a priceless
diamond

Love is as beautiful as a
new day dawning with all
its awesome colours.

Love is as pure as a new
fallen snow on a winter's day.
Love is as free as a bird soaring
in the sky with the wind under its
wings.

My love, my love can be compared to any
of these.
This is the way I feel about thee.

Cecilia Y. Leonard

Alone

As the sun goes down,
darkness covers my town.
Evening has slowly settled in,
and a gentle showering of rain begins.

It is time to draw the shutters tight,
and lay my body down for the night.
Though my tired vessel needs to sleep,
thoughts in my mind still creep.

Late at night I feel alone in the silent,
to have some ones lips to kiss in the nights quiet.
Their warm body next to mine as the night is long,
while we fall asleep to the rains melodic song.

Robert M. Shaddock

Winter In April

I watch as the branches swing and sway
Performing a scene from their ballet
A bird's nest from a winter past
Is clinging tenaciously and holding fast
Already a blanket of pure white snow
Perhaps a good nine inches or so
Soon the shovelers will appear
Dressed in their very warmest gear
They gaze at the mountain of gleaming white stuff
And say to themselves "Enough is enough"

Mary McNamara Hope

Untitled

I'm short, cold tired
expired
fat,
flat...
chested.
I'm invested
in other people's lives. They cry to me,
sigh to me,
tell me what they want to be.
Never once asking me
who I am. Why I'm there,
why I care.
It's all a mystery and they just stare
at me with tears in their eyes.
I've listened to the cries
of people who don't care about me.
Gee,
I wonder why I've never been thanked. I was pushed aside
when I cried
because I was in the path of a really cute guy.

Emily Ackman

Hit And Run

He had contributed much to their lives they said
As they gathered to mourn his death
He lived well, the heir to a fortune
With a passion for speed and fast cars
But those cars ruined him
Hit and run
One man dead
The evidence sat in his garage
A BMW with a broken nose - the car in question
Threatening to turn him in
To tell his terrible secret
And as they surrounded his house,
his fast cars could not get him away
Trapped
So he found a way out
A way they could never catch him
Two men dead

Jessica DeWitt

Waiting

Barren reaches of the heart,
Hands not meeting in the breach
Eyes unfocused on the course of time
As earth's sterility aches with promise
Of seeds unsown; of twisted twigs stripped of grace,
Of moments heavy with the weight of response
And then He comes! - through unreachable reaches.
Hands bridging every breach,
Eyes filled with longing's love,
Time caught in a moment of momentous force,
Nothing will ever be barren again!

Rita O'Connor, S.N.D.

Farewell Dear Friend

A quiet man, my aged dear friend,
Disease had taken so much from him.
His wife so tired, his halting steps,
His shaking hands made such a mass!

He loved his God, he loved his church,
In good health willingly gave so much.
Then come the months with his poor health,
He couldn't even dress himself!

God looked down and saw his suffering
He pain on his families face.
Sent angels to close his eyes in love,
Then gently carried his spirit away.

When his time was up, he was alone,
Helplessly lay in a nursing home,
His family called to find him gone,
They gathered to comfort everyone.

At eighty-four he was so tired,
I know he wanted to be with God.
He is so missed by all who knew
My aged dear friend, till we meet again!
  Mary K. Willey

Unspoken

So many times I've wished I could tell you just how much I really care.
No matter how big or small, for all of us you have always been there.
You have retaught me how to walk a couple of times.
You picked me up when I fell, brushed me off and showed me in which direction to climb.
Always, you have believed in me, even when I no longer believed in myself.
And there has been so many times you have put your needs on the backshelf.
So I felt I needed to take this time and let you know...
I really appreciate and love you, so much more than I ever really show.
  Victoria M. Borjes

Consider The Tree

You have heard the saying
Forty isn't old if you're a tree.
But, isn't forty what we want to be?
Let's consider the tree...and you...and me.

The tree's roots go deep in the ground,
nourished by the moist earth and the warm rain
....as our roots also go deep to the land and to our home,
nourished by family and friends.

The tree's sturdy trunk beckons lovers to carve hearts
and cats to climb ever higher in chase or adventure
...as we also have lovers that carve hearts in our lives
and cats that cuddle in our laps.

The tree welcomes sunshine
sparkling through the frost on its branches on a crisp winter day
...as the sunshine also shines on the frost in our hair.

The tree spreads its branches to welcome the breeze
and to offer shelter to woodland friends
...we open our arms to friends, to love, to life at forty!

Forty is what we want to be!
You and me and the tree!
  Kathryn Mumgaard Martin

Where Passion Lyes

Passion is in the beauty that you see when you look at your trees in the morning right outside the window.

Passion is the bright warm sun on your face, it is in your safe secure piece full home you lay your head at night, feeling everything is all right.

Passion is being so much in love with just one, there face is the only face you see.

Passion is in each and every wave in the ocean or the sea that sways. It is in the cool mellow breeze that blows through your hair.

Passion is looking up into the sky and watching all the stars so bright.

Passion is always there, I will take as much as I can bare. There is passion for me in so many places I can feel or see. If you believe you can also receive. If ever you want it, If ever you need it, you'll find it, if your heart truly cares.

  Because Passion Lyes Everywhere
  Rosie Coleman

Why Mommy?

Mommy, why do you yell at me?
It's hurting me can't you see.
I love you most in all the land,
Why can't you just hold my hand.
Please God can you tell me why?
Why does mommy have to be what they call "high".
Why can't she show me love?
But instead is push and shove.
I wish mommy get some help,
All day long I try to hide my whelp.
Every night I talk to God and pray,
Help my mommy, please don't let her stray.
I tell everyone that we'll take it in stride,
But, when she starts yelling I run and hide.
Please, mommy don't yell at me anymore,
Don't make me run and lock my door.
Please, get help and be here to stay,
I love you mommy that's all I can say.
  Sandy Wright

Storms

The lightning's flash,
  the pounding thunder,
    and the angry clouds rolling
are nature's scorn.

My storms become so insignificant,
my rain so light,
my troubles so small.

I stand amongst nature's turbulence
and feel a power,
a force that must be spent.
It is so far beyond me.
Yet at one within me.
Once spent,
there's a freshness,
a bloom of newness,
it's a cleansing of nature's soul and mine.
  Karen Yokley

Untitled

I reach beneath, and grab a hold-
of a piece of my life.
What is left to be?
Please give me a reason why I lay here-
Why I live. Nothing left of me.

This produces inside my heart:
no partial feelings, no blank despair.
The loss of this life, so close to mine.
No longer bears upon my soul-
For, I no longer care.

Caress me. Comfort me.
Beside me, why are you here?
Why do you love me?
For I am evil,
why do you care?

I hurt so many so long ago.
But, as a friend, you do not mind.
A friend in love; till the very end.
Forever,
and for all time.
Coy W. Yonce III

Untitled

As I contemplate my demise
I see no truth only lies.

There's been no happiness, no joy, no glee
only bitterness and sorrow for me.

To cease to exist would be a win
something to stop the torment within.

I'll not pass gently into the light
but tumble into darkness that
holds a terrible fright

Did I choose this or was it given
to me
Perhaps in death I'll see
Larry McCaslin

Except We Be As Children

We were once children playing in the sunshine.
We did not know life had so much pain.
Laughing and playing, no care, no sorrow.
Living for today not fretting tomorrow.

Where has gladness gone? Isn't Jesus our friend?
Don't you hear the little children? Their joy seems without end.
Oh! how they laugh. That was once you or me.
God give us joy again. Let that be our plea.

Willow a weeping. There are clouds in the sky.
Life gets so weary, sometimes you're going to cry.
But look at the little children. Tears don't linger in their eyes.
Oh! God touch our souls and give us a heart of a child.

Except we be as children walking in the richness of trust.
Believing that God will keep us.
A day at time is the way life must be.
For tomorrow is not ours to see.
Mary E. Campbell

No Flies On Me, Darlin'

It finally happened! I'm over the bumps and on my way again.

My hopes are soaring and my feet are weightless
(except for a few dabs of clay between the toes)

I have divorced the past and unlatched old ties that bind
(like inertia, revenge, fear and other people's agendas)

The "otta be" and the one I am are finally reconciled
(and even like each other a lot!)

The sun shines in, the pores are open and the gut feels great!
(with only some occasional gas)

I throb, I surge, I'm eager to try, to explore new parts and
renew some of the old.

If this is a "born again" happening, let me be the first to shout
"Hallelujah!" There are no flies on me Darlin".
Annette L. Johnson

Prisoner

I gaze down at the vast and lonely moors.
The wind envelops me in a cool wave of misery.
It knows the anguish that possesses my soul.
It knows the agony that grows within my heart.
These acres of wasteland,
Vacant from human sympathy,
Are now to serve as my home.
How long can I possibly live in this wilderness,
Void of any hope or love?
It would be better if I did not live long,
For what good can come from my broken dreams?
My memory of how life used to be haunts me,
And my body writhes in the presence of evil.
One moment of passion
Locked me into an eternal cage of hell.
My sin shall follow me always,
To mock and scorn me,
It has condemned me.
I am no more.
Tricia Fredley

Aids

Tongues wiggling and waggling; Lord, isn't it saddening?
They're talking 'bout someone with AIDS.
How did he catch it—chitter, chatter.
Who knows, who cares; what does it matter?

AIDS — Acquired Immune Deficiency Syndrome
Comes from unsafe sex and can attack anyone.
It comes from shared needles and also transfusions;
It hits young and old whether married or single.

You're married and true; your spouse gave it to you!
Young, innocent mothers bare babies with AIDS.
What of these infants and children so sick
Whose lives are sadly spent suffering with AIDS?

Oh, gosh, she had AIDS; Wonder, how did she get it.
What does it matter; you or I could contract it!
People suffer and die; many go it alone
Till the good Lord steps in and carries them home.

If we cannot help them, we should not condemn them.
We cannot dessert them; we must love and support them.
Think! How would you or I feel in their place?
Suffering with AIDS and looked on with disgrace.
Nancy A. Hammontree

Rose

Alive, alive it grows and pushes from its ruddy head the snow
as up from snow bank straight in line the hearty ruby climbs in time.
Burst forth into sun and mark the spot! Earth's dimpled face
quickly sought to bring in home and life the gift to soothe the heart
and bind the rift. How could a thing with its shape give one the
peace that many take and leave for lost for wants sake all who cannot
endure?
Line and form will suffice the hour and this is found in any flower
but what is it that holds us, trances, imagination dances, and gives
not up its power? Others wilt and die away leaving leavings and
stray decay to line the vase ad senses flay, but the rose in death
still leads astray.
It passes and folds in time as all yet still sublime gives its
final fruit, the perfect scent, the breath of God; still perfect, single,
and aloof.

Andrew Schmit

Monastery Bells

Monastery bells in the distance rang out
My eyes froze to your radiant face as you lit each candle
I knew that smile from some by-gone day
Perhaps it was the carefree grin of an old beau...

A struggle within me occurred as I tried to refrain
From running to you, but each moment my heart
Became more urgent, intense with love for you.
All too soon the service came to a close and
I thought of your eyes-never to behold children of your own and
I thought of your arms-never to embrace the body of a woman and
I thought of you, virile and young, never to experience life
In a make-believe world. And I envied you, and I desired you.

As I took of the bread and drank of the wine
My own life seemed so lifeless. I had everything
You own nothing, yet you were so rich-your joy fulfilled.
The concluding song echoed in my heart, your voice
In melody softly singing "I will see you again."
People filed out of the place of worship. I searched
For one last glimpse of your flowing gray robe but
It had disappeared in the Vermont hills and monastery bells.

Debora E. Wager

"Poppies Perennially Bloom"

Aye 'the poppies still grow in
Flanders fields, 'performing as
surrogate flags their sacred duty
Dear brothers in arms, assured be that
the torch 'from failing hands,' grasping
stoutly the colors to hold them high

In peaceful sleep—rest—you have
lifted your faith to the skies, that
bond between us never to be broken

Sing softly, ye muses, disturb not
their slumber; sleep well, your duty done
Freedom reigns inseculaseculorum

While poppies grow, we with
aging hands pass the baton to
stronger arms with renewed faith,
inspired by you who sleep

Percy Totheroh

Disaster

The ringing in my ear so eternal and strong;
desire and hope muted by the sound;
fear growing with every weakness;
feelings numb to the hearts cry;
compassion bound by angels ties;
the world so turmoiled in denial;
love scampering to find a home;
with hate marching with pride;
the beautiful dove camouflaged;
the precious mind in hiding;
but a thought escapes;
"Why God? Why?"

Cally Wade

Love In Life's Twilight

Our paths crossed ever so briefly,
In the twilight of our lives.
Like an eclipse of the moon, nearly secret,
In the stillness of a lonely night.
Few saw, heard or noticed, then forgetting
Went on their way,
But you saw, beheld and adored me,
That memory I'll cherish all ways,
Then embarking on the rest of our
journey.
Without a single look back,
These memories they cannot take
from us,
Though the moon way, wane and
grow cold,
When you've shared love in life's
Twilight.
You will never really be old.

Mildred Hyatt McLoud

Restless Quest

The run
The hunt
The restless quest
Have you forgotten all of the rest?

A childhood fear
A grown man's dream
The blistering cry of a young woman's scream

The quest for youth
does lack resolve
An uncommon truth
and dreams dissolved

Fear you not
and go your own way
Teach them to run
and teach them to play

Children hoard an abundance of truth
And through them, we
all find our youth

Len C. Glazer

Masterpiece

As the artist approaches the easel, paints in hand,
Thoughts so intricately planned.
The masterpiece about to be sketched; so profound the
Thoughts must surely be to be able to plan so superbly.
Transfer the plan from the mind to the hand to brush
The masterpiece so we can understand.
The sensitivity one must have to be able to follow such a
miraculous plan.

Lana J. Brewer

Lady

Lady, sweet Lady
Ever the sympathetic friend.
Sleek beauty, graceful and white
Running in the wind.

Lady isn't running now
Hopes and aspirations killed.
Cold steel hurtling through black night;
Her legs forever stilled.

Lady isn't running now
Her footsteps silent, past.
Joyful leaping when last she ran;
Freedom gained at last.

Lady isn't running now
Reasons, understanding obscured.
Her grace and beauty forever
In memory's closet preserved.

Lady, sweet Lady
Your running days are through;
Now, ne'er to warmly sit beside me;
Ah, faithful friend, adieu.

Gretchen K. Trace

Dreaming

Lay down your sleepy head upon this fluff of feathery white -
Greeting sweet slumber...leaving days' light -
As my eyes grow weary, heavy with doze,
I contemplate the inevitable - welcoming night's foes -
Drifting into my dominion...accepting my
plight...here I become whatever...invent a new life -
Solving, creating problems...situations galore...
Kings, queens forever here as I drift even more -
Jumping is no obstacle for me - even flying
I can do...this place holds a "wonderful"
magic...undreaming ever knew -
Dawn breaks very quickly...Reality back anew
Once more to face life's sunny day..leaving
'dreams' one might wish to come true.

Margo Culbert

Untitled

You're so close, but yet so far,
Please come and see me as you are.
Each day I pass by, to see if you're home,
I wonder what we would've become.

For in this poem my feelings you'll find.
I dream about you day and night,
Of things you do and who you like.

I hear the songs you use to play,
I think of how I felt on that day,
The songs I hear that remind me of you.
I shed this tear because "I love you".
I want to call you, but I'm too afraid,
Of what you'll think and what you'll say.

I know I hurt you, but you're not the only one,
That has that hurt deep down inside.
Every time I look at you, I just want to cry,
Each time I gaze into your eyes.

Laura M. Webb

Why...?

Why kill the snowy egret?
For feathered hats and pretty looks,
For he's done you no harm.

Why take the life of the thrashing shark?
For his sharp teeth and to make shark finned soup,
He's caused you no trouble.

Why starve the giant panda?
Cutting down his habitat and bamboo forests for houses and towns,
You're endangering him even more.

Why poach the roaming elephant?
So you can make rings and other jewelry from his ivory tusks,
Can't you just let nature be.

Why destroy the playful manatee?
With motor boat propellers and polluted water,
For they have the same right to survive.

Why hurt any living organism?
Hasn't greediness gone to far,
Life is something every living thing should enjoy.

Lauren Mackenzie

Memories

Memories, treasures of the mind
Always gathered, not left behind
They come in many a different kind
Anywhere you look, they are easy to find
A color on a bedroom wall
The brilliant colors seen in the fall
The day you got that special call
Maybe there's one you can recall
The day you met a special friend
It goes with you until your end
Reminds of the package you must send
Of the doctors appointments you must attend
Following you everyday
Never leaving in any way
To cheer you up, you do replay
Your memories, what you do and say
They could be something that you sing
The day you said yes, put on the ring
They're safely tucked under your wing
For a memory is a beautiful thing

Chris Kottke

Armchair Warrior

He draws his sword
and turns the next page
further and further he travels
hunting for his story
What really is this demon
he yearns to abolish?
The illiterate, the un-imaginative
the songwriter, the realist?
As patient as death, loves love,
believes in the fairy tale romance
and all that he has to live for —
islands that never cry
mountains that never go blind
deserts that never die
oceans that never cast aside the dreamer,
the wanna be... the warrior
shadows leaning against every wall
listening, watching, welcoming the next —
to challenge until
life... is over.

Sharon Phillips

The Morning Calm

The calmness in the morning
Is one of everlasting pleasure to witness.
The slow motion swaying of trees in a cool breeze.
The rising of the sun.
The early birds at play yearning for an early rise meal.
A sneaky little kitten lurking nearby
As though he is stalking a prey.
The dampness of the dew lie upon the grass
Like a tiny overnight shower.
The feeling captivates me while I await my loves eyes.
At best it's my sweetest time of day, but nothing next to my loves
Eyes could be more breathtaking.

Anganette Linnen-Fraser

All You Have Given Me Expecting Nothing In Return

On the melody strings of my heart father you helped me to see
Light in the darkest of nights, gave to me fountains of many
Wonderful dreams, a lifetime of endless memories, my spirit you
Lifted above the clouds of the universe, teaching me on the dance
Floors of glory the gracefulness of angels, you changed my life
From one of misery to pure delight, while climbing the mountain
Tops combing the valleys you showed me new and wonderful horizons

Together we traveled on the wings of eagles soaring the skies at
Heaven's gates, you lifted me as strength bowled down and sang to
Me the songs of victory's battles when all I could hear was the
Voices of despair, giving up on life you refused to let go of me
Pouring into me such love of giving, a reason for living, when
Tears of my broken heart flowed as the rivers joining into the
Ocean unending, you dried them with the sweetness of honeycombs

Your compassion engulfed me, covering loneliness, pain and agony
When everything was ripped from me you stayed, holding on to me I
Will always love you more than words could ever say, my life, my
Love, my forever, without you I am as the hollowing winds against
The boundless sea, disappearing clouds of mass non-existent gone
Forever, thank you father for your love, thank you for your care

Betty Jean Booth

Chameleon

Hush little baby don't you cry...
A lyric from a song.
Innocence in a tooth-less smile.
The meaning of birth right.

Who could I have been,
A milk maid, an Indian chief?

There had only been forty-five days.
I ended but didn't die.
Reborn, but with out womb.
Nor with grace of God, or was it?

I had no choice, nor consideration.
Robber of identity, by choice *you* decided.
You placed me in the hands of a surrogate.

To live as another.

Penny Crabtree

Complimentary

I'm a Beautiful Purple Butterfly
Yellow polk-a-dots on each wing
United for clarity as a Lion's eye.
Combined they have strength of a King.

Complimentary colors seem opposite at first
But when they are put together, you can see
They have such added and united worth.

I wish people could see each other this way;
Their value concurrently.

Kathy Borba

Petals On A Blade

Eyes weeping tears of shame.
But there's no way to purify, the withered innocence.
Temptation on the wings of flame.
Tainted ashes fall to earth, and peace becomes torment.
Like a child's untouched soul.
Slowly stained by pain and sorrow.
Like the falcon's broken wing.
And no melody to sing.
When love has been betrayed.
It's like falling petals on a blade.

Sightless is the dismal being.
The virtue of this planet, is ours to fortify.
Mortal man can believe.
Have faith once again, pull the thorn from his side.
As the helpless baby cries.
Wipe the salty tears from its eyes.
And the falcon will take wing.
When there is melody to sing.
Life, the battle we must face.
Like falling petals on a blade...

Connie M. Onjack

Dark And Stormy Night

Feeling like a scared child left in his room after dark,
Expanding like a glowing fire with its burning spark,
Whispering like a comforting mother soothing her baby's cries,
Dreaming like a widow when her loving husband dies,
Scattering like a waterfall as it crashes on the rocks,
Turning like hands on a clock with never ending tocks,
Screeching like an eagle standing on its peak,
Moving like a terrified boy tears streaming down his cheek,
Opening like a screaming mouth crying out in fear,
Dreaming like the elderly knowing their last day is near,
Streaming like a leaf falling off its tree,
Sitting like a blind person waiting for the time they see,
Blooming like a rose reaching for the sky,
Dashing like the tortoise hoping for a tie,
Dancing like the wind after catching a stray kite,
Then the sun calms the rain of this dark and stormy night.

Lauren van Dommelen

Kindness And Modesty

For unto you this day, love shall be with you always.

Pure, luminous, radiating bright, adorned with beauty this
gem of light; is stern, harsh and largely unyielding. The
greatest possible stress lays upon Him this day; that
he have. Kindness, the rest of his life, as he struggles
to maintain good treatment towards his wife.

She wears the proper gown of Modesty, that swept
across the land. Created from this dust of earth, God
formed for her a husband. As she glances at the
clearing sky, she notices her reflection in her weather
warming eyes. In breaths she awes, as the blowing
winds whirl the clouds into wedding rings of rainbows;
circling his faith around her finger.

With this covenant, you have surrendered that love in your
lives. With these rings, I now pronounce you
Man and Wife.

For onto you this day, love shall be with you always.

Dean Johnson

It's At The Cross

Where is that happiness?
Sitting on a star so dull,
Or waiting in a bottle surrounded by sharks,
Maybe dying on a cross
Offered to be free,
But I will yell "Crucify Him!" again and again.
Pick up a hammer
And pick up a nail,
It's so easy to kill
What I so much desire,
To feel that happiness, feel that love
"Crucify Him, Crucify Him!"
Mauricio Gramajo

Something Divorce Can Do

There's nothing that can hurt you more than a divorce.
It destroys you emotionally, and changes your life's course.
It ruins your mind, and destroys your soul.
At times you feel alone; in cold, dark hole.

Your parents say that the other one lies.
Nothing gets accomplished except, that each child cries.
At times I really don't know what to do;
I hear everything and think: What's really true?

Being in the middle is no fun at all,
It is like being bounced around, like a basketball.
Everyone is fighting and you hear what is told.
Your feelings toward everybody turn ice cold.

I tell you from one experience,
Or maybe just a few;
Feeling my life had never made sense.
This is something divorce can do.
Sam Mariani

Soulscape

A soul pure as pedals of a rose which has yet to be born;
Only to wither and fall gently to the ground, rest in peace!

But alas we are awakened for the soul lives on flying
    through the sky beyond the clouds through the shields
    into the stars searching for the light which feeds
    our meager existence.

Falling, falling, falling from the dark, now it is
    bright, and dark again only to be awakened by
    the angry storm of the ocean clutching at my life.
    Can't fight, must escape!

The vision of the light and freedom of my wings rushes my
    soul to move over the oceans beyond the land higher than
    mountains on, on, on.
Who we are is forever yet to be known!
Troy C. Santiago

My Dear Caroline

My dear Caroline, I want you to know that my love for you is deep.
The first time I held you in my arms was the most
    precious moment in my life.
You are truly a gift from God and I am eternally
    grateful to him.

My dear Caroline, I have watched you grow your first year.
I have watched your first steps, your first teeth come in,
    and I have heard your first words.
I have watched you grow day by day and thought how lucky I am.

My dear Caroline, we are coming upon your second year now.
You are becoming more independent and not needing me as much.
I just want you to know that I will be here for you.

My dear Caroline, I will always love you.
Christie L. Thee

Neighborhood

All you have to do is smile at
each other to see how the world disagrees.

They push and shove don't care if they
kill each other and sometimes kill their own brother.

Mother's cry saying why why why did it have
to be my baby that died?

Cries fill the air a fast as a hare screaming
one day your life is going to be a living night-mare.

As people scream because their having bad dreams
of being shot of murdered in the first degree.

Parents are crying because they just saw the man
who shot their son, but the police can't do nothing
because they haven't found the gun. So the man goes free.

Fathers are scared to let their daughters go out late
cause they might get captured and raped

The nights are so silent you can still hear
mothers cry saying why why why did it
have to be my baby that died?
Dana M. Contreras

"The Reluctant Voyager"

A many days, for as long as I can remember
was a shadow cast upon my father's heart
saw it erode his cold stone expression
saw it tear his world forever apart

thrown to the wind, caught by a breeze
was his seaborne vessel in a strange tide
at a distance he saw a city of gold
gone were the dreary echoes he first cried

he was relieved to finally get to shore
time to plant a new seed, and make it grow
but first to reunite with young blood love
still fresh remembered, brown locks and satin bow

with time the merger was fatefully met
and soon enough came a pink blossom
my father became whole again and thickened
then behold, I came feasting on our sour bosom

with his kin close at hand and living
outweighed what was lost back in genesis
he understood that this life ever changing
and that is what bore his exodus
Eugenio Jimenez Jr.

Morning Came

Remembering, past days of solitude
How I feel the wind blow, slowly -
Through the sorrows of time.
Waiting endless and bound
Though only for a moment, the smell of summers past
Live, like I live no more
For these hands a little older -
I move no more like a fresh spring morning
But like a storm, wild and swollen
Empty of the past
Whispering, the sunlight surrounds my days
Though I know not why it is
But feel again, yes, I feel again -
Though only for a moment
Michael K. Russomano

March

The bleat of the lamb, lion's roar,
Grumpy old winter, out the door.
Geese head north, days grow long,
You can hear April in the robins song.

Sun as gold as a buttercup,
Telling flowers, time to get up.
Frisky wind blows to and fro,
Ground, now green, once held snow.

Winds of March must give way,
Fickle April comes to stay.
Sheds tears of gold, and the moment after
Fills the world with golden laughter.
Mary M. Sullivan

I Want To Be

I want to be the sparkle in your eyes
  and the mood behind your smile.
The catchy tune you whistle-
  the one you can't get out of you mind for day.
The sun that parts the clouds,
  when clouds are all you see.

I want to be the sweet scent of new flowers in bloom,
  and when they appear with all their color-
What a reflection of beauty the world seems to project,
  and all seems at peace tranquil and perfect.

I want to be the stars in your sky,
  that guarantee that every wish you have will come true.
The moon that brightens you darkened path
  and the heavens that comfort you and make you feel safe.

I want to be the innocence of a small forgiving children
  who see the world through a kaleidoscope of animation
and the creativity of the younger generation.

As you are my appreciation for life
  I want to be your world.
Laura Fallon

"Down The Road"

He was born on his father's farm,
in his mothers arms.

The siblings he did play
until the toil of land he did bear.

He was there to serve his country,
and render next of kin a life of their own.

His family he holds dear,
though his church is near.

He never know the love of a wife,
for friends he has many.

He gives thanks to the Lord each day,
for land he holds dear.

Music swells the vast of the day,
to bring joy to the soul.

For the joy of sunrise and sunset,
and sounds of the birds to the ear.

Tomorrow be another day,
when down the road his buddy did walk.
Irene Birkner

This Raging War

The trumpet's call covers the land
The battle has begun

Warriors prepare to sacrifice their lives
For the cause is great
But the prize is even greater

Earth is the chosen battle ground
God and Satan send their troops forward into battle

Demons are advancing on the saints
Doubt and fears are infesting their minds

It seems all hope is lost
The demons are growing in number
And gaining strength every day

God in his infinite wisdom
With one final hope for mankind
Sends his son to the front lines

Confidence is restored
Those who doubt and fear infected
Becoming strong and brave once again

Now with Jesus as our captain
We will win this raging war.
James L. Tarter

America's All About

I'm a dreamer without a doubt that's what
America's all about.
Freedom here freedom there
we the people truly care.
Look around at other lands
there's no stars and stripes and cheering bands.
We light the torch that they see
to pronounce welcome to the land of the free.
Take a moment, look around
this is land of liberty you have found.
For this country that we love
pray for strength from above.
Remember not to put her down
for some day on you she may frown.
Walk on high and stand tall
with liberty and justice for all.
I'm a dreamer without a doubt
that's what America's all about.
Denise C. Schoemer

Open Your Eyes And See

**Open your eyes and see
the world in harmony.**
Flowers blooming.
Geese in formation.
A kitten snuggling against his mom.
The chest of the robin red-breast.

**Open your eyes and see
the world in harmony.**
The wild ocean crashing over the rocks
like mountain goats butting heads.
The wind swooshing through
the trees like a mad tornado.
The raindrops tiptoeing over the plains.
The beauty of the dusk sky
like paints spilled over the earth.

Open your eyes and see.
Julia Anne Driggers

Lost Love

We're going to have a baby
in six months or so
I'm so happy
my face is aglow
I sit and I talk
to this baby of mine
telling it soon
and it'll be time
then I can hold
and kiss you too
and we can do all the things
that mothers and babies do
then there's a problem
I'm not feeling quite right
I go to the hospital
and I'm told I lost you tonight
I go through the motions of living each day
wanting to hold you in the worst way
I know that you're gone and there's nothing I can do
but I want you to know that I still love you.

Rose Snodgrass

A Cold Draping Breeze

A cold draping breeze and my hair on
a stranger's shoulder and that
person is standing, looking where
ground meets sky in an eternal kiss
and that stranger is me and I am not
thinking of myself, my life, my
sounds. I am thinking about the
flightless wings on my ankles and my
soul's reaction which needs no wings
to fly, all is good - simple - true, all is
new not renewed - pure, and this
stranger is quite a beautiful person,
with a strong foothold and a good
soul and that soul moves always and is
held, embraced by that eternal kiss
between earth and sky like a kind of
cold draping breeze.

Patrick Gorman Pettis

If Only

My soul stands still as he speaks and silently I dream seeing
the world through his eyes. He is there with me escaping
everything familiar to us. If Only I could think his thoughts.
Remembering the solace of his deep brown eyes returning my smile,
If Only I could alter the condition, If Only I could freely love.
Dreams are but sweet denials of the awakening, and if perchance I
should awake finding him beside me, Love will gently play a sweet
melody in my heart that I shall always sing, and I shall love him
to the very depth, breadth and height that my soul can reach. But
my love has boundaries set by a cruel chance and he is no longer
near. Tears gather in my eyes when parting. The pain stings my
heart and wounds my soul until my eyes are once again mirrored in
his. I walk alone in melancholy mood watching the trees endlessly
exchanging secrets in the soft hush of the wind. The billowy
clouds rest like doom upon my brown and memory invites itself into
the recesses of my mind as I pass a familiar place. If Only I
could love him now. Alone at night feeling the depth of the
shadows and crying out to be embraced and loved, but my morning
sunshine has set into the darkness and the eclipse has once again
overtaken my soul. If Only he could be near, If Only.

Rhonda L. Aquilina

Friendships

The world is touched with God's grace
when He gives a gift of friendship to embrace.
Friendships are taken for granted,
very seldom are the words told,
how much it is needed and valued,
more than its weight in gold.
Not until it is taken from us,
is it realized how much it meant,
and too late to say,
I am glad you are my friend.
Speak your feelings openly,
hold no regrets,
don't be ashamed,
to be open or upset.

For the world is touched with God's grace
when He gives a gift of friendship to embrace.

Tammy Anderson-Schultz

Room

I opened up the door and I stared into my room,
and I stood there with the mop and I tightly gripped the broom,

There were pizza boxes, pop cans and doughnuts five days old
and the sandwich that I had last week was starting to grow mold.

The socks I had on yesterday jumped up and said "hello"
I walked across the room and stepped in month old green Jello.

I sat upon my bed and I heard a real loud crunch,
and I then remembered that I had potato chips for lunch.

I opened up my dresser drawer and there to my surprise,
was a double decker burger and a small order of fries.

I began to pick the clothes up that were all over the floor,
and I was interrupted by a knock upon my door.

My mom was standing at my door looking kinda of nauseous,
as she entered in I wanted her to be very very cautious.

"I can't believe this mess", she said as she glared at me.
"Either clean it up today or you're grounded for eternity".

She left my room and I looked at the mess I had to clean all alone,
so I dropped the mop and broom and thought, "eternity's not that long."

Carla Washington

This Poet's Despair

Please pluck from me, my sweet, this fruitless, dull plum-heart,
For your loving sun I've none, thus brightly bitter turned.
I thought that you I'd have, forever from the start,
Yet failed to tune my tinsel thoughts to match the heart that yearned.
New wishes I'd resign if I could skip reverse through time;
To make your heart rejoin my own would be my quest to fill.
And I'd try anew to turn your love from thyself to be with mine;
Since not seeing you I'm blind to love, cute Cupid's made his kill.
Still, this harlequin hopes your heart's not damaged past repair,
Thus in naming it arctic, denying it's ardent, prithee say the mark's amiss.
All's prima facie, my poring pomp may flow beyond your care,
For this poor poet blends emotions, becomes ambiguous.
  Of your loving years I've flitted five, hereon my poisoned plum's
    purse affords no affect;
  Apologies, poseurs repent, for this prentice prattle send truth
    direct.

Brian P. Howard

Untitled

Where I am headed I am not sure
Will the key I clutch open the door
And if the key does fit and turn
Can I be sure that I will learn

And if my key is of no use
Will I withstand the mental abuse
The fear inside will it overtake
Or will I strive even harder for my sake

And if I strive as hard as I might
Could it be so that I still lose my fight
Would I then decide to give up for sure
Or would I just go and search for another door

And say it's so that I win my war
Would I be content or for the moon would I soar
And if I shot for the moon and I missed
Would I be content with the star that I kissed

And if that star came shooting down
Would I follow it back or stick around
Would I be too scared when I was up top
Would I be afraid that I too may drop

Jess Eckel

Why People Go Wrong

Hear the facts first,
Don't spread false rummer,
That's not a Christian's attitude,
That's not peace, that's not love.

The facts come from the one
Who felt the hurts of many.
But have been silent
As one should know, silence is golden
And so, lots have been holden.

Too much have been said,
Too much have been done,
To manipulate and hinder
The career and progress of one
Who have tried to help so many.

I know in this country
Changes must come to correct
The mistakes of past manipulation
And there shall be no hindrance
 for God will direct my future destiny
  Anonymous.

Ionie Smith-Donalds

"Mom"

You were always there from the time of my birth,
To care for and protect me here on earth.
You were always there in my times of despair,
Always showing me how much you cared.
Even the times when I did not do right,
You turned me around and showed me the light.
Many times my life seemed like such a haze,
Now, all I can offer you is all my praise.
I will never be able to truly express.
Now, that you're on your journey of final rest.
All the memories, Love and Prayer you left me with,
Will always remain my most precious gift.
Mom as I lay down each night to sleep,
Memories of you, will not allow me to weep.
As, my mind slips into its deepest reams,
There you are mom-alive in my dreams.
Now, that you've gone to Heaven above,
You've left me with a heart full of love.
These words are written straight from my heart,
So, I know we'll never be completely apart.

Sheila B. Milner

The Storm

Ominous clouds form on the horizon,
Covering it in a blanket of darkness;
The fresh smell of rainwater fills the air,
The wind whistles through my hair;
Droplets of rain hit me so I go inside;
Hearing the soft "pitter patter" of rain causes me to doze off;
Soon I am awakened, for the soft "pitter patter"
has turned into vigorous drumming;
I see lightning trace the sky like racehorses;
burning everything in its path;
Soon after, I hear thunder as loud as clashing titans;
Then, as suddenly as it appeared, the lightning vanishes;
The reverberating sounds leave my ears;
And the drumming turns to a kitten's purr;
Silence;
The clouds part and leave the sky;
The Heavens are once again at peace

Alexis Justice

Nature

Man has tried to price everything
Yet there are things he cannot capture
Like the freshness after a summer rain
And the rainbow that comes after
These things are here for us to enjoy
Doesn't matter if we are rich or poor
They will be here forevermore

Sunrises and sunsets are a beautiful sight
Reds and blues combined
Spread all over the universe
For any artist to find
Their beauty will last forever
Their colors forever more

Yes, the sky is a lovely picture
Beauty that can't be denied
Thank goodness money can't buy
These things are here for us to enjoy
Doesn't matter if we are rich or poor
They will last forever more

Kay Crites

Remember

Remember their friendly face
Remember their smile
Remember the secrets
Remember the friendship
Don't forget

Remember the fights and arguments
Remember the hours you spent together
Remember the love, the laughter, the jokes
Don't forget

Your best friend has gone, Remember
Remember the one with all the answers
Remember the only one you trusted
Lost in the whirlwind of life, Remember
Don't forget

Remember the Separate Roads taken in
the maze of life, Remember
But, Remember the road where you walked together Don't forget

Remember the shoulder you cried on has led you astray
Remember your best friend has left you, but Remember
Them as if they were here Remember

Meredith Baker

School Lunch

Soggy, stiff, raw, burnt,
Tasteless, chewy, greasy, curt.
Makes me queasy, makes me sick,
Because it is so tough and thick.
Disgusting, unhealthy, unpleasant, gross,
Filthy, unwholesome, and covered with moss.
Food that has more fat than granola,
And probably spawned the virus E-Bola.
Black is the crust that formed on the edges,
White are the organisms growing small ledges.
Food on which bacteria fester-
And I have to live with it,
All next semester.
Bill Steppan

My Mother In Law

What is my mother-in-law to me, now let me think.
She's someone bubbly, loyal and pretty in pink.
She's got long talons of crimson red,
And a heart so soft, that is easily bled.
Her eyes change colour to coordinate her many dresses,
Multi holes in her earlobes and bleached blond tresses.
She turns heads when she is dancing the night away,
In Sam's arms to the music she will sway.
She is not your typical nan who stays in to knit.
And if she didn't work, she would have a fit.
The kids think she's a fairy grandmother bringing them joy.
They make a wish and Hey Presto there is a toy!
I cannot stop her from spoiling us all
She's the bonus in my marriage when I married her boy!
Mariella Cassar

To A Day

One morn I woke with such a weight of misery within my soul
It seemed that everything on earth would keep me from my goal.
When suddenly a still, small voice within me seemed to say,
"Look up and laugh and love and live, this gloom will pass away."

And so I took a look down deep within my secret heart,
And saw all the lovely things in which I had a part;
I bowed my head and closed my eyes, and I began to pray;
And Hope sprang up and filled my soul, and thus I faced the day

The day wore on, my heart grew light, I went about my tasks;
I had my Love, my health, my home - what more could mortal ask?
When evening came my heart could fly! I'd had a happy day,

The still, small voice was right, and all my gloom had passed away.
Marian J. Smith

Gifts

The world was given many gifts;
A Swan,
    the gift of grace.
A Rose,
    the gift of beauty.
A Baby,
    the gift of innocence.
A Dove,
    the gift of peace.
A Heart,
    the gift to love.
And when all these gifts were put into one,
a very special person came forth, and that was you.
Marc David

My Own Secret Place

Cross the grass and through the vegetable garden
is a place where hopes are lifted.
On the fence three wooden beams are shifted.
The grass feels like a pillow,
and the sun is warm and yellow.
My own secret place.

A nice place where I can sit,
and think about life a bit,
Where my frown turns into a smile,
and I can nap a while.
An open entrance where nature would like to stay,
and little ants would like to play.
My own secret place.

Where the aroma is so sweet,
and food is better to eat.
The breeze makes a whistling sound,
it really calms me down.
If you know how to imagine my place is also for you.
If you're one of those that doesn't how life must be blue.
My own secret place.
Suraag S. Patel

Being A Christian Is Not Always Easy

It is so hard to be a Christian.
It is a goal that I yearn to
improve each and every day.

No one understands the pain I go through,
no one cares what I say.

My tears express the spirit that
I feel inside,

The tears are one thing I can not hide.

My friends are always there for me,
with them I am truly blessed,

But it is the sinful ones that
put my Christianity to the test.

Every day I face a new obstacle,
and I pray that the Lord will help me.

Together forever with the Lord Jesus
I will always be.
Celeste Holland

Sail The Unknown

In two seas of Curious Green,
a quiet Enigma sails faithfully,
eager to be discovered and desired,
but still unknown, It lingers,
leaving various traces of sadness.

An infinite fire fed by hope,
swallows melancholy minutes
which exist to hinder firmness,
and create mental tempests,
which wreck remedial fantasies
that generate essential strength.

Yet the humble Mystery survives every obstacle encountered
in the unjust voyage through time,
gaining courage to sail beyond the fog
where it will bloom on the shores of emotion.

And still that pacific Strange drifts,
cautious for that flash of awareness
that will give meaning to a secret
which still dwells among the unknown,
lost in those two vast seas of Curious Green.
Juan Carlos Navarro

Dreaming You Left

I have this dream, it comes late at night
I see a beam of colorful light.

At the end of a tunnel, I see you stand.
My heart starts to rumble, you outstretch your hand

My steps are fast, I run to your side.
I'm near you at last, you are my guide.

We walk along beaches, our feet fall upon sand.
We discover new reaches, together hand in hand.

When the sun begins to fall, the stars start to shine through
You make me cross over a wall, that separates me and you.

I do not want to say goodbye, I do not want to go.
All I can do is utter my cry, as the wind begins to blow.

Suddenly the world goes black, you cannot be found
I sit alone calling you back, upon the vacant ground.
Emmy Lou McCallister

The World Will End Today

The world will end today with a big boom
The world will end tomorrow with a big bang
The world will end in three hours with no bang at all

No one knows when the world will end
It can end in forty eight hours
People say it will end in thirty billion years,
   But is the world a predictable thing?
On course not, the world could end in thirty four hours

We can never predict when the world will end,
   Because if you could good luck to you,
   For no one shall believe you
The world is a very unpredictable thing
The world could blow up thanks to the o' the hat
   to billy mac who lives in the back of a shack
Rishi Roy

Single Person's Lament

When I was twenty and very young,
I searched for love, but did not worry.
After all, I'd marry before thirty.
There was no hurry.

When I was thirty and more mature,
I longed for love and began to sweat.
It wasn't too late,
At least not yet.

Now I'm forty and turning old and gray.
The years are passing by swiftly.
Will my love be there
By the time I'm fifty?
Michael L. Roberts

Forgetfulness

You forgot what I said about God
about what I said about the dog and
what happens to divisions when they are gone
how the night swallows the fiddlehead and the frond.
And you forgot what I said about art
about what I said about the dark and
what you did to me when your heart lied
how glass is the most effective barrier of all.
However, you forgot what I said about hands
about what I said about the empty shells and
what that last mistake killed in everyone and
how every criminal pulled the trigger without one last thought...
Marcella Erb

Untitled

Memories like the flutter of raven wings.
Caws and cackles a reminder in the graveyard.
Winds shift and change under black, velvety wings carrying them this way and that.
They hop from stone to stone like perverse demons searching for a scrap.

"Where you are love?" they crow, as they skip about my bed.
An unholy circle of birds raising my beloved dead.
My severed head-my hollow shell fed
on scraps from the table of the twisted and perverse.

My cup of wormwood wine,
my veins full of arsenic and strychnine.
And a black night hides the sun from my eyes.

Where are you dear, sweet one? Cradle me in your arms tonight.
Look into my eyes and hold me in your sight.
Else I may fall from my bed into Hell's endless night,
and never find you again.

Tell me my love, can you hear my ravens crow?
Can you hear them from your bed?
And if so, would you please send a wren in their stead?
Randy McCowan

My Rainbow

God gave you to me
To make my life worth while
To bring the world a rainbow
And everyone you meet a smile
To see you all my days
To see you in my dreams
To hold your little hand
Make life's worries less than they seem
I tuck you in each and every night
And watch you fall asleep
I dry your tiny tears away
When you've fallen and you weep
I only hope life's good to you
And you won't have to see what I've seen
I hope you can walk in the clouds
And not have to go where I've been
I'll teach you how to love
And to know wrong from right
How to see the world in color
Instead of black and white
Laura Raven

A Single Rain Drop

It rained so much,
no more rain drops left.
The lightening crashed and the thunder roared,
But not a drop fell.

I thought I saw a blue sky today.
But as soon as a smile appeared on my face,
All hell broke.
No more rain drops left.

Confusion and fear swept over me.
I'm back were I started
But I am not hopeless,
I see the raging ocean calm
And the gray skies clear

And a single rain drop rolls
down my cheek.
Lydia Hernandez

My Other Self

This is a poem to my husband Terry
Whom I have loved since ever I can remember.
The son of a quiet, faithful father,
Now too a husband and father like his own,
Whose quiet and tender presence
Calms the tidal waves of my life.
That strength I feel to my very soul
In this humble and unassuming man
Who has taught our Son, not by mighty words,
But yes, by a quiet, faithful example
That living is loving what
God has given.
This alone gives meaning to our earthly journey.
His education in the law is superior,
Yet no one need know.
Everyone draws upon his knowledge and strength.
He listens so well,
And, as I write this poem to the love I will always remember,
I believe
This love was given to me long before I could ever remember.

Martha M. Herron

Growing Up Years

When I was only a little child
Living in the country running wild
I would climb to the top of the mulberry tree
Just to see what I could see
I thought I was sitting on top of the world
Until I looked down, thing started to whorl
With my breeches legs rolled up to my knees
The boys would laugh at me and tease
I did not care I was having fun
At games I could beat nearly everyone
Then I grew up to my middle teens
I traded my breeches for frilly things
With my paten leather slipper and pretty dress
My hair no longer a tangled mess
At last I Had turned out to be
The lady Mama tried to make of me
Now, I'm old my hair turned gray
Of all memories gathered along the way
The ones I hold in my heart most dear
Are the rolled up breeches, bare foot days

Theda M. Russell

38, I, 114

By a twist of fate I have finally seen my face,
It's ugly and depressing and one I wish I could replace,
Time will reap its bounty on the hills when the sun goes down.
But love will never show its face, on a face that only frowns.
And you my friends, troubled and beguiled by the upper level,
Will find my face, and one just like it, and no you will not revel
At the sight of one so old, decrepit and disgust, for tonight my love,
  my face will turn to dust.
And leave you I may for the troubled and beguiled, but the wilderness
  is not one to reject an ugly child
My love for you no boundary will it know, nor melt like when the sun
  hits the cool dry fallen snow.
My love for you so boundless and eternal, will live in flame and
  breath your name, not by day, you night, you are nocturnal.
The ladder remembers every step I took to get to your level.
But will you love me when I say, can I not stand here and revel.
Turn me away just like that, and This, and those,
But don't forget to love me, I'm afraid that is how it goes.
So pack up tight and bring warm things
For snow it has fallen, and you already know what night brings,
For you I am a callin' speak not to others so hold your tongue
And with blessing from the Lord above
See not my face, its ugly disgrace, and you, go live in love,

Eric Larson

Family Ties

Family ties remain with us all our days.
Even though we grow and go our separate ways.
For in life we sometimes do not know where we belong.
But through the bond of our families, we are kept strong.
We can always count on our family to be by your side.
Throughout the ups and downs of life's roller coaster ride.
The laughter, joy, and tears.
The sharing of our triumphs and our innermost fears.
Created memories, we as family share.
Tucked away in our hearts with loving care.
A safe and nurturing place where memories do not part.
The love for our family is there embedded in our hearts.
And although we grow and go our separate ways,
our love for our family will remain with us all our days.

Donna M. Sidney

Silent Night

The night is still.
The sky is black.
A gentle wind blows through the trees.
They are waving, as if saying their last goodbye.
Out in the distance
a series of colors bombards the sky.
Red. Black. Red. Yellow.
The wind picks up gently blowing those fierce colors
closer and closer.
A sudden blast of red and black
fills the area and disintegrates all that is near
The night returns to its natural state.
The ceaseless wind picks up the poisonous ashes.
The only thing that withstood the blast
is a single
solitary
rose,
weeping among the biased dirt,
making us realize
the end has not yet come.

Grace Combs

Untitled

I reached womanhood at age 50,
I acquired a new attitude,
I began to go with my feelings, and
Not look for security.

Deciding to "get what I need" clearly.........
Was another kind of life,

Now, right now, I wanted to experiment
And truly feel in charge........
After all life is only once,
For once, I am making the "most" of it.

Comfortable with my looks,
Assertive in my outlook,
Discovering my many late bloomer talents,
Enjoying the "I'm afraid of you" stares
From authoritative males,
And the "I admire your style" peeks
From younger women.

I have embraced, truly, "becoming a woman"
At 53 and still aging in beauty and grace,

Ana E. Irizarry

An Angel In The Shelter

The sun is glistening on the new fallen snow
Barren leaves of winter and chilling winds that blow

Drifting people outside huddled against the cold
Neither coat nor blanket nor friendships to unfold

Homeless indeed they are, no shelter nor a bed
Asking only for basic needs and wanting to be fed

Can those of us so richly blessed with lovely homes,
good food and wealth
Afford to turn and walk away caring not for our brother's health

Oh, but perhaps we may say, I do not know what to do
Would we know any better if the homeless were me or you

There are questions we can ask and phone calls we can make
And always welcome will be the cookies that we bake

Warm clothing and shoes, soap and shampoo too
What homeless people need is the same as me and you

A good book to read and music to hear
Toys for the children who live in such fear

For we're all God's children and indeed it just might be
There's an angel in the shelter who's speaking to me

So I'll carefully listen and hear with all my heart
For truly now is the time for kindness to start

Ann R. Lovvorn

Beneath The Rustling Leaves

Underfoot, frightened insects scuttle beneath glossy leaves.
Only their tuneless humming is left behind,
As proof of their existence

Overhead, birds scream and laugh to one another.
Crying for help or joy or sorrow,
Their songs merge and intertwine,
Creating a heavenly chorus of song.

Leaves rustle and trees sway,
As though joining in some mindless carefree dance.
Waiting for Sun to adorn then with his golden kisses.
Waiting for Night to wrap them in her cloak of darkness.
Waiting for Winter's chilling touch, and Summer's warm caress.

Sunlight dapples the path.
Bright in one spot, dim in another,
Yet always changing, always transforming.
A forever shifting collage of Light and Dark.

This is how it is,
An undisturbed paradise in harmony.
This is how it always was,
Beneath the rustling leaves.

Kristi Hausman

Reflections Of A Senior Poetry Writer

Writing poetry is fun,
You never know how much until it is done.
But pulling on your thoughts,
Is like making a lot of knots.
The rope can be big and the knots loosely made.
Those are the thoughts that easily fade.
But the tight ones are those that stay.
Secured memories of those days of play.
Seniors can look back and say,
Tomorrows will come, but I had my day.

Hal H. Ebersole

Life

Alpha And Omega
the Beginning and the End.
So simple to conceive; so hard to comprehend.
Everyone sees the warning sign,
once it is too late.
No one sees it coming. It's so f***in' easy to Hate.
But Hate is such a harsh word,
used by little kids;
fighting on the playground. Not knowing what it is.
Anger and Aggression,
brought unto this earth.
Fear of just not knowing, what it is all worth.
But this is all a part of us,
where all the pieces fit.
We just don't understand it all and some just don't give a sh*t.
A little bit of Agony, a little bit of Hate.
A lot of Love and Caring and we just might create;
a Peaceful cd-existence between our bodies and our minds.
This Fear of one another,
still may be left behind.

Joseph J. Biondi

Picture Postcard Meditations

The mist enshrouds the distant dome;
The near hill slopes t'ward palm fringed cone; and here,
Where, in a gentler tone, the river leaves its weight of loam,
   Two little men now cease to roam, and travel home.

Bold stroked, the artist wields his brush.
Lo! Men in action shoreward rush. The proud sea's might
Frail ships will crush; tall masts will break like sand-snapped brush;
For men will fail - God must cry, "Hush," and smooth the foam.

Snow lined like coat of ermine fold, this landscape stretches
Brisk and cold. Strained men - by gentle stroking told -
   go rushing forth appearing bold
'Neath leafless trees now bent, and old, gnarled, stunted, numb.

Trees grown ancient, once were young. And from their branches
Gently hung great yellow flowers with red tipped tongue.
   The birds above them trilled and sung
And swooped to pluck a red-ripe plum mid autumn hum.

Our aging world is past its prime; Yet like this pool,
Smooth, free, sublime, God's peace will stretch o'er sea and thyme.
Proud men will cease their laddered climb t'ward heaven and home.

John Steven Harris

Free

Allow me to run naked,
my vulnerable naked self,
to the open fields of liberty
and inhale the fumes of nature's wealth.

Give me the chance to tumble,
the dark rich soil to my bare flesh;
I'll run through shadows of majestic trees
as I fill my lungs with air so fresh.

I'll exalt as my adolescence is exposed
while being engulfed by the colorful brilliance;
my eyes will capture the resplendent creations
as our Mother reveals her innocence.

Let the sun splash across my skin
as I'm captivated by a world so wild and free.
I'll tranquilly rest with the primitive creatures;
in this deliverance I'll find my solitude and peace.

Sara Mannes

Untitled

Snowflakes falling...
   On the evergreen

Crystalline delight...
   dancing in the blue moonlight

No two alike...
   yet perfect harmony

North wind blows...
   dances with the snow

Frozen subzero night...
   vibrantly alive, winter's delight

Mary E. Robbins

Real

Watering the fake flowers
With apple juice.
It doesn't matter,
neither are real, so
neither exist.
I wish the wind
would blow my name
away so I could
start over, but knowing my
prayers are being
swallowed up by the
swollen emptiness of
hopelessness. Knowing
that hopelessness is only
the echo of a million
different screams, all
running in the same direction.
I exist, but only
my words are real.

Sara Goldshlack

A Feline's Only Wish

Dear old master of mine,
I only have one wish.
To be property taken of,
And warm milk on a dish.
I need not be pampered,
Though a small treat would be nice.
And a couple of toy mice.
Whatever I might do,
Please don't hurt me in any way.
I'll learn from my mistakes,
If you'll help me every day.
I'd like to stay inside,
When it's cold and wet outside.
But when it's sunny out,
I like to run around and hide.
Now that you have read this,
You know my only wish.
Someday soon I hope,
It's this you will accomplish.

Stephanie Gobby

Mother

Mother, God's gift to me
  I like to have her hug me.
I like to have her close to me.
  I like to have her read and tell
stories to me when I was little.
  I like to make my Mother very
proud of me in all I do.
  Mother, God's gift to me

Kari Woodard

Lord From Above

I love you so much
with all my heart
being without you
will tear me apart

Thinking about you
every single night
saying a little prayer
before turning out the light

I'll never be alone
because you are always near
then why should I have
any fears

Deep down inside
I hope you can see
all the joy
that you brought me

You'll be in my heart
with great love
because you are the Lord
that comes from above

Sabata Nunes

Ode To Seattle

Oh, the splendor of your very being
evokes my heart to swell
As I breathe within your bosom
I savor the seduction you instill

Our time as one
Leaves me craving
the moisture of your touch
Submerge me in the taste of you
come now, I'm not asking much

Emerald are your eyes
By height dramatically tall
yet reaching down
you brush the Sound
Could you be real at all?

I'll never know now, I must leave
Beyond the bliss of my dreams
I'll be shrouded in grief

Replacing you will be my
absurd illusion

Debbie L. Stewart

The Dreamcatcher

The dreamcatcher is a hero,
Who saves me from nightmares,
And is always there
to protect me
In those times when
I get scared.

I hate getting scared
in my dreams,
There is nothing I can do,
I can't wake up
to stop the dream,
To make it leave my thoughts,
I try to clear my mind,
But how can you
trick your own mind?

All I can rely on is
the dreamcatcher,
To catch the nightmare
And make the fear go away.

Cinda Dailey

The Unicorn

As he runs beside me,
He laughs.
For his world is different.
With his horn in the air,
He runs toward me.
For our world is strange.
With his horn in the air,
He pierces my heart.
Like a stranger in the night,
He runs away.

Roberta Gorin

"To Melinda"

I miss you in the morning,
  Like flowers miss the rain.
I listen to the wind at night,
  In case you call my name.
And every now and then, I dream
  My touch still makes you smile
And every now and then, I dream
  You're my girl again... awhile.

But ever seasons come and go,
  Like the changing of the leaves.

Still I listen to the wind at night,
  Because I still believe.

John P. Walsh III

Sun Flowers

It's time to warm up,
in the warm sun.
Time to put snow away,
in our mind.
Time to hang up our winter
warm coats,
and time to have fun
in the summer
sun!

Katie Over

A Famous Place

Today a crowd is gathered on a street
That otherwise is empty
And underneath the milling feet
The mindless stones receive the storm
Regardless of who's who.
And like a sponge absorbing water
The street itself absorbs a crowd
No matter why they came.

Irene Ferraro

To Life!

What a winter we have had
Snow and sleet, 'twas very bad.
Hopefully spring will be here soon
And with it we'll see flowers bloom.

Shall we look for sun and glow?
Or, do you think there'll be more snow?
Seems like seasons may reverse
But, of course, it could be worse.

Let us, instead, celebrate life
Even though we know its strife
It's great to be alive and well
Hoping always good news to tell.

Elizabeth S. Bensley

Trapped

They've
Locked me away
And now I can't go anywhere;
I used to be free -
But now I can't go anywhere;
I used to have a soul -
But now it has gone everywhere;
I used to have a mind -
But now it's all used up.
I used to loved a love -
But now it has blown everywhere;
Like so many old leaves -
Dried up, dead in the sun.
I gather the pieces
Of my love -
They're all the same, every one -
Put them back together
As one collage of sorrow;
Look at it tonight -
We'll torch it all tomorrow.....

Matt Leiterding

"I Could Have Been A Canadian!"

I look kinda rough
   hairs a little long.
I turned nineteen and twenty
   killing Viet - Cong.
Kinda hard these days
   to get some squeeze.
What's left of my body
   Resembles swiss cheese.
There are a lot of things
   I'd like to forget.
Like when I got home
   And the people spit.
Well I guess I shouldn't
   Really complain.
I eventually healed
   And got over the pain.
And for my wounds
   And a brand new start.
The army gave me 650 a month
   And a purple heart.

Keith C. Carter

Pain In My Heart

He came around with
Everyday,
I never thought that
He'd go away.
He made me feel so bad
I had to cry,
With each passing day
I felt I could die.
Does he know
He hurt me so,
I always felt oh
So very low
Sometimes he made me
Feel great,
And then I learned
That I could hate.
He is the reason for this
Pain in my heart,
And one of these days
It could all fall apart.

Jennifer Hageman

A Thought

I'm sitting here with the thought
   of a man
And wondering if this is a crush
   I have...
I'm all flustered
   And red in the face.

I have a warm and tingly feeling
   in my heart,
A feeling I thought I had lost
   forever..
Wondering if he thinks of me at all
   And what he thinks of me
   Does he like me.

Kimberly Whitmore

Untitled

Forget the trouble and the strife
Sunny days surround my life

Such a gift to be so blessed
So much different than the rest

Silver lining in every cloud?
I see gold amongst the crowd

So much love, a lot less fear
Surely bring the people here

Remember this, oh love of mine
Nothing heals as well as time

Rhonda K. Allen

The Sunset

I waited all day in the bright rays.
Waited for your longing touch.
I felt no soothing whisper.
You dared not to show.
I just wanted to tell you,
The moment was beautiful,
The rays dipping into the horizon.
But, you laid contempt in your heart.
Everything was perfect.
Yet, one thing was missing,
And that was you.
You should have come for the sunset,
If not for me.

Scott Lambeth

True Love

Like sweet petals from a rose
Your life uplifts my soul.
Even though the thorns are there
Our love will always grow.

On the bush of life
You stand above the rest.
While others will catch my eye
You are still the best.

For in your perfectness
You always will remain.
While the many imitations
Will perish in the rain.

Jeremy P. Moore

Through The Eyes Of A Child

Life isn't cruel
It's only a game
A challenge given
That drive people insane

Love is a pleasure
A hunger in one's heart
A heartache is a need
When lovers drift apart

Sorrow isn't pain
It's only a fear
Sometimes driving one crazy
Or bringing them to tears

If only people knew
That there's no secret to life
Only to learn to enjoy it
Through the eyes of a child

For a child sees
What is innocent and true
And looks at life
With a holy view

Shanda Phillips

Trying Times

School is hard sometimes;
We all have trying times.
Nine-weeks tests are very hard;
But studying will get us far.
We will all go to college one day;
We are all very well on our way.
Everyone gets a job;
Life becomes very hard.
People go out and do new things;
People will always have new flings.
Never give up during hard times;
Everyone has trying times.

Liz Campbell

The Dark Eyes Of The Night

The night is watching me,
With its cold, dark eyes!
I shiver
I'm in a cold, dark house.
I try to comfort myself,
But it's no use.
I hear something;
What is it?
Could it be the night
Reaching its dark claws out to get me?
I curl up in a ball
I hear the noise again.
Dark shadows creep up behind me
The door knob turns
I jump back!
Then I smile.....
No worries,
Mom's finally home!

Hillary Tandrow

On The Edge Of Genius

I aspire to do something Mozartian,
Shakespearean, or Bonapartian.
Creativity surges within me
Demanding fait accompli.
I must do it
or live with my sorrow.
I'll start it —
Day after tomorrow.

A. B. Johnson, Jr.

The Golden Year

From the moment I saw you,
I knew it was love.

The angels had sent you
from heaven above.

Now fifty years have passed,
and what do I see,

that same beautiful face
smiling at me.

We've made it through these
past fifty years,
the fun and the laughter,
the sadness, the tears.

And even though
the children are grown,
we'll never ever be alone.

We've got each other
this is true,
and I want to spend
the next fifty years
with you.
Tina Whittemore

Today

Today is a great day
in the universe.
All of man - made evils
are now but a curse
and all of the wind families
are out a playing;
which is just our
maker's way of saying,
"This earth of mine
is mighty fine
but it's got to be swept
from time to time;
just like some folks
take to praying."
Margie Stewart Johnson

"I Can Let You Go"

When I saw you I thought I could see
Someone who'd always be next to me.
But I guess I was wrong
and it hurt for so long
But I can let you go.
Why did you lie to me?
can't you see?
My love for you is real
but that I guess you'll never feel
but I can let you go
How could I be so blind
to think when I was yours I'd find
someone who'd want to be mine
'til the end of time
but I can let you go
So in the future, I hope you will find
that you can always suture
your heart and mine...
but I can let you go
Erica Haile

"Happiness"

Happiness is the sound of
 Children's laughter new,
 unexpected, excitement
 of what is next.
Happiness, is to see you come
 home at night, with a
 smile, even though
 your day was complicated
Happiness, most of all is
 to touch each other
 before we say, "good night"
Ella Lamadore

Seeing

We look at you and say,
"This is a leaf."
How can we stop there?

For you are wonder, you are magic;
There is not one word to describe you;
Books could not do it.

What botanicus house of fashion
determined your shape, your color?
Who chose the fabric, the design?

Who placed swatches together,
Traced, cut and pinned?
Who stitched the seams?

Why are you called "Prayer Plant?"
When you rise at night
It's not in supplication;

It is to say
"Look at me,
I am the universe!"
Terril J. Young

Secrets In The Trees

The leaves whisper
Telling secrets
They tell the wind
But they don't tell me
When they're old and their colors
Change and they laugh at me
'Cause I don't change colors
When they fall off the tree
And die
No more secrets are told
And I'm laughing at them
Instead of them laughing at me!
LaKeshia Wright

Dear God

If we are all your children and you
love us all so dear; why are nuclear
weapons on the assembly line here?
 If we are all brother and sisters
in you; why are weapons so many
and loving people so few?
 What can we do? What can we say?
 I thank that I have found a
way! We will shelve all those
weapons, yes put them away,
turn to my neighbor, shake their
hand and say;
 "We are all part of one family
and to me that's Okay."
Jeanne Elder

Everything In Time

The spectrum fell today
No one can understand why
Yellow was rising, the rest stable
A spiral of sorts was illuminated
The ringmaster had the key
The map and the legend

A windmill turned

Splashed on the wall
One saw green, one saw black
Yet all that was there was orange
A man from Spain cursed
For him he saw all three

The convention was cut short
By defunct governments
What! Has something been discovered?
Then put it away and let no one know

Yet this could not be contained
More deadly than cancer
The only people immune
Were the blind who could still see
Jeremie J. Dufault

Storming, The Romance

 Haunting face...
Rainscent fills the night.
 Warming embrace...
Droplets swell in flight.
 Tender kisses...
Faster, the storm grows.
 Gentle caresses...
Harder, the wind blows.
 Love words spoken...
Flashing streaks surrounds.
 Boundaries broken...
Raging thunder pounds.
 Heartfelt sighs...
All is falling, breaking.
 Tear swept cries...
Monsoon heart-aching.
 Silent yearning...
The tempest blows past.
 Passions burning...
Dreamy stars, at last.
Carol Cook

Silence

In the years of comfort
In the memories of lies
Salty tears pave roads of sadness
untouched tells a innocents
unloved leaves a familiar darkness
no light, moon light
both seem dark
still time ticks away slowly
why can't they leave me
in the serenity of what
I once was
pain is unreal
but nothing hurts more
than the silence
spoken in the hidden
hells of your heart
burning my desires into ashes
undisturbed heart
silence, silence
unspoken
Crystal Moenius

The Player

The player is back,
back behind the line,
to take a three
and I think that's fine.
Because when he pulls up,
in front of the crowd,
I'll stuff the ball,
and make him frown.
He will be sorry
that he even tried,
'cause he saw me later
and then he cried.
So if you're on the court,
and you think I'm there,
get out of there fast,
or you better beware.

Stephen Williams

It Ain't Wanted Here

Doin' time,
Growin' crime,
It ain't wanted here.
Shootin' guns,
Hit 'n' runs,
It ain't wanted here.
Bein' thugs,
Dealin' drugs,
It ain't wanted here.
Stealin' stuff,
Goin' "puff,"
It ain't wanted here.
Only you can do it,
Make time, think through it.
Then when you're done,
Go out and have some fun,
Increasin' the peace.

Karen Ault

Contact

I hear the rain falling from the sky
But the moisture touches me not
Out of fear
Or respect
I do not know
It settles gently around me
Wary of my movements
An untested trust
It shies around my feet
And I
I bend
Just to let it know
That I am safe

Christian Piccolo

April

April speaks of springtime
With a soft and gentle breeze,
Urging oaks and maples
To put forth their fresh bright leaves.

Awaking plants and flowers
From their damply warming beds,
Reminding all young lovers
Of the june that lies ahead.

It makes the old world new again,
Hiding last years brown dead mat,
With a multi-colored plumage,
Giving earth an easter hat.

Jack Terwilliger

One Thought

If you glance at the morning sky
As all the cotton candy clouds float
slowly by

If you listen closely you will hear
Birds chirping ever so softly, ever
so near

If you glance across the grass you
will see dew spread all around
And in this quiet time of a day,
When there's hardly a sound

If you could think just one thought
in your head
Would you think of cuddling back
up in your cozy, warm bed

Or would you think of me
Your very best friend
Who will be there for you, from
beginning to the end?

Jill Luna

"My Daddy Won't Be Here"

It's almost time for Christmas
and Santa is drawing near.
But the one I love the most,
my Daddy, he won't be here.

But I have a little package
to send you on that day.
And I will ask dear Santa
if he will go your way.

I'll tell him it's important.
Not from the two you see,
for daddy since you went away
God sent my sister to me.

She's the sweetest little bundle
and such a tiny tot.
My mommy says, "in time she'll grow"
and we love her an awful lot.

On Christmas morn we'll open gifts
and sing the Christmas cheer.
But one will be missing.
For my daddy won't be here.

Yolonda R. Grosso

Dreams

Dreams
mysterious, fun, full of hope.
Wondering what's next. How am
I going to get there?

Dreams
discovering, creating, maybe
false hope. Fantasy worlds, people
and things.

Dreams
I am going to be happy!
I am going to get there
with my dreams to carry
me all the way.

No one going to stop
me I am on my way
with my hopes and dreams
to carry me to another day.

Syreeta Hanson

The Healing

During Easter picnic
The crippled kid
Sat to the side of the fun
With meadow-christening tears
Dripping on his chicken leg
When the Blazing Shadow touched him
Hushed his twisted shin
He was rumbling with glory
And stood straight up
His crutch left there
Like a stage prop
In the Act of God
On what became the town's
Most famous day
The boy ran home
The witnesses staggered away...

Charles John Quarto

Time

Swifter than the wind
Speedier than light,
Time breaks the slow promise
She made me last night.
She teases me so,
This quick-witted soul,
She makes me cry
As the faster she goes.
I fear I'll never catch her,
I feel I'll never win.
So as time passed quickly,
I wait for life to begin.

Alisen Down

Shaping Wood

Drawing their words
from freshly oiled stone,
cradling them lovingly,
they peel
skin thin slices
to the ground
in piles, until
blood beads, speckles
to a hard glaze,
whittling me to a shape
I don't even know.

P. Edward Danel

Almost A Yard

There is a pixy in this house.
Little shoes and socks,
and fingerprints.
A naked flash down the hall.
Two and a half feet of light.

Every button a challenge,
And every sleeve a mystery.
Transfixed by snow.
Each time it falls,
And fascinated by where ants go.

To view this universe,
From wide blue eyes,
and long red lashes.
What a gift to see the world
from the short end.

Stephanie Phillips

Come With Me

Come with me,
to a magical, golden place,
where all your wishes and dreams
come true.

Come soar with me,
where laughter is the only
thing you hear.

Come and join me,
where you are free,
free to be yourself.

Joanna M. Schueler

The Late Flight

Geese a late November day
Struggle of gaggle
Ragged to my eye
Gray on gray
Came honking out of the mist
Slid down the Western sky.

Colleen Croson Ewing

Eyes, Windows to the Soul

Eyes, windows to the soul
breaking to the highest one
seeing to reach out...
Feeling of oneness to
encounter an entirely
different world.
Views of thy true self,
watching to get more.
Feel the energy bursting from
the window.
A sense of ones extreme self.
To reach security and
love,
While seeking togetherness of
one's mind and soul.
Eyes, windows to the soul.

Carrie Scott

Your Wings Still Spread

Now I visit you peaches
At this moment to share
Though no longer in presence
The memories still here

You are the birds of my thoughts
That fly so very free
The precious dove of my heart
That keeps you nearer to me

Like a pretty peacock
You're full of many colors
With a humble spirit
That spreads among others

Watching the sun set
As the birds stretch their wings
Flying across land and flying over seas
There is nothing like harmony
Of a canary that still sings

Fly on - precious one - fly on

(Tear Drops)

LaJeune Farmer

My Savior

Countless times this pen has saved
My worthless body from its grave
It spoke the words I couldn't speak
It gave me strength when I was weak

And in a world where trust is slim
I always knew I could trust him
Deep in my heart cold and frayed
He spoke the truth and I obeyed

Amazing how this modest tool
Could make a wise man of a fool
Could with empathetic eyes
Search the souls of those despised

Countless times this pen has saved
My worthless body from its grave

Patrick Joseph Misiti

Tears Of The Willow

Why does the willow weep?
In all her grandeur and beauty
   is she not so strong as she seems?
As lovers caress one another
   beneath her rueful boughs,
   are they thankless
   for the solitude she provides?
Has her heart grown cold
   and her soul become dark?
She stands alone
   and yearns for the embrace
   from one of a pure heart
And her tears feed the river
   which gives her life...

Sonja J. Rees

Blink

As I looked across the land
I saw a small child
running across the land
I blinked and he was gone

As I looked across the land
I saw the beauty
the beauty of the land
I blinked and the beauty was gone

As I looked across the land
I saw the war
that beauty was replaced
I blinked and the war was not gone

As I looked across the land
I saw a small child
dying

I blinked
and never opened
my eyes again

Zachary Shannon

Untitled

Their laughter is constant
Their questions never seize
I sit and wonder, why me?
But when they are sleeping
Quiet overtakes
I sneak to their rooms
To check on my babes
My heart overflows
For what is life
Without them.

Linda McConnell

Snow In July

Another summer's almost gone,
As if it never came.
For now, my life still carries on,
But will it be the same?

I know the Earth will spin around
The golden Sun again,
And there will be warmth abound
And rainbows in the rain.

The fireworks will light the skies
And take my breath away,
But I won't see them in your eyes
On that midsummer day.

You left before the summer did;
You never said goodbye.
And I was marveled like a kid
When snow fell in July.

I know the summer's bell will chime
To give it a new start;
I know your eyes will never shine
To thaw my frozen heart.

Pavel Chernyshev

Untitled

Every time I hear a train
I feel a loss. I feel a pain.
A great writer, a poet my friend
who rode a train right to the end.

But you'll never really die.
Even though you're dead.
You'll never really die
when something you wrote is read

I should have listened more closely
my friend. To all your dreams
and poems. I should have listened
more closely, you said you weren't
coming home.

Smitty

Ghost

Fall asleep the day is gone,
Feeling down and also wrong.
Thinking thoughts of suicide,
knowing what happens when you die.
Hoping that you'll do the right thing,
then all of the sudden...Bang!
You feel yourself floating away
wishing you had waited another day.

You see yourself on the floor,
you see your parents at the door.
Now you know how much they care,
you just wish you could be there.

I sure hope that they will find
the suicide note I left behind.
It says to them to live their lives
the way they did before I died.
I know they will be able to do it,
Even though I went and blew it.
I felt my whole life was a lie,
so that is why I had to die.

Melissa Doak

Jacqueline III

Lost and scared
Was a little child
The fright inside
Wasn't very mild
  "Where is Grandpa?"
As she looks around
But nowhere in sight
Could he be found
  Full of tears
As she starts to cry
Here comes grandpa
To ask her why
  Without a word
He picks her up
And with a hug
He cheers her up
  Any fear inside her
Only he can stop
For the love they share
Can never be topped...

George M. Conney

"Mother"

My mother I love
  So very much
My mother I love
  But cannot touch
Years go by, and I
  Do not see
My mother, my mother
  Where can you be
I lay in bed each
  Night and pray
To see my mother
  When I awake the
  next day
My mother who left
  Without a word
  one night
The mother I love
  But who is
  Nowhere in
  sight

Shawna Preece

Praise God

Some Praise the Lord quite loudly,
And that's all well and good.
I praise Him in more quiet ways
And know I'm understood.

Shouts of Glory Alleluia
May be just fine for them.
God also loves simplicity,
Remember Bethlehem?

Each one of us is different,
And it's really more my style
To Praise my God and Savior
With an ordinary smile.

God knows I love Him dearly;
The Father, Son and Spirit.
I speak to Him. He speaks to me.
Though no one else can hear it!

Ann Yost

The Gift "Fatters"

I once received a precious gift,
It gave my spirits quite a lift.
I found my gift under a tree,
It meant more than the world to me.

He was my companion and friend,
My closest friend until the end.
He filled my life with lots of joy,
He was the sweetest little boy.

One morning I called for my cat,
But as I approached the door mat,
I saw a horrifying sight,
A car had hit him during the night

I felt like my world had ended,
Never again to be mended.
People say, "He's only a cat,"
But to me, he was more than that.

For the six years he was with me,
We were as happy as could be.
I miss him more than words can say,
Still I think of him every day.

Lisa M. Polachek

Unconditional Love

I love you unconditionally,
no matter how you were yesterday,
for the you I have today,
and the ever changing you of tomorrow.
I love you unconditionally,
despite our differences
in attitudes and opinions.
I love you unconditionally,
even during the times when we
might not like each other very well.
I love you unconditionally,
for the positive you have fed to me
and the inner peace occurring within me.
I love you unconditionally,
for the real you I've always seen
that you are beginning to discover.
I love you unconditionally,
with faith and belief in you
until our final days are over,
for you are the other half of me.

Kristi Mossberger

"Losing My Mind"

The other day in English class
(Since grammar makes me yawn)
I went inside my head to think
And saw my brain was gone.

It hated lectures, books, and tests,
And so in indignation
It left its home inside my skull
And took its own vacation.

It took a trip to far-off lands
I always longed to see;
Though I told it we would go someday
It wouldn't wait for me.

Right now it's soaring into space,
Or swimming in the sea.
So if you find my naughty mind
Please mail it home to me.

Gina Beguhn

Tawny Eyes

Tawny eyes looking at me
seeing into my very soul
reading my innermost thoughts

Tawny eyes seeing my
deepest secrets peering
into all the dark corners

Tawny eyes stripping away
all my protective wrapping
leaving me unsure and terrified

Tawny eyes searching out all
of the locked doors opening
the doors to my soul

Tawny eyes leaving me naked
and yet at peace as you
continue to see into my soul

Tawny eyes looking at me
seeing into my very soul
reading my innermost thoughts

Patricia I. White

"At Last"

Jesus One who loves my soul
Jesus One who makes me whole
Jesus you are the Mighty one
The God of love
The Ruler of this earth -
The Strength - of ages past
Your hand stretched out through
all eternity
To help in times of need
A Love beyond belief
A Kingdom forever new
With love in our hearts
With gladness of soul
And peaceful repose
We seek you -
We seek you -
At last..............

Shannon Marie Prichard

It Seemed So Real

It seemed so real,
When we touched and kissed.
It seemed so real,
When we held each other close.
It seemed so real,
When I told you how it feels.
It seemed, it seemed so real.
It seemed so real,
When the place was familiar.
It seemed so real,
When we caressed one another.
It seemed so real,
When we looked upon each other.
It seemed, it seemed so real.
Then I realized it was a dream
and things were not what they seemed.
My longing for you awaits....
In dreamland where things happen...
Until then.....
It seemed......It Seemed So Real.

Jennifer Clark

Untitled

When I dream, I search up in
 the sky
So if you can, please tell
 me why
It's so hard, to achieve those
 things
I see so crystal clear in my
 hopes, and my dreams

May be those clouds that appear
 so soft and ethereal,
are really the misty obstacles in
 which must climb.

For if not for the dreams to
 became who we really are
What is there really,
 Just clouds, no ray of
 sunshine

Susan Linde

Hold My Hand

When we enter this world
 there is someone there
To hold our hand,
 take our problems to bare.

As the years roll by,
 we take on the chore
Just as our parents
 and perhaps a bit more.

Years of Little League,
 Girl Scouts and such
Just came natural,
 it is never too much.

As the twilight hours
 come in to view,
Our hearts are full
 knowing there's nothing due.

Hold my hand,
 Love will see me through.

Eileen C. Bumgardner

Musical Love Affair

Sure it's loud
it's my escape from the atrocities
 of the world
it can say the things that
I can't
it says the words that are forbidden
I love the things it says
the words that enter my mind
relieve me from the stress
the fear
the anger
the personal problems
the agonies are washed
away, old, new, good, bad
it is the universal language

Jennifer Hill

1, 2, 3, Eyes On Me!

1, 2, 3, eyes on me,
Who is peeking from the tree?
It's Seth I see,
Peeking behind the tree!
Now I know who's peeking from the tree,
It's me I see!

Seth R. B. Wilkinson

Higher Places

Why did you create me Lord?
What am I to be?
I search my soul and wonder,
If I'm good enough for thee.

My life is filled with heartache,
And I often stumble and fall.
But you keep telling me to wait
Until you gently call.

You take me and you mold me,
As I yield unto your will
I start to feel the pain inside
Grow fainter, ever still.

I climb up to a higher place,
Where peace and joy abound,
And on my spiritual journey,
It is love that I have found.

Tanya Taure

Love Is Like A Rose

Love is like a rose;
it's pretty from afar,
and you crave to be near it.
But when you get close,
its beauty fades a little;
and your heart just likes it more.
You decide to pick it,
to keep it with you for always;
but when you touch it,
it cuts your finger with one
of its hidden thorns.

Cherri Conley

Retrospective

Later years are peaceful;
No raucous laughter,
No more bitter tears,
Passion's fires have cooled.
Ambition's met reality;
Some dreams were lived
And some were lost.
We have forgiven others' sins,
And also ours.
Hard-won humor softens
Ill-fortune's unkind cuts.
Finally, in our slower pace
we are aware of beauty
We never saw before.

Silvia Schmidt

Untitled

A baby came to this world
his life was a start
and through the years gone by
he loved with all his heart
We cared for him
not to be at last
God I must talk to you
But first forgive us for our past
Tell him we all love him, God
Tell him it's true
Keep him in our hearts, My God
Keep him safe with you
I want him to understand
understand that we care
Take it easy in Heaven, Grandpa
We'll miss you, until we get there.

Jason Riggs

No Answer

I called out to the people,
No answer.
I called out to the birds,
No answer.
I called out to the wind,
No answer.
I knew all I had left
Was the strength in me.

Darkness fell upon me,
Time was running out.
Tears ran down my cheek,
No one wiped them away.
I knew all I had left
Was the strength in me.

Why did no one answer?
People are suffering.
Why does no one care?
Should we ignore what we see?

Quincy Clowe

The Affliction

Quietly time erodes away,
The laughter once freely given,
Before the burden of the spirit,
And tears were a stranger.

Upon these waters stagnant,
With sorrow of demise,
No provision in the wilderness,
Although here I survive.

This thief of my delight,
Left me only with slow decay,
Searching through my yesterdays,
To where desire was betrayed.

Now within this haunted place,
Away from light of day,
The night, my cloak of comfort,
Chained to the shadows, I remain.

Rory A. Robertson

Harlem On A Jet Black Saturday Night

Rainbow images of
lively black, brown
yellow, and cocoanut faces
turning loose corners
to tunes of funky reggae
voluptuous women and
outdoor fires as junkies
warm and hustle men swarm
and ageless grandmothers
keep watch to infants on
roller skates in high
speed chases, as distant
skies overlook this classic
inner city of clandestine
kaleidoscopes, endless
hopes, whispering passions
and fleeting expectations.....

Henry Harris

"The Cave"

The lonely cavern
Howling to the wide canyon
Hoping someone hears

Edward G. Bugden

Deserted

The framework of a city;
Its flesh has long decayed.
Its past is filled with happenings,
of places children played.
Relentless curiosity;
the imagination flows.
no one can ever tell you
its history; its woes.
overwhelming emptiness;
the vastness should be full.
It used to be in color,
but now it is deemed dull.
Roy Layman

Revenge

You drove me to insanity.
You made me swoon.
You seemed to care.

But you lied to me,
And now I'll pay you back.
For now my dreams are shattered,
And it's all you fault.

I gave you my attention,
I gave until I burst.
I made you what you are today,
For what it's worth.

But you are so unappreciative
You were so conceded
You had no feelings for me.

And now dear lover,
As I hold you tight
Remember it is I who shot you dead.

For I have had my revenge.
Leah Winterhalter

Soul Creation

Null and void the chasm
bearing my reflection
soul erratic, never still
restless from inception

Thoughts eclectic, rearrange me
change my mental clothes
inside I'm left in disarray
longing for repose

Affinities emerge, then fade
yet leave an inclination
my mind is clay
my soul is sculptor
I am the creation
Tibor Ouyang

The Wind

There it is,
moving air,
running through the trees,
I know it has a face,
only nature sees.

Look at all the colors,
pink, yellow, and blue,
if you become a part of nature,
you can see it, too.
Katherine Burke

The Last Rose

The beauty of it astonishes me,
It's perfect form with smooth curves,
The bright vivid color,
It's wonderfully pleasing essence,
The natural beauty,
It's meaning as a gift, single or many,
The thin, elegant long stem,
The sharp thorns poking through,
Deep red petals fallen on the ground,
Your sisters have returned to earth,
Wilting and shriveling stems,
You are left to display your beauty,
The chosen one to be the last,
They walk up to you,
They clip you and your long stem,
You are taken in and put in water,
The last rose on the bush,
Clipped and put on display.
Sonja Vora

Untitled

Hey New York let's wake up.
Dreams only come to those who
sleep. Unlike the cat who
has nine lives. We only
Have one so let's not get
high on drugs or play with
guns. Let's just hold our
heads up high and say. Hey
New York I'm no clown I'll be
around - not in the ground.
Louis Anthony Perez

Winter Morning

Cold metallic winter morning snow
shimmering from the blaring sun
shinning like precious metals

Like a mother
caressing a scared child
cool gentle wings
caressed white soft snow

Sea blue sky
blanketed the living land

Clean fresh air
gave life to lifeless objects
in its reach

Burning sun
peeked over an ancient silent forest
spying newly fallen snow
Jason Fuller

Flag

Flowing proudly in the sky,
Never asking who or why,
Just knowing.
A symbol made always to stand,
Marched proudly with a marching band,
Always onward going.
Beautiful, majestic, glowing, proud,
Never too quiet, never too loud,
Just right.
Always knowing every word,
Flying proud, like an eagle bird
In flight.
Jessica Ritsch

I'll Cry When You're Dead

Snowflakes
Fall gently upon your face.
And as I watch them melt
On your lashes,
I long to kiss you
And embrace your warmth.
Veronica Nowak

Untitled

I wonder about Flies
try to kill them
they scatter
seem to disappear
do they come
on rotting flesh of dead stuff
do they gather in gangs and discuss
do they lie awake at nights
disgusted
by swatters and such
indignant Flies
never sorrow for
these expendable guys
while I swat at visions
in my mind's eye
of Flies
I can't help but wonder
about these Damned Flies
Jed Earl

Precious Moment

I held your love
in my hands,
precious as a feather of a white dove,
for only a moment
before time took you away,
just like wind,
lifted you up high above me
and drove you away to foreign shores.

Still I stand here,
my hands held open,
watching you sail far away
and with you
my heart leaves and my love
follows you mile by mile —
yet I live to love you
hoping to meet you there one day.
Susanne Storck

'Off To Work'

It's so easy to drop everything
And think about philosophy
Meanwhile, the rain is coming down
Soon it'll be coming down on me

The buzzer sounds at 6 am
Shocks me from my slumber
Get some coffee, punch the clock
Can't say if it's winter or summer

Don't bother to look at the time
It slips right through your fingers
Tomorrow is already yesterday
And hardly a memory lingers

Only so many days in a lifetime
They're for sale but you can't buy more
Meanwhile the rain's coming down
I can feel it beginning to pour
Rob Byrd

Flame And The Serpent

Scarlet flames flickering from a candle
Like a serpent dancing from a basket.

The fire dancing with the breeze,
The serpent,
Charmed with the sweet melody,
Played by a flute, the twinkling music,
The swaying rhythm.
Both threaten retreat
With the slightest disturbance.

And with a disturbance
The serpent hisses and strikes.
The red flame glitters in the darkness
Then gently flickers out.

Both possess radiance.
The viper's beaming eyes,
The flame's dazzling light,
Each a more hypnotizing sight.

Death by poison, death by fire,
Both grow more deadly,
With every fading hour.

Amy Leiker

Up In The Clouds

   Up in the clouds, I see a star,
beautiful, lost, in winter's night.
   But down here, things are not
so right.
   Loneliness, hurt, and sadness bewail
me, for, a guy who is mine,
who always, has held me, has now
left me lying, here on the floor,
crying, crawling to the door.
But now, I have a new man,
Someone who cares, more
than the other can,
Now stands another star
beside mine, up in the
clouds.

Angel Havens

Untitled

You are my hopes
I lost all my fears
When I wanted to cry
You dried all my tears

How can I prove that
my love is true
When I can't have
  a moment with you
If I had a chance
that chance would be
for me to have you
and you to have me.

Just reach out your hand
I'll meet you half way
Coz my love for you
Will never fade away.

Rod Hogsten

Untitled

I hear myself think
it's so loud
I think the world can hear
but it's muffled by all
the chatter

Cherish Desellier

Give Thanks

From up on a hill
We look to the sky
to give thanks for the blessings
God gave you and I.

From the stream in the valley
Running swiftly and sweet
To the trees that surround it
Standing proudly and neat.

For the fluffy white clouds
That float slowly by
That seem to form little pictures
For just you and I.

Can we give enough thanks
For so many great things
Like the birds, bees and flowers
Or the pretty rocks in the spring.

Then we fall to our knees
and look back to the sky
And thank God for the blessings
He gave you and I.

Tom Cherry

The Edge

Sitting by the edge,
see an eagle soaring.
A crooked stream below,
a herd of horses grazing.
Up above an eagle cries,
then swoops upon its prey.
Sitting by the edge,
on a calm and distant day.

Sitting in a tree
see a sparrow singing.
An anthill down below,
a pair of squirrels chasing.
Up above the sparrow stops,
then starts a song of May.
Sitting in a tree,
on a calm and distant day.

Jennifer Lee Gile

Midnight Longings

The moonlight shone upon the tears,
that trickled down my cheek.
My heart I tried to put to words,
but found I could not speak.

When you left without a word.
Something inside me died.
I could not fill that empty place,
no matter how I tried.

I'm staring now into the sky,
oh! Those words I needed to say.
To let you know just how I felt,
before you passed away.

William F. Quinn

Excuses

Today is slow.
It seems as though
We are machines and
They forgot to wind us up.

And besides,
The weather is sticky
And rainy.

Joanne McGuigan

God's Blessings

On dull and rainy days
We grumble for awhile
Until the sun comes out
And makes us want to smile
We go through life so weary
We miss the joy around
The colors, smells and sounds
Which here on earth abound
There's nothing like a sunset
Or a moon and stars aglow
And who on earth can just forget
The sight of the first snow
We miss the many thoughtful things
That never seem to end
A little word of praise
Or a smile from a dear friend
So don't despair if things go wrong
As on this earth we plod
Just know all things are possible
If we believe in God.

Maureen Konsek

Dodgeball

Stand in the middle of everything,
your enemies are around you.
Run back and forth,
but you can't hide,
hate is after you.

You run,
you jump,
you try to hide,
you can't survive anymore...

The bullet has shot right through you.

Mkhoian Haig

Roses

   What are roses? Are they
Soft impressions of silk
Dresses floating in a spring's
wind of an eagle for the
beauty be the soft lips of
another close to you in
heart. What are roses to
you?

Michelle Pierce

My Patricia

The other night I had a dream
I really don't know why
I dreamed I was in heaven
Away up in the sky

The clouds so white and puffy
The stars so bright and clear
I thought I saw my angel
Her face so very dear

She floated by on gossamer wings
Her gown of silvery white
Her voice was like a little bell
A vision of delight

And to my surprise as I awoke
Lying there beside me
Her big brown eyes and smiling face
My angel - Patricia -
(she will always be there beside me)

Peggy Vincent

Grandma's Rocking Chair

Grandma had a rocking chair
when I was three years old,
she taught me how to sit in it,
she taught me how to scold.
Every time we went to visit
I was by her side, I loved
to sit in the rocking chair
and see who would abide.

When Grandma's time was
near, we always felt some
fear, that grandma would
pass away. We thought of the
joys and the happiness shared,
of grandma's rocking chair.
Aubrey Lappin

Taken So Young

The death of a friend
is so hard to take
One moment we are
playing
The next you're not
awake.
I know they needed
you above
to help and watch
over us below
I just will never know
why so young?
I guess I'm mad
that you're gone...
but understand it's
because you are my
friend, and we will
never get to run or play,
until we meet again
someday.
Alyssa Cowan

The Days And You

The day goes fast,
Not always bright,
But on those dismal days,
You bring the light,
Skies overcast,
Clouds grey,
I'll never leave,
I'll always stay,
When the moon is full,
That's when it's bright,
I'll think of you,
All through the night,
If the stars don't shine,
They'll shine right through.
Through the broken heart,
I broke for you.
Zack Adams

A Precious Gift

Sex is a gift.
A gift from one person
to another,
A man and woman in
Love.
To be shared and enjoyed
equally.
Gary F. Fraker

Untitled

My Life Seems full of hardship
So I pray to You dear Lord
to help me find a better way
to find a brighter road

I pray that You will help me
to forgive and be forgiven
to help my heart be loving
when by hatred it is driven

My mouth does spew contempt
for my neighbors and my life
this heavy heart and soul
can only cause my strife

So if it be Your will oh Lord
please teach me the right way
to appreciate life's blessings
and to find joy in each new day!!!!
Sherry A. Niemer

Nostalgem

He lived his life as though it were
scripted from "Five Easy Pieces",
Rather, he thought he could have.
Those nostalgic nightmares he never
seemed to know, lingered
with him through the daily clutter
of mainstream malaise.
The babbling brook of the stream of
consciousness, over time, erodes...
Frank Noyes

Elf Owl

In that big saguaro cactus,
In that tall sycamore tree,
There lives a little animal,
An owl you can see.

That tiny little owl,
An owl of its own kind,
That tiny little elf owl,
That is very much not kind.

That tiny little elf owl,
With a tiny little myth,
That tiny little elf owl,
Doesn't even miss!

I love that tiny elf owl,
It is so hard to not love,
That tiny little elf owl,
More than a little smudge.
Stephanie L. Shumate

Infinite One

Depth length and heights
East West North and South
The father of lights
So far
Yet so near
He loves you
And does care
Come all who are poor
He will provide forever more
Alberta Deinhardt

Reflections On An Onion Snow

The sky turns slate gray
as brightly colored crocus
poke slender green fingers
through falling snow.

Millions upon millions of tiny
white specks fall, followed by
whirling, tumbling, fat, wet flakes.

And through the silence of
the falling snow, I hear the
happy chirping of robins.

Another winter has passed.
Stephanie B. Reineberg

Farewell

As I leave this world;
I'll think of you.
I'll think of the good memories;
And even force myself to look back
At when you left me stranded and hurt.

My body may be but dead;
But my soul will live on
Through you and all that
Surrounds you.
My soul will be the Eagle
In the sky.

When you see a young child smiling,
Remember, I once smiled as sweet.
When you hear laughter in the air:
Remember, I laughed the same laugh.
Think of the ocean
As my soul dancing for you.

If ever you feel sad for me,
Think-I may never feel pain again.
I am now and forever-Love.
Lori A. Nelsen

"Let's Take A Ride"

Yes we made, no we made not
Yes I can, no we can not
If we do, space is far
Your neighbor is close,

Our minds wander,
But lift is here,

Though we have a tendency
We will have to stay here,

But there is no place,

Here and there and back again,
Where did this all begin
Karl Steen

Stillness

The water moves slowly,
as it drifts upon the lonely beach.
It is total darkness,
total silence,
the beach is still,
motionless,
without a person,
the beach is lonely,
without a voice,
the beach is still.
Kelly Bliemeister

My Falcon

Quickly does my falcon grow.
Someday I'll have to let him go.
Let him go
or let him die.
I won't kill him,
No, not I.
I'll let him go as nature planned.
I won't make him live on land.
I'll let him soar high above
Gracefully like a dove.
I won't kill him,
No, not I.

Ethan H. Kern

The Lady Blue Jay

There was once a lady blue jay
Who lived in an old oak tree,
I climbed the grand oak tree
to see the lady blue jay and
her precious chicks of three.

The sight I saw was such a joy,
a new baby being born.
I think you might want see
this wonderful sight that was so
precious to me.

Beth Douthett

Transmutation

On eagle's wings
I walk the skies
dance on clouds
kiss the stars

On eagle's wings
I wear the sun
taste the moon

I fly, I soar, I scream
I shed my skin
and leave myself behind

On eagle's wings
I laugh with God

Linda J. Edmunds-Casey

Requiem Of A Raptor

Wing, that was a bird.
Ring, that was a ford.

Sin, not in their deaths
But, in their obsolescence.

Mortality is always part
of nature's plan.

The county dump the
plan of man.

And how is it they
come together here?

And will we all this
same fate share.

Sherrick

Emotion

What is an emotion,
Of what kind,
That divides a man from man in
  each one's mind.
We never know what's really
  there that tells us all to be fair,
The love for people,
One and all,
Is what most desire,
Yet what emotions, of what kind,
Divides man from man in
  each ones mind.

Lindsay Rich

Untitled

Some people like to live
Some people like to give
Some people like to unite
Some people like to fight
Some people like to find out
Some people like to hide out
Some people like to say gee
Some people like to say hee hee
But me I just like to be me

Mary Ann Blackwell

"The Tombstone Messenger"

"Greetings William Perseus
  Your brother lies below
I am the Tombstone Messenger
And I have a message all
  should know
Why stand you there gazing thus?
Are you contemplating Eternity
  and dust?
Have you lived a useful life of
  Fire and Gust?
Have you fulfilled your Gods'
  assigned Destiny and Trust?
Know you not that Mortality comes
  to all Creation
And that Return to the Cosmos
  you must?

William P. Spencer

Daddy's Little Girl All Grown

You would always hold my hand
When I was just a little girl.
Around a couple fingers
My little hand I'd curl.

But now that I am grown,
I hold the hand of someone new.
Just now I finally realize
The pain I put you through.

No Longer Daddy's little girl,
No need to rock in Mommy's arms.
Gone the days of laughing
At your silly, little girl's charms.

These are now just memories
As I strive to form some new.
You will not be forgotten
for in these, I want you too.

Allison Walker

"A Message To My Daughter Renee"

I never saw a child
So lovely as Renee.
She walks like the wind.
She's as graceful as a mare.
When in need she's quick to
help in despair.
She has wisdom I cannot
sometimes understand.
But then I comprehend
it must be a gift from God.
She has skin as soft as cotton,
and a beautiful color the shade
of light coffee.
When she smiles it's like
looking at sunshine.

Renee Burdette

Heartfelt

Looking into the eyes of pain
Wishing I could ease the strain
Yearning just to hold her near
Keeping her distant from her fear
Love is what she really seeks
Instead of tears down her cheeks
Being patient and being kind
Are the only things on her mind
I know not what to say
Because I feel, the same way

Patrick W. Bowman

"Different"

Why should I feel depressed,
And mope around all day?
I'm not made like the rest,
And I'm glad God made me this way.

Thou surely had'st a reason,
For my deformity,
And though I do not understand,
Why should I question thee?

My desire to do what others do,
Should never be so great
Be thankful for my abilities,
And not bemoan my fate.

So I must keep my head up high,
And do my very best,
That's all I really need to do,
God will take care of the rest.

Marie Maynard

The Color Black

Why does Black have to be such a
dark and cold color.
I think black, is a beautiful
color. It seems that black is a
bad luck color.
But my opinion is different.
Can you imagine if the world
didn't have the color black?
The world would be blackless,
and there would be no blackness.
Black stands out, that's no doubt.
It's not wrong and it will be
still going on strong.

Diana Coney

finding a green cap

What's that spell?
  Symbol. See me!
I've got it,,
  What are you thinking?
Green.   Look!
      Loop.
What's this?
  Dream, cloud
   Keep it positive
      Continue!
"The next a man, no longer a boy"
    woman   girl
        ruof
Look into the mirror
  and
          Remember-
Keep your mouth clean.
Cascade, sound; Don't be afraid.
Don't deny me! Achieve! dance, love

Christopher Wasson

Remembrance Of Life

Dedicated to the Memory of Lisa Murphy, age 23.

Her beauty, her grace
For she's the one
Whose smile embraced
My empty heart
And weeping soul
In this sadness
I am sold
Though she's gone
Her laughter shines
Always in heart
Always in mind
Yet since that day
When she passed
I often wonder
But seldom ask
Why anyone
So young and bright
Should lose their only
Living Right.

Jennifer Gosney

We Fell In Love, While You Were Sleeping

While you were sleeping,
  I fell in love that night.
While you were sleeping,
  I can't really explain,
  the sounds of your sleep,
  the expressions on your face.
While you were sleeping,
  you held me so tight,
  I knew right then,
  I could not live with-out you.
While you were sleeping,
  I knew you were the one,
  My one true love,
  the one I would marry.
Then when you woke,
  you looked in my eyes.
Then I knew,
  you too, could not live with-out.
While you were sleeping,
  we fell in love in each-others arms.

Gina Marie Sibert

Sadness

The tree with no
  leaves to warm it.
A mother with no
  hair to brush...
A house with no
  roof on top...
A wave with no power
  to wash the sand.
A harmonica that
  doesn't play music.
A hand with no fingers.
A falcon with no wings
  to fly...

Ricky Robinson

The Tango Of Death

  You danced with evil
When you danced that way.

  You pierced me deep
with her sharp red lips.

  Stained cotton collar
was the evidence I needed.

  Sorry to cut in
on the dance I was cheated.

Kim LaFave-Hale

Grace

There once was a girl named Grace
Who dreamed she jumped into space
Woke up in the night
With total fright
Found out she was flying on lace

Eric Peter

Untitled

Black surrounds me,
glowing eyes above.
Quiet and peaceful,
calm takes hold.
Shadows are cast,
dark and mysterious
figures come alive
NIGHT.

Linda Reibsome

Missing Her

Three weeks ago today
Our mother passed away
I already miss her more
Than I ever have before
Life will never be the same
Because I'll always feel this pain
No matter what you say or do
I know that you can feel it too
A better mother there could never be
She was always there for you and me
I thought our mother went away
But I feel her in my heart each day
When the pain begins to hurt real bad
She reminds me of the love she had
No matter what you say or do
I know that you can feel it too
A better mother there could never be
She's still here for you and me

Larry S. Young

You

Your peace is calm, like
the ripples that gently
glide across a usually
disturbed sea.

As may confusion naturally
dwells within myself
I find you harder to
grasp.

You keep quiet with your
emotions stored beneath
your fundamental knowledge
and your emotional intellect

All you bring to me is
grief and mental anguish
with your heart - rending
words but, it's always
been you.

Cheryl Hunter

Ike's Men Came

They came from far across the waters
From the land of wealth and freedom,
Across the wild expanse of water,
The mighty North Atlantic Ocean.

Waters filled with deadly U-boats,
Lurking in the depth below them,
Searching, stalking there to kill them,
In the cold and deadly waters.

To the lovely beleaguered island,
Joined the cousins in their struggle.
Gave their all and never faltered,
Now some sleep the sleep of brothers.

They fought the evil, hated Nazis,
In their tanks, planes, and fox-holes,
Fought them with total dedication,
Willingly gave their last full measure.

Fifty years now they have slumbered,
Ever young, with brows unwrinkled,
Not yet forgotten by their cousins,
Not now, nor ever will they be.

G. R. Ammerman

My Sweet Sunshine

My sweet sunshine
how I love thee!
You warm my heart,
when I'm falling apart
you're here in the day,
during my play.
And I am glad to say,
I'll be there,
during your play!

My sweet sunshine
you are my Joy
every little girl's joy is to
play with you
sweet sunshine how I love you!
You see my good times
you know my bad times
when I go to sleep
you go away
how sad I am
I've lost my day.

Crissy Skusa

Night Frights

The creatures lurk behind the trees
Then I suddenly feel a gust of wind
Something scrapes my bare knees
Oh, it's just some bone-dry leaves

What is that over there?
It is just some eyes
They just gave me a little scare
They are just so gleamy and bare

Then I hear a very shrill cry
It is coming closer
I think I'm going to die
I see something coming closer, oh my

You can be frightened by the night
You could get some kind of bite
something could go out, like the lights
Steven Farwell

Unfinished Journey

In the search for healing,
Pain is telling something,
But what is it?

Hope is most precious thing,
Without hope, no healing.
But what is it?

I envision, I try,
I see healing lights, colors and sky,
But what is it?

To reach the healing symphony,
Barriers have to yield,
But what is it?

Barriers are yielding,
The pure beauty of life is coming,
But what is it?

Soon I can reach and be free,
Positive loving attitude is the key,
In the quest for healing.
Solange M. Bertin

My Love

You are my love my life
my thoughts my dreams my
being my pleasure my hopes
my breath my being, My love
Where are you? My life has
no meaning no desire no fulfillment
my love
Where are you?
Mai Joyce Turner

The Caller

Call me not and then turn away.
You are the night that filtered day
Futile hope is but despair
More than apathy,
Much harder to bear.

Unleashed madness assails the door
Turning away I hear no more.

Crying gently, I close the door.
Judy A. Rogers

Life Is Like a Mystery

Life is like a mystery;
Even though each of us
makes our own destiny.

Life is like a mystery;
Consequences aren't guaranteed
for things that are done by we.

Life is like a mystery;
For everything we want
is never a guarantee.

Life is like a mystery;
We can hope that our
futures will be merry.

Life is like a mystery;
The future of our lives
is truly a mystery.
Jonathan C. Lee

The Tumbleweed And The Vine

A tumbleweed is free
  But lacks direction.
A vine enjoys the wind
  And the sun and the rain
  Just as the tumbleweed
  But with focus, hope, persistence.

Be a mighty vine.
Choose your own course,
  Always reaching higher
  Always facing the sky.
David Hunt

Untitled

The song
The first time ever I
saw your face I saw the sun rise
in your eyes.

The dream
Song - dreams in my
child's eyes of memories
She sang to me
and I knew I would
always love her.
I'll find you
someday,
someway.

The now
"My name is Michael
and I'm a.....
(then I saw your face)
alcoholic."
Michael Reynolds

Anger

Anger is a poison
That is spreading deep inside.
Anger is an ocean
That is moving far and wide,
Anger is a weapon
That is being used to hurt,
Anger is an attitude
That is making one a jerk,
Anger is an illness
That is very sick
Anger is an ugliness
That is beaten with a stick.
Makeba Osayande

If I Were A Animal

If I were a animal,
I'd be a nightingale,
that soared through
the moonlit sky!

If I were an animal,
I'd be a pretty panda bear,
with brown pretty eyes,
that soared with happiness.

If I were an animal,
I'd be a beautiful rabbit,
that has a silent streak,
that, has a nice warm feather.

That is
if I were
an animal!
Shayna M. White

To a Rose

Rose of roses
without an equal,,
Rose of roses
among roses of love.
Rose of roses
that bloom in the Springtime,
Rose of roses
among roses of love.

And even though the butterflies
will take away your pollen,
and the tiny raindrops
will destroy your poise,
You will remain the Rose
among roses of roses,
that will live in my garden
come Springtime or Fall.
B. Grey

Patience

Patience is my daily word
Along with a voice that's seldom heard
For I have four small ones
Who just sometime Obeys...
And then there are our real good days
They are not bad kids most would agree
They just don't pay any attention to me.
Katie Elijah

The Second Chance

The first world too, destroyed by sin,
  Now! A second chance, can we win?
Looks hopeless to us all am sure,
  Everything now is self allure.
Countless idols big and small,
  All the things mentioned by "Paul".
Everything shall come to pass,
  Even though we believe the mass.
Few there be that find the way,
  Sort of scary, the word does say.
Education has come so far,
  Science too, we know each star.
This Love of God to us does call,
  Far more important than baseball.
That beautiful Life outside of Time,
  Who will believe this little rhyme?
This is all to benefit, Man,
  Those who Repent, if we can.
Believe it or not, as before,
  Most of us Know this open door.
Richard H. Swanson

It Tastes So Sweet

It's sweet;
It's neat.
It's warm;
It has no form.
It's sticky;
It's not icky!
It's yummy
In the tummy.
It's brown or tan.
In the Spring it ran.
Pour it in a pan.
Eat it you can.
It's best on pancakes.
It's best on snow.
It's New England Maple Syrup.
  You've got to know!
  Kristiana Wilkinson

Always Believe

Everyone has dreams
within their heart
waiting for that day
to come true.
Wishing upon a star,
dreaming beneath the moon
waiting until the dream
has come true.
Having faith
never giving up
always believing
that the day
will come.
Even if it takes
a year
or a century
be patient and wait
have hope
and the dream
will come true.
  Connie Lee

High School Masquerade

Try to guess who I am
I bet you never will
For I pretend I'm someone else,
Someone rejection won't kill.

The director's shining star,
I jump from role to role.
being what the script asks me to be,
Never what's in my soul.

Lost among so many faces,
Hosting the masquerade.
Dancing with costumes I've invented,
Costumes that won't go away.

Lock myself behind the door,
And throw away the key.
Hide inside my minds castle,
So no one else can see.

Covered by the shadows
Of the dancing masquerade.
I whimper in the dark,
Afraid I've lost my way.
  Stacy DeBlasio

The Monster Under My Bed

There is a monster under
my bed.
He hates oatmeal,
but he makes me feel
eerie and
afraid.
He has 10 claws
and paws
He has sharp and flat fangs
Every night I hide under my sheets
because he gets up and the floor creaks
this monster has no scales
and is my brother
did I tell you I have bunkbeds?
  Brian Webb

My Puppy

He stands and wags his stubby tail
He even tears clothes from the rail
He eats the kitten's supper up
But after all he's just a pup.

He tears our stockings and bites our shoes
He even tears the daily news
What would you do to bring him up
But after all he's just a pup!!!
  Mary Reynolds

The Rainbow

After the rainfall
After the sun
After the clouds
After the fun
Comes the rainbow.

Before the darkness
Before the mad
Before the howls
Before the bad
Comes the rainbow.

The love on this earth
Like fire in a hearth
Has died down.
War and hatred rule the land
But the rainbow will come
And love will come once again
And God will rule a perfect world.
  Genisa Concepcion

Desire

So easily my passions flow,
that burns beneath my skin.
The thoughts I have for you my dear
could be my greatest sin.

Although the threat you feel for me
can not be understood.
You run and hide away from me
as if it does much good.

Yet still I watch and wait to see
if there remains a fire.
That burns the passion deep within
arousing your desire.
  Debra Katrina Martin

Tigertar

Tigertar, Tigertar
What are you?
Tigertar, Tigertar
What do you do?

Are you good with your feet?
Or do you make a nice beat,
Do you sing musical notes?
Or eat Billy goats?

Tigertar, Tigertar
What can it be?
Is it big is it small,
Can it play middle C?

Tigertar, Tigertar
Are you a tiger or a guitar?
Can you play "Green Day"
Or was it you that ate ant mae?
  Natalie Park

Together

As I look in the past
I see us all,
Laughing, crying
As we always have, together.

Today
I see us all,
Enjoying each other
As we always have, together.

As I look into the future
I see us all,
Smiling, joking
As we always have, together.

Though we have flaws and problems
I see us all,
Loving and staying
Together.
  Stephanie Puckett

Love

Nature's Gift
Simple and Free
Starts with the Head
And Ends with the Feet
A Soft Little Head,
And Eyes So Bright.
A round Little Nose
And a Smile Just Right.
Tiny Little Hands So Soft and Warm.
Chubby Little Feet
That Wiggle and Squirm.
Happy Valentine's Day
To a Happy Little Boy.
  Teresa A. Jimenez

Colleen

Truest of these rain down upon my
  soul.
Burning is a flame, where once
  there was no spark.
The visions of you are echoed upon
  my mind,
With every step forward brings
  me back in time.
I give my heart for you to hold
  true.
Where there was love, still
  waiting for you.
  Patrick Lovegren

Forever Mine

Today is yesterday's tomorrow,
As sure as night will give way
   to the dawn.

Thoughts and visions of long ago,
Once so clear and bright,
   are now dimming with each new morn.
Too soon my memories will fade
   and become just shadows of the past.

As I cannot hold back the dawn
That I may savor the blessings
   and joys I have known,
I can only pray that God
   will lock them in my heart,
Where they will live eternally.
Margie Butler

Basketball Game

My favorite sport you can guess
Is basketball
You're dribbling down the court
With a pain in your chest
For if you're going to shoot
Or pass the ball
You shoot the ball with
All your hopes and dreams
If you make it you're cool
If you miss you're a fool
When you win
It's a party
When you lose
It is not so cool
All you can think about
Is how you messed up
But it doesn't really matter
'Cause it's only a game!
Elijah Lefkowitz

Gazebo

Against the bones of Belvedere
on green-skin lawn you rest,
and the swaying tendrils
of a willow catch air and light
Then fall into place like curls.

You shelter the band on July Fourth,
permitting red, white and
blue banners to be threaded through
your white-washed arms as children
sing and dance their tribal jig.

Lovers seek your steepleless frame,
settled under canopy
and hidden from the stars:
huddled in ceremonial embrace
against the night air.
Lorraine Ortega

A Friend Is All You Need

A friend in need,
A friend I will be,
A friend who's blue
Needs a friend who's true.
A friend you need,
A friend I will be,
A friend who shares,
Needs a friend who cares.
Heather Tessen

A Dove

When a dove was once born,
He wasn't forewarned;
Of what he would see,
And it troubled he.

He disliked what he saw
When he flew over all.
Many a sin dismayed his heart,
He saw our world falling apart.

So he took the charge,
To make the hate cease;
His ultimate goal,
Is our holy peace.
Drew DePriest

Grandma

Grandma gold,
Precious gold,
You might think you're old,
But you'll always be gold,
In my heart you're always bold,
You're always warm, never cold,
It's a love story that's untold,
because grandma has a heart of gold.
Audra Meade

Life

You tell me I am only using you
You're right I am
I'm using you like the sun warms
the earth and awakens the tiny
seeds into growing
I'm using you like the wind,
gently blows the seeds of life
over the field
To embellish the land with fragrant
beauty.
I am using you like the soft, clear
liquid drops from endless clouds
As the moisture soaks into the
drenched earth and renews it.
Yes I am using you, only
for my existence.
For you see, Without using you
I have no life.
Sarah Flanagan Williams

"Till I Go"

I'm glad we're married,
I'm glad you said yes.
There may be others,
But you're the best.

I am so proud,
When we go out.
God made,
But one of you.
I feel so loved,
This is so nice.
I'm glad I said,
"I do."

Until God calls you,
I will be close by.
Then when He takes you,
That's when I'll cry.

For I am selfish,
I'll not let go.
For you are mine dear,
"Till I go."
Joe Griffin

Reflections

Each night upon the setting sun
When time slows down and day is done
I sit down in my easy chair
And sip some wine - Reflecting there

I think of you and smile

Remembering the times we've had
I found the courage (I'm so glad)
To tell you that I love you dear
Reflecting now at least a year

But that's just a short while

The love I feel grows more each day
So now I simply have to say
I need you dear, to love me too
But somehow seem to know you do

We do it up in style

When I'm alone and miss you, Hun
I think about the things we've done
Like dancing neath the sky above
And touching, holding, making love

Reflecting makes me smile
Kerry Kniskern

Wave Upon The Sand

Wave upon the sand,
Song in the air,
Smile on her lips,
Wonder in her stare.

Scar on the moon,
Shadow on the sand,
Harshness in his step,
Sorrow in the land.

Whisper in the wind,
Step on her stride,
Tremble on her hand,
Presence by her side.

Cry in the night,
Stain on her breast,
Lust in his eyes,
Mystery on the rest.

Wave upon the sand,
Silence in the air,
No steps on the shore,
This life is never fair.
Michele Beck

Between

    heaven and earth
  conception and birth
      death and life
         and what it's worth

    man and wife
         and what that's about

  a whisper... and a shout

    mother and child
         and which is defiled
    future and past
         and which will last

    submissive and wild
      new and used
  the innocent and the abused
      dances and kegs

      her legs.
Grant West

Someone

What a feeling to know that
someone's there
someone who really cares

someone to trust
someone to adore
someone that you
   know is there
someone to show
   things to
someone that'll
   listen to you
someone for you to treasure and
when you find that special one
who truly knows who you are, and
what you like to do,
then you'll know,
   for a fact,
      that someone,
         really cares about you.
Jamie Pachuta

To my Daddy

For eighty years of grace Lord
I give thanks on bended knee.
For the man that I call Daddy
That you chose to father me.

For the many years I've loved him,
For the chance to tell him so,
For the many ways he's shown me
The things I need to know.

With a full and grateful heart Lord
I know how blest I am;
And I am filled with thankfulness
For you're sharing with me, this man.

For all the fondest memories
In this, our waiting space,
I thank thee Lord, with all my heart,
For his eighty years of grace.
Norma L. Shoop

The Way Of Life

There are things that need to be said.
There is praise to be given.
There are things best left unsaid.
There are things to be forgiven.
There are roads to travel upon,
And ways to go and not to go.
Whether to rest or go on,
Oft times decide joy or woe.
To know the whys and where's of life;
To go through life's scope,
To find peace instead of strife,
To live and learn and cope,
These are the life things we know.
Through which we must all go.
To keep the way true and sure
We must endeavor to endure.
Barnie Lawrence

"The Place"

There's a place where
I can go, where no one knows
during rain or snow, sleet or sun.
   That's where I go
When I'm feeling low.
Joshua Dole

Still Feel Alone

I'm a little child, born unto
a mother and dad, why do I
still feel alone.

I'm a child going to school, I
have lots of friends, why do I
still feel alone.

I'm a wife now, and have a
real fine husband, why do I
still feel alone.

I'm a mother now, and have
three children of my own, why do I
still feel alone.

I'm a grand mother now, and have
three fine grandchildren, why do I
still feel alone.

I'm alone now my children are
all grown, I've had all this, why do I
still feel alone.
Dean Wilson

Kate

Kate's gait was great.
Oft at the gate
She'd wait in state
Her future mate.

His trait was, late.
Kate would berate.
He'd wait; she'd abate,
Capitulate.

He, Kate did sate,
Yeah, captivate.
His weight, bald pate,
Plate, general state

She'd tolerate,
'f he'd stipulate
His vast estate
Would rate for Kate.
Raymond W. Schember

Real Love

longer than eternity
only through the heart
real love endures,
it's unconditional...
it's unexplainable...
loving more than sure.
only through time..as
vivid as a second..
every heart beat for two.
younger is the feeling
older as a number
understanding through and thru.
forgiveness is a factor
often overlooked...but
remains always at peace.
emotions are unstoppable
vibrant as any color
each moment unforgettable
real love endures...
Jun Caraig

Untitled

Why do I write?
So that I can talk to myself
or to people that don't exist
old friends, lost memories
unfinished songs
thoughts of staying together
forever
bus trips
mind trips
broken hearts
the struggle of a lonely girl
trying to understand
the depths of reality
the essence of love
and the telling of stories....
Mysha Christy

Idle Thoughts

Idle thoughts...
...daydreams

Things that catch your eye.
Dwelling in your mind.

Country smells, city smells
Reminding you of days gone by.

Summer smells...
Winter smells...snow.

Childhood memories.
Emotions circling...winding...twisting.
Star dreams! Wishes!
Ruth E. Bonovich

When I Stare At You

When I stare at you,
I look deep inside,
To know the inner person,
Who sits by my side.

I cannot express completely,
The way you make me feel,
But the Love I have for you,
Is ever oh so real.

And as the future days go by,
Some joyous and some blue,
When I want to share my Love,
Is when I stare at you.
Daniel McGuffin

Dolphin

Sea dancers,
leaping joyously
to the dawn
of a new day.

Sea dreamers
swim in the
moonlight for
their midnight
play

Curious creatures
freely swimming
in ocean blue

Curious creatures,
when you discover
them
they discover you.
Jennifer Tate

Hoping, Praying

I sit in my lonely room
I look across the room
And see an empty bed
My Husband used to sleep there
He's gone to war now

Every night I sit there
On the lonely windowsill
Hoping, praying that he's alive today

Every night I wish
On the first bright star
I pray, I hope
I hope, I pray
Please, let him stay alive today

Day after day
Night after night
It's him and him only
Hoping, hoping
Praying, praying
So he'll come back to me
Someday

Karina M. Garcia

To My Sister

Nice to chat with
Good to know
Glad to have her
Where I go

Kind in trouble
Bright in joy
Suits exactly
Can't say why

Sweet and wholesome
Always true
That's my sister
Yes, that's you!!

Shirlee A. McQuown

The Silent Day

I used to sit and ponder.
About this "Golden day",
When all the flock was grown
And gone their separate ways.
Squabbling over dinner.
And who would clean the mess,
I would be all to happy
When the last one left the nest.

Fighting for the curling hair
blow dryers and their dress,
This early morning madness
has finally come to rest.
But that silent day has come now,
And I hate it - for you see.
I wish they were all little,
And in this home with me.

Helen L. Hightower Domenick

Love Pain

Living in a deep dark world,
I feel my mind is dead.
My soul is in a whirl,
With so much left unsaid.
Without you in my arms,
The ache of my heart.
I bid my love no harm,
If only we didn't depart.

John Sweet

Endless Winter

Why is it that
Every single spring,
You never can sit
And watch birds sing?

Even in April
The snow comes down.
On a Vermont Easter morning,
There's snow on the ground.

Maybe someday,
Easter will be green.
You look out the window,
And birds will be seen.

It won't be soon.
As far as I know,
Easter will always
Be covered with snow.

Amber R. Christie

Temper

Down deep below
I feel an ugly
Energy erupting
Red hot lava is
Approaching the surface
Defeating everything in
   Its path
As it travels to the summit
Of the mountain
It produces increasingly
Mixed emotions
Anger, depression, confusion
   fear
These emotions merge
Together until you can't
Tell them apart
The feeling is enormous
Creating so much pressure
Till finally the top explodes
And the hell begins...

Bridget Kolenda

Don't Mourn Me

Don't mourn me when I'm gone
For I've gone to a place beyond

Don't mourn me when I'm gone
For the trees are green
And the grass is lush

Don't mourn me when I'm gone
For the sky is blue
And the sun is bright

Don't mourn me when I'm gone
For no more sorrows have I
But only joy

Don't mourn me when I'm gone
For home is where I'll be

Donna Kurcz

Loves Ending

Love ended quietly.
The peacefulness
Re'echoed its death
Over and over and over
And it was.

Patti Marlow

So When You Hear...
So When I Say...

In a deep wooded forest
A tree hits the solid ground
Does that tree make a noise
Even when no one's around

Though you don't hear these words
As often as you'd should
I really do love you, hon
More than any one man could

I may be a man of few words
But my silence is golden
My head holds a thousand dreams
'bout the treasure that I'm holdin'

It takes more than just words
There's the little things that I do
To show how much you mean to me
To make my love shine through

So when you hear, I love you
Please hold it in your heart
So when I say, I love you
It's only just the start

Rob Brandt

The Sparrow's Song

Fly away little sparrow
Please send him my love
I'm mesmerized by his beauty
And thank the Lord above

Please tell him I am with him
When it seems no one cares
I'll always be at his side
Kissing away his fears

Please tell him he must hold me
Before you fly away
And tell me the words I long to hear
Each and every day

And afterwards my sparrow
The messages you sing
Show all the love
That you've carried on your wings.

Terri Jugila

A Man Stayed Behind.....

When softly, slowly, to you I write
Ink dropped notions soak the page,
A scattering of dark and light
Against whose perfect fate I rage;

Then slowly, softly I whisper here
Forgotten tones inside your mind;
My thoughts my soul, I send them there,
But ah — the body unrefined;

When softly, slowly the seal is kissed
The letter slips itself away,
Remembering how you are missed,
Remembering how I must stay;

I touch and now you touch this sheet
a simple pledge binds us two as We.

Molly Rose LaPorte

Untitled

When you hold me close
My heart begins to pound
My head is like a feather
Floating to the ground

When you kiss my neck or run
Your fingers through my hair
I feel like I'm in heaven
Without a single care

I love your gentle kisses
Caressing me so sweetly
I loved your lips upon my lips
Although it lasted briefly

My thoughts you've totally captured
My heart you truly did steal
I know that I'm in love
But, sweetheart, how do you feel?

Please be my valentine
If only for today
I won't ask for a lifetime
For tomorrow's another day.

Frances Liloia

Looking At Me

I sat looking at myself
Not knowing what to say.
This person looked like me
She spoke like me, she was me.
But if she had come through time
Was she from the future
And was a me that was to be?
Or was she from the past
And was a me that had been?
If she was from yesterday
Then why don't I remember
Being her and talking to me.
But she does not seem to remember
Being here and seeing me.
So was she me or was I her?
Or did it really matter
That the person sitting there
Was a carbon copy
Of the person sitting here,
And neither knew which was real.

Brewer Thompson

Different Colors

We feast our eyes
On a field of wild flowers
Can not take our gaze
From a distant rainbow
Our eyes follow mesmerized
A walking peacock
Pick up humble pebbles
For their colors.
Why is it then,
We can not find beauty
In the different colors
Of our skin?
It seems,
We have forgotten
All these beautiful colors
Were made
By the same hand.

Martha Guardado

Tell Me What You See

Tell me what you see
can you search my heart
can you search my soul
can you search the farthest realm?
Tell me what you see
can you feel my pain
can you feel my sorrow
can you feel my loneliness?
Tell me what you feel
can you?
Do you see it?
Do you feel it?
Tell me what you see
Tell me what you feel.

Jenaire Terry

Patience

Everyone wants to ask me
Do you need any help today?
I tell them all "No, thank you"
God leads me on my way.

I may never walk again
But this, you all must know
If my Lord tells me to
From this chair I'll go.

You see, he's got control of me
He tells me what to do
And, he's the greatest leader
That I ever knew.

He has always told me
From fear you must not hide
And to listen to what he says
He's always at my side.

Jason J. Beaver

My Mother Taught Me

My mother longs to teach me,
  the many things I have not learned.
She wants me to be my best,
  that's all she's ever yearned.

Although she hasn't always been there,
  for me in physical sight,
I know she's always there,
  in heart, soul, and might.

I know she'll have to leave one day,
  that's pretty much understood.
I'll remember the things she taught me,
  remember them for good.

I know she'll still be with me,
  although I cannot see.
She'll always be watching,
  looking down on me.

Heather Duncan

Requiem High

Quicken
  Create
    Animate
      Alive, alive, O!
Discovery
  Hallucinate
    Too late
      Dead...dead...Oh!

Karen Novak

To My Soulmate

Looking into your eyes
I sense you are no stranger
I believe we have met before
On another plane of energy
It really doesn't matter when
Only that our paths have crossed again
It is your energy that is changing
That emptiness in my soul
To comfortable aloneness
It is your energy that is teaching me
A needed lesson of humility
Tolerance and compassion
You are feeding my starving spirit
You are making my soul grow.

Edith Tewich

The Remote Control

The remote control
fell in a hole.
One day I found it
while climbing on the telephone pole.

I turned on the switch
and I saw a witch
screaming on the T.V.
So I turned the station
and went on a vacation
to a place I could float
without a remote.

A "remote" place you see
without a TV.
I can relax,
I can dream,
I can even
eat whipped cream,

But, most of all
I can dream,
I can DREAM!!!

Angela N. Schenck

The Passing Years

The eyes of a child are
  filled with joy
As the years fly by
  for each girl and boy

Now the girl is a woman
  the boy is a man
A new kind of life
  is about to began

The years have their troubles
  some good times and bad
They would not trade any
  no matter how sad

The man so much older
  the end growing near
The woman so fragile
  will this be the year?

They look in the eyes of
  their children so dear
And they know life goes on
  with each passing year.

Barbara A. Hogan

Treasures

Treasures are lovely red roses
Happened upon in the wild.
Treasures are wise words of counsel
Soft off the lips of a child.

Treasures are warm days of sunshine
Following autumn's first frost.
Treasures are finding old keepsakes
After we feared they were lost.

Treasures are flames in a fireplace
And quaffing a goblet or two.
Treasures are good books and music
And treasures are friends such as you.
Lowell Anspaugh

my friend

I want to see myself in your poetry
delight under each stroke of creation;
to smell my sweat on your fingers
as you touch me, form me, turn me.

I want to imagine myself
as I am from left to right and
right to left-
to be imagined and realized.

I want to be the wet matter,
to dry in your presence
completed, said,
unretractable,

Delicious.
Lowell Downey

Submission

Full breasted beauties
line the seashore
sit in silence
wondering which man
will explore them
for free, strip them
freeze their thawed hearts

The have no choice
they must conform
the are the mermaids
the ones who can be thrown
back into the acid sea
the ones who can be locked
behind closed doors
the ones who will be found
dead and washed up on the shore
Lori Hunte

A Song Of Creation

I am the eye of the hurricane and the
    lightening streaking the sky
I am the wind that rustles the leaves
    In the stately mulberry trees

I am the ice and snow and rain
    Renewing the earth
And lessening its pain

I am the morning's first bird song
    And the flight of the bumblebee
I am the newborn babe's first cry
And the new parents heartfelt sigh
I am the roar of the mighty lion

And so it will ever be
For I am life's creative force
And dare not alter my destined course.
Catherine Cahill

Spring

The winter is gone
And spring is now here
Is that chirping
From a bird, that I hear?
The flowers are blooming
And animals hatching
Soon we'll go flower
And butterfly catching
We'll have picnics outside
And barbecues too
I'll invite all my friends
And invite also you!
We'll go swimming and hiking
Play tennis, ride bikes
And soon after that
We'll go fly our kites
There is so much to do
Now that spring has arrived
Come on let's have fun
While the world comes alive!!
Jennifer Greene

The Rain

Rain makes the flowers grow
Rain gives the world a drink
Rain has so many uses
Rain is beautiful, - I think?

Rain springs up life
And rain washes away the death
Rain has so many uses
Rain is beautiful, - I think?

But is the rain what we think it is
Is the rain as beautiful as we believe?
Or is the rain dreary
Or is the rain sad?

Is the rain a way to stop us
And does it get in our way?
Does the rain make us stay inside
When we want to play?

The rain does all these things
And the rain enjoys them all
And when I see a rainbow
The rain is beautiful, - I know!
Cheryl DiLoreto

A Black Rose

A black rose
Represents the way I
mourn.

sadness in my heart
Like a prick of a thorn.

Raindrops of tears
Pour down like a
shower.

As I seek to compare
My life to this flower.

Life is capable of so
many things.

Each morning we
awake, wondering
what the day will
bring.
Dorie L. Smith

Untitled

A day of darkness
A day of death
Life fulfilling
Life's regret
One day to the next
The last of the last

Confusion of pain
Suffering inside
No one to talk to
Nowhere to hide
My soul is sad
Sadness of great love

No one has died
My only suffering
Is myself.
Where do I belong
If I'm not wanted?
Natalie Dybala

Love On The Line

Everything is on the line
In true love;
It's all the time.
In the software of my mind,
I see you!
With your chin up
In the air.
Hope abounds everywhere.
We must do!
We must do our very best;
nothing more, nothing less.
In the middle of the night,
We receive our second sight.
In our dreams ....
Love and hate unfold;
In the stories never told.
Since we don't get a second
chance.
May I tell you in advance;
In my life it's you.
Everything is on the line
In truth, it's all the time!
Benjamin A. Driscoll

Coma

"Rest awhile"
My Jesus said.
And locked me up
Inside my head.

I hear your voice!
I see your face!
I hear you call my name,
and yet
From somewhere deep inside,
I say the things you want to hear.
But words shall never reach your ear.

I try, and yet, I cannot speak.
It's gone, the words I try to seek.
I scream at him to let me out,
To know what this is all about.

And so it comes, this deepening sleep,
And all the while my soul he'll keep.
Till I can wake another day,
And tell you what I want to say.
Carol L. Diener

Let Your Love Shine

When love is just around the bend
In all its sparkling colors
There's only one thing left to do
Grab onto it like no other
Fly on into heartfelt dreams
And caress your love at the seams
Cradle it like you would an infant
And avoid the darkness looming defy it
Trust your heart to lead you through
Times of grief and sadness
And let your love flow for all to share
In their souls alight with gladness
Let your love shine through your eyes
And show in your every word
Spread it round with every touch
Because these days we need so much
But hold your lover dearer still
And keep them warm at night
Share your heart and mind with them
And watch their soul alight
Xavier Alexander Robertson

God Got An Angel

Dedicated in loving memory to my mother, Cynthia Marie Poole.
I lost my mom today Lord
And in way it made me sad
But the more I thought about it Lord
It kind of made me glad

Mom, she meant the world to me
God, you know it's true
But it's real nice feeling
Knowing that she's with you

Making others happy
Was her main goal in life
She was a perfect mother
As well as a perfect wife

You could search the whole world over
And never find another
Who cared so much - and gave so much
As my mom - my dear sweet mother

So God, if you're recruiting Angels
What more can I say
You've really hit the jackpot God
Because you got an Angel today!
Carl Poole

Changes

The age of reason
has come and gone,
the time for rhyme
is just a song.

The heart
is still a mystery,
the soul
is the epitome.

From deep within
there is a surging,
and now
I feel myself emerging.

The cocoon
once well spun,
is beginning
to all come undone.
Janice L. Kiehl

Sadness Within...

Out of the clear blue sky,
the birds sing their morning songs,
songs of love,
songs of hope,
but within these songs,
a sadness dwells,
that tears at the heart,
and in the soul,
nothing seems right,
everything goes wrong,
'cause fate has cursed this soul,
he took away the love in its heart,
never to be opened,
lost in the middle of nowhere,
looking for a way out,
with no keys to locked doors,
so it sits,
singing its song,
a lonely tune for all to hear...
Koji Steven Sakai

The Autumn Sea

The Autumn sea has adopted
A new facade
As its pulsating rhythm
Beats eternally, to and fro.

Its mood is tranquil,
Unruffled and serene,
Yet wary, as threats of storms
Darken its shores.

White grains of sand
Once spread smoothly,
Now stand heaped in terraces
upon the shore.

An eerie feeling
Descends upon one
Seeking quiet repose
Amid nature's beauty.

Has the sea really changed
By the winds of autumn?
Or has the mightiest artist
Painted a scene depicting
The Autumn Sea.
*Peter Paul Rice Sr. and
Pauline Van Norman Rice*

Happiness

Happiness is about caring and
  Sharing with others
Happiness is a smile that
  Stays a while
Happiness is about feeling good
  And not being misunderstood
Happiness is filled with self-respect
  And not with self-neglect
Happiness is about pride and
  Not going on a bumpy ride
Happiness takes away sadness
  And brings along gladness
Happiness can take time and
  It can end up like a sour lime
Remember don't let happiness astray
  Because unhappiness is its prey.
Regena McIntyre

Sunset Years

When youth has gone and left behind,
Its memories and tears.
May you and I, still hand in hand,
Walk through the sunset years.

Tho others may forget you,
As good friends will sometimes do.
May you still love me then, Sweetheart,
As I'll be loving you.

I need you so, My Darling,
Your gentleness, your smile.
I need your understanding heart,
To make my life worthwhile.

So, I send my thanks to Heaven,
Each night before I rest.
That God has chosen you for me,
And made my life so blessed.

There'll never be another,
To replace you, My Dear Heart.
For you have lit the candle,
On the alter of my heart.
Regina Scopelitis

View Point

I am not pretty
My own eyes don't deceive me
I don't envy myself
I don't lie

I'm heartless
My pain is devouring me
My love is almost diminished
I don't care

People don't love me
I'm not for them
They look at me and cringe
I don't look at myself.

My world is grey
I am not happy
My life is dark
I don't want it to change
Meghan Scully

Untitled

I loved you with all my
heart, I didn't think anything
could tear us apart,
But, from what I see I
guess I was wrong you
don't talk to me or, even
call me on the phone I
can't believe, it has finally
come to an end. We are
enemies no longer friends.
My love for you has not
gone away it shall remain
here day after day. As
weeks pass we meet new
friends and try to start
loving once again.
Comarita Alexander

A.I.D.S.

Am I dying?
I am Dying!
Death.
Suffering daily I am...
Tears I fight to continue to
   stand;
Each breathe; a blessing
yet a fight.
To not hold each breath dear
would not be rite!
Though sick I feel, I hope
pray and deal.
As this powerful disease
will NEVER HEAL...
My life it will surely steal.
The sun seems brighter
The birds seem friendlier
It is a beautiful world.

Lahanna Lasher

Dreams

Dreams
are lovely.

Dreams
are terrifying

Dreams
are another world
to explore.

Dreams
are meaningful.

Dreams
are dreadful.

Dreams Dreams

Heather A. Schuchhardt

Untitled

The sun is shining in the morning
Now I'm free to roam
Day has melted into evening
It's time to go home
Look around no one's there
It's so empty they don't care
Light a candle think of me
My most precious memory
Black as midnight hearing voices
Deep inside my head
Stars are shining in the heavens
Like the tears I've shed
Look around no one's there
It's so empty they don't care
Light a candle think of me
My most precious memory
Keep my flame forever burning
Deep inside your mind
I wish you the peace and happiness
That I can never find

Andrea Ercolino

The Teacher

The teacher we had was a peach.
One Saturday, she went to the beach.

   But she slipped and fell in,
   And she couldn't swim.

And now she is unable to teach.

Diane E. Barber

Little Time

I'm a woman;
With some direction;
Some faith;
Some wisdom;
Lots of heartaches;
Only left me with experience;
Little time;
To live my dreams;
Little time;
In which to laugh;
But maybe tomorrow;
I'll live only for today;
And not be so afraid;
Of the past.

Lorie Yeater

"I Have No Clue"

Sometimes I feel your love so
   strong —— as I move along.
Sometimes I think I've figured
   it out — and know why.
Then I turn around and
I'm all confused......again
   wondering where to begin.
Sometimes I feel so all alone,
   drifting as I go.
Then I turn around again,
   and your love is there ——
through a strangers kindness,
my family, my friend, in the
very breath of air.....and then
I feel as though I understand.
Then Dear Lord I'll turn around
again..... I have no clue——

Judith Needham

Childlike Thoughts

Please don't hurt me,
It's a world of hard realities.
Let me keep my childish,
   Wonderment.

Dry my tears when they fall,
Send me kisses thru the telephone.
Lay me down in a bed of
   cotton candy.

Show me your soft side,
Give me your heart.
Listen to my thoughts
Hear my words when I speak
Help me to laugh at the insanity
of life!

Pamela Anne Plouffe

"My Dream Come True"

She was in my thoughts and on my mind
I knew someday that I would find
A kind and thoughtful loving miss
Who greets me with a smile and kiss
She always does nice things for me
To my heart, she holds the key
Everything about her is pure and good
Be mean and bad? She never could!
The best thing that happened in my life
Was meeting Carol, my dear sweet wife.

Frank Rovento

The Gymnast

A gymnast's greatest fear
is a new trick or flip.
And even sometimes
It can make her sick.

Sometimes when she tries it
she does not do it right.
She falls to the ground
from a great height.

It's tough to be a gymnast
no matter what you say
It's tougher than football
and even ballet.

So when you're a gymnast
you have to be tough
And no matter what
you have to show your stuff.

Ann Kingsnorth

The Machine

Minds without walls
a human dream
scarred by the crisp —
cut standards of civilization
unopen to other opinions
we are pushed into paperwork,
   the usual:
   no name
   nine numbers
   sign the bottom
   fill in the spaces
      print:
one quarter inch by one quarter inch
   per letter,
and we'll mail you a life in six to
   eight weeks.

The dream dies.

Sabrina Henry

All Dressed Up

All dressed up
in the shrubbery of adolescence
I hear the battle cry
(Wine, Women, and Song!)

The broken fanfares of birds calls
sprout up like weeds
and awaken the
rash, grumbling beast

A deep N within D
the overgrowth
of pride (Lions,
of passion (Tigers,
and of regret (and Bears,
oh My!)

I hear the voice of God
and pretend it's pan

Joshua Vigil Daniel

Mountain

A gust of wind blows
Stream on mountains flow
And that is where I shall go.
Where I shall go
Up on the mountain.

Dana Lena Davis

Clouded Thoughts

I fight my parents,
I fight my peers,
I fight myself,
I am man-of-war;

Tears are shed
Screams are heard,
Shouts of victory,
But still I am sad;

Winners laugh,
Losers die,
Yet I do not lose;

I do not win either,
Nor am I distressed,
But I am a victor who's heart is sore;

I clash in battle
For a cause of pleasure,
I struggle to survive,
Yet I do not take sides.
Troy A. White

"The Pallid Face"

He fell from his life,
the life he abhorred.
The grievance he felt
was what he couldn't ignore.

The effigy of my heart
was burned as he fell.
I pushed that man,
and put him under God's spell.

The deluge of my fears
came down even more
when I looked down the path
I'd never traveled before.

I looked at his body,
strewn over those rocks.
His face was pallid,
his hair tied in knots.

Shall I admit
what I've done to you all?
Or keep to myself,
and risk the fall?
Meredith Taylor

oh, mother of pearl

the secret of your luster
comes from deep within

truly one of a kind
a like one won't form again

your strength and beauty
wrap around one tiny grain of sand
as we all have our beginning
and form
girl to woman
boy to man

and some form then into a mother
a pearl amongst the sand
Darin Dawdy

The Rose

Our love is like the rose you gave me
Fresh, sweet and soft to the touch
It will always remind me of this moment
For you touched my heart once more
A little deeper every time
A little closer than the time before
Every moment feels just right
While you hold me close and tight
I think we surprise each other
Of who we are and how we feel
And yet we "know" each other
So alike in many ways
Our love is like the rose you gave me
Fresh, sweet and soft to the touch
Jayne M. Witt

Maine I Love

From mountain to sea
Summer sandy beaches
Winter high hills to ski
Spring flowers in bloom
Fall color all around
This state is well groom

Living from coastal fishing
A state that not so poor
Land for lots of farming
Shoes and cloth industries
Money earned by her people
But we are not blustery

You can: hunt, fish, hike,
camp, tinker, snowmobile,
canoe, snowshoe, bike,
garden, boat, swim, dance,
picnic, waterski, rollerblade.
This state is enhance.

But, Oh! How I Love Maine
Florence J. Woods

My Life's Love

You are my day, and my night.
You fill my life,
and make my world so bright.
You give me hope all of everyday.
The best of love
in every single way.
You freshen the old,
and break in the new.
You bring out my smile,
even when I am blue.
Together we will be
always and forever.
Apart is something
we will be, never.
I am yours,
and you, only mine.
For each and everyday,
through all of
life's time.
Sandra Zuri

Untitled

I know it's windy
when leaves are dancing,
when waves are crashing into rocks,
When I get blown away,
and when cool air tickles my nose.
Jake Mazur

Peace

Peace is supposed to be
Like the petals of a flower,
Every second of the day
Every minute to the hour.

People compare it like
A rosebud on its stem,
To fit a person's need
To fulfill every whim.

Every person's problem
Going on and on,
Like the sun will always rise,
Like the dew at dawn.

The terror and agony
But there is no sympathy,
When will the pain cease
When will we finally achieve peace.

But until the day will finally come
Every person will sing their song,
Everybody can talk about peace,
But when will it finally be achieved.
Lauren N. Booker

Beyond The Wave

The potent scent of tide on shore,
bubbles rise from ocean floor.
Where dolphin jump, and Orca dwell,
where midnight sand cast lovers' spell.
The ricochet of sunlight beam,
upon wave's white crest can be seen.
Where thickening reef twist and twine,
mirroring kaleidoscope colors combine.

Creatures sing in harmony,
the song of souls who swim the sea.
Miles below the surface they-
frolic here, and there in play.
Free to call the water Home,
Inside a crested cave-like dome.
Beyond the wave-where eyesight cease,
I find my soul-the sea, my peace.
Brandy Hammack

Teach Me

Teach me to pray
And teach me to love.
Teach me to call on my Jesus above.
If I just fall right
down on my knees.
I know He will hear
and answer my plea.
Now if you are in trouble
I will tell you what to do.
Call on my Jesus. And he will
answer you. If you just call
Him right by His name.
He's the same God
and He will never change
trust in the Savior.
Trust in Him now. Because He
is always willing to come right down
trust in Him. He will never
depart. Because love is always
in His heart.
Ruby M. Williams

Our Friendly Saviour

Christ in all his glory
Shining from above;
He will lead and guide you
With eternal love.

Make a friend of Jesus
Everywhere you go -
If you trip or stumble
He is there to know.

Be a good disciple
In the things you do -
It will be rewarding
Joy will follow you.

Count your many blessings
Show him that you care.
Many more will follow
Many more to share.

Praise the name of Jesus
Let Him always be -
There to love and guide you
For the world to see.

Ferol Elizabeth Lake

Sands Of Life

Sands in an hourglass
   flow from one orb to the next,
time slips away ever so slowly
   until all is gone.
When one chamber is empty
   turn it over,
and start anew.
To some, life is the same way.

C. Heim

The Candle's Plight

Candle—
Once straight and slim,
Bends under the stress of her duty,
Hot waxen tears
Cascading down her tortured body.
Her saucy flame frolics
In blazing jubilance.

Then—
Her body contorts,
Flame writhes in terror until,
When she can abide no more,
She stoops and, collapsing into a
   molten heap,
Summons the darkness.

Lisa M. Holt

"The Country"

The country
is where I live,
The grass so green,
Flowers so red,
Birds chirping oh
so nice, trees swaying
Oh so merrily, with
such a bright blue sky.
Bounds and heaps of
flowers waiting to be
picked and the sun shimmering
off glass like hills. I love you,
mommy, with all of my heart
because nothing compares to you!

Jennifer M. Sotzen

Little Indian Lost

Little indian lost
in a field of weeds.
In a field without harvest
in a field of needs,
little indian lost.

Little indian lost
what is it you are looking for?
Yourself inside yesterdays door
A beautiful night dressed in amour
or a long trip in the grand tour?
Little indian lost.

Little indian lost
in a field of needs.
In an ocean of faces
will they make you believe?

Little indian lost
set yourself free,
little indian lost,
just a little indian be.

Andrew K. Levan Sr.

Where the Wind Blows...

Where the wind blows
It sees and it hears
The laughter of children
Their songs and their prayers

Where the wind blows
People are laughing
New life blossoming
Happiness, great rejoicing

Where the wind blows
There's no peace, only war
Life void of value
What is it all for

Where the wind blows
It must marvel and wonder
Humankind has no purpose
Just greed, fear and plunder

Where the wind blows
The world is more aware
Man cannot rule himself
Free from Gods care

Brooke Wardell

"Carry Me"

Please reach down and save me,
Please come and save me now.
I've tried to learn to cope with life,
But still I don't know how.

I've heard your love is stronger,
Than anyone can know.
So I pray that you'll embrace me,
And get me through this low.

I know I've had much more than some,
But still I feel this need.
To find this joy I have inside,
That's begging to be freed.

And so when you are ready,
To ease me to the ground.
I'll know it's you who carried me,
To this peace that I have found.

Amy Barth

The Pieces

A crack in the mirror
will split you in half
A shattered mirror
will break you to pieces
I keep picking up the pieces
but one is always left behind
My hands are too full
a trail of pieces left
follows me as I get up again....
How many more times can I get up?
Soon there will be too many pieces
left behind
for me to be whole again...

Jessica Marks

Recognize Him

While men stared and mocked,
a brooding sky, dark with sorrow,
draped itself like a black shroud
to cover its Creator
Who hung in shame.

While men pierced His hands and feet
and quibbled over His garments,
a veil was torn, rocks split,
and the earth
shook with rage.

Should the inanimate
have more compassion
than the living?

Let all His creation
recognize Him
and repent.

Barbara J. Penwarden

People Are People

Bears are bears, cows are cows.
Cats are cats, and you are you.
Pictures are beautiful,
Witches are ugly,
but you are still you. Tea is yummy,
Good to drink. People are people,
and that will never change.

Erin L. Cole

Tout à Fait Seul

It is my bliss
The darkness, the moon's soft kiss.
   Longing for feeling.
   The viciousness of my dealing.
The demon in my blood runs cold
My emotions can not hold
   My divine bliss
   The demons gentle kiss.

Nathan Smith

Beauty

I am ONE with it
This Spring breathing flower.
It's looking out at me.

The room is filled. PINK
Crystal bowl holds its LIFE-Force
I'm so peaceful NOW

Edith H. Conner

Goals

It starts out as the spark that inspires the flame,
it's our natural drive to experience fame,
to be more than a pebble in a beach full of sand,
to grow from a regular boy, into an accomplished man,

It was said once that an exceptional man had a "dream,"
yet while he had lived, any change went unseen,
what about us, so called "generation X"?
If that spells out our future, why plan for what's next?

Talent, hard work, giving our all,
is that enough to protect us from an inevitable fall?
And how many times must we pick ourselves up,
dust ourselves off, determined not to give up?

Yet in masses we conform to become someone else,
someone worth more to society, than our original selves,
"Is this all really worth it?", that's the question that I ask...

Then I return to my studies, to once again try to accomplish the task.
Katrina McNaughton

Flight

In all the times I wondered,
I'm still left with a feeling, Why!
Deep inside I can will over come this fear;
the fear that was beaten in;
the fear that must be released, vanquished;
there is only one fear; God;
The intervoice cries,
It cries for release;
cries for freedom;
the need for flight;
the need for spiritual flight;
the life force yearning to be released;
to be free;
when will it come for me.
Philomena Pirolo

Untitled

Memory's harsh but unconsuming fire
Feeds endlessly on deeds not done,
Or simply evil,
In the underbrush of life already lived,
And thus past hope.

But there's a communion
With all those torched by their own fire,
Or yours,
And true love isn't possible
Unless first there's that communion.

So only in the fire of unforgiving memory,
Which will not leave us, ever,
Is love, and then forgiveness
For other burning souls, and yours,
And communion gained brings resurrection.
Warren L. Royer

The Independent Ladybug

  Six tiny legs crawl over the veins
Of leaves that hold the gentle rains
  I'll spread my wings and fly away
to leave the shade and seek a ray
  A light from which the sun must give
and shed some warmth so I can live
  I've found my ray upon the green
The leaf on which I climbed to lean
  And if the rain shall fall on me
I'll regain strength as I fall free
  I'll strive my way...I'll climb and tug...
The independent lady bug...
Alyson Lumenello

Dunblane

So young, so innocent.
All you can say is, "What a shame, it never should have happened", and walk on.
Where are the tears of rage and disbelief? Are we really that cold? When will any of us learn?
When?
Those smiles should haunt us forever but we will soon forget as we have all the martyrs.
Why?
To destroy so many lives with one action and then take your own. To take away the future, the hope, the laughter.
How?
Will it ever end? The death, the destruction. After that day nothing will ever be sacred. What will it take to open your blind, ignorant, indifferent eyes?
What?
How can you not care? When will the pure have to stop dying before you decide to pay attention?
Listen to the whispers of the lost children and cry.
Sarah Lee Cross

Untitled

How canst thou be so close and yet so far?
So hateful is this thing called love, and cruel
That it doth cause me pain for where we are...
For loving one so far I am a fool.
I shall remember always when we met,
We both knew then, alas, t'would not be long.
Our parting moment canst I ne'er forget,
My dread that it be painful far from wrong.
At thine own fault I'm left without a heart,
How empty be my breast with none inside!
I fear I have been torn and wrenched apart,
and from this pain there is no place to hide.
  Yet though I hate thee I do love thee still,
  I've loved thee, sadly, and I always will.
Catherine Russo

What About The Children?

We said "I love you"
We said "I do"
As the years went by
Our love seemed to grow
It blossomed into children
We did our best parents
We gave all of ourselves and more
We forgot the "I love you"s
We couldn't remember the last nice word
Just the latest fight
Our family separated into two
What about the children?
"Why are mommy and daddy so angry"
"Why can't we all live together anymore"
We lost sight, we failed
Our children's little lives are shattered
We never thought they could be so hurt
but, what about the children?
What about the "I love you"s
Nancy Cooper

Sunshine

Sunshine is nice and bright.
It brings the world its light.
Sunshine brings the color to the trees,
And shows the bruises on my knees.
The sunshine warms all of my back,
And shines all over my new black pack.
Anne-Marie Gilpin

"A Tribute To Mom"

You brought a child into the world
  One bright and sunny day,
And suddenly you realized
  She stole your heart away.

You fed her, bathed her, combed her hair,
  And taught her right from wrong.
And when she came with tearful eyes
  You cheered her with a song.

You didn't ask much in return
  Just tender, loving care;
As you saw your daughter grow
  You knew you'd done your share.

Why must I wait for just one day
  A year to say to you,
"I love you, Mom, with all my heart
  May all your dreams come true."
    Carol Rovento

The Rose Of Glass

She weeps softly
this rose of glass.
For she feels the cold of loneliness in her heart.

I look through the window
into her private garden.

I move slowly to the edge of her world.
I wish to come closer,
but I fear the absence of her belief in me.

Gently I approach.
I caress her form
she is warmed by my tenderness.

Before leaving I kiss her softly,
and I see a new glow come to her.

I think often of her alone, in that garden,
and I weep softly,
for that rose of glass.
    Van B. Mahany

Woman To Woman

We are here, you and I, in this time and place for the same purpose, to love, support, and provide what we can for the same man, each in our own unique way.

You are his mother, his first love, you hold a place in his life which will forever be yours are rightfully so.

As his mother, you gave him life, you nurtured him to manhood, these are your gifts to him and your legacy to the female who will someday come to support him in life's work.

I am his woman. I have come to provide for his comfort to a greater extent, now that his needs have grown to include desires nature did not intend for you to fulfill.

I shall respect your place in his life. Will you return the courtesy?

We can work in harmony to create an atmosphere which will enable all of us, Mother, Son and Daughter to grow and flourish, the choice is ours.

Without this mutual acceptance, without this acknowledgement, the triad will be inhibiting and restrictive, like water growing stagnant without movement.

We want the same things for this man, peace, happiness and fulfillment, like you I love him.
    Gabrielle Reinhart

Dreamer

Do you have the lost gazing eyes of a dreamer?
If so, your life hangs by one bright streamer.
A dreamers pain gets deep... deeper.
A dreamers life gets steep... steeper.
A dreamer dreams go through life dancing.
Reality tramples them by prancing.
They often might wish that they were dead.
Only because life hangs by one lonely thread.
A dreamer's feelings are that of a warlock.
Pain sorrow and dreams causes a death-lock.
In my opinion life's only a cloud of rain.
In a dreamers opinion life only causes pain.
My dark eyes are full of skylight.
A dreamers eyes are only full of twilight.
If you dream like a dreamer your only a fool.
You die in confused circles in a huge whirl pool.
    Mellissa Y. Nanney

A Child's Mind

Flying horses and fairy tales,
Wizards strong and helpful elves,
Knights on steed and Dragons too,
These things a child's mind can do

Pegasus on wings of gold,
Carries her to clouds I'm told.
Fairies visit in the night,
Kiss her head and remove her fright.
Wizards strong in casting spells,
Protect her soul and guard her well.
Elves of woods sing her tunes,
Of heroes old and far off moons,
Knights on steeds bow down in praise,
Her honor for, their swords they raise.
Dragons gold and silver tongued
Walk with her while she is young.

As time goes by she looses her youth
She puts them away but holds the truth
She'll see them again through her child's mind
And once again she'll pass through time.
    Wendie Bridge

A Tribute To A Friend

Thank you for always being my friend,
Someone from childhood and through to the end,
  is like a sister only better.
Thanks for the smiles, the fun, the laughter,
And for the confidence to know forever after
  there are more good times to come.
And even in times of pain and sorrow
You eased the hurt by letting me know that tomorrow
  you would always be there.
Thank you for all of the fond memories
But most of all for letting me be
  nothing more than who I am.
It's rare to hold on to a friendship so long,
So many others aren't as strong
  to make it through time.
But we've stuck by each other through all the years
Fortunate to never have any fears of growing apart.
Now we're all grown and our children can see
And inherit from us the rare ability
  to keep a friend for life.
    Pamela Hunt

Sleeping Minds And Dead Souls

"The strong must trample the weak."
My eyes looking, scanning, searching into the bleak
For a face full of hatred to go with those powerful words.
And to think everyone heard.
People blindly followed
As their hearts were gradually hollowed.
Like zombies they marched,
Saluting and calling his name.
Standing behind him
Watching the brutal game.
All that suffering because of one
Wicked face, powerful word,
   And an inhumane heart.
It could have been stopped.
It didn't have to start.
But it did. So people must learn;
Hatred must be deserved
And love must be earned.

Rachel Segal

The Heart, The Rose

The heart standing alone
Without any armor
Tenderly, it grasps the Rose
Trusting, the Heart finds no thorns

The Rose feeling the touch of a stranger
Closes its petals in fear
For a brief moment the Rose is shocked
Finding the touch so tender
Opens its petals once again

The Heart, the Rose sit quietly
The Heart flutters at the Roses beauty
The Rose spreads its petals wider from the
Touch of love from the Heart

The Rose, the Heart grow together
Become one
Causing an explosion, painting their
World with the colors of the rainbow
Paving their path with gold

Kim L. Davis

Rachel Jeanne Ginther

This little girl of Ray's and mine
whom we named Rachel Jeanne
stopped by our Earth one winter's day
to tell us what God means
when he says, Trust in Me, for my ways are higher than yours
some other day you'll meet again
when all Truth will be restored. It's very hard
to let her go to help God with his plan,
but since we must, we thank him for placing her in our hands.
If only for an evening, for we loved her just the same,
as if she'd been with us for years and called us all by name.

But now instead of earthly chat, we'll bow our heads at night
to speak to her through our father to see that she's alright.
Our little girl's an angel now, I do believe that's true.
She's helping others find their way, maybe even me or you.
We're proud of her, our little girl, whose sick body braved
the cold to stop and say thanks Mom and Dad for caring
for me, but God has called me home.

Jeannie K. Ginther

Control

What is control? Where is control?
I have lost control!
I sit and look around me.
Four walls and a window make up my life.
I close my eyes and pretend it is not true.
Why did I have to come here, why do I
Have to stay? Where is my control.
Old, I am old, worn out and ill.
I have no control over things anymore.
Tears, I cannot even control my tears.
They soak my pillow night after night.
Oh, to leave this place and hide where
no one could find me, but I can't
I have no control over my live anymore.
In the last season of life I now realize
only God has the control.
I must wait for his beckoning of me.
Wait within my four walls and window.

Bonnie L. Dralle

"Strange"

Now I lay here in this comforting destitution
And isn't it strange the chilling cold is my refuge

I've been places
Seen things

You'd never like to dream of
And isn't' it strange abuse is a word too commonly heard of

I can't see the truth behind the newspaper headlines
too many people are falling for the "wrong type"

Why are we allowing such goings on in such a "perfect" country?
Strange answers for such a strange world

Ingrid Nelson

'Til There Was You

There were things all around me, unnoticed to my eyes
But then one day to my surprise
a world around me, it came alive.
You see, I saw nothing 'til there was you.

I saw the trees, I saw the water
But not the forest, nor the ocean.
Instead of trees, now I see
The life it brings to all God's creatures.
I see the wood used in houses and the power of the mountains.
The strength, and the grace that was used to create them
and the soft quiet beauty that lies within them
All this was not seen, 'til there was you.

The ocean was big and full of life
but now I see it in a different light.
I see the walks as the sun sets low,
I see us run as the rain came down,
I see the danger adrift at sea,
and I see the excitement of another sunrise
I missed all this 'til there was you

I still look for more, because there is you.....

Douglas Charbonneau

Old-Time Fiddlers' Contest

Thin, wiry farmers...Molded like statues...
Music starts...Fingers begin to move...Toes tap...
Music slows...Then stops...
Only statues again.

Dorothy Young Turner

My Church

As I drive on the church yard Sunday morning
I look up and see the steeple.
I go inside and see a lot of people,
many different faces
sitting in their favorite places.

Then here comes the "Preacher Man."
To be sure he shakes everyone's hand.

The musicians play a verse of two
while offering plates are passed from pew to pew.

The director leads the choir in a beautiful song
that is never too long.

Brother Brown gets up,
A message from God's word he does preach
to help us know better how to live and teach.

The invitation is given to all
to come, join and follow God's call.

He asks someone to pray, then goes to the door
to shake hands with each member once more.

Now, with smiles we go on our way
for the rest of the day.
Imogene Garner Tanner

Metropolis

Urban sprawl with multifarious murmurs of
Multiple tongues; scabby poverty and
Gaudy luxury intertwined with high
Idealism and hard cynicism.
All images of man's age-old destiny
With a pretense of decency, in unseemly
Crawling alleys and deep, fathomless
Trenches of selfish impersonality,
Interjacency, bellacity, rapacity,
Complacency.
All interlaced with chasms of naivety,
Ripples of lucific unreality on
A surface of insentient gelidity
And callous density....
George Klenk

Cold Winds

The cold wind blows,
Bringing the promise of future snows.
Yet, I do not notice on this dark and endless night.
It seems time has died without a fight. When was the last time I
saw the sun? When was the last time I stayed until the night was
done? The end of one day is the beginning of another,
At least that is how I think it was before this other,
But now an eternal shadow is cast upon the ground
And hope is nowhere to be found.
Will there ever be an end to this night?
How many days have we spend without light? One, two, a week, a year.
I cannot remember, all I know is fear.
I walk alone down this barren path in this moonless night.
When is it going to end, this god forsaken night?
I walk alone, but there are people all around,
All around this is where people are to be found.
Yet, they walk alone, too. We all walk in rages without even a shoe.
We are lost and the endless night calls, The night consumes any who
falls. This night will go on forever. Our souls will be ours never,
Never again. And this is the price we pay for our sin.
Tom Olsen

A Prayer For Mommy

With only two hours to live, I helplessly
lay in my bed (wishing I could turn back time)
while listening to my little girl, as she softly
whispers to God:

God, Mommy has been a good mommy,
why must you take her away? She has done
nothing but been the best mommy she could be.

God, please promise me:
you'll take good care of my mommy (she's all I have)

Treat her like she's your mommy, love
her so she'll no longer feel so miserable
and sad. (Wipe Mommy's tears away)...

Please God, take me with Mommy, don't
leave me here alone...

I love my mommy
She's my best friend
Amanda Tank

Poetry Of The Rain

A single raindrop falls and caresses
my cheek as I sit... alone... waiting
for the poetry of the rain... light as
a baby's sigh the earth weeps...
letting its cool gray steel tears
ease the salty ground... a tree gasps
as its outstretched begging arms are
moisten by tears... forgotten brown
leaves laying in disarray dance as
the rain splashes... a new moon laturns
the autumn night as a soft south wind
sings a lullaby though the trees...
whispering, weeping the drops scream
their silent song... forgetting all
behind them... seeing only whats below...
they embrace their last look at light
and fall below the surface... forever
to be hushed by the underworld...
Anna Merchant

A Star

A star is sometimes bright
That shines down through the night.

Some people think it's a guardian angel,
Other people think it's just there to dangle.

Sometimes a shooting star will pass by,
And many children will shout and cry.

Some of the stars are very small,
Yet, some of the stars are quite tall.

But stars will always be there to last,
Even if they vanish by fast.
Holly Snyder

Slave Girl

Working in the early morning light,
wishing someday she could go free.
Working until late at night,
wishing someday she could go free.
Getting whipped repeatedly,
wishing someday she could go free.
Crying softly late at night,
wishing someday she could go free.
Crying, working, getting whipped,
wishing someday that all slaves might be free.
Ashley Ream

My Friend

If you have a friend, work for him,
Stand by him & speak well of him.
   Don't knock or try to pull him down
& wonder why on you fortune always frowns?
     When you have a friend be loyal and
square; don't stand for things that are mean
& unfair. Its better to drop the friendship job
Than belong to an unloyal mob.
   If you accept his friendship stick by him
& strive for him. Make his battles yours.
Add to his might/you'll likely win the fight.
   If you try as a friend, he will try
for you, assist and pull you through and once he
finds your with him to the end, he
has become more than - - -
     Just a friend
Marcella Bodily

Right Foot Left Foot

I'm walking alone the dark corridors of life,
Living everyday as a mother and a wife.

Where am I going, I ask with each step I take,
Being happy, is it always a fake?

Right foot left foot another day has gone by,
You get so used to walking you forget to ask why.

But just when I thought this doom I can't fight,
Along this dark corridor comes a glimmer of light.

Right foot left foot this light I must find,
Faster I walk without looking behind.

As I get closer to the light my pace I slow down,
I'm astonished to see what it is I have found.

There in the midst of this bright loving light,
Was something I thought was way out of sight.

With her arms extended and a tear in her eye,
I looked down at that dark corridor and said my goodbyes.

I ran into her arms into her embrace,
And when I looked up into her eyes, I saw my own face.

With a reassuring smile, she knew I had found the key,
By looking into my own eyes, I found happiness within me.
Christina M. Busch

Remember Me, I'm A Memory...

As you sit by on the beach-and watch-as the salty water
rolls gently over the soft golden sand, you realize the greatness
of its purity. The wave is so cool and refreshing to your feet.
It brings new life with it.
It is all the good times you've shared on that beach.
Then, as it rolls away, with the undertow carrying away some of the
golden pebbles, you sit and think, only to come to the conclusion
that it's a cycle - with all the good, comes a little bit of bad.
Wishing that one cool wave could stay forever at your side,
but it leaves - nothing stays forever. Nature created it to leave.
The stars in the sky then appear-glimmering with hope-lighting the
way past goodness to something better.
But with each new wave comes new memories, and more golden
sand is swept away back out to sea-only to return later, made into
something better. For you are the sand-becoming better;
You are the wave-coming and going; you are the stars-glimmering
with hope; you are the memory-kept forever, recreating yourself;
You are there, you are here, you are everywhere-you are simply you.
Then you shout out at the sea before it can take you away again-
     "Remember me, I'm a memory!"
Katie Hunt

God's Tears

I give to you this promised land.
As I watch you from above.
To see that you do the best you can.
To fill this place with love.

But I get a little pain in my heart.
When I see what you can do.
Let greed come in and tear apart.
This world I gave to you.

You say you'll do better tomorrow.
To try harder than you did today.
To cure the world of pain and sorrow.
If I could only show you the way.

So okay, I'll let the rains come down.
Like I did through all the years.
And when they finally reach the ground.
You can wash the troubles away with my tears.
Ruby Freeman

The Good Old Days

I remember, when I was a lad, I worked in the fields,
to help my Dad.

We cut our hay, with mules and machine,
we got pretty hot, and so did the team.

We stacked our hay, around a pole,
to feed our livestock, when the winters were cold.

We didn't have bailers, to bail or roll,
It was done by hand, around that old pole.

We milked our cows, by hand and pail,
so we could make cream, to take for sale.

We sold our cream, and eggs galore,
drove to town on Saturday, to visit the stores.

Away back then, we didn't need much,
Coffee, Sugar, Salt, and such.

Times were hard, we never got much pay,
I begin working, for a dollar a day.

Yet a dollar back then, was worth much more,
when you bought things, at the grocery store.

Times have changed, and so have the ways,
Yet I still remember, those good old days.
Preston Cape

Quiet Companion

Often acting royal, handsome, and delicate luster
in their prime day.
Suave, pride of our palace.
We as them, loathe the elements, enjoy the Residence.

Pristine and tidy cats
will stalk the dead of night
and the late hour of dusk.

Such a fine companion, always trotting their muse
Only if their stubborn will could be broken
without shattering their grace

Still, as an ancient Sphinx, guarding the lonely days
and somber nights.
Content in a dream with twinkling eyes
that simply see beyond.
Scott S. Yerrington

It

It worked with me secretly as I struggled through attachment
To relationships which were changing.
I thought change meant loss, and in my grief
I did not know what to call it.

I caught a glimpse of it one humid day
As I stood in full rain gear to ward off mosquitos
And part of me reached out to the grandeur that was there.
Only then, I called it patience.

It snuck up on me as I laughed and shared with friends.
As the give and take touched me deeper and deeper
I grew lighter and stronger.
Only then, I called it listening.

It whispered to me in my dreams and contemplation
As I began to work with what truly made me happy
And to face and resolve what did not.
Only then, I called it gratitude.

Imagine my surprise when I awoke one day
And found an old name for something new.
It was always love.
And it is me.
   Nancy P. Carnes

Untitled

People with passion will say the earth will end with fire, they want to share with someone that desire, and need to share that passion with someone, to take the flame even higher. Even when the flame ardently burns, they yearn for the feeling not to end. The feeling of lust and desire, fueling the candle burning. People with no emotions want to stop with ice this earth from turning. The coldness they bring will starve the fire, so they would stop the desire. The ice is worse than the fire, because it brings coldness to everyone, and have no desire for anything. People with desire are always shining, like the sun that warms the earth. The fire in them is the soul of their feelings of passion and lust. They will open doors, for others to discover the same feeling. They try to keep the flame burning so the feeling will never end, because those with this inner fire, fear to be like a beautiful rose losing its petals. It dies little by little for every petal that falls. The people that want this earth to end with ice have no passion and no desire. They can't open the doors for others. They lock themselves in darkness, and don't want no one to set them free. They are always running from the flame that would make them
   Yeneys Marcos

Angie

What started with a crush
   Jumped into a rush
A rush of love and of hate
   Something which I can relate

Oh Angie how I love you and how I feel
   Then why is it that I must conceal
The constant hope of me and you
   Becoming one instead of two

I think of you all night and day
   And sometimes I even pray
So why is it when I reach out to grab your hand
   I find myself in another land
A land of mass confusion and despair
   Something I'm quite use too, as I am often there

If I many never again touch your hand
   Let me be then reminded and
That is I say goodbye, farewell and a deux
   Let you also be reminded that I do love you.
   Stephen C. Rea

The Straw Hat

"Is there anything you want?" She asked.
"Only his hat." I said.
"That old thing?"

That old hat still preens on my shelf
Flashy yet dapper, Dad's creamy white straw.
Five years faded its burgundy band.

I take it down sometimes, touch him —
Feel the rough exterior, scratchy against my cheek
But silky... inside.

I breathe in his scent—woodsy, warm
Then hold it out to him, wait for him
To put it on—just so.

Sometimes I forget... hear his voice, almost answer.
A worn old hat, our remaining bond.
I see it and know he's still—somewhere.

Just a grin
And a straw hat
Coming through my door.
   Judith Noble

Enigma

Nickel.
Here.
In my hand.
Have you traveled to far away lands?
I wonder who has touched you
And where you have been.
Where are you from?
Will you go there again?
Have you traveled far and wide?
How many times have you been multiplied?
Was your purpose ever to fulfill a wish?
Or buy a car, or ring, or dish?
Have you seen the great blue seas?
Or felt the California summer breeze?
Where will you go when you leave my hand?
Will I ever see you again?
   Dana Whitam

Negro Child

Acknowledge your self respect and appreciation for life

Accepting your strife and happiness
To show no regret while looking in hind sight

While I see and open pathways for you to grow

I shall speak and be constantly aware
To give you the undeniable Desire with the tools to know

Appreciate misfortunes and give due respect to them

Maintaining proper internal cooperation
For future misunderstandings and Ni@#erisms

Be mindful of your surroundings,
Challenge yourself to new beginnings
Arresting negative respect for positive wisdom's findings

I shall gain you trust and uphold your identity

While accepting only the best, demand the same

Remember your Past, Future and Present Reality.

Under any circumstances stand up loud and be accounted for

you may give an inch but society will take a mile

But the support of our united Black Heritage is for Negro Child
   Benjamin Grimes

I Think I'm Falling In Love

Everyday I think of you.
Every morning I wake with you on my mind.
Every night I dream of you.
Time after time after time.
And I think I'm falling in love.

You once only thought of me as a friend.
Now I hope your thoughts of me will never end.
I wait for you to make you move.
I seem to wait so long.
I'll be here patiently waiting on.
And I think I'm falling in love.

At first the thought of love just made me cry.
Because I've been hurt before.
But I just can't resist these feelings anymore.
Because I think I'm falling in love.
Samantha Bloomquist

Cooked Carrots

Stand up, you folks!
Your hate, let's bare it,
For the lousy taste of a cooked carrot.

It's not so bad
While crisp and snappy.
But cook that thing — and I'm not happy!

It's mushy, Gooey,
And it changes color.
The taste at best is dull, or duller.

So when you plan
To eat at home,
Just cut the carrot — then leave it alone!
Clyde E. Gugel

A Tribute To Farmers

Up in the morning before break of day.
Bring in the cows - throw down the hay.

Line up the milkers - all in a row.
We must hurry - there's hay out there to mow.

Tend to the livestock - look after the sow.
Now to the house for some good morning chow.

Ma's in the kitchen making good homemade bread.
I bet she wished she could have stayed in bed.

Gas up the tractor - grease up the plows.
Do it with haste before it's back to the cows.

The summers are hot - the winters are cold.
But he wouldn't give up this life for a pot full of gold.

Calloused hands - withered with age
but you'll find the Farmers' name at the top of God's Page!
Marline Henrikson

What I Know

It is hard to hate the man
When I know him as my father.
It is hard to be right all of the time
When he is as stubborn as me.
In our differences
He remembers the similarities
From when he was a child
And thought he was a man
And being punished for what he thought was right.
I am a man, and in his eyes I am a child,
I understand him, but damn it I was right!
Stephen Owen

Untitled

Softy we step, hand in hand,
creeping past still forms,
not daring to breathe lest we awaken
the others who will become unwelcome
guests at our secret meeting.

Down the dark steps we dance lightly.
Freedom and peace and repast
await us if only - if only - the
gods smile upon us and sound sleep continues.

Soft light, hot, strong coffee, muffins and fruit,
the paper shared, life discussed.
It's a rare, special time - just
before morning awakens our babies and
the day erupts in joyful noise and confusion.
Karen B. Munson

The Thief In The Night

Is anybody up? I thought I heard the floor creak,
and it must've been real, because it woke me up out of my sleep.
Oh, hello Mr. Man, in your funny black mask;
what you doing in my house? I'm sorry I've got to ask.
Did you come by earlier, and leave something behind?
Are you a friend of the family, or a relative of mine?
But before you answer, let me close the window;
Pa must've left it open, oh how that wind does blow!
It's funny, how from head to toe, you're all dressed in black.
Well, anyhow, let's go in the kitchen, and I'll make us a snack.
I really should turn on the light, I can't see things far or near,
and I really should wake Ma and Pa, and tell them to come down here.
Well, all right, I won't do neither, so now stop all the fuss.
Well, anyway, I need some milk, and mister, that is a must.
But you should leave the rope and bag and flashlight over there by
    the phone;
Our two pitt bulls, Queen and King, might mistake that light for
  a bone.
Hey Mister, where you going so fast? Our conversation isn't through.
Well at least you could have had the decency, to close the door
    behind you.
Lynn Cato

Heaven And Hell

Far from heaven in the depths of hell.
The reality of being gnaws away at your essence.
Your reality is my elaborate dream,
and my reality is your quest.
To make him real I must first suffer the anguish.
Through anguish I reach heaven,
and passion is all I know of hell.
Through the eyes of passion and anguish I see you.
On one side all of human kind awaits,
on the other persecution.
I will suffer a hundred deaths on the path to salvation.
Salvation is you, and you are salvation.
So what is anguish to me?
The difference between heaven and hell.
Lisa Short

Without Christ

   Without Christ, I am nothing, without Christ, I can be
nothing! Without Christ, I can accomplish nothing of value, so
I will praise him. All that I am or ever hope to be is in Christ
Jesus my Lord and Saviour. So, I will be what he wants me to
be, for my God has created me for all his Glory and Honor. For
this reason, I take no glory or honor for myself. Because I live
and have my being, for without Christ, I would be dead!
So then, I will live for Christ and let Christ rule and reign in
my life.
Rev. Donald E. Battle Sr.

Calib's Burden - A Sonnet

If I should wake and see the morning frost
as gnarl'd fingers reaching for my soul
Will I repent to times gone by or lost
or can I say that I attained life's goals.
When light is bright and flowers seek the sun
will I remember those who spoke of needs
and will there be the thought of deeds undone
or did I help by merely token deeds?
If night should come as gentle evening breeze
and see me as the twilight growing dim
will I be cast as useless autumn leaves,
per chance I might, but life is not that grim.
Wrinkled hands, furrowed brow, old restless feet
Carry me one more mile, make my life complete.

James C. Bruggeman

The Teacher's Prayer

You are my kids and I can't help but see,
How alike you are now no matter what race you be.

It matters not from which country you came.
It matters not which religion you name.

It doesn't even matter if you came from a tribe
and never learned to read or how to inscribe.

Children are children, and God loves you all.
He wants you to know Him, so your name He will call.

You must make a choice to listen and obey
Or live for yourself and so yourself betray.

More than anything I want you to know
The God I serve and whom I love so.

Always remember no matter what your goal
There is a teacher who'll always pray for your soul.

Laurie Stricklan

The Pathetic...Prince Of Poor

With grief stained memories...and his hollow heart,
The old man staggers on...wrapped in rags.
Chasing the ghost of the city...at dawn,
His sunken and swollen eyes, lost...in hate and scorn.

Old tattered photographs...with jagged edges,
Flash like broken glass...that line the gutters.
Gloom like fog, settles over...this broken city.
In his trembling hand...is a cup of pity.

He roams dying streets...in search of aluminum gold.
Gulls with bleeding feet, and heads spinning...watch.
Bending belief brings relief...now swallowed up by fear.
Stand clutching hope in doorways...brushing back a tear.

Morning rays of light crawl up...from the horizon.
Below, the abandoned beach holds...the sands of time.
Another lonely day is born...and will surely die.
His questions left un-answered...begin, and end, with why.

Be brave my broken brother...in your uphill climb.
For you are one, of others...and there will come a time,
When peace will find your soul...and God will adore,
You child of creation...you pathetic prince of poor.

Lenny Daigneault

Reject Of The Depression

Slid down- face down - hidden 'neath the torn and tattered
covers; sobbing quietly.

Thinkin' of the hurts, rejection, poverty - too heavy for thin,
bony shoulders of seven.

Wishin', hopin' dreamin' of the bright tomorrow - thinkin'
for sure - the sun will shine tomorrow.

Tomorrow - again the jeerin' hearin' empty stomach growling,
Classmates peering, shoutin' "here she come without a coat".

"Here she comes in the frost, without shoes".
Without, without, without. Will there ever be a "with"?

Smells from the kitchen - hot soup cookin' - made to feed
Children whose parents dropped a nickel in their pockets.

Another night of hauntin' memories - of children's laughter -
Not of clean glee, but laughter at poverty and rags.

These with other hurtin', hauntin' memories keep belchin' up -
Spoilin' an otherwise childish, peaceful day - at play.

Esther L. Stenstrom

Life

Life begins it starts it stalls
Life gives freedom it disciplines with walls
Life takes us up and gently brings us down
Life wears the mask of serious but is a happy clown.

Life is change but is ever constant
Life is sedate, moving, skipping on this merry jaunt
Life is going somewhere and takes us along
Life loves us, nurtures us, fills us with song.

Life respects and regards us as a jewel
Life guides and teaches us with a compassionate rule
Life is involved but tolerates individual choice
Life enjoys harmony but can discern the singular voice.

Life provides challenge and opportunity
Life gives us purpose, a family, a community
Life will test our ability to give and love
Life allows us to be humbled before our Father above.

Life and what is the meaning of it
Life is a puzzle yet gives us the pieces that correctly fit
Life is precious and life is good
Life is to be here and to be understood.

Vivian Cox

The First Bud

As I awoke this morning
   realizing the tree outside
   the bedroom window had a small bud.
The death of the past months
   were beginning to give birth,
That ol' tree has given the
   small and meek life and
   shelter through the cold
   months, while catching the
   blanket of white snow,
   making prisms of light
   to light the world.
Almost as saying, "I'm always
   alive and serving a purpose.
Soon that tree will be the shade for the tired and meek.
Reunions of roots of generations
   who will retreat to that
   strong ol' tree for the comfort it gives.
Serving humbly to the cold and sweating
Growing never selfish as it gives its
gifts to all the world.

Cheryl Munsey

The Democrats And The Republicans

President Clinton and Senate Majority Leader Dole,
looks good walking on the ground. Which one would you like to
see wearing the crown?

Both will be campaigning from state to state.
Wondering which one will have to give that sad hand shake.

Both of them would like to sit in the chair.
Of course one of them will come up in the rear.

Each of you must get out to vote,
if you don't you will cut your own throat.

We love them very well.
Regardless who win America must continue to sail.
Sail on America, Sail on.
Sophia H. Richardson

Dreams

I fall asleep
A deep sleep,
Because they are not like me.

Is this real?
All these strange feelings,
All of these emotions
Could this just be a dream?

When I awoke I realized something about dreams
You do not know when there coming
or what they will be about.
Or how scary they'll be!

I love my dreams how good or bad.
Because those dreams are the only
things I have to keep me company when
I go to sleep a deep dark sleep.

I've always wondered if I were to
go to sleep and enter the land of
Dreams-will it be full of good things?
or bad? That is the biggest mystery about
dreams to me.
Salvatore Oliva

The Sentimental Road

Bring me not these thoughts in bundles,
place my restless being aside.
Allow myself to rejoice in silence,
and nothing shall make me cry.
Just as the cycle of life begins,
my burdens cease to exist,
and tranquillity wins.
God has given magical tools,
I must not lose them in the insanity
of greed, sorrow or anger, or I, no doubt,
will become my own stranger.
Day after day,
with confidence I pray.
With my whole heart I ask to remain in
peace, love, joy.
For as long as I am capable of these sacred acts,
I give me no chance to walk along the path
of the destructive,
so give me God a life from now on,
ever productive.
Sonia Gill

"Forgiveness Through Jesus Christ"

Forgive me father for I have sinned.
I've done so much wrong,
I just don't know where to begin.
Perhaps I am cursed,
Cause you forgive me now
And then I'll go out and do something even worse.
Your son Jesus died for our sins, I know that this is true
But tell me father just what must I do?

The pain, the guilt, when the wrong has been done,
The begging of forgiveness.
Believe me father it's not very much fun.
Many choosing the easy way out.
But according to your commandments
I very much doubt.

God answered and said, this is the reason
In which I sent my son to die
Believing and disobeying would only be a lie
Follow the teachings of my son, pray and be faithful
And you shall attain all the happiness
in the world.
Cheyenne Bashay

Assurance

My father has assured me that if all I do is done right
With love hope and faith I will be a great light.
No other insurance will I need to be assured of a happy life.
I'll practice this will all my might that I may never lose.
These virtues I'll keep in my mind nothing more do I choose.
A wonderful thing his son has done, he has opened the door
To the greatest gift of all, that we may be with him forever more.
Let us honor him with love and joy for he has put death aside.
Now I've put my life into his hands, that he may guide me as he wills.
As long as I have life my faith in him has filled the bill.
How grand was that deed, that was done for you and me
His love for all will never die, but show itself forever more.
If you believe and practice love like him, life will forever be yours.
Phillip Granado

The Ledge

It's been many centuries since the giant granite rock was formed
Of igneous stone and fiery lava in this wide and wondrous land
But here it lies in glorious splendor like some giant stony stage
Where mighty bear and cougar and other noble creatures stand

Right here on this ledge stood chiefs and mighty Indian warriors
With foreheads covered from the world by weathered Indian hands
Their piercing eyes were sheltered from the cold and driving wind
As they looked upon the beauty of their treasured hunting lands

But gentle whispers in the trees tell a slightly different story
For just a little further down is a somewhat smaller softer ledge
With its warm and grassy sunlit surface all hidden from the world
Where little plants of yellow-green line a partly worn down edge

A place where pretty flowers spread their soft and tender roots
And little rabbits, mice and squirrel might while away each day
Hidden from their enemies and from all danger in their tiny world
Near cozy little burrow homes dug deep in walls of loam and clay

Sometimes it seems like in some dreams that things can be unfair
But who can say just why or where each thing should ever rate
For perfect balance is the catalyst in nature's mighty master plan
And it's often little hidden things that make the great so great
William S. Dvorak

Rise And Shine I Shall

The winter of my life,
Basking in shadows of gloom, and cold hollow
halls of dark shallow sadness. I had expected
too much. Had so many reasons to give up-for
I have said for too many goodbyes, why
was the joy stifled as the dream faded
into silence? My soul and spirit dead.
Oh but I used to dance so, remember me?
Growing vividly with such joy ever - spiraling
up towards the sun and sky, dancing like
a young dazzling jewel in the brilliant
summer haze, pockets full of dreams. Yet die
the dream did beneath the cool evergreens and rushing waters
of a vermont July day. The sundown of my melancholy love, electric
splendor gone. Loss, what is this piercing game you play?
Whatever your ways, I am stuck on you forever. I
only pray that once abundance keeps its promise of
rich harvest and full bloom. Let tragic endings be
my saving grace woven richly into the tapestry of lessons
learned. Clutching my dream like a legend, to my heart, I bid
yesterday's burned out ashes goodbye. Perhaps there shall be
good in my goodbye after all. I tell you now, hear me out —
rise and shine! Rise and shine I shall! A soaring eagle
of a shiny new way is emerging with luminous days on the horizon —
LOOK OUT! Rise and shine I shall!

Nichol Lee Widga

That Rainy Day

The sky is blue.
The clouds are grey.
The rain is beating on my face.
I am reminded of you.
You broke my heart when you left
Because you left me all alone.
Throughout each day,
The thought of you runs through my mind.
I am hoping you can hear me.
Even though you are not here.
I wish you hadn't left
Because there is so much you have missed.
Maybe someday soon we will see each other
Just so I can tell you how much I love you.

Sandra M. Tucker

Please Be Mine

You're as pretty as a flower on a warm summer's day
Not just to hold, but to have in so many ways.
Just say you're all mine unconditionally
My lover and friend for eternity.
Lady of passion style and finesse
You are what I live for to all I confess.
Are the feelings I have the same in your mind?
My darling your treasure was so hard to find.
Heart to heart we are as one
So our future is bright like the morning sun.
Let's make our love last and plant a new seed
Pick out the dead brush we do not need.
Up we will go so high we will fly
The things we have wanted will not be denied.
Pieces of the jigsaw can all come together
And our love will have lasted through all the bad weather.
Make me happy my love, for I am your man
A distinction I cherish let's walk hand in hand.
New beginnings in love are made by design
Start by re-reading the first words on each line.

Richard Wells

For Heather

There you sit, just as any other day,
Just as blind to all my emotions.
I am dying so much, Oh just to say,
That I could love you with such devotion.
I steal a glance every chance I get,
But you still haven't yet figured it out.
I've known you for so little time, and yet,
I love everything that you're about.
Your eyes are beautiful and full of life;
You brighten up even my darkest day,
And give new meaning to my empty life.
I want to take you somewhere far away,
Where we will lie together in the sun
And we won't share each other with anyone.

Mike Mantonya

Can You Hear?

When you stop and look around you, do you listen to the earth
All the wonders you can hear of its life, death, and birth.
In all of God's creation there are many wonders wrought
That this world of noise and turmoil has consumed, and we forgot.

If you stop start to listen with your ear, you'll surely hear
Sounds of life most apparent to those who are near
But have you ever wondered what sound you might have missed
By listening to man made things your world cannot resist.

Turn away from all you know with your mind's eye and ear
And go back to God's creation which He gave us all to share.
Put aside your learn-ed listening and the knowledge it imparts,
Yet seek a better wisdom, and start hearing with your heart.

See the beauty that a child can see, mysterious sounds and wonders
That bring healing to the soul, and peace without measure.
Ne'er forget what was created, and giv'n to man to do his part
To protect and to love, and to listen to his heart.

Jo Barton

Midnight Jewel

Dreysden blue and scarlet red
the turmoil spinning in my head.
While nothings really as it seems,
the answers lie within my dreams.

What troubles in my mind are kept?
Secret sorrows that went unwept.
Lovers lost while never loved,
these are the things that I dream of.

Happiness being the jewel of light,
the gem that I find only at night.
I sleep and my soul is finally set free
to experience what my heart longs to be.

Mark Lighton

A Poem

A poem could be the sun, A poem could be the sky.
A poem could be a girl, A poem could be a guy.
A poem could be the sand, A poem could be the sea,
A poem could be a bird, A poem could be a bee.
A poem could be the moon, A poem could be the stars,
A poem could give off light, but not from afar.
A poem can be a gun, A poem could be a knife,
A poem could be a fruit on the tree of life.
A poem could be a mountain that stands so high,
A poem could make you happy, sad, laugh, or cry.
A poem could be bread, A poem could be wine,
A poem is made up from thoughts of the mind.
Birth of a poem is anything you think it should be,
This is my poem, To you from me.

Craig Davis

Don't Forget Me

My love, my love
Why do you make me cry so?

My love for you is so deep...
Even though I must go.

How will I ever get you to understand?

I am not deserting you,
You have always been my one and only man.

I have given you all my love, my body, my soul,

With your tenderness and all your passion
My heart, so strong....you do hold.

Don't turn your back on me, don't make cry anymore,

I am so scared of leaving, not knowing what's in store.

My darling, my love
Remember all the passion we shared.

Please don't forget me.

Even with your anger.....

Deep down....I know...you really care.

I love you.
Peggy A. Schell

A Race Fact!?

What is race?
... is it the case?
... the shade?
... or the made?

Will it be a vantage?
Or will it be a bondage?
Do you judge?
Or do you justly budge?

Too shallow to care?
Too ignorant to share?
Or too proud to pair?

Which ever you swayed...
How ever you wade...
What ever the case...
Will change the fact of the meaning of race.
Evelyn Sylim

That Feeling Again

The wind is drugged
It knocks the leaves, it knocks the top leaves first
No one, no one thinks of air

I look out as a child
That feeling is sliding as a serpent does
Freeze, can't breathe
The moment bites down hard
When you realize you can't find Mom

I'm too old to play make believe
You can't hand me an orphan cloud like this
You can't hand me a scorched horizon
In frame after frame
Looped venom drops on marble sky
This is my cartoon

Silently I follow a double-cross
looking over my shoulder
Walker, spotted walker

I've seen the sky and my eyes
and I can't imagine them any other color
Matthew Chansky

"Pain"

Yes, pain is only pain,
and nothing ever, remains the same.
So, let us play, life's silly game,
applaud the sun, and curse, the rain.
Our so called goals, we'll strive to obtain,
some ground we'll lose, some we'll gain.
Victory, so sweet, Defeat, such shame,
life is but a dream,
And pain, is only, Pain!
Darrell Ritchison

Autumn's Promise

Softly the leaves float through the balmy air,
Wafting gently, settling in intricate design.
What is the message they have for you and me?
What are the melodious words they sing?
Many are the colors, textures, shapes and sizes-
Quiet, as winter snowflakes covering the ground.
Twisting, twirling, the leaves maneuver into patterns of delight-
Leaving trees bare and lonely as some blow away in sheer abandonment.

What is the purpose of these leaves covering the terrain?
Shall we gather them in baskets or pile on plastic sheets,
Or leave them to warm the earth, preparing it for spring?
Beautiful, mysterious, seemingly without a plan.
But, oh what joy! As the tree remembers other seasons-
New life will come when winter storms are past.
Ah yes, for each tree as for each human there is the Master plan-
That which goes into the earth shall have life again.
Iva E. Steigleder

Hmm...

Scratch...
Scratch, scratch, scratch...
Always, and forever
Scratch!...

Ink wasted black-stained mind opens to
Doors of perception,
Briefly and unequivocally,
confused.

Doodle on forever, my endless love
solidification betrays validation
in my sorry eyes.

Always,
scratch, scratch, scratch, scratchscratch

rip away my brain in sexual sensory overload,
the mind quivers to be stroked in the
nerve-endings dance of love.
Tiny motions and dreamy looks
Catalyze in unintentionally...
Did you mean to?

Do you care?
Thomas J. Cloutier

Freedom

To be Free,
oh, what a thing it would be.
If I could be what I wanted to be,
and not have to worry who might buy me.
That would be the most wonderful thing to me,
because then I could be me
and not have stay up nights crying because he beat me.
Oh, now wonderful it would be,
to only be Free.
Amber Burns

Teachers Are a Necessity

What is a song without words to sing
What is a bell if it does not ring
What is an orchestra without a conductor
What is a classroom without an instructor?

What is a needle without thread
What is a sandwich without bread
What is leaving a throne without a successor
What is a college without a professor?

What is a constitution without any laws
What is Christmas without Santa Claus
What is a lid without a container
What is an athlete without a trainer?

What good is a piano if it doesn't have keys
What is a forest without any trees
What is a goal if you don't try to reach it
What is a lesson if there's no one to teach it?

What is an elevator without a door
What is a beach without a shore
What is a church without a preacher
What is a school without a teacher?

Laura L. Ellison

Cowboy Stan

There once was a man
His buddies all called him Cowboy Stan
Back when Stan was 18 he met Chelsea, who became his wife
They loved through all the joys and strife

They raised three wonderful children: Garret, Cade, and Mazy
Not one of them ever turned out to be lazy
One day when everything was going well
Ol' Stan was riding his horse Apache, when the horse fell

Stan was crushed by Apache's weight
I guess that's where Cowboy Stan met his fate
Right then and there Stan had died
When his family found him, they cried and cried

A few days later friends and family stood around
Watching Cowboy Stan being put into the ground
There were hugs and tears
Worries and fears

However, all of those were taken away
When they remembered that Cowboy Stan was with God on that day
There they stood, thinking of the man
That once was known as Cowboy Stan.

Rhiannon L. Bohlander

Unidentified

I see a light running.
I hear a low "whirrr.."
I'm afraid it's not the wind that chills,
It's not the cold "berrr..."
I see the shadows of shapes.
The "whirrr"...is getting louder.
I turn in endless circles.
My spine has turned to powder.
I feel my knees collapse,
I fall to the ground.
Wait! The "whirrr..." has stopped.
There is no trace of sound.
I see no moon,
I hear no breath.
I smell just one thing...
Death!

Alison Davis

My Favorite Cat

I have a cat who is my friend,
He is the best thing that has ever been.

Although, sometimes he isn't nice,
But some how he catches a lot of mice.

He cleans up his spills,
But he knocks down my pills.

He is a pain
When it come to a game.

But he always lets me win
And that's not a sin.

He is a very good cat
Especially when he's on his mat.

He is my favorite
And he very well knows it!
Oh! I didn't tell you that he is fat.
Do you think he is your favorite kind of cat?

Danica McCleary

Sill

Why that when I hear those sweet words
That slide out of her mouth with elegance
I cry deep within me, inside my heart so full of thought
The way she tenderly speaks, so dear and innocent
So playful yet so much more to me than thought

Why that I cannot bear to think of a life
One without her in the future, in our future
That I know not what will happen to us separate beings
To live a life without that love and advice
Bearing without her heart to cry to

Why that I can feel the hurt bestowed upon her
Not purposed for me, or was that the hidden intent
No one can know, for all that happens God has part in
So maybe we are connected by our inner bodies, our souls
Is it a gift or punishment for me to perceive her pain

Why that my life is all a jumble and will never be clear
Until the days beyond death will I never understand
How much she means to me now and always will
For what we have is special and I deserve the harsh outcomes
For how am I to know what is meant to be, I am only a baby.

Sara Tadikamalla

What Is A Friend

A friend is a term of salutations, some one you support
and they support you
an acquaintance. A want to be friend.

What would you rather have, what would you rather be.
A friend will stand by you thru thick and thru thin
and will be there with you till the very end.

When it's all over and life is thru, will we be able to say
we have been a good friend to you.

Was my face shared with the back of my head, or did I stand
tall and look straight ahead.

You say to my face you are my friend when my back is turned
and my face you can't see, then you are the friend that use to be.

Use to be friends are a dime a dozen, they fold their hands
and look toward the heavens.

When my time comes and life for me ends I hope you can say
he has been a good friend.

Ray L. Myers

Nature's Lullaby

Ah! Majestic snowcapped mountain blessed
Where its birds come home to rest
The doe gliding silently by on her dainty hoofs
No one aware how close she moves
The squirrel sitting atop his tail
probing the hard nut to no avail
While all around the forest green
Nature's Lullaby is quiet and serene
This is the great land of the God of our fathers
The kingdoms of the blessed animals and bowers
And as evening all enfolds, even the brook seems in quiet repose
Then, as if on cue, an orchestrated Hoo! Hoo! Hoo!
The Great Horned Owl with revolving view
Glides silently the leafy monarchs thru
Sending forest folk scurrying for cover
As they see him wheel and hover
The birds' disturbed twitters move among the branches
As the distracting noise of the kill advances
Suddenly all is quiet in the deep mountain glen
Let the Lullaby begin again.

Doris Pronovost

The Eagle

A marvel of nature,
So swift and so true
With massive power and elegance to
It soars up above in the sky so blue
His powerful eyes looking for food
Then he dives to the ground with blinding speed
And when he flies away we can see he will feed
As he travels away to his nest in the blue
He's a marvel of nature I'd say wouldn't you.

Matt McGuinness

"Today Is Our Wedding Anniversary"

Come and let us mark this special occasion,
Let us renew our love and devotion.
Come and embrace me my soulmate,
Come and let us exchange gifts and celebrate!

Our marriage has been like one beautiful dream,
And that's because we worked on it as a team.
Yes and I love you more that ever sweet lady,
Today is our first wedding anniversary!

It seems that whenever you are near,
All my worries just fade away,
It's as if I don't have a care,
For you give me strength to face another day!

My respect for you continues to grow,
I'll worship you from head to toe,
We make such a wonderful pair,
Let us resolve to go for another year!

Let us thank the goddess of love and prosperity,
For her helping hand in our destiny,
Oh I love you more that ever sweet lady,
Today is our first wedding anniversary!

Chateram Singh

Sleeping By A Lake

I can barely hold up my fifty pound eyelids.
Too late-they have found their way to the bottom.
Soft powder presses against my flesh
and I notice ghosts dancing across magic liquid.
Now dawn screams of power.
The sound of peacefulness
and the scent of power ring wildly,
but the liquid stays,
not bothered by anything.

Evan Styles

Seasons Coming And Going

Winter struts her full array, with sun to
tease us on a cold cold day, but we
should remember that snow and rain,
bring us fields of wheat and grain.

Spring brings new life amid the flowers, trees
burst forth with a canopy of green, to tell
us there is much yet unseen.

In Summer everything that grows, for a
time will bloom them go, except those which
were ordained to stay forever green.

Autumn comes upon us gradually lazily as if
to say, wait and watch my colorful array,
the golds, greens, reds of fall, will hold our
eyes, till times passage leaves the branches bare,
not quite all, for some stay green. God's gift
amid the Christmas scene.

Margaret H. Taylor

Heartfelt Love.

Heartfelt Love is impossible for those that
focus upon the "What" aspect of another.
For, as being Soul, Human Beings
can never exist as a "What." Therefore,
in genuine light of Spirit...
A person can only be a "Who." And
to love the "Who" in someone is true for them
as they live on this earth and beyond,
bided in the hearts of those Who felt their love.

James M. Callard

daydreams

and as my feet drag me to my senses
i see the warriors and the dragons
they load my feelings into their wagons
i see that good neighbors are good fences
and onto the sidewalk I draw in chalk
i remember the ashes and cinders
they come to me through third story windows
i remember their fires as I walk
and old women sit in their rocking chairs
i favor them to lumpy old couches
they rest with knitting needles in wool pouches
i favor the way they gather in lairs
my mind is playing mad tricks on me
as all our lives are riddled with ennui

vanessa poholek

As I Pray Before Thee

Forgive me please but if you watch you'll see
my eyes do look
although closed they be.
I see you not now I look upon you when
you shined before all
and were to all a good friend.
Good kind gentle in your ways
that is how I see you
by remembering those days.
I judge a man not by what possessions he has
or by how much money he makes.
I judge a man by how much love he gives
and how many lives he touched.
A truly rich man is one leaves many lives behind
because money can not hold a memory.
So as you leave on the wind here these words as you go.
Because a richer man than thou
I never shall know.

Nick Quadrino

"Rot Before Death"

You raunchy man, you rot before you died,
And long you stunk before the worms were ill
On all the guilt and filth in life you will
To build your vile estate of lofty pride
To peaks which though are high can never hide
Your stench - your rotty taste the worms does kill,
And long they writhe in pain, their cries are shrill
Because the poison of your flesh they've tried.
   So gross you grow, oh man, from first your birth,
   And ever more decay as old you wax,
   And putrify the whole of your small girth,
   So better grow you don't - just less of worth,
   And worse of badness get, and that's the facts,
   And waste to rot you do with loads of mirth.

Jeremy Norenberg

Gratitude

   The Sun rises to the beginning of a
New Age,
   The dew glistens to the reflection of
my soul,
   The air penetrates my skin to
rejuvenate,
   The four directions of the earth offers
new perspective,
   I realize that knowledge flows within
the very cells of my body
   I feel the history of all time by touching
my hand to the earth,
   I hear the secrets of the Universe
whispered by the wind in my ear,
   I am but the matter of the Universe
blessed to house the spirit,
   A creation as grand as all I see,
This is to encompass gratitude.

Kellie Antrim Brown

Raindrops

When it rains, they are not raindrops
but tears from God's eyes.
So many people wondered
and asked him why He cries.
He answers them so solemnly,
"I gave this world my son,
but in return all I got
was hatred, war, and guns."
So, when you see a raindrop,
just think of why God cries,
and try to make this world a better place
so God may dry his eyes.

Jacob Mirabal

Solace For My Dear Love

Aqua cool the light on shines the breath of one so dear,
Immortal soul of dust divine, o pain of bliss so near;
Sacred hollow water springs, the infant cradle boasts,
Emblem queen the sparrow sings, announcing mystery's host;
Darkling ray boisterous cloud, hyperion fallen from grace,
Contraband heaven's shroud, cloven dagger -Garden'
Swollen pools with lacquer view detain the evil spire,
Racket bombast thoroughbred flew, sweet hydrous flask to fire;
O lovely harness unborn to string the liquid ice,
Unshackled Lyra will perform with cupid's pointed vice;
Aqua cool the light on shines the breath of one so dear,
Immortal soul of dust divine, o pain of bliss so near.

Mike Davis

Things That Go "Bump" In Your Prose

Dead metaphors stalk the tender prose
Squeak and gibber in the rows
Among the dark and dank and empty words
When writer's mind is taken unawares,

Enchanted by the ebb and flow
Of the rhythm that you know
Will have you nodding, nearly napping
Suddenly they're everywhere they're not supposed to be.

They're not really dead, you know
Like Brer Fox, they're lying low,
Waiting for a little lapse
To rob your words of life, like vampires in the night.

Not the dawn's early light
Gives these goblins any fright
"Delete this," they quaver
And suck the marrow from your words.

Dead metaphors will not be stilled
Won't stay buried nor fresh ones willed.
So listen for the still, small voice,
And beware of eager volunteers.

Dave Willis

Ocean

I know his color, brilliance of his blue eyes, and his virtue.
I look at him as though at the mirror.
I dive into his waves and as he embraces me,
I overflow I feel warmth.
Nothing, nothing underneath me!
Only the unknown hands are carrying me on a golden wave.
I appear at the magic kingdom, in the palace of miracles.
And it gives birth to days and nights.
The only difference; the nights there possess more
stars and they shine brighter.
The days there are tender and lighter.
There are no dreams, and there everything is breathing free.
And this beauty speaks to me and it's impossible
not to understand its language.
As I hear the tantalizing voice of the waves, I dissolve.
I turn into a slave of the ocean of magic.

Inga Bukharova

Rain

Rain is water,
Rain is sky,
Rain looks like clear glass falling from the high,
Sometimes it looks like snow,
Falling softly to the ground,
But then there may be the sprinkle,
Very few it may be,
But still it shall be rain,
When it hits the ground it looks like shattered glass
has fallen,
But softly though,
It falls,
Rain feels like wet warm showers,
But though sometimes it feels like cold,
Freezing water,
Rainbows appear above,
After the rain is gone,
I am sad because of this,
There is no rain,
But rain is my name

Katie Rains

Adversity

It was raining and blowing.
The wild flowers lifted their faces joyously,
Drinking the drops of life-giving nectar,
Exhilarating in the thrust of the wind.

Some petals were bruised
And some were torn by the force of the rain
As they whipped back and forth in the face of the wind
And pitched up and down with the weight of the water.

I thought to myself, there's a lesson to learn
From observing these flowers rejoice under stress.
No doubt it is hard. Perhaps they feel pain,
Yet they revel in it.

Can I do the same, I muse to myself?
Can I accept pain and stress and grief
As life-giving nectar and trust-exercise
For the growth of my soul?

Yes, I affirm. I choose to receive it
As good, not destructive, with grace, not self-pity.
Head lifted high, shoulders squared to the fray,
I stride down the roadway of life!

Karen L. White

The Poet's Grace

What music fills the poet's ear,
When the words begin to flow?
What sense of rhyme allows the mind,
To reveal what heart should know?

Is it magic - perhaps fairy dust,
That sparks the poet on?
Or is it anguished battered soul,
That writes the poet's song?

Whatever it is, we'll never know,
But we follow where poets lead,
For their words give counsel to arid souls,
That thirst, that wonder, that need.

The wiser the poet, the more we learn,
Of life, of love, and ourselves,
In the hope that we will not spend our time,
Like the dust laden books on shelves.

For once we've journeyed the pages of life,
And the book is folded in place,
The tender words of the meaning of life,
Will remain the poet's grace.

Carole Butterfield

The Lights Of Christmas

If I could only see "The Lights of Christmas"
  through little children's eyes,
I could realize the joy and wonderment
  and see it in the skies.

If I could be but a tiny star
  in the Lord's firmament above,
How happy I'd be just to twinkle
  and reflect the light of God's love.

It is easy to love one another
  with Jesus at the helm,
No hatred toward color nor origin
  just "Love" for each of them.

If I could only see "The Lights of Christmas"
  through little children's eyes,
How happy the whole world and I could be
  if we were really wise.

Lincoln Naumoff

Mr. Wishing Well

I sit upon a park bench, I have but not a care. When wondering what that little boy is doing over there. I watch him toss a penny inside the wishing well. His face looked sad, his hands did shake, as far as I could tell. I wondered what was going on and thought that I would see. So I got up and walked over and he went down on one knee. I stopped and watched the tears toll down his tiny little face. I wondered what was happening and what had just took place. Then his voice did tremble, the little boy had words he said bring my Moma back, this is what I heard. Please Mr. Wishing Well, tell my Moma to come home. The baby really misses her and Daddy's all alone. She's been gone for several weeks now and I don't know where she's gone. And all I know is Moma had been gone for far too long. Daddy says she's up real high and watching from above. So please Mr. Wishing Well send my Moma love. Tell God that we need her home and send her right back down. Cause Daddy can't take much more, there's sadness all around. I can't quite understand all this and wonder don't you see. Why that man was drinking and wrecked our family. If Moma can't come back to us, ask God to set her free. So Moma can keep watching over Baby, Dad and me. The little boy said thanks a lot for all my wishing time. As much as you did listen, I should have tossed a dime.

Darbie Deniz Plumadore

Fragments Of Sunday

They cut — not a painful cut
  like the jagged edge of cold steel —
  but like the healing relief of the surgeon's scalpel
  on an infected wound.

They cut to the soul and allow,

for a moment,

  the purest joy a child of Adam or offspring of Eve can feel.

It is found in the dark tunnel of coal, one diamond,
  concentrated by time
Transforming the opaque
  into a light divider.

Reflecting from the tunnel of black darkness
  a stubborn ray that refuses to be consumed.

More than a ray — a rainbow
  beautiful, brilliant color bursting from blackness
    igniting the soul with new life,
      with new breath

"Let there be light!"
  "Let there be life!"
    and there is...
Thanks to the fragments of sunday.

Nathan E. Steury

Life's Hard

Easy times come and go quickly
While hard times tend to stay
And all the time you're wishing
The hard would just go away.

You want life to be easy
When you know that it's not
You wish the frustration would go away
You wish the pressure would stop.

No one on earth can help what happens
No one makes you sick
No one can change it
By giving their fingers a click.

Sometimes you feel like you can't hold on
But you know you have to
Don't ever give up on yourself
You know what you've got to do.

Jill Kelly

They

They, I say, in every way, to dismiss a conversation that might stay
longer than I want it to. No mess, no fuss- They is a way to say go
away how's the weather? Do I care? They say it's fair, could be
better they says go away

They, the epitome of vagueness, yet a key to conversation
say they to a stranger, they is not personalization
strangers know they
They says go away

They is a state of mind, one that blankets and blinds
a simple word in the back of all minds
don't know what to say?
They says go away

They is a chance, can take it either way
some think it's an invitation to stay
yet, they keeps everyone at bay
They says go away

The bystander effect is the only way to live
the blandness of society, taking nothing, having nothing to give
everyone, everyone, everyone knows they
They says that's my answer, they says go away

Shannan Jahn

Remembrances

The rain was silently falling outside
As she sat and remembered all the things
She has to leave behind.
A young girl waiting for her first dance
Oh so happy she didn't miss her chance.
A young woman just become grown, she's with
a young man she soon would get to know.
A wedding day dawning bright and clear with
memories to make and hold dear.
A baby's first cry, first laugh, first step,
She knows she's not ready to give it all up yet.
The time will come when she won't have a choice.
She can't stop the pain or make it go away,
But she knows her memories will always stay.

Veronica L. Pickett

My Persian Princess

Oh my Persian Princess, how many hearts have you broken
How many others feel the pain that I'm feeling
Your eyes hypnotize me, your beauty captures my heart
Your voice relaxes me, like the sound of a soft waterfall
Oh my Persian Princess, you have me under your spell
My love for you is so strong
There is a fire that burns wildly inside my heart
My heart desperately seeks your love
My heart desperately needs to be with you
I will do anything for you
Please my Persian Princess, please ease my pain
Tell me all of your dreams and wishes
Let me look into your eyes, and see your spirit
Let me hold you in my arms, and wipe away your tears
Let me take all of your pain away
Oh my Persian Princess, how I love you
I will love you for eternity, I will do my best to make you happy
I will shower you with gifts of love
I will give you everything your heart desires
I will protect you like a shield from all harm
Oh my Persian Princess, my beautiful Persian Princess
You have me under your spell

Robert Leon

Cheryl's Children

She is gone
leaving a void in our lives.
The memories not ready to replace the ache.

The elders know
that time will soothe the hurt.
We encircle the family, hug, and share our pain.

To the minors
who watched her slowly die
Whose life had enveloped their lives completely.

She was their rock,
their enabler to realize
the myth of a happy unencumbered childhood.

Numbed by their loss,
the basis of their life destroyed.
Will they artificially numb themselves in years to come?

Or stand up tall
To shout to the world, "I am me!
I'll reach out to life and grab that brass ring"

To become a living legacy
to the woman who only wanted to be a good Mom.

Janet G. McKeown

When You Close Your Eyes

What do you think about
When you close your eyes

Your brand new shoes?
The love of your life?
Why you didn't go out that night?
Why you just walked away from that fight?
Why you cried all day?
How you didn't know what to say?
Why all your friends walked away?
What you could have done to make them stay?
What is wrong with the world?
Or maybe it's just you?

Or do you not think at all
Do you let yourself go numb
So you fee no pain
No hurt
No grief
No love?

Sara Hale

I Wish

I wish there wasn't anything to fear
But fear is why we're here
I wish there was a way to grow wings
So we could fly away from things

I wish there was a way to cry
When you look at the earth all you do is sigh
I wish there was a way to go
But whichever way you go they push you away and say no

I wish there was a way to stop crime
Makin' money, while others are a mime
I wish the country had a good president
But they only make you live with a rich resident

I wish the country had some peace
People putting a room up for lease
I wish that life was good and easy
But life has always been bad and greasy

I wish the violence in the country would stop
But everyone's already been arrested by a cop
I wish people were safe around
But this country has always been bad and down

Jennifer Redmond

How A Writer Interprets The World

Everyday events like conversations in living rooms,
changing positions on sofas and water rings forming
on coffee tables become metaphorical musings
when a writer peeks through windows.
Words become seed offerings, uncrossing of legs
becomes acceptance and water rings become temporary eternity
(when they dry, it's all over). Conversations reap relationship
that root on both sides of coffee tables, wind themselves around
legs, and bloom until the iced tea is gone and no more water drips
from the bottoms of cups (time to leave).
Down the street a couple stagnates at their table.
The paper didn't come, there's only one egg left
and she bought orange juice
with pulp. He hates pulp, but that's all the store had.
Coffee's weak. It's Columbian so it shouldn't be.
Let a poet taste it and she'll swear the marriage is over.
His sweater catches on a nail as he leaves for work and unravels
along the bottom (freedom). Snag a few more and you're
home free. Just be careful where you throw your coat when you
come home. If it lands on her pillow you're not going anywhere.

Melissa Hudler

Untitled

I am from a family of three sisters and a brother.
Our parents raised us with lots of love for each other.

Now we are all married with children of our own,
There's more to love with the way our family has grown.

We've shared Christmas together for 38 years,
But this year, we will hold back tears.

You see our parents will be apart,
They are trying to make a new start.

Even though they have been together all our lives.
Divorce is hard even when your child is 35.

We all will share the pain you two go through,
But remember, we love both of you.

So with the Lord's help,
I know we will survive the painful Christmas of 1995.

Jennifer Mears

The Big One?

Trembling, trembling vibrating shaking faster faster still
Long so long seconds seem like hours
When will it end?
People in shock and disbelief

Where to turn where to go
Destruction and despair everywhere
Dark so dark and silence

Slowly so slowly time moves on
Lives repair, lives moves on
But never to forget no never to forget

Behold life Behold the time we have left
If we could all learn from this tragedy
If we could all be loving
If we could all be humble
If we could all be wiser

But alas as time goes on we go back to our old ways

Some people remember some people have learned
The secret of precious life the close call we
all had the day of the 5.6 Northridge quake

If only we knew this was the big one! Only God knows

Thelma Lyden

Christmas To Me

Does it matter if the weather is warm or cold?
Do you need a tree trimmed in silver and gold?
If your lawn is green instead of snowy white,
Does that make Christmas seem not quite right?

But what does Christmas mean to me?
It's more than presents and an evergreen tree.
It's not about a jolly man dressed in red
Or visions of sugar plums in your head.

Christmas is the time to remember
A baby not really born in December.
That boy was a gift from God above,
Sent from heaven to show His love.

He gave up His life for us on a cruel cross
The righteous one dying for the sin of the lost
But three days later He was alive again
And now He dwells in the hearts of men.

So it's about more than just a baby's birth
It's time to celebrate God coming to earth
This Christmas time rejoice and sing
Worship the Christ, the newborn King.

Cynthia J. Daymon

Schindler's Legacy

The music evokes a certain heartache that can't be articulated or explained
the sadness and desolation of the violin
the image should be of falling snow
and candlelight, and wine, and romance
not ashes

Ashes
the remnants of God's chosen people falling from the sky
ashes of charred bodies
beautiful bodies full of hope
and promise, and love, and fear

When were the Jews to be feared?
After millennia of persecution
when were the Jews to be feared?
How do you fear an ancient tradition that values love,
learning, laughter, music and God?

How do people of vision live in such fear without going mad?
Oskar Schindler pretending to be what he wasn't
protecting a few who would live on to see future generations
of Jews rebuild, and prosper, and grow, and love

Donna R. Bialkin

"War With The World"

The sun is red in the blood filled sky
The heat, like a bronze oven with the world in its belly
We have killed the forest,
murdered the world

In our greed we have destroyed the very thing that gave us life.
We die of thirst,
yet we dare not drink, for fear of a worse death.
Thirst is the bread for our hunger,
for there is nothing else

We have won the war,
though even in our victory we die.
The irony of what was.
Man's war with the world.

Joshua E. Parker

A Christmas Poem

Dear Trav:
The other day a question you asked of me was;
"What's the hidden agenda that lies inside of me?"

I thought and I thought, "How shall I reply", then
the answer came so swift I thought I would cry.

For you to be happy and filled with joy; and to
remember those exciting times I spent with you and your toys;

To share with you how thankful I am, and full of joy,
to have been blessed with you as my boy;

God gave me this precious gift so many years ago,
and because of you, you have taught me more than you know.

We have cried together, and we have played together,
now it's time we enjoy our time in life together;

For all too soon, He says, "your time is past", and
we are quickly laid to our final rest.

So please understand my Dear Son, my hidden agenda is simply done,
"pass on to your son, the gift that will last," for
all too soon and all too fast, "your time will also be past."
Anita M. Davis

God's Miracles

Day by day we see God's miracles great and small
Oh God you are the creator of them all
The cry of a new born baby for the first time
The backdrop of the stars with their heavenly shine

For God produces many miracles as you will see
A ninety year old women holding onto longevity
A daughter with aids who sings her last breath
The hope that God produces in her final rest

Birds that soar to the highest heights
And the last glow of the smallest light
The sun rises and continually sets
The blind man who guides others without regret

The man who sings on the corner and never starves
The child who is homeless with a song in his heart
The miracles of life which are two fold
For a moment you're young then suddenly you're old

The miracles God has is an ever changing view
But God's miracles first have to happen in you
Linda Foster Collins

The Keeper At The Gates

There stands a Keeper at the Gates, the door to Eternal Peace,
　Where all who enter find their Life, and walk on Golden Streets.
"They" say St. Peter's waiting there, on guard at the Pearly Gates,
　To bid us "Enter into rest," or accept our earn-ed fate.
And He could say, "Come, enter in!" Or thunder, "No! Depart!
　Go ye below for your reward, O ye of unclean heart."
Today I reached my journey's end, on my return from hell,
　I met the keeper at the gates, it's someone I know well.
And there I froze, I could not move, I shed a flood of tears,
　Cold chills raced upon my skin, and bells rang in my ears.
Instantly - Truth reigned supreme, replacing all my doubts,
　It was so plain, "How can this be?" my wondering heart cried out.
"O, how could I have been so blind?" My heart sang with such glee,
　As I faced the Keeper at the Gates, I was face to face with - Me!
I'd felt that I was locked inside, while the Master stood without,
　And Lo! These two thousand years, His Truth was met with doubt.
Yes, I'm the keeper at my gate, and you're the guard at yours,
　Alone, we all must find our way to Heaven's Sacred tours.
Don't blame St. Peter if you fail to reach the blissful shores,
　For you alone, can turn the key, that opens Heaven's doors.
Betty Ardis

What's Love All About ???

Do you ever wonder what love's all about,
Can you adequately describe it?
　Is it happy or sad,
　Is it only a fad,

Can We Have A Doctor Prescribe It?

Can you really know what love's all about,
Do you think you understand it?
　Is it ours to give,
　Do we need it to live,

Can Anyone Demand It?

Are you able to show what love's all about,
Could you or I posses it?
　Can it be predicated,
　Will I be addicted,

Can Anyone Assess It?

No one can say what love's all about,
It's total fascination,
　From a baby's coo,
　To an older you,

There's Just No Explanation!!!
Millie L. Spurlin

Bull Rider

He's a bull rider in his heart
He's a winner in his dreams
Although his body hurts he'll keep on going for
his gold buckle dreams
going through each day like a disappearing
song
He'll ros'en up his rope, Just to sing along
He doesn't need the booze or drugs any more
He just needs a good woman to love him
A little bit more
So good night Darling till we meet again
Love isn't like a song
it doesn't always have to end
Rick Oliver McIntyre

Danger

I'm in danger when I walk on the streets
I could get shot and die or something.
When I walked on the street it was like the capacity of
the street felt like a narrow line close to a
cliff and I was about to fall off.
POW!
There goes your life and another, but finally the person
who shot you.
Bianca S. Salas

No Voice

Oh precious baby why do you cry.....
Is it because so many people pass you by?
Oh precious wildlife does anyone care.....
That you will soon disappear?
Oh precious trees cut down everyday.....
is it really true that's progress they say?
With no voices of their own.....
This is the greatest injustice known.
So if you listen close you will hear.....
The cries of God's creation are loud and clear.
Doris Ann Dimatteo

"The License"

As one too young we know not of it,
With time and age we long more for it.
At last the day of testing is now upon us,
To have this thing we've long been promised.
Is it now our key or our curse,
Something of a blessing or something worse.
In our possession we can ride the wind,
Without it we have only time to spend.
A day soon comes when we must show it,
And all our pleading cannot control it.
To save suspension we will not mention,
A revocation, when? In a past dimension.
Then by fate or chance it is gone,
And with it our hopes of holding on.
To get it back we walk the narrow path.
Feeling the pain and the official wrath.
Soon again it is in our possession,
And we now have learned a driving lesson.
Keep it to the right and between the lines,
And the license your future can define.

Danny Westmoreland

The Flood

The muddy waters raging high and roaring across the
   California river's bank
And bag sanding paraded by so many hands no one can
   stop mother's nature on this surface of the land

For the power of man's mind can betray him in the
   depths of pain and in the height of his passion
He tries so desperately with power to control mother's
   nature with failure

For the rivers can flow through with rage and take so
   many men stranded out
To the depths on their eternal rest so speechless to
   see the pain of lamenting cries in so many eyes
We cannot make nor control the growth on this earth

Only creators we could be to invent what our knowledge
   perceive
But not the heavenly science that springs the growth
   of seeds
Through century after century we live with hidden
   knowledge the creation of nature's beauty.

Pearl Rolbinson

Enchanted Memories

Standing on the beach,
feeling the waves crash against you.
The breeze is flowing through your hair, and through your soul,
Making you feel so free, without a care in the world.
You look down to behold a beautiful, blue shell,
it is so soft, so fragile.
You hold it tightly in your hand, yet, so carefully.
You let the sand sift around your feet,
burying them in the sand and salt water.
You never want to leave this miraculous beauty.
The waves inspire you, and the breeze overwhelms you.
It is so beautiful.
Off in the distance you can see the pure, white sails of a sailboat.
You close your eyes and breathe in everything you have just beheld.
You want to always remember the smell, the feel, the beauty.
As you turn to leave you take one last glimpse of this enchanted
island, and to this day that small glimpse is still your memory,
And you vow never to forget it.

Rachel Thomas

Peace On Earth

Freedom.
A wonderful thing.
War.
A terrible thing.
Why do we fight?
What is the point?
All we're doing is killing each other for dirt.
Dirt that isn't even ours.
Empires of dirt.

Freedom again.
After war.
What a mess.
No, not we - they.
Those purple mountain majesties.
Ruined.
Those beautiful for spacious skies.
Blackened.
The best three words in the English language are
Peace on earth.

Elizabeth Snow

Alone

Alone, A small, barely furnished room.
Alone, Light entering through the thin curtains.
Alone, Only she sits in the room.
Alone, Nestled in the corner.
Alone, Emptiness all around her.

Alone, All she can think of is him.
Alone, Love that now has ended.
Alone, Opened was her heart.
Alone, Now nothing but pain.
Alone, Echoing through her head, the thought of the past.

Alone, All light slowly leaves the room.
Alone, Leaving nothing but darkness.
Alone, Objects fade into the blackness.
Alone, Nothingness surrounds everything.
Alone, Everything is gone.

Sean Brady

My Boat

I sail
my boat of faith upon the
sea of truth.

I hoist
the sails of hope, belief,
trust and love.

I tack
into the Gales of difficulties
disappointments, uncertainties and sorrows,
with my hand upon the
tiller of righteousness.

I fear no storms
for he who made
man, boat, and sea;
calms the raging tempest with spoken words
"Be Still."

I arrive safely, into the
harbor of peace;
for God is the
captain of my boat.

Hiram Paul Childs

Flowers And Showers

Purple, red, blue, pink, and yellow flowers, come and go
lightning and thunder and shower's pour down
On the ground it is wet and flower's stir in the wind
I stand on the prairie watching the flower's dance
And in my heart I know nature and man come together

Katie Schultz

"Let The Sunset Play"

After the
day is done and twilight
takes over, the sky is filled with the
glorious sunset. Layers of red, orange, and
even strips of pink are stretched throughout the big
blue canvas. The sun, as bright as it could be, soon
becomes mellow with a dull glow. The flat, grazing land
becomes painted with the colorful rays of the sun. The sun then
begins to rest and hides behind the vast horizon. The bright,
beautiful colors then slowly begin to fade and the darkness of the
night begin to appear. First, shades of purple and gray take the
place of the red, orange, and pink. After a while, little white
dots
are sprinkled onto the dark and cold atmosphere. Finally,
the man of the moon shows off its bright glow
to the dark, tired world below it.
In the distance, a shooting star flies, and the dish
ran away with the spoon.
Good Night.

Jonathan Arteza

Senseless Travesty

Just how can the world stifle your sadness,
as the moon shines golden and mercifully bright;
I can still see you staring into the desolate darkness,
though you're blinded by walls and shielded by light.

Oh goddess of misfortune and damsel of dreamers,
you wished for the love that I could not give.
Though the autumn has ended and the seasons betrayed us,
your memory has faded into the whispering wind.

The answer you gave me was ruthless destruction,
or maybe I dove into the depths of the well;
searching for someone somewhere I knew nothing,
drowning in bottles that emptied and fell.

Your deep dark gaze both penetrating and pensive,
shot through my heart like an arrow and bow,
holding you closer than a bitter illusion,
time vanished in the sunset of a golden glow.

Our journey was long and brutally painless,
as the friends that we knew were so hard to see,
the cliffs that we scaled and the rivers we swam in
lead us to a land called "senseless travesty."

Kenneth Lieberman

The Good Ole Days

Remember when we used to play,
By the old cow creek on a summers day?
We'd fish for crawdads, in the warm summer's sun,
Then we'd run home laughing, when the day was done.
We never worried about drugs or gangs, our world was
filled with pleasant things.
Like slumber parties, hayrack rides, and watching for aliens
in the night skies.
We had lots of fun in so many ways,
We were kids a lot longer in the good ole days.

Mary J. Ockey

Looking Back Can Hurt

I fear the darkness all around me.
It smothers the air that I breathe.
The emptiness I feel inside is even worse.
As if I'm living an evil curse.
If I cry, it will know my weakness.
Laughter tends to cover the sadness.
I try to look for the rainbow at the end.
For some reason the path keeps on wanting to bend.
I look back and see a furious cloud.
As all my problems begin to mount.
A hand reaches out for help.
Hoping to break the continuous melt.
Unsettling water begins to flow.
Gradually the tension begins to go.
I feel the eyes go through me each time.
Always trying to see inside my mind.
Waiting patiently is not my style.
Within a short time I feel I have walked a mile.
The sadness and fear slowly lifts into the air.
Time is what I don't have much to spare.

Catherine R. McArthur

He

I love you is what he said that day
I thought his laughter would never fade
He brought me flowers and teddy bears
He made me feel like I had no cares
I was never bored when he was around
Cause he always turned the scene up-side-down
He acted like he really loved me
But then I found out he was cheating on me
He said it would never happen again
But that's when it all came to an end
Even though I loved him so
I knew I had to let him go

Karla Hansen

Drums

The way a man touches can be a wonderful
thing.
He can make you feel all good inside,
Like a pinkish red rose,
Dancing to the beat of his song
while the green grass blows.
Sometimes when you listen to the wind
emotions can mix.
Getting all scrambled up like a bi-emotional
fix.
The music can slow down to a trembling beat of thunder
making the grass stop blowing
and the rose forget knowing
that simple song,
And how to dance to the beat of her man.

Mirika Andrea Mayo

My Prayer

When my eyes are dry and I can not cry,
I begin to feel real low,
For I wonder if I really love
the one who loved me so.

When I laugh and joke and have a good time
While souls are going to Hell.
I wonder if he is looking down on me
And saying thou art doing well.

My prayer today is Lord help me
To set my affections on things above,
And win some soul to Thee.
Through the greatest of gifts which is Love.

Emery L. Wilkerson

Little Savior

Listen up little boy
I'll be quick and concise
Ambiguity is your illustrious defect
It will be a detriment to your existence
It will prevent you from living
It will murder your personality
To surmount it, you must trample all obstacles.
You must work, practice, conduct, perform, accomplish, complete,
Finish, execute, fulfill, experience, seize, cherish, love! LIVE!
It is your obligation to me. It is your obligation to yourself.
You hold my fate little boy
Mend me, repair my failures
Attach me limb from limb
Rectify me, I want to be able to walk
Nurse me, you own the remedy
Save me, Save us! Only you can.
Please, here me. Assume that I am justifiable.
Have I captivated you?
If I have not, your only destiny is in my reflection.
A reflection that both you and I share.
William J. Brillant

"Why"

Have you ever gazed at the night sky?
Seen the myriad stars, and wondered why?
With luck observed the planets, Mars, Jupiter, and Venus.
Mercury, Neptune, Pluto, and even the strange world Uranus!

Have you ever dreamed of hurtling through space?
Discovering creatures and life in another place?
Would they think and act as we do?
Would they perhaps look like me or you?

Man is always on a quest, his history is one of discovery.
In a millennium no doubt, space travel could be a possibility.
Dreams become reality, imagination spurs incentive.
Man's creativity and intelligence makes him by nature, inventive.

Time is merely a device providing us with orderly information.
As generations progress, as they age and fade into oblivion,
an era may arrive, and those tiny dots of light in the night sky
may be accessible to mankind, giving him answer to the question
"Why"!
Irving Belkin

Shades Of Paradise

As I yearn for paradise
I seek for answers that cannot be.
Is paradise in the sky; beyond the seas;
A reflection of the essence that is me?
Perhaps a vision, a place, a moment in time.
  My soul searches, searches...

Is paradise a journey through time and space
Within my heart - the path I take?
What once was, my soul can see.
What can be is touching me.

Paradise elusive, beckoning onward,
A glimpse of light on uncharted seas.
Winds of hope surging toward the unseen.
Fate is the compass. Faith is the guide.

Paradise - a shade, a beacon or a quest,
A memory, a dream?
The King in me can see.
This is where I choose to be,
Soaring on the wings of angels,
  Shining brightly in the night....
Douglas B. Gordon

Mother Crow

Mother Crow, on windswept snowy mountain top,
  with large pines standing by as you swoop and hover,

Your shiny blue-black fluid form so
  captivating to watch as you hang suspended
    for moments on the up-drafts
     flowing off the canyon of frozen lake, trees,
       hills and granite rocks covered in
         white purity of crystalline coldness.

A rare gift, this visit in snowy Sierra's
  by the Black One.

Mother Crow, Indian spirit messenger
  sharing your oneness-connected energy of the whole,
    bringing a stark contrast in the wintery scene
    where only the wind caused movement
      besides the black winged form.

"Awaken!" her presence beckons,
  with its unusual circumstance.
"It is all ever-changing, fragile in its balance,
  and each one affects the whole, "her message rang out
    carried across the land by the wind.
Jeane Ross

Writing On The Wall

Call out to me stranger no one knows your name
Call out to me lover
In the absence of having the right one to play the game.

I could be the sunshine just if I could memorize the quotes
I used to like on the wall.

I can see the writing on the wall
Turning everything from black to white I guess says it all
I can hear the leaves when October falls
But the tendency is not to see the writing on the wall

Call out to me angel no one knows your game
Call out to the danger and hope ah you hope
Oh it doesn't change

And she could be the sunshine and the light
That shines through my window all through the night on the wall

We began breaking down the silence of the walls
Because the tears have filled an ocean that swelled
throughout the years
The clothes I wear, stained in blood, wrinkled, torn and
  teared blown away
But I can see, I can see the writing on the wall.
Donald W. Mann

Shining Through

The time we spend together is usually far and
in between but to me it's so special though rare
like the rainbow after the rain but are all my feelings
in vain?

My love for you is hidden like clouds that hide the
sun wanting a chance to shine, the thunder is my
heart beat echoing through the clouds the lighting
is the love light wanting to break through somehow.

You have the power to whisk the clouds away for when
the clouds are broken true feelings can show strong
and clear to grow into something beautiful to cherish
for many years.
Paula Fultz

"Uncle Jay's Spirit"

The sun, the sun is rolling now.
The rainbow is coming around the sun.
Then the birds are around the rainbow.
Then, now everything is rolling around.
Uncle Jay sees the spirit.
Now everybody takes his place and
comes over with him.
When Uncle Jay sees them now,
Then he's so happy to see everybody with him.
Then he sees his kids the most.
His wife is coming by, and
He is so happy.
When the sea comes with him,
The sea follows him.
The sea likes him so much
That now Uncle Jay turns around
And goes back with him.

Kelle Ann Richards

I Am Thine

Lord let my heart control my tongue,
and my head control my hands.

For spitteth out of the mouths of fools,
the words of hurt and oh so cruel!

For reacheth out the hands of carelessness,
leaves nothing, but one big mess!

So let me forever find,
the ways to show that I am thine!

Indiana Ellison

Courage In The Face Of Adversity

Numerous clouds whiten the day
The forests are green with exuberant foliage
but the fog sets in any way
Many fruits sadly decomposed from spoilage
The soil rends in a dissentive fashion
as if on the verge of a harsh metamorphosis
Unbeknownst yet severe, a blizzard emerges
Trekking at sporadic speed it razes the land
Leaving all void and barren
as sand slipping through the hand
such a sight leaves a grisly mark
the change occurred without warning
the animals scatter far apart
but all must retreat bereft of mourning
the unexpected change yearns to be rectified right from the start
seeking amendment dissipates into irrevocable realization
that learning, being impeccable comes straight from the heart
when all is said how can this calamity construct a harmonious nation?

Alan Franz

friday afternoon (Leavetaking)

Draw the curtains
Close the door
Won't be hangin' 'round here no more
Toss the books
Say goodbye
I'll never, no never...I refuse to cry

Through the gate
Down the street
Ten years hence, again we'll meet
Turn the corner
Stop the car
But I can't turn back, I've come too far

No, I can't stop nothin', I've come too far.

Christina Corpuz

Seasons

The towering majesty of old, enduring trees
Burgeoning green leaves
Blossoms of white, yellow, pink and red
At dawn the birds celebrate the age-old ritual of spring

Sultry, humid heat
Dew-laden leaves billowing in gentle breezes
Or thrashing vigorously in gray electrical storms
New-mown grass-redolent with the scent of summer

Vibrant vivid colors competing for center stage
Decaying vegetation preparing to replenish the earth
Cool, sun-drenched days
Reaching to winter

Bare glistening branches
Reaching toward heaven in silent supplication
Sleeping tree trunks
Quiet cold days of waiting .... waiting for spring.

Ida Rinkenberger

The Bloom Of Purple Twilight

Dusk was coming still the Old Man sat in his squeaky ol'
Chair...rocking alone in his squeaky way dreaming
The dreams of yesterday.
He stopped rocking and was quiet for a while listening
Intently for the call of a child — But again he nodded
And dozed as he dreamed the dreams of long ago.
His last nod came as his head pitched forward and his
Chin dropped low and the Fairies came in on the tips of
Their toes —
His chin dropped and his head bent low...
— Only The Fairies witnessed the Afterglow
As The Purple Twilight came into Full Bloom.

Muriel Dyar Glaister

"This World"

This world we live in is a beautiful place
It is filled with people of the human race
At times it is hard to understand
As to why things happen to our fellow man

Some of these things are good
I like to see them happen, as we all would
But some of these things are bad
And we don't like to see them happen, they make us mad

This world is a place where we all gather
Some to work, some to play, and to some it doesn't matter
Everyone is different, not everyone the same
One thing is for sure though, we all have our own name

One more thing about this world we live in
Everybody is equal, everybody is human
No one is better than anyone else
This world, a beautiful place within itself.

Richard Anthony Lostritto

Love

Love is a flower opening in June
It stays there morning, evening and afternoon
It makes us smile, it makes us cry
Especially when we say "Goodbye"
It deals with all the hopes and fears
Collecting like dewdrops through the years
Love is a very wondrous thing
It breaks our hearts, or makes them sing
There are many surprises love can bring
Some are happy, some are sad, some
are good, others are bad
If handled carefully, love will stay
and never, ever fade away

Kathleen Welsher

Blue's Song 1996

The drown tone Busy signals sing sweetness to me-This voice sings to me lonely lullabies-My dreams take form only to freeze away-Mistakes that skip like a broken blues record-It was never about that-Never about what that old colored man sings-It's deeper, goes further-Past the two tone-Past those redneck jazz singers-It's all about those cat's, the slick ones on the corner-Talkin that slick jive, puttin on the fake British accents-What do they know about the blues-What do I know-Me the silly ass white boy from the suburbs-What do I know about the blues-Nothin-What do I know about the world-Nothin-Nothin more than those rednecks-Those colored boys-Those smooth talkin rudeboys-I know enough to know there ain't no answers on that vinyl-The turn tables got nothin-Nothin cept vertigo- It's all down hill-But nothing goes down without a fight-Specially me- Skinny blue Irish kid-Holmgang, I go down screaming-Holmgang, to the death-But what do I know 'bout pain-Only those cool cat's at the juice bars, smokin cancer can sing the blues-Not me-Not that silly ass white boy from the suburbs-Naw not him-He can't sing the blues-
Karl T. Eckert

Your Guardian Angel

He's a mighty warrior of God
Standing tall and erect,
For he's a servant of the Lord
Sent down from heaven to protect.

He is your shield, your guide
And your spiritual leader
Placed by your side,
By your heavenly creator.

With his wings stretched out wide
And his heart filled with love,
He's your blessed guardian angel,
Sent from above.

So take hold of his hand
Where ever you may go,
For he was hand picked by God
To lead you to and fro.

Whether through the fiery trails of life,
Or the deep and miry clay.
Your guardian angel will be with you.
Each and every day.
Larry D. Johns

"Alone"

Oh how lonely I am, I am indeed,
Oh how lonely do I feel,
How can one live with no one to care for,
Oh how can one live with no one to ...
Oh how does one live with a soul wish has no love being offered,
Oh how does one stand the loneliness,
Or silentness,
How can one bare with no one aside.
No one can live alone,
Some have no choice,
Some do.
The reason, I do not know,
For I live alone,
For I sleep alone.
For I love alone.
Love what, I know
I too ask my self,
Why I love, Who I love,
My self, my soul, my mind
My only companions.
Giannina Miani

What Is Reality?

Reality is holding you in my arms,
The gentleness of your touch,
The tenderness of your kisses.

Reality is knowing you care for me
As much as I care for you.

Reality is coming face to face with you,
Looking into your eyes,
Seeing the love held there just for me.

Reality is knowing your every move,
Even when you're just standing still.

Reality is the way our bodies join as one,
Each time that we make love.

Reality is the times we sit in silence,
Not needing words to say.

Reality will be waking in the morning
And knowing it's not a dream.
Sheri Nicole Trimble

Shooting Stars

Are shooting stars now false hope?
  In trying times are they ways to cope?
Is it like tossing pennies in a stream?
  Or are they really filled with dreams?

It makes you wonder what you'd pay,
  To see that comet on a given day
Is it worth your mind, your heart or soul?
  It's tough to tell what's destiny's toll.

To a hopeless person it's a sign of light,
  To see on dance upon the night,
But for one to grace a content man's eyes,
  Means nothing to him, it's just the sky.

You may have days that are sad and slow,
  But having stars is good to know,
Because you maybe lucky and see one soon.
  So go out tonight and gaze at the moon.

I'll pray for one to grace your sight,
  I'll hope and pray with all my might,
For seeing one is always great,
  So make a wish to guide your fate.
Shawn Abbott

"My Angels"

I have two children sweet as can be,
though they can create such a catastrophe.
Sometimes they appear to be beautiful angels sent to me.
Other times they sneer at me.
Oh my Lord! Is that the devil I see?
Their rooms are always such a mess.
Although their school work is always their very best.
Sometimes they fight like cat and mouse.
They surely can destroy my house.
Sometimes they support each other strong,
and I know that I have not gone wrong.
So, even when my little devils appear,
I know my angels are very near.
They will return to me soon I hope,
and so I know that I can surely cope.
Lorraine Falconer

To Notice Me

What would it take for you to notice me?
Would I have to climb a tree?
Should I change the way I walk?
How about the way I talk?
Maybe I should take a class,
And learn to cook and sew and make stained a glass,
Or maybe I should let things be
And face up to reality
That it would take way too much
For you to ever notice me.
   Stevie Hille

Unconditional Love

Love is a fragile and tender emotion
So intense and full of devotion
Warm and pleasant, delicate and profound,
Can lift you up to higher ground.

Love can give you complete gratification
The feelings are strong and cannot be mistaken
It brings you joy and extraordinary passion
And also a chemistry that's everlasting.

Love can fulfill your utmost desires,
Coax all insecurities, and set the soul on fire.
This kind of love that I'm speaking of
Is the one we all want ...... Unconditional Love!
   Shanessa L. Fenner

The Unhappy Flower

As a flower wilts, so has my love for you
For you plucked me form the life I knew
You forgot to nourish me and give me my dew
You closed me in a dark room
Instead of kissing me in the sunlight
You did not see my beauty
And make me your delight

So throw me away
And maybe I will bloom again
For someone who knows how to appreciate
My petals and my stems
Someone who knows how to stay
Not leave on a whim
Someone to water and nourish my soul
Even as I grow old

Please throw me away
And let me laugh in the breeze
For this I will gladly take my leave
And try to be happy again
   Lynette Kennedy

The "Not"!

I think - I thought a goodie knower!
About a people, person goer

She thinks she's right, but Ah
She's wrong and doesn't know!

To say and not to do may be right for some,
but not for you!

She goes and goes but not for where
and doesn't care

To say for "what" and think a "not"
must be oh a lot

She's not her mind, if you know-
She thinks a lot...
   Mary A. Frisinger

Carnival

Lost in a fun house of mirrors.
Thousands of "me's"
None of them real.
I smile and they smile back.
Each corner I turn
I am confronted with a different vision of me.
Each vision is one I haven't seen before.
Each distorted image more revealing than the last.
   Rachael Guip

A Friend From God

I had a friend or two when I was in the world.
   I put my heart and trust in each and every one,
I counted on them to listen and care.
   I could not understand why they could not hear my heart,
instead they tore me apart.
   Not understanding anything or even caring,
just selfishly pleasing their own desires.
   It was that very special time that I fell to my knees,
before the Lord with my torn apart heart,
   as the Lord gave me a very special promise,
to mend my friendless wounded heart.
   And you were that very special friend from God.
A friend knowing my heart and caring.
   A friend listening and loving to share their special
feelings with me.
   A special friend hand picked by the Lord,
to love and help me on my way to heaven.
   Oh friend, Oh friend, God has always blessed me so.
And now I have you to share Jesus and our lives together.
   May we two together bloom, into what God wants from us.
   Jane Ellen Wilson

No Boundaries

Love knows no boundaries. Love is
caring for one another. It's free, unselfish
and understanding.

Love is sharing your life with another.
When you cannot be apart a week, a day,
or even an hour.

Love knows no boundaries. It's when you have
a child, then you see that child
smile.

Love is in the morning sun, driven snow,
in mountains high and the valleys low.

Love knows no boundaries. It's found on
the street. In a smile, a nod or even a wink.

Love can be found in the simplest of things
by letting go and accepting life's uneven flow.

Love knows no boundaries.
   Maxine E. Bain

The Peacemaker

She is my best friend,
She is always there for me.
There is nothing greater than
Her voice speaking wisdom and knowledge.

Her touch seems to make
My problems disappear.

She is a peacemaker,

She is my mother.
   Lauren A. Barry

Why You Ask

My heart is filled with so much joy,
but why you ask is my face so poor.
I'm so depressed with all the stress.
I see a dream beyond the trees
that's waiting there just for me.
I do not rejoice and I do not jump about.
For I know how far to go before I realize that nothing like it
ever existed. I feel as though I'm alone
though I know I'm not far from home.
Why you ask is guilt on my mind.
I think about it all the time.
I guess it's the world that's getting worse
or is it me because I put everyone first.
Why you ask is life so violent.
I do not know, but through the years
the world has filled with so many tears.
I feel for the homeless and the children on the street.
Some of which I'd like to meet.
Now ask me again why I'm so depressed
It's because this world is such a mess!!!!!!

Shayla Wallace

Death And Darkness To Light And Life

In this darkness ever binding on a path forever winding,
I walk along the path in a dark world without hope. But suddenly
I look around and suddenly hope is found inside myself and
others. A hope beyond all imagination helps me to cross into
another nation where a light of unimaginable color lights the
path I am taking which is always straight and never curves.
This nation indescribable is always there to go to. All there
is to do is to believe and walk on.

Joshua Moffitt

Puppet

Shattered pieces of a broken memory,
My life is a blur, it's all that I can see.
Seems my whole life I've been trying
To please someone else;
Never once have I done something for myself.

For all the times when it all fell apart,
I give you my all, I give you something from the heart.
All my heartfelt rage, the storms of my soul,
Are handed to you, my friend,
So that you will know how it will end.

I curse the times when I was made a puppet
Of others' dark purposes and what they did covet.
I let them know now that I will no longer serve
Their desires, all of those that were absurd.

For now, I am my own,
No one's servant ever known.
Never more caged, never more enraged,
At those who would control me. I now just scorn
Their attempts to use me, for I am now reborn.

Nick Yancer

Hidden Truths

    A *whispering* breath parched in time.
    Crystalline *beach* immersed with a full moon's tide.
    When love is *called* and hate replies.
    Prejudice of *color* prevails the spirit
of brotherhood *dies*.

Richard L. Griffis

Race For Freedom

What is this marvel racing through the night
muscles surging 'neath golden hide?
What rendezvous must be kept
That merits such devouring stride?

He stops now and snorts and prances
And touches a fine head to his knee,
Then tosses his head again skyward
Offering obeisance to a God only he can see.

Then he's off! Off again running,
Running fearfully, frantically for... for...
Ah! He runs for sweet freedom's sake.
God grant he run evermore

Who would dare tamper with such freedom?
Who could such a demon be?
Would fence and shackle and saddle?
Who but a man, less free.

Judith Gott Clark

Remember Me

Remember me,
The child who cried
the one whose wounds would never die.
Remember me,
The one in shame
who'd cry out tears of pain.
Remember me,
who would run to hide
and would not come out even at suppertime.
Remember me,
the one who grew
to learn that life is really rude.
Look now at me
and now you will see,
how wrong you were to laugh at me.

Karla Suarez

A Bowl Of Mush

Time has a way of making things change
A tall mountain can be ground into dust
Or an ocean dried leaving nothing but sand
Yet the love we share is stronger than time
For it could only change to get bigger and better

But what is this love that holds us together?
It is not a lust that we misconstrue
Nor some hidden insecurity that we try to mask
I know in my heart that it is true
From so deep within and so real
That it takes the place of my dreams

Dreams are just thoughts, but our love is a fact
Something I feel within my body and my soul
A purpose by which to live my life
And strive to build a solid foundation of happiness
In which our love can exist the way it was meant to be

James F. Bellon

Lying

When one Individual
Hears the voice of another,
Our trust are staring at your very eyes.
We turn away for we Believe
Our own reflections.
When we look we realize we never
Did listen to hear what one had said.
So I say
What do we know what one said
To the Individual

Odette De La Torre

Guess What!

As I sit in my chair, watching T.V.
With the newspaper on my lap,
I don't like what I see or hear.
But it fills a well known gap.

Some of the programs are filled with awe,
I don't want to remember what I saw,
It's raining now, it makes me wonder,
Why we all afraid of lightning and thunder,

It helps the flowers, and even the weeds.
The crops grow fast-if the birds don't eat the seeds
If the spring has come why all the snow?
Mother nature's plans, we'll never know.

Before long, it will be wet and dry.
Mow the lawn and rake the hay.
Wash the car, and paint the fence.
We hope for weather that makes good sense.

If this bores you, I'll tell you why,
All my ideas, are old and dry.
But if you do enjoy it, I'll try again
I'll collect my thoughts, but I don't know when.

Donald Willits

Soaring Thunderbirds

Our Thunderbirds reach out to the heaven
   free and soaring through the majestic sky.
Leaving a vapor trail floating so lithe
   making circles of mist appear.
Our Thunderbirds circle back over head
   so close your heart skips a beat.
You spin around to keep them in sight
   feeling the freedom of flight.
The rumble of the jet engines
   gives you a burst of emotion.
They come back and make another pass
   crisscrossing in the sky.
You hold your breath with anticipation
   then let out a yell of exhilaration.
Again and again they pass over head
   each time your emotions run wild.
What the eyes and body have just witnessed
   is American freedom.
Americans like the Thunderbirds have freedom
   to soar and become interlaced in their lives.

Mary Durgan

The Women

An old woman, a woman and a child
Stood together on a moonlit beach,
Watching the waves as they crashed
On the shore, glowing a phosphorus green.

The child sung a song about the endless wonder
Pure as the shells lying broken and white.
The woman sang of her restless longings
Crying like a dove, lost somewhere in the night.

The old woman sang in a whispery voice
That only a few could hear.
A song about wisdom, hope and love,
All that the heart holds dear.

When all is still, I can hear the voices
Singing in sweet harmony.
The old woman, the woman and the child
Are all the inner parts of me.

Delisa Louise Marchetti

Memories

Memories, sweet memories,
Drops of water
Turning to pearls in an oyster,
They are the yesterdays
Enclosed in the heart's cloister;
Colorful and cheerful
Elusive and unreal
Like the cool breeze of a hot summer's night;
For those days my mournful heart bleeds
Be silent, my pitiful tear pleads;
Memories, sweet memories,
Deep down my soul dwell
Cherished through heaven and hell.

Omshanti Mocherla

My Father, And I, Window Keeper

She stood lost inside a window, eyes vacant and staring
there was no energy focusing from them. The panes were
clear inside and out, Her eyes that stared out were shrouded
with doubt. Silence was her only friend, and shame kept
her a liar, lost you might say from day to day, she eluded
everyone who wanted to hold her captive, by being an easy lay.

Silence was His protection, the pane was Her shield,
her hot, prickly tears only meant displeasure for Them,
so close your eyes and let your soul drown, ease the frown
for nothings changed, so cry, cry little child.

Fear not, he's only touching her body, he ripped her,
he tore her until he was spent. She dwells inside the pane,
as she watches him take her body but not her soul, how she
loath's him. Is this all her life really meant, not worth
two cent.

Floods of memories sneaking about, just out of grasp, can
these be dreams or moments of wrath. Who is she, this captive
waif, if not in the window, some looking glass.

Cynthia Reola Taylor

In The Line Of Duty

There was a cop, he was the best,
until a bullet ripped through his chest.

He thought he was cool shooting at his mark,
until a burning pain shot through his heart.

If he was smart, he would have stayed low
but instead he had to let his badge glow.

As he thought, he got upset. If only he had worn his vest,
the bullet would have come to a rest.

But he knew that he had done his best,
during this ultimate test.

It was a stormy night, a stormy night indeed,
but all he could do was lay there and bleed.

As the rain trickled down his face,
he wondered who would ever take his place.

As he lay there in the rain,
he lay there screaming in pain.

A light shot through his mind,
this he realized was his life.

The memories of his kids, and of his wife,
and of the job that cost him his life.

Ky Hamann

Do You Wonder

Do you wonder
What's going on ....
Do your eyes dream
Does your mind scream
Do your lips lie and does your heart cry

Do you wonder what you've done...
Do your eyes call
Does your heart fall
Do your tears fly and won't your feelings die?

Do you wonder what you can do ...
Do your eyes bleed
Don't your tears heed
Does your heart learn and do your eyes burn?

Do you wonder what you are now ...
does your throat ache
But does your voice break
Is your smile fake and does your body shake?

Do you know that guilt is forever?
Brandon Scheuerman

"The Last Days"

It is a time for love.
If we want that gift from above.
And before very long.
And after a while it will only be the strong.
We shall strive for peace,
for which we all shall seek.
Because now it is so much pain.
Yet through it all, there's nothing to gain.
This is now the last "days."
And we must try to change our ways.
For we try to hide our tears.
But then we must face our fears.
We must climb the rough side of the mountain.
If we are to ever find that true fountain.
Lillie Mae Hudson

The Wing Celebration

A special day for angels is the celebration of their wings.
A time to rejoice and happiness for the new angels that came to
the heaven.
After the celebration of a new comer, God came along and had a
talk with him
"For now my dear child you have your wings, you can do everything
including
Act like kings." "For I know you are only seven
And miss your family, you will love your wings."
"So my dear child have fun, be free fly any where."
"Any where in your mildest dreams you would like to go." "For I dare
But please beware of the danger you might get in, "and child of mine
Enjoy your wings and the time you have with them."
Katie Gardas

Ministry Of Class

I have made mistakes in time
learned to love and hate
and looked for guidance through
Jesus Christ my Lord
I have found the way
My life is full of grace
It took only moments to open the door
and find salvation through
Jesus Christ my Lord
Now, everything I do and every thing I say
have spirits of love through
Jesus Christ today.
Joe McGaha Jr.

Single Dad

First light, morning time, get up and start the day.
Check the boys, cover them up, let them sleep some more.
"Rise and shine, rub those eyes, cartoons and breakfast are on."
"Brush your teeth, comb your hair, put down the toy,
where's your books?"
"Have a good day at school." "Have fun at pre-school."
Now's my chance to do what I do.
"Hi Jimmy, how was school? Any homework? Let's get it done.
If you need any help let me know."
"Hi John, how's my boy? Did you paint me a picture?
Let's put it on the 'fridge door."
Free time outside; "I've got the bat, Jimmy's got the gloves,
now where's the - whoops there goes John with the ball.
Sun goes down, toys to put up, "Get your 'nite clothes and
jump in the tub."
"Supper's on." "This is good." Clear the table, now time for T.V.
9:00 "Time for bed." covers up, "Good nites and love you's",
and a kiss on the head, "Sweet dreams little men." Shut the door.
A little time to my self, get things ready for tomorrow,
check the boys one more time.
Little angels asleep, now's my time to rest and get ready
to do it again.
James E. Green Jr.

What Is Life?

Life is a precious gift, given by the good Lord above.
Life is full of wonderful things, peace and joy and love.
What will you do with this precious gift,
for yourself and others? What is your purpose, your destiny,
if not to love your brother?
We tend to cast aside the things we cannot touch, feel or see
The trials of life that we often suffer are
what we made them to be. Though life is full of ups and downs
and you seem to be getting pulled under.
When we show resistance to what we can change,
Well, is there any wonder?
We must accept what we cannot change and
change the things that we can.
Control lies deep inside ourselves and our fellow man.
Search deep down within yourself,
your body, your mind and your soul.
The treasures that you'll find inside cannot be brought and sold.
As much as we wish that the world were perfect,
we know that it really is not.
Just remember that you must humble yourself,
and keep your feet on the solid rock.
Sharon McKnight-Miles

Things Change

My friend called last night
But it wasn't the same.
We tried to talk for a while,
But who is to blame?

Who is to blame for us going our own ways?
As life gets more hectic in these fast paced days
With kids to raise and bills to pay,
We seldom have time to listen to what others say.

We talked about music, about some past fun
We talked about others, and about that "one".
We talked about good times, we talked about bad
But then I realized it's not what we once had.

Am I to blame for leaving our home town?
I tried to stay but it kept bringing me down.
To stay in that town would be such a shame
Is it him or me who's really to blame?

He sees things his way and I see things mine.
Is this friendship over? Is it a matter of time?
My friend called last night,
But it wasn't the same...
Curtis Jones

Escape To Monroe Mountain

When life closes in, my mind runs away...
To the top of the world, to run with the deer.
The trees tower above me, whispering my name,
A message from God that I can't interpret.
I wander across wide mountain meadows
Splashed with a rainbow of dew-tipped wild flowers
Memorials to all who went before.
I stand on a rugged granite ledge
Gazing at the signs of man far below
And stand in awe of the masterpiece I'm in.

Sandy L. Roberts

Oh No!

I tried to fly but instead I jumped right on my father's head.
He fell head over heels, then slipped on banana peels.
He made popcorn which I hit, and it fell on his baseball mitt.
I was punished, sent to my room, had to clean up with a broom.

Courtney Sender

The Eyes Of A Child

Oh, to view the world through the eyes of a child
How carefree and gay life could be
To understand little, but imagine so much
Such wonders and sights we would see.

Consider a boy as he stalks through the trees
He just knows that a tiger runs wild
With a mighty leap he grabs the great beast
Who then barks and kisses the child.

Or imagine the play of a little girl
As she dresses her friends for a tea
Her pink stuffed elephant and calico cat
In her mind are as live as can be.

The Lord gave a gift to the innocent babe
When He did, I'll bet that He smiled
For a brief, shining moment in our walk through life,
We'd view the world through the eyes of a child.

Melody Frerich

Constance

A fair young maid from London, England, sad to leave her land,
Constance Hopkins wore a gold bracelet on her small, pale hand.

All aboard the Mayflower, heading toward a distant shore.
Constance slept on a narrow pallet on a dirty, wooden floor.

Young Francis used some gunpowder to set a storage room ablaze.
He got in lots of trouble and could not sit down for many days.

Finally settling in Plymouth because it seemed so very good,
It had a lot to offer settlers including water, fish, and wood.

The first months were difficult, many got sick and died.
But Mr. Hopkins survived the illness with Constance by his side.

When everyone was better, and the sickness was over and done,
The friendly Indians helped plant crops in the warm spring sun.

Pumpkins, corn, and beans—harvested in the late, fall weather.
Pilgrims and Indians ate the first Thanksgiving feast together.

Minnetuxet, Samoset's girl, wanted Constance as her good friend.
They gave each other presents; their happy feelings had no end.

When Constance got older, and it was almost time for her to wed,
She could not decide between Stephen, Nicholas, or even Ted.

Finally one day Nicholas convinced Constance to be his wife.
She would live with him, have children, and love him all her life.

Julia McIlverey

My Shadow

Tonight I lie in my shadow. I
See nothing. I feel nothing. I know
the only one here is me and my shadow
If I could see it would be your
face. If I could feel it would
be your heart beat next to mine.
But it is so cold here alone with
just my shadow. There's no one
to hold so I do not move. My
shadow lies so very still as though
it is dead in its own dimension.
I feel as though if I were to get
up and leave the room the dark
image of myself would stay behind
in its peaceful slumber, never to move.
The sun begins to rise my shadow
fades slowly away. But I know
tonight I will once more lie
in my shadow.

LuAnn Thomas

Death: 1.2

What would it be like if I died tomorrow?
Would all my friends be filled with sorrow?
Would they be mad, sad, or maybe even a little glad?
Would the people who hate me, smile with glee?
Or, would they wish they'd been a little more nice to me?
What about my girlfriend, would she cry for a day or two?
Or, would she spend the rest of her life silently screaming
"I miss and love you!"
What about my family, would their eyes be filled with tears?
Or, would they wish they'd gotten closer to me in all my eighteen
    years?
What will life be like for my friends when I am gone?
Will it be easy or hard for them to move on?
What will life be like for the people to whom I am dear?
Will they all remember me with every falling tear?
These are the things I wonder being down to my last breath.
Knowing that the next passing moment will bring my untimely death.
The life is flowing out of me like water through a hose.
The world is starting to fade as my eyes begin to close.

Phillip Castro III

Brown Skin Girl

Gone are the days of being brown skin girl!
Gone are the days of being care free!
Gone are the days of being foot-loose!
And fancy free running in red clay of Alabama!

Gone are the days when Mama spanked me and big mama
baked sweet cakes and dried my tears!

Gone are the days of being brown skin girl
running in red clay of Alabama!

Here are your todays, growing up in the big city
with neon lights and cold empty nights.

No one to dry your tears, no one to shelter you
from harm.

Raised to be full of love and grace!
with a heart of gold!

Learning to be cold and warlike, to survive in
the big city with neon lights.

Here are your todays, gone are your yesterdays!

Being brown skin girl foot-loose and fancy free
running in red clay of Alabama!

Alberta Noelle Kent-Martin

Midnight Breeze

The last breath of a dying man
cascades unto the breathless night.
It sails free and unforbidden
out the window and out of sight.
Carried by a midnight breeze
over trees and through hens.
Slowly drifting by a nest of bees
and through a flock of sleeping hens,
It encounters other breaths of other souls
some drifting slowly and others speeding by.
Some breaths whisper about burning coals
and others just don't reply.
Some even sense the timid wind
and others know nothing at all.
When at last it reaches the end
where strange voices alike do call,
it rest upon many a strange voice
to be carried away by choice.

Andy Simmons

Tears In The Night

You see me crying,
And you think you know why,
But, in reality, you only know what can be seen.

Have you ever stopped and asked yourself,
Is this the only time that I have cried?

I cry all the time,
So quietly at night,
That you never notice.

Did you know that?
No! You did not!
You do not know anything.

You see only a third part of me
You will never know me completely.

You think I trust you,
But I do not.

You want to know why?
It's because the things I have to say,
You will never understand.
Therefore why waste my time!

Nancy Sanchez

My Angel

The night is cold and dark as I'm lying here in bed;
The halls are oh so quiet, the sound that I really dread.

The doctors don't have to tell me, I know I'm very ill;
Needles and tubes are everywhere, I must lie very still.

As I stare at the ceiling praying, 'God please see me here;
Please take away this pain I feel, please take away this fear.'

I push the button for the nurse, 'Oh please don't take too long;'
Her shadow appears at my door, her angelic voice sings like a song.

Her love and caring comes shining thru, as a deep inner glow;
The warmth within her was so great, it would melt the falling snow.

Her touch was soft and gentle and oh so very kind;
She looked at me with loving eyes, and eased my troubled mind.

She stayed by me thru those nights, I didn't have to ask;
Thru my eyes I could see, she didn't mind this task.

Her smile protected me, through those long and lonely nights;
God sent this special angel, to ease my pain and frights.

This angel cares for others now, as I know that this must be;
But I know now and always will, God sent her just for me.

Becky Marsh

Tiny Coffin

Wherein a humble heartbeat dwells
Swing softly in the wind
Sing softly in the wind
And on the morrow
With dew drying in the sun
Crack and send forth
Two small awakening senses
Touching first the hardness of the shell
Then the emptiness of freedom
Strength and promise
come out slowly in the rebirth of a gem
Slowly unfurls the light of a thousand rainbows
Following a rain of midnight dew
Dried and kissed by the wind
And lifted within the day to grace
The air and face of the earth
With beauty for as long
As the passing of a whisper

Mary Ann Bryce

Pathways Of Society

Black...
White...
Purity, innocence, angelic, untouched, love
Evil, deception, tainted, unholy, hate
Are the lines visible?
Are the pathways clear?
Do we know which is which?
Is the world really grey?
A painter told me...
Grey is only a mixture of black and white.
What colors do you see?
Which path will you take?
...
Has my pathway already been paved?
Because the patterns on my face?

Joy Hayes

The Land Within My Dreams

I stand without motion and yet I am flying.
I glimpse at a world so lively yet crying.
Of what do I cry has never been foretold.
But out of its whispers comes life of strong hold.
I wonder through a valley so beautiful in sight.
And yet when I touch I feel only my might.
I sense an essence of beauty filled with desire.
And out of its anguish I begin to tire.
Vivid is the image that is seeking its place.
Black is the object that confronts me at face.
What is happening to my state of dreams?
Am I losing control of my own means?
For many years have gone by in spite.
Though I have been here for only a night.
And yet I wake up to start another day.
Thinking about last nights great delay.
And all in all I come to stand.
As a single motion, in one vast land.
The land of paradise I have so often seen.
The land that dwells within my Dreams.

Waldy Charles

Bye

Bye is forever or far, far, away.
Just the same as never ends day after day.
Bye is the moment when everything is over.
When one wish is made on one four leaf clover.
Bye is when you kiss and do not tell.
The word that could send us all straight to hell

Kara Eileen Garrity

To See Me

Surprise!
Surprise, to see me
Do you recognize thee
For I have no tears.
My face has no expression

My body, my mind feels no pain
I'm not sure if I still feel you.
For I am light, I am free, the wind is
beneath me.

My music is like me. Listen hear me sing.
No longer can I be heard.

Darkness, I see is all around me
I'm a woman, a queen. A king by my side.
Happiness is finally approaching

I can be anything I want to be
When death takes over me.
I no longer have to care if love cares for me
   Jeanette R. Kirkendoll

The Raincatcher

He lived in the raincatcher
Up on a puddle upon a hill
From where the told me a lie,

That my life is as short as an oyster shell.
I know it, my love, know too well.

But I remember the day in some forlorn shore,
I screwed off my head with my own two hands
And drinking the fluid warm from my neck,

Rejuvenated.

Softer flesh in the sand, with its squinted eyes,
I have seen the westward sun and its skinny ladder descend.

My God, am I to go?
Yet I heard my little friend call from his raincatcher faraway.

   Where do you think you are going?

My eyes have become accustomed to the rays,
That deflecting my gaze to the earth,
I could no longer see.
   Moéeno Wakamatsu

R.I.P.

A twisted demented body lays upon the green grass ground
Blood seeps from a flesh wound in the chest running rapidly down
A decaying corpse lays paralyzed hour upon hour
Waiting for the starving earth to devour
Pale, cold, flesh lays in a concealed box
Wrapped in chains and air sealed locks
A demented face of our human race
Just another moribund case
Family and friends weep upon this day
For a beloved soul has passed away
Dressed in black and veiled disguise
Dark gray clouds fill the skies
A mystic fog rises from the grave
People walk off into a misty haze
For today another soul was unleashed
May it forever Rest In Peace
   Jason Senior

It's Springtime!

It's springtime, it's here!
The bluebirds are singing again.
It's time to wake up from snowy slumbers,
Time to do things again.

The flowers are blooming,
Oh so pretty they are!
I was waiting for this moment,
When it was so near, and yet so far,

Now the summer sun approaches,
Bugs and bees with it too
"Yea!" the kids say, "There is no more school!"
"No more homework that we must do!"

Here it comes, it's fall.
It's when the leaves turn different ways,
Red, orange, brown, and yellow,
Not green as it was in those Mays.

It's snowing outside!
And it's winter you know,
But now the year is over,
From its head, to its snow!
   Jennifer Alyono

A Christmas Sonnet

An angel spoke that night so long ago.
Appearing to shepherds on the Judean plain
He said, "Fear not," and spoke of peace that reigns
When good will in the hearts of men does flow,
And of a joy for each one of us to know.
Where is the good will that hearts should contain?
Where is the peace that is meant to conquer pain?
The Peace on Earth, among men here below?
Guns still resound. Tears mingle now with mirth.
Our hearts cry out to you, Lord, for release.
Bring peace to our hearts, our time, our earth.
Show men that love could cause the wars to cease.
Oh, let this Christmas time of our Lord's birth
Be a new beginning of joy, of love, and peace!
   Ruth H. Pearson

Along The Colorado

I wandered through this mystical land, just like a Nomad with sack in hand.
   Amidst this tranquil scene of splendor, raging rapids threatened plunder.
Seeking respite from the heat of day, enjoying the beauty of nature's array.
   This panoramic view so splendid, a palette of hues subtly blended.
My body weary and needing rest, I set up camp on a lethal cliff's crest.
   Quietly, like a thief in the night, a curtain of darkness draped over our site.
Do not whisper, for you may miss, smells and strange noises in this black abyss.
   Days filled with wondrous sights, watching in awe at the Bald Eagle's flight.
Artifacts found in red canyons and caves, told visual stories of long-ago Braves.
   I rode that demon river, my canoe and I,
spine running acquiver, for she was not shy!
   A battle we fought. This vortex and me, but when it was over, I was the victor, not she.
   One day I hope again to travel to this magical place in the sun, ride those rapids one more time and when the race is won,
   know in my soul when all's said and done, this is nature in all her glory,
who, if she could speak to me in words, would relate her secret story!
   Joyce De Cesare

Grandmother

Inquisitive fingers
touch the fullness of her long gown
almond-shaped eyes reflect in the mirror
with childish awe

A lacy hood rests atop her chestnut hair
the fragile beauty of her maiden years
embroider emotions, forever gone
    Kathlyn Regina

"Spring Follows Winter"

The days are short and the nights are long,
with many tears cried before the dawn.

The sky is gray when winter is here,
but, sun and warmth will again be near.

As sure as death follows life,
the darkness comes with the night.

But, oh, we know that life follows death,
and joy returns after tears are wept.

Spring will follow the cold of winter,
new life from within, then will enter.

The sun will warm and brighten our days,
God will be with us, in so many ways.

So, as we go through the winter,
with its darkness and pain.

We know Spring will follow,
again... and again.
    Dottie Potter

True Love

I consider the stars
with their raging fury,
and our mighty hand
that made them burn for a million lifetimes.

I consider the sea
with its abundant life,
and our gentle emotion
that formed the delicate shell in my hand.

I consider myself
with my wonderful form,
and our marvelous wisdom
that above all our creation, gave only me the mind to consider.

I consider You
with Your might and emotion and wisdom,
and Your deepest love
that gave me the life of Your only child.
    Dave Carlile

I Remember My Love

I remember the night's cold air
I remember the mist from the ground as the earth cooled itself
I remember the music as it danced around the trees and grass with glee
I remember the lights from the candles as they flickered in your eyes
I remember how the lights in your eyes lead me to your soul and your
   soul to mine
I remember how our souls became one
I remember my love
    Kimberly Castelo

A Different Kind Of Me

I'm so different from all the rest, no one holds patience as I do.
And gives all things time to work out for the best, yet my garments the same as you.
For my eyes, they sparkle with an angelic gleam, unintentionally enhancing those who look.
Open are my ways, conniving deeds aren't me, look inside, inside my book.
For my pages are long with the way I feel, free is my style copying none you see.
Talking to people, finding out what makes them flow, that's what sets me free.
So open your eyes my friend, bats could see my difference, if you only knew.
When you say he's the same, don't second guess, check a little deeper, don't settle for less.
Unique as I am. I'll always be, so different I am, you'll never see————a different kind of me!
    Andre Bel Cher

"Mystery's Shadow"

Worlds beyond and ages passed,
To us a shadow on them is cast;
We cannot learn so easily
Of things that we do know to be.
We know they exist, now or then,
Galaxies are out there, times have been;
And yet our view of them is blocked,
A treasure chest that's sealed and locked.
When will our world find the key
To open up the mystery
And tell of what goes on out there
Far above earth's atmosphere?
Seeing, what has occurred 'fore us
And goes on in what surrounds us,
Can only be images now, in our minds
A mystery unknown, that binds
us to believe.
    Talia Vestri

Mom@AOL.COM

Tears on my pillow, lumps in her bed.
Finding the "empties" is the thing that I dread.

Craving to love her like no other.
But still wondering, "Is she my mother?"

Listening to the arguments over and over.
Would they still happen if you were sober?

I try not to be rude, my feelings I hide.
I try because I know it's her deep down inside.

Her bottle, her companion, alone in her room.
Dreaming the dreams that will never quite bloom.

She says she's going to try to stop, but I know that's a lie.
Although it never quite happens, she always seemed to try.

I know she really cares, but when she drinks it seems to fade.
It's hard to comprehend this with the new mother she has made.

It seems whenever she is angry, she always takes it out on me.
With all that it hurts me inside, she never seems to see.

She blames "it" on my father, the problem she tries to hide.
When you bring "it" up to her, the problem is denied.

Come home now, Mother, before the memories go.
And this will be the tale of childhood- all I'll ever know.
    Robin Mainini

S.W.F.

It's so hard to go back out there
Into the crowd of countless faces
With their painted on smiles and their lists of expectations
All looking for handouts, all waiting for reservations
For a way out here

I've got empathy, feelings, fear and pain
Attachment, comfort, lust, ego, and hate
All of which can pass for love

I've got a listeners ear, a guilty conscious
A plastic smile, and a genuine shyness
All of which can pass for kindness

I've got nice clothing, a nice care
And manners when I need them
I think about presentation, and not only on the weekends
All of which can pass for class

So if there's anybody out there who fits the description
call the number above
I hope you pleased with your decision
I have all that you need, I've made all the provisions
Just make the call and help on my mission
Austin Dames

Love Hurts

You've been here forever;
But only in my mind;
Yet little did I know what a beauty I would find.

You made me feel like no one before;
You made this world seem fair;
Only you could make this happen;
Only you could make me care.

Then I finally realized;
When I woke and you weren't here;
You never loved me anyway;
So I shed a single tear.

I wasn't there in your time of need;
So he gladly filled my place;
Now my heart is aching;
It's broken by empty space.

You were my destiny, that's what I thought;
Now you have said "Good-bye";
A lesson learned, by shattered hopes;
Who says, "It can't hurt to try"?

Love Hurts!
Robert B. Redd

The Flower

The morning sun rises,
The world wakes.
The little flower stretches out its energized arms-
Its petals begin to open, exposing eyes of wonder.
For it is a new day with new experiences.
The soft breeze spreads the wondrous aroma, while the flower just watches the day go by.
It witnesses children's laughter, the innocence of first love and the renewal of everlasting love-
Yet, the flower just sit there. It just watches until it is time to close those tired eyes until a new day.
Tara Blitz

"Love Eternal"

The earth shall be my body,
So that it may worship you.

The night shall be my soul,
So that it may comfort you.

The stars shall be my eyes,
So that they may look upon your radiance.

And the wind shall be my kiss.

These things I promise you
Always and forever.

So that you know that,
My love is eternal.
Dawn LaGoy

The Beautiful Woman

Golden strands...the color of wheat
blowing in the mid-summer, morning breeze.
Brown skin, brushing away the tendrils
that fall, into the pools of...
liquid green.

Like a gazelle...long legs
sinewy muscles,
gracing the earth's crust.
Seeming to look as fragile as a rose,
in full bloom.

Yet...with spirit as strong
as the thorns upon the stem.
Pricking your heart,
to the depths of her love.

She walks alone.
In her world, of beauty
and pain.
Bending down...to touch you,
the lowly dog.

Then rising and walking on.
Marie Theres Heinemann

"Rising Above The Horizon"

Does anybody know when the unexpected might happen?
Like a snow storm in spring,
Or a long shot that wins.
Life is never just the same old thing.

Of course, it is only natural to fear change.
Routine and safety go hand and hand.
Tension fills my veins whenever I meet somebody strange,
And my stomach feels like a feather sucked in by a fan.

Suddenly, the awkwardness is broken!
I should never have worried.
All it took was for a few words to be spoken,
Reducing the large flakes to a small flurry.

Sure, I am wiser for my courageous act
Which brought interest to my otherwise dull day.
Starting a conversation does not require a great deal of tact.
What is the worse that someone could say?

I doubt that anything will be different the next time around.
Shyness will always be a part of me,
But my trait brings pitch to an ordinary sound.
Expanding my small river to a large sea.
Jonathan Plattel

Dreams

Dare I hope?
Dare I dream?
Dare I have a goal to be got?
Dare I aspire to new heights
Though my checkbook dictates not

It is true that life's a stage
An unfinished book
With your experiences to be
Recorded on each page

To strive and achieve
To struggle and obtain
Aah yes, it is one life's sweetest gains

So yes! I dare to hope
Yes! I dare to dream
Yes! I dare to have a goal
For in pursuit of such things
There's a revealing of one's soul

Alasha C. Williams

A Sonnet To My Cat

My dear cat, as I sit and watch you dream,
I often wonder what you dream, you see.
Your eyes sky blue, your fur of milky cream;
Your thoughts continue still to elude me.
You toss and turn and twitch your little nose;
Your face displays a childlike smile.
Contort your body in a playful pose,
I wish to sit and watch for awhile.
Your face reveals curiosity,
Every movement is a trick on my mind.
You paint a picture of serenity,
My heart grows fond just watching you, I find.
   Continue to dream and smile and play
   and I'll continue to wonder and stay.

Margaret Coon

Our Little Patrick

A little boy Patrick has gone to Heaven.
In a couple of weeks he would have been seven.
We wonder why God took him that day;
Why he didn't want him to stay.
He needed an angel, a very special kind,
One that was very hard to find.
A boy with love and a joyous smile,
Who was happy and thoughtful all the while.
One with two brothers who liked to play,
To love and fight and do as they say.
With parents who loved him day after day,
And he cherished and loved them in his own way.
Yes, God wanted a dear little boy,
Patrick was chosen like he'd pick out a toy.
The brightest, the sweetest, the strongest I know.
He was the one God chose to go.
Now he's up in the Heavens so high,
So hold back the tears and try not to cry.
God took him fast that fatal day,
He didn't suffer in any way.
So as he lies in the heavens above —
Patrick will send us all of his love.

Mary Nipper

Valley In The Clouds

Valley in the clouds
Savor the grounds of the great beyond.
Adventure through the valley in the clouds
Essence of the natural.

Alma P. Sanchez

Oceans Of Love

Oceans of Love are either far or near.
There are many oceans full of love,
One for you and one for me.
In order to survive in this world
You must be able to swim in your ocean.
In each ocean, there is a single fish
Which will be your partner for life,
And a lot of others which are merely,
acquaintances.
Your single fish has to be a born swimmer,
in your ocean.
With no oceans full of love, this world
would not continue.
So swim the rivers of hate till you find
you ocean of love.

Christina Baker

The First Crusade

Who can call them by name
the children and aged women
who prepared for war

Who can count the virgins, like
old men with swollen bellies
and serpent tongues, that swore

Who can demean the women's
suffering brought on by untimely labor,
so sore

Who remained all naked on the
plains without bestowing a
thought on their new-born that lives no more

Baron Norman Sylvester III

The Rose

The white rose I place in this vase today.
Is in loving memory of you, my dear Mother who's gone away.
I feel your presence with me looking down from above.
As today you know that my heart is overflowing with love.
I want you to know how special this man is to me.
He's as dear to me as you are in my memory.
I know you would approve of my choice for a mate.
It was God's decision and not just a matter of fate.
I wish you could be here to share this beautiful day with me.
But I am comforted to know that you are at peace with Thee.
You will always hold that special place in my heart.
That only a Mother could possibly be a part.
Thank you, Mother, for giving me my life.
From this day forward my solemn promise to you.
Is to follow your example as a loving mother and wife.

Bev Grossoehmig

Why Are Men This Way?

Why on earth are men this way? I don't know, it's hard to say.
They rob, they steal and act like thugs, they rape, they plunder
and abuse hard drugs. They lie, cheat and kill other men, this
has been happening since way back when...

Some men, they say are bad from birth, do you think that they
will inherit the earth? It seems like the nightly news is just
gore, loaded with violence, murder and more, and where are the
stories of love and good? Surely they happen in your neighborhood

It seems that men are fascinated with crime, gangsters and
murders and guys doing time. Somewhere, somehow we must have
gone wrong, because now we even depict it in song. Are citizens
aware or are they just blind? Could this be the end of mankind?..

What are the answers? It's so hard to say.
I just don't know why,
Men Are This Way.....

Richard K. Miller

"Take Flight"

Sometimes when life brings me down,
I want to soar like an eagle.

I would take off, take flight against the perils of the wind,
Cut through them like a knife, and never descend.

I would dive to meet the waters. Skim my feathers on the tide,
and then rise to meet the horizon meet the moon's crescent side.

I would sweep myself to Egypt.
See the pyramid's mythical sights,
then I'd journey above the canyons.
Roam freely through the nights.

I would ride a deadly waterfall, and drop falling free,
Then spread out my wings catch the breeze,
and follow through to the sea.

I would soar and kiss the sunset
Casting a shadow on the lake,
Somewhere, anywhere at all.
Next I'd romp through the golden haze,
Sit on a star, and then call.

Your dreams are the eagles,
Save the eagles, don't ever let them fall.

Jasmin Azurin Manalac

Evening Star

I sit here in awe as I look out in space,
each star is unique with its own special place.
God must love us dearly to go to such lengths.
whene'er we look up we find his perfect peace,

I'll just follow my savior as onward I pace,
loving neighbors regardless of colors or race.
My Jesus will lead me if given the chance,
so happiness here will be no happenstance.

Each man like the star has his special place,
each peacefully sharing in God's greatest grace.
He'll forgive us our sins if we ask and avow,
that we'll follow his word and trust him just now.

I am thankful that God in his awesome workings,
is always right there to redeem all our shirkings.
He will watch us renege on our promise each day
but his love will forgive each step of the way.

So I'll talk to my Jesus each day of my life,
trying hard to do what we all know is right.
My love I'll proclaim to whomever I can,
so all can see God in my actions and plans.

Virgil K. Brundage

He Was There

He was there that day
When the heaven, earth and the stars were made

He was there that day
When the sands, sea and the clouds were done

He was there that day
Through the hurt, happiness and the fun

He was there that day
When the lion, lamb and the man walked through

He was there that day
At calvary through the hate, scorn and the pain you see

He was there that day
To die on the cross for the sins of you and me

Yes!
He was there that day
Forever the Lord Jesus with us will always stay

Joyce Digges Bontrager

The Legacy Of A Sailor

Abyss to Davey Jones locker, there me bones shall lie;
Stormy sea, a north wind blew, and sunk the ship and I.

Salty wind did we kiss, her lips of sea mist;
And down with the mast she blew, she took our sail,
With a wind straight from hell,
And swallowed me whole and the crew.

Spiced rum she'd not take, she left in our wake,
Our barrels and bottles of laughter;
To fool-hardy men who sing and sin
To find our cheer the day after.

Merry meet again she said, the sea she loves her men;
She'll swallow you whole, 'N'spit out your soul
For true sailors come back again.

Now we sailors return anew,
With respect to the sea we hail;
Naught lesson we've learned,
'Tis the sea that we yearn,
Straight into the gale we'll sail.

Christopher D. Hoover

The Eyes Of My Newly Adopted Son

I showed him the stars and his eyes remained sad,
I pointed out the moon and I did not get a smile in return,
We went to observe the fireworks
And his eyes opened wide with amazement
But when the last sparks went out his eyes were downcast,
As if ashamed of having shared the excitement of the crowd.
I told him about my love for him
And his eyes reflected disbelief and yet a glimmer of hope,
But soon his eyes again lost their gleam
And became indifferent and somewhat mean.
I gave him a hug and his eyes became suddenly relaxed
And filled with sleep.

Who caused you hurt my lovely little one?
How could you be unwanted my dear one?
May your dreams be sweet ones
And when you awaken
May you feel the love, care and trust
That you will always share with us.

Edith H. Saladen

The Morning Of The Sun

Dawn brings the beginning of a new day.
Everything is one day older and one day wiser.
Today is a day to learn and a day to grow.
This day inquiring minds will grow stronger and stronger.

As the sun rises, dew lies on the tips of grass;
A spider web glistens in the sunlight,
And people awaken and begin their daily routines
As squirrels, birds and all other great creatures and creations of
   nature arise.

As the sun rises and daylight becomes more and more plentiful,
The animals conceal themselves from the human world.
Our two worlds do not coexist in harmony.

As evening approaches, the sun begins to sink;
The owl and the other night creatures begin to emerge from their day
   of peaceful slumber.
The crickets chirp their lullaby, and
An owl sings a gentle song in her deep voice.

Mice scurry around and finally lie to rest for the night.
The owl and the cricket perform a serenade as the world sleeps.
The moon and the stars watch over us until the sun rises.

Katrina J. Raser

I Love You

If I said I love you to him,
would it make a difference?
Would he love me back?
Or would it be a mistake?
I can never tell him I love you,
because I can't say it to someone who can't love me back.
Tabitha Hacker

Killings And Murders

The gunshot so loud, I sat up in bed
I wondered whose bullet was in which person's head.
Crimes and killings happen every day.
I wish it would stop, wish it would all go away.

Not all killings are meant to be done.
Some of them happen when people are having fun.
A 17 year old took five lives last night.
Two boys and a sister, their eyes wide with fright.

Is it worth it, a few lousy drinks?
It could have been you! Why don't you think?

I couldn't imagine being that sad.
Not to have a brother and sister, a mother and dad.
Why do they use guns, alcohol, drugs and knives?
Why do they take something from people...
Something as precious as life?
Brittany C. Campbell

Darkest Hours

One day when the sky is full of glistening balls of light.
The moon beams stream across the land in the darkest hours of night.
The people from the stars above look down upon the earth.
They cast their spells toward everyone so no one will be hurt.
Their glitter flows across the land and sets our spirits free,
The sun wakes up our tired eyes and he said "come unto me".
I see a tunnel hollow as I drift through magic skies.
I see a man so peaceful for the give away were his eyes.
He takes hold of my hand but I cannot feel his touch,
And into a world of happiness by a single peaceful clutch.
Cynthia A. Torres

We Sand In The Shadows Of Our Futures

We stand in the sunlight
with the shadow of our future
lying right in front of us

You can't run away from your shadow
it follows you where ever you go

Sometimes I wonder
if my shadow will disappear
when the future comes

Everyone has a future
we just don't know what it is yet
hopefully everyone has a shadow to their future
to lead the way

We only have a few more steps to go
until we reach the end of our shadow
and we reach the doors of our future
although, they are big steps
if we just take our time
and help each other
each and every one of us
will find our future
Mary Katherine Griffin

What Is Hurt?

What is hurt?
Hurt can be physical
Hurt can be emotional
Is hurt physical or emotional?
What is hurt?

What is hurt?
Hurt can be physical
By the man physically beating the woman
By the sexual contact that is harmful
Is that what hurt is?

What is hurt?
Hurt can be emotional
By the man playing mind games with the woman
By the three emotions of the woman
Is that what hurt is?

What is hurt?
Hurt is physical at times
Hurt is emotional at times
Hurt is everything that causes pain
That is what hurt is.
Crystal Soule

Aliens

I had some visitors the other day
They came down from the skies
They spoke to me telepathically
Through their lifeless eyes
They said they wanted to do some tests on me
And take me for a ride
And in the next moment
We were whisked away
Just after I stepped inside
We flew so high
Into the stars
Far from the planet earth
I felt like I had been born again
This was a strange new birth
I had some visitors the other day
I was in for a hell of a ride
They told me they wanted their planet back
Meet you somewhere where worlds collide
William Womack

Nature Calls

The world turns and turns, but I don't feel it.
Why can't I feel the turning world?
Is it true that only with a buzz or more than that
I can feel the world spin around?
Then give me something, I want to feel,
I want to be part of the world.
I want to be able to close my eyes
and feel its roundness rotating in the vast Universe.
I want to fly, fly up high and touch the stars.
Go star hopping, and finally build my nest on the moon.
I want to be free, I want to free my soul.
I want to become one with the elements of nature.
I want to be wind, fire, water.
I want to be a raging storm in the middle of the ocean.
I want to be you, I want to be me.
I want to be free.
Gabriela Lecaro

Oneness

My angel spirit comes to me in brief moments,
At times of waking, I hear her call.
She calls and I respond by knowing that she is there.
A lovely feeling comes over me, like a refreshing breeze,
And I feel a kind of security that only belief can know.
Life goes on, maybe in pure thought —
Maybe in a shadow edged in sunshine —
Maybe only in brief milliseconds of knowing.
   My angel hovers.
Like distant music, I hear and feel the vast existence
Of all the knowledge of the Universe,
And I am not afraid, for I know that all is one,
   And one is all.
Evelyn Lawrence

The flower

It looked up at the sky
tall and proud
looking at all the rain clouds.
It had been awhile since it last rained,
So it needed more water to get on with the day.
It watched and watched as it looked up at the sky,
And at last it saw a flash of light.
Then came the rain harder and harder,
and it dreamed the sensation of getting taller and taller.

When at last the rain quit and the sun rays poured,
It felt that sensation it was waiting for.
Erin Fuhrhop

A Chance

A chance at love so seldom do we get
yet time does pass, unwilling hearts ablaze
for what was meant to be the day we met
compelling thoughts of beauty I do gaze.
A stir to break the silence I did try
but fears arise when love eclipse the heart
emotions fade with guilt; unpleasant cry
ascends to biter heights, I'm torn apart.

A love afraid to carry out its deed
will hide among the shadows of the night
until your love descends to plant the seed
that harbors such young love to soon unite.
Although an interlude is all I miss
enchant me now - for once a little kiss.
Philip Assem

Ladies Of The Season

Spring skipped on the scene
With the splendor of green finery'
Spraying the earth with wild flowers.

Summer danced in, generously yielding
Warm sun rays to mother nature.
Bringing forth the maturity of seed.

Autumn graciously approached the land with
Subtle golden hues, whispering softly,
Time for dormant sleep.

Winter demanded entry with howling winds
And angry clouds, pouring forth heavy rains.
But left with dignity, a white wonderland of snow.
Rosemary Vowell

August 18th, 1993

Tonight my heaven crashed and broke into a million pieces.

From down here, the sky was a pool of shooting stars
for but one person to wish upon.

A Silence, years in the grave, deep below the earth—
deep below my world of existence,
was broken...

And his was too.

Like two veins embracing the human heart,
we once together lived and travelled,

On a journey towards that which gives us life...together,
you and I.

Now we are but lost soulmates, my Friend and I,
linked together by a bond I did not wish for,

I did not want.

And now, I must bare his burden sweetly,
and I must hold his hand tightly,
and I must love his being completely,

My precious love...

And I must let go.
Christen M. Sherman

The Ripple Effect

One by one, gently, that seems to be my call to serve.
Not to make major impacts on society.
Rather, to touch in solitary ways
   that will ripple on and on throughout eternity.

A small encounter here,
A loving acceptance there.
Not concerned with results but attuned to the moment's need.
God will do the rest; God provides the ripple effect.

As in centuries past
   seven loaves became twelve baskets left-over.
Five fish fed the multitudes.

I am small; I am weak.
Just a single, individual human.
But God provides the ripple effect.
Marie R. Petrie

To Love You

To love you, What is it to love you?
The Joys, The excitement, the uplifting rush.
It's the hush in the night, in the quiet moonlight.
It's in the day that all seems to crumble.
I will always love you.
To love you, is to love you the way the are,
not to change any of you.
For I fell in love with you the way you are,
To love you.
I love when you hold me, tender and near.
When I'm in your arms the world's not there,
there's nothing to fear
I will always love you.
To love you is to love you all the day long,
When you're not near.
To hold that little piece of you so close to my heart-
to love you my dear——
I will always love you.
Wanda Jean Lange

Star Gazing

Electric star, very near and so far.
Eloquently wondrous, attired in such glistening dress.
Gleaming rays, kissing nights and days.
Goodnight and good morning, rising and falling without warning.

Living and dying, dying and living again.

Stars up above, in you I sense Divine love.
As the oceans waves roar and heaven's skies pour,
my soul is bequeathed by thee, sweet tranquility.

Diamonds blessed by The Lord; trust, faith, endless sentimental
wonders and soul nourishing treasuries; these tiny radiant astral
afford, while invoking existential memories.

As angels tease and sparkle upon the star's face
   human beings become enchanted and beckoned by their grace.
Electric star, Dear Lord sets thy beauty afire
   knowing full well the magnificence of these beauties, will capture
   the heart's and soul's desire.

To hopefully live life fully, as accomplished and morally as can be,
   while looking beyond the stars of night, into eternity.
To grasp each moment of precious time, which like a specific star
   in heaven, The Lord designated as mine.
   Laurie DuMesnil Reisch

The Loss Of A Loved One

It is hard to get over the loss of a loved one,
You think life is over when actually it's begun.
You think hard and so very long,
To think if there is something you've done wrong.
After a time of crying, agony and pain,
You're weak and all your strength begins to drain.
You think back once again to a time before,
All of the things that you did and once more.
The tears begin flowing not of pain but relief,
Of a time that once was with memories beyond belief.
The walks in the park or singing in the rain.
The picnics in the sand or rolling in the grain.
So keep these memories close at heart,
Never let anyone tear them apart.
Love them always and keep them near,
And if by chance you should hear.
A little voice inside your heart,
Think of that special one and you'll never be apart.
   Cheri Johnson

Because You Told A Lie

You once said your love for me will never end.
You told a lie now, all I do is cry
You said we were through
now I feel like a fool.
I gave you the key to my heart,
you stabbed it, threw it, and tore it apart.
I bought you a ring
and treated you like a king
And in return I was
treated like crap and thrown in a trap.
Even though this is hard for me
I know I have to let you free
Although my love will never die
but now it's time to say "Good-bye"
All of this because you told a lie.
   Monic Chaparro

Ol' Town

Its streets throbbed with life,
It lived, knew laughter, cried tears.
Men fought, lovers loved, babies born,
This sad ol' town of the yesteryears.

Once she was young as a tomorrow
She met each dawn with a taunting eye,
Sheltered its lovers, buried its dead,
All left when it begin to die.

Now she sits with the wind in her hair,
And coyotes play around her fingertips,
She waits for young lovers to come
And kiss her lonely, saddened lips.
   JoLee

"A Life's Treasure"

I've always treated my friends as rare gems that can only be found
in a secluded vault, treasuring each and every one of them,
holding them in the most important and privileged place in my heart,
while at the same time I search for love,
finding that with every broken heart and disappointment my friends
are by my side providing me with a shoulder to cry on
and a hand to hold through the recovery.
More than once I've asked myself
if within those friends I might find my one true love
only to realize that I'm not strong enough
to sacrifice the only sacred thing that I possess,
friendship, to set myself on an adventure
that might end with broken hearts and parted friends.
But once again I'm faced with a choice
that might have a tragic end.
Should I sacrifice a friend for the experience I've always wanted?
Is one of my most valued treasures worth the risk of it not being
love, but mere desire?
Would he venture with me,
or is friendship his biggest treasure too?
   Rocio A. Acosta

Death Is Calling

Death is calling, calling us near
We don't want to go, we have much fear.

Some people see darkness,
Some people see light.

Some see day,
Some see night.

Death is calling, calling us soon.
No one knows when it's going to come,
Morning, night, or noon.

Death is calling, calling out loud.
Will you see yourself in hell,
Or will you be in the clouds.

Death is calling, so you better get right.
People all over are dying, both day and night.

So when death calls for you, be sure that
   right, is all you know.
Because your soul lives eternal,
   where ever you go.
   Tarence E. Johnson Jr.

Silhouette of a Forbidden Love

True love has bestowed upon my heart
Searching for you, only an image appears
So vivid, for I know not who you are
Only who I want you to be
Desperately I reach out to touch you
Visualizing a life with you
A romance so enchanted....
It must be a fairy tale
Only an illusion of what I foresee.
My dream of reality
A tear escapes.....Trickles down my cheek
For too, I realize this is........
A silhouette of Forbidden Love.
Lisa Hedrick

Wild In A Field

I can differ greatly, like day and night,
From the darkest black, to the lightest white.

   Whether, massive in size, I'm tender at heart,
or small in stature, I'm loyal and smart.

   I can help with your garden and carry your loads
over the mountains and down the roads.

   When given the grains to make me healthy,
I can run like the wind, and make you wealthy.

   Shoes can be an option, if you care,
just be sure to buy me a double pair.

   I run and jump, and kick my heels,
as a way to earn my meals,

   Or prance and waltz with great pleasure,
to win the ribbons you so treasure.
Heather Reneé Montey

Who Am I

Who am I, forming from ashes, coming from the grave
Who am I, striped of identity and once a slave
Who am I, living in the dark and sometimes in the park

On the corner, in the projects, in the ghetto I dwell
Watchin' gangs, drugs and violence
What does it take to come up out of this hell

It's like a desert, always thirsty
A drop of water is what I need
A drop of light, a drop of love
Understanding, if you please

Blessed is this day, knowledge has come to me
'Bout some people of my past
Who were Rulers and Kings
Not always in the Ghetto
Not always in the dark
Ancestors, some scientists and doctors
Some even operated on the heart.

So, who am I, is the question
The answer is very clear
I am part of a people of a Great History.
Joan Muhammad

Her

She hath eyes of a raven and her beauty no less
Energy is abundance and her spirit doth show
Her mind is equal to none.
She bares the mark of one with gentleness and care
Yes her soul and grandeur are of the rare
She is one with yonder gift of giving her love so carefree
Now caught in mine own mind I stand decided
That her love has been given to me
James A. Hatfield

Untitled

As He brought forth this soul to be born
A grandfather had long lived forlorn
The years of toil he spent
Solely went to provide for rent

A mother gave her father news
For naught went not the life long dues
For the son he had sought was sent
An unyielding God did at last relent

A mother's youth was spared
By a loving God who showed he cared
A hardened heart's face
Was softened and made to smile by His Grace

A grandmother's loving ways
Shape and filled a life with loving days
Many times this life has flashed before my eyes
I wince as I recall The April eves of their demise

This hardened heart has since grown weary
Of endless nights with eyes red and teary
Pleading nightly on my knees
On the wind I can hear they walk with me thy soul be at ease.
George Falero Sr.

Precious One

What is a grandson? When he seems so much your own.
Then you have him with you for a weekend, then you have to take
  him home,
Oh! I know he hates to go, and yes, then I miss him so.
It's just that there has been so many changes, in his first eight
  years of life.
Bad marriages do put children, into a misunderstood amount of strife.
This little boy lived with us for almost three years.
I guess he loves us so, for we wiped away his tears.
He lives with and loves his mother now, who has another child and
  boyfriend.
He also loves and sees his Dad and new wife on Wed. night and the
  weekend.
Possibly a child to this union we can depend.
This little boy would love to stay here forever we know for sure.
Because, he knows we love him so, he comes first and our love is
  strong and pure.
And in this home with us, he feels at ease and secure.
Oh, my Children, how great it would be.
Two loving parents for you to see.
Together always would be great.
But children just know, sometimes this is fate.
Sometimes parents can't be together with you.
Just know, they both love you, and make the best of what you do!
Janet Druschel

Home For Thanksgiving

The home is a place for families to gather.
The home is for eating and sleeping and laughter.

The home is a fortress for sister and brother.
The home is cemented by the father and mother.

It's the home cooked food that makes one the fatter.
It's all the overeating that makes one the sadder.

It's turkey and dressing and all the trimmings.
It's fussing and discussing the family beginnings.

The table is set with flowers and food.
All the children come home in a good mood.

Nieces and nephews and cousins appear;
Some haven't seen each other in over a year

We almost forget their names and faces;
They are all scattered in so many places.

We will give thanks for everyone here,
And the ones who didn't make it, we pray they will next year.
Ted Parrish

This Will Remain

The joys of life are many if w count them one by one
If we remember for every drop of rain there is also the sun
Often it seems there are more losses than gains
But good always triumphs and this will remain

A heart can break and a tear will fall
And we wonder how to get through it all
Our lives become entangled and subject to change
But if we love one another this will remain

To have a dream is to live and to have grown
Despite discouragement the seed is sown
What we leave behind is the meaning of our name
The deeds we have done will remain

And in the end we know
There is a place where we will go
Where no more tears and only laughter reign
Forever this will remain
Robin Sorrick

Reminiscent

Dear God, I was so arrogant when I was young.
You were patient with me, you let me grow old.

My God, I remember another day,
when the sunlight flourished warmly
against my cheeks, in my ignorance
I was happy, I was so young.

It is evening now, I feel the cold.
The warmth of the sun is gone
and time sits heavy on my shoulders
like a coat too big for me.

I feel the loneliness now.
I need a friend to walk the last mile
with me. Then
I would say to the shadow
"Look! See my beloved!,
can you feel my joy!?"
Phillande C. Jackson Sr.

Poem For Ali - My Precious Dog

Ali, Sweet Ali, my comrade - my pal
your time with me was precious
because we really cared.
Your death was devastating, because
I loved you so. Your quiet acceptance
of your fate made it easier to let you go.
Thank you dear loved one, I wait for
the day, I will lovingly watch as you
Joyfully play. You and me, together
in Heaven, we will be, So Ali, my Ali
please wait for me.
Marie W. Summers

Adolescence

Inside her lies a frail little child
Terrified of life in the world all alone
Disturbed, she awakens yet stays mild
As she is protected by a pure stone
Armor, but one day it won't keep out pain
The armor will crack and abandon her
Trying to hide will perhaps keep her sane.
In need of love, her life remains a blurr
Her cloth of protection torn in pieces.
She is drawn to the unknown-the scary
Abyss. The current of fate now carries
her on flowing slowly-flight not merry.
Her future is unsure, her past is gone
All she has left is the new rising dawn.
Melina Pahigianis

Heaven Or Heartache

After many years of toil and strife,
The Lord steps in and changes my life,
A door is closed, another opened,
A funeral, a heartache, my son and I alone,
So I thought, and to my surprise,
A love I lost is now alive,
Life begins again, a second chance,
Or just faded dreams do I tend to enhance,
The love I bear my son is great,
He does not like the man I choose as mate,
I knew him before I married his dad,
The hatred I see in my son is sad,
Things settle down, a child is born,
Jealous of new brother and father alike,
Now surfaces anger, ill will and strife,
Life goes on you see,
For the Lord is not yet done with me,
From this love, a great pain to be bared,
Again a funeral, alone, two children scared,
Alone am I, no regrets, heaven or heartache I shan't forget.
Donna B. Poulin

In The Mist Of A Garden

In the mist of a garden grew
Two little seedlings pink and blue
Growing their roots firmly in the ground
And always so curious of things around
   Pushing their way up through the dirt
   Teasing each other which would be first
   Too busy to notice there were no weeds
   To busy for most things
   The two little seeds.
How the years rolled to quickly by
It was just yesterday to the Garden Bed's eye
Laughing at their branches playing with the breeze
Time is so short and none to spare
enjoy your seedlings while
They're still there.
   In the mist of the oak trees
   in the garden grew
Two little seedlings pink and blue.
Nina Gower Fraga

The Wind Blowing

   The wind blows backwards, that's what we say,
some remembering times of a long ago day.
One day it blows left, the next it blows right,
you don't know what to think, you don't know how to fight.
You wish it was then, but realize that it is now,
you try to face reality and beat this wind down.
It is too strong for us all,
We seek shelter behind our own wall.
This is because we don't want to see,
what this great mighty wind is doing to you and me.
It's everywhere we go,
we all act like we don't know.
Of the dangers and hardships that lie ahead,
there's no place to turn to, so we've turned and fled.
Suddenly, it's coming from all directions, too much to bear,
so we drop to the ground and pretend not to care.
Megan Stamper

The Comet Hyakutake

It reigned supreme in all ages past
  A billow of white in the space world vast.
Like a mighty bolt from the hand of Thor
  The new found comet streaked by our door.
Stargazers throughout could see very clear
  On cloudless evenings as it drew near.
Like a fuzzy ball in a star lit night
  Our vision was strained as it came into site.
Never a lifetime of one thousand years
  Has one viewed a comet that seemed to trail tears.
Where did it come from, how did it form,
  Perhaps as explosion and great fire storm.
Although lost in eternity in some distant sky
  The comet Hyakutake will surely not die.
For all those that gazed on that wonder to see
  It touched deep inside, I know it did me.

D. James Czech

"Here I Am"

Here I am in my own little world,
surrounded by things I've known since I was a girl.
Sometimes I sit and think about the world ahead,
and I wonder about the things that will be said.

I know I should look forward to being on my own,
but I just don't want to do it alone.
Then I think about all my friends who have to do it too.
But I know that being a follower, is something I just cannot do.

When you are young, you are always protected, but being an adult
and doing things on your own are two things that are connected.
We try to shield ourselves from sadness and ignorance,
but around ourselves, there is no invisible fence.

We go through so many transitions and levels of life, and
sometimes things go right ... But other times all there is, is strife
We try to live up to other's expectations,
but we do always have our own personal limitations.

Life is not meant to be understood,
or lived in a certain way.
But all we can do ..
is just do our best, and live for today.

Kristy L. Autry

Nature...

I took a walk one day, in the power of my subconscious mind
Going any place at any time

This particular day I went to the park
I ran insanely up and down the hills
Every tree I came across I felt its bark
How strange it is I embraced the thrills

Nature didn't seem to mind as long as I took my time she was kind
So, I spread a blanket in her midst and lay cradled in her
giving breast

Giving us what we need to survive
Keeping us well nurtured and alive
All those who don't know her, treat her with disrespect
Unkindness rules the selfish neglect

She gives until she can't give anymore
Now all the avenues of help we can't explore
Her love turns to hate, and God orders her to show you your Fate

Panic and destruction across the land
Help will not come from any man
Come face to face with Fate......
It's all too late!

Zita Muhammad

The Holocaust Of Man

The sand is scorching her feet
Confused and alone
The matter crashes onto the beach
The only sign of life left in the world
It is all gone; everything is gone
Man's ultimate nemesis has won the war
We were oblivious to its power and it went feared by few
Until the nemesis destroyed itself
And left her holding the only beating heart in the entire world
The memory of the light haunts her
The blinding flash that lasted only long enough
To set fear and realization into the souls of man
And the blast that destroyed it all
All but her. One girl left alone to rebuild life
To rebuild the nemesis
She can't do it. Her feet hurt so much
So confused; so alone
She was glad when the blackness came
She slept for eternity. And with her went the world.

Elizabeth A. Kiser

A Feline's Triumph

Who is that kitty,
Lurking behind the door?
Eyes reflecting mischief,
Tail twitching on the floor.
  Who is that kitty,
  Ready to attack on "prey"?
  A swipe of the paws and gone in a flash.
  The kitty's way of play.
Who is that kitty,
Sitting innocently on the chair?
A vibrating purr, an appreciative rub.
"Oh, kitty! You never seen to be fair!"
  Who is that kitty,
  Whose affection is pure as snow?
  "Come here, my sweet little kitty!
  You're my kitty, that's all I need to know".

Olivia Li

Faith

Christ was born but now he's gone
And now we sing him in our song
He rose again on Easter morn
But left again to let us mourn
We pray to him both day and night
And when we die walk toward his light
Baptism to death all in God's name
Is it in God we trust or just his fame
We eat his body and drink his blood
Yet we swear in his name when we feel unloved
His music is played so beautifully
It's what makes the blind man see
Pastor's sermons are done so very well
The people want to hear what he has to tell
From 11-12 we sit there so good
Then after that we're not what we should
Good or bad Christians we are
Not realizing true faith is yet so far!

Jina Evelyn Olson

The Listener

"The Listener" is with me through the day.
"The Listener" is with me through the night.
He answers all my prayers.
He answers all my questions.
But one day he didn't answer my prayer
and I realized that not only I needed "The Listener"
but everybody else needed "The Listener"

Jennie Doris

The Secret Heart

The secret heart holds treasures rare.
Precious moments, beyond compare.
Secrets that are kept so well.
Gems of thoughts on which to dwell.
A childhood dream that time erased,
A sweet young love to take its place.
Friendships gathered through the years,
Treasured by the secret heart so dear.
Sad moments lost in time and space,
When joy and gladness take their place.
The secret heart keeps all these tucked away,
To ponder on another day.

Marie Fallon

Pocahontas

Once lived a young Indian girl who had the name of Pocahontas

She lived in Virginia where it was very mountainous

This young girl, saved the life of an
Englishman, by the name of John Smith

What happened that day was not a myth

She also saved his new English colony by
bringing them food
Without her help the colony wouldn't
have lasted, the colonists would have
unwillingly fasted

Later on, in Pocahontas's young life, she got
married and became John Rolfe's wife

She was baptized as a Christian, Rebecca
Rolfe was her new name, although her
personality remained the same.

Tammie Leonardo

A Special Bouquet Of Flowers

A rose does bloom in splendid beauty
And the fragrance fills the air.
Mary was a bright red rose
And spread beauty everywhere.

Gladiolas show an array of color
Radiant shades of royal blue.
These fragrant beautiful flowers
Gentle memories of mary renew.

An iris exposes dark purple
Displaying soft passionate splendor
When my eyes rest on the iris
It is sweet Mary that I remember.

The day before Mary left us
We talked about flowers of spring.
Now, while I pick flowers alone
Sweet memories of mary it brings.

As I stroll through the fragrant meadows
I can feel Mary's presence there.
The love of beautiful flowers
Is something we'll always share.

Kathleen A. Bruder

On Being Deaf

The ears catch words the mind can't hear
As flowing water meets a wall.
Silence, none but life-long silence,
Never a sound, nor hear a call.

Where lips from words in mottled form,
As speckled light through forestry,
The eyes deceive the lively mind,
Oh! Would not the ears be unchained free!

Frederick M. Brunn

When Our Eyes First Met

There's a hole in my heart so big that you can see,
an empty space in my hand where hers used to be.
People tell me that there's something missing in my smile,
and it's all because we've been apart for a while

When I look up in the sky it just doesn't seem as blue,
and the happy moments in my day are far between and few.
If I can't leave work on time, well I just don't seem to care,
there's no reason to hurry home if she's not there.

Did I speak instead of listen, and not hear what she had said,
or were there times she needed holding and instead I fled
Perhaps we had different feelings, or was it the ones I didn't show,
maybe her parents never liked me, I guess I'll never know

The most painful of all is to say goodbye,
and how it all happened you ask yourself why.
Life seems much too short and the opportunities few,
to find someone special and to say I love you.

But I would never give it back, not the pain or the hurt
and she can even keep my favorite blue stripped shirt.
Because what made it all worthwhile, what I never will forget,
was that wonderful feeling I had when our eyes first met

Stephen Maxson

The Eagle

Soaring high overhead,
I see a noble bird.
A vulture, I dread.

But it is not a feared creature.
It is the Eagle,
And it comes with better features.

Flying proudly around the sky,
He shows his awesome wings to the world.
Come to attack me, he will not try.

I wish I could be free!
Like the Eagle, as I please.
How glorious it would be!

Sarah Della Posta

The Forgiven Society

The children are excused because they are young,
the elderly because they are old.
The men excused by testosterone,
and the women by estrogen.
The killers are excused by abusive parents,
and irresponsibility by adolescence.
The black violence is excused by long, but not forgotten
    slavery,
and whites by greed.
And all we learn from our mistakes is where to put the blame,
and "didn't know any better" becomes a way of life.
Responsibility and accountability have been tossed out the
    window,
and we have become the forgiven society.

Victoria Westenhaver

I Like You

I like you
because beauty envies you;
I like you
for what you do to me when I'm with you;
I like you
because you bring up my inner most thoughts of you;
I like you
because people envy me for knowing you;
Now still I like you
because I never thought I would fall in love with you.

Elcio Chabla

Cobblestone

Never cared much for cobblestone, my boots they shift on the cracks...
Asphalt is hot and sinister, when the sun beats down on your back...
Concrete slabs and concrete lanes only cause feet to ache,
It's time like these when I wish the most for a path in the
   trees by a lake.

A simple path of dirt or sod, rock and bush and leaf...
A secret place of beauty, I know that path would lead...
The ground is softly yielding, to my gentle foot.
The essence is of tree barks, flowers, and root.

The beauty there; a spring, a brook, a gnarled branch of tree...
The beauty there; a searching soul about to be set free...
Then this beauty finds us, so regal yet sublime.
Under every rock and stump, and whispered through all time.

An endless quest of man and God, together they must be...
What a better place to find them,
   Than a path-by a lake-in the trees.
   R. M. Green

The Last Tear

As the last tear rolled off my cheek
I turned away and heard him speak
He told me how sorry he was
And how he would always love me just because
He told me I needed somebody better than him
I told him the chances of finding someone else
are very, very slim
And then I turned and looked at him and began to
speak
As the last tear rolled off his cheek.
   Aimee Wilkinson

Love Is

Love is the excitement I feel when I look forward to seeing you.
It is the feeling of longingness when you are away.
Love is your gentle kisses and soft caresses.
It is my heart calling out to you.
Love is you being the picture of my dreams.
It is making these dreams together.
Love is being crazed by happiness.
It is being able to look into each other's hearts.
Love is what makes me happy even when I am sad.
It is what brings us together as one.
Love is all these things and much more,
But most of all Love is the friendship and
   devotion that I share with you.
   Ronika Patel

Seasons In Maine

There are four seasons in a year,
The longest is when Winter's here.
Winter in Maine is always cold,
But in southern states, is warm as gold.

After Winter follows Spring,
You never know what it brings,
Many changes during these months,
Two more seasons and you can hunt.

It is warm, Summer is here,
To me, the best time of the year.
During this season, there's plenty to do,
To be bored or have fun, it's up to you.

Get out the rake, it is Fall,
Time to work there's wood to haul.
Vacation is done, school has started,
The Summer fun has now departed.
   Ryan Giambattista

War

Combing a path through which many have crossed
lifeless bodies overturned with eyes that silently cry out in fright
foreboding their destinies that others have chosen
to ascend to the heavens of the rich and the poor
hopeful to restore existence to a world in which they have become invincible
the democracy by which they have lived
an authority far greater than theirs
with far less morals than they
have ended a life that was theirs, they thought
to rectify the tears of grief and disillusionment
sounding from the hearts that have perished into the white water brook.
   Jenna Raygada

The Candle

As I watch it burning shorter until nothing is there
I can feel its life flowing into the tranquil air
The light it gives off is for us to take for our own
But nothing can be returned,
For it dies, and it's fire we are loaned
Something that is so beautiful, we take it away so many times
Just watching it wither with the hourly chimes
It's going fast and another we must take
Having the wax flow into another melted lake
Seeing it there I cry into the wind that carries it away
Watching it perish without another breathing day
The feeding of human parasites and I am the host
Clinged onto by society as jelly to another piece of toast
All I have to show for this lifetime of constant attacks
Are the ashes I have given and my lake of melted wax
   Jeremy L. Noland

The Kiss

Twelve o'clock, the noises of the hospital begin to subside
Somewhere a patient moans and somewhere, far away, a baby cries
Silently, the nurses make their midnight rounds, murmuring
   goodnights
the clocks on the wall tick off restless hours and wishful dreaming
   flights
Her room, silent, save for the sound of her measured even breathing
cautious chest rise and fall, freed of ventilator's forced relieving
I watch her heart pausing, fits and starts in the slow downward spiral
I hold her hand in mine, to give her strength, as she walks her last mile
Her family has gone, driven away by their fear, guilt and pain
I hope she understands, they just couldn't watch, there's no one to blame
A peace settles in, her breathing has slowed, soft as a whisper
I say It's alright to go, her face softened as death kissed her.
   Linda Dickison, R.N. ICU

Seeing Your Face With Its Alluring Smile

Seeing your face with its alluring smile,
how I wish I could hold you, if only for a while.
Foolishly I was enthralled by your serene lies,
every time I see you, my heart slowly dies.
I wait and wonder with my heart to understand,
grasping at dreams, waking with empty hands.
Lacking the courage to tell you the way I feel,
quelling my emotion, desperately waiting to reveal.
Tired and tattered my heart grows ever still,
no time to ponder, as my convictions lose their will.
My words have spoken to no greater end,
silence and solitude, painfully left to contend.
   Jonathan Carroll

Grandma

My grandma is very nice.
She gives me lots of advice.

Grandma is my friend.
Just like my dog Ben.

She doesn't lick me like Ben does.
But I love it when she squeezes my nose.

Ben loves to lay on my lap.
But grandma likes to be in her chair to nap.

When grandma snores.
Ben rolls over and sleeps some more.

The three of us like to take a walk.
As we all walk grandma likes to talk.

I'm listening and Ben is understanding.
Because when grandma's talking, her teeth are whistling.

Ben will be my best friend.
My grandma will always be there to the end.
Chari Lynn Rinkel

Ode To My Farm

Farming is fun when you do it every day
Farming is a gift you get your first day
Farming is a hazard to people when they work
But they still continue; their chores they
Don't shirk

Plowing is fun when you live on a farm
Then our tractor is such a charm
You use it for everything but the books
It has nice looks

Harvesting is our favorite time of the year
I get to drive the truck and work on the
Combine Deere
It is a pain in the back to shovel grain
It must be done before the rain

You must dry the grain when it is wet
A drier fire we don't want to get
We all work hard at harvest time
Not to make a buck - just a dime.
Richard Gramlow

Memories

We've been through for a while now
Why'd you have to go away?
It only seems like yesterday
when our eyes first met
and we were lost for words
I remember all the things we did
all the times we had
I thought our love would last a lifetime
but all I have is memories
I haven't smiled for a while now
since we've gone our separate ways
your picture sits beside me
and not a single day goes by
when you don't cross my mind
But that was some time ago
We had to let go
and now there's only memories.
Heath Butler

Friend

To me friendship is important
It's a person you can trust
It's confidence within two people
An understanding which is never lost
A friend is someone you can count on
Who will always be there through thick or thin
Who won't make plans with you and always cancel
And in whose word you can believe
A friend is someone who can keep a secret
Someone you can talk to when you're sad
Someone who can give advise to you and know it's worthy
A friend is someone who won't ever stab you in the back
Yamile Mahomed

In The Closet

I don't remember the sense of your breasts
   as a bundle of laughter and Pampers.
I don't remember your touch upon my face,
   as a stumbling, innocent, menace to my sister.
I don't remember what it was like to have a "mom"
   as a source of strength and compassion for me.

Why did you leave your children to start anew?
I don't remember the facts, just lies and hear say.
   Lies from kin .. rumors from our family's friends.
     I dream of seeing the truth someday.

I don't remember you ever leaving, just that you were gone.
Gone from a first born and little sister, yet time passed on.
But what good is a "mom" to lonely children,
   Once they're all grown and on their own?

I don't remember ever crying like most
   "I want my mommy!"
Rather growing up very lonely.
However, I do remember one bit of reality
   It's a simple and intense thing.
     It was just me alone ... alone and crying.
Frank B. Scovel

"Tropic Of Cancer"

Allow me to think deep
and glance daringly on the brink.
I rise from sleep and the day creeps
from sunrise to noon.
The sun edges tediously towards a zenith,
a zealous height only Icarus knew,
a moment's journey in the stalking of the Moon.

A Narcissistic need to reflect its light,
The Sun brightens the Moon at night.
The Moon may try with results of Sisyphus,
To break the stellar spell.
Futility and frustration,
The Moon tugs at terra firm as well.
Shakes the tides,
Drives wolves to howl,
Haunts madmen into losing that scowl.
All in a last gasp plea,
I feel the Moon staring at me,
Desperate for days of darkness.
Robert Bell

New Shoes

Lend me your shoes, I need a new walk,
I've been wondering around in these old things
I only wish I could learn how to talk
My words are empty and love they can never bring

But new lyrics won't have me sing with a new found glory,
And new shoes will not help me create a new story.
Kristy Wolszczak

"Small Town Romance, Lifetime Love"

In a very small town, many years ago,
a young boy and girl were beginning to grow.
At the age of fourteen they fell in love,
they went together like a hand in a glove.

At the age of eighteen they were married,
and in the next ten years,
they had a boy and two girls
through a lot of smiles and tears.

Now, they're in their fifties,
their children have all grown.
Two of their three children
have children of their own.

I remember how the rumors did fly.
Everyone said, "It won't last."
But, here we are this very day,
way far from the past.

Through all the good and bad times,
we can thank heaven above,
because a "Small Town Romance,
became a Lifetime Love."
Sandra Lynn Wagg Converse

Untitled

Why can't I be with the one I love
Separated never to become one
To be as one like a pair of white doves
I wait alone for someone else to come
Praying they can take me away from this
Yet my heart shall remain for but one soul
death shall come or so I pretend, I wish
This heart has become nothing but a hole
This life-force has become an empty shell
Yet this poor shell has a new chance for life
And soon it unlocks itself from its cell
Growing of a seed dissipates the strife
With death, creates a river of chances
Amongst one is the heart can again dance
Jamie L. Rothrock

What Do You See?

Tell me, my friend, what do you see?
Tell me, my companion, what do you think of me?
Am I a friend to you?
Or am I simply a companion with a smile to lend?

To you, my mother, what do you believe?
To you, my teacher, what do you expect?
To you, my self, who are you?
To you, my peer, tell me, please, who do you want me to be?

Tell me please, so I can start being me.
Andy Blankenbaker

Untitled

I see us as flowers
   We were separate bulbs
   then we grew together
Now, the gardener has pulled us back apart
Only the weather and
   how we are watered
   will bring us the future
Emily E. S. Lyons

Passing's

Is anybody happier because you passed his way?
Does anyone remember that you spoke to him today?
The day is almost over, and its toiling time is through,
Is there anyone to utter now a kindly word of you?
Can you say tonight in parting with the day that's slipping fast?
That you've helped a single brother of the
many that you've passed?
Is a single heart rejoicing over what you did or said?
Does the man whose hopes were fading, now with courage look ahead?
Did you waste the day or lose it?
Was it well or sorely spent?
Did you leave a trail of Kindness, or a scar of discontent?
As you close your eyes in slumber, do
you think that God will say.
You have earned one more tomorrow,
by the work you did today.
Lora Krause

Untitled

Sometimes I think about the way you used to be
I don't know who you were or what you were to be.
But I see you now you're like a dark cloud you don't what to do
you're near love yet you don't rain dark and lonely you complain.
Still to blame for the life you lived.
Such shame for the decisions you have made
How could you say such things to me when you knew all
along it was never meant to be.
You are a cloud, so loud full of all deceit.
I felt the rain falling hard, but I could not see the true meaning
of your smile.
I guess I just believed!
Lisa Marie Freeman

"The Love Which Creates"

Currents drifting,
Pleasing Rhythms, Through Time.
Pulse of Life.
Love..... So intangibly sweet.
A sense of purpose,
Planted from a seed.
Nameless wisdom,
Created By Om sound.
"I am that I am" said he.
The creator, of the World.
Sounds pounding.....
Pounding in his heart!
For Love........
Creating rhythms, Creating patterns.
Waters, Flowing with love-is-Divine.
All Beauty, All grace.
Crystal Waters, Flowing rivers of Love and light.
Dancing with the cosmos.
Finding porpoise, To love.
John Robert Eihem

Dedicated to Mathew Graves

For every life there is a death,
For every death there is a life,
Some come to death before their time,
While others live out life's curious rhyme.
Some people die for reasons of good,
While others die for reasons I have never understood.
From the minute we are born we slowly die,
We learn the emotions to love, laugh and cry.
In our hearts we never see the fate,
Of death knocking so softly at our back gate.
Now it is time to love, overcome and move on to yet another day,
To keep the memory close to heart to never let it drift away.
Tara Smith

A Breeze Of Remembrance

A haunting breeze drifts down from the mountain tops;
It circles my head, whispering chants of remembrance.
The air twirls around my heels like a forgotten cat,
Tempting me to come witness the virtues of my past.
I follow with a vacant stare, I'm lost within myself.
Long ago, too long ago, the stranger I see was me.
Could it really be, we are strangers to ourselves?
I journey further into the bowels of human nature,
To flirt with the actions of my past, to try and change their minds.
I deny what I see, looking the truth in the face,
I'm mocked by the pain.
The world had offered me gifts, I spat in its face.
Revealing what's inside hurts like a knife
That plunges into the depths of one's soul.
The wound coaxes the demons out, they want to play
With the mentality of the weak, with the pride of the strong.
The ghouls dance around my fire of repentance;
Flames of hope lash out, covering my sins in tides of forgiveness.
The past is washed clean, the breeze retreats with my memories.
It drifts back into my history, which I will not repeat.

Jennifer Frances Carter

Summer's Breeze

Wandering through the sands of time, many questions left unanswered;
I look above and see an endless sea of sorrow.
Like a soft summer breeze caressing my every move
And then slowly fading away.
That breeze loves no one but those who choose to walk through it.
And in that moment that someone will know that they are loved by that soft breeze.
But for those who choose not to be loved, even for a brief moment,
Will just stand back and witness such a pure love, that they will wish they could grasp that soft breeze.
And when they find it in themselves to walk through that soft summer's breeze,
It will have already left and died out in search of someone who will open their minds and hearts for it.
And maybe someday, after the cold winter fades,
That someone who wouldn't embrace it, but instead stood back to observe it,
Will be wandering through those sands of time,
Searching and waiting for that soft summer breeze,
They know might never return.

Kathryn Jarlenski

Day Of Heartbreak

If I don't answer when you call,
Or see you if we chance to meet,
Maybe you'll find me staring at a wall,
Or standing on a corner of the street.

You see, I'm not quite myself today,
My life has been torn upside down,
There has been nothing I can do or say,
To get it back on solid ground.

I really thought my heart would break,
As memories keep flooding thru my mind,
Kisses and hugs that were mine to take
And all the hopes and dreams left behind.

This, too, will pass, is the old clique
But how do I convince my aching heart,
When Brooke and Grant left me today
My life is not shattered while we are apart.

Verna Oehlert

Grasping For Your Hand

You seem to be fine, fighting the good fight;
But I wonder if it is really true;
I know that it's different, something's not right;
The cancer is eating away at you.

You have always been the strong one for me;
Now it seems to be my turn to be strong;
God help me, I don't know what I should be;
I have no idea how to get along.

But even still, time seems to be changing;
For everyone else, life keeps marching on;
Before me, my life is rearranging;
So I grasp at life, afraid you'll be gone.

Slipping away through my fingers like sand;
No, stop, wait; I still need my Mother's hand.

Emily White

I'm Never Alone With Jesus Beside Me

I had lived a life that was filled with troubles;
  and each new day would bring me new pain.
I heard about this man called Jesus;
  and then, I knew my life would change.

If you do not know this wonderful Saviour;
  then fall on your knees and pray to Him.
Just let the love of Jesus flow through you;
  and your life will be complete and new.

I'm never alone with Jesus beside me.
I'm never alone when He holds my hand.
I'm never alone when He walks beside me,
And I'll never be alone when He takes me Home.

Valerie Fillers

Reflections

When I was me the world was young
  I struggled with hope,
  my destiny was a myth.

When I was him and the world was wicked
  I felt only pain,
  anger was me.

When I was them there was no world
  no hope, nothing existed
  madness was him.

Then I became you-peace beguiled all that I was
  life existed, love became
  my world existed within a million more
  silently I pray, heard your voice
  acceptance was me, the world is now
  I don't mind living with them.

Richard D. T. Brown

Appreciation Of Your Love

In my days of being a young child,
In my teenage years of going wild,
In all the times I smiled and cried,
You have always been on my side.

When I was in trouble, you were there to help;
When I was hurt, those feelings of pain you also felt;
When you were right and I was wrong;
You were there the whole way to guide me along.

Those times I was blind to your warnings, pretending not to see;
You were there to give me reassurance and security;
In due appreciation of your love, to let you know you're number 1;
And how lucky I am to be your son.

Brian Noel

Grandpa's View

Life at times seems strange to me
It's kind of like the old oak tree.
With arms outstretched towards the sky
As if to ask, must we all die?
From a tiny seed we grew to be strong
We weathered our storms, we sang our songs.
Our purpose we served in so many ways
More often than not on countless days.
Most are gone now who shared in my past
Few memories I have, but will they last?
Our children with little ones that life has brought
Their eyes full of questions, eager to be taught.
So pass on life's secrets, all you have learned
It's part of your love, it's something you've earned.
The day will come when their life is spent
Maybe only then, will they know just what you meant?
So live and learn all that you can
For us, a full life is just a short span.

Robert Edward LaPierre

How Frail I am

Such a worm as I
Weary and worn
Body full of pain
Eyes can't hide the strain
Oh, how frail I am
Trouble on every side
Nowhere to run, nowhere to hide
Oh, where is my strength?
Where is my power?
Heavenly father, be my strength
Be my place to hide, let trouble
Cease on every side. My strength
Be in thee, my hope built on nothing less
Than thy heavenly host. How frail I am
I can do nothing without thee
My earthly body, yet of dust.
Still I am from thee.
Lord help me to know how frail I am
Where my strength comes.

Kendrick R. Douglas

'Thy Sweet Laurel Wreath Of Pastels'

Upon thy head lays thee crown, enhanced circular of wild
flowers, and 'sweet laurel,' evergreen glossy leaves
bestrewed, buds of fair orange apricot colour behold!
Bridal vine barbary, hued by antique lemon yellow pastels,
flocked with crimson blood red berries, fragrance aroma of
earthy scents rising from hon'eysuckel swaying, by shifting
warm breezes, dazzled by the sun, that signals a bobolink
songbirds tune.
Suddenly, sprinkles, moisture, wet droplets dampen thine
radiant crown, limp pale violet ribbons, trail to caress
thou moss green earth, laid to rest, upon thy bare feet —
Twilight, sets against a sapphire blue horizon, wisped by
petal pink angel wings, weaving into the shadows that strew
wisps of golden spun trees, still moist.
A mystic force, thrust an awakening power, that retrieves
restitution thus! A dried revelation of 'thy sweet laurel
wreath of pastels.

Barbara A. Roman (AKA Le Poetess-"Barbette")

Tian'anmen Square

I saw a wildfire in my dreams.
Color red flashed across the screen.
Youth walked to a freedom bell,
Liberty rose and then she fell.

Around the world we heard their spirits cry.
Human rights are denied
Too many die.

Who lit the fire, what fueled the flame?
The Party claims the students are to blame.
Lies in Disguise, what a shame.

Like a sweet song
Peace will enter when hate is gone.

Ain't afraid of dying, forgive me now
Forget me never
A spirit free forever.

Carol Camelio

Sails Upon The Mist

Clouds white oblivion, drift timelessly, through blue.
Delicate color against simulated porcelain perfection.
Reality submerged in misted vapor, drifting...
To glimpses of unstained beauty trailed by foreboding darkness.

Glowing yellow shimmers beneath the depths of the sea. Poseidon,
himself, is the guardian of forgotten sailors snared by the charm of
beauteous sparkling aqua. Like the dark currents hiding treasures,
the unquiet image of a girl mirrors love abolished within. Image
swims just like the tide in a pool, once disturbed by a small pebble.
Look deep, beneath the girl's surface. See the power in the pasty
whiteness of her cheeks, yet feel the pain as bony hands grasp onto
you. Pain, self-inflicted, the passionate compulsion for the lost.
Her own private sail billows in the wind as it travels the inky sea
into the horizon. All the while the mirror which once reflected a
girl wasting away, inside and out, now reflects naught but subtle
shadowed lights.

Into the universe, wings spread for flight,
land just a pattern of lives, close the mind of the future
and leave ajar the door to the present, while the door to the past
is under a rusty padlock.

As one just sails, sails, away.

Allison Lloyd

Spinning Top

Everything is different now,
Life's a spinning top
Always going faster, never seeming to stop
Dizzy from the heartache, reeling from the pain
A never ending motion going insane
We are all puppets waiting in line
To dance to the tune marching in time
Ghosts of the memories floating in from the past
How long will the spinning last
The third dimension is soon appearing
Laughter from another place
Growing louder echoing in space.
Hang on tight to the multi colored top
Praying this is not your stop
Living life to the fullest while you still can
Make each moment last forever, till eternity if you must
For we keep spinning into infinity, a never ending dance
Take your turn on the top while you still have a chance

Michelle Denise (Barrett) Nordlund

"A Black Man"

A black man is strong,
who can be whatever he wants to be,
without the pulls and strains of slavery reigns,
A black man is a descendant of Great African Kings,
whose Royal blood runs through his veins.
A black man has the strength and agility of an African warrior,
who has fought many battles and won,
A black man has the hopes and dreams of an African slave,
But only 'til now be able to fulfill them.
without hearing the rattles from a rusted chain
A black man does not drink, do drugs, or kill;
its the drinks and the drugs that kill, the black man.
A black man is a conqueror, and an achiever
who can overcome any obstacle that may stand in the way of him.
and Greatness!

William Carter

Books A World Of Their Own!

Books contain a world of their own,
Why, can you pretend you are queen sitting upon a thrown.
Books can be funny or sad or glad,
They sometimes may make you mad.
Books are fun to read to me,
No matter if you are a he or she.
Books can take to unknown places,
You might see aliens with very strange faces.
Books can take you on adventures somewhere,
It could take you here and there or anywhere.
Books can be short or long,
But that doesn't make reading them wrong.
You may even like to write your own books,
You might write your own cookbook!
Reading is fun, and I hope you agree,
Because books have spirits only you can set free,
So, pickup a book and read!!!

Lindsey Gamble

Good-Bye

In the darkness of the night I sit alone
I listen to the silence seeing nothing
I hear your voice whispering my name
I can feel your presence in the room

This is the room in which once you sat
Holding me tightly, you never let go
I felt so safe, nothing could harm me
You brought comfort into my life

Too soon your time ran out on this earth
You were beckoned by another
Soon you departed, slowly rising to the heavens above
I could feel you rising above me

Do not forget me, nor our love
You are inside of me, in my heart
The bond between us cannot be broken
Good-bye my love, I will see you soon

Tammy Borgesen

The Frozen Past

I look at a picture on the wall of a small girl.
The little girl is carefree and happy.
She does not worry about the future.
She does not worry about things to come,
But why should she.
She is still sheltered and protected from the world.
As I look at this girl in the picture,
I wonder what it would be like to be there again;
But you can not avoid the inevitable growing up.
I turn away from the picture and cry
Because I now know the pains of growing up.

Amber Millspaugh

Essence Of A Genuine Love

From a far our eyes introduced our souls
And led us into a never ending journey.
Our hands touched,
And you brought out an inner glow.

Captivated by your beloved spirit
You surround my body
With the warmth of your touch,
As I begged for this feeling to never end.

The touch from a passionate kiss
Made my body carefree and uplifted.
My soul succumbs to my conqueror
As I am left breathless in happiness.

Slowly we pull away
Once again our eyes gaze to one another
And our dominate desire for one another
Transforms to the essence of a genuine love.

Cheri Swann

Mankind And A Flower

Decrepit world drifting in space
a flower blooming in the shade
how slowly we cause you demise
bright red pedals with leaves of gold
sickening strangling great mankind
this flower growing pray it ne'er dies
the one in the noose is also the hangman
a gentle wind blows and seeds of beauty fly
like a wild thorn mankind grows
soft rain on this flower liquid life
what beauty quick mankind to crush it
washing away the soot of other life
to fast is mankind taller it looms
this flower so beautiful is surely doomed
as mankind bends over yes to crush it

Timothy Bailey

Our Children (Mine, His And HIS)

God gave to us six children
Who have made us very proud.
We would love to brag about them,
But you can't do that out loud.

So we just sit back and listen
To remarks from all the crowd.
"Yea, they sure have been lucky,
If they had mine, oh, WOW!"

But we don't think we're lucky,
We know that we are truly blessed.
You see, we gave them lessons from HIS book
Which had the answers to all the tests.

Well, it happened like HE said it would,
And we're so glad HIS word is true.
If you stand upon HIS promises,
HE'LL be good to you!

HE'S never broke a promise
And HE'S never told a lie.
So we'll just keep on trusting HIM
With our kids (and grandkids) 'til we die.

Peggy McGahee

Untitled

Running, running, running
past dead bodies of your friends and enemies.
Dodging through stone corridors.
Bullets whistling past your head.
Grenades sailing in the air and ending in a wall of fire.
Human body parts everywhere.
Hearing voices scream in agony.
Try to push all the images out of your mind.
Loading a gun and shooting at men like a heartless machine.
Watching them drop to their knees-
looking at you with such shock on their faces.
With a sigh you come out of the past.
Tears burning your eyes.
You see a hill covered with hundreds of white crosses.
Pausing now and then to read the name inscribed on the cross
Waking up to nightmares of the war-drenched in a cold sweat.
You cannot shake off the terror that haunts you.
Reliving the past-the images so vivid in your mind.
As if it happened yesterday.
Knowing this will haunt you for the rest of your life."

Michele Wollan

Song Of The Soul

I read, but only half of the book
I see, but do I ever really look
At every possibility, every opportunity
Which lies in front of me?

I ask - perhaps the question's wrong?
I sing, but only half of the song
Where is my reality, my own melody
The strains which strain to burst from me?

I hear, with my ears but not my heart
I step, but never truly make a start
Toward the elusive prize. What good to be so wise,
To see through my disguise

For still, I remain still. Until...

Come! Free me from myself
You, Bearer of true wealth
I know I could learn from You

Come and take me to my limit
User, Giver of each minute
I know I should love to love life as You do

I should love to love me as You do

Kate Damman

You Will Know Me

You tease me when you are young
Take one last breath into your lungs
You are afraid of me at middle age.
Be at peace and escape your cage.
You welcome me when you are old.
Forget the stories of me you were told.

I take you from the place called Earth,
And into a new life I give you birth
Either reincarnation, or another plane,
Whether you lived in comfort or in pain.
With me you are equal, rich or poor.
You will not need your possessions any more.

I am clothed in black as I walk the world.
I know every place you may lay curled.
You will know me when you feel my cold breath.
I am what I am, and my name is Death.

Nicholas Martin

Gentle As The Wind

The Wind blows gently.
An Autumn sky is witness to retreating clouds.
Close, I can hear the roar of a lawn mower as it comes to life,
And it quickly mixes in with the sound of a passing plane.
In room windows, tiny suns with golden light appear,
And burn away the darkness.
Quite suddenly, I notice the final cries of the birds.
Finally the mower dies,
And the plane fades with distance.
The tiny suns soon burn out,
And the brilliant colored flowers close.
All is quiet in our sleeping, seemingly peaceful world.
From the plants,
To the animals,
To the traffic, planes, and people,
To the Sun, Moon, and Stars,
All is dead.
Until, once again, the Wind reminds us of what we are.
Alive.

Cheri Stanley

Brandon

A little boy with a plushy toy
for just a moment he stood still.

While the bear hung limply from his arm
he is innocent
he is pure
he is unconditional love.

An angel's smile, a single moment there
then he was gone
to be the child, the man he was meant to be.

Why can't he wait just a bit
for one more day/week/year.

He's here and gone
then we have only our memories
to understand how much we had and how much we lost.

Barbara M. Roque

Multiple Personality Disorder

Survival energy created to change,
from one to another just to rearrange.

The laws of science spring forward to change.
An unknown alliance that I cannot explain.

Imaginary journeys for the ailing mind, a
trip through a jungle of space and time.

Fantastic transformation of the atom self,
hiding from the memories and everyone else.

Flames of anger burning internally,
erupting and protecting the secret in me.

Passionate persons beware of the one, who
sees and shows what the other has known.

Children of the evil may surprise you someday,
uninvited they come with a desire to play.

The skills of life are not easy for one,
looking for peace and finding none.

The animal kingdom says the strong shall survive,
it's my strength to switch and stay alive.

Terri Armstrong

Untitled

The day is early, the sun is not awake,
Your heart is telling you your will can not break.

You pull your strength together for the long journey ahead,
Preparation seems futile but things are still complete with little said.

Even though you have help you realize that it is all up to you,
No one can stop the sequence that you must go through.

You ponder the thought of your job being done,
But with every second the pain is as severe as the previous one.

The events are leaving you pushing forward while your gasping for air,
Praying to the Lord Your God that you were not really there.

You work and push your way through the storm,
Seeking retribution as the hours cary on.

The journey must continue even as your body goes weak,
You grab for pleasant thoughts and for the fortune you seek.

Time has tested the power and depth of your heart,
And when your work is over you find it is only the start.

For even though the road you traveled was long,
The prize at the end will carry you strong.

With the feeling of relief you know you have beaten the world,
When you realize you just gave birth to your little boy or girl...A
MOTHER TO BE
   Shainn Reaves

Flight

I traveled high in the clouds of the sky,
I traveled low the horizon's brow.
And the sweetness of being and the softness of seeing
Engulfed me in ethers of other worlds.
The wings of a bird I used for a sail,
My compass the skill of man's art.
I roared through the blue of heaven's expanse,
And the might of man
And the power of man
Converged in my heart.
No loftier thought, no fre-er stride
Could dwell on the seas and the plains
For the nearness of God is felt in the fog
Chartering my course in the area lanes.
   Justine E. Swenson

Nature's Beauty

Nature's beauty, what a sight,
with such colors bold and bright.
The moon and stars shoot to the sky,
and dance, as nature sings its sigh.

As the day starts rolling in,
the sun comes out with a grin.
The flowers bloom and the trees stand still
at the dawn over the short green hill.

The people wake, and the little ones cry
only to see the clouds drifting by.
The animals scurry to find fruit,
but the owls don't give a hoot.

The day passes on with its charm
not causing anything to be harmed.
For nature, in its special way,
has remembered that God watches us everyday.
   Aihmee Tolentino

Summer

How quickly the warmth of Summer passed
and winter with its cold and dark now cast
the dreary, cloudy, warmless ways
of sleepless nights and lonely days.
The heart still beats but the pain is there
and the soul cries out for Summer's care.
The warm and tender moments known
are now but memories that I own.
And these memories will remain until
my breath is gone and my heart is still.
But my love with no doubts or fears
will not die even with the pain and tears.
For my soul will always be and will recall
the warm and tender times of all
the days and nights of Summer bliss
the warm embrace, the tender kiss.
   Roy F. Cowell

My Brother Tom

He was a four-leaf clover and I a three,
A postwar syndrome, a fallen tree,
A forlorn waif without a mother,
This Vietnam vet who is my brother.

A father softly firm and fair
To three young boys with a lot to learn.

High school typewriter keys he would switch,
Tuning an instructor into a fever pitch.
Wooden eggs turned upon a lathe,
Dyed Easter red for a holiday charade.

A laugh, a grin so much his own;
With all that a tortured soul.
   Vangeli

Girl?

Girl, where's yo momma?
   You, with that short dress on
   and that too much lipstick on
   and that whole can of hairspray on.

Girl, where's yo momma?
   You, screamin and cussing like that
   calling your friends ugly or fat
   letting that man use you like you're an outdoor mat.

Girl, where's yo momma?
   You, telling everybody bout your pain
   giving too much of yourself up with nothing to gain
   losing track of reality and what is sane:

Girl, where's yo momma?
   You, takin things that don't belong to you
   showing your baby sister the things you do
   knowing the road you travel is too much for you

Girl, is that yo momma?
   Is that her? - over there, with that real stiff hair
   with that too short dress on,
   with that too much lipstick on? Girl?
   Naomi P. Smith

Catherine

She Love Me, She Loves Me Not?
My feelings for her are oh so Hot,
The fellas say "You're Whipped,"
I think not.
For Catherine, Oh Cathy.
My love for her runs so deep,
If given the chance I would kiss her feet,
Crazy men talk to sheep.
Boy how I love Catherine, Oh Cathy.
   Errol Fitzgerald Outarsingh

Tiny Thread

The ageless giant, brow furled, capped with a crown of white,
Looms over the landscape an ever-watchful knight.

Awaken the dawn blazing goddess of light!
Envelop nature in your warm embrace, vanquish the solitude of the night.

The morning dew gently embraces mother earth,
Is now a blanket removed as silently the droplets disperse.

Arise, oh creation touched by the sun!
Arise, all creatures that ebb beneath evening tide is done!

The breeze crisp and fresh resonates through the trees,
Leaves bow in reverence, come forth the songs of the season, to the mind tranquility.

The trees boast of contrast, there backs taut and spry,
Stretch forth arms of splendor in dignity and pride.

Incandescent orange, passionate red, visions of beauty before me are bred.
A carpet of yellow mantles the soil bed, sky gray-blue, clouds glide overhead.

The crickets play in melodious unison their harps timed in sweet refrain,
An orchestra tuned to the senses, revives the season again.

The imperturbable solitude, nourishment for the soul,
Fusion of humanity and nature, oneness, a whole.

Shadows creep stealthily, wings spread to feast upon oblivious prey,
All creation dons a death mask, beauty now consumed by decay.
   Carol Monticue

A Walk On A Summer's Night

   I feel the wind brushing across
my face like a feather in the warm
summer night. The clouds looked like they
were as light as the stuffing in a pillow.
As I walk down the sandy beach. The
sand felt warm under my feet keeping
them warm in the cooling night.
The waves started crashing together like
cymbals in a percussion band.
Suddenly cold drops of water came falling
down. Then a flash of lightning bolted through
the sky followed by a roaring thunder. Then
the rain became a light drizzle and the wind
brushed across my face like a butterfly kiss
in the warm summer's eve as I walked
down the sandy beach.
      Meghan McHaney

Peregrination Of The Soul

I saw a man with dead eyes;
His soul was not breathing but he considered himself wise.
His power and wealth was all he pursued,
But peace of mind for him would elude.
He never looked at a person's face,
And was never interested in the pain it traced.
He continued to set up his store of riches,
And never helped those who were stuck in life's glitches.
With all his success he could not escape death;
He still had to face its icy cold breath.
With horror he was sucked into his own darkness of soul,
And his very being was swallowed up whole.
Early in life his soul departed and fell,
And now he has followed it straight to hell!
   Kayembe Henderson

"If"

If you only knew my dreams—based on fairy tales from my childhood long gone. We never really had a childhood; we were just born and forced to be old. Gone are the happy times of laughter and smiles, now just faded memories in a dusty corner of my mind.

If you only felt my pain—would you try to ease the memories of a long and forgotten time? Would you hold me close and whisper, "I'm here forever,"?

If only you knew my prayers—how I ask God to please let me be with you for eternity; how I thank Him every day that I am lucky enough to have you by my side.

If only I could tell you all of the things I want to say— the inquiries, the hidden truths. How they grow into massive piles, never expounded— left to decay.

If only you knew how much I love you—would the past matter at all? No, not if I was with you. Perhaps you could find it in your heart to love me, too.

You will know—because life is one big "if", but it's our "if" and our future, and we'll determine our own way.
   Maria T. Middleton

Hey Daddy

Hey Daddy, look at me, I'm still your little girl.
Remember how you'd pick me up and send me on a twirl?
I'd sit in your lap for hours on end
As you told me old stories again and again.

Hey Daddy, look at me, I'm still your little girl.
Remember how you'd hold me close?
I knew that it was you who loved me most.
You were never too busy to hear my cries.
Then you'd comfort me with your little white lies.

Hey Daddy, look at me, I'm still your little girl.
Am I what you wished I would be?
Hey Daddy - look at me!
   Kelly Elizabeth McHan

House Of Books

Andrew was a canny Scot
Much too far from Camelot
To uncover before the mitered head
And plead his cause with pilot bread.

Of celestial hope and enterprise
He unveiled before hopeful eyes
Of a brave new world trying to read
And raised libraries to plant the seed.

Of ubiquitous truth and trusting guise
Since Adam and Eve broke their ties
And gave the world of coronet
And bade us take care with Antoinette.

In hamlet and town throughout the land
Porticoed doors overawe the band
Of gamins who come to seek
A refuge from the double-speak.

The vaulted ceiling is Heaven's grace
For the dreamer who won't debase
A vision of treats from old Macaulay
And gives back to pudding and Christmas Holly.
   John W. Ceder

Untitled

Dear Friend,
How are you? I just had to send a note to tell you how much I care about you.
I saw you yesterday as you were talking with your friends. I waited all day hoping you would want to talk to me, too. I gave you a sunset to close your day and a cool breeze to rest you - and I waited. You never came. It hurt me - but I still love you because I am your friend. I saw you sleeping last night and longed to touch your brow so I spilled moonlight upon your face. Again, I waited wanting to rush down so we could talk. I have so much to give you. You awoke and rushed off to work. My tears were in the rain. If you would only listen to me. I love you! I try to tell you in blue skies and in the quiet green grass. I whisper it in the leaves on the trees and breathe it in the colors of the flowers. Shout in to you in mountain streams. Give the birds love songs to sing. I clothe you with warm sunshine and perfume the air with nature scents. My love for you is deeper than the ocean and bigger than the biggest need in your heart. Ask me! Talk with me! Please don't forget me. I have so much to share with you! Please don't keep me waiting. I need your love with me forever.

Kathleen Richardson

"It's Through"

What will I tell my six children
Was the thought on mind, at the time

Here I was six years on dialysis
It wasn't the fact, I was bed ridden
on oxygen 24 his day, or even
the wheel chair I get around in

It was the look on these six
small children, ages I though
faces, which kept me going

Doctors gave up loved ones too
Yet here was these children
Not knowing what to do

I had no doubt I'd make it through
Through tears and pain, yet seeing
those lovely faces near

Now after all, is said and done
a transplant, I went through
The children are so glad and grown

I share my tale with you, I pray, if you go down my road
you too will make it through

Connie L. Cochran

Untitled

Spring awakes, dawn is here,
and the seed pushes forth,
into light, and warmth, and life. It struggles to survive,
Fighting against impossibilities.
Finally, its beauty fells an inner strength,
and the bud blossoms into freedom. Freedom to be,
Freedom to have beauty.
The flower caretaker carefully waters its love, every morning, every night.
This flower is a blossom of his love, His care his pride.
One day, he stops the caring.
The flower gets no water from the man.
It absorbs the water from rain,
touchily providing itself with nourishment. But, without the love,
the hardships of life are too much to hear.
The flower slowly wilts, and dies.
Nobody notices the passing of beauty,
The life beauty rots without a tear of appreciation.

John Swindell

"My Friend"

An angel came to me one day, and brought a friend to stay.
The angel knew just what to do, so neither girl would stray.
Many trials and circumstance; caused a great delay.
But the angel kept reminding us; that God planned it that way.
He had a plan to use our lives; and everything that happened.
To make us share our ministry; to all who come after.
The angel knew that we were strange in a silly kind of way.
From others that we're around; each and every day.
"Unique" is our ministry. Nothing can compare!
To the preparation God has made; for his word to share.
He molded us from his clay; in a new and different way.
So we would share what he's done; each and every day.
Thank you Angel for my friend and the music that you bring.
And the joy you give us in our lives. Every time we Sing!

Teresa D. Gilley

Untitled

Many centuries ago
In a star system many light hours distant,
a humanoid life form was walking,
very briskly at first but,
as the twin suns began to set he paused,
and admired the view from the country road.
As he continued,
guided only by the light of the first and second moons,
he watched the third moon slowly climb above the horizon to join
its companions in the abyss of stars and darkness.
Inspired, he thought to himself,
how beautiful it all seemed.
But was it really all a dream?

William S. Marsh

I'm Only Going To Say This Once

I'm only going to say this once
I'm only going to do this once
In my life

So when I take you by the hand
And stand before that holy man
To make your my wife

Know that it's because
You're the one that I love
And only you

With all my hart and soul
The only thing that I know
And believe to be true...

This band of gold that I give to you
Is a never ending circle of love
And a symbol of what I plan to do

To show you that I care and I plan to share
All the good times and the bad times
With all my love for the rest of my life

In sickness or in health
In poverty or in wealth you will be my wife

Joseph D. Anselment

"A Helping Hand"

Our Father in heaven
　to Thee we pray,
　　as we arise each glorious day.
Come into our hearts
　and guide the way,
　　for we are sinners gone astray.

Your footprint path on the road of life,
　helps us follow through every strife,
　　lending a hand when we stumble and fall,
for your Glory awaits at the end of it all.

Karen K. Wendland

My First Balloon Ride

All my life as I looked at the sky,
  I wondered what it would be like a fly,

To float on the air like the little birds do,
  To see through their eyes the wonderful view.

Today I had to chance to see and feel
  An incredible experience that was very real

I took a balloon flight high in the sky,
  And now I know what it is to fly.

To hang suspended with no air flowing
  Quiet and still with the sunbeams glowing.

To look down on the earth like a patch work quilt
  To have peace and tranquility without any guilt

To see for miles in every direction,
  Accept every shift in the wind without question.

In a little basket to soar so high,
  To such great heights up in the sky.

I always thought I was afraid of heights,
  But the joys far exceeded the fright.

So take a chance and you will see,
  Just what a balloon ride meant to me.

Sarah Louise Hickman

Grandma's Quilt

I called you here on this rainy day that we might have some tea.
It was a day just like today, when your Grandma called on me.

She sat me down beside her and told me to take heed.
I pass this quilt now on to you as she placed it on my knee.

This quilt has many memories and tells you of my life.
For here's a piece of my wedding gown when your father took me
  as his wife.

When I became a mother, I let nothing go to waste.
From all your worn out dresses these pieces I have placed.

Remember the time you ran and fell and ripped our favorite skirt.
These pieces here came from it, for I cut a way the dirt.

Mother I asked, "These pieces here, are they from the aprons you
  wore?"
She smiled and said "Yes my Dear, you see there's many more."

We sat and talked for hours as we drank our cups of tea.
She wanted me to pass it on with all its history.

Joseph L. Darnell

A Special Relationship

Sometimes old times are better than new,
For the better times are more than few.
To be with you, all times are fun,
Sitting in the house or out in the sun.
More than a wife, you're also a friend,
Always counting on you everyday to the end.
A relationship in the making, for you and I,
Nothing's the limit, not even the sky.
And to you every day, I grow especially fond,
For what we have is a special bond.
For as we grow older together in life,
Our bond will grow stronger every day my wife.
For our troubled times together we stand,
Fighting them off hand in hand.
For as much in life as we've been through,
I feel so strong when I'm with you.
For in that strength, I know there's a reason,
Loving you more through every season.
We have something special together forever,
I hope that feeling doesn't go away, not ever.

Randy St. Myers

The Perfect World

The perfect world for me would be
A beautiful island under a tropical sun
Stretching as far as one dared to dream
Dreaming, just dreams.

While waves crash upon an eastern shore
The white foam tumbling outward
Palm trees touching the clouds
The distant weeping of sea gulls

Calling; crying for some lost soul
Lost on the ocean never to return
My world; my perfect world?
No; not quite.

Michele Maas

A Marines Manifesto

We are strong in body and mind
We are committed to the protection of the weak and disabled
We are true to the code of "Semper Fi"
We are courage which knows no limits
We are hope and mercy to the sick and needy
We are Hellfire and Brimstone to those who oppose our cause
We are preservers of "Freedom"
We are the Task Masters of human rights
We are the Gatekeepers of Democracy
We are never at rest
We are the essence of victory
We are invincible to defeat
We are the ultimate warriors of our "Great Nation"
We are forged by conviction
We are charter members until death
We are the proudest of the proud
We are the Peacekeepers
We are God fearing
We are the chosen few
We are "United States Marines"

Dennis L. Sheldon

Hopes And Dreams

I get on my knees and say a prayer,
That one day you'll be there.

I lay awake in my bed,
While thoughts of you race through my head.

My love for you is very strong,
I would make sure nothing went wrong.

The only wish I hope to come true,
Is the one wish of having you!

Damon Mellinger

Off To Join The Squadron

Pop's off to join the squadron, gone down to hobnob with the boys.
What new mission he's on, heaven only knows, (sealed orders from above, I suppose).
Yes, it's come down from the Wing Commander, no lights, no instruments,
dead reckoning all the way.
A wondrous flight this must be, into that wild blue yonder, silk scarf flapping in the breeze.
By what star is your course now laid, what measure of distance, if any is made?
Is there a beacon that shines in the night, do you steer your course as a moth to the light?
Does this light guide both your way and mine?
Hey, if you're in the neighborhood won't you give us a sign?
Dip those wings, flash a thumbs up and that old Teutonic grin.
Where you are bound none can say, but where ever these travels lead, we miss you, and God speed.

Jas. H. Stevenson

Poem Taker

One time by many walls.
I wished from the Lord
to bring down happiness from above.
On the streets I walked skipping holes
looking for a circle.
Not aware of any bumps on the road
a tree with a flower broke my stroll.
The closer I got the more my thought went further
and my walk got softer.
My toes quick played in the water.
"Tree why do you cry?"
I asked.
"I have tears and I have nothing to make them dry,"
she replied.
I reached in my pocket
and grabbed a napkin.
Smearing the words of a poem
that I wrote in hoping
it would be giving to the one holding
the happiness I was wishing.

Pedro L. Amaro

Blue Sunday

It's a rainy Sunday
A day that's truly blue
But even worse than Sunday blue
It's Easter Sunday too...
It's rainy and it's gloomy,
and kind of lonely too...
There's really nobody around,
The ones that are about me, are only sporting frowns...
In this place of steel and bricks,
It's a crazy Easter Sunday, what a mix it is, of
Rain and Snow on April 7, 1996
It's a day of rejoice, they say, throughout the world we're told
But in our world behind these bars of fences and of guards.
Our rejoices are so distant, and are only yielding scars,
We all miss our families
Our relatives and friends,
Some sleep away, some are angry!
and can't wait till this
Blue Sunday...
Easter Sunday... Ends...

Peter Simon Buechner III

Days Gone By

The days of your life must not be wasted consider
Each minute a revelation
Use them as a gift, giving them your full
consideration
Study what it's all about as you are part of this
generation
There are no written requirements for personal
creations
Read from your notes or recite a poem at your
next presentation
Tell them about the plane ride that was such a
sensation
Create a pie with an unusual shape of crust, it
could be an artistic revelation
The sensation of just living is a form of
Entertainment and makes a marvelous presentation
All these thing we take for granted even tho
Each one in life is a special situation
"Thank you Lord", let me remember these days, to
Bend a knee and participate in the consecration

W. Drury Clark

Orchard

An orchard is many things, it is a seat in the crotch of
a tree where sunkissed sawdust fell one long ago April,
as childhood questions about the existence of the Easter
Rabbit mingled with the rasping of a father's pruning saw,

or it's a lost, abandoned home place, at the raw edge
of new construction, where father and daughter come to
select scions of a few remaining precious varieties. It is
the transfer of some of the good and the old, by grafting,
to a new planting, in a place that's safe, for a time, for
an orchard.

It is blossoms in spring, on white-garbed ballerina trees
planted with the help of a daughter home on spring break
one muddy, drenching May morning, and, a few years later,
it's HER daughter's pink-parosoled place to dance under
drops, on a rainy November day, while dinner cooks.

The fruit comes in the fall,
but remembrance, in an orchard,
lives and increases day by day, through lifetimes.

Leona Mason Heitsch

A Child Is A Disney World

I like to be the best child in the world.
I need a friend to help me climb the hills
So the world can become a safe place
For the lonely children in the streets.
Sweet as a water fountain flowing in a hot summer,
A happy childhood is the best gift for a child.
But lots of children can't eat, can't smile.
The darkness needs the shine of the sun.
I dream of a time where school will be a paradise
For teachers and students to enjoy the life's wonders.
But for this to happen, society must become
A kingdom where children are kings, innocence is law.
That could never be in a society trapped in
In the web of violence, drugs, and child pornography.
Parents! The choice is yours to make,
Things may look desperate, but remember
Great dreams make great people and great societies.
Please! Don't be afraid to dream of something great,
Mine, a child of the street, is huge and alive,
It's the size of a pyramid.

Herve Florival

Evolution

Grand Dad would read and think for hours,
by the light of a Tiffany lamp.
His father before him had candles,
searching for knowledge and truth
in the damp.

My Dad used a machine. It was keen.
The damn thing would add by itself.
Still once in a while,
he would still have to stop,
and pull down a book from the shelf.

Now days we're not subject
to any restraint.
With a flick of a wrist and the speed of a mouse,
we spreadsheet, we research,
and sometimes we paint.

It's truly amazing
how much one can learn.
Until your hard drive
does a crash and a burn.

D. Edwin Hutchings

Fear And Strength

Did you ever wonder what it's like
to stare death in the face?
To see the cold eyes look at you
and not know it's name.
To feel the hate it brings
from darkness and fear.
It makes you wonder who he is
and where has he been.
To take away your innocence
and give you only pain.
To make you suffer terribly
and you have nothing to gain.
But death will be caught with his greedy ways-one slip
and he will pay for all his evil deeds.
Only time will heal the horror we live through.
Take time out to learn what life is about.
Give strength in number and be brave
in the face of doubt. Help is only a prayer away.
Cause with him he will save the day.
With his Angels from up above, he will save his loved ones.
   Kathryn Keenan

Deep Blue Sea

Let's get lost on an island that's surrounded by the pacific ocean.
And listen to the sound of large waves crashing among the gray
charcoal reef, that were once left behind so many years ago. Where
time is of the essence, and life itself is at its simplest form. Lets
walk along the white sand beach, as we hold each others hand.
And watch as the sun sets along the coast shore, as it timelessly
turns into an enormous ball of luminous fire. Much like that of a
burning flame near the end of a candlelight dinner.

As I ever so gently slide my hand along side her beautiful silky
hair, that now reflects the light of the brightest star in the sky.
I slowly place my lips upon hers and softly kiss her lips, as we both
lie on the beach. While falling into a unwilling and unexpected
fantasy, She unselfishly allows me to explore and enter that
unforbidden cave. For which there is no return, for there'd be no
reason to ever want to leave. As our hearts rush to reach its
maximum heart rate, and the consumption of oxygen is consumed
with every breath

Our bodies now release the purity of life, what is to be the
laws of nature, and what evolution intended it to be. As the
mixture of genes are combined, much liked the process of any other
primates mating. The formular for life is now complete, and life
will begin again on an island surrounded by nothing more than
deep blue sea's.
   Anthony Sanabria

True Night

Tonight is the night everyone wins.
When servants bow, and
Carry out their master's every whim.

But to the true eye
There is only greed,
And the servants rebel
To face their true means.

Ah, but to the master's advantage
They learn of what is about to happen.
So with forces in arm the master's fight.
To the last dying breath with all their might.

At last the war is ended, and to great sorrow,
All are dead none left for the orders, and chores
Of the 'morrow.

In years to come it happens again.
For none the wiser interfere with the sin.
   Jennie Crane

That Would Be The Day

If the dawn didn't break with a warming sun...
to help us begin the day!

If the grass didn't green in the spring....
and the leaves didn't rustle through the trees...
whispering "Hello" to each of us!

If there were no more rainbows to provide us all with a
smile...showering each of us in warm wonderful colors
of life...and in comfort!

If the flowers never bloomed again to welcome us to
summer...to bring us fragrances and sights that
each of us need!

If the moon never rose again in the evening time to
say "Welcome Home"...and the stars didn't glisten with
bright shiny lights of love...to bid us goodnight...
and leave each of us in peace until tomorrow's dawn!
That Would Be The Day:

My heart would shatter in to a million pieces and be strewn
throughout the heavens; and, yes, that would be the day...
I would love you no more!!!
   James Teague

Dinosaur Time

Imagine swamps,
Luscious plants and vegetation,
   and best of all...dinosaurs!
In the smelly swamps are plants all over.
No cats, no zebras, and no store to buy food...oops,
   it's Tyrannosaurus Rex!
The King! Help! Oh, no!
Triceratops on my left
And an Iguanadon on my right.
There's only one way out of this threesome.
Right there on my, my ... oh, no!
There's no way out...help!
Ah, it's only a dream!
   Andrew Fernando E. Quilpa

Sweet Water Valley

Deep in my heart is a memory so true;
   Of my boyhood farm from which I grew.
Of lush green hills and a grassy plain;
   Of a winding brook, like a silver lane.
Of snow white clouds in a deep blue sky;
   Of little valleys with trees so high.
Of orchards in bloom and the butterflies;
   And hummingbirds probing for a nectar prize.
The look of flowers everywhere;
   The smell of roses in the air.
The songs of birds among the trees;
   The buzz of insects and honey bees.
The sound of running water over rocks;
   The freshness of moss growing in flocks.
The gentle breeze so cool and light;
   Scattering blossoms pink and white.
The warmth of the sun from high above;
   The feeling of contentment, the feeling of love.
This was my valley, so sweet and so pure;
   With the grace of God, may it long endure.
   Joseph J. Gruesu

Hope

Cold within the valley of shadows,
Stands a ray of golden light.
One can barely see its brightness,
Whispering softly of things to come.
Yet towering faintly it endures,
And while others overlook its gleam,
It stands a beacon to those lost in despair.
True though it may be dim,
The faith of others will help it grow,
Till at last its graceful beam,
Will outshine even the brightest star,
And become the sun within our hearts.
Alisha Reid

"Shattered Pieces"

I read Cinderella, I wondered if it could be,
That a real Prince Charming would come in search of me.
But Mother always warned me, about kissing all those frogs,
And Daddy said I'd get fleas from sleeping with the dogs.

I've been in and out of love, I've listened to the lies,
And all the frogs accomplished was more tear stains on my eyes.
But I never stopped trusting, in my loving heart,
I'd love my Prince with all his charm and vow to never part.

I never demanded riches, silver, or gold,
Cause a love that can be easily bought, can easily be sold.
I never asked for mansions, just a happy home,
To live, to laugh, and love as one, and a vow to never roam.

I've been used, been confused, been left to cook and clean,
A life of sadness and abuse, was all I'd ever seen.
But I never stopped praying, that a Prince would find,
The shattered pieces from the glass that I had left behind.

So which story do I believe, when will a true love I receive,
A story book ending I conceive, happiness I can achieve.
Happily ever after I'm sure, I will find one day,
I know that I will find my Prince, the frog won't leap away.
Teressia A. J. Wright

Crazy Feelings

Raging Feelings thrust up my spine.
How to define them, "Clouds spinning ever so fine."
Sweet summer sunset burning in the eve,
Secrets buried in the cuff of a satin sleeve.
Crazy the breeze, just in time.
Rinsing my soul from Dew drops,
Fallen from my cheeks.
A feeling of renewal tastes oh so sweet!
Indulging in a escapade, as the noon tide rolls in.
Happiness glazed outside, coming from within.
Beads of sweat clear my brow,
Blades of grass serves as a cool soft towel.
Sunlight to warm me as a warm summer wind.
Naked laughter chosen with whom I pretend.
Caught in a time zone, meant for few.
Sharing a part of me, tailored for you.
Lynn Mandy

The Actress

The actress laughs, the actress more often cries.
Never really loved or understood, the actress; sad,
depressed and lonely makes up her mind and dies.
No one knows why, she decided to no longer be. But,
the best performance of her life was her life, and
she's not even here to see. But, the tears are no
more and the loneliness has ceased. Her academy
award is her tombstone, inscription - "LIFE'S BEST
ACTRESS, MAY SHE REST IN PEACE."
Lisa Gardner

A Lost Hope

As the train eased out of the station
to become no mor'n than a blur;
The last notes of "taps" re-echoed
there wasn't even a stir.
Save a kerchief raised to wipe a tear
or wave a last good-bye.
A voice cried, "Bobby, oh Bob," a week ago
you come by.
Brought us hope,
now you're gone,
and I,
there came a great shout from all about,
voices raised a cheer for Bob and all he
believed and stood for.
So we'll carry on from here.
Your believers,
"All of us."
Myrtle Clark Schulte

What happens when your wishing well dries and your strength dies

What happens when your wishing well
Dries and your
Strength dies?

Do all your dreams disappear behind
The sad shadowed doors
That hold the past?

Does the memory of strengths laughter
Soon change to the horrid
Tears you now shed?

Does the light at the end of the tunnel
Never seem to brighten
Your eyes?

Well than listen to me, your soul, and believe
Love and time
Will fill your well, and revive your strength.
So don't give up even though...

Your wishing well dried and your strength died
Linda June Cox

A New Day

The first rays of light, filling the sky.
Illuminate the earth, bringing forth a peace and comfort.
The dewdrops sparkle on the soft grasses of the field.
Gentle raindrops
While birds fly overhead, graceful wings, playing with the wind.
Down on the ground are mice, emerging from their dwellings.
Scurrying about below, gathering food to eat, listening to the music
of the field.
The crickets are the strings, the bull frogs take up the chorus
The songbirds join in with their lovely tune.
Each part of nature adds a thread of beauty which is woven into an
enchanting melody.
A melody that is contributed to, from the largest of trees, to the
smallest of insects.
A melody showing all that life is, and all that is love.
A melody written thousands of years ago by our Creator
A melody which is, creation
Kelly Walsh

Paradise

As I walked along through the different outside shops on that moon-lit night, friends on either side of me, I realize this is truly paradise. The smell of wonderfully fresh air begins penetrating through my entire body.

That nice, warm breeze blowing in my face removing the loose pieces of hair that are dangling in my way, feels refreshing on that incredibly warm night. The sound of the waves crashing down on the sand sounds so much calmer at this time of night.
I exclude myself from my friends and go on and sit on the beach alone. I sit there in the late hours of the night and stare into the light of the moon. The breeze from the water blows on my bare skin. There is something in this breeze unlike any other breeze I've ever felt. It's a breeze that has a meaning and personality of its own.
I feel someone watching over me. I look into the sky and catch the man in the moon observing my presence. Another breeze rolls in as the palm trees sway gently back and forth in the midnight hour.
My heart fills with the emotions of joy and happiness.
I also feel helpless in knowing that in just a few short days, I would be leaving this wonderful place I now know as, Paradise.
Jenna Finn

God's Feather Bed

I remember as a child
Mom telling me every time it snowed
"God's shaking his feather bed."

God's shaking his feather bed
To make a spot to lay His head.
He shook it here,
He shook it there,
He shook it just about everywhere.
Every time he shook his bed
The feathers fell upon my head.
It became snow so pure and white.
It became snow that glowed in the night.

Now every time see it snow,
I hear my mother say again,
"God's just shaking his feather bed."
Vera Wright

The Memory

I remember the day that's been here
and gone. As I looked all around
and realized something was wrong.
The desperation inside, the pounding
of my heart, as the coldness fell
over me I started falling apart.
I panicked, I wondered, I didn't
think it could be true. In the
back of mind I knew it was
you. They said not to worry that
things would be alright, and I
thought to myself, but I left you that
night. I feel so confused, so hurt, and
so sad. But the most defined feeling
was feeling so mad! As I drove to
the hospital not knowing what
I'd see, all I kept thinking it
must have been me. The memory
still haunts me and I don't
understand why, on that very night you wanted to die!
Chere R. Leap

Blue Eyes

Blue eyes - like ice, angry at you he is
empty, blank stare - no telling what he may do.
Cold and stinging, looking straight through you
your head starts ringing.

Glancing at you, you at him - transceiving passionate beats
Moody and calm, this sun beams on my face.
His glowing radiance I cannot replace.
Warm compassion rarely seen,
When shown I know he knows what I mean.

If you wonder how I read his eyes,
Heartfelt instincts never lie.
Look into my eyes, they tell his story -
You can see him in me.
Danielle Lynn Pinelli Cook

My Child My Son

Long ago a part of me died, at least I felt a part of me die,
my child my son, my first born, choose to leave his earthly home.
His mission here was then compete. The lives he touched so bitter sweet.
The love he gave, was sweet and warm, the love was gone.
I thought, I mourned.
But, when the misty clouds had cleared, my heart was full, his presence near.
His physical being was gone, I know, but the love he left, was still to grow.
The memory takes me day to day, and gives me strength when I feel the strain.

Not long ago a part of you died, at least you felt a part of you die,
your child your son your first born, chose to leave his earthly home.
His mission here is now complete, the memory he left are yours to keep.
Cherri L. Hogan

The Promise

Drop of light fall at my window
rain it is
Bringing the promise of life
To the deep buried roots, soon
To be seen in colors of budding blossoms
And the green of many leaves.
So does the rich beauty of nature
Frame the promise of my world.
Dorothy Darby Smith

The Lost Paradise

Wandering through the hell of paradise
Lost of the love I have yet acquired
Dreaming of the paradise that I have left behind
As I drink from the spout of cain
My abel is in the back of my mind
The bridge in which he speaks of is always in thought,
Yet I always go on
I hope my paradise is not lost for the love
That I love is left alone and unprotected
In the jungle of life
I am miles apart from paradise, but I am in paradise
My mind is bewildered from the liquid of Satan
And my heart is bleeding from my paradise lost
Where shall I go and will I leave my paradise
For the paradise I left?
Kevin Lee Vineyard

Conformity

We're trapped in a world that we don't like.
Changing it is something we just can't do.
Or so we tell ourselves to feel at ease
with dreams we don't try to make come true.
But one person can better another
and so on, on down the line.
Just think of some of the people you've known in your life.
Some brought out bad, some brought out good,
some made you feel real fine.
The world is filled with badness, we know,
but we don't have to conform
to that which we should actually detest
just because it's considered the norm.
Leona Deretchin

Life Goes On...

Cold dark shadows Creep behind trees
rivers flow to Depths of seas
Snow falls
water splashes
the Sun rises and sets
the moon radiates in Darkness
Earthquakes and Ice cream shakes
seasons change
we Dance to music
the Earth rotates (on its axis)
the More we find
the Less we know...
a relationship eXists between Mother Earth
and our Father
People meet, eat, and separate
and Life goes on....
Chrisitna D'Emma

Cloud Number Nine

Seeing you there from across the way,
Feelings I'd never felt before -
I traveled to somewhere new that day
Not knowing what was in store.

"Hello, How are you doing?" I'd like to say.
Your face has the beauty of a snow white dove.
Staring at the stars I'd sit and pray
For you to be my one forever true love.

Cloud number nine what a wonderful place,
You send my heart beating like a wild horse race.
Cloud number nine you're a true friend of mine
You always seem to stop the hands of time
Cloud number nine I need you by my side-
Now and forever until the day I die.

Late at night when everyone is in bed
I thank the Lord for giving me you and-
I take a trip to that very special place.
Christy Eddington

God Gave Me Tools

Healing the hurt of a broken heart,
Where anger and fear all had a part.
So vicious and cruel it tore at this jewel,
Until I discovered God gave me some tools.

His Word pierced my soul and love was birthed.
His Spirit warmed me and brought peace on earth.
New Friendships were formed to give me hope.
Encouragement now, I no longer cope.
   So sweet is my Jesus
   So tender and kind.
   He lifted up me up
   and gave peace of mind.
Kathleen M. Kremers

"A Past With A Future"

We know not what the future holds,
As we choose our path to follow.
Who knows where we will boldly go,
As we step into tomorrow.

One thing for sure as we look back,
As if searching for a clue.
Our past brought us here and that's a fact,
For me as well as you.

Some will succeed and some will fail,
Unaware that "we" have control.
The time is now, we must prevail,
If we wish to meet our goal.

The future looks bright for this nation of ours,
For the past accepted the task.
The heroes of yesterday, today and beyond,
Buys a future that was born in the past.
Gloria Williamson

The Endangered Bald Eagle

I have two legs,
Have wings and lay eggs.
I have hair even though I'm bald.
I eat things that swim and crawl.
I'm endangered you know.
And mostly people are my foe.
Also my favorite dish is poisoned fish.
I don't like it that way but people wash DDT
   in my rivers and it stays.
When I was three,
I almost fell out of my tree.
Now that's the story of me,
The bald eagle who almost fell out of her tree.
Erin Michelle Tinker

Peaceful Poet

When the birds chirp and the doves sing
And it rains outside on the snow
The wind growls and dances in the sky
Something is peaceful I don't know why
It must be that I love chirping and singing
I truly do not know why
Chelsea Marie Hall

His Name Was Otto

His name was Otto, this uncle of mine,
Who came into my life when I was nine.
He was tall, dark and handsome, A German by birth.
And his jokes kept us laughing, with joy and mirth.

A Black Forest watchmaker he was by his trade,
Who was wed to Aunt Ruby, a wise decision he made.
For she would remain at his side many years,
There always to share in his laughter and tears.

On a hot summer's eve, Otto did magic tricks,
Making keys disappear and bits of bread sticks.
He taught us to count in German to ten,
And recite poems about industrious men.

He made lots of money this Uncle of mine,
and was generous always to his very last dime.
My last visit with Uncle, in a hospital bed,
Was happy with songs which he ably led.

Now Otto and his angels are waiting the day,
When we again will join him to work and to play.
Marjorie L. Walker

Angels Are Very Special Beings

Angels, my dear, come in various shapes and sizes.
If this fact is unknown to you, you're due for some surprises.
A pat on he back on a dark, gloomy day, a smile
or a hug or a kiss, can immediately drive the
clouds away in exchange for a feeling of bliss.
Angels don't dwell in outer space, flitting from star
to star, but angels you'll find are wonderfully
kind, reaching us right where we are.
For angels are all around us, neighbors, family,
friends, just open your eyes and you will see
and that's where this story ends.

Happy holidays fellow angels.
Much love,

Fannie I. O'Neil

"If Not For Mom"

What would I do,
if without you?
Who would I be, if you, I'd never see?
Where should I go, if "back home," I'd never know?
When would I have the time
to find the reason behind the rhyme?
How could anybody see my best, my good,
if you had never pointed a should?
Why even think of tomorrow,
if without you, it would be full of sorrow,
If I never saw your smiling face,
nor never been held by your warm embrace,
Should these questions ever be asked,
if, you were only a face behind the mask?
Will you ever begin to know
all the reasons I love you so?
Do you dare begin to count,
All the times I've given you doubt?
Have you ever searched for the perfect clue,
To see me better, still being you?

Christina Kathleen Thomas

My Appalachian Mule

Early to rise, early to shine you lazy mule, you lazy swine.
You're just a beast of burden.
God's servant to man, a four legged creature, long eared funny kind.
For 18 long hot, cold, and dry seasons, you have been a faithful mule,
and friend of mine; helping me plant and raise a poor man's crop at
harvest time. From sunrise to sunset;
we both have marched a million miles through those hills and valleys;
tilling soil, rocks, and roots, and over mountain tops with plow,
and muddy boots.
But now our life's journey and work is nearing an end;
because we are now old and gray, and nearly blind.
"Oh! How I curse Father Time."
So lift up your eyes and ears to heaven, my faithful long earned friend.
Can you hear the Master's voice calling us home to that beautiful
garden in the sky
Where faithful old mules, and poor dirt farmers come to rest in the
great bye and bye.

Mel Johnson

Untitled

She enters my mind strong and pure
like the shadow of a stained glass
church window.
Pulling a true and beautiful reflection
from my memory.
I want to thank her by letting her in,
but it's easier to let myself out.
It's funny how the mind is a terrible thing
to taste.

James M. Barron

The Shuttle Columbia May Lift Off Today

Seven astronauts were assigned to a flight
Originally scheduled for September 28 after night.
The first countdown stopped when a light
Showed that a computer signal relay system was not right.
The second take-off was delayed due to rain
The astronauts tried to take it in vain.
The third launch had to be set back
When a hydrogen tank leak was the attack.
The Columbia tried for a fourth time to lift off in the air
But dangerous cracks in the test engine were there.
For a fifth time, the troubled space shuttle tried to ignite
But this time low clouds interrupted the flight.
Two and a half weeks later NASA again waited for storm after
    storm to clear
The shuttle must launch or the public would jeer.
Columbia had matched its record of six delays
(The last one was in January '86 when they finally got underway).
There on the launch pad old Columbia peered
Sadly watching the Atlantis rendezvous with the Mir.
When will the Columbia lift off?

Joseph Papp

A Friend

A friend is someone that shows compassion,
To others when trouble comes their way.
A friends is someone that listens
To what others have to say.

A friend shows genuine interest, good will and concern,
A friend is someone that is willing to learn
To learn about others and the things they do,
They will be there at times when family is few.

They share the good times and the bad,
They help to comfort us when we are sad.
They take others best interest at heart
That way they are always a part
A part of our lives, actions and ways,
They help us to have better days.

It might come in the form of a handshake or a smile,
It could be just to lend an ear for a while.
But they will never let you down
And you will truly miss them when they are not around.

Carolyn K. Williams

Weeping Willow

Oh weeping willow why do you weep
Do you have some kind of secret to tell?
Do you weep because you might be old and gray?
Do you weep because you might be all alone in the world
oh weeping do not weep you are not alone, you have me
for how many tree's might of shaded a princess
or a wounded knight and his lady love.
Did you shade two lover's as they shared their first kiss?
Were you the tree that shaded a newly borne infant and her mother?
Or maybe a wedding of a king and his new-to-be bride the queen
How many hero's have died and been buried under your branch?
How many princess have cried under you because their father has
banned her lover
How many broken hearts have you mended with your gentle
flowing vines?
Did you see the killings of world war one? Did they make you weep
or maybe it was world war two that made your weep?
Do you remember when I was little and would play under you?
All the places we went all the faces we'd meet all under you!
Now I'm all grown-up, too old to do those things is that why you
    weep
Oh weeping willow, do not weep because of me as you grow older so
    must I!
I'll be back and with me a new friend, my child so don't weep for me
    weeping willow.

Jean Taylor

As One, Our Hearts, "Til Death Do We Part!"

So full of heart,
You have brightened my days!
Showing me a new start,
And brand new ways!

You pulled me out of the rain,
And have gotten rid of my past.
Taken away, all of my pain,
And finally making happiness last!

You showed me a new view,
Of the way relationships should be!
By your sweet words ringing true,
And your efforts to make me happy!

You listened to my cry,
And taught me to hear,
New avenues to try,
And to overcome my fear!

I tasted your wine,
So sweet and full of heart!
And smelled your fragrant roses,
Thank You My Love, "Til death do we part!"

Laurie-Ellen B. Wilkinson

My Hero Too

Fifty three years have passed you see, yet that wide-eyed
little girl I still call me.

Excitement and fear in momma's voice "sit down, be quiet,
hold tight, Grand-mas arrested we're hero's tonight."

No drivers licence, law breaking momma, I heard her pray,
"car don't let me down, we're off to the jail house today."

Me in that black car I did wait, while mamma and the cops
was suppose to debate.

Mistaken identity ———my grandmother freed, we drove home
with a clunk and a jerk and much less speed.

Daddy did I ever tell you of that mid-night ride, "I am
sorry I never told you, I am sorry I lied."

"You mean the broken clutch and what I repaired." Ha, Ha
he laughed, see if I cared.

The joke was on manna and you, —— sweet child she was
my hero too.."

June Moore Langley

War

And so sat they on their mountain high
Above the barren, blighted land below.
While feasting, they, in ambrosial high,
Reclined, and savoured softly the view.
Yet up so very high were they
Away from those oh, so far away,
That the distance did distort in its corrupting way
And make madmen's fancies take to life.

And thought they then amidst visions of glory,
That on the earthen ground so cold
Was etched a crimson emblem of victory.
For this they did rise and give toast.

Yet something purer, held lost within them,
Buried deep inside their cold-grown hearts,
Did perceive this blazoned sign more truly.
'Twas the blood of a million men, felled dead.

David J. Grynkiewicz

Confusion V. Balance

The sum of my emotions is confusion
I seek a balance in perplexed seclusion

What middle ground is between apathy and obsession?
To escape secrecy, must one turn to confession?

If a person's feet aren't on the ground, must they be flighty?
If someone isn't weak, are they always mighty?

I shy from being dogmatic; avoid being too passive
I'd hate to be bored but don't want to be overactive

How to keep from being naive while not being paranoid?
Hate being overworked?—it's no better being unemployed.

Can one's life stay free of clutter without seeming bare?
Can one avoid ignorance and not be painfully aware?

I don't want to be too risky and I'm scared of being afraid
Real honesty frightens people but I won't live a charade.

Can I not be cynical and keep from being idealistic?
May one throw off one's restraints without being anarchistic?

The aforementioned extremes are but a partial list.
How do so many contradictions ever coexist?

Answering such questions is not one of my talents
Still, day and night I yearn to discover *the balance*.

Kelly Paulson

Branches of Life

Chilling on the outside, I warm with a cup of tea.
Pacing within closing walls, may this season pass quickly.
I glance through parted curtains, to view a sight just beyond.
In midst of all the traffic, it is a branch I focus upon.
The twisted, winding structure, reaching out against the sky.
Expanding limbs of welcoming arms as drivers pass on by.
It moves quite slowly, grasping at the winds.
It bends and turns mostly, crackling moans within.
The branch seems deceased, bark is old and chipped away.
Remaining in its lifeless form, till a warm spring day.

Renee L. Fisher

Slowly Say Goodbye

We look back now and think about
    the people who have died.
The men and women, boys and girls,
of every race and every size.

If only someone would have warned them
Maybe they would have been saved.
If only someone had known how to explain
But then again maybe their road was already paved.

We just can't make ourselves believe
That God wanted it to be this way.
Even for the greatest sin
He wouldn't kill innocent people each day.

The human race is greedy and proud
And yet we still want more.
We fight like children amongst ourselves.
Does anyone remember what we're fighting for?

We know you buried your best friend today.
So, close your eyes as the sunset fades.
And we're sorry you had to learn this way
That your best friend had contracted AIDS.

Tiffany Norris

My Piano

Sometimes,
  I think I hear her...
    She cries for me.

Convinced that I have abandoned her,
  She searches the skies for me.

Desperately, she severs the silence with her pleas.
  The wind carries her voice...
    each pitch, more frantic than the one before.

She refuses to believe me,
  I had no choice.... I could do no more.

I try to console her,
  but my words mean
    Nothing.

Only with the touch of my fingers
  will her torment cease.
    My piano...
      My Love...
        My Life...

Nicole M. Casavan

Reason

Why do we rhyme, does it have to do with time?

Shorten this, tighten that, make my reader happy and fat.
Inhibiting our true imagination,
Our true message.
Our soul is not built on rhyming,
But on the wind of the random, more a stream of delights.
A lyric massages our traveler's feet,
Caresses his calloused hand,
Oils and perfumes his long tattered hair.
This traveler wears no shoes, or at least no shoes with comfort.
Endless directions, endless wanting.
So, it is from that, can we see our soul is naked to the night.
Forced to be blended without sight.
His random wishes, touches and quirks,
are left to this forever running band,
Of musical massage, the petulance of the pen in hand.

Timothy Sommer

"My Winter Wonderland"

Gracefully it starts to fall,
Inch by inch it's standing tall
Buried in sea of white,
The wind is blowing cold tonight.

There's frost on the mountains, and a chill in the air.
And hot chocolate inside for everyone to share.
The ice is thick and the snow is deep,
This beautiful scene in my heart, I will always keep.

Now the snow is starting to melt.
When will it come again, it's hard to tell.
As another winter comes to a close
And the rays of sunshine begin to flow,
My winter wonderland and I must part,
But I'll remember it forever in my heart.

Nicole Pfister

Aura

They say the body has an aura — colors of the rainbow yet unseen by
  the naked eye.
Your touch, your kisses draws my aura like the day's sunset:
strokes of fiery reds, of mellow yellows, of lazy oranges, of baby
  blues with a touch of raspberry.
These are the colors of pleasure you give me.
Many sunsets to come.

Jacqueline P. Cabellon

By His Word

As I sit in the quite solitude of my lonely little room.
I slip back in silent memory of days gone by.
In my minds eye I see the turbulence of my life.
Of all the things I've loved and lost.
Of all the sorrow and pain.
Then I reach for his word and find comfort.
And I let go of things from the past.
And by His word, I draw my strength, to face the world again.

Rhonda Blaski

To Ben

You are my future, child,
All my tomorrows,
In you rests my continuation
In you I will go on
Even when long departed

Just as our fore-bears had,
All who had gifted of themselves
To my totality
As well as what you are.

How wonderful it is to know
That there is something in us
Of all who had been here before,
The ones we know and those we haven't heard of
Yet bear their imprint.

Just think that years ahead
In generations yet unborn
Are those who will inherit our make-up
And in whose lives we will continue
You and I - immortals.

Milda Isenberg

An Endless Summer In The Park

Just around the block, it was there.

The millions of tiny pebbles that made up the ground
that got stuck in your shoes, and eventually
scattered around the house.

The monkey bars you'd climb on
until you got a blister on your hand.
The tire swing they'd push you on until you felt sick.
The yellow plastic slide
that was more fun to climb up than to slide down
and the swing set that allowed you to touch the sun

The hills of grass to sit on
and stare into the endless blue sky
or watch a little league baseball game unfold
in a sunny afternoon
of an endless summer
in the park.

Jason Bonine

Friendship

Friendship is love and caring for a friend.
Friendship is letting a friend tell you their problems.
Friendship is being a friend.

Friendship is being nice to one another.
Friendship means being there when a friend needs you.
Friendship is something that you can't buy or sell.

Friendship comes from the heart!
Friendship means sticking up for one another.
Friendship means being there when one is in trouble.
Friendship, you can earn by showing you care.

Amanda D. Bushey

Farewell

The time has come for you to go
The reason why, no one will know
Now that it's time you cannot wait
To stand outside those pearly gates
You walked the Earth and had your fun
Your deeds down here are good and done
The cemetery holds your body there
God lifts your spirit in the air
There you stand without your cane
You'll feel, no more hurt or pain
Now you are able to walk and run
With Jesus Christ, the Holy Son
You will see tears run down our face
but we all know you're in a better place
You think these tears, they might destroy
but these tears are for you, they're tears of joy

Shane Walling

To My Love Laurie

To my wife,
Which I had only dreamed about,
And now is my life!
I could not live without her,
Now that she is here!
Together, we share our hopes —
Our dreams and even a tear!

L is the loving and caring for the family.
A is for always and twinkle in her eye.
U is for the understanding-unlimited time she gives.
R is for the respect she deserves the most.
I is for I will always take her to be my wife, oxoxo.
E is for encouragement and excellence the way she's always been.

Raymond Charles Wilkinson Sr.

A greater passion has filled my soul,
But its blooming I never knew.
For when it had finally pervaded my whole,
It flew with the wind as it blew.

And now that I finally have found a cause
Worthy of such a name;
Soon I'll discover it's but a mirage,
And the wind will blow just the same.

And why can't I give one sincere plight
To a cause that's true and just?
Not rightly a lack of commitment,
But a vein which cradles distrust.

One foot on the shore and one on the stern
As the ship travels out to sea
But I am neither a dweller on dry land
Nor a denizen of water, obviously.

I am content as I straddle the medium
Between two steadfast extremes,
But where the wind blows I follow,
And from the home of contentment I flee.

Charles Adam Miller

Candy

Adults think kids don't need it, but here's
The good old truth: every child needs some to
quench their sugar tooth.
Parents say it rots your teeth and that it's
bad for you, but how would us kids get
along if it weren't for a ju ju or two?
We've tried to reason but enough of that,
now we get our say. No matter if you
like it or not, candy's here to stay!

Phoebe Hastings

Finding My Strength

One, two, three — STOP!
That's all I'll let fall for now.
Tears that flowed freely, choked
Remember anger, hate if possible
His smile is a ghost
It always was chilled, wasn't it Puck?
No.
It must have been real at some point
Powerful drive — just a show?
Throb confused with intimacy
When remembering love — what he called love
Instead I'll remember his hands around my neck — CLENCH!
All that flows is a grunted whisper
"Go ahead you f@%#er, squeeze a little harder
I dare you, my sweet love."
My ace? I always knew he was a coward deep in his soul
My life, my chance prevails
Left him — freedom fight is over
I stand alone
Strong

Maria R. DiCarlo

Spring

Seasons come and go, winter, spring, summer and fall
but to spring is the most beautiful time of all.
The grass which is brown turns a gorgeous green
the trees follow suit and it seems like a dream.
The blue of the sky and the flowers in bloom and
the return of the birds to chase away the gloom.
We spend happy hours working outside all day long
then relax in the shade, listening to the birds singing their song.
Winter is fun, Christmas, New Years, the snow, skating and sledding too
Summer is also fun, vacationing, swimming, boating, and lots of
    things to do.
Fall with its leaves turning colors and falling to the ground
harvesting crops, working late with the bright moon shining down.
Spring brings life to everything and causes everyone to smile
as we emerge from a long, long winter and spend time in the sun for
    awhile.

Ruby Anderson

Sleep Can Be A Beautiful Thing

Being with someone you love is a beautiful thing
When parting, it seems like part
Of your life, and heart are taken
Away, it hurts so bad inside
But not all hope is lost,
Someone supreme has created
Sleep a beautiful thing
And love, I will be with you
Every time I dream

Elizabeth J. Stephenson

Before The End Of Summer

Before the end of summer
Before the end of summer is through,
I will have to say my final good-byes to you and only you,
I will miss your tasty cakes and pies,
And your happy, lovely, joyful cries.

Your presence will be deeply missed,
And all your pains will be healed and kissed.
Your kindness was the very best,
Now your soul is laid to rest.
You're in a better place in the sky,
That is where your soul is left to lie.
You fought your pain to the very end,
But it carried you away in the hot summer wind.

James Ferguson

"Cries From The Earth"

The winds mourn for the fallen trees
   Which once stood so stately in their path
The widened spaces stretching endlessly tell the tale
   Tales heard as in death valleys after an aftermath
Tales of stately timbers clusters of lovely branches
   Fires that came causing them to red in their trenches
How the smoke caused their little ones to choke and gasp
   Holding on the each other during all the earthly blasts
Then came the long blades cutting to their very heart
   Cold steel tearing their trembling, bleeding roots apart
No one heard their cries from hill and plain as they lay
   Stretched our for burial, when the end came
No one would look. No one would hear, no one to grieve
   No one noticed as they lay in death, no one to blame
When the rains would come, washing away every clue
   No one would remember they ever were; only the wind knew.

Bette Lou Antoinnette Jernigan Rogers

On The Threshold

A fragmented soul yearns for the light.
Lost in the shadows and mirrored past
He is frightened by his reflection.

Beguiled and broken, donned in his mortal mask,
The traverse is yet to appear.

Self-proclaimed agonizer, worldly junkie...
Forgetting his existence is not distinguished to this world alone.

Oh, the random mess he's made!
Only to be later hunted down by haunting truths.

Vile and tainted, he walks the same path,
Lessons yet unlearned.

A primordial soup is stirred,
Merging in the harmonies of its eternal existence,
Both earthly and divine.

A taste of the elixir brings forth recognition...
Manifested omniscience.
Anubis summons.

Mary Albanese

"Can I"

I live every day as if it's my last
Can I live my whole life if I hurry up fast
Can I see the whole world with its beauty and grace
Can I see all whom I love, each and every face
Can I fit it all in, do I have the time
Will my life even be long enough to finish this rhyme
We take so much for granted and never finish all our tasks
We greet people and never remove our masks
I want to do it all, see it all, live it all now
Can I fit it all in - will I ever learn how
Can I play in the daisy and sail the seven seas
Count the stars in the sky as far as the eye can see
Can I taste all the cuisine from here and from there
Can I lovingly touch an old person's hair
Can I fly high in the sky and delve deep in the sea
Can I fit this all in and still find time to be me
Can I remember to say I love you to those near and dear
Can I do it all the time and not just once a year
Can I, can I, can I, the question's not this
It's will I, will I, life is something I don't want to miss

Roberta Koehler

The Night Angels Watched

He awakened in the night to the sound of shots
   and broken glass.
His feet hit the floor, hunkering, he squeezed
under the bed and listened to the squealing tires
and bullets trailing off.
Resounding, pounding in diminishing returns
   everywhere but in his mind.
He waited counting springs and studying their
design. Fear had left him long ago.
How many nights had he spent on the floor, he
   wondered.
He was seven years old. Counting the days when
   he could terrorize some kid in the night.
And the angels kept their distance sitting in their
   overstuffed chairs, they watched, exhausted.

William N. Clark

Seedtime

In amazement, I have viewed the changes in you,
As in past years, it has always come true.
Spring, what has awakened you from your winter's sleep?
Was it the song of robins heralding you with their cheep?
Or the warm rays of the sun, that kissed your cool cheek,
Stirring it to melt the frost that imprisoned life and leak
Forth the first green blades of the hardy little crocus,
A sure sign there is more to come, they tell us,
As they open up their delicate petals of varied hue.
Thank God, He made seasons and blessed us with you.

Now that you are awake, there is little time to sleep.
The blue skies will float fleecy white clouds to weep
Rain to nurse the thirsty roots hidden in the ground,
That take their drink and grow without a sound,
Stretching their necks to the sky and faces to the sun,
So very happy just to be alive and seeing everyone.
Oh Spring, it's a very busy time for you,
But we have no doubts that you can do it, too.
Because seasons of seedtime, God has declared,
With tender, loving care, He has always prepared.

Marie Kobi

Verb

I am the kiss upon the lips of the wind.
The rock washed onto beach as sand,
I am the fragrance of unplanted seed.
The song within blue speckled egg.
I am the tear within soft fleeced cloud.
The glow out far unto the East
I am the chill of words unconsidered.
And the warm when love giveth all.
I am the light of gross worlds colliding.
The sweetness aflowing in full bodied tree.
I am the summit of love's rich ecstasy.
The peace of mind when it is still.
I am the promise of all living I am verb.
Always the joy of always beginning

Yolanda Crail

Standing Strong

As I look across the fields and see the trees begin to bloom.
It's like seeing a new life begin. Going from bud to full
maturity and seeing it stand and be so beautiful in its own
way. Like the love I have for you, it started out small like
a bud on a tree and it had grown into much more each day and
as it has grown it has become strong like the roots and the
trunk and when things go wrong we have to bend like the
branches without breakage. Our love will weather all tests,
and will still be standing strong as the beautiful trees
standing in the fields.

Alberta Lynn Bartlett

Daring Choices

Her nearness fills my longing
As fully as a candles light
Embraces the darkened room.

   Sweet, sweet the aroma
   Long lost and covered
   Now caressing heart and soul.

Drawing, calling, softly tugging
Alluring choice must make
The heart long withered.

   Shall I remain behind bars now opened?
   Or daring, fear forsaken, stepping
   Out with mask aside?

Passion stirred on wings now rising
Soaring high beyond past hurt
Shall know again her touch of life.
   Jim Mackey

Oh, You Shine!

When darkness is in the daylight all about
and nowhere I can see
   You shine.

When the brightness is but unlit clouds
and dulled emotions crawl
   You shine.

When with wetness my eyes are blurring
and heaviness weighs my soul
   You shine.

When whirling winds cast me 'round
and no sense in me finds home
   You shine.

Then when I see with clarity full
what you've been through just for me
   You shine!
     Oh, you shine!
   Beth Stevens

Now That Fall Is Here

Summer's gone and Autumn is here,
The Autumn breeze,
Says Winter is near.
The leaves fall quickly down,
The plants and grass turn dark, dark brown.
Young children go out to play.
They place their warm clothes on for the day.
Days are shorter,
And school seems longer,
Now that Fall is here!
   Corin Elise Barron

Death By Bargains

"Oklahoma Bomb Victims Remembered"
"30% off during our After Easter Sale"
Death and sales given the same front-page exposure.
The next page has a full-page spread of women in bras and
panties—
Advertising.
The world of the sublime juxtaposed with the ridiculous.
Life cheapened; sold out; sick with grief one moment—
Excited by bargains the next.
   Karen S. Wolven

I'll Love You In Silence

You came into my life
Quietly, simply, and tenderly
The world stood still
I could not say a period
Nor do a single gesture
To show this feeling deep in my heart
I love you in silence
Love you from a distance
Dream of you from the world of illusions
I wanted to say "I love you"
But I was afraid
Afraid you might ignore me
So in silence, I will care
In silence, I will love you
Cause in silence...
I will find the fulfillment of my dreams...
   Leilani R. Victoria

A Friend Of Mine

In Memory of Pepe Fereira.
A friend of mine likes to go fast;
he very much likes to fly.
He wants to go to very far places;
when he sees you he flies right by.

On a typical day he checks out his boat;
he checks if the cover has a bend,
He checks the motor, meter and everything;
then he washes it 'till the very end.

In a typical race, he puts on his uniform;
and he looks real handsome in it too.
He is also excited and proud;
for he is about to rate the ocean blue.

He flies through the water very fast;
the wind is blowing all over his face.
His hands are gripped to the steering wheel;
You'll be seeing him all over the place.

He's been to pretty much everywhere;
he goes to championships all the time.
For he is never afraid to race;
I'm glad he didn't become a mime.
   Natalie Merino

The Good Samaritan

Arriving on earth/The day of our birth
Becoming a part of God's human creation
The first few years/it does appear
We have very little useful motivation

We than learn to move/and begin to improve
With interest in life and worldly things
Like sports studies/friends and buddies
Striving for progress, perfection brings

'The good old school/and its golden rule
Making grown-up adults of girls and boys
We age and grow/with a desire to show
That exemplary development can be a joy

Giving others a lift/Is a genuine gift
Showing kindness no matter when or where
'There are things to be done/Hard work and fun
Include an occasional needed loving prayer

Giving others a lift/Is a genuine gift
Exemplifying concern for the cares of all
Let our Charity exceed/for those in need
That's truly answering the Masters call.
   Joachim C. Mosbrucker

Winter Days And Little Children

I remember little children on cold and crispy days;
   I stood at the window to see golden hair fly as she ran;
The boys would crush dry leaves beneath swift feet;
   There was so much energy expended in their joyful play.
Time stood so still back then, as winter days often do.
   Stark, cold, but beautiful - and in my heart I thought I could
Keep them as they were when eyes sparkled and smiled up at me
   From innocence and sheer delight -
Sturdy were my little ones, just as my winter tree.

I planted bulbs, raked leaves and felt the joy of rain,
   My eyes drank in the radiance of their faces;
Cold air would fill my lungs, and from both I felt sweet pain.
   In my mind those days are etched so clearly,
As if put there to recall, when other winters were to follow;
   And as parched things would cry out for the refreshing,
So, too, would I have need to see them merely
   As they were before the blossoms came, and green began to grow,
And they did too, in their springtime,
   Back in the many winters, of so very long ago.

Sally Wood

God's Rocket Display

The other morning before the break of day
There appeared in the sky a gorgeous display.
The colors were as brilliant as any could be.
The presence of God you could almost see.
A rocket was launched in New Mexico.
What a beautiful sight, only our Lord could make it so
Arranging the elements in such a way
They showed so many colors in such an array.
He made the gases and moisture just right
So that we could see this marvelous sight.
I would venture to say in the span of our days
We'll never see anything like this at which we can gaze.
I'll never understand how in the darkest of night
Our Lord could show us such a beautiful sight.

Paul Smith

North, South, East, West

East, South, West, North
Through these directions we will sort.
We'll wait until North is fourth.
East, South, West, North

South, North, West, East
Who is going to kill the beast?
When he's dead, we'll have a feast.
South, North, West, East

West, East, North, South
Don't talk with food in your mouth.
If you do you'll go without.
West, East, North, South

North, South, East, West
Which of these do you think is best?
If West is best, what's wrong with the rest?
North, South, East, West

East, South, West, North
Now we're back and North is fourth.
And we're all finished with the sort.
East, South, West, North

Jennifer Dillman

Date Rape Shower Massager

I sit against my slimy wall
Luke warm moisture strings down from my shower head
Tears seem to die as they harden on my pale cheeks
Silly me to think that this would cleanse my body
I can no longer move my arms, my legs
I slowly tilt my head back and press my lips together
Sucking in life, creating a shrill whistle
That manifests into a demonic howl
A cry of pity, only received by the darkness
A small ladybug crawls out from a crack in the sky
Its shining orange light blinds me
A good-luck charm somehow wiggles its way into
This desperate fog filtered dream
It must represent my priest, the one who baptized me
I wonder why it came here, perhaps to save me?
Is this the sign which I have so patiently waited for?
I begin asking these questions
After I crush it between my fingers
I want no salvation
I deserve damnation.

David Bland

Live Your Dream

If the life you are living seems dull
And then world all around you seems small,
Then you must begin trying again
To search for and hold onto a dream.

Life holds no guarantee to success
You must display the willingness
To climb out of the gutter of grief and despair
And grasp for and hold onto a dream.

For dreams are the essence of growth in a life
The treasures we seek as we muddle through strife
While living each day on the edge of the world
Reach out and hold on to those dreams

Start trying today, and dare not delay,
For dreams are sometimes fleeting away
Breath and believe in what your mind sees,
Live for and hold onto your dreams

Zane R. Bollom

The Ageless Reminder

Standing on our deck, I smelled a sweet-scent from early
   Blossoms and hay.
That evening there was a modicum of warmth in the air.
There was a quiescence and silence that night which brought
   An inner peace without delay.
The sky above was clear enabling me to see the stars
   Magnificence before me and I did stare.
Behold! What I saw moving slowly into my sight overwhelmed
   Me with wonder and astonishment.

It was a resplendent, effulgent, beauteous comet sent this
   Way eons ago.
To see this rarity streaking across the heavens filled my
   Mind and soul with great delight and awe.
What fortune and favor to experience this glowing orb full
   Of mystery; with secrets to get to know.
I watched it move across the sky and it seemed to beckon to
   Me, this orb I saw.
God seemed to be telling me, "See! This is my handy work and
   Know it is I who creates all things and gives life."

Joanne Marie Lake

Why?

Why must everyone be a whore
Why do we shove our virginity out the door
What is it with all the "bad girls"
They're so bad it's the only way to get some thrills

A nice girl is looking for a nice guy
She's searched everywhere - down low, up high
One day she said "I'm just gonna have fun"
Today, she decided, she's going to be the bad one

But that didn't work for her at all
She got stranded in a long, dark hall
She tried being bad once, two times, thrice
Then she got tired and went back to being nice

Now she's still alone with a sleazy reputation
Within depression she curses herself to damnation
She is still very naive, but not of the knife
When no one is looking, she takes her own life

Elizabeth Wilkins

"Steal"

Don't steal from the children.
Why leave them alone.
Please don't take away their mother and
their home.
They have no father, that's his greatest sin.
Don't steal from them, they need you and you
need them.
Never give away the greatest love, you'll ever know.
To take away a child's great glow.
I think it's the worlds greatest sin.
They are scared for life down deep within.
Don't lock them out, please let them in.
That love you get, will never end.
Not just for you, but especially for them.

Linda Brown

My Little Angel

I hold my precious daughter in my arms.
Her tiny fingers reach up to grab my necklace.
I touch her smooth, soft face, and I smile.
Gently I kiss her on her head,
Not yet full of hair.
Her eyelids start to fall,
And her baby blue eyes are hidden.
Her weight becomes heavy in my arms,
As she drifts off into dreamland.
Slowly, I take her to bed to lay her down.
She stirs quietly and then rolls onto her side.
I switch off light and walk out of the room.
Slowly, I sit down and ask myself,
Why did I receive such an angel?
Then I think to myself...
I'm a mother, that is why.

Kacy Lengl

The Graduate

Eloquent speeches and gifts galore
Hand shakes, smiles and much much more,
All are conceived thru respect and love
And blessings bestowed by one from above.

All this is true, never denied
And you, reaching out, ventured and tried.
None, no not one, can judge your worth.
You're a queen of many here on earth.

My pride in you shines in my eyes
My respect for you, never disguised.
May your reign at the top never end.
I love you Jo-Jo, my friend, my friend!

Joyce Raphael

Warning You

I see you trying to leave me I've known it for a long time
I didn't pay attention to the move
Cause I never thought you could do something like that.
I only see you with me you know everything you need is in me.
So take a moment to understand me.
Remember a good guy like me is hard to find.
The way I treat you there is no one else like me who will.
I know that you miss me.
Get up, stand up and treasure me.
You know I'm the only one who can satisfy your soul.
Think about the good days and you'll realize
I'm the one don't wait until I change
My mind being with someone else
To say that you miss me.
I know that you are confused there is no need to be confused
Get up, stand up and take your chance.
I'm the one who can satisfy your soul.
The way I'll make you feel
You'll never know if someone could have loved you. So real.

Bernadin Sylvestre

The End

Once long ago when we were friends
We thought our friendship would never end
But time moves fast and things go on
And somehow we proved each other wrong
With words unspoken yet too much said
We let to many things go to our head
Without a word spoken we thought for a while
And our conversation ended without a frown or a smile
We both knew that we could no longer be a friend
So now our wonderful friendship has come to an end

Alicia Brend

Colors

White is like the color of my soul, honest and brave.
But where will it go long from now?
Will I ever know?
Will I have failed, or have I passed?
Will my soul be too scared or will it step out of darkness and into
light?

Red is like my blood - strong and courageous; willing to keep me
alive.
It stands the pain of needles and operations, though it has never
let me down.
I wonder when it will get too old and leave me, but it's still young
now.

Black is like anger willing to come out.
It makes my soul feel weak and my blood feel hot.
I just want to scream, but instead I cry.
As the hot steamy tears run down my face a hot burning cloud of
anger releases.
I think to myself the anger is releasing,
the tears start to fade and I know I am happy again.

Kayla Brooking

"As Dew Does Drop"

As dew does drop and craze along
The lull, lush grass, and bright as days
That gape right into the deep sun,
Like glisten shining off our brows.
And I, my brother's ease, shall work
The winter into tears, until
Our toll will turn with ending toll,
Or dare our drudge not fear its dirge.
Farewell our moor! For toil treads
The tears wept simple and sincere.

Vladimir Bugarski

Today Is Tomorrow

He traded a dream,
She traded a sorrow,
Together, they thought,
His dream could be there tomorrow.

She was like a child climbing a tree,
She was so eager, to believe
There was so much, that she did not see.

The top of a tree,
Has blossoms and clean air.
The top of this tree,
Was empty and bare.

Their dream was made of sand, not clay.
And like sand, it fell and drifted away.
So a woman grew up,
In a strange sort of way.

He'll keep his dream,
And she'll keep her sorrow.
But, at least for a while,
They had a dream for tomorrow.
Dorothy Burgo

Untitled

Not as they seem,
But always as they are.
Their images which are lies;
Their insights which are unimaginative.
The creativity they don't use to express the thoughts that flit
Through their bottomless pit of silence.
Yet they are the ones that prosper.
They are the ones seen to have open minds and willing hearts.
They are the simplicity of the universe.
Therefore they simply are.
Amanda M. Beals

How Do You Know?

How do you know if you're having fun?
Or really having a lark?
A ride at the carnival, a trip on a boat,
Or merely a walk in the park?

A climb up a mountain
To its highest peak,
Sky-dive from a plane
And drop like a streak?

It's but a fleeting moment
To catch if you can
In the web of your memory
As a part of God's plan!
Dorothy J. Izell

The One I Love

This poem is dedicated to the one I love,
An angel who must have been sent from heaven above,
The one whose embrace every night I dream of,
The one whose words often fill me with love,
The one to whom which I feel I belong,
The one whose lips often sing me sweet songs,
The one whose life with whom I want mine to be spent,
The one whose touch is a blessing to be sent,
The one whose eyes I have come to adore,
The one whose loving leaves me begging for more,
The one whose calls I have learned to expect,
The one who sends cards filled with so much respect,
The one who gives blessing for every decision I make,
This little poem has but one point to make,
Because this poem is dedicated to the one I love,
An angel who was definitely sent from above.
Gayla R. Wilson

"The Flight"

We climbed up mountains together, we soared to great heights
Holding each other, we took flight

We found a new world, we caught sight
Of a love others only dream of
Through the depth of our emotions
We began to fly

I wonder, I ask myself why
I replay the thought of you
And once again, I touch the sky

It only takes a little while, and I begin to see
You'll never really leave me
Because it was you who set my heart free

You'll live in my soul forever, you'll be my one truth
My compass when I'm lost at sea
Giving me direction, a purpose and a reason to be

So when I close my eyes
When I need to feel your touch
When I start to wonder why
It's then I reach to touch the sky
It's then you become my truth, and my heart begins to fly
Melissa Peterson

Hills Of Home

At first, I missed the busy street
the hourly passing of the trolley,
the constant hum of city noises—
now the red clay hills are my home,
these woods of lofty pines that lie
beneath a blue and generous sky.

I've grown to love the winds that sway
the lofty pines, moving them as waves
on some long ago remembered city
swimming pool, which I no longer miss
for I have a lake within my woods,
with ducks and singing birds.

Here in this quietness, there's nerve
release. No calming drugs I need.
When the stars appear, bringing the
silent hush of night to the sleeping
woods, there's contentment, a sense
of belonging to the universe in

This small part of the vast creation here.
In these woods, I've found peace..
Ivie Bozeman

My Feline Samantha

Samantha, Samantha, beautiful Samantha
She's a feline, not a panther
Her sly and clever ways always impress me
With a subtle purr is how she addresses me
But don't be startled if this Siamese attempts to strike you
During her playfulness, she will not ignite you
She's declawed at front, as if you didn't know
Beware ... she'll nip you softly and then go, go, go
She'll run and hide for a short while
And later return with a mischievous smile
Her black face and tips of feet and paws
Were described by Anson as being dipped in oil
However, she's my clean, cuddly ball of fur
Always attending that tan, fluffy fur
You can never predict Samantha's daily routine
Because she does so many, many things
I always wondered if life existed without her
How would I compensate for the love that she renders?
No need to worry... she has nine lives and that's splendid!
Roberta K. Hawthorne

Raging Sea

The sailors on board were trembling with fright,
  because of the storm on that cold, wet night.
Their ship was tossed from side to side,
  as the wind declared her power and pride.

Sails and hoists split and came down,
  souls washed overboard where they would drown.
The captain and crew, beyond human power.
  yielded control to the sea in that hour.

Flashes of light brightened the sky,
  revealing the fear in each man's eye.
Waves crashed over the starboard side,
  many were wounded, some even died.

When morning came and all was still,
  the sun brought strength and warmth to heal.
A new day of hope, each man in his heart,
  did learn the lesson the sea did impart.

Brandon Burrus

Piss Syrup And Ground-Glass Pancakes

Ice cold Cow
Egged and Frothing
Battered and Grilled
Hot!
Flip...Flop...Flip
Hot dish
Butter it up
Short and plump
Stacked—
to stay warm,
to stay warm,
to stay warm.
Shiny slivers in Silver Dollars and Short Stacks
Drip...Drop...Dripping
Dulcet Ooze
of distilled rage—
buttered to taste.
All the while
asking
"Ain't Jemima on the pancake box?"

G. Sierra Khan

Bride Of The Morning

The sunrise was splendid. And in a cloud aloft
The "semblance" of a bride was seen in raiment soft,
Her gown flowed with a train borne gently by the wind
The veil puffed, but stayed placed, as if it had been pinned.
She moved with stately grace, quite calm, precise, and slow
Gentle. She was superb! With an aura of glow,
We, my husband and I, today - God's Sabbath Day
Would attend early Church, to thank Him, sing, and pray.
Our souls need nourishing, as well as the body,
God's words as we worships, feed us spiritually
I looked at a window - stained glass - just a mere glance
During the fine sermon. Was this only by chance?
For it made me think of "The Gleaners" by Millet
Showing people gleaning, in a harsh, labored way
We should glean the Bible! Let no word be unread!
There is no greater book! Nor better choice - instead!
As we returned homeward, I prayed God keep from blight
His magnificent gifts - of Speech! Hearing! And Sight!
That bless "Life" with deep joy, and precious peace of mind
For the benefit "and betterment" - of Mankind.

Laura E. Miller

Kick Me In The Head And Stone Me To Death

I sit in a chair
no one is there - here with me
silence screams, deafens my ears
while the voice in the back of my head cheer
but he's always there
in the air - I breathe and feel
watching listening
to me (and only me) and my thoughts
my safety net he catches me when I fall
the cradle I've built has become a nightmare
(or is that just the guilt?)
burning inside of me
burrowing deeper and deeper
imprisoning my hope, my will (my will?)
not anymore eternally nothing forever no more
except for the arms that keep me warm at night
"and/ or" the one-way ticket I've bought out of this hell

Jeannette Lim

Today

Cancer made a call today.
It plans to take my mom away.

Lord I ask a lot of you, and I try not
To question what you do.

But why can't I ask you to explain?
This need you have for suffering and pain.

She's walked a straight and narrow path.
Why must my mother die like that?

I know what I'm supposed to do.
Accept her fate.... and turn to you.

She taught me to believe in you.
She showed me all that's good and true.

There is no question in my mind. I'll hold your
Hand, when it comes her time.

But God almighty up above......... please......
Replace her pain with love.

Bonnie K. Hills

To All Culinary Writers

To all culinary writers:
Spill out your
raw leafy expression
over the meal of words.
Prepare deep-dished action,
though belong it not
wholly to the feeder nor the eater
but to the ingestible words themselves.

Toss it, dish it.
Embellish the wordy paper plate
with meaty nouns
and flowing basins of herbaceous verbs.
Season with care,
using your spice-racks
of adjectives and adverbs.
Remember that you are a chef
and you must prepare enough edible language
to fill the mouth of the eyes
and the belly of the brain.

Nathan A. Howard

A Woman Of Color

Look at that woman standing over there.
She's bold, she's proud, and she shows that she cares.

Cares for her own, and then cares for others,
has no respect of person, for we are sisters and brothers.

Had some good times, and had some bad,
has been at her lowest point, but never got sad.

For if she got sad, she knew it wouldn't do any good,
so she would try again, and do the best that she could.

Even with rapists, murderers, drugs, and discrimination,
that woman recognizes the good things of our nation.

She's not an expert, but smart in her very own little way.
She knows her responsibility, and she knows how to pray.

This lady loves to try, because she knows what's up ahead.
She takes time with our youngsters, and makes sure their hearts are fed.

Some may think she's done little, but I think she's done much,
because just by her showing her love, all she has touched.

So God made a good thing, that's the best that I can say.
She's truly thee example of "Triumphant African American Women"
of today.

Yolanda Whittaker

The Fairies' Ball

One night when the moon was the brightest
On the path by the garden wall,
I awoke to the sound of wee laughter,
The fairies were holding a Ball.

Some froggies sat 'round on their toadstools
Playing gay little tunes soft and low.
And I smiled as I watched the wee fairies
As they gracefully swayed to and fro.

The fireflies hovered above them
Like miniature lanterns aglow,
And an old owl kept track of the hours,
As he hooted the time down below.

Soon the time came for some light refreshment
Which they sipped from a small petal cup.
It was dew from the flowers they'd gathered,
And they drank 'till they drank it all up.

As the moonlight began to fade slowly
And I watched, all at once they were gone.
But I know they'd been there for I'd seen them
At midnight right there on my lawn.

Lorraine D. Rupert

He

For my grandfather

Brown, gray, blue, gold. The colors of the rainbow
you must behold. The brilliance of the sky.
The brightness of the sun. The deepness of the ocean.
See his beauty in everyone.

The sunlight in his face. See the glory in his grace.
Though I whisper in his ear, though I stand before him
in my tears, He doesn't hear me call. He does not see
me cry.

What shall I do, my Lord, before I see him fall? Shall I
tell him I love him? Shall I tell him goodbye?
What shall I do... before 'he' dies.

Julie Ethridge

Don't Waste Your Time On This Precious Earth

Don't waste your time on this precious earth,
  by being an old fuddy-duddy.
Remember life is much too short,
  and there isn't enough room for another duddy-fuddy.
So on your feet,
  and don't defeat,
  your purpose here on earth.
Go see what life is all about,
  become a girl or boy scout.
Earn your badges one by one,
  by helping others in the sun.
Just remember one more thing,
  don't ever be afraid to swing!

Annmarie Barrett

Through It All

I was so lost and it seemed every road
I travelled down these were only tears.
Deep in my heart I felt lonesome;
so all alone just lost in an ocean of fears.
All of my dreams falling down like the autumn leaves,
that die on a cold winter's night.
Just when I thought that I should have given up;
you held me and said, "it's all right,"
I guess I never say I love you enough.
You're that friend that never let me down.
And I thank God for you;
you are the one who makes me shine.
You'll never know just how much
that you mean to me.
I could never make it alone.
When I feel lost all I need is your sweet,
sweet, voice
And I'm so glad you're with me through
it all.

Tom Ciotti

The Prayer

   I bend down on my knees with my hands folded.
I have now learned that I am my worst enemy.
God rescue me from myself so that I don't lose all my
self wealth. At this rate I could never start with a clean
slate. You are the most forgiving even when I'm in this
state. I'll continue to pray for you to bring me through.
On my day of darkness I'll look for you to pass me through
to the light on my judgment day.

Anthony Anderson

Childhood Fantasies

As a young girl, I liked to dream of romance.
When I played with dolls, they always fell in love.
In my world of dreams, no one ever left and no one ever hurt.
Love was love forever and time couldn't erase
the feelings God created.
I'd dream that one day, this would happen to me,
but it was only a childhood fantasy.
Then one day, a man walked into my life and stole my heart and my dream.
On my heart he signed his name and my dream became his treasure.
He took my hand and kissed my lips
and then he gave me the most precious gift of all -
His love had replaced my dream and I came to understand that
even childhood fantasies could come true.

Andrea L. Blanscet

Dying In Love

True love is always me.
A song brought from the deepest sea
follow my path an ocean so pure
a future with love to reach you more
to steal you away from only lust
I would search for you dawn to dust
To see illusions clear but not true
In pain and fear I find I still love you
only to see that woman who's warm and sweat
I find it hard to break down to defeat
To sit alone with your smile in my mind
I see only regions of darkness and that final line
follow my path were love can protect you more
from a man of a heart that weak and sore

Terrance Avis Brown

To The Wall

To the wall one day I must go, before I lay myself down to die; to its surface of ebony I shall travel, even if like a child it makes me break down and cry.

Hundreds of miles I must journey, all the way to Washington D.C.: This monolithic monument before my breath stills I must see.

I'm must with inner dread, look upon its cold, dark face: Where the names are written of lost young men of every race.

To the wall I shall go, with its carefully engraved ebony face: Where friends and loved ones, a name with trembling hand tearfully trace.

To that edifice I must travel, where family and friends stand with heads bowed low: From their hearts and tormented souls, long dead emotions flow.

To that heart rending monument I must go, with a companion both special and real: With me terrible and strong shared emotions they will feel!

To the wall I must go, where the names of long dead school mates are chiseled there: Maybe then I can find the answer, to why for them to die so young and not me was fair.

That herald of young men wasted in a senseless war I must seek, as I have many times in my dreams while tossing in a troubled sleep: There finally to my shaking knees I drop, and with long dammed up emotions weep.

To the wall I must go, there up to my God on bended knee, offer up a desperate plea to hear my agonizing appeal: Then and only then can the lost, wounded boy and soldier within me begin to heal!

E. L. Thomas

Untitled

Only the streets remain unchanged
Even the river is not what it once was
The homes along the streets may come from the past
But the passage of time has made them only memories.
The times that once were are forgotten.
All the landmarks have become museums
It was once the way of life
Now, only a novelty, a quick study.
What was architecture and passion
Is now a closing date and a contract
What was the Ultimate American Dream
Is now another material possession, lacking genuine vision.
Time has left this place behind
The homes and the streets are still here
But heritage and memories are all that is left
The modern city has taken over.

Travis D. Claxton

Answer To A Dream

As I sat staring and dreaming looking out my living room window! What flashed across sent me into total Awe, hundreds of smiling faces of the children whose hearts I reached and touched. With my love and devotion of and to "Old Glory".
Surprising me with words and loving expressions their words straight from the hearts of a nine year old!
Then a flash and a tear! Dream Fulfilled!

Clara Gange

Spirits Illusion

Who are we? We see dimly as our reflection arc from fleeting memories, so frail and clouded in time.

Mind, heart and spirit trapped, but loosed in pain.

Then in veiled passion comes joy so ripe and full, but quickly devoured in delusion, knowing not what we have been.

Are we now, or a million years before; or a space in time we know not.

We search for a misty image to reveal the truth that make us one; but pain and glee mingled with madness and despair transcend other times, and leave us only to grope in shaded illusion.

Alas, we cease to remember as we wait to be.

Glenda Y. Moseley

Canary Yellow Yes But Made Of Gold

How can I subject this person to words
of glory. Though for too long this has been
an untold story. To have the knowledge of this
person in all hopes of being fair.
The only thing to do is recognize this person
and share. Yes share in her love which
you would never forget. With tender
brown eye's and a smile as warm as
the sunset. Responsibility keeps you story
she said. As the tears and sweat ran endlessly from her head.
She may not have the best in life to look forward
to tomorrow. Though it would never
be the fast that she didn't try, to make her tear's and sweat
for sorrow.
So If I'm asked to tell the greatest
story that had ever been told,
it would be "Canary yellowings but made of gold."

Foster Bell III

Dawn Of Destruction

The Flower of the Day arose in glorious splendor.
Vividly, she displayed flamboyant colors, known only when she awoke and before she fell.
She looked over this world convulsed with hate,
and, fearing destruction by this emotion,
the vivacious Flower of the Day could no longer endure this world of wickedness.
So she fell back into the dark
void that is called Night.

The gentle Lotus Blossom of the Night awakes timidly,
to unfold her frail blossom under delicate beams of starlight.
Her pale eyes view with deep sadness,
man's own injustice to man.
She closes her eyes to the wicked plotting in the night,
and slips gently back into the
solitude of the black void of apathy,
before the

Dawn of Destruction.

Misty J. Hammerbacker

Jesse's Rose

The rose petals are falling
Their sweet scent overpowering
They cover the sounds of footsteps,
and the sound of tears being shed.
Petals settle on his face, clinging
so close, covering lashes so long and dark.
He looks so peaceful, so quiet,
can't believe he's gone.
He was so special, so much left to do,
can't believe he left me, what do I do?
We put him to rest on this dreary day,
covering him with petals, shiny with dew
with hopes he's happy in heaven with you.
Nancy J. Schepers

Washing Away The Day

Revolving fury, solving surely
Problems of the dead
The rain comes down on the cold, hard ground
Drowning in a bed
Taught to preach, distraught you reach
Fallacy rules your being
After years of drought, the fog rolls out
Expansion comes from being
Jim Stoutmeyer

When I Came To You That Night

You cannot deny the beauty that surrounds you as the fire burns
  inside
The memory of a passion you try to hide, as you look away from me,
I can see it in your eyes
The touch of a new woman, the scent of his cologne
The memory that takes us far from home
The price I payed for someone who was never really mine
the price we pay for passion, one more time
And as you walk away, were you afraid you would want to stay?
You and I both know we can never be set free
You can never be the man she wants you to be
You wrapped yourself around me like a coat for someone cold
The feeling we knew, never once growing old
And as we walk far away, we can never be that far, for the burning
of a passion, that leaves a long and lasting scar
I can't explain the feeling in the darkness of your room, you and I
both knowing we would have each other soon
As you touched my body, as I felt you deep inside
the passion that was hidden, it burst and came alive
I can't explain the feeling but I knew that it was right
As you stood in front of me, when I came to you that night
Cindy Weinstein

Dance

Dancing is a sport of the arts,
  we always perform from our hearts.
Dancers work together as a team,
  our goals seem unreachable but never
  our dreams.
Dancers practice day and night.
  we never stop until we get it right.
Competition days are a lot of stress,
  but we always come out, doing our best.
When we finally see the competitors we face,
  we all pray that their shoes are unlaced.
Hoping for luck will not get us far,
  we have motivation and dedication to
  make us stars.
So in conclusion, what I'm trying to say,
  reach for your goals and practice everyday.
Laura Paden

Untitled

Dishes are thrown, glasses are smashed, and
  now new holes are in the wall
    I've seen this scene a million times.

He walks in drunk
  close to every night.
    He just wants one thing, but
  she won't give it.

I try to stop him from hollering,
  it's late at night.

She tries to get away, and...
  "My God his hands are around her throat!"
    I ran to her rescue
  showing no fear.

They argue more and more
  his reason is stupid, and
    she keeps covering up.

He's an alcoholic,
  She denies the facts,
    I end up paying the price.
Kelly Tarreto

Grandpa

As we walk down the now familiar halls
We have become accustomed to the calls

The calls of the patients that know our face
They wait for a kind word or a smile, just a trace

We smile and joke with several old folks along the way
As we hurry to see how alert "Grandpa" is today

Sometimes he smiles and we know he knows who we are
Sometimes he looks at us, his blue eyes watching us from afar

Where is he when he isn't with us at all
He doesn't see us or answer when we call

He's in a place God lets him escape to
A place reserved for his "Chosen" few

He has paid his price here in this life
He escapes to a place without pain or strife

His family wishes he would be like he used to be
He isn't as we knew him and it is very hard to see

May God give us the strength, our cross to bear
To know in our hearts, he is in God's care

We can thank God he has very little pain
The storms of life will never trouble him again
Jessie Taylor

Untitled

And sometimes..., sometimes you'll just be sitting there. And
you'll realize, that you'll remember the moment you're in forever.
And just as quickly as you realize it, the moment is gone.
But not really gone, only settled into your mind.
So you know that it will always be there,
always be ready to pluck back up,
and you'll always be able to know that feeling again.
And sometimes, when you realize you'll remember the moment
you're in,
it is these moments you know will be rich and velvety with detail,
so thick, you'll be able to dip yourself into them
and wrap them around you, like your grandmother's quilt.
Those are the moments you cherish.
Not those when you receive material wealth,
not the moment you are the center of attention.
But those moments, the ones you never dreamed could be so magical.
So complete in their utter simplicity.
And sometimes, those moments will catch you by surprise,
Forever.
Annie Terrell

The Heroes

Taking on more than they can,
They rise up and charge toward the goal.
There is no definite plan,
But the cause burns deep inside their souls.
Even though the outlook is not good,
For success, the goal they must obtain.
Each man knows that he should
Endure the hardships and the pain.
As the eternal conflict rages on,
Some men claim victory while others fall.
The crown of righteousness the victors don,
While paying tribute to those fallen who answered the call.
With arms held high in infinite cheer,
The men walk away with no fear.
Trait S. Thompson

"Charm"

His charm and acumen laid waste
to their awareness he is real
but beneath his porcelain surface
is a face of old china cracked and peeled

The vessel which holds his thoughts
has become porous through which secrets often leak
and spread darkly over the glaze
which has been applied with care

Few wondered what was beneath that smooth smile
flat and correct like precision made tile
it gave rise to dulled conversations that seemed lustrous
but on reflection faded, like a cave pearl in the sun

Often times he posed in the half light
so the glare would not reveal
the chips and fissures that comprised this social dream
lest the dream would end

and all that remained would be the shards of a common plate.
Anthony Mastroianni

A Pair Of Shoes

We are inseparable - you left, me right.
It's been a while since that big occasion
When we on John's feet danced all thru the night
And never once thought of another persuasion.

We walked into church ever so softly,
Quite clean and shiny for others to see.
And sometimes went shopping or visiting Aunt Daughtery
'Twas fun to be often where big John might be.

He closed us away in the closet on Mondays,
And of course a rest was always quite good.
We liked best however, to be out for a fun day
And walk on John's feet while he savored good food.

Another persuasion - how can it be
That I'm left in the closet while you're on the go?
There's no way now for big John to use me,
Because a big tragedy took his right leg and toes!

Me right, a half a pair of shoes, believe me
What good can I do? — I feel all uptight!
Can't help big John, but share the tragedy.
It grieves me; he has no need for the right.
Elizabeth H. Valentine

K.K. Hebbar Climbs A Stair

Slow stepped. Room wide as a nation
Crowded with canvasses left sunning
in open Eastern air.
Angular oil men stare a mouthless
Watch. Man in white kurta pajamas
Affixed in missing strokes, his long fingers
Take time to reach his forehead —
Grandchildren squeals and footsteps

Up and down. My Indian elders
handle their dharmas with care.
Carnival tones washed with cigarettes,
Tangerines, mosquito repellent these elements
Chewing on scenes of France in the 40's
or the young one scribbling colors with braided hair.
Cries of "Kakka!" echo under balconies
Over phone lines from a far land, lost time.
Such sorcery of line.
A smile from the pillows he is white against
Talking silk soft of poetry. Next Spring. Long
Sleep in a sea view chair.
Reshmi Hebbar

Kendall

I want to lie in a field with you forever,
Holding you tight to me.
So close, we are one creature with two burning souls.
Hands clasped, hair entwined, we will
hold the storm at bay.
You face both bright sun and soft moon to me.
I will make a home in the hollow of your neck.
Build a temple on the curve of your thigh.
Seek shelter in the cave of your navel.
Rest on the slope of your breast.
And be carried away on the tide of your heart.
I will mark the passing of the days by
the lines that time etches on your face.
Together.
Until we are dust.
Douglas Cross Jr.

The Winds Pump Peace

Winds pump the aided tango.
Sexed-maned riders,
Adrift on the Ilium Coast,
Hide their sated-toady waifs below.
Oh, the aided tango paves aniseed scars,
When tests present that vinyl plasma.
This dried fate burns wheat with chaff!
Restless sixes expose those toady waifs,
But somehow, they elude their epitaphs
In dope-drenched lairs.

Ashore, lyric tones exalt the winds,
And somewhere, inland cafes issue ivies
To pious-shaky males, renewing a tried route,
Acing meals alone.
The winds pump peace.
Hearty belles sing. Their lyric tones
Exalt the named winds. They warn,
"Celibacy, monogamy, abstinence;
Inter, ilium, inert,
Sonde, sonde, sonde."
Kathryn Ceceilia Chancey

A Dying Art

When I was small and all-aware (a long time ago)
my parents used to take me where the bygone people go-
those greeny hills among the stony figures white and gray
of lambs and angels, birds and bones, is where I used to play.
And sometimes when I'd chance to meet a group of statues, I
would sit among them at their feet and listen to them sigh.
I never heard them speak a word, them quiet as the dead,
but now and then I thought I heard their words inside my head.

"He's happy now," one lamb believed, "He's gone beyond the pain."
But next to him an angel grieved, a-crying in the rain.
"No one should go so early on," she almost might have said,
"Young children are too early gone." She bowed her mournful head.
A horseback man, though, was not sad. He boldly held his sword
and fairly shouted, "Charge!!" - I had my ear tuned for the word.
A little rabbit cringed below in fear of hoof and heel-
but rabbits often speak too low to hear, unless you kneel.

My statue garden seemed to be not made of granite stone,
but rather like a family that watched over their own.
It's much more lonely nowadays to go where bygones lay
and find no guardians any more to watch the children play.

Olive West

Untitled

Mother Nature, in the desert
   Is lavish with her touch.
Where else, when all seems sere and bare
   Can beauty thrill so much?

For Ocotillo, when they're blooming
   She forms licking tongues of flame,
The Palo Verde with their lacey dress
   Join in this lovely game.

With flowers of spun gold in their hair
   Their emerald beauty does embrace,
And Chollas' frail and smoke-like blooms
   Chime in with fascinating grace.

The haze on distant mountains,
   Like Mantillas gaily spread,
Is the lace which Mother Nature wears
   Draped in grace about her head.

Owl Clover and Blue Lupins throw
   Colored carpet on the ground,
And the lowly Barrel Cactus
   Wears a ruby-studded crown.

Raymond Knowles

White Face - The Pony

The Pony's name was white face
His hair like silken lace
He once lived on a busy street
Until he was moved to a mountain retreat.

Where he could forever live and roam
On acres and acres of new home
White face live to be quite old
Until the night he was secretly sold

This broke my heart that he was gone
How could people do so wrong?
I wanted him here to live and die
Then I could just say a proper goodbye

If ponies go to heaven someday
White face will be there forever to stay
Yet at times I sigh and almost cry
And ask the question - Why Oh Why?

Esther Perkins Gilmore

Open Your Eyes

The poverty stricken can never be seen by those
   who live in the world.
The pleasures of life blind the fortunate and
   mute and cries of the starving child.
Yet, still, some refuse to close their eyes from
   the pain but instead open then wide and
   absorb the sorrow.
Their mind fills with the heart wrenching cries.
They open their pockets and empty all wealth and
   the hunger stabs at their stomach.
Still the pitiful pleas come and the children pull
   forward more and more.
Tears sting the eyes of the giving for there is no
   more to give,
And the once fortunate now fall to the ground
   withered and poor.
There is nothing left and the cries go on.

Lisa Sorensen

Rural Blessings

Find the places where nature's beauty should surround
Explore the places where rushing brooks make harmonizing sounds
Walk where many wild flowers are around
Look for the trails where solace still may be found

John D. Burt

Wild Goose

Oh, where do you fly the Wild Goose?
What is your destination?
What beckons you go or stay?
What spirit drives you on each day?
Will you not fly down if only for a moment and take this restless
   spirit with you, if only for a day?
To fly with you into the sunrise and sunset.
To pause by a shimmering lake on some far off windswept shore.
To fly with the wind and feel it carry you along your journey to an
   unknown destination.
To fly far above in the tranquil sky away from the noise and
constant
   movement below.
I am with you in spirit as you fly over honking your welcoming and
   lonely call to me.
I am with you if only in a dream.

Windy W. Drury

I'm Still Here

I'm here - Why can't you see me? Why don't you look at me?
Are you afraid if you look at me that you'll look like
me? Why can't you see the beauty inside me?
Look in my eyes - look deep inside me, I'm here - I'm Still Here!

I'm here - Why can't you hear me? Why won't you listen to me?
Do you think I no longer have anything to say that is
worthy of your time?
I still think. I still speak. I still have things that need to be
said - and need to be heard. Listen to me!
I'm here - I'm Still Here!

I'm here - I'm still here. Touch me. Let me feel your arms
around me. Please?
Can't you see how badly I want - no, need you to hold me?
Why are you so afraid of my touch when I so long for yours?
I'm still me and I'm here - I'm Still Here!

I'm here - I still care. I still love. I still feel.
I still crave your companionship, your comfort, your love.
Why do you think that if you don't look at me, that you'll escape?
Look In The Mirror - I Am You!
And we're here - but not for long. We Have Aids.

Paula Gambill

Tomorrow Night

Surrounded by carolling air
My breath wants a shape.
One that would rise in spiral,
But the embracing night would not oblige.

As does she, lips melting
After a moment together.
For eyes closed, generating
Warmth in that future thought.

Then breaking my, their kiss,
All heads turn, some share a gasp,
As a chilling, aching-blue-knuckle tree
Throws four birds to fly.

And without thinking, or notice,
The warmth of the moist lips
Creating shelter, from unobliging air.
My thoughts, a kiss, continue

Brian Tyson

1912-In Memorial-1991

D eeds he did to please the world,
A cting and praying for the boys and girls.
N othing could stop him from going to the top.
N ow he is away but will never be forgot.
Y ears went by with the help of his hands,

T eaching and singing from the grandstand,
H is years went by with a happy heart.
O ver and out to fills his parts,
M aking everyone laugh and smile,
A ll his days went by with great pride.
S o let's all remember him. He was founder of
  Saint Jude Children's Research Hospital.

Matty D. Hadly

Life... Was

Starting to learn at one and two, beginning school at three,
Made 'Responsible' at six... What to expect to be!
  Life... was hard.

Scrubbing and cleaning at seven, lifting and toting at ten,
Constant schooling throughout... What Could a childhood have been?
  Life... was so hard.

Strictly controlled with cruel, harsh words... Forever 'made' to mind!
Constant threats and punishments... Never loved or treated kind.
  Life... was so very hard.

Adolescence hatched monstrous fears, ugliness descended like a cloud,
Never appreciated or stroked... Lonely smothered in the crowd.
  Life... was unbelievably hard.

Admonished at each indiscretion, expected to always be best,
Struggling to appease those around... Seemingly failed for each test.
  Life... was destructively hard.

Surviving college and grad school, adulthood and career a salvation,
Failures turned to triumphs... And retirement an Exclamation!
  Life... isn't so hard.

Della M. Bird

He Cares

I confess and I repent, for I fail God everyday
But I know that He is listening, as I stumble on my way—
Every word and action is known to Him above-
Yet His arms always surround me with mercy born of love,
Praise His name I whisper, you must try again-
For impatience is my enemy, He knows and I do too.
Sometimes my shame engulfs me, I would hide my sin from view—
But then He gently chides me,
Try again, I'll see you through.

Irene F. Baldwin

Never Alone

Before I met Jesus the world was my God
I worshiped the pleasures of men,
But God called to me and I looked in His Word
And found I was trapped by my sin.

  And I cried
Lord I can't make it alone
I've tried how I've tried on my own,
These mountains are steep
This valley too deep
Lord I can't make it alone.

I agreed I was lost and knelt at His cross
Was washed in the blood of GOD's Lamb,
I knew in that moment I had been saved
And the Lord held my soul in His hand.

  And I cried
Praise God I'm not on my own
I no longer face life alone,
The mountains are steep
The valley still deep
But praise God I'm not on my own.

Warren D. Sumrall

"You"

As you laid yourself down to sleep,
you thought about the evenings festivities.
From the kiss hello,
To the kiss goodnight.
From the candle light dinner,
Till the moonlight stroll.
It was a memorable evening,
That shall not be forgotten.
The moment I held you close,
To the time we where hand in hand.
The greeting words "Hello, are you ready."
To the departing words "Goodnight, I love you."
You closed your eyes,
You shed a tear,
I wished you where here.

Daniel McLean

A Child's World

(GIRLS)
  Peanut butter and jelly upon my face
  Mother's trying to teach me grace
  My toys scattered all over the place
  I'd rather wear jeans instead of RIBBONS and LACE!

  Make-up and clothes is what I'll buy
  And I'll do my best or at least I'll try!
  A YOUNG-LADY, I'll be as time goes by
  PRETTY, DETERMINED, GRACEFUL, and SLY.
(BOYS)
  Cookies and milk I like to eat
  Superman and Hulk, I'd like to meet!
  Galoshes I refuse to wear upon my feet!
  FROGS and SNAKES, I think, are neat!

  I'll grow up some day you'll see
  Right now I have no idea of what I'll be
  But when I decide, you can count on me!
  For I'll be a MAN, STRONG, DETERMINED, and FREE!!!
(BOTH)
  But until we do, children, we'll remain
  CAREFREE, HAPPY, NOISY and PLAIN.
  LEARNING, LISTENING, LOVING and TAME.
  For a CHILD'S WORLD, is a world, where LIFE's the GAME!!!

Joyce Marie Reinard

God Blessing On America

America, Jesus stripped Satan
of all authority and placed it
in your hands, America now what
will you do with Jesus? I have
good news for America today;
Jesus is not mad at you.
America at times I guess you
yearn for the youth you once
had when troubles were few.
Prayer has been taken of
our schools, teaching God's word
is against the rules. You must
bloom when you are planted,
in the garden we call life,
but seasons come and seasons
go. My eyes have seen Gods
rainbow; my ears have heard
his voice. And for me there
is no other choice, back to the
good old fashioned when life was lived, in God we trust.

Peggy E. Roth

The Holidays Are Here

Cards to send and gifts to buy
Anticipation with a sigh
The holidays are here!

Family comes and love abounds
The air is filled with scents and sounds
The holidays are here!

Frosted windowpanes and falling snow
Candles warming with their glow
The holidays are here!

Pretty wrapped packages and festive wreaths
The perfect tree with gifts beneath
The holidays are here!

Snow covers the ground where the carolers sing
Hear the church bells as they ring
The holidays are here.

Morning breaks and the children rise
With joyous sparkles in their eyes the holidays are here.

Can we keep this love alive
In our hearts and in our minds
When the holidays are gone???

W. Sydney Rust

The Candle

I was a candle, colorful and tall.
I was a candle, but not solid at all.
I was a candle, smooth to the touch.
I was a candle, who had rejected so much.

I was a candle, cold and dark as the night.
I was a candle, useless without light.
You gave me light, so that I could live.
You gave me light, so that light I might give.

You gave me light, wax now flows down my cheeks.
You gave me light, it's my heart now that speaks.
You gave me light, so that I might know right.
I am but a candle, but I'm also Your light.

Rick Albrecht

Faith

Always have faith in yourself and what you do,
Even though others do their best to sway you,
Give to yourself the benefit of the doubt,
Chances are your instincts will help things work out.

Always remain true to your hopes and your dreams,
Without them, you might fall apart at the seams,
Faith in yourself keeps your spirit alive,
Without it, you might be hard-pressed to survive.

Trust your feelings-put forth your point of view,
Confidence will cause people to listen to you,
A positive attitude changes a "won't" to a "might",
Faith in yourself makes your star shine bright!

Andrea Lynn Mastrobattista

My Beautiful African Ass

"Yo shorty, you got a fat ass"
"Damn you carryin' alota luggage"
"That's alota wagon you draggin"
Stop! Why do you harass my beautiful African Ass
It's hereditary in my family
I can't help it, it's part of me
My lips, my hips, my curves, my switch
My beautiful African Ass!
It's part of my blackness, it's inherent in my past
I am proud of this ass my ancestors gave to me
It has Life, it has Feelings, it has its own History,
It's Bold, it's Stunning, it's not just a body part
I have to love it, it's a form of Black Art

Shareema N. Gadson-Shaw

Interlude

The only sound heard is the gulls above.
A single wave brushes the shore.
All thoughts are dominated by the break,
its silent, crashing yell out for help.

The yell neutralized all the egotism of the world.
A single tear ran down the coast,
slowly and emotionally,
causing all life to succumb, to listen intently.

This isolated feeling of peace
brings rapture and strength for a second.
A blanket has been placed over troubles,
leaving them to sleep, to interlude for a while.

Full concentration on the sound of the gulls.
The realization crashes in; the flock has passed.

Shawn Lynn Ledington

Till Then

Bid you farewell though not gone
Who are we to you, strangers
Can you feel our love behind the tears
Miss your love, it couldn't hurt more
Thank you for the generosity, how you tried to hide
You melted over the years and let in the warmth
Felt your love, caring and goodness
admired your zest for life
Did you know how we valued and admired
Can't let you go, happiness awaits
Till we meet somewhere
It will go on forever
Goodbye, your final party has begun

Irene Murtagh

Common Sky

Inside, my house is empty and dark. There will be no longer ever again. My mother died today. She took with her all that I had inside. My securities, my possibilities, and my dreams.

Holding her head in my lap I ran my fingers through her black and silver curls. No matter how you tried to mess it up, it always held its style. I rocked her gently while singing the words to "Jesus loves me". It was the only spiritual I knew. Mama taught it to me when I was three. Now I wish I had learned more... about everything.

Mama looked up and whispered softly to me that she was tired and needed to rest. She told me that death didn't hurt, it was life that caused pain and suffering. A tear drop fell from my eye and shattered on the floor. I heard her say "I love you". I whispered "I love you" back. Her body went limp in my arms and the rosary beads she was holding fell at my feet. I let out a blood curdling scream as I felt my insides twist in torment. She was gone... as I bent to pick up the rosary, a light so brilliant with colors arose from her body. I watched as this floating rainbow hovered over me for what seemed like a moment. It then rose toward and then went out of the window. Up, up, up... disappearing into the common sky.

My only comfort is knowing that Mama has finally found her peace. Otherwise, I remain a lost and lonely soul in mourning for the rest of my life. I know Mama wouldn't approve, but she was my friend, and it hurts. It really hurts. One day, we'll see each other again, we'll share some of that common sky and then... at last, I will be at peace.

Lisa Anderson

Honor Of Death

The full moon is so beautiful tonight, reflecting
your shadow as you comfort me in this hour of death.

Yes - it is time; to give up this physical mass.
Pour out the best you have, and always be poor-
never reserve anything... "have nothing".

Yes - "You honor me in this time of death;
Do not be sad - Please...Do not." Overflowing is our
love for each other, the metallic of friends.

We are unique - "Sharing energies throughout the
universe, experiencing tranquility."
Do not be sad - Please...Do not; it is time, this flight of death.

Can you feel the presence of an angel? The angel of foolishness;
accept her wings, reserve nothing...the future
holds a higher plane of existence.

I feel your warmth - from the wings that surround me,
claws close in as a ring about me, "Infinitesimal-
this flight of death"; the tactility of warmth is diminishing
as your claws release me.

Do not be sad - Please...Do not, always remember-
"True love-never professes anything."

Robert G. Anderson

A Child To Live Alone

In Memory of Sally Mae Longmire
You brought me here to live alone,
Too little to know what to do
Or where to go.
No one to guide you or stand beside you
What is a child to do all alone.
Placed here and there made it to
　the fair, lied your way thru
　the despair with still no were to go.
Now you're older still on earth waiting
　to go,
A child at heart who's apart that
　called loneliness an art.

Wanda Hughes

My Friend Pat

Over 25 years ago we met and we shared times I will never forget

What times we shared! The good and the bad
The parties and dancing...oh the fun we had!

She was so full of life..helped so many others with their toils and strife

We talked so much..practically every day
Always there for each other...in whatever way

If it meant talking it out in the middle of the night
Whatever it took to make things right

Having someone to listen when you just need to shout
And that someone is always there that's what friends are all about

She was such a kind-hearted soul
Without her in my life..there will always be a hole

When I think of the way she laughed that certain way she held her head
I get that feeling...the one I dread

I miss her a lot and I know she's in a better place
But her passing is still so hard...so hard for me to face

She must have left her essence..oftentimes I seem to feel her presence

Pat was a true friend and those wonderful memories will be with me always... Friends until the end.

Dorris Hameditoloui

Sleeping Bags

They're wrinkled and baggy and oh so much fun
Can be had when you've got one around.
And most people will find that there's lots they can do
When you drop one upon the hard ground.

You can all watch T.V. Until late, late at night.
The sleeping bag never gets mad.
A sleeping bag, you will prob'ly agree,
Is the best friend that you've ever had.

Sometimes you lose track of just what you are doing
And upon it you're jumping and tramping.
And sleeping bags make a most wonderful pal
To have when your fam'ly goes camping.

They'll hide all your secrets, They let you sleep in
When you really should be up and about.
You can hug 'em and squeeze 'em for years and for years
A sleeping bag's hard to wear out.

But in all of the years of my sleeping bag's life
There's one thing that always would make
Me shiver and quiver and mind all my manners
And that's when the Old Bag's awake!

Steve Kraushaar

Morris The Cat

I'd like to tell the story of Morris the cat
He is big, orange, and fat, and that's that!
The house shakes whenever he jumps
or when he runs with a thump thump thump,
and he loves to add to his stomp
when he eats his food with a chomp chomp chomp!
Morris loves to bump heads, the sound is a bonk
If he loves you....Bonk
Oh! He sees me, Bonk!
I could tell you so much more,
but I can't think above his snore.
I love this monstrous ball of fur,
for he has a very loud purr.

Brian Sabo

Trusting

Daddy's gone
Mama cries
So much hurt. So many lies.

Children left
In disarray
Got built in "shut down" to make it thru the day

Oh what long affected grief
Inflicted on innocent minds
Is there any relief in the carnage left behind?

All grown up
Living life
Still dealing with the scars of strife

Learned early on
Not to trust
Doing superficial love rapped up in lust

Healings like
Layers of a onion being peeled away
A refining process day by day

God's love replacing years of doubt
In Jesus, family love is blossoming out
T. Eunice Murriel

Be Real

I am the keeper-I hold the key-only I can release me.

The only walls there are about, are the ones I put up
when I wish to keep someone out.

I answer to no one but myself; I have no one to explain
to but myself.

I can make myself happy, or I can make myself sad; I can
bring out the good, or I can bring out the bad. Only I
can make myself glad.

Look within and open the door; Don't be afraid to go
out the explore; Because you only hurt yourself if you
ignore what is hidden behind the closed door.

So let yourself go, and learn how to know,
whether or not you're putting on a show.

Only you can know whether to go fast or slow. Don't keep
your head low, carry yourself as tho you are the leader of
the show.

So spread your wings, experience new things. Take down your
walls and step out of the shadowed halls.

Love yourself and be who you feel. Only you hold the cards
that need to be dealt. Be real!
Amber M. Sayen

Open My Eyes

Lord, open my eyes, so I may see
And feel, your presence close to me.
Give me strength for my weary feet
As I battle the crowd, on life's busy street!

And widen the vision of my unseeing eyes
So in passing faces - I'd recognize,
Not just a stranger, unloved, unknown
But a friend, with a heart and a soul
That is much like my own!

Give me perception, to make me aware.
That scattered profusely on life's thoro-fare,
Are free gifts of God that we blindly pass by
As we look at the world, with un-seeing eye!
Martha M. Walker

Man's Redemption

High above the city streets
On mountain top solemnly there stands
Three crosses made of wood and nails
Made ready for crucifixion by uncaring hands.

The crowd began to gather there
To watch the scene unfold
As three condemned men were nailed in place
Unmindful that their deeds had been foretold.

The sky grew dark as earth stood still
As our Father reached out to welcome His Son
Who pleaded for mankind's redemption
As they knew not what they had done.

The crowd began to run and clamor
As darkness, rain, and thunder engulfed them all;
And lightening began to flash across the sky
As unbelievers saw the truth this day and on knees did fall.

Because of love so complete and lasting
Our sins were washed anew this day
With Christ our Lord who bore them all
So man could start afresh and with our Father forever stay.
George W. Rogers

God's Voice

Night descending slowly,
a dark shroud around the shoulders of the day.
Fog flowing in a soft breeze
reflecting light from unseen sources.
A distant whip-poor-will whistles a soft good-night.
Quiet signals a time of rest.
Heat lifts mercifully into a vacant sky
taking with it the cares of the day.
I hear God's voice in the silence.
Elizabeth Leopard

Dear Lord Jesus

Lord Jesus, please protect me; please wash away my tears...
   come close and hold me in the night and take away my fears.
Lord Jesus, when I'm weary, when I'm sick, too weak to fight...
   please help me gather strength of mind, of heart, of will for
   might.
Lord Jesus, take Your gentle hand and clasp it into mine;
   walk along the path You've given me and point out all the signs.
Lord Jesus, be my guide, show me the way that I must go;
   speak to me through words of love You think I ought to know.

Lord Jesus, I declare, that I place my trust in You;
   and I put on the shoes of peace with every deed you have me do.
Lord Jesus, with that peace, there is a comfort deep within...
   my mind, my heart, my will and soul that shelters me from sin.

Lord Jesus, be my refuge, keep me safe and make me strong;
   so that I may do Your will and right the world of all its wrongs.
Lord Jesus, send an angel to guard the doorway of my soul;
   let your Spirit flow in through my heart, building memories which
   will grow.

Lord Jesus, intercede for me, if I should slip and fall;
   let the Father know that I am His, and am ready when He calls.
And Lord Jesus, thank the Father for giving You up just for me;
   so that through the Word and by Your grace,
   my soul is now set free.
And finally, dear Lord Jesus, know the love I hold in store...
   for You when we embrace the day I knock on heaven's door.
Cindy Schwieger-Buchholz

Untitled

She sees herself doing cartwheels down the green grassy slopes.
You see her wheelchair sitting in the corner of the cool, clean room.

She feels the soft warm caresses of a springtime love.
You feel the cold, wrinkled skin that has been through too many winters.

She hears the laughter of her children playing mixed with her own laughter as a child.
You hear her struggled breathing accompanied by your own beating heart.

She remembers a long life filled with wondrous sights and emotions, speckled with few disappointments.
You remember her thirst for life's experiences, her love of everything, her ability to deal with difficulties.

And as you look into each others eyes there is an understanding, an awareness, no need for words.

And the circle of life continues on...

Jane Flocks McLean

"A Vision Of Life"

Here I am floating on air
Can't decide whether to come down
I feel totally useless but I can see what's coming ahead of me
I feel like I'm lost somewhere but can't
   detect where I am going
I see total darkness
It seems I'm going and going and I
   can't stop but my sense of direction
   made me feel useful
A vision that I see comes to light —
I hear birds chirping and sounds of waterfalls
   coming down on the rough edges of a rock
Also I hear a river flowing
My body feels so wonderful but numb but why
I feel so alone, so lost, I feel totally overcome
All of a sudden I see something ahead of me
Something that is so beautiful, a vision of loveliness
I feel warmth and a sense of dignity and desire
I felt so alive that I want to come down
   but it was time for me to live

Maria Castanza

Future

How about what you see out there.
Is life in the picture and where?

Take a stroll in memory and search out ahead.
Is there anything in the past make the future as said?
Well life is a dream until we ponder our stead.

All is well if plans are made not by man.
In all profit we gain by an honest plan.

Is the future really ours to seek out a goal?
Or is there another who is all in control?

Well I know someone who cares about me.
I know cause I am special to him you see.
He made day, night, moon, stars, and the little honey bee.

Is there a bright light shining to show the way?
Yes a true light shining so willing you say.

Well follow the future on this good theme.
A light of joy and love and peace within.
Oh! A true stronghold is what we must win.

Something worth holding onto that is right.
And keeping it there so it is never out of sight.
This future I see is wholesome and bright.

Georgia L. Richardson

Where Oh Where

Star light, star bright,
I wish I may, I wish I might,
Find the girl who is meant to be,
The only one for me.
I know she's out there,
But where?
I know I'll find her someday,
And with her my love will stay.
I hope I find her soon,
So my heart can beat to a happy tune.
And when I find her,
I'll know for sure,
Because she'll do her part,
To fill this emptiness in my heart.
I'll want to be with her every hour of every day,
And love you is all she'll hear me say.
I just can't wait until I find you,
Then all my dreams will forever come true.

Rodney Balwinski

Night Prayer

Look into each man's eye,
Do not fear what lies behind;
For each soul wants to cry,
To be freed of all mankind.

Like faith on the wings of a dove,
Send your prayers high into the sky;
Fill them with unconditional love,
Answers are received to the question..."Why?"

If when you wake your heart is light,
Your heart and soul are truly free;
Your purpose in life is clearly in sight,
To be the best person you can be.

Angela M. Soth

Cat With A Big Head

Cat with a big head was sitting in the stairway
He was a massive black one with a tiny white spot on his throat
He had a twin brother of the same size at the main house
They were residents of 45 Ashley Street
So was I
They were fellows of a German shepherd owned by a German woman
He-cat didn't like milk and butter
He-cat shared dog food with the German shepherd
and took himself on a walk daily
Neighbors said he was everywhere
When I returned home he was waiting in the stairway
He ate the fat of my beef steak every evening and never mewed
When I slept he slept under my bed
He was too big for me to carry to Paris
When I left 45 Ashley Street
I left him to his twin brother and the German shepherd
and the German woman
He watched my face but did not mew

Kroy Wen

True Love

I am no artist bold or bleak.
I do not have a form unique.
I have no riches to offer to thee,
Except this one thing that God had endowed o'er me.
The love he created deep within me.
I have only it to offer and no other gold.
But I know you will accept it as I have been told.
Because I am as God meant for me to be,
Just a woman in love with none other but thee!

Ethel Sieczko

Flowers

Flowers, those bright and beautiful things,
Make you feel special in every way,
When you see them they make your hearts sing,
And they really brighten up your day,

Flowers, vivid and aromatic plants,
For whenever you happen to see one,
It almost definitely will grant,
That you will pluck and smell every one.

Flowers when you happen to see them,
Let you go away feelings joyful,
And will make you hum a happy hymn,
So that others will also feel joyful.
Chris E. Matthews

Stars of Dreams

I reach for the stars, each one burning
my hands and boiling my blood. I reach, not under-
standing why, yet not wanting to stop. I reach, knowing
that one of them waits for me. My hands are scorched
black from the heat. Yet, unaware of the pain, I reach
again. Suddenly I am caught up in the fire and fury
of a raging star. I am swirled into the black heavens
of a night. Yet, I let go of the star that soared me
into the sky. I reach higher, never wanting to stop.
Always wanting something higher, always reaching for the
stars. Never stopping.
Sarah Rohrs

Her

Sometimes I wonder what she was like
Was her hair as light as day or as dark as night
Did she sing herself to sleep or did she stay up to weep
Does she ever think about that little child that she threw out
Or is she in an endless sleep giving God her heart to keep

Does she pray to God to forgive her sins
Or does she not care about the way her life ends
Sometimes I think she might miss me but my father is there to kiss me
I'm not saying I don't miss her because I really do

But I can live without her I did when I was two
One day a woman showed up on my doorstep
I didn't think I knew her but I really did
She said "I'm the mother who left you when you were just a kid."

She apologized for leaving me and my dad
But she didn't look too sad
Her hair was a dark gray with a few streaks of brown
Her skin was a dark color it had wrinkles from a frown
Her dress was a bright yellow same as the sun

She talked to me for hours telling me what she did
But I still wish she would have been with me when I was just a kid
Crystal Poindexter (age 13)

Pyong-An At The Local Deli

Breathing an air of peaceful confidence,
against which no conflict could disturb,
he smiles and breaks into his slice of cake,
alone with a contented sigh at the local deli.
"Now this is the way my life should be,"
he muses while brushing away the crumbs.
"To have what I want," as his hand
accepts the check, "and to know the cost
before I'm done."
Wil Simpson

Universal Prayer - Psalm 117

We sing a song of loving praise;
  for God is Love, Who shows true worth.
In faithful, understanding ways
  our Lord will guide our faith's rebirth.
    All peoples and all nations rise
    to praise God's Love, our greatest prize.

We lift our hearts with glorious praise
  for God's continual gifts of grace.
All nations come, each people stays
  and shows God's Love in every race.
    Go out and spread Good News to all:
    God's Love redeems us from the Fall.

God always knows what's best to give,
  as loving kindness shines abroad.
True love embraces all who live,
  reflecting here the face of God.
    Let's witness faith and hope and love,
    brought forth from God's own powers above.
Frank C. Vanden-Eynden

An Even Better Idea

High in the Sierra's, near New Army Pass, with a group of twenty,
The backpacks were heavy, the day long, and the miles had been plenty.
Up ahead, where a hiker led, she yelled and waved her hand.
What we did seek, was Lower Rock Creek, and it halted our little band.

"Twenty feet wide," sighed our guide, but it was a foot deep.
Too wide to cross, with no stepping stones, and too far to leap.
Marching upstream, with our whole team, we looked for a crossing.
We found a huge pine, over a cascade, with white water tossing.

Over the pine, between the branches, with our packs juggling.
On hands and knees, it wasn't a breeze, we were all struggling.
One by one, with screams galore, we crept over the creek's mighty roar.
Tangled in the tree, with scratches on each knee, it wasn't an easy chore.

At the campsite, in the diminishing light, we all began to talk.
At that creek crossing, why balk? It was only a little wet walk.
We went over the pine, without a lifeline, at a great perilous risk.
With water rushing, a little brushing, and one could be gone in a whisk.

The Fathers, and teenage daughters agreed, it is safer to be wet.
In the morning, at the creek, the girls had a better idea yet.
How about, in a turnabout, piggy backing them to the other side?
They were already smarter, than their Dads, who gave them all a ride.
James C. O'Donnell

"Save A Street"

The sweatshirt melts to the carpet
As the interstate yardstick cries for 16
Books end in nothing as schools try again
Boy Scouts building bridges
Girl Scouts selling cookies
Teacher tries to teach
But students just don't care
Light bulb lasts much longer
But darkness is upon us
Save this retched land
By stammering dumbfoundedly
Try to take out trash
But die on the sidewalk
Why do we leave peace
When it's the only answer
Dave R. Wolkensperg

"Unseen Angel"

An angel came and went today
While you scurried at work and play

What? You did not see him, you say
You don't believe in angels anyway

How 'bout the frightened runaway
The loving spouse who's gone astray

Or the family visited by death today
And the hostage imprisoned far away

An abused child, no desire to play
A sweetheart who just walked away

What about that suicide Sunday
The homeless, cardboard for their bay

The unemployed, the bills they can't pay
A fallen believer, a castaway

A lonely neighbor with nothing to say
You haven't seen an angel today?

Consuelo Ramirez McGuire

The Eternal Resting Place

As I remember back on my diseased grandpa,
I notice something different.
When he was with me he was always joyful.
He appeared to be an earthly angel,
   a messenger from the Lord.
When he died I cried and cried,
   but I knew he would never return.
He must be looking down on me
   to make sure I'm ok.
But I never worry about him
   because I know he's with the Lord.
I also know that he's no longer an earthly angel,
   but an angel that of the Lord.
Here on earth he was poor,
   but he's very rich in heaven.
But one day I'll see him again,
   and I know that we'll be happy to be there,
For that is where all great men stop.
That is the eternal resting place.

Scott Whitenack

Untitled

I wish, a dream of mine would come completely true, and never go away.
I like that dream, enjoy it, and that's where I want to stay.
In that dream I was an eagle flying in the sky.
I like that dream and can't describe that feeling of mine.
A graceful bird I was that night,
And now I wish I'd stay.
'Cause in the morning I woke up,
The Eagle flew away.
But I remember it as if it was last night,
And never will, at least I hope,
Forget that wondrous sight,
The Eagle, brave as any bird could ever be.
If storm it sees, it keeps on circling the blue wonders of the sea.
In that dream I was a graceful Eagle,
And part of it will always be in me.

Mikhail Segal

Did You Ever Wonder

Did you ever wonder why 4 goes after 3,
   or why it's dark at night?
Did you ever wonder why mermaids swim under the sea,
   or why wrong is opposite of right?

Did you ever wonder why water is clear,
   or why pebbles are small?
Did you ever wonder why far is not near,
   or why you can bounce a tennis ball?

Did you ever wonder why the earth is round,
   or if bread crumbs can talk?
Did you ever wonder what lies underground,
   or why buttons can't walk?

Did you ever wonder why shoes come in a box,
   or why you sleep in a bed?
Did you ever wonder why keys are made for locks,
   or why words must be said?

Did you ever wonder why people must die,
   or why you put your sock on before your shoe?
If you've ever wondered Why....
   then figure out what to do!!!!

Marina Zhukova & Victoria Vaynberger

Where Trilliums Sleep

Beneath the snows the trilliums sleep
In a bower at the edge of the wood.
Spared for a time from man's clearings deep
Oh, I would reverse that trend if I could.

Secure in there place, where trilliums sleep
Lie matchless unspoken beauty of the past.
Try as he may there, man cannot reap
Until his heart is filled with love at last.

Beneath the snows the trilliums sleep
Those lovely wild lilies of Spring
Until to the sun they joyously leap
When the robins return to sing.

Joseph M. Power

"Because Of A Dream"

Because of a dream, I wait more ardent than before.
I wait, for dreams sometimes open wide the door to
   Love's sure entrance
And to this warm illusion, I hold fast more.

I dreamt you kiss me, and I asked you if you loved me still
Your reply was unhesitant, sincere.
Yes, I love you more than you'll ever know;
And this I know I always will.

A short dream it was, but it made me happy all the day.
So happy, I took heart to pray — for you.

And hoped that through this dream's ending, it could be
Written upon the scene of this life's play.

So, because of a dream, I wait undaunted and patient still;
To share the kiss I dreamed about to thrill to its sweet thrill.

Viola Edmonson

Diversion

Under the dirty streets of New York,
beneath the noise and the ruckus,
lies the dripping, moldy, musty sewer,
with its rats and unknown species.
A little glimmer of glorious, streaming light.
A quarter.

Desiree Carrica

Love Yourself First

If caring too much is an imperfection,
I am as imperfect as they come.
If evaluating this trait is a reflection.
I am reflecting upon this some.

Others have been placed as my priority,
Leaving myself and my happiness behind.
Others haven't always appreciated me,
Leaving my heart crushed and closing my mind.

The lack of gratitude in others is vast,
Realization of this can cause one to weep.
The lack of respect increases as fast,
Realization of this can cause lack of sleep.

Love yourself first before it's too late,
Satisfaction will therefore soon follow.
Love others second and determine your fate,
Satisfaction will progress as you grow.
    Brigitte Armstrong-Sherrill

Thankful Thoughts

One who has never seen
the beauty of a special scene
like the view from a mountain top
or a waterfall by full moonlight,
may have knowledge and understanding
but has no idea of the beauty of life

Without having ever seen
the wonder of a special scene
like frost frozen fat on trees
or a field covered with new snow;
one may have been to the grandest cities
but has no idea of the peacefulness of life.

One cannot have ever seen
the beauty of these special scenes
like the view of the seven seas
or even a large city from afar
without gaining a knowledge of love
and having been given a gift from above
    Eric Pullium

Untitled

Shades of purple and gray
Tis the end of another day
Shadows of figures powerful and black
On them don't dare turn thy back

The rose is held in the light
Tis the end of the endless fight
Dark fog rolls through thee
At last freedom is to be

On the ground a blood stained sword
But, freedom is not the reward
A head hung low in respect
A crushing blow is to expect

Closing the eyes gritting thine teeth
The sword is placed within the sheath
Tired and confused by the twist of fate
There is nothing else left to do but wait.
    Dana Scering

"Why Did You Have To Die?"

You said before
"If I die, I die"
And there in a coffin I saw you lie
Why did you have to die?

You were so strong
You could handle almost anything that was wrong
Why did you have to die?

We all know now you are in a much safer place
But that isn't the case
I will always remember your face
Why did you have to die?

So in your memory I write this poem
And in my memory you will always be
But why did you have to die?
    Sarah Poorian

Enemy But Friend

Looking faintly into the long and abstract dismal mirror
I feel a warm chill
I can't differentiate between life or death
A birth certificate or a will
Time flows with an arhythmic heartbeat
With a tick without a tock
I slowly slumber over
Could I be changing from a son negating a father to a grandpop?
I still wonder why I listen but don't really hear,
I remember peripherally seeing a crowd, but heard no cheer
Death be not proud
The eternal sleep,
I secretly fear.
I am my fiercest enemy and my sweetest friend
Sometimes over judgmental,
The Alpha and the Omega, the beginning and the end—
As I close my eyes, standing parallel to the mirror
I begin to sway
There is one thing important—
I Love Myself tomorrow, yesterday, but more importantly Today.
    John C. Hawkins, Jr.

Children Precious Gifts

Children, one of God's special blessings that He so lovingly lends to us. We are created in the image and likeness of God, as our children are in likeness to us.

They are so precious, so beautiful, what a God given miracle that He has entrusted in our care. They don't ask to be born, they are an alive human being.

We are to nurture them with love and to help their lives. As they grow, our children give us so much in return, their priceless smiles, cute quoteable sayings, their sincere love and dependency on us, with no need to repay. God gave us that responsibility, to protect their precious little being.

The gift of life, created in the likeness of our Heavenly Father. God meets our every need when we depend on Him, with no need to repay, only learn to obey and keep His commandments-just like we expect our children to obey us. Children are truly to be valued lifelong, as one of God's unique specially created handiwork.
    Georgiana Montgomery

The Perfect Gift

If you are looking for the perfect gift, then look in
 the heavens store. The perfect lift that fits all sizes.
Jesus the Son of God. He is the Sweet Rose of
Sharon, He has the aroma that will please any
senses - the very perfect gift.

No size to remember. No wrapping or ribbons to get.
 Only in faith reach out for the perfect gift.
Jesus the Son of God.

He will come in at your beck and call, all in aglow
 With the only salvation that will flood your inner soul.
 He shed His blood on Cavalry, the only key that fits
 every heart, that no on can take part, no sales clerk
 to fall apart. The perfect gift for every heart. Jesus!

It doesn't come in a box. No heavy load to carry - but,
 be merry, because Jesus carried the load of sins
 for mankind to the cross. The perfect gift for any
 boss. Jesus!

When the gift of salvation is accepted, it would be
 perfect to write in your memoirs front page.
 The perfect gift for any age.

No money to spend. No debt to repay. The Savior,
 Jesus Christ, he lays in a manger. asleep on the hay,
 He was born on what we now call Christmas Day.

No need to take out a loan, or wander and roam. He
 gave up the ghost with hardly a groan. The perfect
 gift sits on heavens throne. Jesus Christ can be
 our very own.
  Georgiana Montgomery

In Everyone's Life

In everyone's life- there's a time when you need a friend.
The magic of it all, is just amazingly growing.
A few simple words, or gentle hand, brings out the beauty of it all.
In everyone's life- a little pain must fall, but a friend is there
to take away all.
Their simple words of wisdom, seem to be true. In everyone's life-
a little sun will shine, where you share happiness, hope, an
laughter, each living day. A path that which no one could change,
if it's meant to be. In everyone's life there'll be a friend forever.
  Laurie Butler

Out On Winter's Limb

How does nature's gracious tree limbs endure
 the seasonal harassment?
With the winter's barren, desolate, frigid
 torments!
Frailed after the night's furious winds,
Emptied of snow's white precious
 blanket,
Stretching towards the brightness of the
 day's sunlight,
Knowing the change to greenery is many
 months away!
  Patricia Perras

Untitled

Eyelids weighted with locked away tears
Time has gathered a new set of fears
Ignore the feelings, touch nothing inside
Back away slowly, she's once before tried
Block out the daylight, it's silent at night
Alone in her world she's hidden from sight
Days turned to months, to years, then to black
Gone to her memories, with no way back.
  Pamela K. Pugliese

The Whips And Thorns

As I carry My cross, My body grows tired.
Curse after curse, your angry mouths fired.
The thorns in My head and the whip on My back.
Stripes formed on My body from the whip's thunderous crack.

I look up ahead and I begin to weep.
My everlasting promise, I will keep.
For all of the cheating and for every lie.
Up on the hill, on the cross I shall die.

My friends and family look on with sorrow.
For they all know, I'll be gone the next morrow.
Down on their knees and tears in their eyes,
They follow behind Me and say their good-byes.

I was persecuted and scorn,
With each crack of the whip and the crown I have worn,
For all of your sins, I have died.
Up on the cross, with My arms stretched out wide.
  Kerry Trenholm

Seasonal Love

My love's words are ones which I must abide,
But by morrow she wishes us to part;
I want not to take part in this divide,
For she and she alone doth own my heart.

What could be the reason behind her wish?
Maybe I have done something to offend.
Perhaps her temper's like a broken dish;
Too shattered for me easily mend.

Could it be that her love just runs too deep?
Were the consequences too great to face?
To love completely may make her heart weep;
So she wants to move another place.

For now I may only guess the reasons,
Why her love seems to change with the seasons.
  Scott Perard

On the Path

I was walking down the path
  Suddenly, I stopped.
The grass beneath my feet disappeared
  as did the soles of my shoes.
I stood barefooted on the path.

The brown earth under my feet felt soft and warm.
  I felt the sacredness of the earth.
The earth spoke to me and I comprehended its meaning.

The earth is alive, you know.
  It breathes, it accepts the seed of birds and man.
  It quietly nurtures its gifts, in a special way
Then gives them back to us.
  Helen M. Roe

Why?

You seemed so happy everyday.
Why did you have to go away?
I don't understand why you did what you did.
Was it because of the secrets you hid?
All you could do was try to run.
But why did you have to use a gun?
I know now the pain you went through,
Because now I have to live with it too.
But now you're gone, where did you go?
Only God forever knows.
I hope it's someplace filled with cheer,
Like the days I had when you were here.
  Kristin Cervantez

The Treasure Trove

Childhood on, his ancient soul
proclaimed departure
From ocean's breast, this pearl —
To be waxed luminous by the sands of time —
In quest for self — and quest for "thine."

Far distant shore a gentle
spirit heard her name — his call
and another pearl slid silently
to the deep —
Beneath the squall.

Mindless of the ocean's roar —
Myriad currents swayed in patient dance —
As soul lanterns marked the way —
That they embraced —
was not by chance.

Now sheltered in her hidden cove —
The ocean swelled and thrashed above —
Fierce guardian of these
pearls so loved.
Mary L. Tompsett

Love Is Becoming

I drift
  From one life into another having no purpose
  At times, the loneliness that descends in the middle of my
sleepless
    nights encases me in a gently fog
    Surrounding my thoughts of elusive love

I search
  For something real and find the emptiness of me

I love
  And feel the futility erased
  Love gives meaning to my life

God, Love
  Unseen, Intangible taken on faith become real
  My reality is loving you
  My world comes into focus
  My fantasy world prolongs my time with you

Together
  Reality and fantasy bring time to a standstill
  Love steadies my heart while shaking the core of me
Donna Meakins

Adieu (A French Sonnet)

Friendship is love, only for the sake of caring.
Caring, not for reward, for the sake of comfort.
An open heart, so exposed, with timid daring.
Seeking warmth and tenderness; sending the same forth.
Friendship is a weight; not to be borne by the weak.
Trying times and inconvenience will serve, up, strains.
It will not be maintained by the faithless, or meek.
And words and mistakes, can bring deep, most vicious, pains.
But friendship does not cease, nor fade away, my friend,
with the passing of life's, very short, pleasant, day.
Long will my memory of you, refuse its end.
Fondness, buried in my heart, never to decay.
For friendship is God's gift; the lonely Soul's desire.
The eyes joy, the mind's comfort, the heart's, very, fire.
James McRae, The Nubian Poet

Loon Magic

The manic tremolo floats
Across the storm plowed lake
Melting into the violence
Of grumbling cumulus.

Thunderheads scatter over the water
Hanging so low that their gravid bellies
Decant in pelting panes of fluid
Pummeling the lake's resilient surface.

Lightning spawned peals of thunder
Counterpoint the trembling, laughing loon's cry
As determined waves grasp at the shore
With eroding, foaming talons.

Squalling in anger, the winds
Comb through the pines and
Clean house, then depart as
Playful zephyrs, satisfied.

Cleansed, the air assumes the scent
Of wet earth and bruised firs,
While out on the lake once more
Sounds the lonely wail of the loon.
Irene E. Fraley

Mothers

Mothers have so many wonderful ways,
They help their loved ones when
  they go astray.
Mothers are always near when the
  children have fears at night,
She attends the little ones with all her might.
She is always near to cheer you on
Even when you get stuck with a thorn
A mother is so dear true, we have
to sometimes make a big fuss.
Some of us lost our mothers to the grave
And sometimes the ones that are living
have to be very brave.
A mother is so dear to us,
we have to sometimes make a fuss,
The love that mother gave so honest and true
Will aide and a let me all my life thru.
Alice F. Hopkins

He Is There

Skeptics may say there is no God - but why?
His presence is in all the earth and sky!
A precious bud becomes a rose, full blown;
A newborn calf ere long is fully grown.
The sun, rain, and snow in season flourish
That food be grown to strengthen and to nourish.
All wondrous things, invented by mankind,
Are products of His gift - the human mind;
Yet, all these pale, compared to His creations;
God lives! There are no other explanations!
A tiny babe, of infinite perfection
Decries the lack of Masterly direction;
Mere happen-stance — no that makes reason stare,
And we perceive Divinity is there!
Arleen Dockter

The Demon

I'm waiting... every chance I get, I will drift into your thoughts.
I will make you taste me, want me, and love me. I will slowly bring
myself to you but so sneakily that you won't even realize it. I
will let you think you are rid of me but then I will seize my
opportunity and take you back! I will make you feel like nothing
is more important than me and slowly you will push away everything
else. I will make you feel like nothing or no one can touch you.
You will feel so powerful! Day by day I will become the center
of your life and you will lose everything else. I will be the
only one to stand by you... no matter what. I will be there until
the day you die!

Your demon forever,
Alcohol

Christine Villanueva

Explain Why

Explain to the blind what colors look like
to the deaf the song of a bird.
Explain to the retarded the reason why
their prayers have gone unheard.

Explain to two people who are trying to conceive
a child to complete their life.
Explain to a child born with a drug addiction
of their young parents strife.

Explain the terrorism we face on earth
and the reason some choose to die.
Explain why those who runs this world
have no guilt of a lie.

Explain why the epidemic of Aids persists
when there are precautions to be had.
Explain why some things that we are
confronted with are just too sad.

Explain why children have to grow up so fast
unable to act their age.
Explain why in the worst of times
we just can't turn the page.

Audrey Grote

Untitled

I can remember the kids in the field
running and playing to nothing did they yield.

Always ready for the next day
Thinking if there will be sun and do they get to play.

You and I were once the same
always ready to try a new game.

Candy and cookies were our main course
yes they were just consider the source.

Over the field they go with no worries
their parents awaiting their outrageous stories

So many stories about different things
oh, what joy to our lives their laughter brings.

Seeing the kids makes my heart shine
someday in the future one will be mine.

Christopher D. Adkins

My Mountain Top

Always the mountain filled me with dread
So safely I dwelt in the valley instead,
But when twilight draped the heights in purple and gold
My eyes must look upward the peak to behold.
Deep within me a question troubled my mind.
Should I scale that granite what would I find?

Years of sunshine and shadow passed through my life
Each new year bringing peace or great strife.
At last my mirror reflected a stranger in place,
Silvered hair, darkened eyes, lines on the face.
An unbidden urge sent my thought up on high-
I must climb the mountain and be nearer the sky!

Leaving behind me all I held dear
Without doubt or regret my purpose so clear
Slowly upward I struggled, no easy path this.
On reaching the summit there lay the abyss.
Across the depths stretched a bridge of shimmering rope
With trembling I crossed holding fast to my hope.
All glory filled the sky from the westering sun
Now I knew my Eternity had finally begun.

Poet-Mary Phillips

The Stream

At a picnic last Saturday
Away from my family, far, far away
I heard a noise coming from the stream
It sounded like help or maybe just a scream
I went to the stream to see what was wrong
I looked up and down, but it was too long
I saw a young girl waving her arms in fright
But all of a sudden she was out of sight
I jumped in the water to find the young girl
I looked everywhere, but she was not there
All of a sudden into my hands
Came the little girl like a limp rubberband
I took her to shore, but she was under too long
I told her parents, I'm sorry she's gone.

Jesse Tarter

Path Of Life

A man is travelling down a path,
Soon he comes to a spot to rest.
As he rests, he looks down the path,
Some spots were rocky and hard,
Others were smooth from other travellers.
In some spots he had forged his own path.
Other travellers accompanied him for bits of his journey.
He climbed a titanic mountain. Others turned back.
But he continued.
He was hunting but without guns or arrows,
Chasing but without running.
He was after only one thing:
His dream.

Raymond M. Arnold

All In The Blink Of God's Eye

A baby is born and you grasp his tiny hand
In the blink of God's eye, he has grown into a man,
The child that you love, has a love of his own
In the blink of God's eye, you know that he'll never be alone,
This man has a child a family to share
In the blink of God's eye, you know you'll always care,
The time has come, to meet Him up above
All in the blink of God's eye, and so full of love,
I think to myself, so many memories in my heart
In the blink of God's eye, one life ends and one life starts.

Donna Harris

The Cruzin' Orange Crate

Drivin' down Apache Trail we see him; who could miss that bod of orange.
Old, yet still firm and strong, hangin' out with the "Hogs" in their haven.
Someone pinch me, this must be heaven.
Listen to him roar, sounds so sweet, leaves your ears ringing for more.
Everybody's turnin' their heads; gotta get a quick peak at that orange streak.
Had to have him for our own. Grab him fast and head off to our side of town.
He was a bit run down; didn't have the woman's tender touch.
Worked day and night to get the shakes out, wanted to make him go down nice and firm, holdin' his own on the road.
With me inside sittin' tall and proud in the saddle, grinning ear to ear.
I'm talkin' about our 50' Ford Chop-Top. He's one Hot Rod!
Built Ford tough with Chevy stuff!
Listen for that roar! Here we come, zoomin' by leaving them wanting more.
All they see is a streak of orange and the blue dot tail lights as we disappear out of sight.
There's still a lot to do to make him just right.
We'll keep takin' our time given him that TLC.
I'm we're in no hurry cuz he's here to stay, one day will be real special when we drive down town together even better than ever!

Connie Clark

A Melody Of Phrases

I'm just looking for a place in this world.
A little something that will make me known.
Don't shut me out!
I have a lot to offer.
I've been through a lot.
Haven't experienced enough.
Can I call you, my friend?
(Do you really think you know me)
I can't do this anymore.
I Quit!

Katrina M. Griffin

Nostradamus

He lies with his soul torn by great pains,
Eyes glazed over from lack of sleep.
The thought is imprinted in his mind
In just an hour, their lives they cannot keep.
Nostradamus glides his hand across the paint-chipped globe
Earthquakes, tornadoes, and strong winters he has seen
Probing into the depths of the earth
With this gift of seeing the future before it was shown.
A lone tear falls from his cheek to his map
And creates a river where one will no longer bend.
The unexpected water loosens the ink
And it drips down the side of the table,
Falling to his lap
Where he twiddles his thumbs
For he knows what goes up must come down, and what begins must end.
Is it a gift to know the fate of the land
Or would it be better not to predict God's shifty hand?

Heather Coleman

Last Few Tears

Tommy cries his last few tears,
As he struggles to see and meet his fears,
And battles to control the gears.

All of a sudden the truck veers; into a deep ravine.
As the end of his time here nears,
His life is replayed throughout the years.

Tommy shall cry no more.

Jodi Dickens

"Maturity Flights Of Youth"

Youth—it comes upon us when we least expect it so it seems
Sometimes not fulfilling all our childhood dreams.
One day playing as a child—only to look up, awaken, it's real!
Lost in a field of bewilderment with the unknown emotions we feel.

We discover our new body self, a stranger we yet do not know
Mood swings of crying then smiling; the child is now on the shelf.
Losing trust we had as a child—faltering from outstretched hands
From those who helped us always now they seem to understand.

Then come moments we try things, things that we never would do!
Off in flight with no flight plan—adventure to see us through!
It's fun, thrilling, exciting! We now have the friends that be.
We delight in night, no rules in sight, great it is to be free!!

The world is spinning around us, not knowing the course, we sway.
We want to run home—but where did we come—direction has fallen away.
Surprised! Friends drift from sight, some break—needing repair!
Others drop to earth—no hope for rebirth—we fly in deep despair.

Far away in our conscious mind, feeling helpless, frightened, alone,

We remember, feel our faith renew, it soars us at last to home.
Tomorrow there will be rainbows, flowers, and beauty in sight.
"Flight of Youth" never ending, mature, embraced by the Light.

Marilyn Shurtliff Stacey

Autobiography Of A Woman

Once I was a child so small. Just knee high.
Each year my Mother watched me grow tall as time went by.
God needed my Mother in heaven above. How I did cry.
His need was greater than my love and time went by.
My Father raised me for the next ten years, he really did try.
My three brothers kept me in laughter and tears as time went by.
Then I fell in love and we were wed as time went by.
I had three little girls whom I tucked in bed with a lullaby.
Years later I gave them a brother, the time was nigh.
Now they all have children that call me grandmother as time goes by.
I have seen the mountains and the sea and birds on high.
Enjoyed the sunshine and wind blowing free as time went by.
The strains of music and sweetness of song as time went by.
I have often danced the whole night long and that's no lie.
The sands of the desert and drifts of snow as time goes by.
Miracles of God wherever I go to astound my eye.
I watch the wrinkles slowly appear with a sigh.
But of old age I have no fear as time goes by.
When shadows fall and I am laid to rest, don't you cry.
I have lived a life that is truly blest as time went by.

Helen M. Gecinceis

Song For Mary

I am not here within this silent dwelling
Where shades are drawn and flowers line the walls -

Where people speak in hushed and quiet voices;
Oh no, my dears, I am not here at all.

You will find me now in white gulls soaring;
You will see me in the mist of early dawn.

I am triumphant in the foam of white waves breaking,
I am in the sunset's glow when it is gone.

Look for me whenever loved ones gather,
For I shall love to linger for awhile.

No, I am not here where mourning is and sadness - - -
Find me in the kindness of a smile.

Helen E. Kershaw

Movement

Movement spotted midst the trees,
   stillness captured in brown leaves.
Quietly waiting, what shall I see?

Softly, without sound, a doe appears,
   graceful and small.
Turned her head as though to call.

Invitation answered, joining her now,
   two eager young bucks
   with stubs for crowns.

Moments pass, they seem to stand
   silent and still on my land.
I watched entranced as briskly they danced,
   white tails waving, up the hill.

Movement spotted midst the trees,
   stillness captured in brown leaves.
Quietly waiting, my vision to see,
   white tails waving back at me.
   Barbara Sylvia

Life's Conception

Cold and rainy morning,
lost in my own sensations.
My life is without a warning,
except for my own perceptions.
Sometimes is sad to think we will someday die.
Sometimes is a relief to think we will someday die.

My childhood's obsession,
my resentfulness for one day growing up.
I still revive my joyful memories,
such possessions my soul will never let go.
I see the sky liberating itself from the rain,
and myself from contemplating some tragic end.
Such speculative impression is life's conception.
   Arlon Morales

Warm Thoughts

This world is filled with hopes and dreams,
Yet mine are far away,
I know I will see my spirit rise,
When I am blessed one day.

I sit and wait behind darkened walls,
In a frosty world,
A woman I am not,
I am just a little girl.

A little girl who knows her fate,
Who knows where she will be,
And I will smile and laugh someday,

When the sunlight touches me.
   Theresa Kayzar

Hidden

Darkest corners of the mind
search for the forgotten and you will find
Times has hidden much of your past
painful memories covered by masks
close your eyes and concentrate
the many walls you'll infiltrate
the many pictures that you see
are they real or just a dream?
   Gayle Whiting

Mr. Coke

My name is coke
and I'm no joke.
Come all ye abuser's
come to my suers,
come on and take a ride, I'm coming
in with the tide.
Sell me your love, your life, your wife
I don't care, it's not my thing to be all that fair.
Your life is the key, give it to me and you'll never be free.
Use me once
Use me twice
Look out here comes the vice.
Well, it's been fun, it's been real but now
I must run.
Come visit me anytime,
there will be no denying,
you'll be the one dying.
   Charles E. Gruenewald

Dillys' Tea Party

Winter holds the earth in its frigid grasp,
Bony twigs grate my mind like a cold steel rasp.
Is springs warmth coming soon, perhaps,
The eyes of Dillys' tea party waiting for the hasp.

A flush of warmth blankets the frozen ground,
It's too early yet, but the first stalks abound.
Cups of yellow porcelain dot the garden all around,
Yet the weather's turning soft, spring is yet to be found.

Dipping their heads in the gentle rain,
Dillys' tea party cannot refrain,
The sight is something to behold,
For winter time is nigh, and spring is growing bold.
   Patrick O'Callaghan

Trees

   My love affair with trees dates
back to my youth.

   Climbing trees was a thrill, and
a playhouse in a beautiful maple tree
was a private home of my very own.

   Thousands of varieties and all have
their individual purpose: Some to give
fruit, shade, and a home for birds; timber
for houses, ships and furniture, even a
cross for Jesus.

   Fuel too they provide. Trees control
the purity of the air above and the water
in the ground. They are Earth's greatest
single controller of the climate.

   Trees are a crowning glory of Nature's
handiwork.

   I love trees.
   Lillian Maychick

A Person Who Hurts

   A person who hurts you shouldn't be around.
If the person who hurts you is called a friend,
he should no longer be a friend. If he hurts
you without intent then he should be one who
remains a friend. But if his purpose in life
is to hurt you then maybe you shouldn't be around.
So if you are hurt and he caused it don't be
mad for it might not be your fault.
   Danielle Stern

You're Not Alone

You're not alone
When you have friends
Who care about you
And you can depend on me
To think about you
And how you are
Though you're not here
You're not far from my thoughts
And from my mind
I think about you all the time
And even on this day
I'm thinking of you
And I hope and pray
That you are fine and feeling well
I care about you more than words can tell
Though the days seem long
And the nights seem endless
Just remember
You'll never be friendless

Michelle Ann-Victoria Lopez

A Love Poem

The nights are long and the days are hazy
I like my leisure, but I'm far from lazy
Sometimes I'm serious and sometimes I get crazy
But all times - I love you

Monotonous hours linger during times you're not here
When I explain my empty feelings to your sensitive ear
The words may be scarce, but the meaning is clear
And at all times - I love you

A deep sense of love is felt throughout this man
When you share your warmth as only you can
I look beyond your eyes and squeeze love from your hand
Because at all times - I love you

Vacations from work will come and go all too fast
No leaves of absence from me will be amassed
'Cuz eternal love between us will always last
For at all times - I love you

Other guys will tell you that you're their queen
And the thoughts they project, I can't always demean
For I think the same at times, though strange it may seem
But at all times - I love you

Tom Russell

"Do You Remember When?"

Where was it, that we started from, was it only three?
I remember when I was so happy to learn to climb a tree.

Where was it that we started from when you were only four?
You laughed and laughed at me, when my pants got tore.

Do you remember how fast we grew up to the age of nine?
We held hands and even kissed one time and that was very fine.

At fourteen we found our way, did we finally know the score?
There were differences between us now, we weren't kids anymore.

At seventeen, as the prom queen, you were as pretty as a flower.
On the way home we stopped and parked, oh maybe for an hour.

At twenty-one it was just my bad luck, that I was called to war.
It was pretty hard to loose my leg, but I wasn't crying any more.

The veteran's door said Sonny, "I've made you a perfect leg!"
Now you don't have to sit around or sit on a street corner and beg!

I came home in two long years and found you'd married another guy!
You told me then that you had a son, and that really made me cry.

I'll often wonder to this day, if that fine young boy was really mine!
I just saw him yesterday and he really looks like he's doing fine.

So my dear, although you really are near, to my love, I say goodbye!

Thomas C. Rupert

Power Of The Wind

The wind moves through the trees so bare,
Bending and swaying the tall and the strong.
Such power held in what is unseen,
Yet, display of strength proves it is there.

The wind howls with strong gusts,
Proclaiming its presence to the blind.
It roars with force through the air,
Imposing its will on all of us.

When faith accepts its presence near,
The blinded eye begins to see.
The source of movement in the breeze,
Calls its children to lend an ear.

With sense attuned one begins to feel,
The gentle harmony through the limbs.
Melodies dance on the tips of buds,
Calling forth spring, itself to reveal.

J. Christopher MacDonald

Rage

So much rage built up inside
Trying too hard to hide feelings
That just can't hide

Wanting badly to change your life
Trying to prevent the urges you get
When you hold a knife

Your mind always thinks of everything bad
Trying desperately to ignore it
But it makes you sad

You look in the mirror
Wishing you were someone else
Crying yourself to sleep at night
You just can't help yourself

Natile Bouthillette

Good-bye

I'm saying goodbye to you today,
and hoping the troubles will go away.
The hate will be lifted after so long,
erase all the pain and all of the wrong.
I take back my shoulder and my ear as well,
there's no looking back to no time to dwell.
I'm saying good-bye just giving up,
It's time to say enough is enough.
Forget all the laughter and all of the tears,
forget the friendship after all those years.
I'm saying good-bye there's no looking back,
It's time to say, you're part of my past.

Charlsyee Cordeiro

Dominoes

Zebras are black and white
So are newspapers and dominoes
And lithographs and etchings
Some pussycats are
And Dalmatians
And blackberries with sugar on top,
Tart black radishes inside
Are white and swaying
birches all around are flecked,
    with dashes of black
Lamp posts with their sturdy black roots
    illuminate the night
And somewhere from dusk to dawn
A poet pens the words
    black ink on white paper
    to make her poem.

Karen M. Green

Harsh Words

Too many times, we hurt someone
With harsh words, and we make them blue
Our tongue gets carried away
And these two words "I'm sorry",
Are so hard, for us to say.

After we've hurt someone, with harsh words,
A lump gets in our throat, and makes it dry.
Tears get in our eyes, and we start to cry
But somehow, we can't say,"I'm sorry",
No matter, how hard, we try.

We wish we could go back to yesterday
And, take all our harsh words away
But, somehow our pride gets in our way
And these two words, "I'm sorry",
Are the hardest words, for us to say.

When you say harsh words, to some one
Don't let your pride, get in your way
Don't wait to say, "I'm sorry",
For, there might not come another day.

Nancy Anne Bailey

Petals

In my vision white petals fall from a blooming tree
Covering my head, resting there like seeds
taking root to become thoughts, concepts, fantasies
The blueprints of my future years.

Joseph Sabol

Untitled

If you have ever looked in a child's eyes, even for a moment, and
seen the home of innocence-
You might have understood.

And if you have ever smelt the grass while rolling in the fields of sun-
You might have comprehended what he said as he stood.

If you have ever felt lambs wool, soft and rough on your fingertips-
You might just have a notion.

If you have ever sung to let your spirit free or sat at peace just to be-
His message may have put you in motion.

If you're always striving to be good, if you follow in his
commandments like you should-
You might have heard the sound.

If you smile, you laugh, you cry, and above all love-
The key you might have found.

If you have heard the choir of angels or tasted the joys of life-
You might just have a clue,

That "Blessed are the pure in heart, for they shall see God,"
Might be referring to you.

Sarah Mittelholzer

"I'll Go To Him With A Song"

Some people stand and talk so sweet,
About Jesus whom they hope to meet,
I can hardly wait until my turn,
Because the light in my heart burns.

I sing my song with joy and love,
My song is my testimony and it goes above,
The rafters ring with love, I'm told,
I know I'll walks the streets of gold.

If you want to live forever, say I do,
Take a look at yourself through and through,
Then decide to take the right road home,
With Him on your side, you are never alone.

Patricia O. Patterson

Fire Of Tears

Deep within me burns a sacred fire of tears;
Reflections of my soul, like a hall of a thousand mirrors.

My life has given life, to these tears of flame.
They never die or extinguish, but at times softly wane.

White flames flicker in purest love
flowing gently for all that's divine.

Blue flames trickle in grief or sorrow
and are dried thru only time.

Yellow flames dance in joy
and cry out in pure happiness.

Red flames explode and crackle in anger
but soon dry to less and less

The rainbow flames encompass all flames
simultaneously and all at once...

And may quietly burn and trail
off and on, for months.

I'm so very, very blessed with my fire of tears.
May they continue to burn for me
throughout my remaining years.

Linda L. Lennington

A Long Time Ago

June 1, 1946 - a long time ago,
Two people vowed, "until death do us part".

A long time ago, two people met,
Became friends, then lovers, now man and wife.

A long time ago, two sons were born,
Each with separate goals in life, but loved by both.

A long time ago, these two people vowed,
To love each other 'til the end of time.

A long time ago, now is today, and together still.
And celebrating 50 years, together still.

For all the things that you've done yesterday
For all the things that you will do today
And for all the things you will do tomorrow

With sons, daughters-in-law, grandchildren, family and friends alike,
Mom and Dad, we thank you, and we love you still - June 1, 1996.

Ronald F. Dobiesz

Lights

The doors in town are never open, locked for good.
Dirt from other lands is disdained on clean carpets.

Windows in the homes are barred and shut.
They never want to see the suffering sadistic terror...out there.

The children jump rope in their rooms moaning learned songs:
   "Crime and drugs, gangs and disarray
    Belong not to our town
    But to a town so far away
    So very far away."

Adults huddle together with fingers in their ears:
If I cannot hear it, it does not happen.
Others sit, knees to chest and hands draped over tearful eyes:
If I cannot see it, it will not happen.
The rest cower with fingers dug deep into their mouths:
If I cannot speak it, it shall not happen.

And yet...it happens. Every day in every way,
Through the veil of deaf ears, blind eyes, and gagged mouths.
Inmates of the town, are paralyzed by inactivity, bound by fear.
And when these lights go out in the townspeople,
The Lights go out in town.

Robert M. Sawalski

Death Is Life

The world as I see it,
keeps drifting further and further away.
In my eyes the earth is a demon
and I'm beginning to think we are its prey.
As foolish as it may sound,
day by day we are being eaten alive
and one day before you even realize it,
life will be over no matter how hard you strive.
Death is life and life is death.
Sounds crazy but every one will realize that
once they take that last breath.
What is death? It is the beginning of no end.
Death is a reality, not just a trend.
Life on the other hand is not reality but just a phase.
And once you're convinced
life will be nothing more than a blurry daze.
Start realizing now before it's too late,
or you will be stuck in an eternity of pain,
behind a locked gate.
Launa C. Durbin

I Alone

I need a time when I can be
and sit alone with only me.

If I could have but one thing
this would I choose over everything.

When I'm alone I can cry
I can live or I can die.

You can do things you can't do
when there are people watching you.

You can love or you can hate
or you can sit and contemplate.

How can we live a life
so full of stress so full of strife.

When you're alone in this place
from the world you may shield your face.

From the arrogant points of view
that only seek destroying you.

When I'm old and gray and grown
I hope I still remember how it feels
TO BE ALONE.
Nicole Shelton

Fifty Plus

Who says I don't have the right
   to be on stage!
Thirty years of all that structure,
On call twenty-four hours everyday,
Dammit — I've come of age!

You very young creatures hoot at me,
How do you dare assume my mind
Has gone underground like so
   much garbage.
Don't judge me by my slower step.

Vitality of thought is what
   counts alive,
Imagination to create and experience you see
Is still mine, sure as hellbent
To quiet my rage there's a away,
——SURGE!!!
Stephanie Arden

A Circle Of Friends

I was tired of being negative, I wanted to be free,
to study and to grow for once, to love and trust in me.

"Just look within for what you want and it shall be," they said,
but stubborn me said, "how can that be, I do not comprehend?"

"When it's time, you will know," the words were said again,
"just relax and time will pass, and spirit will tell you when."

Then things began to happen, and I had to agree,
doors began to open, helping hands came out to me.

It seems rather strange now, why I couldn't see,
the ones I had been seeking, were also seeking me.

I meet every week now with my new found friends,
and together we are learning to travel from within.

We link our hands together, we explore the universe,
it's always so different, it's always a first.

We are proud of each other, of how we've all grown,
we don't use the word "jealous," it's a word we won't own.

We are all so special, our timing is right,
to share with the universe, the love of "the light."
"So be it"
Sue T.

First Born

I gave you life, dear child of mine,
Birth pains gave way to joy
As closely in my arms I held
A brand new baby boy!

I watched your growth as day by day
New things became the rule.....
First tooth, first step, first word, and then
It wasn't long... first day of school!

You left my arms, you left my care,
You grew into a man,
Took on a wife!.... then little ones
Soon joined our happy clan.

But love that came with you at birth
Will never cease to grow,
And pride in all that you've become
Makes parent's hearts o'er flow!
Elsie F. Baust

Her Majesty, the Queen

Her majesty Mt. Hood sits on her throne
Buried in blankets of snow.
Her crown is cast with crystal white,
O'er the moon casts a golden glow.

Her attendants in solemn attention stand,
Some thousand or more in woody clumps
Half buried in snow,
As if wonder of it all has turned them all to stone.

Ere summer comes her cloak is changed
From shimmering white to glossy green
Her hair is filled with flowers that spring has brought,
What a glorious change this nature has wrought.

Down through the ages this mountain will stand
Wreathed in the glories of two seasons passed.
Nothing can equal a thing so grand.
Mt. Hood will remain the queen of the land.
Elsie Ryan

My Best Friend

I have a great friend,
Who will stay to the end.
She is so sweet,
Almost like a sugar treat.
I hang out with her all the
time,
Spending every single dime.
She likes to skate
While finishing everything on her
plate.
Her mom and dad are great,
They always let her stay
up late.
That's a great best friend.
Kristie Vaughan

"Stormspell"

Nembus clouded the mist with
   the memory of the past,
That wakes me up in the reality
   of the present..... cause it
rained with the water of the
   early spring,
Giving way for the dew to bath
   at the start of the morning... then
thunder came to threat the unmeasurable
   strength of the past,
By which no one could ever hide
   .....for
Lightning is so dashing yet glaring
   to count the happenings of the
   past, present and the future...
For it was just a stormspell of
   the unpredictable nature.....
Jocelyn Gowdy

Rose

The graceful rose
   is tall and thin.
Her red hat looks lovely
   with her light green
   skin.
When the wind blows high
   she sways and sways.
It sometimes looks like
   she begins to wave.
Her arms are short
   and very thin.
She waves them happily
   in the gentle wind.
The rose is beautiful
   it's plain to see.
Her beauty starts at her
   dark red hat and ends
   with her light green feet.
Felicia Pittman

Oh Where My Cat

Oh where oh where,
Oh where's my cat.
I looked under the hat.
But I think he's under
the big fat mat!
Anya Levine

Remember We Loved

I will sing and dance.
I will write you a poem she said.
Waves of thoughts rushing
on to the years past
beyond words

Mist on the blankets of time
relentless layer over hurt
on to the years past
beyond words

Will you listen to the deep
beyond words

I will write you a poem she said.
Merrilie Camhe

My Home

A place,
where I live,
and where I love;

A land
where I was born,
and where I learn;

That
is my home.
John Deng

Life

In the mist of life's battles
I hear the winds calling my name

The rain washes away my defeat
While cleansing me of my anger

My victories are like sunshine
Bright, bold, beautiful
Always on the horizon

Though I go thru my tornadoes
My hours of darkness and uncertainty
They cease as quickly as they came

For I know with the break of each dawn
I am given another opportunity
Jackie Young-Moore

Everywhere I Go

Everywhere I go
Everything I see
Is a little blackbird
Sitting in a tree.
He's there in the morning.
Sitting in a limb
There in the evening
Undisturbed is him.
He doesn't move
Almost like he's dead
but I've seen him wink
Even turn his head.
The blackest feathers
Pure as night.
Soon those wings
Will put him at flight.
Everywhere I go
Everything I see
Is a little blackbird
Sitting in a tree.
Sondra Biggs

The Window...

If I was a window...
I could be seen from both sides...
The good and bad of my life...
Open for everyone to see...

I could open up to anyone...
Or close myself to the world...
Using only the glass as my shield...
Never letting it down...

Sometimes with pane all around me...
I like being closed...
Letting my heart and soul rest...
A curtain to cover me would be best...

When it's a fresh new day...
I feel open, once again free..
As a butterfly sails the sky...
A gentle breeze blows thru me...
Karen Gowdy

Emptiness

In the light of life, there are shadows
When we enter them, we are empty
At that time we have no feelings
Including Love, Hate, or Sympathy
In this darkness we are alone
There is only me, myself, and I
I can not see the light
Nor the ground or sky
These are the moments I embrace
For I feel no pain
I can have memories
Without having shame
I enjoy the numbness
From my head to my toes
Till it is time to look ahead
Then leave the dark shadows.
Michael Gage

Your Love Is Special

Your love is like a butterfly
with wings spread so wide.
Your love is like a branch
holding on to me.
Your love is like the sun
that shines upon my heart.
Your love is like a flower
that blooms day by day.
There is no other kind of love,
but the love that you've given me
each and every day.
Lori Y. Cordova-Laviolette

One Man

I would love to walk
hand and hand with just
one man who understands.
He sees I have all I need
with just a whisper of Please
He comes from way above
The sky, he's a slave to you
And I. He carried that cross
of so much weight. Across
that land with so much hate.
You don't need a key
to get in that gate
just be good and you don't
have to wait.
Evelyn Caputo

Once Again

In you,
I have seen the real love;
  I wanted to caress it
To get the happiness
  Which I have expected since,
But far from the ocean,
  It's hiding
Forgets all about us.
In you,
I have seen the sunshine;
  I wanted to light me up
To put away the darkness
  All became a nightmare,
And I'm grieving;
  Will you come once again
And fulfill the book?
  Far from you,
I will go, resting
  In your caved heart
To be warm and fortunate.
Benjamin Noel

Complacent By Stone

Rock in hand
Blow to the head

Painted cave wall
Bearing witness of the dead

Given once
By millions taken

Passed in passion
With water breakin'

Bound by honors
Bound by creeds

With a child named service
To cloth their deeds

Administering whose justice?
Protecting what right?

Pray clouds blow away
Save this matter from might
Daniel James Hanrahan

A Poem With No Name

My heart is desolate
and my mind is my only domain
to be free, but are we really free?
You and me
Where will it end
Will you be my friend
I'm going insane from
the madness, the sadness
a world without gladness.

The Lord is my salvation
I hope I shall not die
is that a tear in your eye
don't cry for me mother
don't cry for me and my brother
for the sun comes after the moon
and the sun will come soon.
Antonette Angelique Roche

Angel Of Time

Oh! Angel of Time
Come to me, my force
Come to fulfill my destiny
Come do design my path
And realize my universe!

I am to you
I am from you
Like a seed in the sky
Waiting to bloom!

My thoughts are no longer
My desires...minuscule
For I am only
What you make of me
And forever
I will be for you
And you from Him!
Marcia Souers

Untitled

Smoking cigarettes in a chain,
Trying to kill the pain.
The sorrow I could never kill,
Not even with a pill
Sitting in this place,
Seeing your face.
Not feeling your touch,
Certain I love you so much.

Gazing into your beautiful eyes
I can't see any lies,
If it wasn't for you,
I don't know what I'd do.
Maybe I'd crawl in a hole,
Passing time with a mole.
Victor Caliqiuri

"Surprises"

A pink orange sunrise
Stuns the sleeping sky
With ribbons of brilliance.

A cardinal darting in its
Red flash flight
Awakens the snow hushed land,
Sending sizzles of passion
Along frozen lakes of elegance.

A bouquet of carnations—
Unexpected and unannounced—
Softens my kitchen island
And springs my wintered soul.

These musical telegrams of life
Delight us with arcs of rainbows
And turn vanilla flavored Mondays
Into holly berry Christmases.
Christine Pasinski

My Best Friend

She is nice like sugar
and spice.
She has brown eyes
and she has brown hair.
She's like a big huge teddy bear.
She likes to tweet
and is very sweet.
Sandra Festa

"God's World"

My world is really lonely
I always get real bored,
When no one seems to care
I'll turn to the Lord.

He helps me to overcome
The hurt I feel inside,
Asking him to help me
Lord, please be my guide.

All the pain and sorrow
I've felt for many years,
God has changed my life
He's taken away my fears.

If only you will believe
That he is really there,
Tell him that you love him
He'll show you, he does care.
Jackie D. Young

In The Drink

Once a unicorn
Getting a drink
Unexpectedly kissed
A fish.

Soft muzzle,
Bony mouth,
Touching.
A brief moment
of inter-species delight.

Then:
Fins flicked, fish fled
And unicorn, *quite* red!
Rosalie E. Dunbar

Sharing A Moment In Time

Would the moon be so vast
Or the stars shine as bright
Can the arms of time hold fast
The stubborn advance of daylight
If this time could last forever
Every moment we are near
My love I would endeavor
To always be right here
What pleasures could be offered me
That to your presence would compare
Such happiness would be empty
Were we deprived of time to share
Mark Garcia

The Dream Prince

Weaving tales
Making trails
Keeping me from harm

Always kind
Stands behind
Full of loving charm

The need for help
Does not long stay
As help is always near

Granddad
The prince of taking care
of those that he hold's dear.
Laurie Jean Reese

Free Spirit

A tree has fallen.
Not one branch did stay.
Its time was due.

The sun did shine
this morning new
Its brilliance splendored.

Oh dandelion- your petals
attached to blow.
Gone are they too.

Love- you are here...
Tomorrow?
Still at rest among the many.

A note was sung today.
Quiet heard in evening shadows.

Future's quest?
Not one guess....

Mary Barnes Hiatt

Nosepicker

My brother likes to pick his nose,
And stick on it on the carpet,
When he's feeling really weird,
He puts it in his armpit,
When he feels like a brat,
He sticks it on the cat,
Every once in a long, long while,
He sticks it on the bathroom tile,
And when he feels really good,
He sticks it where he should,
In a tissue!!

Jessica Luedeman

When I Sleep

When I sleep,
I dream about you.
In my dreams I see you.
Do you see me?
I do not know.
But in my dreams,
I see you

When you sleep,
Do you think about me?
Do you see what I see?
Do you dream about me?

I guess I'll never know.
Cause when I sleep I don't talk to you.
Even when I wake I don't talk to you
But some day I'll ask you.
Cause when I sleep I dream about you.

Sarah Macy

Abuse Recoils

My ear hurts
Where I hit you once.
What was it?
A cigarette burn
On a slipcover?
Some momentous matter-
The day's tedium
Made you my victim
God! I hit you/me.
Disbelief and tears
Were in your eyes
But your silence said,
I think, you knew.

Paul V. Higgins

(Missing word it was cut)

The jagged edge of my past love,
Pieces of me all around.
Someday I will regain,
The parts I wish to forget
The surmounting pain
Drives me to regret.
The story unfolds
As truths are known,
Hearts shattered
Seeds unsown.
I beg the Lord
For help to regain
What I once had
As I sit here,
Miserable and alone.

Chris Wilcoxson

Winter's End

Spring is here, and
so is summer.

The leaves on the
trees will soon be coming
out,

Flowers will unfold
from their long winter's
sleep, and brighten up
this old world of ours.

You'll hear bird's
chirping and children
laughing.

And deep inside you,
you'll hear yourself rejoicing
for the long winter's
season has come to an
end.

Suzanne Gardner

Little Angels

Little angels,
Lying silently in bed.
Tucked in tightly,
All prayers said.

Sweet dreams, my angels
Rest peacefully tonight.
Before too long
Will come first light.

Lie still for now,
Tomorrow's a big day,
You can run and jump,
Then laugh and play.

I love you, little angels,
Now sleep tight.
Think only good things.
Don't let the bed bugs bite.

Jennifer L. Robbins

Untitled

Out on the desert
The dry wind blows
Pushing along the dead tumbleweed.
Only the desert
Only the cactus
Flourishes still.

Eric Orewiler

A Spring Day

As I look to the heavens above;
All blue, white and full of love.
The birds sing the song of spring;
Just to welcome all living things.
Flowers have blossomed everywhere;
Just to leave their scent in the air.
The sun shines so bright.
Just as the moon glows in the night.
Thanks to the Man above;
Just another way to show His love.
For this is not just any day;
Just another spring day.

Laurene Tappin

Life!

Life to us is like
a rainbow with no pot
of gold,
you wait and wait
but you always stand
in the cold,
Waiting to see if
there'll be a tomorrow,
or if a headstone
will be waiting
for you,
If you fill your heart
with love there'll be no
room for hate,
We all know life
Always comes to a fate.
Life can be a
wonder so don't fill
your heart with
hate fill it with love instead.

Stephanie Garcia

Joy

In my life I avoided feeling good
For I thought I deserved something
Less. I learned that I want
To feel good. I discovered a joy
That is wonderful and fulfilling.
I smile more and willingly share
That feeling with others. I have
This gift that is impossible
To keep. I must share it. I know
Life in a better way. It will be
Difficult to return to what
I knew. Thank God for the change.
He must have a plan for me that
I am unable to see. I can feel
His love. I seek His will
In life. He gave this joy to me
For some reason. I have
A best friend. Even so,
I am one. Praise be to God.

Dave Stocks

Human?

How long is the
gracing period before
I am human?

Does it take all
my years, or do I
just have to be
numb?

Vanessa A. Glenn

"Man"

Search to share
fear singularity
Here
Drastic theatre of emotion
The test is at hand
Your direction uncertain
Grasp at the physical
Saturate your senses
Do without thinking
As you do
Satisfy your moment
The scales will be
Where is the shelter you seek
Are you sure
Can you be sure
You are afraid

Beau Britt

Betrayal

Destroy my eyes of all that you need.
Erupt your soul,
With a hope of my destiny.

I smelled the stench,
As you entered me.
An essence of blood,
Fallen upon your pupils.

Bellows from your worthless tongue,
Screaming dingy words,
That you use to control me.
I developed a taste,
A thirst for your dirt.

You left me,
Body hugging the floor...

Exhausted,
Empty,
And once again alone.

Kristie Atkins

The Moon

The moon is mysterious
  and an awesome place.
The moon is exciting
  in far off space

You look to the moon when
  you're feeling down.
You look to the moon when
  there's no one 'round.

You look to the moon
  when you're lost and confused
You look to the moon
  and you're always amused.

He'll always keep your secrets
  and he'll be there 'till the end
The moon is your only
  really true friend.

Melissa McKeith

Moms

Moms love us each day
they hug you and kiss you
they take care of us each day
they love us and we love them
we could not split from each other.
But on your birthday I haft to say
  I Love You!

Keshia Lyn Williams

Untitled

Nothing seems clear as the
snow traces the clouds in my mind.
Flakes dance upon the ground
while each blur reminds me
of a separate tear or laugh
that exists in its silence.
The only sound is the crashing
of thoughts as they imbed
their impressions on my heart.
How can a dream possess your soul?
Reality screams coherent
impossibilities at me,
but the only truth is the
aching sweetness that was my heart.
Although opposing thoughts are
warnings of plausible danger,
I cannot abandon the
desire to fly free in hope.
Will you dare to come with me?

Erin-Kathleen McMahon

Untitled

Do not thank me
for I have already
  burned you in effigy
and hunted with glass spears
to shove and shatter
  in your watery mind.
The flowers you sent
  have just now faded in the sun
I've crushed the brittle flora in
  my fingers
hoping to hear your voice
every shred of a petal
I keep bottled with my tears.
I no longer have any dreams,
but you

Tiffany Grace Duncan

Dreams

Dreams are like life,
When dreams die;
Happiness dies;
And all that is sorrow:
Nightmares.

The world would be nothing
Without dreams;
But a black planet
With no life.

With dreams,
The worlds is a better place
Filled with ideas; From

Dreams

Christopher Lee Sevigny

Ode Of Alzheimers

In the attic of my mind,
Tucked away and hard to find,
Many things I used to know;
Like the tides they come and go.

  My memory
  Plays hide and seek with me
  In its place
  An empty space -

Now, that is all I find,
In the attic of my mind.

Gail B. Trunkey

Light

I realize that
through all of this,
he is standing by my side,
the LORD.
Always there,
listening to me,
I have great respect
for him.

He sees what is happening to me,
and it make him sad,
So he is there to get comfort
and strength from, and to make
sure I have friends to lean on.

I can laugh, cry, give, love and share
I have friends.

I am not numb anymore, just tingly,
I am AWAKENING!
I am learning to love myself!
Why NOT me LORD?
I AM ALIVE!!

Rebecca Henry

Sorrow Sleeps

In the dead of night,
I awaken.
My heart pounds,
Sweat pours from my body.

It comes to me,
I am not alone.
Sorrow sleeps,
Alongside me.

As I Lay in darkness,
I hear its plea.
Silent cries,
Cries of pain.

Love inhabits all,
Even the coldest soul.
Souls draped in sadness,
Souls full of Sorrow.

Erin Ledington

Part Of You Will Always Be With Us

In our memories
you will always be,
You open our eyes
to help us see,
The possibilities that
the world does hold,
You kept our secrets
which will never be told,
You filled our lives
with hope and love,
Now you are shining
down from above,
Though you are not
here to see,
Part of you
will always be
with us.

Tarah Lyczewski

Sir Richard Carpetfuzz

Once upon a time there was
A knight named Richard Carpetfuzz.
He could not handle sword or shield
Nor joust or dagger would he wield.

Heavy armor he need not wear,
For many talents he did share.
Rolling on the ground did he
Leave all his foes in agony.

The highest place in court he held
Since many enemies he felled.
And laughter in the air would buzz
For Jester Richard Carpetfuzz.

Andrew Robert Chandler

God

You know what I'm feelin'
   down deep inside;
you are always there to help me
   and right by my side.
The secrets that I've kept
   down deep within my heart;
you have always known
   from the very start.
You know what I'm thinkin'
   each day by day;
so please, help me God
   and guide me your way!

Penny Grainger

once a man...

once a man could walk,
and now he walks no more.
once a man could run,
and now he runs no more.
now a man can sit,
but he only sits with help.
now a man can watch,
but he only watches from afar.
once a man could think,
and now he thinks no more.
once a man could be free,
and now he's free no more.
now a man can cry,
but he only cries alone.
now a man can imagine,
but he only imagines the good.
now a man can be sad,
but he's only sad when awake.
once a man could be a man,
and now he's a man no more.

Leslie Kaplan

Untitled

Through every forest,
Above the trees,
Within my stomach,
Scraped from my knees,
I drink the honey inside your hive,
You are the reason I stay alive,
I will revive the beast inside,
And when I do,
No one will survive.......

Mike Schoonover

My Baby - Girl

She came into my life,
And changed it forever,
Now every moment with her,
Makes my life better,
She showed me she loved me,
She showed me she cared,
She gave me things,
No one else dared,
I love her with every beat of my heart,
And when she is in my arms,
I know nothing can tear us apart,
Every time I see her,
It makes my heart skip a beat,
Her lips are so tender,
She is the best thing,
That ever happens to me,
For she is my life; My love,
And it will last for eternity.

Michael Thomas Pollard

Untitled

I thought of you today,
In each and every way;
Wishing you were here,
To brighten up my day.

When I think of you,
With every beat of my heart;
Thinking, wishing, praying,
Of my life I wish you were part.

But, for now, I can say,
Thinking of you makes me smile;
Just the hope that we will meet,
Is worth to wait a while.

So now, I say to you,
From the bottom of my heart;
I really wish you were here,
So we'd never be apart.

Richard Atkins Jr.

"So"

In the heat of mid life
Terror, no man is kinder and
   gentler, downright truthful
and caring for his behavior
   like god.
Another man, flashing white
   teeth and a large portrait
painted of him a portrait of
   piercing foul vain. A few
Devil's laughter a burnful touch
   sense to seize the
opportunity, the right to
   say he will be better
Than a marching band of
   angels, is he, well he's
   not.

Isaac Munoz

Leaf

Seasons change
freedom at last.
Quietly soaring
gently falling.
calling,
no one heard.
In the end,
silence.

Ken Feese

A Mother's Love

As you grow inside of me, already
I feel the need to protect you.
As you stir around, I lay my hands
upon my womb to assure you that
you are safe.

From the hardness of your kick, I
know that you will have the strength
of a proud warrior.
From the softness of your nudge, I
know that you will have the gentleness
of a fawn.

I feel that I know so much about you,
and yet we have not met...

Now the time has come. I thank God
above. For he has given to me a
blessed gift, which I will
receive with open arms and
a mother's love.

Cherl Smith

Why Me: Ode To The Earth

Why me;
all withered and torn.
How on this earth,
was such disaster born?

Why me;
battered and bruised.
Nature's gifts and beauty,
all crumpled and abused.

Our children have no future,
because their parents didn't care.
When God made this earth,
'twas to pass down and share.

Now your weapons and greed,
corrupt this once great land.
In this tremendous pain,
all had a hand.

Why me;
the earth asks on last time.
Why am I submitted,
to such carelessness and crime?

Jamie Harness

Whisper In The Wind

   When I speak to God
Sometimes I yell it out.
Then I hear his voice with
laughter say you don't have
to shout
   He can hear you clear as
day and even in the night.
He gives you peace and let's
you know everything's alright.
   So if your feeling down
or think that you have
sinned. Just remember
God can hear
   A whisper in the
wind

Khris Woodland

The Chase

Loneliness chases after
As I run ahead
Away from the blues

As fast as my running shoes
Will take me
Around the corner
Down the road I fly

With the wind behind
And no hills to climb
Loneliness chases after
Loneliness chases after
And catches me

Carol Hughes-Rhodes

Life

   Darkness reaches out,
While rain drops crowd the sky.
   Darkness moves about,
And rain drops soon will die.

   Storm clouds are now here,
As thunder rolls around.
   Storm clouds do not fear,
While thunder makes its sound.

   Lightening reaches out,
And brightens across the sky.
   Lightening moves about,
And allows the wind to fly.

Bree Johnson

Math

AAAAAAAAAH!
A typhoon of
numbers is surrounding
me,
Thunder, lightning,
major brainstorm!
the classroom is
spinning
faster and
faster,
until every thing
stops,
great it's writing
period now!

Meghan Farrell

In Memory Of Mom

Almost four years ago, the Lord spoke
and said it was time to go.
I felt like my heart broke into
I kept saying Mom, I miss you.
The angels are rejoicing now,
In heaven above.
Mom you gave me so much love.
I remember your sweet smile and
loving touch.
I knew that I would miss you very much
Mom you touched more lives than
you will ever know
Remember Mom, "I love you", so.
I look forward to seeing you again,
because you are my best friend.

Debra Williams

The Last Leaf

The last leaf of autumn
   fell from the tree by the pond,
Lighting on the gentle breeze
   which welcomed the early dawn.

Stubbornly it had clung
   to that uppermost limb
Through the frost and a dust of snow
   and the teasing, tearing wind.

Why today did it give way
   and release its gripping hold?
We wait for the mysteries of life
   to gradually unfold.

Diane Mahoney

Money, Money, Money

Dollars, Pounds or Yen
I'm still the same to men.
Having me in ones,
needing me in tens.

Some Love me dearly
others scarcely have me.
But beware I'll bring in trouble
whenever I come in bundle.

Kai E. M'bayo

"Always"

I'll not always
Put a smile upon your face
I'll not always
Walk with grace

I will fall
I will sin
But there is good
If you look within

I'll not always
Make you proud
I'll not always
Stand my ground

Temptation will strike
And I will get weak
But I shall always
Keep my fidelity

My love will not fade
When I fall from grace
I will love you and only you...
Always!

Tammy Sue Varner

Raindrops

Raindrops pound on the window,
Trees dance in the wind,
Birds sing out in fright.
Dogs bark as broken hearts are
Lifted and carried away in the arms
of her breath.

Raindrops pound on the roof
As I drift off to sleep.
Relaxing as it may seem,
My soul feels an unrest
As my mind is flooded
...by these raindrops
Falling down my cheeks.

Rachel L. Stevens

Lovers Of The Night

Passion, a rosy evening gown
Confidence, a tuxedo in blue
Both fitted by two common souls
Who found a love that's true

Tangled like two ribbons
Fitting the other's form
Whispers like a summer breeze
Shared to make hearts warm

Taking their place on the dance floor
Surrounded by all, yet no one
Two hearts explode with excitement
Wondering what is to come

Then Confidence takes courage
And Passion gives way
He questions... She says yes
With her glance

And all came to be
When Passion met Confidence
Two lovers of the night
... At the dance

Angela Horn

My Words

My words are mine,
Just mine alone,
And for each one
I must atone.

A world of hurt
Is in my tongue,
Or multitudes
Of praise unsung.

But, oh! sometimes
I hang my head
And wish some words
I'd never said.

Dear friend or foe,
Forgive me, who,
If by my words
Have wounded you.

My prayer is this:
"Dear Lord above,
"Let all my words
"Be born of Love."

Joan Hill

Prayer For Victims Of Cancer

Jesus, ask God, "What shall I do?"
Tell Him I placed my trust in you.
And say I hope it's not too late,
To overcome this ugly fate.
Give the courage you never lost,
When they nailed you to the cross.
You're my hope, the only one
And just like you, I am his son.
I will pray, I will endure,
Now please ask him to send a cure.
If you think I am too late,
Then I'll see you at the "Golden Gate".
If no help can come to me,
Then next to you I want to be.
But if I get some extra years,
You'll see a man who loves and cares.
So please see what you can do,
All my trust is placed in you.

Nicholas C. Depalma Sr.

Untitled

Your smile is so fake,
but I guess it has to be.
So many things in your head
and in your heart.

Your smile is so fake,
yet it's so perfect and right.
I think only you could get away
with just that fake smile.

Your smile means so many things,
so it's perfect for every thing.
Your smile is so fake,
but I guess it has to be.

I know for every smile
there is a sad tear
to be found in this life.
Your smile is so fake,
but I guess it has to be.
Yet it's so perfect and right.

Heather R. Bonney

I Knows What You Sees In Me

I knows what you sees in me.
I knows what it be.

It bez the sparkle of my slanted eyes.
It bez the curve of my thighs.
It bez the ride of my breast.
It bez my high-yellow chest.

It bez the way my voice carries.
It bez the way my mood varies.
It bez the way my hips shift.
It bez the way my cheeks lift.

It bez the way I lick my pop.
It bez the way my smiles never stop.
It bez the way I comb my hair.
It bez the way of my gentle stare.

It bez the way I tease and walk.
It bez the way I sass and talk.
It bez not for what it should be.
It bez not for what is inside of me.

I knows what you sees in me.
I knows what it be.

Sharmane Montgomery

Today

I can no longer see its beauty.
Yet, still I can remember
how its beauty caught my eye.

There it was
as I turned the corner
splendid, shining, glistening
as though making a statement.

Oh, how wonderful it looked.
How it talked and screamed
  and talked again.
It had so much to say.
Yet, I could not hear
no, not yesterday.

Irene Preciado

California Beach

In the water
thru the waves
I'm the sea and all the waves.
I see the sea gulls and the crabs
all the shadows and more crabs.

In the water outside
the waves thru the land
and past the age.
Clams and starfish thru
the day. In the autumn lot's
of waves.

All the colors and all the shapes
look alike without any hates.
All the land and all the pride
I just can't take it,
not even the tide.

In the water
thru the waves
I'm the sea and all the waves.

Chris Yarrows

Untitled

Crazy crazy
Chaotic
my mindless memory
slips me
Crazy chaos
remembers me
caught up like
a dog wound round
a Tree
Quickly quickly
Follow
the chase is free
wound up so tightly
Static jumps from Me

Andrew Lutzky

"To Me"

To me is you whom I could trust.
You always gave loving care.
I could always depend on you,
& you were always there,

To me you're like the light in the sky,
Now my life will never grow dark.
Now I sit here & think dear loved one,
"Why did we have to part"?

To me you'll always be in my heart,
and I'll never forget you. I won't!
And all I ask from you dear loved one,
Don't forget us, please just don't!

Jessica Bednosh

Untitled

I tried not to be too loud.
I couldn't let it show.
But it was coming
I knew
And I waited
And then I let out a cry
Because it hurt.
But it always does.
Doesn't it have to?
Isn't that part of the game?

C. J. Caputo

The Life We Shared

The life we shared together
I thought would never end.
But now my love, it's over
No need now to pretend.
I had you in my arms, my dear
So close but, yet so far.
It seemed you were always miles away
Just hanging on a star.
I never thought it would end this way
But Now babe, it's too late.
By now I should be walking
Thru those beautiful golden gates.
So now my dear, I shed no tears
For all the pain is gone.
Now my life is over
And yours has just begun...

Elizabeth Ann Hennington

My Dreams Have Secrets

My dreams have secrets,
Hidden, even from my wishes.

I can't figure it out,
And I'm starting to get suspicious.

The secrets are shared,
Constantly leaving me out.
Plotting my tomorrow's destiny,
Certain that I'm in doubt.

I can sleep through the night,
Dreams constantly occurring.
I awaken in the morning,
My dreams start blurring.

When I awaken
Before the alarm screams aloud,
Some dreams form into thoughts,
Like raindrops from a cloud.

Yes, my dreams have secrets
To each other, they confide.

Their tales are of spiritual privacy,
And the emotion I keep inside.

Angela Wyatt

Understanding

I saw the sun upon the sea,
A ball of golden majesty;

I tasted salt upon my lips,
A cocktail when the flagon tips;

I smelled the aromatic tang,
Of seaweed and my spirit sang;

I heard the raucous cry of gulls
As they quarreled 'mongst the swells;

I touched the earth beneath my feet
And trembled at its awesome beat;

I knew that He was everywhere
and breathed a sigh, a silent prayer.

Charles Richard Dolan

Finally!

A Blanket of White
What's that? - a Spot of Purple?
Up Pops a Crocus!

Laura L. Tepe

Clairmont's Stream

On the wall of Clairmont
I see a stream
Going steadily on
From the front office to room 23
It goes.
Now and then
Pools of water fill
Then overflow
Causing the stream to keep flowing.
The stream goes through the school
Visiting almost every class.
Nobody thinks about it
But we are proud to see it everyday.
Because the stream means life,
The life in every friendship ever known
To us.
Each pool means each struggle
In each friendship.
And the wider the stream
The better the friends.

Daniel Tao

Golden Sword

When my life is bittersweet
And my soul is on the edge
I think of all the good times
Then I always make a pledge.
To try to live life at the fullest,
And be the best I can
To try to be better than any other man
When friends turn me down
And my family seems not to care
I think of all the happiness
And sometimes take the dare
The dare to try my best
And give my heart to the Lord
And give him my life and soul
Then pull out my Golden Sword.
This sword is all my freshness
And quality guaranteed;
For no one can match the power
Of the Lord God's warranty.

Rose Marie McKillip

The Empty Star

The moon shines upon us
Tonight it leads the way
The stars await their visitors
Soft melodies begin to play
Amongst our sea of blackness
Waits an empty star
To light the tiny structure
The body must be far
The star begins to twinkle
The soul finally free
Here forever after
It will always be
The moonlight grows brighter
With every twinkling star
It's filled with dreams and laughter
Bad memories lying far
The moon will cast a path
When it's time to go
The melodies will play
The empty star will know

Sara Joann Helms

Three Hundred And Sixty Degrees

Unlocking the magic,
Seeking that rainbow,
Wonderful memories,
Warm lights aglow.

Different seasons,
Abnormal times,
Heart-wrenching pleas,
The sour taste of limes.

An open door,
An ancient key,
New foods to try,
Curiosity.

Storms thundering,
Fire and heat,
Hisses and growls,
Things incomplete.

A full circle
Has all my moods gone,
But it's night now,
Sleep, and wait for Dawn.

Ming Chen

Untitled

The clock slowly ticks off
the empty hours of evening tides.
Away from us in lovely pace
a darkened horseman weary rides.
He would not stay with us this night,
he seeks a place to lay his head,
but would not stay with us tonight,
he seeks a resting, not a bed.
"All I ask," the horseman says,
"a place where I am all alone."
"All I need, to be at peace:"
"an empty tomb to keep my bones."
Does he find it in the end?
The clock at silence gently taps.
The only certain answers are
I hope, I doubt, perhaps.
Perhaps.

Stratford

The Poor And Just

In his truth and for his truth
a just man will be blamed, a
poor man shall be slain, for
it has not changed - a poor
man will be blamed, a just man
shall be slain.

His flesh shall lie undercovered
beneath the face of an undiscovered
grave. Yet the sun shines anew
light unto his eyes he sees
another day -

Where is beyond this place
Beyond the scripture of his heart
its cover... the testimony of
His soul its face - the lace of
eternity beyond this place?
A place where God is touching
him when he sleeps and when he weeps.

Where is beyond this place
the lace of eternity, beyond this place?

Dan M. Jones

Mother's Love

Mothers are like a rainbow
They're like a spring flower
And they watch us grow
They have an undying love
As bright as the rainbow above
What do we do without a mother's love
A flower in bloom
Enough love to fill a room
By far, that's what mothers are

Leslie S. Brock

What Keeps

What keeps the stars
from falling out of
the sky?
What keeps the clouds
from falling too low?
What keeps the
earth from floating
off its hinges?
What keeps the
world from being
like a dream?
Like sliding down
a never ending
rainbow of colors?

Celia Collins

P.S.

Pivot
To your creator

Twist
As a creature

Turn
Toward beauty

Savor
An essence

Walters

All Alone

Dark nights,
with soft rain,
loving world
gone down the drain,
all I have ever hoped to be,
all I have ever dreamed,
my face got slammed in the door,
do you worry about me,
did you even see,
I walk alone in this world,
alone, all alone.

Jolee Pizano

Eternity

What is a rose?
  Is it a flower,
Or is it a dream.
  Whatever it may be,
It has great power over me.

  It lays upon a tiny stem,
And drinks one drop of water.
  But when a rose springs
up from the ground,
A new life begins.

Danielle Scianna

Grounding

The miles I walk.
Cracked, broken sidewalks
my feet skim,
and smooth congested streets
they dodge
take me to an
unvertiginous place.

Standing by translucent water
—edge of Klopp lake—
truth is revealed.
Roots ramify from my eyes,
penetrating the depth of the lake,

My soul.
Anthony Meixner

Face Of Fear

To loathe someone,
For whom we hardly care;
Detesting Someone,
From delusions of False Fear:
Evil-Eyed Stranger,
Bearing piercing tyrant's glare;
Napoleon's complexity,
Offensive insecurity,
Is all that's really there.
Heart of Unhappy Darkness,
Cloaked in Habits of the Years:
Dreaded Face of Hatred's Shadow,
From deep within appears.
John Christopher Davis

Untitled

She can only see as
far as she looks.
She can only dream as
long as she sleeps.
She is I
He see's what he wants
to see.
He dreams so vivid so much
He is I
I am both.
Jennifer Parrott

Of Men And Mice

Of mice and men, and men and mice;
which one of them are thee?

And hold before you answer that,
I know it's plain to see.

Now, if I, had to choose, my friend;
you know which one I'd be.

For which one cause's
war and death and hypocrisy?

I know it is not of mice,
that you choose to be.

But rather that of a machine,
and cause atrocity.

And do not think that I am blind,
and that I cannot see.

For which one in the end, my friend,
is really, truly free?
Ryan Wingett

Moonlight And Daydreams

Moonlight and daydreams
Crawl out of their shell,
Soft waterlilies
In a clear water well.

Silently creeping,
The night on the ground,
Chrysanthemums white -
And they don't make a sound.

Simple and plain;
An intricate design
All folded up
In a world intertwined.

Pebbles and gravel
On a long, narrow path.
Oak trees and bushes
Surrounding the mass.

Glittering crystals
Rest on the shore.
What could be less?
And beauty, no more.
Sarah Beth Pobiecke

FEAR

Dedicated to Doris
We've heard it said FEAR has power -
I know it has none -
It rattles and tattles and
has no junction -
It rears and veers with
no compunction -
The first letter "F" means
FALSE to me -
The second letter "E" is
EVIDENCE, of course -
The third letter "A" means
APPEARING, I say -
The fourth is "R" and
REAL it would seem -
So FEAR itself is not to be feared,
for it really says:
FALSE EVIDENCE APPEARING REAL
So go your way, be happy, don't fear,
and your life will change,
I swear!!
Shirley Martin Watson

Love

Love is a strange and
beautiful experience...

Gives meaning to anyone's
existence...

Made to endure and survive
its perpetuated state...

With all its quenching
intensity...

Taking full account of
guests and failures....

Encountering this coexistence
of peace and betterment...

Let it be by making
Salutations to it...

Only growth occurs while
dealing with its beautifulness...
Lady Chaka

Untitled

Where is love?
Does it fall from
the sky up above?
   Is it underneath the willow tree
that was made for you and me?
   Where is he
   Who I close my eyes to see,
   will I ever know the reason
   you are so dear to me?
Kym Gathright

Time

Take time my friend
   to smell the roses
   to see the butterflies
   to hear the birds
   to touch the animals.

Take time my friend
   to love
    to be loved
   to listen.
    to talk;
   to feel;
    to share your feelings
   to care
    and be cared for.

Take time my friend
   to miss,
    and be missed.
Heather Hanna

A Parting Of The Ways

It seems a good-bye is in order,
No use in going on.
You can't ride high in a sinking ship,
So to the lifeboat I'm gone.

Your kisses, so soft and sweet,
for a time made a fool of me.
But now I see just what you are,
And what must come to be.

I let another do to me
What you have in mind;
But I have learned a thing or two,
And this time, I'm not so blind.

So stay inside your so small world.
Wait for another prey.
'Cause this time, my sweet false love,
It's me who's going away
Mike D. Tatum

Walls

Walls surround me,
Closing me in.
Trapped inside,
No way out.
Haven't seen
   the light of day,
Haven't seen the moon,
   that chases the sun away.
Walls surround me.
They forever close me in,
I will never be
Free again.
Nicole Loscocco

The Burden

I had a heavy burden, Lord
   That I gave up to you.
But there are those who think it wise,
   They say that it's my due.

To pick it back up once again
   And carry it along.
I just can't make them understand
   Such thinking is all wrong.

When I gave you that heavy load
   And left it in your care.
I said I'd never take it back,
   But always leave it there.

So as I rise up off my knees
   To walk through another day,
I'll lift my voice in praise to you
   And let that burden lay.

Beneath the cross and in your care
   I'll leave that heavy load.
I'll walk on without that burden,
   In faith on down life's road.

Netty Yount

Untitled

I am truly alone
Nowhere to turn
My plans are gone
I just want to run
He told the last lie
Now he can say good-bye
To the best friend he'll ever have
The only one who truly cared
I thought honesty was top
'guess I was wrong
I've stuck by him
Through thick and thin
I can't believe what
A fool I've been

Sarah M. Parker

"Sweet Serenity"

Serenity
   sweet serenity
Comfort to the soul
   great wonders to behold
No longer blind my mind can see
   no longer cold my heart is free
To love
   the joy life brings
     the new dawn's mist
       as the sparrow sings
So many gifts for me too see,
   when caressed by sweet serenity.

Anthony M. Buckner

Life In Death

Open breezes, winds are blowing,
Over liquid skies of rain.
Vortex spinning, time is showing,
Revealing shadows, lost in pain.
Masking laughter, left unheard,
Crying out to sense its lost.
Screaming silence, without word,
Freedom blossoms, at the cost.
Never knowing outside feelings,
Encased within a private world.
Opened eyes are never seeing,
Life in death, a Fury unfurled.

Dwayne LeBlanc

The Painter

I am organic
like you.
Let's plant a crop
and see what comes up.

Pickles and cabbages?
Paintings and stones?
What's next you darling man?
Man of acrylic and steel.

Your skin smells like
paint
on a warm day
Drying in the sun
Happy and glowing.

Paula Gilbert

Little One

Rest your weary head on my shoulder,
   little one
The day is almost over, the time
   for sleep has come.
You have traveled many miles in
   thought and deed this day.
It is only one of many as you journey
   on your way.
So rest your weary head, and let me
   keep You safe for awhile.
You've slain all your dragons for
   the day
So rest little one, tomorrow you
   can slay mine.

Lesley E. Casey Jr.

The End

Silence.
Peaceful day
Hellish wind, fire, death
Women screaming, children crying.
Devastation.
Evil cloud flying up to kiss the sky
Terror raining down
Death.
Destruction.
Emptiness.
Nothing.
Silence.

Nathan L. Cline

Stolen Moments

The night was clear and cold
With stars galore,
Warmed by heart and soul
Feelings unchecked made bold,
United as one rapture unfolds
Passions promise, needless words of old
When the night was clear and cold.

Full circle we have come
Truer emotions can not we hold,
Stars in their brilliance shine
As the ritual dance arouses the flame,
Love or lust, it is old as time
A look, a touch, the story is told,
The eye of my mind sees what is so
And in my heart I know
Only stolen moments are mine to hold
When the nights are clear and cold.

Bonnie Lowery

"I Feel As Though"

   I am not crazy
just curious.
   I am not lazy
just bored.
   I am not stupid
just simple.
   I am not morbid
just different.
   I am not cold
just emotionless.
   I am not old
just doubtful.
   I am not loved
just tolerated.
   I am not blood
just family
   I am not recognized
just seen
   I am not alive
just conscious

Nylieke Gerkinn

Write Me A Letter

Write me a letter in the clouds,
Swirl a rainbow for your words.

The shepherds staff can be your pen,
The clouds can provide the paper.

Use the sunshine as your ink,
The angels wings can dry it.

The raindrops are not your tears,
Rain is used to seal your letter.

Don't forget to hug our loved ones,
We will be with you someday.

Tell me how beautiful heaven is,
Write me a letter in the clouds.

Tammy Underwood

Beth

Last night in the dark,
Where the stars shine bright.
You left your mark,
In the path of my sight.

Your look was a shimmer,
That blinded my eyes,
Left me to simmer.
With only my lies.

If only for one night,
That we were together,
The memory I hold tight,
Will stay with me forever.

Chris John

Him Again

In my mind I see him near,
Every second his voice I hear.
Yet I see he's fading fast,
I know his words will never last.
His warm embrace I long to feel,
My poor heart I know he'll steal.
Does he wonder, does he care,
How can he know of my despair?
Does he long to be with me,
Will he share the dreams I see?
What are these things written above?
Why, my friend, it's called Love.

Traci Nunez

Untitled

People may laugh
At my gift of gab
And make fun of some of my poems
But, if you could see inside of me.
You'd know what I'm trying to do

I tell em as I see em
I write em as they come
Some are sad some are bad
And some are just plain fun

But all in all they mean the same
To entertain your soul
To soothe the sad and lonely
To make the unhappy glad
And if it tickles your funny bones
How can it all be bad?
Marilyn H. Wills

New Year's Eve

Alone, but not lonely,
I am, a watchful sentinel,
in my daughter's house
where her baby sleeps.

I contemplate my future,
the love that shall be mine,
and the fragile life
beyond the bedroom door.

The minutes fly
toward the midnight hour,
the eagerly awaited moment
of renewed hope and expectation.

Lingering disappointment
is consigned
to flickering shadows
until reflection restores my pain.

Tonight is for the future,
for dreams yet to be fulfilled,
for everlasting hope
which shall sustain me for another year.
Gwen Berkich

"The Incredible Night"

In the dark I hear a lark
It goes, who who who.....
I can't sleep and I take
A peek..... It still goes
Who who who.....

I say to myself, finish the sentence
It still goes who who who..... dawn
comes, night falls, all of a sudden
it stops the who who who.....

I try to get some sleep, but it's
time to go to school. I wasted my
night hearing the who who who.....
Diana Rosario

Untitled

There is no life in life without
the spice of a soon to be wife.
So when that day comes,
when we wed into one,
with you as my wife,
and me as your hun,
the life that we have,
will unite into one.
Steven Stookey

Life's lesson

Life's lesson is really no
lesson at all, with lesson
number one try not to fall,
lesson number two is very
easy to see, always remember
that you can be anything
that you want to be, lesson
number three is not a difficult
task, if you want something
all you have to do is
ask, lesson number four is as
simple as pie, just realize
that you don't have to be high
to fly, lesson number five
is the lesson to always
follow, just remember that
your head is not so hollow,
life's lesson is really no
lesson at all with lesson
number one try not to fall.
Vonswalla Haymond

Life

I was born, not of birth,
But of the rising of the sun,
I could feel, not of touch,
But of the finding of true love,
I could hear, not of the screaming,
But of the panic they'd begun,
I could taste, not of wine,
But of the promises I'd won,
I could see, not of the colors,
But of the beating of life's drums,
I could smell, not from suppers plate,
But of the lies which had been spun,
I would die, not of poison's hand,
But of the setting of the sun.
Jennifer Bree Hugill

Euphoria

To lie among the many sounds,
The ocean's coded message sends;
And see the many jewels abound,
With visual sparkling of its gems.

Serenity has covered you,
A blanket soft of weightlessness;
And lift you up with life renewed,
To know each thought is now suppressed.

Come hither, shores to now engulf,
As where I lie by oceans way;
Suddenly, with great assault,
Massaging me with many sprays.

Entangled in this sensual scene,
Euphoric may your life ensure;
To reach the heights of many dreams,
Departing from so many truths.
Joyce Knodel

Images

Two alike... different
Walk with me. Take my hand.
Feel the sun on our face,
The sand beneath our feet.
Mood ever changing
Loneliness and despair surround you.
Master once again.
Cathy Elliott

As I Waited For You

The trees gently swayed
In that hot summer day.
Nature didn't make a sound
As I waited for you.

Day turned to night
and the darkness fell.
As I waited for you.

8:30 seemed like an eternity
And today was hell.
As I waited for you.

It's 8:29 and the day is done
Only one more minute
till I'm in your arms

One more minute
what could it harm.
As I waited for you.
Dawn Marie Danaher

Alone At Last

As I sit here in silence;
every night and every day.
In the middle of the month of May.
It's a dark quiet place;
not cold but just right.
Where I sit and do nothing
in the middle of the night.
I sit and do nothing;
nothing at all.
It's very tight but not quite small.
This is the place that I come to think,
when I come to eat, and come to drink.
No one else could think such a place.
No one else would think it was safe.
It's only for me just me by myself.
Just me and no one else.
Talisha McGee

Why Me? Why You?

Why me?
Why you?
I'm so confused.
Life is a mess. I'm
going crazy. Don't
Know why I'm here.
I'll figure it all out
Someday. Hopefully soon.
Things never go my way
I'll understand it all someday.
Why me? Why you?
Help me see it through
the good times and the
bad times.
It hurts so bad.
I want out of this mess.
Someone help me.
I'm so confused. Life's
a mess. I want out.
Why me? Why you?
Kristi Jensen

The Funny Poodle

There was once a funny poodle
People said she lost her noodle
You see, all she does
Is eat and buzz
The funny poodle who lost her noodle
Ashley Spencer

Emotions

To touch to feel to embrace
Towering over time
So much we cannot trace
The everlasting grind

More or less great essence
Couragible and timely fears
The test of meaning senses
Throughout remaining years

Never doubt the former
And give them just one chance
Conclude great trace of joiners
For-ever in their trance

B. J. Rockey

Untitled

I am but a Ghost.
In this world but not of it.
A wisp of smoke in the dark.
Wanting to reach out,
Afraid that my hand will pass through.

Hearing voices around me speak
words that make no sense.
Listening to my own voice answer
not understanding my own words
In this world but not of it.

A shadow figure barely noticed.
People walking through me
as if I weren't there.
A Ghost in this world,
but not part of it.

Edward Witowski

My Seashell Heart

Once tiny and shiny
now barnacled and bruised;
blinded by the waves,
tumbled
towards
holiness.

My signature in the sand
through the darkest caves—
Is it brittle bitterness
or only fragile fragments of fear?

Slivers of shell
splintered with pain.
For most of us the pearl
will never be made.

Discovery and collected on the shore
is the best I can hope for.
Now larger and wiser
than I first began—
The purpose of a seashell heart
within an ocean plan.

Beth Ladd

Untitled

Unrelenting unprecedented pain.
Innocence robbed...unable to regain.
Shock, horror disbelief!
Unthinkable moments...so brief.
Loving helplessness...
   Grief.

P. J. Prihoda

My Angel

He made me laugh
He made me cry
My how those Angels can fly

We live our lives to the fullest
we can
He was a very special man

Now that he's gone
Not down on this earth
Apart of him came back
In my baby's wonderful birth

I will always remember him
The funny man he was
My dad that is
With all my Love

Keirsten Schlagel

My Love

You are my eyes, opening my mind
   To the wonders around me
   You are my ears, letting me hear
   All that this world offers
You are my hand, teaching me
   All I can do
You are my feet, leading me to
   Places I never conceived
You are my heart, showing me
   What love is
You are my soul, allowing me to
   Know what life really
   Is

Thomas Meadows

Earth Stood Still

As if life has stopped
A silence drew,
The sun disappeared
As the darkness grew.

As the darkness grew thicker
The silence grew stronger.
Earth stood still
For it moved no longer.

The people are gone
Like the animals and trees,
For nothing is left
Not even the seas.

The breeze that blew
Blows no more,
For time has stopped
And closed its door.

The earth that was
Is now no more.
For it is gone
By Nuclear War.

Danniell Neel

Uncultivated Existence

Not yet captured
By the harsh words
Which fail to define
Wild with freedom
Gentle presence
The poem's still mine.

Rachel Kirk

Companion For Life

Hope,
Love,—both:
for memories that haunt;
taming a beast
Now become a companion for life.

Healing—
no runaway wounds,
Only grateful scars
Walking in rhythm
singing, whispering
of one soul's determination.

Death? Somewhere,
rehearsed but distant—
calling out to the beast,
"No despair is bigger that I am,
But every hope is."

Shug Yagel McBay

Be All You Can Be

Be all you can be;
Be a statue with your head held high.
Push yourself to do the best -
Try your hardest to succeed.

Don't be living with your head
Held down.
Thinking of what you could have been,
Walking amongst a crowd of loneliness.

Take what you have earned,
Take what you deserve.
Hear opportunity knocking,
Be a somebody.

Stand tall, chest out,
March to the beat
Of a rolling drum.
Be all you can be.

Diana Gillespie

"Essence Of A Rainbow"

Red outlines the picture
   hanging in the sky.
   I gaze and wonder why
      there is so much we endure.

Orange brings to me warmth.
   Everyone should know
      the gorgeous afterglow
         of any raging storm.

Yellow is the brightest
   and most beautiful of all.
   I beckon for its call
      to bring me ever highest.

Green and Blue form oceans,
   winding rivers and the seas.
      The amazement never leaves
         as I remember God's devotion.

Indigo and Violet,
   blending all things equal.
   Life's on-going sequel
      will bring more surprise yet.

Doyne Marie Liverett

Silence

It runs with no destiny
It speaks with no sound
It hurts with no pain
It sleeps with no tire
It eats with no fullness
It hears with no sound
It breaks with no snap
It smells with no odor
It is with no being
It watches with no reaction
It is our silence
Aubree Retty

War - Really It's Illegal

Hate, fighting and destruction-
these things are wrong.
War is these things.
War then is wrong.

Death, mourning and sorrow-
these things are sad.
War is these things,
War then is sad.

Killing, murdering and slaughtering-
these things are illegal.
War is these things.
War - really it's illegal.
Joanna Marlene Walters

Untitled

People
so seldom
say I love you
and then
it's either too late
or love goes
so when I tell you
 I love you
it doesn't mean
I know you'll never go
only that
I wish you didn't have to....
Don G. Simpson

Mom

When your eyes closed for the last time
It was as if they were mine
I no longer see you here
But I know you are always near

I see you in my heart
I feel you in my soul
I know that you finally rest
In God's eternal glow

I no longer see your skin
Instead I feel your heart
The strong constant tender love
That will keep us from falling apart

Your soul shines on all of us
Your spirit makes us smile
In God's time we will all unite
Our lives are but a while
Felipe Cardenas

Sadness

I'll save my tears
Until I'm all alone
Then I'll face the pain
Head on

I'll ache inside
And cry my heart out
Seems as if
That's what life's about

Sure, I laugh a little
And I have some fun
But, before I know it
That's all done

And here comes sadness
Creeping back in
It seems a loss
Follows every win

I struggle to smile
In a world so grim
The only real joy in life
Is that of knowing Him
Yvonne M. Bartlett

Sitting

Sitting on the steps
Solitary, speaking and singing
To someone, somewhere.

Perhaps the park,
The place to play,
Is where the people have been put.

But I'll walk in the woods.
Watch wonderful wings flutter
With the wind for awhile.

Mix my mind with miracles,
Majestic moths maybe.
I'll move among many things...

Sitting on the steps.
Bryan D. Raaz

Dream Land

A shimmering light in the distance
Leads the way to Dream Land.
Clouds pick me up and bring me
over to Dream Land.
The doors open Wide
And then I see Dream Land...
A land where
White People and Black People
Are hand in hand.
Where candy falls from trees
And scatters on the ground.
Hope for the future
Is not a dream here in this place.
Hope comes to life in Dream Land.
Life is forever here,
no death, no tears.
This is Dream Land
And
This is where the magic is made.
John Lawrence

Renegade

There's one who wanders from the pack
To roam in quiet solitude
Meanders far, not looking back
Dissident in attitude

He stealthily penetrates the night
Gives pause to sniff the midnight air
And as the wind takes shift in flight
He then can sense her presence there

Quenching that most basic thirst
The pair ensues a liaison
Yet freedom beckons; it is his curse
He leaves her at the crack of dawn
Rebecca Guise

Grand Children

Oh, what a joy
the first grandchild was a boy,
Eyes of blue that sparkled
filled the heart with love.
Along came a brown eyed
beauty, so tiny and beloved.
Not long to wait for
two, It suddenly turn
into identical twins too.
Out of the clear blue sky
came a fair haired lass,
with a world of class.
A small bundle came along,
with a smile that melts
your heart.
The best is last to be
a little angel sent from
heaven above.
These are my grand -
children for me.
Elizabeth Flory

Veterinarian

If I were a veterinarian,
I would save every animal I see,
And people would come from all over,
Just to bring their pets to me.

No animal would be tested on,
To see if the product was dangerous,
I'd find a way to do it myself,
And then I would become famous.

When examined, no bird would squawk,
No dog would ever growl,
And when it's time for shots,
No cat would ever howl.

If I were a veterinarian,
Everything would turn out all right,
For with me standing by its side,
No animal will fight for life.
Brittany Gasper

Hold Love Softly

Hold love softly
As you would a rose,
For love must be free
To bloom as it grows.

If held too tightly
It withers and dies, and
There's nothing left but
A heart that cries ………
— Dolores

The Poet's Wisdom

Flowing, coasting, agile speech,
Rolls like pearls on ocean foam,
The poet strolls along the beach,
And makes the sea and sky his home,
To dare, to dream, to laugh, to know,
The secrets whispered in the wind,
To trace the footprints in the snow,
And be where you have never been,
To listen to the silver throats,
Of birds that sing forgotten songs,
To grasp each perfect music note,
And know when you are right or wrong,
The heart of wisdom always lies,
In silence that has echoed truth,
A light that lingers in the eyes,
Can bring us back our long lost youth.

Suzanne Greninger

Tim

I wonder where you are
I wonder what you are doing
I wonder what you are thinking
And I wonder what you feel

Not always do you tell me
The things I want to hear
But always are you with me
In my mind you are always near

You are part of me, Tim
A part that cannot be removed
A part of myself that I love
Because I love you.

Kristin Fogg

A Bit Of Time

Past tense predicts present
or it the reverse?
Statements of fact
are always terse
   or, the reverse

A present past
perhaps shall last
until today
   maybe, tomorrow

From the eyes of a camera
on a video screen
pasts, presents, futures
are not as they seem
   or, the reverse

The facts of past
are realities of present
and predict future
   or, is it the reverse.

Judith C. Blase

The Garden Of Love

Your love for me was like a beautiful
garden. When you stop loving me this
garden faded away. You were my
angel send from above a gift of
love your the special man that came
in my life now it is hard for me
to let you walk out of my life.
Please take care of this garden
the way I used to, deep in my heart
this garden still exist.

Junia Laura Auguste

The Strength In Love

Love is a vulnerable thing.
It is hard to find
And harder to give.
The risks we take
Aren't what they seem
Until we realize
The things we once had
And finally what we lost.
In the end we have found
That what we gave
Is more valuable
Then what we received.
Yet, with passing time,
Through all our pain,
We come to know
How patience, care, and trust
Lend more security
Than the arms of strength ever will.

Tammy Huisingh

My Skates

Sleek white bodies
Perched on silver blades
Laces seem to smile

Toepicks are mouths open wide
Teeth ready
Awaiting a pivot or jump

They are proud to do their job
Of cutting, slicing, spinning,
Gliding over translucent ice

Without me they lay, waiting
Without them I stand, watching
But together we skate

Holly Masek

Untitled

To look into the eyes of an angel
and see the threads of reality
fall apart.

To hold the hand of pure beauty
and not fear flying to the
highest heavens.

To be kissed by the softest breeze
and not fear the force of
the hurricane.

To be with you and not be alone;
nothing greater could I ever have.

Jeffery A. Scherschel

Fire

Burn.
Let it consume
The void within.

Burn.
Let the chill die down
and the inferno ignite.

Burn.
Let the inner flame
never extinguish.

Burn
Baby
Burn.

Cheyenne Dottavio

One Light

Looking up
into the vastness of the night
I see
a million, tiny
brilliant lights;
Each,
If to go out,
Would make the night
a little darker.
Like our lives...
Each of us
Shining our own light.
When gone,
The empty space
left behind
Can never be filled,
And,
The light that shone there,
will be sorely missed.

Denise Jankas

Mending Fences

We build fences
in every relationship
Some stronger
than the rest
Sometimes the fences
wear and tear
but can still be repaired
others burn down
before they are mended
We must mend our fences
as they break
Not doing so
could be a grave mistake
What a shame
sacrificing a relationship
over misunderstanding
Each waiting for the
other to explain
What becomes of death
when there is yet a fence to mend?

Monica Romano

Guardian Angel

Angel, Angel shine your light
   to keep me safe and warm tonight.

Angel, Angel come to play
   when I awake and start my day.

Keep me safe, keep me close,
   keep my always, Angel Host.

Julia C. Alexander

"Superior Sunrise"

Autumn's down hit the lake,
Although some may call it a sea.
She showed a scene no man can make,
Showed it all to me.

Gitchee Gumes was her Indian name,
But she's called Superior today,
Her size was her claim to fame,
She'd take your breath away

Now the sun is climbing high,
And here I sit alone,
Watching ducks and geese fly by,
O'er this lake that I have known.

Jake R. Brodersen

Untitled

My life is so much happier
Since you and I have met
My feelings couldn't be stronger
Our days I'll never forget

The sun shines so much brighter
The stars have more of a glow
Since you are the wonderful person
I've so well gotten to know

I couldn't ask for more
I feel I have the best
You've won my love and trust
Your tops from all the rest

I know that you will protect me
And guard me from all harm
And walk with me through life
As I rest beneath your arm

Darlene Powell

Grandma And Grandpa

They were there when I felt sad
They made me happy all the time

I miss their hugs
I miss their kisses

He would pick me up at school
She would take me to the mall

Now they are so far away
We have our telephones and notes

I wish they were here to stay

Bethany Beauregard

A Memory

His eyes were blue
His hair was blonde
It's such a shame
my cousin's gone.

He brought me
much happiness
this cousin of
mine, but he
was taken away
before his time.

I love and miss
him in every way
but I know I will
see him again someday.

Julie Friend

Honesty

Sometimes my honesty
Is mixed with fear,
Because I fight the fear
Inside of me.

I know I cannot be without you...
But yet I cannot be with you.
What we are,

Is not what we want,
But then we cannot otherwise be.

We cannot find courage to say,
I love you or good-bye, forever
The way it should be.
We do well to cover up our fear...

But it is not honesty.

Meagan S. Davis

Only You

As you lay your eyes upon
my eyes, I see nothing but
sadness, which is scary.

The sadness carries on
to love, and someday your
eyes, will be nothing but
full of love.

And you'll say "I love
you", and I will say

I will always love
you.

Even if you break my
Heart, I will love you, and
only you. Forever.

Katie Bethard

But Nobody Knows

I flew through the trees,
I went over the sea,
But nobody knows,
But me and the little fishy.

I swam through the waves,
I glanced at the weeds,
But nobody knows,
but me and the seeds.

I strolled on the ground,
I walked over the stones,
But nobody knows,
But me and the tree cones.

I swung on the vines,
I climbed on the trees,
But nobody knows,
but me and the crumbly leaves.

I swam through the water,
I ran on the gentle ground,
But nobody knows,
Because I did not make a sound.

Christine Joseph

Six

That day I returned from school
was the warmest day of my life.
I walked in the kitchen, and there
was my sweet, young mother.
 I was only six.

She took me to the counter
and showed me the bag of flour.
She said, "Cookies or brownies?"
I answered, "Cookies, but why?"
 I was only six.

She said we were going to make cookies
with great big chocolate chips
and butterscotch morsels
on top of each one.
 I was only six.

It was the first time
I had ever made such cookies.
What she said then startled me,
that Daddy died.
 I was six years old.

Beth A. Jueschke

For Sale

The old weathered red barn
squatted silently among the
trees of fall foliage.

Feelings of abandonment and
loneliness etched forever
on its boards.

Fields of golden stalks
swaying mournfully with
the wind, waiting for the
combines with engines halted.

Broken fences along the winding
dirt road where tractor tires
toiled and left their labor
Never To Return.

S. Rae Wirkler

Bright Intrusion

When I awoke this morning
 there was something in my room
That seemed to lift my spirits
 and chased away the gloom.
What's this intruding brightness?
 that made me feel so good
I rubbed my sleepy eyes again
 and then I understood
The sun was shining brightly
 with lots of warmth and light
I had slipped in through my window
 and chased away the night.
So thank you, Mr. Sunshine
 for greeting me today.
Sunshine for greeting me today
Please come again tomorrow
 if you can find your way.
If perchance a cloud should hide
 your golden face from view
I'm sure you'll be returning
 within a day or two.

Irene McGillen

"When I Am Lonely"

When I am lonely,
In distress, and
Cannot find a friend
Anywhere and the
Burdens of life
Get me down;
I must learn to go to Jesus,
Tell Him all my troubles,
And know that He will
Answer by and by.
So, when I am lonely,
In distress, and
Cannot find a friend
Anywhere and the
Burdens of life
Get me down;
I will go to Jesus,
Tell Him all my troubles,
And know that he will
Answer by and by.

Beverly T. Varner

"My Thoughts"

Our "Savior" arose
To save those
Who believe
And get relief.
Our days are numbered
As we go ahead
Trying to please
All that we see.
Yes, it's true
For me and you
We'll meet in heaven
When our day on earth
Are all through
So plan to do right.

Rozella Meadows

"Devil's African-American Advocate"

Why are we still here?
Why am I here, in this place,
On this spot?
Where are all of the Native Americans?
They were the brave-hearted.
I am from the people
Who were afraid to revolt.
They chose their miserable
Life over "Freedom or Death."
Am I to be proud of this?
Are these the kings and queens
Of Africa I have descended from?
If they were a truly proud and
Majestic people, their destiny and
The destiny of the Natives would
Be forever synthesized.
But I am here. Living proof
That the strong does not
Always survive.

Hajar A. M. Nelson

The Sun

The sun is warm,
The sun is bright.
Whoever said the sun was night.
Look in the sky,
And see a fly.
See a bird,
And think of a word.
Can you know the meaning;
Or just think of reasoning.
But only one thing,
Is beyond comprehending.
That is Jesus Christ the everlasting;
The Real Son Of All Being!

Melissa Webb

Untitled

People rush past me
scurrying like rats
who catch a sniff of fresh blood.
They run for a goal
which for them has no name.
But I do not scamper
for though I sit still
I have achieved that
which they so eagerly seek.

Amy Sutton Pilto

My Surrealistic Poem

There's never enough time
  (People not worth a dime?)
Don't have enough time
  (Time to think, time to think)
Feel like a stolid sphynx
  (Is my best plastic smile in?)
Disillusion, delusion
  (Stupidity or illusion?)
Always in a hurry
  (Is there any place to tarry?)
There's never enough time, tho
  (Ho! Ho! Ho!)
To think
  To ponder
    To dream
      To wonder
        To Shrink
        Or
          To
            Sink...?

Gilda J. Castillo

For Sabrina

If I could reach the sky
I would steal the stars
And stitch them together
So that you may have a blanket
To wrap your perfection in.

Eric Koontz

Goodbye To Me

Incline me not to go my will
I fearful, request, this fulfill.
For left alone, I'll surely die
Nevermore to thee rely.
Goodbye to me, ol' wretched vile
God's word grant me compile.
Reach me now, oh blessed savior
I plead this now, to win your favor.
Permission granted, break my deep
Where hidden sin, does rest and sleep.
Open up this dungeon place
Accepting now, complete your grace.

Arthur W. James

"Slipping Away"

The hatred and madness
The injustice she faced
Untrustworthy humans
Her life was a waste

A thunderous voice
Problems slowly arise
The once blossomed flower
Soon lingers and dies

The petals float down
Her heart sinks too low
The seed of her depression
Is starting to grow

The trembling silence
The thorn is her knife
Plunged in her heart
She then takes her life

A soul is now dead
The flower is crushed
Another strange silence
Another one hushed...

Jennifer Dailey

Moonlit Night

So close yet so far,
Its everchanging illumination
Casting shadows through the fog
Of what is so clearly unknown
Overtaken by the darkness
The starlit skies shine with wisdom
Of fate.
Clouds search lost in a universe of
Passion and despair,
As the soft drops of rain fall lightly
Like my heart does for you.

Marcie Lindow

The Flame

How majestic is the flame, perfect
in its own right.
It destroys, it renews.
Come behold its might.
It dances, loosely now tight
with its other selves.
It never changes course.
It's truly wonderful to see.
Come behold its inner
core, its inner core and might.

Wayne Luck

Gifts

Loved ones are gifts
  from
    God
given to us in the form
  of Loans...
    Only
He decides when these
  Loans...
    are to be repaid
So hold on to your
  Memories...
    for they
    are to comfort
    You
  So
God can heal
  your
    Heart...
      in
      Time.

Ann Varnado

Manning Provincial Park

Shadow-speckled and lupine-lined path,
You wind among the pines
  and summer's splashes
  of day lily, aster, cinquefoil.
Dressed to thrill,
Forest and meadow offset
Your needle-matted
  and root-boned essence.
Pungently perfumed
  by rain-showered pine,
You lay out your summer glory
  in this serene valley
  of cool shadow,
  warm sun,
  and glacial streams.

Holly L. O. Huyck

Baby Jesus

Baby Jesus was born
On Christmas morn
And had no place to stay.

But God had a plan
For His newborn lamb
In a manger he would lay.

The stable quite lowly
Became most holy
Because the Christ Child was inside.

His coming brought joy
This small baby boy
Who came to be our guide.

And God sent a star
So that Kings from afar
Should appear in all their glory.

Bringing gifts of love
For the babe from above
To fulfill the age-old story.
Constance Hembree

Expression Of Love

There are so many things
I've been longing to say to you.
If I dare to say them
Would you break my heart in two?
I care for you more
Than I've cared for anyone before.
Each day I fall for you
Just a little more.
When I am with you,
The world will disappear.
Losing you has become my greatest fear.
I guess I am saying that I will always
   cherish you,
Shall I say anymore?
What is the word I am looking for?
Could it be "adore"?
For you, I thank God in heaven above.
Dare I say the word I am looking for?
   The word is LOVE.
Tracy Nicole Tapp

Users

Would you ever,
   lend a hand,
   take a stand.
   Be a pal,
   show them how
   be real nice,
   take a sacrifice.
They turn on you,
   they refer to you as "who?"!
   they don't care.
   It's not fair!
   They're not there for you,
   When you go "Boo-hoo."
So do you still,
   lend a hand, take a stand,
   Be a pal,
   Show them how.
   Be real nice,
   Do you take the sacrifice?
   Now I regret doing it.
Kelly Maxwell

Why Say I Love You

Why say I love you
When I show you every day
Why say I love you
When you can see it in my eyes
Why say I love you
When emotions speak louder than words
Why say I love you
When you know I really do
Why do I say I love you
Because it's really true
When I say I love you
Your eyes light up a room
And when I say I love you
I feel it deep inside
And when I say I love you
You make me feel good inside
So you see
These three words go hand in hand
I love you
Which is very true
Sue A. Neutgens

"Priceless"

Like a diamond caressed in black velvet
Before me does lie,

A lake upon whose face is painted
The brilliant summer sky.

The fawn wander down
For a drink of glistening water pure,

As leafy arms of white birch
Sway gently near the shore.

The blooming flowers scent the air
With a dancing melody,

As butterflies do kiss those flowers
That grow so wildly.

Wispy cirrus clouds crawl by
Like the curl of chimney smoke,

As spider's delicate lace is spun
Over mossy stump of oak.

In this jewel of priceless wonder
Is more I'd love to see,

But hidden in a silver raindrop
Is nature's golden key.
Edward P. Einhart

"The Young Crazed Man"

Who is this Crazed Man
that has stepped into my Air Bubble?
He has taught me how to laugh back
   At Trouble
He has spun me around
like an aerialist with No Net
And he's taught me lessons
   I'll never forget
He has broadened my spectrum of life
and unsheathed My Eyes
   My God - I can see
Can I really be Free
from the traps of the
   Blind and the Damned
Thanks again I say
To this young Crazed Man
Cathy Ross

Show Me The Light

As I wander through the dark
   My eyes grow very wide
Yet, there is nothing that I can see.

   As I wander through the dark
I feel from side to side,
   Yet, there is nothing to steady me.

So I wander through the dark,
   And in the darkness
I do stay;

   Until I see the light —
And with it
   Fly away.

So show me the light,
   The glowing light
So that I may see.

   And I will spread my wings
And take my flight,
   Above every starry sea.
Rachael Elizabeth Eleste

Guest

A poem is an uninvited guest
Breezes in and opens its suitcases
Uninhibited, gets under the skin
And just refuses to leave
The only way to pacify the crying
Child is to push it out
On to the paper. And you are a poet.

To a poet,
A poem is an uninvited guest
Breezes in and opens its suitcases
Uninhibited, gets under the skin
And just refuses to leave
The only way to outsmart the learned
Child is to push it out
On to the paper. Now you are a sucker.

To a suckered poet
A poem is an uninvited guest
Breezes in and opens its suitcases
Uninhibited, gets under the skin.....
Better luck next time.
Venkata C. Majeti

Desert

Vast plains of
nothingness,
stretch across my
life.

My life is cracked
and charred,
like a desert
in summers' drought.
No feelings grow
inside me.

I am burnt
thoughts.
Travis Burns

Untitled

Love is fleeting
like a leaf in the wind.
If not coddled and cherished
it's gone in a whisper.
You must be always aware
nurturing and replenishing.
When you capture your love
give of yourself wholeheartedly.
Offer your very soul
in return for theirs.
Nourish and grow
one from the other.
Take pleasure in together
feeding from each other.
For if it's not equal
one will surely suffer.
Fragile and defenseless
brokenhearted and alone.
While the other catches the wind
and is gone in a whisper.

Susan Parker-Stone

Subaquatic

Float to the bottom
Look up-
an opalescent roof laced with silver
Become sunken treasure
Rest fluid
denying breath
Now burst the surface
spewing diamonds
Gulp and descend
watching pearls drip
upwards from your hands
Swish hollow sounds
in 3/4 time
Bob with the echoes
Fall up! (if at all)
Surge and gush
Forestalling
dry reality

Bonnie Grossen

Beauty Land

It is plain to see
For both you and me
A land that is afar
Over glimmering streams
And through the trees
Where fairies fly
And clouds float in the sky
Blue mountain peaks
And rainbow streaks
Where raindrops plop
And bunnies hop
Where brown deer graze
And children play
In the meadows and brooks
But you can only find this
Beauty land in books.

Hannah Green

Life And Death

Life is but a dream
Thoughts and promises
Told but not always given
Each step forward is a step back
Death comes to all in a false dream

James Robert Ford

My Grandma

Dedicated to my Grandmother, Eva Wintermute

My grandma she was so nice,
She gave her afghans away at no price.
We played games like "Old Maid."
Oh, we were close;
More than most,
And I know my memory of her won't fade.
I love her so much;
And I wish I could touch,
And hold her at least one more time.
Oh, I know I'll be fine,
Remembering these memories of mine.
And time will heal the hurt inside,
I'm so glad I kneeled by her bedside.
And said "I love you,"
Before she died.

Catherine Hodyniak

With My Last Breath

With my last breath
I'll say "I love you"
Proclaiming my heartaches
To hum in your ear
Swearing by my soul
The purest affection
That tugs at my life
Weighing it down
But never being a burden

With my last breath
When I say "I love you"
The moment will pass
Lingering still on my lips
Waiting for you
Hopelessly but not in vain
No sweeter sound remains
To penetrate the numbness
Echoing silently

Marguerite Hogan

You're The Reason For My Love

You're my reason for love,
You're my reason for rhyme,
You're everything to me
You are, you are!

You're the sunlight that beams
You're the rain that falls,
You're all the heavens and more
You are, you are!

You're the one who loves me,
I'm the one who loves you,
You know how to please me,
You know how to touch me,
You know all about love,
I know you can show me
You know, you know!

The lines are many,
The poems are long,
But to me you are the rose,
For long lines will soon bloom,
And so will we.
Our love, our love!!!!

Shirley Ann Stringer

The Dream

There was a night
I dreamed, I died
I went to heaven
To be by your side.

We were walking
By a lovely stream
Then I awoke
It was just a dream.

You looked so real
And felt so good
I seemed to feel
Your every mood.

Then you said to me
You can't stay here
For you still have work
To do down there.

Then I left
That beautiful stream
For after all
It was just a dream.

Dorothy Pearson

Love

My parents' love
is like a ray
Shattering the darkness
Without it
darkness Descends
A bright white light
in My life
Burns out the Darkness
Forever

Michael Binnicker

Living — Pain — Struggle — Gain

Is this life worth living?
There seems to be so much pain.
Is there a reason for struggle?
What do I have to gain?

Yes, this life is worth living -
To stop the tears, death and pain -
There is every reason to struggle
Because I have everything to gain!

Kathleen McVay

Much Beyond Love

It is a time for men
To hide within their own goodness,
Watching.
Guarding the hope of the future.
With all astute awareness and love.
For when neither right nor wrong
Traverses the Universe,
The path to heaven will be strewn
With those that have fallen,
In failure.
Striving in vain, to reach a goal
Much beyond their capacity to love.

Linda Lewis

Nappy Hair

Soft as lambs wool
Black as coal
Sometimes unruly
But always bold

Unique in the universe
No one has it but me
Everybody hates it
But it makes me free

I used to try to change it
With chemicals and such
This made me like you
But I missed it so much

I will no longer deny it
It's part of me
It's wild, it's short, it's different
But it's my identity

Elayne F. Hightower

Enstiwarno

And so we march
step, right
step, right

step, right
  onward to the city;
    that great city nearby.

But look quickly now,
the dawn has come
  please escape, escape from the pain,
    escape from the dragon.
Tomorrow.

James D. Dallett

Rock At The Bottom

Born into a world filled with hope
Grow into a man who relies on dope
Life filled with great expectation
Lost in my attempt at reconciliation
Gun in my hand so I want Starve
Felled at my attempt to hold a job
Fought to achieve this world's success
Felled miserably oh what a mess
Thoughts of suicide I could not hide
Thought of holding on filled with pride
Looking back at my life with a glance
Realizing this could be my last chance

Gregory W. Germany

Dragons Flight

Dragons light
Dragons might
All dragons take to flight

All dragons from brown to blue
Spread your wings
Say your swoon

All dragons from every hue
Fly pass the moon
While midnight looms

Silver, gold, platinum, maroon
Dragons fly under autumns moon

Autumn's twilight winter soon
Fantasy's children must fly soon

DanieLisa Best

Love Is A Splendid Thing

Love is a splendid thing
  At any age in life.
My first engagement ring
  Made Edna my dear wife.
A fifty-two year marriage
  Perfected every day.
Then a funeral carriage
  Carried her away.

Love is a splendid thing
  At any age in life.
My second wedding ring
  Made Virginia my wife.
A twenty-four month marriage,
  Perfect in every way,
Proceeds as a fine carriage
  On life's new highway.

Love is a splendid thing
  At any age in life.
Take heart, reach out and sing;
  Love your wife today!

Raymond B. Knudsen

Only Me

The black ice sweeps around me
Knocking me freezing
I cannot breath under here
I can't escape the fear

I cannot see horizons
Though I know the sun is blazen
I feel I cannot hear
But I can see a tear

Running down my face onto my spine
The days begin to whine
What is this crazy world coming to?
Where have I not been to.

I will not talk till the end of time
I will not speak on your side
I need sometime to my self
But your still high on my shelf

I let the drugs take over
I'm feeling disorder
I can't walk another step
But I'm here flying to my death

Daniel Keaveney

"Waiting For My Lover"

  For I shall wait,
Until eternity if I must;
  I'll look no further,
  I'll look no more,
For you're the one, my soulmate.
  My love is true,
  My love is strong,
I will wait forever long.

Cheryl Kangiser

Sea Of Love

If we all had boat in the
sea of love some would sink
some would float and some have
one to share that boat.
I know I would sink
others float around me and
don't do a thing to help
and so I sink like a rock in
the sea of love

Frank DiGiovanni

A Life of Special Wealth

Sometimes we tend to neglect
The ones we love the most
We take for granted all they give
Because we're just too close

It seems we get too comfortable
To realize what we've got
To appreciate who they are
And —— who they are not

It takes love and understanding
Really of yourself
To give it back to someone else
For a life of special wealth.

Janet Zinke

My Mama

One day God looked down from
Heaven above.
And made a wonderful mother
For me to love.

From the sun He took sunlight
And made her smile so bright.
He took a star from the sky
And put a twinkle in her eyes.

From the angels in Heaven so fair
He took some dust and made her
Lovely hair.

Yes God gave this mother to me
With a heart of gold.
To me, mama, you will never grow old.

In my eyes you will always be
That same young mama
That took care of me.

Mama I love you with all of my heart
And even in death we will never part.
Thanks for being my mama.

Loretta Martin

Thoughts

My present troubles me not
Nor shakes my serious mind
And what may be tomorrow's cross
I do not try to find.
To be the thing we seem
To do the thing we mean
To walk in faith nor dream
Of questioning anyone's scheme:

C. Schillinger

Untitled

I hold you in my heart
When not in my arms,
The sense of your touch,
The thrill of your charms,
and your love that keeps
me warm.

Diana Meyer

Cinquain

Moms
moms are the best
moms are best people
I love my mom so very much

Crystal Garkey

Blue

You know what?
I said
Blue looks good on me
And my smile may be crooked
But it's real
And when it rains
I like to squish my toes
In the mud and ponder my existence
And be an antenna for inspiration.
Because, I said
I'm really starting to like
My split ends and my ugly feet
And my height.
Why?
I said
Because, blue looks good on me.
Melanie Pina

Cats

I love cats,
They are nice,
They catch rats,
And eat mice.

They make me happy,
When I am sad,
Most cats are good,
They're never bad.

But cats need love,
They need to be fed,
They need to be cared for,
And kissed when they go to bed.

Cats need shelter,
Like a warm, cosy home,
And if you want my opinion,
They don't like to be left alone.

I think cats are just like us,
They need a little love,
Just like any animal,
Like a dog or a horse or a dove!
Nichola Taub

Let me be the air you breathe and...

Let me be the air you breathe and
 the world you see.
Let me be the one you want,
 the woman that you seek.
Let me be the shirt on your back,
 hugging you so tight.
Let me be the one who is near you,
 each and every night.
Why can't I be the one you long for,
 lust for, and chase after?
I may not be beautiful, but
 I breathe and I am me
So why won't your memory
 just let go and let me be?
Rebecca Ralston

Winter

Winter rains in with
Christmas lights and
winter vacation
on a rainy, windy day
with trees bare
and cold.
Mollie Chung

Untitled

She sits alone beneath the stair
Breathing dank and musty air
Trembling in the dark of night
Filled with hunger, fear and fright
She listens for familiar sounds
Within despair her spirit drowns
The darkness pulls her in so deep
Her head rests on her arms to weep
She sits and waits for endless days
Her thoughts no more than misty haze
Her body bruised, her spirit weak
The darkness looms immense and bleak
And so she sits, curled up with cold
So young and yet so very old
Here sorrow finds its counterpart:
The breaking of her lonely heart.
Valerie Barta

Requiem In Mother's Hands

A mom, holding our hand,
Walks us to our first day of school,
When she begins to leave
We cry.
She says,
"Feel where my hand held yours,
When you feel lonely or sad
just feel my hand."

A mom pushes us off
Into our lives,
When she finally leaves us
We cry.
We need to remember
to feel her hand in our own
And know she's still there,
Even though she's passed through
to hold her mother's hand
and share the hand of God.
Dennis Schwesinger

What You Can't See

I walk among so many people,
but they can't see my pain.
My heart is filled with so much grief,
I fear I'll go insane.

My mask it covers all my tears
so they can't see inside.
The smile I wear is not for real -
my feelings, I must hide.

I walk aimlessly through the motions
of what appears to be my life,
always wondering about the purpose
since things aren't obviously right.

People cannot feel my anguish here,
nor mend my grieving heart.
They just don't know how hard it is,
to Live - now, that we're apart.

But as I look around myself,
I just can't help but see:
the people that I walk among,
are a mirror reflection of ME!
Ruth Y. Ousley

Season Of Colors

In the shadows of Winter
Spring is only a dream
it soon appears on the horizon
color it yellow and green

Then come the colors of Summer
that Spring's gentle showers have bred
color them purple and orange
fuchsia and bright crimson red

Autumn's bright colors grow brazen
weary, tattered and old
color them light brown and orange
faded yellow with fringes of gold

Eventually Winter comes calling
the ominous season of night
spreading its blankets of coldness
color them silver and white
Rose Favia

"Mama"

For all the years we never shared
I knew in my heart you always cared.

You gave me strength, though you
never knew and with this strength
I grew and grew.

You left me now, forever gone,
but in my heart you will live on.

We've traveled through life so far
apart, sometimes seemingly in the dark.

But through it all there's always
been a precious light deep within.

So for now I say good-bye, trying
hard not to cry.

Wherever you are I'm sure you feel
my broken heart hoping to heal.

I'll take my memories, precious few,
seal them up and always remember you.
Linda McBride

Buck Illusions

Season of the hunt,
They move through the night.

Feeding their hunger,
In the deep moonlit.

If you see his shadow,
Don't blink an eye.

As ghost they travel,
And will fly right bye.
Joanne Schoenberg

Butterfly

Butterfly in the house, house, house.
Butterfly butterfly hooray, hooray.
Butterfly butterfly up butterfly
Butterfly down ok butterfly?
Yes said butterfly. Butterfly
Butterfly fly, fly, fly in the house.
Butterfly butterfly please watch
What's on TV butterfly?
It's Bill Nye the science
guy. What is on next butterfly on
TV? Ads Then turn off the TV.
Marie-Louise Winther

Storied Bedtime

I know a Lilliputian girl
Tucked cozily away.
I climb the stair to muse with her
When dusk has closed the day.

She's seen me come ten hundred times
Yet, always with a smile,
Exacts a fancied tale so I
May linger there awhile.

We weave our dreams of elfin silk,
But, when her lashes fall,
I know my Lilliputian girl's
The sweetest dream of all.
S. Robert Christensen

What Can I Say?

I tried to save you,
But, you did not understand.
I tried to help you,
But, your mind was blind.
I tried to explain,
You acted like you knew everything.
You did not listen,
You did not know anything.
Bang! You kicked my shin,
Then, bumped your own chin
What can I say?
Nothing!
What can I do?
Crying!
C. W. Yang

Friends

As the years go by,
 We tend to lose friends,
That are dear and true.
 But today I hear there
are still a few.
 It brings me back to
yesterday when friends
 were dear to me.
Some have their trends and
 some just pretend.
But for me I have
 found, for ever friends
from the years gone by.
Wanda Goldsmith

Tears And Laughter

In every life,
 there is disappointment,
 tears and sorrow too.
In every life,
 there is joy and laughter,
 fun-filled moments to renew.
My life has seen
 its ups and downs
But the joy of living
 still abounds.
If only this world
 would mend its ways,
And to our Lord,
 give thanks and praise.
The earth could be so heavenly,
 just the way it was meant to be.
James F. Walker

Friends

I had ten light bulbs
And one began to fade
I tried to fix it
But it went out instead.
Now another is flashing
And I'm very afraid
That I may not be able
To fix a light bulb again.
So I sit and I wait
And I try and I try
But I think my nine
Will go down to eight
How many will flash?
How many will fade?
How many will I lose
Till only one remains?
And when that one remains
I'm sorry to say
But that one will flash
And that one will fade.
Pam Sharp

Dreams

Dreams are very important
they are forever giving hope,
like stars in the sky
coming together to form a note.

Many times revolving
around one so very bright,
lighting up the sky
bringing beauty to the night.

Is our dreams no more than fragments
from a hope which shines so brightly?
With their lights sometimes dimming
from their centers fading slightly.

So if stars may fade away
or even fall from the sky.
Will our hopes begin to vanish
from dreams which never fly?
Cynthia M. Adwell

Love Is

I will give you as much as I can.
If you will show me how to give more
then I will give more.
I can only give as much as you need
to receive, or allow me to give
If you receive all I can give, then my
love is endless and fulfilled.
If you receive a portion of my love,
Then I will give others the balance
I am capable of giving.
I must give all that I have
being what I am.
Mary Ellen Bentlin

To A Rose

I've had you on my mind you're like
a rose on a rainy day, yet so close
but so far away. But maybe one day
that rose won't be so far away. Until
that day; all I can do is pray that
maybe on one special day that rain
will go away and then I would know
that my rose isn't so far away,
 from a rainy day.
Larry C. Gunter

Imagination

I have felt freedom
through my imagination
Drifting into realities
through my mind,
my goals have been but dreams
so real,
I lived them.
So alive,
I felt them.
Now I crave peace in reality.
Imagination will contribute to life,
not be life itself.
Sharlene B. Smith

Missing You

Dear Papa I do miss you so
I miss the love you used to show
me as I sat upon your knee
and you played patty cake with me

I miss the sweetness of your face
the special joy of your embrace
the way you bowed your head to pray
when you said grace at meals each day.

I didn't get to say goodbye
To let you know how much that I
would always love love and need you so
Dear Papa, why'd you have to go?
Janice Hullender

Mute

No sound
It's quiet
Visual Stimulation only.

The power lies in the touch.

The touch of one button
located lower center
of black oblong tool.

Weapons
Gangs
Prejudice
Fear

The power lies in the touch.

The touch of one heart
located within the soul
of each human being.

You and me
We hold the power
To touch the button
To touch the heart
To stop the noise.
Michelle Brewer

ABC's and #'s That Speak To U And Me!

O G!
U R 1,
2 C,
Y I 8,
A P,
B 4 T!
Laurel Wilkinson

Untitled

Hush, don't break the silence,
'Tis such a fragile thing;
And only in the silence
can you hear the snowflakes
sing.

Joan Heiman

Earth's Lament

Incredibly neglected
Outrageously abused
Immensely rejected
Forever misused
Unyielding to warnings
With determined persistence
Destroying the source
Of their very existence
Where power and greed
Work hand in hand

Depleting, polluting
Air, water, and land
What lies ahead
For this great planet
And all that grows
And lives upon it
Is up to its caretaker
You will agree
This is nature's code
So - it's you and me.

Erika H. Gould

The Meaning Of Love

Love can be fragile
like a rose pedal at night
Love can be scarey
like a young bird's first flight
Love can be cold
like a winter sunset
Love can be warm
like the touch of a pet
Love can last longer
than shadows at dusk
Love can die quickly
if neither one trust's
Love can be learned
and love can be taught
But the meaning of love
is found in the thought

Paul Brosnan

Lovers Pray

You are my life
You are my soul
You are the air I breath
You are every thing to me....

Claudia E. Craig

Since You've Been "Gone"

I don't remember your voice.
I don't remember your touch.
I don't remember your laugh,
　but I love you so much.
I'm not sure when I forgot,
　but I'll always know...
I'll love you forever, forever I know.

Sharon Gallets

I Love Him

Love is great
Only if you believe in love
Love is sweet,
And so is he
I love him
But he can't know
Why?
Because we're friends
And I can lose that

Megan Schaffer

A Family

A family is a whole,
together one,
a family works together,
plays together,
is happy together,
is sad together,
a family is honest,
loyal,
and loving each other,
together a family is great!

Corin Wilkinson

Tree

A tree is a life
it grows in the day
it lives in the light
while we work and play

A tree grows slowly
but don't be deceived
for a bounty of fruit
will soon be received

A tree drops its fruit
on the barren floor
but it knows what it's doing
it will soon grow more

The fruit on the floor
will soon start growing
it will be a new tree
without me knowing

And there goes the cycle
of a living fruit tree
it live and it dies
just like you and me

Paolo De Castro

Jazz Trio
(Jarrett, DeJohnette And Peacock)

A blur of string fingers
flicking bass fiddle,
upbeat, lowdown, tickling the middle.
Gary laughs through Night and Day.

Smilin' Jack strums drums,
thumbs rides on hides.
Sticks collide and the muse inside
jumps right out of its skin!

Keith giggles, jiggles keys,
improvising pianese.
Black and white he mixes, fixes
our wailing, flailing souls.

Jude Bagatti

Untitled

Waitress warrior
immediate intimacy
bleed your tip
and next...
rhetoric
and my own thoughts
Western thoughts
kill her - revolution
he can't have her
won't share her
must be blessed
touch and succeed
again the next day
and again for years
no individuals
only "miss" or "villain"
tormented and unaware
and still knows no one

Kirsten Parker

I Thought I Knew What Love Was

I thought I knew what love was
Until that glorious morn
It's etched in memory forever
The day my son was born

I thought I knew what love was
Until I heard that first cry
Kissed his precious face
And heard that tiny sigh

I thought I knew what love was
Until I held him to my chest
And felt him snuggle close to me
As he suckled on my breast

I thought I knew what love was
Until our eyes locked in gaze
Such innocence and purity
It shows in many ways

I thought I knew what love was
But now it's plain to see
I didn't know what love was
Until my son was born to me

Mary L. Turner

A Voice From Poverty

Please sir, look at me, though I
am ugly.
Am I a discrace, or
Am I disgraced.?

Please, look at me, or am I
invisible!
Am I as confusing,
As I am confused?

Please, bend to hear me.
I am helpless and
I suffer.

I reach out through the bars
Of your justice, but you look
through me, to far of causes;
And I bleed in the streets of
my poverty.

D. Miller

Sleepless Nights...

Baby - here it is, the middle of the night
  I can't sleep - for you are on my mind
And even when I close my eyes
  It's you, that I still find.

I've been thinking about our future
  of the plans we have still to share -
Of the feelings we carry inside our hearts
  of the dreams we have yet to dare -

Of the family that we will one day complete
  of the things - together we will learn -
Of the laughter that we have to give
  Of the passion that we both yearn -

Of the way our deepest thoughts connect
  of what inside we want to give -
Of the feeling of being united
  in this life we have left to live -

Of knowing that our being together
  will be what makes us whole -
For the love that we both treasure
  Is connected thru our souls -
    Kim Cooke

Maybe Someday

I look at them and wish I was anyone but me.
I cry myself to sleep as I think of how it could be.
I try to accept what I have become,
But sometimes I think I am nothing more than scum.

Life treats me anything but kind,
While I wonder exactly what's going through my mind.
Very seldom do I smile from my heart,
I do what people expect—I just play a part.

I try and I try to find love for myself,
But to me my life is just sad book on a shelf.
I fear the mirror for what I will face.,
When I have to look at this horrid excuse for a face.

It all sounds so dramatic, maybe it's not that bad,
The person I am,
The life that I've had.

I try to think of all the people who have it much worse.
Maybe my life is not such a curse.
I try to think that maybe I can,
Maybe someday I'll accept who I am.
    Alayna Posner

Tomorrow

I feel the warmth of your body, standing close to mine
I see your gold-flecked eyes, once deeply brown
Touch your thinning hair, once thick and fine
Caress the slightly stooped shoulder, still so very strong
I mentally trace your furrowed brow,
  with loving tenderness
Let me tell you how much I love you
Let me take your hand in mine
Let's walk, across the sun lit - meadow
On the high road to tomorrow
You fill my soul with ecstasy
Expand my mind with your dreams
You touch me with your gentle strength
You fire my imagination
Fill my heart with joy
My total being with peace
Let me show you how much I love you
Let me take your hand in mine
Let's walk across the sunlit meadow
Along the high road into tomorrow
    P. L. Meyers

Baby Name

A baby name is the, "Quest"
"Celeste," for a girl to me, I like the best
Sounds superior, from the rest
"Derek Jon," for a boy was my pick
This job was always very slow, far from, "quick"

How about Carrie Ann, Victoria or Nancy
Oh Me! Oh My! How fancy!
Try, Kenny, Steve, or Dan
Oh Me! Oh My! For the little man!

One night, in a dream, the right choice, it would seem
For, the bundle of joy, if it's a boy
"Gregory Allan," rang the bell
Sounds Great! If you repeat it for a spell

Well maybe the answer is buying a name-book
So we all can gander and take a look
How about names, from relatives or friends?
Or names, we can even comprehend
Whatever the child's name, we bless
It will be far from easy, I must confess!
    Nancy Dallmann

Mornings Touch

The morning's distant thunder - Caressing all within reach
Willowed rain - Parachuting to the earth's floor
The trees reach out - Embracing their feathery flight
With blades of grass - Dancing slowly to their touch

The early morning light - Fans thru the clear, misty pane
Its delicate hue - Giving color to the shadows

Time is frozen on mornings as these

The birds melody - Echo of their day coming
My thoughts reach out - Joining their chatter
In hopes to take part in their newly rising day

It's a slow dance with nature and myself

The rest of the world is on hold

For mornings as this - We must embrace the moment of life

Much too precious are these - To let slip away
    Daryl G. Grass

Life's Sunset

Majestic prisms convey the epistle of life's drama,
Look westward toward evening's silhouette of each remembered scene,
They tell the story of this walk along time's eternal strand,
  each moment not clear and tranquil, but rather intermittent
storm clouds conveying both tears of the soul and tears of mortal
  need.
In Death's moment, may the color of my sunset be not clear,
but rather filled with clouds that portray a life immersed
in the sorrows of this world.
And may the Son's rays behind that curtain of sorrow illuminate
and magnify all deeds done in humble adoration to the Author of
  Life.
For it is the Son that transforms a moment of mortality into
a panoramic reflection of his majesty.
For each actor, each life, may we all show forth a prism of
color at life's final sunset, and not just fade into everlasting night.
The colors of the rainbow flow into eternity, and so may
all who trust in the Light, Son, and Creator of Life's final stage.
    David C. Yarborough

Marriage - The Weaver's Loom

In Honor of Jim and Sandra Robinson
They walked through a door called marriage you see,
and set up a loom to weave what's to be -
The pattern of life between them will grow,
And good they have chosen - the threads start to show!

Threads of love bringing children
Threads of warmth bringing friends
Threads of sharing draw together
Threads of giving seem to win.

Their hearts now fully united, their love becomes as one
Truly now best friends and lovers
The marriage quilt may be half done.

Threads of silver are appearing
Shining brightly in their lives
Hand in Hand and hearts together
Weaving softly daily life.

Wonders only love can champion
Strong foundations rule their home
Thus the marriage God has sanctioned
Comes full circle - "from" the weaver's loom!
Rosa Lee Robinson

What Happens When You Fight With A Friend

Now Maria and Jessica were very good friends,
Until they got each other standing on ends.
They fought, they yelled, they
    kicked, and they screamed,
But no one could ever go in between.
Then one day the people said, "How can
    we stop them, they're a horrible dread".
They looked at the two girls pulling
    each others hair and said "We
    should send them to space to float in the air."
So the town's people picked them up
    and carried them away, and no
    one ever saw them after that day.
Sometimes when you look up to the sky,
    you may just see them floating by,
    kicking and screaming as much as
    they please, because they never did
    learn what the people taught, to
    treat people with respect and never tease.
Renee Nemmers

My Sisters Debbie And Veronica

My sisters, you will always be a big part of my
heart, no matter how many miles we are apart.

We grow to love each other for just who we are,
That's why I'm so proud to have sisters who shine
like stars.

My sisters, if you're ever lonely, sad or blue, think
Of something funny that I once said to you, and if
The tears keep falling just let them come out, for
My tears will be falling too and this is no doubt.
After we've had our cry pick-up the phone and tell me hi!

My sisters, how I love you every day. I try to tell
You so, because I'm going to miss you both from the
very first day I go.

My sisters, I love you and will miss your hugs, your
Touch, but most of all I'll miss the closeness of us!
Iris Serna

Love

Love, most beautiful natural instinct life has given us,
Love, mother nature provides the many loves for basic survival,
Love, the greatest demand and motivation within humans,
Love, strongest mental force from these instinctive wants.

Love, the eternal flame of hope human beings wish for,
Love, the greatest physical feeling enjoyed by humans,
Love, compassion of affections for the good of mankind,
Love, romance of humans rewarded by the thirst of sexual love.

Love, in humans charts our course in our daily lives,
Love, in man holds his integrity as a human being,
Love, the pendulum in the philosophy of sanity,
Love, positive traits within humans, to befriend others in need.

Love, the innocent children pure in mind as their faces,
Love, inspiration of man to bring forth new life in humanity,
Love, sharing to give, to be honest, to have faith, to see God,
Love, others' feelings, to understand, to be trusted, to be thankful.

Love, the force of humanity, to live together in peace,
Love, throughout the World keeps Nations at peace,
Love, motivation of human beings for continuous existence,
Love, hope for continual survival of "Worldly Co-existence."
Jim Digregorio

Infinite Sadness

Someone is gone
All over again
Is the pain the worst the first time
Or does it numb through the passing of time
It is the pain we all go through I suppose
We put nothing in perspective
Just our own selfish woes
It's over, it's over, it's over, it's done
There is a certain peace about all of it
You know you can find the light again when you can say
It will be interesting to see what happens next
Classmates—temporary
Acquaintances—temporary
Girlfriends—temporary except for the one
Friends—permanent
Family—permanent
Aaron Maybee

Barefoot Dreams

She longed to take off her shoes and run barefoot through the
beautiful garden of life smell all those sweet flowers
    skip through the babbling streams
    sometimes even dive into the warm
    rhythmical waters of the sea
    then lie on the beach with warm sons
    beaming over her beautiful body.
But the world knew her eyes were open
She had been taught the evils of the sweet apple
and her exposed eye would remain open until she died
There was no excuse for nakedness and child's play
    Her world was one of tight shoes and
harsh words, dark eyes, and jealous, judging minds
with serpents lurking in every corner.
    On the brief occasions in which she dared to reach for the
sweet rose or begin to stare out to sea a harsh reality would slap
her face and warn her not to give in to sweet dreams ever again.
Joyce Dietrich

Unstable Relation

Drifting on a sea of forgotten tears drops
Floating on a cloud of unending bliss
   Never able to find my way
   Never quite able to figure it out
An unending education from a different plane
   An unending relationship inside my head
     She's taken me to heaven
       She's thrown me in hell
I've been alone and emotionless
   Crippled and blind
     lessons are taught
All possibilities of reality are lost
   Light out of darkness
     Beginning at the end
What would life be like without my extraordinary
   Friend?

Ben Shank

In A Cathedral

Life is dead and dark that knows not a cathedral door.
Candles casting countless rays,
A man pinned on the cross,
The arches wide and great and grand,
The ghost of God upon the wall,
An altar of massive ivory melting spirits of stone,
Statues upon saints and Erasmus.....
Mean nothing to an empty church.

Fill it full of people, let them sing as the organ sends
   its screaming message,
Let the priest preach his potent thoughts.....and still
   it is barren.

A ragged old man entered this majestic place one day.
Around him all was quiet.
He was alone in almighty presence.
He poured his heart.....told of the cock crowing thrice and the
   great denial.

He lay there silent and stiff from a stroke.
God listened.....angels sang.....Erasmus smiled.
The cathedral was full.

R. Kenneth Girard

I Know

God, Thou hast filled my skies with sunshine
In December and in May,
Enough to share along life's journey
Even on the darkest day.

Thou sendeth rain in torrents...
In gentle showers to overflowing streams, -
Enough to bathe away my sorrows, heal life's wounds,
And call forth mighty waves to bring ashore my dreams.

O Giver of Good and Perfect Gifts,
Why lovest thou me so?
Yet, through thy bounteous mercy, grace,
I think I know. I know that I know!

Louise J. Thompson

Ever Lasting

Seasons change, friends move away, and life
goes on from day to day
Flowers fade, and streams go dry,
And many times we wonder why.
Yet we can always be assured, because
God tells us in his word,
That unlike changes in the weather,
have goes on and last forever.

Beau Willis

Again

Bright morning buzzard song
Of the hill.
Microcosm landscape on a stone.
Insecticide. Voluptuary calm.

Arboreal thought telepathic and resilient.

Stream speech, incessantly soft.
Its cold-watered tongue
Over teeth of rocky consonances.
Minnow vowels,
Frog verbs,
Prepositions of wide-mouthed fish.
Up-turned hands of leaves
Adrift upon the banter.

Prey-bird afternoon
In the feathery monologue of clouds.
Discover a stool-pidgeon breeze
To finger the departed no-longer pulsing heart of day.

Violining cricket evening,
Set a pace for the sun's orange cadenza
And coda the night 'till dawn sings again.

Robert Birch

The Touch Of A Hand

The sermon seemed short, but the message was strong and realizing,
That I've been living all wrong.

There's this feeling that's coming over me, that I don't quite
understand. A sense of God's presence, surrounding me, and it feels
like the Touch of a Hand.

With just a touch of his hand, he's setting me free. This burden
of shame is being lifted from me. Lord, at this altar, I'm giving you
all that I am. For your love has cleansed me with just the Touch of
Your Hand.

Now there's a joy deep within me, where emptiness, once was inside.
A warmth has replaced the cold, a glow I just can't hide. Why you
stooped to reach for me Lord, is more than I'll ever comprehend.
All I know is you were there for me, when I reached out, you took
my hand.

When I reached out for you, you were there for me. The way you
were there, on the cross of Calvary. Lord, at this altar, take me just
as I am. For your love has cleansed me with Just a Touch of A Hand.

Gerald Rusk

Saver

As I sit here in class
listening to the teacher talk a blast

I think of how many times
I touched people's lives and let them taste the wine

The wine of life
which brings such joy and happiness

The one that I give
That is not like another

I give it to you
and watch you smile wide

It may last for a moment or it might last for months
but you have had it. That is enough.

You have taken a drink from my Canter
and you have sipped it. In full

I hope you will take me with you
until your days of old.

Steve N. Potter

The Days We Are Free

I sit by the shore thinking of you;
Remembering the fun we used to have,
Playing games by this beautiful sea.
Those were the days we were free.

I remember the day we fell in love;
Holding hands as we walked by the sea.
Those were the days we were free.

You stayed with me all my life, my love;
I stayed with you till your death.
Those were the days we were free.

Now I walk to my death in this beautiful sea;
This sea of freedom and love,
And my spirit is free to search for you;
So I go and look by the sea.
Now that we are both free.

I see you standing at the edge of the sea;
Looking on and thinking of me.
This beautiful day at our sea.
These are the days we are free.

Nicole C. Welch

My Daddy As I Understood Him

I was so enthralled with this man in my life
Who has always been so strong and tall
I had no idea this man in my life would ever take a turn and fall
He always had a story to tell, with a thought—just for today
that would last forever and a day
I never had to worry about where I would sleep
I never had to worry about what there was to eat
I never had to worry about what to wear
Because I knew this man would always be there
What a wonderful job this man has performed
And now something has gone wrong, to destroy his form
I miss him and his stories of life
Because they were always so keen and precise
I can't elevate my mind to understand why
But, I know that God will get me through by and by
This is how I understood him to be
And in my life, he will always be

Lynda Moss-McDougall

You Have To Believe

Dedicated to Kathy Minth
By the tombstone where she lay,
They say her soul has flown away.
Up to heaven in the sky,
She is gone, but pleas; don't cry.

She will never feel pain again,
For up in heaven no one can.
She is resting, now in peace,
But her family isn't in the least.

Her family doesn't want to leave,
Her bedroom were she used to sleep.
But they will have to eventually,
She's gone forever, You have to believe.

Kristina Younan

Missing You

I see you each morning in the bed that I make
I see you each night in the dreams I create
Though you're not, I see you here
Awaiting as the day grows near
When you return I'll be able to say
I saw you in memories every moment you were away.

Tracey L. Hawks

No Time

Everyone is so busy. They have too many activities
No time for building friendships
and struggling with passivity.

Everyone is focused on their own needs
No time for building friendships
and forgetting to do kind deeds.

Everyone is allowing time to tick away
No time for building friendships
and not enjoying each day.

Everyone needs close friends.
No time for building friendships
leaves us lonely in the end.

Set your margins. Protect your time.
Start to build friendships
and let God's love shine.

Send a note. Make a call.
Start to build a friendship
and give it your all.

Love one another
and reach out to your brother.

Lorraine E. Beck

The Ocean

I am the ocean...
Dark, beautiful, cool, and incessant
The storms of time, the winds that blow cause not my flow to be disturbed.
For when those storms cease (as they always do) and the winds begin to ease, the original meter of my rhythm returns.

I move methodically along the boundaries of my beaches, absorbing all impurities man puts in my way.
But, ah, my shores remain clean,
For as quickly as man pollutes my shores, I wash all of that dirt away

The strength of my wrath, the serenity of my calmness invoke fear and confusion to all.
But, alas, some mysteries are oft best left unsolved, especially when the solution is inevitably wrong.

Come, drink of my glistening waters, listen to the melodic tones of my tides
Understand me, not control or restrain or second-guess me—
For you couldn't, even if you tried.

I am the ocean.

Olanda Carr Jr.

Life Cycle

As the years creep upon me and wisdom becomes mine
A child is born and the world appears differently to me,
My son's son, it is hard to imagine that this tiny person can illuminate the room
And assure us with a smile that everything is going to be fine.

Everyone is happy and content when he is near,
In his presence we understand the meaning of life,
His inheritance is the unconditional love and support of our family,
We give back the smile that in turn assures him when his life dreams are not clear.

One day my son's world will appear differently to him
When wisdom reaches deep inside the place that he is residing,
A child will be born, his son's son, another soul in the universe,
And we will become part of the familiar life cycle once again.

Jody Baldwin

Mother Like Me

Immaculate one that came to be
You were a mother just like me
You cooked and cleaned each day
Poor in the home you did stay
You knew what it is like to be tired at night
You knew my tears and shared my plight
As you watched your Son Jesus grow
You had to worry where St. Joseph's money would go
You know what it is like to clean the floor
As you turned none away from you door
And like us poor, your Child Jesus was your only treasure
Jesus, Our Lord, whom no one can measure
You too took the mop and the broom
And cleaned each day from room to room
When Joseph was sick you took care of him
And you, too had to be slim
You too knew agony's cost
As Jesus for three days was lost
And lo, for all of the women of the world to see
Our Mother Mary was a mother like me
   Patricia C. Romans

Tear In The Soil Scars On The Planet

We're building smokestacks to the sky, we say it's to re-energize
Don't care who we sterilize, all cost just to minimize

Each day we're wasting away, don't care what they say
We're wasting away

Green water flowing, plants are glowing
Chemicals are in all we eat, there is widespread disease

Our rain forest dying, a greenhouse is rising
Our water ways shining, from sea to shining sea

Ozone layer is getting dark, while acid rain tears us apart
East always fighting with west, with nuclear test

Do all you can, to protect the land!
Do all you can, to help save the land!

Unemployment, welfare lines, people trying to save a dime
Children are crying in vain, please stop hunger pain

Air pollution, revolution, people need to find a solution
If we go on like this we'll cease to exist

It saddens me to see all the time that's been wasted
Let's get together and maybe we'll find a way

Do all you can, to protect the land!
Do all you can, to help save the land!
   Joseph Colangelo

My Sweet Little Son

My son, my sweet little son,
you left your mother and me,
and went straight into heaven,
while we were enjoying your growing age and having all the fun,
My son, my sweet little son.

My heart bleeds and my eyes are full of tears,
as I will not see you now or in the coming years.
Your beautiful smile and laughter filled with cheers,
will always be missed by my eyes and by my ears.
My son, my sweet little son.

At times, I miss you so much
and the agony is such,
that I want to cry loud and scream,
and wish that I could see you at least in my dream.
My son, my sweet little son.
   Abid Syed

Untitled

Dreaming of you night and day
And hoping you'll promise you'll never go away
'Cuz you're the one who makes me laugh
When I feel like crying
Without you by my side I'd feel like dying

Every time I think of you
It still seems like a dream come true
I hope that I'm everything you'll ever need
'Cuz without you I still don't know where I'd be

My love for you is burning hot
And it will never stop
'Cuz there's only one thing I wanna do
And that's... keep on loving you
   Mandy Bruce

Virtual Bosnia

Today the breezes stirred blades of green,
luscious grass, and perfect funk melodies
painted visions in the ocean air.
Curvy island girls with eyes like gemstones
danced along the encroaching shoreline,
while the best of friends swung red-wine jugs
in the moonlight with indulgent verve.

Today in the rubbled Balkan jungle
furious festival roars rang within my thoughts,
in a daydream that raced away from sight
down a mountain, almost flying, only
touching down to swiftly kiss the rocks,
to play upon their edges for moments
usurping moments, mutating into memory.
But swimming deeply in the wind, the dream
laid eyes upon the sun, and missing step
it stumbled into the foothills' gaping jaws.
   D. Patrick Malcor

I Am So Lovely

I say good morning and good night. I kiss my dolls and puppy good night. I am so lovely. I use my hands to plant a seed- my hands to give my friend in need. I am so lovely. My ears to listen and to learn - politeness has taught me to wait my turn. I am so lovely. My mouth and hands and feet are quiet when someone is talking - I run and skip and hop outside- inside is for walking. I am so lovely. I keep my clothing from off the floor. I put them on hooks behind the door. I am so lovely. I wash my hands before I eat. I chew my foods quietly, then I speak. I am so lovely. I say thank you- no thank you - if you please. I cover my mouth when I have to sneeze. I am so lovely.
   Patricia P. Thompson

Masks

You hate him because he
Doesn't look like you. But when you look
In the mirror, do you like what you see?
You teach everyone to hate him
(Because you're afraid of what love might do).
His skin may be different,
But when you cut us, you'll find
We all bleed red.
   Matthew Ratzloff

Death

As Death embraces me with his cold hands,
I do not fight him, I welcome him.
As Death lowers his icy face to mine,
I do not push him away, I kiss him.
As Death picks me up to carry me away.
I do not kick and scream, I go with him.
As Death takes me into his freezing grip,
I do not fuss, I hold onto him tighter.
As Death loves me with cold calculation,
I do not fight it, I'm happy.
I can only find happiness in death now.

Jaime R. Cizewski

Florida II

The road ahead lies flat and straight
Insects unknowingly suicidal rush to their death
Attracted to the lights.
The warm air buffets the car with humidity
Creating a rhythmical sound to accompany the never ending
turn of the wheels upon the road.
The moon almost full in the sky shows the way towards an
unnatural glow in the distance.
The murdering lights stop short of the glow and turn into
darkness, towards sand and water that shine
Equally in their own battle for control of the earth.
The light expires and warm moonlight rushes the senses.
Each sense acting in natural unison, relaxes the mind
and forms a blanket of assurment covering the body.
Nature and human nature have been reunited.

Christopher R. Nigro

Eyes Of Heaven

Someday, in Heaven, I'll find the stars that are in your eyes.
And when there are seven, then maybe you'll realize
That there's no one but you,
And I love you so true.

Just like an angel; so near, but yet so far,
You're the prettiest girl I've ever seen — and you know you are.
And I want to come home
Because without you I'm so alone.

Ronny L. Seres

An Ode To The Bottle

It was supposed to be rainy, but the weather man lied,
It was such a nice day, so they went for a ride.
Mom and Dad sat up front, with Lynn in the back,
To the countryside they drove, with a picnic-lunch sack.
Laughing and singing, all the way there,
They ate and played games, these days were so rare.
They packed up their things, and got in the car,
They weren't in a hurry, their home was not far.
So along home they drove, and rounding the bend,
A car came heading, right straight for them.
Daddy tried as he could, but he didn't have time,
To swerve out of the way, of this one killer's brine.
As she sits in the room, the little girl cries,
There is no one around, to wipe dry her eyes.
Where will she go? What will she do?
Her mommy is gone, and her Daddy too.
Sometimes I dream, that stories like this,
Could somehow be banished; and replaced by bliss.
But the truth of it is, it happens everyday,
And no one ever knows it, until it comes their way.

Amy Harer

Lesson In Life

Mommy, come play with me, please sit down
by my side. Let's listen to the birds
sing, see the sky so blue and wide.

Mommy, let's play ball. Will you take a
walk with me? Teach me how to ride my bike,
help me climb a tree.

Mommy, tell me a story or please read a book
to me. I just need a hug—then I'll let you be.

Mom, can I tell you something? I think you're
pretty neat. Oh, I'm sorry. I didn't mean to
be under your feet.

Mom, I didn't mean to bother you. Sure, I'll get
out of your way. Leave you alone now? Whatever
you say.

Son, why don't you call now or ever come by?
Daughter, why haven't I heard from you? I'm
so lonely I could die.

Jennilee Barnhart

Answered Prayers

When I thought there was nothing left, I turned to God and
He heard me, His promise was kept.
I know my prayers seem urgent at the moment, when others
Have prayers that are more important.
I thanked him for his answer, It came without hesitation.
He has been good to me, I hope that I can live up to his
Expectation.
I guess I am selfish to ask him to help me today. I feel
Better but I still have problems that won't go away.
I am His child, an heir to His throne, and when my time
Comes, I want to live with Him in His home.

Sharon H. Day

Stop The Violence

When the lights go out at night;
two men raise their fists to fight.
Despite the teachings they have heard;
they don't seem one bit concerned.
A small girl 'bout the age of five,
stared at them with big brown eyes.
For the little girl had been taught right;
to talk things out, and not to fight.
She outstretched her fingers and raised her hand;
"Stop The Violence!" she said to the men.
The little girl turned and walked down the street;
All the men could hear was the tapping of her feet.
They thought of the teachings that they once despised;
And looked at each other with guilt in their eyes.
I am sure they'll remember the day;
that they shook hands and walked away.
From this poem a lesson you'll learn;
to STOP THE VIOLENCE, and happiness you'll earn.

Erica Bolar

I Remember

I remember,
thinking of long days in summers past
When blazing crimson sunsets use to laugh
Our whispers beneath the tottering trees
that became secrets embraced in the summer breeze
Twin souls entwined for eternity
Revealing the path to our destiny
Moments of passion frozen in time
Memories of love that will always be mine
that there is nothing else worthy of
the answers I found in the eyes of love.

Marlene Stokes

"An End"

I sit on the lonely beach alone
And watch the sun set into the sea.
The earth, the sky, the sea, and I
Make up the world, alone.

The sun sets lower as the darkness comes,
The night wind blows our time along.
The earth, the sky, the sea and I
Make up the world, alone.

The sun has set, the sea is gone
The wind blows silently on.
The earth, the sky, the wind, and I
Make up the world, alone.

The wind has died, the earth is gone.
My God looks silently on.
My God, the sky, a dream, and I
Make up the world, alone.

The world is lost forever now,
The sky is through with light.
My God, a sigh, a dream and I,
Make up eternity, alone.

Philip K. Nuetzmann

"Back Home On Rainy Lake" (Morning Run)

Jogging along side this lake that I love;
I'm especially fond of the island called "Dove".

One road, with two lanes, surrounded by pines;
Peaceful and lonely, serenity I find.

Clouds threatening rain move in up above;
Humidity, "Heavy" sticks to me like a glove!

Mother duck and her babies are paddling by,
The sea gulls swoop up, then down in the sky.

"Bear Sightings" are common, most every day;
Somehow they elude me, perhaps not today.

Such "Peace and Quiet" seldom are known;
Out in the West, which I once called my home.

Pollution, traffic, and people galore;
That place made me "Crazy" but not any more!!

Good weather, fine restaurants, shops "Extraordinaire!"
Seductive and tempting, they couldn't keep me there.

It's up in "The Bush" where I longed to be,
Instead of "People" we're crowded by "Trees!!"

Roberta D. Larsen

A Day In A Life

Oh peaceful moments of dawn,
I lie awake listening to your calm.
Get up, get up,
The coffee I must make.
Pitter patter, pitter patter,
One must be awake.
Pitter patter, pitter patter,
Oh now, what's the matter?
Oh please, oh please,
Not another one of these.
Hurry, hurry, go to school.
Hurry, hurry, go to work
Hurry home to do more work.
Do the laundry, help with studies.
Stop it, stop it!
How I wish they were buddies.
Cook the supper, clean the kids,
Oh please, just let me close my eyelids.
Oh peaceful moments of dawn,
How I wish for your calm.

Debra A. Cuminotti

Forgotten Love

The old woman gazes into her yard,
Now overgrown, and showing much decay.
She sees the old swing set keeping guard,
Hoping a little boy might still come to play.
The swings were a gift her children did cherish,
And would swing till the summer sky was the darkest blue.
The decrepit set leans heavily, and will soon perish,
Now only frequented by wasps, and a lizard or two.
Then she spies the see-saw, near to tears.
It bring back her children giggling in delight.
The rotting see-saw hasn't budged in years,
The wood is soft and gray, worn by years of sunlight.
Both swings and see-saw are aged and worn with disuse
And soon will fall and finally be seated,
For they have long since outgrown their use
No longer are they needed.
"My boys will visit soon." She says,
Pushing back the hard truth with a shove,
What she has known for countless days,
The truth of her forgotten love.

Michael Gianelloni

A Woman Plight

When I see you cry and voice tremble with pain.
My heart breaks as one in the same I ask God: Am I to blame?
My mind goes back, there was a time when I was contained.
Young, black, beautiful and vain.
I too suffered with no refrain.
And I cried out. Oh God grant me not a daughter to carry this chain.
For woman suffer too much, from the hand of man.
We love them, serve them bare their - children to replenish the land.
Oh what animal this thing call man.
How long must this go on taking abuse from a man.
Where is the love and protection.
Happiness and comfort for us to live.
If this is a woman plight long suffering, child baring,
loveless years. Take back this man today and teach
him some skills, to have confidence in him self
to love, and to give affection to his woman so she
can live and the both can love each other and do your will.
And in a woman plight her pain will heal she'll have nothing to fear
and forever dry her tears.

Loretta Moreno

The Sail

It's only cloth upon a mast
yet it is strong and made to last
wind and rain beats upon its chest
sunshine warmth keeps it blest.
It smiles as we sail along
singing gayly its favorite song
its colors of red, white and blue
means to us it is always true.
We take it down to have a rest
after a long days toil
only to hoist it up again
to greet the morning sun.
It sometimes strains against the wind
but never complains or tears
it just buckles up to every task
and sails proudly along.
I think I've never seen a truer friend than she
my sail, my friend, belongs to me.
After she serves her master well and sails her last sail
I'll put her in my safest place, far away from the sea.

George F. Gettys

She's My Mother

There is a dear lady, alone in her room,
One who still smiles, though her world's filled with gloom.
Awaiting the call of the Master on High
She'll answer His summons, with only a sigh.
Her goodness will brighten the Heavens anew,
The Angels will sing when she joins them, too;
Bless her and keep her, dear Lord, I beg you
She's one of the faithful, one of the few.

Her beautiful eyes can no longer see
Her legs too weak, Lord, to bend a knee.
With heart and soul did she always serve you
Being ever faithful: Ever true.
Seeds of goodness and mercy this Saint did sow,
But that, dear Lord, you already know.
For a labor of love, she asked in return
Only that Heaven she someday would earn.

    She's my mother, dear Lord; have mercy on her;
    She has served you all of her life;
    Love her and keep her in your tender care,
    She never once questioned this strife.
        She's my mother.

Virginia B. Ellis

The Keeper Of My Dreams

When the sun comes up I envision your face.
Your eyes of green pools lift your dreams off to space.

I wonder what you're feeling.
I wonder what you see.
Are you looking into my eyes, or right through me?

I need to feel your arms.
I need to see your smile.
I need to feel the love that I haven't in a while.

We stand so close but you're so far away.
Can I believe the words that you say?

Now that I lay down to sleep,
The events of the day into my dreams will creep.

Will tomorrow be different from today?
Will my love stay?

Toni Fritz

Visiting The Wall For The First Time

I almost saw my dad cry today,
I almost did too,
I heard the sadness of millions,
The walls, the ground, the air,
It all screams out with the haunting of 57,865 souls.
Tears shed on this sacred, silent square
Could fill Hanoi Bay tenfold.
I could see the anger and sorrow in my father's eyes
As he found a childhood friend
Who was whisked away to a far away place.
"Why?" I asked him.
His confusion was apparent, but there was no answer.
I felt like washing away this horrendous past,
Yet my frustration over something older than I.
Brought upon only more confusion.
57,865 children-not men by any account-all lost.
"What a waste..." my dad muttered.
And with our heads lowered to the ground below,
My dad and I left before we added to the flood.
What a waste.

Kevin Paul Hackl

A Sinners Prayer

Lead me, guide me the way I should go.
Help me to understand the things I should know.
Store upon me the ability to forgive.
Teach me, oh Lord, how to live.
Remove all the hatred from my heart.
Grant me, oh Lord, a brand new start.
Show me, oh Lord, how to first love me-
Then how to spread love righteously.
Help me to fulfill what's required of me.
Receive my soul for all eternity.
Bestow upon me a suitable prayer
That covers all things everywhere.
Bless my neighbors, my enemies and friends.
Teach them also to comprehend.
And serve you, oh Lord, twenty-four-seven,
And let it be on earth, as it is in heaven.

Ennis T. Miles

Something Lost

Do you know what's missing in this town
   of wide swept streets and Rembrandt skies,
   jeweled below the mountain rise?
A gallery of balanced power
'til they tore down the old bell tower.

Do you know what's missing in this town?
   No bells to ring out birth or doom,
   no bells of joy, no bells of gloom.
(Perfect bed for a perfect flower)
But no sound from the old bell tower.

Do you know what's missing in this town,
   where latest planes scratch up the skies?
   Where Eagle preens and floats and flies?
No bells to toll or tell the hour.
There are no bells and no bell tower.

Dessie Bryant

An Indian

An old Indian stood on the top of a hill,
By a wild running river one day.
He had come there to feel the days of his youth,
For he knew he'd be passing away.

His hand brushed a tear from a weathered old cheek,
For in his minds eye he could see.
A wild black pony and a golden young boy,
Riding happy, together and free.

He felt once again the breeze on his face,
Smelled the fragrance of wild flowers in bloom.
He pressed once again to his heart the young bride,
Who was called "Sweet Child of The Moon".

He had tasted life's joys and had known its sorrow,
And now he was ready to go.
For his eyes had turned backwards to things that had been,
And his step had grown weary and slow.

Oh God of my father, be with me this night,
Take my hand for I've long been alone.
With a welcome, lead me to the land of forever,
Where an Indian can really be home.

Regina Scopelitis

Life Of A Tree

My roots are old,
and the vines which wrap me
are withering with rot.
For I have lived hundreds of years,
and stood here
through many of your wars.
I've seen many lives come
and go throughout the passing years.
For I live here among my brothers that are left
due to our wars with man, for we cannot
fight back.
I know it is my turn now, to be used as a
structure of man's work.
Only then to be forgotten, for we all were
once part of a beautiful forest.
Russell E. Chandler

Where Fading Flowers Bloom

I wait for her in grass stained harvest gloom
inhaling her remaining shameless grace,
among the weeds where fading flowers bloom.

Like waves from stones cast in a liquid womb
a smile ripples across her age bit face.
I wait for her in grass stained harvest gloom.

Her better threads done weaved into fates loom,
but raveled beauty becomes vintage lace,
among the weeds where fading flowers bloom.

Time's mortal shade shall sweep with tattered broom
and always win the never ending race.
I wait for her in grass stained harvest gloom.

And age has but one boundary, solemn doom.
Her youth is none, but a lingering trace,
Among the weeds where fading flowers bloom.

Let her embering beauty be her tomb
and smolder until I too reach that place.
I wait for her in grass stained harvest gloom,
Among the weeds where fading flowers bloom.
James Trivette

The Hands Of Our People

Look at these hands young man,
touch these hands for they have seen
and done much,
these hands have seen the hardships and
struggles of our people, the victories and
the defeats of our people.
These hands have built weapons, tools,
and the finest decorations for our people,
these hands have built the most
beautiful pottery with the brightest of
paint for my people.
I have built fires, tepees, and even this
community. Now your hands shall take
the place of these hands,
my hands,
for they have started our people,
now you must keep them going.
Matt Mikeska

Wind

Wings on the wind, forever sing to the world.
Watching the flags, slowly unfurl.
Blowing the leaves from the trees in the meadow.
Clouds in the sky wondering why they cast shadows.
Birds in the trees merrily chirping their songs.
Winds in the forest gaily singing along.
Saying to the world, "We all belong".
Patricia Radschlag

O Wondrous Night

One long winter night ago
The moon lit, the stars bright
All was quiet, very peaceful.
So still, a picture of serenity
Only God was working then.
He spread himself as flakes of snow
Over the ground and in the trees
The trees bending over as to reach for more.
A breeze would gently blow by
Like God exhaling a wonderful sigh
For he knew this place was blessed.
The forest animals were in their dens
All snuggled and warm, comfortably tucked in.
There was an air of peace, a taste of hope
For this night was wonderfully safe.
It was the eve of greatness around the world
For the next day a great king was born
A Savior of Grace, so heavenly adorned.
James Hardin Fridy Jr.

The Rawandan Skull

Perched on a hill looking onto the dead land
There is a skull resting on the golden sand
The skull belonged to a human who only lived for peace
But engulfed in war he is nothing but decease

War does nothing but choke human life
Its finger grabbing, mocking human strife
Laughing bullets puncture all that live
We are put on this earth not to hate, but to give

A human skull buried beneath the water
Once lived, surrounded by souls eager to slaughter
But hate took his life and threw it to the sharks
Now he rests alone in the ocean, alone in the dark

Whether on ocean, land, or small place like a hill
War does nothing but to spill blood and kill
Blood which was pumped toward the heart
War does nothing but to break the bond apart

Let the Rawandan skull be a reminder to have peace before war
Stop the slaughter, killing, hatred and gore
Give peace a chance and your lives too
Before on this Earth human civilization will be very few.
Debbie Krug

Compliments

Alex you look very nice today.
Paul you made a huge improvement.
Jane your homework is always so neat.
Hilary you look splendid in your summer dress.
Bob Jr. you got another A in math.
Alice your tan is coming along beautifully.
Jennifer and Peter
I think you both will make fine Doctors.
Gabriel your handwriting
is far ahead of the rest of the class.
Hank what a neat looking lunchbox you have.
Marsha your locker is definitely the neatest.
Billy your haircut looks very nice.
Tom you have such good manners.

Why is it that the only compliments
I ever got were in gym class?
Damn That Little Black Boy Is Fast!
Nnamdi O. Chukwuocha

"Mom"

Like the ocean waves that move in the peaceful calm of the night
So did the life of a beautiful sight
I called her "Mom"
Like the rain that falls from the thunderous skies
So does the tears of sorrow from my eyes
Like the beautiful earth that turns
My love for you "Mom" will always burn
I missed you yesterday
I miss you today
And I will miss you tomorrow
But just because and only because my Jesus is forever real
I will see you again "Mom" I promise I will...
Martina L. Davis

My Dad

My dad, my dad, what a great guy
Everyone loved him and I'll tell you why

Mom taught us loyalty, etiquette and grace
Through dad, honesty and integrity we were to embrace

He gave to so many others throughout his life
coaching, guiding, eliminating strife

All of you know him because of AA
But I'll always know him a different way

He learned to take time for you, for me
He never ignored anyone that made a plea

Among men, I loved my dad the best
He'll always be head and shoulders above the rest

It isn't easy to make amends for your past
But when you do, you're free at last

Dad worked hard to mend his ways
And when he did the Lord gave him praise

So he moved on to a better space
And we have many memories to take his place

My dad, my dad, what a great guy
Everyone loved him and now you know why
Cynthia Harrington

Untitled

Take your fears to the dark nighttime sky
Relinquish your rage to the clouds blowing by.
Deliver your sorrow over the wind whisper gust
let it bare your pain, echoed by lust
To dimmest moon night light morphs shadows like dreams
Drops delicate raindrops of sheen through the trees
And fierce piercing stars explode to vein blaze
As demure revolt prevents you from returning a gaze
A forbidden guilt pursues a veil of delusion
Surrender pale emotion to reap in seclusion
your fantastic like dreams descend into pools of despair
As you're left to inhale to dismal night air.
Scott Gulack

Open Your Eyes And See

Open your eyes and see,
What is inside of me.
Don't judge me by gender or race,
Or the color of my face.
Put aside all of that;
Maybe we can sit and chat,
Become best friends who never part.
That is what I want in my heart,
Not just for me or for you,
But for others who may be different too.
Cassandra Lewis

Raindrops

The loud crack of thunder floods my ears
as lighting illuminates the sky in long,
jagged pieces of light stabbing from heaven to earth
while others slip behind the clouds
like his arrow as it glides into her quiver

Raindrops hard against the window
like first-time lovers frantic, heated,
rapid to reach a climax
I open the door to rain coming in
drops so fast and hard they burn
when I reach to touch them
like the heat of passion when hands caress skin

Sitting on my patio, I surrender myself
Inhaling deeply, I close my eyes and catch my breath
letting it out slowly, relaxing my body
like descending after the apex

Raindrops are softer now,
like a comfortable lover in a tried relationship
relaxed and willing to wait for completion
they touch the ground in a gentle splash.
Barbara A. Jones

Who Hear's Them Fall

Trees that fall all around
Big ones, little ones tall and slim
They crackle, creek and bang
They snap, they crash, they shake the ground
Slowly falling down
They no longer have the strength to grow and to spread
their leaves
No more to shade the woods from heat
No more to sow their seeds
No more to shelter animals in the hollows of their trunks
No more nests built in their branches
No more leaves to grow
The earth has new food to take from the mighty tree
To decompose to feed the land in time to grow again
Who hears the trees that fall
Do you or I?
Linda Carroll

Biscquit

Paint chipped doors hung askew, with hinges that hold rust as well as memories. When it was a bright cinder against the green sea of hills, we played in the angel's hay. Tumble did we; when it rained, snowed, or smiled- the weather never mattered, oh, best friend! We were a body of limbs, now I am just an arm; as loose as a shoe's lace untied. We are not sheltered in the eaves of the rustic barns of made up menagerie. A peach smell reaches my nose, a picture remembered, how empty, how alone can one soul feel in one wrenching, heart-ache pain? So small, so very small... I am so sorry I wasn't there for your last laugh - your last cry. When I visit the paths we've run, the holes we've dug, and the barn we've fled, I can not hold you again, what a cruel gift! When I hear a doorbell ring I expect to hear you reply - silence. Still, no one knows how spiritless, how dead, how alone I feel- as you must have felt until God helped you. Our love was as intricate as a spider's web, as a spinster's bank book records. We had (How? They asked) our own "inside" jokes, we went though so much, as if we were on a trip with Dante' but you arrived (God I prey) in heaven and I on earth. So, would you mind if I talked to your picture - hoping for a reply or if I threw your toy one last time - hoping you'll fetch it leaving me now was hard, but thankful. No pain, but no last summer. But, I still remember, in the rust of the barns in our wit.
Chelsie Hanson

Reality Of Time

Your Baby Book wants my view of the first year,
The thought of it going so fast brings me to tears,
For I realize that your won't need me like you do forever,
Even though we will always have that special bond together.

I remember giving birth to you in the hospital,
Never believing a love so strong was possible.
Holding your tiny body in my arms and never wanting to let go,
Thanking God for the blessing of you and feeling myself glow.

I learned that day just how much love God has in his heart,
Because I too had achieved the greatest love that will never depart.
And as the days turned into months and the months turned into one
    year,
This love I have for you has only grown stronger and my future is so
    clear.
You have grown from a tiny baby who needed so much love and care,
To an independent toddler that crawls and walks without any fear.
You have learned how to communicate in your own little way,
As well, as how to sing and dance, laugh and play.

If I had my way one year would last as long as two,
Just so I could feel that I have spent enough time nurturing you.
Since that is not even a possibility,
I'll just go on loving you and except reality.
Jamie A. Samolej

My Friend

A friend of mine told me some bad news
As a child, my friend was sexually abused
No one believed or paid attention,
No one seemed to care or asked any questions.
As I listened to the story with disbelief
How could a mother, didn't listen, not even blush
A child she conceived was nastily touched?

I cried, and I wondered, how could this be done?
Not to your daughter, not to your son.
As I wipe the tears from my eyes, I realized this wasn't enough.
I'll try to be there for my friend, will be there as much

I told my friend that I understand
As I gave my friend a hug, as I held my friend's hand
My question was to my friend, "What can I do to ease this pain?"
My friends reply was, "It's forever stain."
I told my friend it's never your fault,
but this sick culprit should be taught

I know you hate him, yes you do, but one day the truth will
come through, and if you don't have a parent to hold your hand
You have a friend in me, and I'll take the stand. God will get him,
yes he will, and when you think no one loves you, I love you still...
Grace A. M. Smith

My Prayer To All

Dear Lord who watches all
judge ye not by a crystal ball
Love thee in sin with care
help them through to hang in there.

I love thee my Father
who gave his only Son without bother
let him into your heart
because that's where he should take part.

This is my prayer to all
I judge ye not by crystal ball
I love thee with my heart
Jesus and I will never part.
Marllana Smith

Out On The Front Lawn

On Summer eves in cold, green, mellow grass
In the days of Freeze Tag and Mother-May-I,
We children of thirty years back so often
Espied silvery blimps lumber across the sky.

Shiny specs against fading particles of blue dusk
Took our fascination - stiffened our over charged bodies.
Free from corporate servitude (they were government agents back then),
Free to float, striking like lightning,
We were lifted up by such impossible lightness,
By the innocence of our awe.
On evenings of cool breezes or in calm superb air,
Colossal creatures, as aimless as we,
Clear to see - so out of reach, crossed our worlds.

It could only be in those summer months of fantasy when
In the middle of any game all heads would cock toward the sky.
Then, out on the front lawn, on cold, green, mellow grass,
We children of thirty years back
Would continue to play Spud.
Barbara Glynn Alves

Over The Ice-Cream Counter

She leaned over the ice-cream counter
to tell him hi
the first word she had spoken to him
in over a year
she said she wanted to talk
that is if he wanted to
he smiled genuine
she returned the smile nervously
so much to say
but the words wouldn't come
and the customers were less than understanding
maybe tomorrow, she said
yes, maybe tomorrow, he echoed
she watched the curve of his lips as she turned
and he watched the curve of her body
from over the ice-cream counter
as she walked out the door
and the impatient customers rattled off flavors
to his unlistening ears
Rebecca Pine

Left Out In The Rain

Security is bought, love is not the same,
there's some who know the price we pay when left out in the rain.
Dependent on yourself, or dependent on another,
when day comes can you tell between the lier and the lover?

The lier tells the truth you thought you wanted to be true;
The lover tells the lies of love too common to be new.
But when the sunlight catches them do liers really learn,
it's better to be faithful than continuously burned?

When shadows block the sun, and money is the key,
to desire is human nature not a freak show mystery.
You say you feel it too, the echo of the pain,
the loneliness of all the hearts we've left out in the rain.

Are you here with me today or did you leave the day before?
Can we really see the glass half full when blind behind closed doors?
Say reality's subjective but I tell you I'm no fool,
reality is all we learned from teachings in our school.

Seek the hand you know; take pride in yourself,
for when you're gone, your self is gone, not left for someone else.
I can feel your fear; doesn't it feel strange?
While standing here inside, we'll still be left out in the rain.
Kate Lockwood

If Time Could Be Changed

I wish I were on a plane going down in flames of history over the ocean that holds the key to time and centuries gone by. The triangle between the past, the present, and the future. The magic of it all, the revolutions, the chances that could be taken, things to change, no light beyond death, no disappointments of things done or that could be done. Everlasting time to do whatever, whenever, just turn the key and fly back. Hell fly forward, see what's yet to come. But yet, it makes you think. Life is what you make it and what you've already made. Only you can make the time and that key turn for yourself and it's only going forward. Life was given to people so there would be history, so there would be surprise in the end. You were put on earth for time and most just waste it wondering if they could have changed it all.
Dottie Scalzi

As I Watch

Little people arise bringing the dawn.
They yawn, then scurry about as I watch.
One is the painter, colouring the morning sky.
But why, never the same as I watch.
Another, sits and cries the tears, which scatter.
They splatter the earth with dew, as I watch.
A third, awakens the animals big and small.
With a call, sweet and innocent, as I watch.
The fourth has brushed the stars away, Lit the fire.
Small squire of the mighty sun, as I watch.
They gather to sing the morning songs.
Each belongs, I hear them as I watch.
Suddenly, they are gone, grown to mighty breezes
Like sneezes, four little people, as I watch
The day has begun, gently awake my love.
Gaze above, enjoy this day, as little people watch.
Richard Allen Hendren

I Sea, I See

I sea, I see
A vastness beyond compare
A depth outlasting our care
I am nature classless and free

I sea, Aye Sea! I see
You plunging daggers in me
Thinking you have confined and conquered me
Before I've begun to set my power free

I sea, Aye Sea! I see
Man shrivelled amongst his boats
Reading from historic quotes
Screaming in nature's anguish
With only one Godly wish
To rid the salt from his wounds of me

I sea, Aye Sea! I see
More life than man can give
More strife than he could live
I'm the bearer of life, earth's guard
The cradle and the graveyard
I am Sea and I see, do you?
H. C. Waldt

Lord

Fire, fire everywhere
Dear Lord is the devil walking around here?
Children killing children for no reason
Is this the devil's greeting
Where's the love, hope and charity
Respect, understanding and caring?
"Lord" if we all stop the same time each day
For three minutes just to pray
Maybe it would chase the devil away!
Gloria C. Thomas

Could You Be Love

Could you be loved and give love
The road is very rocky and you need someone too
So why not ask yourself if someone is loving you.

Patience is a virtue, virtue is a grace
Before touching your waist, there must be a smile on your face
Talk really candid but not going too far
Massaging where it hurts and things like that star.

Support you to the fullest with breakfast in bed
Letting you know chivalry is not dead
A Shaka-zulu Romeo will show you how to be living
Sweet heart of mine to be giving.

Love will go on for many days
Could you be loved in infinite ways
The roses are red, the violets are blue
Could you be loved from someone true.

A soul of romance even when all things are gone
In other words, let's get it on
Won't you try this love, try this love
Could you be loved and know of...
Evon E. Simpson

Fear

My daily acquaintance
a lifelong frequenter
fear has been my timidity
apprehension my diffidence
at first thought, a foe to be vanquished
an evil to be undone
but through so many years, so much pain,
no more to be conquered. It cannot be aborted.
Instead, I have given it to me. It is my gift.
I embrace it to my bosom, this motherless child.
I cleave fast to it and make it my strength.
Fear is my friend, my comrade, my compatriot.
Together, we go to war.
This recalcitrant orphan
that no one desires to own
but everyone does.
Donna J. Volmerding

May You Always Walk In Sunshine

May you always walk in sunshine,
May you slumber warm when night wind blows,
May you always live with laughter,
For a smile becomes you so.

May good fortune find your doorstep,
May the bluebirds sing your song,
May your troubles travel your way,
May no worries stay too long.

May your heartaches be forgotten,
May no tears be spilled,
May old acquaintance be remembered,
May your cup of kindness filled.

May you always be a dreamer,
May your wildest dream come true,
May you find someone to love you,
Just as much as I love you.
Brenda J. West

Extra Mile

When you toss out those old garments, and you put them in a sack,
think about the people with no clothes on their back.
While we're rushing here and there friends and family to meet,
think about the children with no shoes on their feet.
We run home each evening to eat a hearty meal,
there's someone who's hungry, think how he feels.
Look into your heart and try to be a friend,
there's someone who needs you around every bend.
The elderly person who's home all alone,
sometime during the day, just pick up the phone.
Say Hi, how are you, take time to share,
and use those precious moments to show you really care.
Don't spend your money on things you don't need,
choose an unfortunate family you can help to feed.
Have a little kindness, be a little bold,
help that homeless victim who's out in the cold.
Then there's the parents that can't afford a toy,
spend some of your money on a girl or boy.
When your day is over and you've help create a smile,
your heart will be contended, because you went that extra mile.

Bonnie LaPradd

Passive Love

I caught myself glancing out the window
    Pondering on the fact that you're gone.
As I linger for tomorrow,
    I stand alone.

Of all the times I could let you see
    That my heart carried an affection.
My love for you burned inside of me
    While my soul was daunted for rejection.

Of all the times I could express,
    So you'd know how much you meant,
That I wanted you and no one else;
    But my fragile heart was silent.

If I could have just one more chance,
    I'd share everything to seize the day.
I'd give you all the romance;
    I'd throw my fears away.

For better or for worse(whether you loved me or not),
    You knew nothing and my heart is dismal.
As your departure came, we reached naught;
    That made me the biggest fool of all.

Matthew E. Kasunick

A Change In The Way That Life Smells

These are the days that love and life
grow like cherry blossoms in my heart
waiting to bloom into delicate, miraculous
signs of life and the tremendous love to come.

These are the days that look back
at the black days of yester years
with tears and sighs of relief; yet, a smile.
A large, grand grin like the Dead-man,
whose life lay out before him
knows and sees good in it.
Like he who smiles at a toothless Death
who comes to carry him away.

And as he sails into the sky,
Death riding his crippled crow
leading the way,
the Dead-man, the Good-man
sails the wind like a kite,
his good deeds like wings
that guide him into
an eternal bright future.

Diane Tajak

The Wind

I am the wind
    Illusive and unseen.
You say you know me
    that I am your friend - your lover
    but do you?

Can you show me to someone and say
    "there goes the wind"
Can you hold me - touch me - comfort me?
    Or do you have only my results
    after I pass by?

I can freeze you or fry you.
I can seduce you or scare you.
I can help you or harm you.
I can torment you or tame you.
I can be your friend or your foe.
I can howl or whisper.
Or - I can quit you altogether.
But you don't know me
    for I am... the wind

Sandy Scheffel

It's Ok

It's Ok to be less than perfect.
To screw up, occasionally goof.
Nobody's going to hate you.
No one will raise the roof.

It's Ok to let people fend for themselves.
You're helping them more if you do.
You can't take care of everyone.
The one you'll be hurting is you.

It's perfectly Ok to disagree.
Who says they're always right?
Respectfully suggest another view.
No need for confrontations or fights.

It's Ok to go with your instincts
Even when proven wrong.
Don't be just another face in the crowd;
Much better to sing your own song.

So now that I've given my lecture
It's time I believe what I say.
It's time to take charge of my life once again.
It's time to realize it's Ok.

Dottie Krug

'Different Perspective'

My Head is spinning, I keep seeing illusions.
Every question I grab at gives me an answer of confusion.
We're seeing things from a different perspective,
and after a while we seem a bit more neglective,
to try and get answers from inside our own minds,
so instead we ask others, to see what they'll find.
They say you're loony and going insane,
"Those problems you've got girl are all in your brain!
Sit down and relax a bit, try on this new jacket,
and when I show you your padded room,
please make a little less racket."
They tell us we're crazy and our heads just aren't right,
but the reality is that they're just not that bright.
You see the problem is they just don't understand...
We think about things differently, so that life's not so bland.

Bobbi Jean Grassmyer

Peace

I live and breathe more steady now for now you're gone,
Where once my pace was rushed it now is toned,
I take up one-time slack to some degree:
For old haphazard ways are now more measured, slowed,

Our bittersweet encounter left me lone on pilgrim's rock,
Free to recall the kinder, gentler you now passed,
Free to miss, to mourn my fantasy warm freckled friend,
Freedom... Bound ... Too long.

Many hours I pressed your recreated flesh anyway I wished, till
finally I sucked your blood and tied your lifeless limbs (now torn),
I packed 'em up, then picked your bones and played as puppy would,
My curious companions, my toys, my sticks - a tune with them I
thrashed, begun as dirge;
Then lively, raucous, frenzied it became till...crash

Wild, unknowing, wanton, I danced, I trod on them
And powder, pumice made ... you're flecks,
Some onto ground, some into water, and most in air,
Dispersed you are, and gone, yet everywhere,
And I can live and breathe more steady now for now you're gone...
almost.

Carole Dombroski

The Lone Cypress

The moon, almost full,
a metaphor for my life.
I need you to hold me, but you're not there.
Who are you anyway?
Friends,
busy with their lives,
can't be reached on a moment's notice.
She calls to me and I go.

The lone cypress, guardian of the purpose, as am I.
I lay my body down on the cool earth.
She wraps her exposed and twisted roots around me
and sings me a lullaby to the rhythm of the flowing ocean.
In these roots her vulnerability is revealed, not unlike my own.
I gaze upward, drinking in the light from the heavens.
Her powerful limbs reach into the night sky
as if to pull the moon into our embrace.
My body softens with the caress of the gentle breeze across my brow.
I melt into her body, my thoughts rushing away with the tide.

Within the solitude I have found my connection.

Dawn Griffin

The Message Of The Rose

In a crystal vase stood a long-stemmed rose.
 Bending slightly in sweet repose.
It seemed to awaken as I walked by,
 for in the distance I heard a faint little cry,
Saying... I have a secret just for you.
It comes from a person whose heart is true.
The message is from the giver of me,
 to add to your joy of my beauty you see.
Its words are those that a bluebird sings,
 and heard in the flutter of angels' wings.
An ancient phrase from ancient days,
 by now you must have a clue.
It's those beautiful words so often heard,
 just a simple "I love you."

Teeny Fulghum Waters

Senior Citizen Trip To Atlantic City

With spirits high and smiling faces,
In numerical order we took our places.
A pit stop at ten - we rushed out in a clump,
You'd think we had entered the castle called Trump.

As we neared the city with anticipation,
They waited with open arms for our donation.

A somber note neath the glamorous facade,
An historic city raped and downtrod.
A vision of blight assailed our eyes,
Diminished us to silence and to sighs.

After cashing our vouchers and dredging up pluck,
We went separate ways to try our luck.

With poker, roulette, black-jack and slots,
The choice was hard — lugging our pots
Of coins around from one place to next,
To find a spot that wasn't hexed.

After hours of poker - with triples and pairs,
I still brought home one buck—of theirs!

Ida Janko Balbirer

North Star

Sometimes we go so far,
Reaching for that gleaming star,
That ever rests in northern sky,
Are we so high, so high we seem to fly?
Look down upon the earth, so pure, so clean,
And think it just another grand scheme,
To which our lives are the script - the parts and
characters ever changing,
The world around us ever rearranging.

Or do we look down to see,
A world containing all that's ugly,
And all the wrongs and faults within,
Watching all the sinners sin,
Sometimes to me it seems that way,
But, then, I think there'll be a brighter day,
When all shall come together in peace,
And in one another, find great surcease.

Larina Crapo

The Question

They see the trees green
They see the sky blue
They see a baby conceived in a womb.
They see it rain then change to sunshine
They see it snow
They see beautiful rainbows
Yet that can't conceive Almighty God who yearns to
love them here below.
Instead evolution is their plan
From monkey to a man
Or a great big explosion that started somewhere
in the ocean.
Let them have their theories whatever they may be
But when they search their hearts they'll find Christ
died for thee.
When times get rough try praying to the ocean
Or to a monkey give him all your devotion
I'll take Jesus who answers all my prayers
I'll take Jesus who was crucified to show how much He cares.

Donna E. Zimmerman

Assassin

I don't like presidents.
It's not hard to see.
The Secret Service was made just for me.

I'm not like Jimmy Hoffa.
I don't try to abuse.
I'm going to make you an offer,
That you can't refuse.

You had better hope I like you.
I have a can of mace.
I might just have to hurt you,
Because I don't like your face.

Don't play nice with me,
Because I don't forgive.
It's no use trying to flee,
Because I know where you live.

So if you ever see me,
You'd better watch what you say.
If you make me angry,
You're going to have to pay.
   Billy Manolios

My Feelings

There you are across the hall.
I can't help but stare
My knees weaken at the thought of your touch.
But shyness has brought me down so low
Even though I don't have a clue.
What I feel for you
Now I'm beginning to see
You've given me friendship, respect and love
I'm not looking for love it's true
But love found me and it's you
Since the day you told me
I've never been the same
Now I'm living with out you
I just can't let go
It hurts so much living without you
Let me take your hand my love
And tell you my feelings.
   Chastity Caton

My Valentine To You

This little poem may be minute and/or far from great.
When it comes to buying cards, I do procrastinate.

I may, at times, seem somewhat petulant or malign.
In my heart, my intentions are nothing short of divine.

My emotions and affection are often blanketed with snow.
Although concealed, adoration and love illuminate my soul.

Romance and Chivalry seldom fit my part.
But then again, you're worthy of a start.

There is never a moment you're not in mind
Whether I'm pressing too fast or running behind.

Seeing your melancholy I clearly detest.
For you, my love, I want only the best.

All I can offer is a simplified I Love you!
What can I say? This is My Valentine to You.
   Donny R. Hearn

The Whole Truth

The truth is like a breath of air. It suddenly comes and goes
Like light that fades into the dark and no one really knows
where it is.
Though people seek it without cease, it's never yet been found.
Real truth is heaven sent while we are earthly bound.
That's why it is.
Like Pilate, we can have the real pure truth standing there before us
unrecognized as the only truth with power to restore us.
We ask what it is.
The kinds of truth absorbed by man and given full dominion
Is what he sets his mind upon, a matter of his opinion.
That's how it is.
Man has opined all kinds of truth that's seldom heard the same.
It's torn, twisted and reshaped into a sport, a game.
A pity, it is.
If one desires to know the truth, the best that can be seen
Is found in the book of John and numbered three sixteen.
And there it is.
   M. C. Van Wagner

The Mist

Mist,
The evil swirling mist,
Forever roaming,
My piercing hush of tranquility,
And my deathly, brutal breeze.
The silence follows,
Echoing soundlessly on and on.
My powerful arms,
Endlessly stretching,
Clothing the entire world of viability.
I spread and disperse,
More malignant and malevolent than ever.
The world of existence,
Is now at its decease.
I leave,
Abandoning the world,
With the presence of life in nature motionless,
Into whatever lies beyond.
   Audrey Bui

Mommies Lap Is Back!

Dad and Mom both truthfully told me,
"Mom will have a baby girl shortly."

While Mom's belly just grew and grew,
Over the months, her lap shrunk too -

I loved to sit and cuddle on Mommies lap.
But as her lap got smaller, her tummy got fat!

My mom's lap's so small now; no longer can sit
The 5 year old Joann, who's having a fit - -

Both Dad and Mom said, "Don't cry and be forlorn"
"Mom's lap will come back, after sister is born".

My sister 'Sedona' arrives - beautiful and well
Mom is most grateful, my Dad's proud as hell.

I do love my sister - - and that is a fact:
"Happy times for Joann again - - - -

Mommies lap is back!
   Richard Blaisdell

What Is Love?

I knew not from where it came or even where it went
I never knew it was something that did not smell of scent,

Searching for the answer of this thing called love
My mind would wonder as I searched the sky above,

Will I know it by touch, by feel, by smell?
Tell me, will I know it in my heart when it fell?

Is it in the hugs and kisses which I never had?
Was it in the scoldings given, as child when bad?

The answer will come inside of me, I felt
My questions are simple, to God I have knelt.

As an adult I yearn for this thing which I missed
What can I do for this thing I have wished?

Searching my soul, my heart and my brain
I discovered the answer through my searches in vain,

Love is a warmth, spreading through you like fire
Emotions are felt, your heart fills with desire,

Compassion takes over inside of you
You can see and relate to the overall view,

Caring for others, yourself is included
That is love, in its fullness exuded.

Roberta Fernandez

Hidden Creatures

Staring at the walls of my room
Corners fold into themselves
Creatures coming out of the creases
The walls are falling to pieces

Heat turned way up
Drinking out of a paper cup
The sea of nightmares and bad dreams
are all coming true

They walk about
and bother you until you die

That is not the last you will see of them
They will be back
When you knock over that stack
They will make you feel bad
Till you change
Then you will be glad
You had a conscience

Carolyn Welker

Untitled

How can I begin to tell of the feelings deep within?
Words alone cannot express all that my heart does hold.
The gratitude and love I feel for my Lord must somehow be told.

Like the morning sun lights the day,
You light my life the very same way.
You are my tower of strength, my source of everything;
It is unto you praises I sing,
You give warmth and meaning to my years and put an end to my
  inner fears.
You dried my eyes that lonely night and whispered "Hush my child
it will be all right."
You were there in my time of need, and anguish began to recede.
You died on Calvary that I might live, and life to me you truly did
  give.
The peace; the joy; the deep content from knowing what is meant to
be your child;
You are my God!

Florence Lunde

The Shadows Of The Storm

Shadows make the day seem so magnificent
Although the shadows of darkness may increase again.
Through the shadows of the storm, the wind may
Blow, it's the sound of the whistling thunder,
The shadow of the storm.
It's destiny to be subsequent to the intense
Of activated magestim makes the environment
Still a day to day living, in which it still
Increases it's intense to the echoes of the
Thunder, you can still hear the cry of the
Shadows of the storm.
The shadows of the storm, is here for us to see
Though it's clear and dark in a gloomy way,
To seek the light of the storm, in pretense it's
The shadows of the storm.
Nor am I beneath you or surround you
For I am the shadow of the storm.
To reach my intense, I may hide in the back
Of clouds, but in pretense again, I am the
Shadows of the storm.

Katrina Diane Smith

Enigma

My heart bleeds for...

   The armless, deformed newborn, famine and starvation victims,
   Widows, widowers, grieving mothers and fathers, orphans,
   The crippled and the maimed of senseless wars.

My heart questions...

   Why? No justice in this world?
   The ruthless live in style; the law-abiding wallow in misery?
   Is there an omniscient but merciless God?

My heart listens...

   This world is only half of your life,
   If a whole life were an apple,
   You are holding only half,
   The other half is with Me!

My heart understands...

   Life is both matter and spirit
   Life is a full life-death cycle,
   Full and complete only with Thee.

Paz R. Dorotheo

Why Do The Willows Weep?

Why do the willows weep?
They are beautiful!

What moon shines in your eyes?
Is he your moon?
As you are mine
A shining beacon,
in the dark, night sky?

And how is it,
that you have reached your moon?
You must be a magical fantasy
For I can't reach you...
My moon...

Now I know why the willows weep
Even when they are straight and stretched
They cannot reach the moon

Kevin Elliott

I Really Don't Like The Winter

I really don't like the winter.
The old barn is starting to splinter;
It turned the butter bitter.
I really don't like the winter.

The minister at church says snow is the worst.
My neighbor almost lost her purse;
Everything is here or hither.
I really don't like the winter.
Michelle Huang

Bound By A Nail

There he hung, each hand bound by a nail.
The man beside him knelt saying: "You're the only one we hail!"
"Let's bury him now, so he's not disturbed,
For he was so kind, and his promise was his word."
They buried him in a tomb, so he could rest in peace.
But little did they know, that he was not quite deceased.
An Angel came, suddenly from above,
Flying like a bird, or maybe a dove.
The man came back as the angel stated at the top of her voice:
"He Has Risen Beside Mankind's Choice!"
For he came back, despite his fall.
Because he came back, to save us all.
Scott Lambert

The Lamb Slain

His purpose was to come one day through channels never tried,
To prove that all men had need of God to sanctify their lives.
With a dialect of wisdom; salvation he proclaimed,
Jesus, the lamb slain; who rose and will return again.

He came with love and brought us hope that healed the multitude,
He taught each man whose ear would hear the only truth he knew.
He beckoned man to heed God's call, and then from sin abstain,
Jesus, the lamb slain; who rose and will return again.

He went through out the land warning men, young and old;
For he knew he'd be the sacrifice that would redeem man's soul.
His destiny was calvary; to give life was his aim,
Jesus, the lamb slain; who rose and will return again.

He found men who believed in him; said by his side they'd stay,
but he already knew he'd be the one that they'd betray.
By many he was ridiculed and scorned to say the same,
Jesus, the lamb slain; who rose and will return again.

Because of man's ignorance and blatant disbelief,
They mocked his name and pierced his flesh; hung him amid two
  thieves.
Yet he's Lord to all who'll give their lives, and loyal will remain,
Jesus, the lamb slain; who rose and will return again.
Christine P. Evans

This African Knot Can Sure Take A Lot

Through wind storms, rains, and falling hail-
this African Knot can sure take a lot.

Through temporary permanents, hot combs, and
brain-tugging braids - this African Knot can sure
take a lot.

When teeth are elongated, and health is fair,
still strong and firm will be this knotted hair.

And when death comes to claim its ultimate prize,
to no one's surprise - the strength of this hair
will still be there.

And even in the end- my friend, this African
Knot can sure take a lot- more!
Sylvia T. Giordano

Smile

A smile is a treasure that is free in the giving,
For those who receive it, a life worth living,
The memory of it will forever last,
The giver much happier as the smile is cast.

It creates a joy that is unforetold,
It's something that can't be bought or sold,
A smile brings peace of mind to the depressed,
A ray of sunshine to those distressed.

A smile that is warm and true,
Is the smile worth giving to you,
It takes so little to impart,
When it comes right from the heart,

There are some too weary to smile,
You give them one it will prove worthwhile,
Broken hearts are again made whole,
By a smile that magnifies the soul.
Edith Madge

Tears For A Friend

Dust settles in corners once filled with life
My eyes wonder around to empty walls and
This is the last time, my friend, it cries
Doors swish and loneliness hides in windows

You were a part of my life
So large and roomy with steps to skip over
and space to run
I learned to love your flaws
steep hill to climb and doors that stick
As you learned to love mine
banging of the walls and running about
But still, we knew this day would come
Never did we think so soon, so soon

Walls of white and halls of gray
Our life was yours as yours was ours
Never will we forget....
Memories will linger
like flashes on the mind to transcend
good from it all...

So farewell, old friend
Vonnie Van Dyke

A Belief

I awoke suddenly.
It was the light that did it; nothing else.
And I jumped out of bed;
ran to the window;
look out and stretched;
because the first rays of the rising sun
had cast out the dread of night past.
And then I smiled,
for the warmth of the sun felt good
upon my body.
And I knew in my heart that this day
would be full of adventure, surprise,
and even disappointment.
But I cared not because like yesterday,
and all the days before;
once again the sun had brought forth
another day for me to live fully;
by truly believing again
that night will never prevail
in its endless struggle against day.
Christopher David Pascal

Untitled

With every passing wind-comes an Old story-
with a New meaning -
a new Thought with the same idea;
the Realization of an old world with a new Generation of people-
with that new generation comes new Ideas and Thoughts that are Yet to happen...
because those who live in the past have no future or no True Beginning-
because life can only be what you make it...

Barbara Guimaraes

Daughter

Daughters I have been blessed with four
Each one I love and adore
They all help to brighten my day
Each one unique in her own way
Through the years I've often been told
Each one a beauty to behold
To help complete this work of art
Each one a kind and loving heart
Best friends with each other is nice to see
Each one a best friend to me
Daughters I have been blessed with four
Each one I love and adore

Marie Paul

Hopelessness

I reach out to grasp life's blessings, I earnestly stretch out my hand, The essence of life just misses my reach, leaving emptiness I can't understand. I find myself hiding while searching my thoughts, perched atop a high wall. As it separates me from desire and hope while I cringe in fear that I'll fall,

The prison that traps and surrounds me, has no real bars and chains, But I'm trapped here nonetheless, by the powerlessness that always remains. The icy fingers of fear grip me, distorting images with nowhere to turn, Hope is dashed like fallen leaves, that wither and dye as they burn.

Somewhere in all the pain and fear is the answer, a vague illusive key
The map that leads me through the maze as the opening is revealed to me. I don't know when it will happen, but I still will faithfully wait, As God will showers me with his abundant grace as he leads me through the gate.

So while I sit in my prison of fear, with eyes that cannot see, I know one day I'll find my reward and reveal in a spirit that is free. For no matter how tightly I am bound, nor how hopeless I can be, I know one day I will walk in the light and joy, together God and me.

Linda Irwin

My Dear Family

Good memories have past, bad memories have past
But we don't know what will happen tomorrow
So say what you need to say before it's all over
The world may end today or tomorrow but within
Your heart you don't want to feel sorrow
What you put off today may not come tomorrow
So give them love that will fade the sorrow
These are the memories of tomorrow

Jalisha Norton

Crucifix Vs Tennis Racket

I claimed the nail to be my own, on the wall next to my bed.
On it I hung my crucifix, devotedly, overhead.

My "heathen" sibling, took it down; in anger tossed it aside.
Shouting, "I'll hang my racket here!" "Find another place!" I cried

The battle started between us, as I threw her racket down.
She snatched it back up and hit me. She was aiming for my "crown"!

I told her that she was "rotten", to cast our Lord, down like that.
And someday in her future years, she'd pay for being a "brat!"

We shoved and slapped each other 'round, fighting for half of the night.
Both of us wrong as we could be, thinking ourselves to be "right!"

Our mother came to end the fight, telling us to go to bed.
Promising stricter punishments, if we failed to do as said.

As soon as Mom was out of sight, our fighting continued once more.
We vowed we'd settle in the morn'... we threatened and even swore.

With hammer in hand, Mom returned, and yanked the nail from the wall.
"I'll have no more of this damned fight...you'll hang NOTHING up at all!"

She shouted as she left the room; my heart was full of sorrow.
Still I vowed, my secret plans to, nail God, back up tomorrow!

Patricia Thayer

This Heart Of Mine

This heart of mine, I wonder why?
Has dreams and visions of beyond the sky.
Of life relit and hope renewed,
Of someone special with the needed food,
To warm my heart and feed my soul!
Who is this one who will make me whole?
Questions and answers I may never know!
But you my friend who I care for so,
Have given to me a part of you,
I know down deep is real and true!
For the times we've spent and the words we've shared,
Are far to precious to be compared
To those before or who may come,
I thank my God from where you're from!
And your friendship's a gift so rare and so fine
You'll always have a place in this heart of mine!

Neil W. Brown

My Life

As I gaze into the stars at night
I realized how good it is to be alive.
I think about my future in living,
What my job will be like, and most of all,
If I can be as strong to myself with the
Flow of motion in my heart which eases my
Pains and gives me happiness.

Through the days that I roam this earth I know I'm not a
Big movie star or just someone important, but I do know
that my life is like a big surprise waiting to happen.
It's like a question in my mind that will be wondering when the
time will come for my first day of death and when that
Time comes, I will have pride in myself and will not be that afraid
To know my life is just beginning.

Michelle L. Grey

Spring

Spring is sunny, but showers may fall,
Pretty flowers pop up and grow tall,
Roaring bears wake up from their sleep,
Insects are eaten by birds that go "peep",
Nectar is moved from flower to flower,
Gracefully they grow after each little shower.
Caitlyn M. Gallagher

Blue

Blue on my flag-
Blue always in the sky-
Blue in my home-
Blue, I see you every day-
Blue so magnificent-
Blue my very favorite color-
Blue, you're so beautiful to me, oh can't you see-
Blue, I don't know what to say
You're in my every day life I hope and pray-
Oh Blue, I really, really love you-
Blue, when I look up after feeding Gertrude,
You're always there-
Amen-
John Morgan III

Pray

Every Night I go on
My Knees and pray.
Every night I ask
Jah Jah, to help me.
Every night I ask Jah Jah,
for forgiveness for my sins.
Every night I ask Jah Jah, to protect me
Every Night I thank
You Jah Jah, for letting me live
Every Night I told you
I love you, Jah Jah.
Every Night I ask Jah Jah,
When are you going to save us all
Every night I pray to you
Jah Jah, when are you going to take me out of hell.
Every night I pray my faith gets stronger
Every night I pray I ask
Jah Jah, to keep my soul in heaven
Every Night I pray
I say. Amen! Amen!
Omar R. Santos

My Favorite Color

My favorite color is blue.
It reminds my of the sky on sunny days with puffy clouds
   that float lazily above my head.
Some days the sapphire ocean turns fierce, with long rolling
   waves and bubbly white-caps like fizz in champagne,
   as water hits the hard, sandy shore.
When storms approach, the atmosphere changes from azure to
   gray and strong winds blow.
I believe the color of blue best describes life.
Some days are the cerulean of sunny days; births, celebrations,
   and special times.
Other days are the silver-blue days of storms; sickness,
   misfortunes, and just plain bad luck.
I enjoy the blue sky of sunny days best!
Jacqueline Moffett

Wild Orchids

Musing and walking step to step on the beach. Rio de janeiro,
Black volcanic sand between our toes. Orchids in your hair,
Corcovado a silhouette in the night wind. Time and distant sky
We walked hand in hand. Faint glimmers of golden orange sky
Peaking between the mountains night face. As the sun sets in
Another place, at the same time with brilliant hue's and hint's of
Aurora Borealis — luminous streamers of light, like memories
Hover in the darkness over head and whisper as flickering lights
Beckon from basic black with amber glow. All light is absorbed
Into nights black abyss, as it is still except for the swish of
Water along the shores where and orchid rests withered. The echoing
Voice's of sea bird's against the moon's night face. Luna Negra,
Black moon like a gleaming jewel hung in the southern night sky.
Black moon, white orchids, rainforest and you. Two under luna
Night's waxing orb, in step into the distance nearer the oceans
Spray. We are prisoners of time's persistence and time is
Persistent — and time does persist.
Waits for none, and like a Dali painting!! Is surreal, abstract yet
Oh so real in it's unreality.
Farrell Hall

Senses

You are not blind.
Open your eyes and see the world in jeopardy.
You are not deaf.
Open your ears and listen to the horrendous cries.
Can you smell it?
The nauseating aroma of anger and fear.
Can you feel it?
The gruesome pain touching your glossy skin.
Can you taste the demoralized words that linger in the air?
You are not moronic.
Open your minds and know that the world has become enraged.
Wars and poverty are in every corner of our lives.
You are not savage.
Open your hearts and feel the world crashing like an eagle with
   broken wings.
Guns and drugs are being sold in our schools and streets.
Open your eyes.
Understand that the world won't mend itself.
Open your minds.
Use your knowledge to sew back the torn earth.
Janise Buyco

Dear Death...

Ah, the absence of light
muffled, deafening
the threshold
bonding what is and with not
comforting pains of the flesh
exposing abstract cuts
drowns sight from thought
Blankets of intense cold
satisfactory remnants of decay
enhance unremembrance within storms
of electricity
of the survivors
of a war deemed life
as disturbed earth lies forever undisturbed upon the grave
a last request
from a dying past
peace
content
and endless rest
Gunther Lipchzech

Escape

I am seven, tiny enough to fit
neatly inside the curve of your belly
where I hold onto you as you shake
lightly in my little arms. Your cries
blow through my chest, make me cry.
My first glimpse, this rite:
swallowing the heavy ache
of loneliness and freedom
following generations of women
loving independence above everything
else they were meant to love, running
as if it were possible to escape
those peculiar places in space and time
holding us together (I am afraid to let them go.)
Abandon them and we abandon ourselves.

Lori Mann

Hold Onto Your Dreams

We all have a destiny
No matter what it may be
Some of us though
Let our dreams go
Because of knowing
The goal is hard going
To get to the top
We might even stop
And never make it too
Don't let that happen to you
Keep your head up high
Always reach for the sky
Never look down
Wipe away that frown
Remember success, it can really be yours
It hard work and determination endures.

Vera A. Hernandez

Memories

I once had a sister named Katie Jo.
I am really sad she had to go.
I have a lot of memories or stories to tell
about my little sister I loved so well.

She was always happy and singing a tune,
even in the garden in the middle of June.
She always had kisses and lots of big hugs,
She even played with toy dishes and little lady bugs.

Oh, how I miss her, and wish she was here,
But, God is always with her, so I have no fear.
Well, all I can say now is "I love you so,"
and, "Gee, I hated to see you go."

Dustin Kovarik

The Baron

I watched him from across the pond,
So statuesque and grand.
My breathing was the only clue
My presence was at hand.

The pond was calm, serene and still—
To make a sound defiling.
This interlude, for both of us
So special, so beguiling.

Where else could someone find such peace?
I dubbed my "friend" The baron
Who fled when crows soared high above.
You see, my friend's a heron!

Dorothy Howlett

Night Sky

At night you should watch the stars.
Sometimes you can see Mars.
You can look for shapes like chocolate bars.
It's fun to look at the stars.

Allie Paquette

If You Only Knew

If you only knew how I felt when I look at you, or when you look at me. You look at me with those sweet, gentle, loving eyes. The same sweet, gentle eyes I wish would look at me the same way you look at those "other girls". If you only knew. If you only knew how the touch of your hand made me feel loved and happy. The touch of your sweet, gentle hands made me feel more happy than I ever thought I could. If you only knew. If you only knew how I felt every time we we're together. I felt like I had never felt before. I always wanted you there, even though I knew you couldn't. You were to busy, but I understood. You had things to do. But you didn't know. How could you? Nobody knows. I never told you. It's not your fault. It was mine. If you only knew. If you only knew how I felt when I finally knew. I didn't know what to do. So I just cried. I could never tell you. If you could know the tears I cried for you. The tears I had to fight back when you talked about those "other girls". The "other girls" that I envied. How it hurt so bad. If you only knew. If you only knew how I felt. So many times I tried to tell you, but I couldn't. If you only knew that I didn't blame you. How could I? You didn't know. Nobody knew. I never told you. If you only knew...

Susan D. Joyce

Lunch Doesn't Frighten Me At All

Teachers scream loud, lunch room all crowd...
   Lunch doesn't frighten me at all!

Milk spills on the floor, kids laugh at the door
   Lunch doesn't frighten me at all!

Kids give me a headache, I give them ten cakes...
   Lunch doesn't frighten me at all!

I eat all my lunch, teachers have their brunch...
   No! Lunch doesn't frighten me at all!

That new classroom, were I have a lot of friends,
   I like the time when school ends...

Lunch doesn't frighten me at all!

Ambar DeLissa Torres

Running Feet

I look out the window
I see your running feet upon the walk
Kaleidoscope scenes of others quickly come
Disjointed happenings -
Unrelated events -
Crowd me with special effects
For the moment
I am out of sync
I stare into the window-pane
I see myself
I quickly smooth my hair
I am back in sync
Running feet are near my door
I wait
Running feet at my door
Shout!
Nana! I'm here

Janet P. Lontka

A Poet

What makes a poet?

It is not scientific
It is not medical
It is the innate ability to capture an emotion at its peak,
 and express it in words or feelings.
The ability to see the beauty not only in one's strength,
 but in one's weakness as well.
Savoring life's everyday experiences as if they were your last.
Retaining childlike qualities, yet tempering them as you grow
 into adulthood.

The power of emotion is what drives every poet.

I am a pure and simple man
yet as I write these words
tears fall from my face.

This is what makes A Poet.
Mark Dempsey

Love Is Like Water

Love is like water so sustaining within,
Water has always been here since the begin.

Like a tender plant that needs sun,
Love is like water cool, refreshing, always lots of fun.

Water and romance liquefying love,
You give it to me like a rain from above.

Love is like water, water is like love,
The two go hand and hand as we travel any barren land.

Yes, love is like water just as love is like many things,
Love will always be dear until there are no more springs.

Water will always flow and so will love,
As long as there's people who trust in the Creator above.
Richard J. Leützinger Jr.

At Heaven's Door

Looking down through his glassy eyes
We knew his time was near,
And all of us around his bed,
Had started shedding tears.

An as he stared up at the ceiling,
A smile upon his face.
He said they came to take him now,
To a far and better place.

So free of pain our father will be,
An that's how I hope we can remember thee.
So let him be free, so we can see,
Him walk through your gates so gallantly.

And as dad slowly slipped a way,
He looked at mom an begin to say,
Cheer up my darling for I'm going away,
But I will be back for you one day.

If it will ease your mind once more,
Just remember darling I'm here at heavens door.
So kiss me now so I can go,
An remember my dear I love you so.
Lori K. Gillespie Maddox

Tears Of Understanding

I can't explain what I feel inside,
There's so many emotions, too many to hide.
A mass of scars from love and life,
A lifetime of dreams lost in strife.

Years of hoping, wondering, and praying,
That someway, someday I would be saying;
'I've been through it all, enough is enough,'
But the days go on, and life is just as tough.

I'm sure it will end one of these years,
And when it does, there will still be tears.
Not tears of hurt, or sorrow, or pain,
But tears of understanding, of all I have gained.
Mary Sluck

She Had A Smile For Me, Yesterday

When the distance is greatest
when the flower is prettiest,
That's when the fragrance is strangest
more profound is love.

Many have said
that distance brings forgetfulness,
but that I'm always thinking
about you, feel that they have lied.

Many flowers in the country
are said to be beautiful,
but none have more enchantment
than the roses in a garden.

That is why I have never forgotten
and even though my resentment is great,
because of the one cupid, would have brought forth
now I remember her beauty and prelude.

What happens with the path
that we have left boarded with, thousands of colors,
others will come and dismay its divine heart
and the only thing that is left is the memory of love.
Jose A. Sagastume S.

Repentance

Will yonder tree replace the cross,
And satan, then, become the boss?
If he rules throughout the day,
Thou might even forget to pray;
Or will God's gift of the holy ghost
Remind thee of that heavenly host-
Singing, "Peace on earth, good will toward men"
Who will open their hearts, and let Christ in?

Which will it be for thee my brother?
One thing sure, It's one or the other.
If thou hast forgotten, this is his day,
Tis not too late for thee to say:
"Forgive Me Lord, I know it's late,
But into thy hands I place my fate;
Include me in that prepared place,
Which began on Christmas, by thy grace."
E. Edward Kipp

Lazy

whatsthepointwhymoveattallimperfectlyfineonthisnice
couchwithmychipsanddipmyclickerforthetvandanicesoft
pillowivegotsomeonetofeedmeandeventhoughtheyreout
rightnowimokwithoutthemittakestoomuchenergytotalkto
heranywaywaitnowimoutofchipsandshesnothomewhat
willIdowelliguessicouldstarvetodeaththatdoesnttake
mucheffort.
Alex N. Moros

Today, Forever And Always

I sit here in the dark, candle flickering down low, sitting with his arms around me our hearts close to each others.

My heart beating one-thousand beats a minute...

Feeling my heart turn to fire when he whispers softly in my ear I love you.

Feeling like jumping for joy, but instead I simply lean over and whisper I love you too.

But today is full of darkness and doom, for today while puffing the pillows, I find a picture of his son and wife.

So tonight I sit here in the dark and weep for we must say goodbye, forever and always.

Not knowing what to say when he arrives, searching every inch of my mind, but only finding darkness and pain.

Wanting to be somewhere else and somebody new, them maybe the pain would go away, today, forever and always!

Angela Smith

Street Ball

To some, it is just a game, to others
it brings fame. You play on the street
or on a field. Watch out for cars or
your fate will be sealed. If you don't
catch it, you'll have to fetch it. You
run bases, maybe a trash can or, a little
boy, they grab the ball, tag you, you
hang your head and walk away from
your defeat, maybe your friends will meet
their feat on some other street.

Adam Summerford

Nathan's Lullaby

I wish I had little Nathan's eyes.
  Then, I'd see what makes him cry.
I wish I had little Nathan's ears.
  Then, I'd hear what gives him tears.
I wish I could hold little Nathan's hand.
  He is Mommy's little man.
I wish I could hold Nathan in my arms
  And keep him safe from any harm.

Nathan, Nathan, please don't cry.
  Mommy'll sing you a lullaby.

I wish I knew how to make him see
  How this world's a better place for me.
I wish I knew the words to say
  How much Mommy loves him today.
Lord, send an angel to watch him close
  And keep him safe where'er he goes.
Give him dreams of sweet things tonight.
  Let him rest 'til tomorrow's light.

Nathan, Nathan, please don't weep.
  You just lay there and go to sleep.

Calvin Ray Turnage Jr.

Satin Flowers

Flowers of gold, flowers of pink,
I wonder why we're made to think.
Flowers of fuchsia, flowers of white,
Is my dog's bark worse than her bite?
Flowers of maple, flowers of gray,
Why is there sudden rain on a warm sunny day?
Flowers of pink, flowers of gold,
Can the answers to these questions ever be told?

Rachel Hock

As I Watch

As I watch he holds her hand,
He loves her so tenderly.
Kisses of passion flow through the air,
As I watch.

As I watch, they walk along the sandy beach.
He sings a sweet love song.
As she listens with her heart, I hear words of love.
As I watch.

As I watch they walk home together,
Talking about how much they love each other.
As they talk I see the fire burning in their eyes,
As I watch.

As I watch he says, "I love you!"
She holds him close and
Whispers back softly, "I love you too!"
As I watch.

Ashley Bergeron

Little Brothers

If you have a little brother, he will be a pain. He will be worse than a day that rains and rains and rains. This is not all I'm sorry to say, all your attention will be taken away, and given to him. And then your mother, will start to forget you.
All because of your little brother.

At the age of three, he will be much worse.
He will not stay out of your room, or he'll fuss, and fuss, and fuss.

At the age of four, more and more bad luck will come your way. You may even have to do something like play-WITH HIM? NO WAY! I REFUSE TO PLAY WITH YOU! SO NOW GO AWAY. If this happens I'm sorry but it's true, he will have to play with you.

At the age of five, it will be the same routine, he will be just as mean.

At the age of seven, he'll be NO heaven. You will have to walk to school with- WITH HIM? NO WAY! THAT WOULD BE SO UNCOOL! But still it is true. He ends up having to walk with you. Then all the kids will laugh, because you are going down the path - OF BEING HIS BABY-SITTER? NO WAY! NOW JUST GO AWAY! Someday this is true.
Probably after school, you will have to baby-sit for him.

But in the end, you will sometimes depend on him.
Then you know you have passed the test of brother and sisterhood.

Kathryn C. Jacoby

A Poet

I would like to be a Poet.
  But that's not really me.
For a Poet must be meek and mild, and have sincerity.
  Me, I have to work hard each and everyday.
So, I have no time to smell the flowers,
  And watch the children play.
And, when it comes to sincerity, hard work get in the way.
But, if I were a Poet, I know how I would be.
For I would write about the things,
  That set my caged heart free.
I would also try to write about,
  The things that interest you.
Some things would make you feel good.
  Some things would make you think.
Some things that on a rainy day,
  Would cause your eyes to blink.
If I were a Poet, that is what I would do.
  Take the feelings in my heart,
And share them all with you.

Clifford Etienne

A Time To Say Goodbye

The news came just the other day
That I was going to be going away.
The tears stung as they fell on my cheeks
I didn't have very many more weeks.
What would I say and what would I do?
I knew I was going to leave all of you.
The years have quickly come and gone
And I loved to see each new morning dawn.
This world gave me loved ones dear-
Ones that now I long to have near,
But as the sun quietly sets today
I sense that Jesus is coming my way.
For my new home in glory I'm bound
A place where no sickness is to be found.
My prayer for all of you that I am leaving
Is that you'll soon stop grieving
And live your life as God would want you to live,
Accepting the comfort and love He will give
And in what will seem to be a short span of time
You can have a home in heaven next to mine.

Linda L. Cottrell

Prejudice And Acceptance

Prejudice is a volcano.
Heat and pressure boiling under a fiery vent exploding into the world.
Acceptance is daybreak.
Growing stronger, brightening the light in which we see ourselves as equal. Prejudice is the swift flow of a river.
Undependable and unstoppable.
Acceptance is the first flower of spring.
Risking destruction to spread cheer to others.
Prejudice is a bitter storm.
Escalating the feeling of isolation and blindness towards its fury.
Acceptance is the shore of Paradise.
Stretching as far as the eye can see, if only we look in the right direction. Prejudice is the wild, frantic accusation towards those that appear to be different. It is the failure to accept those differences. Acceptance is a hole in the wall of bigotry. Starting small, but tunneling through the barriers that have resulted through history and have separated us from understanding.
Acceptance is the destruction of prejudice.
Prejudice is the destruction of our country.

Emily D. Griffeth

My Daughter.. Have I Lost You?

My baby, my child, my daughter!
How could you become so cold,
turn your back and forget me...
How could your loyalty be sold?

My cherished daughter, born unto me
like a miracle or dream come true!
It seems as though I have truly and sadly lost you!

The babe I held so tenderly,
loved and cherished with all my heart!
What have I done or said
that your love and loyalty should depart?

Oh! My darling, cherished daughter!
My heart is breaking,
my mind is torn with grief...
My very soul is shaking
with a sorrow from which there is no relief.

With regret and sorrow I must
let go and say good-bye..
No longer can I cling blindly..
It seems I have truly lost you...Why?

Vickie West

A Child Torn

In the midst of selfish pride
 a precious childhood has died.
Someday she'll search in memory,
 to find - a battle for custody.
All I've taught you will destroy,
 with candy and another toy.
She used to want to hold my hand,
 but I can't go to Disneyland.
Is it worth the victory,
 if she is left a casualty?
A small voice asks, within this war,
 "What are you really fighting for?"
God will be the final judge,
 to show the heart that holds a grudge.
In the end no one will win,
 but her soul will be worn thin.
All you've done with endless scorn,
 is made this child - a child torn.

Kelly Covelens

Flowers

Reared in love, sheltered from harm
Believing in all-to do them no harm,
Beautiful children touched by stars
To all-things are good and not marred by scars.

Scars of dreams, fragments of fear
To be relived when sleep is near.
Angels weep when little ones cry.
Small ones aching, their world gone awry.
Shattered minds, torn hearts
By sick ones with no hearts.
God give them peace and ease of heart
To face each day when the world seems dark.

Give them gentle hands and quiet voices
To guide and help with daily choices.
Become again child of pain
A flower lifting its face to the rain.
Growing in beauty, gentleness and grace
To show the Angels a soul touched by Grace.

Tamara J. Roesly

Just Passing Through

Life sucks, it's a consensus opinion
of all the personalities I have, they keep hintin'
at the idea of suicide, a roller coaster ride
that goes all the way up and runs out of track
heroin looks appealing after all the say no
so I know I'm losing control 'cause I hate needles too
what am I gonna do? Probably nothing
meaning is the prey for years I've been hunting
done nothing but shot myself in the foot so now I limp
through the streets of my life detached like a pimp
from society I live in an alternate world
that others are appalled by or would be if they knew
I flew to eden in a dream that I had
lovely as a new born baby to it's dad
in heaven I was never thought that I could be
I would be happy to have never woken up
struck with the thought of mortality occasionally
leads me to want to live forever or sometimes die immediately

Jeff J. Booms

Silence

Reveal I, piece of silence
Hush all drumbeat escapees;
Releasing inner streams of fear
Releasing inner streams of yens,
Shallow topics, born one day,
Superficial and dread filled.

Opinions, retorts, advises
We drank up the elixir of hypocrisy;
Words, words, words so filthy.
Smarty con-men, we displayed all artistry
Etched words, ink words, settled words
But God-Aper is now damned

Fading on windfalls of satan,
Words have aged, now too slippery,
For human franzy to erase.
Comes the 13th hour...
A call for silence;
Silence a redemption, or else;
Damnation

Nduku Makpaulu

Winds Of Love

Winds of love, breathing their
secrets, in the ears, of all lost lovers.

Singing out the refrains, of fondness, and hope,
caressing our imaginings.

Whispering the promises, of fulfillment,
they carry their sweet joy to our hearts.

Their invisible fingers gently plucking,
our heartstrings, their melodies play in us endlessly.

Singing to our souls, the tunes and words,
that sound so sweet.

"I love you Dearest One, whom
makes my life so complete."

The eddying reveries, swirling
about my soul, carry me away,
enwrapped in their dream

A vision of utter beauty is in the dream and
the embodiment of that beauty is found in you.

Sighing and swaying in the winds, my heart sings,
and I can only say these three words.
"I love you"

Glen W. Porter Jr.

"Saying Goodbye Is Not An Easy Thing To Do"

She was my best friend, we did a lot of special things together.
We told each other secrets but one day she told me
she was Diagnosed with a Disease called "AIDS."
After telling me that my heart plummeted to the floor.
Then I realized that our friendship is limited before
she leaves me forever.
Saying goodbye to her was to painful. I never
thought something like this could happen to her.
Since you left I have no one to talk to about my
problems, no one to play our favorite games.
I'm in pain, I'm really in pain. I didn't want you to
leave me all alone.
I would never forget you my dear friend. And no
other friends of mines could ever replace the friendship we had.
It's so hard to say goodbye to someone you love and someone
you care so much about. Sometimes I wish I could've
done more to help her.
"Because saying goodbye is not an easy thing to do."

Sindy Augustin

Untitled

December, remember, all those
The hopelessness in planning to; next December
Here I be
Causes me delight
My success
How to dress for December; remember
The smallness of attire in those.

Clothed today
Made it
No, I bought it myself.

Those Decembers; dependent on other's wishes
Now rely on couturiers' dresses
Most assuredly mannikined one for me
For December.
I'll watch
For December; remember all those,
the hopelessness—in planning to; next December.

Josefa B. VonBoudenhoven

Untitled

Generations of different families world wide have provided us with their greatness, failure and scandal. From presidents to military, and royalty. The perception from each generation can and is very different world wide. We can read and follow on any given time what a specific generation had accomplished and on any given year. We write about them and add knowledge to their ideas to reach a better way to improve the future of ourselves. World wide creativity is brought forward to be displayed for all to see and explore for the first time. We can never put fault at any generation because it may be our own. Generations of many minds have paved the way to a past that was and a future that is. They come with specific titles to be portrayed as a particular trait of themselves. They have endured many events through happiness and sadness, but will exist forever with major importance. For years to come families world wide will carry on and as individuals we can only make a small participation. For a final note we hope to keep world peace for all to exist on planet earth.

Mary Kjelgaard

insanity

come child, run far away with me
run from bondage of reality
say to hell with life for a while
lay down in the mire and attempt a smile
reason gone, i'm totally bare
time now to throw away all our old cares
where darkness lies hidden in pools
i want to go where insanity rules

Julie Sortor

She

Like the rain that falls from the sky,
Her tears fall.
She hides in the shadows,
Afraid of the light.
She is running from her past,
From those who hurt her.
From those who see her,
But she is really not there.
She is a child of the night.
A child of broken dreams and shattered hearts.
People talk, but she does not hear,
For she is running from the sound.
The night is her only friend.
Darkness comes and she is gone.

Jenny Kiel

Crystal Clear

I am cut to spray colors upon the world...
The sun is my energy and when it sets, I die.
Invisible I am to those who look through,
for they do not know my depth, my feelings.
They cannot see the carefully cut edges that love made.

Amy Hintz

Remembering His Son

God gave us His Son for such a short time
to be born as a baby, just plain, but
sublime.

Mary and Joseph were chosen to raise,
God's Only Son Jesus, later to praise.

His birth gave a hope for people to live,
a gift from God, His Son, to give.

His life here on earth, an example for all,
to love one another and answer the call.

So let's take this time to remember His birth,
also remember His life here on earth, He's
constantly looking down from above, giving
to us, unconditional love.

Sandra Woodburn

Colors in the Night

Green fire burning in you.
   slowly destroyed by the morning dew.
purple agony from which you cannot hide.
   let it flow away with the changing tide.
Orange sadness...turning into fear,
   drained from your thoughts with each falling tear.
Let go of all the feelings,
   yet grasp the colors of bright,
and light shall be shed on your dark and
   hopeless night.

Karla Jane Anderson

Open The Door

Have you ever listened to the sweet song of a bird?
It takes a slow down in the grind of life to appreciate the sounds.
The sounds are free, and they have a special rhythm.
You must quiet yourself, and then these gifts can be heard.

The power sound of wings of the humming bird is for you.
Be aware of soft rain falling lightly onto the petals of a flower
   at your feet.
Gentle wind winding up the cliff, slithering through the leaves of
   the olive tree is yours.
Are you to busy with a given agenda to experience what you're due?

Listening is a skill that rewards all those who seek to unlock a
   new dimension.
Everything around you is just waiting for you to discover the
   mysteries.
Reach for your deepest intelligence and taste the wonders of sound.
Listen for what nobody else can hear and you will become a person
   with a new vision.

Each person listening learns something different just like a
   pattern of a fingerprint.
Step up and take your place among the strong humans today who
   can really hear.
Just the cadence of the wondrous heart that keeps you alive is near.
Take a moment and really live by starting to listen to the moment,
this is only a hint.

Bonnie C. Eriksen

Having Jesus By My Side

I'd rather have Jesus
Than all the worlds gold
I'd rather belong to thee when Growing Old
I'd rather have Jesus
Than diamonds and pearls
A crown of jewels that shines in your curls
I'd rather have Jesus
When going is rough
Than beautiful clothes
And all that stuff

I'd rather have Jesus
Than fame untold
To belong to Him means more than gold
I'd rather have Jesus on the final day
Forever with my Lord in heaven I will stay
So give up your riches
And give up your gold
And belong to Jesus in His precious fold
With doing so you will be richer too,
Better to have Jesus He always is true.

Signe Galdal

Jeremy's Wings

Jeremy's wings went higher -
He thought he could go higher than the sky
But with him on pot,
He just stayed in one place.
No one knew why,
But he did.
Jeremy's wings took him
As high as the sky.
People thought he was crazy
And crazy he was!
He told himself,
"I'll quit one day soon,"
But he never got the chance.
His life was fading fast.
He thought he would recover;
His life went as fast as a dream.
Jeremy's wings took him nowhere,
And in an instant he was gone.

April Turner

In Search Of Love

As I laid down and closed my eyes
I wondered why love was so hard to find
There I was, so deep asleep
Then suddenly I was on my feet
As I opened my eyes, I was at a place far beyond that of mankind.
It was as though I was standing on air
floating on a cloud, but heading no where
Then suddenly a light appear
and said, not to worry, nor have no fear
The light was so bright, that I closed my eyes
And I felt a voice so deep inside
It said, one must not search for love
For it is within you
One can't search for something, that one already has
Then I opened my eyes, I was all alone
There was no light. I was back at home
As I wonder where, I have been
I felt a glow deep within
A blow of joy, and that of love
I finally knew, where I had bone.

John Rosa

Here And There

    Here we sit, stand and scream, Wandering off into
our dreams and the mind believes what you will it
floating away in time searching for how to kill it when
we should just let it go because time always
goes on, until it's gone and No one knows where
    Here we grow old and grey because we've
wasted it all away on wishes, hopes and desires
What a bunch of hypocrites and liars Here
we'll stay and I'm sorry, not for myself but for
everybody else out there
    There is a beautiful place to live, Where
No one takes and everyone gives there's a good place
to start it would be nice but it's a farce
because in order to give there must be from
where to take and that's no mistake.
    Back here in reality away from the dreams
and wishes there is an ugly place not in appearance
but in perception for here truth is hard to
swallow and it hurts and pain is bad it makes me sad
Not for myself but for everybody else out there...
    Gustavo Javier Vitureira Diaz

Infinity

Two harmonious hearts
beating wildly, that were meant for
each embrace.
Falling fate brought them to
-gether lust and love will borrow and bind them
    forgetfully
      forever...
    Samuel A. Bennett

Sipping Ginger Ale In The Dark

Sipping, slurping, guzzling, swigging, gulping
Sipping ginger ale in the dark is a delight at night
Flowing down your throat curing the days blues
Hard day at work? Open the fridge don't go for a Coke
Open a Ginger Ale, why you ask because it's there
Lie in a chair relax your feet and fall asleep
While Sipping Ginger Ale in the Dark
    Mike Cohea

Intimate

Blue skies to gray, Like drizzle to rain.
Most everything in time is subject to change.
The times were many, we shared us
two now so distant, with me and you.
Moments are few and far between.
Worlds apart or so it may seem.
There are reasons to smile, a joyful
tear for special moments throughout the year.
A second, a minute an hour a day
always spent in a caring way and
things have changed, but not to an end
    Just had to tell you.
      I miss You Friend.
    Michael Booker

To Be Or Not To Be?

To be or not to be,
Is that the question?
Is it far nobler
To be real or to be faithful,
To be loved or to be loving,
To be kind or to be good,
To be gentle or to be caring?
It is far nobler to think on these things,
Than on whether you should be or not.
    Melina Rabon

Thanksgiving Day

Thanksgiving Day Is A Day Of Thanks,
And in our hearts thankfulness ranks.
But in our town it's also a day of the game,
In which the Wildcats have the Mountaineers to tame.
And each of their followers stroll to the stadium with pride,
With their hopes and wishes to abide.
And on both sides the stands are filled,
With students waving ribbon and confetti spilled,
And with their spirit and noisemakers, amid the din,
May God bless you and let the best team win.
Because when the great scorer writes in his book your name,
He does not write if you won or lost,
but how you played the game.
    James L. Bove

It's All Down Hill From Here!!

It was not a momentous day, the day that I turned fifty.
I don't care what they say, I didn't feel very nifty.

As I look in the mirror at the body that sags,
It's not a pretty sight anymore, it makes you want to gag.

I ache and hurt in places that I didn't know I had.
I can't do things I used to do and boy, it makes me mad.

What's wrong with those newspapers,
they make that print so small?
I remember it was only yesterday when
I didn't need glasses at all.

My husband yearns for the years when I was vibrant and alive.
The bedroom had that special scent of Channel #5.

It's hard to get romantic like those years of yesterday,
When the bedroom now has the scent and fragrance of Ben Gay.

So people look forward to that day and that special year.
But take it in perspective, "It's all down hill from here!!!"
    Carolyn Becker

March

March is the unpredictable it's true,
Spring is not here yet, winter not through.
'Tho the sun shines bright it's still bitter cold,
So bundle up, don't try to be bold.

The wind whips around like to blow you away.
I try to stay in on that kind of a day.
Showers of rain or maybe snow.
Well it is still March, you know.

We have two parades in March this year.
I'll be watching from my easy chair.
Eat corned beef and cabbage and wear the green.
With my Easter outfit in church I'll be seen.

A new birth, a renewal, a gift from God.
As the Robins return, with the flowers in your yards.
For the coming of Easter, the promise of things,
Green trees and flowers , once more it is Spring.
    Janet Heulitt

"Mothers"

When God made mothers to give us care,
He made them so special they're always there.
He took kindness, goodness, patience and love,
And all of these came from our God above.
The past that you've given me, raising me well
Has helped me through rough spots I never can tell.
Though I don't always show it I love you so true,
And thank God for giving me a mom just like you.
So when I'm impatient, unkind or unseeing,
It's not lack of love mom, it's just human being.
    Theresa McNiff

The Blond People

The people world, have people people
Who once in while produce,
A unique mind that blooms,
Into one of the blond people.
These blond people are unique and special.
Though, everybody has a little blond person in them.
Oh, rare and precious are these blond people
Though you'll never know it,
Till one day when your life is all gray and blue
They'll come up to you, and make you shine through.
There are the yellow ones who do the unthinkable.
There are the silver ones who are pure and through.
There are the vanilla ones who are true and true.
There are the white ones who are humorous too.
There are the ivory ones who look out for you.
But, the gold ones are the special ones.
Though the world would be sad and plaid.
Without the blond people.

Shawn J. Vogel

I Miss You

I miss you in the morning, dear. When all the world is new;
I know that the day brings no joy because it brings not you.
I miss the well-love voice of you, your tender smiles for me,
the charm of you, the joy of your unfailing sympathy.

I miss you in the noontide, dear; the crowded city street
seem but a desert now, I walk in solitude complete.
I miss your hand beside my own, the light touches of your hand,
the quick gleam in the eyes of you so sure to understand.

I miss you in the evening, dear; when daylight fades away;
I miss the sheltering arms of you to rest me from the day,
I try to think I see you yet there where a firelight gleams.
Weary at last, I sleep, and still, I miss you in my dreams.

Jason Russell

Open Your Eyes And See The Four Seasons

Open your eyes and see this splendid world in harmony.
I can see the forest friend gathering up their food, for
now it's winter and animals are getting ready to hibernate.

Open your eyes and see flowers around me, fascinating
colors of flowers that I see, for now it is spring and the
flowers are blooming like diamond rings.

Open your eyes and see the hot sun shining over me. The
bugs and bees fly among the great big trees, for now it's
summer and it's hot as can be.

Open your eyes and see the fall colors falling off the trees.
There are red, orange, yellow brown, and sometimes
green, for now it is fall and pretty piles of leaves are
covering the ground.

Open your eyes and see how good mother nature has been
to you and me.

Marissa Lewis

Forgive Me

The moon shrinks behind the curtain of clouds as the infinite number
of souls looking down upon me turn their rays away. I know they
witnessed my folly and hold their heavenly light from me now to see
only the darkness that I have created. I am stumbling falling but
Father I'm calling please show me the way. The night is so cold, so
dreadfully long, I know I deserve it for I was wrong, Tears are
now what fill my eyes, the moon the stars my actions despise. And
still I wander through the night, the mist around me blocks out the
light. Please Father forgive me for what I've done, I've always
known that I am your son. This one truth I pray it might, save me
from this soulless night.

Michael Brown

At Parting

Perhaps we'll meet again in some far year
And hardly recognize each other's face.

Perhaps we'll grope a moment as we near,
Endeavoring to recall the place
Our ways one crossed, and then, remembering,
We'll let our hands reach out to touch
As strangers might, so brief a thing
One would not guess that once it meant so much.

Perhaps I'll think, "I'm glad he went away,"
And you'll think, "She has aged," and be glad, too;
And then we'll find there's nothing much to say
Beyond the things we've said,
Much less to do.

And so we'll part again and neither guess
The other's sudden sense of loneliness.

Mildred Watson

Revenge

It is arrogant ones like you
Who draw the predator of my revenge.
It is the way you play with the most sincere,
As if all treasures were but your playthings,
That calls the beast of my revenge.

From the deepest, blindest caverns of my soul,
Flashing the blinding white teeth of rage,
Terrible karma springs!
Quavering yet steady,
It leaps at the sight of your patronizing eyes.

Like fangs, let the news of what I've done puncture your frail plots!
When the hot life-blood that is your pride spills from your heart,
Gasp for the pompous words that poured from your throat, now one!
When your vanity has been torn asunder by ruthless justice, in time
My revenge will leave you lying still with all your broken promises.

Have I made all of this sound cold and cruel?
I'm a little shaken myself, seeing the feelings that anger,
That one flaming impulse, can invoke.
With this, never forget how your selfishness
Woke the dormant beast of my revenge.

Angeline Binick

My Friend

Arms open wide you embrace my pain
Only for me to come back again
Hand you my bag of burdens full,
When it's too heavy for me to pull;

Carry it off with heavenly grace
Nothing but love on your beautiful face.
You are my angel sent down from the skies
To fill up my heart and remove my disguise.

"Walk proudly," you whisper, "you're special, my dear."
As your hand gently wipes one more tear.
I look in your eyes and feel so much peace
The guilt and the shame you help me release.

Please know that I love you
Deep in my soul,
And my heart without you
Just wouldn't be whole.

Lynn Surprenant

A Change Of Seasons

The barren trees loom lank and tall
the paths lay hard from winter's cold.
Our thoughts trying hard to bring
to the fore memories of Spring.

Gone now the winter's snow
cold, making movement laboriously slow.
Continually dreaming of warmer things
like the wild pungent odor of Spring.

O, how we long for the hum of bees,
the baby green of grass and leaves,
The promise that natures bounty brings,
with bated breath we wait for Spring.

Now green is the grass o'er the fields lay
where children would romp and play,
with not a care what days would bring,
while basking freely now in Spring.

O, too soon the beloved season pass,
however long we'd like it to last.
Now my heart will forever sing
for the lush breathless beauty of Spring.
   Patricia Farmer

Dreams

Sunny skies and warm winds,
rainy days and cool nights.

Walking on a snow covered walk,
sleeping under a tree on a warm afternoon.

Watching a child play,
planting flowers and watching them grow.

Floating along with the clouds,
able to fly with the birds.

Harmony with each other,
the world growing together.

Peace on earth,
all dreams, Dreams, Dreams, Dreams...
   Norman M. Dillon Jr.

Leaving

No new minds to revolutionize
Or Anglo-size,
Reaching the edge of stir-craziness
As we are.
Time to move on, I'd say,
To you
Or maybe today we'll lose it,
And find it again
And hasten to the door.
If we are late for work
We will not care,
Nor will we cry,
For we have lived
What we were supposed to live,
Eaten the food
We were supposed to eat
And now, our sentence up,
We will step on again
Into a brave new world
With nothing but lost educations leading us.
   Conner Earl

Why Must Winter Come Tonight?

The snowflake that fell,
Changed the motionless world tonight.
It felt like such a pointless trickle,
That would quickly be forgotten.

Gazing down on the depressing Earth.
No light to appear.
Everything was crystal white.
Whips of wind didn't verify till night.

The coats of white, covered the Earth.
Everything slumped to the ivory pavement.
Sunshine vanished to the atmosphere blanket.
Why, I asked, must winter come tonight?
   My-Thuan Tran

Karen

   The Joy of Love, I've found in you can
be measured a number of ways. To get
to the way I love you, we have to leave
the bonds of earth and travel the Vastness
of space itself, across the void, across the
gulf of night, across the endless rain of years.
   Come with me now, Oh Pilgrim of the
stars, for our time is upon us and our eyes
shall see the life before us. The infinity
Of my love for you, which all men shall
see, will be as bright as the morning star
   Were you the star born for me? If so,
here then is our quest, and our world, and
our home. Look skyward now, and forget the past,
for my love for you, shall extend far into
the reaches of space and time. Let the light
of all the galaxies, and of all the sun's
shine down upon our lives forever and ever,
through-out time, till the end of time.
   Dan Bradshaw

Changing Winds

The wind can caress your body
like a gentle lover's touch,
When the winter is on the wane
and you long for Spring so much.
But when the storm clouds gather
and they turn from white to black,
The wind can attack with such a force
that nothing can hold it back.
It would seem that life is like the wind
with periods of calm and stress,
So if you have a home like a harbor that's snug,
you really have been blessed.
   Ruth McMillen

The Poem Syndrome

Words can hurt and words can heal,
words can show how you really feel.

Be they spoken or written bold,
words can calm and words can scold.

I play the word game in my mind,
search for the right word, it's hard to find.

Then at the right moment, at the right time,
out they tumble, the words that rhyme.

It's a challenge but it's so much fun.
conquer the syllables, a poem begun.
   Eileen M. Hector

Untitled

Crash!!! Is that the lightning around me,
or the snapping of my heart
as you crumble it before these eyes.
Boom!!!! Is that the thunder above,
or the sounding of my soul
as it falls to the ground,
felled by your twisted knife.
Bang!!!! The smoking gun is in your hand,
by your design you have murdered my spirit
so that it passes into nothingness.
Why?
Could you not see that you meant the world to me?
I would have thrust my body upon a dagger cold
for the chance to save your breath
from the foul air that surrounds us.
Do you not love me?
I am dust without you,
without meaning,
without love,
without.
Kenneth Giles

This Knows No End

The neglect and the cruelness that animals have to bear
And knowing that mankind really does not care...

The abuse of our children, the pain in their eyes
The deaths that occur before you realize...

The domestic violence between woman and man
The struggles, the pain, death given by the stronger hand...

The wars between the countries, the hatred does grow
Killing off souls that they don't even know...

The inability to control who we love and who we hate
You can't make yourself feel something no matter how long you wait...

The excuse to justify and blame all the bad things on fate
The irresponsibility to take blame before it's too late...

For the Karma that will be that we cannot control
For each and everyone of us to continue playing out our role...

The ongoing tears that our eyes cry in pain
The sun and the moon and the wind and the rain...

The mistakes in our lives in the future and the past
The wisdom to learn but the ignorance to let them be our last...

The feelings in this poem that I continue to write
Is as true as the days will come and turn into the nights...
Maria Moccia-Ball

"Dizzy"

I feel so dizzy - I don't know what to do. Am I
the only that sees the dots in the room? I don't
know what it is - although I know it's not good -
I don't want to feel it - I don't think I should. It's not
me, No - it's this world of hate - damnation seems to
be the only fate. My eyes can't stay open in a
world like this - is happiness there - just something
I missed. Where do I belong in a world of pain -
do I belong anywhere - am I insane? Something
is gone - something is lost - I want to be more
but at what cost? Do people look - do people stare?
Now that I think of it - does anyone care? No one
knows so no one can help - do I cry or do I yelp?
Who do I turn to - to whom do I go ... Is there anywhere
For my dizzy, lost mind and soul?
Nichole Tyner

The Insomniac Returns

Stealthily creeping through the night,
The Insomniac ponders what to do.
Can't sleep. Again.
What to do? What to do?!
Can't sleep. Can't sleep!
The sleep-stealing phantom
Who pesters me at night
Keeps me awake.

The dawn arrives with a sweet
Kiss of gentle light.
She lingers,
Until the morning sun peers over the mountains
And announces the coming day.

Then do I feel the drowsy drug
Of sleep being cast over my entire self.
And just as I begin to doze off,
The alarm screams, and
It is time to rise and face
A new day.
Audrey J. Merriweather

A Tribute To Working Hands

Hey!- Man in the blue,
Did I ever get a chance to thank you?
You patched the tires that grip
The pavement you cemented
Took heed to the tasks at which
I'd so laxly relented.

You; the humble man who rarely complains
Of cracked hands, raw knees and twelve-hour days.
There's no coffee lounge outside,
Just mother nature's abrasively bitter skies.

So they think they've got important places to be -
Noses in the air, they march the streets you sweep.
Their ties are straight, but you've made our nation.
It is you who stacks the bricks and blends the flavors.

Oh, but- Man in the suit,
I'd like to thank you too,
For not seeking that stranger who made you sorry
You double-parked your pride and joy Ferrari!
Lyn Crissman

If I Were In Charge Of The World

If I were in charge of the World
I'd make it so if anybody hurt someone
They'd go to the loony bin.
If I were in charge of the world
Pro sports teams wouldn't be allowed to run up the score,
And they'd have at least 1 child, that actually played.
If I were in charge of the world
There would be machines to do everything for you,
Like brush your teeth, and go to school.
Detention would be on how to do a flip on a trampoline,
Or how to throw the perfect spiral, or how to do monster jams.
If I were in charge of the World
Homeless people would have homes to live in,
And starving people would have food to eat.
If I were in charge of the World
Anybody could have any pet they wanted.
If I were in charge of the World
I would resign in a second, because I wouldn't want the stress
or the pressure
After all, if you were in charge of the World, wouldn't you resign?
Jeremiah Webster

Friendship

Friendship is a special thing,
but you decide the joy it will bring.

You trust in a friend and they trust in you,
and you always share stories and secrets, too.

You have good times and bad times some with tears,
but you're always glad when a friend calms fears.
A good friendship lasts for years and years.

Be fair, honest, and true to a friend,
and the wonders you see in them won't ever end.
Katie Korczykowski

Those Faces

Opening a photograph album, not without dust,
full of a childhood past, so many faces,
captured so long ago, those faces have faded,
forgotten, but all the while existing.

Raise no false hope, release the past,
impress favorably upon the future.
Feeling weak, fearful, but moved,
by the excitement the memories could bring back.

Hoping to remember, all that surrounded,
when searching the plain, and mysterious faces.
Listening quietly for that irresistible moment,
when those faces speak with wisdom and understanding.

In pursuit is the heart, battling not to sever,
and further open in pain in the not knowing.
Give these faces, to the mind, or,
have they floated in and gone?

The mind and body, simply appealing,
not only to remember, those faces,
for they are My faces, but my life memories,
of a childhood past, so I may know myself today.
Lisa M. Siron

A Diamond In The Rough

He was not an ordinary guy.
No, not by any means.
He had a "tough-guy" image.
Yet, there was softness not unseen.

He was the type of friend
you wouldn't easily forget.
He was silly; he was funny.
Yet, there was a generosity inside him,
Unlike anyone you'd ever met.

He was always frank and sometimes loud
and he could put you in your place.
But when he'd write his words in poetry,
Tears would stream right down your face.

So forever will we treasure
this diamond in the rough
And forever in our hearts,
Steven Blackwood
We all will miss you very, very much.
Elizabeth Daly Centeno

Wolf Spirit

Soft beams of moonlight slice through the darkened shadows.
You slink between the forest giants, then, disappear.
Waves of midnight blue lap against the lakeside shore.
Then I hear your chilling song blown across the ages.
Your glowing eyes filled my mind as you stepped from the forest's cover.
Then, like leaving tracks on the snow, you left your footprints in my soul.
Melissa D. Nelson

The Hunt

Waiting silently my taunting mind gives me a fit,
I look from blue to green in the great forest that I sit.

Watching and waiting, he will certainly show,
Red crimson will pour or I will let him go.

I ponder my thoughts; What would the Lord think
For taking his creature without even a wink?

There's a hunger inside I can't understand
As the power of life is held deadly in my hand.

Yet God's creature walks free more than any man,
Should I take that gift to use in my own selfish plan?

The plan of life to live or to die,
His plan is to run, be free, and to fly.

Nature calls him as free as a bird,
He walks through the trees without hardly a word.

He calls to his friends to come run and to play,
His four hoofs stomp the ground on this glorious day.

Finally, he appears with me to determine his fate
I let him walk for I've already ate.

Who am I to take away freedom
From this deer in the woods in his own private kingdom?
Matthew Little

Solitude

Sitting alone,
Staring out into another dimension,
Nothing really exists or does it.
Well not here anyway.
Everything's calm and quite.
The walls appear a bluish color,
The roof is black covered with many stars.
There are decaying corpses under the glass floor.
Maggots are eating out their eyes and crawling out their ears.
You hear a faint buzz, everything is black.
You open your eyes and the journey though your mind has ended.
Or has it?
Matt Green

Ode Of Gratitude From Grandma Unworthy

You've given me accolades and taken me to tea.
You've let me come into the classroom with glee.
You've given me tasks causing me to say.....
"Oh my, how will I ever do that today?"
But somehow I managed, in the workroom zoo,
To come up with something that maybe would do.

You've let me walk into the classroom at will.
And, boy, did I soon learn of your superb teaching skill!!!

When the machine failed I may have been surely,
And then in the door with a smile came shirley,
I knew in a moment everything was all right,
As in would come Melinda and Sandi to help in my plight.
When the copy machine I would view with distrust,
There would be RSP with a "This is a must!"
From Marcia, Kim and Joann I learned to be tenacious.
From Kay, Margo and Connie to be super gracious.

For flowers and knowledge and plaques by the score
Will never replace the PTA, Staff, Students and more.
Through all the stapling, costumes and the rest,
Katie, and I will always exclaim: "Spanger School is the best!!"
Jeanette Thompson

The North

Far up in the frosty north,
Is the land of Midnight Sun.
The bitter cold and shimmering ice.
The days and nights are one.

Sometimes the sun shines so bright,
The reflection hurts your eyes.
Never ending diamonds portray
Silhouettes upon the skies.

You may feel the warmth when you see the light.
Yet when you go outside,
The temperature goes through your being
And you know the sun has lied.

But at that moment, when you go beyond
The bitterness and the cold.
It's the warmth that lies within us,
That keeps us from growing old.
Lucretia S. Mazzei

A Message To You From The Lord

Time is winding up Dear Child, I desire for you to stay a while.
I'm actually thinking forevermore. Come unto Me; The Open Door.
Life is waiting for you in My world of the Spirit.
Receive. It's everlasting. There's no reason to fear it.
All good things are waiting above,
because each and everyone of you is whom I love.
The Good, the Bad...come, I'm able to convert you
Along with your willing mind, you can be brand new.
Don't be ashamed to worship and praise Me;
because, I Am, the One who can save thee.
Turn your life around, don't wait too long.
After a while, I'll soon be gone.
One day My Spirit will be leaving for good,
so I ask you right now to do as you should.
You'll be looking and longing for that comfort I'd sent
All of a sudden, it will have come and went.
Come. Repent. And live for Me now,
No need to worry, I'll teach you how.
Accept Me. Today. The Lord, Jesus Christ,
You'll be on your way to heaven; because I paid the price!
Jackie Harvell

Glory To God, Lord, I Love You

Experience has taught me in every way,
to give God the glory everyday,
I think of my sinful life and let out a sigh for me, why would He send
His only Son to die?
Because He loved me so very much, that's why.
So I won't fret, and I won't cry,
because I've seen the Lord's mercy with my own eye.
He gives me hope, He gives me peace,
and all of my worries cease, when I think of what
the Lord has done for me, and the person He has
yet for me to be. I love Him with all of my heart and
soul, and I want the whole world to know.
Lord, I love you
Jerald McBrayer

A Smile

For so small a gesture
could wake the once still heart
and raise the voice from silence to song.
Would without touch, embrace.
Without word, tell of all,
and warm the chill from an evening sky.
So too, make cool a burning sun by day.
That these eyes may behold
and all thy senses quake,
at so small a gesture.
Edmund Andre'

In The Hyacinth Lair Of The Manticore

Following the ivory palace to its towering destination
I sit in a caravan of robes engulfed by mountains of sunlight
Great blue seas swallowed whole by memories of green desires
Washing on shores of grass blowing gently in the breeze

Sailing on currents of ancient Atlantis and other forgotten times
Talking fearfully to the wind whispering sublime along the waves
I am carried on an unknown path into the depths of a secret sun known
Only to the natives of this watery land where the ocean meets the sky

In the evening when the deep horizon drowns the sun
The moon speaks plainly to the burgeoning stars above
About the smooth gates of pearly exile discovered within the seasons
Holding a fistful of sunlight dreams carried away by the pale blue
    fields.

Sleeping with the stars as my covers and the moonlight as my bed
I walk on marble terraces in the palace of the dancing wind
Through a veil of thin light under a molded sky I reach a hidden lair
Concealed neatly within a great diamond staircase adorned in midnight

Awaking to the immortal cry of crashing waves on a distant shore
I remember speaking to the silver-voiced trees and their evergreen
    house
About the merchant carrying payloads of sand to cover the distant
    shores
Who never once spoke to the earth in all its battalions of moonlit
    wishes
Eric Larsen

I Praise Thy Name By Choice

I praise my Father's Name in the morning,
I praise it again at noon.
I praise it all times in between,
I praise it before the moon.

I praise my Father's Name in the wee hours,
I praise it through the night.
I praise it with a sincere heart,
I praise it with all my might.

I praise His Name when things look grim,
I praise it when things look great.
I praise it for the love of Him,
I praise it with each breath I take.

I praise His Holy Name clearly,
I praise it with heart and voice.
I praise my Father's Name with conviction,
I praise Thy Name by choice.
Linda Vanessa Pope

Elegy

Too brief the time of music,
Of giggling pebbles, chattering like children,
Tumbling to the rhythms of the sea;
When sunlight was a dancer,
Dimpling smiling waves
Whose laughter sang in canon with the shore;
When bright gulls, sounding oboes,
Tuned feathered orchestras to symphonies
Borne on crescendo in the wind.

Too soon the time of muted song and sighing,
Of dances ended,
And of whispered echoings
Of half-remembered melodies
Of listening
To the rising of the moon.
Lillian V. Enright

This England

Here in such endless beauty England lies,
That green and pleasant land which fill the eyes
With meadows lining slowly moving streams
As those abroad remember in their dreams.

The lonely windmill turning empty sails
Looks down upon the fields below, and hails
The rising sun afire with golden ray
Sweeping the dew, like tears from yesterday.

A weathered castle, silent by its moat
Reviews the passing centuries as they float
In endless time before its ancient walls,
Which once knew Kings and Captains in its halls.

This island nation, once by Churchill led,
Paid for the price of freedom with its dead,
As it had done in days long gone before,
When Drake and Nelson manned the ships of war.

Tranquility, and all that it inspires
Now reigns across the countryside and shires,
Its sandy beaches now in peace we roam,
This blessed kingdom, washed by the waves of home.

John T. Saxon

Montana I Love You

Where the lodge poles have rusted out, I've made my home.
Where a valley runs between the hills,
   I've planted a garden.
Where a city rose-garden flowered,
   I meditated.
Where waterless land held pre-historic shells.
   We hunted grouse.

Montana is a land for wanderers,
   And for those who wish a settled home.
Be ready for the sharp-cold winds,
   But be assured of a warm hearth.

Black Angus feed sleek upon green hillsides.
Milking Shorthorns graze contented in deep pastures.
White Charlois stand huge in county shows.
Herefords multiply fat and strong on rangelands.

Cattle, minerals, grains and oil,
   have given the State wealth.
These are the solid foundation of Montana's wealth.
Prosper and grow. As the land matures you,
Give strength to the land.

Shirley L. Luhrsen

Creation In Process

Creation - destruction - two sides of one coin;
   Water and wind destroy stone -
And so are created new formations bold
   That alter each natural zone.

Waterfalls, rivers and lakes bite at shores;
   Wind pushes fire across plains;
Ice cracks the cliffs away, bit by small bit,
   And peaks become hills under rains.

Moonlight and gravity master the tides,
   And the tides create sand of the shores.
Sunshine and lightning can start a stray fire,
   And fire restores forest floors.

A time to build up and a time to tear down -
   In endless and circular play.
Each new creation seems final and strong,
   But then each new form fades away.

Each change in our landscape take eons of time,
   God's time written ever so large.
He makes for us beauty that we may enjoy -
   We know that it's God who's in charge.

Halcyon C. Peterson

In Just Twenty Lines...

I feel like writing a pretty verse
while I make time in just twenty lines...

A pretty verse full of body, like the grape in an aged wine
a wine that breathes, but a verse that dies.

A void in my soul has left me seeking...
I seek answers in my words, but find limits of a poisoned heart.

A verse full of body, like the one that taught me love
but now I make time, to forget my first wine.

Love is real and its roots are made of truths
but tears fall like rain, feeding the planted roots lies.

I seek answers in my words, so I try to write a pretty verse
you were my first wine, and are now the blood poisoning my heart.

You are no longer here to limit my life
time is now born, but I always see it die.

The tears have stopped and I'm alone
my roots have rot, you no longer feed them lies.

Time is a void in my soul, that I try to fill with love
love is like time, it comes so fast and it dies so slow

But now I make time, to write a pretty verse
a verse that dies, in just twenty lines...

Leonel F. Zuniga

The Pain Of Love

The dreams of him
Like her knight in shining armor
And she knows in her mind
That one day she'll conquer.

She'll conquer his love, with mind and heart
and never look back to days they were apart.
She knows in time they'll build dreams to treasure
the strong love between them will last forever.

She has faith in him
everyday it grows stronger,
She knows that in the future
the emptiness will be no longer.

Though she knows she can't tell him,
the feelings start to cause pain.
Her heart cries out for the love of God
and his blood cleanses her in a peaceful rain.

Some say she died in her sleep
yet there really is another part.
The part that took her very life
was the death of a broken heart...

Kimberly Harrison

Thirty Something

Some call it "mid-life crisis,"
but you're not sure that's true.
It's more like a suffocation,
Why are you always feeling blue?

Slowly you breathe in and out;
trying to get your bearings straight,
the kids keep crying, dinner's burning;
you're late for work, that's just great.

One gray hair, no, now there's two;
You're only happy when the sun shines through.
You need a break, but who has time?
You tell your husband, "all is fine."

Just twenty minutes alone in a nice warm bath
could almost surely melt 30's wrath.

Diane C. Calcei

My Friend Kina

Sisters we could never pass, as I am blonde and she is brunette,
But we were alike, her and I, in many ways we knew not yet.

Although our first meeting was not a positive one,
Through a mutual friend we began to have fun.

We began to spend time together night and day,
And then one year I moved away.

Of course there were boyfriends who intervened,
And there were fights though rarely seen.

But we never stopped wondering of the other,
As we grew in mind, and the goals we wished to cover.

And each time over the years we got in touch,
We'd find that we had both grown the same and missed each other much.

We still talk when we are happy or troubled,
And rely on each other when our minds are jumbled.

I thank God to have let me find,
such a wonderful friend who is always on my mind.

Lana M. Stenger

The Power

Beyond the wall which will someday fall are secrets to be revealed... No one knows the power of the men and women to be... Inside their heads are all the answers to all our tragedies... Those that know the answers to all that is to be stand beyond the wall of hope and harmony. I tell you now there is no cure to all that is diseased... The man that holds the power is the man we can not see... He stands before us now as we are on our knees, shines his light upon us and listens to our pleas... Never will the world be free, it will crumble to the ground... And when he sees what we have done he'll take us one by one... As a world we are no more we've done it to ourselves, we took the world for granted and destroyed ourselves as well.
No one knew the answers...
No one knew the cures...
No one knew the reasons, for the reasons were absurd.

Dian Black

I Dreamed A Dream

I dreamed a dream that one day I would meet someone who would make my heart skip a beat. Someone who would knock my soul off of its feet. My dream came true when God blessed me with you.

I dreamed a dream that one day I would meet someone who would be patient and kind. Someone who would love me for me and be mine all mine. My dream came true when God blessed me with you.

I dreamed a dream that one day I would meet someone who would hold my hand tightly. Someone who would never let go no matter what might be.
My dream came true when God blessed me with you.

I dreamed a dream that one day I would meet someone who would be the perfect love for me. Someone who would want to marry and raise a family. My dream came true when God blessed me with you.

I dreamed a dream that one day I would meet someone who would help raise my boy and girl. Someone who would make ours a loving and happy world. My dream came true when God blessed me with you.

I dreamed a dream that one day I would meet someone who would share my laughter and tears. Someone who would ease my fears and stand by me through the years. My dream came true when God blessed me with you.

Shirley Washington-Walls

A Dark Life Lived

I walk several miles to find compassion,
Cold winds rip though layers of coat's fashions.
Snow blinds me and my direction is lost,
I drag myself further, but high are the costs.
The light I once saw forms shapes of a town,
My faith and hope in life, I have just found.
My heart is filled with anticipation,
I hope to receive good accommodation.
I walk up to the first door I come to,
Hateful gestures already, festered and grew.
Door to door I'm lured, the quest brings many falls,
Yet, only the hateful thoughts and gestures call.
Leaving the town to join, shadows of dark,
I will not show pains that live within my heart.
I remain just another nameless face,
Who's wills will wither and wilt within times race.

Nicole Denning

Untitled

No one grows a garden the way they used to do,
With coriander, eye bright, marjoram and rue.
Herbs that served our forebears, helped to
 kill their ills.
Boneset, and camomile, horehound, and squills.
Pungent pennyroyal to clear an aching head.
Lavender that sweetened a white linen bed.
Southern wood for fever, fennel for the eyes.
Bee balm with lemon scent, saffron for our dyes.
Shops are full of remedies, but, wouldn't it
 be nice
To grow our own drugstore out in the sun where it
 would be available to everyone?

Jessie Jones

Just Another Baby

He was born "Just Another Baby" He gave up his Majesty to be born
 "Just Another Baby"
He was God in the Word but born "Just Another Baby". Jesus the
 Lord.
The Angels proclaimed Him—"A Baby Boy was born" "Just
 Another Baby" Jesus Christ the Lord.
People did not know Him—He was born of a Virgin -Mary-and
 born "Jesus Christ The Lord."
Thirty years of silence. Then—Jesus started teaching saving souls-
 and healing.
He was God Almighty-Jesus Christ the Lord-born "Just Another
 Baby".
For three years—He saved-healed—taught through Miracles—
He loved the sinners and the children most of all.
For us—He died a cruel death on the cross—to cleanse us of our sins
 To be worthy and gain our home in heaven—have faith, pray, live
this Earthly live in love and service for Him—"Born Just Another
 Baby"
To know what our Father God looks like—Look to God—"Just
 Another Baby"
Who is Jesus the Lord our God Almighty.

Pauline Brown

Untitled

A sorcerers walk through these dusted roads
I am but a man looking to unfold
The gift we all hold inside
A common love
One day society will rise

A poets wand
Its magic waves
A feeling from inside
All we want to do is explain

Christopher John Palacino

Untitled

At dawn the sun begins to peek its head
Above the tree-lined, horizontal plane.
Through half-slit eyes I watch the ball of red
Arise and kiss the misty, morning rain.
Her subjects — motionless throughout the night —
Awaken from a deep and slumb'rous sleep,
Oblivious to their infernal plight.
These transients then begin, again, to creep
Along the rutted roads and thoroughfares
Restricting them to paths they hope to leave;
Yet when they're speared by words or unt'ward glares,
The fallen and downtrodden can't relieve
Themselves of *all* the pain from sorrow's well...
And so remain they 'neath the gates of hell!
Donald C. Fare

The Book On A Shelf

Like a book on a shelf I stand on the shelf with
So many others, never looked at but judged by
My cover, never picked up, never opened only
Judged by my cover. There are things we pass by
In life every day like the book on the shelf
That we never open up. Had we opened it we would
Have found the riches within the book on the shelf.
So don't make judgment at first sight but look
For the riches within and you will find the
Riches in life like you never had before.
So don't pass up the book on the shelf but open
It up and find the riches within.
Eugene Cazes

Favor For A Friend

They swim through the seas
Like hair flowing in the breeze
Their voices are heard from miles away
Calling others to come and play.
Their bodies and beauty are a big as can be
And no hatred lies in these kings of the sea.
They love us as humans, they love us as one
We love them as lipsticks and kill them for fun.
The lives of these creatures will be at an end
If mankind's ways we do not amend-
A small concession I would say
To hear them sing and watch them play
Save the whales
Brittney Naccarato

Untitled

As the rain trickles down the back of
  my neck
I look up to the sky and feel the rain
  as it pours on my face.
Millions of tiny droplets crashing from
  above.
I twirl around and around letting the rain
  splash all around me.
Laughing not caring who's watching me,
I cry tears of joy, I'm finally free.
Then it stops and I look up
I turn around and walk away.
Kari Swaim

Shadows

there is a house at the end of the street
some say it is spooked
some say there is no such thing
but I say
they are just shadows of the past
coming to dance in the moonlight

shadows of innocence
shadows of love
shadows of heartbreak
shadows of death
all coming to dance in the moonlight

the night echoes of laughter and tears
and by dawn everything is still
just shadows of the night before
dancing in the dawns first glimmer

and so it goes
every night the same
all just shadows
dancing in the moonlight
Ariana M. St. Clair

BONDS

Connectedness so easy to say and see
The cord in a knot
Does not easily fall apart
The links in a chain
Welded in links of permanency
The strands in a rope
Interwoven beyond individuality
Two hands clasp
Bound, connected, eternally

Hands once clasped — slip away, slip away
Bond broken
One hand, alone eternally
One hand alone eternally?
To clasp ——?
To clasp is to risk
The slipping away
To extend ones hand
Is to hope
Hope for a strand
a cord a chain
Rose Stachowiak

Only You

In my history there have been many males,
Relatives, family, and even friends.
In my existence there is only one son,
Who will grow up and mature.
In my life there is only one man,
And that man is you.
You've given me more than I can ever want.
And more than I can ever desire or need.
You filled my home with laughter and happiness,
You filled my life with children and hope.
You give me your heart and your love,
You give me warmth and your humor.
You give me arguments and attitudes,
But you also give me peace and affection.
You fill my mornings with pleasure,
You fill my days with gratification,
You fill my evenings with lust,
You fill my nights with passion.
The more I look at you, the more I love you,
That's why, not only do I love you, but I'm also in love with you
Maggie Orta

What Is The Sound Of Power?

Is it the rumble you hear in the sky
As an enormous jet flies by
Is that the sound of power?

Is it the sound of an AK47 being shot
And someone's being carried off on a cot
Is that the sound of power?

Is it the big bang of a cannon firing
Something that you're not admiring
Is that the sound of power?

Is it the sound of bloody knives knocking together
Leaving behind scars you live with forever
Is that the sound of power?

Is it the sound of a whip on the back of a slave
Tearing off skin he can no longer save
Is that the sound of power?

Is it the sound of a bullet ending a young President's life
Leaving behind his two kids with his wife
Is that the sound of power?

Is it the sound of a hammer putting a nail in God's hand
He's on a cross at the top of the land
Is that the sound of power?

Amanda Wittscheck

Springtime In The Mountains

Winter brought ice, snow and colds
But March show'd, already flowers it beholds
Well, people look for a change,
While ladies will do a flower/arrange.
And families will go out together
In this wonderful, warm'd up weather.
Forgotten are the ice, snow and cold
We're enjoying the wonderful warm'd up world.
Springtime, Everybody feels like new.
It brings new hope, in everything we do
And we make a garden, that is our will
We plant flowers and vegetables, up the hill.
With spade and rake, we prepare the soil
Set in the flowers and plants, with compost to boil
And soon all is in bloom and shine
We feel that is the mountain springtime!
Sure bring flowers on the table, it looks like spring
And wear bright clothing, that is the right thing.

Elli Poller

Disney Blockbusters

Mickey mouse is so funny,
Minnie is his honey.
Donald Duck is a goose.
Simba eats a big moose.
This is a great poem to write.
It might take all night.
Pinocchio has a long nose,
Daisy has no toes.
I can think of lots like me.
Plus the Genie gives wishes
Jasmine doesn't do dishes,
Winnie the Pooh and Tiger too.
Seven dwarfs and Snow White.
But there is no Knight.
Cinderella does the floors.
The little mermaid has no doors.
Dumbo has big ears
Mogily has lived in the jungle for years.
This poem covers Disney glory.
That is my poem and story

Nicole Lucero

Emotions To My Child

My anguish sometimes shows,
My face in its helpless dance.
The anger flashes around me, and I cry.

My heart feels such sorrow,
My mind swirls with riddles,
My arms ache for the touch,
I know I won't have.

I remember our love and lives,
The smiles and repentant words,
The hurtful memories...
The emotions blackened.

Wait... is there hope?
Why no answer? Over time I see smiles,
And love as it boldly triumphs!

Time walks by, my hope dims again,
But in my mind, I see and remember love.

I shall be the champion
She shall see truth
Won't she? Won't she?
Remember my love...

Teresa Symmes

Please, Don't Compromise!

Even if you are very wise,
you still have to deal with daily compromise.

Inside your family, your work, your head
we sometimes get what we want, but often not only that,
and there is a "little something" in us
which refuses that "attached" compromise.

Attached to almost everything
if you take your time and really think!

But friendship - seeing enough far
it's made of people who cross the bar.

If needed: fight, defend and take the stands
and don't loose that precious gift - your friends.
They are your family and more
(Hopefully you don't pick up a "bore"...)

The understanding, discrete and truly loving friend
is what we mostly need now - and at the very end.

Choices shall be made very carefully and kept through the years;
(so often everyone else will have only a couple of deaf ears)

Selecting a friend - be wise and keep remembering:
This may be the only chance when you don't have to compromise!

Jaruska Parente

The Beach

Ocean roaring, moving fast,
trying hard to make time last,

Sea gull's flying through the air,
Children playing here and there,

Clouds in shades of pink and blue,
Sunny days I like them too!

I smell sweet grass as the
sun goes down, on a sand dune I sit,

And all around is the beautiful beach
I have grown to love, and as if saying hello,
a sea gull passes above.

Meghan Mathis

Poetry Land

There is a land where I can go
and in the summer make it snow,
and in the winter I can reach
into the hot sand on the beach,
and I can fly without a plane
through hurricane of wind and rain!

A kid no longer, I am grown
and have a mansion of my own.
You want a truck of candy corn?
Go to the land where poems are born.
It's not too short and never too long-
in the land of poems you can't be wrong.

And if you're feeling really lost and
your brain's in the freezer and needs to defrost,
then ride a cloud to the stars with me
and I will show you how to be free
and the freedom will come when you find -
you can go anywhere - in your mind!
Chris McCarthy

A Widow's Morn

Heart broken of a lost loved one,
that is soon to be forgotten in everyone else's mind but
stays in hers.

Feels alone, feel angry.
For now she is abandoned on this God forsaken earth from
not only a friend but from the most precious thing in
this world. Her one true love.

Always thinking of him. Misses their talks and arguments.
Often thinks of death, for she wants to be by his side
once again.

Always weeping from the hole in her heart that this
tragedy has left her with. So much pain, so much loss that
all she can do now is sigh a silent widow's morn.
Anthony Mascolo

Pollution

I am Beauty, I am Love.
I am what mankind wants on this planet.
Don't ever try to change me,
Leave me the way I am.
I will change your life forever,
Because I have character.
Be careful with my fragile heart,
Because it is on the verge of breaking,
And just now an I putting back the pieces.
I will not tolerate any abuse,
Because I am Strong Willed and I have Rage.
As time goes on my beauty and passion for man,
Has left. I will be strong
For as long as I can,
But with each passing day,
My beautiful clean Face starts to get a little dirtier.
But I will be strong,
Because I am Mother Earth.
Julie Kasdon

"Fire"

A lone solitary spark,
A glimmer of hope,
Breaks away from the group.
Its purpose is to be an example,
To show the way,
But its opinions aren't that of the whole,
It dies away as silently as it came.
Katherine Silvia

Fears Chains

The chains of past bind my soul
reeking havoc as their toll
binding my heart in horrid space
as they feed unmastered on future's face

The chains of past bind my soul
decaying my mind's immortal memories of ole
as once love filled days
are eclipsed by a deep, dark purple haze

The chains of past bind my soul
chains of falsehood black as coal
strength they gather from life's daunting fear
strength that's coupled with a lack in me, a lack to hear

The chains of past bind my soul
in a morbid attempt to reach their goal
festering with unbridled joy
contented to keep my heart a lustful toy

So now you know and see my fate
know why life has encrusted me with hate
to not want love and all its pain
if only in my mind, to keep me here, to keep me sane.
Vergena A. Forbes

Cry Of The Nighthawk

Tis evening - the sun basks in a golden
    glow as the sun lowers itself to the horizon
a wisp of a breeze cools my sticky brow
    as it winds down toward evening
The quite hush is interrupted by the cry of the nighthawk
The barking of some families dog
and the rustling of the leaves beneath an eventide wind
Tis my favorite time of day - this golden twilight
The peace that seems to crawl like a hush
    through suburban hedges
    and fenced in homes
    is like memory
I seem to remember, It will not be long
before I hear my mothers cry
soaring through the wind with the nighthawks
calling me to shower and slumber
as I wind down another day.
Debra D. Scott

Invisible

I looked into her eyes and I could see the pain that I had caused
a slip of the tongue and my mouth breathed life to a word that was
dead. A blade cut through the rubber band that was holding us
together but I couldn't help her because I didn't know how to cry
my heart hurt for her, my eyes burned for her, my mind did
somersaults for her, yet she did not see any of it behind the mask of
silence that I was encased in. She didn't see my sorrow, my tears,
my love. she didn't hear my screams, she couldn't see me cry, and I
could only stand there and watch the torment on her face she
writhed in pain, her pain, my pain. I wanted to give myself to her
in the true sense of the word I wanted to pour out my blood on the
floor and spit in it I could have chopped my heart into a million
tiny, tiny pieces I could have ripped out my eyelashes, strand by
strand and thrown them away, I felt like cutting off my toes and the
fingers on my left hand, if it would have taken her pain away.
yet my body was numb and I was aware that I could not move, I
could not talk, I could not run away and hide, I could not breathe.
she was unable to see what was happening to me, that I was dying
for her, so she just turned and walked away
Aja Horwitz

A Wish Is A Dream

I wish I was rich and had a new car
I wish I could travel around the world and to the stars.
I wish I had a dog, so I could love it so
I wish I was smart and everything I know.
I wish there was peace in the world today
I wish my birthday was everyday.
I wish my dad wouldn't have died
I wish my mom hadn't always cried.
I wish I had a friend that I could talk too
I wish I had a hobby or something to do.
I wish that I could feel loved
I wish I could get hugged.
I wish I had a cabin by a stream
If these wishes don't come true, I could always dream.

Dan Carlson

Restless Winter

Restless pondering memories,
fiery sunsets charring yesterday.
Broken water no rapid flow.
Just a slow trickling stream with very little soul.
Not caught in a current, but gasping for air.
Lost the shine in the silky glare.
Restless pondering days to come.
Hunger embezzled, feeling icy numb.
Dissipated rapture, seizing delight.
Winter chills, not a single sign of life.
Wakened with steaming memories of summer nights.
Wishing winter would come to an end, quietly within a dream.
I find myself wakening with a chilling scream.
Soon Winter will allow Spring to break.
The Sunshine in Spring, will warm my life again.
Leaving the cold lonely nightmares in the Winter Cold.
Where even a small inn
ocean child, grows a scary old.

Lynn Mandy

Play "Malaguena"

Play "Malaguena", let me dream once again;
Let him hold me in images gleaned from my mind.
Play "Malaguena"; he's smiling and then ...
The music stops playing...I'm left far behind.

Softly, play softly; don't scare him away;
His memory grows dearer each time that they play.

Play "Malaguena", let me hear castanets.
He brightened my life with his music and song.
Play "Malaguena"; how I ache with regrets ...
Still his memory stays,
While the melody plays ...
All night long.

Virginia J. Kasza

No More Gray

As the roar of the thunder rings in my ears
the strobe of lightning reveal my tears
never again will I experience these fears
It makes me sick not knowing why I'm here

As I reminisce our memories and ponder our past
I remember all the good times that made us last
Now I'm stuck here in despair, wishing you were here
Trying to escape by drinking whiskey and beer
but, it doesn't replace my loneliness for you
distorting in my heart what I once thought I knew
but, you know, time will heal all wounds, so they say
so now I'm waiting for that glorious day
when the skies clear up and the clouds roll away
and once again there will be no more gray

James Everett Stevens

Goodbye, My Love

As I sit by your side
you reach for my hand
for something to hold on to.
I look at you
You gaze into my eyes
and mouth the tender words, "I love you."
I sit and think
of just how lucky I am
to know that you are mine.
The world's not fair
I know that now
for soon we must say goodbye.
We get to that terrible place where we must part.
We sit in the cold, holding hands
while we wait...
Finally you must go...
You get up, and with a single kiss,
you are gone and I must go on without you.
Until I see you again...

Cassandra Levitt

Untitled

Today I traveled very far,
Tonight I'll wish upon a star.
I'll wish for sanity to come to me,
I'll wish for sanity to set me free.

Today I had no where to go,
I was feeling down and low.
I looked above and saw the rain,
I figured God felt the same.

That night I laid awake in bed,
Trying to unscramble the thoughts in my head.
I opened my eyes to send them away,
I then realized tomorrow was a whole new day.

I fell asleep not knowing why,
I had to live and had to die.
The sun was out and shining bright,
I completely forgot about last night.

Tomorrow I'll travel very far,
Then I'll wish upon a star.
I'll wish for insanity to come to me,
I'll wish for insanity to set me free.

Douglas L. Gamble

This Dreamer's Wish

There are some things I can't erase,
Your special touch, your pretty face;
The way we talked, your soft sweet kiss,
Us together; This Dreamer's Wish.

If there was a potion to change the past,
A potion that could make love last;
I'd search the world for just a taste,
Wishing our love would not go to waste.

It's just a dream this dreamer sees;
Dreams are forever, I'll dream of you and me.
With this at heart, filling my mind,
It's the only way, true happiness I'll find.

As you live your life, in all you do,
Keep within your heart that I love you
You are the best, I gave my all,
And never intended this true love to fall.

Now all my love I am sending with this,
And wishing for yours;

This dreamer's wish.

Mark D. Welch

Mountain Of Love

Here I am lonely on the mountain,
   With a mountain of love in my heart.
Oh! If only I could trust love again,
   But I don't know where to start.

The lonesome call of a lobo wolf,
   As he howls at the silvery moon,
Is akin to my soul's quest for true love,
   So far from the middle of June.

The diamond stars in the mid-night sky,
   Twinkle and whisper this message to me.
"She waits around the bend on the river of life,
   Have strong faith and you will see."
   James R. Madison

Untitled

Today I stop to think and rest for awhile,
I sit under a tree and begin to smile;
I realize something important to me,
That I've been blessed with love through eternity.

It isn't my allowance from week to week,
It isn't my jewelry, our house or my jeep,
I have come to see life's reason for living
It's the memories we make, sharing and giving.

It's small things we do that brings us together,
Done in sunshine and warmth or cold, bad weather,
It's ski trips and car rides for thousands of miles,
That brings us together to share special smiles.

It's time as a family in church and at home,
That have nurtured my life in which I have grown,
For the love we share and the memories we make,
Will always be a part of each passing day.

As I stop thinking of our great of love,
I look up to the sky and thank God above,
For without my family I must say I know,
My life wouldn't know how to love, prosper or grow.
   Nicole C. Blonder

"Trust Has To Be Earned"

Backer, the packer, liars, the players.
Fixing and mixing, cheating and teasing. Causing trouble.
   No honor in the world.
Show boating, mo boating, nowhere to turn, to look for an honest face.
"Trust nowhere to find."
A smile on the face, a pat on the back is not always what it
appears to be.
Talking, lying, joking, signifying monkey, please "Get off my back."
Give me some peace from this; "Miss Shift of Nothingness."
Trust, where are you?
Do what you say. Say what you do.
Words without action means trust is gone bye-bye.
One time only can label you when you are the new kid on the block.
Your track record is black.
Made a mistake?
Build and rebuild a reputation of recognition.
Say what you mean and do what you say.
Then you will reciprocate and give truthfulness and trustfulness.
The trust you earn will be your gratification.
Your masterfication to be among the trusted ones
"Trust Has To Be Earned"!
   Jean Poole

Untitled

Plunging into a deep, dark tunnel,
There is a small sliver of light at the end.
I have only the light to lead me out.
I can hear death creeping up on my,
Hissing soundlessly within my mind.
Seeing a clothed figure with a sickle,
I run faster through the tunnel,
To no avail, I see now,
That I will always be in the tunnel
With death at my side,
And light at the end of the tunnel,
Drifting further and further away.
   Mike Canfield

"Laugh, Laugh, Laugh"

Turn on your laugh...
Turn off your laugh...
To laugh or not to laugh...
To laugh, laugh, laugh...

Threading your needle
And your thread suddenly grows fat...
Laugh, Laugh, Laugh...

When you get in your car
And that tire is flat...
Laugh, Laugh, Laugh...

Your new partial is a food trap...
You open up your yap, You Laugh...
And everything ends up on the
Other guys Lap...

So you call yourself a Sap...
Now look at that and Laugh, Laugh, Laugh...
   Judy Alexander

My Precious Lamb

I love you, my precious Lamb,
My life I gave for you.
I am your Shepherd, trust in me.
Your guide I'll always be.

As you journey along life's winding path,
And loneliness engulfs your weary mind,
Remember, you're not alone, my precious one.
I Love you, refuge in my arms you'll find.

When the fierce storms of life are raging,
And the path you cannot find,
Rest secure, my precious lamb.
I'll still the storm and calm your troubled mind.

When steep mountains rise before you,
And the strength to climb is gone,
Lean on me, my precious one
And new strength again you'll find.

When you come to the end of life's journey,
I'll not leave you alone to roam.
Cling to me, my precious lamb.
I'll carry you safely home.
   Lois Myers King

Butterflight

Behold, a butterfly wings his way towards me whom which to light,
He spreads his wings and stretches them, resting from his flight,
He flies away and I watch and listen, for I am the beholder,
And I'm thankful that his size is small, for he left something on my shoulder.
   Frank C. Williams

Untitled

"Hallelujah! He has come!"
His joyful followers dance and sing,
And strew the palms upon the ground,
To make a pathway for their King.
"Hail! He is coming! Christ Jesus!
The son of God, Messiah, Lord!
From our own sins He will save us!
This man, sprung from the Prophets' word!"
The throngs are jubilant, and well-
Jesus forgives and loves, and heals.
And from His Father, the Word He tells
Of God's true love, which all can feel.
And He has come! All strain to see,
Is he mounted high? Then comes a sound
Of shock, for He's on a donkey
So humble, and so near the ground.
This Heavenly King! The Holy Dove!
So humble, like a common man,
Has come in God's redeeming love,
And He is silent witness stands.

Rebecca Simmons

Gentle Darkness

As the quiet darkness rapes my senses,
  I feel cold and alone.
I look for comfort in the soft down of my pillow,
  but it is no use; nothing will end this sadness.
Then the music starts.

At first it seems to pull me close.
The notes reach my ears as if they were a lover's
  kiss upon my neck.
Then the beat seems to caress me tenderly.

I feel myself being wrapped in the silkiness of the
  rhythm, lifted higher and higher.
At last slowly, gently, I am let down onto a bed of petals.
It is then I realize I am once again alone in the
  darkness.

Something is different.
I am warm and satisfied.
I realize my dark thoughts have been replaced
  with a certain peace, as I drift off to sleep.

Sarah Elizabeth Rovere

Shuttered brain
you blink out unfavorables
and they never were.
Repeat and repeat
positively sure.
Substanced and pure
my corners howl
and cross the path of your haltless trucks.
Hold still
to feel my smooth unwavering edges.
I need no planes nor sandpaper
to be finished and full
but you whisper seeping normalcies
and saturate and drip all over me
and smile in approval,
ignoring the dread inherent
dismissing collapse.

Donald Henry Dusinberre

Autumn

The green trees of summer slowly fade away
As Mother Nature, with paint brush in hand,
Paints the bright green trees into
A rainbow of crimson red, orange and gold mural.
Everything is changing.
The wind blows, as the trees sway.
And the leaves dance and frolic in the wind.
The leaves fall and fall to the ground, forming a blanket of color.
Everything is changing.
The grass, the leaves, and the trees dance to the wind's music.
Fall is like a dance of nature.
Slowly and silently the warm sun says good-bye.
Everything is changing.
The sun's blazing colors slide behind a mountain.
A transition is taking place.
A transition of colors, of harmony and of life.
A new season is being born.
A cool wind sweeps over the land.
Fall has arrived and summer has gone.
Everything has changed.

Angela Forgues

Soul Mate

On the fourth plane of existence,
Souls dance and play after being released from shells.
They exist in love and rescued from moral conflicts.
The souls frolic in pairs and beget in the blue darkness of freedom.

Marie Chambers

Final Wish

I've long wished that when my soul
Is liberated from its flesh
It may join with its sister, the sea.

So please

Unloose my ashes upon the crest of
Surging whitecaps, making my reunion
with marine soulmates and kin complete.

But please

Don't beat yourselves with belated or
Insincere remorse... If you will truly miss
Me, shed your tears for you, not me:

Because my new world has no room for guilt!

Ann Racic

Evil Empathy

Evil empathy holds me back.
A self controlling silence clings to my back.
I feel as though I have wings and I could fly.
But I pull myself down from the sky.
I forgive even those who's anger,
makes me shy.
I do not wish to back off life,
but my heart is pale with fear.
So I take my so-called place,
so close, so near,
to an absolute disgrace.
I stand still;
unmoved in my place,
unmoved in life, and the fake smile on my face.
I am still till no sorrow is blamed on me.
I am not the way life has framed me to be.
How could the joy of my life ever be,
and the confidence I deserve never die,
when evil empathy is the tie,
that holds me to the ground.

Adrienne Joan Staab

"True Trove"

The hail, and snow,
All of these precipitations you know,
But there is one you have not heard,
It is the third,
It is more dangerous than all of the above,
The name of this is the trove,
The trove is a mix of them all,
It ruins the land and tears the love,
So, be careful when you walk,
Just in case the weatherman says the trove is out.
   Brigid Kelly

Daybreak

Morning
The sun rises. It shines on me as I ponder
the wonders of the day.
Birds sing. They know not the dangers
that lie ahead.
Doors slam - dogs bark - horns honk
The city comes alive again.
People bustle about as a new day begins —
And life goes on.
   Eloise H. Macbeth

Moondancing

With sparkling eyes and a tug on my arm,
and a face still clear of let-down,
you announced your intent as if the moon was next door
and the dance floor was clear to the sky.

"Mommy!" You said,
as we "good-nighed" the moon.
"Mommy, listen!" you cried as we peered at the orb,
while urgently tugging my arm.

"Yes, son?" I answered, awaiting a laughable thought,
the kind that makes us both giggle.
Instead I received a wondrous vision
of my son in the future-time, now.

"I'm going to dance on the moon!" You announced,
the moondancing light in your eyes.
"Son, I replied," you know,
I think that you'll do just that!"
   Jan Johnson Wondra

To My Daughter "Michelle"

You're in my thoughts
You're in my prayers
I can't tell you enough, how much I care.
My beautiful caring daughter
The things you do
The things you say
All that you have accomplished large and small,
I will always be very proud of you.
I know we have our disagreements, just a few.
They always pass for me, I hope, also for you.
Life is short, live it to the fullest,
Don't waste it on problems you can't solve.
Now the miles have come between us
and the visits few, but never the love
I have for you.
   Love Mom
   Catherine J. Sawicki

My Walk

As I walked through a farmer's field
I did imbibe God's majesty.
Staring 'cross the great expanse
I realized what I should be.

The grain was waving in the breeze
It called for me to do much more.
The whispers whistled through the trees
Of all God had for me in store.

'Twas then my life flashed e'er my eyes
Of all the things I'd left undone.
The scenes where I had left the path
Created by His only Son.

My knees grew weak as my heart sank
Fast fell I to my knees.
I asked to have yet one more chance-
"Yes" whispered in the breeze.

As then I stood and gazed around
And thought the world was rearranged;
More light and peace were now on earth...
No, it was I that changed.
   Keith A. Richards II

Nature and the Dreamer

There is sanctuary in a lofty dream
Where troubles fade and visions boast
Amid colorful wildflowers and sprouting fields of green...
Where all is perfect with God and man, or mother if you please.

Destiny vanishes for lack of thought or design
Like a ghostly shadow lost in a sudden burst of light;
But with a dash of hope, a moment in time,
One can embrace a reverie that takes you to an obscure place...
There you'll quite often find the one called Me.

Today I'm like a firefly; woe and despair vanish and reappear
But ever so gently, like a fleeting summer breeze.
What tomorrow holds may be unclear;
But today is another beginning of life's journey...
To dream on to a new horizon.
   Jacqueline McElrath

Death And Time On A Day In Eternity

He is black, cold.
He grows not dreary with age.
He lies face down upon the ground.
He lies in the shadows waiting, patiently waiting.

He is not good nor bad.
But he is there.
Time grows old as he does not.
He is quiet waiting, oh so patiently waiting.

Until you can stand no more,
He steps forward and takes the beat from your heart,
And blows your soul away.

He causes neither agony nor relief.
You cannot run or avoid.
Nor are you able to thwart him.
He is Death, and will always wait.

He is everywhere and yet nowhere.
Time and space knows him not.
Yet he shall hold all in his grasp.
For he is darkness. He is.....Death.
   J. Dodson

Shattered Dreams

I built a house of paper once,
And expected it to withstand the rain.
I fell in love with love once,
And expected to withstand the pain.

Friendships have gone stale, you know,
And love lasts but a day.
Searching for the truth, I find,
No path to lead the way.

At rainbow's end, a pot of gold,
Lies waiting for my touch.
Shattered dreams of life sometimes,
It all appears too much.

With beguiling witchcraft and elfin magic,
I search to my dismay.
Only to find my heart's desire,
Gone within a day.

These truths of life that are haunting me,
Can all be as it seems?
When knowing that in my self-deceit,
I live in shattered dreams.
Mario Kiefer

The Search

Have you ever seen the loving side?
Its smell is sweet like roses.
Its sound is a kind seldom heard, yet it is
yearned for.
Its touch gives an everlasting feeling.
Its sight is an ultimate glow that is eternal.
Its truth and honesty and never changes.
It draws you in like the beauty of nature.
Its colors radiate like a rainbow.
Its a security that never leaves.
Its a sense of knowing with no fear.
It is the beginning and the ending.
Its everyone's journey, but sometimes it's forever.
Jennifer M. Galbraith

Some One Cares

If you think that no one cares;
Remember one positive thought,
And, feel the secure comfort that it brought.

Remember a special place;
Recreate it, in you mind, with a lovely trace.

Remember all good things;
And, feel the glowing passion,
That each one brings.

Let yourself be guided through a higher power;
And, let the energy flow;
Wash over you, a wonderful shower.

If you think that no one cares;
Recite this toward a looking glass,
And, the reflection that stares;
With beauty and class,
Is that-some one who cares; always!!
Karen Monk

Alone

Alone she stands on the sandy beach
Her eyes on the horizon, she stands dressed in grey.
While her companions, just out of her reach
In the sparkling waters, frolic and play.
Alone she stands with her head bowed low
Longing for her mate of long ago.
Remembering the day he was taken from her
That early morning in the first sun's glow.
For seven years she has been without him
And when her friends again rise into the sun
She follows far behind in their proud formation
For the gray goose, another lonely year has begun.
Vivian R. Brooks

Colors

Blue, black, purple, and green,
these are all colors of a
beautiful scene.

Beautiful Blue, Precious Pink,
pretty colors, don't you think?

Orange, yellow, red, and white,
plain as day and as the night.

All these colors are where you go.
And all shine brightly through a rainbow.

Peaceful peach, Graceful gray,
Enjoy these colors
because they might be gone someday!
Megan Nicole Kuhn

Remember Me

Remember me with a smile,
how I pushed you to walk that extra mile.
All the joyful times we shared,
true I was,
I always cared.
The struggles in life
the tears we cried
forget me not,
I was always by your side.
Let the spotlight shine on my soul,
to never let the memories grow old.
Remember me with a smile,
I had a heart of gold.
If you cry through the night,
I'll bless you with strength
to defeat the fight.
And when it's time
for your life's journey to conclude,
you too will win
just like I knew you would...
Stephanie O'Neill

That Old Field

I remember, long ago,
that old field was my place to go.
In need or in fun
it didn't matter which one.
It was always there — a thinking spot.
A trusted friend that couldn't be bought

So why, I think to myself, would someone destroy it?

That old field could be many things —
a pirate ship, an eagle's wings.
But today it's one thing and nothing more —
a parking lot and grocery store.
Now that fine old field is gone.
But my memories of her will always live on.
Molly Stuart

The Desert

His touch stones, land marks and mirrors are no more
He is lost

He knows not his name or
what direction the wind

He has only to reach through the veil
and guidance is at his side
But he is lost

She stands next to him waiting

She has been in this desert before him
felt the sting of sand

She knows this abyss of nothingness
and vast empty horizons

She knows the untouched parts of him
But he is lost and does not see

And so she waits
Melissa M. Smith

Forever A Dream

An untouched dream is forever untold, like an answer unspoken or a thought put on hold. A memory impressioned or a footprint left behind, washed away with your touch for someone else to find. A dream of the sunset as it borders the sky, looking out toward the sea as you fall down and fly.

Picturing yourself on a moonlit bay, as you dance through the waters that carry you away. Images drifting as you stand beneath rain, showered with wonder as the sky reviles pain. Seeing a kaleidoscope of everlasting dreams, puts the world in confusion and not as it seems. A breath without air or a minute without time, is this all possible or an illusion of mine?
Hallie Haskins

Sonnet 1

O what wretched Mage now seen before thee,
Trapped self in summoned magical walls,
Walls of such strength one could never break free,
Tired soul yearning for love's tender call:
Inside the walls the mind makes city-states,
Alpha states wish the walls to grow higher
With hope one state sees the wall's only gate,
Yearning for it to burst forth with love's fire.
Then I view thee and all I am now shines
This vision break walls that let not love through,
Waves burst the death gate and to me love binds
Free spirit becomes me when I view thee;
Youth then fills this old wretched soul; I dance;
And my evil heart pierced by love's golden lance.
David L. Wilson

Your Beating Heart

The moon does light the stars at night,
with you in my arms contentment quite.
The kisses like volleys seem to flow,
I feel our love dawning for it's you in my arms I hold.
Our skin touches generating sparks,
like fireflies and starry skies it's we who light the dark.
Our lips do seethe as we cuddle close.
Two young lovers trying in love to make the most;
and as we go to settle down we become one body with love our host.

For you are the one I share my soul with,
through budding dawn, dew and morning mist.
Your body stirs again gently next to mine,
through life's enchanted mornings seem fresh and new each time.
I know when you are with me for I have not a thing to fear,
for I am quite content with you beside me, your beating heart so near.
Robert K. Allison III

"The Devil's Intention"

Seeds of lead now fill the air
like lightening in a storm.
Soldiers wondering if they'll live
to breath tomorrow's morn.
Children who once played
and laughed now bear a knife and musket.
Women who once sang and dance,
bear black, a shovel and casket.
Brothers forced to choose a side
both dying by fratricide.
And this you say, who made this day,
the serpent filled with laughter?
Pride, malice, noxious gases all
form his composition.
Trickery, deceit, pure evil,
there is no resolution.
Just don't invite, receive, believe,
God's hand of competition.
For if you do, you'll do no more,
in war, the Devil's intention...
Justin Mims

One True Love

Our love was meant to be
We both screwed up one too many times
You've moved on
And I still dwell on the past
We had some really good times, we also had some bad
But we always seemed to find our way back
This time it wasn't meant to be.

We use to say 'I Love You'
Now we barely say 'Hello'
I thought we'd always be together
Now there is someone new
The way you used to feel about me will never be the same
We can never take back the things we said or did
At least know that I still care
And will always be there

You were my first and only love
Our love has disappeared, though, never to be found again
But please don't forget me
Because I will always love you!
Stephanie Schmitz

The Betrayal Of Felix

He gazes up at me with loving eyes
And lets his motor of purrs run loud
He jumps in my lap and kisses my face
With his sweet kitten kisses like Judas
Then he attacks my nose with a piercing bite
And bounds away laughing at his new found trick
He sits on the sink and bats me with his tail
Purring as I put ointment on my throbbing face
But when his dish runs empty and his tummy rumbles
The little fiend will have a change of heart
He will lavish his undying affections and sincere pleads for forgiveness
I will forgive him and feed him a meal of the finest milk and tuna
And as I sleep my tiny kitten will warm my feet and lick my cheek
The next morning I find his newest trick and my favorite plant
Brutality murdered and scattered about the rug and shiny marble floor
With the little fiend smiling at me with hopeful eyes next to his empty dish
Amy Hunt

A Different Rainbow

Every star is in its place
Every blade rooted to its determined spot
But where am I?
The blind man had his place by the pool.
Paul had a journey.

My colors are do distinctly different
that I sometimes wonder,
have I strayed from my place?
I am surrounded by red and gold.
My fondness for them cannot disguise
  that I bear the colors of another clan.
I am not one of them.
I am of a different mind,
a different rainbow.
And as I am of separate past,
  I am also of separate future.
Our paths have only entangled for a while
though I so desperately want to believe
  I have only strayed.
But if I haven't, is it too late?

Melinda Chadwick

"Solo"

I stand above the sinister abyss
and watch the vile wraiths pace to and fro,
staring up at me with eyes that pierce my soul.
Daring me to vacillate
from euphony to hellish screams of despair.
To fall headlong into eternal darkness
And die the death of a timorous coward.

I sweat like a vaporous thundercloud.
My tie feels like a hangman's noose
as they cajole, threaten, try to drag me down
as their dark master stands behind me
prodding me with a blazing pitchfork.

Still the words rise steadily from my undaunted larynx
And move the earth to seal the cursed hole.
Demoniac screams fade to enthusiastic applause
And my tortured soul now drifts across celestial waters.

Greg Przywara

Seasons

The sun breaks free of her winter cage, and then begins to shine,
Winter's crisp snow begins to melt, and leaves only green grass behind.
Robins hop around in the sunshine, exposing their bright redbreasts,
In the trees, now green with leaves, they begin to build their nests.

The colors of many beautiful flowers, have now begun to show,
After a refreshing spring shower, the sun begins to shine to create
  a colorful Rainbow.
Animals frolic, happily, to and fro,
Glad to be rid of winter's cruel snow.

Butterflies flutter about in the air,
Making the world seem free of care.
Everything seems so bright and alive, making spirits fly,
But, slowly, spring, and summer too, begin to end, and then pass by.

The warm summer air begins to change, becoming crisp and cold,
The trees' green leaves fall off, making everything seem withered
  and old.
But I know that fall and winter will soon pass,
For when it comes to seasons, nothing seems to last.

Jessica Lahrmann

Little Black Girl

Little Black Girl where have you been?
I have been in slavery with other men.

Little Black Girl where have you been?
I have been with Dr. King marching with other men.

Little Black Girl where have you been?
I have been talking to God with other men.

Little Black Girl where have you been?
I have been earning my respect with other men.

Little Black Girl where have you been?
I have been helping mankind with other men.

Lana Scott

Golden Wings

My heart has harden,
My mind is meek
Cause I'm constantly thinking each day.
But deep down inside I know,
That as sure as the winds do blow,
That God's there where ever I place my feet.
One never knows why he does things differently
Just do right and live life in a righteous way
He don't do this to try to destroy you,
All he wants is for you to obey.
So each day I take life much serious,
I do not talk with distasteful talk
I do not act on devilish thinking,
And I keep peace and love and grace in my walk.
So if you ask why are you so happy?
You ask as if you are heir from a king
I'll slowly turn away and say yes I am heir,
And my father has blessed me with golden wings.

Richard Jordan

Lost Love

Past lovers
forever friends
two different lives, two separate paths
still, always travelers along the same road
Life
evolves in a full circle
Through fate's twist, their thoughts inter twine
A tear falls into an open heart
comforting waves rush toward a lonely beach
Chance then,
to feel the warm ocean breeze on their skin?...
Dare then,
to walk hand-in-hand in the moonlight,
barefoot in the sand?...
Questions ...
for one's mind to ponder
Answers ...
Only the heart can give.

Roger Steven Virata

Wish From The Blind

As the old man stepped - from the cab in the night
  The driver spoke loud - It's such a dark night
I wonder if "God" - sleeps thru the night
  and the devil comes out - and scores on sight...

Shuffling alone - in the stillness of night
  The old man spoke loud - in his broken voice
I hope one day - to see your troublesome world
  up there where "God" may sleep - not from my dark world

Nathan M. LeStage

The Fabric Of Our Worldly Lives

Like an extended embroidery needle pulling colorful strands of thread,
My being is sewn together with all other beings of the world.
I stitch my way through the lands of America, Canada, England,
France, Egypt, and Spain, and discover that the connective threads
ravel the fabric of all the world's people in a multiplicity of
colorful arrangements. Our cloth is bound together,
connected by the threads of life given to us by our creator.
Let not the prejudices of individually zippered thoughts and ideas,
unravel the elegantly embroidered colored fabric of the world.
The cloth has been painstakingly woven, cut, and stitched together.
God's embroidery needle is forever piercing, stitching, binding,
and decorating - with great detail - the fabric of our common
existence.

Merredith Frazier Perkins

Fear -

Sickly whispers faintly fall
From salty painted lips
My frail fingers curl to grasp
For a fleeting feel of loneliness
Dusty debris lingers below
Between the blankets where we lie
In a place where touch cripples hate
We steal feelings floating by
And as lights slide from wall to wall
I'm carried with power from alcohol
Gently stealing your need for more
As you pull me twisting to the floor
Curled embrace I hold you near
Searching sadly through our haze of fear
Empty seclusion in sedated stare
My alcohol screams and doesn't care

Matthew Wood

Old Man Moon

The moon is a wondrous sight
Way up there on high
It beams on the earth and sea
How jealous must be the sky.

Small, large, and larger it gets
Until it fills the heavens with light
What a glorious feeling it is
To be out on a full moon night.

But, alas, alack and gee whiz
It's millions of miles on high
What good is it to me
Way up there in the sky?

It can't get you what you want
Can only make your heart grow sad
So look at the moon, then close your eyes
And dream of what you could of had.

So remember, when you look up high
It's just a light in the sky
For missiles to be guided by, by and by.

Patricia A. Gauss

Untitled

As I lay in this bed alone,
My heart aches to have you home.

You have been gone less than a day,
Yet your return seems like an eternity away.

Our chins are up and our spirits are high,
knowing you'll be back in a blink of an eye.

Don't you forget that We Love You,
And when you get home you'll know that it's true.

Lisa Lemek

Books

Books are strange but yet wonderful.
For they make the world go round.
You learn so many things without traveling around.
Books for children and grown men.
Young and old together.
Many books have tales to tell and knowledge to be told.
Books give wisdom but yet stories too.
Books of love and horror, happiness and the blues.
Yet they are all the same in one way, the powerful
affect they have on you.
Books are strange but yet wonderful.
And now you know why too.

Olivia Keyes

Spirit

On the other side of the door is life
In a reverenced whisper,
I give praise for the here and now
Secretly, I lay down my armor
Gratefully, I open myself to safety
and my spirit is set free
Separated from daily life, I transcend
Renewed, refreshed, refilled,
I pick up my armor and put it back in place
The door opens, I'll face the dragons once more

Secret,
  Separate,
    Safe.
      This!

Cindy Schlossnagle

"Honeymoon"

Listening to his heart beat with yours,
How you and his love soars,
His vows belonging to you,
A perfect life, for you he drew.

Perfect and sweet as honey,
Your love can never be bought by money.
It can only be bought by his protection,
Showing all his tenderly love and affection.

His eyes can burn your eyes to tears,
Protected by his love, you have no fears.
Belonging to each other for eternity, until you die,
Nothing becomes in between because there is a tie.

Michelle Savage

"Mum"

She lays alone awake at night
  Alone again with her past in sight
The memories of days gone by
  Still vivid in her memories eye

Living like this day to day
  Wasting her whole life away

For tomorrow will always come
  And the past should just be that

If you let it fade a little at the start
  It will go were it needs to be
    In the deepness of your heart
    And stay eternally.

Patricia L. Merritt

Untitled

Hello, old self.
Didn't expect to recognize your unfamiliarity
that distinct smelling smoke
heart's incense burning on the
cross that kills
attacked me, leading me to you—
opened my eyes and saw your face
remembered that terminated connection
still associated with
my doubles duties
are intermittently lost on the guillotine's fright
the evening's ignorance knew I was unsettled,
with daytime gazebo dreams
back when your days were candy-coated...
I remember.
I saw your face when I closed my eyes,
spoke with you over the train tracks,
recalled negative regrets of those blissful moments
above the stars and under the clouds—
it wasn't just me in those smoke-filled circles...you were there too.

Kristen Lytvinenko

The Drama Of Life

The murmuring ceased as the lights grew dim.
Slowly the curtains withdrew to reveal the cries of a child.
"The Birth," was written upon a page of white;
held by a man in a black tux seated in the fifth row.

The child grew, into a boy, into a man.
Always saying his lines with precision.
When he wanted the audience to laugh, they did;
and when he wanted them to cry, the tears fell.

Soon the young man grew old and lay upon his bed.
Breathing final breaths, thoughts spiraled back through his life.
So busy was he entertaining others;
the old man forgot to enjoy the life he had led.

The realization came too late for him.
For as he wept, Death stepped onto the stage.
The curtains closed upon the play called, "Life";
and the audience departed, none the wiser.

Kyle Owens

Remembering And The Agonizing Waiting Period

Concentrating on the tick-tock motion
in front of my eyes
Watching the hands move
in slow motion
just as you did moments before
upon my flesh
leaving a tickling sensation
covering me in a blanket
of feverish wetness
I wet my lips
running my fingers upon the dampened skin
feeling the evaporation

I lay spiraling downwards
in a downhill motion
Swaying bits and pieces
of the fragmented swirling concept of time
flying by ever so softly
caressing me with the knowledge
soon it shall be again

Patience Whittaker

The Cloth Of Life

My loom sits idle.
I had trouble with this warp.
The tension was uneven, the selvedge too loose.
As I wound it onto the back beam
One of the threads snapped,
Wrapping around its neighbors.
It pulled from the huddle and through the reed,
Destroying the orderly overshot pattern
Knotted, twisted, snarled, tangled.

Lars sits idle,
The orderly pattern of his brain destroyed
By the plaques and tangles of Alzheimer's.
Knotted, twisted, snarled, tangled.
Can the thread be repaired, replaced?
Can this warp be saved?
Researchers say there's a glimmer of hope for the future.

But it's too late for Lars.
We must forsake this warp and begin again,
New, smooth connecting threads,
An orderly overshot pattern in the cloth of life.

Frances Vadla

Where Does The Time Go?

Could we be considered the future's past
Or maybe the past's future?
Time just can't disappear, it has to
Travel Somewhere.

Does it automatically infiltrate our
Memories, or does it move on to a place
Among then and now?
Maybe it just remains here with us and we
Just don't notice.

Is there a way to go back or a way to advance?
If it is imperative to reside here and we can
Not leave, then the future's not deceit.
Time in the future can only be created if we
Choose it so.

If you please, where exactly does the
Time disappear to? Can it be found again?
Can it be restored? They do say that history
Repeats itself, so when it does, can you trap it
And force it to stay? Maybe not, but you know what?
I'd like to find it.

Clare E. Riley

"Love Garden"

It seems just like yesterday
My grandbabies and I planted the seeds
And then covered them with hay.
Then we took a Little break
We had homemade cookies and cool-aid.
Now refreshed, Brandon said.
Come Nana, lets make another flower bed.
I gathered up the things we needed
Brooke carried the seeds to be seeded.
Hollyhocks, Columbine and sweet Lavender
Brooke's favorite to plant for her mother.

I love the flowers through the years
And worked them by myself with tears
My little helpers are grown up and gone
Away from the flowers we have grown
But the garden of love is still here
Along with all the gray in my hair
But it still seems like yesterday
And the seeds they have planted are
in my heart to stay.

Sue McGraw

Untitled

There are many, many people who have dreamed throughout the years,
A dream to stop all violence and dry the victims's tears,

A dream that men some day could fly,
And explore space beyond the sky.

If you have had a vision of hope,
Hang onto the end of your rope.

No matter what remarks have been made,
Don't let the light grow dim and fade.

Everything is possible to achieve.
The only thing that matters is that you believe.

No matter how impossible your secret dream may seem,
Remember Mr. King's famous words,"I have a dream....."
Emily Windham

My Boys

They are my sorrows, as well as my joys,
They are my sons, two loving boys.
It's true they're responsible for a grey hair or two,
That's because they're boys, through and through.
I've been given roles, I didn't know I could play,
Being me, a wife and a mother, twenty four hours a day.
Either a school meeting, recital or soccer games,
All of these attendance records bear my name.
Whether it's to fight a cause or cheer for a goal,
It's for my boys and is now my role.
There are times I feel worn and wear a frown,
But hugs from my blue eyes, bring me around,
I glow with pride in whatever they do,
Only when they're sick, my heart breaks in two.
There is one thing in life that is like no other,
Having two wonderful sons who call me mother!
Deborah Lapinski

See You Tomorrow

You transformed my religion, you changed my view
You twisted the chains so I could be free
You paid the larks to sing for me
For all of this, I still love you

We talked of little, we learned of myths
My relationship with you was based on ifs
Yet you believed all I said, every word
And now I sit with a fallen bird

Oh how we have changed, me and you
Yet your changes bring me sorrow
I never thought this would be true-
See you tomorrow

You transformed my everything, you gave me my sight
As you fed these ambitions, there was something to live for
Even though this romance was nothing but a folklore
You bought me the stars that summer night

We never could, we never were, so we never will be
This one revelation brings me sorrow
But I can recall the words you gave only to me-
See you tomorrow
Tabitha Gayle Dial

The Meadow

If on the meadow I do stretch
I would seem like reaching for the sky
Oh so blue
It could seem I could catch a bundle of clouds from the sky
Oh me, I sigh
Would it be possible to touch the clouds
And have my fingers go through the clouds
So far up in the heavens
Doris Nixon

You And Me

As friends you and I have been through so much
The crying, the laughing, the playing and such.
With you I cannot remember even one little fight
We are the same but we are different,
   That's what makes it right.
You were there for me every time I needed you,
The problem did not matter, we saw it through.
With you it did not matter if I laughed or if I cried,
Through the good and the bad you stayed by my side.
We were separated once, but not for too long.
That did not matter, we still went on strong.
Now we are faced with being separated again,
But I know you will still be there as my best friend.
No matter how close we are or how far away,
Our friendship will still be there day after day.
I will never forget you, in the future I see,
We will always be friends,
   Together...
      ...You and me.
Heather K. Heers

Images Of Me With You

I am with you now and I have been since the beginning.
You feel my presence, yet sometimes I am taken for granted.
I can be hard to deal with or I can move with ease.
You will see my struggles and feel my hardships,
   but it is through me that you will find happiness.
You will search for my meaning, like a child searches
   for his mother.
Although I will leave you, I will be with many others.
For I am strong and everlasting.
I am life.
Roger Lyle Scott Jr.

Through My Eye

Through my eye I see the world;
   not as white or as black;
   not as man or as woman;
   but as being of nature and God.

Through my eye I see the truth;
   I see the moon and the sun;
   I see the good and the evil.

Through my eye I see the life;
   there is birth and death;
   there is sorrow and joy.
Through my eye and the being of my soul
I see the world and everything of myself.
Tamara Olivia Rooi

God's Promise

I promised you I would lead you out of
Egypt land, And I gave you Moses.
I promised you a savior,
And I gave you Jesus Christ.
I was good toward my world, I
gave you Malcolm, Martin, and Nelson.
I promised hope for a better tomorrow,
a world without sin or without sorrow.
Where crime and execution would be no more.
No drugs, gangs, poverty or war.
Where children can play and walk in peace
But tell me what have you promised me?
Jeffrey Mathews

In The Mind Of A Child

I was watching the tube, enjoying myself
When mom glanced at the clock, on the fireplace shelf
Said son it is late, lets get up to bed
All at once the night things, popped into my head

We climbed up the stairs, and down the hall to my room
To the place where I sleep, and mental demons loom
Mom Kissed me goodnight, then turned out the light
I covered my head, to shut out the night

I stayed awake, did not want the dreams
For fear mom and dad, would hear my loud screams
I waited and listened, for sounds that I knew
Like owls and crickets, my imagination just grew

I lifted the sheet, looked over the edge
Saw something, I think, On my window ledge
But to my surprise, By the light of the moon
Twas the shadow of our cat, invading my room

Then upon the walls, things moving too fast
What I thought was punishment, for things from my past
Turned out to be harmless, so tranquil and mild
But that's how it is, in the mind of a child

Raymond A. Walters

The Embrace Of Loving Death

Never changing
ever aging
this world has evolved around me

To your life I've paid no attention
until I saw it flow from your veins
and into my cold existence

It is this grief I carry
that is my unnatural life
as unnatural as I am immortal

I have beheld with my vampire eyes
all that is human, as I once was human
and now I see humanity clearly

As clear as the hunt
I will see you and I will watch you
and I will embrace you and call you by name

The loving embrace that brings death also is life
forever I will love you
and forever you will not resist

Forever in darkness I will wander
and forever you my love, will be life

F. Ezequiel

Could You Do It?

How many of you could walk down the street
Being mocked by the people you meet
Have stones thrown at your feet
And still love the world?

How many of you could watch your child
Being hung upon a cross
Have those nails drove through His hands
And still love the people?

Now Lord, I'll be honest with You
You did something that I don't think I could do.
You sacrificed your own Son
To gain more than a few.

Well, I thank You.
I love You.

Jody S. Hudson

Your Eyes

When I look into your eyes,
There is a cloaking happiness that engulfs me,
And drains from my body,
The fear, and torment, and rage,
From which I suffer.
Your eyes are the hard-hitting hands,
That gently pull me up,
After I have fallen helplessly,
Into the pits of hate and chaos.
The hands that give me CPR,
After I have inhaled the polluted water,
Of doubt and unwillingness.
The hands that lift me back to health.
Your eyes are a breezy rainforest, peaceful and lush,
Containing the cure to all sickness,
Including the love-sick pain to which I fall prey,
When you are not close to me.
Your eyes are the hug that you give me,
Every time I see you.
I want to see the world, through your eyes.

Stephanie Horowitz

Marionette

Dedicated to Jeffrey Dugdale

The sun is lifted gradually
Drawing the curtains of darkness
To reveal the rising light like days before
The morn is still
But something cries out in silence
Not heard but felt
The cries become painfully familiar
That of which a young one's shoulders
Are weak from the weight of the world
Insisting that the other's tears
Only strengthen himself
Not realizing that it's bringing him down - Falling
So kind so gentle
True pure form of goodness
Sealed and incapable of evil
The young one travels on
The influence is strong
Just smiling leaves a trace in memory
Don't forget, don't let go
Brace the wind and continue.

Nicole M. Bailey

The Day

All the town had come out
on this fine summer morn,
A shine glistening over them
from the sun who'd just been born.
And it filled the day with magic
making if perfect in every way,
and not a sprinkle, nor a shower
would take the beauty from this day.
And if a day could last forever
I would wish it to be this one,
for the happiness that it has brought me
will only end with the setting sun.
Oh, what wonderful a day
yet this didn't seem the case,
for where you'd expect to see a smile
there was a frown upon one's face.
Yet I still longed to be those people
but there was nothing I could do,
If only it hadn't been my funeral
I could enjoy this fine day, too.

Tony Trunfio

Friends

Friends stick by you through thick and thin.
They congratulate you when you win.
Friends are there to lend a shoulder when you cry.
They love to talk with you about the guys.
Friends come over for sleepovers.
They will even pet your smelly dog Rover.
Friends make sure nobody ever hurts you.
They care about you more than you ever knew.
Friends love you no matter what.
They always apologize after you've fought.
Friends could talk on the phone with you for hours at night.
Friends can be your salvation and your light.

Nancy Cook

"Feme Sole"

Your sweet scent wraps me up in the purest fantasy
Love you more then my benefactors,
Want you more then my chosen instrument
Fix my glass cage of endless pain.
Break this reign of unwanted turmoil.
I'm ready to drop, save me
Sealed in your lips. Contract, form
A muscle, dripping your scent. Secretions of your love.
Drink the purple wine of the death-strangled babe
Wish her luck on her washy journey through
The Renaissance of Virginity,
(Someday it will be broken
and innocence will reign in the
filthy streets of ignorant generations,
left behind only to reminisce
about the time aborted from
their wrinkles of ageless confusion.)

Caroline Gabrielli

A Daughter Grieves

Her mother died, and the string was severed.
The daughter floated alone and untethered.
No ties to bind her; no thoughts control.
Just bitter and bereft to her very soul.

Her mother died and comfort died with her.
Now feeling unsettled she tries not to be bitter.
No arms to cling to, no shoulders for crying
No soft voice to tell her to keep on trying.

Her mother died; it would never be the same.
One lost soul awash in life's game.
Her beacon was gone-her guiding light...
Would things go on? Would life ever be right?

I love you Momma with all my heart
And in my soul we are never apart.
I miss you Momma with all my being.
Your beautiful face is the angel I'm seeing.

Send me a message from up above
Awash with hope and eternal love.
Let me know you've a hand in all that I do
And that all my days begin and end with you.

Cheryl B. Frumes

The Truth Lies

The truth lies between the rocks
and is crushed by the descent of the ages.
To all the sinners of the world
the truth is merely a savage attack on society.
Society expects the truth,
and that's why we lie;
to protect the explicitly and divisibility of the world.

Chris Dougherty

Infatuation?

You say my feelings for you are not love,
That they are merely infatuation...
If waking up every morning and you are my first thought
   is infatuation...
If wishing I were your best friend is infatuation...
If seeing your pain and wishing I could bear it for you
   is infatuation...
If imagining "us" together years from now is infatuation...
If trusting you completely is infatuation...
If wanting to tell the world how much I care for you
   is infatuation...
If believing that together we can do anything is infatuation...
Then, Yes, I Am infatuated... Totally and Completely.

Beverly J. Seabolt

Gary (The Place, Where I Was Born)

   Gary is the place where I was born. Messed
up, all tattered and torn. Between two sides good and
evil, Gary is the place where I was born. Children
killing children, children selling crack, these
are things I try to ignore, but Gary, but Gary, the
place where I was born.
   Locked in a cage of silence and death.
Gary is the place where I was born. Oh why, oh why,
do I have shackles on feet. I'm here to stay in
my room I pray. O' God almighty I say, Gary
is the place where I was born, help me, my family
and everyone else, unleash us from the shackles
of pain and death. Let us run free so I'll
be proud of the place where I was born. Oh Gary
oh Gary, the place where I was born.

Michael G. Thomas Jr.

Connectedness

Connectedness...
Can you see, or do you know what I mean?
Bouncing off each other, nothing sticks
except the awareness of something alien between.
Connectedness...
No, it cannot be seen, because there is ever some gloss, or some screen
that keeps us longing for something more serene.
I long to connect, to then be free, not bound...
to love for the moment this friend I've found.
And to know in the depths of my soul that I am not alone is my quest,
to find myself in the presence of some, as yet, unknown guest.

So I grope and I search and then in futility I give up!
Is this the end?
And then there is this surge that comes from within
and I am reminded, that I too, am my own friend.
But my search has not been for me, but for you!
And as strange as it may be, as I looked for you...
I found me.
Connectedness...

Jeff Bates

A Beautiful Lady

In the beginning of this evolving universe, a
Beautiful lady is bestowed upon our souls. Yes, most
distinct and different is her appearance and
personality! As she appears, strolling gracefully
across my eyesight, I speak of her womanhood:
Darkened hair whisking gently in the breeze, eyes
of brown that sparkle as does dew on the early
morning grass. The softness of her skin expels the
sensitivity of her touch. As she reaches out, one's
mind is grasped by a Beautiful Lady!

Stevie C. McLendon

"Especially For You"

I've given you, my love
I've given you, my life
With sincerity, from my heart
I've proposed, and ask you to become, my wife

To be loyal, truthful, devoted and dear

I promise to love you, forever, my dear
Believe me when I tell you that I love you,
Because it's true

You see it comes from my heart,
And it's directed to you, forever and always
I shall love you.

Arthur James Savage

The Forest Beauties

   The Forest Beauties are of the dew drops that
shine like diamonds. It is of the laughing pools
that lap against the shores. It has hidden treasures
of polished beauty that lie under the softly gurgling
brook. It is of the whispering oaks that sway
through the wind. It is the brightly colored birds
that sing their melodious notes as they blissfully
fly through the breeze. It has the bleating fawns
playing in the clearings. It is the wind singing its
soft summer song. Those are what make up the Forest
Beauties.

Leah Michelle Williamson

The Voice

The Voice said, You Must Teach Her
There was no sound, yet I heard it clearly in my mind
You Must Teach Her — but what did He mean?

Teach her what, I wondered
How to talk? - How to walk? - How to eat? - How to play?
I thought long and hard ... but was unsure of my answer
I knew — but I was afraid

I was living in the shadows of myself
My fear kept me from Him, but there was nothing to fear

I know now He was always there, waiting for me to come to Him
And so I did ... with her

You Must Teach Her
That's all He said, but those four words have changed my life
And those of my family and friends — and most definitely hers
Her name is Evan and she's two years old — she's also my
daughter

It seems appropriate that when I heard His message
I was sitting in the dark, in the middle of the night
Now I have been on this path for almost a year
And He has been lighting my way at every step
I truly believe I have seen the Light

Ann Rocha

Playing Hooky

I meant to do my work today
But a red bird sang in the apple tree,
And a butterfly flitted across the field,
And all the leaves were calling me.

The wind went singing over the land
Tossing the grasses to and fro.
A rainbow held out its shining hand,
So what could I do but laugh and go.

Deloris K. Suddarth

For Jenny

Hippity, skippity,
Hoppity hop...
Home from school with a cloppity, clop.
"What did you do today?"
Mother inquires.
"Nothin'..." (the answer seems pulled out with pliers!)
Two hearts with affection
Head different directions:
"What's there to eat, 'cause I'm really starved?"

Hippity skippity,
Hoppity hop...
Bananas are fun with a cookie on top!
"Oh, now I remember,"
... the time's come for sharing:
A feather's pulled out of the pocket with caring...
Hunched over this treasure,
Two heads come together,
And into a lifetime, a memory's carved.

Barbara H. Yarter

Curiosity

Human nature, full of surprises!
Reaches out on a limb to see,
When life tests our curiosity.
If there were a line of doors,
All open but one,
And we had the choice
For all the doors or one.
Curiosity would give up all for one,
To reach out on a limb to see,
Behind the closed door that may be empty.
Regardless if logic would plead,
For the door that offered all we need.

Renata F. Snyder

Love In Their Eyes

She walked in, so gracefully, so deliberately, walker in hand.
He followed; with hands ready to steady her gait; not too
obvious, to allow a sense of dignity.

Her curls, white as snow; his hairline receding, forming a
crown. Their features altered by time. Love was in their eyes.

They chose their meals; vegetarians now — a little bread to top
it off, coffee to warm their cold bones. The young waitress
carried her tray. She followed slowly, deliberately with grace.
He followed, tray in hand — the other ready... she sat, thanking
the young woman; "Remember to come back for your tip
now." He arranged the trays, settling the coats, steadying the
chair as she sat. Love was in their eyes.

He smiled, "I saw a good looking lady in the mirror a moment
ago, and I realized it was you"... She blushed, "Let's move
from under the fan, so you will not catch cold now." He
replied, "That's true honey." She rose, slowly, deliberately
with grace; walker in hand. He followed hands ready...
Love was in his eyes.

Vickie Y. Ogunlade

Untitled

I love to watch the snowflakes fall,
and catch them on my tongue
I like winter best of all,
Gramps says it's cause I'm young

Last night I saw him by the maple tree
His tongue was pointed high
Hey Gramps, I yelled, you're as young as me
I think I saw Gramps cry.

Robert A. Varga

The Canon

Untangle your faith
when villains damn your dreams
and fears seem to lengthen with wrying thoughts

Rise with pride:
Know your picture is not erased
all is not lost for pity's sake
even if it's hard to salvage
something from the wrecked mess
labor not in vain
for success and failure are part of the same

Restore:
Pick up the debris and use it to build
a mightier dream that will stand firm
amidst adversities until reality
breathes life into your golden quest

Rejoice:
More than so is that the dark night
can be your perception of resting light
until the morn' comes again.
Andrea Blackstone

Dreaming

Some say love is a road of treachery
others say it is a road to heaven
The path that I'm taking is giving me memories
a gift that I can hold on to forever
No matter how far apart
or close we are,
In my heart
You'll never be far
Miles turn into minutes,
reuniting has no limits
Valarie Harbaugh

Sight......What Is Right?

Yes, of course, you can see what I'm typing on this white sheet
of paper tonight. But, only the blind have the true eye-sight.

Evil and darkness spread all over this earth. But, only those
without sight know the crying sound of an angel at birth. Wisdom
and knowledge of understanding love is this time.

Joy and happiness do they really help you unwind.
Those without sight were born for a special cause.
And those who cannot hear see life when it starts to pause.

Handicap of different whichever you prefer to say. But, are you
truly normal and the knowing one of this world today. Can you
judge those who cannot see. Not unless you saw yourself and
can say it is to be. Are you honest with your words when you
claimed to have seen or did you lie knowing it wasn't right
and spoke of a dream.

Your mind has sight and can hear very well, even if you yourself
are deaf, dumb, and blind.

With knowledge and sight are caught under Satan's spell so
just because you have sight tell me........does that make you right?
Nabeehah Q. McGill

Is It Spring?

"Is it spring?" "Is it spring?"
I asked the birds and the bees.
I even asked the trees.
But, they would not tell me,
Those grumpy old trees.
Them I asked the flowers and the leaves.
The flowers sprouted out.
The leaves grew big.
Then, I knew it was spring.
Crystal Howard

First Impressions

Your eyes are like the sea
after a storm. They twinkle like the
stars above.
We only met for a moment in time and
the memory of you will last a lifetime.

Another time. Another place.
We shall meet again. Each time shall be
better than the last. For those blue
eyes have melted my heart and have
taken my breath away.

Never before have I seen the eyes
you possess. For with those eyes you
could melt even the coldest heart.

But what do those eyes say about
the man you are.
Are you gentle and kind
Loving and giving.
Or are you wild and fierce.
Like a stallion on the wild plains.
Zenah Leigh Cut

The Bonfire

Blazing fire on a star-filled moonless night,
Flames tripping over logs, licking heavenward,
Sparks sprinting toward the stars.

Three women communing with the elements,
Circle of friendship,
Hands joining across the years.

Crackle, chant of the flames,
Silent starlit configuration,
Balance suspended between heaven and earth.

Different voices blending into a symphonic choir,
Teacher, artist, dancer,
Passion for life — passion for death.

Glowing red hot embers, cool blue hot flames.
Screams in the distance — terror or play?
Cold air, hot flame.

Arms outstretched, black against the sky,
Limbs reaching in reverence
To the night's "Hallelujah Chorus."
Ellen M. Rose

Blessed Destiny

My heart is torn like a highway to nowhere
I'm searching for the right road
But who said finding it would be fair

I dream one day that I will encounter it
My dear friend — do you care?

My conscience essence is gradually effaced
Will I ever find myself
What will end this disgrace

Oh tortured grief
God, it can't be heard!
It's tearing me apart
What have you learned?

You immolated your standing
When I slowly given up
You became my conscience
It's my deserted soul you have won

How can I ever thank you for what you have done
The gift of a poem is simply not enough
Our fearless devotion for each other
Yes! It will never be broken apart
Ivette Palestrant

You Don't Know Me Do You?

As I look into your eyes I know
You don't know me.
As I try to explain I know
You are lost.
My feelings are too deep for you.
They are like an endless ocean and you are a fish.
You swim and swim trying to find the end
But you can not.
I am the balloon that has escaped your young childish hand.
Though you try you can not catch me.
This is not good.
This is bad.
I am alone with my feelings.
A shield stands between us
Like a great labyrinth.
This is why you do not understand
You do not know me.
Nicole Hawley

My World/Our World

Our world consist of 24 hours, 60 minutes, and 60 seconds
Our world consist of the rich and needy
Our world consist of colors and people
Our world has peace makers and fighters
Our world is information and speculation
Our world is work and play
Our world is for all of us,
We see our world as small,
Yet;
My world has no boundaries or colors
My world has need without want
My world has dreams and aspirations
My world has time for joy and responsibility
My world envisions children with no pain, no hunger
My world is for you, and you
Our world my world is always changing
Our world my world has room for a better future.
Allen Dickey

Don't Tell Me

Don't tell me I don't understand,
I understand just fine
You can go and leave us here
And fill our hearts with pain and fear.
You said you loved us all our lives
But then again you're good for your lies
I understand you hate us all,
that's why you go out and do not call
We love you, but you don't care
I'm living out my worst nightmare
You betrayed us all
Now what's to do, but cry and fall
Don't act like you don't know
Now, your family is your foe
Why didn't you just leave,
before I was conceived.
So, don't tell me I don't understand
All the damage came from your hands.
Wendy Kumburis

Tornadoes

April, May and June
tornadoes will be here soon.
Thunder, lightning, rain and hail
thick dark clouds that could lift a whale.
Destroying everything in their way
it will be over by the end of the day.
Melisa Irizarry

Whisper?

A whisper creeping slowly in the night.
Such a frightening experience, that I close my eyes tight.
Voices and scratches heard all around.
My thoughts are racing to the sounds.

My heart beats triple time as minutes pass by.
I need to stay calm and try not to cry.
My body is trembling because of the shock.
And sooner than I'm able to think, I hear a knock.

I slide back further into my covers and sheets,
even though I'm burning up because of the intense heat.
I stiffen up my body and close my eyes tight,
hoping soon everything will turn out alright.

Tears escape when I can't take anymore.
And I hear a noise from underneath the floor.
"Wait!" I say. "There's no need to scream."
"Thank goodness!" I yell, "I'm just in a dream."
Tracie Finley

Getting Old

When you reach 40 years of age,
And wrinkles ruin the beauty of your youth,
Remember how the men used to look at you.
You might be an ugly duckling and not very rich.
People question where your beauty went.
It's where the heart is, where the love is
And your eyes reveal that love.
You keep yourself modest around the praise.
Your beauty deserves more praise.
Your child would say - "This beauty of yours,
Will let everyone know that beauty is an individual characteristic,
I am a new factor in your age of old beauty.
People will say you are ugly, but your beauty will show through.
Erica Gambaro

A School Bus Driver

I wake up in the early morn,
   while most are still asleep I'm up and gone,
On my way to the school bus lot,
   I'm ready to give my job all I've got
I start up my bus, I'm on the road
   house to house I go, picking up my load
Drop the kids at school, my nerves are shot
   I can't wait to get back to the coffee pot
After a couple of cups I'm feeling fine
   Ready to go back on the firing line
Before I know where the day has gone
   I'm back in the bus on the afternoon run
I very carefully get them all home
   now I have a minute of my own
To the bus parking lot once again
   can't wait to get my bus pulled in
Park the bus, I give a sigh, tell the other
   drivers "good bye"
But tomorrow will come, I hear myself say
   I must do the whole thing over the very same way
Dexter L. Strunk

Untitled

As the tree stands alone in its shadow,
we are left to wallow
In the loneliness of life, to live in the fear,
still living to adhere
To what we may wonder at a time,
with all we may deal
Perhaps it's the simplest of all...
Erin Picow

Exit

His only salvation
is the solid iron chain,
that loosely clutches his leg, as he dangles there in the dull
silence

Back and forth, like a metronomic pendulum,
in the eternal darkness
of a million mile pit that has no definite location

All sound is lost in the desolate cavity
not that it doesn't exist,
but it has no reason to surface

For it has been many years
since the slightest flicker of a flame has appeared,
and an infinite period of time will span before another light shall
reveal itself

So there, hanging loosely by a thick iron chain
the man forever swings
within the depths of the silent pit
Ryan Hatch

Best Friends

The music is softly playing, I lay alone on my bed
All I am feeling are thoughts of you in my head
Simple and quiet moments we shared alone
Some of the most wonderful times I have known.

You were sincere, honest, and true
I knew I mattered to you,
You never made me feel lonely or blue.

My knees would grow weak with the touch of your hand
And one kiss from your lips said "I understand"

In heaven I appeared to be
Whenever I felt your arms embrace me.

Our time together was always to short
And so many times in the past we both were hurt
But the hurt never seemed to last too long
'Cause after awhile we were back together
Right where we belonged.

See - Our feelings can never end
because you my LOVE - are my best friend.
Mary Ann Juris

By Myself

If I could be one, just me,
would that be so bad?
It would only be lack of company
that would make me feel sad.
And that would only be Tuesdays.
When I like to speak on movie reviews
and how men are to blame for the world's twisted views
and if asked for donations I'd probably refuse
the local charity.
If I could be one, just me,
all out on my own
would someone I see, see me
and tell me "Go Home!"?
Or perhaps invite me to theirs,
on seeing me lonely and floating in space.
And when I say "no" the look on their face
somehow satisfies me as they're put in their place.
And I'm alone.
As I would like to be.
Aimee Crow

The Love For You

What is this power which burns inside,
giving off emotions my body cannot hide?

Thinking of you has become a habit of mine,
your hair, your eyes, your body so fine.

Like a flower blown away by the wind,
you blossom in my mind again and again.

And now, what can I do?
I start by saying... I have the love for you.
Chris Wright

Untitled

Distorted faces
Looking glass stares
As I stumble past a page of glares.
I'm making no sense
babbling in confusion
The air is so cold and filled with illusion
Detangle my web-
through these words I will swallow
seeking wisdom with in these triumphs
  of tomorrow.
Julie Sacco

Skating N The Ghetto

When I went skating, I saw art on the wall.
I even went skating by the park and saw someone
playing basketball.
My best friend who is dead I could recall.
When I skate in the ghetto it brings me hope.
God helps me cope.
As I skate I saw children trying to jump rope.
And I even saw undercover's bust someone for
selling dope.
I even skated by my best friend's house
Sally my girlfriend who was shot in the alley.
As I skate down the street so free.
His got to be me.
I remember me and Sally crave our
names in the tree.
Now I got to skate home.
Without Sally my soul will be alone.
On my wall is a poetry gold medal.
This was my day skating in the Ghetto.
Tyrell Bell

My Snow White Fairytale

My prince has finally come
My limp arms welcomed him
My blue lips spoke his name
My crystallized eyes looked straight up at him
My dry fingers cracked with anticipation of his kiss
My cold heart fluttered at the sight of him

As he perambulates my glass coffin, he seems satisfied
As he bends down, he looks at my unmoving eyes
As he leans forward, he touches my hard lips
As he stretches out a hand, he feels my dead arms
As he falls in, he holds my parched fingers
As he sits back, he thinks about my unbeating heart

I know what is coming and I fear not
His head goes down with slowness
His lips pucker with eagerness
I know subconsciously that it is all over
I will now live the rest of my perpetual live
In the castles of his body
Jennifer Crouch

Let Me Introduce My Lord

He keeps us safe from all harm,
He wraps us in his loving arms.
He gives us strength when all seems lost,
He gives us hope to carry on.
He stays with us in our darkest hour,
He's always there when we stray too far.

He protects us from Satan's hands,
When we walk on foreign lands.
He will forgive us no matter what,
For all you've ask and even sought.

Because his love is all we need,
Trust in him to plant the seed.
So trust in my Lord to help you today,
He will not leave you but lead the way.

So keep the faith and you will see,
The love my Lord can give to thee.
So when you feel that you may stray,
Listen close and the Lord will say,
"Take my hand for I am the truth, the light, the way!"

Madona Smearman

Jury Duty

We arrive at 8:20 a.m. day after day
Down the hall to the elevator
Day after day
Listen and watch the witnesses
Day after day
Looking at evidence, pictures and weapons
Day after day
Making a decision guilty or not
Day after day
I want to go back to work!

Cindy Strole

Soul

A soul lost,
a soul found,
a soul of good,
a soul of evil.
Who can say?
But one can say.
A soul lost in the trappings of these dark times,
a soul of seething evil, of pain, anguish, and fear.
A soul of pleasure, love, and compassion.
The soul is the body, the mind, and the heart.
The soul of happiness brings day.
The soul of hate brings night.
Take me from these dark days
and bring on the light...

Kris Schultz

"My Heart"

As my heart pounds
you can hear it through the grounds
each minute, each hour, each day, each week
that's what makes our world go round
for I have found "Love"
it was farther than any underground
for I can hear a thump
like I go in the air and pump.
For "Love" is not to dump
love can make you laugh and jump
be careful you won't fall and have a lump
each week, each month, each year
I won't shed one tear
for I have nothing to fear
for I love you dear

Belinda Ortiz

Rise From Who You Are

Rise from who you are
achieve what you must
Soar into the garden of Eden
Each and every petal; red
the color of passion, yellow
the color of friendship, white
the color of sincerity
find yourself as your journey begins
say if you will a line of hope
In dreams you shall prevail
Imagine life as you make it
Loved ones you have forgotten
Create a world of your own
As you are the only one, joy shall come within
As you enjoy you, as you are, weakness is nothing
Your journey is strong and empowered
Embrace your life, it is what you make it
Choices shall control your destiny
Love your self enough
to enjoy it to the fullest

Jeanine Lewis

Silent Mourn

Underneath the clear blue skies
he awakes with a heart of stone
in a city that lies in broken pieces
as winds travel violently from dusk to dawn.

Shines the golden sun of Jerusalem
through his cracked bedside window
he gives a bleary stare
as he witnesses another innocent death.

The blue skies angers to smoke
and gentle cries turn to a howling
as his mother's dying blood sheds
on the pavement ground he walks on.

Visioning a bleak future
where a minimal existence is all there is to look forward to
and opportunities non-existent,
he prays endlessly
as silent tears shed from river to sea

And though they hold the key to set this country free,
he takes hold of the stone for possession of power
and defense of liberty.
With every prison blown to dust,
the enemies walk free.

Zarifa M. Khalil

Sutratman

Each day I cast a thread upon waking,
A string of silk that runs throughout the day,
And then at night, before my sleep taking,
I catch the end and draw the thread my way.

Above my head I see the spark'ling line
Extend beyond the range of birth and death,
And yet it runs for intervals in time
And strings the poles of prayer through desert stretch.

The worldly spider weaves a complex matte,
Her many strands entangle sundry all.
But high above her angel turns from that,
To thread one strand with pearls is her call.

My quest is singular from this day hence;
To find the essence of experience.

Joseph Miller

Regret

I'd like to take an eraser and erase my face
suck myself up into a hypodermic and inject myself
into the veins of some real live person

Just spend one day in someone else's shoes, letting their feet
walk on me, trample me, Move me around without having to
think about it

Would someone turn off these thoughts so I can rest?
I used to say "I wouldn't be who I am today if I hadn't done
what I did"
and "I can do any goddamn thing I put my mind to."
But that's not true.

I'll never be any more than I am already
I've stopped becoming, I simply am

Too old to say "those were childish mistakes, I'll change"
Too late for hoping
Every second counts in the race to the end.

Brindle Cox

"Why Not Today?
A Discovery Of What's Happening"...

Preface
Introduction
...in "the source of our being"
...in "oneness"
...with "religion"
...through "prayer"
...in "Jesus" with "faith" in love
...with "sister and brotherhood"
...to "friendship"
...in "thoughts" in "time"
...in "fear death, doubt, anger and violence"
...to "ecology"
...in "games and role playing"
...in "medicine, food and health"
...in "education"
...in "entertainment"
...in "business"
...beyond "success and failure"
...to "the walls"
...in "world relations and peace"

Herb Brown

A Rare And Precious Stone

That empty stare exists on the face of a beautiful, yet silent, child.
And I know that behind it
lies a window into a remarkable world.

A world of quiet wonder and enormous creativity.
For only an ingenious child
could question her own worth at such a young age.

Perhaps she does not realize the power of her own opinion.
And would rather be the reader
than the heroine in any novel.

They say Einstein didn't speak a word until he was seven years old.
The 'experts' were convinced he was a slow child,
certain he was a half-wit.

So dear parents,
Forget your Psychotherapists, your Healers, your Psychics.
Forget these 'experts'.

Someday her genius and beauty will be heard.

And dear Child, remember this:
The most precious stones are those that are the rarest.

Dana L. Perkins

Recovery

R - is for remembering all my evil ways, then praying to God to help
me make the change.
E - accepting the fact I don't have to live a lie, and with God's
help, I will get by.
C - is for comfort in which we all truly need, seeking only His help,
we will definitely succeed.
O - is for over, for the war is done. Thank you Lord, with You I
have always won!
V - is for victory for it is mine, I have to say God is good, all the
time!
E - is for eternity, I will spend it with You, teaching me always the
right thing to do.
R - is for respecting everything I have been through, so I know better
next time, what not to do.
Y - is for yesterday, for I had say good bye, always remembering
that I need to continue to really try!

Kathy Murphy

Sailing Home

I see the lights from God's harbor gleaming,
As I sail my ship home-ward today,
I must set my sails true,
From the course I shall not stray.

If on this loud roaring sea,
We are tempted to stray,
Then, He in His sweet voice will whisper,
"Sail on, this is the only way."

If we trust Him with patience,
In sweet peace we'll journey home.
For He has said in His word,
"I will never leave thee alone."

God's promise is sure,
Be your heart free from sin,
"Lo! I am with you always,
Even unto the end."

So, "Not My will but Thine be done",
As the harbour lights grow brighter each day,
With the Master guiding our ship,
We'll soon be home to stay.

Macel H. Botkins

Christy

I have a mixed breed dog whose history
Is partly known to me, and a partly a mystery,
She loves people and dogs and going to parks.
She's a good watchdog but never needlessly barks.
I adopted her as a puppy from the animal shelter,
When they let her out of the cage, she ran helter skelter.
Once she dug a hole under the fence and ran away,
She was gone all night and returned the next day.
It had been raining, but her coat was bone dry.
She's very intelligent, in fact, I would say sly.
She has very long legs, and can run like a greyhound,
She used to run laps in the back yard, around and around.
She'll lie on her back for several hours at a time,
To get her tummy rubbed, to her it's sublime,
She likes to be stroked behind her ears.
I hope she'll live at least twenty years.
She wakes me up in the morning by licking my face.
No other dog could ever take Christy's place.

Cheryl E. Henderson

Wait, I Do

Wait, I do, and hate:
Vampires don't expire in this heart,
No coffins going empty, follow Sarte;
This ebb of pain does not abate.

Listen, I do, to golden fairies
Who spin twisted love from ivory wool,
Dressing the heart of the raging fool,
Whose dream the passing storm does carry.

Fire and water, I do iron the ice;
Contaminant poison swallowed by wine:
Inferno entwined in silk covered fine;
Dagger stabbed bosom jaggedly trice.

Bitterly raging, I do, with the beasts of yore,
Dead is the time following life,
Searing silver rings were promised a wife,
A broken heart is the gold of the poor.

Fear, I do, as of late,
When bounds erased by blind emotion
From broken mind and strange commotion:
Wait, I do, and hate.

Roberto A. Contreras

Behind Shut Doors

It's hidden behind shut doors, what we do not know
What we come to find out, the future will eventually show
Nothing is eternally hidden, not what you'd want to be
Because doors can always be opened and eyes will always see.

Sara Ann Lindgren

My Man

He's in my life to stay
   Never to stray

Santa hasn't a thing on him
   With his jolly way

He eats chowder from a bowl
   While the kitty plays with his toes

His soul shines thru his eyes like a light
   Making them easy to read with delight

He's a charmer from a-far
   Dancing around the star

The sun follows him wherever he goes
   Like a candle that glows

Moonbeams racing across his chest
   Striking me like the Goddess of Venus

Waunetta Snell

Brandy

She was gone before I knew it,
Where she went I do not know.
I lost the only love of my life.
She gave me hope, trust, and love,
Which I never knew I had.

I see her in my dreams,
Hoping we will be together again someday.
As she was drifting away from me,
I never realized then how much she really meant to me.

We shared our lives and dreams.
The games we played were make-believe.
She has always watched over me, now, then, and forever.
When the time comes, we will see each other again.

Stacey Ziginow

A Friend Is...

A friend is someone
Who you can count on
When the load is too heavy
When the journey is too far
When the terrain is too perilous

A friend is someone
Who will tell you when you're wrong
Who will help you when you're right
And respect your decision to be either or

A friend is someone
Who knows what you're thinking
Who knows how you're thinking
Who knows why you're thinking
And who knows if you're thinking

A friend is someone
Who answers when you call
Who listens when you talk
And hears you when you're silent
A friend is someone...
Who is my friend?

Frank Buck

With The Turning Of The Globe

How sweet it is when the day begins with the turning of
   the globe.
I wake up with the sun singing to me, while he wears
   his golden robe.
Its shimmering tatters fall upon my dreamy haze.
Morning doves coo when touched by its gentle rays.

By noon the sun is vibrant, in his intense yellow clothes.
Plants all watch him eagerly, each in a receptive pose.
Their hungry green eyes, catch his warm yellow light.
And he runs away down, down toward the night.

Now a silver moon appears, to chase the sun to bed.
He rushes toward the sea; he turns a crimson red.
The sun descends into the cradling waves; he wears his
   evening robe.
How sad it is when the day must end, with the turning
   of the globe.

Conrad Gregory

Upon Our First Night Together

or Can A Man Plumb The Depths Of A Cat's Pique?
Fair cause for funk had Leo (clever cat), who, sensing danger,
His place usurped (to his surprise), and in your bed a bearded stranger,
Hatched evil schemes, no doubt unique, to interrupt post-coital dreams.
With all his might, so great his pique, long past midnight—was it four?—
He leapt as deftly as he could and flung your car keys to the floor,
Which, made of wood, resounded like a slamming door,
Leo thinking (so I surmise), "He'll sleep no more."

Leo's alarms may seem foul dealings,
Yet your sweet charms so sway my feelings,
The praise of each deserves a place—
Your slender limbs and luscious face,
Your gleaming teeth, your winning smile,
Your speech straight-forward, lacking guile,
Your well-toned trunk, your skin so fair,
Your manly voice and soft thick hair—
That were I Leo, declaring war,
The clanking keys would lead to more.

Wilfrid R. Koponen

Back To Oneness

With the combination of affirmation, meditation and concentration,
We will exceed limitation, attaining global purification.
There will be a levitation of our vibration,
That shall lift each and every nation,
Through the transformation, unto divination.
This recrystallization and illumination of the population
Will allow the preservation of the civilization.
With careful preparation, we begin the etheric migration
Of our spirits' elevation,
Seeing the emanation of a heavenly revelation,
That is the visitation of God's manifestation.
Our exploration in this incarnation
Will allow the disintegration
And elimination of any negative sensation.
Assuring the confirmation of our coronation,
Causing the celestial celebration,
Which is the graduation from separation.

For we are all but one indeed!

Jessiah Kneass

Untitled

In a different house, on a different hour,
when the trickling stops from the observation tower,
I will find myself one piece, assured and roused
back to the lifeblood's wake.

In a different space, from another power,
when the darkness fades to reveal pure color,
I will be reborn again, time to make real the other realm.

Unfurled wings of tornado clouds,
this wait so smooth, observe the world.
Manifest the dreams from internal energy,
to make real the wants of the creatures that run wild in me.

Saw a furball with beady eyes,
and a needle demon with a frightened smile,
a little tripper with a swollen head
said to me your heart knows best: Talking of the mystic pass,
the crossing in time when magic is life.
A little fern that moved and spoke,
tripping on his seventh arm: Unite the matter and the mystic self
he said, as he fell, rolled around and laughed.
There's a metal playground in my head!

Alex Gorelik

All About Me

My name is Roshunda, you can call me "Miss Thang."
I love basketball that's my game.
Even though I can't sing playing the clarinet is my thing.
I'm like a rose, something everyone loves.
I remind myself of a rabbit soft, cuddly, and cute.
I like to use my big eyes they always get attention.
Sometimes I get teased about it, I wonder why.
My friends like my friendliness and how I understand.
They also like how I treat them with respect.
I have soft creamy brown skin, long, shiny black hair and dark brown eyes.
My pet peeve is two-face people they don't know when to shut-up.
But I overlook them with my big beautiful smile.
I'm always busy as a bee.
You hardly ever see me sitting on my feet.
My color is black, because that's what I look good in.
I admire Ophrah Winfrey, because she knows what she wants.
I'm an independent black girl who knows what I want, that's why my nickname is "Miss Thang"

Roshunda Jones

Smooth Blue

You
smooth blue stone from the sand
you sing in my hand
never comprehending this audience
of calloused flesh,
hard hands that struggle to feel
your smooth blue water song.
They were soft pink child hands
that felt all the songs
in the dark and green wet places
where blackbirds bathe,
slipping softly on round round riverstones like you.

And you
when the mystery clocks feign speech
you sing in the night
while I sleep.

Lisa L. Frank

Questions

Who knows where the sky ends, or where the night touches the day?
Where broken wings go to mend; where the poet learns his say?

Who knows when time has gone, or when our future flees?
Who knows of the goods deeds done which no one seems to see?

Who knows where the wind blows, fading to a whisper lost?
Or where the closing of the rose is more than gold in cost?

Who knows where stars, like suns, shine their shining light?
Or where the silvery moons glimmer in the velvety night?

Where does the hurt child go to cry crystal tears of pain?
Do sire and dam know that childhood must soon wane?

Where does a foe meet foe, and come away as friends?
Where do lovers cry their woe when true love comes to an end?

Who knows where eternity lies or where the secrets creep?
Who knows if infinity dies or where the forevers keep?

Who can find the brazen key of the lost locked doors upstairs?
Whose answers can pacify me? — A voice murmurs, "No one dares."

Lesa Estabillo

Angeline Nightingale

"Whisper to me," sweetly she says.
Moonlight sonata welcoming secrecy,
Some predestined flight.
Haunted stairway, jagged upon the steps-she steps.
Nightingale shuffled in-heart,
Angeline's sacred dance.

Shimmering eye fascination-
Amusement seems to scream!
Anxious dash - together they seem to speak.
Angeline's soul began to show.

Silhouette moon smil'd in delight!
Cream quiet Pearlman and Angeline preside.
Alive blue drapery,
Gallant gown whips.
Suspended stars to dance in heavens arms
Fantasy, her dance - Angeline.

Undaunted doorway frames elegance, ovalness her face.
Stairway heart, stairway in distance,
Reserved pearl dream heaven
Whispering in a fantasy, too secret...

Rick Goblette Burton

A Tribute To Jim

My husband died a few short days ago,
I loved him far more than anyone could ever know.
I'm sad because I cannot feel grief or tears.
I feel as though he's been gone for many years.
The feeble old man there in the bed that day,
or the form that in the casket lay,
was not my Jim, my life, my loveliest love,
for ages now he's been slipping to that happier land above,
his pain wracked body, at last has set his spirit free
and only in his death can he come softly back to me.
He never complained, though he suffered terribly.
It made me strong to watch his great bravery.
My heart wrenched with tears I could not show,
because I did not want him to know I was hurting so.
Near the end all he knew was ceaseless pain,
yet from somewhere deep within, a glorious smile came.
"We made it love, I see Jesus reaching for my hand
and one day I know you'll join me in that promised land."
Joy filled the room as angels took him home,
Peace fills my heart with memories we've known.
Lillian Martin Johnson

Understand

To understand, is not to comprehend,
But to find an emotional barrier
Which can not be destroyed by an army of a thousand,
But yet, can fall down by the prick of a single pin.

And a lack of understanding of who we are,
And who are the others
Who surround us day and night.

A lack of understanding of who we are,
Where we came from,
What will happen to us, and what has happened to us.

A lack of understanding of what we are destined to do,
And what we have done.
The mistakes we will make, and the mistakes we have made.
An uncertainty of our readiness to find and explore our destiny.

A lack of understanding of our need to
Expand, explore, and to triumph.
But, an understanding that no matter how far out we reach,
We can always go further.
Victoria Unterreiner

Window

She came to me in the still
And sat beneath my window
She whispered words I did not know
I heard her calling
But did not listen when I heard her
I turned my back to face her
So I could see what I had not heard
And listened to her move from behind a shadow
She moved into the light of the dark
And I saw her
It was her in the reflection not my shadow
She whispered again speaking quietly
And I did not listen
I only heard what I needed to hear
And that was her
Moving gently away from me
She came to me in the still
And I did not listen
As I heard her leave the way she came
Gently
Thawny Soto

"Rails To Town"

A whistle is heard in a small town depot,
Lo, what this meant to the community people.
Freight and letters to come by mail,
Also, people would come and go by rail.
To ride the train would take them back,
To the sound of the rail with the clickety clack.
To see the fields and the streams,
Was just the same as in their dreams.
Although there are some who still really care,
The depot is gone and the rails are bare.
Lost in time is the engine's wail,
No more to travel to town by rail.
Marty Schoenthaler

Reality

I will Live
Though the breath of life is an ephemeral gift,
I will love
Though my heart will periodically ache with pain,
I will pray
Though my flesh is weak my soul is worth saving,
I will depart
Though my head may fall in the eternal sleep
The life I leave has been rewarding and complete.
Frenisee West

"The Winds Of Time"

Staring out into the rain, into the
sunless sky, I long for your embrace,
where the sun can break free from the clouds
shining with its pure brilliance.
   Having been touched by your love, my
heart which was yet still a bud, has blossomed
into a radiant flower, yielding a nectar so sweet, no bee
would dare to disturb it.
   For only the graceful beauty of the
butterfly may set aloft on its soft, delicate
petals and drink the fruit of thy love.
   Although the flutter of the butterflies
wings may never pass again, the flower will
bear the seeds of remembrance so the forthcoming
generations of butterflies, for years to come, will stare in awe
of the beauty which had once been, but will never be forgotten.....
Harold Rutledge Odell Jr.

Cigarette

It began with sun-touched passion
surrounding cool blue flames, and I was at once
ignited in fires of brimstone.
The rush burned down throats and breathed hot air,
and swarmed with clotted cries.
I was consumed,
with each take I lost myself,
carried away on blind gray butterflies.
I danced in blue clouds,
mixed with the rain and like tears
I became dust.
Then I was cast aside,
a forgotten cobweb flicked through the air.
Lost in the tangle of dried weeds,
I lay,
melting.
Keith H. Hirata

Evening's Arrival

Shards of sunlight stab at the Earth.
Sun's sizzling rays cease their sting.
Sinking slowly upon the horizon
Golden fingers of energy giving one last power surge into the depths
of the Earth. One last glaring ray — then gone.
Evening begins its vigil.

Sounds of song birds become subdued.
Gentle rufflings of fledglings' wings create a stirring as they fly
to their evening nest
Tree branches sway with their precious package.
To and fro rocks the nest cradle luring the babies to sleep.
Tiny chirps, flutterings, swaying cease and settle into sleepness.
Evening's arrival   all is still.

Sweet stirrings bring honeysuckle fragrance — delicate and
breathcatching
Caught upon the evening breeze to drift for one eternal night.
The leafarms sway in tempo to the breeze become entwined till taunt.
Evening's arrival   all is still.

Gossamer winged dragonfly glides, lands, causing water ripples
Disturbing the silvery mirror surface.
Lotus cupshaped lily pads begin their slow spiral closure encasing
their contents. Evening's arrival   all is still.

Judi Morgan

Your Small One

You tell him to stay.
Still yet he crawls away.
Then you jump and run.
To find your loving son.
Just because he is gone.
Doesn't mean his life is done.
Now he is with the Lord.
Reattach to his umbilical cord.
Now he grows strong under the Lords watch.
The Lord is watching the time on his watch.
He will play sports and have fun.
Because he is your son.

Jeremy M. Jones

L.A.

Mother of pain.
Creator of death.
Maker of blue jeans.
City of brawlers, outcasting the light.
The business of cunning.
The Fat Cats play, while sitting and drinking their Chardonnay.

Some parts are cool and smooth, like a summers day;
Others parts harsh and rough, like that of the salt water crashing
against the bay.
It has a hard complexion which fools many into believing that it can
be saved!
Underneath, in the more relaxed areas, it is just right,
where people don't have to worry about robbery in the night.

Stryder Zalabak

Untitled

Wandering solely thru the halls of despair
Wounded by the one you believed truly cared
Love and fidelity are just illusions
Gathering forth the fruits of confusion
Led by the fires of betrayal
Anger consumes the heart where love once dwelled
Trust no one who swears their love is true
Of the two it is you who will play the fool
When the time comes prepare with hand in fist
For true love between same shall never exist

Federico R. Lastra

Burning Hearts

Of all things going wrong,
Chemicals heated my cavity-
Naturally waking turbulence
In waves of lightning,
Letting universes soar through
Red gashes, and crash

Crash down to collect the
Ash rightfully belonged,
And build in color and smoke,
And fill niches once empty and
Potential

Potential for chemicals
To heat my cavity,
But soot dampers

Dampers spongy groupings
Who grasp at heat

Heat that comforts
Comfort gashes
Gashes that burn
Burn from heat (presumably of course; I'm cold)

Tory True

"Together As One"

Together as one is my only dream,
   both of us happy as a Loving team,

Our trust everlasting in both one another,
   with gossip or mischief well never bother,

For in our hearts and in our souls,
   with this love we will reach all our goals,

To be happy together, together as one,
   getting through the Bad times by jet-skiing in the sun,

Together in love and peace as we should,
   others could only wish that they had what we do,

Every relationship has its good and bad,
   but we must stay happy to get through the sad,

Together as one, in our hearts, we should he able
   to work together on projects right from the start,

In our souls and in our minds,
   me and you together are one of a kind,

This we share so strong and so true,
   I can only feel this way when I'm with you,

Together our dreams can come true, let's stay
   together forever just me and you.

Bradley Gribble

"My Sister Jo"

How did this bond between us grow?
Wherein lies the answer; who will ever know?
How could two different (separate) souls entwine?
Who planned this union, yours and mine?
There was a lot of time and space,
And then I joined the human race!
Solve this mystery,
Transcended thoughts between you and me!
When did this bond begin to grow, can you explain, I don't know!
Time has come and gone, years are passing fast,
This mystical bond will forever last.
But when this bond is broken, as it will surely be.
Standing in that unknown place,
I for you and you for me!

Julia Osman

Dying, Untying

As the house in the dusk was entered,
And the door closed as always behind.
A sense of foreboding overwhelmed me,
With nothing tangible seemingly left to remind,
Me of the union that once lived here,
Not a shred of vibrancy could I find.

His whimper was enough to tell me.
His long-haired coat was many-hued.
As in this humble mongrel lineage,
Even he, the small dog, was subdued.
Sensing through his simple senses,
A terrible sorrow, with which to be imbued.

The tearful and difficult phone call,
Bringing murmurs of the city's finest.
Plans to be made for interment,
And the soul was laid to rest.
And absent the gun, the house again grew silent,
And, going on with life, the final test.
John W. Ridley

Love Lost

She's in a desert;
she's all alone.
She can't find him;
she can't find home.
The Sun, it scorches,
with heat too bright;
but there's no warming
she's cold with fright.

He waits inside;
he thinks she's coming.
The night is deep;
no sign of dawning.
Though hope remains,
his tears are falling.
He only whispers,
yet still he's calling.

They're worlds apart; love's lost forever.
She can't find him — he can't find her.
The sun will blind; the night's unending
Hearts kept apart — there is no mending.
Nicole D. Kalil

I Watch The People Crying

I watch the people crying, the casual tears I feel,
those of Nazis, crying as it should be short
 and strong - tears of superiority,

The Jewish family crying as they should cry, long
 and softly - tears of hope,

The American army crying for what they believe is wrong,
 crying loudly to make them listen,

I hear the shouts, the speeches of beliefs... I listen
Those of Hitler, shouting for the death of Jews,
 his shout is strong,

The shouts of President Roosevelt, pleading for the lives
 of Jewish men and women
 His shout loudly heard, but not loud enough,

I feel the hatred, gestures of anger I see,
those of the Axis Powers,
 showing their hate strongly and powerfully,

Those of the Allies, showing their confidence
 and their hate for the Nazis and their beliefs,

Again I see the crying, with open mouths
 their strong, hopeful cries which cannot be heard any longer.
Alexis Grant

Lonely

In a world with millions of people
I'm alone without a friend
People say being alone is a state of mind
I say the opposite
My version of being alone is having no one to talk to
When I need a friend
Having no one to run to
I think that there is someone to take my loneliness
And fill it with Joy, Happiness, Love
That someone would be to feel my sorrows and pains
Be happy for me when I fulfill my dreams
And in return, I would give her all of me
Two ears to listen to her joys, pain, her life in general
One heart to give her whatever her heart desires
And one mind, body and soul
To make all wildest dreams come true but

It may take all my life to find someone like that
So until then I will always be alone
James Martin

The Tree I Planted For My Grandchildren To See

I am ten today as I plant this tree. I am planting this tree
in the school yard today for all the future children to see.

The children that I especially want to see this
tree are children that will be related to me.

You see, I will have children when I grow up. They will
have children. They will be my grandchildren.

I am planting it in the school yard because children
play there and they will be careful with my tree.

My brothers will start to school and play in this yard.
They will care for my tree while I study in high school.

After that, I will have children of my own. They will go to
school. I will teach them to care for my tree.

You can figure out the rest of this story. My children will
have children of their own. They will be my grandchildren.

I will bring my grandchildren right to this spot. I will
say. "I planted this tree just for you when I was a boy."

You must love and care for my tree. It will give you shade
to play in, branches to climb on, and leaves to study.

Teach your grandchildren to plant a tree. Then the earth
will always have trees for all the children to see.
Weida Carson

Empty Feelings Linger

Empty feelings linger on, I suppose
that once again, I have made all the
wrong choices in life. Or else this
feeling wouldn't be here, right? I'll
put it away in the back of my mind -
acting as if everything's fine. But as
soon as I have a moment alone, I'm
right back were I've started from.
Not happy here, not happy there,
When will it end - How did it begin? I
cease to find the feelings to change,
the feelings that always seem to
remain. Emptiness it lingers on, just
like it did back then. In and out just like me,
if and when will I ever be free.
Free of anger, free of pain, free of
scars that have somehow remained.
Angela J. Pettis

Joe

Your presence fills this space and I know your essence never before
For it touches and takes and rattles my who
In tears and smiles and feelings so real, raw and primitive.

Black night enfolds and my heart wanders...What is it and why must I?
Whispering air creeps up and my skin knows that which is a mystery to my mind
And a song plays on and on and on without a word to repeat.

So Joe? Did you know on some level yet unmined that the stumbling of life and love
Would lead us here? - Asking and pushing at each other until there was emptiness so
Profound and silent that the energy of our souls would shred and cling in shattered patterns?

Dangerous. Beautiful. Unknown?

And in this doing, that I'm getting is there a moment which will rise up from this paralysed chaos of desperate chasms? - Ringing with a clarity and joy
So profound that it will balance the pain of losing you and will it be enough for us all?

I myself want to run screaming into the night and
Lose myself in the desert of the woods which line the shores of my childlessness
Because I threw away that of the most precious out of ignorance and fear so long ago.

And so I fight for those whom you and I have loved
And I will not give up as the song plays on and on and on through the night
One word now heard and repeating in my heart.......love.

Mary Karsten

Soul Escape

The mirror portrays itself.
An empty space without a subject.
Its story cannot be told.
Whatever the surroundings it duplicates.
I survey the emptiness.
But it is I that enters.
My picture is present
But there is also another.
Who is this, friend or foe?
The inner looks out upon the whole.
This must be the everlasting,
The being behind the facade.
Its destiny is in greater hands.

Anthony Green

Grandfather's Farm

I've just been out walking, as I've often done,
Along a cow path long gone, into the rising sun;
With fish pole in hand, down a boulder strewn hill,
To where the stream cuts in and the water is still;
To a place of my youth on my Grandfather's Farm,
Where I felt protected, and sheltered from harm.
The path was worn deep where the cattle had trod,
From thousands of hooves cutting into the sod.
As I skipped along to the songs of life,
Not having yet known the testing of strife,
A covey of quail suddenly took to their wing
And flew right over my head, a marvelous thing.
I stood silently and listened to the whisper of feathers,
tasted the dust of the earth, felt the sting of forever.
Then, as it occurred to me I'd been here before,
It occurred to me also my fishing pole was something more;
The boulders my buddies bodies; the quail, bullets looking for harm;
And it occurred to me I'd soon be back on my Grandfather's Farm.

Dennis H. Bishop

I'll Do It Better Next Time

Clemmie cat died last night.
She was eighteen - frail, painfully thin,
overwhelmed with the miseries of age.

As I sat on my closet floor, her chosen departure site,
I held her head and struggled with my emotions.
Not knowing what to say or do, as usual, I just cried.

I thought back to when I first mourned - for the person who should teach me how.
I was seven, and the house was filled with relatives.
They had come to be with my Mother when she died.
Not knowing what to say or do, I just cried.

Michael found Clemmie cat and me in the closet, moments after she was gone.
He gently picked her up, and carried her around and around the house, murmuring good-byes.
He brushed her poorly groomed fur, and wrapped her in a towel.
Surrounded by our children, he told them about Clemmie cat as a kitten, and then there was the time she ....

Yes, I think I'll do it better next time.

Valerie Walls Riesser

Untitled

The city's digested in accidents
Death's moat waking me up
Her eyes construct a prison for me to dance at will
Alone like a devil's doll
Each night a wrap of comforted loss
I press on to a vision opening up in a ceiling painting
Allowing congress time to set in motion a skeleton exhibit
Lighted up like an orgasm pulse

Tom Roop

When I First Met You

When I first met you,
I was alone at forty-nine,
You were thirty-four, strong and free,
And full of brassy sass.
Your birth into my soul did stir a mournful spirit,
That forced my being to dream the dreams of dreamers,
My feet to dance the dance of dancers,
My mouth to sing the songs of lovers,
And my heart to laugh the laughs of laughter.
Now the sea is restless,
And the boat has set adrift,
My eternal love, farewell,
For a heart too soon you made glad,
Alas! Farewell my love.

BeBe Webster

Thank You

How do I say "Thank You" to a friend
  who's been so dear?
When I need to talk you would always hear.
The things I had to say (whether good or bad.)
You would brighten up my day and
  make me not so sad!

How do I say "Thank You" for all the
  things you've done?
Be it talking or going to the movies,
We always have such fun!

I wish I had the special words to say,
To thank you in a special way.
For always being there for me,
As the best friend you could possibly
  be.

Heather Post

If Only You Knew

A young woman's joy of the expectant new bundle
dreaming of the wonderment of the newly discovered
midnight thoughts.. is it a girl, or a boy
likeness of me or of him
if only you knew.

A young mother's pride of the miracle before her
to hear "Momma" uttered for the very first time
the warmth, the love, the life dedication
of hopes and dreams through each coming year
if only you knew.

A mother's triumphs and trials of raising a child
making choices and decisions, with the best of intentions
in believing and praying that it would all work out
not knowing how abrupt it would close to an end
if only you knew.

A mother's heartache, worry, and pain
of this beautiful child so loved by mother
not knowing, not caring, neglected, despairing
If only you knew.

Angela Rice

My Prayer

O' God help me to walk according to your word.
O' God help me to live day by day according to your word.
O' God help me to love according to your word.
O' God help me to talk according to your word.
O' God help me to be an example to others according to your word.
O' God help me to give according to your word.
O' God help me to forgive and forget according to your word.
O' God Bless and keep me according to your word.
O' God help me to have patience according to your word.
O' God keep me Holy according to your word.
O' God receive my soul according to your word.
Amen

Thenethia Hardy

Pleasure

Pleasure is internal
The illustration no mortal can see
When resistance is down
Feel the essence of its presence
Floating into nostrils saturating grasses of a field
Permeating a soul amid flowers
Blowing between the creases in one's mind
Like the breath of a laughing child
The touch of a cheek
The rush beneath the bones of everyone in love
The cheering notes of a favorite song
Pleasure builds on peaks of hills, it flows in the rivers
It stirs in the valleys like Jesus, the spirit of life imparted
It may come after a long day or short day
It calculates the quantities binding one's soul
Then divides by zero
It is the equivalent of dissociation
The way to pleasure there is none
Don't try to find it
Pleasure has plotted a time for each of us

Hermalena V. Mines

Fate

Walls of glass, a frozen past,
I looked, but could not see.

So I closed my eyes and found disguise,
Hidden in my dreams.

I wished to tell, but talk withheld,
And I heard what was not said.

So much to give, a life to live,
The love my heart has bled.

We said goodbye and could not try,
For no one will time wait.

The unknown has become the security,
To blame this heartache on fate.

Lori A. H. Griswell

The Dream Of A New Dress

To make a dress.
   I have to think very hard.
And look for the best.
   I am working very hard
      And never rest.!
The wish of my dream.
When I was a little girl. I was dreaming
   and always said. If my dreams comes true.
I will try the best, what ever I can do.
   I didn't have a mother, when I was three.
And I had to learn, one two three.
   Now I am over sixty-three.
I should thank the God for helping me!

Pota Stylos

Untitled

She speaks aloud through her dismal mind, yet
so silently the words cannot be heard by others.
She tries to answer the questions thrown in the
frosty air, but they do not understand what
she grandeurs. They only seem to impend her
leaving her speechless, making them believe
that, again, she is without knowledge.
Although it is only silence that overwhelms
the stricken being, she plays the role of
the ignorant one to portray a painting of
prejudice against the unknown.

Phyllis Avila

"Freedom"

A lady that was once a girl,
   will break out of her shell.
But still a little girl,
   scared and trapped in her own world.

Scared and weak with no words to say,
   a whisper; a mumble;
      to ask for the way.
Running and hiding in her world,
A glare of light which she calls hell.
   The light, the light, is it hell?

Strong and fierce as she is,
   outside the shell that's where it is.
Brake the shell and enter her world,
   cross the boundaries of hell,
      there you find a little girl.

Many at hand didn't succeed,
   trust in me and you will see!
Grab my hand and hold me tight:
   I will set you free!

David Hernandez

"Living In Detroit"

Living in Detroit really isn't so bad. Seeing
our city go down has made me dam mad.
Our children are running wild that's just
putting it a little mild. Parents are not
parents anymore they just pack up their
kids and shove them right out the door.
Families are now so distance no-one has
time to listen. It hurts me to my heart to
see everyone so far apart. Guns are everywhere
you could get killed just for being
there. Everyone is blaming someone that's
why nothing is getting done. We have to
pull ourselves together just like the
finest of leather, we have to float high like
a beautiful butter-fly. You see "Detroit"
we have to go back to the old way, and
we shall all have longer days. So let's start
by mending our own ways, you see if we
don't there will be all hell to pay.

Mary Ann Walker

Reality

He who is afraid of reality,
is he who needs to search his soul.
For he who is scared to face life,
Will forever live alone in the cold.
He who is afraid of reality,
Is not only scared of life and death and
in between,
but yet he is also afraid,
of being a human being.
He who is afraid of reality,
Is he who has to accept things as
they are,
For he is physically so close to life,
but yet mentally so far.

Kimberly D. Orr

The Agony And Ecstasy Of Math

Add, subtract, geometry
All these terms are foreign to me.

There's a house in a yard, and feet go in boots,
What kind of plants grow square roots?

Exponents, fractions, words so complex
What in the world will they think of next?

Fractors, radicals, multiplication
I think I need a long vacation.

Imaginary numbers, what a thrill
I'm having enough problems with the real.

Math is so hard, who even cares
All of these numbers give me nightmares.

I've gotten so deep, what will I do
I can no longer add one plus two!

I go to the store, to buy me some bread
And all these equations run through my head!

College Algebra, Trigonometry
What does this math have to do with me

Now you may ask, "What in math could be ecstasy
It's when you finally get that college degree!

Shareon Higgs

Untitled

Twilight just fell, and so did my heart,
Another night and we're still apart.
How I long for us to be reunited
And passion flare like a fire ignited!
My love for you will never wane.
Oh God! How can I stand the pain?
How I rail at fate for taking you away;
And I pray to God to show me the way.
The days pass slow, the nights still slower.
My will to live sinks ever lower.
I remember everything; your last breath,
The second you closed your eyes in death.
I know you're somewhere, waiting for me;
Knowing I'll come, but not when it will be.

Candy Harding

Searching For Truth

We all know we are living in troubled times.
Turn on the T.V., see the hate and crime.
Young boys getting killed on the streets.
Little girls playing trick-or-treat.
Mommy and daddy are losing their mind,
In search of themselves, they will never find.
So much darkness covering the days.
Our minds filled with haze.
A country full of leaders, leading in different directions.
No one bothers to ask questions or make corrections.
Turning our backs on less fortunate and needy,
Because society accepts only the greedy.
There are so many choices to be made.
Is it really the devil underlaid?
What happened to our innocence?
Did we, with all our technology, label ourselves 'duntze'?
Refusing to believe what we cannot see.
Believing, "It could never happen to me."
In a world filled with so much pain and death,
Will the truth come only at last breath?

Tonya Whitetree

Among Us

There are those of an alternate world
who see humans as the animals
that they are all crowded in herds
themselves they are something else
in the mirror they can see it too
and wonder how the others don't
oh, some may think them a little strange
but never guess how strange they are
how different the thoughts they think
pulsing like sore thumbs in their skins
holding themselves still and hard
so others won't hear their hearts
they learn to stand alone without
the need to meet the eyes of men
who might detect the power they have
see the shark beneath the waves.

Albert Goldenberg

The Campfire

The red and purple plumes of glory droop forlorn

The silver morning tramps in gleaming triumph round the world

There is promise in the vast foreboding dawn

A heap of ashes, gray and sodden by the rain
Wind scattered, blurred and blotted in the snow
A black scar in the sunshine by the pine.

Betty Lou Porreca

Love

Love is a treasure that's richer than gold,
Love is finding someone with whom you want to grow old.
Love is like a sunset - and a mountain tipped with snow,
Love is finding someone you can't imagine letting go.
Love is meeting someone you never dreamed you would find,
   And dreading just the thought of leaving them behind.
Love is sharing laughter, troubles and sorrow,
Love is having arguments and being there tomorrow.
Love is when you smile when the other is near by,
Love is understanding and at times not asking "why"?
Love is what I've found in you,
   It's a treasure and a prize.
   And if you ever doubt this,
   Just look into my eyes.
   Honey, I love you,
   In more ways than you know.
Since we met my days are sunsets,
   And mountains tipped with snow.

Jill Amy Band

The Sweet Dream Of Someday

She hardly waits with patience, although there's special care;
   She wants that special someone, although he isn't there

She wants someone to notice. She wants someone to care.
   To her it seems like something almost more than she can bear.

You may often see her dating, though her decision lies in waiting.
   It may seem like it's been forever, though she'd rather it be that
     Than to take whatever

In time she trusts he'll come along;
   At times she fears she could be wrong,
     She prays to God that it won't be long,
       Asks for guidance and to be strong.
         In her heart she wishes he'd soon come,
           But knows it's sooner for others than some.

Someday her search will be through, she will finally stand in view,
   Of that perfect man whom she's been dreaming, that one whose love

     Is full of meaning,

That one whose love will never die, instead getting sweeter by and by,
   From that day on they'll be together, standing as one forever and ever.

Hannah Ruth Morris

My Priceless Gift

The Time had come, it had to be,
The hour itself did not agree!
A Holiday was still in play
But my Darling New-Born was on her way!!!
It was my choice for me to bear,
The happiness I felt was there!!!
Sadly no one else could see...,
The future bright for her and me.
A priceless treasure unforseen,
She came to be a mother's dream!!!
And like a ship put out of sea...
She wavers not and will always be...
My guiding light for eternity!!!

Irene Altken

Mirrors

Mirrors reflect the young and old.
The rich, the poor, the weak, the bold.
Some people thrive off the image they see.
And others just wonder "Is this really me".
For the people who thrive it is a loss in the end.
They never looked at the inside now they are to old to mend.
So if you are young or at least feel that way.
Please look in your heart, you will need it someday.....

Shawna Sopp

Fairy Bright

My lovely fairy with golden hair,
I see you in the early morning light
perched on a flower just sitting there
with sea blue eyes shining bright
you look at me, with love in your eyes
Fragile wings flapping like a butterfly's.

Lovely fairy with golden hair
upon your flower you gently sit
giving of your energy with loving care
as I sit there amazed for a bit
I sigh as I suddenly realize
there's more to life than we see with our eyes.

My sweet, sweet lovely fairy bright
The important lessons you teach
Will always be in my sight
Your loving energy always in my reach.

Elizabeth Berumen

Fade Away

Sometimes the memories are all too clear
The smirk on his face
The tears in my eyes
And, oh, the smell of the beer

Reliving the moment over again
Oh to run away
To crawl in a hole
To hide from a moment that should never have been

I told him to stop and I told him no
The feel of his fist
Hitting my jaw
Will he ever truly let me go?

I know in my mind he'll always stay
Haunting my dreams
Clouding my days
And only with time will he fade away.

Pamela Kay Turner

The Grotto

Here in the grotto, (Lord, built thou for me?)
Is all the answer that can ever be
Lavender bells and golden cymbals in the salt breeze sway
Here, in the gentle dim the ivies play
Peep now between the crags of rock and reach
Clinging across the sharp face each to each

Man is the trespasser and the all unblest,
Unknown, unknowing, by You of Eden dispossessed
All else on earth rests in its certain fate
Interdependent, and in its godly state..
But Man, who tears across beast, field, and mind
Ripping, despoiling, leaving his manufactured filth behind.

Here, in the grotto (Built not, Lord, for me)
If there is answer that I yet may see,
Let me but watch Your lacy fingers turn
Hear the soft icy dripping, watch the strong grasses, learn
How I may humbly leave no scar upon this place.
Comfort my shame, Oh Lord, and give me Grace.

Denise Miller

Phantom

The phantom has now awaken.
It's the shadow of the night,
I'm shackled to the light.
I start to breathe heavily,
Relieving all my anxiety.
Ride the danger into the night,
Watch the moon illumine the sky,
My teardrops burn away the pain,
I'm tired of the world seducing me
Into its lies,
The dying light is calling out to you,
The phantom lives on.
It's all the sins that make you go blind.
Your suffering thoughts are sinking into
The holes of hatred.
In the eyes of the serpent I'm pure.
I've lost the game, reality won again.
The candle flame burns out slowly,
Naked in fear you wait.
The eyes of the storm sees only evil,
   Michelle Lloyd

Someday Soon, Tyler

We will never forget the day
you came to us,
so small, cute and full of charm
your little grin and the little things you did,
to make us smile
We never imagined that a little child
could touch so many hearts like you did
We never thought that you would leave us
so soon, but you have completed the
work God sent you to do.
You have brought us closer than we
have ever been before.
God allowed your life to open a door for us,
but someday soon, Tyler, we'll be together again
all troubles will be forgotten and we'll see
your smiling face.
We'll be in a better place, never
to be apart again.

but Someday Soon Tyler
Someday Soon, Tyler, we'll be together again!
all troubles will be forgotten and we'll see
your smiling face
We'll be in a better place,
never to be apart again.
   Amanda Dewitt

The Star

Believe in yourself and dare to dream.
Remember that life can hold more that seems.
If you keep your chin up and always love who you are,
the chances are good you will surely go far.
You may trip and fall upon rocks and small stones.
But no matter what you are never alone.
Don't let someone change you,
make you someone you're not.
You don't want to lose
the great life that you've got.
Only you can decide
what's wrong and what's right.
Though sometimes you may need
to put up a fight.
But always remember that you are the best.
You don't need to listen to all of the rest.
You are who you are,
and that's forever a star.
   Lisa Gebers

Daddy's Sorry

I'm sorry I wasn't there when you first learned to walk
Nor was I there when you first learned to talk

I'm sorry I wasn't there to tuck you in bed
And kiss you good night on your sweet little head

I'm sorry I wasn't there when you came home from school
And to help with your homework so you wouldn't be some fool

I'm sorry I wasn't there when you fell off your bike
Or to help you catch a nice big pike.

I'm sorry I couldn't get along with your mother
And never had the chance to give you a brother

I'm sorry you grew up not living with Dad
I pray that never made you too sad

But I want you to know as you continue to grow
If you wonder "Did Dad love me?" Don't ever think no
I Love You!
   Garry Habner

Solely Single

I stand in your shade for sobriety's sake
Making miracles to keep you that way
I dance in your shadow of different settling suns
And the night doesn't seem so scary that way
The fraudulent and fierce isn't scary that way
In the dew of the morning you stand in my shade
Hovering miracles about to keep me that way
You waltz with my shadow of different raising suns
And the morning doesn't seem so grisly that way
The rushing of truth into dreams isn't grisly that way
And so is my monogamous and not too bad schedule
And so is my life with a single shadow of choice
A bear, a lover, a drink of water and so
I jig to assortment at the lead of day
And ease to protected sleep when it's dark
I slip into you, you slip into me
This life doesn't seem so solitary this way
This way walking solely sincere
...doesn't seem to unbearable
...not too
   Nancy G. Oxman

Raindrops

The sound of rain on the skylight
Makes me feel so serenely secure
The pellets pounding on the roof
While I'm inside and sure
That the lightning and thunder
In the outside world
can cause me no bodily harm
Because huddled inside my safe, bundled bed
I am totally waddled and warm
Warm as a babe, in my mother's womb
Is this the same feeling I'll feel,
When the raindrops drop
And drop and plop upon my silent tomb?
There will be no feelings
at all for me on that fatal, inevitable day
So why waste my time reflecting
In such a foolish, mortal way?
This moment is precious and loving
And my heart is filled with fun
So rain away, rain away raindrops,
Until you are swallowed by the sun.
   Miki L. Closs

My Hopes, My Fears

First things first, I hope I don't lie down in the Earth.
We first start dying the day of birth.
I fear the people who use dope.
Will I get shot because the color of my coat?
I hope I'll never be alone.
Or to have my son locked up and have no home.
Do I have to work illegally to get paid?
Why is it that newborn babies die of Aids?
I wish everybody didn't have to drink.
And be so drunk that their eyes turn pink.
I hope that I can live one day further.
Fear is found when we hurt each other.
I hope you have fun because you like to play
When the police come you fear you may not get away.
I hope that my son doesn't come home late.
I fear that women living alone aren't safe.
Everybody should get along because we're equal.
But why do police officers like to beat people?
I fear that people will forget how to think.
I hope mankind doesn't become extinct.

Frank Starr

A Little

They wake up wondering
Even a little scared
Yet they must go
Because they know if they can make it through and finish
it's their ticket out

Out of the dark
Out of the pit
Rid of hopelessness,
   fear, entrapment

Into the sun
Into the open
Excited for the future,
   having fun, growing

And for those who did not wake up wondering
Even a little scared
We silently thank the ones in our prayers
that some have returned to that bottomless pit
And help those others who did wake up wandering
Even a little scared

Randall R. Lowery

Casualties Of The Night

Out of the night
Comes the horror and the pain.
Followed by the tears,
Followed by the rain.

"To hell with your values,"
Delinquents yell with so-called pride.
'To hell with our lives,
No rule will we abide!"

And into the day
We ponder those nights:
Death, defiance, deceit, violence.
Has it ever once been worth the fight?

'Peace, love and happiness,
Good luck and good will to all."
Misguiding—we preach throughout the day,
Instead of preparing for their fall.

Morals, virtue, love, spirituality.
All that once was right:
How can it be so easily forgotten?
We're all lost—casualties of the night.

N. Michelle Killgore

Enchantment

Your beauty is as enchanting as a Rose in full bloom. Beauty of the
your outer soul which I Speak, yet it is your inner soul's beauty
which is more enchanting and More extended into the pinnacles of
time

It is your complexity which is confusing but most Admirable.
For the wonders of your mind only captivate my own. For
It is your complexity which embodies your inner soul's beauty.

Like a Rose, you too are special and lovely...Like a Rose in Bloom
You too have grown into a delicate and perfect creation of
God...Like a rose you too have become like a delicate and perfect
part of this Beautiful garden of life... Your enchantment, like a
Rose, Gives off sparks of happiness, warmth, and tenderness...And
like a Rose, your soul's outer perfection shall wilt into the nothing-
ness of that which is endless time, only to be surrounded by delicate
reflections of what once was

You are Enchantment, with an outer soul's beauty which is evanescent...
Yet with an inner soul's perfection which shall exist forever, only to
Be captured and reflected in my own mind and heart...Your enchantment
Is that which is special to a broken dream of my life...

You are Enchantment. The essence of what is you reflects into
what is me...and
So it will only be time that will end your journey of physical
beauty...yet time
Will not end your memory and specialness, the essence of what is
truly inside of you,
And the embodiment of your enchantment shall Live Always...

James D. Ramirez

I Was

   I was young, but now I'm old. I was shy, but
now I'm bold. I was right, but now I'm wrong. I
was weak, but now I'm strong. I was mean, but
now I'm nice. I was dumb, but now I'm wise.

   Do you see what I'm getting at? I was red,
but now I'm black. I used to fly, but now I flow.
I was a fire burning long ago. Do you wish to be
me? Are you happy, or are you mean?

   The way you are, is the way you'll be. Do
not change to be seen. I was selfish, but now I
share. I didn't know, but now I care. I made my
choice how about you? Five, four, three, two,
one, it's due.

Jessie Pelletier

Farewell My Love

I walk through the corridor in a daze,
Remembering the beauty of her smile, to which lonely desperation dies;
All around me there is a misty haze.

The sun beats down upon me, with stained glass rays,
While my heart sings a silent of love, yearning to see her eyes;
I walk through the corridor in a daze.

Praying to succeed before my final days,
Wondering where upon my destiny lies;
All around me there is a misty haze.

Feeling like I'm living one of Shakespeare's plays,
Not to feel love any longer, my lonely soul cries;
I walk through the corridor in a daze.

It's hard to handle, the sorrow that brays,
To think of life without her, it's hard to realize;
All around me there is a misty haze.

For allowing me to know her, to the Lord I give praise,
Though now it's time to mourn, and give her my good-byes;
I walk through the corridor in a daze.
All around me there is a misty haze.

Kevin P. Stanistreet

Our Wedding Day (November 12, 1995)
My Wedding Vows To You Keith
From the first time our eyes met, I knew I had found the man of my dreams. I promise to love you with all my heart, to be your best friend, lover and wife. To never hold on too tight; to allow each of us the space to grow together and as individuals. Never to forget with the love we have to give to each other we will always intertwine our lives to love and live as one. I will accept and love your family as my own. Your friends and family will always be welcome in our home. I will always be considerate, caring, and understanding of your feelings and needs. I will stand beside you in everything to help you achieve your hopes and dreams. To work together to make our love, our family and life be the very best it can be. So with these vows to you I pledge my love, my heart, to share your life to become your loving wife. To love, honor and cherish you and our love for each other always and forever. I will always love you.
Tamara P. Scott

Forgiven
As I knelt down to pray and repent,
Of my passion, my lust, my anger rent,
I heard from lofty skies on high,
Soft echoes of sounds that fly.

Thy piercing tones pricked my heart,
Which gave me comfort in great part.

Thy heavens opened and I did see,
The great, great span of eternity.

And as I repent and wonder in my heart,
Am I forgiven from the start?

Then came sweet music to my soul,
You are forgiven in whole.

Oh such fullness did I feel,
Like partaking a sumptuous holy meal.

Now Lord I pray to make it real,
May thou bind this covenant with thy seal.
John S. San Diego Sr.

An Innocent Man
I had a dream, and I'll tell you what I saw.
I saw an innocent man hanging from the cross.
With a crown of thorns upon his head,
It was there I knelt, and bowed by head.

In prayer, Dear Lord above, I cried to Thee, "Don't
let this be our sinless man from Galilee"

"It is I" a voice said unto me, "It's okay I came to save thee"

When I was born in a stable I knew, my years on this
earth would be very few.
I came for a reason, and that was to save the lost,
and you must help me, no matter what it cost.

Reach out to others, and bring them to me, I came to
save them, and to save thee.

I cried in the Garden of Gethsemane; "Lord let this cup
pass from me, Thy will to be."
My father in heaven sent unto me a legion of angels to comfort me.

I came as prophesy was told in the Old Testament years
ago. To save the lost, that no one would lose their soul.

I had a dream, and I'll tell you what I saw.
I saw an innocent man hanging from the cross.
Fran Brake Arrington

The Gift Of Love
When the clouds of doubts have blinded me,
You shine your Light of Love so that I may see.

When fear leaves me naked, and shivering with cold;
With Peace and understanding, you clothe my weary soul.

When life's lessons make me falter, falling on the road;
You pause with hand extended to
lighten up my load.

When for guidance and inspiration,
my thirsty soul does ache;
You quench it with wisdom dipped
from spirit's lake.

And so I stand here grateful to you
and God above,
That I am blessed to witness the
reality that is Love.
Anne Louise Maloney

Let Angels Sing
T'was a mother's pain beheld by none
  that felled a tear upon the earth.
No words, no plea, no sorrow spoken
  beheld this tear she shed to earth.

A rush of wind gave watch to win;
  A darkened sky gave hush to wind.

With uplift wings full of grace,
  gloriously raised with mercy's strength
  this child of God so stopped by life.

No eyes beheld this upward rise
  on wings of glory, a mother's held.
The tear she felled was all she left.

"Come, my child," she silently said.

"Let angels sing," is what she said.
Ronald C. Moak

Sonnet: She's the One
She's the one I love with all of my heart.
I just don't know what I'd do without her.
I don't know what I'll do when we do part,
But when it happens, I'll hurt forever.

We're still together, and the time is great,
But I don't know how long our time will last.
I'll see her tomorrow, we'll stay up late.
We'll talk about fun we've had in the past.

If it's meant to be, only time will tell,
For the test of time is the best of all.
If we soon must part, I will wish her well.
I'll love her always, long after we fall.

All I know is I love her to death,
And I'll love her until God takes my breath.
Jason Vierck

Terminal
Pain rules all
as the darkness falls
holding myself against tortured dreams of my soul
Jesus Christ why can't I just let go
of the dreams I've had that've died
their slow tortuous death that made my soul want to hide
under cover of unconsciousness
where the pain just hurts so much less
G. S. Flaherty

Infinitesimal Man

As my eyes wander over mountain and sea,
With waters spread over a great span,
A thousand sensations align to enfold me
As I think of the level of man.

When I admire the blanket, colossal and dark,
Gem-studded and cov'ring the land,
The beauty overwhelms me, the vastness compels me
To consider the place of man.

How exalted the seasons, bearing with them
A clime to beckon all hearts!
No human force can summon or send them;
Work done, each slowly departs.

The mighty hurricanes, tornadoes, and 'quakes
Mere mortal is powerless to ban.
The thousand sensations become one revelation:
How infinitesimal is man!

Margarette Combs Saunders

Elvis (The King)

Elvis Aron Presley was the King of Rock"n"Roll
Housed within his body
Was a beautiful heart and soul
He was for every man, woman and child
Animals as well
He was a man for every race, religion and creed
He was a man for everyone's need
Elvis has gone to meet this maker
God, his caretaker
But we must not despair
For he left behind his rock"n"roll along with his heart and soul
He will not be totally missed
For we have all his songs to reminisce
Ladies and gentlemen, boys and girls
Elvis has left the building
But not our hearts, not our minds
We can still hear his music
We can still hear him sing

Norma L. Norris

My Granddaughter - Yet To Be Born

I love you already, child yet to be born.
You have no idea how much you are wanted.

Your birth will herald a re-birth for parents and
grandparents alike. A chance to start over with
the weighty responsibility of child - rearing.

Your father's birth signaled a beginning for me -
it was as if we were both born at the same time.
Your grandmother became a better person then.

Raising your father was a privilege; having an
opportunity to be involved in your life will be
an honor.

Kay Harvin

Mountain Lions

Swiftly running through the desert's sandy floor
Jumps as high as a kangaroo rat
With eyes like a hawk, it spies its prey
Silently stalks
Runs too fast for the eye to see
With its sharp claws it captures
But the meal gets out of his grasp
Finally gives up, not successful
But much wiser

Kimberly Rivera

Em

I came upon a flower one day,
   trampled to the ground.

Its soul was bruised, its stem was bent,
   from elements surround.

A wall was built around my flower,
   so she could grow and mend.

But weeds came round to choke my flower,
   and often to offend.

My heart grew heavy for my flower,
   yet still she did endure.

And as she grew and healed some more,
   she soon become more sure.

My flower stands straight and tall today,
   so beautiful to behold.

She'll leave me soon and travel on,
   to tales as yet untold.

A gift from God, my flower is,
   a gift that can't compare.

A gift from God, my flower is,
   a gift for all to share.

Jerilyn Johnson

Oh Little Baby

Oh little baby so innocent and sweet
Rooting so close to your mom, trying to find that familiar
   heart beat.
Needing a bond only a mom can give
Gotta adjust in this new climate where you came to live.

Oh little baby so innocent and sweet
Before your life gets started you must learn defeat.
For in giving you life, even before your first breath.
Your mom has given you death.
She has given you aids
You're just another mistake she's made.
No matter if from sex or drugs
You'll soon just be a memory of kisses and hugs.

Oh little baby so innocent and sweet
You could have made a life complete.
So many lives you touched.
You've been loved so much.
You never asked to be born
You never asked to be here.

You have made heaven seem so near.

Doris Hall

Mother

Mother, can you understand
There is so much that I have yet to learn
But all of it on my own
There is so much inside me that has never had a chance to breathe
I have to let it out, if only to see if it can survive
Some things won't, but they must be given a chance
Mother, do you see how I've got to change and grow
In every direction, if only to find the way that's right for me
Mother, you know who you are and what
You've already experienced and known so much and so many
But I've barely started, I'm not even sure how to do it
You may not like the way I've chosen to try
But it's the only way I see possible right now
When I know better, I'll do better
But for now you've got to try to trust me and allow me this
There are few things that I am sure of in this world
One of them is you, now let me learn to be sure of me

Amy Sandas

Teens

Why is it that when a child reaches teens
Nothings done without argument, or so it seems
That Parents once looked up to with love and respect
Are now blithering idiots, or worse yet
That rules established long ago
Are stupid and crazy, most they no longer even know
That every request is unreasonable to them
And they haven't gotten along with siblings since, can't remember when
They'll fight with each other like moths flying to light
Neverending battles, morning, noon or night
Money runs through their fingers like handfuls of sand
But God forbid you ask them to give you a hand
Should you say "no", you'll find they'll die
They have to have it and that's no lie
They don't know the difference between want and need
And to dangerous activities, they pay no heed
So trying on Parents, this period of teens
You'll never get through it or so it seems
Best way to make it is to remember when
Your parents were idiots, way back then.

Dianne Mills

A Question Of Romance

Sentiment is old-fashioned;
holding hands out-of-date?
Nothing, but nothing, can save passion
unless it is hate?

Hearts and flowers are out;
sarcasm and whoopie cushions in.
Don't even look, Cynicism shouts,
for love to last. 'What a grin.'

Then why do so many of us long
to find a mate of our soul?
Surely all those poets could not be wrong;
tough or tender, love makes us whole.

Too many ribbons? Too much lace? Not for *my* valentine.
Spirit, desire, and emotion together equal romance.
So here is my tribute with two hearts entwined.
May they flutter forever to honor love's dance.

Phyllis Jean Green

Tiny Tears

   Tears are such tiny things they make no
sound at all, yet I can feel them coming
they're like a waterfall. I wear a smile
upon my face for all the world to see but
the little tears inside of me keep falling
silently.

   They come out on my saddest days and try
to wash away the pain, other times when I'm
full of joy they come again anew, my eyes
will mist, my heart is full, I'm happy
through and through.

   I'll bet I have two kinds of tears yet I
can't tell them apart. Still it seems they
always know what goes on within my heart. So
I'll just keep on smiling through them and
all will surely see, no matter which tears
may fall, I'll know they're just for me.

Nadine Sharpe

Untitled

Rotten is the egg of litany
bound in sinews of reverence
Conglomerate the masses of degeneracy -
the open sores and abscesses of existence
Rows of the chosen many, usurping virtues
   undeniable even to gods
Copulate and multiply does the pestilence
through the diseased biped beast,
jaundiced with syphilis, aids
Heavens cyto-nuclear weapons
the ultimate homo-sapiacides

Matt Miller

Study Of Iris

Irises unfold slowly in the bedroom
taking their own sweet time like true southerners
with an intrinsic wisdom
of selective speed
unfurlment petal by petal
the tight tear of a brazen new bud
opening
ever so gently throughout the long cold night.

I watch them from my high sleigh bed
feel this vibrant envelope expanding
the gap between staid old winter
and rollicking spring.
Did you see that curl of indigo smile
reveal its soft yellow tongue in the waning moonlight?
It is enough to hang a life on
for one more day.

Joanna Candler

Photograph

I looked upon a photograph,
and this is what I saw.

A young man dressed like a soldier
with worry in his eyes,
of those he'd have to fight,
of those who'd have to die.

He has a look of wonder
he has a look of pride
he had a look of fear and death
it shows from deep inside.

He has a look of home
a place he'd rather be
forget this ruthless fighting
with those across the sea.

But duty calls, and he must serve
this Country that he loves,
She's the home of the brave, the land of the free
her honor stands forever with help from God above.

I looked upon a photograph
and that is what I saw.

Richard G. Smith

Sunshine Is Near

As the years pass through dark clouds,
I keep my mind on you.
I've tried my best to stay out of gray skies;
My love for you helped me through,
I have no secrets and no lies.
Just so you know,
I love you true blue....

Dianna I. Ashworth

Years Ago

Years ago I had a mom
a mom who said she cared
a mom who hurt me, but somehow made it seem alright
years ago I had a mom
a mom who had boyfriend
a boyfriend who was very mean
a boyfriend who would also hurt me,
and then laugh
he laughed a laugh that
would send chills down your spine
years ago I had a mom
a mom who has since moved out of my life
a mom who said she loved me
her love also meant pain
a pain I couldn't bear
years ago I had a mom
but, now the ties are severed
severed and never to be rejoined
yet......................
    years ago I had a mom
    Emma Todd

Speak Not One Word

Until it happens to you, you cannot understand
the depth of the pain I feel inside
the words you say so self-assured can only come
from one who's never cried
the tears I've cried.
It could never happen to me or mine
you plainly say so clear and loud
so very proud so proud indeed.
But until you know the sudden jolt
of life gone wrong of endless nights
that just won't end
of grief that just won't mend
you shouldn't speak no not one word.
    Vicki Staffieri

Boxes

Born in big box, buried in a small one,
work in a wide one, live in a tall one,
like children chased bee's and butterflies!
But we are prepared! And we are intelligent,
yes, we leave air holes even for ourselves,
born in a box, died in a box, buried...
we so wish to be out, we punch holes in it,
fill them with slabs of glass and wish,
we see, but can not touch, or smell,
our houses are boards, and posts,
and bricks, and ghosts...
but a box none the less,
like animals, ourselves domesticated,
born in a big box, buried in a small one.
    Kevin Godin

Chronicles Of Fantasy's War

Reality soon descends upon a purloined throne,
A monarch in this vacuous chamber,
No adjutant to assemble forts against the glacial rigor,
They have defected me to parry him alone,
I am certain if I could encounter Strength, she would help me,
but even she has become a refugee too wholly hidden,
I whisper the General Reality has surrendered,
The lie is lost in a mines tempestuous clash,
Now I am too sanguinary to compromise with the realm,
Mirage and Chimera follow their mother Auxiliary to my side,
They succor me with winsome tellings,
Fairytale now dons her licit crown.
    Sherene Rezaiyan

Life As Forgotten

Life is like a cycle,
just like the water cycle.
Don't hop in though,
if you don't know how to swim.

Think that
you always have
a long time ahead of you.
Condensing, precipitating, for years and years
until you finally evaporate.
Take it one day at a time-
not twenty years.

What would it be,
if there was no such
thing as life?
No people, no planets, no atmosphere.
Nothingness,
no such thing as anything?
    Lindsey Silken

The Captive

"Let me go!" she cried, anguished, painfully
remembering her own days in the sun.
Yet he refused, all the while basking in his own
glorious freedom, showered with love, aloft.
The captive waited...waited...

Then he tired of the game,
she was now broken, withered,
no fun even when he deigned to descend
to where she was kept
and so he dropped her -
the chains shattered from the force
of the blow
as did she -
shards of herself littered the room
so he looked for the ancient dustpan
to sweep the untidy mess
into a heap
to dump, out of sight,
behind the rotting stair.
    Elizabeth Shea

Anger

Anger is a delightful manipulator of humanity,
Hot tempered, it is the fuse to a reckless bomb;
Short-lived, it leaves one with endless consequences;
Yet it never takes a leave of absence...

Alone, it is a concentrated evil,
A deep-rooted biological urge,
A primal scream throughout primordial darkness,
However, it is never fully auditory...

It lives in the fathoms of the soul-
Creating a sea of black and red,
Sucking goodness into its whirlpool of pain,
Agonizingly familiar to swim in...

It is present in the Genesis of creation
And the Armageddon of the Earth,
In the violent actions of those who sin,
In the words and silence of those who think they do not;
Anger is the equalizer of all of man -
And forever his end...
    Annamaria Tambone

Mother's Love

No one knows a Mother's Love, the mysteries are untold.
How she bonds to young ones with all the love she holds.
She loves them with a passion and protects them even more,
From dangers they may face, from what the future has in store.

She works so hard to teach them every right from wrong.
But not always can she be there for lifetime is so long.
She doesn't mean to harm them by protecting oh so much.
She doesn't want them to forget their loving Mother's touch.

So she clings on to their childhood where memories keep her bound.
Where dreams for little children and fantasies are found.
To keep her children small in mind, trying hard to let them go.
Hoping that throughout their lives, they know she loves them so.

So as she unties the bonds that keep her children close.
Be patient with a Mother, their future they have chose.
Debra Leeser

I Want You

You are truly so beautiful with your half open shirt,
Your long trousers, your sinewy fingers.
So perfectly beautiful
With your long unrestrained strides,
Which startle the rocks.
You are full of life, full of truth,
And I want you! I want you! I want you!

Beware! Tell me to beware, too!
Your touch will shatter the spell. Stay there nourisher,
Distant, permanent, ideal! It would be wonderful, I know,
To travel the world with you seeing faces, cities, rivers;
Sharing years, kisses, celebrations.
It would be wonderful, I know.

But then my voice would be without lament,
My voice would be without desire,
My voice would not have the inclination it now has,
That you are permanent, distant, ideal.
And I want you! I want you! I want you!

...darling, how do I wish to see you before my departure,
As we were then...Tell me I am mad, I adore you!
C. Markopoulos   (By an unknown poet - translated
from the Greek by Costa Mazkopoulos)

My Mom And Me

I came into this world, as naked as could be.
With a healthy slap from doc, and a loud cry from me.
With out reached arms, and welcomed by my mom to be.
Who all her 87 years thought the very best of me.
I told her often how lucky she was to have a birthday
present like me.
She looked back at me, with a wide smile and agreed.
I miss her so, since she has long passed away.
A void I know, day after day.
Now that I'm getting older, and some day must go that way.
I know once more my hands will be empty like I come.
I only wish every child could be born, and loved the way I was.
For this old world, is big enough for all of us because.
Virginia R. Sieggreen

Friendship

Friendship is a bond
It may last a very long time
Or even a very short time
Friends are two different people,
Who like each other
Sometimes there are groups of
People who like each other
But all that matters is they're friends.
Krystle Hovey

Flight

I let the news of love gone by
Affect my soul after I tried
To find my mate and fly away
As an eagle grown
Now I learn how I will fly
With wings of missing feathers

Altitude is hard to hold
Just breathe in deep is what I'm told
I never will hold her hands again
For I learned late not to touch what burns me.

Feelings continue while I see
How much this person meant to me
Even though I never was
Anything in love to her

My broken heart is bleeding
What I never had still needing
I loved her so, she let me go
And never said a word
Now I feel I'm a broken eagle,
Learning how to fly....., again
John S. Wright

Plea for Understanding

Why does it always seem I turn to you in times of trouble?
Why can't I simply rely on myself and not worry what people think?
It seems as if I have spent my entire life worrying whether I am
doing or saying the right thing.
Who is to say what is right or wrong in this world?
Lord knows that line has been blurred more often than not.
So what do you say — Mother, Fate, God or even you society about
my speech thus far?
Have I opened your eyes?
Have you seen what I have been feeling?
Have you even cared?
After all, each of you is partially to blame for my problems;
All of you had a hand in my growing up.
Then, why does it always seems I turn to you in times of trouble.
Do I blame you?
Should I blame you?
I just don't know anymore.
Maybe, I should just forget...
Maybe I should just quit...
Maybe, maybe I should just accept.
Gabrielle Welch

One Last Chance Gone Wrong

Brief glimpses of the future
Or of the past gone wrong
"It's here they'll be corrected," she says
As she leads me down the hall.

And what awaits me, I wonder,
As no more words pass between
Me, the uncomfortable bastard son,
And her, the beautiful Queen.

She leads me on without a word.
I follow her to my beam ends.
And I stare down off the proverbial plank.
I jump and I descend.

So she leaves it at that point
As my eyes open wide.
I sit bolt upright, stark naked.
With nothing left to hide.

To her, I have bared my soul,
And made a mortal foe.
Even before she turns to leave,
I am alone once more.
Jeremy Rubenstein

The Old Barn

What has happened to the horses I did house
And the many stalls full of cows?
I remember there were many a pig;
One stayed at my side until he was big!
I long to have them all back just one more time to see
If any, or perhaps even all of them, would still remember me.

Now I hear they're tearing me down
All my decaying parts and bits
Will be driven down into town,
and wind up in the old dump pits.
The square nails that held me together
Through rain and wind and very cold weather
Those they'll keep because they're made no more;
They buy round ones now at the hardware store.

My beautiful square logs, best planks and metal roof,
Will all become another barn which will be full proof
That I really didn't die but became a new barn and friend
Protecting my new tenants until their very own end!
Rosebud Elliott Bonar

Father's Day

I never had the chance to say
"farewell" to my father on his final day.
There were no signs, there was no pain,
save for the anguish that is mine each day.

If only I knew his day had come,
I'd have been by his side to show my deep love.
My best friend was leaving;
my nightmare had come;
for the rest of my life, no longer a son.

What words could have shown the depth of my love,
or the courage I lacked to exist on my own?

The days now are empty, as
my soul sits alone,
by the stone that marks him in a world dark and cold.
My fear never leaves me, my dependence so strong,
on the father I lived for, now forever gone.

So on each solemn Sunday, as on this Father's Day
I visit him resting in his eternal bed.
I speak to him softly, then I bid him farewell,
with the tears of my sorrow, and the words never said.
Stephen Samuel Sayad

OKC Bombing

Tick, Tock, Tick, Tock
The time is now nine o'clock.
The morning goes as normal day does,
Head to the corner and catch the bus.
Walk through the doors and sit at the desk,
Drink your coffee, without making a mess.
Tick, Tock it's nine o'two,
Tick, Tock, the sound of KABOOM!
Heads looks left, heads look right
People waking up on the southwest side.
Lives have been lost, loved ones remembered,
Bodies are trapped, and many left injured.
Will they be found before they die?
"Where's my mommy?" Children will cry.
Families will ask "Why God, Why?"
Michael Guthrie

Now That I'm Seventy-Five

I thought when I had reached age seventy-five
There would be little joy to be yet alive.
The world would crowd out life for me
No goals to strive for except aging you see.

But each new day, it seems I have a plan
To fill the hours given unto man,
More places to go, new friends yet to meet
Being amongst the crowds on busy streets.

Many tasks to accomplish, and engagements to keep
Along with numerous hobbies yet to complete,
And now soon the thrill of becoming a Great Grandparent
Will surely be a title and a blessing to inherit.

So praises and thanks be to my God on high
For abundant health and pleasures in unending supply,
To be worthy of all that's been showered on me
I'll be most grateful till Eternity.

So with each new day, another month, or year
That's allotted to me, I want to hold dear,
Making life brimfull of precious memories
What more could I ask than these treasuries.
Eleanor M. Lundberg

Broken

I crumble bits of bread into minuscule fragments;
Chalk color on crimson cloth.
Your words pulverize my heart and soul;
Scarlet drops seeping into white shag
I drain away like the color from my face.
Irreparable, everything stains or is trampled underfoot.
If I were shattered glass, I could fight back,
With even my smallest sliver
As you grind me into your calloused heel.
Bethani Ann De Long

The Life Of The Lost Boys

Life is a springtime - cotton blossoms and pansy petals.
   Escape into Neverland with Peter Pan and
Wendy - stay with the lost boys, tell them a story
   of mothers and fathers and spring's greatest glory.

Life is our springtime - the beginning of eternal.
   Return from your dreamland and let all wounds
heal. Peter and Wendy will always be here to comfort
   the lost child and help her not fear.

Opening to a new world can replace all the past:
   No more Captain Hooks to bring one down;
No more evil pirates lurking behind trees waiting
   to capture the lost child, and tie her
   and then, walk her off the plank into a deep,
endless lake. No more Mr. Snee, no more
   crocodiles. Tiger Lily is safe from these evil wiles.

Bring home the lost boys, teach them and then,
   let them grow up, finally, and win.
Andrea Lauritzen

Life Is Beautiful

Life is beautiful in its own way
Some people die and some stay.
God made birds, animals, and trees
And he made the fish to swim in seas
Each day is wonderful rain or shine
The trees that we cherish are made of pine.
So we should give thanks to his God above
And appreciate his kind and love
Khadija B.

Animal Farm

We the residents of Manor Farm
want a new way of life, free from harm

We want to be rid of Mr. Jones
and all of the things that mankind owns

We all will be equal under our laws
whether we have hooves, claws or paws

We made our Commandments and hope to live by them
our flag flies high as we sing our animal anthem

We do what our comrades say must be done
from early morning till setting sun

We get smarter and better as each day goes by
"Four legs good, two legs bad" is our cry

We wrote a new Commandment replacing the old
"Some are more equal than others" we're told

We seem to be doing what we once thought a crime
the things man did, we do all the time

We now see our leaders on different ground
walking on "two legs" to get around

We didn't mean to do any harm
all we wanted was a better life here on Animal Farm.

Kari Lynn Tannucilli

Rejection And Rebirth

Suddenly my whole life changed,
I wonder if I've gone insane.
Everything is different, yet it's not.
I take a close look at all I've got.
At a time when it's least expected,
I become the one who's rejected.
Should I stop and wonder why
and let time pass me by?
Or do I face this new world with strength
while I try to decide what to think?
I know I have a path to follow,
and in its low spots I shouldn't wallow.
So when I'm confused
and I start to feel used,
I'll stand up and fight
because this is not right!
Then I'll be in control of what my life will hold.
If I make mistakes that's the chance I take.
So I'll walk down that path with my head held high,
and I'll reach for the stars and the clouds and the sky.

Dottie Jones

Lovers Farewell

A wind whistles through the trees,
gentle songs twinkling in moon beams
Crackling leaves under soft little paws,
curled up quietly in one of my dreams.
Memories bring me back to a day, when you held me so tight
Then I recall all my sorrow, when you left later on that night.
I know it was wrong but how could it be,
It felt so right to be with you
Maybe you are my destiny, but there is nothing I can do.
I will always cherish the time we had,
And perish the thought of us apart
You made me beautiful, gave me myself confidence and my heart.
Now it's time to say farewell, you'll always be my friend
I hope that you will always think of me that way until the very end.
And maybe our paths may cross again, "One Sweet Day"
If not I wish you the best, in whatever comes your way.
So many words you have left to say, things to do and places to see
Just make me this one promise...
Take care, if not for you then for me.

Robin Cramer

No Exit

It encloses me within its world.
Not letting anyone or anything out.
Even through its hideous disfigurations,
The others cannot see or hear it,
But I know it is there.
Its gruesome features scorn my eyes,
Its evil voice rips at my ears, teasing me.
They cannot see it, for it is not real to them.
They hide within their homes,
Pretending it's not there.
And when I plead for help,
They leave me in the streets bare.
I have no one to turn to,
No one to listen to me when I cry out my fears.
No one.
I am trapped in this hole I call hell,
Which is filled with the suffering of the world.
There is one door here, but the sign that hangs above is not an exit.
So I plead my heart out to you, to save yourselves.
For once you are in, there is no out.

Heather Noens

Symphonic Sea Walks

Along the misty shore, near ten
the morning sun sneaks thru lofty new day fog
crystalline directed rays, one son
specifically directed, geometric points of reference
alighting unannounced earth treasures
rocks awaiting new headings
old shells left to hear muffled sea echoes
tunnel ear emersion
tiny grains to shuffle for new path patterns
awaiting each oncoming sea print, moon print
imprints to be etched away with each new passing tide
the bay sea foams with memories of warm root beer
over vanilla ice
balmy beach daze of childish summers past down the shore
sky blue hues intermingling with warmer earth tones
and cool emerald algae ripples
pea sea green moss washes up temporarily in respite
anchored by strewn scraps of weathered driftwood
    brought up by another high tide
symbionic symphonic morning sea walks paint portraits of a new day.

Michele Ranta

Untitled

Quietly she sits there, not sure of what to do
She stares out toward the ocean, not sure of what she sees
In the deep dead calm of the night she feels the cool summer
    breeze along her skin, such as a veil that surrounds her
    bare skin
As she sits there and reflects, she listens to the waves crashing
    among the rocks
The memories rush through her mind, leaving her confused
As she walks away, she leaves it all behind
She realizes the past is best left there
And as she takes one last glance out over the ocean, her gaze
    drifts up towards the stars
It's there that she begins to dream of a future full of hope

From the shadows of the night he quietly observes her
He wants to reach out for her, but knows he wouldn't be welcome
So he makes himself comfortable, and remembers how they used to be

As she walks away, he notices her smile, he knows that she no
    longer cries, that her tears have come and gone
And while he wishes to hold her one last time, he knows that
    she is gone.

Nathalie Zuber

The Beauty Of Chicago

I am neither a poetess nor a singer,
   I am only a priest of the beauty of nature.
There is Michigan lake in the east of CHICAGO,
   I am bewitched on seeing the lakeshore beauty of Chicago
The cars are moving in eight lanes on the highway,
   They look like the Yachts are swimming in trims array
on the lakeside there are so many magnificent high-rise buildings.
As Hospitals-Hotels-Business Offices. Companies and
Residential buildings
Among them is a Sears Tower building tallest of the world so high;
It seems as if it is stealingly kissing the sky.
The bright Mercury-Golden lights of those buildings,
   Shine whole night look like as Heaven came down on these
buildings.
Or Chicago Bride wearing a silvery-Golden Brocade's veil,
   Ready to meet her groom stepping in the boat to sail
Or it is Demi God Indra's Ballroom in Heaven,
   Where countless fairies, Nymphs dancing whole the night with fun,
The poets as the great-poet of nature William Wordsworth,
   Shakespeare-Milton-John Keats-Shelley take rebirth on Earth.
In CHICAGO they are fascinated by the lakeshore beauty nature.
   They would compose enchanting poems with great pleasure.0

Shanti Sharma

Open Road

Traveling in life like a sparrow
What path shall one take?
The wide or the narrow?

The wide path traveled by many
Like a mirage in the desert
A narrow will appears to be plenty

The narrow path traveled by few
An abundance of obstacles
A weary traveler what must one do?

Some doors have been opened
Some doors have been closed
Such is the path that one chose

Appearing as if propelled by momentum
In a mirror of time
Like an innate Salmon on a desperate climb

Jon T. Gutierrez

Ever Wandering

Front porch, rocking
Sun hanging low, children clamor in the distance
Ever wandering, ever wandering

Birds flit about, work so hard, yet still sing
Thunder rolls in the distance
Ever wandering, ever wandering

Stars in the heavens, hairs on a head
Colors in an endless array
Ever wandering, ever wandering

New life springs up under death
The cycle continues, age or ageless
Ever wandering, ever wandering

Karen L. McClelland

Wind

Whisping, whirling, twirling,
Through the leaves of the oak trees.
A cool, gentle breeze on a steamy summer day,
Takes all your troubles away.
Back into Pandora's box.

Patrick Toomey

State Of Mind

Terrified, a desperate plot to conceal a shocking secret
for life I tried to keep it - In my mind it would hide
secret's out time to survive the ride
a stout skillfully plotted suspenseful thrilla; mind bendin'
spine chillin' high velocity cap feelin'
like a gift of Black Magic, with slowly growing horror
in order to understand, you must first walk in the shoes
of a dead man; with my heart in my hand cold envelopes the land
No looking back at evil ways, feeling worried as I gaze upon a haze
All still well knowing more than I could ever tell
horror of a six feet present hysterics runnin' wild
The sense of a lost child
When will the terror stop? Who wrote this plot
Lord, please take away the agony, that saddens me
Now I'm branded a beast standing over yo six feet of peace
I can't stand it, I just can't take it anymore.

Gordon Gardner

My Mother

   My mother she is like no other.
My mother, she's one of a kind.
No one other has one like mine.
With a heart that won't grow old.
But that is made of solid gold.
For my mother is the one, that I want to hold and hold.

   My mother she is like no other.
I owe my life to my mother,
For without her I would have no other.
From a baby to a man, I owe my life to my mother.
And when I need that helping hand,
There she'll be like the sand.
Beneath my feet to hold me up.
She's the one that can't be beat.

   My mother she is like no other.
For when I need that special friend,
I know she won't just pretend.
From a baby to a man, she'll always be my special friend.
For when I look into her eyes,
I know she'll always be a part of me.

Leonard Morfitt

Grandma's House

I walked by my Grandma's house today.
It makes me really sad now to go that way.
The trees that I used to climb have been cut down.
Glass from the window lies on the ground.
Flowers that I helped to plant by the door,
Will not bloom there anymore,
The fence where Grandma's dog and I used to play.
Has already been torn down and hauled away.
Board by board will the house go?
Or will they smash it with just one blow?
Stop the destruction! I want to blurt.
I can't stand it! It makes me hurt.

Betty Bitner

Wishing You Were Here

As I sit watching the tide, wishing you were here,
I hear a sound, like a child running from fear.
I turn to listen and try to understand,
And there I see you, dashing towards me through the sand.
You were moving, speaking, but yet silent and still,
Like a man without a passion or a will.
I reach out my hands, waiting, hoping to embrace,
But like a weakened memory, your image was erased.
So here I stare, my eyes filled with tears,
Looking, listening - wishing you were here.

Monica Newell

The Hunt

Into the shivering darkness of the late night,
Stealing quietly through the woods to my perch,
a dead fallen tree, I wait quietly, listening
to the silence of the dark.
Alone. Each minute an hour.
Finally dawn breaks.
I gaze over the small clearing, fingers stiff
on the cold steel of the trigger,
The silence is broken by the snap of a twig.
He's coming toward me out of the dense brush
walking silently, gracefully.
He stops and listens.
I'm ready.
A quick movement alerts him to my presence.
He starts to turn.
Then the crack of the gun.
His white flag drops.
The hunt is over.
Cheryl J. Speer

In Remembrance Of Him

It points toward heaven in remembrance of Him,
The life that He gave and the sin that He cleansed,
The pain He endured and the blood that was shed
It was for us that He died and for us that He bled.
The cross saw it all that broken, dirty wood.
It saw Him gave His life, give all that He could.
It saw the beatings and the pain, the wine that was sour,
The spitting and the mocking, all took the King's power.
He gave up His life to the One who knows best.
It was all over, it was all done, but Yes!
The Lord, He is risen! Freed us from sin!
And it still points toward heaven, in remembrance of Him.
Cassie Pate

The Poet's Agony

I thought it would be easy
I thought the words would flow
I thought I would have the chance to say
Most everything I know

Sometimes it's rather easy
Sometimes the words pour out
But it's really more like pulling teeth
Than stopping up a spout

I thought my subjects were unending
I thought I had a lot to say
What a shock and a surprise to learn
It didn't turn out that way

I know I won't stop writing
I've definitely been bit by the bug
But rather than showing you my work
I think I'll hide it under the rug.
Beth Alderman

Sensual

I'm intrigued with your presence
And overtaken with temptation
I want to fill the night with intense passion
And make you mine for eternity
I want to whisper sweet sentiments in your ear
And caress your body with tender kisses
Images of you encircle my mind, body, and soul
I have seen only you, desired only you, and loved only you
I will show you unconditional love that is immeasurable
We have found true love that will endure
until the end of time
Jennifer McHone

Marie

What has AIDS done to you,
　sweet daughter of mine?
I look into your beautiful brown eyes
　going sightless, and see
　　fear — depression
　　anger — frustration
but also,
　　hope — anticipation
　　love — determination!
You have already received your death sentence;
　So every time I kiss you
　　and hug you
　　and bless you,
　I'm preparing you for the
　　Eternal Kiss — the Eternal Hug
　　The Eternal Blessing.
Diane Reyes

Withered Rose Of Jericho

Waves rise in the East, distant cries of thirsty ancients
　Accusing, blaming, pointing toward me.
　Flooding my dreams, plunging my soul under
　　the drowning echoes of past lives...
　　'It is you!' they scream,
　　weeping tears of sackcloth and ash.
　　The voices are mistaken.
I own no cup that may relieve the parched people,
　My water will not ease their longing.
　You do not know what you ask of me,
　go seek another...
　　'It is you!' they scream,
　　answering any doubt attempted, cornering my fears.
But, my heart is a desert, broken and lifeless
　Searing, freezing, blistering those who enter.
Come, refresh your spirits, fill your hungry hearts,
　enjoy the last meal I can prepare....
　　'It is you!' they scream,
　　drinking the sagebrush and sand provided.
　　The voices are mistaken.
Keith E. Nobles

Destiny

Red, yellow, orange; the Sun sets upon us.
Spraying cascading caresses of dusk,
Touching with velvet fingertips
my inner most person.
Lovingly stroking the depths
of my tender, quiet heart.
I look, I feel your presence
within these beams of solitude.
I sit placidly awaiting your kindred thoughts,
to melt with mine.
Knowing you feel my presence, too.
I reach, I merge,
Your soul to mine.
We are but one...
Only for this moment,
A moment of eternity.
The sun slowly rests behind the horizon of reality.
We are but two...
Alone but together.
For eternity.
Roxanne Strickland

Untitled

I think I shall stand tall through
it all, although not without error.
I'll get though this trial with a smile
no matter what it takes.
How can they judge me so harsh, as if
it's judgement day.
Well, I think the lord let me stand,
so tall, so it will be hard for them to
bring me down.
"Why?", you say, because I'm needed
in many ways.
I will make a difference in this world,
maybe not today, but when the time
comes my way I'll be sure not to miss it.
I'll use all the zeal in me. Eager to
be me, and I'll finally feel at ease
from all the ruse around me.

Lisa Arnold

"Dreams"

While tossing and turning in the middle of the night,
I knew I must take some Alka-seltzer before daylight.

My clothes were messy and my hair every which way,
The "Little Man" inside my head his drums He did play.

When I get to the Bathroom, what do you suppose?
The empty bottle of Alka-seltzer is lying on some old clothes.

For the Alka-seltzer Across the street I must go,
The "Little Man" inside my head is not playing slow.

I grabbed my coat, and put on one shoe
After looking for the other I thought oh! Heck one would do.

When my eyes become accustomed to the night,
In the house across the street, there is no light.

My one shoe comes off and on the cement I fall
My hand is on something feels like a "Flat" ball.

I look in my hand and I can plainly see,
A bottle of Alka-seltzer, I bow my head and Thank Thee!

I put the Alka-seltzer in a glass by the sink.
The "Little Man" inside my head won't let me think.

I drink the Alka-seltzer all down and now I can feel,
It was all a bad dream. It wasn't for real!

Melinda Bentley

"The Perfect Friend"

Today I found a friend
who knew everything I felt.
My every weakness
and all the problems I've been dealt.
She understood my wonders
and listened to how I felt
about life and love.
And she knew what it meant.
Not once did she interrupt me.
Or tell me I was wrong.
She just understood what I was going through
and promised she'd stay long.
I reached out to this friend
to show her that I care.
To pull her close and let her know
how much I need her there.
I went to hold her hand.
To pull her a bit nearer.
And realized that this perfect friend
was nothing but a mirror.

Jessica Kirkpatrick

The End Of The Yo Yo

I'm not going to quit, I'm just going to do better
WHAT FORGOT, IS WHAT I KNOW
And where I was, kept me from seeing where I wanted to go.

I'm not going to quit, I must simply do better
I lost the vision, I couldn't see ahead
I need to open my umbrella and walk through the rain
   And quiet feeling the gloom, and the doom, and the dread.

I'm not going to quit, I will do better
I am me and they are them
I am important to myself and need to take care
So when you're near there's goodness in the air.

I dug my rose-colored glasses out of the barrel
They feel so good upon my nose
And tomorrow when the son shines, I'll take time for that rose!

So watch out world here I come, the dreamer is back
God helps them that helps themselves and all that stuff
Just be a friend and hang on, help me remember what I know
Most important is HOW to get there, not where we go!

Elsie J. Miller

Sound The Trumpet

I walked past the window of the music store one night
Everything was dark inside except for one small light.
Each piece just sitting there in its own distinctive way
As I looked around the room I could almost hear them play.
The piano with its snow-white keys, the harp with silk like strings
The Stradivarius violin with melancholy sounds that ring.
Far in the corner there was something bright
I couldn't see too clear because of the dim light.
I'll come back tomorrow and go in and see
What type of instrument that could possibly be.
There before my eyes I felt a sense of awes
The most beautiful trumpet without even a flaw.
I picked it up and started playing a song
I've always wanted one of these for so very long.
I have only $20.00 and that's not enough
I'm too old to work and times have been rough.
You could clean the instruments at the end of the day
Then you can finish the payments out of your pay.
I played that old trumpet till the setting of the sun
Then God called me home, cause my work on earth was done.

Lois Hugill

The Ride

We took a different desert road
that wound along the edge of Wonder Valley,
east of town where even Mars
would be less barren.
We were taking rides more often now.
You would empty yourself in a steady stream
of out-of-order memory
to me: The child eager for anything.
I would watch you lose yourself on purpose
as the space grew and there were no markers
to tell us where we were.
And as some familiar beast seemed to grow
in the pit of my stomach
you would finally lose control.
There in the pick-up that bounced along the dry and pitted earth
you would explain, Father, that your love was all I had
and I would take your secrets to make them mine
leaving lies and the ghosts of dead kisses
in the road.

Lisa Mann

Untitled

I see her in the distance
She stands alone and looks across the roads blankly, like a snowman
Closer I see her standing still
her face is just as blank as the snow, like a puppet's face
I can't help looking around
there is no seat left for her in the bus

There she comes
With her huge bag, huge body, and her blank face
Everyone stares at her strangely and sarcastically
As if she is a monster on the earth
Giggling, laughing, swearing...
All comes out at the same time
Without any response
She walks to the back of the bus and looks for her seat

Finally She stands still with her blank face
And covers her head by her big hat
Lonesomely she looks out of the window
Across the road, she sees nothing but the snow
Confused, I closed my eyes and
I see nothing but an ugly and cruel society ahead of me.

GuoZhu Li

Surrender To Destiny

No more is everlasting night,
   Come gloom, return to this hell.
The whisper still lingers with the light
   Come darkness, surround the world and swell.
The rising sun no longer disappears,
   Come dusk, envelope me with frowns.
The spirit still flies, causes fear,
   Come comfort methinks endurance drowned
My soul still lingers solitude and still,
   Come melancholy embrace me with your spell
The sound of silence hurts my cursed ears,
   Come moans, shriek and make me yell.
My dream did fade into the lightening sky
   Come destiny, bring me to my grave
The fierce winds did fan the flame of life
   Come death, there's no one here to save.

Samantha Tabacco

Our Children

"Food, food, food please give me food...hungry"
I must say the kid looks hungry.
Eyes well sunken in, sores on his face, lips chapped and cracking.
He says he is hungry and over and over and over again.
Yes, I think he may be hungry.

"Give me pencil, pencil, need pencil - for school, pencil please"
Dressed in rags and shivering she asks for a pencil.
If I was not here looking at her, I might laugh aloud at the irony -
Clothes are what she needs but she wants a pencil for school.
Could she know that the pencil can save her?

"Money, money you have money please, please give money"
Banding together they make their mental assault.
No ear is spared this choir's chorus of begging.
The choir of kids that rarely smile or play.
I know they are kids because they are so much smaller than me.

David M. Lyons

The Search

I traveled many highways
I traveled many roads

I was searching for peace of mind
More precious than any gold

Sometimes as I traveled onward
I felt you in the wind

And the rains that seemed to follow
Seemed to quench me from within

You were the mightiest in the mountains Lord
With your roaring thunder bolts

I had to seek a shelter under the mighty oak
My body took to shaking so I said a little prayer

And I felt your presence near me
A peace beyond compare

A rainbow seamed to follow blue pink and gold
It seemed to beacon onward a magic to be hold
The beauty of Gods love

Yes I found that peace of mind
In the mountains of Gods Love

Gloria Dzwonkowski

Don't Ask Why

There are no words...
Contracted, hyphenated, or expanded upon; that can convey,
The loss of a child, to a Mother...
It is a pain, unlike any other.

A small jagged stone...
Finds a niche in your heart; and takes up residence there;
With no intention of ever leaving...
It's there forever, to keep you grieving.

The stone will stay there...
Causing discomfort when you move, walk, rise out, sit, think, or dream.
When you bring past images to your brain...
It's there to remind you; there's nothing to gain.

You will never find...
The answers to the questions; the meaning of the end,
For life was not designed to be understood...
Only to be accepted; the bad... and the good.

Frances Rethorn

The Burning Feeling

The building erupts into flames,
With outbursts of crackling kindling.
You can hear the frustration
Of the wood as it gets eaten by the fire.
The buildings around don't even glimpse;
Since it is not them, it doesn't matter.

Every once in a while a flame will protrude
From a window casing and show its true horror.
The fighters try to nullify the beast,
But only add to the confusion.

Inevitability the roof will explode,
And the treachery of the orange monster will come out.

Maybe then the other buildings will notice a problem,
But probably not,

Some explode with violent fury,
Some calmly.
But the truth is,
It will explode if the pressure keeps growing.

Most times these buildings are saved, sometimes lost.
I just hope this one can exist until the end.

Brad Kuchinski

Going Home

We never know how long we will be,
With our eyes open and able to see.
The beauty of a sunset, the beauty of a flower,
For the Lord has told us we know not the hour.
When he will be coming to take us home,
Now is the time for us to roam.
And tell all the world of his wonderful grace,
For it may be soon that we look on his face.
He will reach out his nail pierced hand,
Taking us to the Promise Land.
Heaven is where I want us to be,
With our Lord, Jesus Christ, for eternity.

Pamela L. Sestak

The Ploesti Liberators

It was back in 1943, the day was August first,
So many men, so many planes,
Took off and feared the worst,
They left the ground from Africa
And formed a tidal wave,
Flew to glory, pride and pain,
Some to an early grave.

Of all the targets bombed in war that saw liberators fall,
Ploesti was to those who flew,
The very worst of all,
Defending guns and balloons and flak,
Made it far too costly to attack,
But it was thought they could be beat,
By dropping bombs from fifty feet,
So the liberators tried,
Fifty-eight were damaged, fifty-four were lost, over 300 men died.

Let us not let the years erase this battle that was flown,
The most highly decorated American mission the world has ever known,
Lets not forget the sacrifices made by these young men,
The likes of who, the deeds they did, may not be seen again.

John L. Darling Jr.

Tiger Oh Tiger

My beautiful loving tiger,
My precious tiger
Your eyes were like little golden crystals

Your fur silky and shiny as silk itself,
  with a touch of satin

Your movements were so soft and sleek,
  you could catch a bird or lizard in an instant

You brought pleasure to children and adults alike
  Loved by all who touched you

Even though you are gone,
  you are still very dearly missed

Although I have other cats,
  you will always be one of the most precious and purr-fect tigers

Kathryn Paquin

Ode To Dad

Dad is the one with the snuggly hugs,
He's there with Raid when I'm grossed out by bugs.
He makes me frustrated, furious, and mad,
But that's a small price to pay to live with my Dad.
He's not arrogant, vain, rude, or mean,
But sometimes he can be such an old bean.
He is extraordinary, not an ordinary Joe,
And he is a special, if you met him, you'd know.
And so I must end my Ode to Dad,
(If I say anymore, I may make him mad.)

Anna Lane

Blue

Blue is the color of lovely things pretty and divine,
  like mountain streams that flow so gentle and the oceans broad and wide.
Blue is the color of the sky, beautiful and bold,
  it's the color of the arctic ice and sparkles on the snow.
It's the color of delicate violets that make you want to sing,
  and the color of the dew drops on the grass in the early morning.
Blue is the color of a blue spruce tall and mighty in size,
  blue is the color of a steam engine's smoke and a new born babies eyes.
Blue is the color of the earth as you see it from outer space,
  and a color in a triumphant rainbow that disappears without a trace.
Yes, blue is a wonderful color, I notice it all the time,
  it's the color that I always see deep inside my mind.

Marie Patty

Our Great Nation

Many have traveled across our land,
  From the beauty of Alaska to Hawaiian sand.
High in the mountains or down by the sea,
  Our great nation is the place to be.
The sights are magnificent as we look about,
  And freedom and justice prevail throughout;
Making us the very best land of all,
  Upon which other nations can call.
Many times we've reached out a hand,
  For the sake of freedom in another land.
Men have died, these goals to obtain,
  And may their death be never in vain.
Let us be thankful, humble and true,
  Giving our best in all that we do;
And as we give and continue to care,
  Treating all men equal and fair,
Old glory will wave high for all to see,
  We live in a land that truly is free.
Lady liberty will forever stand tall,
  Proclaiming our nation - the greatest of all.

Connie Campbell Bratcher

Untitled

Guiding light
Uriel, Garbiel, Michael, and Raphael
Archangels
Rapture
Dominions and Thrones
Inspiring good will
Angels, principalities, virtues, and powers
Nine choirs remembered in prayer.

A duration for God
Noble
God's heralds
Exaltation
Loving us.

Janet L. Brija

The Lord Is Near

When the sky is black, and the birds fly away.
The storm begins and the whole world is dark.
Clouds surround you, you feel very alone.
Look beyond the clouds, for a rainbow is near.
The Lord never leaves you.
The storm will end, the clouds will go away.
The darkness will disappear.
The Lord walks with you through the snow and the rain.
When it seems darkest in your sorrow and pain.
The sun will rise and dry the rain.
Always remember, the Lord is near.

Sherry Maxwell

Independent Woman

Love bounded me to you.
Habit kept me in your arms.
Strength kept me alive in the end.
  Independent Woman I Am...
  Never saw myself without you.
  Never knew who I was, always living life for another.
    Learned to love myself, be true...
      Cause baby I gave up too much of life for you.
        Living life for myself...
        Taking risks I never took before.
        Learning that before anyone I have myself.
        Crying, dying, but always surviving,
        Pain changing, alleviating, and soon will be no more.
        Independent Woman I Am!
    Sheila Ponce

Hate Is Death Waiting To Happen

Locked in a world of bitterness and lies. Screaming
yelling, and painful cries. Sometimes wishing
the world was colorblind. So the individual
imperfections nobody would ever find. The level
of hatefulness is killing me very slowly. Everyone
has a story to tell me and a broken heart
to show me. People from the barrio to the projects
to the riches neighborhood. Some living with
the troubles and some living good. Don't crush
me with your words of hate. We need to come
together before it's too late. We should live in a
world of love. That's what I wish when
I pray to the Lord above. A last bit of
advice. Peace is something we should live in
not rest in.
    Roxanne Starrett

Darkness

The world is walking in darkness,
not knowing which way to go.
Should I go the right way?
Or should I go with the flow?
I'll take drugs to make me look cool!
Maybe it will just make me look like a fool!
People think we need money and power,
their heads are in the clouds as high as a tower!
Violence is as far as the eye can see,
and all people ever think about is Me!
pollution has filled the air,
when people just sit at home saying stuff like
"It's not fair!"
People are dying all over the world
even in our neighborhood too,
people make up excuses like
"there is nothing I can do!"
The world can make it if we just hold on tight,
then maybe along the way someone will turn on
the light.
    Elizabeth M. Gokey

A Million Things

  I had a million things to say but I said only one,
I had a million places to go but I only went to one,
I had a million people to see but I only saw one,
I had a million things to do but I only did one.
  The thing I said was I love you
The place I went to was your house
  The person I saw was you
And the thing I did was ask you to be mine.
    Megan Radke

To Be Joyful In Whole

Only on a sunny day,
Will the sadness go away,
Rain and thunder misconstrue,
The unhappy demeanor of me and you.

For it continues to storm without a clue,
With its own requisition,
Unaware of our scornful rue.

We continue to loathe,
Through the eyes of its cause,
As the storm shows no signs of any flaws.

If only we could diminish its powerful soul,
We would wish for nothing more,
But to be joyful in whole.
    Derek M. Heckman

"Our Gift"

God in His goodness has given us a gift, and that
gift is you. For He knew when you were born,
that you were meant to be a priceless gift sent
from heaven above.

From the beginning of time He had you in mind
to do a great work. He called you as a young
woman, put His hand of approval on you, set you
apart, and made you part of His wonderful plan.

You have become a shepherd after His own heart,
a Holy and anointed woman of God.
God has given you an understanding heart, He's given you love,
humility and patience for others.

You have given inspiration to many, your life
is devoted to serving God.
He created you with gifts that out shines all others.

Yes, God in His goodness has given us a gift,
and we thank Him for that gift is you.
    Omega Bracey

To Amy:

You are flesh of my flesh and as I ponder my life,
As a watch as you play and you work.
I'm so proud as you grow into one of His own,
an example to all, 'specially me.

You stand firm in your faith,
You respect everyone,
You show love that is hard to compare.
You work hard for the Lord,
Always giving your best.
With the gifts He has given to you.

You never complain when given a task,
You encourage in good times and bad.
You're a letter from Christ written with His own hand.
Bringing joy to all those that you meet.

In these tender years,
May you see His strong hand,
Guiding you on the long way.
Keep your eyes on the King,
And He'll see you straight through.
Praise His name and give glory to Him.
    Donna Hoult

"Happy New Year"

My heart is bleeding, aching, breaking.
A tear falls
My memory recalls
A time of better days, of laughing and creating.

People say that life is goes on,
Their life
But mine is like the lyrics of a sad old song.
You can't freeze time
Or go back,
Just have to face things and react.

A gust of wind, a leaf falls
It's a new season. People say, "Happy New Year"
What's the reason?

Days fade away like the note of a song.
You stop
You look back
But you're still not sure what went wrong.

I'm not sure of much anymore
Uncertain as a sandcastle on the shore.
As I sit here reminiscing,
Remembering.
Christie Klang

My Heart Is Full of Unshed Tears

My heart is full of unshed tears;
The torch I've carried all these years
Has lighted my way dispersed my fears;
The fading song is still in my ears
Ringing deep in my soul like your resonant
  voice
And will throughout my entire life.
How could I know you would fade away
And forget me again in an another day?
Maybe it wasn't all laughter and mirth
But I'd have followed you to the end of
  the earth,
And maybe I shall in another way
When the hand on earth so lightly given
Will be firmly and lovingly clasped in
  heaven
To never again let go.
Helen W. Pabor

Full Moon

The moon shines down with a friendly face,
And brightens the earth with glimmering grace.
The stars twinkle in Heaven so bright,
Ah! Its full moon tonight!

The full moon shines on Harvests of Gold,
Displaying the plenty God hath bestowed.
Corn in rows ready to be picked,
Pumpkins and garden goodies so thick.
The wind so chill, we bundle up tight
To enjoy the full moon this night!

No beauty compares to the winter snow,
While the moon shines down, with a sparkling glow.
The bunnies hop, frolic and play,
While nature all her beauties display.
We stand in wonder at the awesome sight,
For it's full moon tonight!

In winter, spring, summer or fall,
Full moon captures the heart of all.
For this beauty we praise the One Almight,
For those full moon nights!
Martha Mast

We Will Always Have The Moon

You are far enough away,
To be just out of reach.
Yet, when I close my eyes,
You are right here with me.
I wish we could be closer,
So that we would never have to say good bye,
But right now that just can't be.
So at night, before we say our good byes,
Let's look to the moon, and hold each other tight, in our minds.
Distance can't keep us a part,
Because, we will always have the moon.
Mindy D. McStroul

Waiting For The Spring

When spring is slow in coming, when it dies before it's born,
How hard it is to wait, for the promise made when leaves were
  shorn...

When an open hillside beckons, when the stream sends its clear call,
How hard it is to choose one, when both would chase this
  winter-drear...

When weary, dyed-gray days run slowly by, when even trees' sap
  runs dry,
How hard it is to push this tired, trying being,
And not indulge a strangled sigh...

Waiting, choosing, pushing — crocus-like am I
Still waiting for the spring and the robins' first cry;
But as the Creator draws me to His warming light,
I feel the first loosening of the shackles from winter's dark night
And when I burst forth in bloom, how joyous it will be,
To laugh and see the mock-reality of earth's shallow gloom.
Grace Rees

When I Love You Can't Be Heard

  I heard the yelling in the hallway, I saw your face filled with
fear. I wanted to ask what was wrong, but I just couldn't go near.
  I could see the pain in your eyes, from the words she said
that day. I wanted to hold you in my arms and take the pain away.
  I missed the smile on your face. Which way it went I did not
see. You tried to find it but you were just too blind to see.
  I knew your heart was broken when I saw that single tear roll
down your face like an avalanche rolls down a great big hill.
  You think I know everything because my words are clear, I know
only when I see your heart broken and your eyes filled with fear.
My words come from my heart and deep within my soul. I think
that you are beautiful, I just thought I'd tell you so.
  I never quite knew why you said "I Love You," but you did.
Now I know you love me and I want to say it too but I know your
hurting way too much to hear me say the words "I Love You Too!"
Consuelo E. Guzman

Someday

Someday I will be with you.
Someday I will get to see you.
Someday's I wish that it is now.
Someday's I wonder what you look like.
And someday's I can't think of you at all.
Someday's I imagine you are watching me from above.
Someday's I wish that I can remember
the last time I saw you.
Someday I will see you and talk to you.
Someday I will hug you.
Someday.
Michelle Edwards

Lost Memories

I remember those piggy back rides,
and all those times when I would cry,
   You'd lift me up and take me away,
from all the pain and say it was OK.
   You'd make me laugh when I was sad,
You'd make me calm down when I was mad,
   At the world for all those things,
for all those painful things it brings.
   The 2 of us would go out and play, in the sun every day.
And when it would rain and I had to stay in,
   you'd always find a way to make me grin.
Although a lot of my memories were tossed,
   those are the ones that will never be lost.
I would forever have been there for you,
   my only prayer was that you would be there too.
But one of my prayers never came true,
   or else God would not have put me through,
That harsh moment that he did, I was only seven, just a kid.
   Why does God do this to people who don't deserve to be taken away,
who need that time with their kids to play.
   And make them grin when they are sad, all he did was make me mad.
Why did he do it, he made me cry and cry,
   I didn't deserve that to happen did I?

Jessica Tilton

Holding The Key

There's a world all around me which I cannot see
And a place I belong where I so long to be
But instead here I am all alone and afraid
In a prison whose bars are the choices I've made

Each iron rod stands for every mistake
A word I didn't say, or a risk I didn't take
All the things I might be if I only had tried
Every unfulfilled wish, every dream that has died

I was raised to believe that each life has a plan
And the most I could do is the best that I can
If I'd only known then all the things I know now
Perhaps I'd have done it all different somehow

So I sit all alone in my cell and I hide
In a jail where the locks are all on the inside
And I pray to the Lord just to set my soul free
Or the courage for once to let go of the key

Donna McLaughlin

Love

How dear and deep the feeling
when young love comes astealing
binds two hearts with magic strings
sweet the music each heart sings.

Happily hand in hand we go
for time and hearts will have it so
Your love so giving and so rare
Your wisdom so beyond compare!

The heavens did bless me to conspire
to grant me you, my hearts desire
your gentle presence the wild sway
bringing balm 'stead of discord today.

Making my world a better place
for all God's children to embrace
thinking ahead of the world's prospects ample
and Mom and Dad are the loving example.

Irving I. Verter

Mojave Desert

Mustang roam on the desert floor
Over the cliff the hawks fly so high
Joshua trees growing so odd
Arroyos or dry washes in the sand
Vast areas of desert
Even coyotes dig wells

Dry lakes, low places that fill with water after rain
Even rows of creosote bushes
Sand all in the desert path
Even the cacti are very hot
Ravens flying in the hot air
Tumble weeds growing in the sand.

Elizabeth Papp

High Hells

They sat in the closet, banished by their owner.
The joyous sound of click, clack—silence by cancer.

Busy days of working, gay nights of dressing up—
now, only a memory.

How long would they stay in darkness and useless
as cancer took their place?

They shouter to be heard! I can still dance and work.
Please use me!

Their pleading was finally heard.
Her answer came with much pain and she rejoiced!!

Geri Pappert

Moonstruck

Being cold and all alone, I draw to your warmth
Like a tulip forces through the snow

And when you smile your eyes they shine
Like two pearls of wit on this world of mine

For like the tides rise for the moon
My heart moves when you are near

So lured by your beauty till captured by your charm
For a spell so pure there's gotta be a cure

I find the antidote is bitter and it leaves a state of shock
A dose will only ebb the thrill, till the vernal equinox

For even though it ease the pain
And winter hides my heart
The day is sure to come
When I force my way
Back to your warmth
And the tide
Will rise
Again

Casey B. Grant

Choices

There are so many paths to choose from
Yet I do not know which to pick,
For the outcome is unknown to me
They each have their goods and their bads
But with no one to help guide my direction
The choice is left up to me
But I must choose soon
For time is speeding by
And if I wait too long then I will be stuck on the only path I do
   know the outcome of;
The path to no where.

Wendy Gibson

Everyday Indifference

Lustful thoughts had borne the obsession.
Outward appearances veiled the inner connection.
A desire fed by the superficial
Creating a barrier to the truth.

Falsified images cloud the perceptions
Unable to bring light to their darkness of deceptions.
The amazing possibilities are smothered
As expectations build the walls of bias.

Crying out in desperation, one struggles to be free.
Thrusts the dreams and desires before them to see.
Empty eyes, shallow hearts are the recompense.
In misery, the shattered soul retreats behind the walls.

Despair and frustration triumph as the effort crashes down-
Never to discover all they could have found.
Unwillingness, in its ignorance, has murdered a miracle
As the rapture of the light stays hidden in the dark.

Shannon Scott

Naturally Optimistic

What is depression, when the sun is warm
and the grass is green from dusk to dawn.
Consider your hurts and worries and pains.
Is the sun still warm,
Now consider them again.
Many things have measure, but where do they measure
against the sun, and its heat, and its life
comparisons are none.
When it rains it pours, yet the grass is still green.
Even if the storm brings pain,
The birds still sing.
Although the skies sometimes turn gray
In the end they're blue again,
And the sun is still warm
through the thick, through the thin.
Time makes everything alright.
So give a lil time, to fill the negative space.
Then watch the sun shed its light
and except the gift of its daily grace.
Just be naturally optimistic.

Sylvester Bracey

The Frost Of Dawn

Whirlwinds behind me, beyond a placid sea
The fate of posterity turns to dust
And all that is living awakens.

Pale, gray, lifeless creature
barren beside her blooming companions
Inept to love from fears of hate
Free of the pawns of ardour.

Swept through contagious streams
filled with blood and vanity,
Springs of flourishing death deluge,
and Eternity is lost Forever.

Slipping away and never to return —
a spark of ebony, a flash of crimson,
Spiral waves of scarlet
bring forth life as they take it away.

Escaping light through the balloon
the Truth has begun-
It cannot be stopped.
Forever has ended
Tomorrow has not.

Sarah Suconick

The World Today

I'm in a world were things are in closed.
I'm scared, I'm shaking,
I'm hiding away from my fears.
O'please please get me out of here.
Get, get, get me out of here,
the world around us is closing in.
Can't you see it is happening again.
O'please help me, the world
around me is closing in.
Came on, can you see?
There's nothing like you and me,
so keep the earth nice and clean, or
Get, get, get me out of here!

Olivia Summer

Friends Forever

You are there when I need you,
You made me laugh when I cried.
For all the years we've been together,
You've never left my side.
You correct me when you need to, but
never when you don't.
You always make me do the things I
say that I won't.
When something's in my way to where
I cannot move it, you help me clear the
path so that I can see through it.
You are bright and so full of life, you
are brave and you are clever.
And from now on through eternity, we
will be friends forever.

Patrica McCarter

Mystic Proportions

Standing on the quay,
In the cold moonlight,
Seeing across the wharves and slips
The glow of night lamps
Through windows closed
Against the chilled air.

Riding in silence, creaking on their moorings,
Lie the dark schooners, sloops and skiffs
Of men and boys home from the sea.

Beyond quiet shops, the darkened trees,
Barren from winter's drain,
Stand mirthlessly in the night;
Taller that the rooftops
That shelter the night-bound folk,
And not much taller than the masts,
Nor as high as the steeple on the green,
They are the perspective that makes the world
Human size.

Robert F. R. Peters Jr.

The Unknown Face

A beautiful experience happened one day,
As I sat looking in a stream of blue.
I recall it was in the middle of May,
The face was one, of which I knew.
How warm and loving this face looked,
A face I prayed someday to see.
Into my heart its meaning I took,
For I knew, the face was not me.
You see, I have not the face of love,
A face that is soft, warming and free.
Only our dear God, the one above,
In the blue stream was the face of HE.

Linda Orsak Clark

The Ocean

Ageless movement cresting to shore...
It throws itself upon the land,
As might a lover..., caressing and receding.
In rhythm, creating and destroying.
Did this give birth to what I am?

I gaze upon the endless water...
Is this the vast expanse on which Columbus,
Purveyor of spoils for a spanish queen,
Discovered that... Which was always there?

Is this the sea on which Ulysses,
Propelled by winds of dead but living souls,
Ventured from isle to isle
Searching the labyrinth of the gods?
I ask but the Ocean does not answer...

I search the horizon,
An unbending line of distant illusion,
Dancing to the music of nature's instruments...
A gentle lullaby at times..., at times
A howling, shrieking crescendo of decibels.

Raymond Bernard Fink

No Way Out

There's no way out nothing I can do, to make
things right to see it through. There's no way back,
what the hell should I do. Times a wasting I can't wait,
the executioners impatient I can't be late.

Call my bluff, I guess it's fate, the demons will
smile for their new mate. So when its over turn out
the light, go to sleep it will be alright.

Enjoy the night while you still can, I'm one
step away from the gallows stand. Through the trap door,
to the other side, God it's too late to swallow my pride.

Floyd Ortega

A Friend's Love

A friend's love is special, it's something that's unique,
A friend's love is special and it doesn't have to speak.

A friend's love is caring and it always has the time
To listen to a problem, or whatever's on your mind.

A friend's love is unselfish, for it gives and doesn't take
A friend's love is very true, their love is never fake.

So the next time a friend comes to you and you don't know what to say,
Just give them all the love you have, and send them on their way.

Linda Reichard

Forever

To be immortal is to live forever,
Does anyone or anything really die?
Thoughts and memories are never forgotten.
To say they were, would be a lie.

Pictures of history, embedded in minds
Though loving, happy or sad can make us cry.
Truths, lies, facts and fables are passed
through generations forever, we cannot deny.

These things are immortal!
They live in our minds and will
never die.

Maggie Flanigan

Love Is Funny

Love is a funny thing (you know)
Those people out there who were lucky enough
to be or to have been in love know
what I am saying. Love is funny
one minute it's there and it gone
or you may love somebody and they
don't love you back, love is funny.

You may be in love with someone and
they leave you for someone else, love
is funny. You may get married and
then get divorced, love was there and
now it's gone, love is funny.

Don't get me wrong love is great if
you are lucky enough to be in
love it's the most beautiful thing
on earth. But love is still funny.

Anthony Walls Sr.

I Thought I Heard Something There

I thought I heard something there,
Right behind that door.
I guess it's my imagination,
'Cause I can't hear it anymore.

I thought I saw a light there,
Right between the crack.
My mind must be playing tricks on me,
Because I just saw my brother, Jack.

I thought I felt something here,
Aaaaaaahhhh! It's so furry!
Oh, good! It's only my little dog,
I didn't think it could be so scary!

I must move on with my work,
So Mother won't be upset.
I'll try not to be as frightened next time,
I just won't bring my pet.

Melanie Jacobson

Perfect Harmony

When the sky falls into darkness and nature falls to sleep,
The dark clouds overflow in the sky,
Then they begin to weep,

Onto the earth the raindrops fall,
Quenching the thirst,
Responding to nature's call,

Sun rays streak from the sky,
Warming up the air as birds begin to fly,
Babies being born begin to cry,

Children of all colors play and share a smile,
Everyone loves one another,
With respect and gracious style,

The skyline blends perfectly into the land,
The world comes together peacefully hand in hand,

People, fish and animals live together as one,
The miracle of life has begun,

Standing proud and tall like a tree,
With strong family roots extending as far as we can see,

Maintaining our culture and spirituality,
Means living in perfect harmony.

Sherry James Williams

The Fountain In The Park

Spouting from the top
spilling from tier to tier
until reaching the bottom,
beginning its journey again.

The water ripples in the breeze
blowing the spray to the walk
drenched children laugh,
beginning its journey again.

Teenagers wade through the water
their rolled jeans become wet
as parents scold them,
beginning its journey again.

Leaves fall from trees above
plunging, spiraling, dipping, twisting
to drift upon the swells of the small sea,
beginning its journey again.

No water spouts from the top
the snow lies thick in the pond
there is no one to laugh or play around it,
its journey has come to an end.

Caitlin S. Macklin

The World We Live On

No one notices it yet
but fresh air and clean water
will soon be hard to get.
In the future no one will care
if smoke and waste pollutes the air.
That's why we must work now,
and tell people how we can still save the world
if we all say a vow,
That we will recycle more
and make clean air, for birds to soar.
We can pick up litter every day,
or tell children to help the world
before they play.
Now that is all I am going to say
but I hope some day,
you will listen, for if you want to have another
fresh breathing day.

Brian Wood

Telescope

What would your mother say
You bit off more than you could chew
What would your soul say
What are you going to do
We knew we've lost our innocence
But gained what is real and true.

Give me your sadness, I'll take it from here
Take me from madness, under the table, under the stars
Cast out your armor, carve me a stone
Leave it for now, don't go alone

Tempting are the stars, that glitter in the night
To take us in perspective and show
Us how significant is this night
We are juxtaposed on earth
and we dance in step, on land in the spotlight.

We look to the heavens for what they reveal
It's the vastness of living and time can't be real
The wonder of meeting
A mind to be with a soul on a journey
And a heart that is beating to follow our bliss.

Susan Ruzenski

I Shall Be Released

Life is long but is not made to measure
And time will pass through the days and the nights;
Maybe in a dream world time lasts forever
Through light times of birth - through somber last rites.
People come and go - always show their smiles
Filled with laughter, joy, happiness and glee;
Time still runs along - jogging its miles
Leaves one just with memories - lost at sea.
Through the whirling winds of the wintertime
The showers of spring with days washed away;
Days grow longer - onset of summertime
And the threadbare time - Autumn - cold and gray.
Life seems uncertain - no reason or rhyme
Perish into the hands of an old friend - time.

Brendon M. Carey

Nowhere To Hide

Life is such a mystery...
when you blink your eye and you still can't see,
the boundaries are in the air
if it's love, or peace, or plain despair.
All those days that expect pure gloom,
thoughts arise and take up room;
but when all is best,
those thoughts are there to fill your chest.
If only they were as simple as that white lie,
there would be no tears or reason to cry.
The chance to decline on all my ways;
of love...
of pain...
of life...
of strain...
are not as easy as can be,
life's little mystery plays with me,...
you see?

Aimee Gayer

Aloneness

I look through a small open window
  around which the ivy twines;
The rain falls softly through the twilight sky,
  the air breathes slowly through the pines.

An unread book on the table,
  a coffee cup in my hand;
I gaze out through the open window,
  out over shadowy land...

The light of the evening is dying now,
  in near darkness now I stand;
Thoughts of days gone by now rush over me,
  and the rain falls softly on the land...

Marguerite G. Jones

Time

Time passes without markers for me to gauge my life upon. But even if I could stop time for a moment when would that moment be? With the unknown future would it be wise for me to gamble on a moment of happiness and go on further? Is it not the unknown future that keeps us youthful to begin with? If this is true then aging is what would keep us young as time passes ever so quickly. Yet my life is full of uncertainties and although some are letdowns I continue to push forward with hopes that my reward is just ahead of me.

Lois Barton

Simple Things

Life's road is long and the way is rough
It goes onward mile after mile,
With each turn you'll find it's "Simple Things"
That make the journey worthwhile...

It may be just a pat on the back,
Or some kind word that you say;
That will cheer a heart that's downcast,
And brighten a dreary day.

Perhaps it's only a word of praise
Or a hug that says "I care,"
That will make someone who's lonely
Be glad that you are there.

So turn not away from "Simple Things"
To make something great your aim,
For acts of love could give more joy
Than the loudest of men's acclaim.

Myrite A. Brown

Divorce

I'm alone now.
What happened?
Was I too young at the start?
Was I unprepared for the ultimate commitment - myself?

The marriage began in the fifties.
I was pursued, loved, wanted.
The children came, grew up, and left.
I grew tired, bored, unhappy, and unfulfilled.

But the years mellowed me.
Too late!
Someone else took my place.
Now I pursue love, wants, needs.
But......
I'm alone now.
Divorce happened.

Jean A. Scech

Sacred Ground

Here I sit on that sacred ground in front of an audience of trees. Their leaf filled branches flowing in the wind. They are proudly dancing in their sacred dress as the Indians once did. But they are crowded, huddled together, and unable to move freely about. Their roots run deep, but here they are rootless and tired of trying to get over the fence placed around them. The ground beneath them is dark, unfamiliar, and nothing grows. They are not from here, nor do they belong. People have tired to carve customs unknown to them into their wood by force, yet the carving scars over in time, and never reaches the heart of the wood. Of course the carver could never simply accept the tree for what it is. And as I sit here on their sacred ground, uninvited and unwanted, I feel guilt and a sense of remorse. They have been purposely packed and prodded into these small infertile plots, of meaningless ground where no ancestor of theirs has roamed. But why? For the precious metal so many have killed and died for? Or for the thick black liquid that exploded from seemingly useless Oklahoma ground? Was it the malicious, blood thirsty cry for land? Or maybe just because of stupidity; the inability to realize what the land meant to them. I hope that the spring wind will assist these trees in spreading their pollen outside the fence barrier. Giving rise to saplings far away from the reservations forced upon them. Where they can splice their roots with that of their ancestors. Maybe somewhere much like where I am sitting, on their sacred ground.

James Kirk

Emancipating An Angel

Wandering through the wilderness, I came upon a stunning sight.
A pitiful pyramid full of traps, treachery, and boundless blight.
Fabricated from fraudulence, forlornness, and deserted dreams,
I examined its exterior for enervations and sensed a subdued scream.

Years ago I had a dream of an amorous angel who was imprisoned.
Since this vision vexed me, I ventured to where she was hidden.
After an excruciating excursion in a jungle of germinating jealousy,
I spotted this structure and started out to set her free.

Six seasons I spent dusting and digging on and around the walls.
Vainly I tried to get inside and now I was absolutely appalled.
Dejected, I lost all hope and mumbled a primitive poetic phrase.
Looked back at the pyramid and noticed a part of a wall was raised.

Slimy serpents slithered at my feet, as deadly darts dove by my ears.
An arrow was aimed at my heart, yet surprisingly I felt no fear.
I leaped over two trap doors and then freed her from her shackles,
Lifted her upon my shoulders after killing seventeen jaded jackals,

Raced through a maze made of malicious memorials and memories,
Located a door leading to a life of pleasure, peace, and prosperity,
Ran out and her remembrances of ruined relationships were removed
Then the pyramid disintegrated and our hearts hummed in tune.

Scott Dillworth

A Journey

There is a river one must cross,
Oh friend I'm really at a loss,
To point out the path to travel,
Tis a puzzle to unravel.

The trumpet sounds and you must answer,
Was it a wreck, perchance a cancer?
Time so short it numbs the senses,
An open plain devoid of fences.

I hope you've made the proper choices
Listened to the angels voices,
Or when Satan whispered in your ear,
Did you embrace and draw him near?

Now it is your final hour
Subject to a higher power
I hope you've run a worthy race,
To be covered by his grace.

Richard J. Duis

April

Tears of April run down the panes
And water the waiting sail
They're tears of joy that Winter has gone
And the earth will bloom and more
Like night and day it's a happening
That we know will always come round
Our well being always seems to be met
Tho we're prone to complain and to frown
And sure must have patience
With those whom he sent
To tend the earth down below
And to make things better
For themselves and others
To share and to love and to grow
So be happy it's raining and put on a smile
As the rain patters on the glass
Soon you can pick bouquets of lovely flowers
And go out and out the grass

Mildred Kex-Snyder

Let Me Love You

Why do I fight back the tears?
When all I want to do is make love to you.
Why am I alone in this bed of mine?
When all I want is to be there with you.
Come to me and let me love you.
Let me be the one to hold you tight.
Let me be the one you give your love to.
Let me love you tonight.
Let me be the lover you have been dreaming of.
I'll be there to love you through out the night
I'll be there to lay you down.
Give me the keys to your heart and I'll love you right.
I would give you paradise but being with you is twice as nice.
Trust only one thing in this life
Your love is what makes my life right.
Randy D. Buie

I Never Got To Say Goodbye!!!

Some of the only memories I have of you are pictures and others
are gifts.
And yet others were visits to your house when you'd give us candy
and let us draw on paper.
I never spent a night at your house, but deep down in my heart
I knew you still loved me.
I remember you healthy when you could come over once in a while.
But after a while time took its toll on you and you didn't feel
as good anymore.
It got longer between visits and your health only worsened.
Then one night you got worse and they took you to the hospital.
We sat with you for two nights and talked to you; held your hand
and fed you ice from a spoon
Then finally death took you from us quietly and peacefully
without you feeling pain and suffering anymore.
During this time I never said "I love you" or said "I'll miss you."
I never got to say goodbye either and for these two things I kick
myself every time the memories come back to me.
I love and miss you Grandma.
Jessica Baysinger

If This Is It

Your past is something one will never like,
Your past is something one will ne'er forget.
Your past is something remembered as a tike,
Your past is something loved by whom you let.

You have a few once loved amongst the past;
I want thy heart to melt like butter's end
And this to change and love together last
Forever, always have a hand to lend.

And it is wonderful to feel your touch,
Your eyes so deep so full of love and lust;
You will be treated like a queen so much,
Your heart so sweet and soft, you I will always trust.

And I am pleased to know you feel the same,
We feel so much and pray we keep the flame.
Josh Peters

Yesterday

I think of him and I grieve.
I read the epitaph
Of a relationship long since deceased;
A love I never mourned
But had, instead, rejoiced in its demise.
It was right we said good-bye,
Yet I now yearn for
Yesterday.
Kari Malpas

Untitled

Walking up Columbus Avenue, North Beach teaming around us
arms encircled, blurring the lines of friendship —
felt warm, in the chill wind of the city
and blurred my vision to view the future.
It fell to the gutter much later, we wouldn't have guessed
walking so close and familiar.
Waiting outside with the streetlights
casting an unreal sunlight to frame
our huddled bodies —
I failed to think of whomever I should have.
Sitting across the table from his unwavering eye —
I sip Chianti though I don't drink wine.
The noise of the restaurant fails to drown out
the hundred unspoken words
which fall upon the table
as I hide my eyes in food.
Mary Peterson

An Old Friend Named Pain

I have an old friend named Pain, who has stuck by me through the
years, sometimes He's the only friend I have, who brought me
strength through tears.

He is a hard person to live with, so - time to time I run away,
but he always seems to find me, and forces His game for me to play.

He has wasted many hours, with inflections in my mind,
when I could have thought of positive things - instead of marking
time.

He grins His little smile, that shows He's out to win,
but I will always battle Him, and I shall never Give - In.

He always seems to be there, when I least want Him around,
but through my friendship of suffering, I have learned to stand my
ground.

Sometimes Pain overtakes me, but He taught me to Bounce - Back,
from overcoming problems, I counter His attack.

Most people hate and avoid Him, for He's not a kindly Joe,
but he is my friend regardless to the World I'll rarely show.

The ingredients of Pain, to become a grateful friend,
comes from Perseverance, of fighting to THE END.

From perseverance builds Character, of always looking for the best,
and from character comes Hope, of putting Pain to Rest.

Yes, I do have AN OLD FRIEND NAMED PAIN!
Kevin G. Kelly

Dancing

As the clouds covered the sky, and the sun sank into the sea,
   I should have been lonely, but instead, you were with me.
Not a worry in the world came within my reach,
   Because I was dancing with you on a wishful, romantic beach.
The scent of your hair attracted me even more,
   'Cause without you my life would be a bore.
The light from your eyes shot rays in all directions;
   It felt like a tractor beam with all the right connections.
With every slow song, we danced together,
   Hoping the song will never end; we'll dance forever
As your cheeks rose and out came a smile,
   That'll be the same one that appears as we walk down the aisle.
But I won't rush things 'cause it must always be right,
   And since I've met you, I've slept peacefully all night.
Joshua W. Martin

Tomorrow's Dream

I wonder, shall I ever see;
Man treat man decently.
When adjectives by tongue unbound;
Cease forever to be around.
Ah, to live so peacefully.

What matter, my skin be white;
That alone does not equal right.
Nor does black, yellow, or copper tone;
Pigment reaches not, heart or bone.
Ah, to live color blind, night after night.

What matter, whig or Tory;
Listen well to every story.
Then mid profound debate;
Will progress-compromise originate.
Perhaps we can out live past history.

Grant us, control of self;
Leave descriptive comments upon a shelf.
Reach out, to one and all;
Ere tomorrow, we slip and fall.
Unable then, to help even ourself.

Richard E. Beckette

Gift Of Love

He came as a stranger in the night; tranquillity in the midst of the raging storm.

Perhaps a savior of the soul; perhaps a mere messenger.

Love forgotten, until feelings once more procured; like the endless tides of the ageless seas and Odyssey's voyages.

But for how long, the heart cries out?; a moment, perhaps an eternity.

A moment even as fleeting as a candle's flame feels like an eternity.

I long to hear his voice and feel his touch. When he is away, it is as if time stands still; like the endless sands in an hourglass.

I await patiently, longing once more for his touch.

This renaissance of life's most precious joys.

The spark once more rekindled, the flame prevails; passion abounds; true meaning subdues all traces of doubt.

Oh destiny, most profound; prayers answered, no longer disconsolate this heart and soul at peace.

I shall thank God for sending him to me, for freeing my soul, and allowing it to soar like a bird in flight to the heavens above; giving me this most precious of gifts, the gift of love....

Bobbi Roseland

After The Rain

I watched God wash the world tonight
And scrub it quite severely
With wind whipped trees and pounding rain
Then the sun shone through so clearly!

The raindrops glistened on windowpanes
There were puddles here and there
And riverlets running down the drive
Raced on——They knew not where.

Like magic, bright green leaves appeared
On every tree and shrub
And flowers beamed more radiant
After God, His world did scrub.

Wilma Gilbert

In The Wind

My dreams are like rain in the wind,
They can make a ripple or can make a flood,
to change my heart and soul and blood.
My dreams are like the beauty of a Rose,
They can wither and die
or they can burst forth seeds of change
and push me to try
for all the dreams of tomorrow.
My dreams may soar like an eagle looking for its prey,
and change even the clouds and the sky,
or they may be devoured and lie
and turn into sands of glass,
or furnish meals to maggots in the grass,
but if I try and pray,
God may bless and dreams will rain
and ripple even into the sunshine of the day
and cast light into even the darkened clouds of gray night.

Clint Evans

To Heaven

I'm going to a better place,
Where there is no dust
Where there is no lust, and
I know they'll let me in,
And not judge the color of my skin.

Yes, I'm going to a better place,
Where no one is better than me
Where everyone is equal you see,
Where my friend is your friend,
Where love, there is no end.

Yes, I'm going to a better place,
Some would call it a palace
Some would decorate it with lace
But me, I enjoy the slow pace,
No life in the fast lane for me
Because heaven is where I'm going you see.

Where there are no good-byes
Where no one has to cry,
Where you don't feel pain
And everyone is just the same.

Kathy Jones

Just Beyond Reach

By a scrub oak tree she sat on a cloudy, windy day.

A leaf floated from a branch;
And was close,
Almost close enough to touch,
But not quite.

A butterfly danced past her;
And was close,
Almost close enough to touch,
But not quiet.

Memories swept through her mind;
And were close,
Almost close enough to touch,
But not quiet.

A tear fell from the dark sky;
And was close,
It was close enough to touch,
Then she wept.

Cynthia L. Finley

"Clown Of Death"

Clown of death
upon the crooked lane
He'll track you down in one breath
and drive you insane
His glass, black, eyes
hold a thousand lies
His evil smile
will send you on death trial
He's known to be your friend
But he shall scare me from now to the end
He tell's many funny jokes
Only to make you laugh, then choke
So funny till your out of breath
and you fall into your humorous death
A smile painted on the clown
On purpose I am expressing a frown
Mary, Mary quite contrary
Show me where you hid bloody mary
The sky is black, but it's 8 am
Death has come, but I was late

Tia Klienschmidt

Day Dream

Taking off into the galaxy beyond
With hope filled feelings of flying
Reaching a star or maybe the moon
Just waiting, thinking of the sky
Floating in a world with no gravity
Reaching a point where I can't go further
Beyond where I want to go.

Kyle Simpson

"Sleeping Princess"

In the distance, like massive sentinels you stood, in your canyons,
sparkling rivers, on your sides green wood;

Your deep green colors, equaled only by a woman's eyes,
the roundness of your hills, surpassed only by her shapely thighs:

The clean wind, whispering through stalwart trees,
like her voice, rich as honey from your mountain bees:

Oh rocky mountains, with your brilliant splash of red autumn leaf tips,
to match this lavish splendor, the passion of her full red lips:

Snow covers your walls, softly like a fleecy ermine coat,
this splendid whiteness is surpassed, by her smooth lovely throat:

Your thin lonely falls, splashing down through the years,
like her beautiful bowed head, almost sweet as her tears:

Your canyon air is still, as the waning moon above,
the woman's face is pale, could it be from too much love:

Oh, you majestic, magnetic, marvelous rocky mountains:

But, great mountain, your sleeping princess is cold,
where the woman is vibrant, like a flaming statue of gold.

Fred M. Crandall

Lovers

Lovers, lovers that were meant to be.
Shall I be separated from he. In death,
or in life what shall it be. In death it is
such dignity. In life it is such misery. Shall
the pain of living be tested as thee. Please
leave us with some dignity, and with no
misery. Let the pain of living be.

Loni Sullivan

"Signs Of Spring"

The pillowed clouds hang o'er the wood
With blue sky all around
The sun breathes life to dormant rest
From which life will soon abound

The signs of spring are all about
With natures harnessed power
To blossom forth in colored array
With grass and leaf and flower

The snow capped mountains vivid white
Will soon be just remembered dreams
As nature strokes her constant change
To fill the brooks, the ponds and streams

The smoke floats up from the sugaring house
The sap foams up with a billowing white
To turn into a liquid gold
From different grades from heavy to light

The sounds of spring are joyously heard
With the birds and animal voices
To proclaim the season close at hand
In harmony with God it rejoices

Joseph W. Lane

Olfactor 1

The moon strangling life all night long
like a world of lead
where nothing moves except the wind
that falls like shadow
and the smell of the naked earth
innocent virgin male
but bathed in darkness there is life
the smell of skin
fragrant on the wind, fleeting into air
dies a living death
pursuing a capture of an olfactory soul
chase the sun away
Sensual gratification of pure incorporeal odor
lies within the night
Within the skin as delicate as snow
essence of love

Jenna Wiggins

Ten Of Us

We were ten, raised on a farm,
With Mama and Daddy to keep us from harm,
We were raised with goodness and love,
From Mama and Daddy, and the Lord up above,
We're like that old farm wagon, with wheels of spokes,
And like that old wagon, our wheel has broke,
Lil was the first to leave our midst,
And no one will know how much she'll be missed
She's come full circle, and joined those above,
In a place called heaven, filled only with love,
We'll miss our sister, the first to go,
Who will be next, only God knows,
One day we'll all join her up above,
In the place called heaven, so full of love.

Margaret A. Baldwin

Secureness

The lightning thunders,
The wind whistles and howls,
Not a creature stirs.

At first very slow,
But then faster and faster,
Rain starts pouring down.

Tip-Tap-Tip it goes.
As if a monster has come,
The animals hide.

All of this happens,
As I am sleeping in bed,
Being secured by.

Fariha Bhatti

His Journey

He trodded over rocks
Yet he murmured not.
Over seas, and hills and
Deserts, that were very hot,
He healed the sick, and lame,
The way to life was shown,
Because of love, his blessed
Task, though men's rejection
grown,
His temptation in the wilderness
For forty days and nights
His power conquers all
He is the sacred light.
Jesus Our Lord and Saviour
men nailed him on the tree
His 'Love most wonderful and real.'
He did it all for me.

Monica J. Orridge

Dogs

Dogs,
Dogs,
Dogs,
Dumb dogs,
Smart dogs,
Big fat smelly dogs,
Little skinny fragrant dogs,
Those are just a few.
Weiner dogs,
Weird dogs,
Long low thin dogs,
Short low chubby dogs,
Your dogs too.
Their dogs,
Our dogs,
Don't forget hot dogs.
Last of all, best of all.
I like corn dogs.

Phillip R. Burgess

Untitled

Pain in the cold
A child to hold
Glory for the bold
Death to the old
This is the tale
Time has told

Dean L. VanSkiver Jr.

Footsteps

Fading footsteps in the snow.
The softness of the afternoon glow.
Miles traveled with miles to go,
Trading paces of fast and slow.
The snow crunches beneath my feet
As I walk with onward beat,
Warmed only by an inner heat
unaware of what I have yet to meet.
Fading footsteps in the snow.
The wind whispers when it blows.
Grown so much with more to grow.
Learn a lifetime and still more to know.

Cindy Kocsis

Squirrels

Squirrels so swift at work and play,
 Ever seem to whisk away.
Always seeking Meek yet mild.
 To wander about in Nature's Wild,
Searching for a treat to snare,
 To proclaim the victory
 of the Lair.

Margaret Rose Braunberger

The Divorce

When my parents got divorced
I don't remember.
I was two
Now I remember
sometimes I'm lonely and sad
because I
can't see my dad
like everybody else can,
I feel left out,
like I'm sitting in a,
dark, dark, corner
alone.

Rebecca Burd

This Ain't No Football I'm Hiking

"She's nearly
fully dilated,"
the labor room nurse informed
the stand-in
O.B.

Looking away
from the T.V.
The doctor quipped,
"This is a big baby—
around ten pounds.
She'll have a lot of
pushing to do.
Get her into delivery.
Call me when
the head crowns,
and—
try to get her to hold off
for fifteen minutes.
Then it'll be
half time."

Diane M. Weiland

60 And 70

Now is the time
to determine
whether age or sensibility
reign.
Remember,
character - health,
not years,
determine aging.
Seasoned born,
maturity supports
youth. Sidestepping
avoids stagnation
routing failure.
Now is the time
when media
bombard, perplex,
distort, and warp-
embarrassing sensibility.
Time to sidestep, not be
Overwhelmed.

Peter Masley

The Life Of Samuel Clemens

He was born with Haley's comet.
Was just a babe when it passed by.
He grew up to work on a steamboat
And the comet disappeared in the sky.

He wrote many wonderful stories.
They were masterpieces made to last.
He adopted the pen name "Mark Twain"
And the shadow of the comet shot past.

He retired his pen and his paper
And was a happy old man 'til the day
When the comet came down from the sky
And quietly flew him away.

Kimberly DeJoie Hill

Help Me Smile

At a time in my life
I could find no relief,
It now seems like a dream
maybe more, misbelief.

The death of my mother
more than I could bear.
The blest birth of my child,
soon divorce, who would care?

A congenial man
he was burly, yet kind.
Had eyes of compassion,
his work - of the mind.

This man saw my pain
- almost instantly,
my anguish he'd hear,
help me smile, I would plea.

He taught me life's lessons
and how to survive,
I've finally found peace,
I thank God I'm alive.

Debi Bryant

Sssnakesss

Sssilently ssslithering ssnakesss
sssneaking ssswiftly
sssliding acrosss the grasssss

David Adams Jr.

Rape Of A Virgin, 1979

Flow on once virgin river
Whose cycle sought to cleanse
The urine of man's industries
From sea and shore and land.
Flow on once mighty river,
Man's desperate want is great
And the chore far stupendous
For your exact, unhurried pace.
Flow on once virgin river
Whose waters sought to cleanse;
In offering man salvation
Your mortality begins.
Flow on once mighty river
No more baptismal font
Can wash away the sins of man
When your purity is lost.
Flow on once virgin river,
The beings you sought to save
Returned excrement instead;
Your maidenhead is lost.

Kimberly K. Comeau

Question (?)

What is the meaning behind meaningless
how can you exist with nonexistence
can you supply without supplication
is a moment just for instance.

You can write without the right
and leave without being left
"in the pink" is not a color
and ears of corn are deaf.

The English language
is hardly English at all
but slang that's been slung
off some foreign soil.

Can terms really terminate
is a side some way to walk.
Can a substance substantiate
is this any way to talk.

Gary W. Stone

A Wish

Spring Spring
Where have you gone?
Nobody here can
Sing a happy song.

Spring Spring
Where did you go?
Why are you
Under all this snow?

Spring Spring
Why did you hide?
Now, nobody wants
to go outside.

Spring Spring
We can't wait for
You to come!
Hurry and get here
fast, on the run!

Carol Torkelson

The Navajo Reservation

A quiet place, hidden
Decorated with beautiful
canyons and painted sunsets.
Ancient Indian Cliff Dwellings
at Canyon De Chelly—
Voices echo off the deep canyon walls.
A coyote howls.
Imagine: Children playing, laughing.
Listen: Sacred songs of the past,
Prayers to make our nation last.
I open my eyes
Only to see...
Empty cliff dwellings, and
a Navajo grandmother
walking beside a desolate highway,
looking for her lost sheep.

Cynthia Towne

Fields Of People Bending

their hands stained red by the pulp
of fresh strawberries
the hollow snap
as body is torn from stem
echoing through the rows

not quite
what mother used to call
Picking Potatoes
until your fingers were scraped raw
nails worn down to the quick
by the unyielding eyes
blood trickling down to the roots
soaking in
like juices
of strawberries
into skin

Jennifer Allen

"The Perils And Rewards Of Being The First Child"

If you are the oldest child,
It gives you an excuse to go wild.

The worst thing about being first,
I'm telling you, it's simply the worst!
You get blamed every day,
All the time, no matter what you say!

One thing that is fun,
About being number one,
More games, expanded responsibilities,
Much more fun, and so many activities!
You can go to bed later,
Or get to be a skater!

That's why I'm the oldest child!

Meghan Hogan

For My Husband

To most people it is just
A ring on their left hand.
To me it is the most precious
promise in the world.
To me it signifies an honest
and faithful love.
To me it is a comment that
I want for the rest of my
life to be your wife.

Tina Wright

Take Some Flowers To Your Neighbor

Take some flowers to your neighbor
She is old and needs them now
For tomorrow she will leave us
And will rest in Heaven's bough.

She is wond'ring at your absence
She is list'ning for your voice
Oh arise and go now quickly
Don't you know she will rejoice?

She'll soon pass the time of laughter
She'll soon pass the time of fear
She's now waiting for your coming
Knowing you will bring her cheer.

What's so pressing that you can't go?
Could it be you do not care?
Don't you know great joy will fill you
When you with your neighbor share?

Take some flowers to your neighbor
Take them now - oh please, a few.
What? You say 'tis winter season -
Take a smile along with you!

Margaret Guilloud Ashlock

"Abortion" Unborn Heartbeat

Unborn love...I let go of,
My arms are empty,
They long to hold you,

I dream at night about
a little heart beat,

I could hold you against me,
oh, those little hands and feet,

The warmth of mother and daughter
That radiate like a summer sun.

But then a chill runs through me.
Like the day I had to let go of you,

So sleep in peace my little one,
And shine forever as my rising sun.
I'll love you always.

Paula J. Heath

New Shaman Blues

Dragoman
the sound of your walking
sly stride clattering of beads
self stitched from flaps
your tatters and bone drillings jangle,
chink shattering as shards
tip-tapping telling
like fizzled tails
bobtailing the way
as salvadors and seers and sages
go dollied into asylums- and gutters
like wizards wize angus
hoof clattering their sigil beauties
oblivious
to the ancient art
of leather

Anthony John Loftsgaarden

A King In The Jungle

In the jungle,
One foggy evening,
There stood a tiger
In the very center.

Not only was it a tiger,
But it was the king.
The king has a responsibility to do,
And that is to keep peace.

If you dare do anything,
Even eat an insect,
Or kick the dirt,
The king will hunt you down.

After he tries to hunt you down,
You'd better be a fast runner.
Swinging tree to tree,
Just like a monkey you hurry out.
When you leave the jungle
Remember that the king is always there.

Laura Haugerud

Soul Is Empty

Sinking into unconsciousness going
Confused by the matter below
I see it's there but still not knowing
What is it that is so terribly cold?
The blotches on the baby's walls
are hot and breathing steam
The soul has made its final call
Forgetting them it seems
Carried over is the earth
Without a final word
In the deep, dark cell it lurks
Slicing the edge - a sword.
Terror is the final power
It's time I am too sleepy
The stench of earth is far too soar
Hatred forever keeping.

Christina LL. Speed

Nature And Us

The trees are green
The sky is blue
You're part of me
I'm part of you.

When the sun comes up
What a lovely glow
I'm glad we're together
I love you so.

A little creek
Runs swiftly by
Just show me you love me
Until the day we die.

The little animals
Are out to play
Understanding and communication
We need every day.

As the sun goes down
Day comes to an end
Always hold me, caress me
Be my lover, be my friend.

Linda J. Deering

To Be Loved

To be held,
To be hugged,
To be loved.

To have and to hold,
To nurture; to cherish
To be loved.

To be forever on your mind,
To be forever in your heart,
To be loved.

No more tears
No more sorrow
No more pain
Alone with God,
I found love.

Christi L. Salzer

Loves Anxiety

My lady, the ship of my life
   sails this lonely journey
Like a little ship on the largest
   'ocean
As all people do, prayers are said
   for these lonely ships
And, my God, my prayers so out to
   you.
For my little ship, my lady, to
   bring her back.
Bring her back, through these seas
   of anxiety.
Again I ask, dear God, from the
   bottom of my soul.
Bring her to safe port, for
   I love her so.

Leo Hemmerick

Return From The East

She said a thousand wondrous things
about those people: How they had
no language of love, because
no man would speak it. How, then,
missives were in foreign tongues
through which idle dreams passed
more easily. And there was
a woman who screamed out in silence,
like a cobra weaving innocently.
There is, it seems, a away not
to say everything, a way to touch
the stillness of all truth.
Everything seems education:
definition of souls. So, nothing,
there, is everything: a bowl of tea,
space between tepid words, constant
roll of the midnight sea. She
knew enough of them to know their
secret safe from her. But she
could survive...elegantly.

Peter Buttross Jr.

The Falling Dream

We fly
   through a misty
Universe linked
   by our imaginations.
We think we know.
We think
   God loves us.

Merle C. Askew

Untitled

The weather outside is frightful
But the Steelers are so delightful
As they play in the Super Bowl
Let it snow, let it snow, let it snow
They show no signs of stopping
As the Cowboys keep on dropping
It's the only way to go
what a show at the Super Bowl
When they finally leave the game
In awe of the Steelers' reign
Over a team of another name
Now next year they will do the same
So Pittsburgh, let's get together
And forget about the weather
And think of the time next year
When they bring another trophy home.

Ann Kraynyk

Here I Stand

Here I stand
exposed to all who would see me
I am erect
upon this hill I have mastered
My voice raised
to those who pass before me
While I fade
into the grayness of the background
My soul grows cold
as I fight for recognition
And try to keep
my words from growing moldy

Terry L. Rhodes

Untitled

The hate will stop
and love will appear.
A smile will replace
all of the tears.
Out of sorrow,
will come comforting.
There will be no more
pain or suffering.
No more pollution,
crime, and war.
But united we'll stand
forever more.
No more greed,
power, and loneliness.
But we'll find joy
in peace and togetherness.
The day will come
when we'll all be one.
All united in the Son.

Mega Privett

Senior Citizens Apartments

Old Ladies

We cling to empty bottles
Bits of string, tax receipts
And anything to fill
Our rooms; we bring
Old ghosts still nattering
To lives where long ago,
   Children, happily would sing.

Eleanor Skelton Cash (2/16/1990)

Silver Wings

In the frost of winter,
With boughs, laden with snow,
The chilled wind echoes,
High above and down below.
All is white with snow drifts.
All lies in stillness, except the wind.
All the world is frozen in time,
Except the wind of Silver Wings.
Gliding on the wind up high,
Like an aerial ballet.
Gusts of flurry, ever flowing,
Makes Silver Wings twirl away!
The wind is filled with crispness,
As Silver Wings flies on high.
Soaring to the heights of heaven,
Facing God, with Joy and Delight!
Linda Chabot Laue

The Twins

The shadows were falling
and the robins were calling
when Old Mollie came calling
I thought it was funny she
was moving so slow - in the
last pink light of early evening's glow
A step here and a step there
then she would stop and test the air -
She kept looking back towards
the bushes nearby as dark crept
into the evening sky.
Suddenly I knew why
she was dragging her feet
She was coaxing her babies to
come out and eat and out of
the rough tiptoed 8 tiny feet -
Sam Phelps

School's Fellows Friendship And Time

Old school fellow's faces,
beauty and wisdom,
youth and faith...
keepers of the fire's hearts,
that have flown around the sky.

Old school fellow's smile,
sacred lessons, games and fun,
fair, smart, grasshopper's minds,
that have grown over the time.

Old school fellow's hands,
farmers of the loyalty fields,
bold, sprightly, faithful team,
that have sailed, the life's streams.

Old school fellow's minds,
walkers of the lesson's halls,
sowers of the friendship's seed,
bloomy inside and endless dream.
Francesca DiDomenico R.

Kaleidoscope

Spinning kaleidoscope,
She should go to him
Today, tonight, tomorrow,
To tell him...

The kaleidoscope shifts,
Endangered hunter,
Being stalked without mercy;
Pitiful sight.

The colors turn once more,
Unobtrusive life,
Cry that may never be heard;
It matters.

Spinning fast,
The life is now the hunter,
She is the stalker;
Will she show no mercy?

Spinning kaleidoscope,
She must go to him
Today, tonight, tomorrow,
To tell him...
Jenny Solis

He's Not Gone

I didn't believe he was gone
When I cried out his name
I didn't believe he was gone
When we gathered around his grave
I didn't believe he was gone
After everyone had went away
And I still didn't believe he was gone
When I put the flower on his grave

But he's not really gone
He's in our hearts
And our memories
And that's where he'll stay
Until I meet him
In heaven someday.
Sarah Twiner

Flame On

Cat Stevens plays, there's
a closed casket too.
You're home, in your kingdom,
We're alone without you.

Laying off the sauce
We would hear every day.
Unquitting each night, with us,
mean-spirited at times,
but ever-smiling, remembered
in the most perfect picture.

Starlit night, low ceilings
and your friends, cheated
by death as you were
cheated by flames from nowhere.
Mark Gualazzi

"No Inquiry"

Can no one laugh the laugh I love;
Can no one provoke my smile?
My answer sent from up above,
Has been with me all the while.

Look past these eyes my loving friend;
Question not what seems so clear.
Heed this message that I send,
For all the world to hear!
Karina Veronica Molsing

Dreamers

We are all dreamers,
are we not?

Oh, to be a dreamer
in these times,

Where your imagination has
the whole world as its playground;

Where the only limits are the
limits of your own dreams;

Where your dreams can blossom
into a wonderful reality;

Where you can be heard
and understood for a time;

So arise, for this
is the time for
dreamers.
Calista Cahill

Why

I don't understand how a man
of fear can never cry or why
a mother's tears turn into
fears or even why a child has
to grow but covers the body
so it doesn't show

Why should we have to
wonder why our mother
cries our father lies and our
brother dies I don't understand why.

What is it about the laughter
the doubt and all the
leaving out why is it done
why do we run for
what reason is it that
we don't fit in if we
don't give a grin.
Jackie Diaz

Never The Same

The Ocean rolling
the tide in....and out
birds soaring above
thru the changes of the day
thru my changes

Things all slip away to..
violence and passive beauty
the instinct of nature
the obligations of duty

Wind blows sand softly
wind raises the sea
forcing changes
thru aggression

Changes which fall down
all around me
all onto my senses
all becoming my memories

Over the passing of time
it is our nature to be ....
never the same.
Vivian Lee Moore

As Time Goes By

There is beauty in the flowers
There is beauty in the trees
Beauty in your eyes
And up and down the streams

Beauty in the birds song
And the gentle way they fly
Beauty is the baby sleeping
Quiet, peaceful, and dry

The time and sacrifices await you
Turning in the mind
Many have passed
Gotten on through time

Love flows from mind and body
The whole being deep inside
So many loves for each of us
Even as time goes by

The world is so big
And people's hearts so small
I'm glad we could be together
In this life and all
T. R. Edlen

"February"

It's been such a cold and snowy winter
And I've been stuck inside
I couldn't seem to write a thing
no matter how I tried
Today I looked outside and saw
The snow was finally gone
I saw the grassy hillside
And robins on the lawn
So I went out and walked around
And right away it seems
I found my self by flower bed
Searching for a sign of spring
Right away I found them
Those harbingers of spring
Tiny yellow crocuses
What joy and promises they bring
now I can go on back inside
Content with what I've found
And it won't seem near half as long
Till springtime comes around
Marie Cross Pittman

Rebel Waters

Sluicing through the leaden midnight
relentlessly the pounding rains
  mount day by day with flooding might
  and day by day the power gains.
Where yesterday spread grassy loam.
Where once wound the vagrant highway,
  now roils a turbid silted foam
  carving sod to rutted byway.
As battered vales and ledges meld
the furied rumbling beast, uncaged,
  leaves dam and levied farm devoured
  where the rebel waters raged.
Elizabeth Dabbs

Estate Manager

Many things are titled 'Chores'
including dishes, beds, and floors,
cooking, cleaning, all the rest:
That's why I like my 'Work' the best
Joleen Russak

Love For Our Grandson

Dearest Kiefer Lee,
Someday soon you will see,
All the Love we have had,
For you will always be.
Sometimes it makes us sad,
For all the days we did not see,
As you were growing and running free.
It reminds us so much of your Dad.
We can only wait and see,
If someday we will all be,
As a great big, loving family.
Only time will allow it to be,
When all the old times gone bad,
Have faded beyond memory.
May God keep you, Little Lad,
That you may never be so sad,
Because our Love belongs to you,
Kiefer Lee!!
Kathy Wilson

The Pop Quiz

How sad it was for me to see
That I flunked a quiz in history.
It was not France but Italy,
Who took the land of Tripoli
(In nineteen eleven; or, twelve?)
Pop quizzes are fair, I will agree,
It's only that they frighten me,
And churn within a stormy sea,
If I make less than B or C;
(Or, F's not turned so happily.)
Lila Ruth Stokes Matthys

Best Friend

My friend,
My confidant,
Through good times and bad.
My best friend through happy and sad.
You stand beside me
Beside me you walk
You always listen
You're always there when I need to talk
Through happiness, smiles and tears
I know you will always be there
Throughout the years.
Julia Kimani

Stranded

Aboard my ship
away from home
across the Atlantic,
since 1990.
Inside of my cuddy
instead of my house,
because of a shipwreck.
Amid the sharks
outside my boat
beneath the water.
Near to my death
because of no food.
Like to hear from one voice
except for my own.
From a very long distance,
beyond the horizon,
underneath the sunset
aboard a rescue ship - my family.
To save me.
Matt DeMasi

Realities Of Life

The path grows shorter,
With every step I take
And life gets harder
With every move I make

So when I choose the road for me
It will be the one I choose it to be
No one will tell me what to do
That's something only I can do
Jennifer Herbst

Refreshment of Friendship

Like a bright sunny day
with a cloudless blue sky,
As the wind blows on the wavy sea
While sea gulls fly by,
Like a blossoming greenhouse garden
flooded with warm sunlight,
Or a cool refreshing breeze
on a hot summer night,
Like a slow walk through the peaceful,
quiet woods
and fresh clean mountain air.
Is time spent in the company
of friends who truly care.
Tanya Riley

Need

With a hunger startling mind,
prey is watched through the night -
He must detect

A brigade of bushes
conceals a crazy thief
hidden from his prey

A stealth bomber seeking through
the air trying to find his
next victim

Catapulting himself airborne
Descending with
Satisfaction
Jamey Kocan

The Twilight Of Our Years

It was a warm and happy summer
And the world was for the young
As soft breezes whispered promises
Of adventures yet to come.
How beautiful it all seemed then —
No worries then, no fears
When we met there in the sunshine
In the springtime of our years.

In the joyous unrestraint of youth
We grew closer, heart to heart
'Til the longing daily grew so strong
We couldn't bear to part.
So with only kin around us
We soon stood side by side
And pledged our love in vows we made
There in the House of God.

You're still my lover and my friend,
the one who dries my tears...
And I love you more than ever
In the twilight of our years.
Myrtle MacFadden

Enchantment

An aura of winter magic
Fills the frigid air
With the fall of snowflakes
Swirling everywhere
Intricate lace work, iced fringe
Lends majesty to barren trees
Here nature weaves its beauty
For all the world to see.
Earth washed so pure and clean
Within a mantle of white
All bleakness gone once more
To make it all seem right.
Enshrined within its magic
To the full moon's glow
I give a resounding sigh
There amidst the snow.
Enchantment if only for a while
If only it could leave
An indelible message to earth
And ideally earth would cleave.

Rose Marie Thornhill

Dawn

Brilliant pink
To muted blue
Violet.
Deep purple.
Tall, black, pine tree silhouettes.
Feel the quiet stillness.

Ever so slowly
Lighter, brighter
The birds know.
Listen!
Hear the song
Of a new dawn.

Nancy Zeigler

Without Her Near

Does she know that I still love her.
Does she know that I still care.
Must I face another day
Without her near.
Now I suffer now I cry.
Can't go on why should I try,
Can't face another day
Without her near.
If she were here
I would tell her I still love her,
If she were here
I would tell her I still care.
If she were here
I would say please come back today.
My heart is broken
Without you near.
I will always love her
In my heart will always care.
Another lonely day
Without her near.

John Bemis

Labels

Labels, such as "isms" or "ists",
  Genders or hues,
Require of their members
  Quite costly dues!
Genetic or chosen,
  Whatever the cause,
Labels divide us
  Deserve no applause!

Jean Kuebler

The Splattered Box

I made a splattered box for you
to remind you of happy things.
Where there is no need to worry
just focus on your dreams.
Know you are very special,
unique in every way.
I only wish you had never moved
and instead decided to stay.
I'm glad you were rational
about choosing to remain here.
For the destruction of your life
would have brought many tears.
I admire you in a lot of ways
for your friendship and being so kind,
but really appreciate your greatly for
being there when I need to unwind.
We'll always be friends
through the good and the bad.
This splattered box is for you
so you'll never be sad.

Dara Dailey

Always

Are we always hearing ourself say
It's so hard to get ahead today
Do we always seem to have a need
Of needing much more to succeed

Are we always trying to get through
One more thing we have to do
Are we always running to and fro
With one more place we need to go

Do we always find ourself involved
With lots of problems to be solved
Is there always one more weary mile
That never leaves us with a smile

Well life won't always seem unfair
Won't be more than we can bear
If we always find a way
To take the time, slow down and pray

Paulette Howard

A Child's Life In A Peaceless World

This is my child
Full of mischief
And wearing a childish smile

Today he's safe and peaceful
Here with me
But tomorrow, what will his life be?

With hatred and wars all around
No peace nowhere, to be found
Love is gone
It has been taken away
So much trouble in the world
Coming my child's way

I'd like to protect him, forever more
I know I cannot send him back
That's for sure

So what I've got to do
For my peace of mind
Is to take the time to teach him
How to live his life, so he can find
Peace in a troubled world

Earline Rowlett

SCUBA

Flashing, iridescent life
  View me with a cool disdain,
Flawless forms are they, and I,
  Intruder to their deep domain.

And the silence that surrounds me
  Imparts an inner calm,
And a growing sense of timelessness
  The ages build upon.

For the cycle never changes,
  As the waves roll to the shore,
And the patterns that are fashioned
  Are and will be evermore.

And while these coral cliffs I pass
  In the quiet of this vast abyss,
I marvel at each creature,
  And I most truly wish:

That He who formed these myriad shapes
  Will surely grant to me
The joy of coming back again
  To this world beneath the sea.

Eleanor Brown-Dudek

Who Can I Be?

Flitter fuzzy flighty buggy
you are so lovely as you fly
flapping, clapping tirelessly by.

Colorful wings gently kissing
as you lite along the way
bidding one to make you stay.

But it's no lion flyin flyin
cause no one seems afraid of me
so, who can I possibly be?

Barbara Snyder Kelley

"An Ode To No One"

No one is my best friend.
He never speaks his mind.
He doesn't care if I am wrong,
Which I am all the time.
No one is my back up.
He always thinks I'm right.
Even though there was that time,
I got us lost at night.
No one is so perfect.
He's not just a paylay,
And maybe if you're lucky,
You might meet him someday.

Drew Repasy

Snub

I'm a number
I can't be reached
Let the floor raise and fall
You'll never reach me
I will be
I will find a life
I can do nothing for you
I'll hold the dyeing man's hand
Crowds of people scream for hope
As the rain falls apart
How could something so small fall apart
It was so easy for my soul
I need
It's a desire to be filled
Controlled by magnets and vibrations

Branningan S. Cheney

Prelude Of Dreams

As the night approached
the horizon gleamed,
like a lump of gold
in a mountain stream.

The clouds of few
were touched with pink,
for the sun was
surely soon to sink.

The sky was painted
with bright colors so old,
the magnificent shades of
red, orange, and gold.

Then a strange calmness
stretched over the land,
and silence invaded
every creature and man.

The sun's bright rays
faded into the night,
leaving images of magic
for the dreamers up coming flight.

Miranda Moore

If Only I Could Write

Fists clenched,
body tight and tense.

Blackness surrounds,
within the silence.

Mind muddled,
echoes of thoughts
race all around.

With the pen,
in the darkness,
if only I could write
in the solitude
of the sleepless nights.

Diann Hopper

The Mind Is ...

TOO COMPLEX
   for those who are afraid of
     finding themselves
TOO SIMPLE
   for those who think they know
     everything about themselves-
TOO HARD
   foe those who don't even try.
But for those who know
   THE MIND IS.

Carole L. Fritsche

Rose

Flower of thought,
Opening to all life
Through petals of rose.

Spreading her warmth
To all nature,
Only to whether away
Until another day.

Winter has come
To decide her fate.

Melvin Scales

In A Rocking Chair If You Might

Grandma, I know you died last night
even though you tried to fight
As you head toward the light
I ask one favor, if I might
When you do enter the light
Please, see if you can sight
My little, baby boy
Then hold him tight
In a rocking chair, if you might
Rock my little baby boy
For me every night
When you enter the light
Tell him stories about the night
When his mom will enter the light
And then, Grandma, if you might
Hold me and my baby boy tight
In a rocking chair for the night
When I reach the light

Sarah Cox

Do Not Trouble Me With Meaning

I am a man of sense and sound
My coffee and words are finely ground

By the proper measure
Each pleasure
Only is found

Weighed and conveyed
In a careful balance
Ballast and rope
Prudence and scope
Settled and wound
To be said and found
In a manner consistently staid

Lest the debt to oneself is unpaid
When interests are compounded
And reason confounded
Beyond the clean, civil pleasure
Of tea, cream and marmalade

Peter Lange

The Ring

A ring of joy, a ring of sorrow,
Something special ev'ry tomorrow.
As long as dolphins leap
and willows weep,
It is there,
In the land and air.

A ring of pure and endless light,
A haven in the darkest night.
As long as the ring remains,
Each soul proclaims,
"On the Eagle's wings,
All the ring sings,
'I am a light
In the darkest night!'"

Megan O'Malley

Restless

Stay here, sit down I say to thee.
There is no reason for you to flee.
Your eyes are nervous, full of fright.
Be still, soon will pass this night.
Let me make some soothing tea,
to warm your soul and some for me.

Nancy Gaignard

Donna

There's many ways to express
  how I feel,
Each and everyone of them
  is heart beating real,
Thoughts cross my mind all
  leading to your name.
Things we've done leaves no shame,
I have no regrets, no sorrow, nor pain,
With you by my side I'm the
  one who stands to gain,
I've searched for words and
  picked these chosen few.
This poem would not have been
  written if it weren't for you!

Kevin Hugh Gildersleeve

Untitled

I have purged you from my soul,
But, yet, you linger in my mind
To taint the purity of love
That I may feel. From this I find,

To love another, my heart whole,
Is a travesty of some kind.
Withering the white rose, the dove
Of innocence not far behind.

The teeming youth that was my stole
Has knotted and left me confined
To yesterdays that float above
Blocking futures, leaving me blind.

I struggle to attain control
Of severed heart strings to bind.
Instead, they knit to show me of
Coffined love, satin lined.

Rebecca Goodall

Water Colors

Red is the color
of anger and rage,
like a dark rose pressed onto a page.

Orange is the color
of tiger lilies in bloom
bathed in the light of a harvest moon.

Yellow is the color
of tears glistening,
and angels listening.

Green is the color
of a lime
or a clock that whispers time.

Blue is the color
of distant sands;
and the harmony of many bands.

Violet is the color
of a morning glory,
and the excitement of a story.

When blended in unison they form a
rainbow in heaven!

Jessica Lucas

Santa

Santa big jolly and red
Wears a warm hat on his head,
With a long white beard
And sparkling eyes,
On the night before Christmas
He sails across the skies!

Heather Mallory

My Wonderful Lord

When I rise to greet the dawn
   My wonderful Lord is there
No matter what the day may bring
   All my burdens He will share

When coping with the pressures of life
   My wonderful Lord knows best
He will draw me to His side
   Where I shall find peace and rest

When there are times I'm feeling sad
   My wonderful Lord holds me
Safely in His loving arms
   For all eternity

When I close my eyes in prayer
   My wonderful Lord is there
Hearing praise from my grateful heart
   Knowing I'll always be in His care.

Janet Lee

The Dream

I stood alone in the cold sunshine,
the angry wind tearing at my face.
I stood upon the frozen earth,
among the blowing brittle leaves,
among the dead.

I stood in the garden of stones,
where tears well and drop like dew
upon its lonely flowers.

I dreamed in the garden of the dead.

I dreamt that it was spring
and the breathe from your sigh
brushed my cheek,
and it was warm
and inviting.

I read your name upon *your*
granite flower,
and I turned my eyes
toward the brilliant sun,
and stared into the icy rays
so that they might
blind me.

Claudia Canner

"A Rose Unlike Any Other"

A rose unlike any other
Is made from love
A flower to cherish
A gift from Heaven above

Created by a seed
Nurtured through life
A little water and a little love
To keep the petals bright

The petals produce an aroma
So sweet to the air
That brightens everything it touches
And beholds all that is dear

You rose, unlike any other
Are made from love
A flower to cherish
A Gift, from Heaven above

Daniel M. Niemchak

Sharing

A squirrel came through my window
he was as quiet as a mouse
he took all my nuts and berries
and then he left my house

He wasn't very careful though
he left a little trail
I followed him and found him
my tracking never failed

He was surprised to see me there
he was living in a tree
I said give back the berries
that you stole from me

He looked so sad and gave them back
but I didn't have the heart
so instead of taking them all
I settled just for part.

Lloydine Sawall

The Shadow Of Time

Time is very precious
Time is compare to a gold
So time continuous
And never gets old.

   A work that must be done
   Must do it at once
   For time does not wait
   So you must not be late.

It is said that a person in a hurry
Is like a whirling wind
It is always in a worry
For time is coming in.

   The shadow of time is gone
   When yet nothing is done
   Time leaves you old
   For time is gold.

Joan Eileen Sam

Untitled

I'm poor and I'm old,
My hair has gone gray,
My robe is all patches,
My sash is not gay.

The fat God of luck
Never enters our door,
And no visitors come
To drink tea anymore.

Yet I hold my head high
As I walk through the town.
While I serve such a master
My heart's not bowed down.

Justin Delano Walker

Untitled

Butterflies are like happiness.
You can never really grasp it,
But if you wait,
It'll come to you.
Butterflies get happiness from
The nectar they find in flowers,
The nectar is golden
Like the golden happiness inside
Someone's heart

Maggie V. Passione

My Baby's First Words

There are three little cherubs
looking down from above
Each of them knowing
the depth of my love.

They each hold a piece, no,
a part of my heart
Which I will reclaim when
we are no longer apart.

I long for the day that
I can kiss each sweet face.
I know that they too,
have longed my embrace.

They will meet me in Heaven,
as I walk to the Gates.
The sight of my cherubs
will first touch my face.

And all Heaven will cheer as I
hear my baby's first words,
"Oh Mother, how we've waited
for you to be here".

Patty Greiner

Home

I seem to recall, Dad,
On cold blustery days,
You came to take us home from school,
With your horses and the sleigh.

That old fur coat you always wore,
To keep you snug and warm,
And robes to tuck about our feet,
Protection from the storm.

How, as the horses struggled on,
And waded through the snow,
I thought of home, with Mamma's love,
And fires all aglow.

Somehow I knew, as Life went on,
I needed nothing more,
A love to keep me warm inside,
And 'Welcome' on the door.

Florence A. Birdsall

A Valentine Prayer

Forgive me, Lord,
That your teachings, I scorned.
For you knew me and loved me,
Before I was borned!

Although I wandered,
Far out into sin.
You opened your arms,
And took me in!

You gave me friends,
Who understand.
And are always there,
To lend a hand!

A loving church group,
That fasts and prays;
Lord, how do you love me?
Let me count the ways!

Ada Bailey

I Am A Seed

I am a seed can't you see,
Look at me,
I was born a seed

I got roots that look like legs,
I got steams that look like arms,
But I'm still growing,
Just like a seed!

Maisa K. Lebbie

This Hurting Heart

Is this true,
Can this be the end.
I feel so blue,
Will this heart ever be mend.

Goodbye is such a big word.
Why does this have to happen to me?
I pray to you Lord,
Don't let this be.

Love is something I don't understand.
Do your have to go?
Don't you know love hurts this man,
As much as the bullet hurts the doe.

Love makes me sometimes want to die,
Don't let this be.
I know you have to fly,
But stay here with me.

Jeffrey Fitch

I Have The Ability

I have the ability to think
I have the ability to win.
I have the ability to love.
I have the ability to help
   make the world a better place.

Saïeda Lataillade-Lewis

Reality

Dark as the night,
Hate fills the hearts,
Of children who got off,
With really bad starts.

The adults of the future,
The children of the past,
Innocence destroyed,
By the Oklahoma Blast.

The Vietnam war;
America marched for peace,
These children cry out,
'Who will march for me'?

Our troops go off;
To fight foreign wars,
What about the enemy,
Knocking on our doors?

Reality is,
We need to tend to our own!
Before we wake up,
And America is gone.

Susan Sandel

Hopes And Wishes

I sat in my bedroom and looked outside,
what a glorious, twinkling night.
I looked to see all the stars,
but I only saw one.
What is the name?
Ah!
I know. It's the wishing star.
Then...
I remembered yesterday
when I was walking down the street,
I saw all these people without homes.
Then I started to cry.
Ummmm
I have a wonderful thought.
"Why not give my wish to them!"

Sunny Lai

Torn Apart

The Heavens aren't far from me now,
the sky is bluer than ever.
Life can treat you like you're evil,
And death can be your biggest endeavor.
Just soak up your tears with a cloth,
and treasure your moments together.
Make the most of seemingly nothing,
they won't be there forever.
Memories are your sea of joys,
and joys are your lost hopes.
Hopes are your never ending truths,
when you're running out of ropes.
December snow vs. October Fall,
Spring showers shower your heart.
Summer pleasures satisfy your hunger;
Not knowing when you'll be torn apart.

Nikki J. Charette

Untitled

Here I sit with my
Reader's Digest in hand.
Educating my brain,
Gaining laughter so grand.
Small enough for suitcase,
Or purse,
Big enough for the
World to come in.

How many books do you like to keep?
Not to many, you care to repeat.
But readers digest is always a treat.

Jeanette Wilson

Marine Brat

He stands at attention
like one of a sandpiper flock
viewing a horizon.

He stands in uniform
issued by love:
his father's, his country's.

He anticipates the order
of the rumble-car.
His very own Christmas

Eve, with an arsenal
of hugs, a three dog
infantry at his side.

J. Dennis Gillespie

My Husband

I wake up in the morning -
Rub the sleep out of my eyes -

I turn to face the window -
And find the sun did rise.

Each evening as I go to bed -
Never knowing I'll see the morn -

But when I do awaken, I find -
A new day has been born.

I turn to watch you as you sleep -
And then I have to smile -

For though I should be getting up -
I think I'll lay with you awhile.

I count my blessings every day -
And I swell up with pride -

Because the best thing in my life -
Is having you right by my side.

Joyce Montague

Rabi

Down by the river a boy
shall sit... He asked his
Rabi, Rabi why shall we one
day die?
His Rabi flew down on a
golden cloud with words
that would heal.
My boy no one should live
in a fear of death; but
with joy of being blessed!
With those words he disappeared
and the boy found
his death with a tiny tear.
The boy was past and saw
only joy...
You see Rabi is that future
boy!!!

Tanya Wilbert

Spring

Flowers growing fresh from seeds,
girls stringing pretty beads.
Boy are playing with footballs,
while girls are simply dressing dolls.
The trees are wet with the rain,
then the mountains lock oh so plain.
At night crickets sing so loud,
daylight there's not a single cloud.
Snow is going far away,
rain is coming every day.
Summer isn't far away,
hoping it's summer every day.
The sun is coming higher and higher,
we end each night with a warm fire.
Stars in the evening night,
help the people say good night.
Love is coming all around,
and spirits within every sound.

Heather Tinney

Willow

As the brisk wind blows,
Your shade comforts my dark soul,
My Weeping Willow.

Theresa Curcio

International Love

I sensed the love abounding
On my left and on my right
I felt His love descending
Through us, with Almighty Light.

Let it flow gently through us
Anchoring in the earth below
Do you know, it purified us
And our bodies are aglow?

Send Love back to the Source
Surging out to all who need
To our cities, nations, countries.
Help their leaders to believe.

Love the nearest one beside you
They, in turn, shall do the same
The world will soon be perfect
His love will reign Supreme.

Lila Brown

Trick Or Treat

Let's go out and trick or treat
for tonight is the night
When children scream and witches
fly and blood doesn't dry

Let's go out and trick or treat
for there is no other night
Where ghosts glide and spirits
dance and hair flies in the air

Let's go out and trick or treat
for I'm ready to go
When black cats prance and
vampires bite and the moon is full
   Will you go with me?

Melanie Worley

Mask

Life is a concentric circle
with many hills and valleys,
that are hidden
by the masks of peace
and serenity, these masked
hills and valley's are not
revealed until your eyes are
truly opened to the ugliness of the
real world.

Blaine Shaw

A Lost Key

Lies and secrets hidden in the
heart and locked with a lost
key. Stories never dared told
and taken to the confinement
of a grave. Our souls lost
to the wind whispering our
tales that are never told.
Silence broken to the cries
of anger and disappointment.
Our key is found, our hearts
unlocked, our souls released,
and our secrets are lost to
the world.

Anna Wickett and Elise Libby

True Meaning

As I was reading Webster,
I noticed a mistake!
His definition of life,
An error He did make!
He said it was to eat
And also requires growth.
Adaptation to the environment,
Reproduction "Life" must have both.
But, what has He really described,
Just methods to exist.
For "Life" without "True Meaning,"
Is a contradiction, in the Mist.

Gerald A. Torgerson

To My Journal

To where and when my thoughts flow
I write to see where they go
because I can not control this sea
without the pen showing me

I start with a word then phrase
and developing into scorn or praise

Things I can sometimes say to this
I would want everyone else to miss

Richard E. Alessandro

Format

Riding in the red balloon
High above the town
People throwing stones at me
Just to bring me down

Walking in a day dream
Talking in my sleep
Reason is a broken wing
I pray my soul to keep

Wonder why the politicians
Say the things they say
Reading out the verdict
Living life their way

Vigilant righteousness
Ringleader of the riot
Try to silence my unknown voice
You'll never keep me quiet

Christopher Jerald Robinson

Untitled

To whom it may concern
please don't be unset with
my life for it is my decision
to be the way I am.

To whom it may concern
please stop bickering and
hovering over my affairs
for it is my way not yours.

To whom it may concern
stop fighting call me, you know
you'll all equally get my time.

To whom it may concern
don't feel sad for me, for
this is my destiny. Please don't
have pity or sorrow for I know
what I am doing.

Christina Pashalidis

Music

We hear these wonderful
tunes all day and night.
   Pop, Jazz, Rock-n-roll, and
the famous Moody blues also
gospel too. No matter what you
like, love songs is where it's at!
   They all seem to make your
dreams come true, never worry about
being alone, as long as you have
that favorite little song. Like the
moon is white at night, everyone
knows music makes you feel all
right. A time in need then, it's
gospel indeed, songs like an angel's
violin, then you will know this
is where life begins, What is life
without all the sounds around,
and a merrily tune on a merry go round.

Renee Moore

The City

The light of the sun is only a pity,
For only darkness rules the city.
It twists and turns.
For all its lashes sting and burn
No love exists in the city
For only the rough and hardy survive,
So be careful because you're alive.

Kristie Bailey

Your Earthly Works Were Done

You entered this sin-filled world
with a certainty of one.
That surety was realized
when your earthly works were done.

Heaven was your goal,
you trod with a steadfast aim.
You knew the time was near—
that your earthly works were done.

God alone knew that time,
which no man could prolong.
And He alone did dictate
when your earthly works were done.

You ran this race completely;
you smiled and said goodbye.
God opened His arms and welcomed you.
Your earthly works were done.

Theresa L. Cummings

My Cat

My cat Andy
Looks like a piece of candy
He is mostly white
Oh but not quite!!!!!!

He likes to play at night
But with me he likes to fight

With my little sister
He clings to her like a blister

He only eats dry cat food
He is always in a good mood

My cat is so Dandy
That's why we call him Andy!!

Lisa R. Salamo

A Moment In A Lifetime

I held it for an instant
but it slipped beyond my grasp
yet for one precious moment
I held it in my hands.

It felt nothing short of heaven
it glistened like the stars
and if only a moment
I felt it in my heart.

It shimmered like an Angel
as it took my breath away
in that magic moment
there was nothing I could say.

Like a shooting star across the sky
it vanished instantly
I only had a moment
to feel your love eternally.

Dawn Renee Heimbuch

Peace Not War

A lonely quiet sand bar
A crisp July evening
Chirping of birds in the distance
Running water
The rocks under the shallow water
The tiny island
The trees in the river
Lying down —
Slumbering in the soft sand
Listening only to nothing —
Only peace and quiet
Stay by the river for spring —
And summer
This is peace not war
No guns firing
No cannons bombing
No people dying, no people killing
Stay with in peace
Don't go to war
As I say again, this is peace not war.

Johnny Platt

The Times We Had

The times we had,
Some were good some were bad.

Sometimes we were happy,
Sometimes we were sad.

Sometimes in good moods,
Sometimes in bad.

But no matter how the times
were, happy, sad, mad, glad, no
matter how good or bad they were,
We still had one good thing, our
love for each other.

The times we had since the
day we met,
The times we had I will
never forget,

The times we had.

James Patera

At Home

There is a place outside
where Jesus falls
There is a place inside
where nothing calls

A heart full of wings
slowly goes deaf
when a human mind
is beaten and left

I wish the devils would return
to their orgy of clay
so me and all lovers
could come out and play

Jeremy Koelzer

Love

Love can be,
A delicate thing,
As thick as a branch,
As thin as a string.

Love is promises,
Straight from the heart,
Like "No matter what",
Or "Till death do we part".

Love is the strongest,
Thing in the world,
A relationship between,
A boy and a girl.

Michael Diaz

The Wife

And if I said "No", what then?

Would you break apart my soul,
Beat down my every thought,
Awaken all my dreams,
Condemn each strong desire,
Make light of every passion,
Defy my strong-willed notions,
Blow out my burning flame,
Retrieve your kindest words,
Betray my deepest trust,
Quiet my heart-felt song,
Destroy my inner quest?

To you, I must say "Yes".

Michelle H. Wolfe

You're Not Alone

The day is done.
I'm all alone
No one to talk to
No one to phone.
So here I am all alone
The sun's going down
In the West
The moon comes up
Shining its best.
I'm all alone, but I don't care
God whispers to me
I'll always be there
You're not alone.

Irene D. Short

To Mah Lilla Lync'd Boy

Chile, is you gon' tell God
How you was cot an' tied,
O' about the fun we had
Times 'fore you sin' died?

Dis only nine years give
Fo' your young eyes to see
And dis in 'lebben seconds
God done set you free.

Your pah an' me, we come
We bowed and sayed a prayer
I weep to see yo body
Hanging in dat air.

Your shirt was tore off you
Your back was beaten bare
And your eyes, so young, so happy
Give me the strangest stare.

Boy, we's sho' gon' miss you
Dis ain't gon' be the same
But run, now, chile and hurry
So God can get your name!

Doris A. Ezell

Earth Bound

My spirit soars through endless sky
But my feet cling to the ground
I cry my futile yearning cry
While the days fly by, un-bound
Oh come again, lost laughter
Oh come again, wild sound
But the wind is full of silence
And my feet cling to the ground.

Audrey Putnam

Choices: Good Or Bad

Grabbing hold of a life long dream.
Realizing it will never be.
Holding on to the pain inside,
oh will someone help me.

Realizing things that will never be.
Running away from the reality.
And going to a dream.
Of the after effects of the choice
conceived.

Robyn Morris

Ideals Broken

Couples everywhere
Individuals searching...
For the ideals,
they were guaranteed
There is no perfection-
Marriages fail
Hearts break
Ideals are shattered
Souls continue to search
Most desire love
Many need status
Images of icons-
Husband and wife
Only the truth will tell
Two's don't guarantee
Love and happiness

Jamie Chazen

Untitled

Out of the river of waters
Life came gushing forth;
Out of the womb of woman—
Life Eternal.

Were you there in the night
Where I was born?
What did you say then?
Did you ask questions?

Answer me now.
Where did I come from,
Where am I going,
New as I am?

Give me an answer
New and yet ancient
One good to live by
True from the heart.

Where will our love be
When it's all finished;
Will we return then
New-born again?

Edna Earl McGowan

The Sun And The Moon

You are the sun in the east,
each day on you my eyes feast
  Every morning you rise
to open people's eyes
  To my darkness, you are the light
and you are beautiful sight
  Everyday you awake to caress
the earth with your sweet, gentle kiss
  I am the orb of the night,
the moon who leads with gentle light
  No matter how far apart,
we will always share the same heart

I love you

Niki L. Gatewood

Girl On A Swing

I swing out flying
  reach, reach
soar into the trees.

Can I swing over the bar?
A circus aerialist
I am not.

Ecstatic I rise
'til love, like gravity
draws me back.

I swing out falling
  watch the ground move up
with a sinking despair.

I brace my legs
  to fight the fall
skidding to a stop.

Love, like gravity
  draws me back.

Gay Geary

Hold

How old were you
When you ran out of patience?
How old was I
When I learned that embraces
Can merely mean one
Looking for the warmth
Of another?
How old are we
Now
That innocence
Has passed?

Naomi Undine Reiter

I Stand Silence(silent) In The Rain

Standing silence in the rain
To hide these bitter tears of pain

Falling gently upon my head
Blending tears which I have shed

Tears of secrets long untold
Of hopeless fantasies so bold

Anguished tears of a broken heart
Crying silence in the dark

And to live with this pain,
I stand silence in the rain.

Alexander Tumolva

"Thy Face Of Many, Me"

The I you see
The me you know
I am in flesh
Not in soul
A battle of the what and who
Of that I grit
And reluctant do
Thy pain I spare you
Bleeds that of mine
One heart blue
One true
Divine

Niki Agelastos

Love

Love is why we're here today:
  to talk and walk and eat and play.
Love is why Jesus died for you
  because he loved you.
Love is the way you talk with people,
  walk with people, look at people
  and listen.
Listen to people when they talk,
  show interest in conversation.
And you will have love wherever
  you are—over the world or under.

Rachel Claytor

Summer

  The sun is shining
hotter than before.
People sun tanning on the beach.
Lovely flowers blooming by
to see the weather going by.
Birds flying happily in the sky.
Students vacationing by that time
having fun in their lives.

Nathan Noe

Memoirs Of A Lost Canary

  Fluorescent sunlight burns my eyes
As demons dance around my head.
  The rosy truth of yesteryear
Has grown inside my needle.
  My innocence of childhood dreams
Lies lost among the poppy seas.
  Truth flows through and past
My candle has burned too low.
  Too late to save my empty mind
To heal my broken soul.
  Hope left home.
As I stoop to kill.
  I lose myself in yesteryear,
And fall upon my flame.

Leah Kennett

School Years

School years come,
School years go.
You always see them come,
But you never see them go.
It seems as though school just started,
And now it comes to a close.
You make new friends.
You make new beaus.
As the school year closes,
There will be a lot of runny noses.

Frances Bersuder

Friends

Friends forever
Not true
At two.

Give and take.
Sharing and caring
To be loyal/to be true,

Friends forever
Takes time
To age/to ripen,

To share joys
To bear sorrows
a bond.

An embracing circle
Round and round
To begin anew,

Friends forever
A bracelet of gold
a gift.

Bernadette Kelleher

I Wish...

If it was only known by those who love,
Acts so seen by those above.

I wish to tell you,
not today.

They should have seen in other ways.
Still sits the concealed secret.

If only they knew of what I did.
The souls of some might have bled.

Robert Anderson

Thoughts

Thoughts are where I think
That someone is trying to hurt me,
and trying to hurt my friends.
Thoughts of people injuring animals,
throwing trash on the ground,
making the earth full of pollution,
destroying everything.
People getting sick and dying
thoughts that there will soon
be a better place to live.
Nina L. Machado

It Is...

As pure as my mind,
cause it's at its best.
So precious to me,
for you have been blessed.
When dawn sighs,
I watch you rise in relief.
From this partial reality,
that has caused you grief.
An existence of the future,
or so it may seem.
You are my soul,
and this is my dream.
Monica Butler

Stormy Days

You tell me about rain falling down
upon the grass
I say the sun will shine again
you must believe
but cannot hear
through thunderclaps

Was it long ago we
spoke of being together
always warmed by the sun
now it bothers your eyes
you seek the forest
I the desert only hold you here
Elizabeth Fuquay

"Than You Will Ever Know"

You mean more to me
Than you ever know,
You are the light I see
At the end of every road.
You are like the twinkling stars
That light up the midnight sky,
You are always in my heart
Thoughts of you race through my mind.
Sometimes you are as innocent
As a little child,
Every time I see your face
It always makes me smile.
Our love is precious and true
And has been from the start
I will always love you
Those words come from my heart.
I could tell you everyday
Just how much I love you so
But you mean more to me
Than you will ever know.
Jennifer Stone

The Separation

And now that we have gone our way
To act apart our separated plays
The challenge now that we live out
To tread this path but still with doubt

A vine that splits will take its toll
Will not bear fruit without a soul
Unless be tended and well cared
Can both these twigs of life be spared

Until the stars blink and go out
They'll still be life and love about
Forgive, forget, rename the sage
The chapters new, just turn the page

The payments dear but we'll survive
As long as we can both surmise
That knowing this is our new start
We go two ways and heal our hearts
William C. Benesch Jr.

Your Parents

Treat your parents kindly,
  Show them that you care.
Hug them while you can because
  Someday they'll not be there.

Ask them any questions
  Of things you need to know
About their dreams, their future plans,
  And their childhoods long ago.

Iron out your problems,
  Forget about the past.
Dwell only on the memories
  That you really want to last.

Let them know you love them,
  Now the time is right.
You don't know when you'll lose them.
  It could happen any night.
Karen Gunderson

To Be A Kite

A kite is flying
In the sky
I feel alone
I wonder why

The kite is me
My ups and downs
I've lost control
There are no clowns

Tears don't help
They only prove
My heart is empty
I feel no love

I want to be happy
Soar to the sky
Be a kite
But I just can't fly
Beverly De Vito

Life

Love is light,
Life is bright,
and through the eyes
of a child, everything
is fine.
Tammy Priester

People

People can be skinny,
People can be tall,
People can be fat,
And people can be small.

People can be funny,
People can be dumb,
All people have two hands,
Eight fingers and two thumbs.

Many people are blind,
Some people are even deaf,
I write with my right hand,
My friend writes with his left.

This poem's coming to an end,
But people will live longer,
They'll be big, small, short, tall,
And a lot stronger!
David Rossignol

Soliloquy

Together we square handed walk
Nor hesitate, but freely talk
And heed we not the season's lie
Far flung across the April sky

For April's skies are so like Fall
When first we stood beneath this wall
Wind scrubbed, red cheeked, serene
A vision of contentment seen.
Jeanne Hunt

In The Silence

In the silence
in the dark of night
I hear the planet's ringing
and the great coursing
majesty of the galaxy
as the stars
rise and set-
the stellar river
flowing o'er
the
earth's boundaries
Michael Siems

Ragdoll

I am awake
Because I do not sleep.
I am aware
Because I exist.
I stare into space
Because I have eyes.
I know not what I see
Because I do not have knowledge.
I try to speak
But do not succeed
Because my lips
Are but painted images.
I like my life
As simple as it may seem.
I have no troubles
Or a care in the world.
Wouldn't you love to be me?
In all except one child's mind
An insignificant ragdoll.
Becky L. Johnson

Oh Lord I Thank You

I know you hear me when I pray
I know you stop me when I stray
   Oh Lord I thank you

I feel your presence oh so near
You keep the hurt the harm I fear
   Oh Lord, I thank you

I thank you for your Love
I thank you for your friendship
I thank you for your grace
I thank you in this place

I know you loved me before I
I know you help me when I try
   Oh Lord thank you

Don't ever go away from me
Don't shut the door on my salvation
Come closer to me
Fill my heart with adoration

So when I kneel each day and pray
Your love empowers me to say
   Oh Lord I thank you

Gladys Tucker

Patchwork Of Me

Shades of yellow, years past
Sunlight, marigolds, fire
Smiles, sighs, home safe

Green its cool hues spreading
Grass, water, paint
Quiet times trickle on

Red deepest of all,
Anger, stop, cheer
Shining color of love lace

Purple, quiet twilight tint,
Dresses, meadows, velvet,
Dusty feelings of the soul

Blue, history's mistress,
Melancholy, true, weddings,
Porthole of my eternity

Maggie Sikes

Vastness

Staring across and into the room
Beholding a piece of mind
And then understanding it soon
Gradually to create and unlock
Which only my imagination can stop
On an eternal journey within
Going nowhere or some place I've been
Sometimes finding pleasant thoughts
Even when I'm alone
Or on dark journeys to an unknown zone
To this there should be an end
Build a foundation for a goal
Strive forward and lend
Learn to travel and be wise
Do not drown in another's disguise
Be mellow and set a pace
Because us humans are a dying race

Kenneth E. Hyland

American Battlefield

Out of Africa
Enslaved
Into a jungle of white
Concrete wash
Down an alley
Lined with
The feces of debris
Hard eyes
Stare into guns
Shoved into
Each others
Brothers,
  Backs,
    And hearts,
    And heads.
Watching bullets hit the child
  Or mother
    Or sister
      Oh brother!
Dead.

Pandora Rupert

Sky

I am the sky. I am all around.
I house the sun, moon, and stars.
I am everywhere. I am at the
Tallest mountain or the
Smallest anthill. I always was...
I was at the time of the flood and
Will be here forever. The Lord
Has painted me with clouds and
Rainbows and has filled me with
Majestic colors. I have seen you
Change O earth, and I will be
Your blanket of air above you
Forever.

Jaci D'Ulisse

When The Sun Sets

When the sun sets:
Everything is beautiful.
People oceans and even pets.
The sand is a sparkly tan.
The ocean is blue green.
Everything can't wait to be seen.
Fishes squirm all around.
Everything has a beautiful sound.
Roses are a dazzly red,
And flowers have flower beds.
So when the sun sets:
Everything is beautiful.

Korie Caplan

There Is A Balm

Sometimes I am not so graceful
I am clumsy and I trip and stumble over
the few rough spots that crop up
and drop in my path.

So, my eyes lose their sparkle
and my smile loses its warmth,
my hugs lose their passion
and life is absent in my voice.

Oh for the moment that grace returns
to heal the sin, sick soul.
Oh for the moment that grace returns
to make the wounded whole.

Belva Brown Jordan

To Edgar Allan Poe

The torment from your eyes
Is still so strangely streaming
When Night, the Beauty, flies
Spreads wings above the land
In twinkling of the stars
In moon's pale wistful gleaming
Musician of the hearts
Your spirit lives, dear friend

Above your lonely grave
The squadrons raced to battle
While trying to preserve
The country's sacred name
The Union withstood
But fallen from the saddle
The Psyche wounded lies
And hides her face in shame

But nothing's safe from change
The time will play its role
There never was a night
That hasn't brought a dawn
Vulgarity and filth
Can't kill the human soul
The only thing to do
Is hope and hold on...

John Stolyarov

The Wall (An Impression Of The Vietnam War Monument)

Stark
Black
Non-forgiving
Relentless
Fifty thousand souls are on the Wall.

A bleak
Tribute to death
Memories carved on the wall
And who's to say that fifty thousand
Are all?

Walking wounded
Living dead
But—when done and all
Still fifty thousand people are
Forever on the Wall.

Melanie Young Quine

You Say But Will Ya?

You say you want the loving
That others could not give;
You should go out and find it,
And learn how to live.

You say I'm kinda cute,
And you like who I am;
I think that's just fine,
And I'll do what I can.

Will ya give me pleasure,
All throughout my life;
Will ya give me freedom,
Without all the strife?

You say, but will ya?
You say, but I don't know;
You say, but can ya?
We'll see where it'll go.

Jeannie Kincaid

"An Understanding"

Riding a horse
Riding the wind
Through pastures green
And fields of flowers
Sitting high and proud in the saddle
The horse's mane blowing in the breeze
Your feet resting lightly in stirrups
While your beautiful companion strides
You are free
The joy is immense
A feeling of nature
An understanding of life
Riding a horse.
Katie Lester

Inspiration Opus

Art oozes gracefully
From great honors,
Humbled museum walls.

From stone trousers
A scraped knee is
Sculptured in approved pain.

Suffer your toils
To train every target
Build and borrow, as time is tomorrow.

Silence in sight outshines
A heart that glows in
Creating light from life.
David R. Bowman

Untitled

Butterflies are like happiness.
You can never really grasp it,
But if you wait,
It'll come to you.
Butterflies get happiness from
The nectar they find in flowers,
The nectar is golden
Like the golden happiness inside
Someone's heart
Maggie V. Passione

Brothers And Sisters

I often think of who we are
And where it all began.
Products of our lives are we
The woman and the man.

We've travelled many different roads
And yet to have come so far
We've changed in lots of little ways
Though not really who we are.

I remember well the children
We all were way back then
And when I look into your eyes
I still see that child of ten

How fortunate we all are
To have these lines of love
To know that we tethered
To a higher power above

We know that ;we are not alone
For we will always be
Loving close knit members
Of the same sweet family.
Barbara J. O'Malley

Untitled

So many people, so many crimes,
So many people innocently die.
So many tears from family and friends.
So many fears of when it will end.
So many drinkers, who drink and drive
So many accidents, who will survive?
So many memories that we once shared.
So many times that you were there.
So many words I wanted to say.
So many days you were ok.
So many people die like you.
I just wish I had the chance to say
   I love you!
Jennifer Hanna

A Rose Is Me

A rose is me -
That I can see
A simple object
Noticed momentarily.

The softness of the petals
Sprouting from a stem,
Only noticed by the ones
Who care enough for them.

To some they are a thorn
And what they grow on to;
The thing they hate most of all
Reminds themselves of you.

It seems so very odd
What one little flower could mean;
Your inner deepest emotions
Or how the world seems.

A rose is me -
That I can see;
Hated or loved,
That rose is me!
Julie D'Hondt

Of Principles And Power

It was on a cold and wintry day
that God's spirit spoke to me
"Come," He said, "I've much to show,
wondrous things for you to see."

"No longer will you live your life
without purpose, without aim.
Come with Me, My precious child,
and you'll never be the same,"

I saw the Saviour on a cross
suff'ring for my sin
"Only when you give your life
does true life begin.

"The world will be against you,
and hate will pierce you side.
Stand you ground, My love in you
forever will abide."

After all He did for me
on that awesome, awful day
How can I not five all to Him?
How can I turn away?
Sean Wright

Slipping Through

My eyes
live inside
the walls
of my old home.

Each time
I return
I watch
my father vanish
through the keyhole.

My mother
blindfolded
reaches out
for anyone...
and feels
the air
slip
through her fingers.
Sylvia Schuster

Here One Day, Gone The Next

I look outside,
and what do I see?
A sky,
gray,
cloudy, polluted.
I wonder,
what will come,
as time goes on,
and things worsen.
Bombs,
guns,
nuclear war.
How soon will it end?
Years, months, days, hours.
How much longer do we have to live?
Take your life,
see it as a privilege,
and enjoy it.
Because you and I will never know,
when the end may come.
Larry Kravitz

Peace And Beauty

I walked a snow covered road today
I found a beauty there
The peace and quiet of this time
With you I'd like to share
As I walked I looked around me
The trees seemed to bend "Hello"
A snowman smiled as I walked by
A beauty made of snow
I turned to see a little bird
Who seemed to say to me
Come along and fly awhile
I'll teach you to be free
I realized then that I must go
I turned with a deep sigh
The peace and beauty of this day
I'll leave with a tear in my eye
This day will be a memory
Only one of a kind
The artist may capture the beauty
The picture remains in my mind
Janet Putek

Untitled

You knew my life before I was
You know my every error
I was taught of natural highs
And thought life was forever

You let me run the wild path
You let me have the choice
And there you were right by my side
Yet I never heard your voice

I learned of love and learned of hurt
but yet I didn't need
but Praise the lord you still cared
And then I felt a need

And now oh lord you know my life
You forgave on that natural high
And the feeling of life forever
Sharon Horgan

Dream Child

You came to me in my dreams.
  You looked like him, but like
  me also it seems.

I heard your tinkling laughter,
  and even saw your smile.

I watched you run and play, then
  just sit and rest awhile

With chubby hands clasp together
  and a twinkle in your eyes, you
  were watching a butterfly.

As the butterfly flew away, and
  your hands came apart. I heard
  the most wonderful giggle, that
  went straight to my heart.
Robin Hamm

Oklahomans

Reach for one
And then the other
We must all
Come together
Lifting each other
As one does a brother
Holding on
To one another
The babies are now
Little angels
Resting with God
And his holy angels
Pray for strength
And comfort now
All as one
Let's bow down
God will deal
With those men
Who wanted to take lives
By their own hands
Nicole Sandrelli

Winter Skiing

When you ski you go so fast,
You don't even know what you passed.

But when you so really slow,
You can see the winter snow.
Philip Triolo

A Silent Meditation

I'm leaving home today
My first, though I've traveled far
My tears flow silently

My heart asks
Why?
You love it here
This is your place
You grew up
You were nourished here
This is home
The rowhouse bricks are soft, caressing
The people warm
The City inviting

I love you Baltimore for
You are the Best

Yes, I'm leaving home
My first
Polly Fleming

"Unanswered Question"

I went to see her,
just the other day.
I had to ask her,
if I could go out and play.
Not a word she spoke,
but in my heart I knew,
for she would not answer my question
from the morning dew.
My eyes were full of questions
I did not understand.
Why she would not answer me?
As my father held my hand.
I asked my father why
she would not speak.
My father looked down at me
with a tear upon his cheek.
He said, "Just remember my son
all the love she gave."
Then we turned and left,
my mothers grave.
Donald M. Molloy

"Unwanted Shadows"

    Deep within the darkness are
unwanted shadows. Shadows of spirits
from a time long ago. Those that
remain are preserved for the ages.
    The remaining shadows are
those that are trapped under
the darkness of a quiet night.
Unwanted by people who have
no heart. These unwanted
treasures are simply rejected
and forgotten. If you look
long and hard you can see
life through the eyes of an
unwanted shadow.
Phillip P. Aguilar

Winter

Soft, fluffy snow falls
Dripping icicles chatter
Tree tops covered white
Perfumes of pine fill the air
All is quiet once again
Nicole Sczypiorski

Rumors

Black is black
white is white
black is dark
so why not fight
fight against what
  everyone knows
about the past you
  never told.
Who knows this past you
  have not told.
Why is it going around
  like gold.
Why not,
  go back to correct your mistakes.
Cause they are too
  powerful to ever erase.
Mandi Millus

Man's Best Friend

I sit, I wait, I'm so cute!
People walk by, they stop.
I wag my tail, I'm so cute!
Wait don't go - watch me fetch,
The cold, the heat, the sun so warm.
Tomorrow more will come.
Soon I hope to have a new home
But they pass - people always pass
Others leave, why can't I?
I will be good, all I need is love.
We can play, maybe go for a walk
Watch me grow - Become old
They say we are man's Best Friend
But why do I not have a home
Look, the gate is opening
A new home!? I can't wait!
Oh no, the uniform!
I sit, I wait,
Why are there so many in here?
People will not be able to see me!
Cherie Hill

"The Perfect Sacrifice"

Upon his head a crown of thorns
  Cut deeply into his brow
Covering his shoulders a purple robe
  Displayed before the crowd

He carried his cross upon the hill
  Two criminals by his side
"My God, My God, why have you forsaken
  Me?"
  Alas his despairing heart cried

"It is finished" was his final cry
  As the temple curtain tore in two
The Perfect Lamb of sacrifice
  Holy, just, and true

He took the punishment of iniquity -
  A punishment we deserve
He died that we might live
  And lived that we might serve

Every drop of the Savior's blood
  As he hung upon that tree
Cleansed the sins of every man
  For all eternity
Shannon R. Cobb

Untitled

It's been a month since we've
been apart nevertheless, you remain
in my heart. It seemed like forever
back then, it's hard to believe it's
come to an end. At night when I
I'll awake and remember you, I wonder
was our love ever really true?
I just want you to know that
I was always true, but weather
you believe it or not it's up to
you. As I struggle on in life I
finally see that the love that
was given to you wasn't good
enough to keep you here with
me. Is there anything left to say?
Besides your love has gone and
left me a stray. I miss you
a lot, and that's a fact, but one
of these days, you'll get payback!

April Suzanne Faulkner

Untitled

People are crying
Inside we are all dying
With anguish and despair

We miss him oh so much
Yet we still go out to lunch
We still live and have fun
Like we would have done
If he hadn't passed away
That very sad day

People have cried
And he has died
We still love him though
And we all know
That no matter what
He will always be with us
In our hearts

Tammy Hooper

Untitled

Life can be cussed
Life can be kickback
It's darn hard to manage
I've learned for a fact.

The sweat of my brow
is mixed in my heart
Wrenching and screaming
It's pounding the chart.

Loosen, let go
Is all that I ask
Look up, in the sunlight
Drink from its flask

Moments of fullness
Spin through my heart
Reasons of pleasure
fill in my cart.

Enough to maintain
My desire to give
Take more this time
and live.

Cheryl A. Grant

The Wakening Dream

Bottled fingers dream of hair
They never know
But lust for in their etherous dreams
Like worms in white at the foot of God.

Blue like an orange is their mind
And blue is the color
For hair untouched and unlike glass
To fingers lost upon black roads.

Tapping as sightless pink mice
For loving knives
Searches skin the unworldly blue
Floors of her tea steam body.

And lips like His heart flesh of ours
Beat with orange flaw
Their midnight skies of radiant tears
Shed upon the love of worms in white.

Cody N. Larson

Untitled

Open your heart and close your eyes
Feel my hand through dusty leather
Dive in space and softly gather
Hurting question in your sighs.

The only guest in my asylum.
The only face on empty street, -
Through tearing eyes eternal guilt
I see the strings of broken violin

Don't fear walking up the stairs
And crossing threshold of unknown
In here your very uttered "No"
Will mean a thousand of "Yes"

I'll show you things you never saw
You'll hear what no one ever whispered
You are my missed and missing sister
Turned by the villain into crow.
Subtle are the step of dancing dreams
And cold the irony of metal
The touch of beauty is always lethal
Amidst insatiable whims.

Vadim A. Skorupko

Confused

I did it.
Was it good, or was it bad?
What did I do?
How could I do this?
I sat, trying to figure if what I did
was actually meant to be done
and what it was that I had done.
I did the wrong thing.
I know it!
It was bad!! . . .
A voice approached my thoughts.
Not my voice, . . . just a voice.
It said, "Is there enough space?"
I stood there trying to determine what
the phrase meant.
An hour. A day. A week. A month.
It means, if you clutter your mind with
bad thoughts, where will there be room
for good ones . . .
I think!?!

Lindsey Meyer

Your Touch

I cannot let you touch me anymore
you say your touch is gentle
but it is not
your touch to me has only
hurt me
not only on the outside
where it was black and blue but,
in the inside where it's
broken in a million pieces
you have not only hurt
me today or yesterday but,
you have scarred me
for the rest of my life!

Teresa A. Marquez

Reincarnation

When each of us die,
There is a new star in the sky,
And depending on what
Kind of person you are,
Will determine how bright
Will be that star,
So while you're in this world
Try to be the best person you can be,
For when you die, you can be the
Star of stars, you see.

Robert Briscoe

A Friend

A friend is like a flower,
a rose to be exact.
Or maybe like a brand new gate,
that never comes unlatched.
A friend is like an owl,
both beautiful and wise.
Or perhaps like an ember,
whose flame never dies.
A friend is those blades of grass
you can never mow
standing straight and tall and proud
in a perfect little row.
A friend is like a heart that goes
on strong until the end.
Where would we be in this world
if we did not have a friend?

Brandilee Grimm

"Sea Of Ice"

A sea of ice,
The confines of my heart,
It spreads outward,
Limitless as time,
My heart is still beating,
But it is slowing,
And the pain is growing,
The ice begins to break,
The larger the pause,
The bigger the crack,
My heart stops,
Its feelings dead,
The sea of ice,
Is now a home to shards.

Phillip McClelland Ballard

Children Cry

Children cry silent tears
Hiding in their dreams.
No one hears, or so it seems,
All their silent screams.
Lonely, scared, they push away
Ghosts of evening tide,
Waiting hopefully for one,
To calm their fears inside.
Those they trusted gone today,
Who knows about tomorrow.
So they pretend, and play away
All the night's dark sorrow.
Kathy Behnke

Absent Friend

For a moment
  we touched
    you and I.
We shared a small piece of our lives
  one with the other.
What you gave
  will always remain
    a part of me.
Not a gloomy shade
  But a resplendent memory.
And perhaps,
somewhere in time,
  our souls
    will touch
  anew.
Deborah Dorwart

Mental Floss

I need Mental Floss,
Not Dental Floss,
Mental Floss!

My teeth are alright,
It's just that I can't write!

They teach it to me all the time,
But I just don't get it right!

They sell it in a store,
On street 104!

The lady who sells it is Mabel,
It says it on her label!

She wears a big, green hat,
And is a little fat!

She treats you really well,
And you'll love what they sell!
Oh No! Time For More Mental Floss!

Please buy me Mental Floss,
Not Dental Floss,
Mental Floss!
Romina Garber

On My Way

Criss cross the city streets
Hectic, cars stop and go
Closer nears my destination
Trees tall, gnarled with time
Bending in the wind
What tales would unfold
Could only they speak
Thunder breaks my reverie
Rain upon their leaves
The street I call serenity
Monica Jo Horning

Perdition

Those who thrive on greed and lust
are casting their fate to the winds,
like a million grains of dust.

Their days become as twilight
while the sun is shining bright,
they will cry out in bitter anguish
and gnash their teeth in disgust.

Hearts will be full of agony
for evil possessed their spirits
and demons share their destiny,
annihilation their ultimate end.

Death is creeping upon them
judgement day is close at hand,
hell fire will consume their evil souls

Darkness shall enshroud the earth
perdition will soon prevail the wicked
Armageddon is the final conflict
and thus, peace will be reborn.
Jamal M. Bey

"Love And Fame"

When we meet
So silent in the night
You know
We just can't fight
We make love
Until the sun shines bright
Sun shines bright every day
Lets hope it is here to stay
Here to stay
Making our way
Watch out
I am going to be a big star someday
Dale C. Brannan

Choices

It happens just
after the beginning,
marbles and souls.
Buy,
sell,
trade.
Two cents for a
steelie, or
an eternity for
an aggie.
To each his own dealings,
to each his own end.
Frank J. Zoellner

"My Love Is Blind"

My eyes are fine, yet I cannot see.
You have a love that's there for me.

You see my faults.
You see my fallacy.

How can you stand me?

I try to help, yet I do not see.
You squeeze my heart.
My faults my fallacy.

You are the light to me.
Your love helps me to see.
James Clayton Keel

Untitled

Please put away those
old photographs
They remind me of times
I felt joy and could laugh

Where is the time when
Life was so clear
No need for a worry
No use for a tear

But the clock rolled forward
And I didn't know
That a change was coming
The warmth to turn cold

I can only remember I
can't bring back the past
So please put away
Those old photographs.
Gerald Doster Jr.

Reflecting On Spring

Tomorrow is the sunshine
Yesterday was for rain
Surely will come the flowers
Our patience does not wane

Winter was unruly
The snow was quite a sight
We shoveled and we slid about
At last we saw some light

Now April's nearly over
And we are waiting still
For May's abounding beauty
And the scent of daffodils

The seasons are so wonderful
Each one its own array
But best of all I think I like
My birthday month of May
Sandy Wingate

Wistful Dreams

I stare in awe at the
bountiful canopy above me
and listen to the
trembling leaves that
dance on top of the tall grass
that tickles my feet.
A whistling breeze
sweeps through the silent land
bringing the fresh scent
of Fall to embrace
my soul.
The thick dark clouds hide
the heavens above
leaving me to only dream
of the sun weeping
for freedom.
As the clouds quickly
pass over my head,
they take with them
my wishes for tomorrow.
Suzanne C. Costanzo

Spring

Fresh breezes
Fragrant earth
Wispy clouds
Gurgling streams
   It's Spring!

Budding trees
Smiling jonquils
Darting robins
Giggling children
   Ah, Spring!

Clarice L. Johnson

A Stranger's Walk

Walking down the streets
Looking all around
My hands are in my pockets
My head is to the ground
Oh I am such a stranger
A lonely stranger at that
I see an old man walking
So I obliquely tip my hat
Oh I am looking for something
That something I just don't know
So I continue walking
Full of loneliness from head to toe
Oh lonely stranger where will you go
I will continue walking
To where I just don't know

Jeffery J. Nash

My Prayer

Heavenly Father up above
please protect the man I love

Keep him safe and keep him sound
no matter when or where he's bound.

Help him to know and help him to see
that I love him as he loves me,

And then dear Lord help me to be
the kind of woman he wants of me.

Keep us now and keep us forever
happy and loving and always together

For the man I love with all my might
I'll say this prayer every night.

Kathy Norberry

twister

the spinning
laughs me
the dying
stares me
  i turn
  no answer
  turn away
  an answer
   why now?
   i'm ready
   not before?
   wasn't ready
    go away
    i cascade
    come back
    i'm raining
     stay away
     fear you
     come back
     i'm spinning

Mick Cullen

Noise Pollution

The silence
is so
loud
that I can't
hear
a thing!

Kristina Wagner Aubuchon

Selectivity

If thou hast cast a shadow ray
Upon my entwined path,
I may see or blink an eye,
To enjoy the light it cast.

This shadow ray may coolness rare
Provide a darkness sight,
Or may glorious soothing shadow
Bring wholeness and delight.

Rebecca Greene

Lady Raven

And they called her Lady Raven
With her hair of death spun black
and her eyes of hell fire gold.
With a touch as cold as ice
She'll caress you.
With a heart of stone
She'll make you her lover.
With a voice of angels
She'll sing you to sleep
With a sadistic smile
on a mouth of blood
She'll take you to her black clad
bosom singing
"Come to me ye of the flesh, to spend
a wet infinity with a woman they
call Lady Raven."

Teresa Siders

Best Friend

I gave you the keys.
You started your car.
What could happen?
Your house isn't far.

Who would believe
just one bottle of beer,
would fatally affect
the way that you steer.

And now as I stand here
watching you rest,
I know as a friend
I was never your best.

Felicia A. Bartholomew

Untitled

I no longer wear thorny chains
Around my heart-
It is free from the vanquished,
Tainted innocence that has seeped
Through the pores of my soul.

Inside
A Raging River of tears
Floods my heart with peace
And embraces me in sanity...

Rebecca J. Shipley

Mother's Day

That mother's love
you say you miss,
it did not stop
with her passing.
It's there inside you.

It was the gift
that nourished you
and understood you,
still supports you,
advises your decisions,
directs your helping others,
says how nice you look.

That mother's love
you say you miss,
it did not stop
with her passing.
It's there inside you.

Virginia A. Rose-Johnston

whole new

i have been here before
but that time i closed the door
i locked it up and threw away the key
i thought i would never want to see
but now the truth has overcome me
it has opened up my eyes
i'm able to see what was inside
the door has been knocked down
i'm taking a look around
and i like what i have found
i am finally free
there's a whole new me
i've made a new key
i'm in the land of opportunity
for the whole new me
yesterday i was born again
yesterday i became my best-friend
now i think i will begin
my whole new life

willow ambers

"Blind"

If I were young again.
I'd see the birds and the bees.
But being old, I'm lucky just
to hear;
The wind whistling through
the trees:

Happy to hear a child's laughter,
But never to see a child's tear.
The thrill of holding one close
to me;
And feeling they are near.

Living in darkness, with only
sounds around;
You begin to sense the beauty,
that very few have found.

The touch of a hand
and a friendly "Hello!"
Brings to life special things.
"I had seen years ago".

Sharon Delicath

The Butterfly Day

Butterfly, oh, butterfly
so delicate and so shy!
I was wishing today
to have your kind of day!
Not having a care
With God's love to share!
To follow the wind
the whole day to spend!
Butterfly, oh, butterfly
so pretty and so shy!
So fly away and play
and have a butterfly day!

Andrew F. Makatura, Jr.

Untitled

I have no life
but I have death
Sweet death
what would death
be like
would it be fun
would it be boring
like life
do we already know
what death is
are we dead waiting
to be born
Are we born waiting
to meet death
what would death be like
what would being born be like.

Michell Bartelheim

Marshall

Been years gone by since yesterday;
now, this day, too, has passed;
fading into memories
better laid to rest.
Thoughts of loss are more than few
as darkness falls again;
it's always when I miss you most,
now, as well as then.
The day's distractions hidden, by
the shadows all as one;
can't sabotage the feeling that
a great wrong has been done.
I speak to you without my tongue
and, also, pray you hear
that I would be there if I could
and you would be right here.
I thank all Heaven for the time
my life you did so bless;
even though you're long since gone,
I love you nonetheless.

Shannon S. Soder

Why

As I sat on my bed and wondered
why,
I guess I dozed off after a long,
long cry.
I always thought they loved,
each other dearly,
But now I guess I see it
more clearly.
I love my parents and
will forever,
But I guess they really
don't belong together.

Rachel Bailey

The Flight

I was a child
as free as a roaming spirit
I was desire
the touch of a caressing hand
I was fate
meeting you at every corner
I was free
a gypsy wildfire in the wind
Yet I was water
meeting you at every turn of your head

But all I was
was what I had wanted
And all you were was the sky
untouchable as a dream of mine
And what we found
was a touch of fire
An eternal flame
that burned bright...

Janice Marie Napolitano

Past

Never again,
Like never before.
Shall never again,
And never more.

Present and future,
Past and before.
Past and present,
Future and more.

Dwell on the past,
Never more.
Live for the future,
Like never before.

Take hold of the present,
Leave the past behind.
Don't loose the future,
It's so hard to find.

Melissa Jones

Regret

A weaver, working in the dark,
creates a tapestry.
And when he looks at what he's made,
mistakes are all he'll see.
"If I change this, and re-do that,
how lovely it will be."
So all mistakes, corrected thus,
unseen by you and me.
We all are weavers, weaving lives,
all working without sight.
And all mistakes that we have made
are seen, when brought to light.
No change of acts or circumstance
to make past failures right,
life's flaws are not rewoven so,
but lived with, day and night.

M. A. Brown

Pumpkins

Pumpkins give a spook a scare
Out the window they will stare
Pumpkins give a great big fright
Cut them out and what a sight
Look at them; what a glow
All those pumpkins in a row!!!

Fatima Alikhan

Nicholas

An angel from heaven.
Eyes full of promise
and faith,
Laughter full of innocent
joy.

A pure heart
That loves without
Looking too deep,
And arms that hug
With healing comfort.

Thus is the bliss
Of sweet Nicholas.

Sally A. Perry

"Insomnia"

Sleep come take me
To the place I want to be
It is so plain to see
Only sleep can set me free!

Dreams come take me
On a cloud is where I want to be
Going further than the eye can see
Only sleep will set me free!

Fantasies come take me
To the place I want to be
Another time, anther place
Only sleep will set me free!

The night is so long
I wonder what I did wrong
As you lay there asleep
All I can do is weep.

So sleep come take me
To the place I want to be
Yes, only sleep can set me free!

Debra L. Hynum

I Have Finally Won The Chase

As I glance around the vacant room,
My eyes fall on the knife.
I know that I can do no more
Except to take my life.

I shut my eyes to shield them from
Its iridescent glow.
And as I near the silver blade,
I feel the tension grow.

I slowly raise my Savior,
To my trembling chest.
My mind begins to feel at ease,
Knowing soon that it can rest.

Pain overwhelms my body,
As I slowly break the skin.
As it plunges to my heart,
My soul cries from within.

I float above my body now,
Starring at my pale white face.
My expression is not of pain but peace,
I have finally won the chase.

Valerie Stuart

My Friend

My friend a friend,
a friend till the end.
A friend you are now
a friend you will always be
my best friend
for the whole world to see.
You have always been there
in good times and bad
for all the happy moments
and so many of the sad.
You know when to listen
what to say when I am blue.
You are my friend.
So rare. So true

Kimberley Roby

Sometimes

Sometimes the sky is blue,
Sometimes I want to be with you.
Sometimes the rain falls,
Sometimes your popularity falls.
Sometimes you're angry,
Sometimes you're sad.
Sometimes you are mad at the stuff
you never had.
Sometimes you are right,
Sometimes you are wrong,
and there is no way to end this song.

Falynn Needham

"As We Keep Up The Faith"

As you go along each day
ask God to help you pray.
As you continue to seek His face
ask God to bless you in a special way.
As you lean upon the Lord
ask Him to keep us on one accord.
As we know that He's soon to come
ask God to let His will be done.
As we keep up the faith
we must continue to pray.
As we continue to pray
and turn from ungodly ways
the Lord will bless us all the days.

Lagranda A. Dickerson

Mother

M is for the many times
she kissed my tears away;

O is for the open arms
that seemed to guide my way;

T is for the trusting smile
that lit her face anew;

H is for the happiness
that stuck to her like glue;

E is for the emptiness
that was quickly put to sleep;

R is for my radical mother
who is a treasure I'll always keep.

Marianne Podgorski

Blendings

As the darkness of last night
    slowly blends with today's dawn,
    the early risers are at work
Picking bugs from off the lawn.

As the dew on the landscape
    slowly blends with the
    atmosphere,
    the misty clouds evaporate
To let the morning sun appear.

As the sunshine peeking through
    slowly blends with break of day,
    last night was God's refresher
To help all creatures on their way.

As the family stirs from slumber land,
    stardust blends with morning light.
In a way it's sad to realize
    gone forever is last night.

Anna B. Simmons

Clouded Misery

The pinkish purple
shadow of ships,
Collides and results in a massacre,
And ends with a curtain of black.

Cathy Lewis

Ocean

On the end of a long sandy beach,
Children jump and yell
Eager to splash in the water.
A young baby cries out of happiness.
Nothing can compare to this.

Stephanie Fay

The Garden

In my heart dwells a secret place,
Where a flower grows,
The garden is fertile and damp,
All the seeds set in rows.

From the sky the rain pours down,
And the cold wind blows,
Pelting the earth with the rains,
Underground the seed await.

Sun warming the earth,
And the bush shoots forth,
A lush green crown,
Where a single rose grows.

Linda Rose Voigt

Silent Memories

The mother's words,
complete silence in a
trace of eternity.
A solemn smile appears on the lips
of the dying.
The dark abyss of the crashing sea,
a reminder of the comforting womb.
A weak heart, a faithless lover,
and a stonecold stare,
A celestial cloud soon storms, and
the dying remember.

Jill C. Platt

The Autumn Sea

The autumn sea has adopted
    a new facade
As its pulsating rhythm
    beats eternally, to and fro.

Its mood is tranquil,
    unruffled and serene.
Yet wary, as threats of storms
    darken its shores.

White grains of sand
    once spread smoothly
Now stand heaped in terraces
    upon the shore.

An eerie feeling
    descends upon one
Seeking quiet repose
    amid nature's beauty.

Has the sea really changed
    by the winds of autumn?
Or has the mightiest artist painted
    a scene depicting the autumn sea?

Peter Paul Rice Sr.

Tomorrow

We were promised so much happiness
So little hurt and pain
The sunny days tomorrow
Would block out today's rain
Our dreams were filled with love
The future filled with hope
But now we've thrown it all away
We're at the end of our rope
The smiles and the laughter
We thought would always last
Are now just distant memories
A reminder of the past
The sky once filled with sunshine
is grey and bitter cold
We've lost our grip on reality
A grip we could not hold
There's no where else to turn to
No where else to hide
Who knows what tomorrow will bring
Who knows if we'll survive.

Kim Jansen

The Silence

Dark, hurt and betrayed
is my soul
The darkness she has put
upon me
Disrespect, terror and hatred
I have experienced throughout
This lonely depressed thing
called life
The silence calls upon me
calling for the soul that is
withheld, withdrawn and kept within
She calls for it
it is reached
It is torn
then melted away

Kimberly Ann McGowan

Acquiesce

We're strung along like puppets
Connected by a string
We take what we can get
Accepting anything

Not daring to be different
We try to just fit in
We listen to what's in print
Not what's from within

Marching to the beat
Of someone else's drum
Trying to compete
To be the most popular one

We judge by what is seen
Not by what is heard
The outcome is obscene
And also quite absurd

If we all were who we are
And not what our peers make
We could go so far
With what we might create

Adria Siraco

Masterpiece

Soul aflame,
Bleed your color
With a stroke

Sorrow tip-tow into
Shape, line

Slice your fingertips
And paint your passion
Of red

Empty a soul,
Caress the ground
With figure

Heart be lifted
To the creation

Of a Masterpiece

Wendy M. Mossman

A Letter To A Friend

Remember Emma, our Emma
with the soft brown hair,
the freckled face peeling
from a hot summer sun.
Hazel eyes we looked into
and saw a young girl dreaming.

We swam in the river,
raced with the wind.
She could spit like a boy
whistle through her teeth
she learned how to charm.
You took her to the game
I took her to the prom.
She was lovely.

She came home today
in a plain pine box
home from the war,
our Emma.

Fay Drewery

Communication

In Memory of Robert passed on 6/17/96.
It has been with us through out history
much of it is imbedded in love
though tone of voice
speaks from the heart
a hug tells of all the good
and dreams live on forever

Robert C. Rindfleisch

Silver Trees

Silver trees,
all bright and shiny,
some are large,
yet some are tiny.
Hear them creak,
as they glisten,
hear them,
listen... listen.
Watch them sway in the breeze,
watch some more,
watch them touch and tease.
When you watch them long enough,
still to leave, it will be tough.
Silver trees,
all bright and shiny,
some are large,
yet some are tiny.

Douglas Gernat

Untitled

When the moment I saw you
I knew it wouldn't be the same
It was hard that day
Because I wanted to stay

As days pass by
You appear in my eyes
Once again, that very day
I always wonder why
You move me like the River
That runs throw
You make me feel the flow
Ever step that I'm with you
Makes my love feel so true
I just wanted you to know
When the moment I saw you.

Charles Phelts

First Love

She is the most beautiful thing
in the whole world
As stimulating as the sunrise
As soothing as the sunset
My love for her is a wide as the
open night
The stars endlessly reminding of
high times
And like the comfort of the waves
rolling into shore
She is in my life and gone again
Only to appear on a warm summer breeze
In an afternoon daydream beneath the
cool shade of an isolate tree
Peacefully interrupting reality,
temporarily leaving me with a euphoric
sensation
Which never seems to last long enough.

Joseph Michael Paris

Dew Between My Toes

Dew between my toes
Cool sighs on my gravel callused
Sunshine Summer Feet

Dark Night
Warm humid air hugs
me not hot,
but a touch that I revel in.

Wisps of long hair
On a back porch, that
catch the tree's green
tales of when they ruled
the summer.

But we do now,
the hot rocks under my feet
are gone,
only your cheek
breathing as softly as a baby against
my face

And the dew between my toes

Thomas Vandervort

Eternity

I am a body of water,
constant in motion.
The day I become stagnant
Will be the day I die.
My death may come quickly
or it may go slow
time enough for algae to grow.

I am an ocean
moved by the moon and stars
The night they do not shine,
is the end of my time.

Tammi L. Clifford

3-M's

Malcolm, Martin, Mandela
  three good fellows.
One tried to bring peace
  and what happened? More grief.
One had a dream
  to let freedom ring.
One got locked away
  for speaking his own way.
And for the lives they spared
  it was a good share.

Lisa Ann Hill

Suicide

Within my head the options flow,
The choices are evident.
Either continue this life of woe,
Or maybe death will let me attend.
I look at the nature
Of others and see the laughing
At the pain that I harbor.
Why can I find no solacing?
Life has nothing to offer,
I prepare for my termination,
And pull the trigger.
But the choice is not sound,
With life I am bound.

Victoria Murray

No Forgiveness

The thought of you
came to mind.

The good times we shared
and more I know
we should have had,

If I had not picked
the road I chose.

Now I know,
some of the choices
I made were wrong
and hurt a lot of
people, especially you.

I am sorry for the hurt
I caused you
I wish I could make
you see how sorry I am.

The way I feel for you
will never change.

But, I know I could never
ask or get your forgiveness....

Terri Stechmann

Refuge

Out there in the world so vast
The dangers lay in wait
I'm glad my family keeps me in
So safe behind our gate

At times I try to venture forth
They're quick to chide and scold,
"No tellin' what you'll meet out there
Amid the dark and cold"

So I return to our grand porch
Stretch out to feel the sun
I'm free from harm of any kind
From morn 'til day is done

Oh, there's our dog across the walk
He's fleshy, old and slow
I'll just go and tease a bit
No one will ever know

He's laying down, I think I'll sneak
Up to his sleeping mat
I can do just as I please
I am the family cat!

Sheri Carafelly

I Am Confused

Is it morning, or is it night?
Is it day yet or being soon?
I am confused -
  Seems to me, than sometimes
  Is day so bright,
  But then again, the wind and the rain,
  Break on my windows pane,
  Interrupting my sleep,
  I am so confused -
Thoughts are coming and going,
I don't no where to turned what to
retain and what to discard,

  I am confused

Gunta M. Smits

Magdeline

In a small village
Hut made from stone
Under supper table
She huddles in her home

Knocking at the door
Another dying man
She reaches out to touch
His cold lifeless hand

Pictures on a postcard
Dream of brighter days
Someday it could happen
She will get away

Leave behind the fighting
The sorrow and the pain
A miserable existence
Her struggle all in vain

Magdeline was killed
In a bloody raid
Shell that pierced her body
Made in the U.S.A.

Lawrence W. Addison

Saying Goodbye

When someone you love is sick
The Family is weeping inside.
Each in their own way
Telling you to keep on fighting.
And everyone knowing you try.
But the pain you suffer
is too much to bear.

No matter what, you have to keep up
the fight...
To stay with the ones you love
You try with all your might,
yet sleep is hovering above.

But maybe...
you never know.
Your sickness will miraculously
disappear.
And life will be the same again
year after year.

April Hagerman

Ace

I ran above the dune
to find; a breeze
that wasn't there.

And the ace I'd always
carried; didn't seem
as mysterious.

The tidal wake of dreams
I'd sought; receded
solace shore.

But, my ace then parted
sea to find; I'd been
prepared for more.

So help me God...
I think I'm going away
from you.

Cherishing the ace
we'd; always found
on Sunday.

Lee Angel

True Feelings

More of you is never enough
Intensity runs high
Keeping my heart focused on you
Every time we say good-bye.

Wanting you always near me
Enraptured by your touch
Immense feelings captivate me, I'm
Drawn into your clutch.
May I grab you and take you far
Away with me, and then
Never exist to the world we know, we'll
Never be heard from again.

Christine Berghorn

Ode To An Onion

There is a saying - may be true,
About two things - I'll tell to you.
An apple eaten once each day

George D. Earnshaw Jr.

Jeff Stadtherr

For every pedal on a flower,
Symbolizes my love for you.
For every leaf on a tree,
is for all the times I missed you.
For every piece of grass,
is how many times I thought of you.

Sarah Josephson

The Wings Of An Angel

As I slip into the night
  to this far away place
There are people all around me
  but I recognize no face.
Emotions run wild
  from ecstasy to fear
My heart beats much faster,
  for what am I doing here?
On the streets there is turmoil
  I sense agony and pain.
Truly there is nothing here
  for me to gain.
With uplifted arms, I stretch
  my hands to the sky
My feet are swept up
  and like an eagle I fly.
With ease I sail, and with
  confidence I sing,
For I am being carried
  by an Angel on her wing.

Donna Whiteside

Prism

Open the Bible,
From there
  take out a handful of
  sand from Galilee Beach.
Scatter it into the air.
It receives bright sun light
Becoming glittering and dazzling sand.

We are, Today
  a handful of sand
  of Galilee Beach;
Receiving the same light
Glittering in different tinges.

Kim Ingee

Before Me

Look at me and you will see
Others are none, because I am One

But before me were my parents
The clue for you is my parents are Two

But before my parents, my grandparents were more
Now think and think that number comes to Four

Great-grandparents came before those four
You know the Great counted up to Eight

And then there were my great-great-grandparents
Notice that great is now written twice
The number Sixteen is really nice

My family tree goes on before me
It never stops as you can see
Great three times will end my line
Their number was not few
Since the total was Thirty-Two

Rosetta Smoot Roberson

Our Family Prayer

I've just returned from those I love
Though they're not here but up above
Why is it Lord they had to leave
Just when they know were so in need
I know they're "there", and praying too
And asking you to help them thru
So listen Lord to our dear souls
They want, us here, to reach our goals
So many things we always ask
How can you Lord, complete your task?
Please end our special family woes
Or show us how to cope with those
Instill in those who need it most
The spirit of the Holy Ghost
We love them all, as you do too
So show them how to come to you
We thank you too, in humble prayer
For all the good things, that we share
So bless our family Lord - you know them all
And we'll be praying till we hear your call

Anne M. Bostwick

Blue

Blue, one of the infinite colors God allows man to see.
Blue, the color, for now, describes my
personality.

Blue here, Blue there.
Blue designs running through my mind.
Blue, I feel the color Blue.

Blue, within itself, holds infinite shades.
An emotion, emotions, a personality, a piece of a personality.
A color, colors, an event, events.
Childhood, adolescence, adulthood.

A favorite color, for awhile or for a lifetime.
A metaphor, metaphors. A form of communication.

Blue.
Unlike yellow, orange, green, red.
It stands alone.
Its understanding translated through art and
ultimately through feelings.

Blue.
A feeling.

James D. Miller

"Life"

Life is like a flower,
it begins as a small seed.
As a seed you water it,
as life you nurture it so it'll grow.

There are times when the flower will bloom,
the happy times is when life blooms.
A flower may lose a petal or a leaf,
in life there are sad times and grief.

Flowers are beautiful,
and so is life.
But just as flowers wilt,
life may end.

Seeds off of wilted flowers will float in the wind,
and the wondrous cycle will soon start again.

Mary Moorman

About The Sea

A friend of mine he came to me
And asked me news of the sea
I said to him in a hushed tone
One night at a tavern, that I was alone
And he looked at me and looked around
Too noticed that drink and food did abound
I said to him in a quiet tone
That obviously they all were not alone
And then a pirate I think did reveal
That they were dining there too, to understand
And I asked of this man what did he there
And he walked out with them too

So I sat there and I remembered the sea
And too I thought how good it was to me

And I as always wondered why I was
always alone

The answer, pray tell was that I
remembered the River named Rhône.

Karen Seykora

That Night

I think about that night each and every day.
The night you went away, the night you couldn't stay.

You were trying to be a friend, he'd had to much to drink,
If he had just stopped, stopped to think.

So you got into the car, ready to take him home,
It wasn't very far, yet you couldn't have known.

As you began to drive you went a little too fast,
you rounded the curve, as your car began to swerve.

The car flipped over, as he went flying,
you were trapped inside, helplessly dying.

I can't imagine what went through your mind,
as your eyes slowly closed, leaving the world behind.

It was hard for all who knew and loved you,
your fiance, me, your sisters, and mom and dad too.

Now I sit here on the exact day nine years later,
with tears in my eyes, yet I know you're living with our creator.

I guess the reason I wrote this poem is just to say,
I miss you Aunt Lois, and I think of you every day.

Kelly Baker

I Miss You, Son

Almost a year has come and gone
Since Mother's Day has past
And still no word has come from you
My heart is sinking fast

I worry that you'll wait too long
To realize, my son
The war you've waged against your mom
Was never truly won

"Don't contact me!" Your words were harsh
My aching heart won't mend
Can it have been so serious
To lose your lifelong friend?

Your birth was painful for us both
But after, it was fun
We played and cried and otherwise
Were proudly Mom and Son

Appear it does that what we had
Is buried with the past
But how I pray, each passing day
I'll hear, "Hi, Mom," at last.

Barbara G. Ferrell

Love

What do I love? I love family, animals, friends, writing, reading, books, music, and candy.
When do I love? I love when some one is there for me, when I get my wants and needs, when I'm happy and with my family and friends and when I play the piano.
Where do I love? I love home, theme parks, arcades, school, and the beach.
Why do I love? I love because it's a strong feeling, and it describes what I feel when I love where I love why I love and how I love.
How do I love? It's just a natural born feeling, and it's a feeling that I hope never goes away.

Jamarisa Williams

My Way To You

It seems all my life, I've been making my way to you
I know now, I loved you even before I met you,
My life had no meaning until the day I saw you
I knew then it was not chance, but fate that led me to you
When that certain someone comes along
Once in a lifetime, just like the song,
Somehow you know you'll never love anyone else
It's as if you belong to him and not yourself...
Now that it's happened to me
I feel strange yet lucky you see,
That each step, each day I have lived, has brought you to me
It's clear throughout the years I've been looking for you,
I didn't know you, I hadn't met you it's true,
But when that moment arrived every feeling I had inside,
Made my heart stand still and cry...
I saw my life story unfold from my very soul, then I knew,
That all my life I had been making my way to you

Patricia B. Miller

If You Took Away The Means

If you took away the means-then maybe civil hostility would cease.
If you took away the disease-then maybe we could wait for real worth.
If you took away the truth-then maybe suffering would diffuse.
If you took away the skill-then maybe we could dance, from overkill.
If you took away the order-then maybe we would fall, in insignificant mortar.
If you took away the means-then maybe prolonging the dream, would end in effeminate screams.

John C. Neuhaus

Parents

A child needs parents, which God saw fit to give
to help him overcome the disappointments and hurt
this world often gives. Parents are looking
through special eyes, that only God could give.
Children can't see things that hurt and destroy,
they see only pleasure where hurt may arise.
Parents are here to direct us, though we seldom
understand. We question their wisdom,
my logic is better, and without knowing we defy
God's greatest gift to a child: "Parent." So help me
dear God when it seems my way's the best, to open my
eyes and acknowledge you're looking through my
parents' eyes, and with you at the head, how could
they be wrong? Help me think twice, where I usually act
with haste, and see they love me much more than I
know. Maybe then my disappointments will begin to
cease. Then life as it was meant may be happier
day by day just knowing you're watching through my
parents' eyes.

Charles Phillips, Jr.

A Traveler's Nuisance

I'm driving down the street.
I feel empty, no pain, no sorrow sweet.
My soul lies sleeping within my breast.
No surge of anger to speed my quest.

It is lying there, lying in the street.
A silver gray mound my eyes now meet.
Just a nuisance we travelers of roadways share.
Something to swerve about lying, motionless there.

I never stroked its fur, silky smooth or rough.
I never heard its voice, gentle sweet or deeply gruff.
I never saw it run with head held high.
I never saw it leap to catch the morning butterfly.

I thought of the child weary now from walking block to block.
The child who's arms still empty is to tired now to knock.
I asked what emergency had brought it here so soon to die.
I kept my eyes upon the roadway never asking why.

I gave thanks for tears that filled my eyes.
I gave thanks for I remembered how to cry.

Karen R. Mariani

Stems

Grieve with me, for I have lost;
Life has poured its fury down upon me like rain in April.

Comfort me, because fate has turned its tables,
And everything I though I wanted,
Is now out of reach.

Laugh with me, because sometimes the only good joke,
Is life itself.

Cry with me, because the Tulips we planted last fall didn't
Come up, and the tree in our front yard finally died.

Love me, because I am yours.
It began that way and will be so for all eternity.

Accept me, because I am myself,
And not even I understand me at times.

Hold me, because you're my mother;
And of all the people on this Earth,
It is you whom I admire and trust most.

Julia Pleasant

The Passing

History: Might it visit? But to the blind it is no more.
Now there is progress, and upon the past we close the door.

But, alas!, back then, 'twas the land and the hoe,
nature— such a mystery— the ghost of Burke and Cicero.

Then from the north, that terrible storm, enters
"enlightened" self-interest in its most twisted form.

By sixty and five, the world knew it had failed,
destroying our "myths" we so gloriously held.

So is it so wrong to bid them adieu?
For, down here, there remain only a few.

So goodbye to those who believed to the core,
those old Agrarians and a nation no more.

William Alan Polk

A Patch Of Blue

Today is cloudy and dreary
Not like yesterday.
Makes us know that winter has come
And summer has gone away.

Each season has its own beauty
That glows then fades away.
It takes each one to make the year
And stores up memories day by day.

But no matter if the skies are dark
And the rain is pouring through,
Just lift your eyes up to the skies
To find a patch of blue.

Our lives are just like the seasons,
Sometimes up and sometimes down.
It always brightens up again
When we pass on a smile instead of a frown.

When things are dark and gloomy,
Find that patch of blue.
You'll find the hand of our dear Lord,
Reaching down for you.

Ruth Pulliam

My Last Bequest

As for as my possessions left on this earth,
it will take little time to tally its worth.

No I won't be noted for my wealth or fame,
though many surround me, most don't know my name.

As a daughter I know I sometimes left you in a stew,
but I hope you remember my loyalty, and that I loved you.

I hope as your sister, as you remember when,
who was there for you, some fixes you did get me in.

As for you few people, yes you my true friends,
please remember I didn't break, though I did often bend.

And for my precious children and grandchildren, if I leave nothing
else behind, I pray you remember what I said about being kind.

And remember the part, do unto others as you would have them do
unto you, most important of all to your on self be true.

So folks if your searching my estate for my fortune and fame,
my heart aches for you, you've brought me shame.

But to the lives I have crossed along life's highway,
I hope I have helped some make it through another day.

If this was true I will leave here rich and fulfilled,
for it was for you, my life to you I willed.

Diane Rabb

Jo

We met like the first breeze of spring,
gentle, cool
With promise of what summer would bring

Your presence pervaded every fiber of my being,
Slowly, deliberately
Until I was enveloped and full of feeling.

You reached in and opened my soul,
Lovingly, knowingly
Consciousness peaks and interest becomes a goal.

We touched and shared as good friends do,
Tentatively, carefully
Little did I know I was falling in love with you!

Summer is here, the soft breezes flow,
Scented, warm.
Your essence abounds, wherever I go.

Whatever happens is yet to be
Hesitantly, hopefully
Destiny, will bring you, permanently to me.

Ken Swan

Nowhere To Go But Down

The innocence forever lost.
As I sit while thoughts crossed.
Knowing what I was.
Now not knowing who I am.
As I sit amongst hoodlums.
Like a flower that becomes old,
as do thoughts turn cold.
Searching alone in the dark,
waiting for a warm fire to spark.
To find what I need,
As I watched the horn shaped human proceed.
Where he says "I am like him"
Telling me each and every sin,
these he'll never forget,
But I've lived to regret.
The crimes I commit like clothes that always fit.
A feeling of comfort, that shouldn't be.
As he casts his shadow over me.
For he's in control, because he owns my soul.

Bayhun Erpanir

One Love

You once said you loved me and
you'd always be true. You'd never
leave me and I believed you; but you left
me caring alone in despair. My heart was
broken but you didn't care.
Do you sleep well at night? Do
you miss me at all? Was the phone off
the hook when I tried to call? Remember
I told you that you would Regret the day
that you left me for the girl you just met.
You said this is true love, a love that
will Last. Now you're crying it's a love in the
Past. Do you sleep well at night? Do
you miss me at all? Would the phone still
be busy if I tried to call?
We all make mistakes. Some big
some small. Some are forgiven. Some not
at all.

Mary Bigelow

Comet Shine

Oh great comet streaking thru the night
You're so very full of light

You stream above O'Keeffe's Abiquiu
With tail long and marvelous view

Your journey takes you so far
Now drawn into the arms of our sun star

The solar winds blow on high
As you happen to pass us by

You move among the stars so bright
There's not one who can match your sight
William N. Welborn

My Song

She's moving on-listening and singing a song
How ironic-it's describing her life
Who she used to be-that girl, she sounds like me
With great expectations and aspirations of someday becoming a wife
As she reads through pages-depicting her life
She's reminded of how she used to be
Where did things go wrong-this that I've become
No this girl now-she's not me
The things her love's gone through-hearts broken in two
Where does she run-when she's feeling alone
Once to a mother-now to a lover
Where will this woman build a home.
Sorting through her head what she feels in her heart
Is it her feeling, fears, or just voices
Her mind-her own? Still without a home
Life gives her many, but little choices.
Feeling alone-she finds herself in a song
No not this one-this one is wrong.
Don't put yourself here, can't you see-it's clear
You'll always be where you least expect you belong
LaDonna Baker

Standing By The Wall

A place, for the wealthy
Is rich and full of life.
While the poor live in poverty,
A life unappreciated
The poor stand by and watch them go to parties
Wishing they could do the same
Wishing they could trade places
And let the wealthy be poor.

People take advantage
Of what they have
They think they will always have what they have
But then one day
They lose it all
And they will become the poor people
Standing by the wall.
Andrea Lowe

Promised

Beauty we see it all around. From a bright sunny day. To colorful leaves during fall on the ground. Beauty for me is a luxury that I treasure in the things I see. Beauty is in the landscapes such as the mountains and their trees in bloom, it is also the desert on a spring afternoon. Beauty is a gift from the one in the heavens. I can't wait to see the fulfillment of Psalms :37 We think we have beauty and we do. But I look to the bible and its Prophecy to come true. Would it not be grand to live our lives in Jehovah's promised land.
J. T. Waters

The Warrior!

The village has changed, a warrior is gone.
There is no rest, until the dawn.

The village is sad, and we cry our tears.
We all hoped for so many years.

We ride our horses of steel and chrome,
To say farewell, for God has called him home.

But the village elders will tell the new,
About the brave and young warrior true.

How his bike roared in the day, and shined at night.
He was so full of love, and ready to fight.

From the village to heaven hear these words,
warrior true!

From your brothers and sisters,
"Mark, we will always love you."
Gary Prado

The Crying Wolf

As the river flowed gently between
the mountain that was so majestic and clean.
In the gleaming moon beam light,
appeared a howling wolf that was white,
which caused a young indian boy to be in fright
of a wolf that was very forceful and mean.
The indian boy was so keen
in escaping unseen
from the crying wolf.
Victor Walters

Untitled

I see his face and after wave of pure irrational rage hit me with their sickening force
A red mist blinds my eyes, and a whooshing fills my ears
A primal howl burst from my throat, a shiver through me tears

I run at him to do I know not what
My hand rises of it own accord, I try to stop it but...
He screams once it's over, Oh God what have I done
I've signed Satan's contract with ink made of blood.

Then somewhere down deep, down deep in my soul.
I hear someone laughing, I here someone call
He beckons to me with an evil grin
He knows I've been beaten he's seen my sin
and that's all I see forever more, his grin darkness and nothing more
Elizabeth Staley

If You Knew

If you knew how much I love you,
How I cry for you at night,
If you knew how long I've prayed for your salvation,
If you knew how much Christ loves you,
More love than I could ever give,
How He died upon a curs-ed tree,
So that you and I might live,
If you knew how much He cares for you,
If you knew the price He paid,
If all at once you saw the place
Where all my burdens I have laid,
If suddenly you realized what death will really bring,
You'd rush to that wonderful sacred cross
And give Him everything.
Joanna Likness

Grandpa

In every sunrise, every mountain,
   every rainbow, every star,
I'm loving you, I know you're there,
   Yet, I'm not sure where you are.

Are you sitting here beside me?
   Or were you that bird that flew?
I feel the wind blowing in my ear
   And I'm wondering if it's you.

Are you reading over my shoulder?
   Are you holding my hand right now?
I want to tell you I love you,
   I'm not sure if I know just how.

I can feel you wiping my teardrops,
   And asking me, please, not to cry.
But I'm missing you, loving you so much,
   And I'm wondering why you had to die.

Tara Lynne Bryant

Sonnet For Susan

Fair mist of cool morning you bare
special memories to my mind;
near-sacred time together share,
intricate wove tapestry hues
of thoughts of old and learning new
depths unknown for another time.
To seek your eyes and touch your hand
softly caress your gentle skin,
threads of a whole no warmth endow
save chance a gift you left somehow;
sweet essence of you that binds the seam,
fills my senses and sets the scene
act two to this, our passion play.

Scott M. Enerson

To The One I Love

Instead of loving you, I am hurting you...
Instead of protecting you, I am losing you...
Why, oh why, only my heart seems to know,
Is it that I take you for granted, only god knows...

I realize you're hurting; and so am I...
I love you so much, so tell me why?
Why do I do these stupid things...
When I know it brings me lots of nothings...

It's been years I've been like this!
Help, oh God do I know exists...
My mind says no. My body says yes,
I hurt much too, you know, I guess..

We can't, we're on a two way radio,
I say one thing, you do and I go...
We don't get together, I know,
Lack of communications is the flaw...

But please, I beg of you, I hope you know,
I love and hurt and ache for you and you saw,
Let's sit down and talk and we'll know,
Respectively you're me, I'm you and we sow...

I Love You!

Marie-Nicole Dekermarek

Untitled

So happy I cried, so lonely I shook.
So desperate I tried, yet so anxious to look.
To see better days and make today seem so right.
Then the thoughts of you leaving
Just wouldn't come to sight.
Feeling you hold me
   makes it all worth the wait.
For my love for our survival holds the key to that gate.
Yet more than living
   this must be the start
      of our love bringing life...
With this together, how could we ever part.
Growing strong, waited this long...
I love you darlin, sing me your song

Erin Counihan

Starvation Of The Heart

Deep inside my heart
Lodged behind many false fronts
A hunger cries out to be filled
A hunger
An aching tear inside of me
From that single, silent tear
Trickling down
From the windows of my soul
Reveals to the callous world
The malnourishment of my heart
I search my mind for the answer
Capable of relieving the cancerous pain
A longing continually gnawing at my insides
There is not even a morsel for me
While others are enjoying
A feast of success
A hunger forces me
Into a dark world of inability
Where I die of starvation

Kenneth R. Taylor

"Memories"

I make it just find from
9 to 5 because I'm used to your
routine of going to work. I
wait a while. Then my
inner voice says he wont be here
anymore for he is dead. So
where do I go from here my
darling please tell me this won't
be long for I'm used to your
love and kindly advice. Yes people
are helpful and awfully nice
but they can't take the place
of the love of a man for his wife
Lord please hold my hand and help me along
I'll stumpful I'm sure but there
are others who need me and they tell me
in time the grief will grew dim and leave
me with memories that are
lovely and kind.

Arlene Burnum

Words From Within

Please feed me when I'm hungry
Please change me when I'm wet
Please put your arms around me when I'm all upset
Please teach me good manners
Please praise me when I'm good
Please keep the Lord within me, just like I knew you would.

Tammy Meffert

Forgotten Love

He told her things had changed,
She said she didn't feel the same.
He told her good-bye,
And she tried not to cry,
As he took his class ring away.

Months have gone by
And others have come, but it's not the same.
She quickly wipes the tears from her eyes,
And knows she is his
Forgotten Love.
Rhiannon L. Kitts

Tsunami

Wave of destruction, a tide.
Torrents of rain and wind
Like a brutal storm
Caused by earthquakes
Rips through cities sparing none.
A peaceful town will soon be on the run,
From a

Tsunami!!!
Chris J. Lafayette

How Can We Go Wrong

When we look at God's creative paintings in the sky...
And knowing the beauty will surround us until the day we die...
   How can we go wrong

When our years of struggle have weathered the storm...
And our visions, our hopes and dreams have been born...
   How can we go wrong

When the love and caring of others is felt from afar...
And knowing peace will follow when there is an end to war...
   How can we go wrong

When life's large problems turn into something small...
And the joy of living takes priority over all...
   How can we go wrong

When a loved one walks in and your heart skips a beat...
And knowing the love that fills you up will never feel defeat...
   How can we go wrong

When we respect each other from the time of one's birth...
And see the good in someone and account for their worth...
   How can we go wrong

Another glorious day is upon us, another night so long...
Cherish the gift of life, and live it right... How can we go wrong.
Lydia Peterson

Our Country

The Country we love is a troubled place;
No longer friendly, but an angry race.
No longer trusting, but ready to fight;
What can we do to make it right?

Perhaps we must learn to listen more,
Instead of talking of going to war.
Our hungry and homeless are dying each day,
We as Americans must search for a way.

How can we help others when we're not strong?
With our mind and hearts we must right this wrong.
We must learn to love and trust the Lord first,
Before we can ever quench another Country's thirst.
Rose Ann Ray

A Policeman's Prayer

When I am on my duty, Lord
Protect me from all harm
Help me to be alert and strong
To never give cause for alarm.

Let your light be in my eyes
Your wisdom in my speech
Let me live to give honor and glory to You
Help and happiness to others, as far as I can reach

I will try to fill my calling, Lord
To give my best without alarm
To guard my every neighbor
And protect them from all harm

I know a madman's bullet
May some day be for me
Please Lord, keep my wife and family
In peace and serenity.

Grant to all of us, I beg of you
The gifts of tolerance, humility and love
That We may all walk in your way
And find peace from the Lord in Heaven above.
Anna H. Balsinger

Swingin' An' A Singin'

Make you wanna snap your finger
Make you wanna dance along
Got that fever baby, got it all night long

Hearin' those broken chords
Feelin' the jive at five
Gotta dance, gotta snap, gotta sing along
It has to be all night long

Do wop do wop do wop do wop
Mmm that band is hot
Got me outa my chair
With the notes in the air
Play that boys, play it all night long

It's closin' time and the bell did chime
Have floatin' chords in my head
Have them till I go to bed
Told you it last a while
Swingin' an' a Singin' all night long
Tiffany Ann Morin

Let The Walls Come Tumbling Down

As I sit upon a bench,
I hear different and glorious sounds.
The locusts buzz and so do the lights.
The wind carries the murmur of voices and music.
The next sounds I hear are those of joy and gladness,
Along with the weeping of my lonely heart.
My heart cries because I am all alone
Having put up powerful walls to keep from being hurt,
But in building them, I create sorrow and pain.
All it would take to tumble the walls
Would be for someone to seek me out and ask me to come,
...But no one does.

I gaze at the sky waiting for the stars to appear.
They are what I turn to for comfort and love.
When I see them, I feel God's great love
And my walls drop greatly.
His love is unending...like the sky.
His loved ones are as numerous as the stars.
So I continue to wait for someone to ask me to come,
...And for the stars to appear.
Jana Huggins

Paradise Proposal

Paradise, an island of sun
Together, on which, we can have fun
The day fades in to the long cool night
To see the sun set is a wonderful sight

Things such as these I compare to you
I think of you in everything I do
Our love is so strong that it can't be broken
So please accept this golden token

Together we can walk this beach called life
Listen my love, Would you be my wife?
I love you more than you can see
Lover of mine, Will you marry me?
Michael J. Smith

Dream's Door

The dreams that we dream
sometimes seem so vague.
Like being lost in the strangest of plays.
Hold onto those thoughts though
and learn what they mean,
for they influence your world much more
than it seems.
Your dreams are my dreams as is
everyone's.
Since the individuals that we have become,
have never forgotten we've always been one.
So unlock that door and dream a grand dream.
You'll fulfill your desires there,
Ask your soul be your guide there.
A world there awaits you,
With arms stretched out wide there!
Gayle Nutini

Untitled

As my dark days pass still there for me
How can He stand my distorted actions?
While I'm constantly building up stress to bring me down
He helps me through it all and lifts me up to be proud.
This is not so surprising but
I have grown to love him.
I love all his actions, and I love
the way he treats me in his kind and gentle ways
Not knowing if I could ever tell him
but I half to share my thoughts, I do love him.
I talk to him every day in, and day out.
But not yet am I able to say it out loud.
I guess I'm afraid of his reply.
Scared that it will bring a mistake,
one that will move him from me
and that he will never speak to me again.
Even the thought of that hurts
If and when he gets this
I want him to know that I have shared
My very intimate, most treasured feelings with everyone.
Rayan Lockwood

"The World Goes On"

My life grows on misery and complete discomfort
It flourishes on tears of heartache and melancholy
Sad as I am, the Unforgivable seems to be the inevitable.

Weary of body and soul
Tired of merely existing
All have forsaken, Save God
In whom I find tranquility.

Yet, the world goes on!
Carmen Church

Communicator

Recording thoughts is time consuming.
Wave lengths of communication,
filter down the avenues
as we keep the pen in motion.
The philosophers say letters are history.
We are informed.
There is knowledge in words
that balloons into events and feelings,
interacting in dialogue that changes the pace
as they wing their way across the miles.
Does it take a certain setting
to hold a pen and view ones place in history.
Then, why do we procrastinate?—
misrepresenting what truly belongs to another.
In the framework of life
sharing is a
necessity.
Berdelle Kragnes

My Best Friend

My Best Friend will help you out, he can feel your
pain, he will watch you round-a-bout, time and
time again.

My Best Friend will know your dreams, fill
your most desires, he can really help you out, cause
he is higher than higher.

My Best Friend will help you through, when
you're down and out, for he is really watching
you I know without a doubt.

For if you want to have this friend, you can only
seek, hurry now the time is near, that we'll be
at his feet.

If you want to have this friend, just kneel and
pray, cause if you don't the time is near, we'll
be with him someday.

Probably now you have seen who my best friend is, my
Best friend is Jesus Christ and that's the way it is.
Misty Ragsdale

Watching You

When I watch you,
cower before him
staring, speechless by his hatefulness,
wondering if he would ever ...
no, he would never say the three words
you long to hear.

When I watch you,
sit and hold back the anger you feel,
towards a man who is suppose to care for you,
sitting, waiting for the words
you have longed to hear for 17 years.

When I watch you
running to me for the love you ache to be given,
when you used to be as cold as he was.
Now with the confidence
you should of had all your life,
I stand up,
through your pain,
I stand up.
Jenne Vaske

She Is Somewhere Out There

I have hated the day I moved away
From the girl that could not say
She never wanted to be with me
So now I am trying to flee
From the pain in my heart
As it is being torn apart.
She is there and I am here
Standing looking out into the world with a tear
In my eye
As I begin to try
To rebuild my world that was torn asunder.
I just have to wonder
How many times I will go through this
With more relationships that are hit or miss.
I can still smell her perfume in the air.
I know for sure, she is somewhere out there.

Carl Williams

Brains

Well then he said to him
I don't know but you think that I'm just spaced out of my head
and he took his brain and gave it to him
to examine with his microscope.

Well when he took his brain out of his head
he felt dead with shock
cuz his brain was like at least ten times bigger
than his head was
and it had his name engraved upon it
his name only.

Then the other guy he took his brain out,
But he couldn't find it very easily
Because it was so tiny
And he wasn't sure if it was his anyway.

And he said that it wasn't fair.

Terry Foraker

Love Song

From a distance I could see her
For she had been there all along,
But she didn't see me, didn't stir
She just waited patiently singing them a love song.

Her children were awaken,
Their mother had just wanted to hear them speak;
No doubt, it couldn't be mistaken,
It was only their love that she did seek.

As the light brightened and darkness came,
There wasn't much that she could do
It was accepted, there was no one to blame,
The end had been decided, everyone knew.

She knew the day was going to end,
She could feel that it was time to rest;
But it was her children that she had to defend,
So she gave them love, all she knew best.

She tucked them in and turned out the light,
Knowing she'd love them forever, no matter how long;
She couldn't stop it, there was no reason to fight,
So she just waited patiently singing them a love song.

Melissa Wolf

Untitled

I had a good friend named Pat.
With whom I enjoyed a good chat!
A joke I did tell
Made her madder that Hell.
And she took off like the proverbial bat.

Dwight McCleary

"Vigil"

Keeping quite still, I look out my window
At a mockingbird sitting on the telephone wire.
She is there every day, rain or shine,
Outside my kitchen window
Up there on that wire.

What a lonely life
What a lonely vigil,
She seems to keep.

Is that what birds do?
Keep lonesome vigils sitting on telephone wires?
What do I know?
Perhaps she could be waiting for her mate.

So, every day, I see my friend,
Miss Mockingbird, there on her wire:
And I realize, I, too
Keep a lonely vigil here
Writing poems at my kitchen table.
What do I know?

Ashby H. White Jr.

People Watcher

Watching People go by
Everyone different, yet all the same
A people watcher sees.

Some tall, Some short
All going places, all coming back
a People watcher sees.

Keep Smiling, Keep Frowning
Trying to be accepted, trying to find friends
a people Watcher sees.

Working hard, Hardly working
Making fools of ourselves at one time or another
a people watcher Sees.

Trying to find our Independence
While conforming to our friends
The Ironies a people watcher sees.

Cristen R. Dougherty

Journey

Snow
Drifting tenderly, weaving in the open air.
Each flake slightly different from the other,
Travelling gently down the blue-gray path.
Falling, falling through time and space
Resting softly on the quilted earth;
A lonely tree branch, a warm roof.
Gathering to form a feathery plane.
Gentle snow angels appear
Whispering sweet offerings
To those who will listen.

Denise Coen

How Can It Be?

I say how can it be, trying to do what is right,
never being free from the pain of society. Making
mistakes, learning, yet being in a tomb of doom.
Seeing what could be good, but only feeling the
bad. Looking and searching, suspended in air,
wondering if the pain will ever end. Finally I
deaden the pain from within. No longer hurting, no
pain left inside, no more to give, no more to
hide. My body is lifeless, my mind is no more. I
finally died. In my final breath I cried out,
how can it be? I had so much more inside of me.

Donald R. Bosch

Shadow Wife

You gave to me a love so rare
Most lives are lived without it there
If only it were ours to share

Not in the shadows nor the dark of night,
But ever there though in the light
Lest it be but a widow's plight

Now we know all that has passed
Is but the future to be cast
That from the first, it was the last

Though tears, pain, trial, and strife
Are a lover's plague endured through life
I'd choose again the same to live

Even As A Shadow Wife...
Sandi Huston

"Passage Of Time"

You shouldn't have left
when we were so young;
of course back then
we had no say,
we couldn't even ask you to stay.

How do you feel now that we are all grown up
and you've missed so much of our lives?
We never asked you for anything but love.
You didn't fulfill your part of the deal.

Nearly sixteen years I've held this anger
while my mom wiped away my tears.
The sad thing is dad that I never called out for you
when afraid of my fears.

I know you must have had your reasons
and for those reasons unknown to me,
I can't go on feeling this way,
and although I'll never know what it's like to have a father
in its true sense,
I want you to know that I forgive you.
Meghan Ferland

Afro Hair

I had a big Afro hair,
Swaying all up in the air,
Then I saw a blue jay,
Bringing some sticks and hay,
And he and his family were living up there.
Hyuk Kwan

On Stormy Shores

My breath was taken away by the wind
As I stood on that lonely, lonely shore
Watching the thundering waves come in
Taking me back to a time before
When I would go out at night
And watch the menacing clouds draw nigh
With their brilliant beams of light
Flashing through the sheer black sky
Bringing with the pounding, driving rain
Amazed at the fury of the storm
Washing away that great ugly stain
From a land that was savagely torn
Guy H. Anderson

Untitled

My heart beats slowly,
Gently pushing the blood through my body.
My heart beats constant and steady;
A clock ticking away.
That same perpetual ticking
Is the time bomb that you have created within my body.
The instant I sense your presence,
My body explodes.
Oh, I long for your touch.
For you hold the only key
That can unlock my deepest desires.
You create a passion so strong, from the depths of my soul
That it screams to be set free.
Cathy Kenyon

Feeling Free

When I talk to you my heart pumps fast
When I talk to you my foot taps with class
When I talk to you I feel alive with pride
When I have a problem you always by my side
When I pray I feel you coming through
Without you I do not know what to do
You are my heart, my soul, my love, my life
You are the one that will get things right
"I'm Free"! "I'm Free"! As joy as can be
I love you Lord because you have been there for me.
Dale C. Sharp

"Horse Flesh"

Of course, a sword, is a warrior's need.
But oh! The importance of his steed,
so graceful, so swift, none can compete
from, his noble head, to his prancing feet.
White horses, kings, chose to ride,
but a prince, on his black, took pride
Indians, liked the flash of a pinto,
And just see the Arabians go.
Flecks of foam on massive chest
Loyally charging into the test.
Movies always profit, by a great mount
How many in Westerns, do we count?
On fox hunts, their jumping excels,
Their strength great, as muscle swells
Let's all stand and cheer, as they pass by.
Prancing along and keeping Old Glory high.
Horses helped provide food and transportation
To benefit all, in our great nation.
Reita Keeling

An Urge From The Past

Vibrations of immense joy and love,
Always flying high like a dove,
It's voice attracting your mind, pulling your soul,
To a quiet place, where there is surely no toll,

What a wondrous thing,
All the feelings of happiness it brings,
Whether its a bird chirping or a breeze,
It always fills you with ease,

So you must ask yourself one question,
Why we've stood against all the love, I've mentioned,
If only to enter nature's wide open door,
As man has once before.
Robert P. Hansen

Me

Looking around the world
I see
Many things that remind me
Of me

The sky
with all its changing colors
The sea
with its changing tides.
A book
with all the changing words.

But yet,

As still as
a mountain that reaches the sky.
As still as
a boulder in the sea. And
As steady as
the story the words make in a book.
Me,
always changing yet staying steady and still.

Richard E. Murphy

From A Car Window

A single house in a wide open field
A tire swing hangs from a tree in front
A blond-haired boy in a sweater bright red
   On the tire he swings
   Higher, then higher.

Is he lighter than air
Is he one with the breeze
   Or a willow bent and caressed by the breeze?

Is he on a roller coaster dipping and rising
Is he an astronaut careening in orbit
   Or an eagle soaring higher, then higher?

The thrill of the motion
The joy of the breeze
The blond-haired boy in a sweater bright red
   In command of the world
   In a world all his own.

Marie Martz Parry

Waterfall

The waterfall gushes,
rushes and stumbles,
churning, up down, splashing, bending, white frothy,
melody splashing,
sweet peaceful, melody.
The calm, quiet,
soothing, quietly, quietly,
as it slows
down, for the
night.
The WARM
crashing,
waves,
come over me and I,
push myself
further, further....
over the edge, cleansing me, washing me,
WATERFALLS.... are my tears for my life's trials.

Dorothy Kaliati

To Kara, My Special Child

My babe is broken, her wings won't soar,
She tries to flutter but yet stands still
Her gift from God not yet revealed;
Only his grace can save her still.

O what can make a mother's pain
Give her life to yet sustain,
Another bout of endless pain?
What in God's mind is so deranged
To let his children suffer so
When they need strength to thrive and grow?

Yet in her soul still lives the hope
Of yet another life sustained.

I pray for her that in her day
A miracle may be revealed,
That will allow her to grow and heal.
And yet be like a nightingale,
Whose wings can soar and make life real.

At last my china doll will smile.
And know that life is still worthwhile.

Susan Zoni

On That Morning

By the prophets they'd been told
That the grave could never hold
The son of God, and he rose on that third day.
And they found the tomb was bare
For the Savior wasn't there
On that morning when they rolled the stone away.

Just imagine her despair
When she found He wasn't there
And can't you see the tears that Mary shed?
But can't you hear the angel say,
"Fear not, have no dismay
For the one you seek is not among the dead".

Jesus knew He would not stay
Where they laid him in the grave
And He arose and set the captive free.
Some sweet resurrection day
He will carry us away
On that morning when He comes for you and me.

Leona Freeman

A Pear Sunset

It felt my life an overstuffed mess,
   With all that love passion, that burned and bound

The sighing, the dying, the leaving and the lying.
Those familiar mounts and valleys, in which I fed on love's delights,
Until I was nearly dead.

My life was overflowing with love
Great seas of love awash my heart,
Until it spilled over and over.

It is only in later deductions that I realize,
That there was not an inch that palpating chamber for me.

Now I do love the tender of that sumptuous feast,
The beggar's banquet, that I spread before, before you.

I need room in my love for me.
It has come to that.

So hand me that wonderfully ripened pear, over there,
And just a touch of camanbert, if I dare.

Please set it out on the veranda and you sit and watch the sun say
Good eventide to me.

Elizabeth M. Maffeo

The Symphony Of Love

The Symphony of Love is the sound of song and care
Expressed by Mothers everywhere.
It's the gentle breeze alive in the air
Playing the Symphony of a Mother's love.

Her compassion, care, love and concern,
light up the sky in happy return.
Showing that God has a plan
He placed in the Symphony of Love.

She nurtures, teaches, protects and guides
Wherein her heart love doth reside,
She gives of herself to one and all
In the Symphony of Love.

She is rare gift to cherish and hold
Given to us by God
This gift to us can't be measured in gold
It's found in her Symphony of Love.

Therese L. Nitsche

The Facade

As I look backwards in my mind's eye,
I see a little girl happily swinging on a tree swing.
Though she seemed happy there was a cloud over her head,
and she had a bruised heart.
She can't cry, she must hide her feelings.
If she could cry, her not tears would fall like rain.
Her heart felt as though it were a heavy rock.
She must not tell the secret.
When she feels like telling,
She experiences sharp fearful thoughts.
Her anger burned as red as fire.
She wanted to say you ruined my innocence, but her throat was tight.
Her eyes pierced through her guardian as though throwing pebbles at
   him.
It was important that her exterior wouldn't betray her pain inside.
She had to be tough as leather, so she wore a facade of happiness.
Even though years have gone by
she is surprised by feelings of pain, hurt, and anger that still
   exist.

Gisella Clay

A Brand New Man

I knew a man, who knew it all, or so at least it seemed;
Until the day he lost it all, his family, and his dreams...

He awoke one day to find himself, very much alone;
A king without his castle, a man without his home...

He was cast into a dungeon, and the keys were thrown away;
He didn't even want to live, to see another day...

His life it held no meaning, he no longer even cared;
And soon became a prisoner, to depression, and despair...

Just when he had lost all hope, and was brought down upon his knees,
A voice came from the darkness and whispered "Follow me"...

"I'll teach you how to live again, and I will restore your soul;
You'll never have to walk in shame, and you'll never be alone"...

Trembling... crying... he arose, to give life one more try;
To face it standing proud and strong, to put the past aside...

He learned to start each day anew, to cast away his fears;
To overcome the pain and sorrow, and to wipe away the tears...

Today, he is a brand new man, a captive finally free;
Living life for all it's worth, that brand new man is me...!

Christopher P. Corey

Mending Fences

The years have gone so swiftly by...
I know not where, but I do know why.
It's all a part of God's plan, you see...
But why did I let it sneak up on me?
He gave me many chances to prepare...
I ignored the warnings—I didn't have a care.
Now all the time I thought I had
Is mine to use no more...
Like looking through the windows
Of an "Out of Business" store.
Thoughts of many mistakes now occupy my mind...
How to make amends when I'm so far behind.
My advice to you, if you've fences to mend
Is to do them as you go...
Don't wait until the end.

LaPriel Dunford

"Buckskin Johnnie"

Johnnie's a hunter even though he's only two.
His crib is his hideaway
Where he dreams of hunting with you.
When he goes to dream land, He is a big hunting-man.

   Buckskin Johnnie there he goes
   Uses deerhide to make his clothes
   Shoots the dear and tans the hide,
   Buckskin Johnnie's known far and wide.

Now Johnnie also likes to fish
And when the weather's nice
Johnnie likes to catch his fish
Through holes in the ice.

   Buckskin Johnnie there he goes
   Uses a spear to make fish holes.
   He catches fish on every side
   Buckskin Johnnie's known far and wide.

Buckskin Johnnie there he goes
Uses deerhide to make his clothes
Shoots the deer and tans the hide
Buckskin Johnnie's known far and wide.

M. J. McCauley

The Assassination

What a great day it was,
   when it began.
No one knew how it was going to end.

The crowds of people greeting
   the President.
Not a harsh feeling
   was evident.

Driving along in Dallas that day.
No one knew the malice
   the assassin would display.

Shots rang out from the window above.
Then there was a shout for the one she loved.
When the news came that the President was dead,
Jacqueline sat and hung her head.

Watching the funeral procession that day,
The whole world was full of dismay.

When John Fitzgerald Kennedy was laid to rest,
There was only one final test.

The lighting of the eternal flame.
It remembrance of his name.

Jennifer Daniel

God Needed Another Angel

God needed another Angel
So He called your loved one to His side
They will take their place in the Kingdom
To watch over others and also be their guide.

An Angel will watch over you
In your journey through this life
They will often help and guide you
And protect you from all strife.

When you see a miracle happen
An Angel was there by their side
God keeps an eye on people
And Angels are their guide.

To be living there in Heaven
Your loved one has been blessed
For to be chose as an Angel
God only takes the best.
Matthew Scopelitis

Majesty On Ice

Majesty on ice lasts but a few minutes.
Determined by jumps and spins,
and who can get the judge to grin.
Very few make it look easy and many more make it look hard,
falling on a landing or pulling a jump figure skating is not for everyone.

Grinkov and Gordeyeva had such a majesty.
She was a ragdoll easily thrown and he was a boy not yet full grown.
With two olympic gold medals and many World Titles as well,
they were the epitome of artistry and devotion that made anyone's heart swell.

Sadly now their majesty has ended Sergei Grinkov is in Heaven.
All the World came to love these two artisans of the ice,
now we must pull together to show support for his wife.
We will miss watching them perform these two kids who were paired together.

We watched them grow and mature from friends, to a couple, then to parents. Yekaterina and Daria you, have so much support, you and
He will always be in our thoughts and heart,
We will miss him very much but hope you return to perform...your art.
Melanie Tryk

Waking Without You

As the mists of sleep begin to fade
and departs heavenly light,
I'm helpless and afraid,
when slips from deep unconscious sight
the fleeing bliss that was a dream,
that's different every night,
but brings familiar joy supreme.
It happens every morning when,
although you're so far away,
You seemed so near just then...
nearer than you'll be all day.
I shut my eyes and see your face again,
and heartaches kept at bay.
And for a few more seconds, loneliness is gone.
But soon truth robs the dream away
as first light proclaims dawn
that declares another day
and without you, I must somehow carry on.
Stephen Pastiva Jr.

Forgotten America

I had a dream last night
I was in the past
I heard the crackle of a whip
against the slave's back
I saw a mother's heartache
as her only child was sold
I had to ask
could America be so cold
My journey continued
to an immigrant's camp
I fumbled in the dark
for a kerosene lamp
I felt the pain of a small child's hunger
as the neighboring town gorged
I had to ask,
is this the land witch liberty poured?
I fell to my knees,
and there I cried
to truly love America
remember those who suffered and died.
Tina-Marie Cooke

Unanswered Questions

   I have questions that I have
no answers for; I'll ask you just
a few, but I have many more.
   Like why does love hurt when
it feels so very right? How can
someone love someone else when all
they do is fight?
   How can your heart be so full
but feel empty inside? And why are
some people so lonely in life up until they've died?
   They say life is simple, then
why does everyone struggle like they
do? Why does everyone have to work
so hard, except those little few?
   And why do they say, "All's fair
in love and war"? Love is right, war
is wrong, so what's the saying for?
   If someone knows these answers,
I wish they'd let me know; can they
be answered? I don't really think so.
Rebecca Aughenbaugh

Memories

The cold autumn air encased my frozen soul.
With each breath I grew more lethargic.
It brought me back to so many memories.

Trapped in the past I had no recourse but
to let myself be stolen by clouded visions
of fantasy and pain.

Embracing pain as though it were a close friend.
It was a constant companion in the changing
fortunes of time, committing itself to my side.
A loyal and trusted adversary always there
when I needed to be humbled.

I craved the past,
I wrapped myself in the dulled suppressing
comfort of it. Aching for lost companions and
experiences that would never return.
Melanie Heppner

The Flow: From The Stream We Shall Learn To The Sea We Will Return

As I look upon the stream below
I listen to its sounds and watch its waters flow.
Its tempo changes but continues to go
Ripples form when the wind will blow.

Seasons merge from warmth to snow.
Life and the seasons will surely end
But never - never the flow
Even when blocked it can bend
    And around it will go

The water boldly advances and continues
The flows reach out like grand sinews

In the wood the flow starts with a trickle.
Then suddenly it may turn fickle.
In its path a mammoth tree can fall
Its flow turns when a storm will call.

In summer embraced by warm breezes
In winter the stream never freezes.

The flow will not stop till it reaches its dream
Relentless movements flowing
   In a constant stream.

John A. Catoline

Laughing Rocks

And the rocks spewed forth their morning glory
Radiant in their laughter
They had no where to go they knew
But for one crying all alone
Waiting longer than the rest
When was the time that time would bring
Holding fast then moments rising spirits taken away
Some would go and some would stay
Why must I wait here in this jungle of forest and leaves
Dead detritus rotting mournful stench amid
My sky is calling me forth strong and boldly loud
Echoes linger round and round
They said the voices "Your suffering will end"
"Yes be glorified as you ascend!"
Then the small child's hand reaching down
Picked me up, hurling me upward, free at last!
Higher, higher, higher!
Yes! Free at last!

Xavier Le Desma

Bared Tree

The bared tree of autumn
Lay comfortably against the sky,
Making a perfect backdrop for
The great grandmother's wrinkled
Face and sparkling eye.

Her smile told the tale,
The tale of generations of life-sharing,
Shared with the new born infant.
Only love, of one's own, knows this caring!

The sun warmed her face!
It was as if God had kissed them;
Their every breath and very existence
Depending on his blessing them!

He knows them as we can not understand-
Her whole life and the baby's too.
He comforts them with familiarity,
Like the bared tree in the sky so blue.

Betty C. Richey

See The Silence

In the depths of a mind unknown,
thee uncertainty of the man is shown
will he survive or will be break
it is his own future he must make

Deep inside,
lie the unspoken truths
coming from the minds,
of the hollowed youths

What is spoken,
cannot be heard
what it is,
is our eternal word

See the silence,
that we speak
we are the young,
but our minds are not weak

Hear is speak, through our eyes
you cannot see our silent cries
at the dawn, of every day
wake and wonder, if we've run away

Psychically, no.....emotionally scared.
We are the youth's, that you discard.

Jeremy Nord

Me-A Book?

Bring me out when you feel inclined to. I am in the bookcase at the library one of those quiet, kind books, that are there to be used when necessary.

I am happy that I am not a magazine; a few sheets of paper, loosely connected, from which people catch the most sensational things, which turn into gossip. I am proud of my comprehensive, gilt-edged sheets, bound in a dainty cover.

I am not an ordinary book. Cannot be found at all libraries. Those who have access to me are grateful, yet somewhat afraid. Put me quickly back on the spot in the bookcase, so that nobody notices you reading in it. Am I on the wrong shelf? Should I be in the reference room?

All pages aren't read. There are too many of them. But soon, the informative pages are tattered. The more personal and emotional chapters are still almost unread. Only the author and the publishers are acquainted with the contents. Of course, some printer's errors slipped through the presses, but that happens to most writings.

It is okay to look at the cover, then read a little bit on the back, but most comfortable, is probably just to listen to the reviews. Some people have flipped through the book. Others are content with looking at the pictures. Nobody has read the whole book yet.

Is anybody going to do that? Who will be the first one to try?

Anneli Ahlmalm

The Nurse

This tale has been told by many intelligent souls.
Its the grave yard shift and down the hall we go.
It is very quite in the halls yet some strange sounds come from the walls that can even make your skin crawl.
A nurse walks down the hall of the old McAllen Hospital
All dressed in white as white can be.
Some staff even say she seem to be transparent and hard to see.
How could that be?
When the hospital gets busy this nurse will come and walks the halls and then she is gone.
Sometimes she even fades in front of me.
A Ghost!
Is that what I see?

Blanca Estela Gonzalez

Elegy Of A Fool

Sometimes I sit and wonder why life has to be so cruel;
It's like God plays a trick on you the day you're out of school.
You try, you hope, you cry, you pray that soon things will look up;
You wonder how you'll handle things as more pours in your cup.

The days grow short and colder, and the minutes turn to hours;
While all the rich folks look at you from inside ivory towers.

Time ticks on and life goes by without an end in sight;
You wonder what you may have done to deserve such bitter plight.

Faith somehow keeps you going when you're ready to give in;
At least that's what people tell you if you'll just believe in him.

I question my existence; where I fit into his plan;
But, I'm sure he has good reason for me being where I am.

A guess I must accept this life; this hand that I've been dealt;
Although I never asked for more than just a little help.

In this game of life I'm playing I can't throw back any cards;
But why did people lie to me and say "it's not that hard."

So here I sit still wondering why life has to be so cruel;
I think I've found my answer...it's 'cause I'm a trusting fool.

Connie Cummings

American Warrior

I have opened my parachute,
and went into the gates of Hell.

I have seen the anguish of people
struggling for freedom.

I have witnessed the battle-torn people
run over by an overpowering government.

I have seen the people die
in horrible agony.

I have witnessed the cries of children,
Let me be free!

I have used my knife to survive,
I am an American warrior.

No winners, all lose.
This is a thing called War.

Daniel J. Killian

As I Walk On The Beach

As I walk down the beach in the early morn'
I delight in seeing a new day being born.
One minute I am surrounded by no light,
Then next, the sun shines about me, bright.

As I walk along, I have not a care
For I am in awe of God's treasures there.
In the early morn' all the wonders I see
Will stay with me forever and never flee.

As I walk on thru the gentle wind
I know there is not much time to spend.
It is now that I must take it all in.
So later, I can recall that which has been.

As I walk on the beach in life's flow
There is this time that I will always know.
When I chose to seek the beach after the gale.
To see the sunshine on shells bright and pale.

As I walk on the sand coarse and fine,
My thoughts awaken to send chills down my spine,
I knew I came here early to find release.
Little did I know that my answer would be peace.

Marilyn Fouchecourt

The Light Of A Diamond

Her inner light shines brightly like a gem. So bright that I long to nestle close to its warmth.
Her smoothness like a diamond, a beauty like a sapphire does nothing more than reflect her Maker.

Running quickly, I asked my Father if I could hold the gem. There was no answer.
Begging and tugging at His garment, I began to plead for her. He still gave me a silent reply.
Feeling deprived, I left to weep in the garden.

He placed His hand on my shoulder to assure me of His faithfulness;
However, my temper flared and I left to gain the gem on my own.
I was obsessed with her iridescence.
Like a moth attracted to a flame, I could not stand being away.
The thought of segregation squeezed my soul like a wet sponge, and all emotion was drained within.

Finally, I made an effort to hold the gem.
My Father was coming by so I squeezed the gem tightly to my chest.
The sharp crystal edges cut crevices deep within my heart.
At the sight of my own blood I began to panic and dropped the gem.

Loneliness and anxiety came to visit. Envy mocked my every desire of forgetting her.
Doubt kicked my thoughts of mending our friendship, and bitterness plowed my heart to sow seeds of tears.

I knew I would have to go back to my Father to beg for a cure that would heal the void that plagued my soul.

As He bandaged the wound in my chest He told me,
"My child if you would have only waited for me,
You would have seen that I will give you all the pure desires of you heart."

Travis Luttrell

Spring Wind

Angry and fierce, the wind in the spring,
No certain direction, confused little thing,
Cool mist is thrown downward, a gift from the sky,
Relief from confusion - tears in her eyes.

Love comes from the wind bursting high in the air.
Its timing is perfect - her heart needs repair.
The force is demanding, the excitement surreal,
It can't be ignored, its message - to feel.

To trust love again, to open her soul,
Like the wind in the spring
  No direction, no goal.

Open her eyes, make her see what it is,
No reason to fear - the wind wants to give.

Give the smallest of seed
  A new place, a new way,
Love given more chance
  Time given more day.

Nadine Isom

Depression, Despair, Hope And Happiness

You know not the hurt I feel
To you it's imaginary, to me it is real

You know not the demons I face
Fighting them all to hold my place

You know not the dark in which I reside
Fighting the hurt to get outside

You know not the battles I fight,
To overcome my fears and take flight.

I know not where happiness resides,
But I know, I must first look inside.

Tammy Kadrmas

Sinners Prayer

Our Lord Jesus, came down from above
to take our sins, and give us his love
He is not obligated, to hear sinner pray
unless that sinner, is wanting to say
forgive me Lord Jesus, all of my sins
come into my heart, and live within
I give you my heart, and my life I give to
and the rest of my days, I will serve you
you are the potter, I am the clay
Mold me and shape me, that in some way
I can serve you Jesus, both day and night
and in me Jesus, they will see your light

Richard O. Bradley

Coyote Song

When the yodel dog sings his song to the moon,
   I wonder what he has to say?
Does he sing his song to a Coyote maiden,
   A love song, Coyote way.

Some times another will join in,
   and sing a chorus or two.
Their song drifts out across the plain,
   and down the canyons too.

Then a from hill-top, close by,
   another tenor, Coyote way,
Will join the melody, and they will sing
   A Coyote ren-de-ley.

Mavin Sparks

I Am

I am the queen waving to the crowd
I AM
I am the crowd honoring the queen
I AM
I am the preacher standing in the pulpit
I AM
I am the congregation sitting in the pews
I AM
I am the dancer twirling on the stage
I AM
I am the audience applauding the dance
I AM
I AM the color and the sound and the silence

Marcella Socha

"Do You Gang? Or Can You Hang?"

Being in a gang, is like heading for disaster
   You'll be hurt and in trouble, in no-time or faster
If you are so smart, so cool, and so neat
   Then why do you hang out, or live on the street?
If you are so bad, so rough, and so tough
   Then maybe it's time, to call your own bluff
If you are so confident, that you could "hang"
   Then think of your future, and lose the gang
I know you have a brain in your head
   Don't waste it for others, use it instead
Wise up, young ones, wise up while you can
   Stand on your feet, and be your own man
Realize, the gang is not there in the end
   Acknowledge your family as a "real true friend"
If you be your own person, you can demolish the trouble
   You may save yourself, and your family so that goes double.

Kerri Trujillo

Visiting Memories

My brother came to visit me, who died a year ago.
I've never grieved for him like some because I chose it so.

For in my heart he lives each day, he shares my every care.
Before he died, he talked to me and all my cares he shared.

He never said what I should do, but listened with such care.
The days when I would need him still, I know deep down he's there.

He wasn't all that much with talk, that said what I should do.
He listened with compassion and care that plainly said, I love you.

If a lift you needed on a deep depression day, you might get
a chance to talk to him and brighten up your day.

He always had a pleasant way to chase away the blues.
He'd antidotes to share and laugh or tell a joke or two.

No matter what the circumstances, he'd find a brighter side.
Because of such a brother, I've learned how my cares to hide.

No matter what the day will bring, there is a brighter side.
Because of that dear brother, I've an easier road to ride.

A person never dies you see, while they live within you heart.
The body dies, but they live on long after they depart.

Julia L. Dickson

Spring Rhapsody

I survey the beauty of a grassy knoll and upon a blanket
I lie amongst the foliage, closing my eyes, the warmth
of the sun's rays penetrates my flesh.
Hypnotically aware of all vibrations and sounds surrounding
me... I am one with the Earth.
I hear the wind rhythmically whisper through the reeds
as they are gently tossed from side to side.
There is an aroma of blended sweetness that emanates
from the wildflowers scattered throughout, as though
they had been recently placed there as ornaments to
decorate the landscape, and, maybe my senses.
A bee flits from blossom to blossom, humming as
it labors mechanically through the field unaware
of its significance in seasons to come.
The beetles, grasshoppers and fowl miraculously harmonize
themselves to the bass tones of the bee, it's nature's
symphony, I think to myself!
As I listen, the leaves of the trees move in what sounds
like applause!
Ah! Spring! Encore I say! Encore!

Susan St. Jean

The Dancer

Her voice dances in my ears
I can see her, she has no fear
The beautiful dancer
Clothed in silk
And her skin the color of milk
Toes touching the tiny stones
Dancing around for those with
Musical tones
Her golden hair
Dancing on its own
As her feet touch the stone
She sings with a voice of pure gold
A voice that catches and takes hold
Her smile flashes and holds you tight
And her voice holds you through the night

Brett Lashuay

My Son

I had you son, when I was very young,
Not knowing what life had in store,
But when I hold you in my arms,
So small and dependant on me,
I couldn't have loved you more.
I grew up fast, you grew up too,
Thanks to your grandparents, we made it through.
The pressure was rough your teenage years,
I'm glad I wasn't a teenager then,
But you made it through that, and had good times,
that made you lots of friends.
I just want you to know, that your my heart
and my soul, I love you unconditionally,
Take one day at a time, and you
will find, that life is what you want it to be,
Your starting a new life, with a wonderful, loving wife,
And things are fairly O.K.,
So enjoy yourself, we love you son, and have a
wonderful birthday.
Bonita Brown

Dream On

The day is gone, the night is here
To lay to rest your mind and fears.
Sleep well oh soul, rest and gain strength,
The morrow will provide new tests of length.

The hour is near to close your eyes
To look now for sleep's paradise.
To find fulfillment in your dreams
You longed for under the sun's hot beams!

In dreams a new world now create
Where love alone does conquer hate.
Where longing for another soul
Is not in vain, it is your goal.

To dream of happiness and joy
Where true love proves more than a toy.
Where you will join another's mind
And heart and soul of worth will find.

The dream you have might just prove real
And start your heart and soul to heal.
Take courage now and close your eyes,
Perhaps tomorrow you'll find paradise!
Heinz K. Drawe

Poets

I've often been told that Poets are pansies
But here's what I sort of think
That just because guys have a feminine side
Doesn't mean their underwear's pink

Don't think that! Hey! These men are not gay
Some of them even have kids
But because we don't seem to agree
Their thoughts are sealed under lids

I've often been told that poets are pansies
What's that supposed to mean
That these men are gay, for deep meaning they say,
Is in dreams oft left unsaid

They aren't fairies prancing through prairies
Walking around on their toes
There is much more to the men we ignore
Whose words in a rhyme just flows
Robert C. Dunn

Fowl

Baked, fried, boiled, stewed, breaded, mayonnaised, fricasseed,
blackened, barbecued.
Shh... Don't tell anyone the mere thought of it sends chills
up my spine.
Big yellow rubber gloves and goggles.
We are having chicken tonight.
Can't buy it whole
Has to be already dressed.
would you
please carve up
my fowl.

You see I have a
Real Big problem
with the touching fowl
faction.
Thanks.
Perhaps I'll just have salad instead.
No not interested in seeing how they are raised.
Can't even stand to look at them now
faceless.
Lucinda Gilmartin

Listen To Me

I see a baby crying on the floor, but I can not reach her;
We are separated by a wall of glass, six inches thick;
Her parents fight in another room, they do not hear her;
I pound on the glass until my fists are bloody, my cries go unheard
    as well;
If somebody would just listen to me;
She needs an ally, she needs a spokesman, she needs a voice;
The baby crawls over to me and leans against the wall, her little
    hand reaches for mine;
I fall to the ground and place my hand on the glass across from hers;
Electricity flows through the wall as our hearts connect;
She smiles at me and I weep even harder;
And then she is gone, I know I will never hold her again;
If someone had just listened to me, maybe I could have helped.
Rosemarie Dubman

Truth

The search for truth begins deep within;
Exposing itself open to a mind unfettered;
For what reason to seek the truth?
An inspiration or revelation such that the
    mind will know no tether.
In itself - the truth - the source of all
    creation, a chalice of knowledge,
    enlightens through realization.

The truth - an identity;
A source of peace, an essential entity;
A pilot of the soul, navigating to a destination of consummation;
A spiritual magnetism, repelling fallacy, attracting fidelity;
The mind's eye guide - vanquishing mysticism - revealing realism;
A seed of consciousness, lying dormant, waiting to take root;
In no uncertain terms, we are our truth.
Joel B. Makowski

Free...

My heart is so open, so full and deep,
so that I can barely sleep.
My arms are open wide like the rising tide
I fall down and cry.
As the waves come in, our love grows thin,
The Lord forgives us for our sins.
As the birds fly free, so shall we
fly above the open sea.
Carrine Melissa Yates

Love's Path

Beneath the tranquil starry night
We walked hand in hand in the dim moonlight,
We were as two children at play in the sand
We lived only for the moment at hand,
The salty air filled our lungs and blew through our hair
As we strolled along the beach with nary a care,
Two hearts filled with perfect love
Basking in the beauty of the night sky above,
The sea caressing our feet as it washed upon the shore
Covering our footprints where we had stepped moments before,
Cleansing the sand of the depressions we made
All signs that we had passed by would very soon fade,
It's as if the past did not exist
As we walked that night in the ocean's mist,
Two people with one purpose, with a single goal
Walking into the future together as one heart and one soul.

Bob Kyzer

Snow

It falls so silently, drifting in the windless air, so quiet the world, so peaceful. The white rain continues to fall, faster, harder. As small pebbles it bounces off the trees to the rocks, to the earth. Seconds turn into minutes, then hours, this beautiful performance.

The earth becomes a veil that grows to a cloth of cotton that becomes fluffs of fur to mounds of sheep's wool.

Sitting in comfort before the blazing fire, we watch this beauty being performed. It continues with the world at peace with mother nature.

Joanne C. Duxbury

Trail Of Tears

Follow the trail of tears and you will see
To whom happiness is just a memory
Screams and cries full of despair
Are heard left and right, here and there

Starved, thin and skinny as poles
Life, maybe death, who knows what the future holds
Tortured and killed because of your beliefs
Who are the culprits, who are the chiefs?

How long will this masquerade occur?
We don't know; the future is a blur
Tears of pain, tears of fear
From those who question is a brighter future near

The shouts, the cries, the screams, the pleas!
Why did Jews have to pay such a fee?
Ashes falling like precious rain from the sky
Where the bodies of many Jews lie

Children no older than the age of two
Perish before me and you
Follow the trail of tears and you will see
To whom happiness is just a memory

Angela Elliott

Life/Death

Death is a mystery to some
And it provides answer to others
It can be a prayers answer
Or it can be an unexpected cancer
Live can be fragile
So easily taken away
Or it can keep on burning inside
To keep you alive
You can go slow
No one will really know
Except fate who holds the key
To everything that means something to me!

Rachel Crites

Screaming At The Lake

Screaming obscenities to the lake
Those deep emotions no one can fake
The rain cascading down upon my face
Wash away the tears, so much fear
Heart beats a feverish pace
Memories flood as eyes shed another tear
So many things that need to be done
Screaming "Don't go, I need you!"
Helpless, So far from being useful
Anguish wells deep in the soul
Bellow and yell sob and fall
To one knee, whisper to the lake
"I never said I Love You."
Please help me, give some time
Just let her know it is true
I Love You
Don't leave me
Alone.

Sean Steven Braden

Dumped

Dark tunnel passage ways,
black and dreary rainy days,
hoping for a light to guide me through...
nothing just black.

Curtains pulled over my window,
death at the door.
Don't know if I have real friends.
This isn't what I want, but they are screaming for more.

People thinking negative at all costs
and pushing people to the floor.
I don't like this feeling. I want to change.
I'm the target in this target range.

Starry night, come over me.
Shower me with things I haven't seen.
I see a star in the sky falling down,
down on me to help me through this pain.
It will help the pain go away,
wash it out with the rain.

Happy days.....

Erica Burleigh

Survival

Through the eyes of most
Fighting is the brutal machine
Which silences the souls

But if only these tormented souls
Could reach out and speak
They would tell the world of their learnings

The learning of knowledge
Brought the ability to think
Positively about their actions

The learning of precision
Brought the ability
To decide upon their actions

The learning of concentration
Brought the body and mind
Into complete focus

The learning of wisdom
Brought life experiences
Which taught them survival

Juan Luis Montes

The Black Chair

It has its place over in the corner.
Big, black and sturdy, just like daddy.
Two strong arms and a strong back.
The velour texture and feather-filled pillows,
   makes me sink into a security like no other.
There I sit watching daddy stagger across the room,
   yelling through his empty lungs.
My head bowing in shame of a broken curfew,
   trying to think of an explanation.
Listening to every slurred word, his voice grows larger,
   "Where could you have been so late?"
"Out!" I said. I see the backside of his masculine hand
   coming toward my face.
I felt the chair contract, my body trapped inside.
But daddy's slap knocked me out of the chair,
   onto the cold cement-like floor.
Staggering into the next room, he left me there in pain, silent.
My head throbbing, face stinging.
   I look up at the chair through watering eyes.
It could no longer protect me, nor could my daddy!

Kimberly D. Lewis

The Grandfather I Never Knew

Sometimes my mom will tell me
Stories from long ago;
Of a man of great stature,
Whom on this earth I will never know.

Through the years,
I've heard stories of his youth,
How he joined the Navy,
and how he always told the truth.

I've always dreamed of what he looked like;
Tall, nice, handsome, and all dressed in navy blue,
I'm sure he would be so nice to me,
And spoil me like any grandfather would do.

I know that if he was still here,
When I cried, he'd sit me on his knee
And wipe away my every tear,
Until once again I was jumping with glee.

I can't wait until I get to heaven so fair,
For I know that the days left are few;
I'm sure Grandpa will be waiting for me there,
And that's when I'll meet 'the Grandfather I never knew'

Heather Lynn Wills

Butterflies

I met the most precious person I have ever known.
A wondrous experience.
Too soon gone.
But a new one appeared.
Daring and gleeful.
How much fun it was, to know this one.
We played and we talked and we laughed.
We cried and we giggled and we sighed.
One day this one went away.
Replaced by another, I wanted to stay.
But now I knew-she too, would drift.
Away on beautiful wispy wings.
Into the mist.
How my heart sings and sighs.
Too late, too soon, to realize.
The seed that I had sewn.
Too soon to be too grown.

Robert J. Mannen

Sixty-Two Years And Your Free

Oh! The day that we were wed.
I said," that I would sleep in your bed."

Yes, we made a pack.
That in sixty-two years, I could throw you back.

Oh! The years have come and gone.
The work and fun that we have done.

I stand looking at you, as sixty-two pass by.
As we were wed I wondered, oh! I wondered. Why?

Would I ever set you free?
Yes, from me.

Oh! The years have come and gone.
The work and fun that we have done.

Yes, indeed it is time to let you go.
I have to, you know.
Yes, because I'm standing here, as they lower you in the hole.

Nellie Rinkel

Is It The Feelings?

Is it the feelings you have night and day
That words could never begin to say?
Or is it the glow that shines upon your face
That brightens with each loving embrace?

Is it the softness in every kiss
That causes memories to reminisce?
Or is it the tear that trickles from your eye
That expresses the pain in each goodbye?

Is it the times you share together
That will last a day past forever?
Or is it the sweetness in your hearts
That blinded this love from the start?

How is it that you have all this?
Was it a dream or just a wish?
Or was it a prayer to the one above
that delivered you this everlasting love?

Amy Baez

For My Sister

I said a prayer for you last night,
To take away the pain.
For God knows what you are going through,
And how you suffered through the flames.

When all the pieces fall together,
Your life will go from here.
You will have God to hold your hand,
Through heartaches and through fear.

When I think about our life,
We were never close.
Now life has changed everything,
And I love you all the most.

You were always the stronger one,
Now you are fighting for your life.
I am glad I have this time with you
To help you with this fight.

God only knows what is good for us,
Sometimes we do not understand.
For life to us is timeless
When we have it in our hands.

Tina M. Rine

Would They

If I were to leave - go away
would anyone miss me - wish I had stayed
or know how I loved them - how much I cared
and remember the good, the bad we had shared

Would they look at my picture and remember back when
I stood for the camera- I was happy then
and would they all smile a sad little smile
and wonder what it'd be like had I stayed awhile

Would they get on with life- that's what' I'd want
except for those who had trouble being up front
I tried, did what I could - no, I wasn't the best
now it doesn't matter-I've left my fallen nest

I want to pull myself out of this never-ending flood
I've felt pain and shed my share of blood
I don't want to run - but I can't go on
It's uncontrollable - this urge to be gone

But then I wonder if I were to leave - go away
Would anyone miss me - wish I had stayed
or know how I loved them - how much I cared
maybe together we can take on life and remember the good, the bad
we have shared

Maria A. Doran

Spring

Rain is coming down softly, so very softly
on the cold earth and bare trees, hesitantly
because it still is the last day of winter
for budding flowers, a sign of spring, not yet to enter!

Spring wakes up dormant plants and trees
to open the first flowers to the honey bees!
Farther into springtime, the fresh air betrays
evidence what had happened along the ways!

The hills have changed from brown to yellow
California poppies are showing off, their orange in the meadow
The sweet smell of the blue lilacs in the wild
mixes with the scent of cultivated roses, so mild

While spring pushes out all colors in a crescendo
the birth of animals, great and small, are also due
Spring means the beginning of new life on earth
We can enjoy this and admire all new birth!

This is a sure promise from year to year
The magnificence of nature, to us so very dear!
A gift to us all, living on this exotic planet
Let's give it a hand, as to make it even more splendid!

Johanna A. Garretson

The Golden Path

Don't let tomorrow be your last.
For time is fading fast.
Just like it did in yesterday's past.
So kneel at the cross and forget about the past.
Your future lies in what you need best,
From what you learned from your fading past.
It's not too late to take that golden path.
Don't let your past, pull you back.
For you'll fade in eternity's path.
Let the Holy light shine upon your soul.
And take one step at a time in that righteous path.
Cleanse your sins at every stream you cross.
For none is too deep, that you can't cross.
Jesus will be waiting, and standing by that cross.
Just to show you the blood, he lost in the past.
And show you your future in all its Glory.
If you take that Golden Path.

Leonard P. Orr

"The Worst In The Best Of Us"

It isn't the mistakes we make that makes
us seem so small. But the way we grow and learn
from them that makes us stand so tall. Anyone can
fall down as they attempt to run the race.
It takes a winner to get back up and run with
a faster pace. You see no one is perfect no
matter how hard we try. Sometimes we have a
chance to laugh other times a need to cry.
But if we struggle to do our best all along life's
way it seems someone will be there to help us
day by day. Anyone can make a mistake it's
how you turn your life around that counts. Take a
different attitude on life try this and you'll
find out. For if you learn from each mistake and
never repeat it again. The worst will become
the best in you and your confidence will
never end.

Marie E. Jernigan

The Gift

'Twas an angel that touched me late one night,
With wings unfurled bound in glorious light.
From an unearthly fog, a heavenly glow,
Why it came I do not know.

It outstretched its hand and lifted its head,
There for a moment I thought I was dead.
There exploded a light with more power than before,
The blast went through me, it knocked me to the floor.

I rose to my feet and I tried to run,
But the angel had me with the force of the sun.
I wheeled around to look at its face,
But was blinded so much, I had to turn in disgrace.

For my sins, to look, I had not the right,
For it was "HE," with the power, the glory, the might.
I was filled with the "Spirit" on high from above,
The light encased me with "HIS' undying love.

To this day I ponder the events of that eve,
To think of what happened I tend to believe.
I know, I now have to do what is right,
Because, 'twas an angel that touched me late one night.

Douglas E. Lehotay

Soul Mates

Lay down you sword
put away your shield
caress this grieving heart
forget to yield.

Reach beyond your dough
wipe away the tear that lies beneath your eye
shed light on my darkness
hold back your goodbye.

Succumb to your weakness
embrace this impatient soul that stands here
show me what I have not know
do not fear.

Breakdown the wall that blinds you
seek to feel what is there
clothe me with your endless treasures
have no despair.

Ease the thoughts that keep you distant
listen, if your destiny sings to me
follow the star that leads to my path
for soulmates we shall forever be.

Betsie True

Nature, A Person, And The World In Seven Letters, Dannell

If you ever meet a person wearing a charming smile.
If you ever meet a person who loves to talk for a while.
If you ever meet a person who is kind, caring, and sweet.
Then you need to talk to her because she is pretty neat!

She makes the sun shine bright and the birds sing songs of passion.
She makes official dress look like a new statement in fashion.
When you meet her you will realize that she is "the best."
And when her soft voice says "Hi", I'm Dannell" you will feel blessed.

If a picture is worth a thousand words that describe it,
Then she is worth a thousand pictures, and still some more would fit.
She will be the most friendly person you could ever meet.
I know her personally and she is the World to me!

Dawson Kaiser

Memories Of The Old Home Place

It's been years since I've seen the old home place.
Memories still linger that time cannot erase.
My mother would play the organ that was antique.
She played the music by ear and her songs were unique.
Dad loved to work in the garden everyday.
He tilled the ground with the horse and plow the old-fashioned way
Lovely pink and white dog woods covered the woodlands.
I know that God made them with his mighty hands.
He sent many peaceful days there.
And provided us with his loving care.
As the years go by and I dream and yearn.
Wishing for all those wonderful times to return.
Though the old home place is gone now the memories will never depart.
I have them stored deep within my heart.

Dorothy Smith

Ode To April '96

We thought that Spring would bring
pretty flowers
But I awoke to drab, cold snow showers
Trees and sprigs had started to sprout
But now they are in cold storage
afraid to come out
We say that now, the snow won't last
But we are in the middle of a severe snow blast
We pray for sun and warm breezes to bring
The song of birds, a burst of spring
But watching the snow and skies so dim
We'll have to wait... spring is not coming in

Elda Buralli Davy

The Working Girl

She walked the nights through neon lights
Past all the grime and glitter
She plied her trade with manner staid
Though in her soul was bitter

Teeming crowds appeared as clouds
With spirit dampening rain
So many near but none to hear
Her lonely cry of pain

With men she'd known some just half grown
Those many faceless faces
She passed the years in silent tears
With memory's dimming traces

Then on that day she passed away
Came far the saddest dawn
Though she would sin with countless men
Not one would know she'd gone

Del De Shazo

Granddad's Shed

Years ago, when I was just a lad.
I didn't really want to be bad.
But when I did forget to obey,
I can even now hear Grandpa say

Son, I don't want to spank you,
But you must remember lad,
If I don't punish you now,
You will grow up to be bad.

Spare the rod, and spoil the child,
A spank in the right place,
Can really be worth while tho
A pained look would appear on Grandpa's face.

Things have really changed today,
The children aren't taught to obey,
But a spank in the place where they sit
Will bring results in nothing flat.

A lack of corrections is seen today,
Crime has spread in every day.
You mustn't "spank" is what they say
So everyone the price must pay.

Eloise Callin

"I Don't Know How"

The first time I saw you
I didn't know how I felt.
They said you were different,
But I wouldn't believe.
Your china doll face and ever changing chameleon eyes wouldn't let me.
When I see you walk past,
My heart screams Eeee! In an exclamation of joy.
Now I'm certain of how I feel.
My thoughts of you intoxicate my life.
Always seeing your china doll face and ever changing chameleon eyes in my head
Over and over again.
I wish I could tell you how I feel, but
I don't know how.

Becky Aguilar

"A Candle In The Night"

How does it feel to lose a loved one?
That I now know, for I lost my grandpa,
not long ago.
   He gave me a strange shoulder, a kind
word or two, he made me smile, and took
away the blue.
   He called me his chalkeye, I
called him my friend. Like two peas
in a pod, till it came, to an end.
   Through his hands, I felt the
sunshine, his eyes offered hope, his
smile was bright, he was my, "Candle
in the Night,"
   One day I turned to find him gone,
he was no longer there. He had gone,
to the Heaven above, to join my grandma,
who he so loved.
   I dreaded the day it would have to
end, for I lost my grandpa, and closest friend,
   Goodbye, my grandpa, tell I see you again.

Kathy Smith

Some Wonder Why

Some wonder why, that I'm not sad, and miserable such as they,
they gripe, complain, they pay their bill, feeling the same old way.
I counseled with, a person whom, I've known for quite a while,
this person told, of all the woes, that killed a happy smile.
The bills are due, two jobs it takes, to pay the household bills,
this family, of only two, has nothing left for frills.
"How do you make it own your own?" the question put to me,
"I'm as happy, as can be, I've earned the right, you see."
"I don't believe, you feel that way, it's just a 'made up' act,
when all you do, is set behind, that desk and counsel fact.
Come go with me, and then you'll see, none is 'bad-off' as me."
I pushed myself, along the couch, over where all could see.
I pulled up in, my old wheelchair, and settled in the seat;
my crippled legs, and hands and back, and don't forget the feet.
"Come on! Let's go," I kindly smiled, "Just show me what you mean."
"I'm so sorry, I didn't know, your smile is always seen."
"I worry not, about my plight, I'm always at my best,"
for I'll not have, these crippled bones, rob me of my quest.
I strive to make, each day as bright, so happiness you'll see;
there's more to life, than pity of self, others come first to me.

David R. Clukie

Night

The night is like a blanket.
It covers the sky with thick carpets
of blackness.
The night takes its time and moves
across the land.
What it touches, does not speak
but is still in the cold frosty air.
All life stopped as if a spell had been cast
Where thoughts never go away
and dreams never last.
The night is soon broken away by the day,
the spell is over, the night has gone
away.

Kelly Ann Hester

"The Essence"

Your love beckons to me so much
I dare not even touch the emotion's pride,
for there is something calling in its essence.
We will voyage into our heart's infinity to listen.

You are the conscience that guides me
and my desires flourish around it.
I'll climb your ladder - every step.
I will not stop until there is a lesson.
Your cautious innuendoes make me strive
to find the meaning that will allow me to feel alive.

Tears that are flowing to form a deep river
are those we cry together.
Laughter of loving echoes beyond ourselves -
our soul to keep.

I see and feel, in this instance,
what is your and my expectance.
We can achieve through all the pain
and fly through each other again.
I solemnly promise my life to endeavor
to create a spark of light that will shine forever.

Zac Landefeld

Seasons

The leaves fall softly on the moor and plains,
while the late rose blooms.
Winter is next, with snow fall,
spring thereafter, with coming birds.

Samuel Stephanz

The Gentle Hum Of Ten Thousand Years

The white truck just went too fast, crazed...running on and on.
He didn't even slow when he saw her, mutilated her, desecrated her.
Late for jelly doughnut and thirty cent coffee - Fate smiles.

Arcane flash of white dress falling, the caramel taste of her still
  in my mouth,
such a sweet, short life, the gentle hum of ten thousand years going
by and the harbinger of Time is driving too fast.

She wore heavy metal t-shirts and wrote about love;
she shouted so loud and smiled so many, many times before.
Those goddamn eyes were metal...chrome bullets.

A silence in her voice, a wrinkle on my imagination, a stiletto in
  my ribcage,
riding the gentle hum of ten thousand years going by.
The harbinger of Time is driving much too fast. He's late. He's late!

Now, my charcoal mountain of Regret is not a holy place of worship.
Now, while wrapped in a humid wind that speaks of her butterfly
kisses and angel's wings, Fate appears the Unfair God.

Now there's no Time to say, "Goodbye." No Time to say,
  "I'll miss you."
No Time. No Time. No Time.

Nathan D. Huff

Memoriams

When one hears passing of old friends,
comrades of bygone years, one recalls
last moments of greetings.
Memories is immediate
and clear images form and you can hear them speak.
Thoughts and situations becomes reality,
recreating that last moments passed.
To except reality is difficult, as life
moves on until our times is due, then
others will think these thoughts anew.
Passing into memory becomes our way of
life renewed, leaving memories with those
remaining and moving on into our memoriam.

Jack K. Wakamatsu

A Minnesota Winters Night

Windy not quiet, lights low, traffic slow. Some cars that will
not go.

Some people going on buses, trains, planes, heading for a warmer
place this snowy night.

Fireplace lit, wine poured, Bear rug spread out on an old
hardwood floor, a mouse scurries some place.

Drifting snow, shutters flapping, pop-corn popping, roads close
a flicker of a cold in a sensitive nose.

Spark flying in the fire place following the smoke out
in-to the crisp clear sky somewhere. Stars twinkling about.

Jack frost with art on a window pane, a lone wolf tracks his
mate, late night radio talk show running late.

Snow mobile engine echoes across a frozen lake, a chilly draft
floats across a half eaten birthday cake, thought of a warmer
blanket, a quiver and a shake.

Unfinished hot coco in a old chipped mug, dog whining to go out,
only coals left in fire place, a glint of pre-morning light, eyes
with a feel of sand from a restless night.

Lenny I. Lehman

Show Me The Way

Move over sun,
Move over moon,
Show me the way to a bright blue sky.
Take me high above the trees and mountains.
an show me the world beyond.
For I have got me some new wings.
  I am ready to fly.
  I am ready to explore a brand new world.
So, Please show me the way to a bright blue sky.

Donna Lynch

Searching For What Is Lost

  Years ago I had it all,
but somewhere lost it down the line.
  I've been searching for it ever since,
with hopes that it again I can find.
  To know that it once was in my possession,
all of life's bitter-sweet memories.
  To have in my hands again,
no matter when in life it may be.
  A person that had it all,
and that of which I truly did.
  I sat there for years watching,
as life through my fingers had slid.
  A person may never really notice it,
at least not until it is gone.
  Where they will sit empty handed,
heart broken, scarred and all alone.
  But, I must continue my search to find it,
and hopefully will again at whatever it may cost.
  But, I know I'll be forever looking,
For I'll be out there Searching For What Is Lost....

Jimmy P. Hargrove

Memories

You thought the memories would not last
But they still haunt you from your past
They bring back laughter, bring back tears
of friends you've had throughout the years
They torture you with what has been
You want to live those times again
Sometimes they're good, and sometimes bad
The best and worst you've ever had
The blood red tears, the misplaced love
The music, and the moon above
All the stupid things you did
The times you fought, the times you hid
The memories, will not ever go
But then there's always tomorrow.

Kevin Shaffstall (4/18/70 - 12/10/94)

Battling Redemption

The magnificent candle burns brightly the flame ever strong
The statuesque presence picture perfect
But as time goes on changes begin to take shape
The candle begins to diminish
The outsider attempts to mold the melted pieces back up, so the
candle would stand straight and strong once again
Despite the outsiders attempts the candle begins to grow dim
The once strong flame begins to diminish in its own self
Again, the outsider tries to bring life back to the candle
But the candle has won, and finally burns out
All that is left the residue of the once strong brightly burning candle
The outsider has the memory of the once beautiful candle and will
keep it close to them forever.

Teri Ewing

Why?

I heard sad news today of a dearly loved friend
Whose life seems to be steadily nearing its end.
A fast growth in her lungs is impeding her breath,
And appears to be hastening her untimely death.

Such a really true Christian that I had to cry,
As I sorrowed and wept, and I wondered just why
Though it my be untrue, yet it does seem perhaps
That as hard as you try, you still earn life's hard raps.

Now some folks drive like maniacs just for the sport,
While a struggling young Christian speeds once and is caught.
Immoral girls laugh, and view purity with scorn,
Yet one slip by a virgin, and her reputation's gone.

So why, tell me why, God, please explain to me
Why the wicked can sin and get off so scot free;
While those who try to serve You the best that they can
Sometimes suffer and come to an untimely end?

As I wept and I moaned and complained bitterly,
My kind heavenly Father in love answered me:
"My child, though I sorrowed, I never asked why
To save poor lost sinners, My dear Son had to die."

Marjorie B. Richardson

Enchantment

We sat beneath the tree amid the green
The sun's warmth streamed in between the leaves
And clouds in the sky of blue! Nature's
Display in stunning array... spectacular!!

Watch the spider as she weaves her web
Intricate, geometrical, unique in style beautiful!
She drops down on a silken thread... waits!
"Always is tomorrow," and we are part of this too!

Majestic butterflies meet the myriad of spring
Flowers hue of the sun! Red, pink, yellow, white, blue
Songbirds. Jays, squirrels, kittens, dogs nature's path, grand!
Bumble bee pierces the sound they all scatter!

Thank you Lord for our garden and "tree of sharing"
Electro-magnetic forces, earth, wind, fire, water... us!
Strength of care, branch of love from you!
Time is the bond of each, we are the time of bond!

Anita M. Diaz

My Dark Green Forest

Deep in the tranquil woodlands all is peaceful.
I enjoy its relaxing and beautiful lull.
Birds, trees and the sun all work together
To make me as carefree as a flower and as light as a feather.

I like the smell of the warm nighttime campfire.
It makes me feel as though I'll never tire.
I feel a spiritual energy as I dream of my hopes,
That cleanse me as if with a thousand soaps.

I feel a searching of my soul as I soak it all in,
As if it's all inside my heart in a great big bin.
That bin is stored someplace deep; I can't set it free.
And it keeps a record of me under lock and key.

I wish I could just peek at that record book.
So that I could realize all of my faults in one look.
I could make my life the absolute best.
For that, I'd love my dark green forest.

Sara K. Mainhart

Streams Of Consciousness

Thoughts flowing keeping the emotions going
sometimes smooth and serene, sometimes rough and rapid
moving toward the breaks and falls.
If you are lucky there is a branch to hold onto
to keep you from the abyss and help you ashore.
If not then you fall, fall hard dashed on the rocks below
crushed by the weight of emotions
falling over the edge chasing you down to the bottom
pushing you faster, faster toward the rocks below.
Suddenly looms a pool...it's deep, it breaks your fall,
but it's rough in there...your emotions swirl you around
until you find the outlet and even still it's rough for a time.
Then the stream evens out...becomes calm again.
Warm gypsy winds begin to blow and play across the stream
making rivulets as it flows among the fields and flowers.
Then you are joined by another stream...the two of you bounce along
joyfully...playing among the rocks and in the corners of the bows
flowing on together for an eternity to the seas
that are fed
by the streams of consciousness.

Steven R. Johnson

My Love

The soft rain of spring...
Running barefoot in the sand.
With you,
Close by my side...
Watching the stars come out,
Then driving all the way to the beach,
To catch the waves of the rippling sea...
Picnics in the grass.
Gathering daises - a gift of love,
She loves me, she loves me not,
It's all a part of life, I guess,
Joy,
And sadness...
But it all seems so very much more.
Beautiful
With you there
To love me.....

Ricky Fasoli

Today And Tomorrow

As I watch my children today
and plan for their tomorrows
I delight in how they play and play
unaware of the impending sorrow.

God gave me these two children for today
and he tells me not to worry about tomorrow
enjoy them now for they can not stay
they were only mine to borrow.

My hopes and prayers for today
will be the same tomorrow
Lord let me keep them one more day
and please, let there be no more sorrow.

Ron Garza

Love Promises

Promises of love lost in the wind,
turning the torch, life died from flames blown in.
Carrying thoughts burnt from within, running from the light
that flickered again.
Mastering thoughts, screaming for love, lost were the
promises spoke in love.
Flames of love will start again
alive but true to the end.
Deceit still whistles if blown by the wind.
Promises a burden now and then.

Freddie E. Wade

She Was Trim And Beautiful

She was trim and beautiful, and I miss her.
Aye, she was an object of everlasting beauty -
with curves that would catch any seafaring man's eyes.

She was tall and trim, and broad on the beam -
and I loved her.

She was proud and sturdy - yet graceful;
like a moon beam dancing across a calm sea.

Aye, maty. We sailed the seven seas together;
around the horn we flew.

Many a rough water had we seen; she kept me warm, did she.
Then one evening, the seas did come to claim my love, my all.
They took her below to rest, and left me all alone.

Aye, my love is no more. Yet maty, she remains still:
here in my heart: here in my memories.

She was trim and beautiful, and I miss her.

Aye, but a good ship never really dies -
she is here, with me always.

Roy Gerlach

Dropped Out?

So, you quit school because you had no money
　to buy clothes
　　like the other kids wore?
Hello, Stupid!!
　You are such a bore.

Why are schools here?
To develop thinking? To learn?
To do a dress parade yearn?
To belong to a certain tier?

Find yourself a corner.
Fill it well.
Always have a question, an answer,
And yourself you will sell.

Never confront the teacher.
Just ask questions nicely.
Same goes for others.
You'll win spicily.

You don't want any part
　of such a dish?
Alms! Alms! Hasheesh!

Cozette Zahnle

Favorite

Kasandra is my little sister,
Who never does anything wrong,
She torments my cat and brother,
Day after day, all day long.

She jumps on the furniture,
Writes on the walls,
Tears up my literature,
And gets away with it all.

Blonde hair and big brown eyes,
Don't hide those horns and that tail,
Mommy doesn't like it when "her baby" cries.
She yells "whose picking on my poor little girl?"

Little princess, favorite, you spoiled brat.
Enjoy playing kiss-up and angle in heaven.
Remember mom had me first,
I'll be eighteen when you're only seven.

Victory at last.
You want to go where in my new car?
Remember the past,
Looks like you're not going far.

Karina Giamporcaro

Now That She's Gone

She fluttered across the wasteland of my dreamy existence,
And freed my weathered soul with her gentle persistence.
I marveled at the way that she stretched out her wings,
As the essence from her beauty swirled above everything.
Her presence was subtle, yet "oh" so profound,
For she moved me to smile where I once wore a frown.
I held in my breath as she captured my heart,
For I've dreaded that day she'd have to part.
Though my life was submerged like a blade in the snow,
I have blossomed and bloomed with the warmth from her glow.
How I wish she were mine, though she was born to be free,
As she soars through the mist, like a bird off a tree.
But now that she's gone and my life's incomplete,
To the gloom of my landscape I sadly retreat.

David Gonzalez

Broken Heart

Why did you have to leave me,
What did I do so wrong to you,
I wish I knew,
Why don't you tell me how you're feeling,
I'm feeling sad and sorry for the things that has happened to us,

I thought I saw you a few times,
I said hi to you,
Then I haven't seen you since,
I really would like to know what I did so wrong to you,

I never cheated,
Or even betrayed you,
So why can't we be together?

Samantha Goucher

Knowing

   The child within longs to return,
locked between the chambers of mind.
Searching for the familiar scent,
of the ever so faint bouquet.

   Maturity the misplaced key.
Wisdom shall help me overcome,
aide me in my unarmed battle.

   Serenity the merited solo.
Searching for the long ago comforts.
Knowing the images are fabrications.

   My heart motions me forth,
the start being now.
I must move on in search of new doors.

   The master set unlocks all,
using all opportunities.
Knowing present and future are assets.

   Keeping in mind, the past is where it belongs
a memory.

Darcey L. Gray

Evening

Evening brings to the earth quiet rest,
While from a nearby lake you can hear
A loon, winging its way to its nest,
In the distance, an owl's call comes clear.

The grass moves in green waves from the breeze,
Rosy gray clouds slip so shyly by,
Tall dark shadows are cast by the trees,
As the twinkling stars light up the sky.

Margaret Hannah

Reason To Live (In Memory Of My Mother)

So much time on my hands
So many troubles on my mind,
As I aimlessly wander
In search of something to find.

They tell me to "hang on kid"
"But how much longer?" I say,
"From the pain my heart is breaking-
While my strength slips slowly away".

You say that she is with me
Think of her and push right on,
I say no matter what I do
When I'm done she'll still be gone.

Though it may not seem like it
There is always something to give,
Remember how she loved you
And you will always have reason to live.

Katherine L. Harris

April

April is a gift, a prayer, a secret...
Shared by all who love the silence
Of the early dawn, the glory of the sun.

The last refrain of misty rain
Arrives with April,
Wet dust and daffodils...
And winter done.

April is so sudden!
The chilly mornings are no more;
The stun of bare feet on the floor
Has now become the warmth
Of sunbeams...sifting
Through the window shades.

April is a gift, a taste of grace
A promise kept, a giddy dance,
A flight of song
A stir of leaves
Another chance to love someone.

Alberta Quinn

Backwoods Yesterday

There's a cabin nestled deep within the woods
Darkened shadows hover closely neath the trees
Walking through the valley clearly hear
   the rippling water flowing very near
See the lacy patterns shaft of sun, shining
   through the forest dense the trees
Flowers bob their pretty heads and nod
As they feel the soft warm gentle breeze

Feet press gently in the ground, walking
   down that path of years gone by
Heartbeats wildly, Oh the sounds, Captured
   once again, a deep deep sigh
Home again, that home of yesteryears
Where budding trees, a choir of birds do fly
   through the air frame deep blue cloudless sky
Warm sun, oh gentle wind, a whispered sound
It's like a voice from heaven speaks so clear
Where home and God are drawn so very near

Claudine Cerra Blevins

A Special Love Each Day And Night

Everyday and every night.
There's a love that is so right
A special feeling of warmth and joy
Something more than just a toy
Someone to hold you,
When times are not right.
To give you advice, so your day would be bright.
Someone that understands, that love
is not a game
Something that shouldn't be played day by day
So pray to God
Each day and night
For that love, that is so right
And when you find that special love
One that is higher then the skies above
Look at that person, and hold him tight
And tell that person that you always love him
Each day and night.
John Rosa

Laura

Beautiful little Daffodil, resting under the
window sill, petals fair, leaves of green, breathing air
so crisp and clean,

From the ground you gently creep, awakened from
your winter sleep, beckoned forth by natures call, you
seem a martyr to us all,

Through winters snow and bitter wind, you gently
sway, but never bend, standing there so proud and tall,
a gracious look for one so small,

Your tiny head turned toward the sun, singing out
that spring has come.
Debra Hagberg

Us

Violence, crime, war, pollution
The list goes on and on
Some people say it is the side effect of technology
Some say it is the side affect of our ignorance
How can we stop these problems without stopping ourselves?
Killing off species and killing of our own
What's wrong with us?
We make inventions to better our planet
But we finally realize after decades of pollution, violence and hate
It will take more than decades to fix.
Years of killing the planet and ourselves we finally realize we have
to clean it up.
Are we stupid?
What was it like before humans?
Better, worse, who knows?
What some people don't understand
Is why we kill each other
Perhaps it's our destiny
To better our planet
One thing we do know, is that time will tell
William C. Harding

Lessons Life Taught

Take your time examine the way
Life holds great mysteries try as you may
Not all can be seen in a single day
Invest in the future consider your past
What lessons life taught were proven to last
Let love be your beacon while exploring dreams
Abandon the burden of hatred
Your heart will guide the path
That leads to dreams awaiting discovery
Gregory K. Clark

Insomnia

Darkness...but my eyes catch a gleam from a light through the trees
I strain to see what it is, but then the time catches my eye,
an awful feeling of deja vu, and it seems that I never sleep...

I listen to hear another voice, another being, alive somewhere near
  me
I crave another human sound to comfort me, to make me feel less
  alone this night
but there is only this voice, me scolding myself, for being awake
It is awful to be tormented by thought when all I want to do is
  dream

Flipping my pillow to find a cool spot, blanketed by darkness
I lie in the bed, trying to see the cracks in the walls
wishing I could leave, or maybe call someone to talk to
Who might be awake? No one, they're all sleeping

The silence blares against my ears
I tap the wall with my fingernails to make a noise, any noise
I think of all I must do when the dawn comes and the fear of sleep
approaches. If I sleep now, will I wake? I must sleep now!

Force never had much affect on the sandman
I sprawl out on my bed, exhausted from my fight against the night
and suddenly it is morning.
Elizabeth Marie O'Shaughnessy

The Winter Of '96

What seems to go on forever and more
The Winter of 96 has us all chilled to the core
The icy blasts come again and again
Will it ever end
No one seems to know when
The great blizzard has passed
But the snows come still
I think it's a long way to the first daffodil

The groundhog appeared and took one little peek
And said let them have it for another six weeks
I wish he had seen some sun or some light
Which could have meant an end to our plight
But, alas he did not and is back in his hole
So the winter drags on for the young and the old
I know there's life under the snow sure to bloom
But all I can feel is the cold and the gloom

The Summer or Fall would sure be the thing
But just for now Lord
Could you hurry up Spring!
Louis Colabella

Dandelions

Dandelions are a poor man's gold;
Each spring they herald the end of cold.
When winter was long and all seemed dead
Then up popped a dandelion's golden head.

When the sun and rain start them to grow
In profusion their gold they show;
Giving the promise that winter won't stay
And spreading their sunshine along the way.

In a country field or by a city street
A dandelion's gold is a special treat.
No need to plant them or take great care
For dandelions bloom just anywhere.

Blooming dandelions may some annoy
Yet I regard them with great joy!
You may count your riches by other signs
But I'd like my wealth in dandelions!
Betty Daniel Pack

Heavenbound

The silence of life ebbs into eternity.

Hearts heavy give to God
   The babe lent but for a moment;
Arms hungering to cradle sweet innocence
   Ache instead with the pain of hollow emptiness;
Sorrow filled anguish embraces
   The reality of a world gone awry.

Accepting strength and courage to face unsought trials,
   Tears flow cleansing the souls of embittered wonderings;
Peaceful slumberings return as darkness fades into
   The memories and enduring love for this child

Touched by God

And born with angel wings.
   Karen A. Davisson

"Soul Cries Out"

I sit here at the edge of my bed,
Head in my hands.
Tasting every tear that blinds my sight,
I try to drowned my thoughts.
Slowly turning my head
I see my reflection.
A face with no happiness, pale and deadly.
Sunken eyes, weary lips.
They say time heals all wounds
But I think... I'll be broken forever.
The addiction of pain I do feed.
Surrounded by ice cold misery.
I am deafened by the endless song that echoes in my soul.
Quenching every breath, I fall to my knees
My arms held out, my face to the sky.
Questions with no answers whirl in my head.
Unafraid, I cry aloud
Breaking the ties that bind me from the inside.
I finally found the answers
And have been released from the shackles of pain that held me down.
   Jamie Fann

In the Back of My Mind

There you are, in the back of my mind again.
Days and nights lost in a dream state.
The only reality is the love I feel for you.

You are more real in my mind, than to the touch.
Your scent lingers - it fills my lungs and my thoughts.
If I close my eyes and take a deep breath, you are here.

I can feel you caressing my cheek with your lips.
I can feel your strong hands hold my shoulders.
Your legs and feet are intertwined with mine.
We are lost in each other.

No matter where we are, we are together.
Think of me holding your hand, squeezing your hand.
I am there.

You warm my heart and soul.
There you are, in the back of my mind again.
   Jill S. Parolise

'Why I Walk'

I walk for exercise and pleasure.
I walk and don't talk, concentrating on each inhalation and exhalation

I walk for relaxation and expectation.
In nineteen-fifty-five thru nineteen-sixty-five I walked everywhere.
I walked to school monday thru fridays, I walked to church most
Sunday evenings for Baptist Training union, and I walked upon
Minnesota Ave to shop.
In my teenage years walking were wheels, I felt tortuous; none
the less I kept walking. I walked to ball games, I walked to club
meetings, and I walked to parties.
My figure was magnificent and it didn't cost a cent.
In nine-teen seventy-one my medical career begun. I invariably
walked the hospital floors as a respiratory therapist.
I walked briskly and ran on code blues, I walked briskly and
ran to the intensive care units, and I walked briskly and ran
to stat calls and the emergency rooms.
Needless to say, walking was inevitably for me. At time I allowed
humiliation to overwhelm me. I had to keep the momentum.
As I worked through out the hospitals through out the years.
I developed poise upon my toes and grace upon my face.
   Brenda Gregory Polk

Vacation

I do have my pride,
As thru life I do ride,
But I do want to run and hide,
Because with people, at times, I do collide,
That's when I feel that I am on a downward slide,

I just need to go and regroup,
Generate more energy,
Then, again, thru life I can troop,
Plan my life's strategy,

So I'm going on vacation,
And have fun!
Is it a recommendation?
For a while, I can from my daily routine, run,

Just to relax!
And not feel so over-taxed!

So with this trip may I enjoy,
Just like a child with a new toy!

So with my spirit that is torn,
This vacation can make me soar,
So when I come home, I'll feel that I can roar!
And once again stand tall, on life's floor!
   Paula Patterson-Stevenson

A Tear Streaked Face

If only I could choke the tears that come from deep inside.
If only I had a prayer of hope, I wouldn't have to hide.

If only I had a simple gift to keep close to my heart.
I would keep it dear and safe within and never let it part.

I think of people worse off than me but somehow they seem better.
I don't know why I feel this way so I write myself this letter.

I write to myself please do not cry,
I really try, I try, I try.

I tell myself someone will lend a hand.
But till that day, my tears are banned.

They say I'm strange cause I like the dark and candles friendly light.
It's just they give me the strength to give my tears a fight.

I don't think anyone can hear my lonely cries.
I don't think they want to, so I'll just hide them and tell them all lies.

I won't tell anyone about my case.
I'll just hide my tear streaked face.
   Ashlee Springer

The Word (Unspoken Love)

The word you trip on
The word unspoken
The word cuts like a sword

The word hate
The word love
The word diversity

The word adversity
The word releases me from this prison in my mind
The word gives me vision

I revise the word
The words meaning is dead
The threat of the word
The beauty of the word

I bleed the word
I create the word
I delete the word

The word given
The word taken
The word mistaken
Just a word
David C. Ferris

Faded Memories

All my memories a fade
Yet my thoughts as sharp as a blade
I sometimes wonder if I've been there before
So I reach on what my brain has stored
I have the figure in my head
Though not enough for it to be said
The figure comes out then slips on through
I try and wonder if my thoughts were true
I know if I concentrate, my thoughts will appear
I sit and try to bring them near
Thinking again the words do appear
I capture her face and draw the rest near
After thinking and thinking of the thought I would say
I find it's no use for the face is away
Thinking of her my thoughts will soon die
For I realize to myself it was all just a lie
All that was said, all that was done
For all the feelings quickly end down the barrel of a GUN
Joe Sariñana Jr.

I Dream...

I dream of the time when I will live without fear...
A time when a hug isn't a touch that I have to grin and bear.
A time when I can allow other people to come near.

I dream of the time when I will live without fear...
A time when things may get out of my control but I won't despair,
A time when personal difficulties won't affect my career.

I dream of the time when I will live without fear...
A time when it doesn't matter what I wear,
A time when people don't think I am queer.

I dream of the time when I will live without fear...
A time when I won't care if people stare,
A time when I can handle if people care.

I dream of the time when I will live without fear...
A time when 'live life to the fullest' is not just something I may hear,
A time when I can face a peer and walk away with some dignity to spare.

I dream of the time when I will live without fear...
  I dream.
Anne Raffaelo

Fears Within The Mind

Out in the woods
I thought I saw
a ghostly figure walking 'round,
staring with glowing eyes,
as I looked
it turned out to be
only the reflection of me
in the fog that swirled around the trees;
I could swear I heard
someone whisper my name,
but as I listened,
it was only the breeze.
Alynda Cone

After The Love

A sharp pain digs into my heart,
When I realize once again we've been torn apart.

By the same reasons as all the times before,
But this time I promised myself it won't happen anymore.

I can only take so much heartache and pain,
Knowing that loving you I have nothing to gain.

You've set me free and I'm not turning around this time,
I'm erasing you from my heart and my mind.
Janna L. Russell

What You Mean To Me

Some people will stand by you through thick and thin.
You know they will be there until the very end.
All the while knowing that you will always have someone by your side,
To guide you through until the morning light.
Somehow you know that there must have been a plan,
And together we will make it hand and hand.
They've taken away a piece of your heart;
You knew they were the one from the very start.
So together the tow of us will become intertwined
Souls that are forever inseparable in time.
So darling what I've been trying to tell you in so many ways
Is how much you mean to me each and every day.
I may not always be able to say the right things,
But I want you to know to me how much your love brings.
And I'm hoping that always we should never part,
Because I'll love you forever with all of my heart.
Kevin Kutac

My Olympic Run

Oh Lord, I know by your spirit,
The time is drawing near.
The puzzle is coming together,
The picture is becoming more clear...

You said, we see in a mirror darkly,
When you alone are the light.
Help us to put it together,
At last, let us get it right...

We need your wisdom and discernment,
So we can make it thru each day.
The enemy throws up many obstacles,
But your spirit, Lord, will guide our way...

Let us all be single-eyed like the dove,
Seeing, only with spiritual eyes,
As we walk hand in hand with you, Lord,
Your path will materialize...

Through prayer and much supplication,
With correction, from your staff and rod.
We'll keep running the race with hope in our hearts,
Till we kneel before your throne, OH GOD......
Rose A. Benavente

Combat

Warriors gather in a sea of competition.
All fighting for the chance
to woo the sunlit flower.
Can victory be mine?—Will my hope fade?
Lo I the Rock, poor warrior am I.
It is hard for me to defeat the others.
My form hinders combat,
but I have a strong-gentle heart.
I know it will see me through my foes.
My prize is well worth the punishment
this hulky form can sustain.
I will stand aloft the mound of labor,
proud with the Rose in my hand;
Although it will fade, the image of what
it once was will never be lost in the
blue water's of my eyes.
Denos Myrmingos

Open Your Eyes

Look beyond the walls of concrete and steel
Look into my heart and know what's real
Look into my mind at the images that are there
Let our feelings join together as one
Experience that which has been hidden from you
See that which is unseen
Feel that which is unfelt
Late at night my screams go unheard
My tears fall unseen by those around me
My prayer to God in heaven is that I'm set free
There's no real freedom from this for me
This place, this time will always be with me
And as for you my friend, lift your eyes
Fill your heart with joy and gladness
Let your spirit soar
Stay on the outside of jail's door
for what awaits is misery and despair
Amongst those who do not care
Hollis Pete Wilkerson

Dearest Tera

Our thoughts and prayers are with you
And we hope you're feeling better,
We knew a poem would perk you up
Much more than just a letter.

The days will pass by quickly and
You will surely find,
That pleasant thoughts will fill your days
And occupy your mind.

We poets are a special breed
We write of hope and love,
We do our best to say the things
With blessings from above.

So Tera you get well real soon
You life is just beginning,
Do have the faith and look ahead
The game of life's worth winning.
Donald G. Binninger

Braveheart

Wist ye for the Highlands,
  Aflame with heather and gorse.
The banner of cloud and wild grey mist
  That crowns the crags of Norse.
Wist ye for the Highlands,
  The ramparts we stormed on the Heights.
The Sassenach we hurled back again and again,
  From our Kith and our Kin and our Kine.
Leopold Cann

The Single Kiss

As the night wind settled across the lake,
Only one could dare to forsake,
The mystic feeling which came upon her,
Without a word, without a stir.

As soon as this feeling had passed,
All but one remembered the spell it cast,
For the lake that night looked like a gem.
A moonstone with its starry stem.

As the night went on, people stayed on the lake,
Not daring to move, not daring to wake,
For they all thought that this was a dream,
Though it was from the heavens, a holy beam.

What had come upon them that night,
That strange, yet beautiful, ray of light,
Could not be explained except for this,
It was all concealed within a single kiss.
Mary Nelan

Best Friend

Her best friend is always there -
her best friend will always care.

Her best friend will always listen -
her best friend she can always trust in.

My best friend will sometimes care -
my best friend will every now and then be there.

My best friend will listen when she feels like it -
My best friend will keep a secret but only if her mouth will allow her to.

My best friend is lucky she has
  a best friend like me.
Sara Macdonald

Nightmare

Hopes slip down below the horizon,
Setting upon my emotions,
And my torn dreams fade into darkness.
Before you stood as an illusion,
But you dissipated in a burst of light,
Quickly dimming to black.
Running to catch a speck of what's left
Of my immolated fantasies,
I fall into a spiral heading down towards my ultimate desolation.
Your love tainted by reason,
And even the most fervid attempts
To save my love and my sanity
Are shredded by reason's sordid ways.
And at the moment of my desecration,
My eyes fling open to take in the reality
That my pain was all in my mind.
The blurred image in front of me turns pristine-clear.
It's your face with your lips telling me it's all right.
Your merciful hand strokes my hair
To chase the nightmare away.
Michelle McCarty

The Need To Be Free

When I was a boy, I didn't know why,
Why do birds sing? Why do birds fly?
As I was growing, and time spent alone,
I understood why they needed a home
Now that I'm grown, a man of today,
I understand why the birds would not stay.
I often look back at a time gone past,
Where have the years gone and why so fast?
But just as in growing it's clear to see,
I understand why. The need to be free.
Norman W. Rice

Untitled

Night quickly approaches as I retire to my bed
But I begin to hear many voices tossing all around inside my head
I hear the sounds more clearly, now I see the visions too
My father sitting on the couch - mother busy with "work to do."

She said it's time to go to bed, but first she must do my hair
Afterwards, I begged her to no avail to continue to watch TV there
After all of my pleading, I kissed Mom and Dad goodnight
And as Mom tucked me in - I held to my pillow tight.

Ah...to return to those old days all hopes of money I would give
To be a child in her arms again and have one moment I could relive
My eyes open suddenly and I am back here all alone
No one thing is on my mind more now than the want to be at home.

I was only dreaming I will never see childhood again
However, the moments would've been treasured more dearly if what I know now, I knew then
The parents' love for a child is the greatest love I've yet to know
They loved me unconditionally and helped my soul to grow.

I know my parents are still there for me to teach me wrong from right
But I'll never forget the days when they tucked me in at night.
Leslie Chambers

Someday

Set in your ways, yet chance came so sudden.
Mirrors of your memory reflect nothing with each departing word.
Don't attempt feigned sorrow, for pain is a poison I digest.
And as you go forward, leaving empty promises and desperate
Yet useless hope burning through me,
Your image will remain forever.
Someday I may understand, and find sleep without the
Necessary intoxicating dreams which I've come to know.
Someday I will be whole again...
Someday.
Phil Bower

"The Mirror"

In this moment that I share with no-one, relishing that there are no roles to play, I am stripped naked.

Seemingly, less who I am, than the facade that is my life.

Forced to look into the face of pain that is my past and that bleeds, still into my present.

Questioning my choices with my Father's disapproval and apologizing with my child's insecurities.

Analyzing my worthiness for love and the price I am willing to pay.

Longing for the love and assurance that can only come from here, I must return
to this place where no masks exist and squirm through the discomfort of seeing myself, (as I am.)

I pray for a distraction to take me back, where familiarity clouds this mirror,
That I must someday wipe clean.
Annette Slusser

Waking At Your Side

Although, we are not intimate, although, we are not in love;
I smile as I gaze restlessly at the morning sun above.

What I so desire is not be alone.
The warmth of your body insulates my every bone.

It's a crisp, cold morning when I wake at your side.
Under the snugly covers is where I intend to hide.

Content I am, here I could stay.
I wish I was able to wake with you each and every day.
Dawn M. Venosa

The Nursing Home

New beginnings, I was told,
They packed my bags and brought my clothes.
A single bed and dresser drawers..
could never hold for what in store.
My days of sleeping in till late,
ended on that day of fate.
Now I rise before the birds,
and sit and wait till breakfasts served.
The showers may be cold or hot,
depending on who's on or not!
I wait and wait to see who's coming,
yet day by day, the weeks go running.
Thank goodness for the workers there,
whose talents give me daily care!
Christina M. Guk

Wanted

Everyone needs to be wanted,
Everyone needs a friend to talk to,
Everyone needs to feel wanted so that they
can make it through life,
But not everyone does feel wanted
some people are all lonely,
see that person all alone
I bet that she thinks that
no one really wants her
or that no one really likes her
or that no one really cares
what happens to her.
Tiffanie Sorell

My Older Sister

My older sister likes to eat,
But when she does, she's way too neat.

I don't like it, not one bit,
So I decided to throw a Hissy Fit.

I started to yell, scream and cry,
The next thing you know I'm throwing pies.

My mom sends me to my room, Yes siree,
But I don't go, No siree.

I try to reason with her, I really do,
But she always wins, Oh Poop Poop!
Danita Rotella

Grandma's Bible

This book is all that is left of her now,
Unsummoned tears eventually start,
With faltering lip and throbbing brow,
I clutchingly press it to my heart.
For generations in the past,
Here in this book is our family tree,
In my grandma's hands this Bible was clasped,
She, on her death bed, gave it to me.
I remember extremely well those
Whose names these biblical records bear;
As my grandfather read these names, to close
Just after the family's evening prayer.
My grandmother saved this Bible just for me,
Not knowing what a guide it would be.
Amanda Jones

The Dreamer

I know that I must for my heart tells me so.
My thoughts, my dreams, my every emotion.
Stirring in the innermost depth of my being.
As if with a touch of a magical potion.
With whom must I share this variety of dreams.
I have gathered from the realm of the imagination.
Where the spirits of incredulity it seems.
Have punctured my soul to demand revelation.
Alas! When weary I gently succumb.
And my senses turn to dust.
I grope through the mist.
Into the world of words.
And I write for I know that I must.

Marie Ortega

Letting Go Of Lost Home

This seemingly endless search
Will it ever come to an end?
Resources so limited in meeting each need
Is there a place that will truly feel like home?

Perhaps the attempt has been to match the old;
The home once shared with a family so loved.
A house, then much larger and family to greet.
The end of each day is so empty without them!

Filling each new apartment with familiar furnishings,
To a degree that some comfort returns, but not all
Not for the house and its set-up that I longingly ache;
But the loved ones with whom all was shared.

Many dwellings were ours as a family we grew.
In each the ability to find the comfort I seek.
Yes, the ones left behind are the cause of this on going pain;
Not the domiciles at all underlying my struggle and grief.

My task to let go; put the past behind, if I can
Getting my life organized into an element all its own
Comparison being futile; such a match will not happen.
Only my best to make life suitable; forceably formulating new goals.

Susan Limback Rogina

Empty Life

Television flipping, sunbeams exposing dust in the air
Papers and magazines scatter the floor, ash trays filthy
End tables and coffee table with items not put away; who cares?
Bill receipts, books, medication, filled trash bin by the chair.

Finger painting could be done in dust so visible on furniture;
Smears, smudges, and finger prints on mirrors, windows, T.V's
Christmas gifts, though few, wrapped ; but no reason to hide them;
Beginning to get dark, so shades drawn and door locked.

As the darkness sets in, so does emptiness and sorrow fill me.
Little chance of the stillness being broken by the phone or door
Without the sounds of TV, there's just the hum of the furnace and
  purifier
So the television becomes my close friend; my companion and comfort.

This is the grief of not having my loved ones; husband of two
  decades and 14 year old son
At times it's like death, separation from a homelife I cherished
Not being wanted; no reasons, or answers to the future
Pain fills me, yet I'm empty; so back to the television my solace
  must be

Get out and work! Oh, if only I could use that very option
Being limited by a disability has had my willingness ignored
Income so small, entertainment not budgeted; I barely get by
I get out, push my limits; but the biggest majority is a void!

Susan E. L. Regina

Giving Love. . .

Giving love not returned is what women often do.

Giving love not returned is an
empty room void of sunlight filled with tears that fall like
early morning dew

Giving love not returned is a child waiting for christmas
morn...

Giving love not returned is a dark eternity without Christ...

Giving love not returned is facing an empty bed at night

Giving love not returned is a cold January day when snow
covers with its coldness all that you can see..

Giving love not returned is me loving and praying for one
night with you...

Giving love not returned will end when someone loves you

Giving love not returned is waiting for life anew...

Peggy Thomas

Open Your Eyes And See

Open your eyes and see,
All the beautiful colors on that tree!
Colors of red, colors of gold,
Everything new, nothing seems old.

Open your eyes and see,
What the winter has done to that tree.
The leaves are gone, and the branches are bare,
The tree was once beautiful, it seems so unfair.

Open your eyes and see, the tree is looking down on me.
The leaves are green, now that spring is here!
Not a rain cloud in the sky, it seems very clear.

Open your eyes and see,
Now that summer's here, it's a shady spot for me.
The colors of that tree, I hope will not fade,
I love to stare at the neat colors,
I think that tree has it made.

No matter how long and boring,
Those beautiful seasons may be,
You'll find beauty in them some day,
Just open your eyes and see!

Ashlee Watson

Untitled

The sound of your sweet voice makes me quiver
It ignites my heart's internal flame
Your presence in a room sends a romantic shiver
That makes my mind flustered and lame

But ashamed by my appearance
I only long to be near
Close to your beauty and essence
But I flee like a startled deer

If I cannot hold your love
Then may God receive me in heaven up above

Richard Thomason

For Christmas Or Anytime

There is a prayer I'd say for you, if I could but find the words
If secret thoughts and magic dreams and deepest feelings
  could be heard
There is a wish I'd wish for you, but being on the highest plane
And much too fine for common tongues, unspoken must remain
But if at any time on any day for just one moment
One sparkling drop of unspoiled joy finds its way to you
Then at that moment my prayer will have been answered
And at that moment my wish will have come true

Joseph Ray Trainer

Caged

The eyes of the beast scintillate to direction unknown.
Medusa dares not penetrate its gaze.
Hot blood within commutes only between heart and brain.
The heart craves the life saving nutrients that stimulate emotion to revive the beast,
But with each pass the tyranny of the cerebellum prevails.
Neurons are fed to shelter and protect from pernicious obliquity.
Conjunction, sumption, what's your function?
Eradicate the bleating obscenity of these surroundings.
Still my beating heart; pierce it, knead it, wrap it in a bow;
If reason reigns I'll feel no more.

A hand emerges from the clammy stone floor arbitrating habeas impasse.
Wonder twin powers activate circulation alpha and omega.
Eyelids vascillate cornucopia.
The beast sees the geletal observers and springs suddenly to its feet.
A fleeting circumambulation leaves it facing its nemesis.
Euphoria grasps the bars to the cell shaking them with spasmic bedlam.
The words I am not an animal ring with sonorous climax.
That is why we call him the caged animal,
Dr. Detroit casually remarks as the group continues their tour of the facility.

Christopher Edmunds

"When Angels Sleep"

Silently she sleeps
Her head resting on a soft pillow
As angels protect her.

She is herself
A cherub who could have landed
From the heavens

Her face is soft,
Her eyes bright when they're open,
And her laugh like music.

As she slumbers
I'm sure that if I listen close
I can hear singing.

For when she sleeps
Her angels are near her still form
Softly standing watch.

I know one day
I will be able to see the angels
Hovering over her, nurturing.

But for now I'm content to watch the blissful slumber
Of my very own angel on earth.

Jason P. Hunt

"Lionheart"

I am the "Lion" that once roamed the jungle; my head held high and majestically proud. But wandered too far, for now, I am caged. As my manacles and chains hold me, relentlessly in anguish, I speak in my bold and proud voice, but to no avail, in utter shame and disgrace, only to rumble a house cats' sneer.

But "Lo and behold", on the other side of this shady deceit, there are those who pass by. Some of whom I have come to call "Friends", that mock at the greatness I once represented.

Whereas, a barrier stands between myself and the peons, to strike a blow with the power and gracefulness which I stand for. I await for that dreadful day, to be released from my sacrilege and bondage. Yes, indeed a very "Dreadful day" for all those who opposed me and camouflaged their inner being; for on that very day, people around the world will know that the king of the jungle is free once more, and even hungrier that ever before. Nevertheless, the house cats' sneer, will once again become a lions' "Roar"!!!!!

Ray W. K. Montero

An Unforeseen Weekend

Time is well spent without having to make it right.
How well two days were spent when it wasn't supposed to be a night.
It was so calm, natural and joyful.
What was best was that we hadn't breaking any rules.
Knowing that you were there, just an arms reach away.
But still, at the end we had to part, and wait for another day.
Your company, conversation, beauty and touch
is so pleasing that, I don't seem to get enough.
Trying to spend as much time as possible together,
under all kinds of weather.
The people looking at us like fools,
because we act as if we were still in high school.
It doesn't bother me.
It just makes me feel happy and free.
I can't remember when I last felt like this.
Especially after we kiss.
Just the same I want you to know,
that I would like to have you by my side wherever I go.
Yes, that weekend unforeseen,
made me feel like a king and you my queen.

Pedro M. Rosario

A Life Worth Living

The darkness exists in me and invades my soul.
It renders me helpless to fill this vast empty hole.
Where there was once hope, there is now dole.

I cannot contemplate why I must live with such pain.
Always knowing I could end it all, but what would it gain.
Instead I trudge on helplessly living my life in vain.

I am not deterred however from my feelings of inadequacy,
Because I know that hopes exists and it is the key,
To obtaining the happiness I deserve and is due to me.

Debbie L. Uterstaedt

Saved

One day, aside the road, I saw Death.
It beckoned to me, but I refused.
I kept drying "I am to young to die."
But each and every word I said, It seemed amused.
What was I to do?
What was I to say?
I couldn't just leave
And I couldn't let it have its way.
So there I stood
Alone and scared
And then I saw Life.
He looked like He really cared.
Life said to Death
Leave thee alone.
She hasn't done a thing
So just be gone.
Death vanished in thin air.
I just stood there
Kneeling on my knees
In the middle of a prayer.

LeAnne Graves

Jimmy

Your eyes remind me of...
   the bluest of oceans I have ever sailed.
Your lips remind me of...
   the sweetest strawberry I've ever tasted.
Your hair reminds me of...
   the desert of springtime,
   specks of pink in a sandy yellow background.
Your smile reminds me of...
   the warmth and cheeriness from the sun.
Altogether, You remind me of...
   what happiness should be.

Mindy Krovontka

Angel Of Loves

I'm he who holds treasure of love
I'm he who rides the darkest horse,

I'm he who's tears are as red as blood
I'm he who walks behind the roses and carries eternal love.

I'm he who shines upon a star
I'm he who controls light and dark,

I'm he who holds the crown and mysteries of both worlds.
I'm the dark in the light, I'm only one God.

I give life to the past in every men's life,
For them to recognize and learn from their mistakes.

I'm he who holds the power of your soul
I'm he who controls your heart, desires and life.

I'm he who hold the power of love
I'm he eternal as love and everlasting as God.

I'm he who shines in the night
I'm the angel of love
I'm the son of the morning star.
Alex D'Carlo Martinez

Greetings Classmates

As you recall and gather sweet memories of yore,
I am proud to be among you counting the score.
Please keep me in thought and prayer
For I can't in person be there.
I know where every scrap of paper is on the desk
of mine, I confess;
But why doesn't time go slower, go slower...
bewildering, ah yes!
Already I see everyone having fun and wearing a big smile;
Yet, how did it get to be the 60th Reunion in grand style?
In 1995 we've reached another milestone
Never say you're old but rather a polished gemstone!
Things are looking up in pure harmony
God thinks you're special and so do I ... Whee!
Our friendships are a hug from God says a hymn of praise
Thus I ask Him to bless you and give you many more days.
Now as I bid you a fond adieu, may more reunions be
Says your class "poetess," Marie (Parsons) Stucki.
L. Marie Stucki

Perfection

Loving a soul without a body.
Touching a face unseen.
What will this mean years down that road
Looking back at that fork?
Dividing an unknown future,
Confining a way of life.
One way, down an offbeat path-
Hopeful to find that body.
Yet without the soul, is it real to touch-
Or a mere figment of reality?
Lying beneath a blanket of imagination
only to reach a dead end.
Turning around to find the guided path
In all its beauty and glory.
To find that body to match the soul,
Following the flowered way.
Yet stopping, turning down the darkened path,
Searching for the soul itself, satisfied with "It" alone.
Using that same blanket to cover the end,
Propelling past all darkness into undeniable rapture!
Alleah M. Bucs

A Conscience, A Soul, A Man

It comes with me where e'er I go,
but can't be found from head to toe.
A something that I hold within
from a heavenly right, to a terrible sin.
Some people, I wonder, if they dare
to even acknowledge that it's there.

A conscience, a soul - to each only a name,
appear to be different but yet they're the same.

For instance man, one black, one white,
are not as different as day from night.
Both know the difference from right to wrong,
no matter how weak, no matter how strong.
Comes the end and we're all the same -
equality is the name of the game.

Black and white - to each only a name,
appear to be different but yet they're the same.
M. Jeannine Gioia

Watching My Child Grow

Infants are dependent - for their every need
So parents need to readjust - let baby take the lead

Soon they will begin to grow - and they will grow real fast
You watch your child start to walk - the infancy won't last

Your child is so curious - she wants to have all known
And as you answer questions - you realize how she's grown

Time has passed so rapidly - the first day of school you cried
And now you sit and wonder why - 'cause part of you just died

Before you know it, there she goes - out on her first date
You've had that little talk with her - and hope she decides to wait

The big day comes so quickly - you've helped her with her plans
You watch her say her wedding vows - while holding on his hands

Now she has an infant - a child of her own
The cycle starts all over - but your little girl is grown
Terri M. Kuball

Mother

In my life there has always been one
Through every strife and every pun.
From the greatest triumph to the worst defeat.
It started the moment I won to whenever beat.
Always carrying an encouraging word.
That never sounded to absurd.
She's been a part of my life in every way.
Not once letting me wonder astray.
Do you know of whom this message I send?
It is you my mother, my friend.
Molly A. Richert

As I Cross The Street

As I cross the street,
I notice that I sometimes forget to look both ways,
And as I walk down a one way street, I often see that
I am going the wrong way,
I fall into a self-dug hole, and I realize that I tend
to step on people to make a ladder to get myself out.
When I am in a bad, no-win situation, I see myself
hurting other people so that I may avoid as
much possible hurt and embarrassment for myself,
I see these mistakes through the eyes of a human,
Through me,
As I cross the street.
Jessica Hoolihan

Dance With Me

Walk with me
through my own curves
blend into the background
as my one
my one and only
the yearnings have become real
amidst this fairy-tale land
as the protector turns cold
and his lands become fallow
dance with me
through the monochrome lighting
you who are not real
unless I choose you to be
are you walking?
I cannot see you anymore
it seems that real life has made you invisible
   again
   Christine Drake

Friends

We used to be such great friends,
Now we've become enemies.
I sometimes stare out the window,
Wishing to take back all the mean words.
I walk to school alone,
With my friend walking on the other side.
God, how could we have let it happen?
A great friendship destroyed.
I pretend to be so happy with everyone,
But really, I'm terribly sad.
I've tried so many times to talk about it,
But I'm afraid it's hopeless.
God, how could we have let it happen?
A great friendship destroyed.
We use to agree on everything,
Now it's all wrong.
Sometimes we'd tell each other secrets,
Now we call each other names.
God, how could we have let it happen?
A great friendship destroyed.
   Amanda Vastine

Untitled

I must think of good times, in memories past.
I know they're there, but they go so fast.
My son Jimmy was turning five that year,
a little stout, but a lovable dear.
He would play rough, as little boys do,
but his love was warm, sweet, kind and true.
He was smart for a boy going on five.
There was more on his mind, than just momma's jive.
Jennifer Renee, my precious, sweet girl,
if love were a blanket, hers would cover the world.
A sweet two and a half and liked me to hold her.
I'd hold and we'd hug, with her head on my shoulder.
We'd go sit in a rocking chair,
then my lap, with her brother, she would share.
Then the three of us would rock and rock away,
until the two of them, had met the end of their day.
Lay them in bed and tuck them in tight,
softly say I love you, then kissed each a good night.
I love my children, where ever they may be.
Deep in their hearts.... I hope they still love me.
   James G. Stewart Jr.

3108

Everyday when I wake
I see the number 3108.

I look down and remember these,
horrible, painful memories.

The terrible screams, the bad situations,
as much as I want to, I can not escape them.

The deaths and separations of family and friends,
seemed like they would never end.

But one day it did, it came to a close,
"I can leave all my troubles behind me, "I proposed.

However, I forgot, I can not part with fate,
for there carved in my arm is the number, 3108.
   Amelia Heins

Just Friends

As the curtain slowly settles, I soon must take my bow
And bid my friends a fond adieu, my act is over now.

I've played my part, however good, or bad, it may have seemed,
I never tried for leadman roles, perhaps I only dreamed

That friendships last forever, and love is just a tune
We ofttimes play together as we sail beyond the moon.

But dreams soon fade with daylight, for life is real and true,
So nought is surely wasted, if I've been a friend to you.

Hark! the orchestra is playing, see! the lights are all aglow,
Your audience is waiting so continue with the show,

And I'll be down front cheering
Each new goal you will attain
And hoping (though we've been just friends)
As friends we'll still remain.
   Donald D. Miller

Distant Depths

I'm looking down into the distant depths
   of a plashless black lake.
A bitter dry breeze is brushing my skin and
   I still feel the steel in my back from the previous wake.

I'm looking down into distant depths,
   peering for what stands below.
Hoping it's not a crag with homicidal intent,
   fearing how deep I could go.

I'm looking down into distant depths,
   knowing, to flee, is to starve my heart.
I shudder slightly, gulp in a tremulous breath,
   fall toward uncertainty, and security and I part.
   Brent J. Howard

Family Storm

Disbelief blew in swaying emotions
A mist of sorrow soon followed covering all yet foretold
Rumbling sadness sounded off in the distance
Then a flash of fear signaled oncoming pain
Soon the other emotions stormed in with less warning
With a fury not yet understood or controlled
Regrets howled moving clouds of resentment
Guilt rained down and dampened the soul
Anger surged inside threatening to burst down the memories
Yet togetherness brought forth a new calm of strength
Faith had helped them weather their sorrow
Rays of love came thru shining down from the heavens
Carrying a forgiveness that brightened the way
For peace to settle upon the family now knowing
That mother still loves them, even now passed away
   Kevin Lamb

I Can't Find My Way Back Home

She was unhappy with her life, and so she took it.
Funny, but she had said she never would quit.
And so, my life goes on and on,
and only silence will scream at me now.

How could I have seen it? All of the signs were there
But I was done with the madness, and so I made her go.
All the overwhelming sadness, and being all alone
was much too hard to bear, for her there
So she ended it all, for her,
and now I have a cross to hear, an albatross.

I still see her in our children, once in a while
She would have been proud, if she had allowed herself to be,
The joke's on me.
Can you hold me up for just a moment?
My legs gave out on me, just like she.
But, I am sometimes strong,
And I have no choice but to carry on.

I can't find my way home
Can you take me there?
So this is what it's like to be alone.
Tad Sisler

Frantic Green Cries

Thinking of the pain that she felt,
She tried frantically to scream for help.
The pain became deadly as it engulfed her voice,
She became afraid as she heard the horrid noise.
The sudden thought of the terrible lies,
Only brought out the frantic green cries.
All the days that were so flabbergasting,
Made her think this life would be everlasting.
And now she knew the reality of this,
Only death would help seal the pain with a kiss.
The pain she was feeling, she tried to ignore
As she turned her head slowly to look at the floor.
She had given up all her trust,
All these feeling would soon be rust.
The horrid feeling as it began to rise,
Only brought out the frantic green cries.
Standing up top she did not dare,
The feeling of relief as she leap in the air.
To remember the horror and all the lies,
Only brought out the frantic green cries.
Marcela Meletti

I Believe I Should Have Loved You

I should have loved you long ago
  holding all your words dear
  embracing life through your tattered fears
  exclusively hearing the dreams that make
  you who you are — the man I once despised,
  but thank God love I now

I should have loved you long ago
  to feel your gentle ways
  the strength of your arms
  the fire in your eyes
  pulling me away
  from every rugged thought I had
  making you a dreaded soul
  God's time allotted proven sweet
  memories untold

I laugh, I cry
  you wipe the tears with such manly care

I can't help but think I should have loved you long ago
Michelle Blakey

Back To School

In the fall of the year when the nights turn cool
Children's thoughts turn again to the start of school.
After weeks of vacation asking, "What's there to do?"
Now find the days left are all too few
Before school bells ring across the land
And once more they'll have classes, reading and band,
Spelling and science, history and math,
And rememb'ring again as they walk the path
Of learning that studying's always the key
That will open the door to set their minds free
To soar with the knowledge they're learning at school,
When they return in the fall when the nights turn cool.
Carl W. Nicholson

Good News Where Can It Be Found

Today I picked up the paper and read
There's a war in Bosnia - 100 are dead
A mother she beat her child to death
Imagine this woman she took his last breath
I keep turning the pages and what do I find
Four teenagers killed a man for a dime
But where is the good news there must be some
I'm at the end of the paper there wasn't none
But that's not the way God planned it to be
We should pick up the paper and see
A man won a million dollars today
He'll build a big house for all those astray
The sign on the door will say please come in
It doesn't matter the color of your skin
If you're hungry I'll feed you if you're lonely I'll talk
If you're old and you're weak I'll help you walk
So listen let's see what God has to say
Open your bible and read it each day
Find out the Good News and promises too
and have faith in God I know he'll come through
Cathy Andrews

The Passing Of Summer

Summer is swiftly passing us by
The fact is, I don't remember July
I had dreams of what the summer would bring,
And now, I say "what ever happened to spring?"

Oh where have all the lovely days gone?
And soon we shall miss all the birds and their song.
The flowers will fade and the leaves will fall down,
In colorful piles all over the ground.

It soon will be time for the Halloween Parade.
Time for fall harvest when cider is made.
It's a fun-filled time for young and old,
But oh, the weather is growing so cold!

Soon snow flakes will be falling
As we near Thanksgiving day,
And folks getting ready for the Thanksgiving Parade.

So on comes winter with cold winds and snow,
And those bitter cold winds just blow and blow.
The days are short and the nights are long.
So we sit and dream of flowers, birds and their song.

And wait for the winter's cold weather to be gone.
Gladys Olivia Felda

The Great Tide

Eyes that hold, attention caught,
Will you pursue? For I will not,
Out-dated values, a world too fast,
Waiting for love, are you my mast?
I need strength, a sail in the wind,
Harmonious union? Sail pinned?
Will we travel a lifetime? Our love as a guide?
Support me as I hold true, together, side by side,
So I ask you, heart-wide,
Will you withstand the forces....
Of the great tide?
   Karen May

Eternally Yours

Search your soul, if you dare;
For in its essence, you'll find me there.

And in your dreams, where you have wings;
You'll find that thoughts are tangible things.

And know that you will always be,
Within my heart, eternally.

For to yourself you can't deny,
That some things never, ever die.
   Cindy Chira

Our Faith Is Our Own Creator

Last night by the river I was alone walking
A very soft music was in the blowing wind
The fragrance of the trees was so discreetly sent
Through the air that I fell in love with the moment.

As a deeper calm came to reign over the things
My heart and I took a vow to alter nothing
But to leave the slow pages of the time turning
While recording on them everything and nothing.

And as I kept walking enjoying the instant
Inhaling, exhaling the world like an infant
Going through life unknown and stranger to himself
I've come to questioning the life of my own self

(My mind for answer flew to every direction)
So were flown all my hopes and my aspirations
For I have discovered to my own deception
That life will always be to men an illusion.

O divine mystery no lifetime can reveal
O profound secret to all the (God's concealed)
If man's thought is the fruit of his own illusion
What else could make possible the whole creation.
   Robert Esther

God

For our sins his son did die,
And all the people began to cry.
I know in my heart I should confess my sins,
but don't know how,
Although in becoming a christian that is a big vow.
I know I'm not ready to go be with him,
I'm to afraid to make a wrong move and sin.
When it comes time for those special days,
I feel real guilty and him, I try to praise.
He guides me through each day of my life,
And when I'm sad he doesn't let me cry.
Sometimes he grants my every wish and I'm thankful for that,
And when I hurt inside and out beside me he sat.
When I die I'll go and be with him and his son,
And my soul's happiness, I know, has just then begun.
   Kyra Smallwood

Lost Dreams

Some people have tried things that few sane folks would try
Some have built themselves wings, like a kite made of strings
Tried to use them to fly
Some go bungie-jumping, and other foolish schemes
They endanger their life, in their quest, and their strife
Trying to find lost dreams.
Diogenes did search, for an honest man with truth
There was Ponce De Leon, searching every pond
For a fountain of youth.
What makes some people search, for the things they can't find?
They will sail ocean surfs, four corners of the earth
Just to find peace of mind
They will climb high mountains and will forge unknown streams
They will travel afar, and will follow a star
In search of their lost dreams.
Like a brook rolling stone, my life just rolls on by
Now the summer is gone, and fall is coming on
The leaves wither and die
I gaze out my window, as the first snowfall gleams
I can't help thinking of her yesterday's lost love
I still search for lost dreams.
   Russell E. Kidwell

Gifts From The Stable

The son of God unknown to man
Was born one Christmas day,
In a hillside cave so damp and cold
The sages used to say.

His nursery housed a stable
With a donkey, cow and sheep,
But the briskness of the wintry air
Made it hard for Him to sleep

So the animals gathering closer with hopes of warming the boy,
and when the child relaxed with ease they brayed and neighed with joy.
Then the donkey looked upon the babe, and twitched his leathery hide,
He said, "I have no gift for you, but a bony back to ride."

And the cow in all her meekness said, "I'd like to give you silk,
But alas, this comes from humans so I offer you my milk."
Meanwhile, lambs and sheep had gathered 'round his little bed,
Offering Him their softest fleece to place beneath His head.

With this the little boy child cooed and thanked them one by one,
Accepting their gifts as the greatest of all
giving His heart that they won.
   Louise E. Fogell

Contentment

   In fall she wears another face
as summer's season slips from grace
   and autumn comes and turns a page
as youth now greets the handsome sage
   as verdant to vermilion change.

   August remains in memory's eye
as September bids us say good-bye.
   Though youth's excitement now is spent
We dwell in autumn's quiet content,
   Though leisure's offered in July,
on winter's comfort we rely.

   For then we introspective grow
as self's identity, will know
   activities for young and old
and deepening joys our hearts may hold
   as holidays remembered dear
December welcomes yet another year.
   Marilyn Previs

Cloud

I, a robot, imprisoned at work
The window my only escape
Perched atop a grand alluvial plane
Hills in the shape of mountains
Roll toward the pacific sunset

My head tilts back
Behold the clouds
Higher than normal
Motionless

No, wait
They move slowly
Each water molecule flying its own path
White disappears then reappears
Light life
Wandering in unison
To whenever the soul of the cloud decides
Each vapor follows
Or not

Free to be a cloud
I will be, after my robotic life as a human
Drew Searing

Untitled

I have never known any other person
Who is quite as dedicated as you.
Someone who devotes his time and his life
To jobs many others would never attempt to do.

It was hard for me to comprehend
Why you take these things to heart;
But I've come to realize and understand
That it's just the way you are.

There are very few people that I know
Who would put their own life on the line.
But you respond willingly without hesitation;
Bravery such as yours is hard to find.

To be good at what you do is one thing,
But to also enjoy it takes so much more.
Some people sit back and let others take the risks,
Without these risks you may take life as a bore.

So whether you are being a cop, doing CPR,
Or rescuing a family from a blazing fire,
You will always have my prayers with you,
And you will always be someone I admire.
Suzanne A. Jamniczky

Moonshadows

In the Mind's Eye lives the shadows of the soul
The Windows open briefly
And give view
to the evil within
Is this not what the moonshadows see??
They know all in the night
They love nothing
So that soul is bare and without redemption from
The night
The night wanes
and the conscious overtakes
and the moon subsides to the sun
The sun is ignorant to the souls of man
therefor knows not
the violent turmoil that lurks
inside the souls dark presence
Jeffrey Holcombe

Do Not Toss Them To The Wind

Turning around one day to see
A hand touching mine, she looked up at me
The angelic face disturbed with pain
A tiny form shivering in the cold winter rain

Clinging to her side, there he stood, shaking and sad
Tears from blue eyes flowing, oh, so bad
A small body, frail and thin
Imagine, if you can, the trauma he was in

Beaten, molested and left alone
With no one special to call their own
God's precious children anguished by abuse and neglection
Captured and held in the web of rejection

For lack of love and motivation
Their lives are only visions of desolation
Successful, they may not become, not even a circus clown.
Through eyes of frustration, their worlds are upside down

Every child has the right to reach for the stars
And be not hindered by abusive bars
They are the future, not to be tossed to the wind
Rather, walk with them the distance around the bend.
Dorothy Richardson Hiers

Water Our Miracle Resource

Connected is water to all the living
Dependent for even the air we breathe
For electricity, the power we need,
Dear Lord, we humbly give thanks.

Its uses, abuses, are varied and many
The food chain, water renders with plenty
And all our bodies and homes keep clean.

Commerce shipped on oceans and seas
Resplendent beauty in ice and snow
In the sky and all the earth below.

Remember Noah and the Ark he built?
From that great flood his family saved,
Oh yes, our daily menu is water
Dear Lord, we humbly give thanks.
Edna Thurrott

Lessons

Sediment stirs breathed from discontent
Focusing shadowed veining thorns pierced red
Yet blood hath not color crimson plenty
To sheath tales membered those paths have led

Mending fabric tattered in growth regrets
Stitching destined seams cured blindly impure
So bequeath conscious tallies construing
Dreams convicting the immortal voyeur

Vanquished not thy soulful rebirth emerge
Entrancing collapse seedlings to moisten
Spectrums atomize felt that in sadness
To welcome verve learned awaiting lesson
Blair Pettyjohn

The Suicide Of Immortality

On a silvery slant a solitary salty dampness remains
Eye catching the images of a bitter remembrance
Mesmerizing in its majestic madness of memories
Tantalizing the taste buds of hunger stricken emotions
Weening the ridiculous rage ravishing rest from the soul
Flowing falseness, and emptying immortality along its faultless edge
Immaculate impurities of immense integrity balance the nonexistent
Displaying the sins of a deranged divinity
Jason W. Deeds

Mother Earth

Sitting in a secluded corner
Only one of many mourners
I miss inhaling your fresh sweet breath
Low only huffing the stench of death
I recall staring into your blue eyes
Now clouded over with these lies
I'd like to apologize for those like me
All of us blind, no one could see
The cloudy skies, the murky water
For thinking only to sell and to buy her
Cleanse yourself my Mother Earth
Prepare yourself for a new birth
Cristina Hittson

Behind I Remain

Shake my clinched fist in the face of Almighty GOD!
Screaming from the inner most depths of my being.
   Seething with anger, feeling the searing, raw,
twisting pain. Cheeks stained with tears. I clutch my chest as I
   crumple with exhaustion to the ground.
Behind I remain. My house is now silent, no sound.
Shock of my life! HOW COULD YOU YET THIS HAPPEN?
   Was I not a good and loving Wife?
Questions always, answers in this life time, not to come.
   The mystery of "WHY" left to ponder.
Behind I remain. Faint is the whistle of a distant train.
   My mind does wander.
Blaming myself, but mostly God, for I saw the limits of mankind.
   Ironic, it is my faith in the
   "One Divine Deity" that pulled me through my most desperate hour.
Behind I remain. Day to day dealing with pain past. I thank God,
   "His" unconditional love for me will always last.
I have made my peace. Feeling the beginning of "His" healing power.
My turn, may be at hand, soon to see God and my much loved Man.
My heart misses you.
For now, behind I remain.
Judy Winters

A Thousand Faces

The futile hope -
   of those tortured souls.
The scars still bleed,
   from decades ago.
Hopelessness hangs,
   high above the ground.
Sky drop your tears,
   for the lonely and alone.
Desperation's grips,
   like the vice on my heart.
Stealing the lives of those who've come,
   and those who'll soon depart.
But the midnight hour is upon us,
   and death slips in quietly.
Blank are those faces,
   that stand at the grave silently.
Heather L. Mechtensimer

Paul

Speechless, wordless, your eyes belie,
   The silence people know you by
The mystic magic of your smile,
   Your ways so easy to beguile
A moment here, a moment there,
   Searching for reasons, your soul you bare
We search together, you and I,
   Our happiness comes from one on high
You fly while others only plod,
   You are indeed a gift from God.
Sally Caldwell

Don't Leave Now

Don't leave now.... no need to hurry
Time's end is still eternities away
Take my hand...let's walk together
Along the quiet streets of yesterday....
Why not share just one last moment
Remembering the good and happy things
Give our hearts a chance to travel
The dusty paths of our unfinished dreams....
Don't leave now.... that's all I'm asking
Your freedom will be waiting in the end
Stay awhile and let's return to
The places we will never go again....
Close your eyes and take it easy
Don't be afraid of facing what is passed
Nothing's wrong with burning bridges
But is it right destroying them so fast?....
I won't cry.... you have my promise
But still I can't help feeling like I do
Give me time before you leave me
To spend some loving memories with you....
Helen Dodge

The Master Artists

They say a picture paints a thousand words,
But none can compare to the master's touch.
Like the pristine whiteness of a winter's day,
Or the brilliant hues of spring, summer and fall.
The spectacular sun sets and sun rises,
The shining stars and moon in the blue black sky of night,
Even the sun shining in the blue sky of day,
Can not be truly conveyed on canvas of all the beauty we see,
Except for the master artist,
For he's the one who created it all.
Carol A. Fox

Goodbye Love

It's time to say goodbye love to the way things used to be
It's time to live my life the way it was meant to be
There's a reason why and I hope you understand
Why I never let my heart leave my own hands
I've been searching for something that may not be real
It's something that's inside, something that I feel
I've tried to let you in, but our souls are worlds apart
As time goes slowly by I can't deny the feelings of my heart
It's time to say goodbye love it's not what I want to do
But it's not fair to me and it's not fair to you
I'd be leading you down a lonely road where you'd only have part of
   me
You deserve so much more, it's why I must set you free
The tears that I cry are for what can't be
But my love for a friend you'll always hold the key
The questions are so confusing and I really don't know why
All I know is that it's out there, I know I have to try
Treasure what we had and all the memories we made
Remember me always and what we shared will never fade
It's time to say good-bye love it's what we have to do
But know that you'll never leave me and I'll always have love for you
Debi Travers

Ode to Roma

We often thought from time to time
   there should be a poem,
   one that would rhyme
to honor Roma for a job well done
as our Club Secretary she was number one
   her books so legible and neat
   her reports will be hard to beat
We thank you Roma
   you are our special friend
   Our fondness for you will never end.
Doris Lombardi

"Melancholy Flower"

Melancholy flower, then perhaps of the summer, standing alone in the
   sun,
Just that slight bit scorched and showing signs of age.
Making the most of the time it has without any special fuss,
It displays its aging in subtle ways.
A slight droop, colors a little fade, petals a bit wrinkled
It still invites an occasional bee and the occasional eye.
Alone in the rain and wind, bravely raising its leaves to heaven
It gives thanks for what it is, not what it could become.
Soon now it will die.
A peaceful exhalation of spirit and it will be over
A short time of beauty, fragrance and admiration, leaving behind a
   memory
Not of itself as much as what it stood for.
A warm, comforting memory of greens and blue, warm colors and cool
   shadows,
The smell of rain, the buzz of honeybees.
A peaceful exhalation of spirit that remains somehow
A memory of bright things,
Hovering over the spot where it grew
In the cold, hard ground.
   Bernard W. Shwayder

Our Love

Tell me why I Love You and why I truly care,
Tell me why You Love Me and all the thoughts we share.

The time we spend together, the hours how they fly,
Seem like precious moments, as time is passing by.

Two very separate ways of life, most say would be impossible to share,
Our friendship is so meaningful, Our Love so very rare.

Can two hearts really beat as one? Can two minds think the same?
These questions left unanswered, but true feelings still remain.

The sharing, caring, touching and romance, we feel with great emotion.
My heart is bursting open wide with True Love and Deep Devotion.
   Deborah L. Armijo

Friendship

   Every day there is something new in your life, something
you want and something that you don't want. Something you
have and something that you don't have, but life is not
about wanting and having. Life can be about loving, caring
and Friendship, because without these things what is life?

   Friendship is a part of life. It's like taking your
first step, but not as hard. Friendship is like moving up
one step towards life.

   Sharing clothes, studying together, writing letters
to each other, and trading gifts.

   Friendship is something special. It is something that
you give away as a gift, and that is what makes you who and
what you are.
   Yvonne P. Myrick

Peace Within

Confusing as this life might seem, I find my
Peace Within. When times are hard, or
unforgiving, and nowhere can I turn, I look
inside myself and find that Peace I need
Within. Nowhere in this world I've found a
better place I can turn, than to find that
Peace I really need, and seek that
Peace Within.
   Peggy Baker

Roses

Roses of any color,
Are always a welcome sight!
They may be a gift to a dear mother,
A close friend or a loving wife.

Roses usually grow in places that are open,
The plants like a space that is dry!
They bloom beautifully, like words kindly spoken.
Usually they are fragrant even after the petals die.

There are other flowers that I admire!
They, too, have their beautiful colors.
I like orchids and carnations worn with smart attire,
Also there may be bouquets of violets, carnations, orchids and others.

Yet for some reason roses seem to be the flower of universal choice,
Can you visualize a Rose Bowl parade of spectacular roses?
Yes a parade where roses are the boss!
God created and man's to give - never a loss
   Harry B. Harris

The Tenderness Of Love In One's Heart

               Within the shadows
   of a clear winter evening as the brightness of
      the moon shines upon the soul of two when
         joined in harmony, where a serenity and Love
is felt in the heart of one's life.
            As the heart is touched by
   one when two are joined, a warm attachment of
      compassion and tenderness is felt by the other.
         When two feel the attractive beauty
   in the soul of the other, the qualities in a person
become a strong emotional feeling of love.
            With the Love of two the heart
   is gently caressed in such a loving and endearing
   way that a vision of love and happiness are joined
within, so the heart of two will become as one.
   Robert E. Beck

Restoration From Separation

Hovering Spirit of God
Voice calling forth division
Rushing Waters obey
Gathering begins in separation.

Judging Eyes of God
Divided light from darkness
Sun, moon, stars obey and
Evening and Morning become one day.

Shaping hands of God
Formed man from the dry land.
Male and Female He made them
Two blessed to become one.

Walking feet of God
Found the naked couple,
Stripped of commandment covering.
He kicked and cursed the ground!

Caring Heart of God
Protects His jealous creation,
Lest they live forever separate from Him,
He divides Himself for restoration.
   Beth Engel

"Sunsets"

Have you ever seen a sunset at night?
I have never seen such a beautiful sight.
It lights up the entire sky,
Above and between the trees that stand so high.

When you look at one, life and thoughts of war just fade away
Have you ever seen such beauty, you say!
A smile on your face appears,
You know now that night is near.

Colors of pink, purple, yellow, blue, and orange blend together,
It's picture-perfect, especially in fair weather.
I feel sorry for those who haven't seen one,
As I gaze at this sight stretching across the never-ending horizon.

Some are so caught up in life they don't notice mother nature's gifts,
You will notice though that when you see it your spirit uplifts.
I wait to see the sunset all throughout the day.
God I thank you for this, pray.

Katie Noyes

Angels

With so much attention given to Angels today
I keep hoping for a visit or a touch,
To bring some relief to a heart still hurting
Over the loss of someone I loved so much.

I pray for a touch, a feeling, an emotion
To help me know they really are here.
To love us and help when things seem too hard
To help us feel that our love one is still near.

But, while we look for them in the supernatural
We look for them as things hard to understand,
We forget to look around us at the people God has placed
In our lives to reach out with Angel's Hands.

For I've seen them in the eyes of my friends.
I've seen them in a loving outstretched hand.
I've seen them in the deeds of my family.
I've seen them in acts small and grand.

So while living here in our troubles and trials.
Let's not forget to look about us each day,
And see God's many acts of loving kindness
In the Angels He sends along our way.

Shirley Black

I Need To Know

Maybe you love me very much
And I'm your only one,
we've been married nine years,
I gave birth to your daughter and son.

But you do not show your love,
as on with life you go,
maybe you do love me,
but I need to know.

I need to know I'm still as pretty to you
As I was nine years ago.
When you looked my way then
your eyes carried a special glow.

I love you now even more
Than I did nine years ago,
maybe you love me as much;
if you do—— I need to know.

Sunshine

The Attic

Upstairs in a shadowy spot where it's
dark and hot, is a room called the attic. With
flying bats and your dad's old fishing hat.
You stop and wonder where the old
Cot beds are, where you slept when you
were three. You look and look, there
they are, the cot beds full of spider webs,
yuk! Suddenly, you hear your dad
coming up, and the door slams shut. You
say to yourself, what a clutz. All of a sudden,
your thoughts were bent to a shadowy something
far away, towards the window, there she lay,
A picture of your sister who had died, you
held the picture and began to cry.
You thought the house was haunted
with your sisters spirit, and started screaming.
Your mother sat at the edge of
your bed, Aah!! I was only dreaming.

Rian Hunt

To an Ant

Ant, dragging nuthatch feather over pebble-boulders,
however you jerk and falter, you show more grace in the attempt—
carry farther and choose your object better—you learn
more quickly than my awkward bother
with the pseudomatter piled upon carnal concern
that will neither restrain nor exempt
my mind, nor break its connection with the sinew of my shoulders.

Is there any simpler world? I would, like you, programmed,
drag the weightless significance of my everyday through each day
minus this awareness existence is always shammed
and can't ever work another way.
I would, in line or alone, let ethos and dream be damned;
struggle, not knowing struggle; and lay
a leaf down lighter than consciousness or the seed of your father.

Daril Bentley

For Love And Eagles

Some things are so lost to love,
the heavens and the stars above.
Seems to be the only way,
for some to make it through the day.
I find myself seeking answers of the stars,
to guide me down the path so far.
When an eagle flies into the skies,
I hope that love shall never die.
For things like this will be sorely missed,
if people had never had learned to kiss.
Believe me when I say,
that love will always have its day.
As long as people learn to give,
the eagle will fly and love shall live.

Tracy Stevens

"Creation Of Life"

Creation of life, so beautiful in sight,
Beginning a childhood of dreams.

Blanket of warmth for the quiet sleep,
In tears of glidering streams.

No understanding, but soon to be, the child-
will begin to grow.

A maturing apple in the family tree,
From the first strand of hair, to the babies toes.

Troy B. Schuuring

Sick Me

My feelings are controlled by my mind — I wish by my heart.
They are pretty close together, but they seem miles apart.

My past controls me — I should live for today.
I want you to hold me, but I will push you away.

You don't like what I do, I don't even care.
I will do things to hurt you, for less than a stare.

My body needs numbing — my brain needs a high.
These urges keep coming, and now I know why.

My addiction is drugs, I will do what it takes.
So I won't feel the bugs and I won't get the shakes.

A bullet, would be nice, a car and a tree.
Death is a vice, but today not for me.

In my heart there is hope, through God and people I see.
I don't need any dope, to feed sick me.

Dean James Waterfield

Napoleon

Napoleon emperor of the French,
he marched to Russia, he marched
to Egypt, he marched all over
Europe.

He conquered most of Europe and
Africa. He conquered the Germans,
the British, and the Austrians.

He marched and marched till he became
tired. He died and was buried in France.
Hail Napoleon Emperor of the French.
Hail L' Emperor Napoleon.

Andrew Tan

Human Emotions

As I sat in different places with
friends, neighbors and relations
Where is the laughter, joy and graces
For all I see is worry in their faces.

People are wining, dining, and dancing
Not thinking of anything fair
Men and women cheating on each other
Not even caring to love one another.

Children are drinking, smoking and cursing
Moms and Dads are no longer a pair
Where is communication, love and sharing
And where is a family who cares?

God bless America is what it should be,
And only in God we trust
Prayers in schools and church on Sunday
As families were formed in a crust.

I'll take my stand in any land,
A wife and a Mother I'll be
For God made within his plan
A family to hold in my hands.

Jeannette L. Hampton

Untitled

I care for someone who does not know it
my heart beats for her, but I can't show it
I lie awake each night
and I ask myself; Am I doing this right?
What if she knew my feelings for her?
She would just laugh, I'm sure of that.
I tried once but she would not listen
I care for someone
Who would not know if I was missing.

Jonathan L. Pruitt

Two Hearts One Love

When your two hearts came together,
  they became one.
When intermingling of those minds merged,
  the inner heart began to grow.
Then all around a new world flourished,
  in the seeds that were planted by Love.
It is in that atmosphere where true love took root,
  with its vines and branches stretching far and wide.
As the branches of your lives reach out
  and touch new growth,
Let me say Thank-you, for letting that one heart
  touch mine.

Beverly J. White

Time Passages

Let's just have one cup of coffee at a time,
I'll scratch your back if you'll do mine.
I've been in the "likes a lot's" before,
Knock ever so softly on my hearts door.

Come sit beside me upon a sandy beach,
Touch all the shining stars you can reach.
If you'd like you may hold my hand,
But my future written in my heart, not on sand...

I can hear your dreams not mak'em come true,
I will always do for myself what I must do.
Don't run to catch up should I wander away,
If you try to tie me down, I won't stay.

One day in latter years should you hear,
The wind as it whispers my name in your ear,
Look out at the clouds as they drift by,
And see if my pictures up in the sky...

Sharon Ginther

Fire And The Wheel—The Schutzstaffel

    Spiral
     started
      moving
       with
      flames
     down
     the
    hill.
They watched with the fascination of God before them.
     They
      were
     life
    as
     long
    as
  it
crushed.

Jim Cobb

Love's Calling

I must be set free, allowed to be me
Held in your open hand, I can be like
the morning dove or the gentle humming bird
who flies to or away from you again and again...

The unfettered spirit knows no bondages
and withers - when the unthinking, the unfeeling,
the uncaring, would tie my love
with cords of control...

Not so for my kin friend, like the deer
She shies away from the misguided ways
of less caring hands, and harkens only
to true love's nurturing call...

Cathy Lee Jones

Childhood Memories

I first remember my darling mother,
She was in labor with my baby brother,
I couldn't figure out why she was so ill,
Why she couldn't take something to make her well.

But then daddy chased us out to the barn,
Where we all waited for the "all clear alarm,
Then he came out and said we all could go in,
Where my mama was in bed, a baby under her chin.

A little mite, he was, you see, and yet,
He weighed a pound and a half, soaking wet,
But seven of us looked on him lovingly.
For we were happy him and mama was ok, you see.

Last in line, brother Ray, he made eight,
But Dad made us all walk and act straight,
No child abuse, no drug, or no alcohol,
Nothing, but all for one, and one for all.

We grew up poor, but very Richly Blessed,
And we all went our separate ways,
But I shall never forget that day in May,
When our little brother Ray, came to us to stay.

June L. Thomas

When My Life Turned Upside Down

When my life turned upside down, everyone had a frown.
When my life turned upside down, I did not know who was around.
When my life turned upside down, I would sit and wonder why me, why me.
When my life turned upside down, there was no one happy around.
When my life turned upside down, I ended up not looking like me.
When my life turned upside down, I did not know the person I know now.
When my life turned upside down, I thought I walked like a clown.
When my life turned upside down, I had new friends in town...
nurses, doctors and other needle-stabbing friends.
When my life turned upside down, I became a famous girl in town.
When my life turned upside down, I learned about being strong.
When my life turned upside down... I turned it around.

Jessica Rosales

I Am

I am the sunshine to brighten your days
I am the sunlight of four different shades
Early morn, afternoon, evening to dusk.
For all to gaze upon, for all to entrust.

Crimson is for the sunrise of first mornings light,
Yellow is to brighten up the days of our life
Persimmon becomes sunset, which turns grey into night.

Come the beginning of spring, green foliage is born,
Fawn's of whitetail deer, grow into bucks and to does.
Flowers burst with brilliance of colors, birds take flight to soar.

I watch over campers from near and afar
Mankind holds BBQ's, as they play horseshoes and cards.
I enclose families reunions close to my banks.

Near fall I show the most exotic of colors
For autumn withholds the best of all outings.

The sparkling rainbow; of fresh early morn's dew,
Is as lighthearted as me, and within you.

For I am the sunshine to brighten your days
And I am the dusk, which will color the haze

Sharon L. Trujillo

Magic Moments

As magical as it seems
   She watches the sun,
Lower and lower it falls
   Until it can no longer be seen.
Wishing he was there-
   To feel his touch, his embrace,
Remembering his every move
   The way they kissed and made love.
She knows one day they will see each other again.
How will she feel? How will he feel?
They started as friends
   And are who they are,
That's when she realizes that they
   Will always be friends, and
Magic moments they will always share.
As she looks to the sky she says a little prayer:
   Lord, take this heart of mine and show it
   How to love and understand, so that one day
   This heart will find another.

Jessica M. Cablay

Forever Silent

Sometimes, even the silence escapes from the walls of my mind
It spans across the miles that my memories have defined
Just like the flowing river, I find myself returning to the sea
Only to be swept to the shore, where the memories await me
I stand there to embrace the breeze, that time will always allow
For it has blown a thousand miles to find refuge upon my brow
I confront these things that are lost, though they will always remain
As you still rest inside my mind, upon the pillows which I have lain
The silence fills my soul, ever stronger than the walls of this void
But even the sands of time know that our smiles are forever alloyed
I may never understand this, but a friendship I've chosen for thee
This friendship that I have chosen, flows like the river to the sea
And your whisper upon the wind will find refuge upon my brow
As forever I shall embrace the breeze, that time will always allow
The silence that defies my heart is destined to quietly take me away
Forever silent I feel, forever I pray, for the words I could never say

...And so I return with the tide to evaporate and become the rain
As I rest upon the clouds of time, and I silently dream again
Then I'll fall upon the flowing river, flowing forever into the sea
Only to be swept to the shore, where the memories await me...

Christopher Dwayne McCauley

Sister Moon

In the pale
fearful
dark
that makes wolves sing,
I rise to be your guide.
I hear your cries,
I know you're scared.
I'll lead you out of your woods.
I'll meet you in your madness
holding your hand as I walk you back home.
I watch over you
follow you
protect you while you dream.
You look for me when all you see is black.
Keep me for yourself if only for a few hours,
I will tell no one that you cried.
I promise I will never leave.
You won't think of me as the sun will rise,
but I'll keep your secrets
'til we meet tomorrow night.

Johnna Dee Stevens Wrather

Free

From the depths of the black hole
   that is my heart,
I have felt the first stirrings of
   light in years.
It has become a foreign sensation
   to me, after all this time.
The warmth uncurls in my stomach
   and the unfamiliar needle
   of passion runs through me-deep through me.
You caress my skin and the
   game begins.
You kiss my lips and I give
   myself to you,
And my black hole sheds its
   darkness and chains,
And I am set free.
   April Brown

Untitled

I heard the hurricane roaring,
   across the open sea.
Its powerful waves came crashing,
   oh so quietly.
The silence hastened its weary head,
   as it rested on its tomb.
It died just as quickly
   as our souls together: Two.
The time and bitterness saddened my heart,
   but made me strong inside.
"Till death do us part" are just words,
   said by your mouth and mine.
Time heals all wounds they say,
   and life goes on living;
But the pain I feel inside,
   and the loss of your love unchanged;
   will always remain with me,
   just as fresh as a new fallen rain.
   Melissa Pelfrey

Rage

Save me, save me, save me, Oh!
Rage and passion, lust disguised.
Thoughts unfurled like dances, fly.
Questing answers, prose of old. Why don't they now unfold?

Come to me, come to me, come to me, Oh!
Rivers raging rushing so, I though I knew a friends from foe.
Ignorant bliss was best for me;
but now I pray, "Virginity".
Torment, pain, love and fear,
Why is it worse each passing year?

Speak to me, speak to me, speak to me, Oh!
Don't touch me, don't love me....just leave me alone.
Nothing is real, unless it hurts.
It hurts to love when love was best.
Anguish, fear, love and hate;
why was I given such a plate?

Sort this quagmire of twisted dreams.
Open the doors to the imperfect schemes.
Why such a tempest? Why such a whore?
Chase these demons for nevermore.
   G. R. Euwer

Untitled

In this world
all of our own we have let
Love
be the one who is in control In this place
of our own disgrace we have let
Emotion be the one who is in control In our minds
we have never thought that one so
Young
could be the one who is in control In this world
all of on my own who thought
that he would be the one to leave
Me
be the one who is in control
In this world
all of my own
now I am the only
One
Who is trying to be the one
Left
in control
   April Clements

Behind A Name

The beauty of a name lies deep within the soul.
One cannot be recognized by a face or name,
But only can one be recognized by the heart.
Many insights come through the eye,
But one cannot rightly see.
People take advantage of life
Because they cannot realize the essence it carries.
On this earth, everything is beautiful.
Every person and thing holds beauty within.
If only people could see this beauty
and realize how sacred life is.
Life is full of wonder that comes and goes.
One misses what is lost and when one loses,
the beautiful things in life are not forgotten.
Never hold back to something you think you cannot do.
Never forget about the heart inside the soul.
Because at that moment,
You will lose all touch and peace within yourself.
So Live Life
And remember what is in a person's name.
   Betsy Ranae Brottlund

One Small Wheel

Oregon justice, 11:13 am quiet.
Half-suit phone troll; grease to the grind.
"Hesitate in this reason feasible." The judge.
   Cops swear to the judge.
"Written and typed reports match?..." I do.
I now pronounce you order
Mother Judge may I.
"Were you driving under the influence?"
   Guilty 11:23.
"But now I ride a bike."
   Drunk.
Children with the owl eyed husband
   glass, court door... Mirror of a world.
"Thank you."
"When do you want to turn yourself in?.. Friday of Saturday?
..Friday."
"That will be four hundred dollars."
Next...
   Richard T. Shackleford

My Single Mother

The road is long and hard,
It's even harder if you're walking alone.
He left Mom
Left you to raise me alone.
Why, Mom?
I always ask, but I know you don't
Know why.
He was never there for me
I know he never will be.
But you are, Mom
You always have been, and you always will be.
Yes, the road is long, and yes, it is hard.
It might even get harder.
Mom, you'll never walk alone again.
I will walk with you.
I'm not like him.
I won't leave you.
We can make it together.

Michelle Ouellette

November Morning

Brisk Crisp Bracing
These are November-tasting words

But today...ah, today...

The woods are soft, the air is fuzzy
With a sort of mistiness right on the tip of your tongue
The toasted leaves smell like a feast
Of mushrooms
And just-frost-bitten hereby things

The brush underfoot doesn't crunch
It whispers

And the sun, abashed, blushes faintly in the morning sky.

Sandra Kenny

Untitled

The moon at my back,
The clouds at my feet,
and the stars over head.
Up here peace is usual.
If the clouds were firm,
I would stay.
But since they are not,
I can only flow through.
From up here, you can see
the world as it should be.
The oranges, reds, greens, yellows,
purples, browns, blacks, whites and greys...
Just mingling together...
only separated by blue.
It's beautiful from up here.
It was never this beautiful down there.

Korey Dowell

The Rose Of Love

Love begins as a tiny seed;
Firmly planted into a delicate surrounding.
With care and nurturing, it grows a little more each day
Into a small stem of life.

As time goes by, it becomes stronger
And it branches out more stems.
The leaves and thorns are there for protection -
Keeping out the bad things and holding on to the good things.

Soon, colorful petals form.
And, when all of the pieces fit together just right,
A beautiful masterpiece is created -
The masterpiece of love.

Lori Polk

To Be All I Can Be

To be all that I can be
Is the fuel that ignites me
The drive that keep me moving on
The desire deep within me, with which I was born.

I can't settle for anything less than reaching my goals
And as long as I have the breath of life, I've got soul
I will follow my dreams, daring to achieve that which I
Know I can
I refuse to be denied or kept back by anyone

I await tomorrow's challenge
Not knowing what it may be
For the thrill of not knowing what will be
Is what energizes me

So let me move on towards what awaits me
Let me be strong-minded and able-bodied to face my destiny
And whatever the outcome may be in the end
My greatest satisfaction will have come from knowing I stood
Tall and did not bend.

Neville L. Brown

My Fear

My Fear is the deeply embedded terror of hearing footsteps
    walking towards my bedroom door.

My Fear is the looming threat of physical pain when I see
    anger in my abuser's face.

My Fear is in the tears that stream quietly from my face
    when my abuser chokes me into silence.

My Fear is thinking that my mom will kill herself if
    she ever found out.

My Fear is evident in my inner child's eyes when she
    remembers the events of the past.

My Fear is the knowledge that tomorrow I will again
    be raped and abused by my stepfather.

Jane M. Tucker

Desires Within

Reach into your inner mind
Keep yourself wide open, look for any sign
Don't be scared of what you might find
Your souls tied up, need to unwind
Find an answer to any question,
Reaching into your deepest obsession.
Travel to the end of time,
There's no mountain you can't climb
Reach in and pull out all your fear
Now your thoughts are crystal clear.
Fly across the heavens so free....
So much love for the world to see.
You have to swim deep for a vision
To send you off on a Love mission.
Your energy's high, there's enough to lend
So dig deep and find, a loving friend.
Let it out what's in your self,
Stop climbing up a broken shelf.

Scott Smith

Thanksgiving

The scenes of late have been magnificent
I just know they have been heaven sent
the world has taken on a certain grace
powerful as nature-delicate as lace
I come out of myself to look around
and I'm moved by that which surrounds us all
the majestic trees toned with colors of fall
Dear God it is with true Thanksgiving
I thank you for the gift of living
may I take from this some energy
to give all of myself to Thee
   Rosemary Ryan-Koslosky

Portrait Of A Six Year Old

I was in Kindergarten,
Struggling to memorize the alphabet.
Small, delicate hands,
Cutting their way to an award for best scissor user.

Skinny arms like twigs on a tree,
Building towers out of blocks.
Then smirking like the Joker,
Proceeding to destroy the symbol of my expertise.

I dip my fingers in the paint,
Brightly colored tulips on the end of their stems.
That innocent look that dogs give,
Getting me out of many tight places.

That naive mind,
Unknowing of the terrible acts it would witness.
The little body as meek as a mouse's,
Uncaring of the abominations done by adults.

The Sparkling blue eyes,
Waiting in anticipation for Santa on Christmas Eve.
Behind the creased cheek, lopsided eyes and crooked smile,
Sits a boy without a care in the world.
   John Karman

Through The Years

I would like to recognize on your birthday,
The things you did for me without any pay,
When you were about 25, you had me, I was alive.
When I was one, two, not yet three,
You gave me a bottle and nurtured me.
And then when I was a tot, you read to me and taught me a lot.
Through out the years both you and Dad,
Cheered me up when I was sad.
I liked when you came and watched me play,
Baseball at the end of the day.
Even though I'm sometimes bad, and you get upset and even mad.
You come back and do stuff for me, that's what makes me happy.
Through out the years with you,
You bought me things that were very true.
You don't have to do these things, it's all up to you,
But I thank you much for all that you do.
Now I'm a Teenager there is plenty ahead,
I don't need a bottle or get tucked in my bed.
The thing that is important more than all of the above,
The thing I will cherish most is you everlasting love.
   Matt Yarger

"A Dream In A Life- A Life In A Dream"

A beautiful dream
but it can't be held down.

Dreams are free and elusive
like a butterfly dancing on the wind.

Golden wings of visions lightly touching
Petals of our lives but always moving
Carefree through the meadows of our minds.

And so this dream flies on
and I must awake to the truth.
   Elena Malbacias

Depression

He comes like a thief in the middle of the night.
He takes for himself, your joy and your delight.
In the depths of darkness and despair,
  he descends with your emotions - seemingly beyond repair.
Hope goes with him, a willing captive gone.
Now all he leaves behind is emptiness - a sadness,
  neither right nor wrong.
An all engulfing feeling one you never seem to shake.
Is it now really your master and must you dance to his new stake?
Yes, it certainly seems as though has pitched his tent to stay.
And only clouds and gloominess hover over you each day.
But I tell you of a Savior, one who can rescue you from harm.
He restores the broken-hearted and releases them by the strength
  of His right arm.
No more inner turmoil, no sadness will He bring.
For His name is Jesus and He's into conquering.
Not with swords and arrows, but only perfect love.
For He is the Son of God, you see - the One sent from above.
   Susanne M. Downey

"Unknown"

Unknown to man, and all this land
Something so hidden, but yet so grand
Nestling itself in Time's great cradle
Silently waiting, but willingly able
To fight back its fears, and take its stand.

Unknown to me, unknown to you
Unknown to many but yet so few
Never hesitating, nor growing old
Something imagination will never behold
Or find in it any truth.

Until the day that in light it brings
Torment, anguish, and suffering
The day the birds don't stop to sing
And silence falls like a great blanket
Over all the land, turning blue skies green.
   Jeffrey Sothen

Our True Friends

  They love you unconditionally
Lick the tears away when you cry
Mourn when you die

  They have four legs and a tail
They know nothing of human hell

  They tell no lies
Protect us even if it meant they die

  Sad their lives are so short
They are the truest of what the world needs most
  our true friends
   Nancy Smiejek

To Dream

The world is a mindless essence where things of beauty prosper
Sometimes it just takes a moment to stop,
Peer out onto the open sea or the yellow dunes in the desert.

I went for a walk on a mountain top, the air was fresh, the sky blue
Oh, only if those moments could last a lifetime, I would be rich.

People should be more attuned to life's gifts
A child that cuts his hand knows pain
A bird that falls when it's supposed to soar, knows frustration
   and determination.
This world of mine has forgotten how to dream, dreams are the essence
Of the human mind, they are peoples drive when nothing else shines.

To walk yet never get anywhere is not failure, it's the basis of
   reality
I wish I could fly tells a girl to her mother, only ma shakes her head
I know I can fly, I've flown away a long time ago never touching
   ground
I did not become lost, I became found.

I found a land bright and gay
Where chestnuts fall from every tree
No one worries and there are smiles that can be seen from a mile away
This is the land where I want to be
The land where dreams become reality.
   Teresa Beechie

Curcoa

Once twice thrice.
Fluid and pure.
An easy clean.
A calm afternoon sky;
glowing, throbbing yet placid;
over the heads of all whom breathe,
plus those whom do not;
and vessel of the serenity of Sunday drives,
and midday barbecues.

To see one's face from the ground,
from just twelve inches in front of your shoes,
would reveal the portrait of a person,
whose body towers against the background,
of a lustering December jewel.
   Algie L. Johnson II

The Stranger

Is it I, the one that feels such anger? Or could it be the someone
deep inside whom I call the stranger.

Is it I, who feels so destined to die? Or could it be the stranger
making just another outcry.

Is it I, who is doing the falling apart? Or could it be the
stranger
who has the broken heart.

Is it I, who feels so desperate to cling? Or could it be the
stranger hanging on by a string.

Is it I, the one who cries each night? Or could it be the stranger
refusing to give up the fight.

Is it I, who is rising above the sorrow? Or could it be the
stranger
looking towards the new tomorrow.

Is it I, who is opening her wings? Or could it be the stranger
in the midst of her opening.
   Shelley L. Forcier

Life

Out of the silent's of darkness, come's life.
All the protection is gone.
Open to the force of a New World,
love, hate, fear, pain;
The river's of trouble's that produces
The stream of my river of growing
Time is the limit of the avenue of
tomorrow, which never seams to end.
Born to live, and living only to die.
Feeling the wind's of life upon my face.
Like the changing of the seasons.
Spring Ah how beautiful, then
sudden, the cold, winter, the wonder of
snow falling. Unbearable storms,
and then, peace like a river
opens her arms alas, it's over
all at last...
   Alberto Nich Nicastro

When You Love Someone

When you love someone, two hearts become one.
When your heart is broken, you tend to be unspoken.
When you are feeling sad, a friend you wish you had.

When you love someone, two hearts become one.
When you lose the one you love,
it's like losing the mate to your glove.
The day's and nights are oh' so long,
you just don't know where you belong.

When you love someone,
two hearts become one.
I try and try to understand the why,
but all I seem to do is cry.
Wherever your journey has led you,
until I get there I'll be blue.

When you love someone,
two hearts become one.
I see no future here, it's a sin,
because you see I just don't fit in.
I'm wishing someone could explain to me,
just what happens to me.
   Patricia A. Cross

Comfort In Nothingness

Ripples dance on the blue waters of an isolated pond
as I stare into the black sky of a summer night,
I know nothing of what was or what will be,
the present is a chalk drawing that disappears with the mist
of the night and is replaced with the dew of early morning,
the wind blowing through the trees leaves the branches with
a single song to sing,
the stars create a pattern that only I can see.
The flowers sway in the breeze
which steals the delicate petals and carries them off
into the black night,
the fog sets in over the mist like a white blanket
that leaves the dew for the morning to come upon,
if there is anything I desire more
it is to remain here.....
If only it were real.
   Jessica Skura

Forever Young?

"Forever Young" was once a phrase
   That held my dreams inside.
But now it seems so hollow
   And so weak against the tide
Of emotion and reality
   That's inside us all.
The dream must soon crumble,
   Shatter, and must fall.
Life is full of sorrow that plagues
   The strong, the rich and others besides.
The disquiet and depression
   Twist in knots my insides
As I sit pondering why the
   Young must pass away,
Time begins to blur in silence
   And day blends into day.
The meaninglessness of it all
   So weighs down my spirit
That when the stricken cry,
   I feign not to hear it.
Ron Jenkins

The Remembering

Let's go back through the years,
Back through the time,
Let's go back through the fears,
Back through the mind.

Back to a time of yesterdays, faraways and nevermores,
Back to a time of golden youth, silver clouds and copper shores.

In a frame of live when the fear was small,
The world was big and the dream stood tall.
The little treasures brought the greatest joys,
The simple pleasures of sunshine and toys.

Here we sit in the now again.
Searching for our lost dividend.
Old and broken, scared and alone.
In a house full of kids
Looking for a home.
Guy P. Vance

Self-Portrait

Deep in the inventory of my mind,
   damaging memories are locked and filed away,
   causing the fire in the dungeon below
   to crackle and sizzle with fury.
Broken promises smolder,
   sharp words prod the flames,
   and lies spark the pain.
The inside dusted with soot,
   deep scars line the landscape;
   forming a barricade,
   constantly preparing for war.
Broken pieces cover my dungeon floor;
   cracking the surface only in my dreams.
Cindy M. Dichtel

Fear And Uncertainty

I sit here alone, and today I wonder...
Who can I look to for hope,
now that God and his word are dead in my heart?
Who will rescue me from my pain and suffering,
since there are no angels to save me from this personal hell?
When good times turn bad, and my heart grows cold,
who will light the spark I need to heal my frostbitten soul?
When I feel that it's me against the world,
left to take on life's battles alone.
Who will be there to fight this fight beside me,
Will there be anyone beside me at all?
Neal Guernsey

Enclosed In A Box

Enclosed in a box, more is outside.
Caged, yet adrift, no order or freedom.
My mind has power hidden in the mass of tangles
that are my thoughts.
I want to fly but a fall would be hard to take.
Searching for the key that will unlock the door towards
myself reaching me, I find that no one has the answers.
Few seek them.
I want out of the cage, but the disarray of mind
is a maze with only one way out.
The future holds something grand.
That must be the conclusion to this saga of confusion.
The passion in my soul was ignited long ago,
life the spark.
I must plug that spark into outlets from the past
so that I can move ahead to tomorrow.
Answers? More Questions?
That is the glory of each new day.
We live for new experiences and trudge on blindly
through our own mazes, minute by minute into eternity.
Whitney Chamberlin

The Holocaust...

A...dolescents tortured to death.
R...acism increases while population decreases.
E...xhausted parents are torn away from their children.
M...ournful days go by without a bite to eat.
E...xploited humanity pray for a chance to be free.
M...istreated by enemies, the people become too weak to cry.
B...eautiful faces are brutally burned by the prejudice soldiers.
R...ampant Nazis torment human beings for believing differently.
A...ttempted escapes fail along with their souls.
N...ever again will these victims forget about this tragic scene.
C...atastrophe grows in wholesome eyes.
E...motions rumble as martyrs rest in peace.
Melissa Jeanette Padilla

A Fool

When you sit in school complaining
Gee, I hate going to school.
No knowledge am I gaining; I'm just wasting time
like a fool.
You grumble and growl and say with a frown,
if they'd let me have my way; I'd build a big
fire and burn the school down, so I could go out and play.

You shriek and shirk, and say with a jerk,
these lessons don't do any good!
If I could quit school, I'd go out to work,
Learn more and earn money I would!

As people say, every dog has his day, and the schools
at last you leave.
You work very hard, and earn a small pay, and at
night sit at home and grieve.

In school, I could study and learn and play.
Why did I ever quit school?
I thought I was right, and I had my way.
But now I can see I was just a fool!
Ralph Heaton

A Bird

A little bird flew past me
and perched himself up on a tree.

I smiled and sat down so near
but the little bird had No Fear!

All he said was tweet, tweet, tweet
and made his feathers very neat.

He went to his nest that day
and sat upon the grass and hay.

He waited for his mate to see
that what a fine bird was he.

He ruffled his feathers and sat up straight
he looked so handsome to his bird mate.

She flew over to him with lots of glee
and sat next to him on that tree.

I walked away for I knew
that birds need their privacy too!

I remember that bird to this very day
oh, how he sat on that grass and hay.

Jesus made that bird too!
he also made me and you!
Melissa Beth McMahon

A Major Voice

Crowds of windluft tree leaves, more earthbound than their brown
also sparrow brethren, chase each other like merry children,
rustling crinkles and crackling under the feet even of chipmunks
and the squirrels in dry mockery of the woods attempt at quiet,
and solemnity, and deference due the oncome of hoary winter

some of them, in groups, like confident little acrobats, or like
dragonflies ridden by tiny jockeys, do lazy midair turns and
even cartwheel in formation, dashing along currents and rivulets
of nostril clearing spring-water fresh air, kayaks of the dappled
glades, some of them landing with a whoosh of suddenly coming
to rest atop boughs of some grass blades tufts of forest.

That little squirrel takes his distances in leaps of six and eight inches
consolidating each gain by getting up to look around for possible
threats. Cautiously, he gathers his provender caring that the
store place be a secret even from the snowflakes, his kind rodent
eyes now laid over the by the glaze of prophecy.
Gene Simpson

A Brighter Day

We cannot know what lies in store;
We cannot solve life's mystery;
We only know what's gone before -
The future is not ours to see.

This gift of life, from God above,
Is ours to live to full extent;
'Twas given with the deepest love,
Which, through Our Lord, was Heaven-sent.

I have no way of knowing how
The day will start, or how 'twill end;
I only know I hear Him now,
And speak to Him, as friend to friend.

The Light on earth is growing dim;
This life we live shall pass away;
I'm sure that if I live in Him,
I'll be assured a Brighter Day.
Edwin P. Wolfe

Broken Heart

Someone's watching,
Watching from afar.
Watching, wishing on that same star.
No one can see him,
No one can hear
That he is weeping,
Though not from fear.

He has a broken heart,
One that cannot heal.
His body is numb,
He cannot feel.

But maybe there's hope,
Just a small silver
For the love of this immortal giver.
Carrie Johnson

Please Watch Over Me

Jesus, dear Jesus, please watch over me,
Open my eyes, that I may see,
That you were the one, that was sent to save me,
Thank you, dear Jesus, for watching over me.

Jesus, dear Jesus, please watch over me,
I feel so alone, in this troublesome sea,
But safe in your arms, forever I'll be,
Thank you, dear Jesus, for watching over me.

Jesus, dear Jesus, please watch over me,
I know that you know my every need,
They'll all be fulfilled if I only believe,
Thank you, dear Jesus, for watching over me.

Jesus, dear Jesus, please watch over me,
Be my guide daily, for then I shall see,
That God did send you, to watch over me,
Thank you, dear Jesus, for watching over me.
Eunice A. Hommer

This Is Your Season

This is your season,

when fresh silver droplets fall
from pine needles at sunrise,
and the river awakens to flood.

The gentle air will breathe life into us all.
Henry, can you sense nature and her call?

Let the children chase
all the dreams of Spring
that run frantic on the hillside,
sprinkled with poppy and clover
that blanket the countryside.

Henry, soon your dreams will thaw
and escape through the cracks in time;
flitting unseen, gently skipping
from the light sublime.

These Spring months fade
just as soon as they arrive.
We must cherish these days
that keep our dreams alive.
Erik Richards

The Life That Bore, Never More

The grass sways back and forth in my mind;
A picture of beauty captured in time.
A tiny seed in which this life bore,
May the grass live, forever more.

Winter comes with its mighty cold;
Turns dead the grass that once stood bold.
A tiny flake, as it gently lays on the floor,
May the grass live, never more.

My heart beats with the love I crave;
Trapped inside my heart, this hallow cave.
A tiny beat in which this love bore,
May my heart love, forever more.

Troubles come with their souls amourn
To rip my heart of this love I so adorn.
A tiny beat, as it gently lays on the floor,
May my heart love, never more.
Michael Bodenbach

Ron's Poem

I asked myself why?
And was startled with no reply

I looked for a reason to understand
but could find it from no man

I searched for a way to pretend it not to be
until truth and reality finally overcame me

I fought against the love we shared
but that only intensified how much I cared

When I was through blaming all
I suddenly heard the faintest call

I stopped thinking, and just believed
and suddenly my fears and worries were relieved

I asked Jesus is he alright?
And in my dreams, there was a light

Jesus, said he is here, and at peace
so any worries you have my child, cease

You are lucky to have known such a beautiful heart
From his mind and soul your memory will never part

Now go back to the garden, with the other flowers,
and I will bring you up to live with him in your hour.
Lisa DeAngelo

Searching

Lost in a dream,
The search for realism.
Only a sight from within can see the man outside.
Grasp for the lights,
colors so bright.
The pinch, of soothing emotions,
the feeling of ecstasy within.
Let me see for light has become grim.
No hope for innocence once lived,
to far in to get back around.
My pain is a needle,
my fear is control.
Grasp for hate a sight for what's real.
Lost in my thoughts
can't find, touch, or feel.
Be free for once only death so it seems.
The light from above makes all dreams roam free.
The demon that once was is no more.
For innocence is restored,
lost time is ignored.
Joel A. Cullum

Pet Rock

This is my pet rock I take him
everywhere. I tell him all my problems
because he really cares

His name is problem solver he works on
everything. He can not answer questions
because he doesn't sing.

Now that I'm getting older, I still do
love my rock, but I do know something
better I found out I could talk.

I talk to anybody that I really know. I
do not talk to strangers, my teachers told
me so.

Now this was my pet rock, it really was
my friends. I've found some real friends
now, so this will be the end.
Dixie Wirkus

Timeless Love

In this world I find that life is but time,
I have one life to live and but one to give
What pleasure to be your wife and sit side by side
Watching the evening tide
To walk hand in hand
To wear your wedding band
Calling your name
With mine the same
Knowing God's teachings
Are within our reachings
To bear your son
To be as one 'til life is done
If this is God's will
I will love you in life and in death still
If in this life I should find
You cannot be mine
Oh, what a waste of time
I will live but to die,
For my life was but a lie.
Dolores M. McGrew

Beauty - Love

The beauty of a soul is a deep, pure love
Love of God, love of life
It is love for a child and
Of course, love for a wife.

The beauty that shows on the surface, is
As the poet said, "only skin deep",
It is the heart which cannot be seen
Which gives us cause to weep.

The love of a dog for his master,
A young girl's love for her hero,
Love of the wind, love of the rain,
The cold, even when it drops to zero.

It is the love God had for the world
When he created nature
And the love of man for his neighbor
That makes us tall in stature.

The beauty of a soul can only be seen
By a chosen few
Of we creatures of God, and among these few,
One is me, and I know one is you.
Mary Lane Bradshaw

Simple Pleasures

I breathe in the lavender twilight
and let it wash away the day.
The warm evening breeze trails
gentle fingers through my hair
bringing the smell of lilacs and fresh cut grass.
Lightning bugs weave an intricate dance
in the shadows by the hedge.
In the distance, a mother calls her child
to dinner and a screen door slams.
I am alone with the quiet chirp of the
crickets in the deepening gloom.
The evening is a moment trapped in amber,
there is no yesterday, there is no tomorrow,
there is only now... and it is beautiful.
Wendy Kump

The Vessel

Love is like a ship in the ocean,
She bobs and weaves in turbulent emotion.
Creating a wild, swirling, disarray of doubt,
Up, down, in and out, in and out...
Arousing wakes of desire within our HEARTS,
Seizing us with her grapnel, we can't depart.
Her waves entrancing us,
Trailing, from dawn to dusk.
She knocks against our HEARTS,
We grasp at her, and away she darts.
Gail Inez Walker

The Touch

Her beauty lures
my eyes avidly probe
such flesh yet divine
it captures and intoxicates

Laid before me as pasture to gaze upon
is sweet slender softness
touch is transfiguration

She is love divine love...passion
lust has no home here
such darkness abodes not

In such celestial presence glorious light
angels hide their wings hide their beings

She is life eternal life...exaltation
glorious exaltation
basking in her warmth

Roses bow in her presence
breath of spring breeze
I am captured...transfigured
and she awakens
Brady Smith

Heartbeat

In a heartbeat, a baby dies
In a heartbeat, a baby cries
In a heartbeat, our lives have changed
In a heartbeat, the world will never be the same
In a heartbeat, our lives must go on
In a heartbeat, the memories linger on
In a heartbeat, more babies are born
In a heartbeat, we all still mourn
In a heartbeat, a baby cries
In a heartbeat, we still remember the baby that died
Melissa Y. Becker

A Very Dear Friend Named Shawn

Here we are to celebrate a wonderful surprise -
For someone who is special, you can tell by the
look in her eyes.

Her family they are all so special and love every
one so much, that Shawn has come this far in life
because of their loving touch.

Shawn will always have support from friends and
family - and she in turn gives just as much because
she is always filled with glee.

And now this is her special day with everyone around,
you sure can think it won't be long and Shawn will spring
and bound.

She still has pretty rough weeks ahead, but she's prepared
for that - Because Shawn's the type that would think to herself
it's either this or that.

You ask yourself how much more can she take - but knowing Shawn
there is too much at stake.

The thoughts and the prayers will never stop, for someone
who has been so sturdy - But most of all we love you Shawn
today as you turn "30."
Donna L. Wilson

Get Real

Oh, my God, I know not why.
Only that there is a brown spot on my thigh.
What makes it brown only God knows
But why did the deity make fingers and toes?
Appendages protrude in a peculiar way
But you know what they say
You need fingers if you want to make hay.

What is haymaking all about?
Make a million and give a shout
Or maybe it was a golden goose who wove golden thread
Which was tough with webbed feet—and tough with a beak.
So I guess human bodies and minds
Are uniquely configured for cognitive finds.
But why should we think if instead we can feel?
Cuz you got to think if you want to get real.
Walter Ruby

Untitled

To The Rose:
   You are a memory I'll always hold so dear. From each golden smile to each private tear. Of friendship and heartache, love and such hate. Of each simple act that's brought me this fate. From hugs to "I love yous" that have come far too late. The red is a symbol of blood, sweat and tears and I am a product of those many years. As I hear the sounds of water so quick I know the hands of time forever tick. I watch as my friends all come and go. There is pain, but I mustn't let it show. For the rose that neither wilts nor dies, for you only I make my sad lonely cries. Farewell my dear friend I bid thee farewell. Someday soon Rose we'll cry till we're well.
Michelle Anderson

The Biggest Love Of All

The size of the man might appear to deceive,
You may think him hard and seldom at ease.

But it takes just a twinkle from the eye of a child,
To bring to that face a soft gentle smile.

His big hands hold gently the child in his care,
And in the time spent together, he has so much to share.

So though you may view him as just big and tall,
The love in his heart is the biggest of all.
Daphne E. Aguillard

"Life"

Life through out the years will present many hurdles for one to
   soar,
But one will learn from each one hurdled and can earn
   quite a score.

Life will not always be full of happiness and cheer,
   There will be times of anger, sorrow, and at times you
   will shed a tear.

Life will present many different lessons to learn from,
   But you must face each one head on and proceed and
   learn to overcome.

Life may not always be easy or fair,
   But the rough times of life are confronted much easier
   when shared with others who care.

Michael R. Fuller

The Art Of Shedding

I was determined to continue,
   continue collecting the lovely purple shells.
They were perfectly rounded and smooth,
   unblemished, fragile, and still cast aside.

As I walked the beach,
   the rhythm of the waves became my rhythm.
The sun hit my bare back; the wind thrust a mist
   and my body learned to appreciate and reflect.

Treasures of the sea delighted me —
   sandpipers whispering, sea gulls screaming.
Life was simplified at least for awhile
   and civilization did not intrude on me.

Solitude beckoned and I chose a narrow life.
Like playing solitaire on an island,
   I was alone, yet not at all lonely.
The retreat and return of the sea was my eternal light.

The beach taught me the art of shedding,
   shedding clothes, at first, then shelter and vanity.
It was, indeed, too warm, too damp for mental discipline.
Past and future dared not; all that counted was the present.

Connie J. Kirkland

Betrayal

I confessed my love, and so did you
My heart soared high
To know our love would have no bounds
The joy and happiness to be found
You and I entwined together
I knew our love would last forever
My soul sang songs of love united
To touch your hand, to feel your kiss
All these things I might have missed
To look in your eyes and see love shining
But something went wrong
And then I knew
It seems our love would never be
I remember the night
I remember the lies
I think of it still and want to cry
Time heals all wounds by and by
But mine run deep
As deep as lies.

Rhonda M. King

He Doesn't Love Me

What can I do?
I still love him very much.
He has hurt me deeper than
Anyone else ever has.
Why can't I be lucky in love?
Why must I continually be hurt?
When is it my turn to be loved?
Every man that leaves me
Takes a part of me with him.
There's not much of me left.
I feel so empty inside
Except for all of the horrible pain.
I believe there is no greater happiness than True Love.
I want the happiness.

Kimberly McCright

Poem For Raven

I reach inside
And I pull you out
Magnificent and beautiful
I know you love me
Talents demonstrated so unknowing and easy
I take you and display you
Beautifully extraordinary, you seem untouchable
Too lovely, too perfect
So much admired and so, so desired
But I can touch you
Laugh with you and share with you
And you
You stand beside me, walk next to me, and fly with me
And when the rain washes me down
You hold me
Hold me
Falling all around me
Just for a little longer
Hold me...

Laura Miller

Full Moon Adventure

When the moon is full.
The goddess throws her golden scarf
   across the lake.
Its pale light ripples in the wind.
Last night it shimmered at my feet.

"Walk on my path," whispered the Goddess.
I hesitated - would it hold me?
I put out my foot and stepped
Out across the lake on the golden path.
The Goddess smiled at my daring.
Brushing away a cloud, she murmured,
"I knew you could do it."

Carol Baker

My Candle

My candle bright
Gives off a dim light
That is followed by the midnight moon
For now we know that dawn is soon
Half around the clock and a little more
A rooster has a crow in store
He crows it up and then we know it's up and awake we go
Then to work, school, or play on we go in shine, rain, or snow
And then home bound at half past two
Then for bath we undress we do ending with our sock or shoe
Then we all sit at the table of timber to sup up our yummy dinner
At that moment we light my candle shining even dimmer
And as my father says the grace
The light shines on his gentle face

Emily Jensen

"Inside The Mind"

I will wander, and I will travel
And many adventures will unravel
And times will pass
As I search for the greener grass
That lies on the other side of the wall
Where no trial is too great, or achievement too small
In the mind of a man
Who has nothing to lose except the will to have it all

I will always wander, and I will always travel
All my dreams will have been unraveled
Before my own eyes
As I tried life on for size
Life for me was a perfect fit
While on the greener grass I will sit
With trials conquered, achievements succeeded
In the mind of a man
Who had nothing to lose but the determination to see it completed

Steven Gregg

Another Card For Mother

We have all made these cards for you. You'd hang them on the wall.
You probably still have some of them, for they meant the most of all.
So this year I'll make another card, for underneath your tree,
In the hope you'll see, over the years, how much you've meant to me
It came to me, in a moment of knowing, just what I hold most dear,
While trying to find time, to get everything done, and ready for
Christmas this year.
I get out the decorations, I put the cards in the mail.
I do my Christmas shopping, searching for the sales.
I'm really, really trying, to get the feeling of the season.
It seems like so much work, and I wonder, if there's a reason,
Why it doesn't seem like it used to-no matter what I do. Then I see
the tiny Christmas tree.
And the decorations out. But it's not the decorations or a special
  Christmas tree,
I just entered my Mother's home, And there's love in this place
  for me.
No matter how much I acquire, No matter how far I may roam,
Nothing compares to the feeling I have, when I enter my Mother's
  home.
I know how fortunate I am, And I regret so very much,
that there are many, who no longer know, the love of a Mother's
  touch.
There's no stronger love than that, of a parent for their child, For
this I do plainly see,
There's no way I can back to you, Expect perhaps, by passing on
  to mine,
The unconditional love, You've given me.

Joan M. Kelly

Wish I Knew

How many wishes on one point of light
as it falls until it is gone

A sacrifice for selfish thought
this blessed and cosmic wink

A wish, what's this, a search for truth,
the root of religious conception

Is a wish a dream that's out of reach
with a hope one step beyond

Is a hope a wish that is believed in stronger than a dream
and a prayer a hope that is so true it breaks mere mortal
consciousness

Is a prayer a just cause for divine intervention

Is a wish what stars are for?

Travis Robbins

"When Love Is Not Enough"

I tried to love you, I thought
you knew. All you did was make
me blue.
All I needed was us together, you
and me forever and ever.
You told me you loved me and how
much you cared but that didn't
comfort the feeling of me being
scared.
It's not me you want in your life.
You're not looking for a lover or even
a wife.
All you needed was your little white
friend. You thought it was a good
thing, maybe until the end. I
want to stay & help you break away but
you keep going back day after day.
You tried to make me feel guilty by
giving me the blame but it's yourself
you can look back on for why you're so lame.

Carla Glass

My Feelings Go On

A poem may have rhyme or reason
It could be about time or a season!
They are a person's work of art
For it is words which come from the heart!
You may hear or think of a phrase
Which you keep repeating for days!
Those words could be of poetry
Which you shall remember and set you free!
For many they bring great pleasure
As for the poet they are a treasure!
When you feel like you're all alone
Take time and recite a beautiful poem!
Whether it's laughter, trouble or tears
We must always deal with our fears!
For poetry will last through the years!

Tom Unger

I Am

I am an individual
  who spends the years of my life growing up in my home, yet cannot
  relate to anyone else.

I hear the wind wrestling through the trees of the past,
  but I see and feel as though the sun is never shining brightly in
  the future.

I am an individual
  who tries to reach out to other people yet never succeeds.

I pretend as if my life is as wonderful as I dream,
  but I always awake knowing the truth.
  I worry about how my siblings suffer as they grow up and cry when
I imagine their adult lives being like mine.

I am an individual
  who can barely face the light of day when I think about how my
  father treats me, yet I do.

I understand that it is not all my father's fault for his actions,
  but I say that he is the one that needs to open up his eyes and
  see what his abusive ways have done to his family.

I dream of the day when I will be able to leave my worst nightmare,
  my home, but at the same time I try to cope with it as best I can.

I hope my future will bring me someone to love who will love me in
  return, but right now I would just like to pass a night without
  ending the day by crying myself to sleep.

I am an individual who is trapped in my father's world and one day
  hopes to be set free.

I Am.

Sarah M. Ward

Night Owl

Somewhere inside black sky's silence
the night owl spreads her wings to fly.
Somewhere outside the world's violence
is where she goes to hide and cry.
When the pain's too much for her to bear
she flies into the night, so fair
looking for someone to care.
A nocturnal soul free in flight
All alone on a lonely night.
Sensing her only escape is fate,
she envisions the one, her perfect mate.
Needing a soul to be her guide
others the same to fly beside.
Waiting for the elusive cure,
flying along in a frenzied blur,
another night owl, just like her.

Casi Binner

The Room

It holds all my thoughts,
And it knows my feelings.
It knows my desires,
And comforts me in the worst of nightmares.
It holds me within,
Protecting me from the dangers,
That lie on the outside.
The room entertains the sadness,
In hopes to see a smile.
But when in doubt,
The room tries to reassure what's right.
It keeps me warm,
While all around is cold.
It holds all my prized possessions,
And it always has room for one more.
The room could talk forever,
If only the walls could speak.

Lisa Quick

"Because You Love Him"

Everything is perfect,
Picture perfect,
But only to the blind outside,
Inside is harsh and
unmeasurable agony.
You love him,
He seems to love you;
You hate him,
Why does he always hurt you?
From deep within you comes a scream,
"Help us! Him, me, all of us!"
No one hears you,
No one cares.
But then you think,
Maybe, just maybe this time
Someone will hear;
Then maybe just maybe someone will help;
So you keep screaming...
Because you love him.

Brandy Armstrong

Untitled

Letting go and letting be.
We must leave the memory of the hurts in our lives
or we will never be open to anything but the right
  to be unhappy.

Margaret J. Morris

Yesterday

Yesterday, my heart hurt...
I was black and blue from head to foot.

Yesterday, my head was full of rage...
I felt like an animal in a cage.

Yesterday, my eyes were full of tears...
I cried for hours to fill the years.

Yesterday, my mind was confused...
I couldn't stop feeling abused.

Yesterday, my soul hurt deep inside...
I felt as if a piece of me had died.

Yesterday, my heart reached out to you..
I trusted you through and through.

Yesterday, my body and heart became one...
I learned that true friendship can overcome.

Andrea M. Gilroy

Wonders of the World

In the spring of the year,
when the sun is shining down,
the early morning dew is all over the ground.
A light breeze blowing ever so softly
through the air,
all the beautiful flowers without
even a single care.

When I take the time to close my eyes and listen,
it gives my heart a chance to gather
what I've been missing.
The sound of water flowing so softly
down a stream,
I understand for the first time,
that life is such a beautiful thing.
I begin to see the wonderful things
that I normally would miss, and then
I understand why, you are such a
special part of this.

It's only when I have you next to my side,
that all the wonders of the world
can no longer hide.

Johnny J. Mullis

Snow

My memory goes to long ago
To the day I saw my first fallen snow
Down, down the steep embankment we would slide
With graceful ease the cardboard sled would glide

A hazard to drivers, but then
To a farmer becomes a friend
Soaking deep into the plowed furrows of a field
Giving needed moisture for the next crop yield

Like diamonds it glistens through the day
The sun's arrival soon will melt it away
Gone, possibly no to return this year
Going, it leaves the air so fresh and clear

We sometimes cloud our minds like a blanket of snow
And make it hard for it to continue to grow
So just as the snow melts away
Our minds need refreshing day by day.

Pauline Bashaw

The Peaceful Place

As I walked through the mystic shaded forest,
The trees whispered as the wind made its passage,
I looked up at the sky as little rays of the sun streamed down
Through the brilliant leaves as they circulated around.

I heard the sound of water running,
The birds voices rising in the air,
Blending in a perfect unity of harmony.
As I slowly turned the enchanted bend,
I saw water falling with the melody the birds send.

The water cascaded against the rocks
And traveled to destinations unbroken,
As the peaceful place relieved the pain in my soul,
The gentle wind passed through my hair,
To make me a part of this vast knowledge.

As I sat with my feet surrounded by cool water,
In this serene solitude with its hidden power,
I felt whole again: as one being,
Prepared to face the world outside its barrier.
Robin Anderson

Brittney's Christmas

It's that time of year for holidays, family and friends
How many presents are you going to get, well that depends

The question is, have you been bad or good
You know we'd give you the world if we could

Mommy and Daddy love you more and more each and every day
We want to see you happy, and grow-up healthy in every way

I hope your Christmas is full of fun and cheer
I hope Mommy and Daddy make christmas special every year

So listen for the reindeer and their jingling noise
And watch for santa, with a bag full of toys

Well go to bed and curl up tight
Before you know it, it'll be Christmas Eve night.
Jeffrey W. Kessinger

Acid Rain

Breaking through depression
hiding from the pain,
being comforted for every tear,
being sheltered from the rain.

They think they have the powers,
they say they feel your pain,
they have the powers of love and passion,
but not the cure, for acid rain.

As you suffer in its poison,
and you drown in the pools of depression and pain,
It hits you; hot on your skin,
but in your heart, like acid rain.

They make it sound so easy,
and the feelings disappear,
you think the depression is far away,
but, in truth, it's very near.

As, slowly, your heart disappears,
and you just can't stand the pain,
you know the depression you held back for years,
is just like acid rain.
Kelly McCoy

A Soft Rain

The sky screams with thunder
and silence touches the ground.
The dark clouds are looming
while shadow slithers on mound.
All forest grow quiet
flying butterflies disappear.
Suddenly there's a flash
and thunder in the ears.
Sad clouds clear their eyes
water whispers off the earth.
Making a peaceful melody
quenching nature's thirst.
Winged creatures bathe in sky tears
frolicking in the magic mist.
Washing away all fears
feeling like a kiss.
Black vapors vanish from heaven
and blue skies penetrate unnatural night.
Bringing with it the rainbow
and the sapphire beauty of light.
Jason P. Weiland

Country Boy

I was born a poor country boy.
My little heart was filled with joy.
We never had much money.
But we lived in the land of milk and honey.
I remember mother saying,
"For you my son I am nightly praying,"
"That you will grow up to be a respectful man."
I said to mom, "I will do the best I can."
Dad said, "You will never amount to a hill of beans,"
"That is the way with you wayward teens."
My father with love filled my cup,
So to him I lift it up.
With grace love and charity,
All of these things he gave to me.
Now that I am growing old,
I am glad this story has been told.
Francis H. Edwards

Daddy's Gone

I sit and watch the ocean waves.
Caressing and gentle;
rough and majestic.
The continuous pull is hypnotic, riding the wave.

I see my father's smile.
Bright and loving
Strong arms pull me in for a hug.
Warm and secure.

I sit and watch the ocean once again.
Dark and menacing.
A thief among thieves.
Draw and pull.

I watch a full grave covered with flowers of spring.
A presence by my side.
Peace, but yet, resentment.
Elizabeth U. Childers

What The River Says

Sometimes I sit and watch a moody river
water tumbles over rocks stretching farther
and faster into blackeyed woods I wonder
what the water says as it slaps angry curls
in a rapid or what it shouts to the canyon as it slams
against its cold rock wall sometimes I hear the river cry
as its currents amble water sliding over itself
kissing its wet tears breathing a hushed lullaby to the
pebbles as it washes over them again and again
other times I hear the river laugh as it leaps
reaching for willow's fingertips
tickling its lovely bending body
most of the time I hear it rush by me
in a tide of strength fighting to keep up
with the wind and the rain and the watercolor
clouds and the stars that fly with mermaids
up in the high high sky where I touch sun's
face and wander with fairies and angels
scattering tales of distant waters in distant heavens
what the river says is what I say
Alana Schiffman

Rain

As the days go by, I waste my time.
Education is important, but my life is distorted.
I try my best - it's hard to rest.
Life is complicated: I'm always frustrated.
I try to block the evil out and take a shorter route.
I don't gain nothing but pain - my only escape is the rain.
April Ellis

Halloween Night

The ghosts come out, and witches too...
They'll fly around or make a brew.
The Jack O'Lanterns will laugh with terror and fright...
For what is going on this Halloween night?

The monsters and goblins will give a good scare,
For all those who are a part of this ghoulish affair.
The owl hoots in a fearful manner...
Because he is scared of the mad hatter.

Well, who wouldn't be with those glowing eyes,
He always has a great disguise.
The devil laughs with great delight,
'Cause he loves Halloween night.

Halloween is over, all is calm and safe...
On this day a witch and I came face to face.
It is midnight and all the spirits are back to bed,
They were alive...but now they're dead!
Christine J. Tobin

Silence

Silence
a book page slowly turns
 Silence
a cool breeze rustles a stack of papers
 Silence
A bird feeds its young
 Silence
Suddenly a bell rings
Children pour out of rooms
 laughter
 shouting
Then, all of the children disappear into rooms
and now again
 Silence
Chelsea Baker

Father

Respected wise old man,
I'm thinking of my childhood past,
of walks in the park, an appreciation for our beautiful world,
a precious gift, your time.
You gave these things to me;
things that money can't buy.

Respected wise old man,
I smell the bread baking,
I smell the soups and stews,
you sure can bake and cook;
Now I can do this too!

Respected wise old man,
you have a sense of humor-sometimes a joke or two.
Leaving a smile on my face,
without this, it just wouldn't do.

Respected wise old man,
You're reminiscing of things past.
You're getting older,
So am I;
Memories will forever last!
Linda Knapp

Her

I have had many friends in life
they have helped me to bear my strife.
 But of all the things that could occur,
I've never had a better friend than her.

We shared some good times and some bad
I'll never forget the times we had.
We've talked with each other, and bared our hearts,
But a day is coming when we must part.

For though I love her, she must go
And never will I ever know,
Never will I ever see
Why God has given her to me.
Jennifer Tolbert

A Bouquet For Grandma

Went down a country road today.
I might have turned the other way.
Something told me, turn and go.
A whispering wind sweet and low.
Slowly passing shady trees.
Sunshine peeking through the leaves.
Soft warm meadows, wind does blow.
Their grassy fingers say hello.
And flowers, yes the daisy fair.
Love me, love me nots for my hair.
Buttercups, queen ann, and clover sweet.
The trefoil makes bouquet complete.
All my favorite things you see.
Bring you back so near to me.
So many times, I've picked for you.
The wild flowers that God grew.
Each flower's a memory and always will be.
Of the things we've shared just you and me.
I love you Grandma and always will.
And someday we'll meet and pick flowers on the hill.
Holly Massarotti

Highest Hour

When at the Highest Hour
of pleasant muse and after strife
of carnival sounds from whirl to dust
of smiles the color of autumn rust.

When at the Highest Hour
I see the intricate, unstoppable life
from moonlights version of skyline's trust
to the core of earth's amber crust.

What expires my Highest Hour?
Nary higher to achieve?
Lest the Hour I must leave.
Away to grace where I will grieve.

Now I stroll to sightful sleep
upon my pillow soft and sweet
hours past the Hour deep
I lay me down to weep.

Jonathan Kain

Hope

I've come upon a fallen angel
she had a broken wing.

When I drew close, she hissed and snapped
so I stayed away and watched
watched her writhe in pain.

Her eyes - so beautiful,
clouded with tears.

Her face - so pale and smooth,
turned red and shook violently.

As I sat, tears welled and burst,
running down my cheek like a river overflowing its banks.

Just then she stopped
her eyes cleared and
again became the color of lakes.

Her face - once crimson with pain,
lost its frightening color and again became dove pale.

She rose swiftly from her position on the pavement
and soared into flight.
As she disappeared into the horizon,
I could hear her joyous laughter.

Benjamin S. Belletto

A True Friend

   When so many obstacle stood in my way,
right beside me is where you stayed.
   If I need to talk or if I need to cry,
you solve my problems when others wouldn't
try.
   When my grandfather died I was torn apart,
but you put love back into my heart.
   Through thick and thin to the very end,
you have been my very best friend.
   Your advice on guys has saved me from a lot
of pain, and for that my life will never
be the same.
   You were there for me when my other friends
pushed me away, and for that in my heart you
shall forever stay.
   I dread the day when we have to say goodbye,
because a very special part of me will
die.

Jenni Smyth

I

To hold thee in mine arms till dawn's breaking
T'would be a gift of God from heav'n above
Thou dost see in my heart love's true aching
For my longing, a tear comes like a dove.
Thy golden hair which crowneth thee: So soft
The hill of heather canst e'en true compare
Eyes in which mystery is hidden oft
Their color enwraps me so as I stare.
Thy skin so fair, a heart as pure as snow
Grace thou art surely with, and so much more
In thy beauty, God's blessing dost true show
My love for thee: Like waves upon the shore.
   To prove my love, I'd sail the seven seas;
   When death came to take, I'd go forth for thee.

Edward W. McDonald IV

Remind Me!

Holy Spirit, let me learn to know you better.
REMIND ME during the day that you are near,
Waiting for recognition from me.
When I need a steady hand to guide me,
REMIND ME that all I need to do is ask.

When I need strength to get thru the day,
REMIND ME to call on you.
Each moment, if I seem to falter,
COME TO ME, remain near.
YOU know I need you!

When I seem desperate or lonely, be there;
I KNOW you are there, but remind me.
If I am obsessed with troubled moments
Assure me of your presence.
I have a receptive mind, just REMIND ME.

Let my hope be secure
Let my faith be unwavering.
Let YOUR PRESENCE REMIND ME
That you are guiding me
To be my inspiration, MY FRIEND.

Marian Kimpel

Seize The Day

Hold tightly to youth
lest it slip through your fingers
like so many grains of sand
Keep close your ambitions
and follow your heart
to where only dreams may lead you
Cling to your joys
and share them with all you meet
lest joy pass utterly from your life
Grasp to you your life
like the helm of a ship
and steer towards the brilliance of the sunset.....

Deanna Barcus

The Willow Tree

When the sun is out and everyone is playing,
  the willow tree stands;
When the leaves are falling and those
wild winds are blowing,
  the willow tree stands;
When the snow is falling and those
Cold nights appear,
  the willow tree stands;
When the flowers are approaching and
the birds are chirping,
  the willow tree stands...

Kara Boivin

Whitewater Rush

A seven-man rubber raft is placed firmly in the calm waters of West Virginia. All aboard and off we go, swiftly downstream, as the paddlers stroke in unison.

You and six other people are quickly acquainted and bonded for the quick, yet long ride of your life. Suddenly, and without warning, the waters pick up to a fast tempo and your heart begins to race.

Ripples become rapids and calm waters become raging and ripping waves. White caps of mist and spray dance on your face; until, at a moment's notice, droplets become gushing gallons of water.

The paddlers' strokes are struggling to keep their stride. The raft is turning and tossing about like a restless sleeper. The straight calming path is twisted and staggered as a Drunkard's nightmare.

Adrenaline flows from your veins with anticipation of Fatality, capsizing your life and taking your last breath like an intense kiss. Your head is suddenly dipped into the current and you're dragged underwater for what seems like minutes, intently gasping for air. At last, you emerge from the deep — life is leached to a frazzle and all your energy has been frittered away. One last breath fills Your lungs and you realize the ride is over... and you're still Alive.

Jacob W. Burke

Deliberate Intent

One day I up and killed my soul with deliberate intent
My silent cries had gone unheard, my tears had all been spent.
I guess I thought a deadened heart could not feel more pain
But the world I crawl about in now has made me think again.
The pipe became my friend and foe, it was for what I lived
My family needed love from me, I had none left to give
I'd lie, I'd steal, I'd cheat and fight, I'd die to get my high
I lost all I really loved, and don't even know why
I didn't laugh, I couldn't cry, I had no heart at all
I treated everyone like dirt, felt pitiful and small
These things I did all on my own, didn't need much help
My addiction took my fortune, my family and my health
How could I so hate myself to plunge my life in hell?
How could I still crave this drug, its torments I know well
Why would I want to risk my life for shame and grief and pain
And why, when I know the cost, do I do it all again?

Sherry Celley-Lowenberg

The Angels Smiled

I know you're special the Angels smiled the day
that you were born.

Your smile knocks me off my feet, your
laughter fills me with joy.

Your eyes shine like diamonds in the darkest
sky. When I am with you the day and the night
time seem to fly by.

I know that I will always stand by your side,
If you ever need me I'll be right there. I
see the dust from their wings shining in
your hair.

I know you're special the Angels smiled the day
that you were born.

They came to earth and smiled at me and now
when I look at you it's an Angel I will see.

I know you're special the Angels Smiled!

S. L. Mancini

Waiting For Love

"But me, you have not always."
Into your life they will continue to come, waiting to be loved.
See their faces, somehow always beautiful, with
eyes set deep and searching. And whom will the Presence send you?
Sudden strangers, even your children - wrapped surprises, always
looking, passing briefly through your life - undiscovered treasures,
shifting shapes unnoticed, already parting like grains of sand,
so quickly disappearing, sinking into silent deserts of forgotten
memory. The question always returns:

"Did the coils of your heart ever warm and open to the ones I gave
you; how much did you love while we were together; did you care
to stir the flames in which we would have recognized each other?

Love the ones you are given! And whom will you love today?
They will not always be present: some difficult, numb or angrily
remote, others close companions of unspoken mysteries-all are
waiting now, not merely for your knowing mind, cool perfection
like marble, not for easy words, or even for efficient doing,
but waiting for the opening - an open space in your chambered heart
where tears received may find new joy and laughter born of love;
for only love turns tears to jewels and opens eyes to radiant light.

Hal A. Lingerman

Until

Hold my hand until
I'm strong enough to walk alone.
Walk beside me for strength until
I can do it on my own.
I need your direction to get
me through each day.
I need you guidance to ensure
I go the right way.
I need protection
from the outside world.
I need you to stand beside me
and protect this little girl.
I don't always make the right decisions
and I do make some mistakes.
I need you beside me to give me direction
and show me which road I should take.
I need you to love me until
I can love myself.
I need you to stay with me
because I can't do this myself.

Cynthia Irene Thomas

Breakaway

The man skates down the ice to score a goal.
The goalie moves in front to stop the puck.
The man falls down and starts to say "Oh shucks".
When out in front he sees a man named Dole.
He moves the puck to Dole with all his soul.
But he forgot that Dole will need some luck.
For Dole is bad and people know he sucks.
But maybe just this once he'll get a goal.

Dole starts to move his stick to fake a shot.
The goalie moves out front to cut the anglE.
But this was all a part of dole's big plot.
He wants to build suspense and let it dangle.
He wants to show the players what he's got.
Too bad he trips and ends up getting tangled.

Patrick Copeland

A Sleepless Night

    Captured by the sound of silence beckoning inside of me,
What a surprise are the beams of light from the sky that fall
upon the sea.
    The waves roar with passion and force as they hit the shore,
The heat rises, inflections twisted, caught in the memories of
our nights and our dreams from before.
    Such alienated feelings I get when I stare off to the
glistening light,
The darkness around me empties me with a great feeling to fight.
The sea never rests with all the memories it holds,
In the waves are feelings of passion, pain and remorse that it folds.
    To say goodbye to the thoughts that hold us from our sleep,
The sea will always sail and its ships will always weep.

Noel Janssen

Wings Of Love

Indeed, I have found that I have Wings of my own to fly.
Yet, when I dream that I am with you
there are moments when I see myself flying on the back of Pegasus
so that you may be within my arms while I am kissing your soft lips
and leaving behind all concern for where we are going together.

Knowing that together we fly away from old hurts and pains,
and the fears of once abandoned Love. Together we fly closer
toward Love and the freedom "To Be". The freedom to live
safely and joyfully with the Best from within our Hearts.

It is like being able to bring out the Best Wine for the
Good Years.
A wine that was "hidden" until, it was Time.
You and I are free to enjoy the Best of
One Another.
With you, I am Love,
Love to You
I AM

Michael Jacobson Gomez

A Passing Breeze In Time

Seasons come and go
Like a passing breeze,
And I am in the midst of it all.
From shiny green leaves,
To bare wooded trees.
From sweat trickling down my body,
To the numbness of my fingers and cheeks.
Yet what a sight it is to see,
The world revolving around me.
Time waits for no one.
As I find myself standing there,
Gazing at waves in the sea.

Bianca Mozell Gibbs

Jack Daniel's

Jack Daniel's is an old and familiar name,
It makes people feel jolly and happy all the same.
The bottle stands tall and attractive, you see,
No matter how funny and silly it makes you be.

The distillery is big, holds lots of mash,
Which comes in round barrels, like hauling trash.
The taste must be excellent when the process is over,
People go out singing, here comes "Red Rover."

A night cap in the evening will put you to sleep,
Nothing else matters, you don't hear a peep.
But oh! The next morning a headache for sure,
If I had only taken water, it is so pure.

The odor is loud, the spirits run high,
Please don't catch me, is often a sigh.
Keep the cork in the bottle and the lid on tight,
Makes me tell secrets, that might stir up a fight.

Nita Dunbar

Up Here

I'm feeling kind of freaky, a little sneaky.
Somewhat deprived, yet, I'm alive.

I'm ready to dream, I'm willing to scream.
I know I can fly, as long as I'm high.

Just let it be me, let my blind eyes see.
Just let me be real, let my conscience feel.

I'm ready to fight, willing to die,
across this countryside.
Just never let me back into reality,
for it will trigger my insanity.

I'm only sane in this mellow world in my head.
If I come down, my world will be dead.
I'll be lost a far way from home.
And I will never be free to roam.

So to my savior,
let me breathe up in this world of mine,
where nothing hurts me and everything is fine.

Rozanna M. Catoline

From The Window

The night is dark, but cool and crisp.
The tingle of spring tickles my nose,
As it shares its message on a secret wisp.

Catching my eye is one brilliant twinkle of a star,
Far off in the deep universe,
Adrift in a sea of tar.

How would it look, I ask myself, if uncloaked from its disguise?
Or displayed before the bridge crew
On the main viewer of the starship Enterprise?

Slowly the entire scene unfolds before my eyes.
Misty, clouded fingers, highlighted in moonlight
Creep across the black expanse toward the star's light.

Suddenly a dark cottonwood springs up from down below,
Stretching forth its lacy branches
While against a star-lit backdrop, it dances.

I want to stay forever, deep-breathing the clean night air,
Gazing at the simple mysteries
That are around me everywhere.

Ashley Anderson

Wings

When I was just a boy of six
I played with boyish things
Like bows, and arrows, and magic tricks
And believed that boys had wings.

Then, everywhere I went I sang
And strummed guitars
of rubber bands and jelly jars.
I beat the drum I made
And played - for I was just a boy of six
And never was afraid.

But now I am no longer boy,
But never man yet I.
For while the world is surely mine
And will be 'til I die,
Yet every day that passes by
I think back to childish dreams,
And each new day that rushes by
I remember I had wings.

Russell Byers

On Our Way

A gentle hand set us upon our way, long before our feet could stand. Heading down the path of life some for a very short time and some for a long and wondrous trip, we were on our way.

We have seen and heard a great many things of beauty, sorrow, and joy, with a companion, a child, and maybe a friend, to help us our way.

The things we have touched in help or harm and shared our treasures too! We've brushed by His hand, and hem, or may have seen a glimpse of Him, as we traveled on our way.

As the way becomes slower and life's great joy's are remembered, the good times, the worst of times, and more, all tell us just how full the trip has been, as we went along our way.

With hope one day to stand holding tight on to that helping hand that carried us on our way, and look upon His face.

Marita R. Knight

Mikey And Uncle Joe

The winter when I was just past three,
Uncle Joe came to stay with me.
I was happy when he moved in,
Cause I had my own senior citizen.
I liked to walk with Uncle Joe,
He'd hold my hand and we walked real slow,
He wasn't in a hurry like most people are,
And we never got tired, cause we never walked far.
We'd come back and sit beneath the tree,
And he'd sing funny songs to me.
We'd sit by the tree when the weather was mild,
And he'd talk about life when he was a child.
We'd color together and when we were done,
He'd pat my head and say, "Well done my son."
In the spring it was time to go,
And I said goodbye to Uncle Joe.
We promised each other we wouldn't cry,
But it sure was hard to say goodbye.
We were a lot alike Uncle Joe and me,
Though he was "Eighty-Seven" and I was just past three.

Dolores Pouker

For He Sees You!

There is so much hurt
There is so much pain
There is so much grief
Cause the one you lost
Is the one you love
Too much was the cost
And you know how
What path will I take?
There is too much to bear
There is too much to care
Will it ever End?
Endurance Christ will Send
Your wounds Christ will Tend
Broken Hearts Christ will Mend
For He sees you, when you Weep
For He sees you, when the pain is Deep
For He sees you, when the burden is a Heap
For He sees you, when you cannot Leap
For He sees you, when the joy you cannot Keep

Ramesh C. Reddy

Memories

They haunt my days and make a prisoner of my soul.
I want to forget them but that would destroy the "who" that makes me.
I hate them, I love them I unconsciously give them their power.
They are the builders of my strengths and the creators of my insecurities.
They distort and confuse my past. They mystify and glamorize my present.
They nurture my pain. They are the guardians of my joy.
They can live for generations, die within a moment, and be reborn without a thought.
One by one their deaths release me towards freedom and push me a step closer to the unknown.
When they become a mere nothing I will also cease to be and then I will discover the truth; the meaning of me.

Natalie Walker

Love

Imagine love as if a star, whose path bends toward the earth
And though it seems so very far, its light burns like a hearth
And warms the soul with gentle fire, that burns with heavens might
And fills the soul with soft desire, and blinds the keenest sight.

Imagine love as if a flame, who burns a top a wick
And think the candle just the same, as love without a trick
That gives the flame all it desires, and asks it to return
The warmth and light of all its fires, forever may it burn!

Imagine love as falling rain, which causes life to grow
And though this drop appears so plain, this mighty drop will show
That no man can live without, its gentle touch upon His soul
though man would cry and shout, "that he would still live on".

Imagine love as anything, that man could want or have
And to its praise you may sing, for love one cannot save
Until a raining day comes by, when there is none around
Don't break your heart and do not cry, for soon it will be found!

Brian P. Sanker

Lone

Black highways stretch through the desert,
High-tech tentacles break up the sand
But civilization is a relative term,
When your transport's the thumb on your hand.
The road runs on forever, snatching blue sky from obscurity,
With a jump, I can reach for a small piece of heaven.
A Harley streaks by, speeding on through the dusk;
I can tell by the stuttering pop.
coming alive, my senses awaken;
filled by the nature, I stop.
Glancing eastward, I spot a slight glow.
The sun will be rising real soon,
Spreading its brightness to blind me again
and blot out the beautiful moon.
My journey, two weeks now, it seems has just started,
but my destination's yet unnamed.
It exists, a feeling in my mind; to reach it is to be changed
I don't know yet what I will become,
When this transformation is finally complete
But one thing I know and one thing alone,
by then, I'll be used to this heat.

Matthew C. Schierling

Fragile Is This Night

A gentle spirit with noble grace
Surrounds us all regardless of place.
Returning each year for a brief moment,
To awaken feelings put to rest by achieving.
What happens to us,
   On Christmas night.
The table of life that is set before us,
Now suddenly revered like fine crystal,
With the joys of giving and sharing.
But one tear falling, like a stone
Will shatter the beauty,
   On Christmas night.
Weapons laid down in mutual trust,
Enemies do speaketh in gentler tones,
This awesome beauty prevails, peace reigns.
Wrap gently this fragile gift of time,
Open as life demands, not only
   On Christmas night.

Alice J. Macierowski

Dear Friends

Oh my dear friends.
How I thank you all.
It's more than friendship I see.
Always, all my family as well.
I love you.
Fights and talks, we stuck together.
Our care for each other saved us from death.
Different or not, we're proud.
Happy am I that my heart was rescued from sadness.
To the one that changed me, I thank you!

Lisa Van Hook

God One Nation

One nation always raging, if there's gold or oils it's worth racing
into a conflict, even when it will inflict, a young man if he says he
can he'll be pit, against the so called enemy, who it's a sin to be,
for the sake of humanity, he ran with the flag draped over his
shoulders. Raped of sixty years so the older man would see -yet
another day- in an oval room.

One nation, land of the color blind, the peace sign- yet defined a
color line. Runs through each state like an interstate, still I
can't wait, for a piece of uncle's pie. And so I try, I try.
Assimilation, transformation, erasing, reincarnation to be a part of
this nation. Sell out get the hell out, uproot, lost my roots,
replanted but I fell out. I lost something, "Melt son, melt!"

One nation, law abiding—badges and guns, let's start fighting.
The concrete, once was at my feet, but I was grounded and wronged
by the strong- arm of the law.
Who saw E.T. get beat. "Black and blue, the former by virtue.
One cop was too. "That was a big police, all twenty of them" said
Rodney.

One nation!

Jonathan Pope

LiFe

If you think...

That life isn't worth your time...
   What-Ever!!!!

That life is pathetic...
   You're the pathetic one!!!!

That life holds no meaning what so ever...
   Oh Please!!!!

That you should end your life as it is right now...
   GET A LIFE!!!!

Candace Rouse

Weather Friendship

I've often known the storms to blow
And they hardly ever know
Just a fierce chatter of the wind
Some we often call a friend
I want to speak of what matters
But my words get shattered by the wind's clatter

When we often look for a wildless ocean
So gentle, listening, and calm
To hear the silence of its motion
to speak unabridged and quite open
It listens without a word spoken
And I find rest-even-peace-at least of mind

So when the wind blows
As It'll always do
and we need a friend
Somehow who'll listen through
Don't look for a storm
For the ocean's true
And for sure-it will listen to you

Meshante Husband

Jason Tree

When April turns to May
We will see this tree
And will remember.

When weeks fly by and it's July,
We will see this tree
And we'll remember.

When summer turns September
And the chill winds blow
And there is snow,
Even then, we will remember.

Though the leaves all fall and seem to die
Yet the tree lives on, as you do in our hearts.

And when Springs starts, and buds appear
The Jason Tree will flourish once again.

When we are women, when we're men
Years from now, it will remain.
From December to December.
We will see this tree
And we'll remember.

Paula Bowser

The Sea

Early in the morning the sea is enslaved
by wind flowing through the air. Quietly we await...
Crashing and banging people's hearts elate
from the wrath of the sea, plummeting to its grave,
splashing against the stone walls forming caves.
Slowly the wind departs and water permeates
through the sand and silt that the waves confiscate.
Dying down, the waves leave their mark on life's engraving-
Once again the circle is reborn-
charging through the sand, eroding the beaches.
As the moon appears on the glistening sea,
the wind increases, and the water becomes airborne,
Smashing again, a wave triumphs and teaches...
and leaves its mark which everyone can see

Josh Newman

Cathy's Roses

She planted them in a garden and
nurtured them with care and waited
patiently for each blossom to appear.

And when the blossoms did appear,
she watered them with love, for she
knew that beauty such as this can only
come from above.

She shared them with her friends
and with her family. She knew that many
more would bloom, more than she would
ever need.

She watched as the last blossom opened
and the petals fell softly to the ground,
but she was not sad, she knew that
next year; they would bloom all over again

Ann Fugate

Crunch-Time A'Comming

Open up your mind, these words are divine.
Open up your ears, this is, I am, here.
   Jehovah Allah Heim is my name;
keep it in your heart, soon some
will make a new start.
   Pray to me at least once a day;
for there is but one way to get your pay.
   Crunch-time is near. But the
prayerful believers need not fear.
   And, lift up my holy name;
fear not, nor feel any shame.
   So remember, if you want
salvation, pray to me, the maker
and breaker of nations.
   Keep me in your heart and mind,
and graceful salvation, will be thine's.

Newell Michael Evans (The Master Programmer)

The Sounds Of Silence

The sound of his robust laughter
Filling the air with joyous reprise
You can almost see the light of pride
And promise in his eyes.

The sound of his strong voice
Heralding across the years
You can almost feel his strength
Eliminating all your childish fears

The sound of his giving heart
Loving completely a thousand fold
You can almost taste his sweet kiss
Warming you against the night's bitter cold

The sound of his footsteps
Boldly coming toward you
You can almost reach out
And touch his face anew

So listen past the despair and tears
Listen closely and you shall hear
The Sounds of Silence

Chadwick

The Oklahoma Tragedy

It's been a year since the Oklahoma Bombing.
Are we in a state of Calming?
Our lives have no doubt changed
because our fellow employees were strained
By this horrendous planned deed
That grew from a very bad seed.

Today we can only pray
For the survivors and those who passed away
And the loved ones who are grieving
while they are still disbelieving;
How this tragedy could have happened
To a Country that became so saddened.

So as April Nineteenth marks
the anniversary that will spark
A sadness from all our hearts
await the bitterness to depart.
May we as a nation begin to cope
As we find peace through our newfound hope!

Barbara Harden

Wonder

Look around, there is wonder,
Wonder in every place,
Far and near, close and away,
I see the wonder of the world today!
Look at the rock...
Is there wonder in such a thing?
Been on earth for centuries or just since yesterday?
Holding and seeing secrets afar,
Happiness and disaster,
Been through it all...
Nonliving to the human eye
But live in the spirit
That we may never realize!
Wondering, wondering,
Takes us afar,
What is wrong in wondering at all?
For wondering indeed is the nature of all!

Sara-Jayanthi Santhan

This Is Easter

Today we set ourselves aside to ponder
So we can search and look and seek
To find the meaning of our lives
In this The Holy Week

No matter what the Faith of anyone
To some this is the Passover
At the Jewish Seder, we call The Last Supper
Jesus said "Love One Another"

If everyone today would stop and pause
And really and truly live Christianity
There would be so much good and surprise
At the thought of such serendipity

We'll have fun with friends and family
We'll say a prayer at the table
We must think of those around us
Who are not so fortunate and able

We'll rejoice with the message we've been taught
Jesus arose and disappeared forever?
No, we've learned that He'll return
We have no doubt, one way or another!

Maurine Reedy Ruzek

The Gift

God smiled gently on earth this day
and made it perfect in every way.

Because of Him the sun did shine
with rays that warmed each tender vine.

He blessed each flower and each tree
to make them fair for us to see.

He breathed a song for birds to sing
the happy, joyous sounds of spring.

With giving heart, He spread His grace
on every thing and every place.

He touched the clouds with restraining hand
lest they darken this shining land.

Having created the perfect day
He bowed His sacred head to pray
that man accept this gift from above
as a sign of His eternal love.

Ruth Boutelle

Who Am I?

Myself.

A lover of birdsong; a seeker after truth; a child of the elements who
responds to the rain with joyous - yet pensive mood;
to the wind with a lifting heart - yet apprehensive twinge;
to the sun in a deep blue sky with grateful wonder - yet thought for
    shade;
to white, fleecy clouds with childlike joy, yet nostalgic sigh;
to God with adoration - yet trembling awe;
to Jesus with heartfelt gratitude, yet disobedience;

Who am I?

I am Myself. Yet not Myself, but... sometimes One lives in me 'til
I shut Him out.

How glad I am when I hear that familiar knock once more, and
I, myself, run to open wide the door that I may not be —

myself.

Maureen Foster

Angel Of Mystic

Where did you come from my Angel of Mystic
When you walked into my life I could not believe it.
Where were you going on that evening
My Angel of Mystic, so beautiful, so soft with
hair like golden wheat, tanned with the summer
sun.
Eyes so soft and kind, and a smile that would
light up the darkest soul
As you walked by I could not believe my eyes, a
woman, a lady of grace and beauty just walked by
and smiled at me.
Upon the dance floor you gently strolled and
with the grace of an angel you started to
glide, with little or no movement you stated
to grace us with your angelic style of dance
all noise stopped, all eye were focused upon you
an Angel of Mystic, an Angel has walked into
our lives
where did you come from my Angel of Mystic

William A. Baker

Untitled

An Indian's Soapbox Lament
Here we find ourselves again
Doubtful and full of fear
Dubiously we anticipate
As the dreaded day draws near

We've heard all the promises
They kind of hurt my ear
They remind me of the ones I've heard
All broken, from yesteryear

Yet as the time approaches us
It's so difficult not to veer
Its just as hard to watch it come
And greet it with a cheer

But to make a choice and choose we must
A privilege we should hold dear
To place in charge of our affairs
A leader who cannot veer

So now I wonder, "What of Me"?
Had I chose another career
To be a politician in
This coming election year.

J. Marshall

A Little Boy Went A Walking

Once upon a time in a far off land,
A little boy went walking, a pretend stick sword in hand.

He wondered across the meadow and up over a very steep hill,
Slaying imaginary, slimy, green, and purple, fire breathing dragons
    at will.

He grew very tired and sat down on a big rock,
He took off his shoe and contemplated a small hole in his sock,

He soon went to sleep and dreamt of such a wonderful place,
Where not one child was ever judged by appearance, color, or race.

Where every child had a wonderful home in which to stay,
Abuse was unheard of and a chocolate cake desert was the main
meal of the day.

Where the sun shone bright all day and at night came a soft rain,
Where a child suffered no sickness or pain.

He saw no evidence of war and there seemed nothing to fear,
That everyone was ever so happy it seemed crystal clear.

He thought how wonderful it would be to live there,
Where people loved everyone and really seemed to care.

His mother called his name, and he woke and reached for his shoe,
He figured he would leave the rest of this wonderful dream up to you.

Donna Getts

Untitled

To someone who is very special and dear to me,
A pretty girl, who is not told as often as she should be.
A young woman with so many hopes and dreams,
With so many obstacles to overcome it seems.
She has a ticket to a new opening,
And that is exactly where you'll find me.
Standing beside her in every decision she makes,
Giving her strength to believe that she was what it takes.
So, no matter how far apart we are,
Just know that I'll always be with you in you heart.
So always remember that I'll be here for you,
And please don't ever be afraid to come to me too.
Friends for ever, till death do us part,
Cuz you made it in, you have touched my heart.

Kristy Burrell

Lust

What is lust exactly? Is it the ultimate sin that everyone fears, or is it just an emotion that we should all endure? This emotion called lust can be both healthy and unhealthy.

I once knew a man who was basically good at heart but, when he got too close to a woman his brain and his d**k were miles apart. I can recall several times when he would get in trouble for the things he said; he was lucky to wind up only seriously bruised because they wanted to kill him instead.

Lust can be used in a healthy manner as well. I ONCE knew a woman who wanted a certain career so bad, she would not let anyone upset her or make her mad. She went after this job she wanted so bad and when she finally got it she was both happy and glad.

So let it be known that this emotion called lust should be feared, but try to remember it is also an emotion that we should hold very dear.

Danzel Mancour

Untitled

Dream on children, dream on.
For they show hope for you.
In time you'll realize the treasures they hold, and out of them are lessons to be told. In reality it's another life that you can be apart of for a short time. But indefinitely is a no-no.
So you go on the journey but realize what it unfolds.
Oh - oh - oh it amazing at things you'll go through, and wonder why
this is happening to you.
In time realize the answer that's for you and understand the meaning
of it too.
Dream on children, dream on.
For God always watches over you.

Freida D. Smith

The Flight Of A Warrior

The Bald Eagle flies with grace,
His proud spirit gleams on his face.

The sleek feathers embalm his wings,
He flies perpetually and never rescinds.

The wisdom of experience huddles in his mind,
He searches the horizon for the land he must find.

Swiftly sweeping and circling the sky, the rays of the sun blind him,
He pushes and waves the cordons away that bind him.

Soon he is free again to reach his land,
Just a few more flaps and he will arrive at the narrow band.

As the sun goes to sleep the eagle spots home,
He soars to reach the oaks that form a dome.

As he flutters to the bough of a majestic oak he spots a wing far away,
Faster than a speeding bullet he goes to investigate,
What he finds may be his fate.

The scene he witnessed was a disturbing sight,
Four of his comrades trapped in a net and wrapped tight.

So once again the eagle turns back,
He hopes to find a land where evil people are lacked.

Ali Kooshkabadi

My Pillow...

Oh, to my pillow, I love you so much,
Others may think that it's silly and such,
But, I just don't care what anyone thinks.
They are all jealous cause their pillow stinks.

But my pillow and me, we love one another,
We couldn't be closer if he was my brother.
I snuggle him close to me, night after night,
If someone were to hurt him I'd put up a fight.

My pillow and me we go everywhere,
He's private and special, so I don't share.
It would surely upset him to see a new face,
Or wake up without me, in a strange place.

So I keep him at home on my bed where he lives
Cause comfort and love are the things that he gives.
My pillow and me will be in love till the end.
Cause he's not just pillow, he's also my friend.

Lorie A. Potter

Seasons

Spring brings the flowers,
All surrounding the high towers.
The Spring winds get real weary,
And the air gets real eerie.
Then the sun comes out real bright,
The flowers then have no fright.

Summer comes the air is hot,
Then we play with brother Scott.
The Squirrels are jumping from tree to tree,
If you watch you will see.
We run and play in the dirt,
Sometimes we even get hurt.

Fall brings the wandering winds,
The leaves are piled up in bins.
The chilled winds begin to blow,
Then the acorns drop like snow.

I love to play in the snow,
My cheeks and nose start to glow.
Snowballs are flying in the air,
Clumps of ice stick in my hair.

Rachel Boyer

Untitled

What's on the other side?
When you look in the mirror
You see another you.
You see your same world but backwards.
What's it like to live
On the other side?

What's on the other side?
On TV shows, there are actors
Living out another person's life.
They act out their joys, worries, and even their strife.
What's it like to live
On the other side?

What's on the other side?
Some say it's God and Heaven.
It's a place of eternal bliss.
It would be neat to walk on cloud number seven.
What's it like to live
On the other side?

I wonder,
What's on the other side?

Noreen Dacpano

Graduation

I wasn't around for most of your childhood,
there was a story to write.
About a little boy you drew in the sand
and is coming to life tonight.

Hidden between two panes of glass
your future is stronger then your past.
It's never been whether you will succeed.
It's only a matter of when!

As you run through images of my thought-
fast ball, curve, pen and course.
Challenged and blessed in search of self,
you did it on your own.

Now time curves back. We almost touch.
You came out strong and tall.
I may not see all you do, but we share.
I will love you forever. I'll always be there.

William E. Milligan

Untitled

When you are sad the sky grows weary
People are full of hate and greed
There is no sense of direction
No fate—no laughter
The devil himself cannot blink an eye
Because when you are sad
Fish stop swimming and birds can't fly
The world rotates backwards and
It is cold in the summers
Little girls stop jumping rope and
Boys quit playing marbles
Your nose runs and sex is lost from your eye
So please, don't be sad
Because when you're sad
Even the butterflies cry

Roy D. Smith

Space

The drop of dew
Lingered on the daisy petal
Then, pummeled painfully into the ground
Like the words you threw at me.
I tore the flower out of the soil,
Roots and all, to rid it of its agony.
Petal by petal, He loves me,
He loves me not, He loves me,
He loves me not.
Hair in my eyes,
The wind brushed it away
Like you used to do with your sensuous fingers
I lie down in the deep damp grass.
It swallowed me up.
Now you have your space.

Carrie Hockett

The Day

I tumbled in my sleep
like a sharp rock being worn smooth by the water's current
I talked out loud, unaware I was being heard
My heart rhythm escalated into the march of a big brass band
My entire body writhed with tension
"Seize the day! Seize the day! Your life is slipping away!"
resonated in my brain
At last, the sunlight came and shook me gently to consciousness
Even in wake the uneasy feeling lingered, haunted, persisted
I, realizing my fate, felt the urgency to conquer, accomplish, become
Frantically compelled,
I began to catch my dreams
instead of chasing them.

Carrie Merritt

Robbed

Dear little ones now in the cradling arms of the Lord,
The number of you grow so quickly we can't even keep score.
The reasons are many, the solution not a valid one-
You were never given a chance-
A reasonable answer to this, I find none.
Your precious little eyes never got a chance to see,
You yourselves never got a chance to be.
Those tiny little toes on your little feet,
The small little heart that didn't get a chance to beat.
Those beautiful smooth lips that would of loved to be kissed,
For you this is a thing that will be sadly missed.
Those precious little hands that never got a chance to touch,
You poor beautiful children have been robbed of so much.
I'm thankful you're now safe in the arms of the Lord,
I can only pray that people stop choosing to abort.

Tracy Sutton

Momma Sing A Song

As I walked this life as a lad
And time went along, I missed Dad
There were talks that we never had
Momma sing a song for me

Momma sing a song for me
of the one who went to Calvary
It was Jesus the master you see
Momma sing a song for me

Momma would sing a song each day
As she done her work along her way
Then she and I would kneel down and pray
Momma sing a song for me

Now one day Jesus called Momma home
She left me in this old world all alone
I miss her voice and her beautiful tone
Momma sing a song for me

Lewis F. Hampton

"I Am Strong"

My voice is like the force of wind,
I just blow over and over again.
No one can tell me I am wrong,
Because my words are too strong.

My strength is like a charging bull,
And my mouth is very full
Of lightning, thunders, and stormy clouds,
But still I am strong, black, and proud.

I am strong,
No one can tell me I am wrong
Anyways, I just keep on,
Keeping on.

Ameenah Miller

If I Had

If I had a chalkboard
I could show you all the ways to
integrate an equation
I could show you all the ways to find the distance to
the stars, but I don't have a chalkboard.
If I had some paper and a pen I could write you all the
poems that remind me of you
I could write you the scariest stories ever, but I
don't have a pen and paper.
If I had some paint I would paint a picture of you and
me holding hands
but I don't have any paint.
So, what am I going to do?

Kate O'Toole

21 Years Ago

21 Years Ago, I held you in my arms to cherish and protect.

21 Years Ago, I saw the little funny face girl,
that cried anwet.

21 Years Ago, I cried to find out that you had down's syndrome.

21 Years Ago, I said god gave her to me, and does not make mistakes.

21 Years Ago, I was told she would not be very academically inclined, be independent, be able to work, or live a normal life.

21 Years Ago, I ask what is a "Normal" Life? To wake to see the morning sun, run, walk, talk, be loved and give love, having a caring family and friends.

21 Years Ago, I got an angel from heaven who had clip wing, today that clip wing angel has taken flight, and what you see is a beautiful angel by day and night.

All the "Normal" things, we have flew past and beyond.

So, to those parents who may have been blessed enough to have a fallen angel, come their way;

"Help them to fly to better day."
Gwendolyn D. Verner

Forever She Gazes

In darkened corner is where she sits
With a glazed look in her eyes,
Staring into nowhere.
Her heart is beating at a runner's pace,
And her body is throbbing, feeling a million's pains.

    She turns her head quickly,
    Looking over her shoulder
    At yet another dinner-time special
    Her tongue will never feel.

Labeled by professionals—teachers, parents, and priests
As a girl gone mad, a misfit, an experimental tool,
Having no compassion, no emotions to share.
If they would only listen to her closely,
They would hear a whisper
From this troubled, innocent girl...

    "I'm sorry... I'm scared"

Forever she gazes...
David Kinsey

The Bad Dream

There's nowhere I could run to,
There's nowhere I could hide —
The man I love, I took his life,
It happened late last night —
This is a common story,
'Bout a love that would not end —
How confusion got the best of me,
I had no choice, but to set him free —
He had a love that hurt him so,
He would never be the same —
The only thing left was to end his life,
Before he went insane —
When I woke up I realized,
This was all a bad bad dream —
Dear Lord, I hope that he's alright,
I hope it isn't me.
Christine Miller

For The Love Of The Child

With careful planning and much anticipation,
We await the birth of our dear little loved one;
We have all the answers, or so we think,
The color had been decided, it will be blue or pink

The day finally arrives, with much joyful excitement,
Why our labor has just begun and already we're spent;
But soon in our arms, we're holding our little love,
It's as precious to us, as a newborn dove

It isn't too long, before reality sets in,
And we're calling like mad, to our nearest of kin;
Just why won't our baby sleep through the night?
And she cries all day; my what a plight

We think it'll get easier, just down the road,
When she starts crawling, then we'll clean our abode;
And when she starts talking, that sure will be fun,
But no one ever tells us, it's from nine until one

In spite of how our life has certainly changed,
In spite of how our mind has become slightly deranged;
We're thankful for what our eyes are now seeing,
As we embrace this wonderful new being!
Laurie McMahon

A Salute To Mama And Daddy

The whip-o-will sings to the late day shadows,
The strength of his tune startles the quiet.
A bull frog begins his lonely audible,
The welcome of night settles in your mind,
Resting the tired, another day's work behind.

This was a familiar scene for Daddy.
He truly loved the last hours of day.
He mostly sat alone, should you not count hungry hounds
Kept at bay, by an old cat being favored.

Mama would join him when finished with supper chores,
They spoke of the real things that touched their lives,
Crops and harvest, of putting up food, school shoes, a needed rain.
Their conversations were never heated.

We thank you both for bringing us into this world.
Mama, we thank you for teaching the faith, always understanding,
And for always being there.
Daddy, you taught the purpose of hard work,
Of conservation and thrift, and to always look forward.
Our memory smiles,
Our eyes water a salute to both of you.
Jackie Lee Todd

The Book Of Knights

I stand alone beside you,
the waves crash and the wind blows
without comfort or mercy,
But what matters it to me,
every blow is but a kiss, and
every trust is but my answer.
If you feel the chill, you have my coat
If you feel hunger, you have my part.
Every man is not a king, but you're mine,
and to the last breath you have my pledge
Stand with me and every common dog
will meet his God this day.
This I promise on my oath
We will sit in the banquet hall and
boast of our brave deeds
I'll not let a dog lick my boot, but I
will bow to a king
George Eddis

End

Shattered beings lay before me, the earth soaked of blood
A purple haze of victory, shadows where once there was a town
I ask, "Who has won?"
My breath is all to hear, beyond the morose silence
Blanket of an empty race, only my soul remains
The ultimate human destruction, a war amongst ourselves
Blatant ignorance to not have known it was suicide
There remains no one to tell of our stupidity
The wind chooses not to speak
The trees have not strength to grow
My self-starved earth, good and evil has perished
My final dance
I float in my tears, my desolate purgatory
The sun has lost its vibrancy and warmth
My ears forget the singing of a crowd
Not the sweet harmony of life
Not the echoing joys of emotion
The world, its worth of broken glass
My people beckon, projecting their haste
I'd swim the oceans for a smile, I'd suffer the most immense pain
Jani Nucci

Summer Twilight

Plump, purple blossoms litter the ground in fallen glory,
their moment past, like wedding confetti after the event.
Carried on gentle winds, sweet perfume subtly invades my senses
and comforting warmth envelopes me,
turning thoughts to exotic climes as relaxation teeters on lethargy.

I raise a glass to my lips, ice tinkling;
cold liquid in sharp contrast to the fuzzy warmth surrounding me.
Mosquito's buzz and wrr about me with inherent intent,
their frenzied efforts thwarted by pungent repellent candles.
Birds coo softly, as if calling loved ones home to safety,
welcoming them as any other family welcomes its members,
when faced with the end of the day.

Turning to the West, I behold the sunset.
Once a riotous clash of colour,
now a mellow palette before the encroaching night.
Its colour softened by shadow.

The quiet demise of the day is unpretentious, sublime without fanfare.
Languid feelings vanish as I rise to go inside,
my contemplation finished, my soul replenished.
Would that all death could be so beautiful.
Melissa McLeod

She Waits

She sits waiting for your calls.
Wondering if it's over or just on a freeze.
Confused, she can't go on with her life.

She waits to hear you say "It won't work."
Wondering if you love her still.
Confused, of your feelings as well as hers.

She still cares and wants a life with you.
But you haven't made a move in months.
Confused, she sits and waits.

I try to console her and tell her it will work out.
I try to keep her mind off of it.
Confused, she still waits.

I love her, and she is my dearest friend.
I hate to see her hurt this way.
Confused, I sit and wait with her.
Lill Snow

Jeff

Jeff was a very, loving man,
  Always willing, to lend a helping hand.

When ever you were down, or in a slump,
  With the slightest smile, he could cheer you up.

With those funny looking glasses, I loved so dear,
  When he was around, a friend was near.

A card player he was, that's no lie,
  He could always beat you, there was never a tie.

In all of our memories, good and bad,
  When we think about him, we shouldn't be sad.

He will live in our hearts, so deep and true,
  The memory of him, will chase away the blues.

The slightest smile, the gentlest touch,
  I just wanted to say, Jeff, we miss you so much.
Wende A. Lattin

Me.......Struggle

Struggling, for me, me
You,
Were not right
Me
Allowed, lost, settled, settled...me did
Now
Mighty struggle, climb/drown/self-destruct?
Time against.....me.....drifting....
Got to say,
Goodbye, yes, goodbye a must!
Need to climb out of the valley
Back to
Me
Nothing broken but
Me heart
Remember....the one...me
Gave to you...to safe keep
Me...me...me...where are you?
Come back!
Gladys E. Mello

Infectious Love

I surrendered my heart to the devil
I collapsed to his every whip
Infectious love is what he dealt to me
I slowly died as all feeling dripped
I cried as my arms were shackled
And I conversed with those not there
The hour-long minutes consumed me
I had traveled far beyond despair
Lost in a world of misfortune
No love had I ever been close
Twisted thoughts I couldn't unwind
I myself was merely a ghost
Bound to a wall of empty promises
And dreams left unfulfilled
I withered in the emptiness
Of my destiny you had killed
I looked in to eyes of dead light
And what I saw was of nothing true
I suddenly realized after one last stair
That the eyes had belonged to you.
Cassie Andriakos

Comforter

Lord, what would I do and where would I be
If you were not here giving comfort to me
What takes me so long, how often to learn
To rid me of self, to you I must turn
With heart over flowing and eyes wet with tears
Your love is my strength, your presence is here
I'll rest through the night and trust all to thee
Wake fresh in the morning, new blessings to see.
Diane Kemp

Destruction Stew

Begin with one world
   Stir in a large amount of life
A pinch of greed
A dash of fornication
Slowly fold in drugs and alcohol
   to Rid the unwanted lumps
(In another Bowl)
   place racism, in justice, and struggle
   (set aside to rise)
Now mix in Rumors of war with
   the changing of Seasons
Now a dash of homeless, hunger and poor
(Stir vigorously) while Seasonings with
   rival Gangs... And... Wasted Garbage
Finish this Recipe with...
The Killing of elements, animals and people
   And Sit Back
   And Wait!
Felicia Abrams

Nature

I hear the water ripple,
in the silver lake,
after a light rain dribbled,
from when the clouds did shake.

And then the sun come out,
above the valleys rising,
showing off its brilliant light,
which bounced off the cars that were driving.

Then the flowers opened,
this was not a change,
because they do that everyday,
and that was never strange.

Then suddenly the wind blew,
through the trees it danced,
then it went to the bushes,
and in them it pranced.
Sheila Kelly

Me

Lord how I've grown through the paths of my life,
enduring the sorrow and living the strife.

I see brighter skies as the days follow through,
believing in love as I'm looking at you.

Flowers are blooming and trees bare their fruit;
clouds are all smiling and plants take to root.

When I fall down I just pick myself up,
brush off the dirt and then wash with your cup.

Smile for I'm me and I know who I am,
God's little child and man's special friend.
Sandra Brindley

Drive I Say

Drive I say.
On concrete streets of alluring death.
Drive I say.
On four wheeled gas sucking demons.
Drive I say
take a deep breath can't.
Carbon monoxide puffy deadly choking smoking.
Depleting our precious layer of life we call o-zone.
Hypocritical statement.
For I need a car as well.
Carlos Montenegro

Night Walk

Darkness has set upon the cold still night
As she made her way down a lonely street
A faint sound of footsteps are heard from behind.
She turns to look, but only sees a shadow of a stranger
She picks up her walk at a faster pace
The steps go stride for stride with each and every step
Turning to look at the stranger,
She trips and falls to her face
Fear rushes over her, as the stranger gets closer and closer
Suddenly a hand reaches down and helps her to her feet
The stranger moves away, as she looks up to see his face
Shaken from the ordeal, she turns the corner and heads for home
Feeling worn out and puzzled, she turns in for the night
She awakens suddenly from her sleep
With a smile upon her face.
Knowing that her guarding angel walks with her at a even pace.
Dennis E. Potts

Redeemed

He drank water from the cup of deep despise,
   washing clean my sins to their demise.
Suffering He did take for me,
   so that He could set me free.
Glory to His throne of grace,
   my wickedness He did erase.
Pain and darkness did He take,
   that light in me could then awake.
Sorrows carried in despair,
   that my heart could reap repair.
Sickness and disease He bore to their end,
   health anew as our forever friend.
Crucified He died for me,
   sowing life He hung upon that tree.
His grace abounds with love for all,
   waiting for the acceptance of His call.
Linda J. Schwoeble

Letting Go

Letting go is so hard
I see you there with her
You're obviously living fine without me
But I'm not
I just can't let go
All I see is us
Everywhere I turn are the memories of you
The way you held me
The way you used to talk -
so sweetly and loving to me
Everyone tells me to let go
but it's too hard
I guess I'll just spend my life
Just simply
Letting go.
Sabrina Langman

The Angel

An angel came to me one day. He smiled and said he'd seen my pain.
I wept until I stopped to ponder why into my life he wandered?
Now I know he'd always been - waiting 'till I'd stumble in.
Wandering, stumbling, fumbling 'round, he knew I lived and would
be found. 'Till finally that day we met, I never would have chanced
a bet that I would be found bathed in love from this halo-ed creature
born above.

But angels have a way of knowing, into whose lives they should be
going. We all have angels of our own, although we think we live
alone. One must only strain to be the angel they would like to see.
Then, if you try, you just may find that to which you had been blind
the light that guides us all to Him is always shining from within.

So here's a little wing-ed friend to help you when you're 'round
the bend. For when you're blinking back the tears, he'll be there
through many years To help you through your times of sorrow and
find the sunshine of tomorrow. Don't despair or fret or fight. Find
your love, not your might To help you through a stormy night. The
angels watching from aloft are whispering in your dreams so soft...
listen totheir heavenly hymn and follow the light that shines within.

Dawn J. Kimmelman

Death

Death is a grim subject,
It is full of hurt and sorrow.
I've lost all of my grandparents,
But in my thoughts they still live on.
I believe they are still with me,
They love and care for me,
I know I will be safe in life,
For they are watching over me.
My grandparents would have loved me,
Had they got to know me.
Someday I will pass solemnly and slowly,
For they will still be watching over me.

Lance Nadolne

If Only

I love the smell of a fragrant breeze,
A quiet gentle breeze,
It only makes me wish aloud,
To fly among the trees...
But a bird, I am not.

There once stood that tree,
Years ago that doesn't anymore,
But the bark on my hand is enough for me,
To please my weary soul...
If only I kept the seeds.

Now depression rains down on me,
Like a shower of harden stones,
The more bruises and wounds I collect,
The more deeper the cut to the bone...
If only I had an umbrella.

Darryl Jay Moore

Fools Who Fall In Love

Fool's some fall in love or the fun of it
not for the right reason but
wrong choices other's make
a big mistake why because
not for sure who we want
to be with one we pick
is the best thing
two might was the good taste
Three was a big chance
keep was the last hit
no fool really know's why
they ever fall in love in the first
place.

Phyllis Ann Felton

The War For My Civil Rights

The sound of a beating heart,
rings and rings inside a body
that is being destroyed by the boisterous screams
of a fighting nation.

A nation that should be built on equality
and the civil rights of every man, woman and child.

But that nation is a figment of our imaginations.
That dream nation will never come to be,
as long as there is one mind that does not believe.
That one mind, tears down everything that my ancestors built for me.

As long as you look at me as just another Black face,
standing out in the crowd, you will try your best to push me back
   into that hole.
That hole that my people have died over.

But let me tell you something, today is the last day that you
will ever try to push, pull or yank me around.
I am not a toy... Don't play me like a yo-yo.

Jamie Lynn Haines

Untitled

Music is what I like the most.
No matter where I am, coast to coast.
Silverchair is my favorite out of all the groups,
I hope we have the same interests, shooting hoops.
Guitar so smooth, bass so deep,
I play along with the tune as I sweep.
I listen to Silverchair all the time,
I usually wish I could be so divine.
Silverchair poster that looms on my wall,
I paid five bucks for and got at the mall.
Window with the silver chair sticker on the glass.
Took me awhile but I got it stuck there at last.
As you can see I like music so much,
That when I bought my silver chair CD no one could rip it
Out of my clutch.

Lauren Pileggi

Lap Cat

Cat on my lap and I forgot
Blowing rain on the floor, wood will rot
Such nonsense, this cat with one ragged ear
Chosen well he was, God forbid, he has no fear

Cat on my lap, forgot his nap
Nine lives has he, I say thirty perhaps
You'll see him urgently sprint yonder ways
It's not uncommon you know, it's his maze

Cat on my lap, didst twine my heart to putty
Fur groomed wrong way, he looks so nutty
life we unite in part
Freely at will, tail swish, he darts

Cat on my lap
well-tanned, his color
Twisted in strange shape, back alps
Purr, purr

Jean Kaich Jones

The Golden Love

So shiny, so bright it only seems right.
They hold tight to love, that you can feel in the night.
That can take your breath away for the sight of their love.
That is as pure as the night moon that shines in a sliver balloon.
That only follows the golden ones.
Their will never be another that the moon smiles more than,
the golden Lovers.

Susanne Mae McKinny

A Voice From Below

I'm here below, so cast your look down
On a place called earth, I'm here on the ground
Stripped of all hope of a love that is lost
Left with a memory, and wind laden frost
But God is all loving, and I am his child
If this is Hell, how long is a while?
I will endure the loss that I mourn
But why was it taken from me and torn?
What have I done to hurt you so much?
To plague me with this, a withering touch
I ask but one thing, from God up above
From one of his children, a child of his love
Give back to me, the love of my life
What wrong have I done, to warrant this strife?
Hear what I ask, I remind you of me
For I am your child and this is my plea

Richard Reggio

Flowers For Mary

The spirit of her being always pierced through our sorrows and into our souls, with love and kindness which we will always carry.
Today we give a little back as we say good-bye. We do not shed tears, instead we'll send wishes of peace when we bring flowers for Mary.
We'll bring flowers for Mary on this Autumn day.
A dozen soft-petalled torches, each with something to say.

One for the smiles, laughter and tears. Three more for the talks of events past, of children and dreams, and wishes and fears.
Two for loves won and lost for the secret heart's desires and disappointments of risk taken and their costs.
Three represent the human imperfections, arguments, and misunderstandings that only sought to prove the closeness we shared and how much we really cared.

For the sparkle in her eyes that not even the blackest day could dim, we give yet another one.
And one more, for the echo of her voice that will guide us through the rest of our days and has played a role in all we've become.

That leaves a single blossom yet unnamed.

This is a flowers of loveliest hue. Its colors call to mind the tranquility of a warm comfortable flame.
For this is what we hope will prove true: That as you travel away from us to a realm unknown you'll carry with you all that is held within the flame of this last flower yet unnamed.
For this and so much more we will carry.
12 perfect flowers for Mary.

Sandra A. White

Tunnel Of Memories

At the end of the long and dwindled path,
  is a tunnel of worries,
A tunnel of memories,
  that once made you cry.
But, as you look back,
  you stare at your childhood,
You wonder what was wrong,
  but, you refuse to die.
You had run from your problems,
  but, those problems you still have,
You took what wasn't yours,
  but, you still never gave back.
So this tunnel,
  you will never forget,
But all those memories,
  will wind down,
Like a broken clock,
  and you'll just cry,
But, still,
  you'll refuse to die.

Gina Sveda (age 15)

Empty Glass

Eleven broken faces
Eleven broken hearts
Who picks up the pieces
When sanity departs

When did all the glow withdraw
A raging torrent flow
A whisper of past strength
Taking an intermission in life's show

Between the dreams and waves of shame
Lost lovers and children of yesterday
Acting out another's words
Not knowing what he says

No wild horses, no passion
Hidden behind brain locked bars
No hearts to chase, all stopped up
Chasing broken stars

An empty room, no faces smile
No future and no past
I whisper a silent toast to eleven souls
With an empty glass

Walraven Ketellapper

Eulogy To A Child

It's said that when a child is born,
He feels no grief, nor hate, nor scorn.
These things are unknown, as we are told,
A child's dear heart is pure as gold.

His thirst for life, it has no bound,
He wonders at the world he's found.
He runs, he plays, he sings, he cries.
Oh why sweet Lord must children die?

No more to see a winter's snow,
No more his life are we to know.
We miss his laugh, his voice now gone,
He's with the angels in God's bright home.

On wings of joy he soars this day,
Above this world, so far away.
And in our hearts and souls we see,
He still lives in our memories.

C. Shane McMahan

Hope

I feel such, dread but know there's
force, tomorrow will come a
matter of course, one day at a
time, we struggle we pray - you
could be in India, etc., away
We grew in a time when so
much was plenty, expected to
love and never be empty
The future has come, we
throw up our arms, was this
what's expected, no sex unprotected
no friendship to find no closeness
herein, no substance without
A dalliance of sorts, no way to get out. I
live with this hope, feel slightly foolhardy
don't want to go on as the life of the party
My party's upon me and rising within me
I wanted to share all the giving and growing.
Be careful, she says your honesty's showing.

Kathryn Furst

The Legend

Standing tall and proud in the jungles of
Africa our ancestors once stood.

Once we ran wild and free till we were captured
forced to drip into buckets, and taken away,

Through mechanical processes we were made,
stretched and pulled

Now like prisoners we are forced,
forced to carry a heavy burden.

We make possible your transportation,
when we are old and worn we are sometimes used as
planters.

Sometimes we just lie about unused and worn;
we are made to be thrown away.

Serving the world just to be left
in junk yards, and along roads.

We are Tires.
   Mandie Asay

My Sister

My sister is 8 years younger than me,
But we are still best friends.
She cries at night and wakes me,
But I don't mind,
I'll whisper 'I love you' and she goes back to
sleep,
We love each other equally,
She loves me and I love her back,
When she is sick,
I take her in my arms and sing to her,
Her soft breathing and sudden cry fill my room,
Along with the sound of music playing and the
steady hum of the humidifier,
We are bonded by love,
That bond will never break,
A sister is a forever friend.
   Evan Allen

Grandpa's "Missouri Waltz"

That strangely warm November day
   dripping with the nostalgia of a warmer season,
   they laid you to the ground,
   and through the breeze and rustling leaves
   mingled your familiar sound.
A limpid whistling you kept with you,
   the name of which I never knew,
   until the flowers covered over
   and we bid farewell to you.
I still hear it in remembering
   your house, your stories,
   ice cream and anisettes,
   a walk at dawn on a Sunday morning
   and your "Missouri Waltz."
How can I forget?
   Barbara A. D'Annibale

Thank You God

Thank you God for being there, you've always been a good friend,
and thank you God for all the times that you do attend,
but thank you God most of all,
for the love that you bestow,

for it is the true seed,
from which we all do grow.
   Jerome William Tribout

Everyday People Pulling Together

God really blesses when people pull together
Yes, we're cruising with God, like bird of a feather
We are very day people with the mission to fulfill
We can cross every valley, and we can climb every hill

He's a lamp unto our feet, a light unto our path
Soaking our thoughts in his word is like bubbles in a bath
We are building our foundation, come what may
Each stone that build will never break away

I am the vine, you are the branches, remain in me
And the fruits of God's love will take control of thee
Let the tree of prayer grow tall and strong
Focus your thoughts on Him you will never go wrong

True satisfaction is to center your heart upon Him
And you will never find yourself too far out on a limb
Flowering dogwoods light up the forest with bloom
A reminder of His death and resurrection from the tomb

The butterflies are so beautiful to see
They progress in your parts, then they are free
Just as the progression of man comes in four stages
Eternal life is our reward, as written in God's pages
   Jane M. Sandoval

"Human Beauty"

Humanistic beauty and desire is
one's complete acquaintance,
they stricken one's body with
lush vibes that penetrate other
encountered souls. So deeply
they run or how shallow they
are everyone can be as the sky.
When one's soul has been enriched
with happiness and laughter they
are vibrant blue sky, when one has
been familiarized with anger the
thunder and lightning inhibit. When
one is undoubtedly dealing with pain
and suffering the rain comes down as
though there was a drought and dry
land hadn't felt water in years, and when
one is in a hinderant state of peace, then
the snow falls, and every aspect of life
falls into existence.
   Carly Olson

"The Dawn"

Quiet and serene
Beautiful and soothing
I could watch you all day
Your spirit is moving.

As you glide across the sky
it's a natural high
I've been watching you for years
You take away my tears.

Only if I could touch you
I don't want to rush you

The beauty within you can end wars,
me you'll never bore

I think I'm going to buy a plane
so I can ride beside you;
and end my pain

I'm going to grab you out of the sky and make you my wife.
I won't have to get up in the morning
you'll be with me for life.

I Love The Dawn
   David Campbell

"Goodbye Selena"

"Selena to the glory of heaven
you left, now we only have
your remembrance and your songs,
why did god took you with him?
maybe he need an angel with him
and he choose you.
Selena to the glory of heaven
you left, and left and our heart broken.
Selena you were an Angela and
you left to may company to
God, Selena for ever you will live,
with us, although you left next
to God to rest."

Caroline Pacheco

Patience

Patience is a virtue by for to ploy
Patience is not often learned by a little boy.
Patience to a man is a crown upon his head
Whereas, patience to a woman is to have until he's dead.
Patience can be renown if you don't let others get you down.
A judge has to have patience with a trial in his court,
While the accused and his councilor strive to evade a tort.
To have patience at all times is a dream to be desired.
Patience, do you have patience in all of life's cycle?
I most certainly don't
For if I did I would never ever won't,
Patience to sickness is as rain drops is to a former's crop.

Andrew P. Campbell Jr.

Bus Views And Reflections

The river has defrosted.
Distant hills still look like men with crew cuts.
And fields like rows of cornfield stubble.

Tangled fence rows somehow resemble hair-tangled combs.
And brown wind-blown grasses
look like pillow-flattened hair.

Last year's flora is on display
like a countryside arrangement
Including leafless trees with zillions of fingers clawing upwards
to scratch the sky.

White barked birches reveal their slender trunks.
They'd shed their leafage moons ago.

Evergreens, ever faithful to their color, display their pine array.
To match patches of green grasses all along the way.

Some mornings, frost shares the dawn.
Frosted windshields become leftover reminders of the winter past.
But bright sunshine lures us onto warmer summer days in which to bask.

We're all sleepyheads,
waking up from our long winter's nap.

Terry L. Fillyaw

Nature

It's amazing how the little stream joins the larger creek,
  and that one creek joins the big river,
silent, and meek.
  It's amazing how a single seed grows into a
pleasant flower,
  or how a sycamore treeling soon begins to
tower.
  It's all a part of nature, beautiful, splendid,
and great.
  But if we don't stop destroying it, it might
be too late.

Emily Gammel

The "Eagle" Fades Away

The time is drawing closer and closer, as the
"Eagle" slowly fades quietly away
And as for us, it's workers, we'll all have
To hope and pray for a much brighter day.
We have shared tears of sorrow and tears of joy
And we'll remember back when — boy oh boy oh boy!
Some true good friends we have made,
There are some friendships and memories that will never fade.
We have cleaned and polished and worked real hard
And being ever so careful to play the right card.
So here's hoping that after all that has been said and done,
Our "one time" competitor will get the final okay
To come into the plant and their products to run.
The "Eagle" is now fading faster and faster far away
With any sorta luck, we'll all soon be working for number one,

Frito Lay

Untitled

Seeing your beauty and missing you

Seeing your beauty and missing you,
it is more than I can allow myself to
feel, a sorrow so deep without
your touch.

Life's great pleasures are faded,
next to your beautiful soul so
captivating I find life so joyous, with your smile.

Your smile holds me prisoner,
not with iron bars or stone walls, but
a soft velvet prison of
your sweet thoughts.

Your breast's sweet nectar
attracts me beyond measure, others
may try but they cannot compare
with your loveliness and grace.

Your lovely graces are delightful and
it's only a trifle amount that you
allow at one time. With your gift of
patience I wait your fond embrace.

Paul H. Meiers

What Is It?

I come from a planet afar,
when I crashed and landed on this very star.

The first thing I saw
on this strange and wonderful land,

Was something I clearly didn't understand.
It was small and always sat on its butt.

Just please tell me, what is it?

Is it some kind of God,
that humans always pray to.

Or, maybe it is a pet. If it is not,

Please tell me, what is it?

Is it some kind of special plant,
or maybe a great big ant.

It is always talking
and always singing.

Like I said before,
it is some kind of God

That these human things
are always praying to.

Like I said before, What is it?

Marquetta Pride

Timeless Seasons - Forever Love

Songs of love are in the air,
People running to the fair,
What a great romance will bring
This splendorous spring.

Pretty flowers - big green trees,
Swaying with the summer breeze
Sun rays shining on the sea,
Surf and love caresses you and me.

An Autumn harvest-moon shines,
Delicious fruits and aromatic wines,
A gift for a celebration;
Our wedding is the occasion.

Winter's white satin cape covers the land;
In my heart, warm feeling when you touch my hand,
We cuddle up reminiscing together,
That all seasons will be returning forever.
Jane M. Restovic

Untitled

Today there was death. It will come tomorrow.
   There will be no end for the world's sorrow.
The evil is here now. I wish it would go away.
   The wars on earth will make us all pay.
Life is too short. We should try to make it last.
   We need to do differently than we've done in the past.
Joy is hard to find. I'll settle for happiness.
   Unfortunately we can't wipe away all the badness.
Please attempt to try peace. I know it will be hard.
   Just think if you do the world will be your backyard.
Could we be friends? Could we make our peoples see?
   Could we all get along and just be?
Maggie Kollars

Do Not Disturb

May I inquire
Dear Bumble?
I don't mean to pry
It's just that I can't help wonder why
You're clinging here so still
So very quiet
You seem, well, awfully lazy.

Maybe too much honey?
Or have you found euphoria in luscious scent?

You never even budged when I picked your yellow dahlia.
I just wondered
Because bees are always thought so ambitious, busy, occupied.

But then, you worked so hard all summer
Could it be this late September breeze has rocked you
Into slumber?
Sorry if I disturbed you -
I just wondered.
Helen W. Eckel

My Dance With Time

Day in and day out, I danced my tragic dance.
Time drew memories out of me, but at each I didn't dare glance.

Lost time and borrowed time, both I did recall.
Although it greatly affected me, with Time it seemed so small.

More time and better time I uttered in my dance, but Time
answered me "That's my revenge" and drew me into his stance.

Stance, it is, that Time leaves us in when our bitter share.
And then Death will come in its morbid twirl and neither Time or
I will care.
Kelly Wilburn

Imagination

Are you a figment of someone's imagination?
Do you think life is one big aggravation?
Could you make a seed and see a flower grow?
Could you make lightning, rain, or snow?

Do you know how much dirt is in each mountain?
Or how much water is in life's fountains?
Can you make a rainbow in the sky?
Can you make a bird fly?

Can you make a star shine at night?
Or turn darkness into light?
Can you make a monkey climb a tree?
Can you make honey come from a bee?

Could you make a camel with a hump?
Could you make a body from a dirt clump?
Can you make a human mind?
To these answers find.

So if you can create any of the above.
Then you must be bigger than love.
Only the creator is bigger than creation.
And only He can remove your aggravation.
Marilyn Salyers

Under The Ice

Above the water the sun is shining
brilliant colors of red.
Above the water people sing and happy
words are said.
Above the water there is no such
thing as crime.
Above the water people don't run out of time.
Under the ice, There's war in
the Middle East.
Under ice there's children who are
raised to act like beasts.
Under ice there is no warmth and
there is no sun.
Under ice baby's can not play
and animals can not run.
Under ice flowers can not grow
Under ice streams can not flow.
You can save the world and
you can save your life, but you should be
careful, the waters almost ice.
Jessica English

Pains Of Sadness

As I sat just now and watched my granddaughter play,
Sadness was still in my heart today.
Though joy she gives everyday of my life;
Just trying to be happy, for me is a fight!
I feel that I live, each day about the same
Angry and hurt, and wondering "Who can I blame?"
When your health's not so good, and things mostly go wrong;
It makes me feel weak; but I've got to remain strong!
Sometimes the pain is so deep; the sadness fills my soul,
But if I give in; will I be complete; will I feel whole?
Why can't I stop the pretense; and let these tears fall?
Would it make me anything less, could I feel just as tall?!
I wonder though if I would go back to innocence if one
   day I could:
And if I'd change the things I could; and the things
   I should?
But that I guess I'll never know, because I can't;
   and it's too late.
So I'll keep getting the pains of sadness;
   forever that I hate!
Johia M. Lloyd

Sand Between My Fingers

With great sadness, I sat alone on the beach,
Knowing the girl I love was so hard to reach.
She was made up of many emotions,
Each one like a grain of sand from the ocean.

One by one, I placed each grain in my hand,
Until my palm was filled with sand.
Out toward the ocean, I watch the waves roll,
And the thought of this sand; my girl as a whole.

Unfortunately, when the sun came late that day,
And the night had settled dark and grey,
Those tightly held fingers began to widen,
And my sorrowful eyes were left crying.

Within seconds, the sand had slipped away,
And there I was, left to pray.
Hoping the Lord would give me a second chance,
At that newly lost romance.

The Lord heard my prayers, but did not preach,
Thus, one month later, I still sit alone on the beach.
A great pain in my heart still lingers,
Because I let the sand slip through my fingers.
Vincent Scialli

"Promise"

Steven, let me see your smile in every ray of sunshine,
   Your eyes, in the new leaves of the spring.
When I'm loneliest, wrap your arms around me,
   like a blanket of newly fallen snow..
Whisper that you love me, in the sweet smell
   of the roses;
Feel your kiss, with each soft breeze that will
   touch my cheek.
Let me hear your laughter in the rustle of the
      autumn leaves ....
And then, I will have peace.
Carol Anne Letsche

The Day It All Happened

The day we got the call from my Aunt Marylou
She told us what my cousin had to go and do
He had to go off and fight in a war
We didn't think we would see him anymore.

We prayed for him day and night
Wondering why he had to go and fight
The family sat home hoping he was ok.
There was nothing we could do but pray.

I remember the day he got home from the war
We didn't have to sit and pray for him anymore
Grady Pauls a great cousin I love him will my heart
Please god protect him don't ever split us apart

As I write his poem I think of him more
Right now he's off fighting in another war
I'm worried about him I hope he's ok
At this time I need to take timeout to pray.
Jamie Lynn Flowers

Hopes and Dreams

We all have hopes and dreams,
It's like a flowing stream.
We wonder what to do,
Our imagination is clear and blue.
Someday our hopes and dreams will come true,
But only if you want them to,
It just takes the time for you to
believe in you!
Sara Nicole Steele

"Fear"

Fear is something that we need..
For fear is something that we need..
Fear is needed in every day life...
For fear is what keeps the strong alive.
Without fear we have no regard for life...
With it we can enjoy...
life.
Fear is something that we are born with...
For we can not shake it...
Fear is needed in love and in life
in order to make it.
Fear is something that you must
understand, that an abundance of it
does not make you less of a man.
For we know that fear is God given
For if you believe we shall all meet in heaven.
Ismael Rodriguez

Country Boy

I've walked this land for some forty-nine years,
From coast to coast I have seen some tears.
Snow and rain, sleet and hail,
Sunshine and winds from above,
I've done some good — oh yes I've been bad—
But through it all, I am still glad
To be the man that I have become.
I would not change one thing I've done.
Oh there are those that would say,
"You wouldn't change not a day?"
To change one thing that I have done
Would change my life and the race I've won.
So I'll hold my head way up high,
Walk some more until I die.
The things I do are as those I have done;
For me, there is still a race to be won!!
Bill Morris

And Then He Made Arizona

A blinding bright western sky.
The eerie echo of the coyote's cry.

Endless miles of cactus and sand.
Majestic mountains that shadow the land.

Red hot waves of desert heat.
And earth so dry it burns the feet.

The scamper of lizards on the run.
The breath taking beauty of the setting sun.

A sparkling spectrum of stars at night.
Truly the imagination of God all in one site.
Jeanne Guinn

Flames

As the red rose bursts into flames
Which only the few with impassioned hearts can see
It sets the soul into a wild turmoil
To know too much, yet not enough
To cuff fists at every insult
To mope over every short comings
To be what people see
Lost and broken on the waste side
Is that for me, Is that what people see
As the red rose falls to the ground
And the last ash flickers out
With it goes the hopes and dreams of the many
And the life and soul of the one.
Matthew W. Petersen

Confidence

I want to read; that is my need.
I want to learn how; I want to learn now.

The more I live, I want to give,
When I learn to read, I will do a good deed
I will read to others, who perhaps can't see;
I will read to Mothers who have kids like me.

How do I start? I keep asking myself.
I must do my part — take the book off the shelf.
The book that I chose as my number one guide —
The Bible, I won't close till I feel God at my side.

I cannot fear, as the Lord is near;
I know that I am able to get rid of any label.

I am not limited by what men call brain,
I am confident that progress is my natural gain.
God gives me intelligence, ability, and might.
I am inspired to claim this until I see the light.

I am patient and trusting; I am determined to win;
I feel guidance, energy, and strength from within.
All things are possible to God to express,
And as His child, I have my right to success.
Kathleen B. Pierce

Images

I'm wide awake and staring
At the images on the wall-
I wonder why there should be
Anything there at all.

They seem to move so slowly
To the rhythm of the dark.
Do you think there might be a creature,
From a far off zoo or park?

Now the scene is changing and I am on a ship,
Sailing with a pirate crew on a long mysterious trip.
Over the waves and through the gloom-
Twisting and turning and heading for doom.

When all of a sudden the sea grew quiet,
The sun emerged and the colors ran riot.

The harbor secured the ship of my dreams,
And peace and quiet remain serene.

A blanket of calm came over me now
As I drifted asleep for time did allow.
Ruth Arentina Schofield

Thoughts Of A Mariner

Oh vast and understanding sea
I cast my fate, once more, to thee.
Lash out your whitecaps, lash away;
I fear thee not, nor will I — nay,
I've learned that fear will hasten death,
And I'll not have my final breath
At sea, where I have spent life
Escaping mundane stress and strife.

So lap your salty waters, aye,
And swell your waves with foam so high
It swathes me in a briny soak,
And causes me to gasp and choke.
I'll not complain, not I, jack-tar,
I'm hooked on you and ev'ry star;
Your roaring surf calls out to me,
And I am here, eternally.
Bonnie Rogers

For my son, on his graduation

Where are you going, my son, my son
Where are you going, and why?
Will you walk the world wide
Sail bright stars and night tide
Will you travel the depths of your heart?

And will you return, my son, oh my son
And if you return, then why?
Will you come back to hide
In man's excess and pride
And forget the still path of your heart?

Where have you been, my son, my dear son
And where will you go, and why?
Will you seek the dark side
With compassion as guide
And come back to the truth of your heart?
Alice L. Darlington

"Bewildered Child"

I see my Mom,
    I see my Dad.
I remember how it was,
    I remember what we had.

I try and figure out why,
    I have to say to one parent, "Good-bye."
Was I so awful, was I so bad?
    Is that the reason you went away mad?

Don't you know and can't you see?
    I want us to be together,
Not "two" and "one," but "three."
    Which one do I go to? Which one? Who?
Don't you understand, I love both of you.
Jean N. Thompson

Legacy

These things I'll leave you when I'm gone:

A summer lake reflecting dawn,
in quiet beauty shimmering . . .
The mirror of morning's wakening.
I'll leave you stars when skies are dark
and in the rain, a meadowlark;
some violets in forest glades
where sunlight filters soft and fades;
a mountain meadow ringed in blue,
a mountain breeze, dew-washed and cool;
wild strawberries about your feet,
wild roses climbing, pale and sweet,
and in the magic hour of night,
a million fireflies glowing bright.

When you have thoughts you need to share,
come to the woods for I'll be there.
Mary Martin Palma

Untitled

Yes I live for the commend
That's why I go to a private school
So that I may reach the opulent bend

To shine in the shadows of others
And rise against those negative brothers

Keeping my head on the positive side of things
Enjoying the wonders that life brings

No need for the drug, called weed
Cause I'm somebody, who's gonna succeed
Gerard Crichlow

The Cycle Of Life

In the great spinning vase of the earth
One sees the wonder lust of wing. Span, big beautiful wings,
Wings of children Being Pushed out of the cold nest
Instead of falling, They are gathered
Gathered and herded like cows,
The wings start to flap
Flap as the knowledge start to flow
Each room holds herds of children
12 years of them
As the eagle flies high
So do the children of the spinning earth
As they flap their wings
And push their children out
Out in the cold air of life
It starts again
In the great spinning vase of the earth
One sees the wonder lust of wing span, Big Beautiful Wings
Wings span spreading wide
Steven T. Roquemore

Faith, Sir?

The best way I can answer you
what is my religion
is possibly by the following:
I was baptized, catechized
and confirmed in
a 'protestant' or 'reformed'
Christian church
and I call on god
by the names they taught me

And furthermore

In case I lie somewhere dying
I will welcome a spiritual elect
of any recognized humanitarian sane
egalitarian non-fringe religion on earth
to escort me to his faith's judgment, reward -
heaven - hell - howbeit - for my deeds
as readily and openly as to my own
if he accepts me equal as I do him
F. Flickinger

Mr. Muddle

Who invited you inside me?
You were never welcomed.
You snuck in of your own accord.
Perhaps it's because I did not fight off those
who prompted you to enter
that you eventually found a home in me.
The harder I try to fight you
the more you seem to resist.
Victorious in the silence you create,
you distort my view of reality,
like the effect of the haunting hallucination
a bereaved mother has
of her lost child,
calling out to her,
through the darkness,
in the middle of the night.
My mind is my home
and you play with my sanity.
Will I ever be strong enough
to force you out by myself?
Christopher Hamilton

Black Is More Than A Color

What do you think of when you think of black?
I think of soft rich black velvet
so smooth and cool.
It can be in the quiet of the night
When sleep escape you.
What do you think of when you think of black?
I envision Harriet Tubman as she hid
the slaves and of
James Beckwurst who was ever so brave.
I hear W. C. Handy "St. Louis Blues,"
and oh, yes, I hear Marion Anderson too.
What do you think of when you think of black?
I see Bessie Coleman who soared through
the skies and
Harold Washington who was ever so wise.
Black is more than a color to me
It means pride, courage and fortitude
And I hope it means the same to you.
Mary P. Jones

The Spirit

What is the dawn
What is the night
Where is the love that sees through the fight
Who sees the day
Who sees the dawn
Where wanders the motherless fawn
When dawn breaks
And small animals bound
What is he beat upon the ground
It is the silent
It is the night
It is the horse of love and delight
He races upon
An open field
To let his spirits be revealed
I see him
Going to and fro
Oh where oh where does the wonderful spirit
of the Thoroughbred go?
Kathy Janel Sauerwein

Success

I often dreamt of success as,
owning a fine car, a fine home, eating
the finest foods, having a fulfilling career,
and having a fine man at my side...

I worked diligently to achieve my ultimate
goal...
Finally, after several years of struggling,
I own an economical car, I live in an
accommodating apartment, I dine on meat and potatoes
often, I have a decent job - and a decent man
at my side - maybe, I will get those things
I used to dream about, maybe I won't...

But I am happy where I am!
Nothing proves success better than
being alive, and being loved-
And I have both!!
Gwendolyn Yarbrough-El

Val's Angels

Val's angels are with every breath that I breathe,
they encompass the very passages that intrigue,
atop the roof at San Luis Rey Mission,
walking with silver bells of his most powerful permission.
   Not everyone can see them as I have alluded,
just Val and I when walking closely to God as the heavens exuded.
   Val's angels christened my son with gifts from the almighty,
Carrying him through a tremendous battlefield prior his arrival.
   Each day that passes, I thank God for his special hands,
Val too is an angel, so beautiful and free,
   Val is my lovely son, a gift from God to me.
   His light is mine and mine is his,
his spirit flies with the eagles, as he would truly know.
   God's ever presence is amongst us for He had chosen us
to be together touched with the anointing from above.
   When Val was little and was flying afar, I use to recite,
"The Lord is my shepherd, I shall not want."
   Val and I are spiritually bonded with God's ribbons
from the angels and the doves.

Diane M. Newman-Gregerson

Of Mother Grandmother And Me

I grew up in the 40s and 50s with the belief and hope
that assimilation would create a homogeneous society,
the dream still unrealized.
You grew up in invisibility, relegated to less than —
not even a birthright.
Was that your mother's life, too?
And what of your beginnings
where — in what circumstance — by whom — of love or lust
the seasons of your lives were far too short,
33 years 3 months 13 days — 50 years 1 month 20 days,
Shadows seeping into my being to recreate past and future
distilled into subtle seamless folds of eternity.
What made laughter caress your beings?
What happinesses cradled your hearts?
Did hope soar unfettered in your souls?
I see your spirits sparkling with iridescent joys
Tying your hearts to mine.
Mother, Grandmother — finally realizing freedom's authentic truth
Knowing freedom's graceful imperative
Unconditional Love.

Mina Stewart

"I Am Not A Fool"

You think I am fool.
But you're the fool, for thinking you can deceive me!
Even I know you must have you're secrets.

You think I am a fool.
But I love you too much to tell you, you are not deceiving me!
I know you must have your regrets.

Oh..., How difficult, to see it in your eyes, hear it in your
voice, tell it in your actions; You! Trying to deceive me!
And I; Pretending to not know!

You think I am a fool.
Even when you try to deceive me, I know that you love me,
and I love you.
And nothing else matters.
You see I have no regrets.
"I am not a fool."

Patricia Staley

Friends

Friends, you take them for granted,
Whether you notice it or not.

On every holiday you say, "Lets have a party!"
But they can't- they're grounded.
Have you ever stopped to think, what if they never get ungrounded?

Every day you call them up to talk,
But they cant- they're eating dinner.
Have you ever stopped to think, what if they never finish?

Every weekend you ask them if they can come spend the night,
But they can't- they're goin' on vacation.
Have you ever stopped to think, what if they never get back?

Every day you write them a note and tell them to write back,
But they can't- they're absent and out sick.
Have you ever stopped to think, what if it never get better?

What if one day you call them up and find out they're moving?
You'll wish you had thought.

Have you ever stopped to think...

Kristin Werner

A Hypocritical World

Peace is promoted
but still violence is daily.

The people say one thing
but do the opposite.

As examples they teach their children what is right
but at the same time they do wrong.

They want to live in harmony
but use violence as the solution.

The world is contradicting itself.
Does it realize that?

Crime, drugs, gangs, and many more words
are words of hate and must be banished.

They surround the world
they are polluting the air of love.
Does anyone care?

Theresa Ehrenreich

Friendship

Friends like bubble gum
And even cotton candy.
That is what makes
Friends so dandy.

Friends like lots of different dolls
Paperdolls and barbies.
And on that special day of the year,
You could buy your friend one for her party.

Friends enjoy lots of sports
Softball, soccer, and even swimming.
But most of all
Friends like the winning.

Friends enjoy reading
Stories, poems, and jokes.
Sometimes friends go to a movie,
They think is really groovy.

Friends do lots of things together
Weekends, days, and nights.
But, no matter what some may say,
Your friendship will go a long, long, way.

Stephanie Ott

The Outside

Standing among the surroundings, I take it all in.
I am on the outside watching: myself and you alike.
You do not understand me because you do not see me.
You can look but do not touch, I am unable to be reached.
Trying as you may, you cannot see the world as I do.
It is different from the outside.

I wish for acceptance from all; you do not want to.
As I see it, I am alone from my position as an outsider.
You can never come into my mind or my being.
I am different from what you think that you see.
I, myself, am invisible to anyone who is unlike me.
It is different from the outside.

I am not happy; I am not sad; I am not strong; I am not weak.
I do not laugh; I do not cry; I do not believe; I do not understand.
I cannot stand; I cannot lay; I cannot talk; I cannot sleep.
I will not try; I will not relax; I will not live; I Will Not Die.
It is different from the outside.

Rebecca Burns

No More Tears

No more tears, the past defines itself
The fragrance of the orange blossom
is proof enough to rejoice
Celebrate the chance meetings that effect a lifetime
These are gifts. Revisit those you loved at happy times and
Then Set Sail. The scent of sun-drenched skin - the lemon and pine
trees - the honeysuckle; soft wind - the humming of happy bees
golden bracelets on slim tan wrists....these are what I love
I love myself for coming through.

The connecting trust
soul to soul, elements of humanity
the joy of giving

No more tears
The capacity to fall in love
The baby swallows patiently waiting huddled in a nest
These are what I love

No more tears
The ties that bind
The helping hand.

Jennifer Gordon

What Is Inside Of Me

What is inside of me, is a beautiful flower,
ready to bloom.

Behind my heart, is a rose
and whenever I'm sad, it gets weak.
But whenever I'm happy
it lights up like a star, in the sky.

Behind my eyes, is a garden and whenever
I'm angry or sad, it dies and loses all its water.
But when I'm happy it grows and grows.
Inside of me is a daisy,
it's a guide to my life.

Inside of me is a winter storm,
and whenever I'm happy, it calms down.
But whenever I'm sad, it gets worse and worse.

Nicole Di Maio

Thanks, Mama (On Mother's Day)

Thanks, Mama, for all you've done
Throughout these many years,
Your love, your presence, and your drive
Have helped to ease my fears.

Thanks for all the sacrifices
You made to watch us grow,
I've come to see how much you did
And really had to know.

Thanks for all you did for us
We owe it all to you,
For Sis at UGA, Dad at Tech,
And me at L.S.U.

Thanks for always being there
Your help was oh-so-strong,
You helped us all to cope and live
And mostly get along.

Thanks for being just 'The Best'
So don't start feeling blue,
This is our chance to let you know
How much we 'All Love You'!!!

With Love on Mother's Day

Tom Hill

A Summer Sonnet

There drifts from endless time the lovely cry
A shattered shout "Let there be light and life"
The pain wears thin and dull as years go by
as birth bows low to death in endless strife.
The sun beats down on man, the earth is warm
and yet I know this comfort in time will pass.
There is no evil, never is there harm
in summer goods, the love that does not last.
For laughter, youth and love in one short span,
Apollo robed in velvet green and gold
yields place to grey, to wise and aged man
who murmurs life is short and grow old
so take it now this life for us so brief
and build the dream that lasts beyond belief.

Joseph D. Palmer

Untitled

Take advantage of me.
I dare you.
Adopt the restless demon that rattles my bars.
It shivers and moans, wanting out.

Coerce me.
I'll become whoever you wish me to be.
I metamorphose quite easily.
You'll see, you'll see
My many disguises, a theater full of masks.
I'm a mannequin swathed in cowardice.

Mold me.
I'll let you bend my body
Into a sunrise, an ocean, a cesspool.
You choose my identity.

Ravish me.
You stare, never care,
But neither do I.

I belong to no God.
Faith, extraneous, since you consume me thoroughly.
I pray anyway.

Your suit of armor rusts in my rain of tears.

Janet Jachimowicz

Transition

Winter nights are dark and long, midnight peals its lonesome song.
Without my love to warm by breast, sleep will not come, I cannot rest.
Time suspended through empty space, her image fades, how dim her face.
The silence screams beyond belief, eyes red with tears, heart filled with grief.
But wait it seems to me quite clear, the cunning dawn creeps ever near.
Restless slumber in fits and starts, the daylight breaks and darkness parts.
In light of day so fresh and new, I seem to find a rendezvous.
Sweet thoughts of her my mind revive, reminding me I must survive.
My love for her can never part, she would restore my broken heart.
With threads of love she'd mend the break, and grant me peace in sleep or wake.
She'd furnish me with sweet repose, and then would send a single rose.
She'd wish for me my heart to sing, "Have faith my love, it's almost spring."
"In spring you see, life starts anew, the tulips bloom and so will you.
Bright green bursts forth, blue sky above and you shall find a brand new love."

George E. Nancarrow

Gone Down

Far walked the wisp of mantled running,
to smell the sea drip drying,
and lingered once upon a rock,
to taste the salts of crying.

Then off, gone down on green eyes winging,
beneath deep breaths lie gazing,
there wake from roads of sullen gray,
toward words of gentle sayings.

All past the heights stand fast and mocking,
past lowly minds and masks,
gone down now with the maple splendor,
to rest in mine at last.

And when the sea drip rolls grease paint,
to weather another dry soul,
here shall I be to greet their needs,
within my warm eternal knoll.

David E. Wood

Easter Bunny

The Easter Bunny went Hippety-Hop
Delivering baskets in every block
When he passed our house it was like a flash
I wondered why as I peeked through the glass

He traveled up hills and through meadows of hay
While beautiful colors each basket displayed
Making children happy as he went on his way
On this wonderful morning which is Easter Day.

Going on and on Hippety-Hop
One basket left ohooo whom have I forgot
He took out his list starting at the top
I'm sure I'll remember or I want stop.

There's Mary, James, Bill, and John
"Clint Allen" That's him! 1405 Wydham Drive
But that's in Virginia, what shall I do?
I must find the answer before I'm through

I know! "He cried" with a Hippety-Hop
901 E Unaka is my next stop
Clint Allen I'm coming don't be sad
Happy Easter Happy Easter to a nice little Lad

Idia E. Cable

"Mother And Child"

A mother is one like no other,
With no need for a biological connection.
The one who is your mother,
Is the one who gives you direction.

She teaches from her mind and heart.
Her most important endeavor—
To give you an exceptional start;
To create strength, so storms you can weather.

The work of shaping your character,
Requires effort, perseverance, and timing.
But, the person who emerges years later,
Is well worth the years of priming.

The love and the caring she shares,
The self control and the desire to nurture,
The innermost thoughts she bares——
Are all for the one who'll enter the future.

To her you are a most precious gift.
Though at times you push the limits expertly.
She abhors the passage of time so swift,
That will make you an adult too quickly.

Gretha Ruark Lovejoy

A Message

I am a mother, having a child
Who is the father, I never mind - - - This is America

I had a nurse, to look after him
He should be great, that was my dream - - - In this America

My son was grown up, as days passed
He became a saint, working very hard - - - This is America

But I looked like young, known as beauty
I never thought about mother's duty - - - In this America

I had many friends, for my pleasure
To enjoy with them, it was my nature - - - This is America

Once my good son, had come to know
He found in his heart, full of woe - - - In this America

One day he left home and left me too
Since I am lonely, what can I do? - - - Oh! this is America

I lost my son and lost my age
Now I am sad, as a bird in a cage - - - Oh! in this America

Today I repent, for my error
I do nothing but sorry forever - - - Is this America?

If you want to live real happy life
Be a good mother and faithful wife - - - Yes, this is America.

Atmaram J. Barot

Sonnet For Stravinski

Maestro Stravinski, I want to beginski
By saying you don't sound like Irving Berlinski.
No music before yours is closely akinski.

Your chords often make me shudder and winceski;
Your dissonance keeps getting under my skinski;
Your changes in tempo are sharp as a pinski;
Your trumpets and kettledrums make a great dinski;
Your string section sometimes sounds unviolinski;
Your ballet parts must have taxed even Nijinski.

But in view of strong feelings your movements evinceski
And the flat music yours has consigned to the binski
On this closing note no words will I minceski:

You're never committed the cardinal sinski
Of letting musical boredom creepinski.

Philip Schaffner

We Honor And Praise (The Senior Citizen)

Let us salute the past that so triumphantly produced the present by the grace of God.

Let us praise the Senior Citizen who fought the fight and took the blows, and lay out the path for us to travel with less toil.

Let us honor the dignity in the lessons they teach.

Let us reach out a hand of love and understanding. If their greeting seems a little cold, let's think of the toils of getting old.

Let us reach in our hears for a smile, be in control for here is a treasure, its value can't be told.

When a Senior Citizen is near, even in gloom, give a smile, a touch of their hand should give thrills to your mind.

We should pause from day to day to say, "Can I help you while I'm on my way?"

When a Senior Citizen has a smile, you should say thank God its worth my while.
Think of the tears those smiles have halted, broken hearts those smiles have mended.

Think of the hands that touch so gently and wiped away all the fear.

Think of the Senior Citizen as our foundation, for without them there would be nothing to climb.
Matthew Brown

A Person I Hardly Know

Even though you were there for only six years of my life, does not mean anything.

You never picked me up, and played with me.
I guess other people were more important than me.
Now, I have to except my past.

For a person I hardly know, the one thing I know is that you will always be my father, and I will always be your daughter.
Luisa Spadafino

Eyes Of A Child

From lollipops to roller skates, Kites gently floating, high in the sky, to puppies and kittens and county fairs, that's where the secret lies.

From Cinderella and her handsome prince, to their favorite merry-go-round, you can see the look on their faces, as happiness abounds.

To them, life's a bed of roses, so wonderful and carefree,
But as they grow older, and the roses die, They join reality.

Think of the world we could live in, if the fantasy wasn't exiled, Think of the world we could live in, If we still saw life—Through the eyes of a child...
Sherry Keown

The Mistake

Everyone now gives him the cold shoulder
Man, life to him weights like a boulder
thinking all the time of his Great Mistake
of how it cannot be undone, for his and her's sake
Oh! Oh! How to undo the past, he so wonders and wishes
to turn dreary anger into hugs and kisses!
wouldn't that be nice?
If only it could be done in a trice!
but no...
once done, the thing cannot be undone
life goes on...
somehow, someway, he must go elsewhere for his fun.
Sigh...
Joe Korty

"My Life-Long Dreams"

Sometimes I sit back and think of the things that I can be.
I can be anything that I want to be is what people tell me.
I know that I want to be known.
I want people to love me, I don't want to be alone.
It would be nice to be wealthy,
It would be even nicer to be healthy!
I want to have a big family,
I will plan my life sensibly,
I want to get an education!
My dreams will be my motivation.
I want to travel the world,
I want to see everything.
After I've visited many places,
I'll make myself a home,
A home that has familiar faces.
Actually the only thing that matters to me,
Is that I'm happy wherever I may be,
And that I know I can be anything I want to be!
Even though I'm just thirteen
Melissa Mazell

Untitled

The sky cast a purple haze.
While I sat on the beach in a lover's daze.

I thought of my love who had gone away.
While I wished it was just another day.

Reality had awakened me from my sweet dream.
While my life was torn like a ruined seam.

My body ached full of pain.
While I ignored the falling rain.

I felt trapped in a deep grave.
While I hoped to be brave.

I put my head down to cry.
While I let the love we had die

My heart had fallen into a dark hole.
While I could feel the praying of my soul.

I stayed curled up in my little pit.
While suddenly my way was lit.

I heard his voice cut through the night.
While I had about given up the fight.

Their was a lift of all past harms.
While he took me in his arms.
Lacey Luebber

Untitled

Although I do not know you,
I will try to get over it,
although I do not comprehend the things you do,
I will try to understand it.
I do not know why you took my Grandfather.
Why didn't you see that he was needed?
Now I sit here and try to comfort my mother,
because you didn't listen to me as I begged and pleaded.
Do you realize these tears are for real?
You've done it so much, by now I'd think you'd see,
don't you know how you've made us feel,
don't you know how much you've hurt me?
But you can not help me,
all you know is pain,
you do not care about my heart broken family,
and the ones who feel insane.
I can not grasp the things you do,
you can take away a man's last breath,
not for a long time do I want to confront you,
I do not want to face you, the almighty Death.
Lori Wasson

Summer Evening On My Front Lawn

We lie like snakes, eyes level with the green chutes
  That we have covered with a cast away bedspread.

On our magic carpet, bare legs and feet intertwined,
  Tempting the first blood-suckers of the day's closing.

In the shadow of an immense, majestic giant that we have
  Taken for granted because it's home.

Our mouths savor the luscious, ripe red jewels of
  Flavor that quite possibly are nature's greatest sustenance.

Content in our world, warm in the mild air that is sweet
  With my mother's colorful earthen fireworks.

Evening subtly eases into the air, which welcomes her presence
  With layers of pastels amidst its sky.

As we talk about a mystery of the universe, the indigo dusk
  Fills with pinpoints of light.

The navy blue night closes in, wrapping its cloak around us,
  While a voice from inside calls, "time to come in!"

So we gather up the blanket, having lost the battle with time
  (and mosquitoes), take each other's hand and walk into
  The warm glow among walls.
    Megan Long

"If Only"

If only I could hold you near,
clothe myself in your embrace
and drown in the depths of your dark eyes.
if only I could caress your skin
in fading light,
with my trembling hands...

But you are always on the other side
of the wall, insurmountable
thick with thorns and vines, yet painfully transparent
I see you, and I know we can never be,
but if only I had the chance...

The chance that will not come.
I will stay here on my side
and gaze through walls of thorn and vine
admiring the rose
that blossoms
ever on the other side.
    Brian M. Collis

To Greet The Sun

I hear the sound of thunder on the land
As on my horse's back I fly to greet the sun.
The burden on his back is light, and we
Feel the bond of love, my horse and I.

It is the hour before the dawn and then
We see violet and rose on the horizon...
Precursors of the daily magic, the colors
Herald the awesome splendor, the rising sun.

Suddenly we reach our goal and we then
climb the little hill. I stand beside
my lovely horse, feeling the velvet of
his mouth caress my face... tenderly.

Over the horizon looms the first gleaming
of the sun, come to ripen the fruit
for the sacramental wine, giving light
and life in benediction to Mother Earth.

Treasured memories are all I have of
our swift rides to the small hill
to daily greet the rising sun. I rise
to greet the sun, alone, remembering youth...
    Elaine M. Kazen

Untitled

From a distance, I admire her beauty.
I long to have her, but she does not know me.

I move closer and closer, but not close enough.
The closer I come, the more beautiful she is.
Oh, how I long for her delicate touch.

As I move closer, I speak, but she does not hear me.
As I get close enough, I touch, but she does not feel me.

Her skin so smooth, as smooth as silk.
Her eyes so blue, as blue as the sky.

Her hair so soft, as soft as satin.
Her body so beautiful, as beautiful as a rose.

Could such a beautiful woman exist, or is she just a fantasy
  within a dream.......
    Robert F. Barrett

Waiting

Heavy doth my sore heart weigh
within this cage of ash and clay
for yet I wait for Love's fair Prince;
I bid the skies to part for glimpse!

To see his noble eyes, I thirst;
to touch the wounds that n'er were nursed;
to feel his voice upon my cheek;
to know my soul will ever keep!

When all my sinful lusts shall cease
and Love will overcome the beast;
when glories take the place of clay
and all my tears are washed away!

Till then I wrest with death and woe
and wait for eastern sky to show
the face that angels long adored:
Love's fairest Prince and faith's reward!
    Kathryn Slattery

River

The river flows
It flows so cool
I let it take my ankles
The birds sing low — the birds sing low
I cannot feel my ankles

The river flows
It flows so soft
I let it take my body
The wind soars over — the wind soars over
I cannot feel my body

The river flows
It flows so strong
I let it take my will
The sky goes dark — the sky goes dark
I cannot feel my will

The river flows
It flows so clear
I let it take my heart
The water calls — the water calls
I think I feel my heart.
    Rebecca Finley

Elk

How peaceful 'twas in the summer waves
In lake by trees and brush and caves;
The sun beat down, but ne'er was felt
By the elk in the water knelt.

Majestic were the elk that day,
As in the water great forms lay,
As in the water all around,
Sea gulls made a splashing sound

And gentle breeze made pond reeds sway
As hiding hunter stalked its prey
And fell in awe of mighty beast
That would for family prove a feast.

And silent cat it streaked through air,
Its claws and fangs laid cold and bare,
The elk it raised its head and cried,
And lowered it, and fell, and died.

A battle brief was fought that day
Won by hunter, lost by prey,
For such is nature, by and by,
All lips shall sound death's final cry.

Diana Seymour

Pillaged Soul

On the earth I laid and watched you from afar.
Growing as you moved near, broader and taller than the rest.
Flowing over whatever lay in front of you to make yourself
more momentous and prestigious than the others.

In amazement I watched as you rolled towards me.
I wondered why you chose that path.
Was it the easiest way to get where you wanted?
Or did it have the most for you to consume, to build yourself
   yet even higher?

So smoothly you poured upon the shore taking me into your quiet
world.
Then, like in the fit of a raging sea, your waves of love devoured me.
And, drowning in your plentiful force, I lost myself somewhere
   between the land and eternity.

Now, lost at sea with many others quite alike, that I just failed to
   see on the land from which you first took me.

Distantly, I see your shadow surging towards another taste of shore.
For you the build of getting there surpasses the actual reach.
Always anticipating a different way to land.
Dreaming of a better way to steal the sand.

Theresa J. Galivan

Uncertain Love

Bring me back to the waves of keep
to the key of your love I longed to seek
was your heart uncertain before I departed
or mislead into the mist of the secret garden
It was I who gave my soul to the king
my body, my mind, my heart, my everything
is it true you are the queen of love
who sends her beauty as sweet as a dove
was I mistaken to take the wrong key
no it could not have possible been me
to forget your face, to lose a trace
of the warm hold of your embrace
I escaped the demons, the hungry demons
I survived the hell the fiery hell
the jealous Sarah, the angel of lust
to experience the feel of your touch
but now I need the certainty of companionship
the certainty of love
my heart is burning for the desire of you
to make this love come true

Ennis Williams

Forever In My Heart

Forever in my heart you'll stay
Even when I've gone away
I know that you'll be there when I return

No matter how many years go by
Every time I leave I know I'll cry
Inside my love for you will always burn

When the tears start rolling down my face
When I'm feeling sad in some lonely place
When I close my eyes I know I'll think of you

Even when I'm all alone
and I wish I could come home
When I think of your face I won't feel so sad

Robert Williams

A Given Life

An infant's love so small and sweet
With hands so tiny and tiny feet
A gentle touch of a baby's charm
falls to catch a mothers arms
A fathers smile with love and care
A given life only God could share
A love so small only God could give
Remembers this love throughout all its years
A cherished love you will always know
A baby's love will always grow.

Danny Glenn Drew

Red Queen

Another doll to care for, to diaper, to feed
Nothing, teach nothing, to discard in a garbage pail.

Our children are raising the dead. Plastic bones
And snake-like silky styrofoam skin on the faces of
A mannequin nation awaiting and biding its time.

Meanwhile in a faraway field in Arkansas-
In a cabbage patch, a raggedy Anne is born.

In the years beyond years flown by, every one a star-
In the heavens, how lofty their eyes.
Oh, what a generation, a billion points of light.

And where is the love of God for the multitudes
Who wander homeless in the icy grip of winter,
When the Red Queen says: "Off with their heads!"

Robert Mark Erichson

To Mother On Her Birthday

When spun from mud the sculptor cast his clay
And lastly spoke the breath of life eternal
His cherubim, the finish touch, then born unto the day
Newborn, sough not their God on high, but that much more
maternal.
While constellations seemly cheaply bought—
Reflections cast from the skyhung plate—
Within these shining dot shapes wrought
The birth which is thy mother's date.
Beaming banner take alignment, outshine thy lunar part
Pompous lights as there may e'er be
Orchestral moons in chime of time conduct this day to start
For gifted is the day that is our year's first counted quinary
   Some all agog had thought the sainted day one less, at four
   While numinous angels cant forth the fifth, do sweetly praise the
   score.

Josh Lund

Three Cats Of Milan

Three cats lay along the edge of the red-tiled roof
Like fuzzy caterpillars dropped from tenement-trees.
Two black, one tortoiseshell, mottled as the tiles.
Those Italian cats slept separately, silently,
As I looked down on them from a sixth floor window.

> But when night fell, the felines faded,
> Metamorphosed into wakeful warriors:
> Two panthers and a tiger now
> They hurled each other territorial challenges.

> Or perhaps it was another, a rude intruder
> In their urban jungle, a tile-trespasser
> That upset the incumbent combatants
> And operatically howled us awake.

In the warm Milan morning I looked down once again,
Leaning out of our bedroom window, and I could see
The three cats still there as if night never happened,
As if they had always been sleeping, peacefully,
Tame as parlor pussies, on the red roof below.

Barbara Witemeyer

Navajo Marines

Come serve your country, Navajo; you, whom we displaced;
We, who have not learned your ways or speech,
Nor heard the secret nuance of your tongue;
We, who may be over-run by men of foreign mores,
Now need your help!

Men of the means and canyons, will you help us, please?
Your speech will not be ciphered by those alien to your way;
Neither they nor we have learned it.
Your message will be safe with us; secret to your ancient kin.
And so the dineh came;

Helped save the lives of those who claimed their land,
And took the chance of going to their Nataani in the sky.
Who, would you say, was friend? Though late, our thanks is without end;
Our gratitude lives on in men whose lives you saved;
Sculpted symbol placed in Window Rock,

Aperture for all to see and learn of your oblation;
And since we're slowly learning, too, we speak with grateful hearts
To share the wondrous rainbow bridge
In search of finding ways to save
The earth and humbled nation.

Frances-Faith P. Tretton

Water

Standing over it
Almost God-like
Above the innocent pond
A pebble is dropped

The fallen pebble
The rippling water
Like the creation of life
Its size increases

Soon the ripples fade away
As death begins its rampage
It kills at random
And forces caution to be taken

With a cold-hearted grin
It murders with pleasure
No word to take heed
Until time has unfolded

Is death not the demon
But an excuse for our mistakes
Only a reflection from the clearing water is left
A reflection of the dark side within

Ross Kazuto Yasui

Beginning To End

Where there is life,
There is always fate,
Some we will love, some we will hate.

Where there is chance,
We have a choice to make,
Some we give up, some we will take.

Where there is happiness,
There should be romance,
Some we let die, some we enhance.

Where there is love,
There will be a test,
Some we conceal, some we confess.

Where there is a loss,
There will be a win,
Some will start over, and some will end.

De'Lisa Woods

War

War is yet put into effect for good purposes,
but can reveal some of the most painstaking consequences of time,

Though people think we go to war,
we're actually challenging life itself for a better future,

And it may not actually occur in words,
but when war comes to stakes, we are actually,
unconsciously debating between ourselves,
is war really worth all the treasures, it claims to be?

And though the time frames will prevail,
we can only guess what time has for us to come.

Brad Poage

The One In The Mirror

I am a person without a face,
Lost in a sea of human race.
Crying out for someone to hear,
Down from my eyes rolls a single tear.

No one listens to the sound of rain,
Or stops to help someone in pain.
No one comforts one with fear in their eyes,
But they don't mind laughing at someone who cries.

Life to people is all a big game,
Always looking for someone to blame.
Trying to be someone they are not,
They do the opposite of what they are taught.

I wish this world would notice me,
And all of the things I try to be.
But most of all...

When I cry I want someone to hear,
Because the only one who seems to listen is the one in the mirror.

Shawna Blowers

Montana Winter

Grey skies, heavy with snow's portent
   Brooding o'er plains and swelling hills;
Ready to scourge, to cleanse
   Autumn's scarred ground and awkward trees,
Enveloping nature's nakedness with
   Equal white,
Leaving a celibate flow of stillness
   And peace.

Irene Schanche Bowker

An Eternal Impression

As I lay next to him at night
I feel his breath against my skin
I hear his heart beat in my ear
I feel safe knowing he is there

My body seems as one with his
He touches me caringly
Respecting my body and mind
Driving out all the fear I feel

His heart is playful and fun
While his soul seems plagued with mystery
Knowledge feels all corners of his mind
Teaching while at the same time learning

The most intriguing guy I've known
I don't really know at all it seems
But the time I've spent with him
Has left an impression that will last an eternity

Donnette Beawais

Love

When the time is right, you will know
A special feeling in your heart
Will soon appear, before you know it.
A bird will appear, to put a little bug
In your ear and the bug whispers a special message:

Love is true, when you're blue
Love is wonderful, when it's true
When someone loves you
And you love them too!

When you're sad and blue
Just think of love when it was true
When you feel love is real
Then put your heart into it.

Angie Henderson

The Earth

The world changes everyday.
But the changes are here to stay.
Since you have been here and there.
You can not say you do not care.
Clean the earth and make a stand.
If everyone lent a helping hand.
The world would change drastically
so do not take me sarcastically.
I am as serious as a Shakespearean play.
If you trust me that would make my day.
This is the only earth we've got.
So help and clean an awful lot.
Stay with me till I am through
and you will try to keep the water blue.
So love the land and love the water.
Keep it clean for our sons and daughters!

Jill Certisimo

This Gift

In my heart there is a gift that no one can take
The only thing steady and unchanging in my life
This gift is so precious, the greatest gift of all
This gift is free, it will take you as you are
This gift so pure, and so right
will be with me forever, never will it die
What exactly is this gift?
It is the gift of salvation from
my Lord and Savior Jesus Christ!

Alison Kuhn

Sleep Sailors, Sleep

Oh brave men of the sea,
How can we thank you for keeping us free?
But when we stop and pray,
We all will say,
Sleep sailors, sleep; sleep on in peace.

You have served your country well,
And proudly we hail.
For you are not dead,
Because you have made the sea your bed.
Sleep sailors, sleep; sleep on in peace.

Though there is sadness in our hearts,
Because brave men like you had to part,
You leave us here to weep.
But your memory we will always keep.
So sleep sailors, sleep,
Sleep on and on in peace.

Chas Crawford

The Calm Before Desert Storm

A man sits upon a stone of sand and clay,
Contemplating not life but death,
For death stocks this man.

Death does not know the power that this man holds,
When these two meet they will do great battle.

As death approaches he realizes for the first time
Just how powerful this man is,
For lying at the feet of this man,
Is the decaying body of fear.

After the battle is done,
With the body of fear in his hands death retreats,
For he has come to accept his loss this day,
But death will return yet another day,
To try and claim this man once again.

Who is this man?
My God,
This man is me!

Matthew T. Thibeault

Just Before Christmas "67"

To Michael

My tailor bought a pound of magic yesterday, then with silver
   needles, and scarlet thread,
He sewed with scarlet stitches mandarin robes on models made of clay.
   All night, all day, yesterday.

My tailor bought a pound of bread with the profit made, from the
   robes he sold, to the models made of clay, and ate, all day, all
night, yesterday.

   And now my tailor lies in bed, he broke his needles, he used all
His scarlet thread.
   He 's all alone, his model's all went home, to show their robes to
Their friends of clay.
   All night, all day, today, he's eaten all his bread.

Winifred Ackley

Dancing

They heard the music and they danced.
They held and swayed and stirred romance.
His glib and smiling mouth spoke words
   of future promise and
Gave rise to her heartbeats of love,
They walked the life and shared the pain,
Now somewhere, they dance again
From up above to down below,
   they left a part of their
   hearts' glow - and they dance -

Josephine Pappon Keil

"Tears"

My eyes could see her crying,
   Could see her horrid pain.
I watched with stupid cruelty,
   While her tears poured down like rain.

The others had been so cruel to her,
   Had trampled and smashed her pride.
Though I could only sit and watch,
   My sorrow hard to hide.

I could hear her endless sobs,
   So quiet yet so strong.
Why couldn't I stand to help her out?
   Why couldn't I right this wrong?

I've looked back on this horrid day,
   And seen my inner fears.
Though why couldn't I help her out,
   And stop those streaming tears?

Richard Gerke

A Child Was Born

A child was born in Bethlehem
Heaven sent, but no
Room for Him the world said.
Immanuel was His name.
A star of great brilliance guided shepherds
To the little ancient town where in a
Manger they found Him.
Angels and Heavenly Host praised God,
Stable animals adored Him.
That child grew in stature and wisdom.
Our Lord and savior he became!

Dorothy M. Dorsey

Day So Special

The wind blows away the past the sun brings in the new this is why I love you. If I was unable to see I would have still found you. If the sun wouldn't shine and everything as we knew it would change the love I have for you couldn't, it would grow stronger. If the water would be no longer you would be the nourishment I would thirst for. I'd walk burning coles of fire, I'd sleep on beds of nails, I'd except any challenge to prove my love and devotion. You are a temple and I its God, any who would want to try or disgrace its beauty would feel the wrath of its guarding God. My love and strength could move the heavens the mountains and even change the weather, but I won't change and I won't change you. I'll stand along side you I'll stay strong with you, to each a guide. To each a friend to always be lovers to always be with each other to always be there for another no matter whatever. I will always cherish you comfort you praise and honor you respect listen and be patience with you. I'll always bow onto you with all of your needs, and place you upon a pedestal for all to see. I'll never put you in a case as a trophy or a object. You're my love my life. And now so proud to introduce you as my wife.

William G. Bentz

Those Shoes

Those are the shoes that I loved.
Those are my shoes,
That my two feet slid into each and every day.
That I laced up tightly every time
That carried me up the court,
That carried me down the court.
Those shoes, that lifted me off the floor,
That I slid across the floor in defense in,
That I line up with the basket to shoot in.
Those are the shoes that I loved,
The shoes that I cherished.
Those were my shoes.

Mandy Berry

No One Around

If a tree falls deep in the forest
And there's no one around or near it,
The questions's been asked, "Does that tree make a sound?"
If no one is there who can hear it?

If the sun sets orange in the west
And there's no one around to observe it,
Is the beautiful view eternally gone?
Does it need our eyes to preserve it?

If a person feels joy and gladness
And there's no one around to share,
Does the joy have no meaning - the gladness no sense?
Do we need to have someone to care?

If a person feels grief and sadness
All alone in their sorrow and woe,
Are we sure that the grief and the sadness are real?
Does it take another to know?

It seems that the trees, sunset, gladness and sorrow
All need something else to be real.
They're nothing alone - they just don't exist.
Without others to hear, share, and feel.

A. L. Ullrich

The Price

From class to class without a care,
And tonight that special date to share.

She finally made it, her parents are proud;
Top of her class, she stands out in a crowd.

She had to work hard, her family was poor;
Now both Love and Yale have knocked at her door.

The world is hers to do as she will,
Not even finals can break the spell.

She rounds the corner, her last class today,
She hears a loud crack, the world fades away.

She doesn't know what happened or why,
All she knows now is that it is time to die.

The boys were fighting about who's number one;
They never knew the girl they killed with their gun.

To understand why, her parents must try,
For the loss they feel, their tears may never dry.

Our children find pleasure in violence and guns;
But the price is death for our daughters and sons.

Teresa Weber

Life

On a regular dark night I sit and wonder what will happen in life.
I sit on a chair and gaze into the light, pondering the meaning of life.
Although I've never found it, I sit wonder what will happen with me.
I've been through much in my life shall it be death, divorce, sadness, or loneliness.
Neither you nor I can explain why any of these happen, but I have made a guess.
No you can not hear it because it is mine, mine, you must find it out for yourself.
Some take many years pondering these questions of life, some hope to find it out by others.
But what they don't know is that it is different for each person.
I hope you find yours it will be wonderful when you do.
So I sit here late at night and ask myself the meaning of life.

Robert Malgieri

City Kids

Some people say that we are to blame
for all the violence that gives our world shame.
We say we're the only ones left with a flame.
We will ignite that flame and it will not be lame.
For when we ignite that flame it will be like a million lights.
burning out the violence in the streets at nights.
Some people say we shouldn't have rights.
We say that we have kites
and we will fly them very soon.
We will break out of our tight cocoon.
We will emerge with the world in our hands
we will take care of all of its lands.
For the future we do not have sorrow.
For we are the people of tomorrow.
As the people of tomorrow, song is what we will bring.
We will unite our voices and sing.
We will sing a song of love not hate,
a song of how it's not too late
to open your eyes and see
just how the violence came to be.
Anna Tilsen

True Value

Worth of man in life's unknown span
   is something to control.
Whatever you possess in life
   Nothing outvalues your soul.

Fame and fortune are values
   that count for a large measure.
Beauty and ageless youth
   could be certainly considered a treasure.

It's true that these possessions
   always are extolled;
Yet a kind and compassionate soul
   is worth its weight in gold.

Fair treatment of our fellow-man
   during our time on earth;
Our forgiveness and repentance
   set the true value of our worth.
Ann Daly

Glance

Street lights painting pictures in the moon mist
Little girls playing at the river being sun kissed
Flowers strewn across the road of life
And we pass them all by with a loving glance
   Stop admire the beauty around you
   Stop and smell the fresh morning dew
Nothing is more beautiful than the simplest of things
And we pass them all by with a loving glance
   A loving glance, a star dance, maybe a little more romance
   tear down your shrine take a little more time
   We don't need reason or rhyme just a glance
David Ross-Smith

Rebirth

Rebirth is an excruciatingly painful process.
Wrenching, writhing, fighting to survive.
The old being refuses to die.

Screaming, kicking, clawing, tearing for its life,
Grasping to re-establish control.

The final gasp for life dearly threatens the new creature.
Struggling to assassinate the suckling.
Surrender the only option;
Truce not possible.
A slow painful death to deliver a new vitality.
Lynn Vrany

Dreams In A Satchel

The mellifluous naiad releases free
The diminishing penumbra it foresees

A sibyl dances chimerously
As I dream quite charily

Of a shiver that pulsates inside
A shiver of love, beside

An unforeseen love token
Youthful splendor forever broken

A labyrinth of sensation quickens
To encompass my essence and core, deafens

A suppressed voice of peace
That weeps for release.
Krista Bot

Understanding

Our lives are like a book in this day
and age, because everyday is like a
new page. To be able to go that extra
mile on even having to take a smile.
Somehow, we seem to make it through
the good and bad times as we struggle
down the long path. A path that will
always make us feel safe and secure
and only to know that it will endure.

In the end, knowing that there will be
a new page for tomorrow, still we can
only worry about today. For the good
and the bad will never go away. Having
someone like you around helps to make
turning that page an easier task, rather
than having to do it alone.
Dendee Keltz

Love In The Garden

Two lovers together hold hand in hand
but their differences part them.
They seek a passage to a secret garden
where they wish they could be together forever.
They marry in secret and die together with love
in the beautiful garden.
Natasha Spence

Color Of His Soul

   What color is his soul? Is it black and decaying? Eating up his heart and mind? Is it silver? Electrifying everything it touches and shocking rounds of fantasy into the innocent? Is it violet? With viciousness and raw fury lashing out at everyone? Forever tormented by his tainted love of fantasy?

   Is it red? Like the scorching rage that flows through his veins? Does it penetrate and darken his soul? Like that of a dead being? Is it azure? Like something that is always reaching higher, whether what they're wanting is good or bad? Is it orange? Like a signal flare warning others to back off, get away, leave him alone? Is it pink? Like the gentleness that once was there? Loving his parents, his friends, and reality?

   Or is white? Pure, unscathed, from the harm he has done himself? From the pain he has inflicted? Safe from the fantasy, the fears, and the problems of reality?

   Does the true person lay inside his soul? Lay open and honest? Unafraid of what the world will think? Will his soul ever see the dawn? The death of the true love of life has already be fallen within him, but can his real life be saved?

   His life could be so innocent, never pure again, but true.
Ashley Dionne Waugh

Bouquet

Standing tall in the vase of the world
There is nothing so lovely as you bunch of color girls
Mahogany skin of reddish brown
From the garden of love is where you were found.
Mellow Yellow, my lady fair
with a radiant beauty that fills the air.
Teasing Tan, caramel rose
Elegant and class is what she shows.
Cocoa Brown, chocolate chip.
Sweet as sugar, honey drip.

Black Orchid, true flower of the nile
Winning ways, lasting style.
Standing tall together to make up this bouquet
For sure, you are the greatest
You bunch of intellectual, variegated ladies.

Dorothy Ann Garth

"Giving Your Child Life"

Where has the time gone my child, it seems we've just begun.
You are so mature in your eyes, and yet you are so young.

This day you leave behind, adventures of younger days,
"It's in the past" but don't forget, what you've learned along the way.

We hope we've done our job, preparing you for this day.
Believe in yourself, family and God and you will never go astray.

Hold your head high in all that you do, be proud of each day that you live.
Life is a circle in one sort of way... you get back from what you give.

We'll always be proud of what you do, even when we don't see eye to eye.
As a parent we have one small hope... it's a faze and in time will pass by.

Keep smiling, trying and doing your best. Be caring, loving and giving.
The years to come belong to you, as you pave the road you'll be living.

We'll be "Here" to help you grow, like the sun and rain for a seed.
Follow your heart when making choices and you are bound to succeed.

Renee Meyer

Down Hill Racing

Just the thought of racing makes my toes tingle.
When I hear the word "racing", I think fast, fast and faster!
Downhill skiing is a great sport but racing is Awesome !!

Just the chair lift ride makes you feel splendid, but once you get into the starting gate and hear 3-2-1 Go! You are off like a bullet shooting out of a gun. Then you pass the first gate, you start feeling the wind whistling and howling through your ears trying to scare you off like a monster. Instead you challenge it.. To its Doom! Going faster and faster dodging gates at the same time.
Until you're thinking about "one" thing - the finish line.
You get into the tuck position and burn it until you pass the finish line.

You are stopping to the sound of friends and family cheering and applauding you.

Don't you think down hill racing is great!! Maybe one day you will feel the glory of crossing the Finish Line.

But for now, just practice so you can cross the finish line.

Lydia Coverdale

Forever

Singing songs and laughing.
Going to the doughnut shop and playing scrabble.
I will never forget.
Then the day you got sick,
I read to you, and pretended nothing was wrong,
But there was.
Only a few months, maybe weeks or even days.
No one could tell, but the One above.
Only one wish; for you to never leave me.
September 6, 1993.
Didn't get to say good-bye.
But in your heart and mine, we knew the suffering
Had to come to an end.
Now I go to your home, the wonderful memories,
The times we had all full of fun and laughter
But the memories will never die.
I will love you
Always and forever!!

T'lene Greene

Take Away The Pain

Once born to life a happy child
With hopes of even chances,
Had since grown up with memories,
And scars from childhood glances.

A teen-ager, unknown to me
I grew up all to fast
The shattered dreams and hopeless thoughts
Just kept me in my past

As growing old is near to me
I've done my very best.
With, struggles, flash-backs,
Painful thoughts, I've put them all to rest

You see my dear I know the pain
We share from all our past.
Through loving, learning, many tears
We've broke the chain at last.

Toni Lynn Botelho

Santa Barbara City Beautiful

We rode in early twilight hours
   Along the cliffs and curving shores
Past Eucalyptus, staunch and tall
   Standing guard, by garden wall
Graceful in the blue of night
   Sentinels, in the fading light.

Scarcely heard the ocean's roar
   As we followed cliff and shore,
While gently laving wavelets raced
   To fringe the shore with frothy lace
The gulls their plaintive calls subdued
   In magic stillness, flight pursued.

Along old Spanish, friendly streets
   Still softly trod by padre feet
The village folk who ply their trade
   Stroll quietly in the evening's shade.
Protective hills beyond the town
   Reach down and gently drop, night's gown
Upon St. Barbara far below, and houses
   Stretched out row by row.

Edwina N. Beilman

My Princess

My princess thou art like an angel divine
With wings made of gold and a halo so fine
From a dream come true thou art here with me
My princess, my lady, I bow unto thee.

Julia Alcala

"Till The Last Drop"

My mind begins to race.
My heart begins to pound.
Hushed sounds grow stronger
with my every heartbeat.
As I look around,
the room seems to spin about.
Then, the lights flash off.
I like it that way.
Not seeing my mirrored reflection,
allows me to concentrate.
Nothing but the cold object
within my hands is of importance.
My grip grows stronger with the sensation of pressure,
yet my shadowed figure begins to tremble.
I permit myself
to think of everything, but
I realize I have nothing.
Red is the color of my fate,
and now drips the last drop of
my ever existing essence.

Meredith Dickman

Freedom

I lay,
Staring at the moonlit sky,
Thinking,
Wondering,
In a world of my own,
All alone,
Nobody around as far as the eye can see,
To distant shores,
To the highest heights,
I can be whoever I want to be,
See whatever I want to see,
Do whatever I want to do,
I can be free,
I can be me,
No troubles,
No worries,
I'm free,
Free at last.

Lauren Firewiez

Daddy

There is this man from my past,
who you need not ask.
It's been eight years of pain,
Since he left me that day.
Although time has gone by,
still sometimes I cry.
A little girl alone and scared,
to me my father didn't care.
I knew not why my father left,
the hurt and pain inside I kept.
I see other kids with their father at their side,
and still I wonder what happened to mine.
If only I could tell him how much I care,
Yet I can't seem to find him anywhere.

Kristy McCay

A Son

A baby boy, all dressed in blue
To love, to hold, a son always true
A wonderful gift from the Lord high above
Someone to cherish, someone to love
To share with each other, family and friends
Loneliness of heart never again
The joy you'll feel, the pride, the love
Are gifts to you from the guy up above
Love him cherish him, never let him go
Without telling him, you love him so
How important he is in your life
Even when he's grown with family and wife
Your heart will ache when once he's gone
But your love from him will live on and on
Will it be worth it, you bet it will be
A love so great only sets you free
To love even more, whatever it brings
To your life and your heart, so many things
Things that might never have been
If God had not chosen you for him

Mary Salazar

Finally Leaving

It's time to go - we're finally leaving
But memories we will keep retrieving

We have spent twelve hard years waiting for this day
To make our parents proud in so many ways

We have had a lot of fun with our friends
    from class to class
Now the time is almost here, don't let it pass

The friends we've made here, will remain in
    our hearts
When the sad, yet joyous time comes for us to part

The memories we have made here, we will take
    with us always
The tests keep coming as we count down our last days

For those we leave behind, these words are for you
Your dreams will come true, and someday you'll be here too

For those who mean so much, and have encouraged us,
    We thank you for everything
They call our names, we turn our tassles,
    a tears falls- we're finally leaving

Teresa A. McDuffie

A Precious Gift

Life is a gift so precious and rare,
each sunrise one is blest with should be treated with care.

The sound of a heartbeat, the rhythm of the sea
the sway of the branches of an old climbing tree

The awesome wonder of the night sky
a young child's question always starting with, "Why?"

Each heartbeat should be treated as life from the start;
our home, mother earth, should be respected like art.

It should be treasured, protected, cleaned and preserved.
Each being on the planet should be cared for and heard.

Appreciate the things one takes for granted each day
one never knows when it will be taken away...

Life is a gift so precious and rare.
Each sunrise one is blest with should be treated with care.

Rachele Wehr

Old Ivory Keys

Whispering melodies
Golden dreams
Floating, high above
Cut like a knife to my soul
Leaving nothing but a wound
Infected and plagued. Screaming inside
The ivory keys play a familiar tune
The tune of my life.
Listening, I walk through my soul
To the minor chord seeing only dust left behind
From years of abuse and shattered glass.
Picking up the glass I move to compose a major chord
Only to find no other tune could be played
On the old ivory keys snuggled close to my heart.
Utterly confused I search for a new piano
Only to find that there is no room for one
The one with a familiar tune,
A minor chord, and faded memories.

Jennifer Cook

"My Shining Soul"

The tears of my Heart
Are silent and slow
They drown out the voice
Of my solitary soul;

They weaken my resolve yet strengthen my need
They give voice to my wants
But muffle my plead;

The tears of my Heart
Are selfish and vain giving credence to pity
And compassion disdain;

The tears of my Heart are soft and new
Teaching things of life
Which are both sad and true;

The tears of my Heart are a unique possession
Alone which is mine to learn of its lessons
Discovering among them my own shining soul
And washing it clean as I conquer my goal.

Karen Louise Hicks

Untitled

We stopped loving the other night
when power mowers of reason stripped
our delicate green fields
mercilessly
when foreign winds sifted our protective
clouds of hazy mist and heavens,
when reason triumphed
and emotions fell
dead
we stood naked the other night
on hard ground, in hot sun
and faced each other
(for the first time)

and parted
with passion
and sadness
(and most of all relief)

Peter W. Livingston

"The Man Of The Moon"

The man of the moon is the very polite man that lights up our warm summer nights with a very soft inviting glow

But we are not always graced with his glow but that time is only when he is asleep

Then there are times when he is only partially awake those times he is what I call half awake

When ever you see the moon I hope you see his polite glowing face grinning at you as he cheers you up

I know it cheers me up to look at the Man of The Moon.

Steven Lyon

Music

There are different kinds of music.
There is jazz and pop.
It doesn't matter what you listen to,
As long as it's at the top.

There're many different composers.
From Beethoven to Mariah Carey.
They are all very good,
Even if they are scary.

Some music is romantic.
Some music is just plain fun.
It can sometimes be sad,
But it's always on the run.

Music can be soft.
It can also be loud.
If you listen to mellow music,
It might cause you to think you're on a cloud.

Some people just love music.
Others do not.
Some people think music is rotten,
Others think it's hot.

Christa Smith

Open Your Eyes...

Look at me, I look a mess.
That might be your guess.
But that's not the truth, I'm not uncouth.
What you see on the outside is not the real test.

Inside, I'm very clean.
A lot cleaner than what you've seen.
Open your eyes and see, what's inside of me.
You can't see, but if you could,
you would want to be more like me.

If you were more like me, you would be my friend.
Happy, and sad, all the way to the end.

Open your eyes and see...inside of me.

Isaac Smith

Angel Friend

I put my hands where your wings should be
But it's not the only thing I can't see
My guardian angel, sent from above
Always together, but bound from your love
I try hard to find it, but words can't express
All my life, and my love, to you I confess
Scared to admit it, or not there at all?
There's nothing to say, I can't break the fall
Scared to death, can hurt no one else
I take a deep breath, can't hide from myself

Leslie Houser

The Swan And The Saint Of The Night

A sphere of time suspend and serene
  Embraced my forlorn soul swift the cascading stream
Carrying me backwards bathed in celestial light
  Drawn by ancient chariots the legend Saint of the Night

Fueled by embers glowing into slumbering dreams I sink
  Fanned by horse's wings transparent tipped in pink
Chimes ran in my arrival archangels fluttered round
  Singing songs of distant memories to another dimension found

My will became consumed by a spirit light that shown
  Into it I sought asylum his warmth became my home
Rapture emblazed my heart full and warm and bright
  You've resurrected hope my Savior of the Night!

My eyes have never witnessed the apparition drawing near
  But my soul knew the rhythm of the saint from yesteryear
I've waited all these years transcending times of yore
  The moon and sun align eclipsing our bond once more

The promise is kept scared an oath of silence reigns
  Sequestered by the cadence from the land of the ethereal plains
Each star blinks triumphant a cathedral torched with light
  Nature's forces converge the Swan and the Saint of the Night
    Desiree Vassios

The Light

There is a light upon the hill
Which beckons to me each night.
It's calling me for some unknown reason
To come and explore its simple world.

It continues to call out to me through the night.
Should I go or should I stay?
I finally give in and let myself drift,
Drift away to explore a world of simplicity.

This simple world which I have entered
Makes me forget all my troubles.
Both past and present are forgotten.
For there is no room for troubles here.

As I sit here feeling free
Someone enters the room and
Pulls me back into reality;
Where I am only trouble free in dreams.
    Eileen Karol

My Relations!

Oh my relations, I salute you
Those who have come before me,
Those who have come with me
and those who will come after me,
I salute you!

For your blood is my blood, and my blood is your blood
and your blood is BLACK blood
and BLACK blood is RED blood
and RED blood is MIXED blood

And MIXED blood is WHITE blood
and ASIAN blood is RED blood
and RED blood is mixed blood

and MIXED blood is INDIA blood

and INDIA blood is RED blood
and RED blood is MIXED blood

And MIXED blood is MY blood, and MY blood is YOUR blood
Oh my relations, I salute you!
    Juanita M. Nowak

When Comes The Light

A face against the window pane
  smudges of small fingers on the glass
The child within us all
  does not wish to see this world
  but the stars that glitter
    just beyond its grasp
If one star should fall tonight
  and simply disappear
  then would the wish
    upon it made come true
The child gazing on the skies
  who hopes for things unseen
  may never touch the fallen star
    but always see the dream
Oh little one who now looks out
  upon the endless night
  believe in dreams
    now wished upon
They will be
  when comes the light
    Joleen Chamberlain

Touched By The Holy One

Loneliness and sadness beyond compare
Disillusion and destiny into despair
The pains and sufferings wracked on and on
And then, the touch of the Holy One.

The mists and clouds became a joyous site
The gardens of life all filled with delight
My life became a precious thing
Given, by the gift of the Holy One.

And as I walk through each and every day
I know now love and hope to play
Within my life each day and night
For I, have been touched by the Holy One.

And Angels dance and merrily sing
To the joyousness of life in everything
Their song of love rings in my ears
For I, am part, of the Holy One.

When my days are finally done
You'll find me following the setting sun
With love and happiness beyond compare
For I, will live, with the Holy One.
    Linda Lee Hibbett Poland

Crossing The Terminator

When I cross the terminator and fly
into gentle bliss, I shall greet
the eve of my days with no regret
but this.
We began our journey through life,
hand in hand side by side,
but somewhere along the way you were taken
and we no longer walked in stride.
If only you could have been with me
as I continued on my flight, alas it
was a long and lonely journey and now
I finally cross the terminator and fly
with you into the night.
    Houston T. Reynolds

The Child

He sits there with an inquisitive
look upon his face,
With his deep brown eyes, like
an endless pit of wonder.
Amazed by what has taken place
with new questions to ponder.
Questions, of curiosity and
amazement.
But most of all, that satisfying
look is the result of his
Deep thinking of his child-like mind.
You cherish this moment, for
You may think it's all
Over, but there's still more to
come....
Later.

Christina Zolezi

Untitled

A person unknown to me,
but seemingly kind.
I open up and smile
afraid of rejection
A smile back
I feel so good.
So warm and open.
My fear of you creeps
   silently away.
Knowing your feelings
   match mine.
Warms me inside
If nothing else
we can be friends.
But no matter what happens
I will love you for your
   warmth and friendship
And because you are real
   and just you.

Ellen Moss

Yesterday

A man is sitting on the grass
reflecting upon the past.

Suddenly — running toward him
his son smiling
so he reaches to hold him
only to grasp a breeze

The man and his dreams are sitting
reflecting on the past

When they see — running toward them
his son smiling
and the man waving — sighs

While his dream wipes away a tear

Carolyn Custer

Friends

Best friends are something
   That come once in a life
Sometimes they're more important
   Than even a wife
You tell them secrets
   And your every thought
Friends like these
   Just can't be bought

George Wagner

Cry To The Lord

O Lord you know my heart
and all its deep desires.
Fill me with your peace,
to quench my fleshly fires.

I stand before you Lord,
my face stained with the tears
of not releasing all to you,
and living with my fears.

O take my burdens Lord
that I can no longer bear,
for I know that in your hands
they'll receive the best of care.

Patricia Castline

Shadowboxing

I shadowbox
in my kitchen
late at night.
I am a relentless
opponent. I throw
hard shots.
I drop men
with a single punch.
My nose was broken
twice
in Golden Gloves
boxing.
I am entitled
to these
thoughts.

Peter Martin

To Live Again

Sometime ago I wondered then
What it would be like to live again
To live once more
Just to see
If I would change
Or still be me
Would love be more than starry eyes
Would there be a reason why I cry
To be left alone in deep despair
Hungry for understanding and care
Only time will tell
If I'll live again - or go to hell.

Kelsey Donwen

Immense Love

As the sun is the gold of the world
because it illuminates the planet
As the silvery moon
enamors the earth
As the sea separates, although
kissing with salt every shore
As the stars that sprinkle
with diamonds the sky
As the air that gives
life to the universe
So is the strength of mother's love
more immense than the sea,
the air, the sun, the moon
   and all the stars.

Josephine Goizueta

Under the Overpass

Under the overpass
where my soul screams its cry
to the thoughtless cars
that drive on by

Against my soft corner
made of dirt and rags
I stumble over lyrics
from old paper bags

My mother is not here
to me she is blind
Alone I struggle
with the monsters in my mind

I have no one here
Just you and I
My heart hurts so bad
but it will never die

Under the over pass
that's where my heart leans
when I look at my reflection
in an old can of beans

Joshua Hofford

The Forest Of Daydreams

She haunted the Forest of Daydreams,
The blithe of her Spirit to find.
That gleeful, frolicking dryad,
   Who danced on her soul
   And made her life whole,
Then vanished, a victim of time.

Discovery betrayed the searching,
For carelessly had she tossed
Her treasures, immortal, about her—
   (The things which she seeks;
   The secrets she keeps).
Her Spirit was never lost!

Carol K. Berry

Home

Dedicated to Amanda Querry
Music drifts into my ears.
It echoes in the chambers of my
Heart,
Coursing through my
soul.
And for a moment, I am in the
Past.
I am with you, and I know
That wherever and whenever
I am with you
Then
I am
Home.

Zack Ira Phoenix Shaffer

Jessica Dubroff

   There was a girl who
loved to fly. She had a
dream to learn the sky. She
would have been the youngest
kid, to fly in the sky like
no one else did. With her father
and teacher she flew through
thunder and rain. Now they
are resting in heaven until we
can meet there again.

Krista Shields

The River

Frothy, icy-cold bubbling by the
mountain road,
Clear and cool like a pool
Fast and furious-
Oh so curious,
The whirling swirling never ending
In and out from rock to rock,
Heaven knows where it will stop
Sliding over slippery moss,
As a finger over frost
Swollen sides that wash the shore,
Taking with it more and more,
Grasping rocks out of fear,
For all to soon the end is near.

Marianne Flores

A Tear In The Sand

The tide of time will erase,
The pain of sorrow today I must face
My tears that fall the sands embrace
The deep choking despair
Will give to my mind the solace
that I care.
Now that life has ceased,
My tears and sorrow seek their release.
I will travel the road of time.
The choice is mine.
Tie my love to a tear in the sand.

Ruth Snell

Angel

Our little angel has arrived,
big blue eyes and golden curls,
Lord, how we love her, no one
will ever know, but as you
all know, a lot of little problems
come along with angel so, when
the two o'clock feeding comes, and
you are fumbling in the dark, trying
to find out what is going on, just
stop and think, oh, well next year
this time it will all be done, cause
our little angel has changed from
infant to one, always cherish these
fond memories as the years roll along,
cause one of these days, your angel
will be grown.

Eloise Lillard

My Child

Her love unfolds my heart
like the dances of flower
pedals. Smiling. She is pure
and free like the wind.
I adore her. She is as
beautiful as any butterfly.
As sweet as any honey. Holding
me through grey storms and
blue rapture. She is my life's
blood. I pray for her future.
Love is wonderful. My child.
So beautiful. So innocent.
So kind. My child is my power.
She gives reason for tomorrow.

Sheryl Quinones

Untitled

Benny Hines was a frustrated guy
When he looked at his lifestyle signs
For no matter how much he forged ahead
He'd always be known as B. Hines!

Allan Fraser

Stars

Twinkling softly into the night,
Stars are shining oh so bright

Their soft gentle glow
Will start to show.
As night comes so do they
Sparkling as children pray.

Twinkling its last tonight,
Stars are leaving left and right.

Meg Young

Untitled

Love is like a poison
that creeps upon you
without inception.
A passion that
burns like fire.

A passion baring
with what's inside.
Like a heart burning
with desire, needs,
and wants.

A competition so great
the heart cannot fight.
A poison a love
so strong

Alexiss Jones

Dad

Still crying from so many years ago,
or was it tears of joy remembering
memories of a man who helped me
become what I have become.

Of course I was in my own carefree
world where I only cared about
infant worries.

Nowadays I see my Dad in a whole other
story of life, but a close friendly
stranger to me.

Jacob Young

Bird Upon The Wind

The darkness is not gone
although the rain has stopped.

The sun shines down upon the land
the stars have all come out.

My powers moved inside me
I control the rain no more.

All of this because of you
because I see your joy.

I realized you are happy
so now I'll set you free.

Like a bird upon the wind
like a whale out on the sea.

Barrie Rudisill

Your Touch

When you touch me
My heart skips a beat.
My mind wonders.
My soul is set a flight
My core is warm,
My muscles relaxed.
In just a passing touch
My body is not my own
It is mesmerized by your Touch.
Such strength and power
In such small hands.
Such drive and force
In such a small body
Such power to have in just
Your touch...

Jennifer Blose

Rebirth

The knowledge of the ages
Employs a gardener's theme
Transplanting ancient wisdom
In each succeeding dream
The hybrids, too, containing
Old seeds of basic truth
That blossom in new versions
New concepts taking root
Though each emerging petal
Of ideas, fresh and clean,
Hint gently of ancestors
Whose traces can be seen,
Still, more and more unfolding,
Combining with the Earth,
A new thought brings rejoicing
At its unique rebirth.

Betty McMillen

Death Angel

When the bell tolls midnight
All's quiet 'cross the town.
When the night sounds cease,
Death Angel is around.

He'll make His mark
On the old the weak,
And especially the unfortunate,
He'll most willingly keep.

With wings like sails,
Skinless bones of steel,
Hooded head, vicious laugh
His ax won't make a deal.

But don't get me wrong,
He does have a friend.
A brimstone serpent.
That could make it all end.

So heed my word,
Listen to my advice.
Sleep with no regrets,
To keep from paying the price.

Gregg Pesek

Stressed Out

he nibbles and gnaws
the thick hard whiteness all the
way down to the quick

Suzanne Bayard

Angels Kiss

When an angel sends
a kiss your way
the sweetness of its
love will stay.

As it blows into
the wind and you
feel a gentle touch.

Remember it's your
angel saying,
"I love you very much."

Marie Ortiz

When I'm Alone, I Think Of You

When I'm alone, I think of you.
You make my world a little less blue.
The cheerful smile across your face
Sends me into outer space.
Your loving ways make me glow
I think of you, and then I know.
Without you there'd be no place
For me to go and be embraced.
Friends may come, and friends may go
But with you I will always know.
I hope that we will never part
'Cuz if you leave, you take my heart.

Christine Schull

"Rippling Waters"

Rippling Waters,
Take my message
To my loved one far away;
Swelling Waters
Bear this message
To my sweetheart light and gay:

Rippling Waters,
Sing to me now
Of my darling on his way;
Tell him softly,
I am waiting
On your brink for him each day:

Rippling Waters,
I am lonely;
For he's far away from home;
Ask him gently,
Shall he hear me
As o'er land and sea he'll roam?

Ivy Constable Richards

Untitled

This man we see before us,
 Has lived a happy life.
He has four beautiful children,
 and a loving devoted wife.
This man we see before us,
 works very hard for a living.
But this man we all know so well,
 never grows tired of giving.
This man we see before us,
 has changed throughout the years.
And the hardships he has left behind,
 No longer are they fears.
This man we see before us,
 has shown us all great love
And we shall forever remember him,
 when he is up above.

Sara Ann Warren

I Bow

I bow before your brilliant light
I bow before your awesome might
I kneel beneath your righteous gaze
Knowing my ungodly ways

You rise to pass the judgement true
When someone else approaches you
"Father, wait! I beg, I pray;
Please listen now to what I say."

"This one who stands condemned to die
Is really righteous in your eye
Please look again upon her head
My blood is sprinkled there in red."

"I bought her from the arms of death
And brought her here now to rest
Today she dines at banquet fare
To her I pledge my love and care."

The father smiles at His son
"It is good what you have done
Take and seat her by your throne
To you, dear child, Welcome Home!"

Teresa A. Birket

without warning

a sturdy evergreen
surrenders to
icy gales and gravity.

failing to bridge the ravine,
the tree tumbles
into the frothing river water.

constellations and the
pale moonbeams alone
bear witness to the fall.

such is my sorrow.

now on a splintering wooden swing,
i pendulum
perpetually to and fro again.

lost in a desolate playground
forever stretching
from horizon to horizon.

silence softly hums and buzzes
in my ear -
an insistent reminder.

such is my sorrow.

Matt Christian

Ho, Ho, Ho

Life's laughs are
but few
with the whole
world feeling
blue,
becoming rude in
the eyes of
scrooge.
25th myths only
minutes away,
ropes hang,
feet dangle,
eyes fold,
the movement comes
to a close.
Merry Christmas!
to all who remain
bold.

Stephen Izzo

Untitled

Time was the paths where petal laden
 Swirls of laughter filled the air
Clouds of hope across the sky
 Steps were straight and sure.
Tomorrow's promise graced the table
 Dreams of joy blessed sleeping eyes
The seeds of earth lie waiting
 As the tears of God came gently down
Flowers raise their petals to the sky
 With sorrow comes the growing.
The shadows lengthened
 Sunlight hid neath sorrow's gown
Left a deep, deep longing.

Juliet Warren

Loss

A cross to bear have I
A heavy cross,
'Tis one of loss
And loneliness.

But with each dawn there's work to do
A busy day,
And so I work,
And pray.

But startime only brings again
A lonely night
And so I pray for light
And strength to bear my cross.

Kathleen McDonald Callahan

Tricycle

No,
I won't let her ride
my tricycle.

I like her fine
and all, it's just...
my tricycle is mine.

She has her *own* tricycle,
new roller skates,
View Masters and fingerpaints,

Charlie's Angels van, big Barbie head
with hair you brush
and lips you paint red -

and all I want
is a little ride
by myself,

around the block
and past my
house.

Sarah Elisabeth Freeman

I Have A Little Rose

I have a little rose
which always grows,
and I take good care of
it when it's cold. I love
it and it loves me
and I won't sell it, because
she's as beautiful as
can be.

Susana Sayles

Alone

Do not come knocking at my door,
if you do not plan to enter.

Do not come courting me,
if you do not plan to take my hand.

I am not like the others,
I don't play those silly games
like all the rest.

You have deceived so many,
and so many are yet to come.

I don't want to fall
into the mindless trap.

Soon you will find your youth gone
and your life growing short.

Then you will ask yourself:
Why did I not enter that door?
Why did I not take your hand?

Why am I left here to die? ALONE

Amity Magner

Winter

Winter white is pure delight
When the sun is shining bright.

Winter gray is. . .Well, Okay
With the hope for a better day.

Winter pink is great I think.
But Winter Black is awful!

Verla Lind

The Mother's Song!

You think our day is over
when the children are all settled.
Well it's only just begun.
Don't forget the wee hours
when the hungry cry is sung..
That could be at 2 or 3
no one knows just when.
And don't forget the cough and sniffle
get out the medicine.
The cooking, cleaning and laundry
that's done all day long,
cannot compare to the evenings
that's a Mothers song
So when they say 'how was your day?'
just smile in return.
And say it's only just begun.
Because you know later on
the Mothers song is sung.

Paula Palladino

Untitled

With such sorrow that I say
   goodbye.
Death is not the end of
   my Love for you.
Even with us apart my
   Love will never die.
We haven't seen much of
   Each other in this life.
We will see each other again
   And more in another life
As each day passes I will
   Think of you.
I will never quit loving you
   Grandma.
With all my love.

Chyanne Miller

Battle Of Strength

I was the fool;
I played your little game.
I tried to be the perfect friend,
But nothing was the same.

I began to wonder if it was just me,
That I deserved the wrong,
But then I began to see
Why I had put up with you for so long.

What is the power that you seek,
To rob the poor
To hurt the week,
Or just to lie some more?

I myself am strong.
You will not break down my walls.
My soul will live long,
And shall not suffer the falls.

Stephanie Schraven

Angels Among Us

Are you an angel in heaven?
Are you looking down on me?
Do you watch me night and day?
Are you proud of what you see?

Could you come and talk a while?
For tonight I can not sleep.
I try remembering you,
And the memories so deep.

Could you visit me in my dreams,
And hold me in your arms?
Cleanse my heart of the hate I feel,
And keep me safe from harm.

Come sing me a lullaby,
And strum your harp of gold.
Come sit by my bedside,
And tell of stories untold.

Could someone please explain,
Just why you had to die?
Could someone please say,
It's all right for me to cry?

Julia Ann Rugg

Me

There's a kid inside me
Who's dying to get out
There's woman inside me
Who no one knows about.

There's a romantic there
Who loves satin and lace,
There's a loner somewhere
Who has a sad face.

There's a daredevil here
Who loves to have fun
There's a hard worker too
Who tries to get things done.

All of these people
Are inside of me.
They are who I am,
My personality.

Sara Nelson

Untitled

Me and boo-daddy blazed up a trail
   down 64,
hazing up the car
   lazying our eyes.
"So tell me a secret"
   we'd say,
tiptoeing into each other's lives.
Barging into my brain,
   he did
and made my ice melt,
   my wall fall...
And I loved him for the now and
   thereafter;
loved him for lovin' my soul.

Sherri M. Arnold

Discovering Me

I have a compulsion
to save cardboard tubes
from saran wrap
from scott tissue
from bounty towels
from Christmas gift wrap
as if to deny
Their used up usefulness -
like me.

Donna M. Roberts

Mom

In a circle of uncertainty
There is some light
A helping hand that
Always reaches in hope

Someone always stays by my side
Takes me in stride
Part of my pride
Lift the darkness away
Place the fear at bay
Watch over my dreams
Tenderness hath no extremes

I toss and turn at night
Nightmares come to roost
Suddenly agony subsides
You are there at my side

I wake to flares of glorious sun
Leave the room
To see you there for me
Even in blindness
I could see...

Joshua Kaufman

What Is Love?

What is love?
A deep sensation that causes
hate or deep relation?

Does love consist of tender emotion?
Caring, kind, thoughtful devotion?

Or is it a feeling concealed
within a heart,
endlessly beating for new hope,
fresh start?
What is love?

Kathleen Riedstra

No Apologies

I talk to you, on this cold day.
The sun shines bright,
But it's not the way..
...the way it's supposed to be.

I ponder my actions
Pleading for forgiveness.
If only what I did to you,
Your mind,
Your soul,
Could be disremembered
By all.

Do you accept my apology?
Do you hear me?
Will the pain ever go away?
I wish you could answer me.

But I know you never will.
I realize you can't
I'm Sorry.

But sorry doesn't count Anymore.

Stop the Violence.
Joel Ortsman

The Dressmaker

So slowly sensibilities
become
pale white
parcel dancers
with graceful fingers;
stepping back,
gently
withdrawing touch,
watching
modest bits
yield one beautiful
shape. Inspired,
God will
often
embarrass reality so.
Keith V. Andi

To A Diamond Above

We have many lifetimes and many bodies,
We have but one soul.

This soul will affect the lives
of countless others.
Some more, some less.

Paul touched my soul
Will he again?

I pray
He is at peace, his soul has
joined the sky and become

A Diamond Above!
F. M. McBride

My Goal

The firm belief that sets me apart
from those who can't understand.
That passion for which I am willing
to ignore fear and pain.
The reality of failure.
The stubbornness to risk it.
My goal.
Wendell V. Troullier

Thank You

You may have sent a pretty card,
  To brighten up the day.
You may have called to talk awhile,
  To hear what she might say.

You may have come to visit her.
  And brought a little gift
But just the fact that you were there
  Sure gave her heart a lift

So many hearts reached out to her,
So many teardrops fell.
The love that came from all of you,
  Rang clear just like a bell.

She knew each one who held her hand,
  She felt your gentle touch.
And though she couldn't tell you so,
  It meant so very much.

To all who kept her in their prayers,
  Or helped in any way.
Our heartfelt thanks and gratitude,
  Are more than we can say.
Mary Reisinger

My Grandfather

A man tall and thin
Always dressed as neat as a pin

A man full of joy
He even made a rocking horse as a toy

He never would laugh when you
wanted to have a serious talk

So instead he would take you on his
favorite walk

My grandfather wasn't famous
and did not have a well known name

But to me he could of been
in the Hall of Fame
Tammy Paulish

Dreams

I feel you walking behind me
Watching the sunlight on my hair
I let you for awhile,
Enjoying your eyes upon me
Then I turn...
Only to be held in the arms
Of my shadow

I hear you calling my name
Your deep voice melting my heart
I savor the mellow sound
Then smiling, I turn around
Only to be caressed by the wind...

I feel you inside me
Your firmness once again
Leaves me breathless
Tingling to my inner soul...
And as our lips meet
I awake from heavenly dream
Phasha

Sunset

Blood red sun,
Low on the horizon.
Grasses twist
And bend, and weave.
Sitting here,
I'm lost in the madness.
Face the sun,
I beg for reprieve.

So they say,
Look to the horizon.
Horizon...
Look as if you don't care.
Past shades haunt
Tap me on the shoulder.
When I look
I see no one there.
Michelle Booher

The Destruction

The sky is falling
Lightning crashes
Mountains roar
Meteor smashes
Animals that murder
A psychotic killer
Drugs taking over the minds
Grunge taking over the skies
Darkness is all that can be seen
Where is the light?
The holy being?
Disasters that destroy the bonds
Children are killing their moms
Nuclear warfare
Germs, disease
The whole world,
Been brought down to its knees
A frightening poem that says it all
No one lives we all shall fall
Mike Lockhart

Barbara

The girl looked away
her blondness setting
into the Vienna sunrise
with unfading laughter
and undying smiles
locked into my tortured mind
looked away
Eyes wild;
the past blue night
Skin so white:
reminder of the morning light
Hand in hand she looks away
She'd utter no concerns,
cry about no worries
while she is mine
Strong sighs regarding pain gone by
become weak sobs on the receiver
when I hang up a tear stained phone.
Erin V. Kyle

A Rare Bloom

I discovered you there
Brave and uncertain...
The first bloom born
A fleeting moment of tender beauty
In a harsh solitude
A fragile gift to an undeserving world.
Martha Renner

A Man

A man must stand alone to be a man
Abuse never escapes a man
Reality is when a man must be
Security is man's goal
Crying is his silence
Wandering is when he is forgot
Remembering he will always be true
Loving he is always filled
Regardless a man must stand alone
A man is a man

Spencer Colburn Scarborough

"Reality Of Fear"

Sometimes I am afraid...
Afraid to be alone,
For when I am alone,
I close my eyes and feel
  your presence.
Then, I open them that and
  you disappear.
When, I realize that you
  are not there,
My world turns to darkness,
  and I am afraid...
Afraid that you are gone forever.
Then, I wake from my dream,
And my fear is a reality.

Sharon A. Burke

Untitled

As I sit with the "Thing" so near
next to me.
I wave and I smack and I Yell
just to see.
To everyone's surprise I've changed
its demeanor.
All I wanted was for the children
to watch something cleaner.
Now they've all quieted down their
activity on pause.
Their vision is rivited by the
animal with great claws.
Quickly they forget the violent
show they had just seen.
They opt it for this show
now all is serene.

Frank M. Christofano

The Consummate Angel

If God were to create
A consummate angel,
Then grant her
The great gift of life.

He would not construe it.
He would just simply do it!
Then bless her,
With the great gift of life.

And should the breath
Of God's Angel,
Come here unto me,
And kiss my dark days
Into heavenly light.

Could I not help but worship
This angel so perfect,
The saviour of lost days
And lonely nights?

Diamond David King

At Times I Think I'm Crazy

Sometimes I even wonder
Why God put me here.
At times I think I'm crazy
That no one even cares.

I feel as if no one listens
To anything I have to say.
At times I think I'm crazy
That I'm not even here today.

I wonder if I left this world
If anyone would know.
At times I think I'm Crazy
That someday I may just go.

I realize this is an easy answer
To just go and take a dive.
At times I think I'm crazy
But I'd rather be alive.

Tiffany Kouri

Condemned

Their screams are silent,
Their thoughts ring out.
The dark so violent,
The day they shout.

Out of the light,
He must surely fall.
Into the night,
Blackness and all.

Judge and jury,
Guilty as sin.
Too much fury,
About to begin.

An angry glare
From sinner to saint.
The oddest pair,
Their contrast so faint.

Finally the end
To a tragic mess.
Our prayers we send,
May his soul be blessed.

Crissa Martin

Curtain Call

"All the world's a stage",
That's what some folks say;
And all of us are actors,
With parts in life's grand play.
Some think, all there's to it
Is wearing the right face;
Knowing our cue and lines;
Where to stand in place.
But, when the play is over,
And there are no curtain calls;
The crowd makes for the exit,
As the footlights brightness falls,
Thinking, we're just actors,
Only acting in a play,
"None of this is real;"
It doesn't matter anyway."
If that were true, we'd all be heroes;
Not a villain, nor a clown.
Life's real, get your act together,
Before they bring the curtain down.

Robert Keller

"Oh Dear Lord"

Oh Dear Lord, our prayers
please hear,
Today is the day, that
marks one year.
Since Jaycee Lee
was taken away,
from her friends and her family,
on that warm June day.
Our hearts still ache,
our eye's shed tears,
Oh Dear Lord be still our fears.
We must keep the faith,
In our hearts the hope.
That the day draws near,
when we will shed a different tear.
A tear of joy, upon Jaycees
return.
So in our hearts, we shall pray,
That soon we shall be blessed,
upon that day. Amen

Ranee Hinshaw

A Blackened Cloud

A blackened cloud
Has brought darkness
Into my world.
The once happy soul
Now mopes about
In utter silence.
A salty tear
And a quiet sigh,
Has escaped my tired body.
An agonizing pain
Is all that lurks
Within my weary heart.
A chilling breeze
Is all that flows
Through my weak veins.
No more use or time
To cry for help
Or even attempt to escape,
Because a blackened cloud
Has taken over my world.

Erin Marie Poma

Always

Yesterday -
I say I hate
you, I am hurt.

Today -
I say I want
you, I am playful

Tomorrow -
I say I need
you, I am scared

Always -
my heart
says I love
you. I just do!

Bridget Yakes

Victoria

Quite fair of face
With gentle eyes
Whose shy, retiring smile disguised
A lonely, lovely girl abides
With heart of peace
If opened wide
So we could gaze in, deep inside.

Graceful; Sensitive is her name
Softly, she is always there
With voice of love
She speaks my name
And I am gifted from above
My lovely, golden child of love.

Kay Martin

The Storm

There are no pinks and blues
   the sky is full of grays
The quiet sea is calm no more
   as it breaks on through the haze
The gentle breeze of yesterday
   is now a howling roar
The waves keep pace and crash
   upon the rocky shore
The sun has now decided
   to sleep a little late
"I'll warm the earth later;
   for now, it will have to wait!"

Andre P. Lavigne

"The Gift"

If I could give the world a gift,
It would be the gift of love.
All those who are sad,
I would make happy and glad.
All those who are ill,
I would create a fix-all pill.
All those empty tummies,
I would fill with lots of yummies.
My gift is one
That is sure to be fun.
The need for money wouldn't be,
Because my gift,
Would be free.

Krystle Robinson

Foxes Run In The Wild

The bluejay does not
Soar overhead like
The eagle. Rain falls
on the graves tonight.
Ghosts float through
the stones. Calling
upon your innocence.
Telling you to rescue
them one last time.
In a flash there
is lightening and
the graves are
illuminated and I
see her message
scrawled-come and
drink sweet
wine with me.

Jean Fitzgerald

My Heart

My heart is like a trampoline
bouncing love up and down
My heart is like gold
very great to have
My heart is made of emeralds
elegant and delicate
My heart will shine forever
like the sun and stars
My heart explodes when I'm sad
and glows when I'm happy
My heart beats hard and loud
like a drum
My heart is priceless
just like you and me

Daniel De Maria

Times Of Our Life

The first love we shared:
   Blissful.
The hours we were apart:
   Sadness.
The ever growing love:
   Warmth.
Days we let anger enter in:
   Estrangement.
Great comfort we gave each other:
   Strength.
Times we communicated tenderly:
   Maturity.
Touching the smiling face:
   Hoping.
Silent gaunt face of the last days:
   Fear.
I can only hope to remember all the
   times gone before.

Mildred I. Autio

Retrospect

A yellow room turned sour
and I
wished I hadn't closed my eyes
again and again and I
miss warm lips in the nape of my neck
and the hand that softened the day

But (strange) I don't mention the face
or remember colored eyes.
and I lost nothing
that I remember giving

Like the bills I found
in my winter coat
seasons later

Kendra L. Peyton

The Sundial

Time's frisbee,
Destiny's doorstop,
Fate's pizza cutter,
Life's frying pan,
Death's coat hook,
Reality's paperweight,
Just another little symbol,
For a big idea.

Brian J. McFillen

Still Life

Beautiful flower
Dead flowers
Masking your grave
We die among you
As you reach for the light
We sigh at the futility of your plight
Strangled as you grow
We mark ourselves so that we may know
Your elegant beauty
Leaning to the light
We are as one - we know now your might

Sharon D. Jones

Untitled

The birds were singing
The trees swaying back and forth
Everything peaceful

The cloudburst ending
Flowers beginning to bloom
Animals playing

Everything was great
Until mankind came along
Mother Nature weeps

Trees being cut down
Birds shot out of the blue sky
Animals dying

Ozone has a hole
Exhaust fumes from vehicles
All from pollution

The sky rains acid
Oil leaks killing animals
Damage, destruction

Lora Beth Seiverling

The Search

For eighteen years
I searched and looked.
I don't know
how many hours it took.

But I knew
deep down in my heart
that someday I would find you
from the very start

Then one morning
In late July
I stretched out
before my God and cried

God
In His great mercy and His grace
He lifted me up off my face

And before that day had become another
He reunited me
with my sweet mother.

Carol McClure

Riding

Some want to ride in tight, itchy
clothes like bobbing boards on a
rigid, perfectly trained animal.

I'd rather be riding in my loose
jeans and cowboy hat on a wild
stallion into the last few burning
red rays of a perfect sunset.

Jacqueline S. Campbell

Dreams

In a dream
   with my fear
All alone
   except for a tear

Frightened, I stood
   searching in the mist
I felt the warmth
   of your loving kiss

Unknowing -
   of what was to be
I finally woke up
   you were with me

Time went by
   so quickly in the wind
Escaping back -
   to what should have been

Again I awoke
   alive with the pain
Fearing forever
   never to see you again ...

Jode Cooley

This Gift

If I die in sleep tonight,
and I never see the morning light,

Please carry out this wish from me,
and take this gift I give to thee.

I wish to give you all my love,
and tell you you're from God above.

I wish you joy don't cry for me,
For in a Holy place I'll be.

Peaceful there forever more,
Lying inside heaven's door.

Robin Willson

I Loved You Very Much

Remember the time when we first met?
   The month of April wore pink blush.
Your eyes said, "I adore you."
   I loved you very much.

Remember when we married?
   Leaves of yellow danced in glee.
You vowed to loved forever,
   And I softly did agree.

Remember when you hit me?
   You said I was to blame.
You told me I was stupid,
   That my actions brought you shame.

Remember when I left you?
   And the children came along?
You had to know the plans you made,
   Were oh-so very wrong.

Remember when you killed me?
   And your money was your crutch?
Your tears of grief fell on my grave.
   I loved you very, very much.

Doreen Jones

Strength Within

One says "I am he,"
   But that's not who we see.
Each day goes by, he says "Hi."
   But as you walk,
He's there to stalk.
   Watching you as you go,
And you never know.
   You think a friend is he,
But that's only what the eye can see.
   Underneath it all,
He wants to see you fall,
   Down, down, beneath his feet,
Never in the victor's seat.
   But defeat him you will,
For your heart is not still.
   On the beat goes, the blood flows.
You will overcome and rise above,
   You have love.
Your heart beats to live, not to die,
   You will survive.

Tania Meck

Jesus Is The Light

Jesus is like a lighthouse
That stands upon a hill
And you can always see that light
While you are in his will.

Herod tried to put it out
But it was to no avail
And many since has tried it
But all have seemed to fail.

It was in the Garden of Gethsemane
That light shown bright as day
He prayed all night to his Father
To bring us a better way.

And there in Pilate's judgment hall
He could have been set free
But Jesus uttered not a word
And died for you and me.

But many years have come and gone
Man's life is full of sin
And when we see and obey that light
Our life will then begin.

Edward G. Ellifritt

Love

Love is a precious thing to
Start,
But, then again he always breaks
Your heart.

He thinks that you mean not a
Thing,
But, to you he means
Everything.

To you love means a
Lot,
But, to him it is
Not.

In the end it is all a
Mess,
But, after all it started
Like this.

Lisa Lindler

Alone

Alone in the dark
with no one to see
a soul with a heart
that has no where to be

She has no one to talk to
no where to cry
alone in the dark
living a lie

People want to care
and she knows they are trying
alone in the dark
just crying and crying

Everyone has someone
close to their heart
alone in the dark
with no where to start

Eileen Aki Marceau

Love Gone Wrong

It seems that it was only yesterday,
when I first loved you.
I tried always to be strong.
I see you now and wonder
why you stayed so long.
Did I take time to show
what you meant to me?
Did I take the time?
Was my shadow so great that it
was overpowering?
Was my shadow so weak there
was no form?
Was the man there?
Was the fear so great that my love
forgot to shine strong?
Where did I go wrong?

R. D. Schwartz

My Sister And The Telephone

   My sister and the telephone,
She won't leave it alone!
   "Bla, Bla, Bla, and Blee, Blee, Blee
Boys, Boys, Boys, Hee, Hee, Hee"
   My sister and the telephone,
She won't leave it alone!
   Not for 1 minute,
2 minutes,
3 minutes top,
All she does is talk, talk, talk!
   Take a walk,
Cheerlead,
Do something pleeaasee!
   My sister and the telephone,
She won't leave it alone!

Dominique Capone

Heart Puzzle

There was a time I felt sure of things
   that went through my mind
A roller coaster of emotions seems
   a little more down in motion
Devastation, puzzle pieces scattered
   of a whole heart that I continually
   gather to save every piece
I hold on to the pieces in the dark
One tiny piece stays lit enough to see
To rebuild the hearts of you and me.

Debbie Pont

Untitled

The left is seductive a safe haven
The sweetest of fruit, dark tabu
A constant whirl pool of thought have I
I'm sucked to the Bottom, yet I breathe
My lungs LAUGH and STING
The painted one draws a frown
and from his cheek -
Plummets a salty likeness of reality
The pure at heart are wolves within
See the demon cast a grin
Strangulation of a clown

Brady F. Robinson

Borstch "A La Russe"

To prepare a good borstch "a la Russe"
Just one dozen components you use:
WATER, SALT, HERBS, POTATOES,
ONIONS, CARROTS, TOMATOES,
LEMON, SUGAR (this last don't abuse).

(For "abuse" (overdo), by the way,
"Over-borstch" Russians normally say.
This linguistic digression
Should complete your impression
Borstch deserves a poetic essay!)

In a separate pot boil some MEAT.
To the vegetable add some READ BEAT
And some CABBAGE (cut both).
Stew them all. Add the broth.
All you need after this is: to eat!

Vladimir Strelnitski

Shadows In The Mind

At night I see her dreaming,
I reach, but she's not there,
I want to stop and tell her,
How much I truly care.
The mists of night descending,
Thru vapors I can see,
Her lovely face is smiling,
She means the World to Me.
Her image now grows clearer,
My heart begins to pound,
I seem to see her speaking,
Thru lips that make no sound.
The harder that I struggle,
Tho futile it may be,
I see her mouthing softly,
Sweet words, I only see.
I've finally come to realize,
It's Faith that I must find,
Our souls were always touching,
Like SHADOWS IN THE MIND.

Charles Costello

Untitled

   Last night when you held
me in your arms. I wished the night
would never end. Your touch was warm,
your kiss was like heaven. It was
all golden and precious memories.
   Today you're gone and I have
nothing to hold on too, but our
memories. I don't know for sure
if I'll ever see you again. But
I do know for sure that I will
always love you.

Donna Kay Cox

Untitled

This is a story about
   Our granddaughter
Kristen Elizabeth Dodd
Who is in the first grade.
She is seven years old,
   Is learning to read
And to print letters.
   She makes a perfect "m."
I told her I thought
   The letter "k" was wonderful.
I could hardly wait
   To learn how to write "k."
We were not taught to print.
   We were taught cursive writing.
Kristen does not live in a city.
   She lives in the country
Where her family has two dogs
   And four cats.
Kristen has a little brother,
   Matthew Aaron Dodd.

Dorothy Bieber Bliss

My Flower Garden

Out in the garden
Beneath the apple tree
Flowers grow
Just for me

There's purple ones
There's red ones
There's yellow ones too
There's pink ones and orange ones
Some are even blue

I planted them myself
One by one
People are quite impressed
By the work I've done

I will pick some out
To make some bouquets
I will put one on the table
To soak the sun's rays

Sara Forman

The Monster In My Life

The monster in my life
Annoys me everyday
It's crying all the time
If it doesn't get its way.
The environment's a disaster area
There's trash everywhere
Dirty dishes piling up
Its clothes show a tear.
Listening on my phone calls
Eating like a horse
It's pig style living
Is done with such a force.
Jealousy takes over
A smirk on its face
Screaming all to loudly
It's heard from anyplace.
Getting on my nerves
Its voice cuts like a knife
It's my little sister
The monster in my life.

Jessica Grisham

Untitled

Singing
of sweet sorrow
trebled voice like a songbird
tells of unseen feelings
A heart breaks
like the clinking of crystals
a piece forever gone
a bell tolls in the distance
the final embrace
of two lovers
the wind whistles
and adds to the song
by bringing cold rain
to dampen our warbler's throat
now aching with tears
Shadows fading
in to the distance
as the once lovers part
a dark, stormy night.

Sarah Williamson

My Sons

Sometimes I wonder
Where the years have gone
It seems so long
Since you guys left home
Sometimes I get lonely
Sometimes I'm sad
I wish I could go back
To some of the days we had
Cause all of you brothers
Were really such a joy
I didn't know how much
When you were all just a boy
But times marches on
And mines almost run out
But I hope you guys will try
To understand what life's all about
It's loving and caring
For your fellow man
It's not doing great things
But just the best that you can!

Helen Carswell

Fallen Sound

From where do I roam
When I have no home?
To whom do I speak?
I don't hear a peep.
Who is it that cares
Or meddles in my affairs?
What is it you desire
From one whose soul is on fire?
Do you dare to enter my world
Of the deceptions of a little girl?
Can you hear the screams
That come from my dreams?
I warn you not to open up!
Is it too late? Her world is corrupt!!

Heather Crowell

Spring Has Sprung!

One morning I go outside,
I see some things that weren't
There before. Flowers are in bloom,
Trees are green, and it is Spring!
It is warmer, not cold like in,
Winter.
Why yes, yes, it's Spring!

Adrienne D'Ulisse

Rift

Creeping
Crawling
Falling through the cracks
Fingers' cuts gaping
Grasping for a hold
Clawing at the earth
Barren of purchase
Dirt, sand, rock
Sifting
Drifting
Past my eyes
Closing my lungs
Raking my throat
Choking on my panic
And plummeting deep within myself
To die

Kenneth F. Penttinen

Accept Me

For what I am
not what I could have been
or even will be
Accept me.
Acceptance must be present tense,
   with no conditions,
     and based upon reality.
If windows of your heart
   must rosy - tinted be
     you have not accepted me.
See me as I am
   without distortion of your dreams...
A human being, beautiful, unique.
Free to grow
   according to the seed within myself.
Accept me
   so I need not twist myself
     to fit your pattern...
But resting in acceptance,
   can grow.

D. W. Pullin

Someday Soon

As I sit here on my cloud
I look down and think aloud
Maybe one day they will see
And they will truly come
   to me

I came down and gave
   them love
I came down just like
   a dove
I came down and died
   for them
And somebody soon I'll
   come again.

Renee N. Benson

So Called Planet

Good men die most everyday,
while bad men always get their way
and all of us, confused since birth,
on this so called planet Earth.

Poor men die with humble cries,
all from others greed and lies,
and our life, what's its worth?
on this so called planet Earth.

Adam Halverson

Untitled

My days of happiness
seemed at an end
till I saw the beauty
within.
I never did see
one pretty as she
who captured my heart
with a posing part
I never believed she
would love me
till I asked her to be mine
she said "that would be fine"
And to this day
Whatever may be
will always
live in my heart
as she lives in my mind
which would be just find
if only it weren't a dream.

Loren Stanley

Return

The soft green hills
Clothed extravagantly
with stately trees;
interrupted beautifully
with jeweled lakes,
lured me deeply
as medusa lured the seaman.
but my treasure
is pure delight
not a sirens' song.
A beloved embrace
tried, not found wanting
only waiting
to fill the void
created by my absence.
my heart is still
and in the stillness
listens to God's voice
where first I heard it
here in Shangri-La.

Carol Guild

The Mighty Man

The sun like a pierced heart
bled across the heavens,
spilling over the mountains
into the valley, where death
was not haste in its merciless
hour, nor lacking in its
primordial power.

No breath did stir,
save for the breath
of Eleazar, who, still
cleaving his sword,
swaying on a heap of twisted,
battered, and butchered
Philistine flesh and armor —

Parted his dry, blood cracked lips,
his utterance rising above the
black smoke of burning chariots:

"Hear, O Israel, Jehovah our God
is One Jehovah!"

Jesse D. McGowan

Shattered Heart

My heart is like broken glass
shattered upon the cold, hard ground.
Its pieces are sharp,
and stab the insides of my soul.
If that there was some force
to mend the broken glass.
You would find the empty space
where one heart's piece once was.
The place where love's loss
struck the shattering blow.
A piece, whose being gone,
Lets love's sweet life run out.
Leaving the empty shell of a man
you see before you.

Timothy Bailey

Picture

A moment in time
  One moment
    Held
Held captive in a picture
Feelings felt
(Missing line it was cut)
Feelings captured in a picture
Feelings never again felt
  The same way
    But yet
Forever captured in a picture
Feelings other's didn't feel
  But yet
Forever captured in a picture

Bridget M. Bird

Untitled

I have spoken words of wisdom,
But you did not hear.
Have I not shown you the way?
But you could not follow.

The angels sang in harmony.
You didn't sing along.
And when prayers weren't answered
Your anger became strong.

Feelings from the heart
That must come from within the soul;
Like a lost sheep
Not knowing which way to go.

I am always here.
Your faith you need to find.
And I will always love you
Till the end of time.

Joseph Dowdrick

Covenant

Your saintly scholars penned your deed
"O saving victim" to behold

Pray come to we so much in need
Unworthy letters' glories told

Of humble heart and manner meek
Eternal gift we long to own

Of your great source we dare not speak
The father's wheat so loving sown

Body- bread of life the sacred host
Blood- shed before the ages
Soul- we take you in we dare to boast
Divinity-Rule us bring us near
To lose you now our greatest fear

Michael A. Gibson

Death

A million ways to die
I think all the time
But one to choose
Is so hard to decide
Maybe I'll drink some pills
And sleep my life away
Maybe I'll slit my wrist
Till my blood runs away
Maybe I'll take a gun
And put it to my head
Then pull the trigger
And I'm instantly dead
But that's too much blood
And a hassle to buy
Cause I know a guy who did it
Did he really want to die?
A million ways to die
In this world today
But to choose one and why
Is hardest I say

Victoria Rodriguez

Road To Nowhere

Where does the road to nowhere lead?
No one really knows.
Though many travel down its path
We don't know where it goes.

It doesn't lead to good or bad
Or right or wrong decisions.
Although I think it may fulfill
What each of us envisions.

Maybe the road to nowhere
Is a tool for us to use
To take a rest while we decide
Which path that we should choose.

One may not fare too well if he
Should choose to stay too long
On the road to nowhere, though.
It's not where we belong.

To me the road to nowhere,
It leads everywhere, you see.
But the somewhere that it takes us
Is up to you and me.

Darlene W. Stark

Short One Angel

I saw you for the first time
Standing near the hall
Your spirit took control of me
Nearly walked into a wall

I wanted to meet you soon
A mutual friend we had
My mind wouldn't let me forget you
And I'm sincerely glad, cause

Short one angel, darling
Heaven has got to be
But I've been blessed, oh yes
Cause you've been sent to me

I did something that
I've never ever done
Proposed to you immediately
I still think you're the one

So if that wonderful day ever comes
If you decide that I'm the one
Be ready to accept all my love
Cloudy skies will give way to the sun.

Perry Farmer

When I Was a Child...

When I was a child
I had peaceful sleep
Uninterrupted by dreams
Except for those of Santa Claus
Now I hardly sleep at all
I toss and turn
Caused by an active mind
Wondering about things undone
And those that cannot be changed
Things that were said
And the moments of silence
Of what life has in store for me-
And the secrets it still holds

Rachel Thompson

The Orphan

It's lonely being an orphan,
Not knowing where you'll be.
Will I be here tomorrow?
Will I be going away?
I hear the kids at school say,
"What place does she call home?"
I get my things and walk away,
I feel so all alone.
The kids whose parents keep them
Are as lucky as can be.
But someday soon I'll have a mom.
A mom whose just for me.
So parents please, take time to hold
the hands
Of husbands, wife, or child
And let them see and feel your love.
In kisses, hugs and smiles.
Be grateful that you have a child
And keep them by your side.

Vivian B. Caldwell

Changing Of The Seasons

Now that summer has passed,
The cold brisk air sets in.
The leaves change from...
Green to yellow;
Yellow to orange;
Orange to red;
And red to brown.
Winter is approaching fast
And soon all will be lost
Under that glittering blanket of snow.

S. A. Hoover

A World Without Love

Love, there is no such thing,
It is only an illusion,
one person's fantasy,
everyone's dream.

How can it be...
A world without love?

But as long as there are dreams,
Illusions, and fantasies,
Everyone will hope to find love...
The impossible link
between illusion and reality.

Crystal D. Trivette

Flower Power

I am a little flower
Imbued with flower power.
Artists like to paint me
With as many faces as Eve.
In colors of the rainbow
I freely my beauty bestow.
In green kingdom on earth
I preside over new birth.
My task is making seed,
A miracle the hungry feeds.
With our Creator's help, we know,
Farmers plant seed in fields to grow.
With work, sunshine and the rain
There is harvest of fruit and grain.
I breathe the air that you breathe.
Please keep it pollutant free.
Drink from same cup of water,
Purity is need of flower power.
Take care of the environment,
Your children's future endowment.

Rachel Stephens

I Have

I have openly challenged
both earth and sky
without ever once
stopping to ask why

I have taken on mountains
in full force
I have chased distant rainbows
to their very source

I have moved like the wind
upon magical skis
And have felt the cool crispness
of a winter's breeze

I have traveled slopes
where virgin powder ran deep
And those too far to reach
I have traveled in my sleep

And I have stood on endless mountain
with foot in ski
And gazed in awe
at all this - that God has given me

Jeffrey A. Jackson

The New World

Imagine yourself in a world
with no sorrow.
When present day problems will
not be remembered and joy will
abound for every tomorrow,
The sun shines brightly all
over the earth and mankind
is freed from sin's ugly curse.
See the children playing until
their heart's delight stroking
the lion's great mane without
any fear or dreadful fright.
Envision people of all races living
and working as one while basking
under the sun.
Hear the birds melodious tunes
as you behold your friends and
loved ones rise from the tombs.
This is the new world.

Damian Aguila

The Slaughter

Millions are slaughtered,
millions are slain.
They may not be talking
but I know they're in pain.

Butchered in minutes,
what purpose is life,
if all they have to look forward to
is misery and strife?
Michael Rusinko

Teasings

Like the seasons,
Life is teasings.

After winter,
Comes the Spring,

Hopeful of what,
Life will bring.

Summer's exciting,
Warm and inviting.

And when autumn sighs,
We harvest our lives.

And like the seasons,
Life has been teasings.
Michael G. Andrus

A Message To The Great Lakes

I sing my praise high to thee,
O, Great Waters of the North.
In unison with the sea gulls
that govern thy brilliant sky.
Mine is but an insignificant voice
among those of living things
whose bodies and souls
thy generosity has nurtured.
Fly high, all of you in flocks,
soar to the clouds,
you guardians of the Great Waters.
Tell your Master of my message.
Come back,
and bring your Master's words,
for I will be here,
waiting faithfully
on her white sandy beaches.
Anna Maria Siti Kawuryan

Two Hearts

I think of you often
More often than I should
I met you ago
Though it seems like a lifetime
You loved me for who I was
I loved you back
We were together, forever,
I hoped.
But someone came between us,
Someone, I don't know
And drove the two of us apart,
Away from each other,
Breaking my heart.

Now we're together again
Each day I learn to love you more
Once again, more than I should.
I hope to stay together-forever-
With no one in between us,
Between our two hearts.
Toni Lee Krafft

A Fool Of A Friend

I have a friend
who is doing some bad stuff,
Oh, how do I tell him,
he no longer looks buff?

By doing these things,
he thinks he is cool,
I try to tell him,
but he is such a fool.

A fool not to listen,
A fool not to care,
I know I will lose him,
and it does not seem fair.

He thinks they will do no harm,
-but they will,
and he doesn't even stop,
to see how I feel.

I don't want to lose him,
He is such a good friend,
but if he keeps this up,
I will in the end.
Brandy Wood

Mother To Child

I am you.
You are me.
　We
　Are
　One.
When we were born,
Our world began.
When one dies, the other cries,
"I
　Am
　One."
And my world goes on.
Joy McQueen

A Single Rose

This perfect rose so
Beautiful and bright,
Stands straight up
With no problems in height
Each petal is perfectly formed
Each thorn is perfectly
sharp in every way
Its leaves are so
Green and full
But as the days goes by
And the rose is beginning to die
The petals begin to drop
And the leaves begin to flop
Soon this perfect rose
Has disappeared in life itself
Sandra Middleton

Untitled

She lies beneath a willow tree,
Thoughts, mind, vision.
Wind breaks,
clouds collide, rain.
Rainbow color dimension of time.
She lies understands little a man.
Eyes swirling piercing colliding aging.
Time, place, middle a race.
Hair a flame gold shiver no pain.
Love, respect.
Yellow a color. Joy.
David De Assumpcao

I Wonder

I wonder why men of today,
Wonder why men of yesterday,
Named the sun, the moon
and stars.
And many other things
there are.
I wonder why they named
the trees.
The birds and flowers, ants
and bees.
I wonder why they named
they fruits
and vegetables that don't wear
boots.
And as I wonder and look back
To many, many years ago,
I seem to wonder why
they lacked
To say, I wonder why I
named it so.
Violet Forrest

Sugar

Curved tail
Sharp toenails
Loyal and loving
Playful and shoving
Bad and naughty
Short and haughty
Mysterious eyes
Full of love that never hides.
Kathleen Frey

Easter Morning

Bells chime and tell a story
Hail Jesus birth, and holy glory.

We love you Lord, how sweet you are
Radiant, pure bright as a star.

Oh Lord, so much you did love us
Nailed to a cross and died above us.

A huge round rock has moved away
Christ had risen on this day.

Hearts singing with heavenly praise
Upon this day he did raise.
Freeing us all from mortal sin
New life received just from him.
Cleanse me Lord, my heart today
Forgive my weakness I do pray.
Blessed Lord, our mighty king
In humble song and praise we sing.
A loving God always be
Crucified for all and set us free.
Jack A. Rogers

Shackled

Stifling steel boxes,
Iron igloo transports,
No clarity in confine,
Behind the cold glass shine,
Hunting hollow obligations.

Childhood's end of fantasy,
Flashing youth, fleeting dreams,
The surround of clocks are clicking.
The toil and folly are found.
False passion to fire the line.
Click ta ta... Click ta ta
Am I to follow in time?
Simon Gordon

Untitled

I write because
   You can't read

I sing because
   You can't hear

I scream because
   You can't listen

You think they are
   On your side

But they laugh at you because
   You can't feel
Jessica Guerin

Verity

Your hand hath taken me
to an ardent place of solitude,

Tranquil running waters of Life
Compensate for the roughness.

Passionate thoughts of us has
caused an eruption of emotions
which cannot be held back,
the surge has taken its toll
upon this tabernacle.

The mirror of life hath reflected
verity therefore I have peace within.

It was then at that moment
I realize love has its own touch.

The mark of perfection
The embodiment
The superlative moment
is now
Maxine Brockington

Nature

Lies down a lush rich carpet of
emerald over the coppery earth, and
paints the night sky a brilliant
sapphire. Bright metallic stars border
the night, brightened by the pale
golden moon. A bundle of soft
smoky clouds blanket the earth,
lulled to sleep by the soft sighs of
the night wind. Twilight tags
along with the moon, tip toeing
across the sky, hiding from the
sun peeking above, the horizon.
Aroused by the sunlight, blossoms
stretch and yawn, greeting the new day.
Rachelle Gines

I sit

In the tree,
I sit.
Watching the
leaves blow by.

While I sit,
I feel the breeze.
All alone,
I feel so free.

All my problems
are carried away.
So where I sit,
I will stay.
Phyllis Burgess

Haunting Flames OF The Past

While sitting in my chair,
My eyes wondered in a great stare.
The fire, the source of light,
Danced with flames of the night.
My eyes began to see,
Faces of the past in the red flames,
That dealt with me.

Oh' the past came back!
There I see their shadows in black!
Pain, suffering, and the joy I lack!
Was in my mind.
It all came back!

Sorrow was with me,
It was always to be.
Before there was joy and love.
Then came death and over took
My dove — along with me.
All has haunted me,
And the past will never leave me,
Without she
C. Jared Ragsdale

Pain

Pain, pain, pain -
How can we remain sane?
There is medication for certain places,
Pain decreases in some cases.
Treated with medicine may cure in time,
Without recurring down the line.

Pain, pain, pain -
How can we remain sane?
No cures in sight,
Which would give us delight.
There's suffering that's never gone,
Until our duty is done.

Pain, pain, pain -
How can we remain sane?
Researches give us hope,
So we can cope.
Faith in our God Being,
Helps us in our seeing.
June E. Smith

A Shadow

A shadow moves
in the dark it doesn't
talk it just does what you do.
Natalie Prouty

Future's Chances

As the current quickly drags you
and you try to gasp for air,
you are pulled back in life's forces
with tender loving care.
You will take the chance of downfall
as you look into the depths
and you know you can't resist it,
so you take the next few steps.
You're fragile and uncertain,
but there are possibilities.
So grab the future's chances
and see what you're to be.
Theresa Courteau Moore

The End

Trust,
Understanding,
Caring,
Sharing,
Happy,
Loved,
A sudden change.
Confused,
Alone,
Depressed,
Hurt,
Unloved,
The end of a relationship.
Jodi Scheff

If Only I Had A Chance

If only I had a chance to do
it again,

I would...

Walk a little straighter;
Talk a little softer;
Smile a little more;
Work a little harder:
Live a little sweeter;
Endure the task,
   without reasons to ask;
Not complain
   when times as blue.

But most of all,

I would say,
"I Love You"
Every time I had a chance.

If only I had a chance.
Jeffery L. Hariston

"Theater Of The Absurd"

The bakery is out of watermelon,
And my pockets are full of rain,
The whole world has gone crazy,
No normalcy remains,

It's the dogs that walk their masters,
And books that read themselves,
There's pepper on the ceiling,
And buildings on the shelves,

The world is really flat,
I know, I've sailed the edge,
It's 120 degrees outside,
But still, snow on the hedge,

The guns all committed suicide,
At the state of world peace,
The rich lock their cardboard doors,
As the poor sit down to feast.
Nichole D. T. Greiner

God Saw Me An Angel

God send me an angel
With golden wings sand halo,
One with caring eyes
Of sympathy an love
Someone to hold me an rock me
Take all my fears away
Show me the way to tomorrow
Away from the storms of today
Sara Cook

The Rainy Day

The sky was dull and gray as lead
As far as I could see,
And heavy was my soul with dread
As rain fell silently.

It never stopped, it never paused
All through the day it fell,
And all this gloom and grayness caused
My deepest fears to swell.

But while my fear increased in size
The rain began to stop,
And in my dark and weary eyes
The sunbeams gently dropped.

Away with dread! For as I gazed
Above the stately trees,
I stood with awe and in amaze...
A rainbow smiled at me!

Leah Vincent

My Uncle Jason

I do not understand....
Why my Uncle Jason got cancer,
Why he had to die,
Why I never got to see him
But most of all I do not understand why
my grandma gives me his old things,
because I think she should keep them.
But what I do understand most is
heaven, because he has somewhere
peaceful to go.

Emily McKay

Trapped

They usually just
Yell and scream
He's a walking nightmare
Not just a bad dream

We are held here against
Our own free will
With an occasional threat
To strike or kill

I wish the pain would
Just go away
Me and my mom, I know,
Will leave him someday

Ba-bye Daddy
There is no doubt
Three strikes and
You're out

ShaRhonda Rushin

Jacqueline

Tell me if you believe in magic
And I will cast you a spell
Tell me if you feel love in your heart
And I'll know I cast it well
If I could wave my magic wand
And make everything all right
Would you give to me your love
Would you walk into my light
My magic is neither black or white
I'm just a wizard of the heart
I know you can feel my energy
Yours is as strong as mine
Together we would both be stronger
Let us sip on life like wine

Jeffrey S. Grow

Two Brothers

Two brothers once served in sequence
   to implement a dream
of brotherhood for all men
   within our national scheme.

To right injustices wrongs
   was the work that they began.
But death which canceled fruition
   in truth revealed each man.

Twice a cruel assassin
   submerged this nation deep in grief
Stilling voices which had taught us
   to "believe in belief."

They rest, preceding destiny,
   beneath a flickering flame.
Two hundred million mourners
   deny guilt and share the shame!

Lois M. Williams

Night Rain

The wind
like a lover's fingers
rustles my hair
and sends silly shivers
down my neck and spine

Sweet deodorant from earth
flares my nostrils and channels
electric messages of rain

Night echoes
doors bang
lightening flashes
and dead leaves dance in the air

With swift determination
nature assaults this silent night
and sends me cover-groping
huddling in the corner of my bed
wishing you were here

Karen Ann Burke

Do Cowboys

Do Cowboys have to clean their room,
Or straighten up their bed?
To hold a mop in calloused hands
must fill his heart with dread.
A cowboy's hands were made for
ropes, for branding, building fence!
Not cleaning floors, washing clothes,
waxing, dusting vents.
When I grow up I'll be a cowboy
ornery, strong and tough,
But as for now my mother says
I have to do this stuff!
I clean my room, I brush my teeth
I even comb my hair.
Do cowboys have to do these things?
Do the dogies even care?
When I grow up I'll do the things
that cowboys like to do!
And when I have kids they probably
will ask these questions too!

Rick Beckner

"Conflict"

What was
And what is
Mix not
What was is past
With hope
Remaining there
What is presides
Yet what was lurks near

Ambivalence rules

What is must reign
What was must disappear
With faith
With love
With prayer
What is overpowers
What was
Fades away

Jason P. Geoffrion

Heaven Is My Home

The time is drawing nigh
For God's children to go home

The gates of pearl are opening
As the Angels sing their song

Weep no more my children
For the streets of gold are warm

Your house is lit with laughter
And your family feels no harm

There will be no more suffering
As Gabriel blows his horn

The gates of pearl are opening
For God's children to go home.

Wanda Williams

The Park

I like to play
at the park everyday.
It is fun
especially in the sun.
I like the slide
because down it I will glide.
On the swings I go high
it feels like I can fly.
The merry-go-round goes around
by feet that touch the ground.
I also like to climb a tree.
When I do the whole park I can see.

Denise Hickman

Untitled

Dear Lord, you brought a lady
named Debbie into my life.
She is full of smiles and
an appreciate of life.
Her eyes are like smiles;
never a frown, and if you
guide her my way,
I'll never let her down.
So, if you give her the
confidence to trust in
me, that would make
me so very happy.

Scott H. Bremner

Our Country

The crown of justice
There is a lack, I dare to say;
Under the sun, this cloudy day.

Bring forth your light my
precious moon, I fear
the sun attacks you soon.

Freedom lingers, somewhere in
between, just rest a while
and gain back your self esteem.

Say, I like the way look behind
that fancy book. But
aren't your pages a little
torn and scattered?

Hurry, hurry precious moon,
there is a lack, I dare
to say, I feel the heat,
under the sun this cloudy day.

Betty J. Tennyson

Seven Fifteen Four

Seven fifteen four
 we need you
Seven fifteen four
 Where are you?
Seven fifteen four
 Do you exist?

Seven fifteen four
 Why are we down?
Seven fifteen four
 Why aren't you around?

 We need you now
 All of the people know how.
 "It's that simple."

Seven fifteen four
 we need you
Seven fifteen four
 Where are you?
Seven fifteen four
 Do you exist?

Joe O'Cañas

"One Perfect White Rose"

I only have one true love,
He's Perfect in every way.

My love for him is unique,
Just like the white snowflakes.

Every moment I think of him,
My heart blossoms like a rose.

So, I give to you my love,
"one perfect white rose"

Jeanine Gacek-Marcheschi

The River

There's You.
And there's me.
And then there's this river.
And just like the river
We don't know where we're going.
Fate will take us to where were going.
And we will end up in the same place
As the river.
Somewhere.

Amanda Sheley

Us

What will become
become of Us
with U I have no worries-
no cares

When it's over
all I think
all my thoughts are Us-
what will we become

Forever I wait
eternally I'm patient
till I die-
I'll think of us

Laura Grant

Love Is Free

The love of the soul
Is very hard to show
For when we love
From deep within
It's hard to let them know

We've made these rules
And standards
Of just how love should be
When God gave of his
Love he meant it to be
Free!

Terri Muraoka

"T.V. Screen"

Box you in my living room,
not so much that lives here now,
cherished knowledge we assume,
the chance to never ask.

Wooden box,
brass gold handle,
station break,
break my concentration.

And my fixed stare relaxes,
into a tear,
pry away eyes,
I cover my ear.

Words in and out, what do you mean?
What our thoughts have expressed,
what our eyes have seen,
wasting the moment on a T.V. screen.

Lawrence Mark

Why Lord?

Why Lord did You let me stay
When all things said I'd go away?
My heart and brain were all worn out
I could not talk or laugh or shout.
Within the hour my time would come
And You would gently take me home.
The room was filled with tears and Love
My family tried to rise above
The fact that Death would soon be here
To take me to that other sphere
Where I would be forever free
To answer only unto Thee.
I need to know what I must do
To dedicate this life to You.
I need to find Your plans for me
From here until eternity.

Elizabeth A. Terwilliger

Mr. Kurt Cobain

Inside myself I hold you tight,
for your death is around me tonight.
 I can feel the speed,
you said you once need.
 As they report your death,
I lost my breath.
 You had moved me with your words.
I wipe my tears away,
 Now I can't choose my way.
I followed your songs until the end,
 my heart shall never mend.
Now that you're gone,
 I still can't say so long.
So Mr. Kurt Cobain, here I come,
 because without you,
I'm going insane.
 Oh, Mr. Kurt Cobain.

Nicole Gigliotta

"Heavenly Nest"

Under your wings
is where I want to be
hiding in the shadow
of the "Almighty"

I place my trust
into your hands
growing in faith
I will learn to stand

Keep me protected
O' great "I am"
Cover me with your blood
O' "spotless lamb'

Guide me Holy Spirit
lead the way
help me to follow
until the day,

My soul reaches Heaven
And I can rest
in my new home,
my "Heavenly Nest."

Tracy Ward

Maybe Tomorrow

Maybe tomorrow
I'll take a walk
I'll ask you to join me
so we can talk.

Maybe tomorrow
we'll see what we've missed
we may even remember
the first time we kissed.

Maybe tomorrow
we'll talk about why
we've let so many moments
just pass us by.

Maybe tomorrow
we'll see how fast
our present becomes
our distant past.

Maybe tomorrow
lives only in dreams
tomorrow is never
as close as it seems.

Shelly Hepp

The Diminishing Light

The fire was diminishing
one day in our lives
So we tell our selves
it is not real, But we don't know
what the future holds for us!

The fire was gone
for the both of us now
Lord tell me what to do now
I miss her so much!

"Now I am trying to
get back on my feet
one step at a time
I tried to get over you
someday we will be together
in the Lords home"

"I know that
the diminishing light
is like a door in the Wind"
Patrick Cannon

The Breath Of God

Have you ever felt really sad
And you didn't know what to do?
And then all of a sudden,
Strange feelings came to you?

Did you ever ask yourself
What was it that you felt,
That made you want to talk to God
And on your knees you knelt?

Have you ever stopped to wonder
As the wind whispered past your ears,
That it might only be God speaking
That you actually did hear?

Let God be the master of your mind;
For if to this you yield,
No matter what you face
With love you shall be filled.

So do not fear when you feel it.
It's everywhere you trod.
Accept it for what it is.
Tis only the breath of God.
Victoria Rende

Nature

Nature lifts our spirits
In a quiet sort of way.
Just by being there for us
On each and every day.

Flying birds and budding trees
Fill up our world with joy.
Showing us rare beauty
That we can all enjoy.

Listen to the whistling wind,
Or the hum of rustling leaves.
And hear a meadowlark in song.
What beauty its song weaves.

So always turn to Nature
When things get out of hand.
And take the time to look and see
This gift that's oh so grand.
Sheila B. Roark

Untitled

I long for love
I long for him
For some reason
My soul is drawn towards him
There is a part of him
That makes me whole
I can't give him up
Even if I get hurt
He is something I dream about
My anger towards him
Ceases when he smiles
My lust for him
Grows when he touches me
My heart aches
When he walks away
When I am with him
I am happy
I long for his
love.
Devin Chase

I'll Ride On

The wind is blowing through my hair
As I race through the valley.
My hands sweating
As I hold the reins
So tightly.

I'm going so fast
That my heart skips a beat.
The breath has been taken from my body.
I feel like I'm racing the wind
On my horse.
We are one together.
We are going much faster than the wind
And Ohhh! We've won!

I close my eyes
And let my horse take control.
With the wind blowing
Through my hair,
I'll ride on.
Amy Dutil

Await

To she who knows my soul
A rose who fills my life
You've touched my lonely heart
And calmed my inner strife

I long for your embrace
And though to war I'm sent
My thoughts are always of you
For my body holds your scent

My dear Princess beloved
Though apart our fate is such
I'll return to our kingdom
And relive our music's touch

Be still my cherished Eve
For soon with you I'll be
A symphony will I write
For your heart doth rest in me
Antonio Tambunan

A Place Called Mother

I'm spoiled not of mind
Given to me by
The most beautiful
Of my kind.

Taught myriads of lessons in life,
I am your neophyte. For I
Adhere to whom negates my strife.

It is you, one of many
But when I take notice
You are not just any.

For my blood is yours
Sacred and rich, from the
Source of which it pours.

A land of no other.
But that which is fertile,
A place called mother.
Beynamaan Dominick

Sky

Ocean in the air
bearing waves of white smooth foam
swimming fish with wings
singing their beautiful songs
and waving down to the earth
Monica Galarneau

Befriending Death

I know not where
or when she comes.
I only know the sad sacred mark
She leaves upon her leaving.
Her name is death.

I know her well.
She is my steady companion.
Enemy to the young and vibrant.
Friend to the old and sick.
Her paradoxes confound me.

I both love and hate her.
I welcome her at times
with open arms.
I berate her with curses
when her timing is cruel.

In my line of work
I have no choice
but to befriend her.
I hope she will befriend me
when my time comes.
The Rev. Joan E. Beilstein

Owl

In the darkness of the night
An owl flew
Across the sky
His silhouette
Barely visible
In the darkness of the night
His call
So clear
In the darkness of the night
He's gone
By first light
But he will be back
Tomorrow
In the darkness of the night
Kymberly Markowitz

My Confidant

My friend, my confidant
   Where have you come from
   Where will you go
My friend, my confidant
   How long have you been there
   How long will you stay
My friend, my confidant
   Why do you treat me so good
   Why do you care
My friend, my confidant
   Some days you bring a smile
   Some days you show sorrow
My friend, my confidant
   My angel in disguise
   My reason for tomorrow
My friend, my confidant
   Please stay right there
   at least for a while

Tammy Lee

Walk Through A Child's Mind

Come with me my child,
and I will show you many things.
For there are wonders in this place,
like a sailing fish that sings.
Just walk with me awhile,
and open up your mind,
and if I seem a little harsh,
please know that I am kind.
And when I let go of your hand,
let all your senses free,
and experience all the wonders,
even though you cannot see.
Let me lead you through,
the deep recesses of your mind,
and know the images you see,
and transcending space and time.
Let the aura that surrounds you,
lead you to the light,
and when you open up your eyes,
truly know the gift of sight.

Gerard Walker

When The Sun Goes Down

When the sun goes down,
Shadows and sorrow
Fill the cold crisp air
Of a winter night.

When the sun goes down,
I wait...and I wait
For the coming dawn
that seems far away.

When the sun goes down,
I glance at the sky
To look for a sign
Of our last sunset.

When the sun goes down,
I recall my friend
Whose pain and sorrow
Were too much to bear.
He went to his sunset,
When the sun went down.

Catherine Rutherford

Angel

Who saw the
swan floating by?
Who saw the
stars in the
Bright sky?
Who saw my
Father pass
away! Die?
Who saw my
family sit down
and cry?
Who saw the
tears drop from
my eyes?
Who saw the
Angels drop
from the sky!
To pick up his
soul and say
goodbye!!!!

Crystal Neiderman

Soulful

Mountains so high,
   but not high enough.
Your eyes, set fire to my soul.

Blooms of roses,
   dripping with rain.
Your heart, springtime unfolds.

Ocean waves,
   moving endlessly.
Your touch, my spirit controlled.

Separation,
   for untold memories.
Your kiss, one I behold.

Esther Ilosky

Flickering Fire

Flickering fire,
Jump and dance.
Casting shadows on the wall.
Burning slowly through the night.
Slowly but surely everything falls.
Jump jump fizz and pop.
Jump jump burn and fade away.
Flickering fire,
Jump and dance.
Burning around the ring.
Around the circle of life we go,
And never say a thing.
Jump jump fizz and pop.
Jump jump burn and fade away,
Like the flickering fire.

Owen Patrick West

Thistles In The Wind

A moment ago, was now.....
... just a moment ago.
Why do we let these moments slip away
Like thistles in the wind?
Never to return.
Other thistles come...but not the same,
And then move on, the way they came,
These Thistles,
in the Wind.

Joylette L. Portlock

Daughters

No longer my small children
Adults you have become
Young men have come to claim you
As wives you're now to be

The chain of life continues
Each link a place in time
Now your small children we do love
The joy begins anew

I've been a daughter, wife and mother
Now grandmother I am
The chain of life continues
Goes on and on and on

Lorraine Probst

Untainted Kiss

Your smile is like a cup of honey
   Smile again,
So I can taste the sweetness
   of your
   lips...

Nonie J. Wishon

Black Fear

Her life is black,
like tainted blood,
she stole from me,
more than she understood;

It hurt so much,
it was pure pain,
it nearly drove me,
completely insane;

She has no conscience,
she has no fear,
I loved her once,
ever so dear,
but then she betrayed me,
she left me for dead,
lying hurt,
in that black bed;

Now one of these days,
I will make her pay,
then what will she do,
then what will she say?

Brian Steinbach

Wolves In Sheep's Clothing

Wolves in sheep's clothing,
with picnic baskets,
standing along the lane.

Offering goodies they know
that you want, they try
to seduce you to sin.

If, you take the first bite,
it's to their delight,
you'll sin again, and again.

Wolves in sheep's clothing,
with picnic baskets,
look like ordinary men.

Stephanie C. Nosacek

Thankful

There is someone very dear
Someone who is always near.
As we work and as we play, he is
watchful through the day.
The beauty of his wonders
surrounds us,
The sky he paints will always
astound us.
So let's be thankful from day
to day
For just as long as he lets us
stay.

Margaret Riley

Ode On Sure

I assure you
I am unsure
Shall I ensure
Or insure?
Y sure!

Dorothy M. Seipel

Look Up - Look Down - Look All Around

What keeps the flame burning
I wonder day-to-day
The sun has the answer
No words, just warming rays

Before day breaks, I think
What draws me to my feet
The earth knows where I stand
And where the lines will meet

I feel the answer's near
Gazing through childish eyes
Watching my children play
Puts to rest all the why's

David A. Bolks

The Robin In The Snow

Which way to go
The robin in the snow.
North, South, East or West
I wonder which way is the best.

I know it's time to build my nest
To lay some eggs, and all the rest.

But Mother Nature has her plan
To keep snow on New England land
The daffodils and crocuses try
To open up and see the sky.

I'll have a chat with Mother "N"
To bring the spring up here again
And make the snow go far away
So all my friends and flowers can stay!

Lea M. Neal

Beauty

Unseen beauty is beauty denied.
 If it can lift us to untold heights,
Then why not capture
 The moment of rapture.

Man trods too close to earth
 And cannot lift his spirit.
Then nature's design bestows
 That rare elixir to all mankind!.

Michael Garfield

Cocaine

We were in the abandoned
  warehouse;
It was silent, too quiet.
No one moved, we just listened.
The white powder tingled;
It hurt the very first time.
He sniffed it off the table
He choked.
"It feels nice, "he said." It
really makes me fly."
He said to try it.
I told him no!
He pressured me again.
I still said "No"!
I ran out of the warehouse,
As fast as I could.
Only to awaken to read
the newspaper;
And find him dead.

Emily Lukitsh

Vanishing

There is a special type of person.
They are becoming few;
who are immense,
and equal no other.
They are the vanishing.

Aside from the necessity
they have no opposite side.
They are unbeatable in bond and trust.
Their absence is the norm,
which will crash from existence
at first down of hope and trust.

The absence is extinguishing
our special ones fast.
They break down all the love,
which holds our world as one.
Be a vanishing.

Save us!

Brandi Phipps

Fancy Colours

Purple is the color of Lent
Yellow is what Easter sent.

Red is the wine we take
Tan is the bread we break.

Green is around Christmas time
Gold is the color of a church's chime.

What do colors remind you of?

Emerald is my birthstone
Olive is the money you loan.

Bronze means your in third place
Silver is kept in a glass case.

Which colors do you like?

Sara Schmidt

Clouds

Clouds so fogged so soft
fairies living in the sky
no dust to be found

Anthony Carl Puccio Jr.

Friends

I go to his house,
Or he comes to mine.
We play together
Most of the time.

When we're not together,
We talk on the phone.
Because of my friend
I'm never alone.

My friend trusts me,
And I trust him, too.
To trust is the best thing
That we've learned to do.

Matthew Tan

A Rock In A Waterfall

I am but a rock,
standing in the rain.
I am but a rock,
feeling so much pain.
Water trickling over me,
trying to reach the sea.
As I slowly trudge,
from day to day,
I wonder if I'll make it okay.
Just like our country,
I won't give up.

Ashley Braun

My Lord

Hair black as a ravens wing
Eyes blue as the depths of the sea
Fairest amongst 10,000
Yes My Lord Is He.
When He walked into a town,
people would stop and stare
wondering.
Could this be the one they call Jesus?
The one with the raven black hair.

Joseph M. Bourg

My Mother, She's In Heaven

It was on a cloudy morning
As I sat down by her grave
The tears came without warning
For I knew below she laid

When suddenly the sun shone
And I looked up to the sky
My Mother, she's in Heaven
And tries to tell me why

She's helping God to make a home
For each of us on Earth
A place where there will be no pain
It is our second birth

No wars, no hate, no killing
Just love for all mankind
to know my Mom helps build this place
Gives me my peace of mind

Barbara A. Shugart

Silent Love

As we speak...............
We seldom reach.........
The point or place.......
To voice our love........
A love unspoken..........
Expressed in silence....
We look to listen.........
As we tend to reason...
We choose this season.
A time revealing..........
A day for many...........
A place of one.............
A place you have........
I love you Dad.............
On this day.................
A Father's Day............
As every day...............
I need your love just the same!

Whitt Phillips III

I Had Fun Being A Child Again...

I had fun being a child again
if only for one brief night
the clowns brought me joy
that I had forgotten was possible
and I almost felt it was I
taming the savage lions and tigers

when the trapeze artist flew
gracefully through the air
the wind was carrying me too
safely above the world below
and anything was possible
in that moment of flight

but the circus is over now
the tents have been folded
the clowns have wiped off
their greasepaint smiles
and the elephants are
sleeping in their iron cages

Pauline Francia Martin

Our Song

Blind love directing moves
That selfishness eventually soothes
Trying to be a Mother, a friend
Lost in a battle of right and wrong
I sadly write a Mother's song.

Looking for guidance not around
Only silence within the sound
Trying to be a daughter, a friend
Confusion mounting for so long
I sadly write a mother's song.

Surrender only a matter of time
Reality and sadness becomes mine
Trying to be a Mother, a daughter
Our love remains for ever long
As Divine Truth unveils or song.

Marti E. Brandtner

I'm Going Home

I'm going home. I'm going home
  to my Lord.
Where I can see his smiling face
And have happiness forever
I'm going home. I'm going home

Annie Down

My Dream

My dream is that
Maybe someday
The world will
be more peaceful
And violence won't exist

I wish to live in
A safe environment
Where respect is given
And people know
What "peace" means

Freedom is very meaningful
Without it we wouldn't be
Able to be happy or to
Know what happiness is

Freedom and peace
Are important to me
Are these important
To others as well?

Cecilia Doina Iosif

I'd Go

In the blink of an eye,
In the beat of a heart,
I'd go.

All you'd have to do
Is say the word,
And I'd go.

I want every moment
That I can get.
Just let me know, and I'd go.

Anywhere you want,
Anytime you say,
I'd go.

Susan Gertsch

The Fall

Shouldn't have got so
                    loaded
    the gun
            eye aimed
                    for the sky
but only shot an angle
                (4° below) down
I fall as
    a leaf of
            orange and re(*a*)d
flames
    of passion
            rage
                    w(*h*)ine
to my self
        -is*h* ow(*e*) ne(*a*)r
: heaven
        ly   pi(*p*)er
                    hope
(*of*) hE.R.
        (*leaves*) love...

Dustin Arellano

Ebon Gale

I never took the time
To see the moon glow.
I never took the time
To watch my son grow.
I never had the time
(At least that's how it seems)
To take a few steps back
And see what "It all" means.
I tried to take the time
But man's not here to stay
And in the twilight of my life
My Lord took me away
Children of the earth
Heed well what I now say.
Make time to enjoy your living
Waste not your life away.

Bryan Courtney Burke

Loves Offset Memory

Stilled by a jagged shoreline,
waves engulf minds thought.
Empty sails wait in silent hunger....
the endless horizon so near.
Without concept of future
known only by its past.
Encounter visions of time
losing sight to the blessing moment
consume the overwhelming pain.
Having not known its bitter taste,
heartfelt sorrow alone in my dreams
brings the awakening of...
    loves offset memory.

Andrew Sullivan

Friends

Friends may come
And friends may go
But our love for each other
Will always show.

Together forever
Through thick and through thin
Sharing our laughter
And dreams from within

In good times and bad
I'll always be there
To be right by your side
Showing you I really do care.

Alyse M. Burrows

That Curve Rings A Bell

That Chapel of intellectual thought
Those hallowed halls
Where no one questions
Whose wisdom
Is truly being taught
Isolation of fears is impossible
Perpetuation of false ideas
More than possible
Hate is not a so silent
Partner of fear
The cloaked words
Are very clear
Justification for Genocide
For a simple race of fools
And no one will shed a tear

Keith Jones

Perfect Harmony

In the early morning
I have seen
Nature
In perfect harmony

Facing West I see
An incredible sapphire blue sky
In it
Glowing and translucent
A perfect full moon
Setting on the horizon
In front of me

Turning to the East
The same shape I see
This time
The brilliant orange sphere of dawn
Surrounded by
A sunrise sky
Rising up to end the night

In the early morning I have seen
Nature in perfect harmony

Amy Jorgensen

Restoration

Night turns to day
humans change their ways
love enters and leaves
people learn their pet peeves
hearts break and scatter
new pieces are found with flatter
every night changes to day
with love never going away

Adam Hudson

Breath of Spring

In the magic
black as pitch evening
the second of the first warm evenings
to touch us in whispers
after the bitter unmerciful February,
we weave like fancy ribbon
through the star struck darkness
embraced by the triumphant
Hello, Hello, Hello of the peeper frogs
who have crawled from the winter mud
in exaltation.
The scent of the
sun warmed, snow melted, moist earth
rising up and breathing in
swirling around my soul.
This perfume
is like the breath of an angel.

Tracy Teuscher

To My Son

  Once there was a little boy,
he was my greatest pride and joy.
  Many years went by since then,
much too fast my little boy
  grew up to be a man.
Not any more is he a little boy,
  but still my greatest pride and joy.

Hildegard Gagnon

Shark Attack!

Some sharks are dangerous,
you must know
they could gobble you up
from head to toe
if a shark is hungry get out of
sight,
or you'll be its dinner
tonight.
Sharks can eat anything
anything at all,
Something big,
Something small,
they could eat you
if they wanted too!
So you better watch out
if a shark's about!!!

Frances Devine

Untitled

When we raced through the desert sand
The heat draining with in the man
I look and I wonder what lies ahead
Will I make it to the end
Who will be the first to go
Down that dark path of death
As my comrade holds on tightly
We both ride ever so silently
As the oil turns day into night
I see the tanks burning bright
Will the bodies stay out of sight
As we search with anger and fright
Will the gases fill the sky
Is that when I will surly die
Or is it years from this date
When we finally meet our fate
From the days in the past
When we raced through the desert sand.

Daniel A. Brown

Arthritis

My Spirit just flies from me,
  Like all winged creatures do -
It travels through the lanes of trees
  And meadow sparked with dew.

My Spirit world is not confined
  With work in house and yard-
The weeds grow tall in just no time
  And my Spirit doesn't mind.

It dreams of fun things easily done
  And trips so dear to heart,
But this crippled body I am in
  Holds my Spirit 'till death we part.

Zella Lorenzen

Loves Broken

When you hear those words
After loving him
Your heart feels like it collapsed
Those words were all pain
He doesn't care
He's off with another women
You thought he was the one
That special one
You were wrong
He's just another one of them

Lisa Robinson

A Landlord's Lament

A landlord's all smiles
  When the rent comes 'roun'
But speak of a leak
  And then there's a frown.

Forget to mention insulation
  And you're his bosom pal.
'Course he can't feel the cold;
  He winters in Southern Cal.!

Paying rent is a waste
  Over many a moon,
But ask him to sell to you
  And he'd call you a loon.

"Consider depreciation,
  Interest, and tax,
A fall in real estate,
  And other solemn facts.

"No, it really doesn't pay,"
  Drones he, "these days;
Why, to figure my income tax
  Takes four C.P.A.s!"

Mary B. Parrott

Middle-Aged Syndrome

Shattered dreams
Upon my brow,
Speak no more lies
To the living dead.

Heart throb memories
Just now
Impart my lips,
Whispering to the winds,
Who with shrilled laughter
Mock my pain,
Only to remain
the same.

Adelia Wood McConnell

Untitled

...stars...spots...
...spots...stains...
...stains...dirt...
...dirt...earth...
...earth...moon...
...moon...stars...

Circle, circle all around
Until we land upon the ground.

up in the sky and down below
we spak and spek until we flow
back again from whence we started
an ellipsoid joined and never parted

Circle, circle all around
Never shall a thought touch ground.

...stars...moon...
...moon...earth...
...earth...dirt...
...dirt...stains...
...stains...spots...
...spots...stars...

Christopher S. Powers

Seeing Eye To Eye

A visit to our parents,
Is a source of bringing joy.
Especially, if we see things
Eye to Eye.

The joy we share in feelings,
Is not measured by what's done.
It's simply, are we seeing
Eye to Eye?

Life here on earth forms patterns,
That extend beyond the veil.
Joy here or there, is seeing
Eye to Eye.

Our reference is to scriptures,
As we learn what's right and true.
They show us, how to see things
Eye to Eye.

It's hands involved in service,
And a heart that's turned to love.
Combine, assure we see things
Eye to Eye.

Alton J. Mathie

Untitled

I know I am brave
for I keep falling in love,
My heart flies away
on the wings of a dove.
If the dove dies
and falls to the ground,
battered and bruised,
a few tears to be found,
I pick it up and nurse
it to health, to wait
for another to bring
it loves wealth.

Mary Lakner

Love

Is it sloppy or neat,
Is it strong or is it weak,
Does it last a long time or
forgotten in a week,
Is it pure or fake,
Is it lustful or Cuddlie,
Does it make life complete or
do you wonder all the time if
it is right for you,
Who knows?

Michelle Waltz

The Prisoner

It's strange how many would deride,
the one who smiles with tear dim eyes,
and verily tries in vain to hide,
the burning pain that never dies.
But somewhere deep within the soul
remains an ever glowing coal,
that brings the tear drops to his eyes.

For those who laugh have never known
the bitter pain of parting tears
or faced an empty world alone
that has but long and lonely years.
Where the dawn of each tomorrow
lies within deep folds of sorrow,
beneath its vale of on shed tears.

James G. Gostlin

Today

It's a time for healing-
It's a time to be patient-
It's a time for a penny-
  To call upon our thoughts.

It's a time for giving-
It's a time to be thankful-
It's a time for a song-
  To sing within our hearts.

It's a time for growing-
It's a time to be living-
It's a time for a future-
  To hope beyond our souls.

It's a time for honesty-
It's a time to be truthful-
It's a time for a poem-
  To recite between ourselves.

Susan Otani

"I Wish"

I wish you were here to watch me
Every move I make
A simple walk across a room
Every step I take
I wish you were here to watch me
Shake and sway and dance
To glide across the floor
What I would do for just one glance
I wish you were here to watch me
Laugh and smile and play
When I crinkle up my nose
You know, that special way
I wish you were here to watch me
I say it everyday
I wish you were here to watch me
And would never go away.

Lynn McKenney

Untitled

Am I the only one
  am I
  A solo duet
  Just I
  I have strutted
  I HAVE FRETTED
  But when my hour
  Comes
  Will I be
Alone
  A solo duet

Zachary Kirk

Untitled

Illusions mixed with reality
Just dreams or maybe destiny
Cloudy rivers of emotions brought
to be run parallel to sparkling
streams of certainty, feelings of
waves crashing are at the
mercy of time but not everlasting,
like imprints in the sand
that never stay,
we must learn our lessons and
leave or the heavy price will pay.

Joshua Meneshian

Ages

When I was one I just started
  to have fun.
When I was two I two I started
  to say I love you.
When I was three I planted
  a tree,
When I was four I learned to close
  the door.
When I was five I learned to
  spell bye-bye,
When I was 6 six I was just
  six.
When I was seven I thought
  the world was heaven
When I was eight I learned
  how to paint the gate.
When I was nine I thought everything
  was mine.
Now that I am ten I found
  a best friend.

Chrystina Burner

Freedom

"Nothing left to lose,"

I've heard it said, but,
I feel fear inside, instead.

It lies before me glistening,
While I, no longer listening,
Keep searching for my guide.

I have it! I nearly have it!
My senses almost salivating
The taste and I both captivating
The glow within kept...yet...there.

So, who's to say it shouldn't be?
It's sure the answer's, only me.
And why do I deny myself?
That fear inside exerts itself
To keep me here beside myself.

Break out! Break out! My light
Freed now, will banish winter's night!
To fly in the dark!
To aim for the mark!
To hide not the spark
Of love that is freedom!

Sherry Powell

Regret

She came so many times and said;
  "Please mother, play with me."
But almost crossly I replied,
  "Run child and let me be!"

"I've work to do; the house to clean;
  The beds to make; a meal to cook;
Go find your dolls or color crayons;
  Or sit down with a book.'

And now I'm old and she is grown
  And gone too far for me to see.
It's just in dreams I hear her say
  "Oh, mother, play with me!"

If I had only taken time
  To help my baby play,
The tears would fall less freely
  And my heartache less today.

Vera Bell Lewis

Sticking It Out

Through thick and through thin
That's where it begins
To start building a foundation again
Through all that's been done
For all it's been worth
I will stick with you until the end

I could never replace
the feelings I have
for you and only you
But if you were to ever replace
the love that we share
I wouldn't know what to do

As far as I can see
The stronger our love
The happier we will be
For all that I know
For all I can tell
There's no one but you for me

Monna D. Bari

Birdie In The Sky

Birdie birdie in the sky,
come right down from the sky,
birdie birdie way up high,
don't you feel good in the sky?
why I do does it matter to you?
well no, did you ever know?
I like you, do you like me?
   No!
  Said the bird and it flew away.

Lorin Eggering

Freedom Runner

I am black and I ran as the
wind,
I gave you pride and glory,
Yet you still don't recognize me.
I gave you honor beyond glory.
And you still shackle me.
After all this
I came out in glory.
I'm a runner for freedom
I'm Jesse Owens.

Joseph A. Carrero

My Wish

I wish I may
I wish I might
Wish my life away
This very night.

I lay me down to sleep
I pray never to wake
My soul God to keep
Never another breath to take.

To end this daily torment
And mental anguish
No more days in battle spent
No more invisible demons to vanquish.

Over and done
The battle is never won
The final setting of the sun
No more races to run.

I wish I may
I wish I might
Wish my life away
This very night.

Eleanor D. Brown

Untimely Critic

In a censorious mood, the judge in him
bade Haydn take up scores he wrote in by-past years
and toss them in a surging stream
there to be borne away
in runnels of water and of time.

Another day he might have heard their magic.

Too quick to judge, the critic in me surfaces
to censor and reject dear thoughts
I yearn to say to those I love.
I pitch these to the winds
where thermals dip to bear them off in space.

Too late now for both the music and the words.

Bette Fauth

Untitled

Morning, evening for setting sun.
All the day is fun.
Tomorrow looms just once the evening.
And well he all sing
To each day new.
Many not few.
The air is crisp, cool for clear
And my loved one is near.

Sylvia M. Schusky

A Friend

Take time to love
and time to care
Take time to feel
for others fare
Just let them know
that even when
Their world goes wrong
you'll be a friend

Karen E. Teague

The Long Dark Tunnel Of Race

Racism is a long dark and dreary tunnel
Towering cold stone walls represent the hearts of all who are racist
The overwhelming length is representative of its journey through generations
Bitter unforgiving and black because of derogatory remarks
Made by those who don't understand the beauty of difference

Peace is a radiant shimmering light
Making the towering cold walls of the tunnel warm and welcoming
Shining beaming light through the once dark tunnel
Creating a glistening golden door at the tunnel's end
The end of racism; the beginning of a beautiful peaceful nation

Maryann Matera

Storm Song

Gentle bells chime while
lonely raindrops plummet.
Glossy trumpets drone while
winds scream out in malcontent.
Quaking drum rhythm quickens while
thunder builds and rumbles.
Golden cymbals collide while
brilliant lightening flashes above.
Whispering flutes grow distant while
tranquility conquers all.
Nature's orchestra takes a bow.

David Sapp

Miss Him

I miss him.
When I think about the things we did in the
past I begin to cry.
When I think about what we were going to
do in the future I begin to sigh.
I miss him.
He was my brother and my best friend, I know
someday my heart will began to mend.
I miss him.
We were as close as water is to the ground.
When I'm alone...looking at his picture I
hear a certain, little, sweet sound.
I miss him.
At times I even hear his little, soft words
like "I love you."
I like to listen to them while I watch and
listen to a tiny little bluebird and a beautiful
white dove.
I miss him.

Kelly Patterson

On Children Having Children

Conceived of despair and cloaked in love's dominion craved,
Nurtured in a milieu of requisite passion depraved
To vile addiction the derelict fetus be slaved.
The tender madonna sacrificed, indeed,
Over whom the exalted matriarch supersede.

Patricians scorn the blighted seed,
The ministerial devout condemn the deed,
Indulgent avant-garde her choice applaud.
Paternal sovereignty recompenses the fruit of God
And, in so doing, the progeny's sire displace.

The moment comes: Oh heavenly grace!
Fair progenitor's quandary the gentlewomen debate.
Dupe or defiler? That and nothing more!
Alas, too late, the errant father paces the floor.
The suckling babe discovers a breast to adore.

Love found, soon gives way to love's heavy weight.
Life's conundrum thus does kismet employ
Against the fair maiden who envisioned a toy.
Conceived in despair for love's dominion she'd await,
Sweet maiden your childhood is lost to fate!

Seamus O'Toole

You're Special Too

Sometimes we look upon yesterday with envy for times gone by,
While today dark clouds fill the sky.
Yesterday was a day of great joy and happiness to all,
But how tragic it seems that all good times must fall.
Couples may part and people may die
But someday those dark clouds will leave the sky.
Do not long for yesterday but long for tomorrow
And don't let your heart be overcome by sorrow.
It hurts me so to see you cry for I can see the sadness in your eye.
Don't be sad for these clouds will clear and the happiness of
tomorrow is very near.
Do not bow your head in despair for tomorrow will come and I am
sure you will be there.
Good times must go for others to come and bad times, yes there will
be some.
Forget about the bad times and live for the good, then happiness
will find you just as it should.
Remember someone will always be there for you and that you are
special because you are you.

Brandon Avery

Spit

Sickening sweet,
like a drop of dew.

Tantalizing my tongue,
Rolling a trail down the back
of my throat.

Oh Love, The Kiss

Opening of souls,
Unification of bodies,
Portrayal of deep emotions.

The Kiss

A reaper of joy or sorrow.
Touches all with birth, climax, or death.

Affection, The Kiss
Entanglement of legs, arms,
curling of toes.

The Life,
A Kiss,
Through Us.

Melissa Fanelli

The Real World

Reality is a mystery,
Strangers pass by circumstance.
Day echo history,
They somehow took a chance.

They walk, and talk,
　Alone United in Happiness.
Think Alone, Dream Alone,
　Almost in complete bliss.
Strangers have a system...

Maybe a world of their own,
Living within self reality.
　The Art of Happiness..... Alone.

It's the real world,
　That allows the self to flourish.
It's allowing everyone to take control,
　That rapes the mind of courage.

The strangers are the brave and strong,
Living a life by chance.
Ignoring simple barriers,
Please sustain that horrible glance.

Kristine Honnila

The Mirror

I caught your eyes in the mirror today, they held me there.
Still with amazement, like a child looking thru a toyshop
　Window.

In that mirror I see us as one. Oh! to cross over into
the world on the otherside of the glass, where the only sounds
that are heard are the songs our heart sing and the soft
whispers of love that caress my ear.

You caught her watching you in the mirror, you must know
about that woman in that piece of glass, how she wants to
cradle you in her arms and keep you for her own.

Some days I wish to shatter and release these lovers from
behind the glass that holds them, framed, like an erotic painting.
But I dare not destroy it, I need it. I look into that magical
world when my heart and body are longing to be with you.
I see them there in a passionate embrace, then I remember you
are still with me.

The mirror, the lovers, your eyes are my assurance of
　our Love.

Lorena M. Davis

Enchantment

You -
Wrap me, encompass me,
permeate and entwine me -
into and around you, through and within you...
So easily, so fearlessly - and expect me
To believe - this is you, this is me
this is us... And this is real.
Then-when the wings of my heart
flutter their fear of ensnarement
and move with faintest breath
Around the periphery
You reach out... No!-No... Don't leave me...
And I cry within,
I know... I know... I don't want to go -
Catch me... Please catch me, and
Still the madly beating fear within me
With your eyes, your voice
Your arms that reach out to hold me
gently... And rock me slowly
into surrender.

Susan Storms

Early Morning

In the early morning,
I'm laying in my lover's arms.
My head is resting on his chest,
and my breasts are pressed to his muscular torso.
His arms are encircling my waist,
and our legs are intertwined.
Our breath is quick,
and I feel his heart beating in tune with mine.
His eyes spell out his love for me,
and mine mirror the same.
His lips gently find mine,
and I know this is not wrong.

Jessica Heneghan

No Love Involved

Whore, that is all I am
He knocked and I opened the door.
He said "want to?", I said "okay",
And that is the night I gave my virginity away
I was drunk and stoned
His body perfectly toned
I gave in
No words did he need to say to win
But when you can do the cutest guy in school
Who needs all the bull
No one can I tell
For why should I dwell?
He's trying to win back an old flame
Why should he get the blame?
He ignores me in the halls
Doesn't return my calls
But that's what happens
When he's a f***ing player
And you're a stupid whore.

Melissa Geldermann

Thanks To You

I felt like a little bird who was so scared.
You nurtured and you cared.

I felt like a little bird perched on the nest.
You encourage me to take the test.

Now. I felt like a little bird soaring to the blue.

Thanks to you.

K. Borba

Our Dream

As the beads of sweat glisten off your shimmering breasts.
Your brown nipples protrude toward the sun.
The heavenly scent that permeates from your loins.
Drives the poor beast inside to pure ecstasy.
As my eyes glide over your suntanned body.
I find myself mesmerized by such beauty.
And your eyes of brown, match the sand on which you lay.
Your fiery personality, matches the thunderous roar of the incoming
   waves.
The golden glow, that radiates off your hair.
Gives off a serene feeling, that fills the air.
I ask myself, could the two of us stay forever on this island's shore?
She turns her head towards me saying, I'd love nothing more.

Wayne Dimitri

Requiem For A Wedding (For Shawn And Sabrina)

It is like the candystore,
belly laughing its colors upon entrance.
It is like sex,
not the first fumbling f*@%,
but the art of making love
when your tongue becomes the brush,
your breath the sun.
It is like a dog's breath,
scratching at your neck on winter night.
It is like a child,
nine days old dreaming of things
it could not possibly know.
It is like a sheet of paper,
clean and crisp,
no wrinkle or blemish.
It is like the cool breeze
after the hot shower
running along your skin making it reptilian.
It is like that,
beautiful to those who know what it is.

Kirk Everts

Her Fantasy

Thrusting and pulsing, pulling him closest
receive him politely and be a good hostess
panting and raving and calling his name
Not like a lady but feeling no shame
Brushing him softly with meadows of flowers
and smoothing his restlessness through the hours
Lighting red candles and playing a chorus
of violent music that enhances love for us
Blanketing the bed with petals of soft roses
which tickle the skin and clear up our noses
Setting the room at a hot heavy setting to make us sweat through the heaviest petting filling my cheeks with fruit from fine vineyards and tongue-kissing gently until he is hard perfuming my neck with mild spices and watch to see how much it entices Hand feeding him warm poultry with hollandaise sauce and hoping she realizes the nature of my cause Scratching and pulling his face to my body and hope he doesn't think I'm too rowdy Hunger his flesh and thirst his juice pray he catches on, or is it no use? A woman, I'm truly no need to offend but clear-cut curves that taper and bend do nothing for him, on even the stormiest day if I knew him better, I'd know he is gay.

Marcy Platt

Second Day Of Spring

I hear the blue bird singing up in the weeping willow
Where his house swings in a gentle breeze,
That my Kenny made for me
Right this second a bluebird came,
And flew at the window as I sat in amazement
Right in front of me —
Sitting quiet, gathering my thought's
Thinking on what to write next
It seems a moth was inside the window pane
And this is what the bluebird sought in vane,
Right in front of me
He looked real sweet struggling for his footing on the sash
You see I've ran out of seed, I hate to say,
The birds I've given my banana bread
There's nearly a foot of snow lying on the ground,
And more is now falling, It would be fine with me
If this wasn't the second day of spring!
What would you say if I told you
Now he's back perched on the pergola
Looking for that moth I killed

Susan R. Layne

Absolute Love

Absolute love is the deepest form of human adoration.
It is more than the meeting of hearts and the meshing of flesh.
It is the bonding of Souls that makes the circle of love complete.

The coming together of two souls that are meant to be; forms a bond of eternal oneness.
It is a love that springs from the beginning of time and will go till the end of eternity.

Many who Live and Love, never know the truest Love.
However, there are a special few who are lucky enough to live to Love, as we so intensely do.

Absolute Love is the combining of heart, body, and soul.
It is a feeling of freshness; like everyday is a new day with anticipation of things to come.
It is a feeling of agelessness; like something that has been around and a comfort forever.

Absolute Love is You and Me,
For we exemplify the emblem of Love Everlasting.

Emma M. Cook

The Lottery

A knot of anxiety me as I sit and hear the tragedies
  of another life, another time.

But the time is now.

As children die, their last breath stolen too soon,
Cries and helpless screams echo from those not prepared to say
  goodbye.

Across the sea, hate of incompassionate brothers
  flood the street with innocent blood.

Bodies, like rag dolls, tossed and forgotten,
  Their souls searching for beauty.

And here I sit, surrounded by plenty,
  and wonder how I was so fortunate
  to have opportunity and freedom
  in the lottery of birth.

Diane Joyce Mehagian

Conductor

The stick glides effortlessly through the air
And etches its shapes with the utmost care.
Directed by a disembodied hand with relative ease
Instruments follow while it dots i's and crosses t's.
The baton languidly floats through space thick with suspense
The audience shifts uncomfortably as the situation begins to tense.
Trombones bellow and tubas release a low growl
While a single flute goes on the prowl.
The conductor tightly grips his wand
While clarinets and drums begin to bond.
Urgency builds as the stick waves in frenzied motions.
Similar to the unrestrained fury exhibited by the ocean.
The conductor begins to thrust and parry
Like the sword fighter cornering its quarry.
The jabs punctuated by the timpani
Mimic the fencer fighting within me.

Laura Naomi Leeb

Born Out Of Time

I was born late.
When I came in the world my parents knew I would never be great.
My father ran away.
My mother struggled to make it every day.
She worked her fingers to the bone
I ended up all alone
They moved me from place to place
Each time I put on a different face.
I finally grew up.
I never had any luck.
I made a bad choice
because I wanted people to hear my voice
I had too many scars
I ended up behind bars.
My life was pure hell
My soul people tried to sell
Nothing was ever right
I had to fight for my life.
Born out of time
Will I ever get what's mine?

Sophia Signal

Rest Easy

Rest easy, my sweet one, my dear
With my arms holding you tight
There is nothing for you to fear
For I will be with you all this night

But should your dreams be troubled
Wake and tell me what they meant to you
For while your joy shared is doubled,
Your sorrows shared are cut in two.

Rest easy, my love, my dear one
Sleep long and deep by my side
Don't fear the fruition of what has begun
Nor the washing out of evening's tide.

Let the morning bring what it may
For we cannot halt Time's Sun above
And though we must part our separate ways
Know that you go always bearing my love.

Robin Siddique

Untitled

Down in a hole so close to the top,
Just reaching out almost over and out,
Just pushing everything behind,
What a great moment!
Then to be thrown back down, deeper than ever before,
The hole seems endless,
Till I crash to the bottom.
With everything and more on top of me.
How do I get out now?
After all the time spent to get out,
Just to be thrown deeper into it,
What a punishing moment.
Help is needed,
But who can help?
When people try to use you,
When people just lie to you,
Just to get themselves out,
But when I stand up,
I crush those people,
What a relieving moment.
Cody Rothrock

My Heart Was Broken Once

My heart was once filled with love,
   then he came my way.
He said I was as pretty as a dove.
Then he left that day with my heart behind him.

He said he had used me,
   when he told me I could not bare.
I did not want to see him walk away.

I thought he was sincere,
I thought his love was true.
All I had left was a single tear.
I only wanted to pursue my happiness of love.

He made me feel as low as dirt.
He made me feel so used.
All he did was flirt with other girls.
My heart was so abused and he still kept smiling at her.

So now the relationship is over,
If I could only have my way,
To wish upon a four-leaf clove,
   and find true love one day.

Because my heart was broken once.
T. Bailey

Peace Of Life

I was walking for a long time.
I walked until I reached the top of the hill.
There the green grass touches my feet.
I can feel lady bugs crawl on me and fly away.
The breeze touches my face and wraps around my warm body.
The sun shines through the wind breezing on me.
The Sun wants to have a chance to touch me deep in my soul.
I stood there on top of the hill; I didn't move.
I couldn't speak... to wake up the peace all around and within me.
I just stood there, with my arms open wide,
Feeling the heart of the earth beating.
When night comes, I am still standing on the hill
Waiting for the next day of peace to come again.
Toya D. Jones

Finally

Without grudging or complaining I can wait the cold chilly winter
with a ray of hope and joyful anticipation.
I'll not complain.
I'll wait until GOD promotes me.
Until He puts the finishing touches on my character and personality.
I'll wait this one out.
I'll be restituted and in due season will get my reward.
I'll get him who is prepared for me.
I love winter now, for if there is no winter, spring cannot come and
flowers cannot blossom.
The love of my life cannot be rewarded until I have had my winter.
Life blossoms in the spring.
Now I understand.
Finally.
Constance Rena Poitier

Snow

The sharp wind blows against the trees.
The geese winging south along their way.
The endless falling of the bright colored leaves,
and the quickly cooling evenings and balmy days.

I know that the cold winter is on its way.
I can't look forward to the mounting snow
When even the sun shows no bright array,
an the bitter cold seems never to let you go.

But I recall way back many years ago,
when my sleigh was my favorite toy.
When I was young I would pray for snow
for it must be the dream of every boy.

Oh! Just to find that perfect hill,
the one that climbs half way to the sky.
To know that once in a lifetime thrill
of teetering on the edge, then letting fly.

I still hate the thought of winter days.
But with a smile of a youth I know,
winter becomes nothing but a passing haze.
So with a shiver, I must say "let it snow."
Robert E. Jackson

I Can Make A Difference

I am only one person, one in a billion,
Fairly insignificant,
But I can make a difference.

People say our nation is falling apart.
I do not think this is true.
No nation is perfect, and ours is no exception.
There is room for improvement,
And I can make a difference.

To start it off, I can try to be a better person.
I can influence my peers to do the same.
I can make a difference.

I will speak out for what I believe,
And I will not be alone.
For all it takes is one voice, one believer
That turns into a hundred,
That turns into a thousand,
That turns into a million.
I can make a difference.

I am only one person,
But I can make a difference.
Erin Nolan

Lost Friend

I had a friend
She was more essential to me than life itself
One day she became ill
And we lost her

Yes, I grieved
And a dark cloud settled over my existence
I feel her warm my heart
As I cry these endless nights

I feel her spirit with me
Even though I cannot see her face
I know it will be alright
And go on like I should
She will forever be with me
And wait for me at the gates of heaven

Sandi Liniewicz

Sisters Three Are We

As sisters we were born as three
   Our Mother and Father have been there repeatedly.
We're each different in our own way
   Our lives are intertwined each and every day
We each have our own family we love in a special way.
   I thank God, mom and dad for each one of you.
I know we have a special bond that keeps us strong
   which keeps our hearts together forever.

Twila South

"Now Before I'm Gone"

How I wish you could realize,
The emptiness when I've gone.
The time that is so precious,
seems so unimportant in your young mind.
I know because I've been there,
No time for my Dad.
Depressingly now I miss him,
the Pain is Always there,
Not to mention mother, who left me way too soon.
I hope I've earned your true love
And not just bought it with the gifts.
For it's my loving heart and kindness,
you're too young to comprehend you'll miss,
Please Love me for today,
before on to Heaven I'll pass
I'll Always Look down upon you,
Your Daddy, each and every day.

Ron Haggard

My Blessings From You

Thanks so much for all that you've done, for all my experiences in life and have won.
You've been the strength behind my success, when God gave me you, he granted me the best.
If I had searched the world around, it would be you I prayed that I found.
For all of life's lessons that I've been taught, it was always your baggage of wisdom that you brought.
When those nights refused to give me rest, it was your gentle touch and sweet caress.
Although there were no words to say, you were my sunshine on a dreadful day.
The gift of patience is like no other, but the real blessing is having you as my Mother.
Always by prayer we'll be together, with every breath of air I take, forever and ever.

Lisa Conroy

Ornaments

Everything, everybody, every existence needs something.
What is a flower without its stem?
A pile of color over time blending with the
dirt on which it lies.
Yet what is a flower without its petals?
A lonely stem independently standing alone out
of the ground.
But united as one, the flower becomes a
beautiful ornament of nature.
In the same respect, what would you or I
be without family or friends?
Friends being the petals of our flower.
Without them, we are no longer beautiful.
Family being the stem of our flower.
They help us stand tall among the other
flowers in the garden.
Both friends and family being rooted by love.
United with them, we become a beautiful
ornament of society.

Cynthia Matje

Home Away From Home

A little bit of solid air, a mixture of Earth and fire
leads to a night of ecstasy.
A world full of promise, never on the same day,
always for the night;
Once in a while forever.

This is just another Home
away form home;
Where you are not so responsible
for everyone life,
and everything that you can't change

You can see the sun rise
from my bedroom window.
You can build your castles
in the Sun-
You can be most anything;
You can be my everything
for the night

Laurada Devers

The Poet's Art

To pen a line that will flow and glide,
   to unwrap one's thoughts boxed up inside,
   to no longer make one's feelings to hide,
That's the poet's start.

To relieve ones dread and dry his tears,
   to help a friend overcome his fears,
   to inspire the listener with the words he hears,
That's the poet's heart.

To have something to say and say it well,
   to cast upon the reader a spell,
   to frame words so they settle and dwell,
That's the poet's part.

To learn the adventure of pursuing a goal,
   to plumb the depths of the inner soul,
   to find in life one's final role,
That's the poet's art.

J. Thomas Duke

Only For One Night

I met you at the convention,
Totally thrilled and totally heated by your stimulating appearance;
Turned on by your walk and turned on by your talk...
Woooo...I'm gonna make you mine.

SHYLY, you express your fantasy and, BOLDLY, I execute it;
Never a care, nor a worry about the true me or you;
Just my desire to be all that I can be to you...
Just only for one night.

The caress of your hand, the soft touch of your kiss...
Hmmmm..... I must be in heaven;
If only for one night, surely, this ecstasy cannot be real;
My will to behave cannot suppress my fleshy desires to misbehave;
To feel your countenance, to explore your manly being,
To reach into the depths of your soul.

Yes.....only for one night is the truth of the matter;
'Cause I'm not living a lie, but truly enjoying the moment;
Tomorrow's a new day and we're back to reality.

You have a life and I have mine;
Only for one night, we shared that special magic;
Unbeknownst to your wife! Unbeknownst to the world!
Only For One Night...it was Me...and only Me...
Who became your true dream girl.

Wardella Reese

Fragments Of Leukippus

To jump into a volcano is not the act of a God...
but to return [is]...[and] who has seen Empedokles lately?

Who would I worship?
Zeus and power? Aphrodite and love?
... the wind ... or Chronos and time
— for time holds all power and love

The gods evaporate like clouds
they came from nothing and left nothing
behind not thrones or texts or ruins or treasures
what man now petitions their return?
if we exist in the image of our creators
then we are merely clouds

Let the caduceus be our symbol
as mystery is based on knowledge based
on mystery ... through all levels
in a ever-recurring spiral

Ecstasy is a heart in which the sun distends

One records the most profound meanings the most ecstatic
visions clumsily ... occasionally ... in fragments

Maolanaithe Rian

That Last Blast

I would like to share a story that is all so true,
Don't turn your back on God or the devil will try to destroy you.
My facts are based on heart ache and pain,
While watching my life fade away, by partying with cocaine.
For the trouble it causes seems unfair and unjust,
But there is no one to blame, no one, but us.
While trying to get high with others and live life so fast,
Not knowing one day it could be "that last blast."
At first it looked cool to run wild and feel free,
On the other hand it was the devil preparing to kill me.
Cocaine will ruin your image and make your money fade to dust,
And through all that agony, the devil is laughing at us.
I thank God Almighty I'm saved and this story is now past,
My life could have been damned forever, if I had taken " that last blast."

Keith Coleman

Yester Years

I saw a little boy the other day
Who reminded me of you as I watched him play.
He was with his mother at the fountain square
And I watched her lovingly stroke his hair.
His hair was the color of bright, golden wheat
And I observed him closely as he dangled his feet.
His eyes were blue, the color of the sky.
They twinkled and danced, this cute little guy!
The complexion of his was snow, lily white
With tints of pink from the bright sunlight.
His busy little hands skimmed the water without care
and I watched him with fondness splashing with dare.
His dimples were indented in stone on his cheeks.
How he looked like you and it only seemed weeks
That I was the mother there stroking your cheek
Watching you splash in the water and looking so meek.
As they turned hand in hand and slowly disappeared
I thought how I wish I could bring back those years!

Kelly J. Kent-Parcell

Women And Love

A split second yawns between Heaven and Hell,
The ocean of Regret pounds upon the sand. Is this our world? I ask,
I cry.
IT pants, beckons then retreats, whispers to those who venture near.
Teasing, tantalizing, a test, a prayer, a dream.
Molten and freezing by turns,
Scalding, searing, sublime and sudden, stabbing,
Stagnant.
All this and more, if you can grasp it;
All that and less, if it eludes you.
Lost forever in gazes, empty gestures; caressed and then demeaned,
exalted, but defiled.
For this treasure, this modern Holy Grail: We quest;
Better a piece, a fragment of an illusion than all of nothing,
Better to lie to ourselves than be deceived.
Tortured, restless, vengeful knights with clutching, trembling empty
  hands
Come away with savaged hearts, scarred souls, cursing
Cure and pestilence with no distinctions drawn.
In this loveless world,
This is desperate
Enough to die for.

Marjorie Hale

Life

Open up your eyes
can you see?
What this old world - has done to us
"you and me"
The good old days
are gone!
Far far away
From all of our happy home.
"So please" let there be peace -
And open up our heart,
To all - and everybody
Right from the start.
There is so little time
Left in our lives:
To truly be happy
While we all are still alive.
All he ask - is for us to accept his love
That he shall send to us all
From above...

Nova Norman

Circumstances

A new day is born,
darkness, always falls,
and draws each day to a close.

Flowers always bloom in springtime,
Bringing their unique beauty
that was at loss, during the cold of winter.

Love.
The flower of unique beauty.
Plucked from the unknown forests of life.
Shall one admire its beauty from afar?
Never truly, and completely touching,
Nor letting oneself be touched
by the beauty that lies hidden, unknown, within.

Can this flower of admiration be lost forever?
From standing alone.
Fighting the changes in seasons...
Lauran Du Breuil

"Owed To Frustration"

As I sit down to write I stare at this paper,
   And nothing will enter my mind.
I search all around for somewhere to start,
   But I think I'm just wasting my time.

I try to envision a scene to begin,
   This essay that I have to draft.
'Cause in trying to write it sinks or swims,
   So somebody toss me a raft.

Now my head has begun to be filled with frustration
   No comfort in paper that's bare.
The best part of my life slowly drifts into space,
   While I sit petrified on this chair.

As each stroke of the clock passes seconds away,
   The pressure mounts upon my nerves.
A deadline to meet with nothing to say,
   Because I lack knowledge of verbs.

But just as I start to lose all composure,
   And give up my writing career.
Written down on this paper miraculously,
   The poem you've read right here.
Melvin McDonald

In Love

There is no greater bliss than love
When two people are right for each other
You always feel great peace from above
To know he cannot be replaced by another.

There is no greater pain than love
When everything seems one-sided
Missing is the peace from above
And you're not sure what will be decided.

The joy of love brings smiles and laughter
The pain brings tears and sorrow
I'll accept the pain if it means love after
And a happy blissful tomorrow.
Darlene McGillick

Forever Dreaming

Gazing past reality, into a world of dreams,
Where to love one another, is the highest of all means,
People loving, people sharing, without any recall,
In a world of harmony, there's no need for hate at all,
People living side by side, willing to share the land,
Everyone is growing together, always hand in hand.
Peter Lee

I Love Only You

There's a moment I pause, in this life of mine
There's a moment I remember, all our good times;
There's a moment I can recall, all dressed in lace
There's a moment I remember, that look on your face;

There's a moment I sleep, but just for a while
There's a moment I can see, your beautiful smile;
There's a moment time will pass, and you are not here
There's a moment in my dreams, I try and change that my dear;

There's a moment this old house, is just not the same
There's a moment my thoughts, seems to play a little game;
There's a moment in my heart, I cry very loud
There's a moment plus a moment, for you I'm very proud;

There's a moment people say, are you all right
There's a moment in my bed, I think of you all night;
There's a moment feelings show, when I'm all alone
There's a moment I catch myself, and remember you're gone;

There's a moment I watch and wait, looking at your picture on the table
There's a moment I pray to God, to please help when I'm unable;
There's a moment you gave me, a new life and that's true
There's a moment you need to know, I Love Only You;
Leatrice Williams

I Held Jesus Hand

I saw a star hanging in mid air,
I went to see why it was just sitting there.
Out of that star, there came a man,
I asked him if I could please hold his hand.

I went and told everyone what I saw,
They said I was lying and that's against Gods law.
So I prayed to the Lord from up above,
Please let him come back on the wings of a dove.

I wanted to prove to every one what I saw
To let them know, I didn't break God's law.
A few days later, I looked out to see,
That same little star in front of me.

I cried because I couldn't go with that man,
I didn't want to let go of his heavenly hand.
I hope when I die, I'll see him again.
So I can thank Jesus for always holding my hand.
Sharon Rhodes

Contractor

You ask me what happened to the windows of my soul
   He took them.
They'd look better as a skylight down the street
flanking the new bay window out facing the lake.
   But either way
if he built them into someone's house
or threw golf balls at their glass
they are no longer mine, he took them.
I hope he keeps them clean.
Doesn't let the grime from urban streets
gather and block the view
Streaks them with the Windex and fresh paper towels.
I doubt he remembers, they were once mine.
   He took them.
They'd look better in a kitchen down the block
opening into someone's foyer over looking the garden.
But either way they are no longer mine.
Chole Ferguson

Life

I am human,
  though you say my thoughts are not always down to earth.
I am human,
  though you say I am as different as an alien.
Even though I am human,
  my thoughts can sometimes be strangely different from yours.

I am one person,
  though I see things through many different eyes.
I am one person,
  though my personalities are many to discover.
Even though I am one person,
  I can realize the thoughts and feelings of millions.

I have a soul,
  that is as strong as my will.
I have a soul,
  that I rely on as my guide.
Even though my soul in one is itself,
  It is connected to you and everyone in the ring of life that keeps our world alive.

Anna Strimaitis

Night So Long

Yesterday your yellow veil seemed to darken with the sunset
Today your face reveals more expressive features
eyes that speak louder, lips that seem fuller
Was the night so long?

I too have chattered with the moon
Endless talks bathe in revelatory light
I too was hypnotized by figures dancing around stars
and swept onto a threshold of self

Where cataracts of age peeled like pages in a breeze
And I watched the wondrous tot, bold explorer of new worlds
I listened to the questioning youth, convincing soldier of his day
I observed the grown warrior as he maneuvered reason and logic
in the eleventh hour

And I came to know the Sculptor better
He who eyes transparent souls and moves decisively across the board
And I knew that I was the core of all and a particle of each
and that each tiny life was but a spark in totality

And I too have risen enormous with the sun
Eyes that speak louder, lips which seem fuller
Billowed with the luster of a
night so long.

Gloria Evangelista

The Past

Is the past the present; which makes the future?

It is said, "The past is the past" So...
Everything I think,
Everyway I am...is contrived from
the past.
Good or Bad - Pretty or Ugly - Up or Down - So...
is the past really the past,
or is it
the present?

It is also said, "The future is unpredictable" - So...
Everything I think today.
Everyway I am today...is creating
the future tomorrow.
Happy or sad - Positive or Negative - Right or Wrong - So...
is the future really the present,
or is it
The Past?

Michelle M. Mize

A Single Pane

Yet to what fate doth err befall
This sorrowed heart of mine.
The clicks, the clangs, of broken strings,
An empty-hearted stall.

A revelation of the past,
Which stops the forward flow,
A choosing choice, that choosers choose,
Has placed the hopes and dreams below.

How close to souls desire,
In my thoughts have I become,
But nothings there, there is nothing,
The hand of jest again has won.

This wall of glass, this single pane,
Is placed before my Juliet.
How true and tricks, black and white don't mix,
Tis best she stays a Capulet.

J. B. Wells

Black Is Beautiful

"Black is beautiful!"
I heard the shout at the
demonstration.
But that is not what I was taught.
No, black is ugly, inferior, ignorant,
unintelligent, untrustworthy, easily scared.
So they all said. When I asked why they believed
those things, told me that everyone knows that's the Truth.
But I know that's not the truth. I know and I'm certain.
It was a hot New Orleans summer day and I was
trapped, cornered in the garage by a
Rabid dog.
Frozen in terror.
The hands holding the two-by-four
were black hands, the hands of Gladys,
my aunt's maid hired just to clean and cook.
As I watched the mad dog run away howling in
pain, I knew they were wrong and that Gladys was
brave, faithful, loving, lovely and
Beautiful!

Jack Gordon

In Memory

The only thing I know for sure is where I'll be tomorrow.
While during my life, I have experienced love,
I find it's not forever.

I have my boys to comfort me, such joy they surely bring,
but one day soon, they will be on their own,
no longer dependent on me.

As I have detoured from my path, the purpose I still do wonder,
There is lots to do, the challenge is set,
I accept and will be eager.

I try to keep my thoughts complete, in hopes that memories won't fade,
a roller coaster ride I find,
although it too will end.

I never know just what to expect or when certain things will happen,
Life will go on, but for just how long, is still most uncertain.
I will endure what lies ahead, and happily I will go forth.

There is a place upon the hill that patiently waits for me.
Reassuringly, I feel that the only place the peace will be,
is where I'll be tomorrow.

Rose Basil

A Rose Is A Rose

A rose is a rose of such exquisite beauty,
It sits on its long stem throne
As, if, in celestial duty.
Glorious colors in mass array
Gloriously blooming day by day.
Vibrant wine red, rich ones so velvety
As if saying, pleading, "Oh Please! Oh Please! Pluck Me."
Lacey breathtaking white ones oh! so rich and pure,
Thoughts of filial love do occur.
Ravishing hues of purple and pink,
So simply ravishing, they almost wink.
Gorgeous strains of oranges and yellow
With their divine scents and aromas so sweet and mellow.
Now tell me: is not a rose, a rose of such exquisite beauty?
To cultivate them is almost a God given duty.

Amy Juarez

Art

Feelings can be expressed in forms of art.
This is done with an initiative.
A way to expressed feelings is to dart,
Abstract and freely, but conservative.

The many styles of art can be used
To express other feelings you may have.
Sometimes people have this talent abused
By others who don't have it, and get mad.

Least specific styles of art include
Painting, drawing, sculpting, and frescos.
More specific styles of art include
Mosaic, modeling, and stained glass windows.

When I draw, I become content inside,
After that my friends and I will abide.

Allyson Roy

"Hannah"

Hannah's house is on fire!
People say she's a liar,
Puritans accuse her,
They call her a witch,
But I don't believe it,
Nosiree,
Hannah is a nice old widow,
Who needs some help,
She and her cat are the only ones there,
When puritans think people are witches,
They hang them and drown 'em,
Poor old woman,
Will Hannah be hung?
She's just an old quaker,
Not a witch,
Just believe me,
I know!
I could tell the jury,
(For the trial she'll have),
Hannah's not guilty!

Jessica Lund

Alone

I notice him from afar, but he never glances my way.
When we pass one another our eyes never meet,
   were just two strangers among many.
As time passes, my heart grows with deep emotions for him,
   but it will always remain a secret locked away.
Time cannot unlock or break away the
   chains that keeps my feeling of love buried.
Knowing deep within, I'll always be alone.
Too shy to tell him and too afraid of being loved
My love for him will still remain a secret for now
   and for all time.

Susannah B. Rayoan

A Wasted Life

Vincent, the rage in your brush, the peyote in your colors.
Why did you crucify yourself to the tree? Was there no one to bring
   you to the stillness of the beginning...before all creation was.
   The Supreme Ego, that is, the never ending space,
   as the infinite Heavens. Misused truth had poisoned your mind.
   Victim begets Victim!
So young a man with such torment in your soul.
The compensation of Art as a means to an end? Damned if I do,
   damned if I don't.
Was there no one to open the prison gates silencing judgment?
So young and innocent. How Rachel cried for her children!
Woe unto you, scribes and Pharisees, hypocrites!
Theo, you meant well, but the brush of "impressionism", did it
   make the blind see? The deaf hear?
The light shine out of darkness? One day these paintings will be
   thrown out in the streets!...For lack of bread.
No Vincent, the gun was not the end, but the light, and the
stillness from the beginning.

Dennis Pelliccia

The Growth Of Love

As you grow older sometimes love sneaks upon you. I am in love
and my eyes have opened. As the sun rises a new dawn awakes and
then I think of you.....
All I want, all I get, let it be captured in my heart, what you
are to me is my smile and my strength.
Still what I feel towards you I protect inside,
scared to let go what has been faithfully mine.
Do you feel as I do...so confused at times?
The time has come and I now do not watch from the distance as I
did before. I hand over my precious body and spirit. I shall
give you everything, my sweet everything. A started friendship
just turned into love. The stars that twinkle alongside us
shall not fall. Shackles and chains can't hold my feelings back.
I'm riddled by you. We need each other to hold onto. Some of
the sanest days are mad, so hold onto your friends. Still we
watch another beautiful day pass like a dream. But how long can
this last?

Samantha Sickles

Blindfold

This love inside is what tries to escape
Trying to jump out and pull down fate
Only time will tell before it gets too late

Love is blind or is it just wearing a blindfold
Peaking out from underneath to see what its eyes behold
Finding out what is sometimes better left untold

Tie a blindfold around my eyes
Make it black it never dries
So you don't have to see me cry

Speak softly into my ear
Anything that your heart holds dear

Kiss me softly on the lips
The way to my heart is by your kiss
When you're gone that's what I miss

Dance with me just one last dance
Who knows we might still have a chance
At what is known as romance

I could walk alone and you would be therein
In my heart with all my love and caring
Even with a blindfold on I could see you within

John A. Balulis Jr.

It Didn't Matter At All

Two little men sat on a hill, discussing the ills of the earth,
Said one, "It seems the problems today are worse than the
Day of my birth."
Blinking his eyes, the other replied: "How long would you say
that has been?"
The answer came, "not long enough to change a thing
by deed or word or pen."
And so they argued, pro and con, of matters great and small,
While a thousand years later, neither argument was greater
Nor seemed to matter at all.

Jack W. Carmichael

Winter War

Ah yes, here they come
Marching in one by one.
With their approach they shine and rattle
For they're preparing to do battle.
Above the land they mass and thunder
The gloomy clouds of the month December.
Each year the winter comes to fight
With all its forces and all its might
Again I wonder will it succeed
With cold and dark and violent need
The freeze a soul, to break a heart
To end a life and then depart
Or will there be a brave return?
Electric storms, cold winds that burn
Another year of valiant fight
Another quest to find the light.

Lana Aoude

An Ending Day

The street globes are glowing with flickering lights
As the night sets in, it's a glorious sight.
The birds have nested, as the stars show their glow
And youngsters are tucked in, their dreams all in tow.
In the distance the breezes are singing their tunes.
With flowers of the day leaving off their perfumes.
It's relaxing, refreshing and restful for all
As out in the darkness the owls make their calls
The quiet sets in as the day comes to an end
And at last it's a time for all to just rest
And to look towards tomorrow, hoping it is the best

Melba Morris

Iaco Dreams

I dream of soft sea sides sometimes
And wonder if I
Could ever dream of a softer side
Or inhale, then float into the sky

I dream of quiet quilt hugs sometimes
And wonder if I
Could ever dream of a more quaint quilt hug
Or sleep forever within the arms of time

I dream of green grass beneath my feet sometimes
And wonder if I
Could ever dream of greener grass
Or stand alone in it all... and smile

I dream of sweet symphonies sometimes
And wonder if I
Could ever dream of sweeter songs
Or conduct all the birds in a tune in my mind

Sometimes I dream when I'm with you
And wonder if, I
With my dreams will come true
Or remain my haven, when skies are not blue

Meliesa Ross

My Father's Worship

The night I caught him with the needle,
He reminded me of a witch doctor summing up the
Evil spirits, as he sat there,
One arm tied with a leather belt.
There were no volcanoes in which to throw
Vestal virgins; no goat hearts to be drained of the blood.
Just some mystical potion
Too evil for my innocence to understand.
My heart pounded at what I saw.
His eyes rolling in the back of his head,
As the potion entered his blood stream.
And engulfed by the rapture, he sat there
Motionless, as if praying to some ancient deity.

Tyra Cooper

Broken Heart

I never knew my heart could be broken,
I've heard many times that "It will happen"
I've also heard the "It happens to everyone"
But I didn't believe this until you left
Now I know all of it is true
Tears come to my eyes when I hear your name
I picture your handsome face,
My heart feels like glass shattering piece by piece,
It's falling apart, I just know it,
My pain will never stop,
I never knew my heart could be broken.

Morgan McGuire

A Parent's Reminder

A child is a gift from God above,
That is sent to us to nurture and love.
Cherish each moment as it goes by,
Because they are gone with the blink of an
    eye.
Love them and hold them and tell them you
    care,
Let them know you have time to spare.
For the time with your children goes by
    much too fast.
Before you know it will be part of your
    past.

Cheryl N. Stonborg

Granddaddy

   She tells you were handsome
Golden honey brown hair curling around your ears
Your eyes she said were deep blue oceans
That could freeze like ponds
When the snow first hits and melts with the sun
Warming her nervous childhood making her a queen
When you voice raises its tenor
To the lull-a-bye of praise
She told me that you loved me
When you were a jolly elf
Full of pride
Beaming with hope
When you held my tiny body
In gracious, round arms
Smoothing the satin gown
As the picture was taken
But I lost that sacred photo
As time went running by
Faster and fast
And I lost that memory in my mind

Tina Towles

Lost Love

The wind, the rain,
The hint of spring,
The remembrance of winters past,
Bring back memories that last,
The thoughts of yesteryear,
With excitement once again,
I wonder of a past love,
Where the love has gone,
Where the love has been,
The lost love that passed we sorely blundered.
The love may have became like a gentle breeze,
Or maybe, just maybe a clap of thunder.

Harold R. Lewis

He'll Always Be There

The Lord has always been so very good,
He's gotten me through things when no one else could.
I love Him, I praise Him, and make no mistake
That He's why I can take each breath that I take.
I know it's hard to know what to do
When asking the Lord to help get you through.
There's a few simple things you can do for a start
Bow your head, close you eyes, and look down in you heart,
So dig deep, just let go, don't hold anything back
Where you're weak and unsure, God will take up the slack.
If you are searching for peace that comes from within
Giving trust in the Lord is where you'll begin.
Don't give up, it's not easy to get in the door
But anything that's worth having is worth working for.
Place your life in His hands, and you won't miss you call
He welcomes you in and there's room for us all.
Let your faith be your map that you follow each day
And by trusting in God, you can't lose your way.
When your love and faith in the Lord are sincere
If ever you need Him, He'll Always be There.....

Freda Hand

Untitled

I have this feeling of having
traveled a long distance
but yet not gone very far.
Of drowning in my own thoughts
and trying to grasp something
that's within my reach, but being
afraid to grab it. Who knows I
just might turn to dust if I reach it.
Trying hard to keep my sanity, at times
I feel so alone, so powerless. I see
Everything that's happening around me and
I have no control over it.
Fighting back the tears and the pain
I continue through life with a mask
hiding my feelings, I use my smile
to cover up the pain. And fear of
someone looking deep into my eyes
and seeing the darkness.

Abigail Alberto

True Feelings

   With a pure heart and a clear mind
my spirit travels to another place and time,
I soar like an eagle with grace and pride
free from all conflicts that hurt me inside.
The backdrop of a sunrise as I fly with
magical colors that lite up the sky
   Floating on a gentle breeze I glide
across the water and see the reflection
of my God my father there with me. To help
me this day guiding my way for without
his love I would surly go astray.

David Wayne Kynerd

Friendship

Friends have a relationship,
where you love, and share, and care.
A friend can give a loving tip,
or give a smile to wear.

A friend will never let you down,
if they're a loving friend.
Sometimes a friend becomes a clown,
and your friendship starts to end.

Once you find the love is gone,
it will not be much fun.
If you're patient and be kind,
you'll soon find another one.

Don't ever think all your friends will let you down,
soon you'll learn to come around.

You can have many types of friends,
be open and be a friend of anyone.
With many friends it never ends,
and before you know it you'll have fun.

If you have a friend or two,
you'll have a lot of fun.
So my advice to you,
is to be a friend of everyone.

The limit of the amount of your friends,
will certainly never have an end.

Jesse Dresbach

My Country

Within my heart there burns a love
For a country far away,
Australia dear, my native land
Where I'll return some day
My country is so proud and fair
To conquer her let no one dare
She abounds in rarest fruits and flowers
Thriving in warm tropic showers,
Silver, gold and cattle land
And sunny beaches with yellow sand
Sweeping golden fields of wheat
Swaying and bending in the heat
Sparkling lakes and tall gum trees
Mountains, rivers and wide blue seas
Australia, land of the ANZACS brave,
Long may the flag of the Southern cross wave.

Lenore Vigil

Night

Standing on the threshold, excitement fills the air
As I peer around the corner at the light that shines in there.
Fear leaps out and grabs me, an icy chill invades my soul
And I turn my head and crawl back into my dark familiar hole.

And somehow as I lay there in the comfort of my fears
Somehow as I look out through my streaming, steaming tears
A hint of love comes sneaking in to tug on a heartstring
And somewhere deep inside of me a voice begins to sing.

But quickly as I hear the song of laughter bubble up
Swiftly as I feel myself being lifted from above
I wrap myself up tighter still, 'til that voice is no longer heard
And listen to that voice, instead, that kills with ugly words

And as I struggle and suffer pain in profoundly different ways
I want so much to take that step on the road to better days
To a life that's filled with friends and love and usefulness ahead
And yet, in spite of all of that, I run and hide instead.

Oh, will I ever find the strength to step fully into that light
Or must I always look at it with fear, frustration, fright
My heart will soar for a second or two when I think someday I might
But most of the time spirit dwells in sadness, darkness, night.

Bob Farrell

Union Of Souls

Will you let your soul fly free with mine?
Even for just the slightest moment.
Come close on silent wings;
free of your programmed mind and structured being.
I promise you worlds with no boundaries - weaving and darting
through myriad moving molecules—reaching and touching.

Let go of what you can see with your eyes and reach beyond the
unknown with me.
Look at a leaf bud and see the promise of life;
listen to a bird sing and hear the song of the ages;
taste the honeysuckle and know the sweetness of youth;
smell the closeness of a summer shower
and inhale the perfume of the Gods;
touch my hand and feel the joy in your heart.

For an infinitesimal second share the spirit of your soul;
free the ecstasy like sparks from a million shooting fireworks.
Fly with me if you will, touch with me if you dare.
I'll not hold you.
My heart will treasure yesterday's memory,
my soul will keep tomorrow's promise.

Jane Hagedorn

I Love A Rainy Day

As I stand at the window and look out at a rainy day.
I ask myself, "Why do I like a rainy day?"
Then I see a raindrop running down the window pane.
I guess this reminds me of a tear that runs down my face
when I am in pain
The clouds are sometimes so dark and gray,
I ask myself, "What is it about this rainy day?"
I think it reminds me of some dark day
When a storm blew all my dreams away.
But just about then I see a small light,
and those dark clouds seem to break away.
I see a ray of sunlight like the break of day,
and I ask myself, "Do I really need these rainy days?
Do I need these tears on my face?
I think I know down deep inside there may be
Someone out there who understands why I love a rainy day.
Yes, someone who would listen to why I have these rainy days.
When that tear starts to roll down my face, he will be there
With a soft touch, reach up and wipe that tear away.
I know he understands why "I love a rainy day".
And I feel with each touch of his hand on my face
My dark cloud may someday go away.

Robert Timms

"Mount Fuji Spring"

The world has many things of natural beauty,
one of my favorites being Japan's majestic mount fuji.

In the spring, the slopes covered with snow,
Reflects in the mirror clear water of Lake Yamanaka-ko.

Cherry blossom petals, their breath taking beauty spent.
Rush away in a gentle breeze as if late for another appointment.

Colorful birds perch in the surrounding trees,
Welcoming the warm weather as they sing their melodies.

The frogs around the lake have awakened from their winter rest,
And seem to be competing as who can be the loudest.

A lone hawk silently glides by in search of food,
Causing all the smaller creatures to quickly develop a quit mood.

The bees are busily collecting nectar for honey,
From a flower covered bush in an area that is sunny.

All of these events are repeated year after year,
And are thoroughly enjoyed by those visiting or living near.

Michael Dale McDonald

"Say A Little Prayer"

Say a little prayer, to God before you rise,
To help you through the day, let you
have blue skies.
Say a little prayer, for the ones you love so.

For God, too watch over them,
wherever they may go.
Say a little prayer, to help them on their way
For it never hurts anyone to take time to pray
Say a little prayer, for someone
somewhere, may he sad and blue,
Because someday, it could be you

Say a little prayer to God, to forgive
us for our sins.
Lead us to straighter pathways
our ways to amend.
So say a little prayer, each night
before you sleep. To God up in heaven, our
souls to always keep.

Marie C. Rawls

Follow Me

You can hunt rocks and nature things up and down the brooks
and ditches.
You might even get briars and stickers hooked in your britches.
And as you follow the creek very far. Remember you've got to
follow me if you want to be a star.

You can sit in a porch swing and let the wind blow through
your hair.
You can gaze across the country side on a day so fair.
But as your thoughts drift away out far, know you've got to
follow me if you want to be a star.

You can drive your jalopy over the country roads.
You can wave at all the farmers carrying their loads.
But as your mind wonders away out far, you've got to follow
me if you want to be a star.

You can live in the big city and shop in all the large stores.
You can sail on a ship or fly from shore to shore.
But as your thoughts wonder away out far, you've got to
follow me if you want to be a star.

Now, I'm not talking about the stars in the heavens above,
But on a stage of life with the people that you love.

Yes, you have followed me very very far and in my heart, you
have always been my star.

Larry L. Smith

Prayer

My spirit is troubled, my soul not at rest,
I look to my Lord, and make my request.
Send down your spirit and fill me with peace
Wash me with love, my anxiety cease.
I know I'm unworthy, but humbly I ask,
Be kind with me Lord, don't take me to task.
I offer my love, such an imperfect gift,
It's all that I have for the burdens You lift.
Your mercy, patience, and kindness abound,
No greater love could ever be found.
And though I am selfish, sinful and weak,
You still always listen whenever I speak.
Though I never can give proper thanksgiving,
I'll continue to praise You all the days I am living.
Your humble servant, all the rest of my days,
Every word and action, my song of praise.

Barbara L. Vesey

Happiness

Happiness, is finally breaking through the pain of past abuse.
Learning to live from the other side of the coin;
   To be able to trust again!
   To be able to laugh again!
   To be able to take back control of your life.

Happiness is finally being able to reach out for the brass ring;
   To grow and learn how to live again,
   To forget the past, and get on with the present,
   To believe in oneself for the first time,
   To know you can contribute something worthwhile,
     to humanity, before you die.

Happiness, is learning how to hug in a good way,
   and enjoy the warmth and comfort it can bring.
Finally, it's the love, understanding, and friendship you share
   with those who have walked down the same road of life,
And have survived,
   just like you have!!!
   Jacquie Wrolstad

Flowing River What Have You Seen

Flowing river, what have you seen,
   On your long, quiet journey to the sea?
Have you seen an ancient willow,
   Weeping as it hides lovers stealing a quiet kiss?
Or is it dusty pink rose petals,
   Thrown carelessly away by a playful sprite?
Have you seen morning mists,
   Dissipate gracefully, with the afternoon light?
Or the sun glimmering on little waves,
   As light shines on watered silk?
Maybe you haven't seen any of these things,
   These wonderful, romantic things.
Could it be, the only thing you have seen
   Is a pair of beautiful green-blue eyes,
With huge silvery tears, forming a river,
   On a long quiet journey to the sea?
   Marie Perkins

A Lover's Pose

Eyeball to eyeball, nose to nose,
here we lie, in a lover's pose.
I don't know what you're thinking,
your eyes are closed.
Breathing evenly, arm draped across my thigh,
here we lie in a lover's pose,
and I don't think I feel anything at all.
I can feel your breath, upon my face,
smell you, upon the sheets,
remember words murmured, before we fell to sleep.
Here we lie in a lover's pose,
I don't think I meant any of them at all.
Your eyes flutter open, they stare into mine,
I know that you're thinking,
I don't like this, at all.
Eyeball to eyeball, nose to nose,
here we lie in a lover's pose,
and I really wish, I was alone.
   Onishia Noland

A Whisper In The Wind

The twinkling of stars on a peaceful night.
The way was clear, their journey was right.
Guided by a star for all to see.
A wonderful miracle was soon to be.
A whisper in the wind proclaimed so clear.
Their prayers were answered,
The savior is here.
   David Rodriquez

The Shelter

From dawn 'till dusk,
Your face I seek,
Your are my strength,
When I am weak.
You are my rock, my shelter, my savior, my shield,
God, unto you only do I yield.

When life's torrential rains pour down,
There will I be found,
Standing under a shelter sent from above,
Provided by a God whose heart overflows with tenderness and love

Though I may fall during this grueling race,
I keep my eyes fixed upon God's holy face,
One that speaks mercy and grace.

Hail to the Lord,
Praise to the King,
For when we are in God's mighty shelter,
Evil has no sting!
   Brad McMahan

Salvation

I remember how once you could read my thoughts
And I could read yours, too—
When I wanted to
Then he came and bought your soul
Took you back with him to hell
Like Hades and Persephone
While I stood idly by, simply a spectator
The only one who could have done something
The only one who could have saved you
Now, today, we sit alone together, like strangers
I can no longer fathom your mind, your world—
Am not sure I want to
But at least your soul is yours again
Fought for and recaptured without me
You found salvation without my help
While I burned the bridge between us.
   Jody McNeese

What I See?

The wind blows though the trees,
making a faint whispering.

The waves stir in the lake,
making a faint roar, like the lion.

The mountains stand guard,
over everything below.
As though they are the father of all.

They all create a scene.
They play their part.

As I sit and think,
they come alive in my mind.

The wind my mother,
the one who loves me most.

The lake my father,
the one with all the power.

And the mountains, Oh those sweet large mountains,
my brother, saying I will always be safe.

I see a tranquility undisturbed by anyone.
I see a family,
living happily as the untamed wild.
   Joleen J. Sorensen

My Greatest Blessing From God

Poetry for my wife, who is poetry in the flesh and spirit.
I thank my Heavenly Father for you daily.
My greatest blessing from God is you, for
My greatest gifts from God came from you,
You gave me three beautiful children, thank you.
Thank you for forgiving me when I'm wrong.
Thank you for standing by my side when I'm weak.
Thank you for your support in making my life a success;
Now, let me make yours an equal success.
Whatever your desire, I will be there for you,
I will give you and do all I can to make it happen for you.
All I want is what gives you happiness, joy, peace and love.
All I want is to love you all the days of my life.
Let us both rejoice in the Lord together and be
His example of the perfect marriage, the perfect family.
I love you Honey, because you loved me even in the worst of times;
Because of your loving spirit, you brought me close to God.
Don't change; stand strong in who you are. You touch more people
Than you know, and God is well pleased with you, He will say,
"Well done, My good and faithful servant."
David Lee Fouché

Time Will Heal

The past is past so let it lie. That's what they
tell me believe me I've tried. But flash backs
occur and cannot be controlled of the things
untold.

Try as I might to keep them controlled they
come to the surface wanting to be told.

If I had done this or I had done that I feel as
though I was the one attacked.

These feelings are real there's no denying, but
we must never stop trying. Things will get
better one day you will see as long as there's
hope in you and me.
Diane S. Bernier

Homocidalmanicat

My pet, a cat, is a wild as wild can be.
I pick him up, he runs away,
and the next thing I know
he's eating me.

He likes me though, I know it,
Although he chews on my favorite hat.
He's a true Homocidalmanicat.

At breakfast he's at me the most.
He acts like I'm his host.
But when I leave the table,
he creeps and steals my (now dead) poor meal.

He likes me though, I know it.
Although he chews on my favorite hat.
He's a true Homocidalmanicat.
Colin Arden

Looking In The Picture Window

There is a face at the window.
It smiles at my catch.
I run toward it and wave.
Then about-face — go for the touchdown!
    Roll down the hill.
I come back up the hill.
The face gone, the room dark.
The end zone overgrown.
I bushwhack to the faceless
Window where my grandfather
    Used to stand.
W. Wright Dempsey Jr.

To My Love

Roots holding firm within the ground, source of love, beauty, and wisdom.
A stalk slender and strong, holding hidden thorns to guard against those who wish it harm.
Red petals of desire, feeling so soft and tender, I long to know.
Each one holding, embracing, spiraling to the garden center, source of the sweet smelling fragrance which dulls the senses, loves sacred nest.
Flower of immaculate love, petals of enticing desire, cannot I become a drop of purity amongst your luscious garden.
Wade Bacun

Twilight

During twilight hours,
When the sky flushes with a dying glow
With shades of all flowers,
With endless colors all in rows,
With restless clouds,
Upon the dark twilight hues
With stars standing in crowds,
Upon those sparkling blues
The heavens are cloaked by a burning sun,
Tones of yellow and orange are stealing the show
You pray for it never to be done,
As it sinks down very low,
Soon the darkness of night
Assumes its plight,
With an occasional star,
Poking through from afar.
Annie Calamari

Tony

I held him in my arms
    when he was only twenty minutes old,
his eyes squinty and blurred,
    already a dark chocolate color.

A tiny cap perched precariously on his head,
    to keep his body from growing cold,
the blanket wrapped tightly around
    for the same purpose.

As I held him close to me
    my heart forged a bond
of love with him to last our lifetimes.
    His and mine, together.

My tiny puff of life and breath
    has grown to half a man
with thoughts, ideas, and emotions.
    The bond of love even deeper between us.

My grandson, light of my life,
    apple of my eye, holder of my hand,
he growing up and me growing older
    it will end someday, but not now.
Marion L. Gartman

Untitled

Mother's hands are special, their worth cannot be told.
For with that wonderful touch all pain and fears will go.
They feel as soft as delicate silk, though lined and made rough, for they have done so many things that other hands would not touch.
They have dried many tears and given a gentle caress, nursed wounds and fixed countless meals never taking a rest.
They may not hold diamonds and other precious stones, for their strength and solace is more valuable to soother and console.
So when you look at Mothers hands the story can be told,
God gave those hands to a Mother with a heart of gold...
Robin Radcliff

He Is Not Gone

His face is missed at my table today.
Ron, my friend, has just stepped away.
He visits a place so majestic and grand.
A beautiful valley in a glorious land.

Peace goes with him and love guides him through.
My friend is whole, his body is new.
God serves his banquet, seasoned with love,
My friend dines with angels high up above.

Someday, my friend will greet me again,
God, in his wisdom, knows the hour and when,
Ron and I will talk like before.
Until our reunion, he watches the door.

My friend looks down from Heaven, I know,
His love guides my steps wherever I go.
This I'll remember and continue to pray,
My friend is not gone, he has just stepped away.

Brenda Ann Pirtle

Tell Me About Myself

There was a lady at the bus stop.
Who told a tale I haven't forgot.
About her friend whose doing wrong.
Seems to me, causing her much harm.

She told a tale of a man gone astray.
Seems to me, she still wants him to stay.
I say, "Pray For Him. Maybe He'll Stop Doing Wrong."
But I can't help but wonder, "Is he causing her harm?"

There was a lady at the bus stop.
Standing on one foot, then the other.
Telling a tale that could be about my brother.
My sister, my mother, my father, it could be.
But, she told a tale that could have been me.

There was a lady at the bus stop.
Who told a tale I haven't forgot.

Robbie White Woodson

The Reaper Comes

The reaper came but he wasn't so grim,
Say "Goodbye" to you father now, because I have come to take him....

I looked at him dying in his bed,
As I watched helplessly, I saw his soul lift gently from his head....

I didn't know at that moment what it is to die,
I only knew I lost my father and all I could do was cry....

He still calls my name and I hear him loud and clear as day,
His voice stays gently on my mind and it never goes away....

I miss you so much Daddy, sometimes the hurt is so deep I don't know what to do,
The only consolation that I have in my aching heart is knowing
This world was never meant for someone as beautiful as you....

Sylvia La Barbera

My Parents

My parents are very special to me.
They are there whenever I scrape a knee.

If I have a problem, we talk it out.
They never scream and shout

We love to spend time with each other.
I love my mother!

We never - well, almost never - interrupt and bother.
I love my father!

They'll always have a special place in my heart.
And we'll never, ever part

Marlow Riedling

Eddie

His hair, lusciously long
His muscles, boldly strong
His eyes, piercing blue
His clothes are worn, even his shoes

He shouts his anger into the mic
Oh to see him, it is a sight

Sweat rolls down his face
His mind is lost without a trace

To see him is to want him
To want him is to love him

Despite his frustration, anger, and rage
He is the voice for our age

Laura Beth Stubblefield

Final Goodbye

It's time to say "goodbye"
The light is growing dim
I can't control the feeling inside, the terror down within'
Oh how I shall miss the warm summer days
The chilly nights of winter, they're vanishing in the haze
My family oh so dear, my friends are always near
My time has come too early, but please don't shed a tear
"Why me" I ask inside, I'm too young for this to be
I only had one sniff of It, but now look what it's done to me
Oh how I wish I could take back that one day in my life,
    How I wish it so
I will never see what it's like to live a life all of my own
I'll never start a family, or marry someone nice
Oh God why did you do this to me, did you just go and roll the dice?
The time is coming closer, I can feel it in my heart
Just hold my hand and stay beside me
I promise you we'll never part
I'm saying my "goodbye" now
The light is fully dimmed
I don't have to control the feeling inside
For there is no more terror within'

Corinne Thumm

Ode To Vietnam Veterans

Let this wall be your shrine and our touchstone
So that we may always remember
What we once forgot:
To give one's life is no little thing.

Our conscience looking backward;
Forever onward, remembering a time,
When things were not so good; when
A total conscience wavered, flickered and nearly died.

Our apathy developed into an indifference for our defenders.
Remorse, reach out, striving to touch the souls of the departed.
To express: the loss, the pain and the extreme regret.
This stark wall intensifies the anguish of this era.

And there, in the background, those anxious figures,
Graven in the cold of metal
They serve to compound the tragedy of it all.
This spot is heavy with remorse and our extreme regret.

Phyllis L. Gaiotti

The Little Boy!

When I was a little boy people used to laugh
and pick on me , they would call me names like wimp
or siss. (Sissy)

When I got a little older I learned to use my fists.
   Now that I'm a man I've learned
not to raise a hand.

   Now if people treat me like the little boy,
      I look at them and wonder, -who the little boy
really is?

   As a man I ponder, how do you defend yourself
      from the little boy?
      This my friend is how you should defend.
When someone acts in ignorance simply ignore them.

Charles Palmere

Teenage Suicide

Past all that has been unsaid
I come to wonder if I'm dead
Everything around is sending me vibes
Now I wonder where I stand
Is this life lasting through eternity
Or do we come and go as they please
Only the strange can tell you the truth
But lies is all that they receive
And all are triggered at their consent
What will happen to all around
We act as if we don't exist
But every little one has a tear tumbling down
And now the parents have a frown
Where can we go with all we know
Seems as if we know too much
And now we wait to see if we are right.

Rob Parisi

Lasting Time

Centuries have passed, but it's only been hours.
Sitting in this cell I start to ponder.
Eager to leave, but going nowhere
I start to wonder
If I will slumber and it will all be a bad dream.

Curt Johnson

Perfect World

Come with me to a world of sunshine, love and unity.
No one here will hurt you, let your imagination go.
What do you see in a perfect world?
I see rainbows, sunlight, puffed clouds,
People smiling and laughing.
No worries or arguments.
A bridge over there in a meadow.
It stands over a crystal stream.
Wildlife all around it.
Flowers sweet smelling, colors so bright.
Soft, gentle animals drinking the clear water.
A couple stands on the bridge.
Waiting?
No, just taking in everything they can with one look.
Their life is simple.
Love rules their world, happiness,
Something most of us can't even understand.
But wish we could.
So, what rules your world?

Debra E. Nelson

Our People

Our black race can't seem to come together
No matter the conditions or even the weather
Our main objective is to hold each other back
That's not fiction but just plain fact
We step on each other to get ahead
We sometimes leave our victims for dead
So we ourselves can get ahead
Sometime we try to hide our color
We even try to take on another
For it will never do
For we are black through and through
Until we except who we are
And work together we won't get far
Our black race must work to come together
Or our condition will get worse
They'll never get better.

Alicia Riley

Sharing

The dimensions and definitions of myself,
change and shift to such an extent
that is has been difficult to
"find myself"

Yet, I persist.

For if I do not struggle with the attempt,
who shall challenge on my behalf.
For if I do not endure,
how shall I ever share that which I am, with
another.

However, the possibility of sharing
that which I am with another,
is not the motive of the struggle.

The possibility of sharing that
which I am with me,
is the essence of the thing.

Janice L. Burns

The Lonely Call

I did not hear the lonely call,
My ears were filled with future sounds—
Of love, strange places, happiness and joy,
Children's voices, mine and more.

Through the years, the sound was there,
Touching faintly through the tears—
Children's laughter, love and life,
Kept the barrier fairly intact.

The years passed by, one by one,
Chipping away the edges of serenity—
The hurt, the loneliness and the words,
Wore thin the shield of love.

The eyes that were so bright with hope,
The heart so full of love—
The lonely call had finally touched,
Absorbed the shield and dulled.

The lonely call was always there,
But happiness shut it out—
Finally destiny intervenes and the
Loneliness is in-not out.

Norma Alliston

A Special Pony

Dippy is a good horse
Especially on the jump course.
He is a Dapple Gray
Not a dark Brown like a Bay.
Dippy has the courage of a horse
But actually he is a pony.

Dippy had ulcers and he was old. Then one
Night he got a cold. Now he's gone and left me
lonely. But I'll always remember that pony.

I remember him well, and he is one thing I
would Never sell. He was a little speedy and a
Little fast. My memory of him will always last.

When I visit his grave I think about him; fast
And brave. I will always love and miss him, I
will never forget him, especially his cute,
And trusting face. No other pony could ever
Take his place.

Jeana Atkins

Untitled

When I look in the mirror,
I don't know what I see.
I am confused,
Would you please help me!
I am looking to be my own personal self,
But who am I really?

I want to be happy and free,
But will my soul let me.
I have to take on my own identity.
Let me look in the mirror and see me.

Michelle Dettling

Amy

Your lips are so sweet, while your hair is like gold,
I have wanted for years, to grab you and hold.

My dream has come true, in my arms you will stay,
It's weird how fate works, in its mysterious way.

While once we were friends, with our feelings inside,
I know now you care, so I'll no longer hide.

My feelings for you, burn with such a great heat,
I wait for the moment, when our lips again meet.

The feelings I have, are not just of lust,
The feelings I have are respect and of trust.

I bid you adieu, while my feelings are strong,
I hope our relationship, is loving and long.

Taylor Scott

Memories From Afar

He left this world to enter anew
It does not seem right but it is true.
It was his time I guess you could say
even though we may not like it that way.
In the sky we see above
He is there sending all of his love.
Although transparent he may be
he is there for you and for me.
He is not there to hold or embrace
yet in the shadows we see his face.
Here we sit and morn his death
although he is not dead, he took his first breath.
A breath into a magical life he shall now live
but to see him again there is nothing we would not give.

Nicole L. Parris

Life's Like An Ocean Of Seas

Though it roars
Though it flows
No one knows where it goes

Though it flows
Though it roars
No one knows how it flows

Though it's sometimes calm
Though it's always cool
The waters too have their moods

Though it's sometimes full
Though it's sometimes blue
No one knows when it blows

Though it's sometimes high
Though it's sometimes low
Who can tell of its source?
Who can tell the power behind the force?

All I know is, it has no end
All I know is it's full of mysteries
Life's like an ocean of seas.

Joyce Asabor

The End

He put a round in the chamber as he
Contemplated the deed.
　Hearing objections in his head but
Paying them no heed.
　Facing the sun with a smile, a haunting
Deadly grin.
　Gathering up the strength to commit
The ultimate sin.
　Faced with empty dreams and the agony of
Regret.
　A mountain of pain impossible
To forget.
　Driven by his thoughts into the
Depths of Hell.
　A place where he can no longer
Stand to dwell.
　Closing his eyes and fighting back
His fear.
　He slowly pulled the trigger and
Watched his life disappear.

Jake Trimm

To Be Free, Suddenly

I can feel it moving upon me suddenly I'm free,
free to cry to laugh to sigh...
then suddenly all those highest mountains don't seem so high...
I'm suddenly head over hills where times are low, I can help
myself because I'm in control. Suddenly I have given
control of my life over to God who receives us (his children)
willfully and at all times unconditionally.
(Thank You, Oh Lord) Heavenly father, so Divine who I
adore all of a sudden, I'm not so sad anymore, pledges of
truth of acceptance are sure as change is a coming...
suddenly, it takes its place and oh how now I can feel it
suddenly I see and understand that we can choose to be
foolish, we live in a world which now has many foolish
people with many foolish things. Always and suddenly the
master and creator of all Greatness and goodness has shown
his Grace upon the face of this place we know as Mother Earth
suddenly and always it is our responsibility to treat each other
righteously, for it's the way we want to be treated
suddenly and always we should keep our mother earth
because she is of God's universe....

Chun-Tay Hodge

The Game

I sit watching the smoke rise from a cigarette
Like a soul rising from a lifeless body
I fall into contemplation of life
With all its twists and turns

Watching people as they walk by
Knowing that every second that slips away
That time is cut away
From their earthbound existence

They become older
They try to keep their youth
And it becomes
Just a game to stay young

But they know that in this game
There are no winners
But still they play
The game
Christopher H. Rider

The Truth Hurts

Each day you act like nothing's wrong
but each time I kiss you, your stomach turns
because deep inside you know the truth hurts.

Each night you stay up thinking of what
you've done today. When you sleep you have
no dreams to dream and no hopes to hope.

Each time I talk to you, I don't know
what to believe anymore because you've only
told me lies. I don't understand why.

But when your friends stop the lies it
comes down to you and the truth then both
you and I know: "The Truth Hurts".
Paula Solorzano

I Love You Cuz

I love you cuz, you're my angel
I love you cuz, you're my friend
I love you cuz, love never ends

I love you cuz, you're my mom
I love you cuz, you're my dad
I love you cuz, you give me a life to live

I love you cuz, you're my sister
I love you cuz, you're my brother
I love you cuz, I'm like no other
Douglas E. Young

The Girl

She remembers when she was small,
Full of joy and love all around her,
Curious about everything, No worries at all,
   She remembers, who is she? The Girl.
She remembers when she was a little more tall,
loving the outside and the wind in her hair,
She's screaming but no one will hear her call,
   She remembers, who is she? The Girl
She remembers when she grew up a little bit more,
Confusion sets in and the world is changing,
She's sad and her heart is very sore,
   She remembers, who is she? The Girl.
She's grown up but it's already too late,
Memories will be with her forever,
She wants to love, but she only feels hate.
   She remembers, who is she? The Girl.
Kim Clark

The Housewife Blues

Up from your bed at five o'clock. Turn out the cat. Turn off the clock. Rush to the bathroom to wash off your face. Snatch off your gown with its ragged lace. Put on your dress; a button is off. Don't look for your shoes for you know they are lost. You look all around you and gosh what a sight. You must have had visitors some time through the night. For certainly a family of four or five couldn't make such a mess. Good heavens alive! You do the laundry, you sweep the floor. You wash the dishes by the score. You mow the lawn and run to town before the morning is half around. Then junior rises; what a tart. He wants his breakfast ala carte. He wants it served cafe' style; served right and with a smile. He wants his clothes, a certain kind. To form and fashion he is blind. Faded jeans is all he'll wear. Then you have ruptoins with his hair. Then sister bounces down the stairs with many curlers in her hair. She can't find this! She can't find that! Then she and brother have a spat. Now, to the aspirin bottle go. No, make it Bufferin, aspirin's slow. You check the clock; it's after four. You hear your family at the door. You wonder where the day has gone. You feel another headache coming on. Now hubby, he comes dragging in. The toys are strewn all over the den. He saunters to his easy chair. "Bring me a cup of coffee, dear. I have worked eight hours today, and I'm too tired to work or play". Your hands are red, your eyes are too. You ache in body through and through. Your hair strings around your face. Your tired body has lost its grace. You have got to make it one more day. So, please be careful what you say. You must stop and realize you are only looking through your eyes. You're his doctor, his lawyer, nurse; you're his cook, his wife, that's worse. Don't touch the strings on his purse, because if you do, a fuse will burst. Now. a man's work is from sun to sun, but woman's is never done. So don't expect too much from life, because honey, you are someone's wife.
Beatrice Cockrell

Sonnet To A Psychopath

The mask you wear belies the barren soul,
Evoking trust, securing aid to ply
The plans and checkered patterns of your role,
And leave aghast the bonded friends to sigh.
How soon the gleam that shimmers in your eyes
Betrays the hope to plumb a deeper vein,
The charm and grace and wit in quick surprise
Upstage the heartless player's sad domain.
With glib barrage of words a fort you rear
'Twixt proffered love and earnest, heartfelt rune.
Nor hope, nor faith, nor enervating fear
Expect incursion there for soulful boon.
   How strange to know and not know indeed
   A mortal blind to life's primeval need.
Norman Ellis

Virtual Reality

As we seek to personify our intentions
   We fail to observe the transient dimensions
With every step in cadence strides
   Voluptuous ego in vanity prides

As we try to exonerate the past
   Desires endlessly seem to last
In infinity existence is bound
   But nowhere is there time to be found

As we transcend this illusory existence
   We approach the divine in vain persistence
Virtual is to be human in nature
True reality is non-dual in nature
Ashwin B. Mistry

Am I Old Enough?

I thought I was old enough to be out
on my own, and to have a child at
age sixteen I felt more like I
   was grown.

And the day my man, the father of my
child did not turn out to be what I
thought he would be, was the day
he walked out on our child and me.

  So now I am finally paying the price,
to know that being a teenage mother is
not nice. I had to quit school and worked
two jobs to keep hope alive for me
and my child, because the life I had
out there in the world was pretty wild.
  Sometimes I wished the day would come
back when I had listened to my mother,
but I have already messed up so why bother.
So now I have to continue to live the life I
have now, and I hope and pray that things
will work out for me and my child somehow.
    Cheryl Jackson

Thoughts Of Him

He stirs the soul —
Visions of his goodness
Spreads the wealth
And leaves my grin to linger.
A good friend —
Touching hearts and
Asking for nothing.
Misunderstood by those
Who need to see to believe...
But I can see.
Those sparkling eyes of a child!
He is playful and kind,
And caring, too much, maybe
Sometimes to unveil a facade of ugliness —
Brief, but impressionable.
Only those who search within
Will know his true convictions.
I know, and I believe.
He has shown me his sweetness,
And my heart is at peace.
    Jennifer Wolfenden

Lion

A mighty King
His name is gold,
Stillness shudders at his blatant roar
The Lion comes.

The Lion comes
He calls for food,
His choice appeased
Midst his kingdom's shade, his hunger ceased
The Lion rests.

The Lion comes
And life is back,
Shrieks from big birds
An elephant's wail
Laughs from hyenas and their pack
The Lion comes.
    Lottie Lee Mason

Passion Unspoken

What shall I say to him.
   the object of my affection?
My love for him burns brightly
   I do not understand how it escapes detection.
So enraptured am I that the words fail
to fall from my lips.
Yet I can hardly contain this passion.
Imprisoned am I by my desires.
Terrified that he must surely realize it.
Fearful that he may never acknowledge it.
I love this man with my entire being.
A passion so intense that I fear it will
destroy me.
Should I reveal these truths held captive in my mind?
If spoken and he denies me, what would become of me?
My heart would break in an instance
yet I will not go one moment longer
without confessing.
This love shall not be denied.
This passion must be spoken.
    Kathleen Hammes

Flood

Her old life flees along with the orange rescue boats,
Chased away by a deep river and torrential rain.
Filthy muddy water washes her dreams away
And leaves her alone with two young brothers
All in one night

How can a newly orphaned girl achieve her dreams,
Stranded on a lonely rooftop with her sobbing siblings?
All in one night

She ponders her old life-
Filled with all the wonders of childhood;
Trees to climb, flowers to pick, sweets to savor-
A life changed by water gone wild,
All in one night
    Elaine L. Hornby

If I Were A Snowflake

If I were a snowflake,
I would drift from the sky,
and land on a place as cold as I.
I would watch the people shovel the snow
and wait for the wind to blow me away
to a place where the children would say,
"We will build a snowman today."
And the children would pack me on his head
and I would never be led away
from the snowman which was my bed
and I would enjoy my time
in the snowman's head.
    Deborah Guiffaut

"As Strong As The Love Will Glow"

Wondering where you have been all my life
From the very first time I laid my eyes on you,
Spoke to you, I knew that you were that special person
By your disguise, Oh how I want to show you what love is
And I babe will always be there for your comfortness,
Like the sunshine glare coming from the skies,
You can declare that my love will always be glowing for you,
As more of the days to go by day by day
My love will always be stronger for you
    William P. Johnson

Real World

In the real world,
Children cry at night.
  White and black cross into gray.
Wrong suddenly becomes right.

In the real world,
Upon souls the devil does feed.
  Hearts are viciously broken,
Leaving the lonely to bleed.

In the real world,
People's dreams are shattered.
  Death replaces life,
And existence becomes scattered.

Why is love so hard to hold,
And feelings cease to exist?
  It seems the true meaning of life
We have looked past and missed.

  So, I unsheathe my sword
And set out upon the great quest.
  To find again peace, harmony and love.
Virtues hidden, but still found among the best.
   Troy L. Mendenhall

Struggle

Women black and strong
stately and defiant
baskets on your heads
child in your belly
Marching towards the city in search of equality

Women old and gnarled
scrubbing steps with distant eyes
Which tell stories of years of pain and suffering

Woman-child you have the story
of two generations behind you
LEARN FROM THEM
   Patricia Rodney

Help!

Where to, I ask,
What hidden place is there for me to hide?
To lay my daily burdens down for just one
Moment,
Casting cares aside
Please God, I beg
Gently take my hand and lead me there,
Then as a child, I'll humbly go to rest
And given strength, go on to
God knows where.
   Madge Westendorf

In The Eye Of An Eagle

In the eye of an eagle, I would be free. I would fly so fast that the wild winds would blow my gold and white feathers and as the wind, hits my fragile face it would make my eyes water. The feeling of being free; to spread my wings and fly; to answer to no one; to be able to fly and see everything that man wishes he could see. The feeling of being independent and not having to deal with guns, gangs, and violence. To be in the eye of an eagle would be like holding a great big precious jewel in my hands. In the eye of an eagle is like being a wild animal that can never be captured. To be able to see the world; to be able to escape from the world sometimes. In the eye of an eagle...
   Wauneta Louise Vann

Railway Children

Pulling into a train station, at a town we
didn't know, would this be the time of separation?
The look on your face told me so.

  Mixed emotions were among us, as we stood
there in a line, smiling faces there to greet us,
but...... not every time.

  I kissed you goodbye at the station, as you got
back on the train, just a young boy without
destination, I didn't understand your pain.

  Where are you today my sister, and are you
still alive? The day they took you from me, I was
a lad just barely five.

  I still have this old picture, of you and me
from long ago, and with it and your memories, I
still cry from missing you so.
   Ron Krout

Mourn For Childhood

So much a child, yet so old,
  where did all the time go?
The time when there were no cares is gone.
   It flew away.
   It left too soon, only to allow the pain.
The tears that fall from my eyes,
   the knife that makes me bleed,
and the bowl of ashes that remain.
   Ashes to ashes, dust to dust.
The time has come for me to die.
   For, without innocence I can no longer live.
I cannot watch the horror,
   I cannot hear the screams,
I cannot taste the tears,
   No more shall I endure.
   Vanessa Larson

Kitchen After Dark

In a kitchen after dark everything changes
Like an ordinary stove transforms into
Stuart the stove who is a very sweet young
Man until someone starts pushing his buttons
That's when he gets all fired up. Or the ever so
Sweet Samantha the stove hood who defiantly
Knows what is love for she is ever so in love
With Stuart the stove and is constantly
Hovering over him. There's also Freddy the
Fridge who thinks he knows what he's talking
About, but everyone knows he's just full of
Bologna. Of course there's Sally the sink who
Loans out her extra room for weekly utensil
Meetings. So whenever you find yourself in a
kitchen after dark beware!
   Jackie Guiliani

God's Hands

That night in the hospital
Hearing everyone cry,
Not believing she would really die.
Her thick, brown hair surrounding her pretty face,
Now she's gone to a better place.
Her dreams to go to college
Her dreams to be successful
All in the balance of God's Hands.
Now I wait till I see her again
My sister and my friend.
   Eva Bass

Until My Ship Is Anchored

How can I help not missing you
For the pain never goes away
As sadly my ship leads me
To you... as I place flowers on your grave

Yes, I recall each moment
And every small detail
All... now a memory
As swiftly onward I must sail

And though... time cannot be erased
Nor started over again
Neither can it be forgotten
It just becomes my closest friend

So, onward I'll keep sailing
Oft' times docking at your grave
Until my ship is anchored
On that last eternal wave

Constance M. Bernhard

The Eye Of The Cat

A big brown eyeball shines like brass
As it peers through the big clear looking glass
It sees the black cat sit and stare
As he attempts to give the victim a scare
Crouched like a panther he's ready to kill
He's thinking much thought but yet he stays still
Then pounces his victim persistent to death
Claws in the rat until his last breath
A stalker sees himself as a cat
Sees a victim as no more than the rat
The blue moon shines as the stalker awaits.
The victim knows nothing of his deadly fate
With the greatest of ease the stalker attacks
And takes his victim down from the back
The stalker finds being the cat isn't fun
When the victim fights back with his handgun

Ares Joe Casarez

Qs And Answers

If procrastination be the thief of time
  Why?- With so little left
    Don't we share more now
    With those we'll leave bereft

Is it - mindless - we feel invincible
  To the forces of life's battering
    or find
    Thoughts of departure too shattering

And as we pray for strength today
  To do what needs be done
  Give of ourselves along the way
    To every needful one

Please: Grant us that the wasted years
  Gone - "With not enough of"
  Are forgiven to become
    A heritage of Love

Terry M. Greene

Eternity

Pour yourself into me and feel the love I wish to expend.
Together, we gather thorns for flowers, and lies for happiness.
I call to you from afar to raise you from your dreary sleep.
To unite our souls and swim in the lakes of each others' minds.
I yearn for your presence and need your touch.
Often I get so cold when you are not near.
For you are the only one who helps alleviate my fears.
We burn in our lust, we die in our eyes, and drown in our arms, for eternity.

Derek Damico

A Place In The Heart

  There's a place in my heart where the air is pure,
and the water is still so clean.
  There's a place in my heart where you look out your
window, and the world is a beautiful scene.

  In this place all people are loved, there's no such thing as abuse.
Prejudices do not exist, for here they have no use.

  The children never starve from hunger, they do not cry from fear.
They're always fed and there are no wars, for the world has enough
to share.

  Guns and bombs are not a threat, people don't kill they live.
When someone's in need a stranger will help, and everyone knows
to forgive.

  If all of God's people could open their minds and realize what
life is worth.
We could pull this place right out of the heart, and make it be real
on earth!

Tammy Silva

Devil Go Away

Devil go away
  I do not want, your evil in my world today.
Devil go away
  For I have prey today.
My pray is here to stay.
Devil go away
  "You"! Will not have
My soul today.
  My soul is here to stay.
For I have prey everyday,
  To keep you away
Devil! You will go away.
  For I have faith in him.
For he paid the way
  It was him, who died
for my sins today.
  He arose on Easter Day.
He lifted me up, and gave me wings.
So I could fly far away.
  .....So devil you stay away

Cheryl Reese

I'd Like To Know

I was reading a prophet and it said
One day human race won't see a sunset
It said our morality would be dead
I asked myself if it could be true,
And so I walked down the avenue.

I saw children coming home from school
I guess I must've been a fool
Because at first I was stoned
I saw a boy who carried a gun
But this is how today things at school run.

So now I ask how we became this way
Because there is a huge price we must pay;
Would someone tell me, I'd like to know
Are we coming to a death row?!

Would someone tell me
How a mother kills
Would someone tell me
How a lawyer steals
If our morality already dead
Will we see a peaceful sunset?!

Angela Vasserman

Wooden Ships Asleep

Quiet of water... gently holding each shape.
Still of night... no abuse 'til dawn.
Held in check like tender lace...
Hemp and nylon has its place.
Oceans pound us to and fro...
Men push beyond our control.
Victims of wind and whim...
Wearing us from thick to thin.
Flags of full colour... we carried with pride.
The lights, the lights... they're bringing us home.
Still of night... our only song.
Modern men, have no idea...
There was a time, when daylight was dearer.
History has dealt us a terrible fate...
Ships of plastic and men with no faith.
Wooden ships, we are getting old...
Wooden ships, that can't be sold.
It's better this way...even though we must rot.
Sawdust to sawdust...we were and are the best of the lot.

Louis Gilmore

The Sea

A strange land to be sure
Where mist and sea and wet sand are one once more.
The eyes beguiled
We stepped out upon the shimmering surface-
A carpet of welcome unfurled from the deep.

Down into the watery tunnel we went
Drawn deeper within exquisite crescendos of harmonies
Yet unheard by the human ear-
Thunderous basses, angelic choruses entwined in unison
The song of the sea, the soul's own song.

Then with a tumultuous roar the stallions emerged
To crest the waves, eyes watery wild with passion.
Pearls and shells in garlands adorned their necks
Seaspray their manes, but none so splendid
As golden Neptune strident at the reins.

God of the Ages
What celebration to dance in your kingdom
And witness mermen sounding sea horns
To pattern out of the ethers silver spires-
At last to be within the castle of all dreams.

Fiona Douglas-Hamilton

Mother

I heard your tender voice
through the darkness where I grew,
you nurtured me and shielded me, as only you could do.

I saw your tears of joy
as I took my very first breath,
your eyes were wide, your face a glow, a sense of happiness.

I felt your will and liveliness
as I took my very first steps,
you gave me spirit, encouragement, although I felt inept.

I observed you from a distance
as I grew into a man,
you were amiable and meek, unwithered by demand.

I sometimes see you in myself
as I search my heart and soul,
you're a true humanitarian, how much, you'll never know.

I found in you great strength
as I've found in no other,
you love me unconditionally, you're an angel...you're my mother.

Lesli Lynn Sadakane

Born Is Beauty

Birth is the beauty from which I came,
a seed which bore no other name.
No one can ever be what became me,
but this is what gives the world its beauty.

All quilted patterns of human traces,
make up the globe with many races.
A spectrum of light brings out the sign
that the wonder of creation is human kind.

We are what make the world go 'round,
'cause in each of us beauty is found.
Masked by a grace which unwraps the dawn,
our human spirit will always live on.

If we see what lies beyond one's image so bold,
their soul will reflect us in its mirror of gold.
We'll never be alike but the same from the start,
'cause the beauty of life was baked within the heart.

Now we know the answer to the secret of peace,
it lies within us....
the mystery of life that will never cease.

Frances Hergan

My Son Of The Nineties

It seems like only yesterday
You were innocent and small.
You're grown up now and on your way
And I don't really know you at all.

I spoke very often of right and wrong
And about making good decisions.
You haven't been away from me that long
But you certainly have different visions.

I don't think I like the Nineties much
Living together is just not 'my thing'.
There are precious moments in courtship
Love grows—a proposal—a ring.

I'm sure you're in love with this woman
And for you life is pretty certain.
But, I haven't been to a wedding
And my heart can't seem to stop hurting.

Linda A. Reilly

Who Am I?

Who am I? That's the question I ask.
As I look into the mirror each day,
I see a lost little girl not knowing who she is.
As she envies the woman on her
wall she wanders, "She is no different
from me!" "We are both human!"
"We eat, drink, and breathe!" This lost
girl I see in my reflection is longing
to be loved and like for who she is
and not by appearance. She is lost in
curiosity. "When will I be able to know
and find out who I really am? I have
been waiting for so long and for what?
To be taken as a joke? I don't know, but
one day I will be discovered!

Emily Yung

Royal Robin Upon His Throne

As the sun doth take its place in the sky,
And the dew settle fresh on the ground,
A robin peeks out from within a wee knothole,
And silently looks around.

As it doth not see one from the outside world,
It spreads its wings and taketh flight.
It perches atop the towering sycamore tree,
And washes its wings so bright.

For at this time there approaches no man,
To fall his magnificent throne.
No man nor maid doth now advance,
To claim the forest as his own.

The tiny robin looks down upon,
Its royal subjects whom boweth low.
He cheerfully chirps a merry tune,
As his subjects gaily dance below.

Debra Guzman

The Touch Of A Hand

It's smooth as silk and it glides evenly.
As my eyes close I can feel the touch that soothes
and heals
It rushes in like a mighty wind,
that blows the fresh air and
whirlwind dreams in my mind.
It carries strength as strong as a
mighty storm, but yet it holds on
to me like a mighty thorn.
Oh what a joyous thrill,
to know it's not over the hill,
but right within my reach,
So I dream dreams upon the sand,
of just a little touch of a hand.

Earlene Coes Lester

Vision

I had a dream or vision of which I can't be sure,
Appearing was my Father attempting to assure,
Son he said, I love you and please do not grieve so,
Some day we'll be together in the next world this I know,
Don't look at this dead body as if it were the end,
We both have responsibilities that we must surly tend,
We brought each other happiness and now we must go on,
You to live in this world and me the world beyond.

God granted us this meeting for you to put to rest,
The fear that my departing would make your living less,
Do you think for just a minute our Creator could have planned,
For us to spend these few short years and it would be the end.
Hurry now, you must return, until the day we meet,
When your wife or son or daughter has a vision just as sweet.

Keith Williams

Family

From the drawing of life at the birth of a babe
til suddenly it seems you've reached middle age
Until death takes its toll on the sick or the old
A family will stand together.

Molded and Bonded by generations of love
Strengthened and guided by grace from above
Welded by faith, compassion, and trust
Giving one to another that which is just
A family stands together

From the roots of our beginning to each twig on our tree
This love is unshaken through eternity.
Nothing can break us or tear us apart
For each to the other we've given our heart.
And our Family will stand together.

Estelle M. Lovette

Breath from Heaven

I am so forlorn and yet with faith can be reborn
Help me God in my grief enrich me in my belief
For I am called to die
Yet heard the voice call in the night
Focus on the truth the Christ the light....
Then came the lie
So I focused on my own self-worth
and lost the chance at my re-birth
falling and falling to the heat of hell
I cried, I screamed my plea
'Twas just my humbleness he'd asked from me
I bowed my head into my shame
And once again called out the savior's name.
Before the final burn, the grip came firm
His hand was gently lifting my head
'Twas he, the one whose very blood was shed
He'd bought my life
who fought again, so unworthy of such love
Telling you this from heaven above.

Gale Cetto

Cherry Blossom

I dream a
Japanese Summer...
Of breeze-blown field paddies under cotton wind-wisps,
Floating upon sun-kissed sea of gold in blue.

I muse but awaken to a sardonic soft-scent of
Ginkgo and Cherry Blossom,
Matrimonially coupled as Buddha's beloved Shinto.

I reflect contritely among hills and valleys,
Sea's mist,
Marveling at autumn's ignominiously
Dissonant anthem, heard solely
Within allusion's prophetic chamber
Winter's Spring heralds its cyclic rendezvous, crying shrill-toned
up my spine.

I find comfort, though, despite
Ominous chill-tongued whispers,
In single Cherished Blossom glide over moss-glazed rock on
rippled glass.

Fragranced soul beckons
Summer slumber-intoxication.

I dream a heaven upon a bed of blossoms.

Mario C. Davis

A Poem For My Loving Father

A lasting love for you,
You will never be alone;
You have left us now:
You are going home to join
Your loving wife and mother.
Sleep in peace sweetheart.
Love, love, love forever
It's not good-bye....
But sleep in peace.
I will see you when I get home!

In loving memory of my father, Mr. G. W. Russell,
and mother, Mrs. Adell Russell,
and grandmother, Mrs. Idella Russell,
and all my loved ones gone before me.

Bettye Russell

Eyes Of Love

The photo was of a young girl on the beach,
Skin gleaming with oil and sunlight.
The old man said proudly, "This is my wife,"
A smile on his face and eyes bright.

You can tell from the picture how fair she was then,
This girl who now is his wife.
They've always been close, but not only friends,
He calls her "the love of my life".

The picture he holds has been his companion,
His precious possession for years.
They've travelled to far away places and back,
Shared laughter and often some tears.

The man's wife, now aged as he is and slow,
Has wrinkles and hair mostly white.
Her mind's not as sharp as it was on that beach,
Her memory's gone and her sight.

No matter her creaking old bones and sore knees,
For him she flies free as a dove.
She's still the young girl that she was long ago
As seen through the eyes of his love.

Jeanne D. Gunning

Untitled

Song of last Shitacawa Sioux they march on and on.
Endless days, endless nights.
Sad, empty eyes, down cast,
one strong born remains.
All others, dead, dead
She returns, returns
To home, to home.
She seeks always
A people no more, there voices stilled.
All is gone, All is gone.
Who will teach her now?
She cries, she cries.
For people who are no more
White men came, death came
Mother earth cries out.
Her children's voices stilled,
White men hands, their blood,
who listens now, to her now,
Mother earth knows.
She knows, she knows.

Brenda Clarke

An Ode To Oklahoma City

The horrible, horrible plot,
It hurt our country a lot,
So many lives were taken,
So many dreams forsaken,
The building so quickly came down,
The whole world seemed to frown,
While the survivors list was still at zero,
Ordinary people risked their lives to become America's hero,
The women, the children, and men,
Their lives won't be as they have been,
So many people had come to the call,
To lend their love and support to all,
And until they found the guilty human,
The police had to keep movin',
A teddy bear was given to all,
Who had lost someone in this senseless fall,
One year later the pain is still deep,
And the sorrow inside we will always keep,
All Americans must know,
The sadness caused by this blow.

Kari Day

Magic Roses

A rose, just one rose
I'm asking, yes, I'm asking from you
A rose, just one rose.
From you, yes you I know I'd cry,
For I've never yet gotten a rose,
Not even one rose.
As I leaned against the wall and watched as you walked by,
Wishing you would grab my hand and walk me by your side.
The second that I saw you I knew I had no chance,
The fancy car, football games, and high school king at every dance.
Many years later as I walked beside that wall,
I glance back at the memories of that young man that I saw.
As I slowly began to walk, lonely through the night,
A dark shadow behind me, came into my sight.
A rose I always asked for, A rose I then got.
I don't know how to thank him for that miracle that he brought.
As I slowly grab the petal and all my prayers come true,
I finally get to tell him those three words of "I love you."

April Aynes

A Single Rose

From the rarest rose in thy hand can not begin to compare to your beauty only introduce it. The beauty of a rose cannot be compare to any other flower, and like a rose, your beauty cannot be compared to any other woman around. Like a fragile unbloomed rose, your eyes propel me into a trance where I can only see how attractive you are and how nothing else matters. Compared to the blooming of the rose, your smile makes my heart skip beats. Like the fragrant of a rose, you leave me gasping for more air every time you go by because your beauty takes the breath out of me. Your long hair reminds me of the green stem of a rose and how it brings out its beauty as thus your beautiful hair does for you. However, the thorns of the rose reminds me that I don't have the courage to speak to you. This brings a single tear to my eye that waters the rose I embrace in my heart for You!

Mike Trotter

The Egg

An egg once sat upon a wall,
His name was Humpy Dump.
One day he tilted too far back
And landed with a thump.

The men and horses of the King
Converged upon the spot.
They thought they could repair the egg,
But really they could not.

An egg is scientifically
A chicken embryo.
Inside old Humpy was a chick-
Outside it didn't show.

But bird or man it matters not,
You think no one will know?
Just when you think you've fooled them all,
Your inner self will show.

So when you scramble to the top
And mock those down below,
Be careful that you do not slip-
Cause when you go-you go!

Greg Miller

Untitled

If life was like the blades of grass,
we would continue to grow.
If life was like the old willow,
we would be able to bend in time.
But we're not the many blades of grass.
We are not the old willow.

If the soul was like an open book,
we would be there for all to see.
If the soul was like a gentle breeze,
we would be eternal.
But the soul can be closed to all,
and the gentle breeze can cease.

But through time a life might bend,
and we will continue to grow.
We can learn to read what's in our hearts.
And with love the soul will be eternal.

Rosemary Miscovich

'Momma'

I can recall a lot of times,
I said I hated you.

I'm sure you know, but I must say,
That isn't very true.

Our friendship has grown into a thing,
So great I can't explain.

It's kind of like a rainbow,
After a treacherous rain.

Our argues are thunder,
Our shouts the rain.

But friendship and love have colored the sky,
We've overcome the pain.

I need you and rely on you,
I'm sure you know that now.

You'll always be 'Momma' to me,
Though I can't say just how.

I'll love you throughout my entire life,
And in the great beyond.

It's like a spell's been cast over me,
With the simple wave of a wand.

Sheana R. Director

Ode To Mom And Dad

In this old world so full of strife
My good dad found quite a wife
And the wife how smart was she
To find a man such as he.

When we were young and very small
They always answered our beck and call
Now we are grown and still have trouble
But they still come on the double.

When troubles and crisis come our way
They are always there to save the day
When sickness or sorrow do descend
They are always there to lend a hand.

Babysitter, shopping pal, advise in need
They are always there for every need
Just even need them for help or fun
They always come on the run.

There is so much that I could add
Some of it funny some of it sad
But for a starter I hope it will do,
This "Mom and Dad," my ode to you.

Betty J. Nash

Untitled

Last night as I got down and prayed, the Lord became so real,
He said, "My child talk to me, tell Me how you feel,"
I said, "I don't know what to do, my life has fell apart,"
He said to me, "that's why My child, I want to renew your heart,"
I said, "but Lord, I love him so, but no-one seems to care,"
"they care my child, more than you know, they tell Me in fervent prayer,"
"still Lord I'm so unhappy, it shouldn't be this way
"then do my child that which is right, turn and walk away,"
"but I feel that once we're married, then he will start to give,"
"My child, I died on Calvary, so a lie you would not live,"
"but Lord, to turn and walk away would cause such pain to me,"
"My child am I not able, to strengthen and comfort thee?"
"I love you more than you could know, I want to set you free,
that's why I say with out-stretched arm's, My child,
return to me....

Linda Mullins

I Think I'll Go Fishin'

The roof's fallin' in and the bills are all due
And I can't even smile, I'm feelin' so blue.
My boss let me go with a little pink slip
And I lost at the track on another bad tip....

The kids are all sick and in bed with the flu
And my wife just told me that she's been untrue.
The house is dark, guess the bill wasn't paid.
The dog had pups and I thought she was spayed...

I called my brother and asked for a loan
But laughter was all that I heard on the phone.
So I'm packin' my truck, headin' out of this town,
And if I am lucky, I'll never be found... so...

I think I'll go fishin' - way up on the hill
Where everything's quiet and peaceful and still.
I'll pitch me a tent and get away from it all
And if things calm down, I'll be back in the fall.

Sandy Fischer

Treasures Of Love

I wish that I were rich for you,
To buy you dreams untold.
Sleek racing cars of trips to the stars,
Or ships with sails of gold.

Days without toil, just idle bliss,
To do your heart's desire.
To swim, or skate or fly away,
Or just dream beside a fire.

But all I have is a wealth of love,
And this I gladly give.
I'll lay its riches at your feet,
As long as we both shall live.

Phyllis Dilts

White Owls...

If I could say any-thing and thus be discreet,
hidden by the misty air of the night.
Complacent of thought no matter, your heart
whispers theory,
my intuition of scholar are right.
To reiterate or interpret a perception of fire,
brilliance,
splendor, and spirit, in awe, true blue.
Comprisal and wisdom in vision known by so
many, yet none can jest or fathom such
celestial alliteration of one,
"All Of Which Is You"

Kenneth E. McDowell

Smile

Wouldn't it be wonderful even for a little while,
If most of the people around us would break out into a smile.

Start your day as pleasant as you can be,
The rewards are wonderful and you will see.

Why be gloomy and why be sad,
Life is so short, so why be mad.

We should show kindness to one another,
This way, believe it or not, we'll appreciate each other.

A little smile will go a long way,
And make people happy each and every day.

As long as we try to do our best,
We could set a good example for all the rest.

Control your anger no matter what people say,
And try your best to have a nice day.

If you and I would do our part,
It would give us a good feeling from our heart.

So I remind you, even for a little while,
Don't be afraid, break out into a smile.

Frank Wypych

Hallelujah

We are the creation of the Lord our God
The sheep of his pasture as we travel this sod
Be thankful with our praise as we come to his throne
Because we know heaven will be our last home

Hallelujah! Hallelujah! Praise to the Lord
Hallelujah! Hallelujah! All the earth sings
Hallelujah! Hallelujah! We worship our Lord
Hallelujah! Hallelujah! Earth his praises rings

The Lord is merciful praise his glorious name
His love is for ever and is always the same
His faithfulness continues throughout all our time
He is the creator and he is all mine

Hallelujah! Hallelujah! Praise to the Lord
Hallelujah! Hallelujah! All the earth sings
Hallelujah! Hallelujah! We worship our Lord
Hallelujah! Hallelujah! Earth his praises rings

Lee Stuck

The Visiting Russian Navy

The green-gray ship of Russia's fleet lay moored beside our pier,
Its guns and missiles in full view, in confidence, not fear.
They came in peace to meet our men; returned each one's salute;
Our thousands came and lines the dock to board and meet her crew.

The pink-cheeked men, those mothers' sons, shook hands and greeted all
Along the rails, their fervent hope of making peace, not war.
I gave bandanas to some men—a mother's touch for sure,
Then gazed below at waters blue, not red with blood of war.

The sky was clear, not pocked with bursts, but calm, soft clouds above;
This mother's heart was full of hope; and overhead, a dove!
It sat upon the upper part—the crow's nest of that ship.
I felt a drop—a tear of joy—on my own quivv'ring lip.

Lee Fleming Reese

Passing Season

Through the Appalachian mist I flew
To a place that I once knew
Under low lying clouds and rain I came
I knew it would never be the same
The dreary weather echoed what was in my heart
A sadness realized when we did part
The autumn colors faded in the darkened skies
While vivid memories flashed before my eyes
The cold wind caused the leaves to fall
Somehow I understood the permanence of it all
As the familiar mountains stood agelessly there
All I could do was tearfully stare
At the change that this season signified to me
A time of passing in my family
I knew that this would happen someday
That all the skies would turn to gray
I wore black to show my emptiness
For a father I truly miss

Virginia M. Vaccaro

It's Over

We met so long before.
From then I've only cared about you more.
We've had together so much fun.
Now you've disappeared like the setting sun.
Laughing, joking, driving in the rain.
Oh, how remembering brings such pain.

It took so long for us to realize.
We were such a big part of each other's lives.
It only took just one kiss.
Now your love is what I miss.
Your arms around me holding me close.
That feeling of warmth is what I miss most.

Now you've gone like a winter's storm.
In my heart the hurt begins to form.
I've known for so long it's true.
But it's over now and how can I say...
I love you.

Jody VanHout

The Night Breathes

And so the night breathes,
    with the wind a gentle tease.
The ocean a distant rumble,
    my mind starts to fumble.

As the coating of the night surrounds me,
    the weight of the day drowns me.
A sigh of relief escapes my lips,
    into dreamland my mind slips.

My eyelids have gained weight,
    once again it has gotten late.
With my soul I appease
    and so the night breathes.

L. A. Vogel

The Shadow Horse

A mysterious shadow is what it is
A horse and its baby on a rocky ridge
Some cows surround them on a foggy morning
And they munch on grass just ignoring
As birds fly past they stay very peaceful
A beautiful scene early in the morning

Megan Watzin

How Sweet The Sound

Hours of struggle to enter this world. How sweet the sound of a
   baby's first cry.
Days of study and earnest striving, How sweet the sound of a
   final school bell.
Weeks of seeking that "hoped for" job. How sweet the sound of
   "You're hired!".
Months of searching for that "special one". How sweet the sound
   of wedding fun.
Years of labor for life's needs and pleasures. Experiencing pride
   in one's accomplishments and endeavors. How sweet the sound
   of a retirement gala.
A decade or so later, when the reaper calls...may his voice
   resound as sweetly.
Can the unexperienced "sound of silence" be less sweet - than
   what has been?
    Gwyn Esch

Untitled

I walked once with head held high
Through war torn jungles that reached the sky
A young boy only days before
now a tested man in time of war
Fighting not for glory nor for fame
but for country and in Gods name
feared or scorned by fellow man
But I stood once where heroes stand
To take the life of another man
would be an act I could not plan
But to serve my country and questioning ask
I feel to be my patriotic task
To defend her in time of war
against enemies on foreign shore
is not popular throughout the land
but I stood once where heroes stand
    Roy L. Cranford Sr.

Top Dawg

He prances up and down the street
Looking for somebody to eat.

He bites his T-bone till it cracks,
Then he goes and rounds up his packs.

He likes to terrorize people's houses,
He ain't no cat, he don't chase no mouses.

He does very bad thangs,
Especially with his fangs!

This dog don't listen to your cry,
He will pass you by and by.

If he comes around your neighborhood,
You had better run for good!
    Matt Mitchell

The Family Tree

It's an amazing thing to me -
   The family tree.
From grandparents and parents before,
   To my children and the offspring they bore.
I watch as they grow and personalities flow;
   Before my eyes - a resurrection of those
Who came before, ancestors of yore.
   It comes to mind how quickly passes time.
How deeply rooted is the Family Tree!
   Its revelation never ending
Till mankind ceases to be.
   On-going - the Family Tree.
    Genevieve Tesche

End Of The Road

As you walk the road of life
There are many paths to take
Each one poses a different problem
Another decision to make
No one knows which trail to choose
For the ends have all turned black
But once you make a certain choice
There is no turning back
As I walk my own small road
It hurts for me to find
That shattered dreams and painful thoughts
Are all that's left behind
As we stare into the dark
We can't see through the night
We try to find that certain path
That will lead us to the light
As we wander in the darkness
On this road that can't be named
We go and take the final step
To find the end the same
    Thomas Narcisi

Mystery Girl

   There's this girl on my mind 24 hours A day.
As I look into her beautiful blue eyes, I see A glimpse of
hope for us but none, none at this moment.

   I do everything I can to get her to notice me but nothing,
nothing at all is working none, none at this moment.

   As I treat her like a Queen with all of my respect, while I try
to get her to notice me but nothing, nothing at all is working
none, none at this moment.

   As I love her with all my heart and I've made my decision
that I'm going to wait for her, while hoping just one day she
will notice me but nothing, nothing at all is working none, none
at this moment.

   As I look up into the sky and the sun sets and the stars
come out, they remind me of this Mystery Girl her beautiful blue
eyes covered with glasses, her brown hair, but she is not
noticing me, nothing, nothing at all is working none, none at
this moment.
    Chris Medley

Spring In Snow Country

A squirrel is chirping outside
And chickadees are at the feeder.
Auntie called today and reported the crows.
Now crows really mean Spring!
But looking out of the window,
Snow is piled all over.
Most folks enjoy tulips and daffodils,
And warm days with trees budding,
And blossoms and raking the yard.
Fortunately! There are crows, black as they are,
That bring a hope of Spring to arrive,
About the same time the places south are heading into summer.
For now, we in snow country can hope
To have shoveled the last of the winter's white cover,
And wait for the piles to melt away.
This my friend takes patience!
    Joan Lasanen

Remember

It lay upon the floor
Broken, beaten, gone forever.
No one would know what it was before.
I held the pieces in my arms,
I cried as I tried to fit them together,
It would never be the same.
I took the pieces and put them in the box,
Someday I would find and put them together,
Then I would remember his face and eyes
and his gentle voice.
I would never forget again.
Glenda Lamb

Untitled

After all the pain and sorrow, after all
the time spent wishing the day would
be tomorrow. There are still feelings
gleaming through all of the mess,
shimmering and shining, not becoming
less. So many tears shed, as his image
drifts through my head. Yearning to
let the feelings I have for him
out and dance among the wind. Even
if it demands falling apart, I just
want him to know how I feel in
my heart. Some of these expressions
raging against the currents of which
they were sent. These feelings not
only held in by skin, but also by
fears of rejection. These feelings
cannot for eternity be held behind
bars, for they will remain forever
as hidden scars.
Kira Shoemaker

Finding True Love

Before I had years of endless anguish and pain.
Then like a guardian angel you were at my side.
So I knew all was not in vain.
That the true person I was no longer had to hide.
At first it was very rough indeed.
Frightened I believe to think what it was like to be tied down.
To your words often I did not heed.
Then I realized I was meant to be found.
Because the patience and love you showed was and still is so strong.
Even I can understand that you pulled me from the drowning depths.
To let me know it was with you I belong.
Theresa D. Eckard

Heaven Opened Its Doors Again Today

Heaven opened its doors again today.
The dew drops fall off the roses on the grave.
The wind seems to have become still
The Emptiness of my soul seems only to
have froze in time
The thought of tomorrow coming, there doesn't
seem to be any reason to look forward to it anymore.
As I look around I see evidence, that
life is forever and so is death.
I'm surrounded by hundreds of years
Of memories of all of the people who
were here before.
Were they all as lost as me.
How did they mourn, was it as hard for them.
There it is again, the dew drops keep sliding
Off the petals on to the grave.
That's all that remains of the event today
Because Heaven opened its doors again
Maria Shonka

The Storm Is Descending

The storm is descending from the mountain
like a curtain on the stage
exposing an unfinished choreography
of human tragedy and confusion
of actors without a part, a song, or a dialogue.

The storm is descending upon a valley
of blooming flowers and singing birds
of children playing and lovers dreaming

The storm is descending with a mighty roar
like a lioness pursuing a gazelle
or a youth in search of freedom.
It comes into a desolate valley
seeking playmates and finding none.

The storm has come into my soul
and cleansed me from the dust
of my travails, but left me trembling
like a leaf in cold rain or a child in the dark
a helpless prey of my loneliness.
Joseph F. Velez

The Earth Is Alive So Many Ways

The Earth is alive in so many ways! The mountains are faces that can see the entire world. The rivers that run from them are the tears that they cry; all because of pollution that fill the sky.

Cacti are prickly people with bad attitudes; if you cross them they'll stick you. Their bad Attitudes are from the pollution in the air that they breath.

Bushes are the mothers who protect the weeds and saplings which are their children.
They must protect them from destruction which probably will come.

Trees are tall, tall, people whose branches which are their arms, sway in the wind trying to push away the pollution.

The sand and dirt is a blanket that protects the plants' roots, which are their tender feet.

The sun is the Earth's giant heater which turns on and off with day and night. But when clogged with pollution, the heater will no longer work.

The clouds when not polluted keep the heater from overheating and charring all the earth's many people.

And the beautiful blue sky is a spectacular blanket that has gray stains where the pollution got to it.

The night sky is a rhinestone studded coat, which wraps itself around the earth to keep it warm during the cold.

Oh yes! The earth is alive in so many ways!
Mandi Goretcki

"Long Gone Navy Days"

Be proud my military man, for you did what was expected and did all that you can. I met you in December of 84, and traveled many roads, until March of 94. You served on many navy ships that were so tall, and strong, and you never did anything that was wrong. We played those scenes so often that was told, and going away wasn't always easy, and you tried to be bold. Our times spent being apart was often painful and enduring to me and your heart. Your phone calls long distance in the middle of the nights, was usually unexpected, and with much delight. You're a desert storm veteran, who you should be very proud, because it was your duty, so please don't frown. You gave me the best years of being a wife, and although it will sadden me, I'll miss the navy life. So dear husband, go forward with all of your might, and be all that you can in civilian life.
Mary R. Moseley

Questions For Answers

The muddy waters of the unknown urging you not to move on
The absolute obligation pushing you forward
The fear of the obligation wears a sinister smile
The constant isolation seems as if it will only multiply
The uncertainty crushes down with its unbearable weight
The absence of answers brings only more questions
The pursuit of knowledge leads to infinite ignorance
The end is waiting to strike and overpower
The end is said to be a new beginning
The end, however, may be just that.

Charles T. Rafey

Thoughts Of You

Whenever I miss you, know that I do?
I let my thoughts wander to spend time with you!

I hear your friendly voice and see your sunny smile
Even though our distance apart is many a mile.

I soak up the silence that somehow surrounds me
As I recall the happy and sad times that used to be.

The years have a way of separating friends —
Circumstances, age, jobs, it all depends!

Yet memories have a power that somehow start
Within our lives, and stay, though we are far apart.

They recall reminders our friendship brought —
It's so nice to be together if only for a visit in thought.

So, when I miss you, wishing won't do as
I just let my thoughts wander and think about you!

Marguerite LeBlanc

Real Woman

A real woman to me is a woman who is loving, kind and understanding and to my brother and I she is the best mother in the world. My mother Kerry Carroll is a real woman to me, because she has taken care of me since I was born and has always been by my side. I feel my mom is special in different ways. She is not only a great mother, she is also a hard worker. She work very hard to support my brother and I. My Mom is always helping to solve my problems. She inspires me to obtain my goals in my future and fulfill my hopes and dreams. If it wasn't for her I would never be who I am or where I am today. My mother taught me how to do things for myself, so I can be a responsible young women and follow in her footsteps. My mother taught me to never give up even if I have to try continuously.

Jolene Samson

The Infinite Sea Beside Me

The sea and I have a great relationship-
For we two contain secrets from within.
Shall we stay in this together?
Seems as not, it would be a sin.
We both try to reach for the shore,
With our mighty and powerful waves.
It only makes it harder and harder-
For there are some presences of shallow caves.
It will try to stop us from reaching our point.
Each of us seem under a gradual grace,
To find your place in this confusing world.
However, were almost like were in a maniac race.
We will prove to the world that,
Our quest will soon hit a stop.
Which is not intensely far off,
With the time that we had just got.

Navdeep Singh

The Run

I was working in the kitchen and when I looked up,
out in my flower bed digging away, was a pup.
As I went running out the door just as fast I could.
The pup saw me coming and, with his tail wagging, he stood.
When I got close, he took off up the hill,
I was an old lady, should I follow him? I will!
So follow him I did and as a runner, I was slow,
but he would stop and wait for me, smiling, don't you know.
Then he would take off again when I got near,
he kept in the lead with me bringing up the rear.

As we started back down the hill, much to our surprise,
we slipped into a mud hole which the rain had caused to rise.
The pup he was happy, he'd had a good run,
he looked like he had never had so much fun.
I guess he enjoyed the race and I must confess,
I enjoyed it too, although I was a muddy mess.
As in times of trouble, I started to sing,
I begin to pray we had not broken anything.
As he licked my face and wiggled, I had to admit
this run was one bit of foolishness, I would never forget.

M. C. Davis

"Unifications"

Two bodies, apart, each half of a whole,
Working together, toward a unified goal.
Before passing one night, their lives were both droll.
Now they're sharing the joys of a unified soul.
   Two bodies, now are but one.

Each night in her arms, he thinks of the first.
How she captured his soul, and quenched its deep thirst.
She remembers his words, like a poem well versed.
Did she choose to be his, or was she coerced?
   She chose him to join her as one.

Though his words are hypnotic, she gives herself freely.
And he knows what he's done, but she makes it so easy.
When she flashes a smile, or a wink so discreetly
He's glad they've united, for he loves her completely.
   Two loves now united as one.

Their love will be blessed, and often put to the test,
   But as one, they will meet all occasions.
Two bodies, one choice, two lovers rejoice...
   These are life's unifications.

Octavio A. Villalona Jr.

"Egypt"

A land so barren, dry, destitute, old as time
Lay lost from the blessing of the master's hand,
Standing still like the pendulum of a worn ol clock
Quiet and stilled, this hot parched land.

You hear the moans from her histories grave
Cut deep are the wounds of her pain and agony,
The marks are visible you cannot deny
Etched upon her face for all the world to see.

The wisdom that raised the ancient pyramids
And preserved the bodies of her rulers and kings,
Is locked in the darkness of their souls and minds
The lament of her hurts and loss continually rings.

There's a stream of hope and life
Coursing its way through her heart,
God Himself must have named it the Nile
All will be gone if its waters ever depart.

The children, oh the precious children
If eyes are the windows of the soul,
The sadness and hurt you can see there
Is the message through them told.

Lennie Whitt Carroll

A Fly In The Paint

I came upon a fly one day, sitting on a wall.
A closer look revealed to me, the choice was not his call.

Did he go there in the paint by choice or just by chance?
How or why he's in this mess is of no consequence.

What is running through his thoughts, now that time is near?
Doom, self pity, and powerlessness are ringing in his ear.

I feel so sorry for this fly, he seems so much like me.
Fate just jumped in one fine day and made life misery.

Situations, other people, drag me to my knees.
I can't be who I want to be all because of these.

All the outside influences are pulling me apart.
So many things are asked of me, I've lost what's in my heart.

We're powerless to free ourselves, the prison's much too strong.
We can't get out, we must give up, it's where we now belong.

Just standing there and watching him, there's something that I find.
His own prison is the paint and mine is my own mind.

By blaming fate for my own state, I give up my control.
It's not fate's fault how I turn out, it can't see my soul.

I'm glad I saw the fly that day in the paint upon the wall.
I realize, we can free ourselves, the power's in all.

Judith M. Westfahl

Understanding Me

I have a chemical Imbalance in my brain.
   Are you Understanding Me.
Sometimes say, Sometimes I speed.
   Are you Understanding Me
Psalms 65, seems to calm me down, I have faith in God.
As Jesus says in Mark-Chapter II Verse 22.
   Are you Understanding Me
So wake up everybody as Teddy Pendograss says, reach out and
touch somebody's hand, and make the world a better place.
   Are you Understanding Me
I also have anxiety and confused, so I pray to Father God for
guidance to help me, through the traffic, to save my soul from
sin, to Love, to Pray, so my mind won't wander off.
   Are you Understanding Me
For one sweet day, sings Mariah Carey and Boyz II men.
   Are you Understanding Me
One day we will meet in Glory, Oh! Yes this Poetry is about me.
   Did you Understand Me.

Jean A. Streat

"Pain Drops"

Throughout life pain comes along.
Sometimes I can barely feel it,
but other times the feeling is too strong.

It causes a pool of hurt to well up
in my eyes.
Then the pain drops roll down the hill
of my cheeks as I begin to cry.

A puddle of pain drops in my hand is what I see.
Suddenly, I realize the hurt is now outside
instead of within me.

God has once again replaced the storm of hurt
formed from the pain drop shower.
With an ocean of hope and a field of faith flowers.

Earlene Boykin

Untitled

God never closes a door in over face,
But he opens another to take its place,
Sometimes we can't see the reason why,
And we show our resentment in our tears
  and sighs.

If we just dwell on the woes of others,
Delve into the troubles of sisters and brothers,
We'll find that our burdens do not compare
Maybe we even have less than our share.

If we can just learn to accept what comes
And never to conquering "self-pity" succumb,
Then the blows we receive as we travel life's road
Will strengthen our backbone and help us
  carry our load

Virginia M. Volzer

I CRY BUT ALAS, I GET NO RELEASE

I cry but alas I can get no release
My heart is heavy
Within my breast
But still I get no release

When will my mind be well?
That I might at last be happy?
Happiness is fleeting, unreal like a mist,
A puff of smoke

Still I hope for release
From this life of torment
The sky is blue
But all I see is black clouds of despair.

Grace Cooper

Fear

I stand on the battlefield.
Bombs are dropping like rain.
I am scared.
I want to run, but I am petrified.
The sound of gunshots drums in my ear.
A dying man calls out to me, but I can not see him.
Suddenly I feel a sharp pain in my arm.
I look down and see that I am shot.
I scream and start to run.
I run, and run, and run.

Rebecca Livengood

To My Stranger

  I see you everyday, but only from a distance,
visions of you flood my mind, yet I don't know who you are.
  Your hair is the color of death and your eyes the color of
emeralds. When you smile my heart skips a beat, and the plunges
into a sea of hot lava where it melts.
  Your laugh brings me a feeling that couldn't be expressed in a
thousand words, I only wish I could be laughing with you.
  But... that is child like dreaming in a fantasy world, let now
my dreams extinguish while I retreat back into reality.
  I wish I knew you, and everything about you down to your darkest
secret but.....
    What I know now is all I will ever know,
     for no one will know my secret.
    Although my dreams
     may
      die, I have myself to blame,
because, for as long as I shall live, I may never even know your name.

Sabrina Shore

The Last Season

Autumn's leaves are falling
How quickly the seasons have past
Before you know it, winter's snow has come
You cannot make time last
Spring, Summer, Fall, Winter
Your final day has come
No more to see the summer's sun
Once this winter's day is done

Carrie-Ann Cariglio

Book I: A Parable Of Spirit And Truth

I looked for God recently and He did not find me.
I wanted to talk with Him.

I tried to get His attention and sadly concluded, after some time,
That I was not in a place where He would look for me.

And then a voice inside of me said, "Rejoice!"

You will not find Him in comfortable places.
He has already been there and
Mended broken spirits.
Healed the sick. Given sight to the blind.
Provided food and shelter to those who sit under the sound of His voice.
Given wisdom from on high to those in danger of stumbling.
And made a way out of no way for the sightless.

Go, look for Him in a place called
Oklahoma.
Call out His name in a place called
Bosnia
Whisper His name in His hearing in a place called
Liberia
Wait on Him in a place called
Montana.

Elaine Sykes

In The Heart Of The Seed

In the heart of the seed, buried deep
so deep. Lay a little plant, fast asleep.
Wake: Said The Sunshine, Creep To The Light,
Come And See What A Beautiful Sight.

Cheryl Asiq

And The Angel Said

And the angel heard the cry in the night
The sweet voice softly whispered
do not cry tonight for the Lord has heard
He will mend your broken heart
And all the sadness that has entered in
Wipe the tears away for you are beginning
a new day.
Let it go and start to laugh again
Even one little smile will make the
day even brighter
For you are beginning a new day
and the days ahead will be clearer
Start to laugh start to smile start to be
happy again
For the Lord has heard and He is answering
your prayer
This is what he wanted me to whisper
in your head

Debora Ann Pamplin

Nature's Blessings

The Great Spirit is our father. He is in all things.
He is beside us at all times. We may not see Him. But He
is there to guide us.
He is in the air that we breathe.
The Earth is our mother. She nurtures us and gives to
us the nourishment we need to survive.
The sun is our grandmother. She basks all living things
in warmth. So that we may continue to grow.
The moon is our brother. He gives to us the light we
need at night to make our way.
The rain is our sister. She brings to us water so that
we may quench our thirst.
The thunder and lightning is our grandfather. He
brings his wrath and fury down upon us when he is angry.
to cleanse the land.
The sky is our blanket of wisdom. It is always above us
to remind us that we are of one Great Spirit, Great Earth
and Great Nation.

Brenda Golden

The Struggle

Fleeting thoughts of love and passion
crash in her head
like the surf against the bluff.
Leaving her with an emptiness
she never dreamt possible.
She tries to rise above the hollowness,
but something pursues her.
She can feel its grasp upon her.
It is very strong, very powerful.
She knows not how long she can
battle the demons, before they triumph
over her. She can hear their cries of
victory, feel their mastery upon her flesh.
Her body weary from the struggle,
her mind almost in total surrender.
With one last desperate attempt,
she fails to be the victor.
She has acquiesced to the incubus,
never again to be.

Cathy L. Becker

"Hand-prints"

I remember the tousle haired boy
    dropping by with flowers picked along the way,
    eager to share his wondrous world.
He blew through my days like a gust of wind,
    bring the sweet sounds of laughter,
    handfuls of daisies and tad pole or two.
When he completed kindergarten he rang the bell,
    diploma in hand to show me,
    and I poured Pepsi into wine glass
    to toast the graduate.
The screen-door closed with a bang behind him,
    leaving silence in its wake,
    and I saw the hand-print on the wall
    where he stopped to fumble with his shoe.
Today when first I heard the news,
    I remembered that wall
    and all the hand-prints he left,
    dropping by.

Alison Conley

"There's No Such Thing As An Empty Nest"

As when robins believe their lives to have just begun,
from what seems to appear from the heavens, comes a little one.
To provide for this new joy, the new parents construct a home a top a tree.
Only to enrich their lives even more than before, come two more, making three.
These little ones soon start learning from their parents.
Never realizing it to all be preparance,
for the way of life that yet lies ahead.
Clinging to every word that their parents said.
Always minding everything that they have been taught,
mistakes that have been learned and fears that have been fought.
Instructing them how to use wings that would someday enable them to fly.
In mastering these skills, they realized that there were no limits to the sky.
Through this, the once young of life, but now mature robins,
knew that they could no longer stay.
And the parents knew that all they had taught, would one day
help their off spring to fly away.
But this is not to be worried about, for these birds of flight are
out to do their best, and they will always remember that
"Home" is where the "Love" is, and "Home" is at the nest.
Airman Ryan M. Booher

"The Immortal Beloved"

Hope is engulfed and strangled by Life...
She smells the love; once so robust,
now faint as the distant bell that rings between them.
Air so heavy it forces Her down...
down to Her knees as She grasps for
Her neck as she's trying to breathe,
but Life is too strong...She
feels Herself becoming limp;
Numbness crawls from Her toes throughout
Her distilled body-She can barely feel
Her blood stopping, slowly....

Life laughs, as Hope dies helplessly.
He kisses Her now becoming cool and pale lips,
and whispers in Her lifeless ear-
"I am the Immortal Beloved; you have craved my tasted,
now fear my gaze,
you wanted me-the sinful apple,
now Forever will you have me."
Alison Fantozzi

Summer One Million BC

Eons ago, was this a real bummer
  or was it the same...
This season called Summer?
A time pterodactyls could get very touchy,
And brontosaurus were enamored and mushy.
It's a time when the king, Mr. Tyrannosaurus Rex,
Gets itchy, and twitchy with thoughts about sex.

I've just answered my question...
  it is still the same;
The yearning, the romance, and the mating game.
Robert W. Dixon

Revelation

I can no longer stand the same old thing.
I want something different,
a change to stimulate the mind.
I cannot continue to follow those
before me, their paths having
already been beaten solid.
I need to find an expression,
without it becoming a tradition.
John Deglow

Hole In My Pocket

I got a dollar for my birthday,
50 cents for sweeping the floor.
What happened with all my money?
For I have no more

I think I bought a Hershey's bar,
a sucker and ball.
Now I'm searching through the couch,
and up and down the hall.

What happened with my money?
It just went down the drain.
I think I have a hole in my pocket,
or maybe something's wrong with my brain.
Joy Morris

Clouds

Clouds up in the heavens, soft and floating, palest blue
rolling with the winds across the sky;
casting tranquil shadows, sheltering our lives
masquerade as love from out my eyes.

Everpresent, loyal; through storms and sun and rain
clouds presence never faltering at all;
never hesitating to offer their protection
like love, cloud's devotion builds a wall.

Clouds withhold no secrets, no shame is theirs to grieve
true attributes of love given freely;
they ever share their credence asking nothing in return
acceptance is the lock that is love's key.

Clouds up in the heavens parallel my life
and the love I feel sometimes makes me cry;
reflecting on cloud's beauty, for I know without love
there would be not a cloud in the sky.
Gail Rheaume

To Chris

More than a brother, More than a friend,
A childhood playmate, A love that will never end.

Our lives intermeshed, Like fine silken threads,
Woven together, A part of the whole.

A garment of caring, A deep understanding,
Without look or work, A river that's felt.

A gold tinted memory, Or newly shared laugh,
Threads side by side, Running together.

A compassionate sharing, Of happiness and pain,
An outstretched hand, Fingers just touching.

A give and a pull, Yet never a tear,
Bound close together, As ancient book pages.
Elizabeth Sawyer

Lost And Found

I lost my way some time ago.
How it happened I do not know.
In my youth life was grand.
Hunting and fishing across the land.
My father and I stayed side by side.
Our being together filled him with pride.
Then somehow we slipped apart.
With him gone I was off to a bad start.
Slowly life meant nothing to me.
I wanted to die just to be free.
When life wasn't living, and I wanted it to end.
My father showed up, I found my best friend.
Wade J. Gilson

To Those Who Fall

Don't move me to pity you with sorrow,
Yesterday you made your choice for tomorrow,
Although through many moments of laughter,
In view of the downward spiral hereafter,
   you cried,
So sum up your past, give meaning to the present,
   and pave a path for the future.
To those who fall, I offer my prayer,
For having fallen myself, my plea, "I've been there,"
But the road unwinds the farther you crawl,
You're lifted to leap, to clear any wall,
All obstacles die from the rebirth of your soul,
The obvious becomes a story once told,
Hence the greatest reward as now you
   stand tall,
Is commitment to self and to those who fall.

Deborah Foster

Childhood Memory

I was once a small girl curled in a ball
with knobby knees and eyes incredulous
the kitchen floor cold on my heaving soul
I listened; terrified of the upcoming fuss.

My mother is waiting, daggers in her eyes
her body is quivering with tension and anger
mother is a silent stone, a thundering sky
her body emanates a tangible ire.

What I remember next is black and white
like a still dream pierced by fragmented yells
he is leaving. Guilty, he will not fight
I see him crying dry, his body swells.

So long ago, but the kitchen holds ghosts
of a small girl crying and the man she loves most.

Cristy Alger

Letting Go

Letting go is so hard to do
   especially if it's someone you love.
But let go we really must,
   if indeed, "In God We Trust".
The one you love will be in a better place,
   where there's no pain or sorrow.
Yet, will live within our hearts
   for all of our tomorrows.

Beverley F. Riley

Partners

Life alone, without you, would not be.
For each day the sun, I would not see.
Life alone, without you, could not be.
For each lonely night, the star's, I could not see.
The day's would go on, with not many smiles.
And the sadness would grow like the snow in big piles.
Before I'd know it, spring would be here, along
With the blossoms, each day, would bring fear.
I don't know what I would do alone, on my own!
For we can never be prepared even if we were shown.
As Life goes on and you think of that time.
I'll pray everyday that I'd go first, so that I can
Say, that you'll always be mine till my dying day.

Lynn E. Swager

Interlude

We walked upon a hillside green
And paused beside a mountain stream.
We listened to a thrush's call
And climbed above a waterfall.

At times we walked beside the sea
And talked of life - and you and me.
Yet knew not how - or when
Fate would let us meet again.

Thrice we climbed a mountain pass
Struggling up the rocky steep.
Then rested at that thrilling height
Wishing we had wings for flight.

These are only memories, dear
And 'tis not these that keep you near.
"Tis your heart reaching out to mine each day
Which helps me travel my separate way.

Surely 'twas no caprice of fate
To across our paths when it was too late.
Divine wisdom alone knows when and the way
But I know our paths must merge someday.

Hazel M. Denning

Black Poplars

Guarding orchards on the highway
one row parallel, the other angled acutely,
poplars - a phalanx ready for assault
against the wind - a flying wedge

Afternoon sun crouches behind the lines
lighting their consecutive spines - throwing bars
across the road

One drives over these weightless bones
before the exit

In winter red-tailed hawks, sentinels
in the highest tips of slender branches - ice-blackened:
permit our passing
in gray frozen dawns

Evenings - as we are questing home -
these dark shimmering trees, are checkpoint
to the dwelling - where proper rituals -
sacrifice of the black ewe's blood
and the ram's prepared with a bronze knife;
white barley, honey and wine - are offered
for conversations with remembered shadows.

Pat Morrison

Mystic Man

   You are my mystic man and with your magic
touch have given my soul more than any mere mortal
can. You have cast your spell and rescued my
heart from it's hell, my fantasies, my passions,
no one had ever been shown, but like magic and
with no words spoken your soul had already known.
   My hearts wishes fulfilled by your sweet
kisses. In your strong arms I am sheltered
from all of lifes harms and transported to a
higher plain, far away from sorrow and pain.
   Oh mystic man, what powers you possess,
ask of me any want or desire, any request.
You will never be denied, about this I would not lie.
   You are my mystic man and I, I am your woman.

Carolyn Gunnoe

Tears Of Christmas

People look and me and say: "Why she is doing fine."
But, deep inside the pain is there each and every day.
The years have passed and still the tears they flow.

We lost our son, age twenty-five, in Ninety-Four.
He was so very special, bright, cheery, and full of news.
He filled our hearts and home with love and warmth that always glowed.

Now he's gone and Christmas is here and I go on for others in the world.
I dress so very cheery - tie bows and ribbons in my hair to bring cheer to others who are dear.
For Christmas is just a job, an act and I try to do it well, so not to burden others with my woe.

Christmas cards and Christmas songs brings us joy and also pain.
The hurt is great when you hear or read Have The Merriest Christmas Ever and I wonder how?
A Christmas tree has many memories from generation to generation plus, much more.
So, when our tree is put in place, the pain will start to flow.

Our son would want the tree the same, as his brother told me so.
An angel I will place upon the tree in memory of our loving son.
A job I must do each year to justify the tree a glow.

For all my years, Christmas has been special with magic in the air.
The magics gone, but Peace, Goodwill, and Gobs Blessings to all -
Is what I have to give at Christmas time to everyone I know.

Eleanor Adams

The Mark Of Cain

One marvels at the babes so young, and the wondrous ways their mischief runs.
Sweet young voices of youth divine, charging through Mom's laundry line.
Is it in the air or what they ate, perhaps visitors from outer space.
Or could there be a darker scheme, something lurking in their genes?

When I look upon my boys, I see them with a tempened joy.
Is it as the poet says, the mark of Cain upon their heads?
It could not have been so long ago, that boys were not allowed to grow,
And cause their father's eyes to roll, making airplanes from his papyrus scrolls.

Did he pause and breath a sigh, and wonder at this mark from birth,
The way that man will scourge the earth, and build his temples to the sky?
This poet of the plight of man, in a kingdom of the sands,
Who wrote these words so long ago, does touch my heart with thoughts I know.

Jas. H. Stevenson

Life Moments

An endless road which our feet must trod.
Time moves along, yet we stand still.
A destiny of uncertainty. Our minds, how they are baffled with intrusion of destruction.
I speak to you, my mind needs to be free.
Release the bond, release me.
Listen to my thought, my mind, as I speak.
With my heart I cry.
Please do not turn away. Beneath the surface, in the depths there is pain.
Pain from the agony and suffering I have contained.
Tomorrow my path shall be straight, the road a journey of peace.
My burden shall be light, and no more pain will I suffer.
Tomorrow my days shall be bright.
I will release the pressures of the burdensome load.
For I will be free.
Free at last to just be me.

Margaret Gowins

A Child's Winter Play

Soft flakes falling, light and gently, large and slow
Snowsuit, scarf, and mittens to keep away the cold
Each step promotes the imagination of walking on the moon
Not another footprint in sight; only those of your own

Sun sparkling brightly off the tiny, new-fallen flakes
Like little stars having landed; there for no one but me
Over boot-tops walking with 'giant' steps to a big, roomy spot
Then turning and dropping, spreading arms and legs back and forth

Most carefully arising; not to disturb one segment of the design
And there, on the ground, the likeness of a small angel is found
Such delight; so exciting this creation in this world I call mine
A few more steps at a time, more angels to make, all of them mine

Knocking on the window, this splendor to share with family inside
For a smile of acknowledgment; that confirmation so gratifying
A bottle of colored water, now fulfilled with angel making, I had
Squirting carefully what I thought was my name, and many designs

Shaking the snow from the mittens; wrists stinging from the cold
Headed for the door, and a blunder never forgotten nor repeated
Snow mounded fresh on the doorknob, tempting eagerly to taste
Ouch! Stuck, pulled, bled; but lovingly comforted, outside again.

Susan E. Rogina

Pages In My Mind

There was a time when I feared my life was finally at an end.
There was no one for me to talk to, for I didn't have one friend.
I had always been told since not very old, that all I believed was wrong.
I was afraid to believe in myself too much and I couldn't sing my song.
I would never amount to much, that's what they used to say.
and I believed in what they told me for it seemed to me that way.
Then just as I had accepted that this was the way it would always be,
you came into my life and changed it so drastically.
You lit up the darkness that was deep within my soul.
Tenderly nurturing my heart as you were helping it to grow.
You taught me how to stand as you revealed each golden strand,
while helping me to see that there are wonderful things about me.
I guess I could never find another friend like you,
but that is fine by me, for no one else will ever do.
You showed me things about myself that I could scarce believe.
You were there through the pain and sorrow, for you're not the kind to leave.
You opened up my heart and soul, you let my spirit soar.
You helped me to know when to speak softly and when it was time to roar.
You have always made me feel so special in ways I could never define,
so all I can do is say thank you to you for unlocking the pages within my mind!

Julie Durham-Holupka

Winter Silence

In the middle of the winter
With silver leaves upon the trees
The wind blows, the snow falls upon the branches
Of the trees with silver leaves.
When the ducks in the cold
Sleep in their nests in the reeds,
When the deer with quiet passion
Run through the silent snow,
When rabbits, squirrels, and chipmunks
Go for shelter in their homes,
When the birches, willows and maples
Stand in silence in the snow
In the middle of the winter
Where the trees with silver leaves grow.

Deirdre M. Rippe

Watching A Baby Deer

While slowly strolling beside a creek, I stopped to watch a baby deer,
It didn't see or hear me, it didn't know, I was standing near.
It looked in wide-eyed wonder, at every thing it saw,
It would nibble at grass or sniff at a rock, being careful not to fall.

It tossed its head, it kicked up its hoofs, following Mom to a big pine tree,
Then along came a beautiful Butterfly, bobbing and darting, flying so free.
The deer stopped to watch this beautiful creature, flying along with ease,
He wondered if some day he could fly, and go where ever he might please

It looked so easy, it looked like fun, he couldn't wait to try,
Then he could help Santa, by pulling his sleigh, flying across the sky
Now!!! you know how it could have happened, or, maybe it came about,
On Christmas Eve, as they travel across the sky, listen for a shout.

Of, "Merry Christmas To All, And To All A Good Night."
As they travel up-ward and out of sight.
And think of the baby deer that wanted to fly,
While watching a lovely, Butterfly.

Alma F. Dye

A Fiery Fourth

Framework decorates the sky.
Red, white, and blue.
Humid night in dawn of July.
Painted patriotic hue.

Any night in America cries Sovereignty.
Each sight of splendor does declare.
The grace that others have died for.
Many a year ago in the fateful air.

Everything in abundance and much more.
From barren plains to the rocky shore,
where waves echo an assisting roar.
For others to wax the freedom we know.

Foolish dream of liberty understood.
By a determined minuteman long ago.
Makes the worst of America seem good.
And a beautiful legacy yet to bestow.

Marcus Elias Colonna

Winter's Last Hurrah

Old Man Winter came with a blast,
Though we knew he would soon be past;
The snows he brought were pretty and white,
So schools were dismissed to the kid's delight.

Then he sent us winter from the North Pole,
That chilled us in body and soul;
He held us in a long harsh grip,
While we watched the temperatures dip.

Finally there came some warm sunny days,
And we were led to believe he had changed his ways;
But oh, how mistaken we surely can get,
For Mister Winter wasn't through quite yet.

He answered the curtain call yet again,
And sent us some zero weather with a grin;
But then he took a bow and fell dead,
While jonquils and tulips bloomed by his head.

Soon he was buried beneath the grassy sod,
That had so long know his chastening rod;
We know he will return with his ways so raw,
But for now we rejoice that he has his last hurrah.

Will H. Havens

Inside My Room

I sit surrounded by all of my stuffed animals on my bed.
My two goldfish swim about in their bowl on the shelf above my head.
My favorite book, Sesame Street Dictionary, sits on the shelf
My secrets are hidden in a box under my bed, but nobody knows but my imaginary friend, 'Self.'

My favorite game is Candyland.
But my time is spent mostly with He-Man or G-I Joe's in hand.
As soon as I can save more quarters in my big Coke bottle on the floor,
My Mom will take me to Toys R Us to buy Skeletor.

From my big window I can see,
Many squirrels running through the trees.
My Big Bird swingset and my treehouse sit quietly in the woods,
But I hear them calling for me to come play if I could.

I really want to go outside and play.
But my Mom said I was bad and here I have to stay.
On my bed I have to sit for I fear,
The monster hiding behind the door in the closet I will not be able to steer clear.

My decision is to stay and play within my room,
Until Mom decides not to lower the boom.

Jeremy Martino

Fire's Light

This dagger drives far into the soul.
Slowly, it takes its toll.
The wound is so deep.
Yet, some may smile or stare as you weep.
They do not feel the pain.
Though your struggle is not in vain.
The blade's wound burns like fire.
It moves within you, only to inspire.
This is the finest hour.
Pain becomes your strength and power.

Carmela Cantone

The Sun Sets on the Shore

I walk along the sandy shore
Hoping to see this beautiful sunset once more.
The waves crash up against the rocks
As the sailboats sail to the docks.
The glorious sun is setting.
I think of all the beautiful places I will be heading.
I see the dolphins gliding on the water so free.
Oh, how I wish that could be me.
I have never seen such a beautiful sight,
Not even at night.
The sky, with all its colors, symbolizes so many things,
Like a bird flying free flapping its wings.
And I can never hope that I,
Will ever have to say goodbye.

Kristyn Mount

Peace Of Mind

I do not ask for kingly crown, or flowery beds of ease,
I care much less for fame, renown, to do just as I please;
I only ask, that while I'm here, the chance to seek and find
The thing I cherish most of all— and that is peace of mind.

To gain this there is much to do, and struggle though I may,
I turn to him who knows my faults and helps me on my way;
I stumble, and then rise again, the flesh is weak indeed,
but somewhere and by faith I know, is peace of mind, my creed.

How vain we humans are at times, and often we are blind,
Far more than any earthy prize is what I hope to find;
Elusive though it seems to be, yet free to all mankind,
In faith, and hope, and clarity I'll find my peace of mind.

Charles Morrison Sr.

Levi

He was a handsome blond headed, little boy.
Always filled with exciting ideas, his eyes
danced with joy.

He was such a sweet bundle of energy, playing
and having fun.
I couldn't of loved him more if he were my own son.

He was such a loving little guy.
When I think of his little face, it brings a
tear to my eye.

The last time I saw him I hugged him goodbye.
A few months later, I found out that through a
senseless accident he had died.

His death was totally unfair.
Hit by a drunk driver who didn't even stop,
to drunk to even care.

When will these people learn not to drink and drive?
How many more little children will have to lose
there lives?

Julie Crafton

'Great Grand Mother's Big Black Iron Pot'

We watch as great grand mothers cooks,
from an original generational family cook book

"It's Slum Gelly yum today,"
Great grand mothers says."

Magic seems to go into that pot,
because the alcoma means a lot.

Grand mother calls this recipe x.y.z.
It's all the same to my sibling and me.

Soup is what it is to mom,
And that's okay to me my sister and brother Tom.

So a sour family sits down to eat,
Rusty runs to the table awaiting his treat.

Down Rusty great grand mothers colds
The only dog I've ever had that is so bold.

Great grand father leads,
And we all bless the table
Thanking God for Slum Gelly yum,
That makes our body's able.

Jacquelyn Ortega Wilbon

A Run'n Spirit

O'Lord: Please let my spirit run free: When I stumble please let my spirit pick me up, and turn me around, and allow me to stand as tall as a tree.

Because; I've a prayer for, my spirit to run free; without any harm done to me. O'Lord: Only you know when that will be.

I know I've a strong spirit to run free: And; allow your love to be in every part of me; I long for my heart to have joy in abundance please.

I would like to be able to know, that it's perfectly okay to have a struggling spirit, and I know difficulty is merely a part of my spirit run'n free.

O'Lord: I know that gratitude is what makes difficulties depart from me; and all because of you "O'Lord" I've a joyous heart, and with Happiness intake of Life's Strugglogistics and its difficulties of a run'n spirit to be free.

I want to be able to turn my free spirit into beautifully of Glorifying Thee!

Dorothy Lewis

"The Window Of A Black Woman"

Looking out of the window of my heart, life seem
hard I can do it. Life is fill with joy, sorrow and
heartache, can we grow and become all we can
be without it all.
Out of the eyes of this black woman, there are many
reason to be strong, life would bet you down. My
head is high, I walk tall, my back is straight, my
eyes on the mark ahead of me.
Can I do the job? Yes I can. A great job, a won.
direful task of raising my children, all nine of them,
alone. Working, cleaning, all that consist of being a mother.
I keep my eyes on the mark.
Looking out of the window of my heart, life was
hard, I did it. Life was fill with joy, sorrow,
heartache, but I did it. Children are grown,
I fell alone but I'm never alone, my heart is
fill with contentment, yes this is the heart,
the soul of the windows of a strong black woman.

Earline W. Frazier

Bye Daddy

The crash of waves upon the shore
Will they cease and be no more?
The sea of love and happiness
soon to be that of emptiness?
The river of truth and hope and dreams
will it dry out and cease to stream?

No

The crash of waves upon the shore
will surely be forevermore.
The sea of love and happiness
will open up to us embrace.
The river of truth and hope and dreams
will glitter still by loving sunbeams.

So

Life will go on and wounds will mend
and memories become our friend.
And soon enough, we'll learn to know
that joy yet in our heart can grow.

We'll meet again, of that I'm sure,
as sure as the waves crash on the shore.

Lesley Robinson

Daydreams

I stare out there...
Far out into a giant void
That I subconsciously fill
With colorful imaginings
Of mega plans and dreams fulfilled.
What a wondrous sight
This tableau of my life...
So perfect, so bright...
With gaze transfixed, I smile contentedly,
But a prick from my conscious self insists
That what I'm having in my mind's eye
Is just a phantom mirage
In the desert of my life.
Yet — steady within my sight — the tableau remains
As if urging to have faith...
To believe that I have the means
The power — to make my dreams come true...
That I can strive to attain my goals
And enjoy those tantalizing treats
That always seem to be so out of reach.

Paulina C. Cabral

Homeless Soldier

A homeless soldier lying beneath a tent cut out of card board box,
an open fire for his fire place
A mattress on crates, a blue blanket that covered nearly all
his face
An abandon lot where houses use to be
All gone now except one old dead tree
His battle field is the streets of New York City, trying to
keep alive
He receives no medal for being able to survive
He cuddles himself beneath his blanket trying to keep warm
The radio continues to forecast of a coming snow storm
New York City in this great land of plenty
Won't you share even but a mere penny
How can we be content in our warm homes
While a homeless soldier lies beneath a cold winter sky
shivering in his bones
Let us help the homeless, show them we care
They are God's children you know, so precious and dear

Blanche McLeod

I Hope To Cope

There must be trust
in the expanse of suspicion.
There must be pain,
the pain that necessitates compassion.
The lone star must glimmer
in an infinite vacuum of desolation.
If not, let us prepare
for the great Orwellian despair.

Why should one block
the overwhelming torrents of
materialism, madness, and mediocrity?
Why should one prolong life
in the face of inevitable death?
For the sole of reason that
the baby cries,
the light shines in your eyes...

And for the belief in that eternal hope
that allows us to cope.

Sapna Shah

My Fairy Tale

I never believed in fairy tales
Until I was blessed with you.
Now my soul is filled with happiness
And my spirits are renewed

Each moment is a dreamy moment
When it is spent with you.
Our every move and conversation
Takes on a fairy tale hue.

This is how our lives should be
As we prepare to walk together.
Enchanting enough to charm the world
And strong enough to withstand the weather.

So at this moment I pledge my love
My heart and soul I give completely to you.
I'm grateful for the part you've played
In making my fairy tale come true.

Vickie J. Sims

Above

Above the clouds,
the sky is blue,
you can see all the mountains there are to view.
If you look down,
you're sure to find,
a blanket like cotton you've left behind.
Your worries are gone,
your mind is clear,
and there is no fear to find up here.
You don't want to go down,
'cause this is like heaven,
and it doesn't matter if you're 100 or 7.

Robin A. Gow

Credit Cards

Credit cards are tokens, of companies who love;
They make it easy, they give credit a big shove;
You'll whip out that old card, whenever you're out of cash:
But watch out when that bill comes in, you'll see a money crash.
A plastic card for this, and a credit card for that;
To put them in your wallet, it hurts you if you sat;
Beware of the credit card, whatever you do, for if you get behind,
The company may sue;
Or in a collection agency you may see yourself;
The safest place for credit cards, is just right on a shelf.
To save face, and not disgrace, here's what should be done;
Pay in cash, for if you do, the battles finally won.
All who own these cards, simply on loan,
   and want to save the human race;
Just cock your arm, and let it go, out there in outer space.

Shirley Allen

The Ravishing Flowers

A breezy summer day brought happiness and the
Delay of sadness,
When flower met a flower,
They grow near each other, becoming friends during
the long summer days,
When fall came and the leaves started to turn,
Poison ivy interfered with a Judas like turn,
When winters long days came,
Ice cubes interfered,
Not with a Judas like turn but with another
flowers evil frost,
They soon became weeds,
No longer together,
They freshly bloomed again with hatred against
each other.

Elizabeth E. Hall

Untitled

The words blow in my ear like the howling of a violent wind.
I remember the words in my mind;
They are bullet wounds in my heart.
Why do they torment me like they do?

I huddle in a ball like a sleeping cat.
The tears run down my face in shower of pain.
The walls watch me and silently whisper, "It's okay."
I know they are right...or I hope they are.

The words linger in my mind like a terrifying picture.
I wish they would leave me and let me be.
The words have hurt me long enough.
I lie down and sleep... the silence has finally come.

Hannah Smith

Help!

Taken from and destroyed, our Mother cries,
as corporate scum rapes her open sores,
of many lifetimes hope. The justice lies,
kills, and steals man's freedom like greedy whores.
Choice means nothing to the powers that be,
conditioned to think what they do is right,
by the media preaching apathy.
All that's left to do is to stand and fight.
Corrosion of the power-hungry minds
is destroying us wherever we stand,
shallow discrimination of mankind,
the blower that keeps the fires of hate fanned.
While many don't care and it in silence,
what is fair is fair, take back with violence.

Mike Smith

Death

Just like an eagle
Death soars above,
He knows he's not wanted
He knows he's not loved.

But still he seeks his victim
And moves in for the kill,
As we stand aside and wonder
Is this really God's will?

Death takes control,
Sometimes with one swift blow
And no matter how strong we are
On that never ending journey, we all must go.

The thought of death gives
New meaning to life
Because we all want to live
And enjoy this paradise.

So keep you door closed,
Both day and night,
Because we will not surrender to death,
Not without a fight.

Gairy Spence

An American Soldier

An American boy who just turned eighteen.
Ahead of him lies his life-long dreams.

Like going to college and being on his own.
Hoping he could make it living alone.

All by himself, how would it be?
This notice came from the army.

He was being drafted in case of a war.
And this was something he could not ignore.

He registered at the nearest base.
He never thought of it as a scary place.

Next week was when he had to leave.
This news was just too hard to believe.

He became a man, in a short period of time.
Soon he would fight on the firing line.

He was trained very well, he matured to a man.
Then off to war in a foreign land.

On the firing lines with his enemies near.
He tried to deny his feelings of fear.

The first shot was fired; the war had begun.
There goes the life of America's son.

Lauren Brooke Tobey

At Sunset

The evening shadows begin to fall
Yet the wind and waves hurry inland
To greet the announcement of dusk
The sun shines sparingly through the haze
That captures the sea
As a prelude for night

My eyes peer through the thin, grey-green
  and blue hazy silky screen
On evening's ebb tide
As pink soft shadows
Kiss the earth goodnight

Susan Smeltzer

Night's Messenger

Calls the voice of Mother Night
For all her children time to rest,
And what better messenger sent than the flight
Of she who knows it best.
Cry loud and spread thy feathers far
And gleaming eyes to light your face,
Silently soar as a falling star
As you glide through darkened sky and space.
Time cut short and shadows fade
Morning hues the sky does make,
Night's will spent, her power played,
And now will the messenger her rest take.

Kevin D. McFillen

My Tools

Nothing's too big, nothing's too small,
  I am fix-it woman, I can fix-it all.
I can swing a hammer as good as any man,
  I can fix anything because I believe I can.
I'm a tinkering fool, I like to take things apart,
  I'll even try with something close to your heart.
I can put on a tab-roof or shingles on a house,
  even for a girl I ain't no wimpy mouse.
I know about points and plugs and about timing,
  nothing bugs me more than a motor that's whining.
I've got screw drivers, pliers and my own tape measure,
  but my hammer is what I mostly treasure.
My own tool box is quite full and doesn't lack,
  but if you use it, would you kindly put it back?

Danene Whitney

The Power Of Chance

Life is a game, it's full of chances,
Jobs, friends, and many romances.
You can have joy, everything going your way,
All that can change, it's like night and day.
The power of chance, you never know what you'll see,
It may send the song of a bird, or the sting of a bee.
A bad choice, step if you will,
Causes you to stumble, time won't stand still.
Chance, it so delicately holds your fate,
Some you many like, some you may hate.
No matter how weak, no matter how strong,
You must pay the price if your choice is wrong.
Your life is a game, it's already been played,
Your destiny's set, it's already been made.
There are choices to make, lives to live,
Fun to have, presents to give.
All that's for one special reason,
Your reason not time, you have your own life to be in.
You must be careful, you never know when the end is near,
Life is a game of chance, a game, with a lot to fear.

Casey Allen

Moonlight With Kisses

Moonlight with kisses
a charm bracelet, too
is a moment of madness
with a girl I once knew

her taste was of essence
with a smile like pure snow
she was my sunshine
wherever we go

her hair was like silk threads
of a softness, I know
she was always full of laughter
to make my days
so much more

so,
when I think of moonlight
with kisses, it takes my mind
back for more, of that moment of madness
from a girl, I had to know

Danny Williams

A Ronsense Nhyme

I ponder as I wander through the garden gate out yonder,
Why do carrots, corn and cabbage start with "C",
While the turnips and tomatoes and the parsnips and potatoes
Start respectively with letters "T" and "P"?

Would it not be just as well if we changed the way we spell?
Pronunciation then would change to coincide.
But then, if we changed the spelling it would cause disputes and yelling,
And confused misunderstanding far and wide.

For example, if a "B" is used instead of "P"
We'd be eating "Beas" and "Beppers" and "Botatoes".
And if we substitute a "D" in the usual place of "T"
We end up then with "Durnips" and "Domatoes".
In place of corn and cabbage, cuke and carrot
We could be growing "Porn" and "Pabbage", "Puke" and "Parrot".
Doesn't sound so appetizing, it would take some analyzing,
We'd have to look into it, search and ferret.

So, after all this weighty conversation
It seems most beneficial for the nation
If we keep the status quo, let "B" be "B", and "O" be "O"
Or we'll need a lot of keen interpretation.

Alice B. Miner

Being Myself

Who am I? I begin to wonder.
As the sun rise and set and people enter and exit my life.
I wonder, who am I?

The person that I once knew no longer exists.
With every experience, every new event, a new personality is formed.
A personality that reflects the pain, joy or sorrow that has been felt.

A new event, a new personality.
New event, new personality.
Event, personality...
And on and on it goes.

Layer after layer is formed.
The original surface... Never to be seen again.

It once shined, now the surface is dull.
And I wonder, who am I?

Elizabeth A. Olton

Maybe You Could Love Me

Between all the cries and
Between all the laughs
I still found the time to love you
Between all the fears and
Between all the thoughts
I stayed
Something inside told me "no"
And me being me, didn't listen
Now I sit and wonder what's gonna happen to us
I sit silently many days, my heart aching
I cry silently many nights till I fall asleep
I can't let go
When I close my eyes, my thoughts often wonder far
I have this close knit feeling you do care—
But not much
If you could hear my cries
If you could feel the wetness of my tears
Maybe you could find it in your heart-
To love me.

JaNae Griffin

The Shadows

One day when I awoke I thought of this recurring dream I have had. In this dream I see myself looking in a mirror. I looked very deep into the mirror. Beyond my image, I could see that there were many shadows. I could see shadows of darkness and shadows of light.

I kept asking myself, "What was this dream? What are these shadows I see before me?"

My day went on busy as every other day. Again that night I had the very same dream. So in my prayers I asked the Lord...

"Lord, I said, "I am troubled, why do I have these dreams of shadows continuously?"

The Lord answered, "My child, the shadows you see before you are the goodness and love that you have shown to your fellow men."

"But Lord," I said, "There are many shadows I see."

"My child," the Lord answered, "You have mocked and passed judgment against your fellow men and yet you yourself are not perfect. For it is written let he who is without sin cast the first stone."

Rose Giovinazzo Mahoney

Secrets

Secrets..... are troublesome fog that clouds one's mind,
These dark, endless blocks are hidden for no one to find.
How can they be eliminated so they will not taunt,
They come and spread when least expected, their purpose to haunt.
You can defeat them, innocent honestly is the key,
Though if you tell your forbidden truth, your respect will break free.

Secrets..... are incurable diseases that feed on fear,
Beware of this contagious plague, it surrounds your peers.
You can easily run, but you can not hide,
For this indomitable fog dwells perpetually inside.
It is stuck to you so you may fret,
The words of pain will make you regret.

Secrets..... don't have them wrong, they can be destroyed,
They can be rid of as fast as deployed.
You can fight them, secrets might go away,
But, in some form a secret will stay
This translucent mist will cause war and crime,
Secrets disperse only in the toll of time.

Zach Klein

Nature

Let us be washed over by the rain
fall. Spring gave flower and live again...
When renewed the light shone, freely.
We acknowledge this infinite joy!...
Where all was treated like a boy...
Divine was the good looking lady!
Enchanted to serve them with great love;
that bring peace and comfort to us, all,
went forth to celebrate this nice dove.
Whom was the Bride, so long blessed, actual
for human being rejoice, redeem
their heart; grave not, deep gratitude seem
full of happiness. For gentle groom.
Where flower on hand greatly bloom...
All that was sacred liveth freely!...
redeem their "heart" in harmony...

Claudel Jazon

Deep

You made me die,
Each time I read,
You made me cry,
The words you said.

You made me black,
All promises cost,
You made me lack,
All love I've lost.

I thought I'd find you in my dreams,
You said forever, it didn't keep,
I thought you loved me, it's not what it seems,
Keep falling deeper, deeper, deep.

Why couldn't you show,
I love you once more,
Too old, too far, too close to know,
Deeper, deepest, deep no more.

I wanted to, and just couldn't quite,
It took so long, completed a one,
Should not have followed such a light,
It was too dark, I have fallen dead.

Bethany Schmidt

When He Came

When He came there was only a bud
Struggling in a cold harsh world
And losing the battle.
It had almost given up.
But with a lot of care and a little sun,
It began to struggle less.
It started to fight.
After a long time, little by little, it began to blossom.
Now it is a flower living and growing
In a world that doesn't seem to harsh anymore.

When He came there was a little girl, meek and frail,
Struggling in a cold harsh world
And losing the battle.
She had almost given up.
But with a lot of love and a little push,
She became less meek.
She became stronger. She started to fight.
After a long time, little by little, she began to bloom.
Now she is a woman living and growing
In a world that doesn't seem so harsh anymore.

Shari Wilson

The Perfect Dream

To never feel a kiss,
Oh, what do we miss?

Is it like watching the sunrise?
Try to imagine seeing it TIME AFTER TIME.

Hear the oceans crashing to the shore,
Reach beyond the horizons for life beholds so much more!

To savor the taste of something sweet,
Life is much too short, never miss a beat!

The times we feel as if we're climbing a cliff,
Remember the moments that truly do uplift.

Just sit and listen to the birds,
They are talking too, can't you hear their words?

Breath the aroma of a rose,
What could that propose?

Crying of a newborn child,
Sometimes life seems like such a trial,
But we are only here for a very very short while!

Where will it all lead? What does this all mean!
Possibly that life + Time = our own PERFECT DREAM... ... ...

Donna Jean O'Hagan

Maybe

Maybe,
My grandparents were like the Israelites,
Enslaved!! By ignorance and tradition.
Maybe,
My parents were like Moses,
Struggling, traveling, to see the promised land.
Maybe,
I am like Joshua,
Leading the next generation to that place,
Where hate and prejudice no longer exists.
MAYBE.

Brenda J. Zeigler

Alone

I was walking around a well,
With my shadow one day.
Only one was hurt when I fell,
And my shadow had nothing to say.
Then I ran into the dark knowingly so blind.
When I glanced back,
There it stood,
I had left my shadow behind.

Chadwick R. Swetnam

Rosebud

I have longed for you beautiful rose
You give me love with the scent of happiness that is induced
    by your beauty
There have always been too many times in which you have died
For I do not know if it was negligence in not giving you
    more love
Or if it was that you had no love for me
Perhaps it was failing to hang on to that thin thread of life
    you caressed so motherly
I am lost without your natural beauty my rose
So please, come back to me...

Jackson David Newton

Do It Now

There's no need to sit and wonder,
There's no time to wish and ponder,
Life will not wait for you
No matter what you say or do,

  Do It Now

When you're young, the world's gigantic
Parents worry, life seem frantic
Before you know it, you has vanished
Plans and pleasure almost banished,

  Do It Now

Saving for joys when you have time
Time and money will never rhyme,
All that you saved won't cure your ills
Most of it's spent for potions and pills,

  Do It Now

Dreams of the future stay afar
Things you would do, seem like a star
So do each day, fill full each hour
With all joys of living, with all your power,
  Do It Now
William C. Glenn

Not A Deadhead

Poetry in motion sways within my head.
Syllables in linedance wake me from my bed.

Basic conversations march in metered verse.
Words once left discarded do not seem perverse.

Rhyming lines of couplets romance thoughts profound.
Consonants and vowels waltz creating sound.

What's caused this commotion to bombard my brain?
Might it be love's longing to write this refrain?
JoAnne D. Johnson

Purple Mountains Toppling

In the fertile folds of the valleys of this planet is where I build
my palace.
The animals are my followers, and the trees my army.
But my enemy slowly defeats me, killing off my army one by one,
weakening it before I can train more. The people of my village are
left with nothing.
Each morning as I stroll among the community I see my starving
frozen children.
Everyday more, more to bury.
Left without the protection of the army we will all surely be
destroyed.
Who gave ultimate power to my enemies,
  my enemies the..........humans?
Carrie Woodrum

The Greatest Gift

You give so much to others, with everything
  you do.
It does not go unnoticed, it touches my
  life too.
You have given me the greatest gift that I
  could ever have.
To love to live, and live to love, to touch
  others as you have.
Eternal life is yours to be, a gift of you,
  passed on through me.
Ellen Greenlee

Children All Children

Most precious life children
Most precious love children
Most precious friendship children
Most precious caring children
Most precious brave and daring children
Most precious innocent children
Most precious loyalty children
Most precious free spirited children
Most precious laughter children
So remember, we were all children and what
  lies in children lies deep within us as
  not children
We have just forgotten.
Santo Fusco

"Sleepless Nights"

On sleepless nights, I lie awake.
I cry and think of you.
  The memories keep flooding in,
of things we used to do.
  I cannot sleep; impossible!
The thoughts they just rewind.
  It hurts so much to be alone;
to me, you were so kind.
  I toss and turn, and turn and toss;
no comfort without you near.
  How I long to hold you in my arms,
to soothe your every fear.
  Yet, one day I know I'll get some rest;
with you, I'll be alright.
  But until that day I'll think of you
on all these sleepless nights.
William Alan Graham

To The End

Into the moon and starry night,
as I rush down and through the bite.
That you left with your tears,
you gave me your silent screams and sneers.
Your soul never left with mine,
you made me lost because you weren't my kind.
Trapped by the very day of the land,
you never should have stopped holding my hand.
Through the trees and deep forest in your heart,
did I search from the start.
Jenny Manolis

Rachel's Poem

This stream of consciousness is for you,
  at your request.

Right now, this moment, the world is yours.
  Run with it, while there's still time,
  Don't look back.

Now. Everything your senses perceive is yours;
  Your kingdom to rule as you wish.
  Stop — don't think — absorb.
  Sit and contemplate the silence.

This instant in time was created for you.
  You exist in it. Live
in the time you have been given.

A stream of consciousness for you,
  at your request.
Megan Gorsuch

Love

Love is very funny,
Just like a silly bunny.
You never know when you're in love,
Because it is hidden like a dove.
You look far and near,
But it will take you more than a year.
When you find that special one,
You know that you are done.
But beware,
Because if you know you're in love
You must really care...
So if you think you're in love,
Think again,
Because somewhere down the road it will all come an end.

Justin Alberto

Anniversary

Insects of lightning circled
Delirious in the haze of the Buckeye night
Reeling in the evening heat and love
Beginning more than half a century ago

Spring born soldier beside
Delicate August flower
Pressed uniform and pure white
Stand against bluegrass in fortress

Love loom spun
From Kentucky to Ohio
Illinois to California
Growing over time
In two beautiful children

Love they have created
Strengthened, spawned
Does not fade
And in the starry humid nights
The fireflies still circle

Terrance Robert Terich

A Graphic Description Of Someone I Love Debra

Do you know what love is? Is it possible to describe it? I can describe it. She is five foot and three inches tall and blonde. Debra is a young lady I met five months ago. When I first saw her, I was in love. Debra is shy, quiet, and basically a total sweetheart. She is also short, thin, beautiful, and is a total babe. I asked her out Saturday night; she had her doubts, but decided to give me a chance.

We are having a date, this Saturday night. I am glad, over joyed, head over heals, and basically excited about Saturday night. She decided to give me a chance, because I have waited five months for her. She is impressed, because I have waited for her, without giving up hope, that she will be mine one day. In return, that proves, admits, brings out, and shows her, that I love her.

My love for her is big, giant, huge, and out of this world. I hope everything works out between me and her. To be truthful, honest, and straight to the point, I hope this relationship lasts forever, till the end of eternity, which never ends, and for now.

If you don't think I know what love is, you're stupid braindead, and six cans short of a six pack. I know what love is IT'S DEBRA.

Jamie P. Frauendorfer

I The Earth

Is man so blind that he cannot see
I The Earth - what have you done to me

You have taken away my clean fresh air
And replaced it with clouds of despair

You have polluted my waters all over this land
I am at the mercy of your treacherous hand

All of God's creatures both great and small
Will become extinct, there'll be none at all

How will you ever reap what you sow
When on this earth you'll have nowhere to go

For all I have given and for all you have taken
It's because of your deeds that you'll be forsaken

Teach your young before it's too late
So that they don't repeat your fatal mistake

For If I The Earth you do not cherish
It will be by your own hand that you will perish

Penny Cole

The Moment

I think back to the sound of the water running under the road.
To the walking and how cool you were.
Leaving, standing at the open door to my truck,
not wanting to leave.
Caught in the moment.
Knowing you were moving on, missing you already.

Steven Buccellato

A Poem for Phillip

I do recall the days gone by,
Our broken hearts, why do they cry.
Is it from something we thought we've missed,
Or just his little hands, and a big fat kiss.
We loved him more than he'll ever know,
And I really wish I could watch him grow.
He conquered all the dreams he had,
And for this I shouldn't be mad.
I'll miss him now for the rest of my life,
I'm glad he's found the most perfect life.
He's in the hands of God again,
At least I know he's with good friends.
But I know the pain will never end,
And so I guess I'll cry again.

Phillip E. Hammond Jr.

Make Believe

Have you ever found yourself wishing
That instead of working you could be fishing?
Or in place of cleaning house
You could spend the day with your spouse?

But maybe instead of being with him
You could take a trip on a whim.
Just pretend that for the day
Everything could be your way.

The costs of things wouldn't matter
All things would come on a silver platter
Instead of playing make believe
All you asked for-you would receive.

But as we know this can't be true
Expecting things out of the blue
But just for once, wouldn't it be nice
To have these things without paying a price?

Kathy Pope

Look In My Heart

I don't always do what I know I should:
And I know I don't do things the way that you would.

We don't walk, talk, or look the same:
And we don't share each others name.

We have different hopes and different dreams:
Different desires for different things.

I know we don't always see eye to eye:
Things that make me laugh may make you cry.

You may wear diamonds and strands of gold:
You may have wealth and riches untold.

But, I place my value on the simpler things:
Not on a mansion or on diamond rings.

I have my family and the Lord above:
A peace in my soul and a heart full of love.

So if you judge me look beyond what you see:
Look in my heart and find the real me.

Linda Sue Gillum

Dancers In The Fog

Winter haze enshrouding all it touches
Creates a world of measured fantasy.
Skeletal sprites cavort with arms
Raised in joy to their existence;
Formless behemoths in stately polonaise
Lumber to places unknown;
Flat bottomed boats with graceful arches
Glide aimlessly on a sea of cotton;
Wispy fairies swirl and eddy with abandon
Upon their streams and rivers;
And beleaguered travelers, for a brief moment,
Become dancers in the fog.

Patricia A. Cultice

Spring

Spring is fun,
Feel the warm sun.

There's a breeze in the air,
Better hold on to your hair.

Flowers bloom, grass to mow,
Thank goodness, no more snow.

Girls jumping rope, boys playing ball,
Such a good time had by all.

Lots of sunshine, plenty of daytime,
Warm weather is a special delight of mine.

Children laugh, birds sing,
Everyone loves the time of spring.

Victoria S. Mitchell

"Lady Eternity"

She came and touched my shoulder
  I lingered at her door
She put her fingers to her lips
  And whispered "One minute more."
I hadn't seen her face before
  And looked around to see
If someone else could recall
  This lady of mystery
But no one else was there but I
  To hear or even see
As her sweet face appeared once more
  And said, "Come - My names "Eternity"

Rosemary E. Butler

Blessings From Above

Whatever blessings God gives you
Be thankful and use it well;
Be it small or something big
Be content and do not beg,
Good deeds are always rewarded.

Do not let vanity engulf your pride,
Modest man does not talk of himself,
Never think of yourself to be above others,
Just remember you are blessed
God will only give you the best.

Remember that the good Lord
Will always be there looking after you
You might probably stumble on the way
But cheer up... Your guardian angel
Will be there too, to help you.

Impossible it is to predict what lies ahead
Have the courage to go forward and strive hard,
Healthy attitude helps you reach your goal,
For something could be done,
Think of the rewards of labor, love and wisdom.

Natividad F. Bacalzo

A Thought Of Fear

Living outside yourself
You only turn to stone
Killed during your first life
Cutting through all flesh and bone
While hands break to hold all energy
You're born so mysterious
I just can't hear what you say to me

Where is your soul
Where is your love
While cold and darkness rise above
A feeling of conquering will
Down inside me
I use the strength of many
To crush who might stop me

Your brutal curse a reflection of shade
This shadow of darkness I don't want to fade
A hollow light my soul just passed through
All in a memory you killed what I knew
A dream of all hate I rise up in fear
Waking in silence I just disappear

Susan Allen

A Boy And His Wonderful Kite

Out in the broad, treeless meadow
In the early spring weather of March;
A Boy brings his kite, to send Flying,
High in the azure blue arch.

Holding his craft with boyish pride
A spool of twine, tight in his grip;
The kite gaily spins in the zephyr,
Its tail gives a bounding skip.

Bearing his kite against the breeze,
Running, he lets the taut cord unwind;
To gaze while it climbs ever higher
Leaving him waiting behind.

There on the ground gazing skyward,
Viewing his kite, as it flies in spring;
Little bird you can go no higher
Held fast at the end of a string.

The kite linked by a twirling cord,
Flutters, and suddenly breaks free;
High overhead, a wavering plane
Now beckons, come fly with me!

Mary E. Nagode

Relapse

Come with me don't be afraid
There's nothing to fear when you are brave
The sounds of the silence float about your head
But you are secure with the things you've said.

Listen awhile and you will find
All roads lead back into your mind
The world is a sheet of molten glass
Through which all of this must pass.

Can you recall the moment when
The sun burnt out and lit again?
The river was flowing right into your grasp
But it all dried up when the sun relapsed.

Listen awhile to the passing day
Tomorrow awaits for those who stay
Dance while you can for the time is near
When all this will fade and disappear.

Mike Lavoie

"The Wind Cries Back"

Hypocrites have constructed a mock funeral,
in the pseudo hope of our saviour's procession.
The caskets lay closed except for the in-between.
Mother Earth cried out for reform,
and the wind cried back.
Our beloved human race stood with jaw agape.
Marvelous visions and unbelievable actions.

The train rode through at dawn.
Spreading bland emotions and delirium about the town.
The mayor and his six wives danced naked in the lawn.
His daughter, his lover, perched on a swing wearing her bridal
uniform, with a clown nose obscuring her precious face.

When will we catch up with the dream?
Will we remain crouched and tired?
Saving pennies to buy next week's groceries.
The children all ran for the hills to hide.
A mutiny of tiny infants, our future committing suicide.
Too much doubt for my young mind to handle.
I cried out for assurance and hope... and the wind cried back.

Ben Pesta

The Vigil

The sky is gray,
As gray as last night's fireplace ashes.
The trees are bare and gaunt,
Like old bones in the desert.
The dog huddles in his house.
The cats hunt for a small ray of sunshine.
I turn from the window,
As gloomy as the day.
Suddenly, I spot a robin tugging at a worm,
A smile tugs at the corners of my mouth.
I waited and watched and was rewarded,
Spring is here!

Roseanne Bradley

The Crowds

Crowded
Crunched
Crammed Corners

   Picturesque
   Peaceful
   Planned Corners

     Decadent Delightful Damned Corners.

Eileen T. Green

It's My Dream

I'm gonna take care of you it's my dream you're my mother
cause it's your love that get's me through hard times and
my troubles. I know I put you through some hurt and pain
you still took care of me despite the shame you endured the
pain you placed no blame you believed in me and you see
a success in me so mother I say to you you're my life and
I love you and I'm gonna take care of you no more hurt only
healing and I'll be your security no more struggles or
worries only flurries of the love I bring cause you're the
best mom any son can dream I'm gonna take care of you
till the morning turns to noon
till the noon turns to eve
till the eve turns to night
and again in the early light
I'm gonna take care of you it's my dream I love you.

Wade Tapp Jr.

Near, But Yet So Far

Where can this elusive treasure be
I have searched everywhere, it seems to me.
I felt it touch me as the morning sky turned bright
I heard it whisper, as from the forest, birds took flight
The gentle morning breeze, the sun dancing across the pond
All gave me a special feeling of which I was so fond.
The warmth of the sun upon my face,
A walk through the woods to a special place
All gave me the feeling that in some way,
I had found that treasure for which I searched today.
While I sat on the porch as night grew near
I remembered the many sights and sounds so dear.
Within my heart grew a feeling of great release
I knew I had finally had that precious treasure, peace.
This wonderful gift for which I had searched many a mile,
Was here within my soul all the while.
I realized that peace is not something you must find
Because it is really a state of mind.
At myself, I had to grin,
I knew peace was something that must come from within.

Brenda Green

Bic

A man with an invisible energy
detector walked along the beach.
He was a scientist of ambitious
personal pursuits who had, in his
unique and unprecedented research
and experimentation, discovered a
highly fragile but sophisticated
system of detecting invisible energy
sources present in the environment,
which was worked through a small,
handheld scientific instrument.
He called it an invisible energy detector.

It looked like a pen.

Matthew Seeley

I Loved You

You said you loved me, you said you cared.
All of the times we spent, all of the love we shared.
I thought they would last, that you would never go,
I thought that you were true, how was I supposed to know?
All of the time you said those things, all the times you lied.
I tried to understand you, oh how hard I tried.
But I know I can't make you change, I know you'll stay the same.
Just remember I loved you, that will never change.

Shera Garcia

Untitled

I awoke this morning, my eyes still weak
My mind knows that I am sad.
My love for you can not compete
With the beautiful feelings that you have.
The words in my heart I can not speak
For my love for you I can not explain
Although, I know we will never meet
For this love, I live in pain.

Tomorrow, comes another day
Maybe then the pain will cease.
If they do not I will pray
For my life to live in peace.
I love her with every breath I take
I will always kept her in sight.
Her love I will not forsake
Because she is my light.

Richard Ory

Driving Down A Western Kansas Road

Gliding, swirling, floating effortlessly,
One of many birds of prey.
So many years it's always been the same,
Another rodent will die today.

Now he's perched upon a telephone pole.
Proud and bold as can be.
In Kansas, he's the reigning king,
And that's all right with me.

An ocean of wheat expanding on for miles
With one or two islands of trees.
Midwest wind whips the grain to waves of green
Like a tossed and churning stormy sea.

Sunflowers aligned so straight and evenly
Like soldiers before a head of state.
Clouded shadows play tag with all below.
The eagle watches and waits.

The eagle and hawk are flying free.
It may sound simple, but it means so much to me.
May they fly eternally.

John E. Myers

The Bobby E. Moore Jr. Story

Dear Lord hear my plea,
　Open my mind so I can see.
Change this heart of stone,
　Help me to make heaven my home.

The road I traveled has been so long,
　Because it's you Lord who I have never known.
I have drifted so deep within my sins,
　Fighting a lost battle that I can never win.

I have many a time wanted to give up,
　but, the desires of sin kept filling my cup.
I don't know how I made it his far,
　With a gun, knife and crow bar.

I don't regret the things I've learned,
　Lord help me to make a brand new turn.
Lord give me a new heart and mind,
　So I can be just like you and your kind.

Give me the knowledge of your word,
　So I can teach other who have never heard.
Dear Lord let me stand tall and honor your sake,
　Please dear Lord anything but the Fiery Lake.

Bobby E. Moore Jr.

Ms. Cat

One blustery February day
Something black came my way
No larger than a baby's mitten
That ball of fur was a baby kitten
The kitten had a little girl at home
But that German Shepherd was free to roam
After running away time after time
The little girl said the kitty was mine
She soon established who would be boss
She would meow I want nine lives tuna in sauce.
We lived in the country so I let her be free
When a dog came by she would head for a tree
It will rain in the south at the drop of a hat
She would pounce on the screen and looked like a bat
She is now an uptown cat
She lives in condo healthy and fat
She still hears the dogs, but on TV
She will stretch and meow you can't get to me
After twelve years we have a language we alone can understand
She's still the boss and I have her tuna in hand

Appy Jo McDaniel

All Of This...

Your eyes speak to mine
In their silent, eloquent language
They tell me what words could never express
Of unshared dreams, and hopeful plans, and
hurtful memories

All of this they share...and more

So, with my gaze
I try to communicate to the depths of your heart
All of my compassion, my love, my understanding,
and recognition of your soul

All of this I share...and more

With my mind, I will you to understand that my
heart is sincere
In the crowded darkness, amongst the sun-kissed
beams of light that fall on your face
I see you smile

And my heart declared my devotion, my need, and
my faith in you

All of this it shared...and more

Christina L. Garris

Ode To A Stranger

Was it hard for you to leave your home carrying
The shame of your swollen belly at only sixteen?

Who did you stay with? Were they kind to you,
Or did they fuel your pain? How did the long months
Of waiting pass for you, young, frightened, forced
To watch your beautiful adolescent body grow
Into an unknown thing?

Did you cry often, hating my conception? Or did you stroke
Your mistake with uncontrolled love and compassion?
And when you expelled my life from yours, did you sigh with
Welcome relief, or did your arms long for me in the stillness?

Have you ever thought of me in the dark night, as I
Have thought of you? Forever separated, forever intertwined,
Distance and ignorance too weak to deny our bond set in blood.

Are you happy now, content with planned children by your side?
Or do you see me in their eyes as I have often seen you
In the eyes of strangers? Yet, I have grown to understand your
Silence. — Even welcome it —
For you gave me what you could in giving me life,
And life is good enough.

Conneen Dewey

Eternity

Tonight the moon's light guides me to you
I can see your reflection in the water, but
yet when I turn around, you're nowhere to
be found.
Your sweet, tender voice fills the air
sometimes I feel like reaching out and
holding you.
The earth is spinning and I'm getting
nowhere
Oh, how I long to feel your body touching
mine.
Just to feel your touch, to hear your voice
that's all I need to make it through the night.
I feel you looking at me through the moon
and stars,
Your eyes piercing right through my soul
a chill goes up my spine as you caress my
skin.
You put your arms around me, and hold me
for... Eternity.

Francisco M. Ayala Jr.

"Katherine"

Katherine,
A beautiful name for a beautiful person
A name I will never forget
A name I will always love
And a name I will always cherish

I hold your picture close to my heart
And think of you every night
You are in my mind and in my soul
I have to tell you I love you so

I hope nothing comes between us
and nothing break us apart
Because if it does,
I will break my Heart!

Sam H. Thai

Dungeon

Darkness,
Chains,
Odor of Ages.
Where am I?

Silence,
Trapped,
Doomed for Wrongs;
Who am I?

Broken,
Weak,
Full of Years.
What am I?

Lost,
Unforgiven,
Nothing.
Why am I?

Wilbert Evan Hauch

Spring

Spring is when things come to life. Everything
is very nice. If you can come to play, we
will have a very good day. It's when the
flowers bloom, and the sky is never gloom.
Everybody loves spring because I say it is a
very wonderful thing!

Krista Roscoe

America

The home of the free and the brave.
I remember it well,
we landed in Harlem, New York
A place called little Italy.
I remember it well.
My father was a bricklayer
and landed a job.
I remember it well.
Education was the main thing
in my father's mind
I remember it well.
I became a lawyer
and my brother a barber.
I remember it well.
God bless America
for I will remember it well.

Salvator Ferello

When My Sister Died

O greed how can you be so great?
When someone dies please, please wait.
Don't take her things and walk away.
There will never be another day.
To sort out all her precious things.
To know what joy her memory brings.
I need time to pick and choose.
What did she love that I can use?
I know, I know, I'll take her cat.
There is no doubt - she would like that
Her cat was her great joy, her love,
And when she looks down from above
She'll know that every meow and purr
Will make me always think of her.

Tobista Fichera

Flirt

I knew from the start
that you were just a flirt.
And yet I fell in love with you
knowing I'd get hurt.

I hoped to tie you down
and make you love just one.
But how could I do something
no one else had ever done?

Now I know you'll never love me
and I'm trying not to cry.
For I've got to find the strength
to tell your lips good-bye.

If you ask for me again
you'll find I won't be there.
I need a love to call my own,
not one I have to share.

I'll hide my broken heart
behind a laughing face.
You may think I never cared
but no one can take your place.

David A. Brence

Freedom

Freedom - I think that I
Could never give it up.
It permeates all
I think and do.
Anything less
Would not be enough.

Jeanette Rhoback

Ascending Fog

As each moment goes by
I ask myself
how painful is my life
is my spirit at ease
have I fulfilled one
of my dreams
they are just distant recollections
from my time since past
give back youthful body
I am tired and beguiled
even hard for me to smile
I was only twenty six
my muscles torn
bones out of place
this I can't face
as each moment goes by
I ask myself how

painful is my life
come back tomorrow
you can pull out the knife

Robert H. Wade

For God's Darlings

The big fours can open many doors:
   1. Education
   2. Good grooming
   3. Good manners
   4. Be professional
They are right for you and me
And how smart you will be.

Other steps are:
No jumping, no bumping, no climbing.
No running while in the house
And that's the way it should be.
By no fighting, no biting,
No hitting or kicking,
You are blest and nice, I see.

Elva S. Fried

"Once We Were A Family"

Once we were a family,
then suddenly it was gone.
Each has went His way
there's not much left of yesterday.

A generation lost,
that only God can save.
The World has claimed our young
Lost in worldly fun,

Eyes that cannot see,
Ears that cannot hear
Hearts that have,
been turned away.

Once we were a family,
If only it could be a gain,
But only "God", can save
It, from this world of sin.

Gladys M. Garske

Winter

Winter comes in white
Puts a chilly blanket down
Earth's meadows so green
Dressing trees with lacey flakes
No more flowers to be seen

Lisa Ma'ree Anderson

Distant Love

He's captured all my outward thoughts,
   and inward, all my heart.
I look of course upon this child,
   a human work of art.
It's hard to love from far away,
   but I love him none the less.
As I look upon this child of yours,
   I know we've all been blessed.
I'm looking at this paper,
   with an image very clear.
And wishing that this image
   could be standing here.
To hear him laugh, to see him play,
   to sit him on my knee.
These, of course, are simple things,
   but mean so much to me.

John Swanson

I Wonder If God Cries

I wonder if God cries
when we do the things we do.
I wonder if He bows His head in shame
when we down His holy name.
I wonder if God cries
when we fail to read His word.
I wonder if God cries
when we deny His son lives.
I wonder if God cries
when we abuse the ones we love.
I wonder if God cries
when we destroy the nature He created.
I wonder if He ever wants to throw
up His hands and say I give up.
I wonder if God cries
when we do the things we do.

Margret Wilcox

Autumn

Flowers Dying,
Leaves changing color,
People getting out their mittens,
Children playing all day long,
Cool breeze against their cheeks,
Eating warm meals everyday,
Having friends who care,
Colors here, there, and everywhere,
Birds sing all day long,
Touch of wind against my skin,
makes me feel like part of Autumn.

Sarah Violet Cole

The Dance

Come dance with me my love
To the melody I know so well...

These burns do I deserve
from living through such hell?

Keep dancing with me my love
I feel the comforts of home...

You feed me the fire
Which fuels this desire

To master at last
the unknown...

Dana Tomei

The Hunt

Hunt,
A term of such diversity.
What is this hunt?
Why is it so hard to understand?

People who don't like the killer,
Kill the killer.
Now they are the killer.
A circle that will never end,
From one hunter to another.

The attacker must be dealt with,
But who will be the revenger?
You will.
But now the revenger will be after you.
A life long process that will kill you.

The hunter, who is no different,
from the thinker.
All want peace,
But what price will they pay?
Who will go next?

Christopher M. Worthington

Undying Friendship

The roses will bloom
   With fragrance so sweet;
We care for them gently,
   Their life is a treat.

There are some close friendships
   Which as roses, bloom;
They make our lives cheery
   And dispel all our gloom.

But as time fades the roses
   Our friends often die;
But their fragrance still lingers,
   Their memories won't die.

We praise God for roses
   Which brighten our day;
Much more do we praise Him
   For friends sent our way.

Jim Dickensheets

Old Fashioned Love

Old fashioned friends
spending old fashioned time
doing old fashioned things
the old fashioned way.

Old fashioned couple
holding old fashioned hands
under the old fashioned tree
the old fashioned way.

Old fashioned boy
gives old fashioned ring
to old fashioned girl
the old fashioned way.

Old fashioned wedding
on an old fashioned day
in the old fashioned Church
the old fashioned way.

Old fashioned couple
spending old fashioned time
doing old fashioned things
the old fashioned way.

Lisa Ann Eaton

Love Is...

Love is just a four letter word
   but it means so much
Love is caring and sharing
   and feeling that special touch
Whenever your relationship gets
   in a bind
Love is always there to help
   you unwind
If you treat given love with
   respect
Then respectable love is what
   you'll get
Love is kind, love is true
Love is more beautiful when
   it comes from you...

Tashira McCollister

"Frontier Woman"

I stand proud and tall
   (for one so small)
Packing a knife and gun
With a hand on my hip,
   (don't give me no lip)
Or a mother will mourn her son.

Clad in boots, jeans, and shirt
(why in hell wear a skirt)
With eight hungry kids to feed,
I harvest the crop
(with the pigs still to slop)
That callused hands started from seed.

I lay alone in our old feather bed
(my mind conjuring up Ned)
Feeling the dark and the cold
Hating the war that took him away
(No lovin' for many a day)
And killed half my soul.

Judy A. Egan

The Night

Twisting in the breeze
Dying in slow continuity
Forming the other worldly shape
Darkness mounting light;
Preparing the seed
Something abrupt
enter exit
enter exist.
The shadows fade;
nightmares are apples glistening
falling from the early morning sky.
Dawn of time;
It ends;
Only to begin again

Steve Villafranca

Untitled

   Sleepless, speechless, it's time to
go on. I think to myself how has
it came to this, alone as I cry out
please doesn't someone feel my pain,

   I'm a man who is too full
of pride to acknowledge another man's
plea. Does he not see that I know,
or does he not care. If indeed this
is the case, truly you have no friend,
but a jealous enemy!

Clyde Sanders

There Is Something About Snow Hill

I know a group of people,
    Who are striving to do God's will;
They are in the body of Christ,
    And they're members of Snow Hill.

There is something about Snow Hill
    No matter where I roam;
There is something about Snow Hill
    That makes me glad to be home.

My mother and my father - Lord,
    They taught me how to pray;
They said, "In times of sorrow
    The Lord will make a way."

My mother said, "Child, remember that
    God is real;
No matter where you go,
    Stay on the battlefield."

When I see the empty pews,
    Where my loved-ones used to be,
Then I know, I must keep on striving
    To win the victory.

Al Horton

Vernal Equinox

Could there really ever be
happier songs than Chickadees?
What heavenly garment vests
better than red Robin's breast?
Might colors be more refined
than Jay feather, blue-sky-lined?
Sun sunk into Buttercups?
or, Tulip bowls opened up?
What bride could wear finer lace
than Cherry tree's floral grace?
Symphonies of Willow-wind
dark's forebodings now do mend.
Welcome, we our One True Light.
Resurrection comes to night.

Dianna Drinkard

A Precious Gift

There's a love in my heart,
    a love you can hold,
but be careful because
    this love is as precious as gold.

When you've held this gift,
    of love close to your heart,
Sometimes you'll feel like,
    it is very hard to part.

And when you've finally gasped,
    this love that's in the air,
This love that is precious,
    this love you and I share.

And every minute of the day,
    I want to have you near,
For I'm not ashamed to say,
    "I love you dear".

Tiffany Nichole Fitzwater

A Farmer's Spring

I wish everyone could know
    Spring's coming as I do
Sights and smells and sounds all flow
    Green grass and sky so blue

The sight of a newborn calf
    With mother close beside
Brings joy within to a laugh
    Warmth overflows inside

The smell of fresh turned soil
    Praying our seed will grow
Our work is not a toil
    Within it our blood flows

The sound of the birds singing
    Is sunshine to our ears
The sounds of children bringing
    Treasures they find so dear

Spring brings us a brand new start
    A chance to start anew
The season close to my heart
    Can be close to you, too

Susan Johannsen

We Hold In Our Hands... Life

We hold in our hands
    a life that's full of treasures
Like a walk through summer sands
    we control life's many pleasures

We hold in our hands
    the power of our dreams
Like uncontrolled laughter
    that bursts at the seams

We hold in our hands
    the direction of our children
Like the winds of a fall day
    we let them lead the way

We hold in our hands
    the plan for life's future roads
Like the map that's used for travel
    we deserve the life we chose

We hold in our hands
    a life that will be no more
But in the end
    the life we led was truly our own

Candace Brown

God's Small Creature

Out my window
every morning
Sometimes noon time
And sometimes night
There is one of God's
Small creatures
Feeding nectar while in flight
There I'm staring
With amazement
Careful not to say a word!
For I know God's
Given nature
Of the lovely Hummingbird.

Hettie Hoy Rice

If

If I could hold you once again
The changes I would make
Things to do much differently
If my hand you'd take
If we could travel back in time
Past the anger and the tears
If we could put our lives in reverse
And bring back the forgotten years
We'd be each half of a whole
As we became man and wife
The adventures would be unceasing
As together we shared a life
But has it been too long
Have too many tears been cried
If we could forgive and forget
I'd be unfailing by your side
If you would promise me forever
I'd return without delay
If you would promise me forever
Then forever I would stay.

Lori Ann Nerge

Good-Bye

If I shall enter my soul
Upon the end of mortality
Then this world
Shall be a better place without me

Will they mourn
This lost confused soul?
Cherish it forever
And never let go?

Or will they forget
And never realize
Upon all the reasons in the world
Why I had to die

Never understand
The way I felt inside
Never understand
The feelings I had to hide

They will see me once more
And have one last cry
Without a chance to be heard
The world: Good-bye.

Syvanna Roland

Coming Home

Seeing your sad, young man face
Remembering youth, another place
Torn shins, broken tooth and nose
Little boys growing, as life goes

Heartaches taken in such stride
Deeming life's game, a wild ride
Drinking and playing every game
Pleasure taken, however it came

Habits made at such early age
Not broken, bringing such rage
Destroyed body, mind growing weak
Absorbing cravings addicts seek

Dreams of places, that perfect job
Such fine things, addiction did rob
Will taken, falling ever so deep
Little pride for this man to keep

Future and dreams seeming long gone
Mother hoping he'll soon come home
Knowing prayers, miracles do make
Repeating many, for all their sake

Yvonne Cole

Commitment

Since I live my life for thee,
my dreams can never be.
For you many things I have done,
without you I can not be one.
The life I live belongs to you,
I remember this in all I do.

Why do I live my life for thee,
do I feel what no one can see.
You are no longer here,
I live at once my deepest fear.
Does my sole now come apart,
does lost love shatter my heart.

Worry not of my pain,
I have learned to avoid the strain.
Although I am now alone,
morbid is not my tone.
I no longer live my life for thee,
for once I live my life for me.

Russell Robert Ohlrogge

Branches Of Love

Whisper softly in my branches
whispering winds calling to me
Whisper softly that you're beautiful
through and through, is she?
Whisper softly I my branches
whispering winds calling to me
As you sway in the moonlight
A little sprout I do see,
Then one day in the sunlight you
will be mature like me
Whisper softly in my branches
whispering winds calling to me
Go Whisper that I love her
whispering winds calling to me

Janice Berry

Lord

Here I am; come take me by the hand
And
To the end of the road we shall go
Side by side
Please come talk to me; I'm afraid
Of the dark world I see coming at
Me
When I'm asleep I lose control of
The dark dream,
It's hard to let go of that hurt
That pain, so I ask you again
Why did you go?
Come stay with me and together
We shall sit on the sand and hear
The ocean waves come in.
Lord, tell me it's going to be OK
Please
Lord, answer me somehow.

Carolina Rivera Streetman

Untitled

There was a man
he had a gun
his butt got burnt
and the story is done.
   Needle and pin
   Needle and pin
   When a man
   gets married
   trouble begins.

Chandai Raghunauth

Untitled

Our love knows no beginning,
it will see no end - it is infinite.

The path we have traveled
has been rough, but never rocky -
allowing us to strengthen and grow.

Now as we bond together - the future
holds nothing but promise,
because we are as one!

Joyce Schneider

What Is Love

   Love is the ingredient that wipes
away the tears from the eyes of the
broken-hearted. And heals the soul
of those who are affected.
   Love covers a multitude of sin
which wars against us in our minds,
holding us down like chains.
   Evil is Curse, but love has the
power to look into the eyes of a
human and see the soul.

Debra L. Fonseca

Words Of War

I sit and try to pray,
But my mind is full of sorrow.
I killed a man today,
And maybe another tomorrow.

Marching with eyes full of tears,
While seeing young soldiers die,
Loud explosions hurting my ears,
Grown men break down and cry.

I wonder what the enemy's thinking,
Will I again see their faces.
I wonder what the futures is bringing,
Maybe war in other places.

This war so full of agony.
Come see and lose your sanity.

Felix Vega

Untitled

Just before I go to bed,
Every night I lay my head,
Stare up at the stars above,
Unbounded is my Love.
Someday I shall know that Love,
Love that even now knows me,
Over oceans far and wide,
Valleys traversed, mountains climbed.
Early I shall rise and see,
Someone that's so good to me.
Yesterday was not a dream.
Owning up to my true Love.
Understanding what's above.

Michael J. Schafer

As Blue As The Ocean

There are two things that I have
and they are as blue as the ocean
and as light as the sky.
They glimmer in the sunshine,
and sparkle in the moonlight.

These two things are my eyes.

Colleen Sanders

Here

Here, I sit alone
While my love for you has grown
Here, I sit all day
And think of something to say
Here, I sit all night
To think of a way to make it right
Here, I think of you
And what I should do
Here, I sit all the time
Wishing you would be mine

James W. Kipler

The Price For Beauty

What can you offer me?
I asked Life one day.
What would you like?
I heard a voice say
Oh! I'd like beauty
Please make me fair
So those who meet me
Will stand and stare
Then quickly offer
Friendship to share.

Then life looked puzzled
And began to smile
Beauty shall be yours
With a price my child
A price for beauty,
How much shall I pay?
Then Life gave an Answer
You must love some each day.
I paid the price each day a part
Now beauty dwells within my heart.

Ruth M. Overcash

Storm Clouds

Storm clouds on the horizon-
   What shall they bring today?
Are they full of rain or snow-
   Will they keep me from my play?

Storm clouds on the horizon-
   What do they mean for me?
Will they bring trouble?
   In time - We shall see!

Storm clouds on the horizon-
   Have beauty of their own.
They turn and toss-
   Where next - will they roam?

Storm clouds on the horizon-
   Will they arrive today?
Looks like they are breaking up-
   They've decided not to stay!

Rosetta Ewing Schemenauer

Butterflies

Butterfly flying high in the sky,
I'm going to catch you when you fly by
As you fly so far and near
Out of sight you disappear.
With flashes of gold, blue and yellow,
You're a lively little fellow!
I can see you at a glance
As you spin around and prance.
So be gone with you, my little friend
Wish I had your wings to lend!

Neloise K. Medeiros

The Evils Of Poetry

Poetry is a monster,
LURKING in the glen,
Creeps up and consumes you,
Before you lift your pen.

Poetry is vile,
The rot that rots your brain,
For all this endless rhyming,
Can drive a man insane.

Poetry is nasty,
It speaks of greed and lust,
Of kingdoms, reputations, people,
Soon reduced to dust.

Poetry is seductive,
A star-crossed lover's trance,
A wordy web of putrid fantasy,
That rip's out a heart like a lance.

That, my friend, is poetry,
Not a limerick or pun.
A thing that I would vindicate,
If it weren't so much darn fun!!

Philip Andrew Wesley

Empty Endings

It's sad how things end
without a final ending
Like a card that you buy
without ever sending

You end ever seeing
and eventually talking
You just say good-bye
and keep on walking

The memories are still there
and may make you wonder...
will the sun come back
Or will you hear only thunder

Though times seem stormy
and there's no one to hold
It takes time to heal
to shake off the cold

But remember when life
deals empty endings to you,
The rising sun of tomorrow
may bring something new

Dawn Barnett

Core

Defend me yet you cannot hate,
Surrender not for any fate,
Devoid of life, ashamed to die,
You dine with death and still you cry.
Running will not save you now,
It never saved you any how.
Imprisoned here for all of time,
Paying for another's crime.
This is the way that it must be.
Your empty songs won't set you free.
Pretending that the life you lead,
Will satisfy some worldly need.
And all the time you know inside,
That once was life has all but died.
You covet such a blissful pain,
And seek to find the truth in vain.
But what's this now? A speck of light.
Is this supposed to be your fight?
Endure, escape, and persevere
Or stay and live your life in fear.

Joshua J. Freeze

A Secret Place

There is a secret place
where I can find a tender face
and a warm embrace

When no one else is around
and there is barely a sound
I listen to words so profound

Here my tired soul is renewed
and washed from sin's residue

Daily I go to abide
here my spirit comes alive
Oh yes, I am satisfied

A tender face, a warm embrace
His amazing grace is in this place...

Valerie A. Knight

A Corporate Woman

She learned to dress mannequins,
then to dress herself.
Her perfume became subtle,
her accessories vibrant.
She captured the look of each season.

Playfulness yielded to sophistication.
Even her embrace became ceremonial.
Her kiss reluctant.

Promoted to buyer,
she decided what they would wear.
They waited, naked, poised
for her selections.

The transformation complete.
Her laughter gone.
Only the demure smile,
and expressionless eyes.

William D. Smith

One

Petals of a Rose
from an angel be born.
Petals from heaven are you,
I am a thorn.

One alone
not a garden be.
But a thorn and a petal,
becomes a garden free.

Together a flower
we become.
The Petal, the Thorn,
a Rose as one.

Our love is the stem
growing long and bold.
Thorns on its spine
but, petals behold.

A flower from above,
a part given to each.
Requires only our love
to heaven a Rose reach.

John Karst

Untitled

Who next will the wind blow?
Into my path, through my door?
Will it be friend or stranger or foe?
Who next will the wind blow?

What next will the sun shine down?
Upon my face, upon my toes?
Will it be blessing or burden or clown?
What next will the sun shine down?

Where next will my feet wander?
To a new city, to a new world?
Of those lands will I be fonder?
Where next will my feet wander?

To which heights will my mind travel?

Shakhi Majumdar

"Star" Of Jan 27, 92

You were a shinning Star;
And you fell from The Sky:
And you fell to the Earth,
To become, Grandma's Little Guy.
Now you, twinkle and you shine.
With your big Green Eyes.
And you're mine, All mine;
Cause you're Grandma's Little Guy.
And as you grow I'll watch you shine:
With those Big Green Eyes.
And some day you'll be;
A Big; Big; Man:
But, you'll Always be Grandma's
Little Guy, with those Big Green Eyes.
God; sent you to me, And you're
Grandma's Little Guy, Mine All Mine.

Bess Ahten

That Boy Justin

Tousled mop of soft brown hair
Freckles here and there
A scientific turn of mind,
Ever curious and curiouser.

Steady green eyes
Of unwavering gaze
Fix a questioning look,
Then head for a book.

Little blond brother in tow,
To the beaver ponds they go.
Barefoot - and pale from winter
Soon sun-browned - and late for dinner.

Quick deft hands
Small brown helpful hands
They fix most anything
And catch frogs and toads of spring.

Mud, snails, bird nests
In a wonderfully unorganized mess
Under his bed - his prized collection
For a rainy day's recollection.

Mary Holm

Day After Day

One day I felt
you with my eyes.
I saw you I loved
you so much.
It was not a dream.
It was real.

Arianna Reich

Memories

She had her memories,
My mother said
On turning eighty
And I just half that.

What did I know
Of her dreams and wants?
Years of child-rearing
And sacrifice.

Growing-up so long ago
Working and playing
Or were they the same?
I wish I'd asked.

But I had my dreams
Now turned to memories.
Joanne Sly

Forgotten

Shivers of the long lost
Lost in a world of illusion.
Self-sacrifice of my happy smile.
Self-sacrifice of my ever desire.
To forget my euphoria,
To forget my desire,
To forget my distant love.
Hallucinations of the meeting.
Will it be what was expected?
Lust, energy, relief,
Or will it be the nightmare of
Hatred, confusion, digress?
Or rather, Will it ever be?
Will it ever be?????
Winde Stark

A Lesson From Nature

In the midst of daffodils,
one chilly summer eve.
She waves goodbye with hesitance,
with a teardrop as he leaves.

A little girl with heartfelt love,
a bird that could not fly,
Now stands alone ambiguously,
as the bird migrates the sky.

Her care, devotion and love she gave,
unaware of a need to part,
Now faced with the reality,
and left with broken heart.

And as I watched I realized,
with a teardrop from my eye.
I too will feel the loss, she feels,
when it's time for her to fly!!
Teresa M. Combs

Rainbows

You'll never see a rainbow
  without the rain.
You'll never appreciate joy
  without the pain.
You'll never know good
  without the bad.
You'll never truly be happy
  without ever being sad.
I never knew love until
  I meet you.
I never knew sorrow until
  you said we're through.
Arlow Bailey

Alone In A Crowd

To: Lydia Vazquez Rodriguez
Alone in a crowd
So you believe.
The pain in your
Heart you try to deceive.

Alone in your birth,
Alone your departure.
The many between know
This sorrow.
We hold this pain
Through tomorrow.

Alone in the dark, we
Will light the way
And see you through
One more day.

Alone in the light,
Then God is with thee.
Alone in a crowd.
You will never be.
Anibal Ventura Jr.

Nothing But Hope

We come into this world with
Nothing But Hope
We live on borrowed time
And the time allotted to each of us,
Is Cleanly up to Fate...

We all have roles to play,
"Purposes for Being"

And though we sometimes think we know,
Just what our purpose is,
Fate has a way of shifting roles,
And it's not for us to question why,
But we must duly comply,

Because the path we take in life
was defined for us,
Long before we came.
And we cannot Fight the hands of Fate.

Fate will always win.
Sandra Joy Baronette

Two Hands

Two hands folded
  asking God to help me
But as I went through the day
  this is what I did see

Two hands to speak
  for people who can't talk
Two hands to roll a wheelchair
  for people who can't walk

Two hands comforting someone
  when a loved one passed away
Two hands begging for food
  on a cold and rainy day

Two hands holding a baby
  whom they can not feed
Two hands asking
  to give to those who need

Two hands folded
  thanking God for all he has given me
I have plenty
  but just couldn't see
Nancy Willerton Soto

Mindless

Dark as the night
I walk through the shade
I think of ways
To bring back yesterday.
But it is gone
and can't be revived
The passion I feel for it
flows through my mind

I bring back the pain
that I feel inside
I am my enemy
no wisdom resides

But as I recall
the memories I've hid
I know of the darkness
that lives in my mind.
Carly Shirk

Happy Holidays

Holidays are a time of joy
and a perfect time to get a toy.
A time to light Menorahs or decorate
  a tree.
Some people may even go across the
  sea.
Car, ship, or plane, it doesn't matter.
  They are all the same!
A time to love and a time to care,
A time to give
And a time to share.
A time to be very, very happy,
Not a time to sit and be sappy.
The most important thing that your
parents always make you say...
Is.....Happy Happy Holidays!!!
Susan Gilman

Neptune

Who is this ruler of the sea
Is he just a myth
Or real, like the ground
Underneath me

Does he rise like the wind,
With his golden spear of three

Some say he lives in a vast
Beautiful, palace
With the help of his trident

Mermaids, mermen
Servants of thee
Who scout the land of the big sea

He controls the oceans climate
From high tide, to low
From the many wondrous animals
And plants down below

And his wife, with so much might
Her name is Amphitrite
With her by his side
Nothing else will ever collide
Jared Drury

495

Lost Love

Oh, how lonely it can be,
To lose someone's love,
Either by death or divorce,
Both are heartbreaking.
It's hard to lose your loved one.
The tender kisses,
The hugging and the sweet smiles.
The time that was shared.
It's now lost and gone forever,
You can't turn back time,
Just keep precious memories.

Tina Fitch

Free

Like the butterfly
who flies so free,
That is what
I long to be,
Free from worry,
Free from sorrow,
So free today
and for every tomorrow,
Free from pain,
Free from stress,
Free from heartache
and loneliness,
I'd feel the wind
upon my wings
I'd think of only
beautiful things,
But since I am
who I must be,
I can but dream
that I am free.

Karen J. Chavira

Nancy Dances

Nancy dances through my mind.
I see her strong jawline
Reflecting back the light.
As she waits, muscles tense.
Then she moves, precise.
Her cascading waterfalls of hair
Accentuate her liquid movement
And as Nancy dances through my mind
I fight to find the words
To bring the motion to life.

Rodney R. Jensen Jr.

The Sweetness Of The Dawn

Shattered glass and Silent Screams
   invokes the pain that
   life will bring.
Disillusions of the past
   grab us within its
   clasp.
Acid, reeking, rotting breath
   holds the reminiscences
   of death.
Bold in hope, and Blind in
   Faith
With bated breath we
   do await...
The Sweetness of the Dawn

Melissa Jefferson

The Battle

The battle's raging,
Men are dying;
Everywhere you look,
Deadmen are lying.

Many men gave their lives,
Their beliefs were what mattered;
Many more made it home,
Their hearts and souls shattered.

It's a free country now,
And no one remembers
The battle's rage,
Or victory's splendor

But was it all worth it?
The fighting, the blood?
The great men that were lost
In death's evil flood?

Would you give your life
For what you believe?
Would you stand for what's right
If death you'd receive?

Autumn Johnson

Dreams

There's a place your mind can wander
There's a time it takes control
The time is while you're sleeping
And the place is in your soul

You create your own festivities
Sometimes you're wide awake
Through nightmare creativities
It wasn't real for heaven sake

You drift off into daydreams
Though your eyes are open wide
Conscious and aware you seem
Subconsciously daydreaming inside

Your body stores a spirit
Which someday will be gone
The dreams your spirit takes with it
In others will live on

In life you'll have some dreams
Unexplained beyond control
In my personal opinion
Unbodied spirits have found a soul

Louis Bianco

I Wish...

I wish....
That you were here with me
The way it always used to be
Good times, bad times...made it through
Why you left I have no clue
Was it me, or was it that... You
Changed your mind away from me
Oh, dear Lord, how could this be?

Tears are falling, hail and thunder
On my mind, I often wonder
Why love hurts, when it ends
I feel that we could still be friends

A childhood crush
I've known so long...
Something so right, slowly went wrong
I bid farewell to yesterday
Open up my mouth to say
"I wish"

Gisele Winston

The End Is Here

The end is near
I can feel it in my heart
She was the best
Though she suffered so much
I have to let her go.

Now it's over
She's gone
There is nothing left to do
I can't go with her
He won't let me
She can't stay here
He won't let her.

But there is nothing I can do
Nothing left for her
I won't say good-by
I'll see you soon
But for now my friend
The end is here.

Dawn M. Meadows

Why

Why must I fall for you?
Why can't I get over you?

Your brawn hair,
Your brown floppy hair.

Why me,
Why can't I get over you?
Why,

I know why,
I care for you, that's why.

Jessica Ritter

Harmony

Come dream with me,
Open your eyes and see,
How happy you can be.
Trees swaying,
Kids playing,
Grass growing
Sun glowing,
Open your eyes and see,
If the world were in harmony,
It would be a happier place to be.
Sunset falls,
Quiet walls,
Cozy shawls,
Sleeping calls,
Under your covers a place to sleep,
Wiggle all your little feet,
Safely sleeping in our beds,
Dreams are floating through our heads,
Dreams about kids playing just like me,
We can live in harmony!

Sarah Petruska

The Grizzly Bear

Once I was behind a bush,
when I felt a great big push,
I turned and saw a grizzly bear,
right behind me, just sitting there.
I screamed and ran away so far,
and jumped into my mommy's car.
She drove away in the night so black,
and we never, ever, ever went back.

Megan Danielle Tillery

From Nags Head

Whenever I go to Manteo
Along the beach road
I go by Jockey Ridge
A dune so bare and bold
People always climb this dune
So shall I late or soon
For at the top I'll stop
And gaze across the way
To view a house a weather beaten house
A lonely house along the way
Harbouring memories of yesteryear
A better life with friends so dear

Ivy C. Philbrook

Moving On

As the days go by and
turn into years,
We try to be brave
and overcome our fears.

The world in some places can
look cruel and mean,
But sometimes things aren't
always what they seem.

We all move on
to go our separate ways,
Even though we wish
we could stay for always.

Growing up as kids we were
always together,
But everybody knows that
nothing lasts forever.

We want very much to make
something of our lives,
And we can reach our dreams
if we work hard and strive.

Christie Dolliver

Untitled

I need your smile, your warm
soft stare.

The beach, the stars, the warm
night air, are little things that show
we care.

The kids, the home, our family are
small examples of the love we share.

So show me my lovely man, that
you do care for the woman I am.

Mary Orihuela

I Wish...

I can hear you talking to others, and
I will listen. I can see you in a room
with others, and I will watch. I can
feel you in my dreams, and I will
wish. Even if we were together I
would still dream about the way you
smile, the way your sweet, tender lips
could be pressing against mine, the way
I feel when you are near, and the way
light would sparkle in your eyes.
But, even though I know there's
never going to be a "you and I" my
love for you I shall never deny.

Jeanna Kemp

The Silence

Not a sound around.
You can hear nothing but the air.
No one says a word.
Only thoughts are read.
What is that we want.
We do not know, but to only think...
The silence that speaks our mind.
To wonder what happens next...

Cindy Toy

Love Hurts

Have you ever loved so much
before that your love is lost
with a single touch?
Your heart grows hard, your
mind goes sad and all that
seemed before is gone so fast.
You try it once, promising
never again, trying to chase
away the hurt still there.
Trying to change the past,
the promise broken, you try again...
fail again.
Learning from these mistakes, you
take it slow to show you care.
True love will come eventually.

Lisa Mott

Love

Love is great, but sometimes confusing
Sometimes you think you love,
but you don't.
Love can be fantastic
if you just think.
Love is like a rainbow
It suddenly appears.
Love brings happiness, hearts, and
even sorrow
Love is terrific
But don't break a Heart!

Nichole Paige Foreman

A Message

Angels, Angels
all around.
Messengers of God
While we're Earth bound.
Sent to help us as we stay,
here to guide and brighten our way,
to shows us love and happiness too
Supply our hearts with
goodness and truth, reveal
to us, what we're to do.
To live as one, not as two,
Join together is the truth.
Love one another that's all there is.
Is started with Almighty and that's
Where it end.

Beth Clay Logan

Untitled

Look towards the future,
And celebrate the past,
But live each day until the next,
As if it were your last.

Robb Witte

I Have To Be Free

I love you BUT I have to be free
I love you but I have to be me
I need you and I want you to need me,
but I still have to be free
I don't care what anyone else needs
I don't care what anyone else thinks
I know what you think is
what matters to me
I will love you always whatever
may be
But there will come a day
when you will set me free.

Rosalie Frentiero Nelson

To A Child

Rain is splashing on the ground
forming a curtain all around.
Come with me to stomp in pools,
and shake the bushes free of jewels;
for this is the kind of day
meant for little boys to play.

Ernestine E. Dvorak

Repose

When through the glass
I see the fading sun,
When all the tasks I have
are done,
When fevered brows no
longer need my touch,
And I can say my chores
have been too much
I'd like to close my eyes
and just pretend
That all good things never
end.
The bad will pass away
as morning dew,
And loved ones pass before
me in review
Then I can sleep at last
and say
I've had a happy day.

June R. Martin

One Day

One more day until tomorrow
One more day until the end.
One more day until it's over,
One more heart you'll have to mend.

One more day until I'll miss you,
One less person to defend,
One more heart gone and broken,
One less letter you'll have to send.

One more day until we're through,
One more day I have to prove,
One more day I have to tell you,
One more day to improve.

One more day for you to love me,
One more day for you to care,
One more day for you to see me,
One more day for you to stare.

One more day for me to say good-bye,
One more day to be with you,
One more day until we leave each other,
One more day to say I love you too.

Jennifer Hague

Look Beyond

Look beyond the visible
  Surface and see what
  You can find.

Where do I look? You may
  ask. Well, look inside
  your mind.

Focus on the future and
  the joy that it can bring.

Today, we all know that to live
  life to the fullest is a
  very special thing.

Follow your heart and follow
  your dreams, no matter the
  obstacles you may face.

Look beyond today; prepare for
  tomorrow, and find your
  permanent place.

Kimberly A. Welch

Nowhere

Dark, broken windows
Closed, boarded doors
Dirt smothers everything
That covers the floors.

Shelter for the homeless
To keep from the snow
Feelings of desperation
They try not to show.

Taking in handouts
Other peoples trash
People are afraid
And don't give them cash.

No place to live
No place to call home
No place for their children
To say is their own.

Lost lonely people
No one to care
No job is available
To someone that lives "Nowhere".

Tanya McGlade

Women

Women can be really cheap
even when they rob you
in your sleep.

They always use you for money
and all they can say is
thank you, honey.

Sometimes they can be nice
but other times
they can be as cold as ice.

They're always in a bad mood
and most of the time
they can be rude.

They always argue, fuss, and fight
they hardly ever
do anything right.

So, when your women tries
to put you down
just tell her who runs this town.

Chris Clark

Wherever I Go I Am

I can't get away from myself
I tried and tried and tried
I cried and cried and I cried
I take my pain wherever I go
I carry it deep inside
A geographical change is no cure
That I am sure.
I tried
I take me with me wherever I go
A very complicated life I know
Trapped in bondage by my own making.
Mistakes of the past
creating my pain
I know I must forgive myself
Then I will be free.

Helen Anderson

I Wish There Was A Way

I wish there was a way
a way for you to understand
if I could just show you
but how

The emotion the character
the dreams the imagination
the heart of my very existence
I wish there was a way

To show you my mind
the colors my world
to let you see me
I wish there was a way

I could give you paint
and paper the size of the sky
but my mind wouldn't fit
I wish there was a way

A way for you to understand
for you to see, to see me
I wish there was a way
a way for you to understand

Frankie Sanchez

Lost Love

Who would have thought,
It would turn out this way?
To see the man you love,
Fly far, far away.

It only took a second
to take his life.
No time for "I love you,"
or even "Good-bye."

You wish you could see
his beautiful face.
To even make a bargain
and take his place.

You miss those moments,
That you were in his arms.
To look into his eyes,
And see his charm.

Even though he flew away,
And now you're far apart.
He will always remain with you,
Forever in your heart.

Elizabeth Waters

Hope

Slowly sinking
into a pit of darkness
the musty air pervades my senses.
Absolute solitude
laughter, heard no more-
Replaced by the sound of falling tears.
Desolation; despair
they are my companions-
A shred of hope pierces my heart.
Invading white light
blessed relief-
from all the anger.
Singing, laughing
Love grabs my soul-
All pain is released.
Loneliness lost forever
Undisturbed tranquility,
peace

Jennifer Thurmon

Untitled

Escape with me,
Escape with me to paradise.
Come with me,
Come with me to happiness.
Flee with me,
Flee with me to safety.
Experience with me,
Experience with me peace.
Invite me,
Invite me into your world.

Jennifer Horon

Till Death Do Us Part

I was so lost; you rescued me.
I was afraid; you held me safe.
I was sad; you lightened my heart.
I was lonely; you held my hand.
  But now you have gone.

I am lost; I can't find my way.
I am afraid; no one holds me.
I am sad; my heart is heavy.
I am lonely; my hands are cold.
  Why did you have to go?

Catherine Scudder

Yesterday's Door

I have shut the door on yesterday
Its sorrows and heartaches.

I have looked within its gloomy walls
Past failures and mistakes,

And now I throw the key away
And seek another room,

And furnish it with hopes and smiles
And every springtime bloom.

No thought shall enter this abode
That has a taint of pain

And anger, malice and distrust
Shall never entrance gain.

I have shut the door on yesterday
And thrown the key away.

Tomorrow holds no fear for me
Since I have found today.

Nell DuPay

"Love Or Hate"

My question for the world;
  Goes like this,
    Is it easier to fight;
Or make love not a fist,
  To love someone;
You must help one another,
  But to hate someone;
You just kill all your brothers,
  To kill don't take effort;
Just one simple thought,
  But to love someone;
Is like a war you just fought,
    Sometime's you win;
Sometime's you lose,
  But the prize, prize for your hate;
Is the life that you lose,
  So you make the choice;
To love or to hate,
  And remember your prize;
That awaits at death's gate.

T. Y. Conley

A New Land

I hear you waking, America.
  The waves of Watergate
Spill over into listening ears.

I hear you scolding, America,
  Because of lies and hate
That magnify your fears.

I see you girding, America,
  To meet this awful foe
Who storms your capitol gates.

I see you kneeling, America
  Before the God who
Governs all your fates.

I see you repentant, America;
  With all your guilt
Bared for God to see.

I see you free again, America:
  You're still the mighty land
You started out to be.

Oh, God Bless America!

Evelyn M. Rambo

Stardust

Another year, another tear
Another enemy, acting with vile
Another victory, another cheer
Another smile, and another mile

As the year comes to an end
We think of more years to spend
Wandering through eternities
Of unknowing
Hoping to find new knowledge
Showing
Never quite understanding why
We are
But a
Bit of dust...
In an endless sky.

Katy Marie Dorr

If Only He Knew

If only he knew,
That as I sit here and listen,
I hear his voice comforting me,
But it is only as a friend.

As a friend he thinks,
But to me I think of love.

If only he knew,
Where my tears are from,
They are from my heart,
I cry only because my heart does.

If only he knew,
That my heart cries for his.

If only he knew,
The reason I cry,
But it is that I love him.

Delesha J. Lineberry

"Repent"

Her love dear as the life I hold
Like a divine angel sent
From the Heavens to bless my soul
I only feel repent.

She starves me for the love I need
I yearn for heart - filled love
A touch from her will make me bleed
Her soul as free as a dove.

Power of Zephyr can not compare
To passion felt for her
To the stars I see, my heart will tear
I can't resist the lure.

Only the Moon and Stars compare
The wonder of her scent
I know I will never have her
I only feel Repent.

Alfred Fung

After Beethoven's 9th

An eyelash
Leaves its owner
Tumbles like a tree
To the cliff below
Its staggering weight
Minuscule
To the mountain that moves
In a Universe that sings

Madeline F. Weaver

Secrets In The Wind

The wind blows from the mountain
Touching me softly with its secrets
Of rushing rivers being born,
Of dying trees and fresh new growth,
Of baby creatures romping,
Of predators, the old, old cycle
Of birth and life and death.
It whispers softly of its secrets
Then hurries on.

Elaine Varney

"Blinding White"

The snow quietly falls,
covering the flaws of the Earth,
taking sharp edges away,
creating soft flowing scenes,
what once was harsh and hard,
is now gentle and serene,
what was dull and colorless,
now is clean and peaceful,
moon lights tiny sparkles,
light the field of white,
trees denuded by nature,
show off white coats,
fences the only interruption,
in this endless white world,
don't spoil what God has given,
walk the fields with your eyes,
run only with your mind,
step only with imagination,
the snow quietly falls,
covering the flaws of the Earth.

Howard D. Hughes

The Ocean

The ocean is a life
of ageless wonder,
When we are no longer here
she will live on.

Her body has many secrets
that we have yet to find,
She has also told us many secrets
of times long before our own.

At times she can be
as gentle as a lamb,
She can also release her anger
and crash down like a wild beast.

Within her depths
we find life in incredible amounts,
Somewhere from those depths
we must remember we arose from.

So treat her well
and cherish her purity,
For once she is gone
we will be no more.

Peter Pasterak

Evening

A sputtering flame,
  Handel's chorus,
A solitary rose dressed in somnolence,
Evening wanders in and out
  Of amber streams
Until ominous clouds roar,
I know them well,
  We've met many times before
  On dusty back-roads,
They no longer threaten,
  Only illuminate the sky
  With scratchy lace,
  Billowy smoke.
I light the flame again,
  Listen to Handel's chorus,
  Place the rose in fresh water.
Old enemies speak in half voice
  As evening wanders on.

Marjorie Roberts

Untitled

The words I write
Upon this page
About the hurt
The hate and rage
This world we know
This world we see
Someday we'll know
Someday we'll be

We hold the power
To create a place
A place where war
Has no face
We have to work
To do our part
Add some hope
And a bit of heart

Dina Kahnovitch

Tomcat Man

Won't you be my tomcat man
Together we will roam the land
We'll make a vow and join our hearts
From you I know I'd never part
Your stripes are cute
You look so tough
Honey I just can't get enough
Midnight screecher
Tiger pal
Darling you're the cat's meow

Sheila Webb

Death Or Life

In an instant, one who you
have known all of your life is gone.

What was is gone.
What I am and who I am are
questioned. All I can think is
who will be next, for I don't
know what the future holds.
I choose to hold the present.

Mia Mesches

The Flood

The water was raging
  Like angry storm clouds.
The water was swirling
  Like leaves in a windstorm.
The water was cold
  Like the first fallen snow.
The water was muddy
  Like dirty silly putty.

The water created destruction
  Like a bomb during construction.
The water carried debris
  Far and wide as one could see.
And when all was said and done
  And the water had subsided.
All was left for people to do
  Was to help each other thru
To face the next day too.

Carol Lawrence

Evening Song

Twilight reaches out tonight
With fingers soft and gray,
She gently picks the sunbeams up
And tucks them safe away.

A star comes out and twinkles
Like a candle in the night.
And, in response, a firefly
Sends back its little light.

A night bird croons its lullaby,
And then it goes to rest.
I think that in the evening
God loves this world the best.

Maithel M. Martin

Lapwing

Lapwing, take me beneath your wings
And teach me how to fly
Do you hear the song the songbird sings
It says I soon shall die
But before I go away from you
I'll swear my love is real
The lies you heard were never true
And no death shroud can conceal
Love blessed by the song of a bird
And christened above the sky
By this lapwing I have heard
And her song that cannot die

Billy Middleton

Blink Of An Eye

How elusive are peace, love,
  joy, and happiness,
And yet, how permanent are
  their opponents.

Wars, hatreds, suspicions,
  jealousies and envies
all seem to be with us
  forever and a day.

But peace, love, joy
  and happiness last
but a moment, and then are
  a passing dream.

All the ugly things are
  as solid as walls.
They are as the immovable
  Rock of Gibraltar.

All the lovely things,
  though, are as perfumes,
Here in an instant, gone in a flash;
  vanished, in the blink of an eye.

John F. Tashjian

The Storm

A spectacular sunset
On a cumulus precipice.
A foreboding sight
Of ominous beauty.
A drop of forethought,
A mist of apprehension,
A sprinkle of hope,
A shower of passion.
Then it poured.

Gary L. Herrig

Puff Balls

Do you know those
round fuzzy forms
a sort of weed
that children catch
mid-air
to make a wish
and blow away?

I just saw one
from my boat
in the middle of
the lake
pass me by
climbing the crest
of each endless ripple
working so hard,
working so hard.

Margaret R. Duensing

Treasure In Love

Treasure the golden love
With silver anchor cord
That binds the two gold hearts

When apart the heart knows
The other heart pines for the one

Each one's heart is
Each others treasure
The treasure in love.

Whether new or old
The heart melts heated gold
The eyes shine fiery diamonds
The hands fold in rare silk
When love treasure is near.

My love is my treasure
Treasure for all eternity.
It is pure gold.

Toni Thomas

Spring

Spring is what heaven ought to be
In awesome wonder life we see
transformed in fullest majesty
awakening the flower and the tree,
the promise held within the seed.
Celestial sweetness beckons me
to witness Eden's creativity,
together, Lord, we reverence Thee.

In Spring we glimpse eternity.

Elaine Carol Harvey

The Second Birth

Sun upon the pane,
  melts the shell of self.
Inside the casing lies,
  a tiny bud of life.
Patience, love and care,
  nourish the embryo.
Watered with faith and trust,
  growth begins anew.
Time has moved ahead,
  true selfhood has emerged.

Rosemary Schram

Homecoming

The long stretch
  of road awaits.
The years have caused
  the aging of form,
and of memories?
  Warm welcome
will I receive,
  or the memories of
past injustices return?

I cannot know,
  till I return
the deep fear within
  shall haunt me.
Within reach of the door
  where I stand there will be
open arms,
  or the cold remembrance of me.

I knock.

Peter Rifkind

Winter Grass On Assateague Island

Fierce unruly winds
whip your hair
into thick clumps
springy enough to hold
the dead weight
of dreaming ponies
that fold themselves
in your wild mane
and listen to the sea
lumbering beneath them
the sun lodges
in your matted nests
tawny in the morning
burnt rust by evening
I want to burrow in your heat
your salt-clean straw
below the wind's bite
unwind into sleep
and wait for a delicate hoof
to part my dreams

Marilyn Lerch

Sandman

We watch with eyes that
  look through gates.
It's human lies that
  drive our hates.
And yet we gaze upon
  the night,
To see the stars that
  shimmer bright.
So look within to see
  your fear;
Hide your eyes so you
  can hear.
The Sandman comes to those
  who sleep;
For those who don't...
  their souls, he'll keep!

Dean J. Pettine

The Unknown

A love of life,
A respect for nature,
All these reflect on thee.
A truth in words,
A hope for perfection,
A never ending jamboree.
A wish of savory,
A longing heart,
A lingering cheery spree.
A yearning soul,
A doubting core,
For as long as we could see.
We can never determine,
The quest of life,
So it is an impossible plea.
For the way God planned,
Isn't known to man,
We can only pray on knee.

Katrina Garner

Ode To Longevity

When Life's cycle exceeds the norm
A gift from Heaven takes form
And enjoy in years long
The satisfaction of our needs.
This gift, this reward, this favor
Of the Gods, to what merit or conduct,
Or deed, do we in obeyance bow?
To nature's multiple laws?
Hearken! Fellow members of our species
Do not deprive others of this Gift.
Make longevity a universal shift.

Edward de Brito

Light

Light moves around in my house
Like quicksilver.
Tall windows invite light inside
To scatter patterns and shadows
On the floors and walls.
Prisms on the windows catch sunlight
And splash rainbows across the walls.
As day moves from East to West
So too does the light.
East rooms become shadowed and dim
While West rooms revel in light.
As day flows away and becomes night
Lamps turn on and once again
My house is filled with light.

Louise Norman

A Poem

A Poem resides
In the mind where it hides-
Is given birth
From the heart's worth.

A poem lives eternally
Touching you and me-
Reaching far and wide
From city to countryside.

A poem can communicate
Words of love, words of hate.
Bringing thoughts to your mind,
A poem can make time unwind.

Diane Ryan

May

The breeze has laughed the clouds away;
The sun's come out to play.
The crocuses now dance again.
Rejoice! At last, it's May.

The tulips bow and weave in time
To May's ballet of spring.
Its melodies reverberate;
'Tis time the earth to sing.

The weeping willows spin their threads
In tapestries of green;
The dogwood blossoms' blizzard storm
With wonderment is seen.

The azure blue of pond and lake
Throws out a welcome cry,
As homeward glide the ducks and geese
Announcing spring is nigh.

The artistry of sunset's glow
Paints pictures in the sky;
The earth below reflects their hues
This May to glorify.

David A. Kelly

Orange

Orange is the sunset,
  In the afternoon.
Orange are the poppies
  Asleep under the moon.

Orange are oranges,
  With lots of Vitamin C.
Orange are the pumpkins,
  That are bigger than a Kiwi

Orange are pencils,
  That write very well.
Orange "Cheez-Its,"
  That taste just swell.

Phillip Villalobos

Suppressed Love

I love you for a thousand years,
Held back my thoughts and my tears.
Wondering if you'll ever know,
Hoping that my love will show.
Seeing you every day,
Not wanting you to go away.
Wondering if I said too much,
Always hoping for your touch.

Michael K. Schwartz

Our Children

Blowing bubbles, having fun,
making mudpies in the sun.
They can laugh, they can play,
they can chase your blues away.

Playing mommy, playing dad,
learning to know good from bad.
Wearing hats, wrecking ties,
asking questions, telling lies.

Growing up, leaving home,
having children of their own.
Hear them laugh, feel them cry,
hope they never say good-by.

Tricia L. Sprague

The Evergreen

In the evergreen you can be alone
you can find a place that you call home
you can find someone that really cares,
in the evergreen.
In the evergreen you can be a star.
Sit on a blue moon and see near or far.
You can write a book, a poem or two,
but mostly you can just be you.

Rachel Rivers

Loud

Turn it up loud
   I've got some feeling to kill
Turn it up loud
   I've got some emotions to still
Turn it up loud
   Give me strength and will
Turn it up loud

Turn that volume clockwise
Till it strikes twelve
Feel the beating music
Moving inside yourselves

Engulf me in your melody
Make me feel your tune
Fill my mind with the words you sing
Forgetting my misfortune

Block out today's reality
Make it all fade away
Call it mood music
But that the way I like it - OK

Turn it up loud

Rhonda Haas

Introspectives

When all seems for naught
and life is fraught with pain,
you must look deep inside
and discover that which remains.
Only then will you find
everything that you are,
that you were,
and everything you may yet be.
For in these times of trouble
only you can find the way.
Let your heart, your soul
your mind be your guide
and set yourself free.

Jason A. Barros

Beloved

I saw the sun, rise in your eyes-
and felt your heart radiating a
warmth I'd never known.
A blanket of comfort wrapping
around me, body and soul, till
I felt no more pain.
I saw then where rainbows hide
to break through on the rainstorms
of Heaven, and caught a glimpse of
Heavens' weeping Angels-drying
their eyes on September breezes.
Frozen in this moment of time and
all reasoning for loving you peered
through a misty morning sunrise—
amazing me!
How I know you, my sweet breath
of springtime! And knowing you
is all there needs to be.

Kathy Twitchell

A Shell Exploded

A shell exploded
Wrecking a small farm building
Killing some people;

Medics! Hey medics!
An injured soldier pleaded
Help that young mother;

And the medic saw
The woman was in labor
Ready to give birth;

And in that battle
A little baby was born
As the soldier died;

So reminded be
The Lord gives and takes away
As we come and go;

Grant therefore that we
May make the most of our lives
Helping those in need.

Hiroshi Minami

The Color Green

Green can be a fast Kawisaki
dirt bike. It also can be
slow like grass growing.
Green can be
cool like
the shade of
a green leaved tree.
Green is monster blood.
Green is a hunter's camouflage.

Jonas Stomberg

Cymru

Land of bards song and harp
Cambrensis sang thy praises
Rome hath heard thy melodies
And Caesar came to Dolaucothi
Thy fame did he behold but stole
Thy treasures of buried gold.

David Olsen

The Savaging Of The Plum Tree

When the plum tree swayed its blooms
the old man said its shape was like
a foaming wave that sprayed the stars
against the night-

But in the night a white chameleon
rode the plume tree's wave
and perjured it with black
transparent tears-

Was it the black rain of tears that
marred the plum tree's shape?
"Oh no!" the old man cried, "The night
was calm- No one heard the rain!"

But when the children played beneath
the tree, it was they who saw
the shadow underneath- It was
black and ate the grass-

It was the lover of the tree.

Sarah Wormhoudt

To My Precious Daughter, Brittnee Chyella

I never held you in my arms
Or saw your precious smile.
I never got to feel your warmth
Or hold you close, dear child.

I never got to hear you cry
Or wipe tears from your face;
And say how much you mean to me
And make your world a caring place.

I wonder how our life would be
If you were with me now.
I long to have you close to me.
To share my love somehow.

Of all the things I never did
The most important that I wanted to do
Was hold you close inside my arms
And tell you that I love you.

But since that never happened
And you've passed on out of sight,
I'll tell you in my prayers
That I love you every night.

Carla Diahanne Brown

The Perfect Gift

Everybody has one special thing in
their life;
a puppy, a flower, a special memory
but I have something better.
Better than the first ray of sunshine
each morning;
better than the rainbows God has made;
more precious than a fresh cut gem,
and the smell of a forest after a
rainstorm;
With all the perfection in the world;
God did his finest work when He
made you!!

Linda Acquafredda

Grandma

Always busy, never at rest.
Making home a cozy nest.
Working hard doing chores.
A gentle smile you adore.
Playing cards, baking pies,
Rocking chairs and family ties.
Making crafts and baby sitting.
Sending cards always fitting.
Mowing grass and bailing hay.
Going to church on Sunday.
Humming birds, kitty cats,
Warm hellos and welcome mats.
Praying hands and heart of gold.
Loving stories often told.
Always giving without a thought.
Important things you've taught.
Now I know what's truly meant.
When I hear the words "Heaven sent."
Heavenly Angel above,
You're missed by all we send our love.

Sheryl Uhlott

Forty-Two

41 years have come and gone.
42 I'll be with the coming dawn.

Many are blurs,
   memory serves me not.
But a special few,
   I have not forgot.
The times of trouble
   and sorrow fade,
But I'll remember
   the joyful times we made.

We struggle through our daily trials
'Til we stop to look back
   on our many miles.
A wrinkle here,
   a gray hair there,
Signs of aging
   we can share.
But call us old?
   You won't dare!

Glenda L. Weeks

Sleep

The realm of sleep
where safety reigns.
Sweet is the silence
so quiet it rings.
Secure in aloneness.
Solace in singularity.
Rage in the mind.
Battlefield that is the brain.
Motivation dead.
Imagination dead.
Stories without words
Paintings without imagination.
Casualties in the war of
insecurity.
Solidarity.
Dancing with the Angel of Slumber,
the savior.
Hurry sweet sleep,
bring your peace.

Bryan W. Gildea

Heavens Above

What is this business
Of seeing the future
By viewing the moon and the stars?

In the dead of night
A twinkling light
Could be Jupiter, Venus, or Mars.

How can you tell
By looking up there
That my future holds beauty and love?

Is it allowed
If there is a cloud
To misread the heavens above?

Tell me your views
Not only the news
Of what this is all about.

I'd like to say
I believe you today
   ...But I have a wee bit of doubt!

Carin Carrigg

Kevin, My Son

With vacant eyes
He'll gaze at me.
With trembling lips
He'll disagree.

His voice is harsh,
His words are cold.
I wish I knew
What thoughts unfold.

"Why do we fight —
Is there no love?",
I pray each night
To God above.

My little boy
Has grown too fast,
His childhood gone,
His life has passed.

Someday he'll know
Just what he's done.
I'll love him still,
Kevin, my son!

Vikki Liverpool

Come Forth My Song

It cries for release
This song that's within me
But the words to the song
Seem to evade me
Why is it there?
Why does it haunt me?
Is it my soul?
Or is it my story?
Like the wolf sings his song
Onto the moon
and the night hears the cry
of the mournful loon
Come forth my song!

Ben Mallory

The Day Grandmama Saw Red

Nobody told her...
She thought she surely would die.
She became a woman!

Phyllis Sue Newnam Sand

Calling All Angels

We're calling all angels...
with all the violence and the pain
this world is dying
We need your help...
can't you hear us calling?

We're calling all angels...
pollution and decay
is destroying us
Can you help us today...
help us to live?

We're calling all angels...
we have to fight this sin
Though slowly we are dying...
we are dying from within!

We're calling to you angels...
tears are falling from on high
Can you relieve us from this sorrow...
from this self-inflicted Hell?

Nikky Affolder

"The Predator"

Time is a predator
A predator that stalks us eternally
stalks us without mercy
We have learned to control so much
Yet, time is beyond our control
We are unable to turn back time
Nor jump into the future
Much less put time on a standstill
Time is the predator
We are the prey
Time is the single predator
that we cannot escape
A soundless predator
that many of us are unaware of
Time never ceases
Each of us will die
Yet time, this predator
is eternal, infinite!

Mirjam Troesch

Football Season Opens

As the fall of year approaches
I look forward to the day,
When the football season opens
And the games that come on Sunday
Though sometimes they're on a Monday.

There are quarrels for the TV
So I guess we need another,
But in fall it seems it's me
Who will watch it without falter
And I don't want it to alter.

For they know it'll soon be over
And no more will they as whole
Have to suffer suffer suffer,
For I've finally reached my goal
To enjoy the Super Bowl.

So with that ends all the quarrel
That there seems to be in all,
Though I have to give a farewell
To the fun brought by that ball
I'll be waiting for next fall.

Mario Torres

Re-Birth

I feel the morning sun
as it beats upon my face.
The glory from the Lord above
He shows His loving grace.

The beauty of the rain
as the drops fall gently down.
The smell of moistened soil
as it lands upon the ground.

The coolness in the air
as the fall says "hello".
The colored leaves upon the trees
that gently fall below.

I feel the love from God above
who gently tends the earth.
How blessed we are to share all this
and feel our own re-birth.

Nancy Drury

Play Tree

We were put here to play to dream
  We all have our fate it seems
A tree that god put on our green earth
  That we have seen since our birth
A tree to climb to sit to dream
  A tree with limb to put a swing
We have gods hand that created us
  We have gods hands to put our trust
We grow up all to soon at last
  Then our dreams are in the past
So if it's Gods will I'll dream and play
  Until it's my time for judgement day

Terry A. Gruenholz

Mountains High

I stand on mountains, some are tall
for no more fear that I will fall
you know the answer is no no no!
Once you're off the white white snow
The alcohol was bad enough
but white white snow was truly tough
I kicked the habit that is true
the fact myself I must now chew
The plain is flat the mountains high
I love life better high and dry
you love the plains I love the sky
I love the mountains high and dry
We bit off more then we could chew
I'll try to help you make it through
The days are tough the night are long
all you need is help-be strong
I'll hold your hand when you are weak
for Gods inside, we'll have to seek
You'll love yourself when day is done
for then you say oh! yes, I have won

Nancy Rae Dehne

Together, Me And You

We vowed to love each other
Long ago when love was new.
We pledge to honor and cherish
Together, me and you.
We've had our share of good times
Made a home had children, too.
All the happy hours we've shared
Together, me and you.
And, yes, we've had some rough roads -
Did the best way we knew -
Hard paths we've had to travel
Together, Me and You
For the Lord joined us forever
Love honest, tried and true
A love that last a life time -
Together, me and you.
And when sun sets and day is done
Both our lives are through
We'll stroll the streets of Heaven.
Together, me and you.

Lynn Stuard

Us

You hold me in your arms,
You gently kiss my hair.
Our bodies lay close together,
Warm with the love we share.
I long to stay here forever,
Let time stop now and stay...
Always in your arms,
You whisper, "Can I keep you?"

Laura Van Domelen

Feelings Of The Garden

As I walked down the steps,
I took a look around.
I see something beautiful,
a beautiful place I've found.
This place gives me joy,
and it fills my heart with glee.
Here is a place that will let me
be free.

Jayne Kildow

Little Man
Dedicated To C. Browning

Little man who goes before me
Staring up with opaque eyes.
Do you see the starlit wonder?
Are the answers in the sky?

Little man who goes before me
The strength you have puts me to shame.
While others rage and cry around you
Your soul stays gentle like the rain.

Little man who goes before me
With simple mind and open heart.
How is it that you're my beacon
When all around me is gray and dark?

Little man who goes before me
Your tiny hand so lost in mine.
I hold a little tighter now
For the enemy is Time.

Little man who goes before me
The sun is setting-it's time to sleep.
I guard your laughter in my soul
The day is done, - and now I weep.

Kathy Herron

Sister

No matter where I go,
You go with me,
No matter what I do,
You do it with me,
No matter what I choose,
You support me,
No matter what happens,
You are with me,
If not physically,
Mentally,
You are my friend...
My family...
My sister.

Sarah Heider

My Grandmother

Her eyes give me everything
I needed and still do. She
and me forever together and
always will be. She's my grandmother
who means everything to me.
And when she's gone I will have
my questions, but for now she's
here by my side. My grandmother
and me forever together. I look
like her. I know her. She also know
me. We are the same and yet different.
And when that day comes when
she is no longer with me. I will thank
God up above for giving me her special
kind of love.

Qurratulayn Abdur-Raquiyb

Bodypart

Need you here
  like I need
my heart to beat
my lungs to breathe
my eyes to see
my feet to walk
my brain to think

My eyes need you to be
  the only beauty they see
My hands need you to be
  the only thing they caress
My lungs need you to be
  the only aroma they breathe
My mind needs to think
  you are a part of me

You are a body part
a part that I
cannot live without

Michael L. McEvoy

Junior's Taste Test Guide

Delicious?
  Nutritious?
    Suspicious!
      Judicious!

Anita Rickert Meier

Soft

How doth the light glimmers
extravagant beauty outshining
the Sun.

Wind wakes the willow as if
to part for Beauty.
Ah, but, soft!
Shadows sprawled on bodies.

Dream, even the moon
is doomed,
becomes a grove of
Fantasy.

Sleep doth the body good
as the soul rest his
head quietly, ever so softly
on his pillow.

How doth the pale moon
reverse the Sun!

Stefano Marzoli

I Can, I Can

As I walk down the road of life
I can't make it up the hill
But on life's roads
I will still face problems
Unknown
I can, I can
I can't sail across this ocean
It's too long and wide
But no matter how long or wide
I will find land
I can, I can
I can't get through this desert
It's dry and hard
But I will find water
I can, I can.

Sarah Kalkbrenner

The Lady

She gracefully performs her
ballet through my head;

Each display becoming more
perfectly detailed;

I warmly embrace her, and
explore, finding daily that I
know less and less;

Constantly venturing into the
abyss known as everlasting
 knowledge!
Shelbe J. Whitaker

Dragons

Dragons can be mean or nice,
Feeding on bamboo or mice,
Hiss and grunt and roar and scream,
What's that in their nose? It's steam!
Inside mountains, underground.
They don't go there to be found.
Yellow, black, silver, and green,
They use these colors to be seen.
Dragons may look frightening,
But deep down enlightening.
Heidi E. Schmid

Dive Into A Dream, Jump Into Reality

Dive into a dream,
Fill yourself with glory.
Jump into reality, and
And live to tell the story.

Dream a dream of wondrous things,
Of Kings and Queens and soldiers.
Find a treasure of rubies and rings,
Of jewels and diamond boulders.

Dive into a dream
Find the power in you.
Jump into reality,
And make your dreams come true.
Renaite C. Ellis

In A Church

In a church
A restless
Congregation
Of Schoolchildren
And their
Stifled giggles
For no reason
At a girl
and Classmate
For being
Shy
A swift pinch
The girl's
eyes
Sting
with Tears
Innocence and Cruelty
In a church
Samantha Nicole Barrio

The Fear Of A Soldier

Excited! Yes that's what I am
Nothing at this moment means a damn
Nothing except for what I've longed
to see is all that's important,
important to me.

I can't wait until the next day
I can't wait until I find my way
To and fro is where I'll go
until I just can't go no more.

Excited! Yes that's what I'll be
until this moment has passed and
left me. Right now that far I
cannot see because fun is all
that matters to me.

Oh what a time I plan to have
Oh what a story I have to tell.
but let me not forget why I am
here. But let me not forget about
my fear.
Patricia A. Scott

Alignment

Alignment...
 the greatest sacrifice
 the greatest reward

Thinking your highest...
 most ultimate thought

Living it - step by step
Then feel the joyous spirit
 arise within

The warmth of integration
Light of self-knowledge
 shining through

The boundaries that illusion
 separateness becoming
 transparent

Union visible for those who see
 beyond the eye's focus,
 or just for this day...
Lynne Riedy

R_P_D

It's dark as dark can be
I can hardly feel me anymore
Dirty as dirty can be

I didn't even know what it was
Bang bang bang

It was in me
Up me
Knocking every part of me

To young to know what it was
To scared to face it
Stripped inside and outside

It was cold and hot
And yet I couldn't feel it
I can never decide for me again

Up up up - back and front
Bang bang bang

I thought it was safe there
Everything around me suggested love
Up up up - back and front

I can never decide for me
Averi R. Roberts

Destiny

When we make love,
I feel the earth move.
Like a dove,
Skin soft so smooth.

Our souls are as one,
And our minds are the same.
It may seem as only a game.

I want you,
For eternity!
I want you,
For the world to see!
I'll have you,
And you will be.
My only true love,
It's destiny.
Gregory Aron Smith

Untitled

Three little lambs on
an Easter Day,
All join together in
a family way.

One blue with kindness
in a young man's hands,
One pink with love as a
woman commands

One white and pure with
mothering stride,
Bore forth the love and
kindness with pride

So all join together in
a family way,
Three little lambs on
an Easter Day.
Judie Sowa

Untitled

The same eyes
The same hands
Different views
Different stands
One is calm
One is wild
One is the mother
The other the child
Elizabeth K. Gailey

Born Again

Lord before you came into my life
I was half and now I am whole.

Lord with you I am Born Again.
Lying safe in your arms.

With you Lord my life has a new
meaning you would never leave me
when there is trouble and I would
never be alone.

 Lord I am Yours

 I am Born Again
Kerilyn Gomez

Inner Piece

Carry this in darkness,
My thoughts are never found.
When this tree falls in our woodland,
Will you run to be hear its sound?

The deaf ears hear a baby's cry,
The blind eyes see its pain.
I've heard too often stories told,
We lose so we may gain.

Come over here, but not where I am,
It's already far too busy.
To understand the balance,
You must first be very dizzy.

If I gave my heart a song,
Of this balance it would sing.
And way upstairs, 'tween the rafters,
You could hear the madness ring.

I have not understanding,
Nor wisdom do I wield.
But you, my love, must have faith,
For your Heartsong all will yield.

Bibo

Love

Some thoughts came into my head,
One night while lying in bed,
Read them slow - read them fast,
The meanings will always last,
The message is for you from me,
Please, oh please - can't you see?
Love is people, love is places,
Love is smiling - laughing faces,
Love is happy - love is sad,
Love is never getting mad,
Love is seldom - love is rare,
Love is tender loving care,
Love is truth - love is blind,
Love is always on your mind,
Love is many things you see,
All of which you mean to me,
Love is Love - but every day,
For your love - I'll hope and pray.

Merl Pritts

Untitled

The swallow flies
The baby cries
And summer dies

Storm clouds billow
Like a feather pillow
And weep like the willow
Snow in the dale
Soon will prevail
And cover the trail

The swallow flies
As summer dies
And again the baby cries

F. W. White

Tribute

O tragic day come claim your loss,
And seven souls take away...
Destroying bridges as yet uncrossed,
Delaying our triumph for another day!
To mark this sad occasion,
I give a somber sigh and nod
For those who painted the icy blue sky,
And touched the face of God!
Such a fitting name, the challenger,
For it's been ten long years...
And what a challenge for us all,
To stop the flow of tears!
But isn't life itself a challenge,
With each a different road to trod?
And like those seven astronauts,
We too must touch the face of God!

Dennis Dale Popham

Him

I see him only in my mind
For he is gone
Not forever mind you
only never to return
Why I ask must he pass
The only answer
that can be given
is only never to return
But only to join him
In peace forever again.

Elizabeth Brook Hayes

The Gift Of Sharing

Sharing brings a good feeling
Anytime day or evening
Whether for joy or for sorrow
There are many feelings to borrow
Sharing is beautiful
It shows not greed or jealousy
It reveals the beauty of the soul

Meredith Gayle Billington

My Very Special Rainbow

Red is for the love in my heart
   That I feel for only you,
Orange is for the sunsets, dear
   With me you've shared a few -
Yellow is for the sun's shine
   That glows upon your face,
Green, the grass, we've dreamt upon
   In Spring, it takes its place.
Blue is for the skies so clear
   As we begin each new day -
Purple, my love, for the memories
   The part in life they play.

Sharlene M. Evers

Mom And Dad

  They're not bad
The only parents I've ever had
And I'm glad.
To me they are the best
For they always help me without rest
And for that I thank them
And give them my love.
The four of us are a glove
Bound together by love.

Selena Medrano

Rainbows And Butterflies And Horses With Wings

I ask Angels to bless you
and to hold you tight
and to whisper "I love you"
into the night.

They keep you safely
as you sleep
and kiss your eyes,
your nose,
your feet.

So watch closely for traces
of angel dust and glitter
as back and forth they flitter
carrying rainbows and butterflies
and horses with wings...
and all of the happiness
that angels bring.

So sweet dreams my baby
and know you are loved
by me and all of the angels
in heaven above.

Sandi Moren

The Answer

I have never felt so alone,
I have never felt so afraid,
But I know my God is with me
And by His grace I'm saved.

There are wings around my shoulders,
There are hands holding mine,
I feel tempted now to question
But it's Thy will, Lord, not mine.

Voices are gently praying
While I cry in tears of grief,
But He holds my broken spirit
In Him there's sweet relief.

God is listening to my heart
And He hears each lifted prayer,
I know wherever I go
I will always find Him there.

Many nights I have cried,
And trembled deep with fear,
But I know by His sweet grace
He will bring the Answer near.

Melinda Gray Cooley

Endangered Species

What have we done
  to all the little ones?
Gone is their chance
  to sing, laugh, or dance.
No taste of life,
  or to love a wife.
Nor to see the sun,
  to play and have fun.
What have we done
  with all the little ones?
Taken before their prime,
  by people with no time,
For what God has given
  tho' they were sinnin'.
What have we done
  for all the little ones?
Trying to legalize,
  by those with lives,
What will be done
  to all the little ones.

Monty Klatt

"Family"

Family is there when you need them.
Your family will never leave you.
They will never forget you.
When someone dies in your Family,
and you feel like you've lost
them forever, you haven't because
they live inside your heart.

When you need comfort, Family is
always there for you.
When you need to know if there
is life out there, your Family is
there for you.
One thing that no can change,
is that your Family will always
Love You!

Lillian McRoberts

Quiet Thoughts

My eyes had opened
with quiet thoughts
and
Dreams still on my mind,
Then Sunlight brought
As the day began,
Sweet warmth,
A breeze,
While early signs of Spring,
Had tenderly turned blades of grass,
To deeper shades of green.

Outside my window,
A child's kite,
drifted lazily overhead
The clouds rolled by,
One by One
As Robins sang their songs of Joy,
While we made love,
Or was this just a Dream?

Beverly L. Hamel

Hero

My fallen hero
His glory expelled
Shining no more
Away he went
Asking for nothing
Giving everything
Listening always
Never complaining
But now I see
In the dead of night
A new hero has emerged
And he will do
All that my fallen
Hero has done.

Andrew Joseph Civettini

"Guiding Light"

Teach us not to fight,
The guiding light,
That shows us day and night,
The Lord is such a wonderful sight,
That we must not hide from in fright,
His power is full of might,
That shines ever so bright,
may we pray with hands so tight,
And the Lord will hear our plight.

Mike Moon

Nocturnal Visitor

You came upon me suddenly
In the silence of my room.
Stealthily,
Noiselessly,
You plotted my doom.
Why? Why do you choose to harbor
Ill feeling?
For what reason, I don't know.
Is it because I have no wings,
But am grounded,
Does that make me foe?
Little mosquito - why must it be?
State your case against me.
Let me know your grudge.
(Ouch! He bit me!)

Jo Elizabeth Gergoff

Daddy's Lament

A smile,
to light the night from afar.
Eyes a twinkle,
as the brightest star.

A hug,
to take away my fears.
A kiss
to dry my tears.

A life,
with hurt around every bend.
A love,
so life can mend.

A yearning,
to be always near.
My love,
my life,
my Dana.

Anthony Marino

What if...

What if children were allowed to rule
the classroom or the world?
Perhaps unitedly and strategically an
unyielding system could be vanquished
and unlimited possibilities unfurled.
Envisioned is a standard of truth and
purity for all to see which would
propagate a future pearled.

Rachel (Holweger) Norman

The Whisper

Sadness is like the color gray.
Sun's stored away on a dreary day.
Weeping willows blow in the breeze.
Storms coming in, in from the seas.
Leaves falling down,
Orange and brown.
Winter's coming in,
Thunder is coming,
Lightning is striking.
But can you hear?
A whisper that's near?
Whispering: Sadness is like the....

Christina Sun

My Castle Of Webs

Inside my mind, a castle
Built of webs through time
One by one each day
Another thread I bind.
My silken threads glisten
As each knot is tied with pain
From dreams taken away by storms
And clouds overran with rain.
Each room in my castle
Closes in, as a silent wind blows
Spilling thoughts through the cracks
As voices whisper in the windows.
These webs are strong
Strong enough to hold the morning dew
But not strong enough to hold the tears
That life has harshly threw.
And for now this castle keeps me same
From all the sorrow I carry
These precious webs of pain
Maybe someday this soul will bury.

Debra Millican

The Aftermath

A single Rose from the
waste has
Risen
and it happened sofast,
I can scarce
remember
The Chance Meeting.

Thomas F. Quitoni

Sometimes

Sometimes we sit and cry
  about the times we let
  slip by.
We sit and think of how it
  could have been and think
  our sadness has no end.
But one day all the hurt and
  sadness will be done,
And our well earned happiness
  will "overcome."

Shawn Burgbacher

Listen To The Stillness

Listen to the stillness
at peace with the world.
No trickles in the pond.
No sound of the bees as they whirl.

Listen to the stillness
of the sun at bey.
And the silence of the soft white
clouds as they drift, drift away.

Listen to the stillness
of the genteel breeze passing by.
Look at the daffodils bowing
softly, as if to say hi.

Listen to the stillness
of the blue bird in flight.
Not a sound they make
as they flow out of sight.

Listen to the stillness
of the sleepy summer day.
All seems to be at rest
and nothing to disturb what may.

Paulette Downey

Playtime

Oh, if only I could stay,
and watch my child as she plays.
To be a fly upon her wall
seeing her; nothing else at all.
For I know that soon will come
the day when all her playing's done.
But now, in my room so quiet,
I listen to her joyful riot.
Not to intrude, or ruin her fun.
My time is when her playing's done.
My heart, though, would be full today,
if I could watch her as she plays.

Cheri L. Rohan-Chesley

On Returning Home

I thought to go back home one day
Not so very long ago,
And important though it seemed to be,
I could not make it so.
Driving down familiar streets
Past the house where I was born,
It somehow looked so different now;
Old and tired and worn.
I sought out childhood faces
For old memories to rest upon.
But even that was not to be;
They'd all long since moved on.
Sadly, I soon gave up my search,
For nothing there remained
Of the little town I once called home,
Save the sign which bears its name.

Dan Hergenroder

I Never Thought It Would Be You

I never thought it would be you,
Who would make my head spin,
Stop me to think,
To think about you.

I never thought it would be you,
Who would make me happy,
Stop me to talk,
To talk about you.

I never thought it would be you,
Who would make me need to love,
Stop to love,
To love only you.

I never thought it would be you,
Who I am falling in love with,
Stop me to dream,
To dream you.

Travis 'Son' Hanson

Freedom Set Free

Freedom in the air
Walls crumbling
Hopes and dreams alive
Freedom of thought
Equality becoming a reality

Freedom in the air
Bird in flight
Freedom set free
Glorious free world coming
Freedom in the air

Phyllis Payne

Downward Spiral - Or The Life Of A Flower

Petal
to the floor
I wonder
What was wished for

Drop, dropping
fluttering down
downward spiral
forgive us all

Sins of the Father,
convey to the daughter
each of us sinners
hell bent all

Look, looking,
for the key
to unlock Heaven's door,
always hidden inside me.

Petal, petal
to the floor
I know
of what was wished for.

Crissy Lee Burroughs

No Place In Time...

I can think of no place in time
I'd rather be.
Your warm touch...
Your soothing kiss...
I have trouble
Sleeping at night
Without you near.
You're so far from me.
So far from here-
Where I want you to be.
I want your warm touch.
And though I've never felt it...
Your soothing kiss is what I need,
To put my troubled soul at ease.
My mind is torn,
My soul is tormented,
My heart only knows.
It only knows...

Jamia Marie West

Edicius (All I Feel)

Gloom
impending doom
hopeless
helpless
deepest sadness
buried alive
alone
utterly alone
afraid
numb
giving up hope
nothing matters
nothing helps
painfully alone
endless suffering
leave me alone

Sandra K. Ostergren

Untitled

Love me like you used to
I don't want us to be through
You and I we have a history
let's not turn our love into
misery.
Please work me and your family
for you will have all the
stuff dreams are made of
till each and every night,
I shall hold you in my
heart; so you will never
have to part...

Linda Johnson

Earth

Our Earth is so grand;
so lend a helping hand.
Stop the pollution;
that's one solution.
Earth was just fine,
then came mankind.
All Earth has done is give,
and all it wants to do is live.
There are so many things to do,
now Earth needs help from you!

Michelle Graham

The Bowling Tournament

My son just lost the tournament,
Please let him see my pride.
I know how much he's practiced,
God knows, how hard he tried.

His eyes are downcast,
As he shakes the winner's hand.
Let him know his day will come,
Please, just let him understand.

His head is bowed his shoulders bent,
I feel how he must hurt,
As he packed away his ball and shoes,
And changed his oily shirt.

And as my soul was aching,
And my heart began to bleed.
I turned around, and there he was,
Rooting for the second seed!!!!!

Marilyn Flynn

The Beach

Wade in the ocean wide
get splashed by its mighty tide
duck in the waves to hide
nothing but water by your side.
Jump out and dry your feet
tons of people there to meet
in the sand, take a seat
sand everywhere, no concrete.
Stomp in a wet sand mound
kick your feet, on the ground
dance and run, all around
listen to the beach's sound.
Up you get
wishing you didn't have to go yet
yelling good-bye, to the people you met
as you run inside, watch the sun set.

Holly C. Spencer

"Mother"

For giving me life.
For taking care of me when I was
too small or too sick to take care
of myself.
For picking me up when I fell down.
For drying my tears.
For hurting with me when I hurt.
For helping me fix my mistakes.
For making me try my best.
For taking the time to give me
advise even though you knew I'd do
what I wanted.
For being there when I need you.
For giving up things you
could have had.
For loving me all of my life.
For being my mother.
I will always love you.
James A. Starr

"You Are My Dream ... My Love"

Did you know, I am here?
Could you possibly imagine?
But could you tell ...
I watch you from a far?

Stars in my eyes,
Love in my heart,
Every time I see his face.

Hope in my soul,
Dreams in my mind,
With one single glance of him,

And with my heart, lonely
I stood. Wishing I could have him.

So I cry and tears
Roll down my cheeks.
As some tears stay in my
Heart. GOODBYE LOVE...my LOVE.

No point to anything,
No point to Life!
But live to Die,
And DREAM to CRY!
Monica V. Alvillar

Children By The Sea

The sun has risen
The sand is glistening
Waves are gently flowing
Playing are children by the sea

Time marches on
Thoughts of sadness gone
Life has drawn
Children by the sea

Care is in the air
Parents taking care
of smiling faces of
Children by the sea

Castles being made
of children who have stayed
from dusk till dawn
all their energy has gone
How I love the
Children by the sea
Debra M. Haynes

What Is It?

Stare into the black
here it comes
knocking on my mind
pulling at my heart
pain like a dart

Found or lost
was it ever
memories in my mind
emotions running high
buzzing like a fly

Breathe a heavy sigh
here it is
always running wild
hiding like a child
Jim Ward

What Is War?

War is dying
war is killing
war is bleeding for hours
war is seeing your friend die
war is madness
war is cruelty
war is attacking a base
war is glory
war is crying in anger
war is a challenge
war is a struggle
war is training day and night
war is never-ending
war is hatred

That is what war is
Tom Langford

The Old Front Parch

When I was a kid down
Tuckhahoe neck,
Mom and Pop loved me
like a brushed and a peck.
They would work all
day, to finish their
chores, then they would
run for the old front
Porch, through the old screen door.
They would sit and
talk, until around
about Eleven, Boy I
thought I was in heaven.
They would sit and make
plans for the next day
all I had to do was run and play
It brings back memories
that makes me sad.
I'll never forget the old
front Porch, and my Mom and Dad.
Sallie M. Everngam

Butterfly Dancer

   Oh my beautiful dancer
come dance for me. From flower
to blossom endlessly! You dance in
the air like a beautiful song,
and no matter what, you dance
all day long. Like a leaf blowing
in the wind, dancing beautifully.
Over and over oh butterfly dancer
come dance for me.
Amber Shackelton

Trips To Ships

Our bus trips to ships
Are interesting and great.
Seeing familiar faces and friends
We look forward to the date.

We have good drivers
And arrive safely there.
We leave our problems at home.
Our money we bet and dare.

We go and spend the day
Having fun and know
We are not the only ones
Who lose all their dough.

Our leader, Pauline,
Starts us on our way,
With a smile and prayer
Asking for safety all day.

We hope she will continue
To keep our trips going,
It's not fun to go alone,
We get to hear others moaning.
Ruth Faggard

Endless Holiday

Endless holiday
Everlasting fear
Can't find the way
Think I'll let you steer

My life stinks
Not like you care
But it's what everybody thinks
I know they stare

My life has no direction
you're the lucky one
No one shows me affection
Go on without me your vengeance is done

My life has come to an end
My extinction your reincarnation
I'll be the one without a friend
you'll be the one with a destination
Alicia Ybarra

Rose

Love is like a rose
it has a love within
for a special person to
share again and again

It will bring you joy
It will bring you pain
It will bring you sadness
but all will be good.

When you give him
this special rose
his hearts will melt
as will yours

But only the one
true love of you
can share this
special rose.
Christina Paradee

Thoughts

They race through the mind's eye
Focussing on the past that
Looms larger as Time cruises
Relentlessly without asking why.

Yesterday appears and often beckons
As Today's concerns crowd Life
And its stresses seem to overwhelm
The foundation upon which it reckons.

Past performance crowds its way,
And conjures up those images
Of a day O, once so smooth,
Now cast aside and saying nay.

Yet, Life's experience tends to offer
Help to those who seek its benefit
From conversation with its possessor
And calls upon that one to proffer.

Sifting well the chaff from the wheat
Is a delight as the distance Past
Offers its thoughts and character
To the Present in an effort to repeat.

Daniel E. Lewis

Untitled

How precious life is this adorned!
Tears like diamonds in the grass.
What treasures here inside this chest!
Present, future, past!

The veil unfolded yet finds crease
And stills my refuge cares.
Lessons learned
Trees climbed-all bare.

And now joy I find in smallest flower;
Well as things undescribed
Emotion boundless
Alive.

Oh, still my heart to earthen murmurs
To hear Gods voice arise;
In silence-deadly calm.
And echoes far from I.

Bernice A. Jalbert

Grandpa

Who will tell jokes to Ellen?
Who will rock and hum to me?
It's hard tellen
Oh it was so hard to see
Moaning, groaning, crying
I would sit and hold his hand
My grandpa was dying
It was so hard to understand
Oh how I will miss his love
I long to see him someday
in the heaven above
I hope to say
Lying there ready to die
It was so hard to say
Goodbye

Laura M. Sheetz

Untitled

A poem must start
low,
unobtrusive.
Then.....must....Leap!
Catching eyes,
hearts,
souls.
It must be a
hawk.
Soaring, flying, bringing
pointing,
people's eyes.
Then must slowly,
spiral,
down,
Tempering the flames.
Then must become the
solitary,
crystal rose.
Capturing hearts, minds.

Allison Erb

On Viewing The Stars

By the light of the moon
I sit here and watch
As the light lingers on
With the tick of the clock

Everything is quiet
only the wind is awake
Another day passes on
As I sit here and wait

I thank you God
For the stars this night
A million shining symbols
Of your goodness and light

What would this life be
Without your small little gifts
To give hope to our spirits
And truly uplift

Help me tomorrow
As I go through the day
To count every blessing
That you send my way

Terri Townsend Day

The Moocher

Josh, the little moocher,
whines at me.
Any time food is near,
he is at my knee.

Josh is so cute,
he's my little chum.
He's a bottomless pit,
better give him some.

Food in the mouth,
forefingers follow.
That makes food better,
maybe easier to swallow.

Umm he says,
then he whines and begs.
Umm he says,
and he plays with his pegs.

Mona I. Brown

No One Can Imitate My Grace

I was in a fog and I was lame
Then, out of the mist I slowly came
Only to find everything the same
My outer - my inner - my healing shame
Who I am - I find - is eternally bound
To search - to seek - to understand the ground

To stand alone, yet choose a friend
To be a companion - until the end
No one, but no one can imitate my grace
I make mistakes I can't erase
I am a human - I'm in the race
But no one, no one can imitate my grace

Joannah Hall Glass

The Compromise

Like old pigeons in their coats
With ruffled feathers, keeping hold
Or bees in Winter, seared
By the cold
Dropping one-by-one from the hive
To die in the snow,
The three old ladies
Hold fast to their place
In the corner of the room.
They slowly nod and smile
Whispering
While the party flows
Rum-te-tum, rum-te-tum
Around them.

Robert I. Katz

Grandfather's Advice

There sat Grandfather
in a soft chair
There sat I, a maiden-fair,
With eyes that held me
by wisdom's glance
he spoke these words
sharp as a lance -
"Wear not thy faith
one day in seven
but ever weave
a garment to heaven."

Carmelita R. Simila

Poetry

Poetry is as pretty
As can be
Poetry can help people to see
To See
To Feel
To Love
To be Happy
Poetry is there to help us
Feel our feelings thoroughly
It could be sad, mad,
Or even glad
But it's there for us all
To see individually
Poetry

Jane Brancato

"Life"

The leaves rustle,
   and the winds blows.
The moons shines,
   and the sun glows.
The seasons change,
   and the Earth turns.
The day dies out,
   and the fire still burns.
The cars pass,
   and the planes fly.
Things change,
   and people die.
Matthew Karp

Dust On Water

Pine trees wave a whisper through
its voice, on breath delicate as hue,
suggests a tale of syncope
and none is in the dream but me.

Upon a pool, the whisper grows
a whirlwind 'cross the water blows
frenzied waves lash at the air
blindly seeking redress there.

But now lie calm since breath withdrew
their greater self at once renewed.
I pray that sleep, when soon away
delivers me to such a day.
Darrel Matteson

What Is Blue?

Blue is the sky,
also my nice bootie
it is the ocean fresh
and clean blue is mostly
what a boy would
wear or a funny
clown's hair. It is a
crayon that people
use to color a house
or a mouse that fell
in blue paint. A car
can be blue, the car
could go voom! Voom

   Blue in the zoo? That
would be new! Blue is
Blue and that might
make it cool!
Thomas Wood

The Wind

The wind will blow.
It's often still.
It carries a message
On how I feel.

If in the wind
You should hear,
Words of love
Whispered in your ear.

Just smile and grin,
I sent it from within.
The words, "I love you"
I whispered in the wind.
Mary F. Docherty

I Wish I Could Go Somewhere

I wish I could go somewhere.
And just die.
Without anyone asking
how, or why?
Nobody loves me,
So where do I turn,
when my heart and soul start
to burn and to yearn?
No one knows the sadness,
that I feel deep inside,
I bet hardly any one'd care
if I took a leap and died.
What goes on in my head,
no one can figure out.
But yet they don't care,
how I'll eventually turnout,
I bet they'll be sorry,
once I am dead
But no tears,
Do I want to be shed.
Krystal Moore

Had I To Do It Over Again

Had I the chance to delve into
The pages of my life,
And go from 20 back to one
Rub out err and strife.

Stepping out and looking
On the back porch of my time
To grasp the overview back then
And flip the thin fine dime.

Knowledge is a precious gift
Gained from time and pain,
Now turn the page to 20 and one
Let your memories remain.

Renew and tilt your footsteps
Grind a fine tuned path,
Let looking over your shoulder
Be a learning aftermath.
Sally K. Van Zomeren

Battle Between Father And Son

I found an old drawing
   of yours the other day
It took me years back to
   adolescent days of
   war and peace.

Your sketching of a dragon,
   fierce and prehistoric,
Entangled with another,
Meshed in design.

Armoured heart, silent and blind
In combat with the tyrant
   whose iron hand
   was too trampled
   to conquer the invisible sword
   that slayed
   the heart
   of the warrior
   or the
   villain?
Lynda D. Peters

"The Dance"

A touch of glistening bronze
A whisper of golden glow
A kiss of fiery sunset
Creating a masterful show
Somber as a darkened sea
And radiant as a candle flame
Fluttering, sailing, floating, waving
Whispering, rustling, echoing my name
Huddled in mass commotion
Upon the sleepless ground
Until heaven's breath uplifts them
They joyfully abound
Skyward whirling, clapping, twirling
Dancing as they fly
Nestling again to earthly slumber
Fall to sleep with a sigh
Karla Jo Mason

Untitled

I look up at your steel towers,
And I feel like a child.
Car brakes screaming-people cursing,
Noises my ears don't understand.
Everything is grey-streets, sidewalks,
Souls.
Crowds of people-wind up toys,
Moving too fast to feel.
What is there to feel?
Cold wind and solid cement,
Unresponsive to emotion,
Unfeeling.
Who is there to feel emotion?
Suits and skirts of black,
Cry only over losing green.
Not for lack of grass and trees,
But falling numbers-Black Monday.
Hot tears from ruined man,
Who sleeps in streets-unseen,
Dying.
Alicia Camigliano

LaMoille

There is a town called LaMoille
Where ranchers ply their ceaseless toil
And rivulets purge the fertile soil.

The craggy tors above the town
Release the tumult all around
As winter sheds her snow - wet gown.

As springs doth bring the sap to rise
And green abounds to hurt the eyes
The flowers rise to many sighs.

To those of us who live so near
This is a treasure held quite dear
With awe filled silence one can hear.

Then the mines did open up
The people came with kid and pup
Our quiet peace was then disrupt.

Snowmobiles did then abound
The silence wracked with awful sound
Around the mounts the racket wound.

Please give us back our solitude
Mom Nature thinks you are quite rude.
Deborah L. Burdic

Dear Grandchild

We went today to a quiet place
Marked only by a stone
And wished that we could raise you up
And gently take you home.

We yearn so much to hold you,
To kiss your tiny head.
To rock you softly in a chair,
Then tuck you into bed.

Your stay with us was very short
And we were torn apart.
Now you only live and grow
In dreams deep in our hearts.

There is much love that can't
Be spent
On one so sweet and dear.
But we shall never more forget
The visit you made here.

Jean N. Lind

"The Whispered Secret"

Our days are ciphered indefinitely.
Each day we're growing older, closer,
and more in love.
Together, joined in promise -
Promise,
of love eternal.
Spoken silent words -
in the mind, but never heard aloud.
Words from the heart,
echoing in memorable sound.
An actor's smile,
painted, now erased.
True emotions flowing,
rhythmically.
A secret kept -
inside,
Told aloud -
in soft whisper.
A sacred friendship...
forever.

Adrianne Cattoni

This Man

A red-tailed hawk soars
through the line of vision
and his heart leaps
at the sight
of its casual grace,
effortless feats of strength,
and beauty.

Bound by the earth,
he stands on the overlook
above the river
savoring the bird's-eye view;
races along the country roads
reveling in the power of his machine
and companionship of his son;
wants to have the wind in his face
experiencing a glimpse
of that hawks nature given freedom.

This man's spirit,
no longer grounded in flesh,
is released to soar upon the wind.

Laura Dowd

Untitled

It is not for us to know
What God has in store for us
today.....
For a time to wait is
sometimes His way of
blessing us with another
one of His special blessings
another day.
For God tells us in His
Word.......
Every time has its SEASON.

Kay Stafford

Summer

Summer
nice and warm
when flowers bloom and fruits ripen
Just to see the little
squirrels
running around pine trees
Playing and chatting
would bring a special
gleam
to a child's eyes
Summer oh summer
you are so cheerful and warm

Patricia Onuegbu

Dreams

I'd like to be inside of you
to see and feel your dreams
for when I saw your deepest fear
Id be there then to calm your screams

Your dreams they mean, a lot to me
the things you think or feel
so just to be inside of you
would make me feel so real

And if I was, seeing these things
I know for sure, I'd see
many thoughts and real sweet dreams
of yours so truly, Me!

So if you're ever down and out
and nothing just wont do
I'll tell you now, without a doubt
I'm always there for you!

You can always know I'm in your heart
and I'm surely your best friend
we know inside, we'll never part
and our love will never end.

Teresa Hamill

Run

Run.
Run far,
Run free.
Run from all your fears,
Run from all you expect to be.
Run from your sorrow.
Run from your pain.
Run fast.
Run until the sweat comes like rain.
Run to forget,
Run to remember.
Run.

Brian T. Jason

Layed Down With Roses

in a time so long ago when life
in all its magnificence made
you mine i
layed down with roses
that time when your velvet
touch and scent so sweet i
layed down with roses
the golden hue of happiness
shown all around and
that wispy mist wrapped us
as lovers entwine i
layed down with roses
now in this time there is
no you and i have naught
but a pricked and bloody
soul that runs red remembering
when i
layed down with roses

James Robinson

Dad

Of all the things I try to be.
Being you're daughter is one of the
   most important to me.
Since being my "Daddy's little helper"
   way back then.
You've taught me so much through
   all that you've been.
I know you're not perfect, but is
   anyone?
To me you're the greatest; all that
   I want to become.
In all that I am, and all that I do.
I hope people always see a whole
   lot of you.
I know this is short, but I hope you
   heard what I wanted to say:
I look up to you and love you
   more and more each day.

Christine Hogendobler

Storms

Flippant remarks,
tossed across the void
like peanut shells
or empty cans.
She catches them
as one might catch
an eel, still wet
and slippery.
Her fake plastic smile
sickens me,
though my own lips
are contorted
in a semblance of a grin.
As I watch her,
I cannot help but think,
somewhat hypocritically,
how much I hate her.

John A. Melson

Cornered Destiny

Be calm,
There is nothing in this smile.
But there is more,
More than you and I can take.

In the dim shadows,
Of a cornered destiny,
Fights a victim,
To keep awake.

But still,
The pain numbs the wound.
Left open,
By an uncaring fool.

And all eyes close,
On a world,
That breads devils,
Without rule.

Joseph A. Mira Jr.

I Will Never Leave Thee

Jesus spoke these comforting words
"I will never leave thee"
And I remember with thankful heart
My Lord, is always with me.
As I walk in Christian faith
I have no doubt or fear
Christ, is my constant companion
He is always near.
And with love and certainty
Step by step each day
His light shall be my guide
To lead me along life's way.
For I walk by faith in Christ
And rest in His care
Always drawing closer to Him
In love and thoughtful prayer.
For Christ, gives me life and love
He has made me free
And I remember His faithful promise
"I will never leave thee."

Jane F. Seigle

Searching

I look all around
And there is darkness
Searching I came to you
You turned away
I reach out
But there is only emptiness
Joy surrounds me
Like a cloak torn to shreds
Happiness is the friend
I've never met
Life's pathways
Lead only to despair
Where is love?
It is gone
Where is hope?
That too is gone
There is nothing left
But longing
The need to belong

Julian Walters

By Gone Days

Sometime I wish I could go back
  To days of by gone years,
When we could walk or drive along
  Without so many fears.
What's happened to the youth today
  That makes some act so strong?
Or are the parents not around
  To teach them right from wrong?
They use a gun instead of fists
  And hijack cars galore,
And then they say they're innocent
  And turn and do some more
Let's teach some morals, pure and sound
  Not fear to walk alone,
Let's turn the fury all around.
  And make it safe for all.
But time goes on and all things change
  Let's hope for better, soon-
I thank the Lord for all I have
  Let's sing a different tune.

Angela J. Scardino

To Dream

When I go dreaming
I find a place
Out there in the world for me
With cool streams flowing
Blue skies soft
Pure water
Wind so free
Rocks of gray
Short and tall
Wild bears roaring
Roads so small
Winding - weaving
Paths of stone
Carry me to a place
I call my own
A place where I can smell the beauty
Of life as it should be
Without a care or worry
Life's little cure for me

Gail H. Wagner

A Special Touch

There is a love one cannot compare
The love a mother and daughter share
Mothers possess A Special Touch,
One we desperately need so much
She has a sparkle in her eye
Assuring you it's all right to cry
She holds you close when in despair
Letting you know she's always there
All the love she has inside
Fills our heart with lots of pride
Always working, never at rest,
Mothers deserve the very best
Yes, she has A Special Touch
And I love her very much

Michelle J. Willette

Room Of Dreams

Tall Arches
opening to grand

Clouded Windows
moving with light—

Whispered Airs
breathing of bright

Spectrous Dust
moving ethereal pulse—

Shadowed Columns
marking space

Deep Silence
swooning...shimmering—

Incandescence

Clifford Davoli

"Coming Home"

I'm coming home to you,
in need of a prayer.
I stand before you - Lord
because I know you Care.

I'm coming home to you,
feeling weighed down,
looking for a smile,
and not a frown.

I'm coming home- Lord,
without a dime in my purse.
I need to be Blessed,
and not to be cursed.

I'm coming home,
because you are my friend.
I'm standing before you- Lord
this is where my new life....Begins!

Donna Reed

Celebrate

Our celebration at birth, shouldn't be,
for all our hardships we've yet to see.
But when our name is called up yonder,
our work on earth is but a wonder.

We leave behind, for those we care,
all the memories, we love and share.
Now the celebration should take place,
and thank the Lord for all His grace.

We were chosen to be the ones,
to share the years, one by one.
The window of our life is such,
as though a magic wand did touch.

But now safety, in his care,
all our woes with Him we share.
As we watch from above,
we wait all those we love.

A new beginning, That's what this is!
We are waiting in our bliss.
The pain and suffering is gone of late,
now is the time to celebrate!

Matilda M. Segura

Oklahoma City

She wore bells on her feet
her shoes neatly laced her
face glowed like candles in a
darkened world she was my girl
and she wore bells on her
feet she marched in circles
around the monument of
death the wind blew yet she
marched yet she marched
out there upon the
prairies quiet silent are
the souls asleep among
the monument of death.

Jimmy Grady

Hell

Within darkness
What can I see
Someone locked the door
and threw away the key.

A fire now burns
it hurts me within
A horned fellow appears
he tells me I have sinned.

Pain now fills me
I only wanted to get away,
A mistake I can't correct
I didn't know it was this way

God help me please
This man tortures me so
Pull me from this fire
Tell him to let me go.

Richard Wilder

My Baby

The softest skin ever,
The cutest little face,
And warmest heart,
It was my baby.
Full flesh and all,
She was mine.
To care for,
And to love.
Mine to hold,
Ever so tight.
She was my little baby
And always would be.
For me to love,
Endlessly......

Colleen Murphy

When I See Behind The Sunset

When I see behind the sunset
I think of you.
I know a new day has come to stay
With the new beginnings with you.
Because when I go to my peaceful place
I begin to realize who I really am.
And each time I'm there I see your face
So behind the sunset I'll stay
With warmth, happiness together
To get us through this life
Just as day to day

Alan Manning

My Family

I never had children of my own,
The seed was sterile that I had sown.
I married a family of five,
I worked hard to keep alive.
A mother and children of four,
That welcomed me at the door.
Glad to see me each night,
Working every day was a fight.
Cutting meat day by day,
Every Friday got my pay,
Taking home groceries by the arm load,
Driving home an a rocky road.
Listening to the children happy at home
After working myself a rest
Proud, I did my best.

Richard W. Luedtke

Singularity

California mellow sun massages
wannabee brown bodies
lounge lizards in an outpour
frenzy of still acceptance;

Oxymoron to the nth power
explore the five
w's and get no answers.

Oh well:
bodies and shells,
oceans and deserts,
satie and sartre,
etc.'s and i.e.'s;

Left with rights
and wrongs,
we stand in
tread waters of
singularity.

P. J. Van Niel

"Comforting Owl"

When Earl brought me here
as his bride
You came whoo, hoo, hoo, whoo, whoo
That is what you cried
We snuggled together
The moon was so bright.
Many years have passed
Now I am alone
When the moon is bright.
You come whoo hoo hoo whoo whoo
And it seems so right.
Like a lovely prayer
All thru the night.
I thank you in my sorrow
For your every whoo whoo
You are so comforting
All the night through.

Mildred Clauff Jemison

Untitled

   Witnessing the murderer being
caught.
   Hearing blood-curdling
screams.
   Waiting to see what happens
next.
   Jumping at the slightest
sound...
   Then you awake, wondering
if it really happened.

Jeannette Thomas

Where Are They

Where are they
Who fill our hearts,
With that sense of love?

Where are they
Who make our hearts,
Flutter like a dove?

Where are they
Who know us well,
In all of its meaning?

Where are they
Who make us laugh,
Leave us smiling, gleaming?

Where are they
We love so much
We know we're far apart.

Where are they?
Where have they gone?
They who hold our hearts.

Emily Sattazahn

Welcome The Morning

The morning has come,
the day now is new.
This peace, now so simple,
is noticed by few.

The night's pressing hardships,
have now passed away
revealing grand new potential
mired in today.

One must look forward;
to the future unknown,
while always knowing,
the path seen is his own.

Memories are blessed;
thoughts of those we held dear
but to never look forward
only strengthens one's fear.

So take hold of the moment,
seize ye the day;
For death is but a price
we all inevitably pay.

Matthew Leavell

To Catch A Dream Of Love

On the wings of an eagle
I send my sweet Love
Listen to the music
Thrumming across the miles
Sending a message of yearning
To touch and see you smile
Reach up and catch the Dream
And hold it to your heart
Why must we be apart?
Send for me my tender lover
And in the twinkling of an eye
I will be with you forever
Until the day I die!

Anita M. Plouffe

"The Bell Calls"

I see the leaves,
Appear in the spring,

How clearly,
The bell does ring,

I see the leaves,
Change color in the fall,

How clearly,
The bell does call.

I see the leaves,
In winter, fall and die,

How clear,
The bell from the sky.
Mattie M. Stewart

Tears

They speak a language all their own
And stand for how we feel
Whether they're used with joy or sorrow
These tears are very real
You use them when you're happy
You use them when you're sad
They go along with big old grins
And many are shed when you're mad
We share these things with others too
They teach us more each day
A special part of great big hugs
And fill our eyes when we pray
So though you cry a little
Or cry an awful lot
These funny things called tears
Are sometimes all we've got
To share with grief and sorrow
Or share with joy and love
These tears that speak a language
Are sent from God above
Renee Pemberton

My Nearness

My footprints wear no skin
wear nothing weigh nothing
are visible on granule lid of earth,
spread out are dried
by the nearness of the sun's tentacles

I turn back to find one, then another;
the innumerable traces of myself
that have no relative shadows
Each print halts my nearness

I watch them crumble
from the tentacles' touch
Pieces are driven into hungry sunlight,
acquainting in the air

Naked bits of life dash in brilliance
through swatches of evening
I look through night windows
The night crowds my closeness

I listen to the swish of wings
that with sleep will close the night
Francesca Aragon Azevedo

Charlene Can

Congratulations!
Charlene Garrett,
Receiving teacher support
Becoming "Teacher of Year".
Grant.

Grant,
"I Can",
Believing in self,
Shaping destiny with books.
Reading.

Reading,
Racing teams,
Winning in classrooms,
Achieving success with teamwork.
Accomplishments.

Accomplishments,
Steadfast motivation,
Working extra hours,
Receiving well-earned rewards.
Congratulations!
Betty Luddington

You

I want to say how much I care.
And I always will,
You'll never know how much of my life
that you have fulfilled.

I always have a smile on my face
when ever you are near,
With just a touch from you
that's caring and so dear.

You make me feel like no man ever has
with jut being who you are,
I hope I can return the same
and be your shining star.

You don't say much to me
of how you really feel,
but your eyes and touch tell me
there is more of you to reveal.

Maybe someday
it will all come around,
That you will finally realize
how much you have truly found.
Laura L. Keys

No Hat Hanging Here

Bastards stole my only grocery cart;
Almost all I own has gone crash.
Another trip to place near B.A.R.T.;
Lining up to beg a new stash.
Must find different place to hide;
Sleeping with one open eye.
Those S.O.B.s have no human pride;
Oh, for one true friend afore I die.
Catching sleep during the safer days;
Surviving can have many faces.
At least asleep avoids the ways;
Those fat cats stare at my places.
Better stares than averted glances;
Snotty smug ones never helping free.
Still there are some hesitant advances;
Like those ladies at the food pantry.
If only I could clear my topside;
Perhaps work would be a possibility.
Once again to have a home and fireside;
No longer a life of certain futility.
J. Warner Ralls

He Learned To Play

He learned to play the guitar
When he was just a kid,
So he could stay up late at night
Like all the grown folks did.

He watched the magic fingers
Of his uncles and his dad,
Move fluently across the strings
Of the instruments they had.

Upon their knees he sat amazed
For hours they would stay,
And when his hand could reach around
they taught him how to play.

Some disappointing days of loss
Have come and gone since then,
But memories of those days gone by
Shine through his gentle grin.

Then born one day, a little child
A son sat on his knee,
And he told him as he's since told more
If you want to play, watch me.
Cynthia D. Hyatt

Cocoa, Why Do I Love You So?

Cocoa, why do I love you so?
Is it because your bark
Is as sweet as the meadow lark
I hear singing in the nearby park?

Cocoa, why do I love you so?
Could it be because you have a
Soft gentle soothing touch
That to me means so much?

Cocoa, why do I love you so?
Maybe it is because you took your paw
And rubbed it lovingly on my right jaw
then kissed me thrice tenderly.

Cocoa, why do I love you so?
It does not really matter.
So let's stop the chit-chatter
Because your love for me you daily show.
Florence M. Jones

Ode To A Desert Rose Garden

I dream of fields of daisies
I dream of big shade trees
But what I see are tumbleweeds
Blowing in the breeze.

Lots of sand and cacti
A roadrunner, wren or bee
So a visit to the rose garden
Is what really pleases me.

The roses seem to beckon
Come forth and look at me.
Pink and red ones
Yellow, blue and white
And when the sun goes down
Their fragrance lingers in the night.

A gentle blowing wind,
The dry desert air,
And ever blooming roses
Make me happy that I'm here.
N. Loy Higgins

For I Am Small

When I survey this thing called life
What part is there for me to play?
For I am small,
And do not understand my role;
Too many isms for me to comprehend.

It has been said that we are as stars,
Each with some light to shed,
But where is mine?
For I am small,
And have not much glimmer.

Perhaps each one of us is a universe,
And deep within our cores
A thousand galaxies shine
Like brilliant suns.

But I am small
And don't emit much light;
O Lord, increase my candlepower
And cause my beams to stream
Upon some darkened hope;
Then what was small has grown.

Gordon Deau Schlundt

Of The Rain

Rain is raining
    all around,
raining on trees
    and on the ground.
Trickling rhythmically
    to and fro,
branches to leaves
    downward flow.
Drop-by-drop gather
    in small pools,
sparkling in brilliance
    like many jewels.
Rain continuous downhill,
    gravitating on its way
to a stream, a river,
    and seaward to a bay.
There, to be absorbed
    by sun again,
to begin a new cycle
    of-the-rain.

Cesarina Maria Rossetti

By The Fireplace

As each flame warms my heart
I see a glimpse of you
Within each glowing spark
Lies memories fresh and new.

Flickering, fleeting flames
Some orange, some blue, some gold
All telling bits of you
Nostalgic thoughts of old.

As embers faintly burn
Fading to ashes gray
The glow in my heart remains
Treasured deep to stay.

Mada Scott

Just The Way Things Are

I like things just the way they are
But they could be better with a car.
I would like a million dollars
Then I could buy a million cat collars.
I would keep giving my house an expansion
Until it was considered a very large mansion.
My amount of pets would be much more than few
Until my house could be considered a zoo.
I also think it would be cool
to have a personal swimming pool.
School hours would have a big change
They would be in the ten to fifteen minute range.
The world would see no more fights
From the beginning of morning till the end of nights.
There would be love and kindness everywhere
Along with happiness, loyalty, and the will to share.
Everyone would be in a happy mood
Because pizza would be the official food.
I think these things would improve the world by far
But I guess things are all right just the way they are.

Brian Golden

Color Me Beautiful

Don't look at me as a pigment of skin
Color me beautiful and be my friend
When I need a job don't ask why
Color me beautiful so I qualify
We are different yet still the same
Color me beautiful so you'll know my name
Tragedy strikes and we let down our guard
Color me beautiful everyday is hard
Children play as children do
Color me beautiful as the child in you
It makes no difference what your eyes see
Color me beautiful see inside me
More that hues of a spectrum old
Color me beautiful to cleanse your soul
Evil arises with a lash of the tongue
Color me beautiful as we are one
Beautiful color that I am
Color me beautiful as a strong man
Color me beautiful like children do
Color me, color beautiful, I'm part of you.

Gregory Cubit

Fearing Society

Alone in a place unknown,
Fearing what is out there.
Stuck in a hole like a man without a soul.
Not knowing where and not knowing why
mankind is so far behind.

Free me from this cell that entraps me so well
This cloud over my head that fills me with dread.
The fear within my mind that makes me go blind.

I do not fear what is out there, but what is within my mind, body,
    and soul that makes me whole.
When did I become trapped in this world that is about to snap.
I have tried to escape this hell like place.

But I can't leave because I live and walk and talk within the soul
    of society.

Alex Sessions

Your Choice

In loving memory of my mother's sister, Glinda.
You thought the choice you made was right.
You weren't aware of the disease you'd have to fight.
But now you're gone and it's too late,
To warn you of your awful fate.

If I could go back in time,
I'd give every last penny and dime,
To see you home and healthy again.
Back to your husband and children.

But it's good to know that you've fought your fight,
And you've finally gotten to see that bright light,
That so many of us wonder when we'll see,
The day we lie down and go to sleep.

Sommer Daun Reprogle

The Loss Of Someone Very Special

Upon this earth there did walk a man, along
the way he made a plan.
To seek and find a special friend, who would
keep him company until the end.
When he did, he took her into his care, gave
her his love and all he had to share.
He planted his seeds within her pouch, then
watched over them as they did sprout.
Into the air full bloom they came, one by one
with them they carried his name.
He felt he had more to share, for this was a
man who was wise and fair.
He decided to represent the elderly that were
not receiving the proper care.
He entered a career that many would not dare.
A world of stress, bitterness, and hate.
He carried with him, his confidence and faith.
He touched the lives of many people small and
great. Soon he became the man to represent our
State. His death was hard for all to take.

Marilyn Kalina

My Thoughts Are Of You

Moonlit night, dinner by candle light
   Music fit to soothe
The stars are bright, the mood is right
   My thoughts are of you

Sipping champagne by the fire, unspeakable love is what I desire
   In a bed of roses for two
As the flames grow higher, Suddenly I'm inspired
   My thoughts are of you

A stroll through the park, Sharing Kisses in the dark
   Trading secrets all night through
A Sky show Starts, as my heart ignites from a spark
   My thoughts are of you

As the night comes to an end, I recap where I've been
   Actually I never moved
My mind starts to spin, I'm lost in the wind
   My thoughts are of you

Katrina Chestnut

Born Free

Until I'm born again free someday there
is no life for me this way. I'll never smile
again until I win the freedom I long for
each day. You can't be the man or woman
you want to be until you can say you're
free to live your life your way and be
born again free someday.

Anthony J. Romero

The Carefree Boy

There he goes with his long cane pole,
Heading down to the fishing hole.
He knows his day will be filled with joy,
Because he is a happy, carefree boy.

He knows every bird by its melodious call,
Knows how the squirrel hides nuts in the fall.
He knows that nature was made to enjoy,
Because he is a happy, carefree boy.

He'll fish awhile, maybe swim about noon,
Maybe just rest and whistle a merry tune,
All nature, and all it holds, is his toy,
Because he is a happy, carefree boy.

He knows each animal and tree by name,
Knows where to find the sweetest sugar cane,
Knows every bloom and plant, and much, much more,
Because he is an expert in nature lore.

Oh, yes! He is wise beyond his years.
We would have no need to shed so many tears.
If we only hand the wisdom it takes to enjoy
The things that are almost a part of happy, carefree boy.

Aleta M. McRae

Through All The Years, Trials And Tribulations

Queen - Strong, Intelligent, Warrior
Child Bearing, LOVING....

"Black Woman"

Kidnapped, Raped, Beaten, Field Worker,
Maid, LOVING...

"Black women"

Timid, Scared, Frustrated, Confused,
Left Out, Over Looked, Ashamed,
Embarrassed, LOVING...

"Black Woman"

Back Bone, Looked up to, Home Maker, Intimidating,
Bold, Vivid Colours, Astonishing, Amazing,
Calm, Outgoing, Still Strong,
Not Shy, Real,
Beautiful, LOVING...

"Black Woman"

E. Janean Mitchell

Heart Break

As I sit here pondering on the past, our close relationship I do ask,
through good and bad times things have passed,
One of these days together at last.

Hurt and pain had touched our hearts,
Misunderstanding tore us apart.
time has come for us to start, mending all our broken hearts.

Life's too short to hold a grudge,
some of the strongest don't ever budge,
but when it comes to those you love,
it's time to thank the Lord above.

We never know day after day, if on this earth we'll forever stay,
so before the time we have to lay, for you and the boys I do pray.

For whatever pain that came from me,
the hurt of course I did not see,
so to you I say I'm so sorry,
and best of friends again we'll be.

The only guarantee that I will make,
through months of pain and true heartache,
on this earth it's never too late,
these arms of mine won't let your heart break.

Shannique R. To'omalatai

Time

Time is slipping out of my hands.
I don't know where the minutes have gone
and I don't know where they're going.
Maybe they'll go to a needy person
or maybe they'll catch me later.
When love finds me time,
hopefully will slow down
so that I can be with love forever.
If not, then let time end
and go somewhere else.
Because I don't want time on my hands
if I can't share it with someone else.
What is lonely time worth anyway?
Does it even compare to an ounce
of passion or tears?
Through the year
time has been slipping out of my hands,
but those minutes will be back again someday.
Hopefully I will be with him on that day.
For this time I pray.

Stacey A. Shaw

And So It Is

   The sound is soft,
And so it is.
   The ground is wet,
And so it is.
   The light is dim,
And so it is.
   The leaves are kept up by the branches,
And so it is.
   The wind is blowing up the trees,
And so it is.
   My heart and mind are full of words and notions,
And so it is.
   The flowers in color, red, orange, pink and purple,
And so it is.
   The coffee sends out a quenchable aroma,
And so it is.
   Grey and black and white wings flutter in the air,
And so it is.
   Our Father looks at his children with love and adoration,
And so it is.

Peter Lampros

Every Night

After the day is gone.
And the night has come.
I go into my room.
I lay on my bed and only think of you.
I wonder if you ever think of me.
Every night is the same,
I'm here with nothing but a memory.
I can't get you out of my head.
Every night as I go to bed.
I remember your eyes, your hair,
Your touch, your kindness to me.
You are more than just another man to me.
You'll never know how special.
Every night as I go to bed.
I know it's all just in my head.
I'm probably never in yours.
Every night as I go to bed,
I long to be in yours.

Betty Jean Hill

Dear Friend

It warms my heart, when at times
Through you I can see myself.
The times when I can touch
Those invisible, but searing emotions,
The fearing but caring heart
And a persistent but unsure thought.

It makes me grow a little fonder
To know through you I can realize,
That a day fulfilled is only a day
When a part of me I give away.
The times when time is unimportant
And a pertinent but pleasant thought.

It revives for me elated pleasure,
To see you feel, and shy, and shield,
And then you smile and that is real,
Life is simple, yet serious, and chaotic,
And painful, and sad. But also,
Calm, and joyful, and glad, and sweet.
Especially when the one that makes you
Smiles, is often in your thoughts.

Lingsworth B. Pendley

Angel Of Mine

I have my own little angel
So fair, beautiful and radiant,
Never aging forever young.

God carried he down to earth
Especially meant for me,
During time of trial, tribulations
My little angel is there to comfort me.

Not uttering a word just feeling he presence
Her silence is peaceful and refreshing as a breeze
We have talks and listening,
I thank God for my little angel

For without her, life wouldn't be the same
I see her when least expecting
Feel her presence, needing a friend
A special Angel she'll always be.

For she's God's little Angel sent to me
That makes her precious and dear
God knows we need special Angels

For help through life's way
We all need special Angels along the way.

Kathy Haeni

A Walk In Time

If you take a walk around in the 1800's
you will find it's nothing like today.
Back then the land was used wisely
you could yell and yet none would hear.
If you walked, way back when
you would see a special balance
a balance that unites the animals and the trees,
and you can see them living in pure harmony.
Today that balance is almost gone.
For about 70 years we've said, "No harm done."
Now people are seeing what they have done.
We have destroyed everything.
From the ozone to the water it's all being destroyed.
While some say, "Oh, Well!"
I hope most say, "Farewell."
Farewell to all we have destroyed,
and that those who care save what we haven't destroyed.

Eric Pirtle

Dedicated To Harmony

When the angels have all left...
And no life exists here,
When all the water has dried up...
And mankind is just a memory.....
...I will think of you

When all the stars have a number...
And one of them is you,
I will gaze upon your glory...
Until I am consumed by the fire....
...I will be with you

When all else has failed you...
And you feel all alone,
Know that a whisper of my name...
Will inspire legions to your rescue...
...I will come for you

When they put the final brush strokes...
To the canvas of eternity,
They will not be able to complete the picture...
Without a little harmony...
...I feel it from you

Steven K. Breck

Christ And Beautiful

Look at that Sunset, isn't it beautiful?
This is what I always say
Why does it make me happy,
At the end of each day?

As I pondered this over,
In breath of REST,
I noticed the colors,
They were GOD's best.

First I saw Red,
The Blood He eagerly shed,
Then Yellow the color of the sun (Son)
Thus, the sunset of Rest.

I thought, CHRIST AND BEAUTIFUL
That's what you are,
You did all this for me
You have the scars.

As I gaze at the Sunset,
At the end of each day,
I'll say "CHRIST AND BEAUTIFUL"
That's ALL I can say

Claress Ann Sarvello

February 25, 1978

We waited the sign of spring
The pussy willow, the children soon will bring
  Then the trees will bud, red and green,
The ground will have lost its covers of white
  To dirty brown, then green to sprout to our delight.
By now the sky have cleared, and grown warm,
  Lazily to drift by, a sky watches delight.
The lawn have long since turn green,
  Trees too have all there leaves,
Birds have build their nest, and flown,
  Squirrels bring out there young so small at
First, to shiver and shake, soon to grow bold
  And skimper about.
Warm breezes, from which strong winds blow,
  the night grows warm, with millions of
Stars to light the way.
  This we waited for, thought long winter days

Donald A. Flaherty

The Observer

A man was sitting across the way
Looking at she with eyes of gray

While he looked, I could plainly see
That he was in love with the beautiful she

She gleamed at him, he fell apart
As if beautiful she had stolen his heart

He stood with pride and lingered near
The sound of her soft voice, I could not hear

It looked like inside him there was a fire
And it's true, the flames of a burning desire

He touched her softly with gentle hands
She looked at him with the eyes of a lamb

So passionate, so soothing, so soft were her eyes
Telling him that she speaks no lies

He realized this and sat to talk
Gleaming at her with the eyes of a hawk

I saw this feeling come down from above
When it landed on them, 'twas the feeling of love

All I saw this beautiful, starry night
Was observed greatly with all of my might

C. J. Johnson

Peeking Out

It's pretty cold in here.
Oh, I've made believe it's warm, but it isn't.
The warm fuzzies from others penetrate only skin deep.
Because if they knew. If they really knew.
But I'm afraid it's even colder out there.
The weird ones are out there. I'm not like them.

Then I meet one. Then another.
Different they are, yet the same.

We're queer. We're really queer.
Not in the mean, ugly way the word is used.
But in a gently descriptive way.

Like the four-leaf clover in a field of "normal" cousins.
Or our dog with his singular lower canine
That pushes his upper lip into its characteristic, lopsided grin.

Queer.

Yet beautiful.

I push open the door. No more peeking out. I step out.
The warm sunlight of truth drenches my soul with its
Soothing balm of boldness.

I'm finally finding home.

Jeffrey W. DeVore

The Homeless House

There once was a house
That lived in a mouse.

Why would a house
Live in a mouse?

One day the mouse
Got too big to live in the house.

The mouse wanted to be nice
And pay the price.

So, he let the house live in his tummy.
And he said it was very yummy.

Jessica Lee

Good-Bye Isn't Easy

Saying "good-bye" isn't easy,
in fact, it makes me queasy.

Saying "farewell" is terrible
in fact, it makes me miserable.

Saying "I'll miss you" is bad,
in fact, it makes me sad.

Saying "keep in touch" is such a chore,
in fact, it makes me miss you more.

Saying "I'll see you" is a dream,
in fact, it makes me want to scream.

Saying "good-bye" is always hard to say,
in fact, it makes me wish that you stay.

Marcus Harris

Seeking

Man is a pilgrim
journeying on an eternal river.

He exists,
a dropped anchor on a rough sea.

I am still running in darkness,
as if a bare wintery tree.

But there is a hidden color,
waiting for green spring with great hope
while intensively struggling inside.

Sitting in a log cottage
silent at midnight,

As if making tea with spring water,

Let us have
a pure and clean heart.

Wintery night
looking at a starry sky,

Praying silently
like wintery bare trees,

Let us have a deep and humble mind.

The future to run is there.

Ock Kyu Yoo

Carpe Momentum

Once, when time was still young,
I was not unlike yourself.
I went to school, and played
The games children play,
Then went home again.
When once I stopped
To catch my breath,
Time passed me by.
It did not stop to take
A rest or look at what went by.
On it went, slow at first,
Then faster by the day. And when I
Tried to begin where I'd left off, 'twas
Not time enough. I couldn't go back to what
Had been; I had to go on to what may be. Now
Here I lie, a lame, decrepit man, and so here I too will die.

Erik M. Filipiak

"Hazed Into Oblivion"

Drifting like romantic ship captains
   through caressing waters
   and lonely fog

swaying in a light breeze
   like in Virgin Mother's arms

enveloped in the safety of lower quarters
   ensconced in faded bed sheets

   off to unknown regions
   uncharted and unnamed

   A guiding crescent
   assures a wide-open fate

   as open as
   the violently raging waters below

Greg Svitil

God's Country

Echoes call throughout the valley
   Smoke rises from the river
The sun fades behind a cliff
   People sigh and stare at
    God's work

Swift raindrops fall on the dry land
life abounds in the newly discovered wetness
flowers spring up, quenched with strength
   God's love radiates from beyond
    the sky

Michael Held

Untitled

You picked me up, and you let me fly,
Your steel hands squeezed me, until I cried.
You sent me on a journey, far, far away,
Although I still love you, till this day.
I'll always remember, that day you chose your fate,
You didn't know I wouldn't be waiting at that gate.
I recall, how you blamed it on your disease and
You would tell me to forgive and forget.
But I was freezing inside.
Was it because of the coldness of your heart, or your belt.
No matter whatever it was, I dealt.
You seemed to think it was my fault, your life was falling apart.
These reasons, I wished, I could run somewhere afar.
You kept me confined, to do your trash,
You were ungrateful, so you bashed.
I tried to make you happy, but of course you didn't care,
I started to see that your insides were bare.
Oh please tell me, is there a better place than this.
I can't really remember, when you gave me a loving kiss.
I'll never know, what love is all about.

Michelle Pinelle

"Purify"

Let my passion be washed by the churning sea,
And my desires cleansed by your legacy.
Let my intentions drown in the galaxy
As angels look down from above.

Let my wickedness cease in the bitter fight
For my soul from the thoughts that control at night.
In my dreams I dance within shadows and light
On the shore of the northern cove.

But I cry for the girl who left years ago.
If I saw her today I would never know
Which one, if not both of us, had transformed so.
In heaven I will see my love.

Christine Shukailo

Crocus

Therapy is similar to the growth process of a beautiful
crocus unfolding after lying dormant for many months.
When the crocus receives nurturance from the rays of the
sun, the struggle to break through the hard-crusted
winter's earth begins. The warmth from the sunlight gives
the crocus strength and courage to start its long journey
upward. Just when some sense of progress begins to take
hold, a cold dark night arrives. The crocus shrinks back
inside, to the world that feels comfortable and familiar, to
the world that has provided protection for so long. It takes
many more days of feeling the gentle caresses of the sunlight
and many times returning to the safe earth, before the crocus
begins to trust the light and summon the courage to
emerge. Finally the long awaited birth of the crocus,
complete with its magnificent color and full bloom lifts
its face unto the light and gives of itself to the world.

Joy Allison

Cascade Of Domain

The sun shining
like a candle in the dark,
Clouds overhead
blanketing the sapphire sky.
Marshes swaying
with the southward breeze,
Long green branches
greet the shimmering pond.
Birds calling
for their early morning ritual,
A glistening trap
just awaiting a fly.
Young popping out of eggs
to receive new life,
Insects too frigid to move
except for those desperately searching food for winter.
As I was sitting up on the hill covered green,
I knew this cascade of land
would prevail through the end.

Mary Winn

My Love

...The first time I ever saw your face,
No doubt about it, Love was the case.
The electricity I felt that was in the air,
Those eyes, those lips, and beautiful hair,

That smile that could light up a city,
Your presence was felt, bright and witty,
Young and voluptuous with a strong will to live,
You are a wonderful person with so much to give.

That beautiful glow that shines on your face,
That beauty that surrounds you from place to place,
The sweet tone of your voice, just as you talk,
The world shines around you, every step as you walk,

Your kindness and flair to know what to say,
You make life worth living, from day to day.
Is this Love? The court is out,
The jury convicts me, there is no doubt.
The thought of you, my heart breathes a sigh,
Until we meet again, a tearful good-bye...

Adam Abdallah

Untitled

The starlit sky twinkles ever so gently
An instant flash of lightening interrupts-
Peace and harmony falls back into place
A streak runs against the black foreground
Slowly clouds overcome and rule the night sky

Anna J. Prince

Angel

I am an angel, I follow souls
I followed a soul labeled 11413
he grew up in violence
he was in his thirties
and shot a man in the night
never found by the police
lived in fear and died a cruel death.
I took his soul I am an angel
I take souls for judgment
I took a soul labeled 11413
through time and space

I am an angel, I follow souls
I followed a soul labeled 11413
he grew up a fine man, a rich man
he was in his late forties
having a face in his head
in his early fifties and found the face
the face was in its thirties, it was night.
I am an angel
My friend labeled 11413 found peace.

Joel R. Priddy

"The Children"

What have we given the children
What have we shown them of life
How will they handle the pressure
The heartache, the pain, the strife
How do they make their decisions
Which the right way to go
Do they follow the river of others
Or turn and create their own flow
It's said you're as good as your promise
Well what do we tell them now
We're sorry it's not like it should be
But we'll make it up somehow
Then we turn and go back to our own world
And they feel they've been turned away
We live in our own world of problems
And they don't know just what to say
When my children have grown and I'm older
Will they really believe that I tried
Will they understand like I hope that they can
It was for them each time that I cried.

Ronald W. Sandnes

Gravity

Gravity is an invisible force
You can't really see it of course

You can see the result of gravity
It pulls down on you and me

Gravity is one of God's forces
That doesn't give man any choices

The rules of gravity are very simple
If anything goes up it'll come down and make a dimple

Man has tried to defy the forces of gravity many times
And most of the time he injured his spine

Gravity is one of God's absolute forces
No matter what man does it takes it courses

Can you imagine if gravity wasn't here
We'd all be floating in the atmosphere

But in the reality if there was no gravity
there would be no life for you and me

God is the engineer of life's plan
He thought it out before he created man

Ajamu Bandele

The Paradox

Love can be both kind and cruel, happy and sad, elation and madness. It can truly be the very best thing and the very worse thing that could happen to you.

Love...the tender hand that strokes you with a softness like that of a gentle breeze, caressing and carrying away the sweet aroma of a spring flower.

Love...the rigid fist that can destroy you with a thunderous force like that of a hurricane, stripping away and uprooting everything in its path, showing no mercy.

Yet to avoid love for fear of its destructive potential would, to us, be unthinkable. To forsake love in the interest of emotional sanctuary is far beyond our capabilities.

So we go on loving and loving. Baring our souls to the threat unabated. Many of us losing only to love again. We are undaunted by the pain for the fear of losing the pleasure.

Our souls, rudderless ship, tossed in an endless unpredictable sea of emotion. Helpless against the current, and content to be so. We are fully aware that the waves will indeed go on forever. The thunder and lightning will come and go, we will press on, without a momentary thought of retreat. For we know, more certainly each time, that the calm that follows is worth a thousands storm. Love is truly eternal, as is its........PARADOX.

Brian Cross

The End

Darkness settles creeping in like a blanket of fog on a river in autumn, penetrating every pore of my soul. Reminding me of unfulfilled dreams, time lost, energy spent. It takes one half of every breath and allows it to collect in a place that even I know nothing about. It festers there, growing without notice. Shadowing every hope, every thought, smothering every possibility for inspiration. Until it's large enough to bare itself. When released it soars, creating a wind felt through blood and tissue, down to the very marrow of every bone. Its ugliness is as pure as the thoughts of a child and even then it remains silent. More powerful than even the greatest of empires. Many phrases describe this and it has many names; the lack of thought, the judgement of others, fascist regimes, ceasing to care, maybe it is hell or just vast evil, perhaps Mephistopheles, I do not know. It is the seed of the apocalypse and the beginning of the end...its name is ignorance.

Scott K. Russell

Never Meant

My wishes are that I could forget
Some horrid memories that have been set
Upon my mind, upon my time, in the past,
Which linger and linger and always last!!
My heart cries out - the pain runs deep
But most of all my sorrow seeps
Deeper and deeper into my soul
Stop these thoughts before death takes its toll.
My future is here: Some say it's been blessed
With children, with love and happiness.
Beneath all this, my cries are to you.
Please help me forget why my past was so blue.
The lessons presented and learned before
Have troubled me so, they touched my innercore.
My struggles and struggles are to forget the dark times.
My desires, to trust life again, to move down the lines.
Just help me forget: Don't hand me false hopes,
Don't judge me or control me or give me the ropes.
Bring me love and happiness; and to be content
Help me to forget what was really never meant!

Betty Yount-Perry

Untitled

Tears are not going to bring him back,
  so please don't cry.
I understand that it is hard to smile,
  but we all have to try.
That is what he would want to see.
Just let him know he's in your heart,
  and will always be.
Memories of him will always be here,
  his body is gone, but his soul is near.
His long stressful days are over with and done
He was a husband, father, brother, uncle,
  a friend and a son.
So when you cry over him day or night,
  just remember he is alright,
And please wipe away those tears.
To realize he is now away from all his fears.

Kelley J. Flavin

Wishes

I'm wishing you happiness and joy that
you must wish for, too,
With happiness and joy you'll succeed in
everything you do.
People who bring joy to you in many big
and small ways.
Keep pride in being who you are
Today, Tomorrow, Always.
May all dreams you have today be reality
tomorrow.
That you'll face each day and goal never
knowing any sorrow;
Best wishes on reaching out to become
the best at what you do.
Accepting every challenge to make your
dreams come true!

David Norris

Eternity

How cold it is
on this lonely winter night.
Me, myself is alone
fearfully afraid in fright.
Eternity is to Eternity
like darkness is to death.
This cold winter wind
just took away my breath.
I gasp and I struggle through all this snow
crawling and searching for a warm place to go.
Darkness has reached my last destination
as I pray and pray for my only temptation.

Stacy N. Coleman

The Dandelion

Crowding sterility out of the green expanse
A vibrant yellow fills my nose with
A pleasant sound,
And I marvel.

An under appreciated, misunderstood beauty
Resilient but gentle stands proudly,
Resolutely, though deemed a nuisance
In Spring.

The same who in Fall sends a message
Spread by wish seeds,
A message of defiant hope sent on the wind
Of a close-eyed kiss.

Sarah Michelle Poletti

Memories Of Dad

It was a cold winter day the
29th of December a day in my
heart that I'll always remember
A call came to my home to
tell me that my dad was gone
I brushed back a tear and hung
up the phone just at that moment
I felt so alone. But God gently spoke
do not fear for you're not alone
my child I'm here. Over a year
has gone by since that dreary
day when God he called my dad
away. Although were not together on earth
anymore someday in heaven our
spirits will soar. He was a great
man while on this Earth he trod
but now he's in heaven at peace
with God.
   Sharon Muncy

Transition- Excerpt From Six
Dedicated to the Memory of Kahlil Gabron, Teacher and Friend

After an age of vast searching
   realized in naught, but a twinkling
did I catch, even then for the barest of moments,
a clear illumination of my heart song
reflected from the depth's of eyes baring
   moments before belonging to mine enemy;
In that fractured second, he struck me down
   with furious vengeance, as of one betrayed
      yet even still I lived, thought my soul, for a time
         wounded East with a camel
and upon waking found the spoor of my ethereal companion
   heaped on my head and nothing more
While profound, as this revelation was,
   I had a matter of being open to
      choice.
   Wyvren Dean

Dream Whispers

Sleepy eyes close for the night
Anticipating peaceful flight
Menacing shadows suddenly appear
Forming terror, faces real
Bring forth deep, inner reserve
Dormant dragons ready to serve
Unrecognition the ultimate fall
Of never knowing the universal law
That conquers, slays unmentionable dares
Brought forth from a haunting nightmare
Still lingering in the bright of day
Where dreams really have no say
To frighten and torment those who recur
Bits and pieces of an eerie slumber
Learn to understand the shifting secrets
That reveal themselves to those who will seek it
The inner voice that is trying to say
Take back your life, be stronger today
When subconscious speaks, be good listeners
And dare to believe in subtle dream whispers
   Stephanie J. Routte

Autumn Society

Wind whispered through the towering trees
   as the clouds cried ...
for the falling die-ing leaves!
   Henry L. Hollingsworth

Love Yourself And You Will Never Be Alone

Our journey in life begins deep inside,
show your true feelings, don't let them hide.

Begin by loving yourself and your love for others will flow,
just then you'll notice your strength start to grow.

You won't be afraid when you're at peace within,
all your walls will come down and you'll know you can win!

Self-love brings about a positive change,
you won't fell alone, you'll start to feel strange.

Deep within you will discover a white light,
peace and tranquillity will guide you through your darkest night.

Love yourself, for there is no greater feeling,
the rewards will be rich, all your wounds will start healing.

You will never be alone as long as your spirit is alive,
take one day at a time and you will survive!
   Jodi Cross

Quite Honestly

For centuries it seemed I was lost in those turbid eyes
I might have and could have always been
quite forcibly and quite honestly
Near to him felt his heartbeat
like it was upon my skin. The blood
in my veins danced to its rhythm
Always is he drawing me from the truth
and the world and the karma of it all
only as if the wind knew, as close to me as it was
I could weep a thousand words because the sight of him
bites into me like a shovel into the soft earth
Dream of songs to brush of the dirt
...to send me into oblivion
as it has always been my only sanctuary from him
   Amy Price

Untitled

You have the power of two men
You know you're bound for greatness, only you don't know when
Living two lives simultaneously you must choose
One seems to be success, the other pure happiness, you can't lose
You need to get ahead of your dreams and go for your goals
The simple taste of victory can give you infinite souls
Find it in yourself to put fourth the face value of your life
Expressing your feelings to others about having a wife
Be like the rest and go for both without looking back
Plan your moves carefully then go for the attack
Let your greatest ambitions soar so they can grow
When you're on top of the world, the wind will blow
Persistance is the key made of gold
In the making of something greater, you will break the mold
   Mitch Keller

Little Child

My little child, where do I start
   It all began with a zing to my heart.
How was I to know, from that point on
   My life forever was to be a "mom."
The first time I held you and looked at your face
   I was full of content and I loved my place
You were precious and tender and oh so small
   You are my child, life's greatest gift of all
As you grew my little one, so did your love
   I thank you and the good Lord above
Thank you for all the joy and happiness
you have brought to me
   My little child you will always be
   I love you, Love Mom
   Sheila Griego

"My Life Is The Sea, The Sea Is Me"

As I stand and look at the sea
I reflect on my life
Doing a day's work
Pulling nets, baiting lines, setting lobster pots
Going through the roughest seas
To survive for my family and me
My life is the sea, the sea is me
To all who lost their lives to the beast
To all who survived the beast's bite
We all know that there will be another day, and another fight
My life is the sea, the sea is me
To the people who think that home is on the sea
Or that home is on the land
Either way people sure miss the sea or the land
But when I die, where is my real home?
My life is the sea, the sea is me
  Scott F. Paladino

To My Mom

As I grow up, I see that we drift apart
No more hugs or kisses goodbye
or I Love You's as we leave for the day
coming home and saying hello, how was your day
Then leaving with friends
we don't even think twice
You just think of when I was young and how my face
would light up when you walked through the door
and giving you a big hug and kiss
before you even got a chance to take off your jacket
how you hated it but now you miss
You were always there for me when I needed you the most
We fought and things were said that neither of us meant.
But in the end I still love you
and love is forever
For you are my mom, the most sacred thing on the planet is your love.
  Kevin Gray

My World Is Mine

At dawn
The window opens on the deep quietude of
My world,
Smaller yet than yesterday but still
My world;
When sunset comes
What remains today of the full life
I once knew?
Children at play,
Friends coming by to pass the time of day,
Bringing bits of news, breaking up
A now endless of seconds, minutes hours.
But, today, between the dawn and sunset,
That time is mine to cherish, savor and enjoy;
For my world now is mine alone
From dawn to dusk;
From dusk to dawn
To do with as I will.
  Phyllis I. Dalton

Retirement

An ending—a door—opportunity—
  relaxation—catching up—rest and
  chores—travel—concerns

Boredom—in a rut—dissatisfaction—low
  energy—no meaning—no value—internal
  strife—life is tiresome

Plans—what's next?—looking—changing—
  dreaming—challenge—small steps—
  giant steps—the world!
  Nancy M. Lindsay

The Unborn Star

The unborn star
Who is the unborn star.
Is it the man who has never worn a crown.
Is it the man who has never recorded a sound.
Is it the young girl, everyone says is so cute and talented.
Or is it the women, who doesn't know where to start.
But in her heart, she has always known she is star.
Are they the lonely people, who no one understands.
Or the people never taken seriously.
They are the people who feel each tear, an actor cries.
Chills run up and down their spines.
With each word, with each sentence, with every glance.
With each kiss.
Though many are born, and many are scorned.
Few shall know the hurt, or feel the tear; rolling down the face.
But only felt in the heart and soul of the unborn star.
  Marilyn M. Cruz de Guy

I Don't Want To Be Cinderella

If I could talk to you
If you could only know
The pain I've lived with all my life
The pain that seems to grow

Was I that big a failure
as daughter or as friend
How do I earn a place within
Your heart won't even bend

You tell me often that you love me
We share a laugh and tears
But on the outside of your warmth
Is where I've spent my years

My birthday shared with your paid guests
No diamonds of yours on my hand
No trips with me for time alone
No boats stayed parked on land

I may not need you as the others
It's not the things I envy
But if your gifts equal your love
Then where does that leave me
  Lory Warren

On A Beautiful Autumn Morn

On a beautiful autumn morn
I saw a baby bird being born
It was born in a golden crop of corn
Its egg was hatched and torn
And every day birds blow their horns
to remind them of the baby bird being born
On a beautiful autumn morn

On a beautiful autumn morn
A wonderful cotton dress is worn
Because birds feel they are forlorn
as if their soul had been pricked by a thorn
Birds feel they have to kick and scorn
Because they think there is no hope of life being born
On a beautiful autumn morn

But on this beautiful autumn morn
When the cotton dress is worn
Make sure you blow your horns
Because inside the birds, something new is born
It's like receiving a new brass horn
On a beautiful autumn morn
  Melissa June Gifford

Reflections

And are sisters just reflections of their
   Parents' selves, or each one of the other?
My hair is dark and eyes are green; she is fair.
   Her hair is light and eyes are blue; furthermore,
Her nature seems so bright while mine is dark.
   If we mirror one another, it must
Surely be to show the other what might
   Have been; some retrospect of life and love.
Almost a mirror image, my sister stands
   Before me smiling, reaching out with love
She pulls me through the mirror with soft hands
   And standing side by side reflect on life.
Each stronger for the other; able and bright
   Gifted with love and patience, graced with light.

Sandra Hudgins

Midnight Shadow

Amber glow from the fire
While black hearts ache at the funeral pyre
Misty wind blows through the air
Let the child say a prayer
A bloody rose may kiss thy soul, just like sunshine on a grassy knoll
Deep within the depths of our pain lies the weeping child again and
   again
Crystal thought clear as day
Let the child pray
Walk into hell without a glance back
Like a carnival monster with a child in a gunny sack
Devil's dance before your sight, to try to dim your soul's light
Listen to the crow sing the song of what we do right and what we
   do wrong
Mock the fallen angel without a fear
Put your ear to a grave, what do you hear?
Spent my life locked up in a cage where I nursed and fed my rage
To let it out with a pen like a sage where it flows like blood onto
   the page
What do the angels see from above?
A sight filled with hatred rather than love
Like a demon in business with a soul to sell
The view from heaven must look like hell.

Brandon Like

Let It Go

I watched it daily, some called it "The Trial of The Century"
I missed my Soaps, Luncheon dates, Meetings and lots of Shopping
sprees

It was a Who Done It, another sad mystery
The children sleeping upstairs that's what convinced me, that it
surely was not he

Each evening on TV a lot of careers got a boost or start
Picking the daily court proceedings apart

I wondered did all of the Analysts watch as I did
or did they rely on the sound bites, God forbid

Books, Talk Shows, Ratings, for many it was beneficial
But boy, oh boy shamefully superficial

Well the Trial is over now, the verdict was Not Guilty

Talk Show Hosts, Journalists, Pundits, haven't you heard you can
stop the illusions
Someone please tell them that the trial has reached a conclusion!

Ann Allen Urban

True Love

From the depths of the ocean it rises, and
lies softly upon the shore.
It glistens on the water to live forever more.

Tis a star that falls from heavens sky,
casting its last glean of light.
Grasping wishes of a heart, to keep its soul
abright.

Guarded on an eagles wing as it soars
the mountain high.
Only the strong will journey through
his majestic sky.

Brilliant as the colors of heavens who join
and come together as one.
True love is rainbow, that can never be
undone.

Steadfast I hold to my true love, for
he is my gleam of light.
For him I'll journey the realm of storms.
Till a rainbow is in sight.

Lisa Clarke

The Foundation

I see a well structured house in the distance.
As I get closer I can tell its foundation is solid.
I walk in and look around,
The walls in each room are strongly made.
I walk upstairs in the bedrooms, they seem warm and gentle.
I can feel a peace like no other around me as I walk through each
   room.
For this house is a house of God
But you cannot tell from the outside until you look in.
The deeper you look the more peace and love you will find.
For this does not need be a house,
But each person's perspective on themselves.
Continue to look in deep and you shall find our Lord ready to give
   you
A solid foundation on which to live,
Also safe walls on which to protect you, and the warmest, gentlest
rooms on which to give you his love.

Mary Beth Deery

What Are We Here For

I've often wondered why I'm here,
The purpose of my life.
I somehow feel there's more to it,
Than being a Mom and Wife.
Now that's a very important task,
One that I dearly love.
But, is that all that were here for,
Or should I dare to ask?
Our obligations never cease.
We cook, we clean, we wash, we sew,
It's true we aim to please.
But is that all; is there no more,
To what us women are put here for?
If it's true, don't let us know!
But tell those men instead,
To LOVE their Mom with all their hearts,
And also the Woman they Wed.

Elizabeth J. Dickens Thompson

The Hill

I sit below the hill,
Watching shadows play upon the hill.
Rays of silver figures,
Misty, wet and cold,
Dancing, laughing and crying upon the hill,
Watching me below the hill.

Tall trees towering high above the hill:
Roughhewn bark of rust and moss of mold,
Pins of needle green erect,
Blood of honey sap,
Smell of tangy poison from the trees above the hill.

Fallen, tender grass of green,
Teardrops on their faces,
Gazing up toward the sky,
Always, always wondering why.

Inky black sky; silver eyes of shark,
Piercing the very soul of the hill,
Glaring
  Down
    Down upon me
      Below the hill.
    Carmen Casanova

The Window

The scene outside my window repeats itself
In different patterns
The strange trees highlighted by a distant sun
Strange to think
My same sun
Brothers to warm this secluded little continent
And my same sky
Watches even this place too
It's foreign life
Normal on earth
Strange to me
We only know such a small part of this planet
Only he stars know all there is to see
    Amy Colla

Rewards

The stout, hard working man stood on the slightly
raised ground, overlooking his pride and joy,
while the sun slowly crept below the horizon.
His rigorous day was over, and silence was overtaking
his farm. As he watched the fiery sun plunge
below the horizon, he thinks back to the effort
he puts into his day, and how there are no
obvious rewards of his labor.
But, he knows in his heart that there are
deeper rewards; because he knows he is doing
what he loves most.
    Burton W. Post

No Fourth Wall

I'd like a room with no fourth wall
Seldom too big and never too small.

To read a book or sing a song
Imagination to come along.

I'd make my way from end to end
Stopping to work, or chat with a friend.

To rise in the morning and sleep with the eve
Having nothing in mind, but whatever I please.

Having a guest could be quite a chore,
How could they enter, without any door?
    Laurie B. Hayes

Witness

If you hold still, you can be a witness to this enveloping death.
I must take the gun and hold it close to my crazed little mind.
No, the knife is too sharp,
  too tempting to swim in, not mourn for the crimson rivers that flow
    from my veins.
I know that somewhere there is a gun
with my name etched upon it in tiny golden letters, inviting.
This hunger for death is inherent; we all fear what we want the most.
I think I'm starving...
Are you coming along for the ride?
Be wary; no roller coaster ever tasted like this.
I am afraid that this blanket I am hiding under is suffocating me;
I have made no attempt to pull it off.
I want you to be there when I go to the velvet fields where,
when I fall, tender head, tender little rotting mind will not feel the
  pain of the crash.
Pack your silver bag with tiny corrupted trinkets,
reminders of the mortal world.
Are you ready?
It is time for me to unclasp my chains; go forth.
Hold my hand tightly as I leave you.
    Alyssa Russo

My Highland Home

I dreamt last night of fen and moor,
Of thistled down and heathered hill,
Of fog enshrouded highland lochs
Where ancient beast breed still,
Of weathered cliffs and rock strewn shores,
Of forest, sombre green,
Beyond the threshold of the
Highland home I've never seen.

I saw the sheep and cattle
Led down winding country lanes
And claymores drawn for battle,
Sunny dells and gentle rains.
Far off I heard staccato drums
And mournful pipes which sing
Of half remembered highland homes
Which stand in Scottish dreams.
    Mark F. Owens

The Heart Speaks

A man does not
Need freedom until he sees it.
Dreams have the best sight in existence.
These eyes can see through any wall
No matter how thick.
Captors shut their prisoner's eyes
But who can shut the mouth of the heart?

The heart speaks in only one language:
It is the dream,
Reaching out to our otherwise deaf
Ears telling them things only
The soul knows.

Dreams are our silent transport
To the gates of worlds that
Our conscience could never open,
Showing us experiences that
Make us both joyous and frightened.

On the whole we would be nothing more
Than sand on the beach without dreams.
    Tess Tubbs

Reflection In The Pond

The thunder crashed and my dreams it dashes.
I awaken and rise from my bed as dark clouds roll overhead.
On such a day so dank, dark, and dreary,
I step out into the rain while the weary.

I walk through the forest as the rain pours down,
the light of my soul extinguished when suddenly I found,
in a clearing a pond with rays of sun glistening,
as I lay by the pond and the waves I am listening.

A gentle breeze caresses the water and I see,
in the still blue water a reflection so serene.
A vision of beauty, mind, body, and soul,
eyes of sky blue, auburn hair of gold, and skin of a deer foal.

She smiles so sweetly and to the water beckons me in,
for in the circle of life we all are but kin.
I step into the water, so calm, cool and blue,
to my Little White Dove and adventures new.

The sunshine fades and the day turns to grey.
It's down, down, down, to a bright new day.
Through eternity we will wander into a new life,
where there is so pain, no pain, suffering or strife.
Richard D. Blake

Untitled

Frigid air flowing above a warm tropic tide.
Dust moat floating free on a vagrant breeze,
wafting upward over tropic seas.
Droplet forming 'round condensation nuclei with
independent identity.
Rising upward on columnar air.
Other droplets collide, first one, then two, then three.
Gone forever is self identity.
Higher, higher!
Faster still, striking others, gaining energy.
Clouds form joining forces.
Now falling, now rising, faster still...wind, rain and hail.
Positive, negative, electricities flash.
Clouds ripped asunder shout their protest in claps of thunder.
Deluges fall, soaking a grateful earth.
Saturated rivulets forever wind
their way toward waiting seas
in search of a dust moat
seeking identity
on a vagrant breeze.
John J. Humphrey

My Renaissance Song

Let us dance by the river and the fountain on the green;
By the banks of the Tennessee, we gather to hear;
The songs of the troubadours of yesteryear
Oh! Bring back the magic like the druids in the spring;
And let us have new life again;

On the court of regal splendor, the Lords and ladies behold;
They belly dancers, jugglers and poets of old;
And the women will no more be prisoners inside their wall,
Because their knight in shinning armor will surely fall;
So, now, all my children; Jonathan and Ashley, Melissa and James;
play in the gardens and dance in the lanes!
Joice Royal

Only You

Joey, only you can bring the happiness that adds a touch of spring to any season Joey, and to any little thing. Joey, only you can bring the sunshine to my heart when clouds are gray, and give a special feeling to that most uncertain day. And Joey, that's the reason my dreams have all come true. My heart has been the happiest loving only you.
Dawn E. Kakley

You Became

You became the light of my life
You became my days and night
You became my joy and sorrow
You became my gift for tomorrow
But nature has come and taken you away
And now I'll have no brighter days
To a better place you have gone
From up above will you sing me a song
To ease my pain and my sorrow
To bring me back a brighter tomorrow
In my heart you will always be
The only one that was made for me
When I need a friend, or you will I call
For you are, my true friend, friend in all
So keep watching me from up above
Because all for you there's nothing but love
Michelle McCormick

Near Tears

We have come, my love, to a crossroads.
There will soon be choices to make.
Whichever path we choose to follow
leaves another we must forsake.

From the first time my eyes beheld you,
I knew beyond any a doubt
you were the one of my hopes and dreams.
The warmth I could not live without.

Through your eyes, I've seen the honesty
from friendship plentiful and deep.
Through your smile, I've felt the happiness
from a heart I so hope to keep.

But rare are the days we're together,
as too far we remain apart.
So to you I send on the breezes
my love, my life and my heart.

You must now follow where e'er love leads,
as light follows the dawning day.
I pray you'll forever remember
our memories along your way.
Dean L. Wooldridge

Ode From Mother To Daughter

On Her Approaching Wedding
My darling, daughter dear,
Since your birth I have had no fear;
I knew that you would grow up to understand,
That life is not always easy in this land.

As a pretty, little tiny tot,
Oh, how sometimes you did plot;
To get what you wanted in any way,
But you learned that this did not always pay.

With love and patience, I guided you,
To accept life and not get blue;
Sometimes there were many nays,
But you adjusted through the days.

Soon you will put on your wedding ring,
I know I'll have to cut the apron string;
But even birds from the nest must fly,
So, it is for your happiness that I will cry.

Go with your husband and forever be true;
I realize I am not really losing you;
I am just gaining a wonderful son,
Remember, I will love you both as one.
Dorothy D. Morrow

Hope

She quietly walked into my life; rarely speaking, only sometimes
    smiling.
Her eyes were mysteriously empty; her gaze was blank.
Such a young life, terrorized by unspeakable violence.
A mother and a father - meant to protect...
    Instead, the source of great pain.
One wielded, the other stood by.
Now, neither parent remained in her world.
Others reached out - relatives, teachers and neighbors - to the
    distanced corners of her soul...
    Offering understanding, acceptance and love.
Slowly....very slowly......life began to return to her eyes.
She smiled more; laughed more; cried more.
She had turned a corner; she had begun a journey along a new path -
A path towards light and life...freedom for her soul.
My heart joyously leaped as she embarked on a journey towards a
    better life.
My heart also ached....
Her path had been hard, but hard it would continue to be.
I will never forget that young girl...
Her strength was remarkable - her courage great...
she will prevail. She renewed hope in me...
And, for that, I will be forever thankful.

    Stacy Thacker

Come At Least To My Dreams

Come at least to my dreams, love,
If we can not meet when I am awake.
Far and near searched I have,
No sight of you is my heartache.

I have behaved and I have done my best,
I have even vowed to wait for you only;
Yet my youth will stay forever not,
It pains my heart to see it fade barrenly.

Come dance with me, after the night falls,
No more will life be an empty dream;
'Cause when I hold you in my arms,
The holder of the world I shall become.

Let me hold you longer in the moonlight,
Let me taste more of your sweet breath;
For when the dawn comes and the dreams fleet,
Only the memory of your smiles I'll be left with.

    David S. Chong

The Dying Society

    As I walk down and dark empty road I can smell the
death of a society. I see a man on the corner drowning in
his own blood, he was shot and left to die as his body lays
in the mud.
    In the dark shadows of a run down building I can see a
silhouette of a man, not knowing what type. Then I see a
bright yellow flame inhaled into a pipe, the man blows out
the dark smoke of death. He goes to grab his chest and
struggles for his last breath, then his hands fall to his
side and his body lays down to rest.
    I see a young child playing in the street and then I
hear his mother calling. Gun shoots ring out from a house
I turn to see the young child has fallen. I go over to see
if the child is ok, there is a puddle of blood by his head,
it's just another innocent life wasted away.
    I begin to walk up the street and see a man with
clothes that look like a bunched up rag. He asks for some
spare change while he sucks on a bottle that is wrapped in a bag.
I walked pass paying no attention, he stops me to ask me a
question, "Did you know that our society is dying?

    William S. Heron Sr.

My Kauai

Air sweetly caressing, cooling, lovingly
Holding you gently
With the tenderness of a lover.

Palm trees gracefully aspiring, swaying high
into the clouds that slowly drift by
Soothing the bruised spirit.

Multiple shades of green strewn on
hills and valleys pleasantly unfolding with splashes
of quiet morning glory blue, fragrant yellow and
fierce passionate crimson — a feast of visioness.

Sounds of ocean rhythm touching the shore with strength
and depth adding richness and substance to the soft
subtle melodies of the winged and hidden creatures.

Long curving beaches of soft sand and penetrating heat
on tired bodies yearning for peace and quietness of soul.

How I love these moments in this place —
To rest my eyes on the beauty of it all and feel the
wonder and connection with a greater beingness

    Melody Kelley

Serendipity

The weak sun beat down upon a park
bereft of laughter, smiles, and noisy children.
Only the cooing of a sole, famished pigeon
belied the message of taciturn winter's advent.
Yet, a young child sat down in the park's sandbox
to dig a tunnel to China.
The sky had pelted semi-frozen meteorites upon the coarse sand,
which collated into chilly sand balls.
Her fingers grew numb; she wanted to go home,
but she decided to dig five minutes more.
Her cheeks had just become ripe cherries,
and her ears had just become icicles attached to her head,
when the skin of her palm hit a rough, parallel surface.
Was it part of the Great Wall?
With failure weighing down her heart,
she thrust her nearly paralyzed hand into the abyss once more.
Unexpectedly, her forefinger felt a slick, smooth object.
In daylight, the face of George Washington appeared upon it.
She left the motionless park, by the way of Montague Street,
heading for the closest candy store.

    Ileana Ciobanu

Cows In Queue

Veiled spawn of dawn, dim mist of morn,
Wet wisping clouds, limp fields of corn,
Through bleary fog, on grassy dew,
I saw them there, the cows in queue—
slow-lining forward, drudgery.
Perhaps just dull complacency.
Greasy drops fell from the gray
Chasing all the gnats away.
Though they mulled on soft green chew,
They stayed in form, the cows in queue.
Their plastic eyes had glanced at me
With guarded curiosity.
A hollow thud, a sterling glint,
Into the slaughterhouse they went.

    E. Kevin Kreps

The King

The lion stands atop the mountain
Tall, Mighty, Proud
He regards his kingdom carefully,
amber golden eyes filled with wisdom.
Tall and mighty he walks, he circles his palace
Like lighting he jumps to the next mountain top
With a spirit of electricity he flies and lands lightly,
Lightly in the deep green valley below
The moss soft beneath his paws
Animals look through dark eyes, eyes filled with respect
The lion continues to run
His mane becoming one with the golden sun
Running again to the next mountain top
Tall, Mighty, Proud
The King

Jocelyn Olick

Pine Tree

I stood at the old pine tree,
And watched the World go by,
I talked to the old pine tree,
In hopes it would be my friend,
I cried at the old pine tree,
And no one would listen,
I walked to the old pine tree,
In faiths my savior would be there,
I took a rope to the old pine tree,
And I tied it to the branch,
I watched the rope swing on the old pine tree,
I stuck my head in the noose,
And I jumped from the old pine tree.

Niki Lightcap

Memorial Day

On memorial day, our respects we do pay
For our soldiers, in their grave,
Who have fought, for their country, ever so brave!
These soldiers fought with guns,
Always had the enemy, on the run!
On this day of memory:
Soldiers are still fighting, the enemy,
All the world is fighting, for land control,
Which will be won, by our patrol.
Some of our soldiers, are now killed,
And their fighting, is now stilled!
Soldiers are prisoners, behind enemy bars,
While on yonder hill, their country flag is full or stars.
Our soldiers, who death, have meant,
Are now buried, in six foot depth,
Where their souls, shall be kept.
They fight in winter, summer, spring and fall,
Not just one, but them all.
God bless these soldiers, dead or a live,
Before and after our goal, they revive.

Virginia Hunsinger

To Wound A Man's Spirit

To wound a man's spirit is a terrible thing
For there is pain and anger in this.
So when your time comes around,
You surely won't be missed.

But the man filled with hope,
Shall recover from his pain
Because his heart is like the soil,
And his tears are like the rain.

Clifton Franklin

A Better Place

How lonely she sits there by the still water
Feeling a pain only she can feel;
Telling herself over and over again,
"This is not Happening! This is not Real!"

But as life spills
Through destiny's doorway;
She raises her eyes toward the sky
And wishes herself as a cloud to fly away.

Pleasant sounds of laughter and singing
Move through her mind as these weeping clouds do;
"Be not of heavy heart, but rejoice," said the voice of the Lamb,
"For there is a soul in heaven new."

Brett Hayes

Dreams

Dreams. A mystery to the dreamer itself. How? Where do they happen?
It's a mystery. Some true. Some will come true. Some funny. Sad.
Scary. Some ridiculous. Deja Vu. Has it happened to you?
Seems like a routine. Go to sleep. Dream. Wake up. Forget about it.
Some linger on to you. You could never forget. Some of people
you've never met. Fantasies. Dreaming. beyond reality. Planned?
Puzzling.
I know. Dreamer? Couldn't possibly make it up while being asleep.
Or could he? Does it seem real? Reach for heaven. Touch His face.
Kiss His hand. Wake up. Reality check. It's not real. An
unsolved mystery. Nightmare. From movies? Or from the
Nightmare himself?
 See it after you? Hungry. Waiting. Hunting you. Wake up.
Just a dream. Close your eyes. Try it again. Dream of a far, far......
 Oh no! It's after you again. Hide. Try. Try. Push it away.
Wake up. Shh! Listen. Hear the beating. Feel the chill down your
neck. Drip! drip! Sweat pours down. Trickles. Lay back down.
Motionless. Re-runs. Forget.
A test. Good versus Evil. A Dream versus a Nightmare. Determine which is which. Seem to real to happen? Seems it will
happen because it felt so real? You'll find out. What does the
night bring you?
Dreams? Fantasies? Can you determine? Only the night will tell.
Sweet Dreams!

Nicolette Weintraub

Forsaken Baker

I'm making the guilt again
preparing it like some unholy grandmother's recipe
in a wooden churn with holes and rust
and a splintering rod that pokes my hands with slivers:
"Pour the oozy soup of responsibility
that makes everything stick together
add a dash of illicit pleasures for flavoring."
My hands are raw from mixing.

"Pour the white-hot mass into a cauldron
for the final ingredient."
The yellowing liquid foams over the edges
spills onto my soon-to-be-anointed shoes.

The steamy stench delights my nose—
a tendril of desire sneaks into my pinkish brain.
The heat melds it all into a giant needy bubble
begging and ready at last
to accept my soul
for a coating of candy-apple hell.

Bryan VanDyke

My 30th Birthday

When I was 15 my spirit was free
Then I was 18 and there was knowledge in me
I started to Med School, my future in mind
Leaving the joys of boyhood behind.

I worked and studied my knowledge to gain
To become a Doctor was my greatest aim
I graduated with honors when I was 27
God surely blessed me with a gift from Heaven.

I am 30 now with a Doctor's degree
Using the talents that God has given me
Older and wiser, more serious you see
For the patients I treat depend on me.

The 30s must be the prime of my life
As I work and toil for my Baby and Wife
May I grow in wisdom as the years go by
For the weeks and months they seem to fly.

The Lord bless and keep me in His protection and Grace
Until I meet Him face to face
Welcome home, my Son, I can hear Him say
Your battles are over and this is where you stay.

F. Ruth Myles

The Mighty Men Of God

The mighty men of God full of power and might
armed with the Holy Ghost and fire
always ready to fight
enemies on the left and all on the right
what will I do?
Well!, it's time to fight
No time to run I must stand my ground
no devil in hell is going to take my crown
I have been here before maybe you can see
with the same old enemies facing me
They charged with their weapons
fears, temptations, and snare
all I can see is the enemies glare
But this time is different I have lost to much ground
I will not, I can not I refuse to turn around
so it's off to war just Jesus and me
and all I can see is victory!

Herman Edward McDonald

Mother

Day in, day out, my mother works,
Works her life away,
Just for love of her children,
Whom she loves more each day.

She works and works,
Each day and night,
Her work is never done,
Never putting up a fight to do the things she's done.

She never asks repayment,
Never asks a share
In the profits of her work,
So loving, so much care.

When her daily work is over,
She tucks her kids in bed,
And then she asks of her God,
No harm upon their heads.

Kaylie Miller

The Moth

i am the Bombyx mori,
the silk-weaving caterpillar of China's glory.
i, the ghastly and unholy plait
the purple robes of China's glory.

i am the ever-changing, i am the never-reigning, i am the
always-hidden, hidden among the floating sun and fire harlots of
the sky, consuming gray.
i fly at night, afraid of the light. i am the want-a-be butterfly,
i listen as their bells pluck the same and lonely song. i reach for nectar
but drink gall and vinegar, bitter aftertaste in my selfish mouth.

The sun is buried 'neath the fleece of clouds, the burrow i poke,
I can do something the Dancing Ones cannot, in my Cocoon, I can
spin silk, though course as rye's chaff to the touch, it is mine, and I
spin and will spin till i die, dreaming of weaving braided gold
thread and twisting the corkscrews of the Night off for the Stars to
view My Masterpiece.

i am the Bombyx mori, the silk-weaving caterpillar of China's glory.
i, the ghastly and unholy plait, the purple robes of China's glory.

Erin Gallis

"Words From The Poet's Mouth"

   Poetry is a beautiful collection of words
that can make you laugh or cry.
   It can be about a wonderful time
or about someone who will die.
   Poetry is about nature —
of the world's and of men.
   Good poetry will fill you with the desire
to read it over again.
   Poetry is about emotions
that cause feelings to rise or sink;
   But the most important aspect of it
is that it requires one to think.

Devon Amanda Rush

A Piece Of Hope

There is a small room with darkness all around.
Sunshine, happiness, and smiles are not found.
Every single corner's filled with hatred and fear.
Everyone thinks the world's end is coming near.
All four walls are holding poverty and war.
Not ever a ray of light shines through anymore.
Crime is in the air from the bottom to the top.
Murders and thefts just can't seemed to be stopped.
Suddenly, a flame from the center bursts forth.
It is a tiny candle burning for all its worth.
Even though the flame and the amount of light is small,
It signifies as hope, a piece of hope for all.

Kim Naguit

For The Poets

Time for the poetry contest again
And you all know that this sonnet should win.
The lines flow smoothly with cadence and rhyme
And alliteration in perfect time.
But there are hundreds for judges to read
With wordsmiths writing at stupendous speed.
Penning odes and ballads and epics too
Iambic pentameter and haiku.
Yet the winner is often some drivel
That causes the real poets to snivel.
Precious works from the heart are cast aside
And all hopes for recognition have died.
Who bestows these critics their credential
To quash the bards with so much potential?

John Demske

They Don't Whistle Anymore

Sultry, Manhattan days so long ago;
moist bodies glisten, dresses cling,
and sidewalks shimmer -
steamy mirages.

Raven hair sways to the rhythm of staccato
high heels. She smiles as his sensual
whistle floats over her on
soft kitten paws.

Season pass. Time holds her hand and
writes its musical score in her eyes,
lining her face, dulling the lyrics
of her being.

Skyscrapers pant in the heat. She moves easily
to his music - he, so lithe and young,
eyes of liquid fire, free of time's
unyielding grasp.

His embers sear her soul, and she moves in
rhythm's past. Is the low, sweet whistle
she hears, only the windsong
of her memory?

Elaine Lawrie

The Death In The Night

The vast night encloses the silver moon
the fog smothers the breath of the trees
the fierce tide breaks hard with cold rocks to wound
thunder pounds deadly with lightning to seize

He lays in darkness surrounded by fear
killing the spirit that wants to get near
evil rises from its grave to be found
in cracks and spaces where life is a doubt
those with no hope, the thoughtless and raged
get swallowed by this most hideous thing
loneliness, from which each victim is staged
the rape of the sinner, the pain of the sting
blackness forever, never to forgive
'tis the death of the man who never lived

Kathleen M. Coulson

A Dream

A dream is there to wish on.
Some dreams are good, some are bad.
The good ones are the best!
You can fly through the sky, in a dream.
You can be anything you want to be.
You can be anywhere.
You have a dream to wish on.

Ashley Rhodebeck

"The Sun Still Shines"

Pain and sorrow - death and despair
the agonies of life are shown everywhere.
Poverty and sickness - loneliness and grief
day end and day out no encouragement no relief.

Unemployment, teen pregnancies, suicide unchecked
single mother, single father - the world is in a wreck.
A vicious cycle round and round we go
one thing can be certain - one thing we know,
as long as the sun still shines
we still have hope.

Gloria Hunt

Lydia

Gentle lady, full of grace
heaven holds a special place...

For one who lived these words-
it's true
"Love one another as I have loved you..."

Always counting her blessings
looking forward to tomorrow
Filling hearts with joy,
overcoming life's sorrow...

A strong willed woman,
a guiding light
To follow with such a zest for life...

Never tired of doing what is right,
A true example, forever pleasing in
God's sight...

Who loved God's creatures, great and small
An angel on earth, most of all...

A woman who blessed each life she touched
Though on earth near a century,
will be missed very much...

Diana Honstein

Life

Life is precious, from the time it begins.
A gift of love that can be held in your hands
with Daddy's hard work, and Mother's frail look
you wonder how much of their life you took.

Because now they work harder to meet all your
needs. I hear Mother's prayers saying,
Dear Lord, please watch over my baby, come
day and night - it doesn't matter about us,
make sure it's all right.
With each baby born, there's less time for themselves
their hopes and their dreams go up on a shelf.
They are always giving, one way or another
but there is nothing quite like the love of
your mother - so when you're all grown up and you're feeling blue,
take a long look at your baby shoes, and you will say to
yourself these don't even look worn - then
look at a pain of your mother's because they're
all tattered and torn. Because the load was
heavy, and the miles were long, - her shoes
wore out, but her feet went on.

Tom Cook

Alternatives

Our thoughts bloom while living.
Our energy is sparkling bright.
Each day's drama directs us through
The challenge or the fight.

The struggle of sadness or joy
Is merely a choice to get right.
If we gaze too long at darkness
We lose the fullness of light.

Then live and learn through sorrow, to
Adapt beyond each plight.
For if our plans have failed us another
Choice is right.

With wings of hope we are lifted so
We can see with clearer sight.
That endless springs are blooming and ours
When our thinking is right.

Richard B. Johnson

Message Of Peace

My mind's full of wishes and dreams:
I am quiet, but it shouts and screams...

What is the existence-
A universe with stars, land, oceans, rivers and streams?

What is the meaning of life-
Is it reality or just a dream?

I don't know what I should believe-
evolution or the story of Adam and Eve.

If the story of Adam and Eve is right,
the human race should be either black or white.

When one story in the holy books is incorrect,
Many others stories fall in doubt and defect.

It is a big question-who we are,
and from whence we came.

And a bigger question: Where are we going
and what is the name of the game.

Since all myths are illusion mistakes;
For the sake of humanity and for God's sake,
Let us all be one and work for world peace,
Let us give up our stupid pride and prejudice.
Reza Soltani

God's Finale

In the coarse of my existence
I have never seen so much hate
The stars are blacker and the moon is fading
I see there is nothing I can do
All I can do is subject myself to watch
I don't remember what the world was like before
I want the children to live again, laugh again
No one see's what they are doing
He has always taken control
But it's gotten out of hand
All I can do is comfort Him
He watches His world, His creation, fade
I see Him cry sometimes
The Angels weep with Him
He knows the end is soon
That when people stop caring
When it's all over, thy kingdom come
He will be done
Here on earth as it is in heaven
Melissa Zurcher

Deadbeat Daughter

Put a pie in the window
And she comes runnin' for miles
Put a roast on the table
She'll sit down for awhile
There's biscuits in the oven it's plains to see
She's deadbeat daughter her husbands name is lee

Now that girl she works in a grocery store
Stockin' shelves sweepin' and mopin' floors
Now she threw here poor old grandma into the street
She's deadbeat daughter her husbands name is Lee

Now old lee he works for a plant
He gets all the rubbers that he can have
Now deadbeat daughter she damn well likes that
Because half the time she's flat down on her back

Now deadbeat daughter her brain is dense
She's real ignorant and she doesn't have sense
Deadbeat daughter she's as dumb as can be
It's a miracle and a wonder that she doesn't have fleas!
Steven F. Pourner

My Ghetto

In my life I have seen peace, in my life I have seen war.
People have been nice to me, while others tear down your door.
Things are kind of funny in life, and other times quite sad.
The ones that make you the happiest, are also the ones who make
  you mad
Growing up is hard today, to put it in perspective.
What to be? And who to be? Is every ones objective.
Look around at all the hate that passes around the globe.
Forget about the melting pot, racism turned off the stove.
In school we're taught to love each other, that is what I learned.
But on the street where no one cares, you'll find that you'll get burned.
Doing drugs or doing crime, to me it's all the same.
Whether you know it or not, you're playing the devil's game.
Folks don't know how to read or write, and frankly don't even care
You smile, laugh, and talk a lot, but can you count bus fare?
Women are having babies before they can even cook.
At twenty-five you'll realize, your youth that baby took.
Aids is on the hunt and your age it doesn't mind.
If you do drugs or sleep around, aids is all you'll find.
This is what my ghettos made of drunks and welfare cases.
In my ghetto nothing changes, just a few new faces.
William Gonzalez

A Lonely Man Wanders The Street His Story Untold

A lonely man wanders the street his story untold: In his mind going back a few years. He is seen a young and innocent man. His sky blue eyes sparkling with the magic of one who is about to make his fortune. A determined look set in his face and a wild dream in his heart, he sets on his way.

Faces long forgotten and hopes crushed long ago roam his head. He settles on an image of the same young man the sparkle is gone with hard work and his mind not so innocent with greed and the promise of a love that is not there to fill his empty heart.

Again an image of appears of a man not quite as defined and humble as the last. His eyes dull and dead. His face mean and ugly. His once gentle hands now rough and covered with blood. Not blood as red as man's but blood black as guilt.

Older yet we see him having realized the death he bears. His heart is filled with guilt and his once beautiful blue eyes filled with shame. Sorrow is set in his face now and forevermore. He enters a room of cold faces, ones he once loved. The girl he was to marry, his children and friends now gone. Only the cold hard faces of enemies remain. They turn away from him with disgust.

We see him slowly turn and leave with a heavy heart. So I a lonely man wander the street, we share a common guilt. This man's name and mine are one in the same, for we are one and the same.
Kristen Kartchner

Release

Some things are best let go after a while:
A grown-up child,
An injured animal, sheltered while it's healed,
Grief over a loved one gone on ahead,
Unfulfilled dreams,
Unanswered prayers (which God may be answering
In ways we know not of),
Lost love, no matter what the reason.

Let go, and cherish the memories,
Bright threads through life's fabric.

Life goes on, life changes; God is constant;
And God can take our hopes and dreams,
Our memories and heartaches
And turn them into a new Way:
Life indestructible, strong, sure,
Immeasurably peaceful and satisfying.
Elaine W. Miller

Riches

Folks often ask what God has given to me?
Why, He's given me eyes so that I might see
The beauties all around this land,
and oh; I think it's simply grand.
He's given me ears so that I might hear
voices of those I love so dear:
Sound of birds, on the wing, and the beautiful melodies they sing.
Then He's given me a mind so I can choose the way
I want to live from day to day.
I can choose the one way and walk with Him, or choose the other,
   the way of sin.
"Then He promises me a home in the sky where I shall never never
   die."
So although my riches you may not see, God has been real good to me,
He's given me riches that could never be measured with silver, or
   gold.
I am rich indeed I have (wealth and riches) untold...

Marie Keenan Swartz

"Memories Of Dad"

It is getting along toward evening, and the crickets are beginning
   to sing.
The neighbors have been clearing "New Ground," for the crops
   they'll plant in the spring.
The dusk of evening envelopes the mountains, the animals prepare
   for the long night.
A big orange moon climbs over the ridge tops. The valley is bathed
   in soft light.
In the ponds the frogs sing love songs, the turtles hide deep in
   their brook.
The sage fields move restless in the moonlight. A baby owl takes
   his first look!
Fireflies, tiny flashbulbs bring dots of light to the glen.
A 'possum chews on a saw briar, and offers the world a crooked grin.
Night wraps around like a blanket, and the dew feels like a soft tear.
Far away in the valley of deep shadows, there's someone, I wish
   could be here.
An old dog bays off in the valley and the sound leaves me so lonely
   I groan.
Like a lifetime that's been lived and is over, It's time I moved
   closer home.
Together we use to walk in these valleys, the hills would sing out -
   never sad.
The wind would softly caress us, just me, my old dog, and My Dad!

Bobby J. Combs

Crashing Reality

Moving in and out of those dark corners
I see things I never have before
And those lights get brighter and brighter
But we're not too concerned tonight
Our love will never be understood
Others tell stories but ours are aaalll true
I'm having doubts - 'cos living with you could prove scary
No time to think, mental people stop me for one
Reason or another
But we all want the same
How good we are for each other could never be known by them
Someday soon I will have to tell my mother about those
Walls closing in
This town is depressing me again - I have to get out
Somehow today
Twisted laughter still echoes over and over in my head
But there's nothing to do
Summer is coming and that's when all my fairies come
Out to play
Who knows sickness in a world just like this

Nicole Leary

Second Chance

In the place where I am now,
   I think of when and why and how.

I think of all the damage done,
   lying and stealing and pointing guns.

My family and friends that have always cared,
   I used and mistreated beyond repair.

I sit alone within these walls and think,
   and think of what went wrong.

There's no excuse for these faults of mine,
   so now I'm in here doing my time.

Words can't express how glad I am
   to know my health and family again.

I am grateful for this new beginning
   to live without my minds constant spinning.

What irony to say that now I'm freed—
   freed from all the drugs I used to need.

Someday I'll walk outside these walls
   and feel the happiness of my second freedom.
A freedom I failed to acknowledge
   until it was taken away.

Kenneth James Stoltzfus

The Friend You Truly Are

A friend you truly are,
Always there to hear the gripes.
Never complaining, rarely asking, seldom taking.

Caring, understanding ways are clearly see
Always there to lend a helping hand.
Giving smiles to those in need.
That is the friend you truly are.

You see in others, what is normally hard to find.
Many say you live in a dream world.
You know where you have been,
and where you want to go.
Yet, always caring, always giving.

Few friends I have made through the passing of time.
What a pleasure it is to say you are one.
Knowing you has been such a delight.
You will be treasured forever.
For true friends like you are hard to come by.
That is the friend you truly are.

Kim Zappa

Love After Death

To Jim a true and favorite bunny
   I write to you with love my honey
This life of ours we do not choose
   Hard it is when we lose
From guilt to anger, the pain is great
   Reality, dictates our fate
The love you had no one can replace
   Or love less in any case
Grow with the time that passes
   Pray and heal through the masses
You're not the same guy as before
   But the man I now adore
A single man in love again
   Should always cherish how it's been
A new someone to unfold
   Hopefully helps lessen the load
Companionship, a fresh feeling indeed
   Makes life worth living, a definite need
The future and life, I don't have a clue
   Remember only, "To thine own self be true".

Sharon M. Caruso

Mirror Maze

I started, wandering aimlessly
Drifting in circles, roaming the same paths, finding only dead ends.
I looked up to the phosphorescent moon, to inquire for guidance
It only gazed down nonchalantly, and left me all alone, lost in darkness.
I began to cry, the clouds above felt my sorrow
And sharing my pain, sprinkled soft dew drops, that tasted sweet like strawberries.
A faint melody whispered in my ears - Beethoven's Moonlight Sonata.
A Russian Blue kitty cat, seductively stared at me, with its pale sea-green eyes
Beckoning me to follow.
I saw in the distance, a flame flickering on a single candle.
These sensations subtly grew stronger
Leading me to you.
Dawn broke as the sun started to rise
My darkness disappeared, your love was my light
Leading me through the labyrinth, as you gently took my hand.
I felt a warm fluttery feeling inside
When we reached paradise at the heart of the maze.
I saw in the mirrors, so many reflections of you
And I know that represents your love
Magnified and multiplied all around me.
   Amy Chang

Life

Life is great while it's here.
Life can get confusing,
But don't live your life in fear.
Life is full of many ups and downs,
But be happy and live it good.
Life is sometimes sad but do not frown.
Life is full of regrets,
But always look toward the future not on the past.
Life might get you down sometimes but do not fret.
Life is full of accomplishments and goals,
But don't let anything stand in the way.
Be good in life, in your heart, and in your soul.
But do not be too good.
Life is great while it's here.
   Lindsey Dehl

The Thing On My Windowsill

I stare intently at the thing on my windowsill.
It sits motionless.
The sun's radiance illuminates the tiny hair-like spines.
Gently, I touch it.
It feels as fuzzy as a peach and as soft as a feather.
Its breath is inaudible.
Nonetheless, it is alive.
I put my nose to it.
A trace of dust is all I detect.
I pick up this thing and pour water over it.
As it drinks, I bring it close to my ear and listen.
A faint crackling noise, like the sound of dry leaves is all I hear.
I put the cactus plant back on my windowsill.
   Karyn Ihara

Singled Out

Hearts in my eye's could not catch your fall.
It's so sad to hang yourself standing over the wishing well.
Nobody want you to see what their running from.
Standing out-side of you, laughter is a point of view.
Can't you fell my fears, couldn't you see my tears.
All I can do is stand here next to you.
All I needed was some love and affection,
send me in the right direction.
Won't tell you when I go ..,
It's the life you lead,
when it's the life you leave.
   Gregory G. Haats

"Through A Bullet"

Screams shout from the 3:00 a.m. sky,
another soul is ready to die.
Caught in the crossfire,
it's all the same.
Just another pawn,
in this deadly game.
Lights flashing,
sirens blaring,
paramedics fighting,
to save the innocent soul.
The darkness sinks in,
they arrived too late,
the shadows take their toll.

The sun rises,
the mourners gather,
with heavy, weak hearts.
The bell declares another soul has past.
Brought into the world by God,
Swallowed by Death....

...Through a bullet.
   Jeffrey S. Sheehan

"Just The Other Day"

Never thought I'd live to be this old
the earth still turns and I'm still standing

Just the other day I sat down to take a look
   asking if and where did I go wrong
Did I forgive I never forgot

Just the other day, I though I had it tough
then I tripped over a child who hadn't eaten enough
   her skin draped over her bones
a cardboard box for a home

Just the other day I started to live
   never living up to my full potential
only worried about the things that were essential
I finally listened to what someone else had to say
it could have been a life time but it was
Just the other day
   Timothy Hesselink

River Of Life

The river flows
To where it goes
And there it leaves behind
Something to remind
   An engraved path, of aftermath
For someone else to find

   A life of precious worth
   Will leave its mark upon the earth

It will erode, a definite road
And carve a unique route
Of what life is all about.
   And left in the ground, could it be found
That your life had been poured out?

   Will the surface of the earth
   Tell the purpose of your birth?

The river bleeds, to where it leads
Into the ocean vast, while time is slipping fast
   But will you live, enough to give
An impression of your past?

   Now that you exist, how will you be missed?
   John Gregg

Untitled

Dear Grandmother:
   We are all so glad that we could have this day. To show you how much you are loved as you struggle along your way. We are here in love and admiration. We have shared and cared throughout the years without much concern about tomorrow. We wish with all our hearts that there was something we could do. But hope and love is all we have to give you at this time. The hope that our love will give you strength and courage to fight for another day or even another hour. We write this because We Love You! And want you to know the best years we have shared. Our concerns are for you tomorrows. Life may seem unfair right now. But we will always remember your strength, your courage and your love that you have given each of us as we struggle along our way.

With love,
Deborah L. Borton

Retrospect

Vision if you will...a field amidst wood...
Snow blankets all...quilting what it could.

Yonder, a lassie with mittens donned...
She comes to a stop at a frozen pond.

The child sits on snow-covered ground.
Nary a soul...for miles around.

Our maiden minds neither...the snow nor cold.
...She looks to be...about nine years old.

We observe the lass now...laced up in skates.
Over the pond... she swirls figure eights!

She moves so quietly in this winter scene...
Her feeling...her face...so serene.

Her blades cut grooves deep into ice...
Its surface is taking slice after slice!

The skin of her face feels the biting chill!
But going home is against her will!

Winter sky darkens! It darkens its shade!
Moonbeams pierce thru...To the heart of the glade!

The girl keeps dancing across cold, cold lake...
...To take leave of her sport...what will it take?

Marion Blair

Listen To The Silence

You sit alone in an empty room.
The roar of the silence surrounds and envelopes you
And the silence is complete.
But through the din a voice calls—
"My beloved child," it calls to all who will hear.
The voice is that still, small voice that cries out to your spirit.
At times you may listen.
At others you won't understand.
But still that voice calls to you in earnest.
The voice encourages and sympathizes,
Rejoices and grieves with you.
Whatever the occasion, the heart of that voice
Is right there with you.
So, keep your feet forward
And slow not your pace;
For the One who guides
Will always keep you straight.

Michelle S. DeBoer

All Alone

Falling stars upon your head
Thinking of the worlds you had read
Little whispers echo through your mind
Thoughts of those you had left all behind
Suddenly things become crystal clear
As though the existence of you were never here
You may be a memory or just a thought
All of the arguments you wanted to be fought
You pushed and tried to get me to leave
Why the answer is a thought I just can't conceive
You led me to believe that I was the one
In the end you said it was all just in fun
You wanted to leave so you could roam
So now I'm left standing here all alone

Kristine Kraslen

To My Mother On My First Mother's Day

Now that I'm finally a mother
I can finally see
The great love you have for your daughter
no matter how young she may be.
Too bad this new job has no instructions
to study and follow through,
The only example I have to follow
is the mother I've had in you.
The love you raised me with
has been the most valuable lesson of all,
and I love you most for always being there
to catch me when I fall.

Alisa Gonsalves

I Am Happy

I am happy.
Why you say because:
I have no man by my side,
I have no children in my arms,
I have no mansion, but a small cottage,
I have no money,
I haven't eaten a king's feast, but a small dish of vegetables,
I haven't any fancy new clothes, but my modest old worn ones,
I have no talents really to speak of,
I am not famous, but known only to friends and relatives.
So why am I happy?
Because I have come to know the greatest person in all the universe.
He is happy, a God, and I am happy.

Karen Alfreda Ford

Amy

Amy, when we met I knew you were the one for me from the start,
Days, weeks and months passed, then you gave me your heart.
We were so happy as we looked forward to our future together,
You are my angel and you will be with me forever.
As we sat and talked I felt your warm body next to mine,
You were so sweet, loving and kind.
I had no way of knowing God was going to call you home, There are no words to express how much I miss you now that you are gone.
I still have memories of you and me planning our wedding date,
Not knowing we were planning it too late.
I thank God for letting me have you even though it was for a short time, When I look at your picture I know you loved me and you were mine.
It was so hard Amy, my love, to say goodbye, But I will always love you until the day I die.
Then we will be together again and never have to part,
Because God planned our future from the start.

T. Ann Jones

Heaven Hears

I call The
Night and day to help me.
I call The
Now and then to guide me.
He listens.
He protects.
He directs.
He knows that someone somewhere cries for help.

So many times I have encountered
graces and blessings He bestowed.
Smiles replaced sadness.
The struggles encountered met.
And worries were painted with easiness.
It's surprising, amazing.
Emotions soar, unbelievable.

Oh The I see I feel
Let me say this,
thank you so much,
Your love, Your presence unremarkably
forever forgotten.

Carolyn P. Macabeo

"Life"

We all received the greatest gift of all
The gift is life
Thru life there is love
Thru love there is hurt
Thru hurt there is caring
Thru caring there is sorrow
Thru sorrow there is happiness
Thru happiness there is pain
Thru pain there is growing
Thru growing there is mistakes
Thru mistakes there is knowledge
Thru knowledge there is failure
Thru failure there is success
Thru success there is struggle
Thru struggle there is achievements
Thru achievements there is giving
Thru giving there is receiving
Thru receiving there is life
Thru life there is the greatest gift

Sheryl L. Goedken

Snow

The days are shorter and the cold descends, the winter time comes here
The skies and heavens open up from end to end, dropping white
   flakes far and near
A virgin blanket covers the ground, so pure and new
I often say nature's best show, along with frost from frozen dew
A silent shroud everywhere, all around pure white
It reflects in the days sunshine and sparkles in the night's moonlight
A blizzard comes, a storm that shows Mother Nature's savage power
So much snow falls and covers the trees some of them look like an
   ivory tower
The color white, cold and wet, the feel of snow
The color I like, for the flakes to fall the temperature must be low
There's moisture on the windows, forming crisp white frost
Seems kind of a shame it melts and the beauties lost
Ice forms on the streets and sidewalks, take care not to slip slid away
It melts and goes until it's nothing but foggy memories of a by gone
   day
Crystal flakes no two alike, a mystery of the ages
The snow the color of white, like papers blank pages
The snowy scene comes with all the beauty winter can bring
It will end when the weather gets warmer and life begins again in
   spring

Robert G. Baynum

A Moment In My Life

You shared a moment in my life,
the time it passes quickly.
You shared your time, you gave your love,
we had a few laughs too.

And now it's time to say Good-Bye,
but all is not forgotten.
The time, the love, the laughter shared
will stay somewhere within.

And when I'm grown and reflecting back
on moments in my life,
I'll think of you and feel the joy
of the days that we did share.

Vivienne Weinreb

"The Rose"

A lovely rose opened, alive and new,
yet not unkissed by the sweet morning dew.
It was a meager bush, all alone
How it got there, nobody knows.
Yet there is stands, just the same
The child of sunshine and soft, summer rain.
And so it has grown each day on the hill
And if no one has harmed it may be there still.

Becky Dye

Untitled

The evil of its black wings over you,
Watching and waiting to makes its attack,
Coming in closer and closer with each kiss,
The kiss of death,
Ripping at you,
Dark as the devil's eye,
Bright as the blood dripping from your heart
In sequence of the tick-tock of the clock,
Watching and waiting for it to stop,
Once it stops the blood will fall as cold as death,
Never dying,
Shaping you until you are one with them,
Soon your black wings will spread,
Falling into a pattern of evil,
As blood falls into a puddle beneath the clock,
The clock stops.

Tara Renfrow

Tales Of Moshup

Of the cliffs our tales were spoken
Stories of the life of Moshup
Messy giant here was living
Squant his wife and all their children
In the den they called the Devil's.
Caught the whales and spilled their life blood
Till the cliffs with this were stained
And black charcoal from his fires
With the red was intermingled.
Long ago a fear approached him
Sensing trouble to his people.
For the aliens were coming
Bringing with them time of sorrow
Then did Moshup change his children
Into whales within the ocean.
He and his wife then departed
For the unknown worlds around them.

Jacqueline L. Childs

"I Remember Mother"

I remember mother, that day in her garden, her private retreat
Sped tumbling soil, tears that glisten her cheek
I'm in touch with her feelings, this day I'm aware
That the woman who is kneeling has so much to bare
Awakened within me, finally I see
Not just mother, but friend, the closest to me
This woman, young and lovely, everyone's strength
Forgetting herself, our needs she will tend
And of dad, why, they're lovers
How thoughtless I've been
Not seeing one to the other, only each there for me
Tears overcome me, how do I begin
But words are unspoken and as her eyes meet mine
We embrace in understanding, our hearts then entwine
Now mother and daughter are woman to woman, friend beside friend
I remember mother, that day in her garden, her private retreat
That day in her garden, forever ours to keep

Pamela Leolani Tiogangco

Porcelain Doll

Oh porcelain doll
   as I sit and watch you sleep,
I wonder what your symbol is
   with your face so innocent and sweet.
Could you be someone's love
   who, in the end, has faded?
Or are you just a forbidden love
   waiting to be awaken?
If you were mine to label,
   I would have to say
That your symbol would be, without a doubt,
   for a love I lost today.
You would be enclosed in glass
   to preserve the memories
And hold behind your sleeping eyes
   the emptiness inside of me.
Oh porcelain doll in a box
   you are now mine to keep.
Please remember the love I had
   and never let me weep.

Aline Munro

The Telephone

Well I had to leave and I was in a hurry.
   The telephone rang and I started to worry.
My worries were well founded as you will soon see.
   The wife answered the phone, then handed it to me.

It's the same all over and it's without debate.
   When the telephone rings everybody has to wait.
I went to the bank and it just had to be.
   The telephone got the attention, not little old me.

How bad is city government in a crucial debate?
   They answer the telephone, while they make you wait.
Go into a parts house, the worst of all time.
   You stand around waiting while they sell on the line.

I'm a paying customer, cash in hand I bring.
   But my money's no good when the telephone rings.
I stand around all day, till I want to cry.
   I've got everything in my hand that I want to buy.

Now these are examples, I've just given a few.
   It's happened all my life and you know that it's true.
Well I was finally fed up, so determined and bold.
   I ordered by telephone and they put me on hold.

Warren E. McDaniel

Forgiveness

It doesn't come easy.
By far, it is one of the most difficult feelings to
acknowledge or accept.

Its arrival brings no formal announcement.
It sort of creeps up on you and
reluctance greets it at the door.

How it manages to come inside is beyond me.
I'm still trying to figure that one out.
And while I'm discovering its clandestine intrusion,
it's already moved on to the next victim, leaving behind
a bigger heart and a grateful soul

Christine Rios

Untitled

I walk my feet through wild grass
And feel the sun slip down my neck.
The air is filled with tawny leaves the winter wind has cast.

My feet are bare, my hair is wet,
The time of day I'll never know.
Nor can I know how long I'll wait before the sun will set.

I never to the world have shown
The notes that I alone do sing.
The notes that ride at midnight through where apple trees do grow.

My eyes were dry when in the spring.
In the morning I was young.
When mid day came they cried a bit and aged an autumn's wing.

Eyes that dim for one more time cry tears on wild grass.
So silently has winter come.
Now slowly sinks the sun whose golden rays will be my last,
And in apple groves with tawny leaves my song no more is sung.

Amanda G. Mabey

Perspectives

We each have different perspectives
About life and truth and man
Some perspectives make sense
Many are hard to understand

Many perspectives are valid
Some perspectives are wrong
Some have a measure of truth
But we have to get along

Each person has a different point of view
And still there's universal truth
And how opinions mean to you
I'd like to ask for proof

Criticism doesn't help you to grow
We're all just sisters and brothers
We need to teach what we know
And learn to help each other

Opinions do not matter
It's just somebody's pain
And when all is said and done
Only your real self will remain

Tim Pearson

A Bend In The River

A bend in the river
I sat on a rock on the bend in the river
I watch the water run in the
bend of the river
I watch the birds look for food
in the bend of the river
in the bend of the river the
water was so clear
at the bend of the river my river

Clarence Dickerman Jr.

"Lord Help Me"

Dear Lord help me to be
All I need to be, show me how to love him
Place strength inside of me
For I feel so all alone
In this world of defeat
Traveling by myself
Going down a one way street
Lord help me to see, continue to care
For life seems so cruel
So many times unfair
Lord have I failed in every single way
Would you show me my purpose
On this earth today
The very one I Love I hold to me so dear
I seem to drive away
Instead of drawing near
Lord would you guide me
Take my hand, dry my tears
Teach me what to say and do
I feel so lost and full of fear

Shirley A. Bascko

Midnight Lamentation

As dark as night, the clouds roll by
And drift to lands of sleep;
Where slumber lays and beauty stays
And sorrow the heart keeps.

Midnight lulls and serenades
The dreams of hope and peace...
A state without pain; a state without gain;
A state of long-last release.

Coldness chills and surrounds my mind
And pinches my anguished heart.
It's frosty and stiff; brittle and thin,
For my youth never had a start.

As silent as death, the wind mourns for
And caresses my empty life.
It floats on songs my heart can't sing
And stabs me like a knife.

My vacant tears fall like the vastless sea
And drown my weary heart.
They flood the dams of my reserve,
And control just shreds apart.

Eliana Capri Dunlap

The Looking Glass

Easter present and Easter past
Roland, pick-up the looking glass.

What do you see, how far does it extend?
Forever and ever, without an end.
Can you see along the way,
What lies ahead of us today?
Hardships, trials, sunshine and laughter,
A struggle with tears and life ever-after.

Can you see beside the path
Is it shallow, what type of math?
Beautiful trees and colorful flowers,
Rolling acres and mountains that tower.
Rampaging rivers and roaring seas,
Snakes alive and killer bees.

The path is not straight, it bends and winds
The degree it seems is all in our minds.
To be endowed is more hardship than naught,
The bends in the road are curiously wrought.
What can we do, but accept the task,
To plow straight through and forget the mask.

Roland B. Davis

Junk Drawer

Opening my junk drawer - what a sight!
Things popped out at me - what a fright!
It's only been several weeks
When in this drawer I did seek
One single black shoelace
Put there so I'd know its place
Among safety pins and rubber bands
Coupons for the pizza man
Scissors, screwdriver, recipes too,
Crayons, red, yellow, blue,
Baby's rattle that fell on the floor
A key for the car and a key for the door,
Now, I search to my dismay
Can't find my pen for the mess in the way,
Company's coming, alack and alas,
Must hurry, hurry, must act fast.
I can't have anyone see this drawer
This disarray of objects galore,
So here I go in a frenzied way
Clean that drawer if just for a day.

Eleanor F. Basinger

Memory

In the deepest part of my memory, I see a light that used to be, oh so bright and full of glow, like a thousand candles burning in my soul. It would light the way for you to see, that used to be my love for thee.

In the deepest part of my memory, like an early morning day in spring, when the flowers bloom and the birds would sing, the sky so blue, the grass real green, when the morning sun kisses the deep, blue sea, that used to be my love for thee.

In the deepest part of my memory, I would hold you close and you would see, that warm embrace, and gentle kiss, like a sweet warm breeze across your lips, it's something special that would touch your soul, and tell your heart, that you would know, that used to be my love for thee.

In the deepest part of my memory, I remembered when you left me, and how I hurt the pain so deep, and how I cried myself to sleep I remembered how we touched at night and how are love was always right, and the little things that would make you laugh, and then I though how this could be, I'll always be in love with thee.

Larry D. Smith

The White Snow Owl

On a cold wintry snowy day
the white snow owl landed at my feet.
He looked at me with his dark brown starry eyes,
a beauty hard to describe.
I was startled by his surprise,
it was a vision from the sky.
We stood silent for a moment and gazed at each other,
then the snow owl turned his head
and flew away over the shed.
We both said our goodbyes.

Charlotte Burke

Untitled

You're losing me again.
I came back, hoping you changed as you said you did.
Yet the you from before still lives inside
the nice picture you painted.
The real you still has the shades of black and gray
that push me away.
I can't do this much longer.
My loyalty and love for you wanes greatly.
I can't tell you how sad it is for me to tell you
you're losing me again.

Rob Diesel

Elsie

Her eyes were blue as the summer sky.
Her laughter rang like music from on high.
Her skin was soft as the petals of a rose.
She was beauty, beauty the spoken word cannot disclose.

We walked together arm in arm along life's many roads.
We sang our songs, cried our tears, we shared each other's woes.
'Twas she who lighted our path as day gave way to night.
She was the staff I leaned on, she was my very life.

She could touch a brush in winter and cause the flowers to bloom
She was a gentle, caring soul who did not dwell on doom.
She was many things, this lady, this lover of life.
Who is she you wonder? She was my beautiful wife...
   R. C. Cornwell

Moment Of Yesterday

Just a moment of yesterday
What would I give?
What would I say?
What moment would it be?
Would it be when we met?
What magic or electrical moment?
There are so many! Which one would you say?
Which one would, or could it be?
Maybe there are so many - I could not say.
But our love is so true, a moment would be more that just a yesterday,
with you
   Donald L. Archer

This Too Shall Pass

So many evil things happening in this world,
This too shall pass

People killing, stealing lying, destroying others dreams,
This too shall pass

Too many wars going on throughout the world,
This too shall pass

So much hate, mistrust and deceit going on,
This too shall pass

So much illness and pain, people crying out in vain,
This too shall pass

We live our lives worrying about our tomorrows instead of enjoying our todays,

This too shall pass

Let us enjoy the beauty of the sky, sun, moon, stars, oceans, flowers and so much more,

This to shall pass
   Barbara A. Cooper

Jacob's Well Kenya

God took us far out into his fields that day
to a wind swept hill no trees for shade.
Dirt paths snaked down into lush valleys below
winding into thatched hut villages built long ago.
Near us a faucet rose up from the ground
the only water well for many miles around.
To the well they came unaware God had chose this time
when they would hear of His free gift to all mankind.
Empty pots on their heads, empty souls so lost
we told them of Jesus and how His life sin cost.
Tears flowed freely as they said, "Yes" to Christ
All rejoiced as He gave each eternal life.
Christ knocked and they opened their heart's door
to the Living Water of Jesus our Savior and Lord.
   Janice Peterson

Our Brothers

Our brothers were all courageous men
they always did kind things
They tried to help, they did their best
they died for what was good.

Why they had to die, I do not know
Maybe God had a war in heaven

But our brothers will always be remembered
On special days shared by all.

Our brothers were the men who died
for this country
Our brothers fought to give us our
freedom, our life and our liberty
They won this fight but
we lost them.

So their memories will live on forever
And on this day, this Memorial Day
Their memories will be
shared and honored.
   Lottie Howell

What's Wrong With You

You hurt me— I'm in pain
All promises broke.
You declared me disabled
Took away all good I'ld done

I was good with people
Cared and did my best for the lot
Yet you replaced me by a grocery clerk
From the trash aisle.

Studied in school I did, memorized each word
Took two courses and passed I did,
When Doctor's said I couldn't
Listening to you, and now I'm a waste,

They talk about you and it's so unfair
Put down the best and keep the trash
What's wrong with me? It's you.
What's wrong with you?
   Ellyn Guppy Hook

Absence

The illuminant cradle of the everchanging stars.
The shadowy effect without the sheltering tree.
The prowling territory of the cat.
The home of the bat.
The ancient ballroom of all parties.
The lovers sweetly needed paradise.
The shrouded gift for the thief.
The horrid monster beneath the bed.
The savage creatures within the closet.
The absence of light.

Is it bad or is it good.
Should it be trusted, should it be mistrusted.
Is it with character, is it without character.
Is it horrific, is it terrific.
Should it be yearned for, should it be hidden from.
Is it wonderful or is it wonderless.

Phases pass, phases come.
So mysterious, so peaceful, so silent.
The absence of light.
   Rodney R. Ruble

My Friend

"Beneath The Cross Of Jesus"
I hope to make my stand.
To testify to love and truth
As "My life goes on as planned."
say "Yes to all God promises"
That they will "All come true"
He will send you "Peace and happiness"
In all you seek and do
"First and last in all my dreams"
"He guides me on my way"
He will provide if you confide
The greatest dreams your way
He guides and guards you all life through
No piece meal will he send.
If you pray aright both "Day and night"
He will always be your friend.

Alice Kell

My Queen

If I were a king's servant, and commissioned by my Lord to find the fairest maiden in all His kingdom; for Him to love, cherish, and share His kingdom with; I would have to say, "My Lord, I know of such a one of whom you speak, for her beauty is spoken throughout the land, and she is one who would please you and have a desire for you and your kingdom."

Then with haste, I would come to you and take your hand and present you to our Lord and King.

Then, if I were the King, I would take your hand, look into your eyes and say, "She is more than I could ever dream. Only God can create the beauty that I see in her."

Then as king, with your hand in mine, I would bow my knee before you and say: "I see such beauty in you, that I give you my love, my kingdom, and will spend the rest of my life to please you."

Then, I would rise up and take you in my arms, and hold you forever.

"And thy desire shall be to thy husband,
    and he shall rule over thee."

Paul Lucia

Plans For Me

Shall I be, a missionary?
A preacher endowed with words,
A teacher of God's Word Holy?
What does my Lord want me to be?

A missionary in far away lands,
He can live knees deep in local sand,
Seeking out the brave,
He can call to take a stand,

A preacher with words so endowed,
Can God's majesty un - shroud,
He can with keen words,
Lift a man's soul above the clouds.

A teacher of the Holy Word, it's said,
Needs to remember all he's read,
In the teaching of Word,
He finds. He has taught himself instead.

What does God want me to be?
In this rhyme it's plain to see,
His plans included, not only me,
But you, too, we are all of these.

william wilder

Me??? A Country Queen???

Some say I have a way with words, and I should write some Country songs, The kind that make you happy, or just want to sing along!! The kind of songs that make you sad, and sometimes, even cry, songs about those cheating men songs about good-by! Somebody done somebody right, or done somebody wrong, The kind of things that always make, the greatest Country song! I've never thought about it, I just write the way I feel, I write about my life, my loves, it's nothing, no big deal!! But, wouldn't it be something? If songs I chose to write? If I ended up at the C.M.A.?? Countries best awards, one night? Nominated best new writer, of a Country song, sitting in the front now, of course, Mom would come along!! Imagine, hearing, Garth Brooks say, "And the winner is?? Kathy Dean!!! I could be famous, just like Dolly?? Me?? a Country Queen??????

Kathy Dean

"Homeward Bound"

Out there beyond the sky
    are worlds I know only with my mind's eye.

Worlds that someday other men will truly know
    when man finally begins to grow.

Man will grow within and without.
    Of this I am sure. I have no doubt.

Since his fall man has travelled far,
    but he's still only halfway to his star.

Throughout the Universe will spread Mankind,
    but greater than numerical growth will be the growth of Man's mind

Truths will come to him that we may never know
    for Man's present mind has a decidedly dim glow.

At last Man will reach the evolutionary end,
    and homeward bound he will meet his One True Friend.

Edward G. Donnelly

A Box Full Of Dreams

Here in this box is all I've ever wanted
Here lies all I've longed for
Things now stored on a shelf
So neatly packed away
A box full of dreams
Tucked out of sight
But not out of my mind
My heart still holds the longing
For my box full of dreams
For whatever the reasons
I've let them slip away
Or they have fallen apart
So here they lie protected
A box full of dreams

Rosslen S. Houser

Sunshine

Sunshine is a wonderful thing
You see it at the crack of dawn
You wake up and hear the birds sing
And you just know it's a beautiful morn
Every morning the sun brings light
And you see the gleam in people's eyes
Although they know that it soon will be night
Sunshine, oh what a beautiful thing!

Jennifer Bullock

Quiet Moments

Quiet moments are
precious jewels of rest
scattered in the rocks
of daily responsibilities,

colorful blossoms of beauty
sprouting in the garden of weeds
of troubles and despair,

sparkling stars of hope in the ebony void of space
that peek out from behind the cloud cover
of illness and injury,

sweet smiles of joy and happiness
found in the bustling crowd's faces of frowns
of worry and anger,

refreshing visits with God
when one finds space to stretch and relax
amid the clutter from everyday life.

In quiet moments
one finds peace
with oneself
and the world.
    Fran Bock

To Those Less Fortunate

Give to those who hurt you
They are the ones in need

Always remember, before a flower became a flower
It was once a seed

Give to those who quit
Before they try their best

Always remember before the bird learned to fly
He was stranded in his nest

Give to those who have no harmony
And can not feel to sing

Always remember the butterfly was only a caterpillar
Before he grew his wings
    Lenore Tsai

Love And Its Ways

Love makes a way,
Love permits a ray,
Love spent away,
A time that is to pray.

Oh love to where is your immortal soul,
Oh love that lives up to the grave,
Show me how to crush you too,
Oh love show me the way until your
  essence will have no day.

When love soon decays,
And a lover soon dismay,
A test is seen and on,
That makes a lover moans,

But when love is pure and true,
That lovers share and do,
This makes us everything,
And paints this world a pink.
    Diadema Tor Mansour

Cherished

Memory bits...melting together.
  Focused...heart's pure image...flows in view
Total acceptance...loving presence.
  Matching...awe inspiring...wonder...you.

Living within my heart...unfettered.
  Pungent memories...perfume each room.
Poignant...purging teardrops...now priceless.
  These emotions...will survive death's tomb.

The spirit of you...encased in flesh.
  Abides with me...wherever I roam.
Warm soft touch...feminine's tenderness.
  Tells me...I'm not...exploring alone.

You have become...prime part of my life.
  That never can...nor will be...erased.
No matter what...my future...may hold.
  I possess...what cannot be...replaced.

Dedicate...devote...nurturing love.
  Nourishing soulmate...commitment to.
Valued times we've spent...talked...reviewed.
  Albums of joy, tears, cheers...First Love...you.
    Virgil Nabity

Flying Cross Country

Flying under a deep blue sky filled with sunshine and over a cloud ocean of rolling waves, the plane bumped along on the invisible potholes in the sky. Bumpity bump, bumpity bump I'm having trouble drinking coffee from my cup.

Smooth flying at last. Now the clouds are like a huge arid desert of rippling sand. I wish I had a cup of coffee in my hand.

Now the clouds look like snow covered land, with rolling hills as a background for the snow covered mountain tops. Oops! That is not a cloud formation! That's the rugged snow covered Rocky Mountain Range. Bumpity bump, bumpity bump. I'd better finish the coffee that is left in my cup.
    Alyce M. Nielson

One Afternoon Of Late

This afternoon I do not need
anything but this book of poetry
and tea and fire in the fireplace.

This book, hard-backed, deceptively small,
can be held in a single hand
and read at leisure without a dictionary.

The thoughts here contained are accessible
on a variety of themes to pluck
like chocolates—an assortment of pleasures

that require solitude, a soulish stillness,
far from the demand of days. Quiet —
to hear the poet's imaginings.

I find waiting inside this house of crusty cardboard
a recluse, rich, bidding me

I enter, losing thought of banal things
and take my tea with him. He speaks
of wealth of other places.

We visit for hours, this wordsmith and me,
'til I must leave. I rise reluctantly, but restoke the fire.
    Margie McClure

Remember The Dead

Abandoned bodies lay among the grass and grain,
shouting cries of endless pain.
Lives were lost, Lives were saved
blood soaked bodies lay decayed.
Remember the dead, the fallen, the weak
one moment, one bullet gave them eternal sleep.
All gave some, some gave all
imaging what the soldiers saw.
The crimson ground, the crimson grass
the soldiers hoped the war would soon pass.
War is physical, yet fought in your head
so take some time to Remember the dead.
Matthew Zimmerman

April

Dogwood is wearing her best white lace.
Violet is showing her quaint pixie face.
Wistaria has climbed the Tupelo tree
Flaunting her purple - panicled drapery.

Shy things are peeping from cranny and nook,
From the top of the hill down to the brook.
Squirrels are leaping from tree to tree.
Birds are singing a new melody.

Clouds overhead are like cotton candy,
But your umbrella you should keep handy,
And go spread the word around
Capricious April is back in town!
Willette Caudle McGuire

Beauty And The Beholder

It was once said,
That beauty is beheld in the eyes
And this you may believe
For there are so many beautiful things
Which the eyes may perceive.
But for one moment, refrain from this perception
And allow your thoughts to reflect
For the realm of beauty, is much more complex.
The fragrance of flowers
As they bloom in spring,
The sweet melody of the mockingbird
In the song it sings.
The caress of a lovers hand
By the fire on a cold winter's night,
The texture of Chardonnay
On the palate, ever so lite.
These are beautiful things
Which bring pleasure, and appease
But they too, are sensations
Which the eyes cannot perceive.
Daryl E. White

Spring Wonderful Spring

After winter's cruel cold and depressing days,
the earth awakens and shows signs of spring.
It comes slowly in various ways.
Breezes are soft as a taste of wine,
the promise of clear skies and sunshine,
beckons the flowers to come forth without fear.
Birds appear in feathers of colors so bright
to sing a chorus of "Spring is here."
Our hearts beat faster, we're energized
with rake, hoe, denim and boots were a sight
we are ready, willing and able to exercise.
Children laughing, flying, a kite.
Smiling faces turned to the sun, we shout
"Spring wonderful Spring".
At last spring is here!!!
Virginia J. Brady

To Mansford

A little white house stood
On a tree lined street yesterday
It was built with a heart of love.
The strong hands never grew tired
As they labored day after day.
<Body Each nail was carefully placed.
By the hands of the builder.
For it was not a house. It was to be a home.
If that little house could talk.
It would tell of the love shared.
Of singing, laughter and tears.
There was a lot of living there.

Sometimes I feel much sorrow
The builder and the house are gone.
But I'm sure the builder is busy.
Helping to build a home.
This vision I keep in my heart.
Someday I will hear the call.
Mother come all is ready.
And in my heart, I will know. I will be going home.
Thelma Barnes

He And Me

The shoes that move us
are polished, but creased.
Laces gray, our double knots, long ago, fastened
securely.

Foot sounds create our private rhythm
in their passage of time,
moving us forward into a mint fresh meadow.

Decades of years together and now
our hearts beat as only one.
Poised, heads high, no matter and forever,
perpetually paired.

The world we know has been refashioned.
That once important, seems less.
Visions forgotten and postponed, now within reach,
glimmer in our glow.

I move with you, oh love, hand in hand.
Aged images project the trail of time, we, still expectant
supporting forever, one to other.
Worn shoes advance, dancing into a new overture.
Happy, we eternally, oh gifted love of ours.
Eileen Yarnutoski Raymond

Thoughts Of Others

Have you ever been poor and forlorn
Deny your child food who's just been born
Many souls in our world today
Are forced to face these trials everyday
There is but one thing we can do today
For these dear souls we must pray
Whether Indian, African, Japanese, or Chinese
Jesus said."...Unto the least of these."
After they are fed and clothed
They are ready to receive God's Word
Our prayer and giving will not be in vain
For someday these souls will Heaven gain
When we reach Heaven's shore, gathered by the Crystal Sea
We may hear a soul say, "Thank you for helping me."
Shirley Pieri

We Are Blessed With Beautiful Memories

There will always be a special place in our hearts
Time takes away the edge of grief.
But memories turn back every leaf.
Think of us on your journey and be at peace.

Our live will never be the same.
For a cherished link is missing beloved husband:
From our family chain.
Death causes heart ached no one can heal.

We have out share of thoughts.
Of laughter and cheers, we cannot
Live those days over.
With each tomorrow that comes along.

We will remember you and the yesterdays
Memories of you will never grow old.
They are etched in out hearts with letter of gold.
No longer in out lives to share.
Nestled in our hearts, you are always there.
Sadly missed along the way.
We know that you are resting.
And that someday we will meet.

Evelyn T. Tallman

My Comet

You suddenly appeared in my night sky
and brightened my life for a week
trailing a tail of charms
to captivate me
and dreams to entrance me
Then you streaked away into space
Have you gone to gleam at other globes?
Sparkling at other spheres
Dazzling other domains
Pleasing other planets
Whistling past other worlds where women wait?
Don't leave me in the dark
scanning the sky
I know you couldn't stay
but please try to come back
I'll be here
I'll wait forever for you
My comet.

Barbara R. DuBois

Uplifting

When you look into someone's soul, what is it you see?
What's really there could you accept them as they may be?
Why do we feel that's a place that should open, when another person
    seeks it out?
Should it not be uplifting in our whole self about?

Sunshine, laughter, sadness and empathy.
These things we wish to find in you and me
For without them, what would it be like?
To soar for goals we've planned, we'd have to fight.

A soul is something from within
It should be shared only if one dares,
It should be uplifting; not full of sin.
We should be very cautious opening to only someone we will allow in.

Uplifting people have souls that are special
Watching for people, who are only on the prowl
For a person's soul to open it up, make it play
To try and take all the goodness away.

Shirley J. Bierly

A Faithful Friend

A sad little boy who sat all alone
With tear-filled eyes said with a moan,
"I have no friends so I can have no fun."
While there at his feet sat the forgotten one.

Now little boys who wish to play
must have a friend and a sunny day.
If friends are gone and there is a cloudy sky
Then little boys are bound to cry.

So if friends won't play or don't appear
Perhaps it's time to wipe that tear.
For when skies are grey and friends are few
Won't your friendly doggy do?

He is a friend that's faithful, true and kind.
He forsakes all others with just you in mind.
This faithful friend I'm speaking of
Will fill each day with puppy love.

Leslie A. Cole

Summer's End

Climbing up the molten lass of a withered treetop.
To spy on the jungle far up ahead.
The sun takes me sixteen years back.
In the corner of some decrepit hut lies the
afterlife of a human soul.
Strewn to the ground searching for a place.
To be buried beneath the stars, nourishment
for the sick and dying.
Accomplishment for the living and those to come.
Beheld by a thousand strangers and a thousand
moons, guided by the hand that turns the
mountains to the sky.
Up ahead the street comes the band of
wanderers and townspeople gathering
at the doorstep of a lonely couple.

Mary Duque

Silence

The silence announces itself.
Transparent shades slowly descend.
Emotions crawl upon a shelf.
A heart knows not what to defend.

Tears flow over a once smiling cheek.
Eyes rummage for what cannot be seen.
Angers' rage becomes meek.
Silence begins to humble and demean.

Questions drown in the quiet sea.
Answers are veiled deep inside.
Silence casts off loves' plea.
The heart is exposed with nowhere to hide.

Silence drives all away.
Loneliness engulfs those who dare to resist.
The distance grows between those who stay.
Their only hope is, love will persist.

Gary H. Long

You Were A Good Man Billy Jones

How very short the span of life
Years of joy some of strife
What does one do as the final bell tolls
To sum up his life and achievement of goals
Dwell not on the sad but rather the sublime
Events of which proud over passage of time
Youthful endeavors, accomplishments of note
In service of country and fulfillment of hopes
The essence of which could be etched in stone
At the final resting place of one Billy Jones.

William Henry Jones

"A Seed"

A seed, a tiny thing,
It is even smaller than a ring.
A seed if you plant it will grow a rose,
And give off a fragrance for your nose.
One in the ground will feed us all,
Making corn grow ever so green and tall.
One is even the father of the clothes we wear,
And ends up in the rags we tear.
The nastiest is started from a seed
And that we know is an old weed.
A seed can start a child agrowing,
And later on he'll do the sowing.
A seed will make us grass so green,
That our mowers will hack off so clean.
A seed planted between some friends,
Can sometimes end up lovers in the end.
What value can this little thing be;
It's a miraculous gift from "God", given to you and me.

Philomena Rossi

Zuma Rock

Symbol of new capital — Zuma Rock
With a face that changes with drops of tears.
On Southern entry, sad tears on the rock,
Uninviting, threatening, full of fears.

Why should Zuma Rock wear so sad a face?
But tears of joy drop as Northern roads wind —
Welcoming, reassuring Zuma face,
Like a chameleon on a magic wand.

Why does Zuma present conflicting hopes?
May be our insensitiveness to sin.
The assassins, the armed robbers, the dupes
Whose praise we are always eager to sing.

May be our lulled sense of security
As we struggle to procure daily meals.
Silent, hungry, jobless majority
Now turn to God to heal our inner ills.

How incomprehensible our God is!
Whose great triumphs rise from great tragedies
And from defeats rise His great victories.
Our unchanging solid "Rock of Ages".

Priscilla Oguine

Shalom

she stood in the sultry
sun   alone   yet with everyone   dignitaries
from every peace loving land   she clung
to the mother's hand

an attack left Rabin shot in the
back   guests praised the peacemaker
so brave   the killer didn't care who was there
to honor a fallen Jew

then a hush   as a wisp of a girl   dark
hair framing a face not easy to forget
forgive me she said   I don't want to talk about the peace
process   I want to talk about my grandfather

grandmother cries and I cannot comfort her
I remember when
we sat around our campfires   laughing at your
stories of by-gone days and our tomorrows
now your light is gone
grandfather   I miss you already
she started to cry
I love you grandfather   until the day I die

Mimi Eagan

Nature

Winter approaches
Stealthily.....
...In a feline manner
Leaving small clues as footprints.

Crisp mornings: Dew to Frost
Knowing, Flora Bloom. Spawning Salmon.
They themselves sacrificed to Grizzly jaws.

Sudden...Abrupt...It's here!
Flowers Stand: Crystals in Time
Nature-fattened Ursus scurries to sleep.

Winter's Arms envelop me
No luxury of struggle
Sweet, cold embrace
Acceptance.

Kimberly S. Gregory

Thank You For The Middle Years

Thank You for the precious imperfections
That enhance the beauty of the perfect.
Thank You for adversity and life's large frustrations
Imparting patience with small daily irritations.
Thank You for the priceless privilege to err
That bestows the hard-won wondrous wisdom of experience.
Thank You for illness profound
Making more dear health refound.
Thank You for tragedy and the painful sorrow
Making more meaningful the happy tomorrow.
Thank You for the faithful friend.
Thank You for the false one too
Teaching for the treasure more the true.

Thank You for these middle years
Free from youth's fettered fears
Of passions aflame, wildly untamed,
Now sweetly tempered, quietly restrained
When neither dreams nor regrets master me,
Believing still in miracles to be!

Emma Mai Ewing

Heartache

The mate you thought to you was true,
Boasts that he has found someone new.
The world that you knew, has just crashed,
Dreams for the future are now bashed!
Pick yourself up, do what you must,
Why should you lie there in the dust?
Take hold, plan a life of your own,
"So what?" If you go on alone?
When you are forced to be single
Find others with whom you can mingle.
Establish yourself on new ground,
That's where happiness can be found.

Bernice DiBernardinis

My Father

   A Proud Man . . . A man whose pride for his family outshines that of a Marine for the Corps.

   A Man whose Drive is so Strong that it still Remains unchallenged

   A Man whose love for his family even Cupid can't match.

   As a father, I can only pray that I ran raise a family life my father did.
I love you dad.

Steven Ary

Credit Cards

Credit cards are tokens, of companies who love;
They make it easy, they give credit a big shove;
You'll whip out that old card, whenever you're out of cash:
But watch out when that bill comes in, you'll see a money crash.
A plastic card for this, and a credit card for that;
To put them in your wallet, it hurts you if you sat;
Beware of the credit card, whatever you do, for if you get behind,
The company may sue;
Or in a collection agency you may see yourself;
The safest place for credit cards, is just right on a shelf.
To save face, and not disgrace, here's what should be done;
Pay in cash, for if you do, the battles finally won.
All who own these cards, simply on loan,
   and want to save the human race;
Just cock your arm, and let it go, out there in outer space.
   Shirley Allen

A New Leaf

There is much in life that we have to deal with
Although it seems a shame that it can not be a gift
Each time we gather our wits
It can remain a challenge to remain fit
What we take in can be a new trip
It will serve us best if it's sip by sip
When we realize there is much to gain
It's less likely that we have room to complain
Each new trial sometimes needs a little pump
But in the long run - we need this to avoid a slump
It does no good to thump, thump
Because we could be knocking on the wrong door
Which generally speaking will only make us poor
Anytime we get a new head of steam
It gives us the cool breeze of the stream
It does not matter that we succeed
But, alas we unknowing have planted a new seed
With this seed we hold in our hand
We could move from the bland to the grand slam.
   Edward T. Philpitt

The Death Of Innocence

I used to believe in so many things, never questioning why. What was the reasoning behind these belief's, or if some of them were even a lie. Then without warning the sword of truth, had slain my ignorance bliss, and though it was necessary thing my innocence I always have missed. The truth is true power; I have heard people say, but I must ask myself what's the price we must pay? For knowing the truth has given me strength, but it's left me alone with no one to thank. So many people I used to hold high, but now with the truth I have to ask why. Because these people in whom I believed, I found they were only trying to deceive. This deception has been practiced since the beginning of time, but in my ignorance I knew of no crime. And now that the truth has opened my eyes, I can never believe in their terrible lies. It is good that I am no longer deceived, though now I find I have nothing to believe. With eyes full of truth I examine all I see, while sadly I mourn all of life's mysteries. For no longer will I see the world with eyes full of wonderful bliss, and I think that this is what most I will miss. And even if occasionally truth shines in their eyes, I can never trust anyone whose been telling me lies. And though I still miss my innocent days I can never go back to those ignorant ways!
   Julie Durham-Holupka

Reflections

In pecan trees and palm trees
Wind and rain do as they please.
But without the sun
to warm their leaves
There would be little there to please.
As I look down through the trees
I see a butterfly dancing
to a midday breeze.
But I have shot down the angel that sang
life is good, a wonderful renewal, like spring.
'Cause sometimes life is just a bitter thing.
When fire and rain encounter
nothing remains to keep.
As I have encountered
and turned to fall asleep.
But these things mean nothing.
They do not matter to me, my dears.
'Cause I know that I am safe in God's love
today, and in future years.
   Michael Green

So Kind, So Sweet

When I think about my life complete,
   it includes a woman so kind, so sweet.
One that I can call my wife,
   and to her dedicate my life.
Who will love me not for what I say and do,
   but for the man I am through and through.
To hold me close if tears I cry,
   and know the love I speak is never a lie.
Who will bear my children though in pain,
   with understanding all the same.
For her, I will protect and defend,
   standing my ground until the end.
With her, I will love, honor, and obey,
   for by her side I will forever stay.
   Tony E. Dummermuth

Ode To My Disease

   You can rob me of my riches, and take all of my gold
My dignity however will stay as I grow old.

   You can eat at all my senses, my limbs make oh so weak,
My will to go on living for it shall stay at peak.

   You can try to break my family by taking all my time,
It seems as though we persevere, through love that's so divine.

   And here you are with all your pain, my morals you will
Never stain, I'll battle you with all my will, till day of Jesus Reign.
   Lucia DiSabatino

A Feline Muse

Many tales of Cats are written,
Of rough old tom, or tiny kitten.
But still, of Cats the authors speak
Because the Cat is so unique.

The Cat seems always bold but shy;
Warm and friendly, but also sly.
When one has once resolved his brain,
The personality might quickly change.

No single Cat can set the tone
For every breed of Cat that's known.
Suffice to say they are diverse,
Or why would man resort to verse?

With lucent eyes and silken fur,
No sound more pleasing than Kitty's purr.
A joy to have, much grief to loose,
The Cat's the pet that I would choose.
   Keith C. Chastain

Biographies of Poets

ABBOTT, SHAWN T.
[b.] July 12, 1977, Springville, NY; [p.] Timothy and Ginger Abbott; [ed.] High School Diploma at Corey Area High School and I now attend Edinboro University; [occ.] None (Little Caesar's); [memb.] Saegertown United Methodist Church, Coach of Corey Area Big League Team; [hon.] Who's Who among American Students (Academic/Athletic); [oth. writ.] None, so far; [pers.] Things always get better!; [a.] Corey, PA

ABRAMS, FELICIA ANN MARIE
[pen.] Filly; [b.] August 19, 1958, Ithaca, NY; [m.] Robert V. Abrams, May 16; [ch.] Chacora, Halique Abrams; [ed.] Ithaca High, Empire State College Associate in Science in Human Service; [occ.] Unemployed Student Mother, and Wife; [oth. writ.] 1. A Dying Poet, 2. How Little of Faith, 3. Mirror on the Beach, 4. Lonely Boy, 5. Death Comes Knocking, 6. Brunetta's Child, 7. Chocolate Lady and many more; [pers.] I have written many personal poems since the age of ten, in hopes that the child who lives within can express her pain, fears, love and anger through our lives together; [a.] Rochester, NY

ACKLEY, WINIFRED
[pen.] Winifred-Conrad-Ackley; [b.] February 3, 1971, Vallejo, CA; [p.] Charles and Zelma; [m.] Herman J. Ackley, January 17, 1944; [ch.] James W. and Sandra G.; [ed.] Graduated High School; [occ.] Housewife; [oth. writ.] Book containing 30 spiritual prayers and talks with flower children-Black Wall's and Clay Man-Cassius Clay to fighting hand's to be mail Trip To The Moon-G13 All Find God And Home; [pers.] I awoke from 3 day out of body becoming my mother and my self when she left her mortal being. I found my need to find the motherhood of God's love. He told me to write and love and care for His children not made of clay; [a.] North Hollywood, CA

ADAMS, ELEANOR B.
[b.] August 9, 1947, Georgetown, DE; [p.] John L. and Grace Briggs; [m.] George A. Adams, July 24, 1967; [ch.] John L. - Alphie; [ed.] Georgetown High Sch. 1965; Pierce Jr. College, Philadelphia, PA 1967; [occ.] Officer Manager; [pers.] Plan to write poems and short stories for families and children to cope with grief and normal daily life; [a.] Seaford, DE

ADAMS, ZACK
[b.] April 13, 1980, Canoga Park; [p.] Lowell and Jane Adams; [ed.] I've only made it through Junior High and now I'm a Junior in High School; [occ.] High School; [memb.] NRA, Safari Club International; [hon.] Just the Trophies they give out for playing Little League baseball and soccer; [oth. writ.] Several poems that I wrote in my spare time or when they "pop" in my head.; [pers.] I write to let my feelings come out and the feelings that came out in this particular poem were those for an ex-girl friend.; [a.] Simi Valley, CA

AGUILAR, BECKY
[b.] May 3, 1982, El Paso, TX; [p.] Luis Aguilar, Barbara Aguilar; [ed.] Eastpoint Elem. Eastwood Middle School; [occ.] Student; [memb.] Achieving Writers of English Society; [hon.] A.W.E.S., Outstanding Jazz Musician, Academic Achievement, National Junior Honor Society; [oth. writ.] Various Short Stories; [pers.] I think writing is the key to the human soul. When I write a piece, I write from deep within my soul.; [a.] El Paso, TX

AGUILAR, PHILLIP P.
[b.] February 4, 1982, Pasadena, CA; [p.] Patti Aguilar and Vincent Stevenson; [ed.] 1 grade - 5 grade Byron Thompson Orthopedically Handicapped School 6th - 8th Appling Middle School; [occ.] Student at Bolton High School - Freshman; [pers.] All though I'm physically challenged, it hasn't stopped me from following my dreams.; [a.] Arlington, TN

AGUILLARD, DAPHNE E.
[b.] March 9, 1968, Baton Rouge, LA; [p.] Eddie and Sandy Ellis; [m.] Jessie Dusty Aguillard II, March 2, 1991; [memb.] Southern Poetry Association; [oth. writ.] Several poems published through the Southern Poetry Association; [pers.] The inspiration for my poetry comes from the people and things that I love. The main inspiration in my life has been my husband, Dusty. He fills my heart and my soul with the love and support I need to keep writing poetry; [a.] Erwinville, LA

AHTEN, BESSIE M.
[pen.] "Bess"; [b.] January 23, 1949, Peoria, IL; [p.] Woodruff and Viola Lippert; [m.] William H. Ahten, October 29, 1966; [ch.] Johanna M. Bushong; [ed.] Have just returned to school for more training; [occ.] Housewife; [hon.] Won 1st place in 7th grade, for a poem I wrote about spring, in English class. Was put in display case in hall, by front door of schools; [oth. writ.] "Spring Has Sprung", "Upon Your Death", "You're My Loving Friend", "My Dad"; [pers.] I wrote this for my grandson on the day he was born; my mother influenced me in a lot of my works.; [a.] Creve Coeur, IL

ALBANESE, MARY
[b.] January 26, 1959, New York, NY; [p.] Laurette Plaige; [m.] Jack Albanese; [ch.] Justin George, Simone Rose, Dakota Irene; [ed.] Walt Whitman High School; [occ.] Freelance Artist; [pers.] As all that exists is connected in the great circle of life, when we reach beyond our ordinary daily existence to find the spark of wonder inside each of us - humanity and the horizons of our universal spirituality expand.; [a.] East Stroudsburg, PA

ALBERTO, JUSTIN
[b.] July 21, 1982, Danbury, CT; [p.] John Alberto, Lucille Alberto; [ed.] St. Gregory the Great School, Immaculate High School; [hon.] Honor Roll, Best Defensive Lineman at Joe Namath Football Camp; [oth. writ.] This is my first poem ever published.; [pers.] I would like to dedicate my poem to my best friend, Ivy. Without her I don't know where I would be right now.; [a.] Danbury, CT

ALCALA, JULIA L.
[b.] December 9, 1962, Chicago, IL; [p.] Domenick and Bianca Del Seni; [ch.] Danielle; [pers.] "My Princess" is my first poem to be published, it is an honor for her to be displayed for all to read, you now have a piece of my heart, cherish her as I do.; [a.] Brooklyn, NY

ALGER, CRISTINA DE MARIGNY
[b.] February 20, 1980, New York City, NY; [p.] Josephine Romanach Alger, David Dewey Alger; [ed.] Chapin School (NYC), (Kindergarten - 9th Grade), currently in 10th Grade at the Groton School (Groton, Mass.); [occ.] Student (High-School); [pers.] I have always had a tremendous love for writing poetry, an interest inspired by my father. I hope to continue to evolve my poetry as I finish high school and then college.; [a.] New York City, NY

ALLEN, EVAN
[pen.] Evan Allen; [b.] May 24, 1986, Portland, ME; [p.] Scott Allen and Jessie Thuma; [ed.] Attending Merry Mount Elementary School, entering 5th grade; [occ.] Student; [memb.] Quincy Youth Soccer, Unitarian Universalist Church, Speechwood Knoll School Band; [hon.] Elementary Laboratory write. Center for gifted students first place in Woody Allen Road Race; [oth. writ.] This is my first one that is getting published, but my brother and I are working on a newspaper together.; [pers.] I read all the time. I love my little sister Jessie and we play a lot. I like to write.; [a.] Quincy, MA

ALLEN, MARK
[b.] Salt Lake City; [p.] Alan K. Allen and Sharon Hatch; [pers.] Special thanks to my inspiration: Jenelyn, love always.; [a.] Salt Lake City, UT

ALLEN, SUSAN
[b.] February 28, 1981, Hubertus; [p.] Gloria and Bob Allen; [ed.] High School 10th grade Hartford Union High School; [occ.] 15 year old student; [oth. writ.] I have written many other poems and I keep them collected. Born in Beaver Dam, WI moved to Molalla, Oregon 1982-1988 now reside in Hartford.; [pers.] To me, poems are my way to bring out thoughts and any opinion I have. Poems are good ways for expressions.; [a.] Hartford, WI

ALLISTON, NORMA NOVELLA
[b.] January 3, 1923, Brookport, IL; [p.] Hale and Ethel Kerr; [m.] Howard Alliston, April 23, 1941; [ch.] Lee, Sue and Timothy, 12 grand, 15 great; [ed.] Eastern Michigan University Graduated 1970 - Master Science Deg. Speech Therapy; [occ.] Retired; [memb.] Belleville Church of Christ; [oth. writ.] Only special poems for special people and special events; [pers.] Niece of Nell Modglin, who belonged to many poetry organizations.; [a.] Ypsilanti, MI

ALVILLAR, MONICA V.
[b.] October 13, 1982, EL Paso; [p.] Rosa and Frank Alvillar; [ed.] St. Joseph's School, I am going to be a Freshman at Loretto Academy High School; [occ.] Student; [memb.] National Junior Honor Society, Junior Olympic Volleyball Team Bordercity Eagles, Kids and Company Playhouse; [hon.] President of National Junior Honor Society (NJHS); [oth. writ.] Short stories in the school paper, The Soaring Eagle.; [pers.] Life is lived to love and hate. We only accomplish what we love and truly desire, and we hate the obstacles that try to stop us.; [a.] El Paso, TX

ALVIN, BAKER WILLIAM
[b.] July 1, 1948, Rochester, NY; [p.] Arnold, Edith; [m.] Becky Wood, March 29, 1993; [ch.] Jenny, Billy, Destinie, Jeremy, Teddi, and Whysper; [occ.] Househusband; [a.] Mesa, AR

AMMERMAN, GALE R.
[b.] March 6, 1923, Sullivan, IN; [p.] Lyman and Iva Ammerman; [m.] Jane L. Ammerman nee Burke, September 26, 1943; [ch.] Kathleen, John, Joe, Mark and Chris; [ed.] Ph.D. Purdue Univ.; [occ.] Professor Emeritus, Miss State Univ.; [memb.] Institute of Food Technologists, Council for Agric. Sci. and Technology, Phi Tau Sigma, Phi Kappa Phi, Gamma Sigma Delta; [hon.] Alpha Zeta Honor Society, Member Phi Kappa Phi, Fellow of I.F.T., Member of Gamma Sigma Delta, past Pres. Phi Tau Sigma; [oth. writ.] 200 scientific papers, book Careers in Food Technol. author of Your Career in Food

Technology, Richard Rosen Press, NY., author *Home Canning* Wimmer Bros Press, Memphis.; [pers.] A scientist turned author, I have two completed manuscripts which I hope to publish this year.; [a.] Aliceville, AL

ANDERSON, ANTHONY
[p.] Daisy Anderson, Perry Anderson; [m.] Anna Marie Anderson; [ch.] Khaleel Amir, Anthony Jr.; [ed.] Jamaica High School, Lamar University, [a.] Queens Village, NY

ANDERSON, HELEN
[b.] April 2, 1946, Brooklyn, NY; [p.] Olof (Deceased) and Halfrid Anderson; [ed.] West Hempstead High Adelphi Business School; [occ.] Secretary in a law firm; [hon.] Winner of Communal poem at Borders Books and Music National Poetry months (April 1996) won $15.00 Gift Certificate and a bookmark. I bought a dictionary with the certificate.; [pers.] My poetry brings great joy into my life. What a surprise to discover as an adult that I could write and that people take an interest in my poems. To see my words in print is so special to me.; [a.] West Hempstead, NY

ANDERSON, ROBERT
[p.] Richard Anderson, Sylvia Anderson; [ch.] Larinda Kelby Anderson, Jason Daniel Anderson; [ed.] Oklahoma State University; [occ.] United States Postal Service/FSM Clerk; [oth. writ.] "Warriors Dream," "Last and Final Battle," "Creation," "Warmth from Within"; [pers.] Looking through the windows of heaven, seeing the fairest among all daughters, and the noblest of all young knights. Love to both my children.; [a.] Oklahoma City, OK

ANDERSON, ROBIN
[b.] November 22, 1963, Rutherfordton, NC; [p.] Larry Mull, Barbara Waters; [ch.] Joshua Brooks, Skylar Brent; [ed.] Chase High School, Isothermal Community College, Montreat College; [occ.] Data Entry Operator Shelby, NC; [hon.] Dean's List; [a.] Forest City, NC

ANDERSON, RUBY A.
[b.] January 9, 1915, Morris, IL; [p.] Deceased; [m.] Deceased, August 3, 1938; [ch.] Three children, seven grandchildren and three great-grandchildren; [ed.] Jr. High School; [occ.] Retired; [oth. writ.] Two Christmas stories I wrote when I was 14, Received a doll as one first prize and a train set for the other. I love to write poetry.; [pers.] I was raised on the farm, married a farmer and lived all my life close to God and nature. The country is a beautiful quiet spot to think of all see all God's wonderful creation.; [a.] Newark, IL

ANDRUS, MICHAEL G.
[b.] July 22, 1952, Provo, UT; [p.] Clair and Ruby Andrus; [m.] Treasa Andrus; [ch.] Wendy, Jeffrey, Richard, Russell, Angela; [occ.] Hospital Administrator; [a.] Preston, ID

AOUDE, LANA
[b.] December 29, 1964, Beirut, Lebanon; [pers.] The one goal worth striving for is the pursuit of truth in all things.; [a.] Roslindale, MA

AQUILINA, RHONDA L.
[b.] November 28, 1969, San Francisco; [p.] Tom and Jean Aquilina; [m.] Gary D. Saballos; [ed.] High School, some college, court reporting school (High School, St. Paul, USF, Court Reporter Training Center); [occ.] Court Reporter; [pers.] "If Only" was created in 1988, when I met my significant other, Gary, who inspired me to write this poem, and it is to Gary that I dedicate "If Only"; [a.] Chicago, IL

ARDIS, BETTY
[b.] July 14, 1927, Ruth, MS; [p.] JC and Ethel McCullough Coghlan; [m.] Deceased; [ch.] Seven; [ed.] College; [occ.] Nurse; [oth. writ.] An unpublished book of 100 poems for children

ARMIJO, DEBORAH L.
[b.] September 18, 1955, Covina, CA; [p.] George and Bee Armijo; [ch.] Justin Waldon, Katie Waldon, Jedediah Waldon; [ed.] Glendora High School; [occ.] Manager Escrow Officer, Home Escrow Co, Inc.; [oth. writ.] For friends and family.; [pers.] All that I have written comes from my heart, whether it be love, pain, or just because.; [a.] Hesperia, CA

ARNOLD, LISA
[b.] January 24, 1966, Denver, CO; [p.] Carolyn Blough, Larry Herrera; [ch.] Stephanie (9 yrs.), Zachariah (3 yrs.); [ed.] Abraham Lincoln High School, Denver, CO; [occ.] Photographer for Nationwide Studios, Pharmacy Tech.; [hon.] Semi-finalist in the National Library of Poetry contest 1996; [pers.] Live for the passions that burn inside yourself. It never dies. It just burns forever.; [a.] Denver, CO

ARNOLD, RAYMOND MORRIS
[b.] April 24, 1983, Baltimore; [p.] Melinda Arnold and Jerry Arnold; [ed.] Dublin Elementary and Southampton Middle, now entering 8th grade; [occ.] Student; [memb.] 4-H; [hon.] Young Author's Conference Award 1994; [oth. writ.] Several short stories (Sci. fic./fantasy); [pers.] Instead of sitting around forgetting dreams, people should follow their dream wherever it may lead them.; [a.] Street, MD

ARRINGTON, FRAN BRAKE
[pen.] Fran Brake Arrington; [b.] March 18, 1947, Waverly, TN; [p.] Jack and Arbie Brake; [m.] Cliff Arrington, November 23, 1982; [ch.] Traye, Chris, Tim, and Johnny (Aric); [ed.] Maplewood High, Nsg School; [occ.] Disabled Nurse due to severe spinal disease; [memb.] Goodlettsville Church of Christ. Past Matron 1986 Madison Chapter #479 O.E.S. Worthy Matron 1996 Madison #479 O.E.S. Past Matrons of Middle TN; [hon.] Lettered in drama, speech, and poetry.; [oth. writ.] None published, those I share to my friends. "This Land Was My Land" for my Indian Ancestors.; [pers.] Dedicated to my best friend, my Amy Lowe and Edna St. Vincent Molay were great influences to me. Since my body is racked with pain every day, there are days you don't think it is even worth going on. I think of Job and Jesus suffering, and I go on; [a.] Goodlettsville, TN

ARTEZA, JONATHAN B.
[b.] August 1, 1982, Miami, FL; [p.] Gloria and Alden Arteza; [ed.] Sunset Preparatory School, St. Timothy School, St. Thomas Aquinas High School; [occ.] High School Student; [memb.] NJHS (National Junior Honor Society), Student Council; [hon.] Salutatorian (1996), Citizenship Award, second honors, first honors, Presidential Academic Excellence Award, Presidential Physical Fitness Award, Principal's award, Spanish award, Service award.; [oth. writ.] Several poems published in School Magazines (St. Timothy): Metanoia ('94-'95), writings ('95-'96); [a.] Lauderhill, FL

ASABOR, JOYCE
[pen.] Joyce Osakwe; [b.] March 16, 1961, Lagos; [p.] Phillip and Monica Osakwe; [m.] Rey Timothy Asabor, March 16, 1991; [ch.] Emmanuella 4 yrs and Joshua 12 months; [ed.] Bachelors Degree in Journalism (College of Journalism, London) 1981-85; [occ.] Freelance Journalist; [memb.] None so far here in the US, in Nigeria (Nigerian Institute of Public Relations (NIPR), Nigerian Union of Journalists (NIJ)) Member of the Editorial Board of West African Bankers Association News; [hon.] Ordained Pastor (Nov. 1993) Lagos Nigeria; [oth. writ.] Various poems and a book on my experience since coming to the US as an Asylee (yet to be published).; [pers.] Always look unto God the Author and finisher of our faith and to be used as an instrument of hope to those who have lost hope in everything.; [a.] New York, NY

ASHWORTH, DIANNA IRENE
[pen.] Solitaire; [b.] January 19, 1962, Hammond, IL; [p.] Maureen James, Daniel Lievers; [m.] Robert Charles Ashworth, February 12, 1994; [ch.] Constance Sharp, Patrick Sharp, Gabrielle Sharp, Desirae Sessa; [ed.] Manchester Regional H.S. Haledon, N.J.; [occ.] Competitive Shopper Tax preparer.; [memb.] Suncoast Chapter Red Cross volunteer, St. Patrick's Church; [hon.] 1975 - Track 'n' field 1st and 2nd place High Jump. 1976-78 N.Y.S Swim championships 1st medley relay - 2nd 100 meter.; [oth. writ.] Several poems, but never published.; [pers.] I wrote this particular poem in memoriam of the pressing times of my life, and the losses yet to regain.; [a.] Tampa, FL

ASKEW, MERLE
[b.] August 29, 1928, Visalia, CA; [p.] Jimmie and Mary Askew; [m.] Judith Askew, May 29, 1952; [ch.] Tina Suzanne, James Mitchell, Lisa Jeanette; [ed.] College of the Redwoods, Mendocino, Coast Education Center Fort Bragg, California; [occ.] Communications Operator II 911 and Dispatch, Calif. Hwy Patrol; [memb.] Oakland Police and Fire Retirement Assn., Disabled Fire and Police Assn. California Callback Assn., "Radio Dispatchers Assn. Cause"; [pers.] "Love one another!" is the best advice I've heard.; [a.] Grass Valley, CA

ATKINS, KRISTIE
[b.] December 1, 1977; [p.] Theresa and Bill Atkins; [ed.] University of Maryland at College Park; [pers.] We often go through life chasing after stale things, so we may assure ourselves that our needs have been met. We are left to realize, we can no longer hold onto the things we shall never have again. We must then face the things left for us and move on from the things dwelling in our pasts. To my angel brother who is dancing amongst the clouds of heaven, I thank you for your strength.; [a.] Silver Spring, MD

AUGUSTE, JUNIA L.
[b.] May 29, 1982, Haiti; [p.] Joseph, Paulette Auguste; [ed.] 9th grade; [occ.] Student; [a.] Brooklyn, NY

AUGUSTIN, SINDY
[b.] November 17, 1976, Haiti; [p.] Darnel Augustin, Marie Augustin; [ed.] Edward R. Murrow High School; [pers.] I try every day to do the best because, since one of my best friends went on to a better place, I think if there's other people with the AIDS virus, don't give up, keep fighting and that's why I wrote this poetry.; [a.] Brooklyn, NY

AUTIO, MILDRED I.
[b.] August 11, 1927, Finlayson, MN; [p.] Ernest, Jennie Belling; [m.] Ray J. Autio (Deceased 1989), November 2, 1946; [ch.] Three sons, one daughter, six grandchildren; [ed.] 1-8 Country School Dist. 36, 9-12 Willow River High, Elder College Lakewood Community College, all in Minnesota; [occ.] Retired; [oth. writ.] "Dance of the Winter Winds", "Farewell to Autumn"; [pers.] My married life gave deep thoughts and some ideas for writing. I write about the great outdoors. The weather fascinates me, it is one element that humans cannot alter. Where I live we get all sorts of storms winter and summer, I love to witness all types (violent or just rough) and my life also.; [a.] Saint Paul, MN

AVILA, PHYLLIS ESPERANZA
[b.] July 28, 1975, Northridge, CA; [p.] Karen Davis and Tony Avila; [ch.] Aric Kratz; [occ.] Retail; [oth. writ.] I have a personal collection, just gathering dust.; [pers.] Always be at peace, and show kindness to those around you.; [a.] Santa Monica, CA

BABB, KHADIJA L.
[pen.] Dee Dee; [b.] September 14, 1987, Nashville, TN; [p.] Nieta Babb, Rod Edmundson; [ed.] Gateway Elementary School grade 4; [occ.] Student; [memb.] Youth Choir; [hon.] Honor Roll, Achievement Award; [a.] Nashville, TN

BABIN, JENNIFER T.
[b.] September 25, 1970, Baton Rouge, LA; [p.] Warren and Anna Thrasher; [m.] Barry J. Babin, December 9, 1995; [ed.] Bachelor of Science in Psychology at Louisiana State University in Baton Rouge; [occ.] Nanny with Almost Mom in Zachary, LA; [oth. writ.] Several poems published in my high school newspaper.; [pers.] I am happiest when I am doing what I enjoy and that is being creative. Each person has a gift that God bestowed on us at our birth, yet it must be constantly nurtured because each gift is precious and should be cherished.; [a.] Brusly, LA

BACALZO, NATIVIDAD F.
[pen.] Nat de Leon; [b.] June 25, 1917, Manila, Philippines; [p.] Fermin and Dolores Fabico (Deceased); [m.] Anacleto Bacalzo (Deceased), August 18, 1937; [ch.] Benjamin Bacalzo MD; [ed.] Bachelor of Science in Education; [occ.] Retired; [pers.] I wanted to test my intelligence of years past, that is, if I could still bring out the glitter of an intellectual gift, and with this honor, I feel strongly that I still have the wit or mental capacity to compete.; [a.] Tamarac, FL

BACON, ROWENA L.
[b.] October 26, 1923, Kentucky; [p.] Henry and Mollie Fields; [ch.] Tawny Hale, John Mack Brown, and Perry Robert Moore and 3 Grand children; [occ.] Retired Grandmother; [oth. writ.] Writes poetry for entertainment of family and friends. Always striving to point out the wonder of God.; [pers.] He's always there the river of life Home Life, outside my window many others.

BACUN, WADE
[b.] June 19, 1976, Clewiston, FL; [ed.] Currently in College, Attending Colorado State University; [occ.] Student; [pers.] The imagination is the key to the soul, pen and paper is merely a door.

BAILEY, ARLOW
[b.] September 15, 1953, Iowa City, IA; [m.] Divorced; [ch.] Mark Bailey; [ed.] AA Degree Park and Natural Resources AA Degree Orthopaedic Physician Assisting; [occ.] Orthopaedic Physicians Assistant; [memb.] ASOPA, FAOT, NAOT; [oth. writ.] Unpublished book "Lovecycles Here's How I See It", over 70 poems on religion, Looking for Love, Finding Love, Losing Love. Then doing Positive Affirmations in order to cope the loss and start over.; [pers.] I imagine myself as a coal miner's light, shining love on all that I see.

BAILEY, NICOLE M.
[b.] April 13, 1980, SLC, UT; [p.] Cory and Gloria Bailey; [ed.] Graduating with honors from Jordan High; [occ.] Free-Lance writer; [memb.] International Thespian Society, Artistic Honor Society; [hon.] Theatrical Letter, Thespian Membership; [oth. writ.] Several poems honored by local contests; [pers.] I don't write for fame, glory, or recognition. I write for personal satisfaction and that's taken me places you can't go with any other motivation.; [a.] Sandy, UT

BAILEY, TERRI LYN
[b.] December 12, 1977, Bay City, MI; [p.] Thomas and Nancy Bailey; [ed.] Graduate of Central High School, current freshman at Delta College; [hon.] 2 Savings bonds and a gold charm for 1 year perfect attendance in high school, certificate for a tutoring program; [oth. writ.] National Library of Poetry's *The Rippling Waters* poem - "Graduation Day" Crest books from Central High School; [pers.] I write about things that have happened to me, because it helps get my feelings in the open. People should do what they can to get their feelings out, it helps.; [a.] Bay City, MI

BAILEY, TIMOTHY
[b.] May 23, 1975, Kentucky; [p.] William and Cathy Bailey; [ed.] English Major at Kent State (Stark) Fairless High School; [memb.] Rhetoric Society; [oth. writ.] Working on a book *Song Of A Turmoiled Heart*.; [pers.] I believe that knowledge is the key to everything, and the way to truth. Writing is the first thing I truly fell in love with.; [a.] Navarre, OH

BAKER, CHRISTINA J.
[pen.] Christina J. Baker; [b.] June 11, Tucson, AZ; [p.] Joe Baker and Pam Rauch; [ed.] Marana High School; [memb.] 4-H Raising Lambs and Pigs; [hon.] Honor Roll; [a.] Tucson, AZ

BAKER, LADONNA
[b.] July 22, 1974, Jackson, MS; [p.] Jo Baker (Mother) and LaDon Baker (Father); [ed.] High School: Woodland Hills Baptist Academy graduated: 1992, College: Holmes Community College and Hinds Community College, presently (College) University of Southern Mississippi, Major: Microbiology; [occ.] Bartender; [hon.] Mu Alpha Theta; [oth. writ.] Personal diary of collected and created poetry and short stories; [pers.] One must connect the heart, the mind, and the soul for the harmony of the self and for loved ones, in order to live a successful life. Find the goodness of your soul and pass it on to others through your kindness.; [a.] Jackson, MS

BALBIRER, IDA JANKO
[b.] January 14, 1916, N.Y.C., NY; [p.] Sam Janko, Sarah Janko; [m.] Hyman Balbirer, July 19, 1937; [ch.] Ralph, Susan; [ed.] High School and 80 years of living; [occ.] Retired musician and bookkeeper; [oth. writ.] A number of poems pertaining to family birthdays, anniversaries, etc. Am now working on an autobiography for the family and am being encouraged to have it published.; [pers.] The word "can't" is not in my vocabulary.; [a.] Woodridge, NY

BALDWIN, IRENE F.
[pen.] Irene Baldwin; [b.] September 7, 1911, Sturgeon, MO; [p.] David, Alice Roberts; [m.] Roy Willard, September 4, 1938, Fred Baldwin, March 31, 1973; [ch.] Charles, David Willard, Karen Polchek; [ed.] Sturgeon High (Mo), Chillicothe Business College and courses Med. Terminology at ASU; [occ.] Retired Medical Librarian, Mesa Luth. Hospital (10 years); [memb.] Faith Community Church, Eastern Star, New American Heart Assoc. Hospital Auxiliary; [hon.] Valedictorian (Class 1929), Mesa Lutheran Hosp. (On Retirement), Pres. Missions (Church), various comm.; [oth. writ.] Valedictorian Speech (Prose), writings in Auxiliary Paper, Poems for Guest of Hospital Writings Church Chronicle; [pers.] I want only to serve God and love my neighbor. To be a blessing to "someone" each day.; [a.] Chandler, AZ

BALL, MARIA
[pen.] Maria Moccia-Ball; [b.] November 18, 1956, Worcester, MA; [p.] Michael F. and Cecelia G. Moccia; [m.] Stephen Ball, September 18, 1993; [ed.] Grafton High, Quinsigamonn Community College 1 year; [occ.] Secretary; [hon.] 1st Degree Black Belt style of Martial Arts: Shaolin Kempo Karate; [oth. writ.] I have a manuscript of poems I have written. I have never submitted any of my work until now to Nat. Lib. of Poetry. I would like information on how to publish my poems.; [pers.] All of my poems came from within, everything I write comes from my heart.; [a.] Rutland, MA

BALSINGER, ANNA
[b.] October 28, 1920, Brentwood, MD; [p.] John P. and Ruth C. Hoffman; [m.] July 14, 1941; [ch.] 7, 39 Grandchildren, 52 Great-Grandchildren; [ed.] GED - 1969 Statistical Asst. Amer. Univ. Wash, DC; [occ.] Correspondent (Herald Standard Newspaper); [memb.] Fayette County Community Action Agency Inc. on the Advisory Council and Senior Citizen Center; [oth. writ.] "Day's I Remember," "Remembering Mama," "Immortality," "We Only Have One Mother," "Just For Today," "Childhood," "Our Sorrows;" [pers.] I am the type of person who makes friends easily and I have lots of them in both PA and MD and enjoy my friends and my life.; [a.] Uniontown, PA

BAND, JILL
[b.] May 19, 1971, Livingston, NJ; [p.] Jeffrey Band and Ellen Band; [ed.] East Brunswick High, University of South Florida, National College of Chiropractic; [occ.] Doctor of Chiropractic; [memb.] American Chiropractic Association, East Brunswick Jewish Center; [hon.] Dean's List; [oth. writ.] I am in the process of writing a children's poetry book titled "Just A Kid I Am"; [pers.] Poetry has always been my escape and hobby. I have gained great confidence in my writing through my mom, dad, brother Kenny and companion Michael.; [a.] Oak Park, IL

BANDELE, AJAMU
[pen.] Ajamu Bandele; [b.] February 20, 1946, Tolleson, AZ; [ch.] Five children; [ed.] Glendale, AZ Elementary Unit I, Glendale High, Glendale Community College; [occ.] Quality Engineer Ipec/ Planar; [memb.] TNBA - Bowling Assoc.; [hon.] Baseball scholarship - GCC, March 1, 1966 inspiration to write books; [oth. writ.] Think About It (unpublished), Adult Jokes and Poems (unpublished), A Book Of Short Stories And Trivia (U.P.), A Book Of Poems, A Black Man's View (U.P.), A Book Of Poems - Vol. 2 A Black Man's View (U.P.); [pers.] I write my material for people to learn from, es-

pecially young children and teenagers. "Success is the rage but success comes with wisdom and wisdom comes with age."; [a.] Phoenix, AZ

BARNETT, DAWN
[b.] April 22, 1968, Milwaukee, WI; [p.] Joseph and Linda Fate; [m.] John Barnett, August 26, 1995; [ed.] Oak Creek Senior High, University of WI - Oshkosh, B.A. in Journalism; [occ.] Marketing Manager Attalus, USA, Chicago, IL; [oth. writ.] Several human interest stories published in Community Newspapers, Inc.; [pers.] Classic American Literature and poetry have always inspired me. To me, writing poetry is the key which unlocks the door to your soul.; [a.] Deerfield, IL

BARONETTE, SANDRA JOY
[pen.] Esjoi; [b.] February 14, 1964, Jamaica, WI; [p.] Gloria Andrade; [ed.] Mount Nebo Elementary School, Haile Selassie High School, Liguanea Adult Learning Centre Kingstown J.W.I.; [occ.] Child Care Technician; [oth. writ.] I write a lot in my spare time and over the years. I have developed quite a collection of unpublished poems and lyrics.; [pers.] I get much joy from living I want to give back as much as I get, but I wonder if that's possible, because life is such generously given.; [a.] Brooklyn, NY

BAROT, ATMARAM J.
[b.] September 6, 1936, Nisraya, India; [p.] Jivanlal Barot, Maniben Barot; [m.] Niranjana Barot, February 28, 1960; [ch.] Kandarp/Yagnesh/Nilesh; [ed.] M.A. (Guj Uni A'Bad), B.Ed. (Guj Uni India); [occ.] Retired as an Adult Education officer Gov't of Gujrat (India); [hon.] Honor was given by K.M. Munshi - a great Indian Author; [oth. writ.] Some poems and articles were published in Gujarati (India) newspapers.; [pers.] I like to write on beauty, nature and social problems.; [a.] Chicago, IL

BARRETT, DESSIE
[pen.] Dessie Bryant; [b.] December 14, 1928; [p.] Wade Bryant, Agnes McCarrell Bryant; [ch.] Karoll Smith, Gretchen McCormick, John Bryant Guza; [occ.] Retired; [oth. writ.] Freelance and staff newspaper writing, poem in voice, Eastern Arizona College Publication. Several poetry anthologies.; [pers.] I grew up in the Rio Grande Valley of New Mexico. Much of my writing has a Southwestern flavor.; [a.] Safford, AR

BARROS, JASON
[b.] April 25, 1924, Brockton, MA; [p.] Arthur Barros, Peggy Barros; [ed.] Bridgewater/Raynham Regional High School, University of Amherst; [occ.] Student; [memb.] International Tang Soo Do Federation; [pers.] Writing is the window to the soul.; [a.] Bridgewater, MA

BARTLETT, YVONNE M.
[b.] October 25, Detroit, MI; [p.] Ms. Thelmarie E. Johnson; [m.] Rodney H. Bartlett, March 27; [ch.] LaCicely Nicole, Tequila Brandyce, Rodnica Jeanee; [ed.] Cass Tech. High, Detroit College of Business; [occ.] Administrative Secretary 2, Wayne County, Detroit, MI; [memb.] Moses Temple Baptist Church; [hon.] Dean's List; [oth. writ.] Several poems published in the Moses Temple Baptist Church bulletins, songs; [pers.] "With God, All things are possible..." (Matt. 19:26); [a.] Redford Township, MI

BARTON, LOIS
[b.] July 21, 1951, Elmhurst, IL; [p.] Harry Gerlich, Lillian Gerlich; [ch.] Richard Young, Lisa Young; [pers.]

Thanks to my family who allowed me to express myself and stood beside me in both good times and bad. Their continuous support has prompted me to share this poem with others.; [a.] Villa Park, IL

BASCKO, SHIRLEY ANN
[b.] August 24, 1946, Augusta, AR; [p.] Monteen McCurdy - Roy Elvin Murray; [m.] Richard Bascko (Deceased), September 28, 1973; [ch.] Regina Bascko, Kenneth Bascko; [ed.] Searcy High School, Searcy, AR, La Salle University Chicago, Illinois Artex University, Beverly Enterprises Little Rock, Arkansas; [occ.] Ancillary Clerk for Beverly Health and Rehabilitation Center Searcy, Arkansas; [memb.] Jesus Name Church Patterson, Arkansas, International Society of Poets; [hon.] Arkansas Children's Hospital Little Rock, Arkansas Leisure Lodge Nursing Center of Searcy, Arkansas (1 year of service); [oth. writ.] Life Is Too Short For Hang Ups, Love Can Hurt, Pain Of A Mother, Happy Father's Day To A Loving Father, Love Sick, I Need You To Love Me, A Dad Like You, All The Little Things, You Can Always Find A Way; [pers.] I would like to dedicate this poem to James C. Smith Sr. of Searcy AR, the man I love, who is so dear to me. Many of my poems revolve around J.C and my feelings for Him.; [a.] Kensett, AR

BASHAY, CHEYENNE M.
[b.] April 4, 1976, Trinidad, Pos; [p.] Morris Bashay and Elisha Bashay; [ed.] Arima Senior Comprehensive High School, Trinidad West, Indies; [occ.] Security Ramp Agent and Officer at J.F.K. International Airport; [hon.] The United States Armed Forces; [oth. writ.] I've also written lots of poems for churches, schools and concerts, but none ever to be published; [pers.] Over the years I've been deeply touched and inspired by poetry written about God or to God. This great talent has been brought about by the help of my father, and by the great talent he also possesses in poetry writing; [a.] Queens Village, NY

BATTLE SR., REV. DONALD EDWIN
[b.] February 24, 1950, St. Petersburg, FL; [p.] Christine Neal; [m.] Cordelia Elaine Battle, June 21, 1969; [ch.] Donald Battle, Jr., Celeste Battle; [ed.] Delaware County College 1971, American Institute of Banking 1975, International Bible Seminary 1982; [occ.] Founder, President and Director The International Evangelical Mission; [memb.] Living Waters Community Worship Center, (Assoc. Minister) International Seminary Ministerial Assoc.; [hon.] Dean's List Honor Graduate, International Bible Seminary 1982; [oth. writ.] Bible Commentary Articles, Journalist - The Good News Christian Journal, Song Writing, and Poetry.; [pers.] Love is the greatest Power in all the universe. Its Power has no limit, so Love will never, ever, fail, because God is Love!; [a.] Swedesboro, NJ

BATTS, JAMES
[pen.] James Clark Batts; [b.] June 1, 1941, Melrose Park, IL; [p.] Harry Batts, Elizabeth Batts; [m.] Karen Batts; [ch.] Allyson, Erik, Christopher; [ed.] Proviso East High, Drake University, Northwestern University; [occ.] English Teacher, Niles West High School; [memb.] Ivy Lynn Chaplik Award Committee, National Honor Society Committee; [hon.] Monroe Dram Scholarship, Outstanding Junior Award, Outstanding Senior Award, Notre Dame, 1988, *Who's Who Among American's Teachers*. Trustee to Village of Kildeer; [oth. writ.] Poetry published previously in The National Library of Poetry.; [a.] Kildeer, IL

BAYSINGER, JESSICA
[pen.] Jessica Baysinger; [b.] August 19, 1981, Denver, CO; [p.] Evelyn Krus and Randy Baysinger; [ed.] Brighton High School; [occ.] Student; [oth. writ.] None published 2 books - Cafe Jeans, One Eye Always Looking, many other poems that weren't published; [pers.] A good friend told me, "Persevere, it will be worth it - not just for you, but for the rest of us."; [a.] Brighton, CO

BEALS, AMANDA M.
[pen.] Cheyanne; [b.] November 13, 1976, Madison, WI; [p.] Judy Beals and Rellis Beals; [ed.] Ball State University, Ohio State University, Major Journalism.; [occ.] Student; [pers.] Rarely does one have an original thought that has not been inspired by another, thinking is just the uniqueness with which you express those thoughts.; [a.] Chillicothe, OH

BEAUREGARD, BETHANY
[pen.] Beth Marie; [b.] March 1, 1988, Woonsochet, RI; [p.] Edward Beauregard, Cynthia Beauregard; [ed.] 2nd Grade Student at J.F.K., Elementary - Blackstone MA; [memb.] Blackstone Little League - Blackstone Youth Soccer; [hon.] Superstar Student - 1995; [pers.] "I write poems to make people happy with happy thoughts." "I Write How I Feel."; [a.] Blackstone, MA

BECK, ERIKA
[pen.] Judy Fuller; [b.] October 2, 1927, Germany; [m.] Ronald E. Beck, December 19, 1948 (Deceased), March 15, 1992; [ch.] Gary, Robert, Ronald, Irene, David; [ed.] Germany; [occ.] Retired; [memb.] Ladies Aux. Taylor Hose Co. No 1 Eastern Star, Meth. Church Moscow; [oth. writ.] 25th, 26th 27th Ann. Stewardship Project, essays, poems 1959.; [pers.] I strive to reach the heart of mankind. To bring out inner feelings. I have been writing poems since I was 9 years old. Personal, to specific family members and friends.; [a.] Moscow, PA

BECKER, CATHY L.
[b.] September 17, 1954, Syracuse, NY; [p.] Paul Bowker, Jean Bowker; [m.] Jack, August 20, 1976; [ch.] Sara, Jennifer, Anthony; [ed.] Liverpool High, Kent State University; [pers.] I strive to integrate my personal experiences and emotions into my writing. I have been influenced by the writings of the great William B. Yeats.; [a.] North Canton, OH

BECKER, MELISSA Y.
[b.] June 28, 1960, Wis. Rapids, WI; [p.] Mavis Ann Kuehl, Raymond C. Kuehl Sr.; [m.] Kenneth A. Becker Sr., March 31, 1990; [ch.] Cory (Roo-Roo) Christopher and Kenny Jr., (Twins) Nicole and my heartbeats; [ed.] Wautoma High; [occ.] Sewing machine operator; [pers.] Dreams can come true, maybe not the way you imagine it but sometimes better. Never give up hope or belief in God even when it seems He is not there.; [a.] Oshkosh, WI

BEECHIE, TERESA
[b.] September 21, 1979, San Jose, CA; [p.] Jay and Mary Beechie; [occ.] High School student; [pers.] "Nobody knows exactly how fascinating you are, because they can never see inside your mind". So I make it a point to tell aloud what others cannot see in my mind.; [a.] Bakersfield, CA

BEGUHN, GINA
[b.] September 28, 1980, Waukesha, WI; [p.] David Beguhn and Denise Beguhn; [ed.] Oconomowoc High School; [occ.] Full time student graduating in 1999; [a.] Oconomowoc, WI

BEILMAN, EDWINA N.
[b.] May 18, 1910, Sagamore, MA; [p.] Charles and Genera Eldredge; [m.] Edward V. Beilman, November 3, 1945; [ed.] Grammar (Sagamore) High (Bourne, MA) Fine Arts Graduate of the Swain Sch. of Design New Bedford, Mass; [occ.] Retired Supervisor of Art of Grades 1-12 Biddeford ME, Hamilton Hon Mass Hampton NH 12 yrs. Private Sch. Riverview; [memb.] E Sandwich (Special Ed) Music Sch. Centerville MA Artist at Disney Studios, Calif. Employed Artist by Domestic Thermostate Calif. Employed by U.S. Engineers, Manhattan Project 3 yrs during (war); [hon.] U.S. Eng. Award for saving life of 3 yr. old in water Richland, Wash, Received prize for watercolor painting Sturgiss Library of Towne Barnstable Cape Cod. Mass and Plaque hangs in Hyannis, Mass selectmens office. Cape Cod; [pers.] Sometimes ago I read and I believe there is a rhythm of universal law. This rhythm sets vibrations in motion around me (us) bringing back to me (us) what I've set forth, with God's help.; [a.] West Barnstable, MA

BEILSTEIN, REV. JOAN E.
[b.] December 14, 1960, Washington, DC; [ed.] Master of Divinity, The General Theological Seminary, New York, NY.; [occ.] Episcopal Priest; [hon.] The church and society award for master's thesis entitled "The Message of Job in the age of Aids" Dean's List, Alpha Kappa Delta; [oth. writ.] Articles for the Washington Diocese of the Episcopal church newspapers, contributor to homily services.; [pers.] I strive to be a vehicle of God's all-inclusive love, care and compassion in the world.; [a.] Springfield, VA

BERENS, JUDITH ANN
[b.] March 4, 1949, Clarksburg, WV; [p.] David O'Brien, Carol O'Brien; [m.] Jerome Berens, February 2, 1974; [ch.] Christa Kay, Danielle Christine, Amanda Joy and Veronica Ann; [ed.] Waukegan Township High, Blackburn College, College of Lake County; [occ.] Graphic Artist; [memb.] Calvary Temple Church, Lake County Fighting Back; [hon.] Lake County Fighting Back Chairman's Award; [oth. writ.] Article in Spirit newspaper.; [pers.] My poems are inspired by love, beauty, observations and emotions. "The Hug" was written for Christa, my first-born baby woman.; [a.] Wadsworth, IL

BERNHARD, CONSTANCE M.
[b.] February 1, 1957, Reading, PA; [p.] David Seyfert, Janice Seyfert; [m.] David R. Bernhard, November 17, 1993; [ch.] Casey R. Bernhard (age 22), Mickey D. Bernhard (age 20); [occ.] Hershey Chocolate, USA; [oth. writ.] "Angel In Disguise", "Your Hand Is Not A Weapon", "I'm Only Two Feet Tall", "Birthday Tears"... and many others...; [pers.] This particular poem was written for my brother. David Seyfert Jr. who was killed at the young age of 29. He had made plans to help us move into our new home on Sept. 28 & 29, but his plans were never fulfilled, because on this day he was killed in a tragic car accident at 4:05 a.m.... killed instantly. So, I write for my mother... she places the poem in the newspaper on special occasions. This poem, one of many short I have written... is in memory of a beloved brother, friends and son. My poems do not always pertain to death, but they all do reflect upon God. My goal in writing poetry... is that the reader will in some way think about God.; [a.] Denver, PA

BERNIER, DIANE S.
[pen.] D. S. Bernier; [b.] September 17, 1944, Bridgewater, MA; [pers.] Dedicated to my Michelle with love, Mom; [a.] Danielson, CT

BERRY, W. RICHARD
[b.] February 26, 1945, Madison, IN; [p.] Russell and Alice Berry; [m.] Judy, February 12, 1966; [ch.] Carmen and Melissa; [ed.] 3 yrs. College; [occ.] Indiana Kentucky Elect. Corp, Personnel Dept.; [memb.] I.S.P.; [hon.] Distinguished Poet of I.S.P. Award Of Merit, Editors Choice; [oth. writ.] Published "Rhymes with reason," "memories", and two (2) more in publishing process; [pers.] My poems are to star memories of poverty and friends now and many years from now.; [a.] Hanover, IN

BERTIN, SOLANGE M.
[b.] August 4, 1925, Paris, France; [ed.] International Institute of Reflexology (Florida), Acupressure Institute of America (Cal.); [oth. writ.] Several poems, unpublished yet.; [pers.] 26 years surviving three cancers.; [a.] Anchorage, AK

BERUMEN, ELIZABETH
[pen.] Elizabeth Berumen; [b.] August 9, 1965, Long Branch, NJ; [p.] Clara Delpizzo, Peter Pine; [m.] William Berumen, December 21, 1995; [ch.] Michael Pine, Christopher Pine; [ed.] Mercer County Comm. College, Our Lady of Enchantment Seminary of Wicca; [occ.] Registered Nurse, Seminary Student; [oth. writ.] Numerous unpublished Childhood - Teen Year poems, nothing previously published.; [pers.] This poem Fairy Bright has special meaning to me. I believe in Angels, Fairies and other nature spirits I hope this poem will inspire those who read it.; [a.] Sacramento, CA

BEY, JAMAL M.
[b.] September 3, 1943, Canton, OH; [p.] Mrs. Lyria R. Walters; [m.] Darla J. Bey; [ch.] Six; [occ.] Carpenter (Retired); [memb.] American Legion, A.L. Brooks Post #157, AARP; [hon.] Honorable discharge US Army (6 yrs.); [oth. writ.] Just recently completed book, entitled "The Self-Destruct Syndrome, the African-American Dilemma," still seeking publisher.; [pers.] The utmost praise is due to the Almighty God for He is the master potter, and I am the clay! "Blessed are all they that put their trust in him."; [a.] Columbus, OH

BIGGS, SONDRA
[b.] April 30, 1984, Brownwood, TX; [p.] Cindy Steel, Alvin Biggs; [ed.] 6th Grade, Early Middle School Early TX; [occ.] Student; [memb.] 4H, Boys and Girls Club; [hon.] Science Fair 2nd Place, Art Show 5th Place; [pers.] Sometimes the best things happen when you least expect them.; [a.] Early, TX

BILLINGTON, MEREDITH D.
[b.] March 27, 1975, Washington, DC; [p.] Errol and Marsha Billington; [ed.] High School and 2 years in College; [oth. writ.] Several unpublished poems and a couple of fiction works in progress; [pers.] I want my poetry to illustrate how nature works. I also wish to express human characteristics in animals living in the wild.; [a.] Silver Spring, MD

BINNICKER, MIKE B.
[b.] February 20, 1982, San Antonio, TX; [p.] Jim and Jan; [ed.] Judson High School, 9th grade; [memb.] NJHS Member, BSA Life Scout, Soccer for San Antonio Heat F.C.; [hon.] Super Honor Roll; [pers.] Anything that is worth having, you must work for.; [a.] University City, TX

BINNINGER, DONALD G.
[b.] October 1, 1928, Cleveland, OH; [p.] Amy and George Binninger; [m.] Helen E. Binninger, March 24, 1989; [ch.] Three - 1 son and 2 daughters; [ed.] Bachelor of Science in Journalism - 1952 University of Wisconsin; [occ.] Retired in 1995; [memb.] Editor of Village Newspaper "The Villager" in Desolo Villas in Bradenton, Florida; [pers.] Have written poems and short stories since High School, but haven't attempted to publish anything until now.

BIRDSALL, FLORENCE A.
[b.] November 3, 1912, Caro, MI; [p.] Chas F. and Atha Rosebush; [m.] Widow - J. A. Salswedel, December 10, 1930, Howard O. Birdsall, May 6, 1972; [ch.] Duane, Dale and Judy Salswedel; [ed.] Graduate Oxford High, June 1930; [occ.] Retired Bank Teller; [oth. writ.] Just my poetry which I titled 'Fond Memories'.; [pers.] I have never before submitted any of my poems. My family and friends have been my only inspiration.

BIRKET, TERESA A.
[b.] November 14, 1960, Florida; [m.] Bob L. Birket, November 14, 1988; [ch.] Brian (6), Heather (2); [ed.] Graduated High School, Graduated from Trade School - Medical Secretary; [occ.] Mother - Full-time and House Wife; [oth. writ.] In my High School Literary Magazine about 4 other poems; [pers.] Any recognition for any writing I do must be directed to Jesus who gives me any talent I may think I have.; [a.] Mesa, AZ

BIRKNER, IRENE
[b.] July 24, 1934, Paderborn, IL; [p.] Fred and Anne Wachtel; [m.] Zeno G. Birkner (Deceased), August 17, 1955; [ch.] Thirteen; [ed.] High School Grad.; [occ.] Child Care Center Cook; [oth. writ.] "Sweet Music" to be published.; [pers.] I write poetry as I am inspired, it's like inner reflections.; [a.] Millstadt, IL

BLAIR, MARION
[pen.] Granny "B"; [b.] September 10, 1938; [m.] Elige W. Blair Jr., September 14, 1957; [ch.] Bethanie Lyn (Blair) Godsey, Lance Everet Blair; [occ.] Poet, Author, Songwriter, Inventor; [oth. writ.] Finished manuscript - full book "Hillbilly Rhymes of the Blair Clan Tymes" by Granny "B." Contains 30 true stories of an early pioneer family who settled in East Tennessee. (Seeking Publication).; [pers.] This writer prefers to use poetry to portray true life experiences capturing poignant human drama in all phases, considering hillbilly/country her specialty. Particularly interested in genealogical work.; [a.] Knoxville, TN

BLAND, DAVID JOSEPH
[b.] August 31, 1976, Fairmont, WV; [p.] Pamela Kay Bland; [ed.] Sophomore at Fairmont State College majoring in Commercial Design/Graphics; [occ.] Freelance Artist/consultant at BDM Federal of NASA; [oth. writ.] Poetry published in *The Whetstone*, an art and literary journal of Fairmont State College; [pers.] My poetry is a collection of raw, unbridled, sometimes misguided emotions that depict scenes as unusual or unique as myself. (Some utterly beautiful, others grotesquely insane). Each one guaranteed to implant explicit visions inside your skull, or your money back.; [a.] Mannington, WV

BLEVINS, CLAUDINE CERRA
[b.] September 6, 1928, Schell City, MO; [p.] Walter and Frances Snider; [m.] Clyde Blevins, April 15, 1989; [ch.] Eight children; [ed.] 8th grade; [occ.] Writer, Singing, Ministry, Homemaker; [memb.] Word of Life

Church; [hon.] Top 3 of a finalist for poems "Quietly Waiting" "Hearts Cry" Best Poems of 90's - Semi-finalist "Bookwoods Yesterday" Library Poetry Award - Art Scholarship.; [oth. writ.] One poem book "Wings In The Valley", Two other books published. "I Watched God Make A Saint" and "Trophies Of God's Grace" over 300 country gospel songs.; [pers.] Born back in the hills of Missouri 1 of 16 children. Attended 1 room school house 1st and 8th grade - walked 3 miles going and coming, born poor. 1 room Baptist church I attended had great influence on my life where I learned you are rich if you have Jesus.; [a.] Kansas City, MO

BLONDER, NICOLE C.
[b.] November 16, 1969, Fresno; [p.] Gene and Patricia Blonder; [occ.] Elementary Teacher; [pers.] In loving memory of my little brother, Beau, who taught me how to live and love through God.; [a.] Fresno, CA

BLUESTEIN, CHERYL
[b.] January 22, 1953; [p.] Molly Mahl; [m.] H. Jack Bluestein, July 24, 1985; [ch.] Korrie, Andy, David; [ed.] University of Maryland Baltimore County, George Mason University, Southwest Missouri State U; [occ.] Gerontologist; [oth. writ.] Used to write weekly column on aging for a Gannett newspaper, associate editor *Aging Network News*(McLean, VA).; [pers.] Enjoy the human side of people of all ages - particularly those 80's!; [a.] Columbia, MD

BOCK, FRAN SPEARS
[b.] June 18, 1947, Tulsa, OK; [p.] Ace and Nina Spears; [m.] Russ Bock, June 3, 1969; [ch.] Tammy Bock, Sheila Bock; [ed.] North Texas State University, California State University Long Beach, Eastern Hills High School; [occ.] English Teacher at Torrance High School, Torrance, CA; [memb.] The Neighborhood Church, Covenant Choir; [hon.] *Who's Who Among America's Teachers*; [a.] Palos Verdes Estates, CA

BONIDIE, TRACEY
[b.] August 6, 1972, Pittsburgh, PA; [p.] Ronald and Loraine Leith; [m.] Steven R. Bonidie, February 26, 1994; [ed.] Woodland Hills High, Forbes Road East Votech School; [occ.] Office Representative State Farm Insurance; [a.] Monroe, MI

BONINE, JASON A.
[b.] February 1, 1980, Cottage Grove, MN; [p.] Gordon and Sheila Bonine; [ed.] Currently a Jr. at Park Sr. High in Cottage Grove, MN; [occ.] Student at Park Sr. High in Cottage Grove; [oth. writ.] The Fanged Hunter a short story published in our local newspaper, The Bulletin.; [pers.] I believe that people should have as many experiences in their lives as possible, and never sent a minute getting for the mundane.; [a.] Cottage Grove, MN

BOOKER, MICHAEL
[b.] June 27, 1960, Newark, NJ; [p.] Eugene Booker, Esther Booker; [m.] Juanita Booker, August 5, 1987; [ch.] Michael Jr., Shanita Michelle; [ed.] Malcolm X Shabazz High Springfield College; [occ.] Adoption Social Worker; [oth. writ.] "Reality" - "A Child's Heart", "Brother My Brother", "Dreams Come True"; [pers.] Live by your heart and truth never lies, because who you are within can not be disguised.; [a.] Springfield, MA

BORASH, JOSEPH
[pen.] Joe; [b.] March 7, 1979, Little Falls, MN; [p.] Jerome, Debra Borash; [ed.] I am a senior in High School Holdingford Minnesota; [memb.] Member Sportsmens Club, Member FFA; [hon.] I had my poem published in a book of high school students from Minnesota, 1994-95 and 1995-96 Multiple year award for *Who's Who Among American High School Students* State FFA Award; [a.] Rice, MN

BORBA, KATHLEEN D.
[pen.] Kathy Borba; [b.] August 20, 1955, Tulare; [p.] Bill and Agnes Newman; [ch.] Cory Douglas Borba; [ed.] AA Degree from Liberty University, AS Degree from College of Sequoias, I'm working toward my BA Degree at Liberty University, VA, Graduate from The Institute of Children's Literature in CT.; [occ.] Entrepreneur; [hon.] Tulare Emblem Club No. 217, Scholarship Award in High School. The name of the high school was Tulare Western H.S.; [oth. writ.] I've had two (2) poems and two (2) stories published in the children's magazine, "The Young Crusader."; [pers.] I strive to reflect the ways of Christ not only in my life but in my writing which is loving kindness to all.; [a.] Tulare, CA

BORGESEN, TAMMY LYNNE
[pen.] Tammy Borgesen; [b.] May 10, 1979, Dallas, TX; [p.] Paula Helena Borgesen; [ed.] Ursuline Academy - High School Senior; [occ.] Student; [hon.] English Honor - Sophomore Year, Member of Jesuit Thespian Society; [oth. writ.] Other poems I've written.; [pers.] I have always believed that love was at the root of all true happiness and love can never die.; [a.] Dallas, TX

BOURG, JOSEPH M.
[b.] May 26, 1960, New Orleans; [p.] Eli Bourg, Velma Bourg; [m.] Elizabeth Bourg, November 6, 1992; [ch.] Chrystal Hale; [ed.] Archbishop Shaw High, Phillips Junior College.; [occ.] Electrician; [hon.] Associate's Degree Electronics Engineering; [oth. writ.] Many more Christian poems not yet published; [pers.] My poems are God- inspired. Expressed in the forms of God. The Father God, The Son, and God the Holy Spirit; [a.] Gretna, LA

BOUTELLE, RUTH
[b.] December 18, 1917, Brooklyn, NY; [p.] Mabel and Harold Spangenberg; [m.] Gregory Boutelle (Deceased), April 22, 1950; [ch.] 4 son - Donald and Paul, Matthew, Gregory; [ed.] Erasmus Hall High Brooklyn College 1978 Summa Cum Laude; [occ.] Retired AT&T; [hon.] Phi Beta Kappa Alpha Sigma Lambda; [pers.] Writing poetry demands that you think, and analyze your feelings and attitudes. It provides an emotional and psychological catharsis.; [a.] West Palm Beach, FL

BOVE, JAMES L.
[pen.] Jim Bove; [b.] August 9, 1935, Hazleton, PA; [p.] Genevieve C. Bove and James V. Bove; [ed.] West Hazleton High School, West Hazleton, PA, Central Police Training School, Virginia State Police Academy, Richmond, VA, Northern Virginia Police Academy, Pope Road, Fairfax, VA; [occ.] Retired Fairfax County Virginia Police Officer; [hon.] Life saving award from the State of Pennsylvania, Honorable Discharge from United States Air Force; [oth. writ.] Wrote for School Newspaper and Literary Editor for the yearbook.; [pers.] I have always lived my life according to my Father's philosophy. He always said, "Anyone can do anything they want if they put their mind to it."; [a.] Alexandria, VA

BOWER, PHILIP MARK
[b.] March 21, 1972, Costa Mesa, CA; [p.] Dr. Douglas and Glenna Diener; [ed.] San Joaquin Valley College, University California of Riverside; [occ.] Real Estate; [hon.] High School Valedictorian; [oth. writ.] We're Going To The Beach Tomorrow.; [pers.] Life is a gift, not a promise. Happiness is achieved only with an individual's contentment.; [a.] Riverside, CA

BOWSER, PAULA
[b.] October 26, 1951, Monterey, CA; [p.] The late Lt. Col. Henry J. Picard Sr., Emma Didier Picard; [m.] Thomas L. Bowser, June 10, 1977; [ch.] David (born September 4, 1982), Laura (born May 17, 1985); [ed.] Graduated Woodbridges HS 1969, BS in English James Madison U 1973, M Div. Eastern Mennonite Seminary 1982; [occ.] Campus Minister, ISU through July 1996; [hon.] Outstanding Creative Achievement Award from the English Dept. at JMU 1974; [oth. writ.] Jonah: God's Global Reach (Brethren Press) part of the Covenant Bible Study Series C. 1992.; [pers.] Jason Tree was written for a friend of my son David, who died suddenly of a brain tumor. A tree was planted in his honor, and the poem is read each year by his friends and family to help remember him.; [a.] Ankeny, IA

BOYD, STEVEN
[pen.] Steven Dewain Boyd; [b.] September 8, 1979, Tacoma, WA; [p.] Robert and Deborah Boyd; [ed.] Cascade Christian High School - 10th grade completed; [occ.] Student/Courtesy Clerk, Safeway; [memb.] Boy Scouts of America, Tacoma United Pentecostal Church; [hon.] Life Scout; [pers.] If the grass is always greener on the other side, then stay where you are and you will always be happy.; [a.] Tacoma, WA

BOYKIN, EARLEN
[b.] September 6, 1969, Brundidge, AL; [p.] Evelyn Boykin; [ed.] Pike County High, Concordia College, Alabama Agricultural and Mechanical University; [occ.] USAF; [memb.] Alpha Kappa Alpha Sorority Incorporated; [hon.] Alpha Kappa Mu, Phi Theta Kappa, Dean's List, *Who's Who Among College Students*, Society of Presidential Scholars; [pers.] I strive, "Minute by Minute," to allow faith, hope and love to reflect in my writings. God is my greatest inspiration along with Maya Angelou, Helen Steiner Rice, and Susan L. Taylor.; [a.] San Antonio, TX

BRABO, LYNNE KAY
[b.] August 13, 1945, Ann Arbor, MI; [p.] Carl and Mary Isaacson; [m.] Ronald, June 1, 1985; [ch.] Darren Scott Jones, Krystyna L. Jones, Wendy A. Jones, Step Children: Marian L. Miller (Reynolds), David R, Brabo, Frank E. Brabo, Grandchildren: Dusty (Darren Robt Lee) Jones, Taylor Rebecca Lynne Edwards, Ashley Dawn Miller, Ariel Nicole Miller, Max (David Maxwell) Brabo; [ed.] Graduated an average student from Whitmore Lake HS - Mich. Attended Business Mgt. College Course; [occ.] Housewife - waiting for job opening with Frito Lay Chip Co; [memb.] Methodist Church, Past - Girl Scout Leader, Past Officer in 2 different Workers Unions; [hon.] High School PTA Achievement Award, Grade School Spelling Bee, Winner - 2 times; [oth. writ.] Limited to friends' and relatives' special occasions.; [pers.] If each person in today's society would take time to be more sensitive to others' feelings and perhaps more friendly towards others, the love we all share could make a difference in our world.

BRACEY JR., SYLVESTER L.
[pen.] S.C.B. II; [b.] October 2, 1971, Chicago, IL; [p.] Sylvester C. Bracey, Angella Williams; [ed.] Rich South H.S. University of Arkansas Pine Bluff, Tennessee State University (Engineering Major) (Mass Communications Minor); [occ.] Collections manager for people Gas at the Law offices of Heller, Shapiro, Frisonel Ferleger; [hon.] Poems published in the Chicago Defender Newspaper as well as "For Romantics Only" a newsletter of poetry based in Chicago. I also participated and placed in the "Sprite Rhymes for the Mind" contest, 1996.; [oth. writ.] "How Are We to Compete", "If A Man Shares His Strength", "A Mother Love", "Anniece", "Colorful Souls", "Nostalgia"; [pers.] My poems are composed to capture and animate your mind's conception. Ignited by visual imagery, colorfully illustrated by way of written word. My greatest poetic influence was Sylvester C. Bracey Sr. in my opinion one of the best poets to date.; [a.] Chicago, IL

BRADLEY, RICHARD O.
[pen.] Kojack; [b.] October 1, 1927, Indianapolis, IN; [p.] Clyde L. and Myrtle M.; [m.] J. Joyce Bradley, May 9, 1952; [ch.] Richard R. and Deborah M.; [ed.] 8 years; [occ.] Retired; [memb.] Full Gospel Business Men's Fellowship International; [oth. writ.] Some 60 to 75 unpublished.; [pers.] I love God with all of my heart, and all of my work is dedicated to God.; [a.] Poland, IN

BRADSHAW, MARY LANE
[b.] November 13, 1928, Lynn, MS; [p.] Daniel and Mary Collins (Dec.); [m.] Albert H. Bradshaw, June 2, 1966; [ch.] Lane M., Bryan C., David L.; [ed.] 8th grade, 3 yrs. college; [occ.] Homemaker; [hon.] Honorable mention World of Poetry ("Song to a Sailor") Golden Poet, 1992; [oth. writ.] "Persistent Yearning," "My Three Sons, "Ode To My Child Who Will Never Be," "Sequel," "Our Lives" (written for my husband with love); [pers.] I have been blessed with many talents and a loving family.; [a.] Keystone Heights, FL

BRADY, VIRGINIA J.
[pen.] Virginia J. Brady; [b.] November 8, 1924, New Canaan, CT; [p.] Anthony and Margaret Savatsky; [m.] Peter R. Brady, April 22, 1946; [ch.] Virginia, Patricia, Peter, Margo, Katheryn; [ed.] New Canaan High School, Kings Country School of Nursing Life Experiences; [occ.] Retired; [memb.] KCSN Alumni Assoc., US Army Nurse Cadet Corp., St. Mary's Church Scholarship Donor, International Society of Poets, Horticultural Society; [hon.] 3 Editor's Choice Awards 1995 and 1996; [oth. writ.] Poems written for bereavement groups, local senior citizen groups, and for public middle school poetry classes.; [pers.] I try to write simply about emotion and some controversial issues that we face in life that both adults and children can relate to and enjoy.; [a.] New Monmouth, NJ

BRANCATO, JANE
[b.] March 24, 1951, Brooklyn, NY; [p.] Belle Katz, David Katz; [m.] John Brancato, May 10, 1980; [ch.] Joseph Damien; [ed.] P.S. 222, Marine Park Junior High and James Madison High; [occ.] Home maker - Avon Rep

BRANCHE, ANNETTE M.
[pen.] Annette M. Branche; [b.] February 23, Savannah, GA; [p.] Chappelle M. and Inez Smalls; [m.] Divorced; [ch.] Two all grown up; [ed.] West Phila High School-Grad-Attended Central-Penn Bus. School Bus. ADM. N. VA. Comm. College - Divine Higher Consecration Science Church Graduate; [occ.] Memorial Consultant, Founder WACUP, Inc.; [memb.] AARP-Capitol City Task Force for Penna. Board Member The Black United Fund For Pennsylvania; [hon.] Giraffe Commendation-1991-Certificate of Loyalty 1958. P.G. County Civic Association Federation. President Award - 1995, Outstanding Citizen Award 1992, Journal Cup Nominee 1993.; [oth. writ.] "Warnings Against Cemeteries Unfair Practices" (1993) First and Second Editions (1996) Article for Local Newspapers and "Warnings Against Cemeteries Unfair Practices" brochure; [pers.] Each and every day is special - ignore the dark clouds accept only the light! With good health and faith in Universal Love you are in control!; [a.] Highspire, PA

BRAUNBERGER, MARGARET ROSE
[b.] March 24, 1950, Tacoma, WA; [p.] Louis and Katherina Lindauer; [m.] Clarence Braunberger, December 31, 1977; [ch.] Arron, Danny, Terry, (Braunberger); [ed.] Sumner, High School, Clover Park Tech. College, every life is an education, in itself!; [occ.] Housewife, mother and grandmother; [memb.] Swiss Ladies Society (Lifetime), D.A.V. Auxiliary (25th District Democrats (Past Secretary 2 years) Precinct Committee Officer - District Precinct 25-165, Volunteered for Mike Kreidler U.S. Repres. (Wash.), Volunteered for Senator Calvin Goings (Wash.); [hon.] 6th Grade (Blue Ribbon) Perfect Attendance, Edgemont School (Wash.), Member Washington State Deca. Club - State Secretary (1969); [oth. writ.] 1 Small Article (1963), Western Farmers Magazine, Small Article in Deca Magazine (1969); [pers.] I love my husband, family and friends and I enjoy helping people! Keeping the "balance" in Nature is very important! This one's for the Animals! God Bless.; [a.] Puyallup, WA

BRECK, STEVEN K.
[pen.] Steven Kimmerling; [b.] August 15, 1959, Danville, VA; [p.] William and Deanna Breck; [m.] Harmony Lauritzen, September 28, 1995; [ed.] 1 year college; [occ.] Film Industry Driver/Art Dept; [hon.] Honorable Mention, Poetry Contest 1989; [oth. writ.] "Children at Risk" poetry book for charity "Friends and Lovers" book (poetry) "Letters from Utopia" screenplay.; [pers.] You can pretend to be anything you wish, but eventually you must be who you are.; [a.] Salt Lake City, UT

BRESTAN, MARIA
[b.] August 17, 1979; [p.] Donald Brestan, Lydia Brestan; [ed.] West Leyden High School; [occ.] Student; [memb.] Ecology Club, M.H.O., Clowning, Key Club; [hon.] National Honor Society, Fern Award for English; [oth. writ.] "The Cancer" won in a poetry contest at my school called Prize Write.; [a.] Northlake, IL

BRIDGE-LAW, WENDIE S.
[b.] February 1, 1962, Helena, MT; [p.] William and Mary Ann Bridge; [m.] Don Law; [ch.] Amanda (10), Jon-Ryan (4), Crystal (14), John (13); [ed.] Eastern Montana College; [occ.] Housewife/Mother; [pers.] My family is the only thing that has meaning. I believe that the basics of responsibility lie in the family and their values. Family is our future.; [a.] Flint, MI

BRILLANT, WILL
[pen.] William J. Brillant; [b.] July 19, 1977, Brunswick, ME; [p.] Paul Brillant and Doris Brillant; [ed.] Brunswick High School, Framingham State College (currently enrolled, Freshman); [occ.] Dishwasher, Cooks Lobster House, Bailey's Island, ME; [memb.] Maine Writers, Publishers Alliance; [oth. writ.] "Dark Dungeon," "Weak," "Filth," "Obstruction" "A.D.D.," "And I Fall."; [pers.] I have been greatly influenced by my High School Teacher Mr. Richard Wile. He encouraged me to give "this poetry thing" a try. I realize that life is a journey and not a destination. Procrastination only leads to frustration...tomorrow.; [a.] Brunswick, ME

BRINDLEY, SANDRA M.
[b.] February 1, 1950, Newberry, MI; [m.] David A. Brindley, July 23, 1988; [ch.] Rene' Brindley - stepdaughter; [ed.] Newberry High, Northern Michigan University; [occ.] Cosmetologist and Student; [hon.] Federal Women's Program Woman of the Year 1989-1990, USAF Angel Award - 1990 - Decimomannu AFB, Sardinia, Italy; [pers.] My writing has been greatly influenced by the places I have lived and the people who have touched my life over the years.; [a.] Marquette, MI

BRITT, BEAU
[b.] June 17, 1964, Los Angeles; [p.] Mr. and Mrs. Leo Wyler; [ed.] Menlo College A.A. UCLA (withdraw) Pasadena Art Center (withdrew) Robert Louis Stevenson High School Pebble Beech Ca.; [occ.] Artist (contemporary) varied media; [memb.] Influenced by Franz Kafka and Edgar Allen Poe; [hon.] Dean's List, Honor roll, Menlo College; [oth. writ.] Working on science-fiction novel; [pers.] I promote the awareness of the possibilities regarding life and its vulnerable dimensions. Observation is the jewel of life.; [a.] Los Angeles, CA

BROCKINGTON, MITCHELL E.
[pen.] Sea Sight; [b.] January 19, 1948, Baltimore, MD; [p.] Mrs. Victoria Brockington; [m.] Sandra Brockington; [ch.] Lakia Antonio and ten step-kids; [occ.] Writer; [hon.] God has surely blessed me.; [a.] Baltimore, MD

BRODERICK, T. M.
[pen.] Timothy Broderick; [b.] April 9, 1927, Chicago, IL; [m.] Mary Phelan Broderick, May 29, 1966; [ed.] Work in Progress; [occ.] Retired; [pers.] I believe God wants to be obeyed not worshiped. If you do your best you meet all His expectations.

BROTTLUNO, BETSY RANAE
[b.] July 31, 1979, Minneapolis, MN; [p.] Barry and Shelli Brottluno; [ed.] Hopkins High School, Senior in 1996-97; [occ.] Student - High School; [memb.] *Who's Who Among American Students*, Team Leader for Teens at St. Stephens Episcopal Church; [hon.] National Honor Society selected as a Member; [pers.] I believe all people are good at heart and can achieve what the soul is put into, for it will not fade into nothingness like physical things will...but will endure forever.; [a.] Minnetonka, MN

BROWN, CANDACE E.
[pen.] Candace E. Brown; [b.] May 31, 1966, San Leandro, CA; [p.] Caroline H. Beebe and Gordon Willey; [m.] Alan I. Brown, February 22, 1992; [ch.] Taylor Grace Brown, Mackezie Lynn Brown; [ed.] Hartford High School; [occ.] Albank, Marble Division - Head Teller; [oth. writ.] First publication.

BROWN, DANIEL A.
[b.] June 11, 1969, Sayre, PA; [p.] Jack J. Brown, Mary Ann Musto; [m.] Elizabeth Ann Yohon; [ed.] Notre Dame High School, Corning Community College; [occ.] Deputy Sheriff; [memb.] VFW, American Legion; [hon.] Southwest Asia Service Medal with 2 Bronze Service Stars, Kuwait Liberation Medal; [oth. writ.] No other writings; [pers.] Think Safety; [a.] Bath, NY

BROWN, ELEANOR
[b.] April 15, 1963, Fort Riley, KS; [p.] Dorothy Hensley; [ch.] Shannon and Ethany Brown; [ed.] Manhattan High School; [pers.] Writing is my release from the stress of real life. It enables me to express my impression of those things around me.; [a.] Marysville, KS

BROWN, GARRY C.
[b.] November 22, 1965, Brooklyn, NY

BROWN, LEA A.
[pen.] Lea; [b.] October 26, 1948, Richmond, CA; [p.] Bertha E. and Fletcher P. Wilbanks; [m.] Ernest P. Brown, May 18, 1968; [ch.] C. Michael; [ed.] Hinkley High School Metro State (one semester); [occ.] Retired Customer Service Manager; [oth. writ.] Several poems published in AOL newsletter; [pers.] I wish to bring a better awareness to man about the plight of this planet and all the animals that live with us. Part of my heritage is Cherokee and I draw from the Native American ways; [a.] Aurora, CO

BROWN, LINDA
[b.] June 26, 1953, Tampa, FL; [p.] Thelma and Johnny Brown; [ch.] Olivia Homesley, Tracy Medina, Michael Homesley; [ed.] 12th Grade Turkey Creek High School I.C.F.M.R. Lic. University of S. Florida Asst. Nurse (Training School Erwin College); [occ.] Homemaker, Grandmother; [memb.] Victory Baptist Church, School P.T.A. Head Start Program Mem.; [hon.] Working with handicapped - children and adults center "Golden Heart Award"; [oth. writ.] School paper, now pub. manuscript of poems, waiting to be discovered; [pers.] My poetry comes from real life itself. I strive to reach out and touch a soul, to let them know they're not alone.; [a.] Plant City, FL

BROWN, MATTHEW
[b.] June 11, 1939, Statesville, NC; [p.] Verlon and Ocie Mae Brown; [ch.] Brian and Verlon Brown; [ed.] Morningside High School, Burke Trade School; [occ.] Building Maintenance, Florence E. Smith Community Center, NY; [memb.] NAACP, Nation Action Network, The Afrikan Poetry Theatre, Inc.; [hon.] Adult School Essay winner, local radio poetry writing winner; [oth. writ.] Several writings and poems. An essay written up in a local weekly newspaper, *The New York Voice*.; [pers.] I know with faith and understanding you can triumph over difficult and seemingly impossible problems. With faith in God, I triumphed over illiteracy. We must understand the power within us.; [a.] Corona, NY

BROWN, MONA I.
[pen.] Monica Blair, Lakota; [b.] March 5, 1966, Search, AR; [p.] Otis S. and Lola I. Brown; [ed.] Salem High School '84, Tulsa Jr. College '86, and University of Missouri - Rolla B.S. in Psychology '93, applied for M.A. in Counseling at Webster Univ. in Rolla; [occ.] Disabled; [hon.] Psi Chi (Psych.), Sigma Tau Delta (Engl.); [oth. writ.] Editor-in-chief and writer for *Um-Rolla Psychology Alumni Newsletter* - "Minds Eye" - from to '93. I also achieved a writing minor from Um-Rolla, in '93.; [pers.] My inspirations and aspirations in writing (and life) have come from the encouragement and influence of S.H.S. teacher Joyce Inman, Um-Rolla professors Mary Boyd and Gene Doty, and my friends - Karen S., Janet H., Robin C., Charla S., Mary S., and Janey B., their support means a lot. Thanks everybody!; [a.] Salem, MO

BROWN, NEVILLE LORENZO
[pen.] Nabil Zenubio Kuti; [b.] July 17, 1941, Ancon, Canal Zone; [p.] Amabelle D. Brown, Sherman R. Brown; [m.] Divorced; [ch.] Derrick L., Melanie A., Neville L. Jr.; [ed.] Paraiso High School, Balboa, Canal Zone Brooklyn College, Brooklyn, N.Y.; [occ.] Administrative Assistant Department of Health, Brooklyn, NY; [memb.] Viet-Nam Veterans Association Society For The Right To Die, Association Of Black Journalists, National Rifle Association; [hon.] Award and letter of Appreciation from Dept. of Defense. Award and Certificate from Veterans Leadership Program N.Y.C.; [oth. writ.] Poems published in *New Voices in American Poetry*, several magazine articles and poems, articles in local newspapers. *Kingsboro Psychiatric News Letter*, Poem entitled "Dedication" to Cheryl Westbrook Coordinator.; [pers.] I strive to be all I can be in this life and try in my writing to inspire others to follow their dreams.; [a.] Brooklyn, NY

BROWN, TERRANCE AVIS
[pen.] T. A. B.; [b.] December 29, 1971, Philadelphia, PA; [p.] Marie Brown, John Smith; [ed.] Murrell Dobbins A.V.T.S. High School; [occ.] Electrician Sub Contractor; [oth. writ.] Wrote several poems, never published; [pers.] Love inspired me in writing, many could not survive without it, and many died of it. We must understand the power love has.

BROWN, TOMMIKCO T.
[pen.] Thoughts worth thinking; [b.] October 12, 1969, Los Angeles, CA; [p.] Paul Brown, Barbara Brown Carlisle; [m.] Daryl Stevenson, still waiting; [ch.] Mercedes, Soncearea, Anthony, Daryljuea; [ed.] 11th Grade, Non Graduate; [occ.] Mother and Hairstylist; [memb.] First Church of God; [oth. writ.] I have many poems that I write when I'm sad, happy and trying to make a point. They all sit in my notebook. I pour out my emotions through poetry.; [pers.] I'm always thinking about life and my poetry comes from my spirit. I haven't studied or read poetry before, I just write it. It only takes me 5 to 10 minutes to write a 30 line poem. They're my thoughts in rhythm.; [a.] Long Beach, CA

BROWN JR., JOSEPH R. D.
[pen.] Richard Taylor-Brown; [b.] May 24, 1963, Honolulu, HI; [ed.] H. L. Ferguson High, Embrg - Riddle Aeronautical University, Community College of Air Force, Thomas Nelson Community College; [occ.] Juvenile Counselor; [memb.] World Victory Church outreach Center, Air Force Sergeants Assoc. Air Force Reserves; [pers.] My writing reflects the man behind the name. I realize that I cannot reflect the essence of humanity as a whole, only as an individual and from my view and experiences. I see myself as an enlightener, not a writer.; [a.] Newport News, VA

BROWN-DUDEK, ELEANOR
[pen.] Eleanor Brown-Dudek; [b.] August 26, 1926, Argusville, NY; [p.] Alfred and Joy Green; [m.] Hubert C. Brown (Dec.), M. Wm. Dudek, April 25, 1947 and July 25, 1980; [ch.] Leslie Joy and Christopher Heal; [ed.] Gloversville H.S., B.A. English, Skidmore College, Saratoga Sp., NY; [occ.] Retired Exec. Sec. to the V.P. for Dev. and Alumni Affairs Skidmore College; [memb.] Former Sec. and Newsletter Editor, Saratoga YMCA Scuba Club, Literacy Volunteers, FM Radio Rise on air Reader, Skidmore College Alumni Club; [pers.] Nothing could have prepared me for the beauty and diversity of life under the sea. We take very seriously our responsibility to protect and preserve this fragile and priceless environment for future generations.; [a.] Schenectady, NY

BRUNDAGE, VIRGIL K.
[pen.] V. Brundage; [b.] December 10, 1922, Wichita, KS; [p.] Harley, Mabel Brundage; [m.] Virginia (Ginna) Brundage, April 4, 1942; [ch.] Virginia - Michael - Sharron; [ed.] High School; [memb.] Past Pres. Hexart of Amer. Fed. Square Dance Club Past Editor HAFSDC Fed Facts Magazine. Member Teamsters Union.; [hon.] 30 Years Award a Truck (Diamond Ring 1/4 Carat) Line Hall Motor Transit; [oth. writ.] "To Ginna," "Our Son," "To Leah," "Today," "My Vision," "My Church," "Friendship Song," "His Gift," "The Spirit Like Me," "Ozark Peace Volunteers" (Meals on Wheels); [pers.] I try to show love for nature and fellow man in all my writings.; [a.] Kansas City, NY

BRYANT, DEBI A.
[b.] May 9, 1962, Winfield, KS; [p.] Joe Yount, Cathy Yount; [m.] Jim E. Bryant, June 25, 1988; [ch.] Daniel James, Taylor Ann, (step-children: Ashley Nicole, Nicholas James); [ed.] Winfield High School, St. John's College, Wichita State University; [occ.] Nuclear Medicine Technician Galichia Medical Group, Wichita, KS; [memb.] Lutheran Church Missouri Synod, Leukemia Society of American; [hon.] *Who's Who Among American High School Students*, Dean's List, Outstanding Student Award - Rotary Club; [pers.] God, family, a simple life - these bring contentment.; [a.] Wichita, KS

BRYANT, MICHAEL F.
[b.] May 8, 1952, Fort Wayne, IN; [ch.] "Son" Harley Michael Bryant; [pers.] This poem is dedicated to all the men and women who served and died in the Vietnam War.

BRYANT, TARA LYNNE
[pen.] Rain Amber; [b.] November 13, 1979, Toledo, OH; [p.] James Bryant, Patricia Bryant; [ed.] Barrington High School, Browning Academy in Cancun, Mexico, Wayland Academy College Prep.; [memb.] Student Impact/Student Insight at Willow Creek Church, Pittsburgh Project Missionary Trip, United States Gymnastics Federation; [hon.] Gymnastics Trophies Diving Medals and Ribbons; [oth. writ.] A few poems published in magazines and a school literary book called *Nuance*.; [pers.] I believe nothing in the world has happened coincidentally. We are all a small part of a master plan. There are no accidents. The Lord has us all in the safety of His hand.; [a.] Barrington, IL

BUCCELLATO, STEVEN
[b.] July 2, 1961, Queens, NY; [p.] Anthony and Elaine Buccellato; [ed.] Andrew Warde H.S., Fairfield University; [occ.] Supervisor United Parcel Service Stratford, CT; [pers.] Early influence - Thomas Mann. I believe in the struggle to rise from loss and disappointment to further the soul.; [a.] Fairfield, CT

BUCHHOLZ, CYNTHIA SCHWIEGER
[b.] December 7, 1962, Medelia, MN; [p.] Roscoe and Sylvia Schwieger; [m.] John Scott Buchholz, August 19, 1995; [ch.] Caleb John, Michaela Joy; [ed.] Anoka Senior High School, Anoka, MN; [oth. writ.] Forget-Me-Not child, I beseech thee today, Do not forsake Me, though you be dismayed. Reach up with your hands, and I'll greet you with love. I'll recapture your heart from the heavens above. Just call out My name when your sorrows are high, I'll shower your with mercy, until victory is nigh. Use this flower to remind you that you are My Own, So delicate and beautiful... a treasure I hold. The pedals so pure that burst into life, Is your soul, that with love, will bloom from My Light. Forget-

Me-Not child, I beseech thee today, For without Me, your life will just wither away. Be anxious for nothing, for as I care for this bloom, I will keep thee, and guide thee, and return for thee soon. Until the time of the end, hold fast to My ways, Learn as much as you can without any delay. Stand firm with your sword anchored deeply in love, Rest in the faith until My kingdom come. Love, Jesus.; [pers.] My inspiration comes fellowship with my Lord and Savior Jesus Christ. For the miracles of healing to my body, the countless blessings of His redeeming grace, and the inestimable compassion He has shown me: To Him alone I do I give the glory. Jesus truly is faithful, even when we are not.; [a.] Saint Paul, MN

BUCK, FRANK
[b.] May 21, 1958, Detroit, MI; [p.] Joseph and Beverly Buck; [m.] Linda S. Buck, February 4, 1978; [ch.] Brady and Brandi; [ed.] 12th Grade; [occ.] Factory worker/Brickmason; [oth. writ.] None published Portfolio of Poems and Songs.; [pers.] "A true Poet writes from the heart and not the head".; [a.] Meridian, MS

BUCKNER, ANTHONY M.
[pen.] "TB"; [b.] January 25, 1966, Washington, DC; [p.] Father Deceased, Brenda M. Buckner; [ed.] H.S. Grad. 7 years in the military also a veteran of Desert Storm, attended Police Academy in June 92 Lawrence, KS.; [occ.] Retired/Disabled due to PTSD Post Traumatic Stress Disorder and DJD in lower back hips and knees; [memb.] Veterans of Foreign Wars (VFW) Disabled American Veterans; [hon.] Military Campaign Ribbons for Operation Desert Storm. Letters of Commendation from the Major's office for Outstanding Work (2).; [oth. writ.] I have written almost 100 poems in the last year. They (some) are in my books, "The Willow Try" or "A Cowboy Tail" both of which I am trying to get published.; [pers.] I write so that people can read and see that they are not alone. I hit bottom and am coming back. You see "Every Day of Living is a Life" I live by that Motto.; [a.] Topeka, KS

BUCS, ALLEAH
[b.] July 13, 1976, Trenton, NJ; [p.] Jim and Elaine Bucs; [ed.] Rider University; [occ.] State of NJ, Office of the Governor, Aide to the Governor; [pers.] Life is so much, like looking into a mirror. Everything there is a reflection of one's existence. Only when you are looking in the mirror, you need to stare through the glass and find out what is really there...; [a.] Pemberton, NJ

BUECHNER, PETER
[pen.] Peter Simon Buechner III; [b.] May 23, 1959, Long Island, NY; [p.] Peter and Doris Buechner; [m.] Colleen White; [ch.] Paul; [ed.] Babylon High School; [occ.] Cabinet Maker, Frustrated Artist (hee hee); [pers.] I thank God for the time I've had to reorganize and rectify my life, to begin anew in September of '96. With all my love to Big D, my sisters Jean, Doris, and Pat. Most of all, my love to my "Starr" — my soulmate Forever and Eternity!; [a.] Medford, NY

BULLOCK, JENNIFER
[b.] September 10, 1981, NYC; [p.] Terance and Sonia Bullock; [ed.] St. Vincent Ferrer High School; [occ.] Student

BURDETTE, RENEE
[pen.] Renee; [b.] June 2, 1954, Detroit; [p.] Joann Burdette; [ed.] A High School Mumfare High Diploma,) (An Associate's Oakland Community College Degree in Liberal Arts,) and a training in X-rays, Mary Grove College; [memb.] The annual song contest. (The Billboard); [hon.] Awards for song writings - "Since You're Gone" and "Remember When"; [oth. writ.] "The Flower", "God Fill The Earth With Love", "I Love America", "I'm Burning Up The Road To Get To Your Love", etc. (unpublished poems); [pers.] In my songs and in my poems, I strive for the love of God, my mother, and myself. I love writing for the entertainment of others as well as myself; [a.] Detroit, MI

BURDIC, DEBORAH L.
[pen.] Deborah Logan; [b.] February 29, 1944, Bethlehem, PA; [p.] Carter and Margaret Kendall; [m.] Billy Laram Burdic, December 31, 1987; [ch.] Two stepchildren, Colene and Bradley Burdic; [ed.] B.S.Ed. Elem. Ed. Master's Credits in Guidance, Co-op Voc. Ed., and Elem. Ed. Courses; [occ.] Small business owner and aspiring writer/poet; [oth. writ.] "October," "Imagine Magazine Paradox" *Imagine Magazine* (poems), some erotica submitted, status as yet undetermined, humorous article, submitted status as yet undetermined; [pers.] I have always been eclectic in my tastes, life style, and attitude, so I write, anything and everything that comes to mind in hope that what I have to say will ring some bells with all people, in every walk of life.; [a.] Elko, NV

BURGESS, PHILLIP R.
[pen.] Phillip; [b.] March 27, 1986, Sacramento, CA; [p.] Steve and Lisa Burgess; [ed.] Completed 4th Grade; [memb.] Club Scouts of America, A.L.P.'s Accelerated learning programs, Young Authors; [pers.] Stay in School; [a.] Abilene, TX

BURGESS, PHYLLIS
[b.] August 20, 1979, Bedford, IN; [p.] Asa Burgess, Caroline Burgess (D. 1989); [ed.] BNL High School; [occ.] Student at BNL; [memb.] Future Homemakers of America; [hon.] Bedford Swim Team; [pers.] Live each day to its fullest. Never put anything off for tomorrow.; [a.] Bedford, IN

BURKE, BRYAN C.
[b.] November 20, 1978, Metter, GA; [p.] Bennie Burke (Mother); [ed.] Emanuel County Institute; [memb.] Beta Club; [hon.] Region Debate Award, Region Drama Award, Region Quartet Award, Honor Roll; [pers.] In a world so full of darkness, lucky are those that find their light and blessed are those that share it.; [a.] Twin City, GA

BURKE, CHARLOTTE
[b.] January 25, 1924, Astoria, NY; [p.] Thomas and Charlotte Winkel; [m.] Jerome, June 28, 1947; [ch.] John, Robert, Paul, Michael, Thomas, Rosemary; [ed.] Bryant High School; [occ.] Retired; [memb.] Notre Dame Choir, Herrics Community Teacher, Sing and Dance at Resorts; [hon.] New York University, Goodwife Award, Diploma in Guitar Playing; [oth. writ.] "Log Cabin" The National Library of Poetry, "All Of A Sudden" *Poetic Voices of America* numerous others in *Susquehanna Transcript*; [pers.] Inspired by scenery, singing, playing guitar; [a.] New Hyde Park, NY

BURKE, CHRISTOPHER DANIEL
[b.] June 22, 1985, Houston, TX; [p.] Michael & Connie Burke; [ed.] J.F. Mendoza Elementary and currently attending O'Callaghan Middle School; [occ.] Student; [memb.] DARE Program, Star Trek Club- (USS Columbia II), Orchestra program at O'Callaghan Middle School; [hon.] Student of the month, Graduate of DARE, Graduate from Elementary School; [oth. writ.] Was invited by Mendoza Elementary School to attend Southern Nevada Young Writers Fair -(Once Upon A Time)- theme, in 1996; [pers.] One writer who influences me is Shel Silverstein. He is my favorite author and he has given me many ideas for my funny and seriour stories and poems. I hope to become a good writer and to have more poeple look up to me and my writings; [a.] Las Vegas, Nevada

BURKE, KAREN A.
[b.] March 18, 1953, Los Angeles, CA; [p.] Bi-Cultural (Bahamian-American); [ed.] M.A., New York University, NYC; [occ.] Educational Facilitator/Writer/Performer; [oth. writ.] Several essays and poems published in local papers and institutional in-house organs; [pers.] Poetry is a powerful prism that can illuminate our lives. I strive to use poetry as a vehicle of truth.; [a.] Washington, DC

BURKE, KATHERINE
[b.] January 1, 1987, Cooperstown, NY; [p.] Michael and Roxanne; [ed.] Seaford Manor; [occ.] Student; [memb.] Jr. Girl Scouts; [hon.] Certificate of Scholastic Excellence; [pers.] I would like to thank my teachers, I could not have done it without them.; [a.] Seaford, NY

BURLEIGH, ERICA KENNA
[pen.] Kenna Lee Burleigh; [b.] October 13, 1981, San Diego, CA; [p.] Ken and Barbie Burleigh; [ed.] Graduated 8th grade 1996; [occ.] Dancer, Cheerleader, Poet, Student; [hon.] Honor Roll; [pers.] Luck may bring you money, but it will never bring you wisdom. Kindness is a gift everyone can give. It's never too late to reach for your goals. I could only do it with the support of my mother and dear friends.; [a.] Chino Hills, CA

BURNER, CHRYSTINA
[p.] August 6, 1985, Toledo; [m.] Robin Burner, David Wojo; [ed.] Hawkins Elementary 6th Grade; [hon.] Honor awards, Learning Olympic, Student of the Month, Citizenship, Perfect Attendance Awards, Certificate of Achievement on Martin Luther King (poem); [oth. writ.] "I Have A Dream" project for school on Martin Luther King.

BURNS, REBECCA
[b.] December 5, 1979, Butler, PA; [p.] Kathleen T. Estes and Warren A. Estes; [ed.] The Mathematics and Science Renaissance Program at Clover Hill High School (High School); [occ.] Student; [memb.] Students against Drunk Driving (SADD), Forensics, Drama; [hon.] Honor Student at High School, attending "Magnet" School for the gifted; [pers.] Everyday I create memories. Everyday at least one of those memories is happy. Everyday is a good day if I can find the happy memory I made for myself.; [a.] Midlothian, VA

BURNUM, SELENE
[b.] 1913, Sayre, Oklahoma; [p.] Jessie and Alice Robison; [m.] Roy Simmons (First husband), January 18, 1930 and Roy Burnum (Second husband), December 15, 1960; [ch.] Terrel Simmons, on first husband, I have one grandson and 4 great, 1 boy and 3 girls, Saren, Beth, Rhianon, Swain; [ed.] Sophomore High School; [occ.] Retired; [oth. writ.] No. Only wrote poems, for fun and self satisfaction, never thought I was good enough for publishing; [pers.] Went through dust bowl 1934, move to Oregon, in 1945, did sewing for public for 16 years, also worked in school cafeterias for 10 years. Also growing flowers. I really shouldn't order the books I am

on a limited income but guess I can cut corners somewhere and this has never happened to me before.; [a.] Canyonville, OR

BURRIS, PAMELA S.
[b.] May 23, 1961, Woodland, CA; [p.] James and Penny Burris; [ed.] Dixon High School, California State University, Sacramento (Ethnic Studies - Native American Studies with Anthropology Minor); [oth. writ.] Other poems not published yet, and some other stories about life.; [pers.] I write my feelings and thoughts. I have been influenced by many current events and also a lot of Third World writers. My poetry and other writings reflect my current moods.; [a.] Dixon, CA

BURROUGHS, CRISSY LEE
[pen.] C. L. Burroughs; [b.] January 18, 1978, San Gabriel, CA; [p.] Michael A. Burroughs, Reva C. Caskey-Martell; [ed.] High School Graduate; [occ.] Student; [hon.] English, Science; [pers.] This poem was written for the memory of my father Michael Alan Burroughs. I want to say I love him, and I'd like to dedicate this poem to my mom and sister Karen Sue Burroughs-Gryden. With Love always.; [a.] Ontario, CA

BURTON, RICK
[pen.] Goblette; [b.] October 25, 1974, Salt Lake City; [pers.] Poetry is the Rational Creation of my soul, the fine ability of words...; [a.] Salt Lake City, UT

BUSCH, CHRISTINA M.
[b.] September 24, 1966, Chicago; [p.] Holly Przeniczny; [m.] Anthony Busch, March 7, 1986; [ch.] BriAnne N. Busch; [ed.] Barrington High, Barrington, IL; [occ.] International Export Manager; [a.] Carpentersville, IL

BUTKUS, CHERYL L.
[b.] June 11, 1973, Stevens Point; [p.] John and Barbara Butkus; [ed.] UW-Stevens Point, Mid-State Technical College; [a.] Stevens Point, WI

BUTLER, CAROLYN LORRAINE
[b.] October 17, 1956, Bogalusa, LA; [p.] Rev. and Mrs. Tom Bailey Jr.; [ch.] Eric Maurice and Bryan Lee; [ed.] AA Pearl River College - Poplarville, MS, BA Southeastern Louisiana University Hammond, LA; [occ.] Business Owner Knoxville, TN 37923; [memb.] Knoxville Christian Center, Knoxville, TN; [oth. writ.] Poems - "In Troubled Times," "Fly Little Bird Fly," "Whispers In The Dark," "Man Of God;" [pers.] My poems are about real life situations and are written to inspire others in the storms of life.; [a.] Knoxville, TN

BUTLER, LAURIE A.
[b.] April 13, 1962, Connecticut; [p.] Mr. and Mrs. Louis H. Goulet; [m.] Thomas L. Butler, November 1, 1986; [ch.] Amanda, Stacy, Marcy, and Michael; [ed.] North Attleboro, High, No. Attleboro Mass.; [occ.] Mom; [memb.] Thalia PTA; [hon.] Outstanding Achievements with working with Handicapped Child. Also at school with reading.; [oth. writ.] Been published in home town paper, poetry corner in *Sun Chronicle*, Attleboro; [pers.] All my poems come from my life's happenings, when I feel something and words come from within I write them down. It's as one in a life time thing.; [a.] Virginia Beach, VA

BUTLER, ROSEMARY E.
[b.] May 27, 1938, Brooklyn, NY; [p.] John E. Bergen, Elizabeth C. Whelan Bergen; [m.] Patrick J. Butler, December 27, 1985; [ch.] Debra Scherick, Marianne Porcaro, Daniel J. Scherick, Brenda Sommer; [ed.] High School graduate; [occ.] Customer Service Rep for Internal Revenue Dept.; [memb.] Women of the Moose; [hon.] 1975 Clover International Poetry Competition Award for The Seed of Life by Rosemary Scherick (before remarriage); [oth. writ.] "The Seed of Life," "Let's Look a Little Beyond," published in local weekly; [pers.] This particular poem was written during one of the times when my oldest daughter, Debra was very ill. Debra was born with Spina Bifida and was always very sickly. On May 24, 1993, Debra took Lady Eternity's hand, and held tight.

BUYCO, JANISE MAE
[b.] January 21, 1982; [p.] Romeo and Ramona Buyco; [ed.] Holy Name School, Lowell High School; [occ.] Student; [hon.] First Honors Mercy High Second Place poetry; [oth. writ.] Poems published in *Mercy High Legacy* and *Panther Press*. Articles for *Panther Press*.; [pers.] If you want to leave an imprint on earth speak out your opinions. If you want a big dent stand up for them.; [a.] San Francisco, CA

CABLAY, JESSICA
[b.] September 4, 1972, Hilo, HI; [p.] Perlita Cablay; [ed.] Hilo High School, Hawaii Community College, International Air Academy; [occ.] Accounts Payable Clerk at All About Travel, Inc. in Tigard, OR; [memb.] Volunteer at Oregon Food Bank; [hon.] 2nd Runner up in Miss Hawaii-Island Filipina Pageant '93-'94, Dean's List, Service Award; [a.] Milwaukie, OR

CABRAL, PAULINA C.
[pen.] Paulina Dela Cruz; [b.] June 22, 1919, Philippines; [p.] Segundo Dela Cruz and Mansi Silvestre; [m.] Fidel M. Cabral (Deceased), 1948; [ch.] Connie, Dionicio, Rey, Tony and Cesar; [ed.] Just about enough to light up the path of my simple life.; [occ.] Retired; [hon.] Poems published in *Edge of Twilight*, *Best Poems of 1995*, *Between The Raindrops* and *Best Poems of 1996*.; [oth. writ.] Several short stories in Tagalog (National Language of the Philippines) and some essays and short poems published by Ramon Roces Publications before and after World War II.; [pers.] Came to the United States in 1974 to be with daughter Connie, who was then on the staff of the Philippine Consulate General in New York. Decided to stay, now proud of being naturalized U.S. citizen, though I'll never forget my roots in my native land!; [a.] Teaneck, NJ

CAHILL, CALISTA A.
[b.] October 10, 1978, Carbondale, IL; [p.] Francis and Sharon Cahill; [ed.] Lincoln Community High School; [occ.] Student; [memb.] Girl Scouts, Natural Helpers, Peer Mediators, French Club, The International Thespian Society, School and Church Choirs; [hon.] Central State Eight Conference Music Award solo - first place ensemble - first place; [pers.] For a dreamer like myself, friends and family are very special. When my father died earlier this year I found this to be true.; [a.] Lincoln, IL

CALLAHAN, PATRICK M.
[pen.] Patrick Michael James O'Callaghan; [b.] February 2, 1961, Harbor City, CA; [p.] Patrick Callahan, Mary Callahan; [m.] Deborah Lynn Callahan, April 16, 1988; [ch.] Patrick Jeremy, Meaghan Marie; [ed.] Los Altos High, College of the Redwoods, Calif. Dept. of Forestry Fire Academy; [occ.] Retired Fireman; [memb.] Knights of Columbus; [hon.] Dean's List, Scholarship; [oth. writ.] Many poems about nature and children, my Irish ancestry, two books, *Irish Ancestry*, *Death of a Loved One*.; [pers.] Teach your children about their ancestry!; [a.] Anderson, CA

CALLAWAY, JAMES T.
[b.] March 7, 1958, Milford, DE; [p.] Nyle and Lillian Callaway; [m.] Linda Callaway, February 16, 1980; [ch.] Mickey J. T. Beth; [ed.] Lake Forest High School; [occ.] Plant Engineer; [memb.] Odd Fellows; [pers.] As newborn children we possess all of God's gifts. As we grow and learn we slowly cast them aside. The world through a child's eyes is wonderful. And it's the same world we live in.; [a.] Frederica, DE

CAMHE, MERRILIE
[b.] March 1, 1946, New York City; [p.] Ruth and Paul Camhe; [ch.] Brett Rabbat; [ed.] Brooklyn College, The New School; [occ.] Graphic Design; [memb.] SEGD (Society of Environmental Graphic Designers), NEWH (Nat'l Executive Women in Hospitality), BOMA (Bldg. Owners Mgmt. Assoc.); [hon.] Strathmore Certificate of Excellence, Association for the Graphic Arts Special Merit; [pers.] Life is but a dream.; [a.] New York, NY

CAMIGLIANO, ALICIA
[b.] May 24, 1976, Warren, PA; [p.] John and Joyce Camigliano; [ed.] Warren Area High School currently at Malone Christian College; [occ.] College Student; [hon.] Dean's List; [oth. writ.] Poems published in both high school and college literary mags. Also, a poem published in church newsletter.; [pers.] I believe literature is a vital part of life. My greatest influence is the work of William Blake.; [a.] Canton, OH

CAMPBELL, DAVID
[pen.] David Campbell; [b.] September 11, 1974, Germany; [p.] Carolyn L. Campbell; [ed.] Clark Atlanta University, Electrical Engineering; [occ.] Supervisor in the 1996 Olympic Games Airport; [hon.] Honor Student; [oth. writ.] I have many other poems that I want to be a best seller. I know I can be, if I just get a book out.; [pers.] I love writing poetry, it releases my mind from my Brain. To travel the galaxy and discover new creations.; [a.] Columbus, GA

CAMPBELL, LIZ
[b.] June 1, 1981, Jackson, MS; [p.] Bill Campbell, Anita Campbell; [ed.] I will go into 10th Grade at Terry High School for the '96-'97 school year.; [occ.] I babysit and help friends with school work.; [memb.] I am in the High School Band and on the flagline. I was in the Gifted Program through 8th grades.; [hon.] Honors Student, participated in Duke Univ. TIP program for academically talented students.; [oth. writ.] Local newspapers have printed other poems.; [pers.] My poems come from the heart and nowhere else. Teachers and loved ones are my inspiration.; [a.] Jackson, MS

CAMPBELL, MARY E.
[b.] February 14, 1942, Detroit, MI; [p.] Jesse and Lola Peterson; [m.] Jesse Campbell, June 20, 1964; [ch.] Tiya, Lance, Kobie; [ed.] Southeastern High School St. Clair College Windsor Ont. Canada; [occ.] Self Employed Company Name, Marca Interior Decorator to Personalize Care; [memb.] Ciem Church Intervention Economical Ministry - CIP Church Intervention Project World of Faith Church; [oth. writ.] "A Time To Remember," "Ford Time," "To Have and To Hold" (Standard Publishing) "China Trade," (Reference Booklet); [pers.] To share in my writings that which God has so richly shared with me.; [a.] Detroit, MI

CAMPBELL JR., ANDREW P.
[pen.] Perk Campbell; [b.] January 22, 1938, East Saint Louis, IL; [ch.] Andrew P. Campbell III; [ed.] San Francisco State University Southern Illinois University Foot Hill College, Los Altos Hill CA. College of Marin, Kent Kentfield CA. Taught Creative Drama to Elementary Children; [occ.] Disabled, Hair Stylist; [hon.] Received various reference for stage plays - T.V. Performances Educational, Francisco Bay Area Girl Scout (Seminar); [pers.] I have to relate my poem with every life and something for my son Andrew III to learn from.; [a.] East Palo Alto, CA

CANNER, CLAUDIA A.
[b.] November 24, 1952, Brooklyn, NY; [p.] Anita Canner & William Canner(Deceased); [ch.] Vanessa Sabatino (B) 1976; [hon.] Editors Choice Award - National Library of Poetry; [oth. writ.] "Across The Line" Historical Novel of the American Civil War, unpublished. Political articles and new releases while serving as legislative assistant in the New York State Assembly; [pers.] I am profoundly moved by the Abraham Lincoln and heartwrenching poetic diaries of battle weary civil war soldiers, prisioners and loved ones left behind. I honor all those who have sacrificed so greatly, by committing my writing to their plight and remembering our Vietnam soldiers in my poetry; [a.] Woodhaven, New York

CAPE, PRESTON
[b.] July 12, 1937, Adair Co, KY; [p.] Finis and Emma Cape; [m.] Ruth M. Sneed Cape, February 6, 1960; [ch.] Leonard Cape; [ed.] Grade 4 Grade School; [occ.] Retired; [memb.] None other than churches; [oth. writ.] Poems and some gospel songs; [pers.] Never did any writing until January, 1996, Bought my first used typed writer.; [a.] Columbia, KY

CAPUTI, MICHAEL JAMES
[b.] November 3, 1977, Port Jefferson, NY; [p.] Wanda and Joseph Caputi; [ed.] Chaminade - Madonna High, University of Miami; [occ.] Student; [memb.] Project Graduation Reunion Committee; [hon.] Silver Knight Nominee in Science, 6th place in FBLA district competition.; [pers.] This poem, "Reunited," is dedicated to my one true love, Silvia Maria Domenech.; [a.] Hollywood, FL

CARAFELLY, SHERI
[b.] February 5, 1943, Dearborn, MI; [p.] Jacob and Doris Broth; [m.] Dennis, February 18, 1966; [ch.] Amy, Roy - Grandchildren: Chloe; [ed.] St. Lawrence Inst., Northwood Inst., Central MI. Univ; [occ.] Bible and Music Teacher; [memb.] Metropolitan Tabernacle A/G Church; [hon.] Christian Ed. Director of year 1993; [oth. writ.] Poems-Local Newspapers; [pers.] We need to be concerned with God's word and people.; [a.] Macob, MI

CAREY, BRENDON M.
[b.] December 31, 1979, Lynn, MA; [p.] Barbara H. Carey, Leonard Paul Carey Sr.; [ed.] Our Lady of the Assumption, St. John's Preparatory School; [occ.] Porter/Service Dept., Star Market, Lynn, MA; [memb.] American Diabetes Association; [hon.] Delta Epsilon Phi, National German Honor Society, Physical Education Silver Medal Award, (2) Goethe Institute Awards for German Excellence; [oth. writ.] Several unpublished songs and poems, article published in *The 21st Century* magazine; [pers.] "I'll never forget who I am, where I came from, where I am today, and who put me there, God and all of you." James Brown.; [a.] Lynn, MA

CARLSON, DAN
[pen.] Dan Carlson; [b.] February 25, 1980, Saint Louis Park, MN; [p.] Rob and Cindy Carlson; [ed.] Osseo Senior High - 11th Grade; [oth. writ.] I have written a couple of poems that I have gotten great feedback from, "A Teenage Mother," and "A Silent Secret."; [pers.] I don't base my writings on anyone or anything or even a certain topic like other writers do. I write naturally from my heart you could say. I know I have written something good if they either cry, smile or even sigh. I love to write poems, it relieves some of the pleasures in life. I'd like to thank Janet and Broke Johnson, Chandra Shaw, and Jessica Stevens for always being there for me.; [a.] Maple Grove, MN

CARR JR., OLANDA
[b.] March 6, 1972, Charlotte, NC; [p.] Olanda Carr Sr., Delia Carr; [ed.] West Charlotte High School, North Carolina State University; [occ.] Senior Vendor Relations Representatives at Belk Stores Services; [memb.] Kappa Alpha Psi Fraternity, Communications and Shepherding Committee, Men's Council at First United Presbyterian Church, Cities in School Tutorial Program; [hon.] 1996 Pacesetter Achievement Award Belk Stores Services, 1996 Certificate of Appreciation - Cities in School Program, 1993 NAACP Youth of the year; [oth. writ.] Several poems and articles in school newspaper (NCSU, *The Nubian Message*), church newsletter (*The United Voice*); [pers.] With every poem I write, I strive to give honor to the beauty of nature. My poems relate the similarities among mankind and nature, and all of the lessons we can learn from God's creations.; [a.] Charlotte, NC

CARRERO, JOSEPH A.
[b.] February 6, 1969, New York City; [p.] Fulgencio and Frances Carrero; [m.] Divorced; [ch.] Alec and Camilla; [ed.] Saint Raymond High School Milit.; [occ.] Student (full-time) at Devry (Brunswick, NJ); [memb.] DPMA: Data Management Processing Association, Sierra (Environment Group) Club, The Nature Conservancy; [hon.] Military Achievement Medals (for excellence); [oth. writ.] "Freedom Runner" is the only poem I managed to hold onto, the others are lost for good. Strange how I always had this poem with me throughout all the years and travels.; [pers.] A saying I believe in, "A dreamer lives forever; a toiler dies in a day." Believe in your dreams, but most important believe in yourself.; [a.] Bronx, NY

CARRICATO, AARON
[b.] January 6, 1979, Harrisburg, PA; [p.] Charles F. and Micky L. McDermott; [ed.] 11th Grade Central Dauphin High; [occ.] Student and Lifeguard; [memb.] Member of Central Dauphin High School Wrestling Team.; [hon.] Presently nominated for *Who's Who Among American High School Students*; [oth. writ] Several short stories and poems; [pers.] Poetry to me is an open door through which thoughts and experiences of both triumphs and tragedies are expressed. Poetry is truly only written from the soul, either by one or many.; [a.] Harrisburg, PA

CARROLL, LENNIE WHITT
[pen.] Lennie Whitt Carroll; [b.] November 27, 1935, Attalla, AL; [p.] Knox and Stella Whitt; [m.] Wayne Carroll, May 21, 1954; [ch.] Mike Carroll and Crystal Gazaway; [ed.] Etowah High School; [occ.] Pastor, Sand Valley Assembly of God, Teach 4 and 5 yr olds at Harvest Christian; [oth. writ.] I have written several poems that tell a story.; [pers.] I love to paint pictures with words. Writing poems is another way for me to minister to people.

CARTER, KEITH C.
[b.] June 30, 1952, Midland, TX; [p.] D. Keith Carter and Judy Carter; [m.] Divorced; [ch.] One daughter, Myriah Tess Carter; [ed.] Graduated High School, got drafted, and went on to be "All That I Could Be"; [occ.] Furniture Mover and Daddy; [hon.] The only honor I consider worth mentioning is that of being my daughter's Daddy; she is 10 yrs old and the pride of my life.; [pers.] "Being All I Could Be Left Me Less Than What I Was" but I'd do it all over again, even knowing what I know at 44 years old; [a.] Arvada, CO

CASANOVA, CARMEN
[b.] August 14, 1962, Murrayville, BC, Canada; [p.] Wanda de Boer, I am also a descendent of Swiss poet and novelist Carl Spitteler who won the Nobel prize for Literature in 1919; [ed.] Langley Senior Secondary School, American Academy of Dramatic Arts (A.A.), British-American Acting Academy. I am currently completing a B.F.A. in Theatre (Acting) at the University of Victoria; [occ.] Actress, model and fine artist; [memb.] British Actors' Equity Association (BAEA), the Alliance of Canadian Cinema, Television and Radio Artists Performers Guild (ACTRA Performers Guild) and the Union of B.C. Performers (UBCP); [hon.] South Coast Repertory/Professional Conservatory (Tony Award-Winning Theatre) Scholarship Award, Tom Steele Memorial Scholarship Award and Langley Arts Council Scholarship Award; [oth. writ.] Several poems published in local newspapers.; [pers.] Lift the veils of the mind and you shall find the treasures of the soul!; [a.] Salt Spring Island, British Columbia, Canada

CASAREZ, ARES
[pen.] Ares Casarez; [b.] November 3, 1978, Santa Barbara, CA; [p.] Joe and Martha Casarez; [ed.] 12th Grader at D.P. Continuation High School; [occ.] Employee of Taco Bell; [memb.] L.A. Church of Christ Santa Barbara Sector Teen Ministry; [hon.] Poetry published in a High School Poetry Anthology Book, Excellence in English Award La Cuesta High School; [oth. writ.] "The *Purpose of Life,*" book title: *12th Annual High School Poetry Anthology.*; [pers.] I write for the art of it and to express powerful messages.; [a.] Goleta, CA

CASEY JR., LESLEY E.
[pen.] Casey; [b.] December 16, 1940, Texas; [p.] Gene and Ethel Casey; [m.] Jillayne Louise Casey, March 8, 1962; [ch.] Denise-Laura-Shawn-Teresa; [ed.] High School; [occ.] Retired; [pers.] As insignificant as we are as individuals, we can still make a difference in the world around us.; [a.] Dearborn, MI

CASH, MARY ELEANOR SKELTON
[pen.] Mary Eleanor Skelton Cash; [b.] December 9, 1926, Eldorado, IL; [p.] Joseph and Mary Plunkett Skelton; [m.] Ex-Norman Everett Cash (Divorced 1971), 1949; [ch.] Keith, Craig, GiniLou and Mary Cash; [ed.] B.A. Social Psychology; [occ.] Poet; [oth. writ.] Six books, two plays, est. 2000 poems; [pers.] With minor access to poetry, my first poem came to me in Quaker Meeting, Schenectady, NY (1957) "Treasures Life Surely Brings To Those Who Joy In Simple Things" still a family favorite, professionalized at WRFG Radio, Atlanta, GA where known as political street poet, also self-publ. selling 3000 copies my poems walking door-to-door, lifetime diaries kept at Harvard University, Schlesinger Library, Cambridge, Massachusetts.; [a.] Saint Petersburg, FL

CATOLINE, ROSANNA
[pen.] Rozanna Catoline; [b.] March 6, 1977, Youngstown, OH; [p.] John A. and The Late Caroline Catoline; [ed.] Poland High School and I am going to start maybe at Pittsburgh University in the fall; [occ.] Writer; [memb.] Carnegie Art Museum and was an active member of a literary magazine in High School; [hon.] Was published in Literary magazine at Poland High School; [oth. writ.] I am currently writing a book, titled, *A Cigarette By Sunset*. And am working on poems.; [pers.] Writing is the details that we sometimes ignore.; [a.] Pittsburgh, PA

CATOLINE SR., JOHN ALLAN
[b.] October 14, 1937, Youngstown, OH; [p.] Felix J. Catoline, Mary Clare Esposito; [m.] Caroline Deblasio Catoline (Deceased), July 8, 1973; [ch.] John Jr., Rosanna Marie; [ed.] Kent State Univ., Middlebury College VT., Rutgers Univ., N.V., Univ., of PISA (Italy), Bach. of Arts, Master of Arts, M.Ed; [occ.] Retired teacher of History, World Cultures, Italian Language and culture; [memb.] Audubon Society, Sierra Club, Carnegie Museums, Butler Institute of American Art; [hon.] Fulbright Research and Teaching Grant - Scholar to Italy 1967-1968; [oth. writ.] Essays on Travels, Reflections and Meditations Memoirs; [pers.] My focus is Tolerance - acceptance and comprehension of other cultures and mentalities. I strongly believe in the environment - the balance of nature. Humankind's role - to enhance nature not to destroy or manipulate; [a.] Cranberry Township, PA

CATON, CHASTITY
[pen.] C. C.; [b.] July 9, 1980; [p.] Greg and Annette Caton; [ed.] High School Greenfield McClain High; [occ.] Waitress; [oth. writ.] Just my personal stuff; [pers.] I always try to write about what's inside. I have all my feelings down on paper.; [a.] Greenfield, OH

CEDER, JOHN W.
[b.] July 21, 1918, Moline, IL; [p.] Louise and Hjalmer Ceder; [ed.] Univ. of Washington - BA Stockholm's Hoqskola - Certificate Butler University BA Indiana University - MA University of Kentucky - MA; [occ.] Retired; [memb.] Prince of Peace Lutheran Church, 88th Infantry Association; [hon.] Bronze Star; [oth. writ.] *Butternut* - (novel) *The Hook and Eye* - (novel) I have written two more unpublished novels and some epic poetry. I am currently working on another novel; [pers.] Robert Burns is the poet I most admire.; [a.] Martinsville, IN

CENTENO, ELIZABETH DALY
[b.] December 13, 1964, Brooklyn, NY; [m.] Rick Centeno, May 28, 1988; [ch.] Patrick Arthur; [pers.] This poem was written as a tribute to the deceased because of the tremendous creative, spiritual, and emotional effect he had in my heart, in my life, and in my soul.; [a.] Brooklyn, NY

CERNY, MATILDA
[pen.] Matilda Segura; [b.] May 6, 1941, Hale Center, TX; [p.] Anastacio Segura, Juanita Segura; [ch.] LaJuana Marie, Gregory Anastacio, Connie Lynn, Tracy Ann; [ed.] Hale Center High, Los Angeles City College, Glendale City College; [occ.] Retired, 28 years, Pacific Bell, Test Desk Technician; [oth. writ.] None published; [pers.] I take pen in hand to express what I feel and hope I've helped someone along the way.; [a.] West Covina, CA

CERVANTEZ, KRISTIN
[b.] March 26, 1981, Nashville, TN; [ed.] Ninth Grade Lavernge High School; [occ.] Student; [memb.] Lavergne High School basketball team; [pers.] This poem is written in memory of my good friend, Bobby Hornick, who passed away suddenly.; [a.] Smyrna, TN

CETTO, GALE
[pen.] Terry; [b.] September 26, 1946, Bethel, PA; [p.] Mary C. Price; [m.] Richard M. Cetto, April 21, 1969; [ch.] Timon and Michele; [occ.] Vol. work old Folks home, pet Therapy; [hon.] Some for painting, some for writing, some for volunteer work.; [oth. writ.] Write for religious mag. last June "These Days"; [pers.] "To glorify my Heavenly Father is my only goal".

CHANSKY, MATTHEW
[b.] December 16, 1964, Raleigh, NC; [p.] Norman and Elissa Chansky; [ed.] BFA Tyler School of Art, MFA Stanford University; [occ.] Artist, Illustrator; [hon.] National exhibition record noted in New York Times article by Vivian Raynor - Nov. 5, 1995. Several purchase awards and private collections.; [oth. writ.] Compiling a book of drawings and poems, currently unpublished.; [pers.] Beauty has always been a commodity. However, in the '90's, face value has hit an all-time low.; [a.] Philadelphia, PA

CHARETTE, NIKKI JEANINE
[b.] October 26, 1981, Marysville, CA; [p.] Nancy and Wayne Charette; [ed.] Currently in 10th Grade at St. Michael's H.S., also taking College Classes in Journalism; [occ.] Student; [memb.] Guide Dogs - 4 the Blind; [hon.] Nat'l Convention Center of Music in San Diego awarded top 50 best Piano Players in California 1992; [oth. writ.] 1 poem published in *Reader's Digest*, and several in local Newspapers.; [pers.] Poetry is a journey not an action. It is accomplished with the many steps and wonders of the mind and the minds pictorial achievements.; [a.] Window Rock, AZ

CHARLES, WALDY
[pen.] Waldy Charles; [b.] July 23, 1981, Worcester, MA; [p.] Waldeck and Carole Charles; [ed.] Lindenhurst Senior High; [occ.] High School Student: (Just completed 9th going on to 10th.); [memb.] French Club, Fellowship Club, Key Club, R.O.T.C., Band, L' Atelier, Environment Club; [hon.] Received recognition in *Who's Who Among American High School Students*, Honor roll; [oth. writ.] I have made a couple of poems. Two were published in school.; [pers.] In my writings I try to create a world where emotions carry out the tone or expressions of my feelings.; [a.] Lindenhurst, NY

CHAVIRA, KAREN J.
[pen.] K. C.; [b.] July 30, 1949, Illinois; [p.] Al and Dorothy Geiger; [m.] Divorced for 18 years; [ch.] 3 and 5 grandchildren; [ed.] High School - Camelback - Phoenix, Arizona; [occ.] Day Care Operator and Apt. Manager; [hon.] Poem won contest in Local Newspaper contest. Raising 9 ½ yr. old grandson Michael to become a doctor and writer.; [oth. writ.] Write poetry as a hobby. Would like to write a book someday.; [pers.] The person I most admire is Whoopi Goldberg, who is very inspiring to me. My best friend of 20 years, Tricia McGinley, has been my great source of encouragement.; [a.] Logan, UT

CHAZEN, JAMIE
[b.] August 2, 1968, Buffalo, NY; [p.] Mel Chazen, Dotty Chazen; [ed.] Sweet Home Sr. High, BA Psychology from Cal. State Long Beach, Paralegal Certificate from UCLA Extension; [occ.] Paralegal; [memb.] Toastmasters, Board of Directors, Comprehensive Child Development Center, Volunteer for Harriett Buhai Center for Family Law and Make-A-Wish; [pers.] I write about situations that affect myself, friends, and society as a whole. I believe only through our mistakes do we evolve, grow, and finally realize what life is about.; [a.] Long Beach, CA

CHEN, MING
[b.] January 14, 1981, Pasadena, CA; [ed.] High School Freshman; [hon.] Several awards in Piano Competitions in California, Scholarship and "Outstanding Graduate" in Junior High; [oth. writ.] Executive editor and writer of Junior High Newspaper; [a.] San Marino, CA

CHENEY, BRANNIGAN S.
[pen.] Key; [b.] July 21, 1956, Ogden, UT; [p.] Steven J. Cheney, Debbie D. Cheney; [ed.] Evanston High School; [occ.] Two year Missionary for the Church of Jesus Christ of Latter Day Saints; [hon.] Eagle Scout for the Boy Scouts of America; [oth. writ.] Published state wide high school contests. Other minor winnings.; [pers.] Life is what we make it, good or bad it's up to us. We have an ability in all of us to make a difference. I hope for a better world, I hope for a lot of things that now seem hard to accomplish, but I know I can make an impact.; [a.] Evanston, WY

CHERRY SR., THOMAS M.
[pen.] Tom Cherry; [b.] April 5, 1936, Clermont, IN; [p.] William and Jessie Cherry; [m.] Diann K., February 17, 1990; [ed.] 12 yrs. H.S. Clayton H.S. - Ind. Presbyterian College S. Carolina; [occ.] Retired Military; [hon.] Outstanding Basketball player, 10 yrs. in Europe, Coach in youth Athletics, Math instructor Military; [oth. writ.] Several unpublished personal poems.; [pers.] Stop and smell the roses. Appreciate what has been given us in nature.; [a.] Martinsville, IN

CHILDS SR., HIRAM PAUL
[b.] November 23, 1919, Gray, GA; [p.] Deceased; [m.] Margaret Eloise (Mayo) Childs, December 1, 1940; [ch.] Hiram Paul Childs Jr.; [ed.] Jones Co. High School, GA, State University, Texas Tech. (Air Force Cadet Training); [occ.] Retired - Lockheed Aircraft Corp. - 30 yrs. - 3 mos. Quality Control; [memb.] American Legion, Veteran WW II and Korean Wars, Member Prince Ave. Bapt. Church Athens; [hon.] State award, Freedom's GA Foundation 1976 - National Editorial Award, Freedom's Foundation 1977; [oth. writ.] Book *Paul's Treasures*; [pers.] I give credit to God that I am able to write love God and all people.; [a.] Hartwell, GA

CHRISTOFANO, FRANK M.
[b.] September 25, 1961, Jeanette; [p.] Frank L. Christofano and Hazel Yurt; [m.] Terri J. Marietta, August 6, 1983; [ch.] Sarah, Frank, Cassandra; [ed.] Jeannette Sr. High, Class of 79, Edinboro University; [occ.] Heavy Equipment Operator and Artist; [memb.] Theta Chi Fraternity; [hon.] Several Art Club Awards. Many of my drawings and mirror etchings are hanging in my friends' and families' homes.; [pers.] Sometimes I see things so vividly that I must put it down on paper with the hope that others may enjoy it too.; [a.] Jeannette, PA

CHUKWUOCHA, NNAMDI O.
[pen.] Twin Poet; [b.] November 16, 1970, Wilmington, DE; [p.] Mary E. Jones, William Hicks Anderson; [ed.]

Senior at Delaware State University - Honors History - Major, Kiswahili - Minor with 4.0 GPA; [occ.] Youth Advocate at Kingswood Community Center; [memb.] Twin Poets - performing group, Alpha Chi National Honors Society, Phi Alpha Theta, International Historical Society - Sigma Tau Chapter Delaware St.; [hon.] Dean's List, Odunde Poetry Slam "96" Grand prize winners (Twin Poets) with Brother Al Mills, Mayor Sills Service Award "96", Nation Builder African Rites of Passage; [oth. writ.] Poems published for local newspaper, *Drumbeat Newsletter, Know Thy Self Newsletter, Del-State News Million Man March National Newsletter*; [pers.] The purpose of my writing is to awaken the revolutionary spirit buried deep within the souls of an oppressed people. My inspirations are my Mother, Twin Brother, and the struggles of Urban Life.; [a.] Wilmington, DE

CIOBANU, ILEANA MARIA
[b.] November 4, 1978, Boston, MA; [p.] Dan Ciobanu, Sharilyn and Geary Keeton; [ed.] Green Mountain High School/Class of 1996, Harvard University/Class of 2000; [occ.] General Office Assistant, Lakewood City Attorney's Office; [memb.] Mensa, Kiwanis Pediatric Trauma, Institute Key Club District Chairperson, Division Key Club Outstanding Lieutenant Governor, National Honor Society President, Speech and Debate Club President, Spanish, French, and German Honor Societies, Teen Court Defense/Prosecuting Attorney, City of Lakewood's City Attorney's Office and Probation Office Volunteer, Government Club Vice-President; [hon.] Valedictorian, National Merit Finalist, *Who's Who Among American High School Students*, Green Mountain High School's "top student in the graduating class of 1996" for News 4's "Class of Colorado", United State President's Youth Service Award, Member of Science Bowl team placing 1st at State and 6th at Nationals, Science Olympiad National, State, and Regional Medal Winner, Tandy Technology Scholar, State Finalist in International Extemporaneous Speaking, Top of the Mountain Senior, Outstanding Advanced Placement English Student/Social Studies Student/Foreign Language Student, Top of the Mountain Speech and Debate Award, Optimist Club Honoree; [oth. writ.] My school newspaper published the essay I wrote the U.S. Institute of Peace National Peace Essay Contest entitled "Maintaining National Security and Global Stability in a 'Polyarchical' World." I was the Colorado State 1st Place Winner and the 3rd Place National Winner. Because I placed in the top three nationwide, the Institute placed my essay on the Internet.; [pers.] My poem "Serendipity" is very symbolic to me. When I was little, I did find a quarter when I was digging a hole to China. However, I would not have found that quarter and bought the lollipop if I had not dug diligently, despite the cold unyielding sand. I have noticed that throughout my life I have become the person I am today because of this magical combination of serendipity and hard work.; [a.] Lakewood, CO

CIOTTI, THOMAS J.
[pen.] Thomas J. Ciotti; [b.] January 16, 1948, Flushing, NY; [p.] Peter and Angela Ciotti; [m.] Claudia Ciotti, November 1995; [ch.] Two Girls, 8 and 3, One boy, 27 in college; [occ.] Was Musical Director at St. Brigid's Church; [hon.] Wrote and sang the song at the Waldorf to Nancy Reagan; [oth. writ.] Many of my lyrics put to songs also used his songs and tapes were made and played at other churches.

CIVETTINI, ANDREW J.
[b.] November 13, 1979, Mount Lebanon, PA; [p.] Grace and Michael Corba, Joe Civettini; [ed.] Carlynton Jr., Sr. High; [memb.] Boy Scouts of America, Students Against Drunk Driving, National Brotherhood of Scout Campers, National Honor Society; [oth. writ.] Published in local teen newspaper; [pers.] I strive to convey emotion in my writing while blocking out rationality. I have been most influenced by my friends who have helped me discover true emotion.; [a.] Carnegie, PA

CIZEWSKI, JAIME
[b.] August 29, 1977, Michigan, Novi; [p.] George Cizewski and Cheryl Parry; [memb.] World Wildlife Fund, National Wildlife Foundation, American Kennel Club; [pers.] I find that poetry is an extension of your soul. It's an excellent way of sorting out your feelings, and a perfect and easy way to tell the world how you feel. Edgar Allen Poe has been a great influence in my writing.; [a.] Harrison Township, MI

CLARK, JENNIFER O. N.
[pen.] Jennifer Clark; [b.] June 29, 1964, Danville, IL; [p.] Otis and Marie Nelson; [m.] Ernest Clark (Deceased), June 14, 1986; [ch.] Vincent and Marcus Clark; [ed.] Danville High School-Grad '82, Illinois State University Grad '86, Waubonsee Community College '95 I took additional sign language classes; [occ.] Sign Language Instructor; [memb.] Church of God, IEA, NEA; [hon.] Dean's list '86 Dean's list '95, Parent volunteer of the year '96 at Good Shepherd Head Start; [oth. writ.] I have produced a sign language video "Learning with Sign Language." I also write music.; [pers.] If I take care of God's business, He will take care of mine. I must keep Him first.

CLARK, JOHN STEPHENS
[b.] August 8, 1975, Morristown, TN; [p.] Patricia D. Clark, John M. Clark; [ed.] Alcoa High, Pellissippi Community College 2 yrs.; [occ.] US Army; [hon.] Gift of Life and the eyes to hear her and the ears to see her sing and dance; [oth. writ.] Many other poems and a few short stories which have not been published yet are screaming out for recognition.; [pers.] Writing poetry is an awakening, a musical chorus of the soul, from the inner depths of the bowels, the emotional climax exploding in rhyme and prose.; [a.] Alcoa, TN

CLARK, W. DRURY
[pen.] Drury; [b.] June 10, 1913, Owensboro, KY; [p.] John and Annabell Clark; [m.] Katherine Meehan, August 6, 1940; [ch.] Two; [ed.] Ex Circular GNI-Tech taught night classes Anderson Ind. owned Clarke Associates; [occ.] Retired; [memb.] Elks -Gamma Mu Tau; [hon.] Safety Director of Year GM "Guide Lanip Div,"1940-44; [oth. writ.] None published - collection of my own and friends about 150 or more poems written for special occasions for friends.; [pers.] You are never to old to learn Poetry - A Hobby; [a.] Kalamazoo, MI

CLARKE, BRENDA J.
[pen.] Mom; [b.] January 22, 1961, Hillsboro, OR; [p.] Sally, Richard Brown; [m.] Edward Clarke, April 18, 1980; [ch.] Shawnay, Linda, Jessie, Shannan; [ed.] Grammar Gaston, Cornelius Junior High Neil Armstrong. Forest Grove High School; [occ.] Community Support Specialist; [memb.] Indian Education Title IV; [hon.] Art Award 76-77, Y.C.C. Certificate Completion, Nursing Home, Mighty Midget Award, Golden Poet Award 1990; [oth. writ.] "Last Mustang"; [pers.] Nothing in life is impossible unless you make it impossible.; [a.] Saint Helens, OR

CLARKE, LISA
[pen.] Lisa Clarke; [b.] November 25, 1960, Terre Haute; [p.] Beverly Lynch, Kenneth Lynch; [m.] Robert Clarke, October 23, 1979; [ch.] Jessica Lynn Clarke, Lindsay Jean Clarke; [ed.] South Vigo High School; [occ.] Teacher Aid; [oth. writ.] Poems I have written about my family and friends.; [pers.] I write what is in my heart. God and my loved ones are my inspiration.; [a.] Crawfordsville, IN

CLAXTON, TRAVIS D.
[b.] September 1, 1971, Jacksonville, FL; [p.] Patricia Thompson, Jack Thompson; [a.] Jacksonville, FL

COBB, JAMES C.
[pen.] Jim Cobb; [b.] December 30, 1975, Flint, MI; [p.] James R. and Carol A. Cobb; [ed.] Pella Community High School, Iowa University of Northern Iowa; [occ.] Full-time student; [oth. writ.] Several notebooks of various prose, poems and songs currently being reorganized for book publication. I am currently working on my first screenplay.; [pers.] "Fire and the Wheel — the Schutzstaffel" is a short piece about comparing our recent past to our initial origins. Mankind hasn't changed. This piece symbolizes that many times, our ignorance is false strength. Such was true for early man, such was true for 1930's Germany (P.S. The poem is shaped as S because the Schutzstafel's symbol was SS.); [a.] Otley, IA

COCHRAN, CONNIE
[pen.] Irish; [b.] July 7, 1947; [p.] Eleanor and Larry (Passed away); [m.] Widow; [ch.] Six; [ed.] Nurse-Same, Mang.- Sales - Writer (another view of ones self) briefs; [occ.] Disable transplant do briefs now and then; [memb.] I am a member of National ABWA (American Business Women's Association) also the Rubber City Chapter; [hon.] 5043 Landscaping Awards for garden of Akron Word. From Mayor and Governor George U. Voinovich of state of Ohio.; [oth. writ.] Another view of one's self (briefs) I've done many briefs to help others; [pers.] Thank you for the pleasure of your kind words. I hope the poem which I wrote will touch the hearts of many and help others. Thank you.; [a.] Akron, OH

COHEA, MIKE
[pen.] Mike Cohea; [b.] January 13, 1982, Anaheim, CA; [p.] Robert and Lyn Cohea; [occ.] Student; [memb.] Junior Latin Classical League; [a.] Vancouver, WA

COLABELLA, LOUIS
[b.] January 4, 1936, Brooklyn, NY; [p.] Frank and Josephine Colabella; [m.] Maria Colabella, September 15, 1962; [ch.] Paul, Louis and Julie (Paul and Randy Colabella are parents to grandson Ryan).; [ed.] St. Francis Preparatory High School Brooklyn, NY, NYSE Securities Training (Registered Representative); [occ.] Retired - Telephone stock order clerk on Floor of NYSE for 35 years.; [oth. writ.] Various poems and writings, none of which have been published.; [pers.] I only recently began writing poetry as a hobby and really enjoy the challenge of putting thoughts together and seeing them actually become something. I get my inspiration to write from nature, events that happen, and often other people, but mostly just when the Spirit moves me.; [a.] Brooklyn, NY

COLEMAN, KEITH W.
[b.] March 29, 1960, Richmond, VA; [p.] Charlotte M. Coleman; [m.] Kym Y. Coleman, January 20, 1990; [ch.] Billy Davis; [ed.] Henrico High School; [occ.] Fire

Fighter III, EMT City of Richmond Fire Bureau; [pers.] Since I have dedicated my life to Jesus Christ, I was delivered from Substance Abuse. I am now a living testimony that with God all things are possible.; [a.] Richmond, VA

COLLINS, LINDA F.
[pen.] Linda Collins; [b.] March 10, 1959, Washington, DC; [p.] Paul Foster, Jennie Foster; [m.] Terence Collins, May 15, 1984; [ch.] Patrice, Ryan, Terence Collins; [ed.] McKinley Sr High, Morgan State Univ. Maryland Univ. and International Correspondence School; [occ.] Federal Relations Rep; [memb.] American Heart Association, Lincoln Vista Civic Assoc, Mt Calvary Baptist Church; [oth. writ.] "The Doorkeeper," "Running The Race"; [pers.] Nothing in life that is worth having is easy to obtain. I give all honor and praise to God, who inspires my thoughts and my written words.; [a.] Lanham, MD

COMBS, GRACE
[b.] May 26, 1979, Alaska; [p.] Felisa and Ronald; [ed.] I'm still in my senior year at El Cajon Valley High School; [occ.] High School Student; [oth. writ.] Unpublished: "Unborn Dreams," "Winter's Joy," "Shattered Tears," and more.; [pers.] Even though I'm young and never before have had any of my writings published, I have one thing in common with most poets. That is to paint pictures and feelings into minds with words as my brush.; [a.] El Cajon, CA

COMBS, TERESA M.
[pen.] Traci Combs; [b.] March 22, 1967, Greenville, OH; [p.] Eric Hughes, Aleda Hartzell; [m.] Randell M. Combs, December 31, 1994; [ch.] Kimberly Jo and Kelsey Renee; [ed.] Greenville Senior High School; [occ.] Secretary/Bookkeeper, Iowa Roofing Co., Des Moines, Iowa; [pers.] Expressing my feeling through poetry has always been easy for me. "A Lesson From Nature" came to me by the love of my beautiful daughters. They are my biggest inspiration.; [a.] Des Moines, IA

CONCEPCION, GENISA
[b.] February 20, 1986, Providence, RT; [p.] Rita Lynn Concepcion, Eugenio Concepcion; [ed.] Children's Discovery Center, St. Lucy School, Rotella Elementary School Waterbury, CT; [occ.] Student; [memb.] Girl Scouts; [pers.] I love reading and writing, I hope to publish many books and poems. My philosophy is: Remember the Magic Word: Attitude; [a.] Waterbury, CT

CONEY, DIANA
[b.] August 26, 1974, Panama; [p.] Edmundo A. Clarke, Diana Clarke; [m.] Corey A. Coney, December 29, 1994; [ed.] North Miami Senior High; [occ.] Up coming Writer; [hon.] Certificate for helping kids in English. And also certificate for my English class in High School; [oth. writ.] Poetry book comic strip; [pers.] I love to write the reason of doing so. Whenever I write about life, relationships and love, my heart really enjoys every bit of it.; [a.] Broward, FL

CONLEY III, THOMAS YOUNG
[pen.] Ty Conley "Yoyo"; [b.] October 20, 1970, Baltimore, MD; [p.] Marie K. Stuart, Thomas Y. Conley II; [ed.] General Education Diploma, waiting to start College; [occ.] Mineral Wholesaler - Retailer; [memb.] Rainbow/Grateful Dead Family; [hon.] This is an honor to me; [oth. writ.] "Wings of a Dove," "Salvation," "A Prayer for Change," and many many more. "Love or Hate" is to all the people who suffered from the Rodney King Riots; [pers.] We are all living pieces of the earth, we are all one. We must love one another in order to change the problems of today. Love Has No Color, Humanity Does, Rainbows are all colors combined as one; [a.] San Francisco, CA

CONNER, EDITH HENSLEY
[pen.] "Gavin Lewis"; [b.] February 9, 1912, Lemon Cove, CA; [p.] Wm. H. and Nora C. Hensley; [m.] Deceased (Gene Conner); [ch.] Harry G. and Trudy J. Coleman; [ed.] College B.S. at U. of T. (Knot) Plus a variety of Short Courses, regularly through spring '96; [occ.] Retired (winter: S.C. Ctr. Fl.); [memb.] A.A.U.W., (Assoc. Member: Unitarian Church) member in (Oak Ridge TN. and Assp. The Community Church, SC Ctr Fl.); [hon.] My niece told me I was her Mentor.; [oth. writ.] None published, but have "book" of Haiku writings ready (almost) to be edited and published. Another: About *Episodes* in my grandson's life. Will be a young child's true stories. Short "thought" called *Coffee Talk*!; [pers.] I think there is Beauty in all people, nature and rocks, if one observes quietly and "polishes" each, the reward will be also, in one of Deepak Chopras books: "When you stop learning you stop growing."; [a.] Sun City Center, FL

CONNEY, GEORGE
[b.] September 12, 1968, Staten Island, NY; [p.] Jacqueline Schreiber, George E. Conney; [ed.] Brentwood Ross HS, Brentwood, NY; [occ.] Carpenter; [memb.] B.A.M.D. - Bay Area Musicians Organization, Panama City, FL; [oth. writ.] Numerous unpublished poems, song lyrics for personal enjoyment and sharing with others; [pers.] I would like to thank Kathren Miller for letting me share my poems at the Bayview Cafe, my mother for encouraging me to never give up, and my niece Jacqueline Sfreddo, for making "Jacqueline III" possible.; [a.] Panama City, FL

CONOVER JR., KENNETH R.
[pen.] Jonethon Verrnerok; [b.] July 2, 1966, Seoul, South Korea; [p.] Kenneth R. Conover Sr., Kyong Hwa Kim; [ed.] Rutgers University, School of Business; [occ.] Financial Accountant, Merrill Lynch

COOK, DANIELLE LYN
[pen.] Dani Cook; [b.] April 29, 1964, Dearborn, Michigan; [p.] Janice & Cliff Hullender; [ed.] Atlanta Art Institute Drama Major/University of Tennessee at Chattanooga; [occ.] Actress-Artist-Writer; [hon.] Was given "Mentally Gifted Minor" Award in School in California; [oth. writ.] Several poems, Children's Stories - was working on a Screenplay when she died (August 7, 1996); [pers.] Dani was the perpetual little girl, always trying to bring love and joy into every life she met. We miss her and thank her for the wonderful memories! She was our angel; [a.] Chattanooga, TN

COOPER, GRACE
[pen.] Sharon Cooper; [b.] February 1922, Jamaica, WI; [p.] Nelson and Hattle Cooper; [ch.] Sabrina and Jelani; [ed.] Kingsway High, West Indies College; [oth. writ.] Several short stories and poems unpublished; [pers.] I credit any talent to my father, the gifted artist and writer Nelson Cooper.; [a.] Queens, NY

CORDEIRO, CHARLSYEE M. P.
[b.] April 10, 1978, Ewa Beach, HI; [p.] Angelita Cordeiro and Callen Cordeiro Sr.; [ed.] 1996 gradate of James Campbell High School; [occ.] Student; [memb.] Quill and Scroll (International Honorary Society for High School Journalist); [hon.] Editor's Choice awards, for "Someday" published in *Where Dreams Begin* and for "Letting Go" published in *Best Poems of 1996*, Editor in Chief of the *Ewa Naupaka* (James Campbell High's Newspaper) 1995-1996; [oth. writ.] "Someday" (published in *Where Dreams Begin*) and "Letting Go" (Published in *Best Poems of 1996*); [pers.] A really good poem is one that is felt by the heart and soul.; [a.] Ewa Beach, HI

COREY, REBEKKA LYNN
[b.] March 4, 1979, St. Clair, MI; [p.] Thomas Corey, Margaret Corey; [ed.] Marine City High School; [memb.] National Honor Society, Students Against Drunk Driving, High School Band; [hon.] National Honor Society, National Science Merit Award, All-American Scholar Award, National Leadership and Service Award; [pers.] My poem, "Don't Be Afraid" is based on how I believe people of today should live their lives. Life is complex enough, be yourself and it will be easier.; [a.] Marine City, MI

CORNWELL, ELSIE V.
[b.] May 6, 1921, Ona, OR; [p.] Chub and Tency Ryan; [m.] Russell C. Cornwell, August 13, 1954; [ch.] Patricia, Sheryl and Terri; [ed.] Waldport High School; [occ.] Homemaker; [a.] Hillsboro, OR

COSTANZO, SUZANNE C.
[pen.] Suzie; [b.] August 5, 1984, Pittsburgh; [p.] Samuel A. and Barbara C. Costanzo; [ed.] O'Hara Elementary School, 7th Grade St. Scholastica School (current); [occ.] Student; [memb.] Participant in Carnegie Mellon's Investigation of Talented and Creative Elementary Students, Aspinwall Softball League, St. Scholastica Basketball; [hon.] Published in *Kidsburgh Press* and *Kids Today Mini Magazine* - High Honor Roll; [oth. writ.] I have written a various collection of poetry of all types.; [pers.] Creative thoughts very often run through my head - even causing me to awaken in the middle of the night to get my thoughts onto paper.; [a.] Pittsburgh, PA

COSTELLO, CHARLES
[pen.] Chuck; [b.] January 19, 1952, Washington, DC; [p.] Helen Costello, Charles Costello; [m.] Pam Costello, January 28, 1983; [ch.] Patricia Gale, Charles Vincent Jr., (Stepsons) Clay and Jason; [ed.] High School, School of Life; [occ.] Automotive Master Tech. retired, Security and Marketing Strategist; [memb.] Sierra Club, Georgia Conservancy; [hon.] ASE Master Technician, AT&T Security Marketing Mgr. for 1993 - Central Florida; [oth. writ.] "Automotive Computer Diagnostic Techniques" - many, many poems; [pers.] I write what comes to me from within, very inspired by nature, I try to be the husband that a very patient wife would want to have, as she is my inspiration.; [a.] Douglasville, GA

COULSON, KATHLEEN M.
[b.] March 9, 1975, Indianapolis, IN; [p.] John and Margaret Kennedy; [m.] Travis Coulson, November 5, 1994; [ed.] Brownsbury High School, IUPUI; [occ.] Student; [a.] Indianapolis, IN

COUNIHAN, ERIN
[pen.] Elise MacNaughty and Peter Robert; [b.] December 10, 1957, Cumberland, MD; [p.] Joseph and Dolores Counihan; [ch.] Brandy 16, Monica 11, James 7; [ed.] 1975 Carlynton Grad. Associates Liberal Arts Culinary Art Grad.; [occ.] Culinary Arts Domestic Engineer; [memb.] North Shore Animal League, Audubon Society, VVA; [hon.] I've been awarded the honor of express-

ing these thoughts, emotions, and attitudes in our rise of *Frost at Midnight*. Dew meet me at sunrise!; [oth. writ.] "Da Risen Fall of Siggyls Czar Dust Sand Box to Castles," (Nar-a-Non) "Back in The Saddle," "Trap Called Love," "Morning Manshine"; [pers.] One life to live so precious time too fast, thou shan't return the present from the past. Eternity comes soon enough of all...past, present and future last!; [a.] Pittsburgh, PA

COVELENS, KELLY
[b.] May 27, 1962, Milwaukee, WI; [p.] James and Janice Marlowe; [m.] David Allen Covelens, October 24, 1992; [ch.] Henry, Nicole, Taylor; [ed.] Hartford High School, Secretarial and Computer Programming Training University of Wisconsin - Platteville Business Administration; [occ.] Homemaker, aspiring writer. Ex-office manager; [oth. writ.] I have written three children's stories and currently am trying to get them published.; [pers.] I have dedicated this poem to my stepdaughter Nicole Rose Covelens for the pain she has endured being involved in a custody battle.; [a.] Milwaukee, WI

COWAN, ALYSSA
[b.] June 13, 1985, Newark, DE; [p.] Karen Cowan and Michael Cowan; [ed.] I will be in 6th grade at Bancroft Middle School; [pers.] My mom has inspired me to write poems, it helps with my feelings.; [a.] Newark, DE

COWLEY JR., RICHARD J.
[pen.] Seamus O'Toole; [b.] January 22, 1944, Elmira, NY; [p.] Richard and Sarah Cowley; [m.] Catherine, August 20, 1966; [ch.] Jeff and Jam; [ed.] Masters Degree - Elmira College, Bachelors Degree - Mansfield University; [occ.] Teacher of "at risk" student; [memb.] Watkins Glen Writing Group; [oth. writ.] Several articles in Business periodicals, numerous poems and short stories. Completed Novel-working title, *The Furbishen Affair*.; [pers.] The American Culture is in the midst of profound changes. Poets and writers need to understand the import of these changes on the collective American psyche and confront them.; [a.] Elmira, NY

COX, BRENDA
[pen.] Brindle Cox; [b.] December 10, 1957, Louisville, KY; [p.] Charles S. Kaltenthaler and Patricia Ann Bryan; [m.] J. Darryl Cox, December 31, 1993; [ch.] Kendall Christine Hedges (11); [ed.] B.A. in English from Centre College of KY 1980. MBA from Univ. of Louisville 1982; [occ.] Controller, oil and gas; [memb.] Dallas Area Romance Authors-DARA, Romance Writers of America-RWA.; [pers.] Each person has a darkness to navigate. The soul is black and white.

CRABTREE, KEVIN
[pen.] Cosey B. Grant; [ed.] High School, School of Hard Knocks; [occ.] Carpentry, Victorian Specialist; [oth. writ.] Personal essays and poetry. I can not write to please others and so I write to please myself. If other people enjoy it, so be it.; [pers.] I like to think of writing as an art form more than an intellectual process. I feel my work is still evolving ever happens by force.; [a.] Hampton, IA

CRABTREE, PENNY
[pen.] Boggs, Charlotte; [b.] April 10, 1951, Canton, OH; [m.] Dennis, May 14, 1987; [ch.] Melisa Williams; [ed.] Ohio University, University of South Carolina; [occ.] Designer; [oth. writ.] Poems: "Analogy," *Shadows* Editor, *Nutshell News* Author: Faux Book and Design Literature.; [pers.] I write because I have something to say. My heritage and my family are my inspiration.; [a.] Columbus, OH

CRABTREE, STEPHANIE
[b.] June 13, 1979, Nashville, TN; [p.] David and Cathy Crabtree; [ed.] Student in High School; [oth. writ.] None published; [pers.] I have been inspired by a traumatic automobile accident which resulted in the death of a friend, due to the use of alcohol and drugs.; [a.] Nashville, TN

CRAIG, CLAUDIA
[b.] March 17, 1972, Durango, Mexico; [m.] Jeremy Craig, December 16, 1993; [ch.] Kerry; [ed.] High School graduate and currently in School, McLain Community High School; [occ.] Student of the Colo. School of Travel; [oth. writ.] I gave a speech in my High School graduation entitled "Coming to America".; [pers.] Give love, and you'll receive love. Take care of our Mother Earth; without her we wouldn't be here.; [a.] Arvada, CO

CRAIL, YOLANDA
[pen.] Yolanda Flowers Crail; [b.] February 25, 1946, Belize, CA

CRAWFORD SR., CHARLES E.
[b.] March 16, 1933, Louisville, KY; [p.] Josh and Julia Crawford; [m.] Annie J. Crawford, August 27, 1966; [ch.] Seven, Four Grandkids and One Great; [ed.] 12th Central High 1950, Louisville KY; [occ.] Retired from Chrysler due to back injury 1970; [oth. writ.] "What a Question to a Friend," "What Good is Life," "Don't Wake Me," "Prison Bound," "Want be Home for Xmas," "As I Got One Wish"; [pers.] My greatest wish was to see some of my writing in print; now my wish has come true.; [a.] Detroit, MI

CRITES, RACHEL
[b.] August 24, 1980, Marietta, GA; [p.] Mr. and Mrs. Crites; [ed.] Klein High School hopefully Stephen F. Austin; [occ.] Student; [oth. writ.] I've written many other poems that I keep to myself, sometimes I share them with special friends.; [pers.] Life becomes much more enjoyable when you have a positive attitude.; [a.] Spring, TX

CROSS, JODI
[b.] July 18, Rochester, NY; [p.] Joan and Harry Cross; [ed.] BA - St. Thomas University, Miami, FL - MBA - Nova Southeastern University - Ft. Lauderdale, FL; [occ.] Director of Marketing for a Golfspa resort; [hon.] Dean's List - St. Thomas of Villanova Univ. Notable Woman in Business feature story; [oth. writ.] "Rollercoaster," "The Dreamer," "Edge of Darkness"; [pers.] My writing reflects deep emotional feelings and life experiences.; [a.] Jupiter, FL

CROSS, SARAH LEE
[b.] July 25, 1980, Santiago, Chile; [p.] Walter and Margaret Cross; [ed.] Currently a high school student, finishing 9th in the USA and will be returning to Mexico City were I've lived for 9 yrs.; [occ.] 10th grade student at Logos-Escuela de Bachilleres.; [pers.] Never stop being outraged at injustice...the day we forget is the day everything is lost.; [a.] Lake Ariel, PA

CROSS JR., DOUGLAS
[b.] November 13, 1973, Newburyport, MA; [p.] Mary Higgins, Douglas Cross; [ed.] Newburyport High Fitchburg State College; [occ.] College Student; [oth. writ.] Poems published in school anthologies; [a.] Newburyport, MA

CROSSMAN, NICHOLAS W.
[b.] January 13, 1982, Orlando, FL; [p.] Bruce R. and Katherine A. Crossman; [ed.] Elem. Park Maitland School, Maitland, Fl., Middle and H.S., Trinity Preparatory School, Winter Park, Fl.; [occ.] Student at Trinity Preparatory School, Winter Park, Fl., will be attending 9th grade; [memb.] Trinity Aquatic Team; [hon.] 7th Grade Honor Roll, Math 7 Achievement Award, 3rd Grade Science Fair 1st Place; [pers.] I hope for peace throughout the world and for all corruption to cease. I hope that one day mankind will be more loving, kind, and truthful towards one another and not so judgmental.; [a.] Maitland, FL

CROUCH, CELINDA M.
[b.] April 10, 1964, Gilmer, TX; [p.] Charles and Jean Upchurch; [m.] Arthur Crouch, November 1, 1986; [ch.] Dogs: Lucky and Tuffy; [ed.] Brinkley High - Brinkley Ark., Cedar Valley College - Lancaster, TX; [occ.] Veterinary Technician; [memb.] North American Veterinary Technicians Assoc.; [hon.] Certificate for Completing Annual Continuing Education program. (CVT); [pers.] I have written several poems for friends and family. Most, are all my personal feelings. I write how I feel.; [a.] Harleton, TX

CUBIT, GREGORY
[b.] May 17, 1963, Jersey City, NJ; [p.] Mr. N. R. Cubit, Mrs. Elizabeth Cubit; [ed.] Southwest High School Mercer University - B.A. Degree; [occ.] Art Teacher; [memb.] Alpha Phi Alpha Fraternity, Inc. B.M.I., Institute of Children's Literature; [hon.] *Who's Who Among America's Teachers*; [oth. writ.] Five years writing as lead writer - local entertainment paper, songwriter for one concept records; [pers.] I write with a deliberate power and sincerity that touches the soul of the reader. My influence...Life itself.; [a.] Macon, GA

CUCCIA, CATHERINE
[b.] May 11, 1980, Port Jefferson, NY; [p.] Salvatore Cuccia, Elvira Cuccia; [ed.] Ward Melville High School, currently in grade 11.; [hon.] Was awarded the First Annual Marvin Palmore Poetry Award, won 1st place in Hadassah Tolerance Poetry Contest, placed twice in Living Authors Literary Contest; [oth. writ.] Several poems published in newspapers, poetry anthologies, and literary magazines.; [pers.] Words have meaning and beauty unique to every individual. I write with universal themes of hope and unity, for I believe that there is always a light in the darkness.; [a.] South Setauket, NY

CULBERT, MARGARET M.
[pen.] Margo C.; [b.] August 11, 1946, New Orleans, LA; [p.] Mrs. Gladys Mack; [ch.] Kevin Culbert; [ed.] John Mc Donough #35 Senior High, Southern University, B.R.; [occ.] Secretary, L.A. Superior Court; [oth. writ.] I have many poems, although I have never attempted to publish them.; [pers.] My poems usually come to me as 'visions' - visions that are pictures in my mind, then put to words on paper. They're written to enlighten the spirit as well as cause one to be observant, therefore to 'think'.; [a.] Ontario, CA

CULLUM, JOEL A.
[b.] April 27, 1969, Memphis, TN; [p.] Russell and Jeanette Cullum; [ed.] Bartlett High, State Technical Institute at Memphis, Crichton College; [occ.] Manufacturing Engineer, Witt; [oth. writ.] All poetry is unpublished and the entire collection I have called *Something To Think About*; [pers.] I believe there is but one God who created all and a piece of Him is in everything we see, feel, and taste. Omni presence is not impossible.; [a.] Memphis, TN

CUMMINGS, ANGELA
[b.] June 17, 1967, Pontiac, MI; [p.] Daniel and Mary Pruente; [m.] David Cummings, December 3, 1988; [ch.] Brittany Arryn, Danielle Alyssa and Austin Charles; [ed.] Rochester Adams High, Macomb Community College; [occ.] Wife and Mother; [oth. writ.] One other poem published in *Forever And A Day*; [pers.] I strive to reflect the value of children. I believe no greater treasures exist. I am greatly influenced by my children. It's an honor to be their mother.; [a.] Rochester, MI

CZECH, D. JAMES
[b.] January 20, 1933, East Liverpool, OH; [p.] Elizabeth and Waldemere Czech; [m.] Nancy Butcher Czech, November 1, 1956; [ch.] D. James II and Jacquelyn; [ed.] East Liverpool High School, Kent State Univ; [occ.] Retired, Baker Engineers; [memb.] Masonic Lodge #662, 32 degree/New Castle Consistory, Syria Shrine Temple, Alaska Pipeline Builders Assoc., Underground Tech. Research Consul; [hon.] First Recipient, Baker Eng. "Total Quality Management Award"; [oth. writ.] "Man On The Moon" July 1969, published in *Baker Eng. Mag.* and several other unpublished works.; [pers.] All that I have accomplished in life, I owe to my loving wife and family - thank you.; [a.] East Liverpool, OH

D'ULISSE, JACI
[b.] February 16, 1984, Hamilton, NJ; [p.] Joseph D'Ulisse, Lynn D'Ulisse; [ed.] Life Center Academy - 1996/97 will enter 7th grade; [memb.] JH Cheerleader, Capital Assembly of God "Y's"; [hon.] Academic excellence with a grade average of 95. Several dance competition awards.; [oth. writ.] Started writing first `book' at age 7; [pers.] I enjoy writing short stories and poetry. It is now a hobby but I look forward to being a writer/journalist when I grow up.; [a.] Hamilton, NJ

DADOLY, EVANGELOS ANGELO
[pen.] Vangeli; [b.] May 7, 1925, Lowell, MA; [p.] Costas and Efthemia Dadoly; [m.] Marjorie A. Dadoly, June 29, 1952; [ch.] Karen, Janet and John; [ed.] Boston University, B.S., 1961, Boston State College, Masters in Education; [occ.] Retired University of Lowell, MA, Math professor; [memb.] National Education Association; [hon.] American Legion, School Award at Dracut High School, Recipient of Trustee Scholarships Boston University; [oth. writ.] "My Mountain Spirit", "Ode To The Retirement...Of My Wife Marjorie", "A Light that Burns"; [a.] Dracut, MA

DAFORNO, MICHAEL
[b.] September 28, 1975, Boston, MA; [ed.] Cardinal Spellman High School; [occ.] Self Employed Vending and Arcade Games; [oth. writ.] Several unpublished poems "Never Feel Alone" June 12, 1996, "Together" June 12, 1996, "Girl-Friend" June 12, 1996, "Baseball" June 13, 1996, "Blinded By The Light of Fate" June 14, 1996, "Puzzle Poem" June 13, 1996, "The Day Will Come..." May 27, 1996, "I See More..." May 23, 1996, "I Could Imagine...", "I See Her All The Time...", "Why Do I Feel..." October 2, 1995, "How Can You Be So Kind..." October 3, 1995, "Sheila", "Can It Be..." February 16, 1996, "Did I Ever Say `Thank You'...", "I Can't Believe...", "Shattered Dreams" May 27, 1996, "The Final Tear", "Mystery In The Night" May 1996, "The Book In Your Head" April 1996, "Mystery In The Night Part II" May 22, 1996, "I Will Never Be Dead" May 27, 1996, "Death Of An Innocent" (Rewritten in different form and text April 10, 1996. Original available, however the original author unknown), "Lady Killer" May 26, 1996, "Dream" April 13, 1996, "Helper Forever" April 3, 1996, "Why Do You Go?", "I Could Describe..." April 1996, "True Friend", "Jury" October 3, 1995, "Slip Into The Nighttime" October 3, 1995, "The Lifeguard", "So You Say...", "She Was My Girlfriend" March 19, 1996, "The Angel I Knew" May 22, 1996, "Crash" March 19, 1996, "When She Was Pulled From The Sky", "Heartbroken" June 25, 1996; [pers.] The poem in this book was written for my girlfriend at the time. Thank you Nora for the inspiration. Special thanks also to everyone that has been there for me when I need help.; [a.] Randolph, MA

DAIGNEAULT, LENNY
[b.] January 7, 1958, Worcester, MA; [p.] John Daigneault, Betty Daigneault; [ed.] Continuing on a Daily Basis; [occ.] Jack of All Trades, Master Of None; [oth. writ.] Some Done, Others To Follow.; [pers.] Thanks to family, friends and especially Sue, Katie, and Mo for a chance to wake up every day happy and loved.; [a.] Melrose, MA

DAILEY, CINDA
[b.] May 10, 1984, Tulsa; [p.] Randall and Sandra Dailey; [ed.] Now attending 7th grade at Homing Middle School in Hominy Oklahoma; [memb.] Native American Ball Team and Basketball Team, (AISA) American Indian Student Assoc. Cheerleading; [hon.] Honor Society, Reading, Spelling, Social Studies and English Awards. Indian student of the month. President's Award Music Award. Always been on honor roll. Most improved cheering squad; [pers.] I am very interested in my Native American heritage and will hopefully continue writing so others can be able to see the beauty I see in my heritage; [a.] Hominy, OK

DAILEY, JENNIFER JEAN
[b.] May 15, 1982, California; [p.] Paula Dailey, John Dailey; [ed.] St. Pius V School; [occ.] Student; [hon.] Principle Honors, USAA National English Award, School Writing Award; [a.] Buena Park, CA

DALTON, PHYLLIS I.
[b.] September 25, 1909, Marienthal, KS; [p.] Benjamin and Pearl Bull; [m.] Jack M. Dalton, February 13, 1950; [ed.] Marysville, Kansas High, University of Nebraska BSC, MA, University of Denver, MS in Librarianship; [occ.] Library Consultant, Freelance; [memb.] National League of American Pen Women, American Association of University Women, American Library Association.; [oth. writ.] Book: *Library Service to the Deaf and Hearing Impaired* Oryx Press. Numerous writings in Books and Journals on the subject of Libraries and the subject of Disabilities; [pers.] I try to live each day to its fullest. I try to be helpful to people with my writing.; [a.] Scottsdale, AZ

DALY, ANN
[b.] September 11, 1938, Montague City, MA; [p.] Chester J. (Alyce Giknis) Sokolosky; [m.] Robert G. Daly, August 4, 1962; [ch.] Colleen, Susan, Katy; [ed.] Elms College, B.A. French, Summer and graduate studies Laval U. (Quebec City, Canada) Middlebury (A.) College; [occ.] Volunteer for charitable organizations; [pers.] Kindness to others should be expressed in personal interaction and through the beautiful positive power of written expression.; [a.] Old Lyme, CT

DAMRON, TAMMY
[pen.] Tammy Lynn; [b.] June 28, 1967, Las Vegas, NV; [p.] Diana Zakrysek and Art Pacheco; [m.] Jason Kosera, July 3, 1990; [ch.] Adrian and Amber Damron; [ed.] Graduated in 1985 went to college for one year; [occ.] Writer and Homemaker; [hon.] Received three certificates in English and reading; [oth. writ.] I am in the process of writing a book that contains ten short stories.; [pers.] With my writing I want my readers to experience the Nirvana of life not to hide behind a close door but to open a door. You may only live once but you can live it openly?

DANDO, STACEY L.
[b.] May 6, 1959, New Castle, PA; [p.] Rodger Swogger and Madeline (Perrett) Kreslick; [m.] September 19, 1975 to December 1, 1995; [ch.] Randy Jason (RJ) Bradley, Phillip and Katie; [ed.] Union Area 10th Vo-Tech G.E.D. diploma; [occ.] Baker for Marriott at Westminister College New Wilmington, PA; [memb.] First Baptist Church New Castle, PA; [pers.] I kept journals of my divorce until one day they were gone. It look 1 1/2 yrs. after that to start writing again, choosing poems instead of journaling. G.E.D. testing I scored low on reading and writing skills; [a.] Edinburg, PA

DANEL, P. EDWARD
[b.] August 19, 1957, Windber, PA; [p.] Paul and Helen Danel; [m.] Kathy (Bencie) Danel, June 21, 1980; [ch.] Ryan 13, Breanne 11; [ed.] BA - Secondary Education (Univ. of Pittsburgh at Johnstown) currently working toward MA in Teaching English (Indiana Univ. of PA); [occ.] Teacher - Secondary English, Windber High School; [oth. writ.] Poem previously published by the National Library of Poetry; [a.] Windber, PA

DAVIS, AARON KYLE
[pen.] Short Stuff; [b.] August 19, 1983, Iola, KS; [p.] Keith and Gaye Davis; [ed.] Remington Middle School; [occ.] Student; [memb.] Saint Vincent De Paul Catholic Church. Entertainment this month Comic Club; [hon.] 4.0 student. All "A" Honor Roll in 6th and 7th grades. 5th place in the American Legion Essay Contest, in 7th Grade. Lettered and medaled in track in 7th grade. Participate in the Gifted program at Remington.; [oth. writ.] Have written several other poems and essays.; [pers.] You can do whatever you want to as long as you believe in yourself and do your best.; [a.] Benton, KS

DAVIS, ALISON
[b.] March 29, 1980, Tampa, FL; [p.] Larry Davis, Shirley Davis; [ed.] St. Petersburg High School; [occ.] Junior in I.B. At S.P.H.S.; [memb.] Ambassadors of S.P.H.S., Church Folk Group; [hon.] Young Authors, 2nd place Catholic Daughters of American Educational Contest.; [oth. writ.] My young author's poetry book. Short story that got 2nd place C.D.A.E.C.; [pers.] May all your dreams come true 'cause to dream is to be or not be.; [a.] Saint Petersburg, FL

DAVIS, ANITA M.
[b.] January 11, 1939, Boise, ID; [p.] Earl and Helen Worthington; [m.] Jack L. Davis, August 26, 1955; [ch.] Atina M. Davis (Wiese) - Travis J. Davis; [ed.] Background: Personal Development Training; [occ.] Training Consultant V.P. People Make America, Inc; [oth. writ.] None published; [pers.] Corporate America Begins at Home. Our nation's future depends upon our leadership and guidance of our youth today. It must begin at home.; [a.] Tualatin, OR

DAVIS, CRAIG A.
[pen.] Cad-Berry; [b.] April 19, 1966, Brooklyn, NY; [p.] Louise B. Davis; [m.] Tiffany (Up and coming); [ch.] Craig Jr. - 10, Tatiana - 7, Jahlique - 6 months; [ed.]

Well, I dropped out of high school in the 12th grade to support my family and been doing it ever since.; [occ.] Auto mechanic, but want to direct a couple of movies I wrote.; [oth. writ.] (Screenplays) "What The F— Am I Supposed To Do," "Crime Wave," "Under 10 over 100."; [pers.] I guess it's the same thing I tell my kids every time they say life is too hard for them, I believe in my self, my self I believe in.; [a.] Brooklyn, NY

DAVIS, DANA LENA
[b.] January 4, 1985, Hopkinsville; [p.] Joyce and Dan Davis; [ed.] Graduated from 5th grade; [occ.] Student; [memb.] Duke University Talent Identification Program (The Motivation for Academic Performance Program); [hon.] President's Education Award for Outstanding Academic Achievement, Citizenship Award, Certificate of Scholarship for making Principal's List all year, Computer Achievement Certificate for highest reading average, Reading Achievement Certificate third place in Regional Governors Cup Competition; [a.] Gracey, KY

DAVIS, JOHN CHRISTOPHER
[pen.] John Davis, John Christopher; [b.] July 20, 1954, Mobile; [ed.] McGill Institute Spring Hill College; [occ.] Entrepreneur; [memb.] International Traders Association.; [hon.] B.A. English; [oth. writ.] "Monochodum Mundi" a docu-dramatic treatment about the possible effects of nuclear testing in outer space.; [pers.] "Treat people as if they were what they ought to be and you help them become what they are capable of becoming." Goethe, 18th Century, poet and dramatist. The Self Fulfilling Prophecy, or the Pygmalion Effect, never ceases to amaze me.; [a.] Mobile, AL

DAVIS, KIM L.
[b.] March 23, 1958, Fort Worth, TX; [oth. writ.] Self published book titled, *Heart and Soul*; [pers.] I always try to remember a lesson my father taught me: The most precious gift we can give ourselves is the gift of humor. "Humor can take you through the hardest times. It will always bring you out of the darkness and into the light."; [a.] Longview, TX

DAVIS, M. CAROLYN
[pen.] M. C. Davis; [b.] October 20, 1937, Elkhart, IN; [p.] Allen Hobart Meador, Wilma Lotus Clark; [m.] Paul E. Davis, May 30, 1958; [ch.] Edward Lee Davis; [ed.] Dexter City High, WVU - Parkersburg, Wash. Tech.; [occ.] Retired; [memb.] Fairview United Methodist Women; [hon.] None published; [pers.] Just wanted to have fun with this poem and others!; [a.] Washington, WV

DAVIS, MARIO C.
[b.] September 8, 1979, Beaverton, OR; [p.] John and Maria Davis; [ed.] Evanston Township High School; [occ.] High School Student; [memb.] Lacrosse Club and Golf Team, Jazz Band and Orchestra, World of Difference and School Improvement Team, School Newspaper, Radio D.J.; [hon.] Justin Wyun Memorial Fund Award Recipient, 1st place in Jazz Improvisation, Illinois Music Educators Assoc. 1995, Hon. Mention IATE Poetry Contest; [oth. writ.] Several unpublished poems; [pers.] All praise be to the Creator, through whom and with whom all things are possible! Glory to Kahil Gibran and Countee Cullen for their profound influence. May life be a river flowing, with banks of mud and gold; [a.] Evanston, IL

DAVIS, MARTINA L.
[b.] July 11, 1971, Wilmington, DE; [p.] James R. Davis and Bernice L. Davis; [ch.] Arian D. Davis; [ed.] Howard Career Center, Long Island University; [occ.] Information Specialist Peterson Consulting L.L.P. - New York, NY; [hon.] Dean's List - Long Island University; [pers.] "Mom" was written in loving memory of my mother, Bernice L. Davis, who died on April 7, 1991. Her death was sudden and disheartening, but her birth has been uplifting and inspiring. For that "Mom" I say, "Thank you."; [a.] Brooklyn, NY

DAVIS, ROBERT OTTO
[pen.] Robert Otto Davis; [b.] June 20, 1975, Columbia, SC; [p.] Otto and Ann Davis Jr.; [ed.] Richard Winn Academy, Winthrop University, transferred to Coastal Carolina University; [occ.] Roofer/Student; [memb.] Sigma Phi Epsilon; [pers.] All praise and credit goes to God. Without Him nothing's possible. Also, my heart goes out to Mrs. Arnette for believing in me when I didn't believe in myself. This is an example of you not giving up on me.; [a.] Blythewood, SC

DAVIS, ROLAND B.
[b.] August 24, 1934, Cleveland, OH; [p.] Roland (Hallam) Davis and Elizabeth Zelenak; [m.] Marie Jane Szalay, September 15, 1956; [ch.] Bernadette Marie Furlong, Deborah Anne Blatnik; [ed.] East Technical High, Cleveland, Ohio Cuyahoga Community College, Parma, Ohio University of Notre Dame, Notre Dame, IN; [occ.] Engineer; [hon.] Eagle Scout, BSA Scouters Award, BSA Scarabaean Honor Society, East Tech National Honor Society, East Tech. Steuben Society of America Award, for Excellence in German. Good Conduct, U.S. Army; [oth. writ.] *Simply Blue, The Garden Of Life, The Two Sides Of Life, Best Poems of the '90s, My World, Lyrical Heritage, The Looking Glass, Frost at Midnight*, Recorded on Cassette "Sound of Poetry"; [pers.] I am a romantic that finds pleasure with people and machines, and I write what comes from within, the solitude of a moment can turn into an eternity of life, enjoy the moment.; [a.] Stow, OH

DAVIS, WILL
[b.] October 30, 1959, Scranton, PA; [p.] Don Davis, Marion Davis; [ed.] West Scranton High; [occ.] Asst. Manager Automotive Parts Department; [memb.] Heritage Baptist Church; [hon.] Although when I wrote "My Last Breath," I didn't intend it to be read at funerals, it has been read at many in my area and I hope my writing gave a little comfort in a great time of need; [oth. writ.] Several other poems, unpublished. I am a new author, this is the first poem I have ever submitted.; [pers.] I hope all of my writings will give some a source of comfort, but what I strive to do is give honor and glory to my Lord and saviour Jesus Christ.; [a.] Scranton, PA

DAVISSON, KAREN A.
[b.] May 28, 1958, Coronado, CA; [p.] Gerald Adams, Carole Adams; [m.] Michael A. Davisson, June 18, 1976; [ch.] Ryan A. Davisson; [ed.] Granby High, Norfolk, VA New Mexico State University, Las Cruces, NM; [occ.] Secretary; [memb.] Sandia Baptist Church, Albuquerque, NM; [hon.] National Honor Society - 4 Years Crimson Scholar - NMSU; [oth. writ.] "Quiet the Pain"; [pers.] I was once told by a teacher that the best writings come from life experience, and have definitely found that to be the case. My poetry has been the means by which I deal with the emotions of the life God has allowed me to experience.; [a.] Edgewood, NM

DAY, SHARON H.
[pen.] Tony Day; [b.] November 24, 1947, Bay Minette, AL; [p.] Harlon and Reatha Quinley; [m.] Divorced; [ch.] Abbey and Colter; [ed.] Graduated from Baldwin County High 1966; [memb.] Order of Eastern Star; [hon.] Past Matron of Ella D. Chambers Chapter #26, past grand representative of New Brunswick in AL; [pers.] Most of my poems come from personal experience and all come from the heart; [a.] Bay Minette, AL

DAY, TERRI
[b.] April 16, 1965, Evansville, IN; [p.] Ray and Sandra Townsend; [m.] Edward H. Day III, February 16, 1985; [ch.] John Woodson Day; [ed.] In my junior year of college working toward a B.S. Degree in Criminal Law and then on to law school in Delaware, Webster Co. High 1983; [occ.] Mother, full time college student.; [hon.] Wayland Baptist Universities President's List; [oth. writ.] Several poems published in church bulletins.; [pers.] I am moved to write by the small pleasures in life such as, "Viewing the Stars". Everyday life is my inspiration.; [a.] Eielson Air Force Base, AL

DE BRITO, EDWARD
[b.] May 10, 1910, Iquitos, Peru; [p.] Guillerme Antonio and Maria Eloysa; [m.] Vivian Catherine Von Bartheld, 1942; [ch.] Edward W., Catherine Vivian, Richard Bartheld, Elaine Castillo; [ed.] Grade School in Peru, High School in Brazil, Seminary in Brazil Various Courses in Sociology Chapman University in the USA; [occ.] Retired from State of California as Minority Specialist; [memb.] American Legion; [hon.] None except the usual medals for four campaigns in the European Theater of operations 1942 to 1945; [oth. writ.] A novel not yet completed; [pers.] Veteran World War II 3 years United States Army Air Force.; [a.] Santa Paula, CA

DEAN, KATHY
[pen.] Kathy Dean; [b.] April 21, 1955, Inglewood, CA; [p.] Marcia Colbert, Dennis Hanley; [m.] Jack L. French, September 4, 1983; [ch.] Lisa M. Dean, Wayne A. Dean, Derek S. Dean; [ed.] High School; [occ.] Apt. Manager; [hon.] Honorable mention for "Tears of a Fool"; [oth. writ.] "Tears Of A Fool," "A Choice," "Money Wouldn't Change Me?," "Lend A Helping Hand"; [pers.] For my beautiful granddaughter, Kayla Marie Wolff.; [a.] Bakersfield, CA

DEBLASIO, STACY
[b.] February 8, 1976, Glen Cove, NY; [p.] Diane and Alberico DeBlasio; [ed.] North Shore High School, State University of New York at Fredonia; [occ.] College Student Genetics Major; [hon.] Dean's List, American Legion Scholarship Award, AP Scholar with Distinction, National Honors Society; [oth. writ.] This is my first publication.; [pers.] Every word that drips from my pen, takes a piece of my soul within it.; [a.] Glen Cove, NY

DECKER, MICHELLE
[b.] November 30, 1985, West Palm Beach, FL; [p.] Lisa and Ronald Decker; [ed.] Lighthouse Elem. School, 5th grade, Mr. Peru; [occ.] Student; [memb.] Girl Scouts, Reporter for kids newspaper- *Kidzette*; [hon.] Honors student, received perfect score on Florida writers test; [oth. writ.] Published in *Highlights* magazine and *Kidzette*; [a.] Palm Beach Gardens, FL

DECOLATI, JOHN J.
[pen.] "Dino" "Deco"; [b.] April 17, 1962, Glassport, PA; [p.] John & Thelma Decolati; [f.] Carol N. Giannandrea, October 1998; [ed.] B.S. Finance & Ac-

counting Bethany College, Bethany, WV; [occ.] Sr. Asst. Mgr./Sr. Staff Accountant - Tube City, Inc. (Glassport, PA); [memb.] Amateur Softball Association (A.S.A.) Softball Umpire (21 years) Fairfax Softball Umpires Association (Fairfax, VA) (10 years); [hon.] Bethany College Alumni Award for outstanding senior. Numerous "Pat on the Baul" awards/ 2-time employee of the month @ Honeywell Federal Systems, Inc. (McLean, VA.); [oth. writ.] Several poems written for weddings and given as "Toasts" by the "Best Man". Poetry writings span 3 decades in counting (70's, 80's, 90's), Most recent: "Friendship", "I am Santa"; [pers.] My motto has always been and will continue to be; "If you see someone without a smile.....Give them one of yours!!"; [a.] Glassport, PA

DEEDS, JASON W.
[pen.] The Journeyman; [b.] December 6, 1978, Alameda, CA; [p.] Charles and Mary Deeds; [ed.] Graduate Patrick Henry High Class of 1997; [occ.] Owner of local recording studio and Independent record label, Student; [oth. writ.] Various other poems, none published as of this date; [pers.] Be happy as long as you live, and live as long as you are happy.; [a.] San Diego, CA

DEERY, MARY BETH
[pen.] Beth; [b.] March 18, 1961; [p.] Agnes and Eugene Deery; [ed.] Narragansett High School and CCRI, CHA; [pers.] I feel my gift of poetry is inspired by the Holy Spirit.; [a.] Narragansett, RI

DEHL, LINDSEY DARLINE
[b.] September 3, 1983, Soda Springs, ID; [p.] Barbara Hemman Dehl, Curtis R. Dehl; [ed.] Currently in 8th grade West Junior High School, Nampa, Idaho, K-6 Soda Springs School District, Soda Springs, Idaho; [occ.] Student; [memb.] U.S.S. Swim Team, National Honor Society, Head First, 4-H; [hon.] 4.0 Presidential Award, Academic Excellence Award, Athletic Excellence Award, 1st - 3rd place at State and Multi-State Regional Swim Meets; [oth. writ.] Poem "If I Could Be A Flower" published in the anthology of Young American Poets.; [pers.] I truly believe in life and living it to the fullest and I believe that if you can hear and understand nature you'll know poetry!.; [a.] Nampa, ID

DEHNE, NANCY RAE
[pen.] Nancy Rae; [b.] August 27, 1943, Norfolk, VA; [p.] Marcella Tobin and Linsey Alton; [m.] Richard L. Dehne, March 21, 1980; [ch.] Four own, four step; [ed.] High School Grad - Wash Park Lakeside School Natural Ther. Massage Ther.; [occ.] Massage Ther.; [memb.] Amta; [oth. writ.] Some - not published; [pers.] I have feelings and thoughts from within and I write them on paper.; [a.] Racine, WI

DEMPSEY, MARK STEPHEN
[b.] September 14, 1958, Washington, DC; [p.] Patrick Dempsey, Natalie Mancini; [ed.] Frostburg State College; [occ.] Amtrak (Auto Train); [oth. writ.] My own personal writings on record.; [pers.] I can honestly say that I have not been influenced by any one poet or author. I have just been blessed with the most wonderful family a man could want, and friends I have learned to love. I do not crave riches or celebrity status. I just want to express my feelings in the best way I know how.; [a.] Frederick, MD

DENG, HUANWEN
[pen.] John Deng; [b.] July 13, 1975, China; [p.] Zhao Ji Deng, Hui Chang Deng; [ed.] Sterling Hts. High School, Macomb Community College; [occ.] Second year of college; [pers.] In the past 4 years, I crossed the Pacific Ocean and traveled half to the country. Finally I realized that the best place for me is my home.; [a.] Sterling Heights, MI

DEPALMA, NICHOLAS C.
[b.] May 1, 1932, Newark, NJ; [p.] Domenic DePalma and Joseph DePalma; [m.] Stella DePalma, May 15, 1955; [ch.] Judith, Diane, Nicholas Jr., Joseph; [ed.] Boys Vocational, Newark, NJ; [occ.] Retired; [memb.] Knights of Columbus (Avenel, NJ), VFW, Avenel, NJ; [hon.] 35 years - Safe Driver Award for Tose Fowler Trucking.; [oth. writ.] Several poems, mostly for family birthdays, anniversaries, also friends of family.; [pers.] This poem I wrote ("Victims of Cancer") is written for all people in dire need of prayer for the suffering of Cancer.; [a.] Avenel, NJ

DERETCHIN, LEONA M.
[b.] August 23, 1956, Altoona, PA; [p.] Robert Theodore Thompson and Leona Hardt; [m.] Jeffrey P. Deretchin, October 11, 1994; [ch.] Shawn Michael Thompson, Amanda Lynn McClelland; [ed.] Graduate of Logansport High School - Logansport, IN '74, currently a student at Greenville Technical College, Greenville, SC; [occ.] Student and Housewife; [hon.] The National Dean's List 1995-96, Phi Theta Kappa; [oth. writ.] I am currently in the process of preparing a collection of poetry for copyright in hopes of future publication.; [pers.] Jehova's will, conveyed through His word, the Bible, is the key to finding harmony among ourselves and with the universe.; [a.] Taylors, SC

DETTLING, MICHELLE R.
[b.] August 3, 1976, Pittsburgh, PA; [p.] Mr. and Mrs. Russell Dettling Jr.; [ed.] Montour High, Robert Morris College; [occ.] Student; [pers.] Thank you to my parents Russ and Roseann, for encouraging me. To Sharon, Rusty, and Jeff - I love you. My grandparents D and B you are very special to me. I love you too.; [a.] Pittsburgh, PA

DEVINE, FRANCES
[b.] September 30, 1985; [p.] Gerard and Joyce; [ed.] Bishop Parker (Miltow Keywes England 1989-1994), St. Lawrence School, Towcester Northampton, England 1994-1995, St. Lawrence, Pingree (Weymouth, Mass. 1995-96); [hon.] "A" student; [pers.] I write poems because I love the English language. Inspired by my teacher Mr. Nightengale, I had in 4th grade.; [a.] Dorchester, Boston

DEVORE, JEFFREY
[b.] May 8, 1951, Ironton, MO; [p.] Wolden and Frances DeVore; [ch.] Nicholas, Brad, Kate; [ed.] Doctor of Chiropractic, Logan College of Chiropractic, Masters of Divinity, Fuller Theological Seminary; [occ.] Clinical Associate Professor, Ordained Minister; [memb.] American Chiropractic Association, Eastern Assoc., So. Cal. Conference, United Church of Christ; [oth. writ.] Professional Chiropractic Articles, monthly church newsletter cover articles.; [pers.] I seek the good in others as evidence of God's creative power.; [a.] Whittier, CA

DIAL, TABITHA
[b.] February 22, 1980, Grand Jct., CO; [p.] Floyd and Neila Dial; [ed.] Honors Lit./Comp., Adv. Lit. Themes/Comp., Journalism I and II, Marching/Symphonic Band, Jr. at GJHS, working for academic excellence, planning for college; [hon.] First place in the Catholic Daughters of America Essay Contest, Four Superior Solo and Ensemble Music Awards; [pers.] My greatest influences are the times I have had in my family/school life, the study of music, and the works of Emily Dickinson. I hope to continue writing poetry and prose, as I can not escape doing so.; [a.] Grand Junction, CO

DICKENSHEETS, JAMES
[b.] December 1, 1948; [p.] John, Ethel; [m.] Linda Dickensheets, March 10, 1972; [ch.] Sara Lynn, Brian James; [ed.] Lee High, Grace Bible College, Davenport College; [occ.] High School Custodian; [memb.] Berean Bible Church, Christian Education Committee; [pers.] Jesus Christ is the Author of my faith and my talent. His presence in my life influences all writings.; [a.] Wyoming, MI

DICKERSON, LAGRANDA
[pen.] Vicki; [b.] July 6, 1971, Gainesville, FL; [p.] Sandra B. Davis; [ed.] Miami Edison Senior High School; [occ.] Parking Attendant; [memb.] The Church of God Tabernacle (True Holiness); [hon.] Certificates for - Child Care of Miami Dade Community College. Certificate from my job.; [oth. writ.] I have a lot of other poems that I have written up. I have presented them to an Elementary School that I used to work at. Some were also typed on quite of few of our church programs. I have made up one for that school name.; [pers.] Poetry has always been one of my goals in life. I enjoy writing poems and anything else. Poetry is one of the talents that God has given me.; [a.] Miami, FL

DIENER, CAROL L.
[b.] May 30, 1941, Detroit, MI; [p.] William and Cleo Cain; [m.] Dennis W. Diener Sr., October 12, 1962; [ch.] Dennis W. Diener Jr. and Lori Lynn Diener Rathje; [ed.] Bad Axe High School currently enrolled American College, Bryn Mawr., PA, for CHFC/CLU degrees. Dearborn Financial Institute, Inc.; [occ.] Insurance Agent and Investments Registered Representative also own and operate bookkeeping and word processing firm.; [memb.] Cross Lutheran Church Pigeon, MI, Pigeon Economic Development Corp., Pigeon Chamber of Commerce, GFWC Pigeon Worth While Club, NALU, Serve as Sunday School Teacher at Cross Lutheran, past 4-H Leader for 16 years - served 13 years on board of Directors Scheurer Hospital, Pigeon, MI; [hon.] Paul Harris Fellow Award from Pigeon Rotary Club; [oth. writ.] Only short stories and poems for grandchildren, children and family members - nothing sent for publication.; [a.] Pigeon, MI

DILLMAN, JENNIFER
[b.] June 22, 1976, Waterloo, IA; [p.] Jeff and Sue Dillman; [ed.] Currently enrolled at the University of Iowa studying Ancient Civilization; [hon.] *Who's Who Among America's High School Students*, Dean's List; [oth. writ.] "The Boy Who Ate the Sun", "No Trees", "Because the World's in Utter Chaos", "Beneath Her Window"; [a.] Newton, IA

DILLON, MILDRED M.
[b.] February 26, 1926, Franklin County, AL; [p.] Robert Michell (Deceased), Virginia Bell Draper; [m.] William Herbert Dillon, October 21, 1945; [ch.] David Dillon, Ann McGhee; [ed.] High School, Nurses Aide, Hospital Housekeeper; [occ.] Retired; [hon.] First poem I ever submitted my husband saw your ad in newspaper and told me I should send one of my poems.; [oth. writ.] Started writing poems four years ago. Most are long ones about people that are dear to me.; [pers.] I enjoy

writing poems for birthdays instead of buying ones that someone else wrote.; [a.] Rocky Mount, VA

DISABATINO, LUCIA
[pen.] Lucia; [b.] January 24, 1966, Brooklyn, NY; [p.] Charles and Josephine DeMarco; [m.] Frank A. Disabatino, July 1994; [ch.] Steven Bruce Reed II; [ed.] Christiana High, Delaware Technical Community College; [occ.] Property Manager; [oth. writ.] "They Care," "Inside Me," "Little One"; [pers.] God Bless All who suffer from any disease or illness. Please try to fight, and I pray for all who are ill. Keep your heads up.; [a.] Wilmington, DE

DIXON, BARBARA ANN
[b.] August 1, 1942, Pennsgrove, NJ; [p.] Athur and Clara Jones (Deceased); [m.] Ethean Dixon, June 3, 1961; [ch.] Kim, Leslie, David, Ethan; [ed.] A High School drop out who completed and obtained a GED cert. in 1976. Became a Licensed Practical Nurse, 1978, at Salem Community College Carneys Point, N.J. Became a Registered Nurse, and degree 1982 Delaware Tech. Comm. College Stanton, DE.; [occ.] RN, Homemaker; [hon.] On the dean's list all years at Salem Comm. and Del. Tech., Employee of the Year Mem. Hosp. Salem County 1987; [oth. writ.] "Daybreak," "Christ to Me," "I Watch"; [pers.] My greatest desire is to walk worthy of the vocation wherein I am called, and to share some of the grace, beauty, and hope that is in Christ Jesus my Lord.; [a.] Carney's Point, NJ

DOCKTER, ARLEEN
[b.] March 25, 1914, Ogden, UT; [p.] Sarah Elizabeth, Goddard Sessions; [m.] Parley P. Sessions, November 5, 1938; [ch.] Jacqueline, Sharon and Gary; [ed.] High School Grad.; [occ.] Housewife; [memb.] Church of Jesus Christ of Latter Day Saints, Relief Society, Choir, Chorister for our ward; [hon.] Honor Student Award Pin at Graduation, Editor of Quarterly Classicum (Year Book) Lead in Operetta in Jr. Year at High School, have written music and poetry for many special occasions by request.; [oth. writ.] Close to 100 songs - words and music, have written poetry since I was a very young child. I am still at the age of 82, writing poetry for my grandchildren and great grandchildren.; [pers.] "It is not important how long you live, but how you live." My husband and I walk four miles every day to improve the quality of life. We celebrated our 50th Wedding Anniversary in 1988. Still in love!; [a.] Ogden, UT

DODSON, JOSEPH K.
[b.] March 13, 1977, Nevada, IA; [p.] Joe and Vicki Dodson; [ed.] Nevada High School, Marshaltown Comm. College; [occ.] Cook at Indian Creek County Club; [memb.] Elder at Central Presbyterian Church, Dean's List; [oth. writ.] Has written several "A" work stories and papers since elementary, currently working on a Science fiction/horror novel.; [pers.] "Since the 7th grade, I have been greatly influenced by Stephen King, Donald P. Bellisario, and my Grandfather. I try to project the pain along with happiness I have experienced in my writing."; [a.] Nevada, IA

DOMINICK, BEYNAMAAN
[pen.] Bey; [b.] June 8, 1971, New York, NY; [p.] Barbara and Bertrum Dominick; [m.] Michelle Dominick, Infinity; [ch.] Gabrielle Amber Dominick; [ed.] Self-educated; [occ.] Poet/Essayist; [hon.] First and second place Awards for Poems and Essays; [pers.] I seek to teach the abundant truth which is within the light of wisdom and knowledge of self.; [a.] Bronx, NY

DOROTHEO, MRS. PAZ R.
[b.] January 24, 1929, Philippines; [p.] Gertrudis Visarra and Pacifico Ruiz; [m.] Richard S. Dorotheo Jr., April 19, 1952; [ch.] Six (3 of whom are Physicians, 1 in Management, 2 in Computer Science); [ed.] Bachelor of Sc. in Education, Summa Cum Laude, Master of Arts in English, Magna Cum Laude at Univ. of San Carlos, Cebu City, Philippines; [occ.] Retired after 30 years teaching English in College; [memb.] All canceled upon retirement; [hon.] M. S. Citizenship on February 24, 1994; [oth. writ.] 1. Speech Improvement, 2. College English, 3. Compassion of English and Cebuano Verbs (Master's thesis published by the University of San Carlos); [pers.] Profoundly influenced by my strong family and Christian values in my random reflections - poems looking for a publisher for someone who is long on ideas but short on funds. Can you help?; [a.] Tampa, FL

DOTTAVIO, CHEYENNE
[pen.] Phoenix Starr, Darien Luna; [b.] August 20, 1979; [p.] Patricia and Jack Dottavio; [ed.] High School; [occ.] High School Student (senior year); [memb.] Happy Tails Pet Sanctuary; [hon.] Honor Roll (Jr. year); [oth. writ.] "Mother Earth", "Unstable?!", "Wild Wimmin", "Red Letter" and Freelance Screenplays and community theatre plays.; [pers.] My greatest influences on my writing have been my 9th grade English teacher Ms. Crosby and my 11th grade educator Mrs. Applegate. Thank you for the push.; [a.] Sacramento, CA

DOUGLAS, KENDRICK RAY
[b.] June 5, 1977, Texas City, TX; [p.] Martha and Kenneth Douglas; [ed.] Freshman at College of Mainland, Texas City, Texas Majoring in Microcomputer Applications; [memb.] Mt. Carmel Missionary Baptist Church. Jr. Deacon Former Member of the High School Teen Out Reach Christian Club; [hon.] $400.00 Scholarship from above-named Church, Diploma Dickinson High School; [oth. writ.] "Peace Over There" June 18th 1996, "Together With God" June 20th 1996, "In Prayer" June 8, 1996.; [pers.] I can do all things through Christ, who strengthens me. Phil 4:13.; [a.] Dickinson, TX

DOWD, LAURA
[b.] October 4, 1955, Hastings, NE; [p.] Dr. Eugene and Mary Moschel; [m.] Larry Dowd, April 28, 1990; [ch.] Anna Virginia Dowd; [ed.] Edmonds Senior High Univ. of Washington (2 yrs.); [occ.] Aspiring Children's Book writer, Mom, Housewife; [memb.] Meridian United Church of Christ, Society of Children's Book Writers Illustrators; [hon.] Best Director 1988-89 Season, Best Supporting Actress 1988-89 Season (Grande Olde Players - Omaha, NE), note: Best Director for "Annie Buddy's Christmas Fantasy"/Best Supporting Actress for the role of Ida in "See How They Run"; [oth. writ.] Poem published in *Oregon Coast* magazine, "Annie Buddy's Christmas Fantasy" - a play co-authored and produced in 1988; [pers.] The exploration of relationships, within and without, has been my strongest inspiration. The expression of myself through poetry has been and will continue to be my lifelong avocation.; [a.] Tigard, OR

DOWELL, KOREY CHRISTOPHER EVERETT
[b.] April 17, 1979, New York, NY; [p.] Kevin and Valerie Dowell; [ed.] High School, St. John's Preparatory, Morehouse College (Fall 1996); [occ.] Student; [memb.] World Tae Kwon Do Association, Student Council President ('95-'96), Peer Counselor ('95-'96); [hon.] Thomas J. Manton Congressional Leadership Award, Service Award, New York Urban League Scholarship, Black Cancus Scholarship; [oth. writ.] Poem published in anthology for poems by Young American's 1992; [pers.] "The journey of a thousands miles must begin with a single step." -Tao Te Ching; [a.] East Elmhurst, NY

DOYEN, RENEE
[b.] January 12, 1945, Gary, IN; [p.] Joseph J. And Marylou Doyen; [ed.] Indiana School for the Blind, Atlanta Christian College; [occ.] Darkroom Technician at Elkhart General Hospital; [memb.] Central Christian of Elkhart, IN, American Council of the Blind, YWCA; [oth. writ.] Over 20 unpublished poems; [pers.] Bachelors degree in Christian Education, interests are reading, playing a keyboard and swimming. My poems reflect realism and concern over world events.; [a.] Elkhart, IN

DOYLE, KATHLEEN
[b.] October 11, 1978, New York; [p.] Patricia Doyle and Stephen Doyle; [ed.] Graduate of Hudson High School; [memb.] St. Michael Youth Choir, "Expressions" Singing Ensemble; [hon.] $20,000 Scholarship through the Army; [oth. writ.] One published in a local newspaper, many unpublished writings; [pers.] A thank you to all the special teachers and mentors who have helped me be who I am.; [a.] Hudson, FL

DRAKE, CHRISTINE ELISE
[b.] May 19, 1976, Stanford, CA; [p.] Jay Worsley, Mary Kay Worsley; [m.] Joshua David Drake, May 6, 1995; [ch.] Joshua Alexander; [ed.] Portland Community College, Western Business College; [occ.] Mother; [memb.] CBN, Mom's Club, Tigard First Baptist; [hon.] Western Business College, Graduated with honors; [oth. writ.] Http: //www.europa.coml Elise; [pers.] My poems are always about my own personal experiences. I write in the hope that others will be able to relate to, and be moved by what I have said.; [a.] Tigard, OR

DRESBACH, JESSE AARON
[pen.] Jesse; [b.] September 7, 1982, Mt. View, CA; [p.] Diane and Jim Dresbach; [ed.] Graduated 8th grade - June 1996 from Rogers Middle School, San Jose, Calif. attending Prospect High School, Saratoga, Calif. in Fall 1996; [occ.] Student, to date my career choice - architect; [memb.] Cub Scouts in Elementary School. Honor Band in Middle School - played Clarinet. Also play piano. Clubs in Middle School - Spirit, Yearbook, Uniform, Student Council; [hon.] Honor roll 16 quarters 5th grade to 8th grade, Block R in Middle School for volunteer service outside hours, Band Awards for 5 years in band 4th grade to 8th grade. President's Award for outstanding Academic Achievement; [oth. writ.] Various essays, poems, papers and letters during last 4 years of school. Short stories written on own time, outside of school.; [pers.] "I want to thank my mom for sending the poem in, and all of my family for all of their influences. I would like say to everyone that what has helped me, is to do whatever you like to do, as long as it makes you happy, and that it is right. Listen to that little voice we often ignore."; [a.] Campbell, CA

DREW, DANNY GLENN
[b.] February 12, 1947, Longview, TX; [p.] W. L. and Ida Mae Drew; [m.] Ruthy A. Drew, December 11, 1965; [ch.] Rickey, Randy, Lana, Jennifer; [ed.] Longview High School, Kilgore College, Collin County Community College; [occ.] Management; [memb.] Plano Lodge #768; [pers.] I wrote this poetry in front of my wife in about 5 minutes, for we were in a hurry to get it to a baby shower. I pinned this poem to a basket we were taking.; [a.] Dallas, TX

DREWERY, FAY
[pers.] A poet is a thinker and a dreamer who sees clearly the heartbeat of the people and nations of his or her generation. In a few words they speak sorrow, joy, strife, the running of the lonely and the anger of the many. Dear Poet, never give up writing words that move the soul and strengthen the spirit. Your words may be the only truth history will record.

DRINKARD, DIANNA P.
[pen.] Dianna Might Press; [b.] April 2, 1947, Detroit, MI; [p.] Nathan and Nancy Dworin Salicoff; [m.] David Roy Drinkard, Vernal Equinox, 1979; [ed.] B.A./M.A. The University of Michigan, Ann Arbor, MI., M.A. Herbal Medicine, Emerson College, Ontario, Canada, Soul Therapist/Minister, The Universal Life Church, Modesta, CA., Reiki Master, Reiki Center Southfield, MI., graduate studies, English Literature, Fareleigh Dickenson University, Banbury, England; [occ.] Healer, Teacher, Painter, Poet; [hon.] *International Who's Who in Poetry*, many Certificate Awards from First Place to Honorable Mention; [oth. writ.] "Vernal Equinox", Anthology at *Frost at Midnight*.; [pers.] If the word was the beginning of creation, then it is incumbent upon those who are talented in the use of the word to use it for the benefit of all life, everywhere, raising it to an appreciation level beyond the ordinary or mundane.

DRISCOLL, BENJAMIN A.
[pen.] B. A. D.; [b.] March 12, 1944, Ypsilanti, MI; [p.] Adam and Edith Driscoll; [m.] Deborah A. Driscoll, November 25, 1983; [ch.] Benjamin Jr, Priscilla, Dadra, Jamin and Nimaj; [ed.] Barstow Elementary, Miller Jr. High - Cass Technical High - Wayne State University; [occ.] Color Lithographer; [a.] Detroit, MI

DRUEDING, JUSTINA
[pen.] Willow Ambers; [b.] September 10, 1981, Miami, FL; [p.] Rita French, Edward Drueding; [ed.] Entering 10th Grade at Springfield High School; [occ.] Junior Civitan Club, Beta Club; [oth. writ.] Poem published in Zest fest. Unpublished poems, novel, screenplays and short stories.; [pers.] I like to write about issues facing people my age and even older in hopes that they will read them and not be so judgmental.; [a.] Springfield, TN

DRURY, NANCY E.
[b.] October 16, 1963, Flint, MI; [p.] Burl and Violet Hawes; [m.] William T. Drury; [ch.] Joseph William Drury and Katherine Michelle Drury; [ed.] Hamady High School, Ross Medical Education Ctr.; [occ.] Homemaker; [pers.] I am thankful for this opportunity to be published. My poetry reflects the love of the Lord, from which everything we have comes.; [a.] Flint, MI

DRURY, WINDY
[b.] November 16, 1943, Houston, TX; [p.] John and Asenath Albers; [m.] Charles E. Drury, August 26, 1977; [ch.] Shaun (son), Charles, David, Becky (step-children); [ed.] Pikes Peak Community College-Colorado Springs, Co-AAS Degree-Early Child Development.; [occ.] Retired Secretary; [memb.] Coventry Cross Episcopal Church-DAV Member-Veteran Hon Disch. from U.S.M.C. and U.S. Navy; [hon.] Phi Theta Kappa, Dean's List; [oth. writ.] Unpublished "Ghost By The Sea" - "The Clock" - "Billy, The Lonely Boy" - and others; [pers.] The spirit of man I find cannot be conquered as long as he has hope.; [a.] Gardnerville, NV

DUBENSKY, JOHANNA A. WOLFE
[pen.] Johanna Wolfe Dubensky; [b.] Alomogordo, NM; [p.] H. Joseph Wolfe, Clare C.; [m.] George E. Dubensky; [ch.] Geo Jr., Jim GC-Mike Shelley, Kristen and Jan; [ed.] Three years college and continuing CED for permanent Deacon and spouse; [occ.] Volunteer Pastoral Care; [memb.] Literacy Teacher for (GED) each member accomplished goal. Three year Facilitator for Parish Renew "Program Own Biblical Writings (Bible Ref.)" used in class; [hon.] Recognition of service-Command Headquarters Kelly AFB, Randolph (MPC) Defense Mapping Agency 2 years Brooks AFB. Certificate Outstanding Service and Courtesy Pastoral Ministry, Seminary 1985; [oth. writ.] poems published (by Johanna A. Wolfe) 1946-two year books The Exposition Press. NY 1st in "Renew Program" Local Church, 1989-1993; [pers.] My dream is to bring some sunshine, hope, and cheer into the hearts of all of God's children; [a.] San Antonio, TX

DUFAULT, JEREMIE J.
[b.] May 9, 1978, Yakima, WA; [p.] Joseph and Joan Dufault; [ed.] High School Graduate pursuing College education.; [occ.] Student at the University of Pennsylvania; [hon.] National Honor Society Scholarship Recipient.; [pers.] In my writing I attempt to reveal the intricacies of aspects of life that are taken for granted or overlooked as commonplace.; [a.] Yakima, WA

DUIS, RICHARD J.
[b.] May 24, 1924, Chicago, IL; [p.] Richard Duis, Mary Duis; [m.] Marilyn G. Duis, May 26, 1951; [ch.] Sherry, Gail, David, Randall, Daniel, Andrew; [ed.] Niles High School Capitol Radio Institute U.S. Army International Correspondence School; [occ.] Retired Plumber; [memb.] American Legion VFW NRA AM Vets SDA Church U.A. Plumbers and Pipefitters; [oth. writ.] Newspaper and church publications.; [pers.] Looking forward to eternal life on recognition of the Trivia connected with this one.; [a.] Niles, MI

DUKE, J. THOMAS
[pen.] Jonathan Teague; [b.] January 15, 1963, Berea, OH; [p.] Tom and Genny Duke; [m.] Lori Lee Duke, August 21, 1982; [ch.] (2 sons) Jordan (Age 10) and Jared (age 8); [ed.] Attended Lee College (Cleveland, TN); [occ.] Ordained Minister with the Church of God (Cleveland, TN); [memb.] State Youth and Christian Education Board of Churches of God in Southern Ohio, Warren County Mentor Program; [hon.] District Youth Director of the Year 1995; [oth. writ.] Poem: "A Prayer for Words" published in the book *Listen With Your Heart* by Quill Books (Harlingen, TX); [pers.] "We can never have enough beautiful words in our vocabularies or our libraries".; [a.] Lebanon, OH

DULMAGE, DORIS R.
[pen.] Doris Daniells-Dulmage; [b.] April 7, 1919, Dorking, Ontario, Canada; [p.] Maurice and Lydia Daniells; [m.] Harry B. Dulmage, August 11, 1945; [ch.] Five boys, one girl (1 set of twins), nine grandchildren; [ed.] Writing for Children and Teenagers Institute of Children Literature; [occ.] Retired Business Executive; [memb.] Auxiliary of Gideon's International in Canada; [oth. writ.] Poems, children's stories, articles; [pers.] I like to show appreciation and wonder for God's marvelous creation.; [a.] Prescott, Ontario, Canada

DUMMERMUTH, TONY E.
[b.] September 3, 1970, Kansas City, MO; [p.] Charles Dummermuth, Shirley Decker; [ed.] Pleasanton High School, Barton County Community College; [occ.] Machine Operator, Century Manufacturing, Ellsworth, KS; [memb.] United States Junior Chamber of Commerce, Ellsworth Church of Christ; [hon.] Local Jaycee Presidential Award of Honor, Local Distinguished Service Award; [oth. writ.] "Loving Night...Cherished Night" in *Memories of Tomorrow*; [pers.] In my writings I find a place of comfort where I can truly express my deepest feelings for what is around me. My hope is that all who read it may find it too. My dearest friend, Dana, thank you for all your encouragement.; [a.] Kansas City, MO

DUNBAR, ROSALIE E.
[ed.] B.F.A. (Radio - TV), A. M. (Educational Anthropology), Ph. D. (Religious Education), New York University; [occ.] Editor-Writer; [memb.] The First Church of Christ, Scientist, Boston, MA, Cornell Lab of Ornithology and other bird-watching organizations, Hancock Shaker Village and Canterbury Shaker Village; [oth. writ.] Published in The Christian Science Monitor, The Christian Science Sentinel, and The Christian Science Journal as well as a few other publications (mostly in prose); [pers.] I believe that life is full of the unexpected - the moments when joy, beauty, and excellence break through in ways that crack open the shell of daily routine and that we have to keep our hearts ready to receive them.; [a.] Dracut, MA

DUNFORD, LAPRIEL BARTSCHI
[b.] November 10, 1927, Georgetown, ID; [p.] Frank and Gwen Bartschi; [m.] Ray Dunford, May 1, 1946; [ch.] Cheryl Rae, Marian, Teresa, Mark B.; [ed.] Georgetown Public School, 8 years Georgetown High School, 4 years; [occ.] Housewife, wife, mother and grandmother and great grandmother; [memb.] Church of Jesus Christ of Latter Day Saints (Mormon), Positions Held: R.S. Homemaking Leader, Y.W. Speech Director, Activity Counselor, YWMIA Secretary, YWMIA Treasurer and Ward Librarian for fourteen years...; [hon.] I also served as a Cub Scout Den Mother for four years.; [oth. writ.] I have a portfolio full of poetry, mainly about family and fun. But I seem to become emotional, when for proofing, I read to my Hon. I have a disease called Parkinson, and a happy traveler, I'm not. So writing keeps me quite busy, and my husband keeps driving while I "Jot"... I've written about the Golden Years, and a tale about the crow.. There is a lot I need to write about and time is getting short, so for this opportunity I thank you, from the bottom of my heart.; [a.] Georgetown, ID

DUQUE, MARY
[pen.] Maria Augusta Duque; [b.] August 28, 1979, Quito, Ecuador; [p.] Isabel and German Duque; [ed.] Clements High School; [occ.] High School Student; [pers.] "I have been and still am a seeker, but I have ceased to question stars and books, I have begun to listen to the teachings my blood whispers to me.".; [a.] Sugar Land, TX

DUXBURY, JOANNE C.
[b.] December 24, 1939, Granton, WI; [p.] John C. and Guyla V. VandeBerg; [ch.] Lana M. Stenger, grandchildren: Amber Renee and Jeremiah John; [ed.] Beaver Dam High School, Beaver Dam, Wisconsin Fresno City College, Fresno, California; [occ.] Antique Dealer with a shop in Chowchilla, Ca., and Temporary Services doing miscellaneous clerical work in Walworth County, Wisconsin; [memb.] Phi Theta Kappa, Theta Beta Chapter Fresno City College. Soroptimist of Mariposa County, Mariposa, CA.; [hon.] Bierkoe, Most Distinguished

Member Award from Phi Kappa.; [oth. writ.] Many other writings, but still in the closet, with this kind of encouragement I'll have to dust them off.; [pers.] At this time in my life I don't know where I want to call home. I have a business in Calif, but came back to my grass roots in Wisconsin, with a stop over in Arizona to visit the grandchildren. I hope to do more writing and in listening to my inner self I feel I could do well. I feel it is God's hand that leads me to whatever my purpose in life may be. I like the saying "Let Go, Let God", and with this bit of poetry being published, I have another signal that my writing will be accepted.

DYBALA, NATALIE R.
[b.] July 18, 1980, Chicago, IL; [p.] Bruce and Theresa Dybala; [ed.] Currently enrolled in Peotone High School as a Junior, Study Ballet at American Dance Center in Olympia Fields, IL; [memb.] Quill and Scroll, Thespians; [hon.] Scholastic Honor Emblem for Scoring among the top 10% on the Plan Test. GPA: 4.7 out of 5.0 scale.; [oth. writ.] Written for personal enjoyment, no publications; [pers.] I've learned to enjoy life as it is, try to make the best of it and don't be afraid to achieve your goals.; [a.] Peotone, IL

DYE, ALMA FRYE
[b.] December 6, 1934, Parkersburg, WV; [p.] Lula Hammons and Clarence Frye; [m.] Harold Holten Dye Jr., September 16, 1950; [ch.] Sheila Dolores, Althea Diane, and Kenneth B. (Deceased); [ed.] High School; [occ.] *Mount Vernon News* and Self employed; [hon.] Poems published in: *Mount Vernon News, Coshocton Tribune, Sparrowgrass Poetry*, The National Library of Poetry; [oth. writ.] Children's books, compiling a book of poetry, compiling family recipes for a book; [pers.] Any honors I receive belong to my mother, she believes in me. I thank Pearl Moravy, she encourages me. My children, they listened to my poems and loved me. My creed: there is a way, I will find it or I will make one.; [a.] Mount Vernon, OH

EAGAN, MIMI
[b.] August 28, 1926, Syracuse, NJ; [p.] Leo and Eleanor Eagan; [ch.] Margot Papworth, Muffie Wilson, Chris Cheney; [ed.] Georgian Court College - BA degree; [memb.] Several local Clubs; [hon.] Editors Choice, Distinguished Member of International Society of Poets, International Poetry Award 1995; [oth. writ.] Poems that have been published by National Library of Poetry, Book titled *Bittersweet*; [pers.] I write about everything I love; I write about women and how we are treated. I'm very anti-war, so I write about the waste of war. I love to write Haiku for the discipline of imaginary.; [a.] Fayetteville, NY

EARNSHAW JR., DR. GEORGE D.
[b.] February 5, 1924, Elverson, PA; [p.] George and Elizabeth Earnshaw; [m.] Dorothy Earnshaw, August 10, 1946; [ch.] One son, six daughters; [ed.] Coatesville, PA. H.S. - 1941, John Brown Univ. - B.A. - 1949 N.O. Baptist Theol. Sem. 1964 Covington Theol. Seminary New Orleans, La. Ft. Oglethorpe, GA - D. Min.; [occ.] Missionary-Preacher-Teacher; [memb.] Highland Park Baptist Church; [oth. writ.] Sermons, poems none published except in local church papers; [pers.] Have been preaching since 1945. In my ministry have taught in churches and in both public and private school part time or full time in grades K-12, College and Seminary; [a.] Chattanooga, TN

EDDINGTON, CHRISTY
[b.] March 19, 1974, Longview, TX; [p.] Mike and Jamie Jameson; [m.] Jason Eddington, May 14, 1994; [ed.] White Oak High, White Oak, TX, Kilgore College, Kilgore, TX; [occ.] Laboratory Aide, Good Shepherd Medical Center, Longview, TX; [oth. writ.] Several articles and poems published in local newspapers.; [pers.] My writings reflect the beauty, innocence, and simplicity of life and nature.; [a.] Gladewater, TX

EGAN, JUDY A.
[b.] July 23, 1940, Ashland, KY; [p.] Maxwell and Evelyn Otis; [m.] Divorced, February 14, 1958; [ch.] Erin, Diane, Shari, Mary, Kim; [ed.] High School Grad; [occ.] Retired; [memb.] Boys Town; [oth. writ.] Articles published in senior high school newspaper.; [pers.] A truly young person is one who always looks at the world with eyes full of questions and asks them.; [a.] Tacoma, WA

EGGERING, LORIN
[b.] October 23, 1989, Kingston, NY; [p.] Robert and Carol Eggering; [occ.] Student; [memb.] Brownies

EILTS, SHARRY
[pen.] Sherrick; [b.] July 22, 1963, Aberdeen, SD; [ed.] Bachelor Fine Arts 1995, MSCD College, Denver Co., 3.65 G.P.A., Major Advertising Design; [occ.] Artist/Student; [memb.] Denver Art Museum, Denver History Museum, Denver Zoo; [hon.] Several of my Art Works have been displayed at Metropolitan State College; [oth. writ.] Several fine art books. Senior thesis: "The Preservation and Restoration of Art Masterpieces." A children's book - Design Intern at the Children's Museum. Design Intern at Westword Paper.; [pers.] Shortly after graduation I was involved in a car accident and was injured. My psychologist, Helen White, suggested I should write. Several professors believe I have writing talent as well. Webster defines design as creation - working out the details of. Almost every religion from ancient to modern concern themselves with creation. Is it true that "nothing is new under the sun?" That a static society is a dead society? If so, and I believe it to be, then one of the most important functions of any artist is to create and present ideas, concepts, and products in a new and exciting manner to interact with the universal energy that unites all life worldwide, to be a part of the continued forward and artistic mobility of society. I chose to be a designer because it is a fascinating field that infiltrates every aspect of life. The design arena is very broad and that allows me to explore my paths of creativity freely. It goes beyond boundaries and gives me flexibility, which empowers me to reach more people. I, like most designers, am very excited over custom publishing and addressing specific audiences, however, it is my intention to retain the power of personal creativity and not allow it to be overshadowed by computers. I work in a variety of media, because I believe that all the arts should be integrated into society to create a unified environment. Most people see design as style, function, or communication. I prefer to approach a project with no preconceived style and hope people will value me for my ideas and sensibilities. In today's fast-paced world a designer must be a "problem solver" and "communication manager" who understands contradiction, diversity, and ecological responsibilities in order to improve the quality of life for present and future generations to come. I agree with Aristotle's statement over 2,000 years ago that, "Life is doing things not making things." Design affords the opportunity for an artist to do things and not just make things.; [a.] Denver, CO

EINEM, JOHN ROBERT
[pen.] John Robert Von Einem; [b.] May 20, 1963, Minnesota; [p.] Sonja and Bob Eugene Einem; [ed.] College student currently attending CR Art/Computer Science Major plan to attend HSV; [occ.] Self employed artist, photographer etc.; [memb.] At planetary society and health sport. Arcata First Baptist Church; [oth. writ.] None published yet so far; [pers.] I believe in the unity and interestedness of everything, everything in the universe is both connected and yet separate continues and discontinues - a fractor!; [a.] Arcata, CA

ELLEN, NANCY
[pen.] Nan-See Ellen; [b.] July 28, 1942, Pueblo, CO; [ch.] Rene, Michael, Harron, Shane; [ed.] Bachelor Degree in Social Work, A.A. in Business; [occ.] Pueblo Country Club Restaurant and Banquet Waitperson; [memb.] National Humanist Society, Women's League of Voters; [hon.] Several Awards for my Handmade Dollhouse Furniture and Dollhouses; [oth. writ.] Several poems published in newspapers. I have written several children's stories, none as yet have been published.; [pers.] Nature and life's simple things have the greatest influence on my writings. Giving peace a hand, in a time when society is so full of anger and turmoil, I do by volunteering or in my writings.; [a.] Pueblo, CO

ELLIOTT, VICTORIA A.
[b.] January 5, 1974, Warwick, NY; [p.] Lucien and Ruth Elliott; [ed.] Currently pursuing a BS Degree in Business from Mississippi University for Women in Columbus, MS; [occ.] Full-time Student, Part-time Clerk; [memb.] Blacklist Honorary Social Club, Highlander Social Club; [oth. writ.] *Victoria's Vagitus*, unpublished collection of poems.; [a.] Columbus, MS

ELLIS, RENAITE C.
[pen.] Sara Remi; [b.] January 4, 1983, Buffalo, NY; [p.] Thomas and Susan Ellis; [ed.] Eden Elementary and Eden Jr./Sr. High Schools; [occ.] Student; [memb.] Girl scouts, Soccer, School Newspaper, Stage Crew, Concert Choir; [oth. writ.] A few short stories, other poems for school.; [pers.] "Dreams are the material that reality is made of."; [a.] Eden, NY

ELLISON, INDIANA
[b.] June 19, 1938, Etowah, AL; [p.] Fred Couey, Myrtle Couey; [m.] Donald K. Ellison Sr., July 7, 1964; [ch.] Donald K. Ellison Jr., Daniel Ellison, Robert Ledford, Roger Ledford, Dianne Logan; [ed.] Cedar Valley, Meggs County Tennessee; [occ.] Disabled/retired, Seamstress; [oth. writ.] I have many other poems and songs that haven't been published. Also I had a letter to the editor published in the *Gadsden Times* newspaper.; [pers.] My writing is influenced by my love for God, and my family. Also, memories of my late husband inspire me greatly. To me poetry is as beautiful as the face of a child.

ENERSON, SCOTT M.
[pen.] Matthew Stevens; [b.] December 6, 1956, Denver, CO; [oth. writ.] Compiling a collection of original poems for publication tentatively titled *Initials In The Sand.*; [pers.] To read my words is to know my heart.; [a.] Addison, IL

ENGEL, BETH ANNE
[b.] July 11, 1949, Valley Forge, PA; [p.] Herbert Ford, Romaine Moore; [m.] David L. Engel, August 13, 1977; [ch.] Emily; [ed.] S. Horace Scott Senior High School, West Chester State College, Lancaster Theological Semi-

nary; [occ.] Seminary Student; [memb.] Upper Octorara Presbyterian Church Parksburg, PA; [hon.] Scholarships from Lancaster Theological Seminary; [oth. writ.] This is the first piece I have sent for publication. Currently writing a book about the life and death of my son at the age of 11 from cystic fibrosis. Other poetry pieces.; [a.] Parksburg, PA

ENRIGHT, LILLIAN V.
[b.] August 14, 1933, Stoneham, MA; [p.] James E. Viola, Lillian G. Viola; [m.] James J. Enright, July 4, 1956; [ch.] Andrew Gerard, Karen Marie; [ed.] B.S. Mus. Ed., Lowell State, M.Ed. Boston State, Doctoral Studies Completed at U. of Illinois; [occ.] Retired Teacher, Musical Director of Chatham Community Chorus; [memb.] Phi Delta Kappa, Phi Kappa Phi MTA-R/NEA-R; [hon.] (National Federation of Music Teachers) NFMT - prize winning pianist (Association for Community Theater Excellence) ACTE Award for Musical Direction 1994; [oth. writ.] Primarily texts for original music compositions unpublished; [pers.] I have always been fascinated by the sonority and rhythmic cadence of words and word combinations, and I try to use them to create poetic visual imagery; [a.] West Chatham, MA

ERARDI, JEAN
[b.] August 18, 1961, Kinston, NC; [p.] David & Peggy Prince; [s.] Robert Erardi, April 26, 1983; [ch.] Matthew, Amber, Frank, Jake; [ed.] Watauga High School; [occ.] Housewife, mother, Home-schooling educator; [pers.] I enjoy many different avenues of writing, but my first loves are poetry and children's books. The loss of my oldest child, Matthew, has been one of my strongest motivating forces behind my writing. My other children continue to inspire me daily; [a.] Boone, NC

ERICHSON, ROBERT MARK
[pen.] E. L. Speer; [b.] November 30, 1953, New Orleans; [p.] Fred M. Erichson, Anna L. Erichson; [m.] Dedicated to Debra Brady and her fine family; [ed.] Private Elementary School, Henner, LA, graduated from Subiaco Academy Ark. took degree at William Carey College in Gulfport MS, May 1995; [memb.] Was a member of Southern Poetry Association and published; [hon.] Crackenack Telemarketer Received Sales Award 1982; [oth. writ.] Four published works 1991-1992. S.P.A pass Christian, MS Dedication poem for Polo Tournament New Orleans, Nov. 1989.; [pers.] Sounds and Sights are never lost, but carried upon the winds, in the trees on the tides, in the rumblings of air and sea, no matter how ancient, waiting for the right eyes and ears.; [a.] Bay Saint Louis, MS

ESCH, GWENDOLYN
[pen.] Dr. Gwyn Esch; [b.] June 23, 1937, Greenville, NC; [p.] Aileen Hurst Clark Dilda and Curtis Benjamin Clark; [m.] Walter Philip Esch Sr., July 15, 1967; [ch.] Walter Philip Esch Jr., Eric Clark Esch; [ed.] Greenville High School (1955), (1959) B.S. Degree - East Carolina Univ., (1965) M.A. Degree - Nova Southern Univ., (1991) Ed. D. Degree - Nova Southern Univ.; [occ.] Retired Academic Excellence Team Program Teacher Miami (Dade County), Florida; [memb.] East Carolina Univ. Alumni Assoc., Nova Southeastern Univ. Alumni Assoc., Jarvis Memorial Methodist Church, American Assoc. of Methodist Church, American Assoc. of Retired Persons; [hon.] 1972-Received an Outstanding Elementary Teacher of America Award. 1988 - Specially selected and appointed for the position of Academic Excellence Team Program teacher. 1991 - Gwyn's doctoral dissertation on nurturing second grader's literacy and language development received Nova Southeastern Univ.'s Practicum Award and was selected by the Educational Info. Center for inclusion in their ERIC database.; [pers.] It is my belief, that "words" offer us our most widely used form of communication and greatly influence our existence. Thus, all mankind should be nurtured and strengthened by wisely expressed "thoughts"-spoken, written and read.; [a.] Miami, FL

ESTABILLO, LESA
[b.] July 12, 1980, San Fernando, Philippines; [p.] Rudy and Luningning Estabillo; [ed.] Beginning my junior year at Kadena High School in the Kadena Air Force Base on Okinawa, Japan; [occ.] Student; [hon.] Principal's Honor roll, first place prizes in 3 local essay contests; [oth. writ.] One article in *411 Teen Magazine* an essay in *This Week* (local Okinawan Magazine) and an essay in a compilation booklet commemorating Black History Month; [pers.] As I journey through the swift years of my youth, I wonder about questions and discover answers which reveal even more questions. I hope I'll never stop my wondering and wandering.; [a.] Okinawa, Japan

ETIENNE, CLIFFORD
[b.] February 25, 1949, New Orleans, LA; [p.] Edward and Ella Etienne; [m.] Rosemary B. Etienne, August 13, 1993; [ch.] Erica, Clifford Allen, Richard, Jessica, Johnether, Tracey, Rochell; [ed.] G. W. Carner Sr. High School; [occ.] Towboat Pilot; [memb.] New Israel Baptist Church; [a.] New Orleans, LA

EVANS, CLINT
[b.] October 19, 1976, Denver, CO; [p.] Richard and Patricia Evans; [ed.] Soda Springs High School, College of Southern Idaho; [occ.] Student at College of Southern Idaho; [memb.] Member of Hope Lutheran Church, Soda Springs Idaho, on Youth Council and other Church positions, involved in some Community Projects for Youth and Adults; [pers.] I try to put more into writing then just words or single meanings and I try to add visual enjoyment (a mental picture) to what the reader perceives. I enjoy classical poetry, especially Shakespeare.; [a.] Twin Falls, ID

EVERNGAM, SALLIE M.
[b.] July 9, 1914, Denton, MD; [p.] William and Sallie Satlerfield; [m.] Lester K. Everngam, October 22, 1932; [ed.] Denton Elementary and High School; [occ.] Retired housewife; [oth. writ.] Write as a hobby, poems, songs, music

EWING, TERI
[b.] December 19, 1953, South Bend, WA; [p.] Edmund J. Walsh, Lillie Walsh; [m.] Richard Ewing Jr., June 6, 1995; [ch.] Melissa Cooper Ewing, Richard and Wendie Ewing; [ed.] Raymond High School, Grays Harbor Community College, Western Washington State College; [occ.] Warranty Administrator, University Volkswagen-Audi-Subaru, Seattle, WA.; [memb.] John Wayne Pioneer Wagons and Riders, Washington State Horse Council, Washington State Horsemen; [hon.] Foundation Member of the "John Wayne Pioneer Wagon and Riders" Club; [oth. writ.] Just for my friends and myself; [pers.] I write what I feel inside.; [a.] Renton, WA

EZELL, DORIS A.
[b.] March 10, 1950, McConnells, SC; [p.] Stanley Ezell and Nellie Lewis; [ch.] Tina Ezell-Hull, Nikki Meeks; [ed.] Education Specialist, 1992, M.A., 1975, B.A., 1973, Writing Consultant Certification, 1986, attended Oxford University/Lincoln College, 1996; [occ.] 7th grade language arts teacher at Chester Middle; [memb.] Bread Loaf Rural Teacher Network, Alumni Association of Winthrop University, National Council of Teachers of English, Poetry Society of South Carolina, National Education Assoc.; [hon.] Write Teacher of South Carolina, *Who's Who Among American Teachers*, 1995, 1992, 1990, 1989, Chester Middle Teacher of the year, 1988-89, Fulbright Award to China, 1991, Fulbright-Hays award for tour and study in Indonesia, 1994, Dewitt Wallace, Reader's Digest Fellowship to attend Bread Loaf School of English in Middlebury, Vermont, 1995 and Oxford, England; [oth. writ.] Point of South Carolina, articles for *Just Good News* magazine, *Blue Parlor Readings* of Bread Loaf School of English, *Pegasus, Art Summer* literary magazine; [pers.] I beckon for poetry to scratch the inner itch deep within my soul, without tearing a hole in its unassuming origin. Its melodic legacy composes the song that makes my life golden and the original dance which propels my dreams into silver flight. Poetry is my panacea...; [a.] Rock Hill, SC

FANN, JAMIE NOEL
[pen.] Jamie; [b.] November 3, 1977, Newark, OH; [p.] James and Holly Fann; [ed.] Graduated from Schaumburg Christian School in May of 1996. I will be attending Cornerstone College in Grand Rapids Michigan in the fall.; [occ.] I am a sales associate for Gap clothing store in Schaumburg, IL; [hon.] I received state runner-up in oral interpretation of scripture and 2nd place in creative writing my senior year of high school, 2nd place - creative writing poetry my junior year of high school; [oth. writ.] I write for my own personal pleasure, this is the first time anything of mine has been published; [pers.] I give all the glory to Jesus Christ because He has given me all my talent and I will use that talent to praise Him.; [a.] Hoffman Estates, IL

FARE, DONALD CHARLES
[pen.] Miles Merwin XII; [b.] January 20, 1949, Greenville, MI; [p.] Lavon J. Fare, Marian Hoopman Fare; [m.] Barbara J. VanDyke, September 19, 1996; [ch.] Sarah A. Sheneman, Barbara L. Coleman, Donald C. Fare II, Timothy Ryan, Alexander Fare, Heather Mellisa Fare, Charlotte E. Fare; [ed.] Central Montcalm H.S., Aquinas College Ferris State University; [occ.] Medical Technologist/Entrepreneur; [memb.] American Society of Clinical Pathologists; [hon.] National Honor Society, Valedictorian, Rho Chi, Dean's List, 25K Old Kent River Bank Run (1989 finisher); [pers.] My poetry, at times, reflects my deep, personal relationship with Jesus Christ, yet, I also allow my many life-experiences conduit to creative, cryptic expression.; [a.] Grand Rapids, MI

FARMER, LAJEUNE V.
[b.] June 16, 1964, Washington, DC; [p.] John Farmer, LaVerne Farmer; [ed.] Crossland Senior High; [occ.] Data Entry Operator; [oth. writ.] Several poems writing to be published.; [pers.] This is God's gift that I am able to express my feelings in the form of poetry, letting others know we are never alone while experiencing life's situations. Early on I read many nursery rhymes. Later I was inspired by Maya Angelou's books: "I Know Why The Caged Bird Sings," and "Phenomenal Woman."; [a.] Capitol Heights, MD

FARMER, PATRICIA
[b.] July 24, 1943, Chicago, IL; [p.] Cleveland and Nannie Taylor; [m.] March 26, 1960, (Separated, April 26, 1970); [ch.] Keith, Greg, Chris, Cindy, Marq's Nessa.; [ed.] AAS - Comm. College at Forest Park - 1978

Criminal Justice some College Credits toward my BA; [occ.] Retired CNA; [memb.] AARP; [oth. writ.] I usually write poems as gifts to my loved ones.; [pers.] As a single parent I strive to let our young people understand how sound judgement and a positive self are the keys to a rich and rewarding life.; [a.] Chicago, IL

FARMER, PERRY
[b.] March 22, 1957, Washington, DC; [p.] Virginia and Perry Farmer Sr.; [ed.] One year college, Bethune-Cookman Daytona Beach, FL, Univ. of District of Columbia - Wash., DC, Ballou Sr. High; [occ.] Assistant Mailroom Manager, PT Private Investigator; [memb.] International Freelance Photographer Organization, N.A.A.C.P.; [oth. writ.] About 50 song lyrics registered with the Library of Congress. I hope to collaborate with a musician to add music to my lyrics.; [pers.] I believe man must walk by faith and not by sight. I also believe being self-employed is better than being an employee.; [a.] Washington, DC

FARRELL, MEGHAN
[pen.] Meg; [b.] October 15, 1985, Manhasset; [p.] Josephine and John Farrell; [ed.] Attending the 6th grade year 96/97; [memb.] International Society of Poets Distinguished Member; [hon.] Editor's Choice Award; [oth. writ.] "Dancing in the snow," "the clouds," "Untitled," "Lacy Snowflakes," "Open Your Eyes And See," "Sadness," "Runaway," and "Across The Moon"; [a.] Baldwin, NY

FAULKNER, APRIL S.
[b.] April 2, 1980, Memphis, TN; [p.] Susan and Tim Faulkner; [ed.] H.W. Byers High School

FAUTH, BETTE LAVERNE
[b.] November 18, 1919, Catasauqua, PA; [p.] Wilbur Nuss and Bessie Kurts; [m.] Warren W. Fauth, April 19, 1947; [ch.] Nadine Edith, Bonita Marie, Heather Suzette; [ed.] Thiel College, PA B.A., Gallaudet University, M.A., Claremont Graduate School, MFA; [occ.] Assoc. Prof of Art, Emeritus, Riverside Community College, Director of Art Gallery, Riverside Community College, Painter; [memb.] Riverside Art Museum, San Bernardino, Co. Art Museum, Oak Glen Dulcimer Players, Art Matters; [hon.] Work represented in Riverside Art Museum Exhibitions, San Bernardino Co. Museum, UCR Faculty Club, Riverside Community College Gallery, Solo exhibitions in Riverside, Long Beach, Designer of History Walk of Riverside, Riverside Community College Lecturer, 1985, Riverside Art Foundation Award, 1975; [oth. writ.] *China: Close Encounters In An Ancient World*, Chapters in book: "Movement For The Developing Child", "Folk Art Of Brazil" articles in grade teacher magazine on art; [pers.] Admirer of Robert Frost, Emily Dickinson, Sara Teasdale, Wordsworth. My aim is to create paintings with words, poems that contain emotions of universal significance.; [a.] Riverside, CA

FELTON, PHYLLIS A.
[pen.] Phyllis Ann Felton; [b.] April 21, 1965, Elizabeth City, NC; [p.] Hattie E. and Wesley Felton; [m.] Michael Tolliver Jr.; [ed.] Hempstead High School Hempstd D., New York 11550 Airline Training Thompson Career Prep 59 Main St. Port Washington N.Y.; [occ.] Produce Supervisor of a Supermarket also Ladies Sales Person of High Fashion Ladies Clothing Store; [memb.] One Member of the Chamber Commerce for 6 years; [hon.] No awards yet.; [oth. writ.] Had a couple of writings in Grammar School Fulton St. School Hempstead, N.Y. 11550 but was never awarded anything.; [pers.] I am a quiet person, love to travel, shop, and go to different countries, my Sister Rosetta Felton inspired me to go on writing poems.; [a.] Hempstead, NY

FERLAND, MEGHAN MARIE
[b.] August 26, 1976, Manchester, NH; [p.] James T. Ferland, Charlotte L. Ferland; [ed.] Junior at University Systems of NH; [occ.] Student; [oth. writ.] This is my first published piece, but I have written several others. I began writing poetry in a creative writing course I took last semester. This is the first contest I have participated in and the first poem I ever submitted.; [pers.] Thanks to my entire family who have all inspired me. Special thanks to my mother for her unconditional love and for supporting and urging me to write, my brother Tyson for teaching me some very important lessons on life, my brother Ian for being my best friend and for always finding the humor in everything, my grandmother Marie who has always been there for me, my father, who after reading this poem, will know that I do love him. I am truly indebted to you all and love you with all of my heart.; [a.] Manchester, NH

FERNANDEZ, ROBERTA
[b.] April 11, 1938, Monroe, GA; [p.] Howard-Stancel, Roberta Anderson; [m.] Silveriano Fernandez, April 1, 1969; [ch.] Teresa Wert, Leslie Loja; [ed.] 1 year college - Business; [occ.] Retired; [memb.] VFW Auxiliary, Sheriff's Volunteer Association - Investment Club; [hon.] One award for poem in 1989 - Did not get copy of book in which it was published. Have other awards not pertaining to writings; [oth. writ.] Have written my Autobiography in rough form. Write for local community newspaper.; [pers.] I write what I feel.; [a.] Anderson, CA

FERRELL, BARBARA
[pen.] Valentina; [b.] February 14, 1933, Tampa, FL; [m.] George Ferrell, June 2, 1989; [ch.] Claudia, Clarence, Timothy; [ed.] 2 yrs. College; [occ.] Writer; [hon.] Creative Writer of Year. Most Popular Contributing Columnist, Poet Extraordinaire *Stars and Stripes*; [oth. writ.] Contributing columnist, special feature writer. Book *Marriage, Motherhood and other Embarrassments* Technical writer, numerous poetry offerings.; [pers.] Pleasure, by way of accolades come not from public awake, instead, from having put into words what others think and wish to express, yet cannot.; [a.] New Port Richey, FL

FERRIS IV, DAVID C.
[pen.] The Kid; [b.] September 9, 1974, Newhaven, CT; [p.] David C. Ferris III, Karen Santamaria; [ed.] Graduated Guilford High School Class of 1994; [occ.] Stock clerk for Edward Syper Markets and a short order cook for a restaurant; [memb.] CPR group A Peer Connection Group; [hon.] 2 English Awards 1 Social Studies Award William Home Award for most all around improved student.; [pers.] Always keep your eyes open, mind open to new ideas even if you agree or disagree, knowledge is the ultimate power of an open mind.; [a.] CT

FESTA, SANDRA
[b.] September 8, 1986, Smithtown, NY; [p.] Aldo and Denise Festa; [ed.] 5th grade (as of Sept. 1996) Canaan Elementary School Patchogue, NY; [occ.] Student; [memb.] Peer Leadership, Band, Math Olympiad, Show Choir, Chorus

FINLEY, CYNTHIA L.
[pen.] Cynthia Finley; [b.] September 17, 1961, Des Moines, IA; [p.] Ora Kuhns and Peggy Kuhns; [m.] Donald Finley, July 6, 1991; [ch.] Christian Michael and Tawney Ann; [ed.] East High, D.M.A.C.C. (short for Des Moines Area Community College); [occ.] Medical Office Manager; [oth. writ.] None published. Currently working on several children's stories; [pers.] Writing poetry gives you a sense of flowing onto paper your inner-most feelings, thoughts and dreams. I thank my mother for passing on to me a love for writing, and I hope my children will follow in this.; [a.] Jenks, OK

FINLEY, REBECCA
[b.] August 15, 1975; [p.] Judson and Alice Finley; [ed.] Ashland High; [occ.] Senior at Southern Oregon State College; [hon.] Phi Kappa Phi, Dean's List, Presidential Scholarship, Lee Mulling Scholarship; [a.] Ashland, OR

FINN, JENNA
[pen.] Jenna Finn; [b.] May 1, 1981, Northampton, MA; [p.] James and Louise Finn; [ed.] Russell H. Conwell Elementary, Gateway Regional Middle School, Wahconah Regional High School; [memb.] Girl Scout for 9 years; [pers.] I feel that you can express your feelings and emotions through poems and short stories.; [a.] Worthington, MA

FIORELLA, ALBERT
[pen.] A.J.; [b.] November 8, 1975, Huntington, NY; [p.] Albert J. Fiorella Sr. and Cheryl Gray; [ed.] Sophomore - Fordham University, New York City - Anthropology major; [occ.] Student - Anthropology B.A. '97; [memb.] Guitarist in "Drill Press"; [pers.] "To find yourself in the music, you must first lose yourself to the music" - G. Densley.; [a.] New York City, NY

FISCHER, SANDY
[b.] March 6, 1944, Steamboat Springs, CO; [p.] William MacFarlane, Wilma MacFarlane; [ch.] Anthony Curtis, Timothy Wayne; [ed.] Soroco High School - Oak Creek, CO; [occ.] Data Entry Operator; [oth. writ.] Poems published in steamboat pilot *Gen Gaea* newspapers, *Stars and Stripes* magazine; [pers.] Poems that raise the awareness of the general public on environmental issues, the plight of the American Indians and the breakdown of moral and ethical values in the family today, are my way of contributing to the consciousness raising of the American people.; [a.] Grand Junction, CO

FISHER, RENEE L.
[b.] October 8, 1961, Bucks County, PA; [p.] Augusta E. Richeal, Francis E. Richeal; [m.] Michael F. Fisher, September 3, 1995; [ed.] Woodrow Wilson, H.S., LaSalle University; [occ.] Admin. Assist, for President of A Home Builder Company, Fairview Village, PA.; [hon.] Certified as 1st Degree Black Belt in Karate (Tae Kwon Do), *Who's Who Among American High School Students*; [oth. writ.] Misc. items published in Local papers and magazines. One item published in a book *Fall Condours*, 1988.; [pers.] Life is a gift, Embrace it, Enhance it, and truly treasure it.; [a.] Jeffersonville, PA

FITCH, JEFFREY E.
[b.] February 10, 1981; [p.] Marlene Fitch and Jeff Sadler; [ed.] Still in school at Key West High; [occ.] Work at the Key West International Airport; [oth. writ.] I have written other poems called, "Alone," "You," "Always Together," "I Wish You Were Mine," "The Chance," "Bloody Night," "This Little Dream," and "A Lot of Love."; [pers.] I write poetry all the time. Most of my

writings talk about things that happen to me. My poetry is usually about love and pain, the two main things in my life.; [a.] Key West, FL

FLETCHER, KORESSA GREGORY
[pen.] Koressa Gregory; [b.] December 10, 1959, Lorado, TX; [p.] Ben Gregory Sr., and Doddie Kirschner; [m.] Bobby Darrell Fletcher, August 29, 1987; [ch.] Chad Ryan Johnson; [ed.] Brazosport High School, Houston Community College; [occ.] Mental Health Student; [memb.] Texas Paraprofessional Association, Harris County Juvenile Court Volunteers; [hon.] Phi Theta Kappa, Dean's List, HCC Foundation Scholarship; [pers.] My soul has traveled a long journey and will someday reach an ultimate state of enlightenment, where everything is possible.; [a.] Houston, TX

FLORIVAL, HERVE
[b.] August 15, 1955, Ouanaminthe, Haiti; [p.] Tina and Germain Florival; [m.] Magda Florival; [ch.] Lizz Florival; [ed.] Master of Science in Education; [occ.] Teaching; [memb.] Association of Haitian Educators; [oth. writ.] My other writings are in Creole. They are: Poems, stories etc.; [pers.] If we want to build a better society, we have to give back to the children their naivete and their innocence. My other goal is to provide to Haitian students children's literature; [a.] Miami, FL

FLORY, ELIZABETH
[b.] May 10, 1933, Hoopeston, IL; [p.] William and Leota Bradshaw; [m.] Carl Flory, October 11, 1953; [ch.] Michael, Jeffrey, David, Grandchildren: Matthew, Kara, Joshua, Jason Krista, Derek, Tyler; [ed.] Grade School Honeywell School Hoopeston, Ill. and Danville Ill, St. Paul's Lutheran Napoleon O. High School Napoleon Ohio plus GED from Napoleon, O.; [occ.] Housewife, also retired Inspector from manufacturing writing company; [memb.] St. Paul's Lutheran Church Napoleon, Ohio; [hon.] GED Award GED is the equivalent of a High School Diploma, but I would recommended every one staying in school to begin with; [oth. writ.] I entered a contest and wrote a short story about my experience in a Girl Scout camp. It was in a literature writing. I never continued with it.; [pers.] I have enjoyed writing different things about my Grandchildren and sons, also I write about my pets, 2 dogs and 3 cats, plus different other subjects.; [a.] Napoleon, OH

FLOWERS, JAMIE LYNN
[b.] August 10, 1979, Lee Memorial Dowagiac; [p.] Mark and Drewetta Flowers; [ed.] Still in High School. I'm only a Junior at Decatur Jr/Sr High School; [hon.] Awards on an Essay about my aunt. Also an award from another poem entered in a contest.; [oth. writ.] A poem about my favorite math teacher Miss Jennifer Brown and a poem about my grandma; [pers.] My writing is always to people about how they make me feel or help me out. Also most of my writing is to or about family members; [a.] Decatur, MI

FOGELL, LOUISE E.
[b.] May 14, 1928, Michigan; [p.] Deceased; [m.] Retired; [ch.] Girl Marianne David; [ed.] 8 yrs. Country School Inactive WAAC 5th Army "Medics", "Self Taught"; [occ.] Retired and Medically Handicapped and Retired Certified Religion Teacher; [memb.] Lifetime Membership in the International Clover Poetry Association and the International Society of Poets also the Daughters of Isabella Our Lady of Sorrows Circle #0617; [hon.] Honorable mention award 1969, International Poetry Competition Clover Collection of Verse 1970 "Life Dance", member in the above mentioned Editors Choice Award in 95 and 96 the National Library of Poetry; [oth. writ.] *Clover Collection of Verse Vols 1-2-3-4* also the *100 and 1 Best of Clover*, 2 books in Sparrowgrass Poetry Forum *Treasured Poems of America* the National Library of Poetry, *East of Sunrise* Columbia, SC. Newspaper and our Church Paper the *Saint Agathe Hour*; [pers.] God is my ghost writer. I ask Him to choose the topic and give me the wisdom and knowledge I need to write and He never lets me down.; [a.] Redford, MI

FONSECA, DEBRA
[pen.] Dreamer; [b.] November 20, 1974, Bronx Lebanon; [p.] Coral D. Fonseca, Jose L. Fonseca; [ed.] 12th grade Fashion Industries Artist; [hon.] Art/English/win a bond from the government for writing; [oth. writ.] "Who Are You," "Falling," "The World," "The Voice In My Head"; [pers.] Life is a gift so praise it. For when it's gone it darkness the hearts of many.; [a.] New York City, NY

FORAKER, TERRY
[pen.] Robin Lewis; [b.] September 17, 1968, Everett, WA; [p.] Shane Foraker, Janet Foraker; [m.] Dolores Marquez Foraker, August 8, 1992; [ch.] Marcelle Brooke, Jaclyn Renee, Logan Terence; [ed.] North Kitsap High School, Stonington High School, London Central High School, Ricks College, Brigham Young University; [occ.] Accounting Clerk; [hon.] Barn Island Essay Contest winner 1989, first place, Ricks College Poetry Contest 1986; [pers.] Poetry is a Godsend, establishing a point in space and time for the conscious and subconscious to join hands briefly. Through it we can express the seeming unreality of our condition with a raucous horse laugh.; [a.] Federal Way, WA

FOUCHE, DAVID L.
[b.] January 21, 1956, Davenport, IA; [p.] Harold L. and Patricia Fouche; [m.] Elynn D. Fouche, July 26, 1975; [ch.] Justin, 17, Taylor, 15, Erin, 13; [ed.] B.S. Education Fly F-15 Fighters for the Air Force Pilot T-38 Flight Instructor Pilot; [occ.] Medically Retired Capt; [memb.] Officer's Club, too many medals to list; [hon.] Officer of the year at Lowery A.F.B. and Officer of the Quarter at Air Force Academy; [oth. writ.] "Have Pain, Will Play" "False Prophets, They're Among Us"; [pers.] Everybody has a story to tell about their experience in life. Everybody has had some form of success to tell the world about. People should not cut themselves short!; [a.] Colorado Spring, CO

FOX, CAROL
[pen.] C.A. Fox; [b.] January 24, 1950, Ashland, OH; [p.] Rex and Vesta Bowman; [m.] Daniel, September 21, 1990; [ch.] Tina Marie; [ed.] High School Graduate; [occ.] Secretary; [memb.] Gold Wing Road Riders Assoc. Honorary member of the International Society of Poets.; [hon.] Editor's Choice Award for poem "God's Hand". Nominated as Amateur Poet of the year by the International Society of Poets for the past 2 years.; [oth. writ.] Several poems published by the National Library of Poetry, one of my poems, "With You", was wanted to be made into a song,; [pers.] Most of my poems are about God's creation or the way I feel about very special people in my life.; [a.] Salem, OH

FRALEY, IRENE E.
[pen.] Rene Fraley; [b.] February 24, 1939; [m.] Albert M. Fraley; [ed.] Wells College, Aurora N.Y.

FRANKLIN, CLIFTON CHARLES
[b.] August 24, 1959, Milford, TX; [p.] Blanche, Glover; [m.] Divorced; [ch.] Carlissa Franklin, Michael Franklin; [ed.] High School Diploma Roswell State Board of Education Roswell, New Mexico; [occ.] Store Clerk; [memb.] Church Kehilat Ben David El Paso, TX; [hon.] Honorable Discharge U.S. Army Aug. 1980 Highest Rank Sgt. E-5; [oth. writ.] Several unpublished poems and book; [pers.] Freedom is something that we don't have, but some thing that we should continually pursue.; [a.] Abilene, TX

FRANKLIN, SHARON
[b.] January 8, 1970, Canlon, OH; [p.] James and Carol Franklin; [ed.] Martin County High School; [oth. writ.] Two other poems published by the National Library of Poetry, "Father" and "The Windmill"; [pers.] "Silence is golden, never fail to share it".; [a.] Stuart, FL

FREY, KATHLEEN MARIE
[b.] November 19, 1982, Athens, GA; [p.] Mary L. and Edward E. Frey; [ed.] Student, Oglethorpe County Middle School; [hon.] Straight A's in all Elementary grades, Basketball Award, Track Awards, Honor Academic Program Awards; [pers.] I hope to make a difference to others and my world.; [a.] Arnoldsville, GA

FRIDLEY, COLLEEN ELAINE
[b.] April 5, 1965, New Iberia, LA; [p.] Chery Greenberg, Kenneth KuyKendall; [m.] Stephen Kent Fridley, July 15, 1985; [ch.] Contessa Marie (11 yrs.), Stephen Kyle (7 yrs.); [ed.] MacArthur High, Richland College; [pers.] This poem is dedicated to my loving husband Stephen, who inspired this poem, along with the encouragement and love from my whole family.; [a.] San Antonio, TX

FRUMES, CHERYL B.
[p.] Lauren S. Frumes, Arlene W. Frumes; [ed.] University of California Santa Barbara, San Fernando Valley College of Law; [occ.] Attorney; [memb.] California State Bar, Arizona State Bar, Los Angeles County Bar; [pers.] "A Daughter Grieves" was written in honor of my mother, Arlene, who died of metastatic breast cancer on December 15, 1995. This poem is dedicated to my father Lauren, my brother Cary, and all famous families whose lives have been irrevocably altered by this devastating disease.; [a.] Woodland Hills, CA

FULLER, MICHAEL R.
[b.] October 29, 1955, Concordia, KS; [p.] Keith Fuller Sr., Pauline Fuller; [m.] Denice A. Fuller, February 5, 1977; [ch.] Gary Dean, Dustin Ray; [ed.] Jamestown Public Schools K-12th, Cloud County Community College; [occ.] Unemployed; [hon.] Phi Theta Kappa, *Who's Who in American Junior Colleges*; [oth. writ.] Several written since my severe vehicle accident and near-death experience on April 7, 1993; [pers.] My near-death experience I have lived my second chance at life with "Family" being the number 1 Priority.; [a.] Lansing, KS

FULLER, SIDNE
[b.] May 30, 1935, Honolulu, HI; [p.] Charles and Marie Countryman; [m.] Dean Fuller, November 24, 1963; [ch.] Kevin Hardin and Joni Siebers; [ed.] Bellingham High School Washington State College - University of Hawaii - Bachelor of Fine Arts; [occ.] Volunteer at Mary Moor Park Eastside Museum. Paint and Sell Children's Chairs. Also work with acrylics, watercolor, landscape and portraits; [memb.] Mary Moor Museum, Redmond Senior Center, Square Dance Club; [pers.] After years of creative expression...drawing, painting and crafts, I

now find a new outlet for my artistic endeavors. My 1st poem - what fun! I hope to further challenge myself with this new avenue of expression; [a.] Redmond, WA

FULTZ, JUDY
[b.] November 10, 1949, Cleveland, TN; [p.] George Crego and Grace Crego; [m.] Wier Fultz, December 10, 1991; [ch.] Nicki L. Hockett, Mark Van Hoose, Dale Van House; [ed.] Fairborn High School Kings Hwy. Bible Institute; [occ.] Baker - Meijer Inc, Dayton Ohio Store #101; [oth. writ.] "Your Wedding Day" (For Mark), "You Know You're A Baker If...", "The Storm Is Over"; [pers.] If I can make life more pleasant for those I cross paths with, by helping them find humor, even when they think there is none, and to make them laugh when they think they can't, I have succeeded.; [a.] New Carlisle, OH

FURST, KATHRYN
[b.] February 17, 1959, US Air Base Wiesbaden, Germany (US Citizen); [p.] Dr. Stephen W. Furst and Barbara Furst; [ed.] B.A. Psychology Hofstra University; [occ.] Sales; [oth. writ.] This is my first publication since childhood.; [pers.] I dance with the embers of life. Artistry moves through my body and spirit in the form of words and dance. My greatest influence is the eternal love of my departed sister Athena Furst 1964 - 1994; [a.] Boca Raton, FL

FUSCO, SANTO C.
[b.] August 16, 1953, New York; [p.] Nicholas and Rose Fusco; [m.] Brenda A. Fusco, June 22, 1985; [ch.] Jessica and Michael; [ed.] High School, St. Anthony's Grammar School, Holy Rosary; [occ.] Senior Finisher Howmedica, Pfizer; [oth. writ.] "Chosen One" published in local newspaper; [pers.] All things come to those who believe, for me, for you, and every one in need.; [a.] Lyndhurst, NY

GAINES, REGINA A.
[pen.] Lady Chaka; [b.] Htfd, CT; [p.] Mr. and Mrs. Annie Gaines; [ed.] B.A. U. of HTFD; [occ.] Operations Director the Joe, Picture This Show, Inc.; [memb.] National Urban League Allen Chapel AME Church; [hon.] Sterling's *Who's Who* Executive Edition. New Voices in American Literature Outstanding Young Women of America Award; [oth. writ.] Several poems published in local newspapers, articles for the *City Beat* (regional entertainment magazine) short stories published in *Joe's Kids Page* (regional children's newspaper), published *Naturaltivity* poetry collection.; [pers.] I strive to reflect the resilient spirit of mankind in the face of adversity and challenges in life; [a.] Hartford, CT

GAINES, WILLIAM W.
[pen.] William W. Gaines; [b.] February 4, 1925, Temple, OK; [p.] Wes and Molly Gaines; [m.] Rosemary O'Tremba Gaines, September 23, 1958; [ch.] 4; [ed.] High school; [occ.] Ret.; [memb.] American Legion; [hon.] Victory Medal Mediterranean Middle East War Zone Bar, Atlantic War Zone Bar, Asiatic Pacific War Zone Bar, Korean War Zone Bar, China Service Medal, Japanese Occupation Medal, Graduate Under Water Demolition US Navy UDT #5; [oth. writ.] Poetry - Armed Forces *Stars and Stripes* news sheet several dozen others poems I'm still holding.; [pers.] Know it, if you don't know it.; [a.] Citrus Heights, CA

GALDAL, SIGNE
[pen.] Sonja; [b.] September 3, 1937, Kvinnesdal, Norway; [p.] Oscar and Gurine Galdal; [ed.] Grammar and High School; [occ.] Songwriter; [hon.] Song are listed with B.M.I.; [oth. writ.] I have other poems on hand if you wish to have me send them to you.; [pers.] I wish to have my material published to bring out a message in my religious writing of poems and lyrics.; [a.] Brooklyn, NY

GALLO, PETER
[b.] February 26, 1961, San Francisco, CA; [p.] Anthony and Alice Gallo; [m.] Roni, September 12, 1987; [ed.] B.A. Whitman College, M.A. Portland State University; [occ.] Writer/Ph.D. candidate with Wits University College Dublin, Ireland; [pers.] Session #24 is part of a much larger project which, though psychologically oriented, is ultimately concerned with the evolution of a personal mythical consciousness - in other words, comprehension spiritual healing.; [a.] Sandy, OR

GALLOWAY, JACQUELINE
[b.] May 23, 1965, Baltimore, MD; [p.] Thomas Bazemore and Claudia Bazemore; [m.] Mr. Osceola M. Galloway Jr., July 30, 1988; [ch.] Ashley, Ametrius and Miandra; [ed.] Southwestern High, Morgan State University and Watterson Career Center; [occ.] Cheshire Machine Operator; [memb.] Truth and Love Christian Fellowship; [hon.] Servant of the Year, Good Samaritan Award, National Honor Society, *Who's Who*, Academics and Writing Competition; [oth. writ.] "A woman," "There's Relief," "What Education Means to Me," and poems during times of bereavement; [pers.] I aim to reach out to the world with a message in my writing.; [a.] Baltimore, MD

GAMBILL, PAULA
[pen.] P. J. Sandy; [b.] April 29, 1948, Illinois; [p.] George R. Binkley, Dorothea A. Sandy; [ch.] Amy Louise, DeAnna Jennifer, Travis Randall, Nicole Brianne; [ed.] Temple High School, Tempe, AZ, Children's Institute of Literature currently attending Yavapai College, Prescott, AZ majoring in Sociology; [occ.] Legal Secretary - Yavapai County Attorney's Office, Prescott, AZ; [memb.] American Red Cross HIV/AIDS Instructor; [oth. writ.] Children's stories and articles. (Published include "Penguins - Birds that Fly Under Water", "Smog Pie" and "Jack-O-Lanterns-They Weren't Always Just for Fun", *Legions of Light* Magazine, 1995).; [pers.] Poetry is the expression of all feelings - be they happy or sad, loving nor loathsome, obscure or profound, sensible or nonsensical - written from the heart to be read from the heart.; [a.] Prescott, AZ

GAMBLE, DOUGLAS
[b.] October 5, 1970, Indiana, PA; [p.] Michael and Karen Gamble; [ed.] McClintock High School, Mesa Community College; [pers.] I believe poetry comes from the heart of the dreamers.; [a.] Chandler, AZ

GAMBLE, LINDSEY MARIE
[b.] September 23, 1985, Glen Rock, NJ; [p.] Geraldine and Jerry; [ed.] 4 grade Memorial School, North Haledon; [hon.] First place winner of 4th grade poetry contest, first place in "create an ad" contest; [oth. writ.] "Space," in the *Anthology of Poetry by Young Americans*; [pers.] I love to write, and I hope others enjoy my work; [a.] North Haledon, NJ

GAMMAGE, DANNY L.
[b.] May 25, 1957, Phoenix, AZ; [p.] Floyd Leodist and Mercedes Gammage; [m.] Sharon Gammage, April 21, 1987; [ch.] Dana, Dominique and Shane Gammage; [ed.] B.S. Zoology (Northern AZ Univ), M.A. Biology (CSU Dominguez Hills); [occ.] Environmental Management and Radiation Safety, CSU, Dominguez Hills; [memb.] Kappa Alpha Psi Fraternity Inc., California Environmental Health Association, Health Physics Society; [oth. writ.] Poems: "Boys in the Basement," "The Prized Bull." Technical Writings: South Bay Los Angeles Hazardous Materials Transportation Studies, Los Angeles County Hazardous Materials Transportation Risk Analysis; [pers.] Education of our children and the full economic participation of all Americans in the enhancement of our great country. May the future hold no limits to progressive, creative thoughts for any American.; [a.] Long Beach, CA

GARBER, ROMINA
[b.] August 25, 1984, Buenos Aires, Argentina; [p.] Dr. Miguel Garber, Liliana Garber; [ed.] Bay Harbor Elementary, Highland Oaks Middle School; [occ.] Middle School student; [hon.] 1st Place in The Youth Fair (Miami) Fl 1994, for a creative writing poem; [oth. writ.] Poems and stories submitted to several contests; [pers.] Everything I write has a message, inspired by my feelings.; [a.] North Miami Beach, FL

GARCIA, MARK ANTHONY
[b.] July 16, 1955, New York, NY; [m.] Divorced; [ch.] Elizabeth "Amy" Garcia; [ed.] MBA from Tampa College; [hon.] Graduated Cum Laude; [oth. writ.] Several yet unpublished poems; [pers.] I receive inspiration to write from my loved ones, especially my daughters.; [a.] Tampa, FL

GARCIA, NICHOLAS
[b.] December 25, 1928, Detroit, MI; [p.] John Paula Garcia; [m.] Billie Garcia, May 19, 1947; [ch.] 5; [ed.] 5th grade, Self Educated; [occ.] Retired after working 43 years; [a.] Clinton Township, MI

GARCIA, STEPHANIE MARIE
[pen.] Sissy; [b.] September 22, 1983, Chandler, AZ; [p.] Larry and Faye Garcia; [ed.] 7th grade; [occ.] Honor Student at Kynene Del Pueblo Middle School; [hon.] I have been on the Honor Roll for 6 years; [a.] Chandler, AZ

GARDAS, KATIE BETH
[b.] April 18, 1983; [hon.] I am on a B Honor Roll, and am known as a Student Leader in the School, I am only 13; [oth. writ.] I am currently writing a poem book.; [pers.] I love writing stories and poems.; [a.] Arden Hills, MN

GARDNER, DEANNA
[pen.] Deanna Gardner; [b.] October 15, 1982, Oakland, NJ; [p.] Anne and David Gardner; [ed.] St. Elizabeth School Wyckoff, NJ; [occ.] Student; [memb.] St. Elizabeth's Basketball Team, Art Student, Volunteer at Ramapo Bergan Animal Shelter; [hon.] First Place Awards at the Young People's Art Show in Oakland and the Ringwood Manor Art Association, 1996. Bergen County Interparochial Basketball League First Place Championship for 1994 and 1995; [oth. writ.] A poem published in *A Celebration of New Jersey's Young Poets* 1996; [pers.] I strive to do my best.; [a.] Oakland, NJ

GARDNER, GORDON RAY
[pen.] Green Giant; [b.] October 13, 1975, Houston, TX; [p.] Kenneth Gardner, Brenda Gardner; [ch.] Jasmine Marie Gardner; [ed.] Thomas Jefferson High School Lamar University; [occ.] Produce Manager - Trainee, Market Basket #45; [pers.] It never seems to fail, walk-

ing in the trail to the gateway to hell. I'm watching people fry, dead die, dead men tell no lie, when swimming in the ocean, with boots full of lead. I really never could understand how to the blind could lead the dead.; [a.] Port Arthur, TX

GARDNER, LISA
[b.] July 31, 1965, River Rouge, MI; [p.] Willie and Fannie Gardner; [ed.] Graduated from Ecorse High School in 1983. Attended Community College and Business School after high school. Currently taking a course in Children's Literature writing.; [hon.] Associate Degree in Child Care Technology; [oth. writ.] I have one Romantic fiction story soon to be published by a known subsidy publ. company. I have submitted my second story to publishers for possible publication, also. I am currently writing my third fictional story. I write poetry and songs as well.; [pers.] Why put others down because they're different? While you're putting others down so that they will feel inferior, some one up above is putting them up for superior ground.; [a.] Lincoln Park, MI

GARRITY, KARA EILEEN
[b.] November 6, 1973, Indianapolis; [p.] Thomas M. Garrity and Kathy Brinley; [ed.] I am starting my Senior year of High School this fall 1996. Sheridan Christian Academy; [occ.] High School Student; [memb.] Christ The Savior Lutheran Church; [hon.] Creative Writing Award Honor Roll 94.5 average; [oth. writ.] "Angels"; [pers.] "I write about my feeling on life and hope that I can touch someone through my writings". My reflections have been influenced by my brother, Lee Thomas Garrity who passed away in 1989; [a.] Nobblesville, IN

GARSBE, GLADYS M.
[b.] February 4, 1927, Erie, PA; [p.] Lenora and Nelis Ploss; [m.] Edward W. Garsbe, December 13, 1946, Second time, February 28, 1972; [ch.] Bonnie, James Edward, Kathleen; [ed.] 8th grade Academy - High quit to work - to help mother during war; [occ.] Housewife; [hon.] "The Glory of Heaven" written 12 yrs. and 50 stories - "Daisey's Dream" and "Woodland Retreat," three golden poet awards, award for Poetic achievement several certificates for other poems "The Roots of Home" (Stars) "Anniversary," "Winter Time Dreams," "First Snow," published in newspaper.; [oth. writ.] Horse story, "For the Love of Pleasure," dog story - "A Boy and His Dog," a few other stories, one "The Faith of a Child"; [pers.] My love of poetry began in English Class, where I memorized poems and recited them. My poems are Heart poems, of Country, Loved ones, Friends, Humorous Sweet and sad.; [a.] Wimauma, FL

GARTH, DOROTHY
[pen.] Lester Mason Jr. Sayisha Allen; [b.] July, Phenix City, AL; [p.] Queen Estella and Jake Smith; [m.] Melvin Garth, March 16; [ch.] Melvin II, Nichole; [ed.] South Girard High; [occ.] Secretary for D and D Trucking Co.; [memb.] American Red Cross, The Artistic Women Club; [hon.] A honorable award given to me by my elementary principal Miss Susie Allen for writing "My Old Horse Bess".; [oth. writ.] "My Old Horse Bess" a play I wrote at age eleven and performed on stage at Phoenix City Elementary with other member of the sixth grade class. Poems published in local newspapers.; [pers.] I love to write, maybe one day I'll pull all the papers from underneath my bed and find in them a best seller.; [a.] Detroit, MI

GARTMAN, MARION L.
[b.] April 14, 1943, Portland, OR; [p.] Laurane and Frank Armstrong; [m.] Otto A. Gartman, March 2, 1963; [ch.] Debra Fenton and Alan Gartman; [ed.] Graduated H.S. 1961 - from South Hadley H.S. in S. Hadley, MA; [occ.] Wife, Mother, Grandmother, Conservation Commission, - MACC, M and Tom Range Study Commissioner, - Smith's Ferry Conservation Commission Professional Volunteer; [memb.] First Lutheran Church-Clerk Holyoke Conservation Commission - MACC, Mt. Tom Range Study Commissioner, - Smith's Ferry Conservation Commission Sec.; [hon.] MACC 1995, Environmental Service Award as a "Special Conservation Commissioner"; [oth. writ.] Columnist for the *Holyoke Sun* on Environmental Issues. Several poems published in various Newspapers - writer, editor, reporter, publisher of *The Fog Horn* - a neighborhood newspaper; [pers.] Have been writing for more than 30 years for personal pleasure - have just begun to explore serious writing - Most writings about family, friends and environment - currently researching history of Smith's Ferry in.; [a.] Holyoke, MA

GEHRIE, ERIC A.
[b.] September 13, 1982, Evanston, IL; [p.] Mark and Cynthia Gehrie; [ed.] 8th Grade; [occ.] Student; [hon.] Honor Roll (School) Service Awards (School); [oth. writ.] No other published writings.; [a.] Winnetka, IL

GERKE, RICHARD JON
[pen.] Richard Gerke; [ed.] South Kitsap High School; [occ.] Pattern maker and fantasy/sci-fi writer in my spare time; [oth. writ.] Published: none, unpublished: Wings Fury, Gateway 1 & 2, Flood Things, A.I.D.S., Technosound; [pers.] "We cannot discover new oceans unless we have the courage to lose sight of the shore."; [a.] Olalla, Washington

GERMANO, ANTHONY J.
[pen.] Ynohtna Onamreg; [b.] August 24, 1926, Providence, RI; [p.] Anthony A. Germano, Cora (Woodlock) Germano; [ed.] High School Mount Pleasant attended Our Lady of Providence Seminary; [occ.] Retired; [memb.] St. Philips Church (R.C) NCSC National Council of Senior Citizens IAM International Assoc. of Machinist; [hon.] Veteran World War II Served on CVELL U.S.S. Card Eto medal 1 star; [pers.] If respect is desired, then respect must also be given.; [a.] North Scituate, RI

GIAMMALVA, BARBARA S.
[b.] July 25, 1943, Chicago, IL; [p.] Leo Hawryszkiw, Catherine Folwarski; [m.] Sam Giammalva, February 25, 1961; [ch.] Daughter, Pamela Eve, Son, Philip Samuel; [ed.] Steinmetz High School, Numerous college credits; [occ.] Procedural writer for a bank in Anchorage; [pers.] I love to write. I desire to write all manner of truths.; [a.] Anchorage, AK

GIBSON, MICHAEL
[b.] May 14, 1951, Pasco, WA; [p.] John and Freda Gibson; [m.] Edna C. Gibson, August 16, 1972; [ch.] Robert F. and Andrew A.; [ed.] Bachelor of Arts from California State University Long Beach; [occ.] Postal Employee; [pers.] I have always been deeply moved by the writings of the doctors of the church. I think that their contribution to the deposit of faith has been of unmeasurable value to moral society as well as to the faithful.; [a.] Brea, CA

GIGLIOTTA, NICOLE
[pen.] Erica Jon Austin; [b.] February 22, 1982, Milwaukee, WI; [p.] Luanne and Greg Stuckert; [ed.] Waterford High; [occ.] Poet, Writer, Author; [hon.] Graduated 8th grade; [oth. writ.] None, besides a story that's not quite finished; [pers.] I have gotten influenced by my big brother, Kurt Cobain's music, and all of my friends. My English teacher, Mary Lofy, and Math teacher.; [a.] Waterford, WI

GILES, KENNETH
[b.] December 1, 1977, Charleston, WV; [occ.] Student - University of Delaware; [pers.] I believe that happiness can only be achieved through personal insight and reflection.; [a.] Wilmington, DE

GILLESPIE, DIANA MARIE
[b.] June 24, 1980, San Jose; [p.] B. Gillespie; [ed.] Ceres High School; [pers.] I am a full-time student at Ceres High. This is my first publication. I hope to have many more.; [a.] Turlock, CA

GILLEY, TERESA D.
[pen.] Teresa Gilley; [b.] May 20, 1958, B'ham, AL; [p.] Alfred (Dot) Davis, Shirley Peoples Davis; [m.] Gregg Gilley, June 14, 1974; [ch.] Rayburn Craig (1976), Wesley Brian (1979); [ed.] University UABI B'ham Bachelors and Masters Degree in Education.; [occ.] Elementary Teacher, Moody Elem. School Moody, Al Jefferson St. Junior College, Samford; [memb.] Happy Home Baptist Church, Leeds, AL; [hon.] High School Beta Club, Top 1/4 Senior Class "1976" Cum Laude 1989 UAB B'ham. AL; [oth. writ.] Several poems and songs but none published at this time; [pers.] I owe everything I am or everything I become to my savior, "Jesus Christ", who died for me. All of my writings have been inspired by God.; [a.] Moody, AL

GILLUM, LINDA S.
[b.] December 27, 1957, Montgomery, WV; [p.] Joseph Johnson, Loris Nidiffer; [m.] Douglas B. Gillum, January 15, 1983; [ch.] Jami Lynn, Douglas Burl, Amanda Kay; [occ.] Homemaker; [memb.] Woodhaven Freewill Baptist Church; [hon.] I have been given the greatest honor of them all, the honor in serving a true and living God.; [oth. writ.] "Memories" and "Mommy," I'm sorry neither of which have been published.; [pers.] I would like to dedicate my poem ("Look In My Heart") to anyone who stands in judgement of another.; [a.] La Salle, MI

GINES, RACHELLE
[pen.] Starshine; [b.] May 14, 1980, Gardena, CA; [p.] Dominador C. MD and Leah Gines RN; [ed.] Sacred Heart Elementary, Notre Dame High School; [memb.] Writes for the Notre Dame Newspaper, *The Messenger*, Member of *Summit* Yr. Book Staff; [pers.] I write for others and not myself. Great influenced by William Wordsworth's use of natural imagery.

GINTHER, JEANNIE K.
[b.] April 7, 1961, Altoona, PA; [p.] Harold and Louise Lloyd; [m.] Raymond S. Ginther, December 27, 1992; [ch.] Matthew, Rachel (Deceased) and Elizabeth; [ed.] B.A. Penn State University; [occ.] Owner/Operator, Ginther's Bed and Breakfast, State College, Pa.; [oth. writ.] Several unpublished poems and an unpublished feature length screenplay titled "The Silent Voice"; [pers.] Always try to focus on the positive outcome of a seemingly negative situation since there will always be enough good to outweigh the bad.; [a.] State College, PA

GIOIA, JEANNINE
[pen.] Jeannine Gioia; [b.] December 26, 1953, Dearborn, MI; [p.] Jack Bass, Olga Bass; [ed.] Cody High School, Detroit, MI; [occ.] Territory Manager, ConAgra Retail Sales; [oth. writ.] As my first poem submitted for publication, I am encouraged to pursue other ventures.; [pers.] Anything I accomplish in life is due to my family whose values, love and support encourage creativity and confidence.; [a.] Clinton Township, MI

GIORDANO, MRS. SYLVIA
[b.] June 28, 1972, Memphis, TN; [p.] Rolanda and Larry; [m.] Mr. David Antonio Giordano, September 28, 1992; [ch.] Malcolm and Maryann; [ed.] Hillcrest High School, Southern University at Baton Rouge, State Technical Institute of Memphis; [occ.] Homemaker and student; [memb.] Hillcrest High School/National Honor Society, Hillcrest High School/ Hall of Fame; [hon.] Golf Scholarship for Southern University, all District Volleyball Award for the City of Memphis; [oth. writ.] "I Would Like To Sing"; [pers.] I wrote "This African Knot Can Sure Take A Lot" while pregnant with my daughter, Maryann. I was eight months pregnant and had allowed my hair to suffer. My husband, David, pointed this out to me, and that was my inspiration for this poem. I sincerely hope you "get it".; [a.] Memphis, TN

GLAISTER, MURIEL DYAR
[b.] January 24, 1928, Hamilton, AL; [p.] S. C. and Bulaf Dyar; [m.] Joseph W. Glaister, January 26, 1952; [ch.] Ira Glaister, Jerome Glaister, Debra Glaister, Shervic Hendriy, Melissa G. Pereira; [ed.] B.S. Liberal Arts, BSN-Nursing, MA Education, MA Clinical Counseling. U.N.A. Florence, AL, UAH Huntsville, AL.; [occ.] Retired R.N. Clinical Councilor; [memb.] Al made Aux National Med Aux. Biology Honor Soc. Ed. Honor Society Highland Baptist Church, American Nurses Assoc., Ala. State Nurses Assoc.; [hon.] Deans List UNA; [oth. writ.] Short stories, poems.; [pers.] As I am in the Late Autumn of my seasons I work out of my home which is located in the North Western Hills of Alabama and I gaze into the giant Oak and Hickory Trees all ablaze in a burst of the many hues of color. I then look up and beyond those magnificent forms of life and I am satisfied for I have witnessed the various hues of color.; [a.] Florence, AL

GLAZER, LEN C.
[b.] October 16, 1971, Boston, MA; [p.] Lloyd and Lois Glazer; [m.] Johanna Glazer, July 6, 1996; [ed.] Beaver Country Day School, Brandies University, Massachusetts School of Professional Psychology (MSPP); [occ.] Psychologist Intern Martial Arts Instructor; [memb.] International Kokondo Association (IKA); [pers.] "Rudeness is a weak person's imitation of strength." Shihan Paul Arel, IKA.; [a.] Canton, MA

GOLDEN, BRENDA
[pen.] Taylor Golden; [b.] January 11, 1961, Florida; [p.] Ray and Mary Brown; [m.] Stephen Golden, August 11, 1990; [ch.] Sierra and Nathan; [ed.] High School; [occ.] Own Sign Business; [oth. writ.] Romance novel *Mountains in the Sky* (1st and just completed) Thriller Novel - *A Model's Nightmare* (Script for movies - currently writing); [pers.] Thank you!! None for my writing began writing in Oct 95. I have many unpublished poems that I have never before submitted. I just thought I'd send in two for this contest. I was surprised! My widest and most important goal in life is to teach people to respect the earth our children.; [a.] Orlando, FL

GONZALEZ, BLANCA ESTELA
[b.] October 14, 1957, MacAllen, TX; [p.] Argentina Alvarado Gonzalez, Marcelo Gonzalez Jr.; [ed.] PSJA High School 1976, Pan American University 1980 BA Psychology and Elementary Education Texas A and I University 1985 MA Reading, Texas Teaching Certificates Elementary Education, Psychology, Reading Specialist, Supervision and Mid-Management; [occ.] Reading Specialist, Teacher at PSJA North High School, 15 years teaching experience in elementary, secondary, and college; [memb.] Texas Computer Education Association, The International Society of Poets, Poetry Society of America, Texas Class Room Teachers Association; [hon.] Editor's Choice Award 1994 and 1995, 1995 International Poets of Merit Award Poem published in *After the Storm*, first division of two year in ensemble band, second Division for one year in ensemble band Psychology Scholarship for tuition, President honor roll; [oth. writ.] Article published in local paper, poem published in the following books: *After The Storm, Best Poems of 1996, A Delicate Balance, Beneath the Harvest Moon, A Tapestry of Thought, Carving in Stone*; [pers.] I believe that through education anything will be achieved. A goal is accomplished through hard work and determination. The stars can be reached.; [a.] San Juan, TX

GORDON, DOUGLAS B.
[b.] February 17, 1960; [p.] Thomas L. Gordon, Virginia B. Gordon; [ch.] Chandra Rochelle; [pers.] Our destinies are experienced progressively like stepping stones to the future. The sum of our experiences awaits us.; [a.] Gainesville, FL

GORDON, JACK
[b.] June 11, 1933, Saint Louis, MO; [p.] Unknown - Adopted; [ch.] Jacqueline, William, David; [ed.] ABD (all but dissertation, Philosophy, V.C. Berkeley); [occ.] Claims Authorizer, Social Security; [memb.] Pax Christi, Call to Action; [oth. writ.] Articles for Local Union Newspaper; [pers.] My spiritual commitment is to Liberation Theology. My intellectual commitment is to expose the cognitive and moral errors to fundamentalism and the religious right, especially the latter's inability to discover the true nature of the Christian Gospel. I also want to fight racism and sexism.; [a.] San Francisco, CA

GORSUCH, MEGAN
[b.] December 20, 1979, Rushville, IL; [p.] Lynn and Randy Gorsuch; [ed.] High School; [occ.] Student; [hon.] First place pen and ink category in school art show; [oth. writ.] Poem and editorial in school paper.; [pers.] Go forward - don't look back. The past is behind you. Instead, live in the moment and dream with a smile.; [a.] Dunlap, IL

GOWDY, KAREN L.
[b.] March 6, 1952, Portland, OR; [p.] Howard and Patsy Farquhar; [m.] Joe I. Gowdy, February 12, 1972; [ch.] Brian and Erin; [ed.] A High School Graduate; [occ.] Home Day care Provider; [oth. writ.] I have done a few poems for News Letters to Hospice and Compassionate Friends.; [pers.] After the loss of my son a year ago, I began to search for the truth in life. Through my poetry I have uncovered and discovered a light that brings me some peace.; [a.] Redmond, OR

GRAINGER, PENNY LONG
[b.] May 5, 1971, Tampa, FL; [p.] Wanda Turbeville Tedder, Noah David Long; [m.] Jimmy Franklin Grainger, October 25, 1991; [ch.] (Step children) Tara 15, Jeremy - 10; [ed.] Graduated from West Columbus High School 1989 and Graduated from Southeastern Community College August 1996 with an Associates degree in Applied Science; [occ.] Lab Assistant a Southeastern Community College and Micro Computer Systems Technologist for Mickary Mill Day Care of Whiteville; [memb.] Member of Macedonia Baptist Church of Evergreen, Old 74 Saddle Club of Chadbourn, American Quarter Horse Association, National Wildlife Federation; [oth. writ.] Several other poems that I put together to make the book entitled *Feelings*.; [pers.] I love to write poetry. I try to take what I feel and put it into words. I enjoy reflecting on God in some of my poems, because without Him, none of this is possible. I enjoy sharing my feelings with others.; [a.] Chadbourn, NC

GRAMMAR, SAM
[b.] February 27, 1980, El Paso, TX; [p.] Gary Grammar, Debbie Grammar; [ed.] Currently a Junior at Andress High School; [occ.] Student; [memb.] *Who's Who Among American High School Students*; [hon.] *Who's Who Among American High School Students* (top 5% academically of all American High School students); [pers.] I am concerned by the general lack of care for mankind's home, the earth. My writing is an attempt to instill some desire and action toward preserving our planet.; [a.] El Paso, TX

GRANADO, PHILLIP R.
[b.] September 6, 1943, Denver, CO; [p.] Manuel Granado, Mary Lou Granado; [m.] Maria Granado, June 6, 1976; [ch.] Goose, Mario, Elena, Staven, Karen, and Virginia; [ed.] Sacred Heart Elementary Westminister Jr High, Santa Monica Community College; [occ.] Disabled; [memb.] World Wide Church of God, Top Records Songwriters Association; [oth. writ.] "How Great You Are", "I Want to Make You Mine", "When You Left Me All Alone"; [pers.] To help and love my fellows and try to be a good example to the younger generation.

GRANDINETTI, DENNIS L.
[b.] September 12, 1951, Mt. Pleasant, IA; [p.] Betty and Phillip Grandinetti; [m.] Shelly Grandinetti, February 3, 1982; [ch.] Elizabeth, Victoria, Phillip, William, Caroline, Jacob, Alexander, Denny; [ed.] Wentworth Military Academy; [a.] Blairsburg, IA

GRASS, DARYL G.
[pen.] Daryl G. Grass; [b.] December 22, 1957, Lyons, NY; [p.] Gerard A. Grass, Joyce M. Grass; [ed.] North Rose - Wolcott H.S., Erie CC. Empire State College (Rochester, NY); [occ.] Developmental Aide, Personal Trainer; [memb.] The Cousteau Society, Institute of Poetic Sciences; [hon.] None to speak of in writing, Various Photos Published and Award Winners in *Gannett Newspapers* Photo Contest; [oth. writ.] A few short stories, various other poems about nature and life's wonderments.; [pers.] If we as Individual experience our true inner self and live it day to day, the possibilities for true happiness and meaningful Existence would be endless.; [a.] North Rose, NY

GRAY, DARCEY L.
[b.] October 16, 1970, Illinois; [p.] Daine and Roger Baker; [m.] Christopher Gray, September 1, 1990; [ch.] Brett, Kevin, Dalton; [ed.] Belvedere High, San Antonio College; [occ.] Forklift Driver Chrysler; [pers.] I have been writing poems for years, thanks to the support of my family I now am able to share my work with others.; [a.] Belvedere, IL

GREEN, ANTHONY
[pen.] Zane Green; [b.] May 14, 1968, Richmond, VA; [p.] Kenneth and Patricia Green; [m.] Janine Green, August 19, 1995; [ed.] Meadowbrook High Longwood College, Virginia Commonwealth University; [oth. writ.] Hobby Poetry; [pers.] I want to convey that all living creatures were put on earth for a specific reason in my poems.; [a.] Richmond, VA

GREEN, KAREN
[pen.] Karen Ina Margulies, Olsen Green; [b.] January 27, 1939, New York City, NY; [p.] Roberta Goodbinder and Irwin Margulies; [m.] Divorced (Leonard Green), 1963-81; [ch.] Garth and Allison; [ed.] American Community School of Paris, Duke Univ. '59, Boston Univ '60, MA Psychology Amer. Univ. '73, MA Literature; [occ.] D.C. Licensed Psychologist - private practice Psychotherapist (1968 - present), also adjunct Professor Lit.; [memb.] ASSOC APA, Intl Council of Psychologists, Natl Register of Health Serv. Providers.; [hon.] Phi Beta Kappa, *Who's Who of American Women;* [oth. writ.] "These Dead Ladies Are My Friends" - Winner Drama Competition Source Theater D.C. 1983, arrayed and directed "Song We've Never Sing" and "Where Has Love Gone" 1985, poetry readings participant.; [pers.] I am concerned with crossing boundaries that divide - racial religious, political, sexual. I want women to find their voice and to be acknowledged and I want to celebrate love and it's vagaries, yet keep a sense of irony.; [a.] Washington, DC

GREEN, MARY FRANCES
[pen.] Mary F. Green; [b.] November 7, 1910, Bay Minette, AL; [p.] Edward Joseph Green and Willie Byrne Green; [ed.] Baldwin County High, 20th Century Business College, Special Courses at George Washington University, Washington, D.C.; [occ.] Retired, after working 23 years for Office of Naval Intelligence, D.C. and 7 years for Brookings Institution, D.C.; [memb.] Daughters of the American Revolution, The Mayflower Society, Colonial Dames of the 17th Century, Order of the Crown of Charlemagne in USA, Spanish Fort United Methodist Church; [hon.] Nothing significant.; [oth. writ.] A few poems published in *Westminster Village Chimes,* my retirement home publication. An unpublished genealogical pamphlet distributed to relatives.; [pers.] Hopefully, interest in poetry will help keep some of traditional values alive.; [a.] Spanish Fort, AL

GREEN, R. M.
[b.] January 29, 1953, Spokane; [p.] Henry and Linda Aman; [m.] Christine Marie Green, November 7, 1992; [ch.] Megan Marie, Rachel Katrina, Joseph Aaron, Hawken Foster; [ed.] Cheney High School E.W.S.C. (Eastern Washington State College) (Cheney) (1 year); [occ.] Heavy Duty Mechanic and welder - Instructor; [memb.] International Union of Operating Engineer's #370; [hon.] Being published by the National Library of Poetry; [oth. writ.] Numerous writings in personal journal. Story base lines for a series of educational children's book.; [pers.] "To capture a mood by writing....is all I really want to say."; [a.] Spokane, WA

GREEN, VIRGINIA ANN
[b.] February 28, 1932, Red Elm, SD; [p.] Orville and Anna Minnig; [m.] Richard G. Green, June 17, 1949; [ch.] Kathleen V. Gardner, Jeannine Hill; [ed.] Lincoln High School, Lincoln Nebr., many college classes, Community College classes, adult education courses; [occ.] Enjoying painting, writing, reading, traveling, volunteer work; [memb.] Berean Bible Church, Hospital Aux, Legion Aux, VFW Aux, Christian Women's Club, several volunteer organizations; [hon.] Honor of being a wife for 47 years. Awards are our two daughters!; [oth. writ.] *Scribe* (Lincoln High School Publish), I have written poems all of my life for myself, children, friend's birthdays, anniversaries, etc. When the mood strikes — I write. When the event is here — I write.; [pers.] I love life and enjoy writing poetry for myself and other people. They are simple writings, easy to understand and enjoyable. It's enjoyable composing poems and giving them away.; [a.] Torrington, WY

GREENE, JENNIFER
[b.] February 5, 1985, New York, NY; [p.] Joanne and Howard Greene; [ed.] Completed up to 5th grade; [occ.] Student; [hon.] Gemini Club, Safety Patrol, Math Olympiad, L. I. Trivia Challenge; [oth. writ.] Poems and short stories; [a.] Roslyn, L. I., NY

GREGORIOUS, RONDA ANN
[b.] January 29, 1962, Salt Lake City, UT; [p.] Ronald Hunt, Shirley Hunt; [m.] William B. Gregorious, November 26, 1982; [ch.] Ann Renee, Andrew William; [memb.] The Church of Jesus Christ of Latter Day Saints; [oth. writ.] This is my first published poem.; [pers.] I write poetry to put important messages into perspective.

GREINER, NICHOLE D. T.
[b.] March 9, 1976, Austin, TX; [p.] William Greiner, Maureen Agger; [ed.] Nazareth Academy H.S., Archbishop Ryan H.S.; [occ.] U.S. Coast Guard; [memb.] Camp Fire Boys and Girls; [oth. writ.] Volumes of things unpublished; [pers.] My pen has no capacity for drawing on paper, just sketching in the minds of those who read its scribbled madness.; [a.] Alameda, CA

GREINER, PATRICIA M.
[b.] March 8, 1961, Iowa; [p.] Mary and Lawrence (Spike) Davis; [m.] Jerome J. Greiner, September 5, 1986; [ch.] Angela Hartman; [ed.] Hamilton College; [occ.] Sales and Marketing Director, Computer; [pers.] This poem was written as a part of my grieving process after the loss of my babies. I have dedicated it to them, Abby, Jerri and Aaron.; [a.] Cedar Rapids, IA

GRIBBLE, BRADLEY
[pen.] Bradley Gribble; [b.] October 3, 1964, Santa Monica; [p.] Nancy Hunt, Tim Gribble; [m.] Margaret Ann Gleeson (girlfriend); [ed.] Silverado High School; [occ.] Energy Management Technician; [oth. writ.] This is my first poem I've ever written and I wrote it for my girlfriend; [pers.] I just wrote what I was feeling at the time and what was in my heart!; [a.] Mission Viejo, CA

GRIFFIN, JAMES EZRA
[b.] November 2, 1941, Rocky Mt., NC; [p.] David S. and Mary Lou Griffin; [m.] Suzan Arntson Griffin, June 17, 1972; [ch.] Sarah, Matthew, Rachel; [ed.] PAD, UNC-Chapel Hill, Latin American Literature; [occ.] Assoc. Prof. of Spanish American Literature (College of William and Mary); [oth. writ.] Poetry: Currently revising Memorial Day Poems (Series of 4 poems of which "Wall Within" is one). Short stories, currently revising "Acts of Kindness" and "The Locksmith and Joe-Joe", and in Spanish "Amor De Angel", "En Este Pueblo No Pasa Nada", and "In Memoriam".; [a.] Williamsburg, VA

GRIFFIN, JANAE L.
[b.] September 10, 1979, Chattanooga, TN; [p.] Darryl and Lorine Griffin; [ed.] Rising Senior at Lakeside High School; [occ.] Student; [oth. writ.] Various non-published poems.; [pers.] My inspirational writings are internally spun by the emotional roller coaster we call life.; [a.] Evans, GA

GRIFFIN, MARY KATHERINE
[b.] March 10, 1982, Mission Viejo, CA; [p.] Powers and Sandy Griffin; [memb.] I have joined poetry clubs at my junior high school, where I can share my poems with some of the peers; [pers.] Poetry is a way for me to express my feelings, thoughts, and opinions. I feel it is a wonderful way to let out your anger, and most importantly be yourself.; [a.] Laguna Niguel, CA

GRIFFIS, RICHARD L.
[p.] Nixon Griffis, Anne C. McGuerin; [ed.] Tallahassee Community College A.A., Florida State University: School of Theatric, Technical design; [occ.] Woodcrafter - Monterey Boat Co.; [hon.] New York Zoological Society working department of Herpetology; [oth. writ.] "Blues" eyre literary magazine at Tallahassee Community College; [pers.] Perpetuate a writing tradition established by William Elliot Griffis. Emulate the vision of "Americana" posed by grandfather, former U.S. Ambassador Stanton Griffis. Incorporate the free spirit of my Naturalist father Nixon Griffis.; [a.] Williston, FL

GRIMES, BENJAMIN
[pen.] Benjamin Grimes; [b.] May 8, 1968, Troy, NY; [p.] James Henny Grimes, JoAnn Grimes; [ed.] Pacific High School, Carroll Hill Elementary School, W.H. Doyle-Middle School, Hudson Valley Community College; [occ.] Student; [hon.] Language Arts Award, Special Olympics Gold Medal, *Who's Who Among American High School Students,* Academic of Excellence Award, Minority Honors Scholarship, Metropolitan Life Foundation Scholarship Award; [oth. writ.] My other writings included with my achievements are "Why African Americans Need to Stay in School"; [pers.] I try to live by the divine law - `what you sow, you will reap'; [a.] Troy, NY

GRISHAM, JESSICA LYNN
[b.] March 14, 1983, Burlington, WI; [p.] Daniel and Tammy Grisham; [occ.] Student; [memb.] National Junior Honor Society; [hon.] National Junior Honor Society; [pers.] I express my thoughts through poetry and hope to succeed one day.; [a.] Burlington, WI

GRISWELL, LORI A. H.
[pen.] LoriAnne; [b.] September 8, 1967, Summersville, WV; [p.] Floyd D. and Linda M. (Summers) Hypes; [m.] Jerry J. Griswell Jr., June 14, 1986; [ed.] Saint Leo College, Fort Eustis, VA (Bachelor's in Criminology due Spring 1997), (Associate of Arts received June 1995), also attended North Georgia Military College 1992-1994; [occ.] Paralegal for Local Law Firm; [memb.] Delta Epsilon Sigma, National Scholastic Honor Society; [hon.] High School English Award on Senior Recognition Day; [oth. writ.] Won 3rd place in Easter Essay as a High School Senior. Compiled family history and journals into a 'book' at age 16 for future generations.; [pers.] Nothing else quite takes you to another place and time as a well written poem or story. May we not forget this historical process in the technological wonders yet to come!; [a.] Newport News, VI

GRUENEWALD, CHARLES
[b.] September 2, 1967, St. Louis, MO; [p.] Wilma Luciono, Nick Luciono; [pers.] Life is good. Live it well for it is the only one you have; [a.] Las Vegas, NV

GRUENHOLZ, TERRY A.
[b.] June 17, 1950, Greencastle; [p.] Mary Ann and Jack Gruenholz; [m.] Divorced; [ch.] Heather, Jerod, Ryan; [ed.] Greencastle High; [occ.] General Telephone Facility Main; [memb.] Moose Lodge, Elks Lodge, American Leg; [oth. writ.] Nothing else has ever been submitted for publishing; [a.] Greencastle, IN

GUARDADO, MARTHA
[b.] August 16, 1945, El Salvador; [p.] Andres Leonor and Leonor Merino; [m.] Luis Guardado, October 24, 1970; [ch.] Katherine; [ed.] Eleven years; [occ.] Office Clerk; [oth. writ.] Poems; [pers.] I am a dreamer, who Hears the songs of the silent bird and feels smiling angels standing by her side.; [a.] San Francisco, CA

GUM, W. LOUIS
[b.] June 8, 1968, Illinois; [pers.] No guessing. No second-guessing.; [a.] Quincy, MA

GUNDERSON, KAREN
[b.] October 6, 1947, Great Falls, MT; [p.] Clarence and Lois Stephens; [m.] Robert D. Gunderson (Bob), July 13, 1969; [ch.] Sara Gunderson, Rob Gunderson and Wife Dawn, Kristin Neil and husband Karnes and son Karstin (grandson); [ed.] Great Falls High School, Montana State University, Northern Montana College Graduate; [occ.] First grade teacher; [memb.] Good Shepherd Lutheran Church, Delta Kappa Gamma; [oth. writ.] Several poems, many personal ones written to and about individual friends of family members.; [pers.] Some words and phrases just tumble out that I feel I must do something about. I can't seem to let them be until I've arranged them into poetry.; [a.] Polson, MT

GUTIERREZ, JON THOMAS
[pen.] John Gutierrez; [b.] September 27, 1962, Carmichael, CA; [p.] Edward Gutierrez, Lucky Cook; [ed.] Santa Maria High, Allan Hancock College, Sac City College; [occ.] Oil Refinery-Industrial Maintenance; [memb.] Sacramento Area Regional Theatre Alliance (S.A.R.T.A.); [oth. writ.] One other registered poem, compilation, and a short story in process; [pers.] Within our lifetimes, we all experience adversities. I feel the arts are a thermostatic form of expression. During the highs and during the lows, we can be imaginative and creative!; [a.] Sacramento, CA

GUZMAN, DEBRA
[b.] December 27, 1984, Des Moines, IA; [p.] John and Maria Guzman II; [ed.] Clarke Elementary; [occ.] Student; [memb.] Clarke Elementary Band, First Assembly of God, 4-H, Missionettes, School Newspaper Staff, Talented and Gifted Team; [hon.] Band Competition Award, 4-H County Fair Awards, Honor Roll, Student Council, Talented and Gifted Team, Young Writer's Conference Participant; [oth. writ.] Local and school newspaper writings; [pers.] I believe the gift of writing your feeling, hopes, and dreams on a single piece of paper is the greatest gift of all.; [a.] Osceola, IA

GUZMAN, JORGE LUIS
[pen.] Pocho; [b.] June 21, 1964, Milwaukee, WI; [p.] Francisco, Milca Guzman; [m.] Carmen Cuevas, November 6, 1982; [ch.] Jorge L. Jr., Ricardo; [ed.] LPN, AAS, EMT; [occ.] SSG, US Army; [hon.] Kuwait Liberation Medals, Meritorious Service Medal, Army Commendation Medals, LPN of the Year 1991 and 1992; [oth. writ.] "Together", "I Think of You"; [pers.] Make life fun, you only have one.; [a.] Fort Lewis, WA

HAATS, GREGORY G.
[pen.] Toyota; [b.] August 6, 1961, Vancouver, WA; [p.] Ms. Shirley Ann Arionus; [ed.] G.E.D./92; [hon.] Hazelden, Educational Materials. Portfolio Graphics, Inc., Letters of Recommendation, My Work on Saynoway, Foundation New Verbal War Against Drugs and Alcohol. Primarily Developed to Raise Money for Deaf and Blind Schools Special Olympics, National AIDS Foundation; [oth. writ.] Poetry, dedicate, singled out. Dedicate (Video) 100% proceeds goes to United Way foundation and Dornbecers Children's Hospitals.; [pers.] I'm just a little person doing and saying the right thing.; [a.] Vancouver, WA

HAGBERG, DEBRA A.
[b.] November 8, 1965, Middletown, CT; [p.] David Taylor, Grace Clark; [ch.] Christopher Paquette, Matthew Hagberg; [ed.] Mohican Community, College, Norwich CT, Wooster Beauty College, Wooster Ohio; [occ.] Corrections Officer D.O.C. Niantic CT; [pers.] To create a work of art that touches one heart, is true grace, a moment of joy, in the most of all your sorrow.; [a.] Colchester, CT

HAGERMAN, APRIL
[b.] August 1, 1982, Naples, FL; [p.] Colette and Ron Hagerman; [ed.] North Country Road School, Jr. High; [occ.] Student; [hon.] Honor Roll; [pers.] This poem was written in loving memory of my Uncle, Gilbert Lehman. who died June 17, 1955 of Cancer.; [a.] Miller Place, NY

HAGUE, JENNIFER MARIE
[pen.] Jennier Marie Hague; [b.] September 7, 1979, Orange, CA; [p.] Donna and Jerry Hague; [ed.] Graduate June of '96 at age 16 enrolled in Saddleback College for Doctor Degree; [occ.] Hostess; [hon.] Graduated high school at age 16 with 3.2 G.P.A.; [pers.] Was inspired by father at age nine to write poetry and play guitar. Now at age 16 enrolled in college to become an O.B. Doctor

HAIG, MKHOIAN
[b.] February 20, 1978, Armenia; [p.] Mkhoian Stepan and Louisa; [ed.] Graduated from El Camino Heal High School 1996, planning to attend College, an transfer to C-Sun; [occ.] Working in a flower shop part-time (Aida' Flower and Paradise Garden Flowers); [memb.] I am currently sending my writing into light.; [hon.] Have a poem published in Anthology of poetry teen-writers.; [oth. writ.] "Secrets," "The Grave," "Mama," "Death," etc....; [pers.] Writing is not my career choice, but a friend I have come to talk to over so much pain.; [a.] Los Angeles, CA

HALE, KIM LAFARE
[b.] October 5, 1962, Flint, MI; [p.] Rod LaFare, Joan LaFare; [m.] Darryl Hale, May 16, 1992; [ed.] Bachelor of Science in Elementary Education. Associate in Applied Science in Sign Language Interpreting; [occ.] Teacher; [memb.] M.E.A.; [hon.] Certificate of Achievement in Deaf Studies - High Honors; [oth. writ.] Several poems, unpublished at this time.; [pers.] Creative people focus not so much on meeting deadlines, impressing people, or making money, as on the pleasure and challenge of their work - (anonymous) I am one of those people.; [a.] Flint, MI

HALL, DORIS S.
[b.] Henry Co, VA; [p.] Mr. and Mrs. A. A. Staples; [m.] Jay H. Hall; [ch.] Janet, Tammy, Carolyn, Penny, and Angel - 5 girls, one dozen grandbabies; [occ.] Housewife; [oth. writ.] Independent Label "Truck Driving Mama," an "Mr. and Mrs." used to be country songs that are recorded by my daughter Angel Dawn and see being played on radio.; [pers.] I love to write anything. I am a very shy person, and I don't talk so I write because I have a lot to say, or I think so. That needs to be said.; [a.] Elkin, NC

HALL, FARRELL
[b.] August 10, 1943, Aiken, SC; [p.] Joseph and Blanche Hall; [m.] Brenda Joyce Hall; [ch.] Khadija, Sharief, Krishna, Eric, John, Sasha, Rana; [ed.] Philadelphia Community College, Temple University, Hillsborough Community College, Pre-Law Curriculum (Minor Education); [occ.] Child Care Supervisor; [memb.] Phi-Theta-Kappa, National Honor Fraternity, Free and Accepted (Prince Hall) Freemasons; [hon.] Phi-Theta-Kappa (awarded for a 3.5 GPA) Dean's List. Several poems published by local papers and author of news column titled "Consequence".; [oth. writ.] "Prelude," "Galvanized Man," "Juzz Jazz," "My Lady," and "Remembered," influenced by Langston Hughes, T. S. Elliot, Edna St. Vincent Milay, Garcia Lorca; [pers.] I love English as a language. I feel that our language is maligned and put to dis-use in film and in song. If you read James A. Michener you will hear the love of English by Michener.; [a.] Tampa, FL

HALL, REBECCA
[b.] July 1, 1974, Jacksonville, FL; [p.] Lester J. and Sandra E. Hall; [ed.] Godby High, Florida State University; [occ.] Elementary Education Student; [memb.] Northwoods Baptist Church, F.S.U. Marching Chiefs; [hon.] F.S.U. Marching Chiefs' Medal of Honor Dean's List; [pers.] Life to me is like a box of jewels, with each jewel kept so safe inside the best stuff (the Diamonds) are my most secret dreams...my ideals, philosophies, and beliefs. Yet sometimes my diamonds seem to be more like Cubic Zirconia (as my ideals mix with reality). Through trial and error, I try new things in new lights (sometimes Ruby, Sapphire, or Garnet works just right). Yet through it all, I grow and I change. I try to keep my heart pure as gold and my actions just the same. Then, I look at my jewels and reflect on my past. What could I change? What worked the best? The box which holds my jewels is my outer appearance...my cover. This is what other people see. I wonder to myself, is it only my outside or can they really see what I keep hidden inside of me?; [a.] Tallahassee, FL

HAMEDITOLOUI, DORRIS
[b.] Cleveland, OH; [p.] Ruth Palmer; [ch.] Dino; [ed.] John Adams High School, Cleveland, OH, Heald's Business College and Laney College Oakland, California; [occ.] Executive Legal Assistant; [memb.] International Society of Poets, the National Authors Registry, International Society of Authors and Artists; [hon.] Editor's Choice Award from the National Library of Poetry, Accomplishment of Merit Certificate from the National Authors Registry, listing in the 1996 edition of *Who's Who in New Poets*; [oth. writ.] Several other poems published in seven anthologies, three poems released on two cassettes as song lyrics.; [pers.] I was inspired to write poetry by my Theater Arts instructor who taught me how to focus on my innermost thoughts and feelings and how to bring them to the surface. I have a goal to write a book for children and teenagers based on my life and experiences.; [a.] Alameda, CA

HAMILL, TERESA
[b.] January 16, 1965, Dallas, TX; [p.] Wayne Villines, Jeanette Pogue Shaw, Wilson Shaw; [m.] James Hamill, April 27, 1990; [ch.] Trevor James; [ed.] Duncanville High School, Eastfield College; [occ.] Drafting, Barry Rhodes Land Surveyors, Rowlett, TX; [oth. writ.] Many poems, novel (in working); [pers.] I greatly admire books and poetry and hope that my work will be an inspiration to others as well.; [a.] Mesquite, TX

HAMILTON, CHRISTOPHER
[b.] December 12, 1975, Laconia, NH; [p.] Robert and Lindon Hamilton; [ed.] I Graduated from Spaulding High School in Rochester, NH in 1994 and am currently a Junior at the University at New England; [occ.] Student; [memb.] UNE Men's Volleyball; [oth. writ.] Nothing else currently published.; [pers.] I have been greatly influenced by the music of Pink Floyd. I've found the profound meanings underlying their songs to be inspirational and the sheer complexity of their artistry to be nothing short of captivating.; [a.] Rochester, NH

HAMMES, KATHLEEN M.
[b.] March 27, 1960, Springfield, IL; [p.] Abraham Wood, Wanda Wood; [m.] Anthony Hammes, October 3, 1987; [ed.] Lanphier High, C.A.V.C. for LPN; [occ.] Medical Records Processing Clerk; [hon.] National Honor Society Senior Year High School; [pers.] God has blessed me with a talent for writing. I want to share this talent with others.; [a.] Springfield, IL

HAMMOND JR., PHILLIP E.
[b.] April 25, 1957, Fulton, NY; [p.] Phillip and Mary Ann Hammond; [m.] Theresa Gigliotti, November 20, 1976; [ch.] Chatherine Marie, Cristina Marie Phillip E III; [ed.] G. Ray Bodley High School; [occ.] Painting Contractor, Musician (Bass Guitarist); [pers.] "I do recall the days gone by," was written for Phillip E. Hammond III who passed away in 1987 from a Brain Tumor at the age of 6 years old. I will always love you, Love Dad; [a.] Minetto, NY

HAMMONTREE, NANCY
[pen.] Nancy Gibbs; [b.] August 5, 1944, Newport, VT; [p.] Gordon L. and Theresa Alexander; [ch.] Two; [ed.] High School of Commerce, Springfield, MA., some College, Palm Beach Community College, Lake Worth, FL; [occ.] Administrative Assistant, Bethesda Memorial Hospital, Boynton Beach, FL; [hon.] Gold Star of Excellence and Tiffany "Manpower" Pendant for Outstanding Work for Manpower Temporary Agency; [oth. writ.] Several poems a few published in church Advent. Booklet and one in *Our World's Most Treasure Poems*; [pers.] My self expression is in music and poetry. I hope someday to encourage and inspire others through them.; [a.] Delray Beach, FL

HANNAH, MARGARET
[b.] April 23, 1925; [m.] Glen G. Hannah; [ch.] Mark, Sharon, Clinton; [oth. writ.] I have written several poems and short stories. I have a small book now on sale.; [pers.] I love the sounds and sights of nature and the beauty of God's world.; [a.] Rural Peoria, IL

HANRAHAN, DANIEL J.
[pen.] James; [b.] August 27, 1957, Woodstock, IL; [p.] James and Frances Hanrahan; [m.] Mary P. Hanrahan, October 26, 1980; [ed.] High School grad 2 yrs College; [occ.] Journeyman Electrician; [oth. writ.] Other poetry; [pers.] I became interested in poetry while working in remote parts of Alaska and after hearing some of Robert Service's works. Even with 17 years in Alaska I still have a little Sam McGee in me. But train Iditarod dogs anyway.; [a.] Palmer, AK

HANSON, SYREETA
[b.] October 19, 1980, Flint, MI; [p.] John and Peggy Hanson; [ed.] Flint Central High; [occ.] Student at Flint Central High; [oth. writ.] School writing contests; [pers.] I really enjoy writing, it gives me inspiration and a chance to express my thoughts!; [a.] Flint, MI

HANSON, TRAVIS
[pen.] Travis 'Son' Hanson; [b.] December 21, 1980, Aberdeen, SD; [p.] Belinda and Ron Hanson, Garry Hanson; [ed.] I am currently in my sophomore year in Highland, when I graduate I plan on attending Huron University in Huron, South Dakota for two years, then transfer to Paris to study literature.; [occ.] I work for my step father on his farm; [memb.] I am a member of my high school's all state chorus, I also participate in sports such as wrestling and track. I am a member of the Doland FFA chapter South Dakotas Association.; [hon.] I have Lettered in wrestling track, chorus, band. I placed 32nd in crop identification at State FFA convention. My team placed 10th. I received the star Greenhand Degree at our chapter banquet.; [oth. writ.] I have written many poems. One of them was published in the Modern Poetry Society's anthology *Heirs to America*.; [pers.] Many of my poems are about someone in my life or an isolated feeling or thought. I don't follow a pattern or form. I write what comes to mind.; [a.] Doland, SD

HARDEN, BARBARA P.
[b.] July 26, 1942, Bay City, MT; [p.] Frank Swiatowy, Emma Swiatowy; [m.] Thomas P. Harden, July 26, 1985; [ed.] Bachelor of Secondary Education, Central Michigan University, Mt. Pleasant, MI; [occ.] Tax Account Representative Internal Revenue Service Detroit, MI; [memb.] Past member of American Business Women's Assoc. No current membership at this time; [oth. writ.] Nothing published, poems for family members on occasions.; [pers.] I strive to write a message to portray my inner feelings. I learned to write poetry in grade school and have written poems more for my pleasure and now would like to branch into writing for others.; [a.] Washington, MI

HARDING, CANDY
[b.] June 22, 1970, Jamestown, TN; [p.] Earl Brown and Shirlene Cooper; [m.] Shawn Harding, May 15, 1993; [ch.] Justing, Jacob, Samantha; [a.] Jamestown, TN

HARGROVE, JIMMY PAUL
[pen.] Toy; [b.] April 5, 1965, Houma, LA; [p.] Johnny and Lucy Green; [m.] Darlene K. Hargrove, June 11, 1993; [ch.] Rodney, Amy K, Jacklyn; [ed.] Graduated Lee College out of Baytown TX with a degree in welding in 1990. Also on A.A.S. in CAD from ITT Technical Inst in 1994; [memb.] National Vocational-Technical Honor Society, American Red Cross; [oth. writ.] Several poems published in the 1985 American Anthology out of California.; [pers.] I have learned that there is a little boy inside of all of us "grown men."; [a.] Dayton, TX

HARRIS, DONNA L.
[b.] January 26, 1954, Chicago Heights, IL; [p.] Mervin and Wanetta Davis; [m.] Bruce L. Harris, March 31, 1972; [ch.] Nathanael, Andrew, Philip, and Jessica; [ed.] Homewood-Flossmoor High School, Private Art Tutoring; [occ.] Artist, Children's Books Author; [oth. writ.] This is my first, but I have plans for many more. I also write children's books.; [pers.] I believe that every person we meet places a mark on our lives, as we place a mark on theirs. So let your mark be one of compassion and love.; [a.] Homewood, IL

HARRIS, HARRY B.
[b.] May 10, 1921, Brunswick, GA; [p.] Taylor Harris, Jannie Harris; [m.] Anna Cooper Harris, September, 1988; [ch.] Cynthia, Candice, Jeanette, Tammy and John; [ed.] MBA, Southeast University 1988; [occ.] U.S. Dept. State (Ret) U.S.A. (Ret); [memb.] 15 Various Organizations; [hon.] Veteran WWII, Korea and Vietnam; [oth. writ.] Professional Papers and Several Poems; [pers.] America is a great country where a person can express him/her self, freely, in poetry.; [a.] Silver Spring, MD

HARRIS, JACQUELINE RAE
[b.] November 22, 1978, Independence, MO; [p.] Jack and Denise Harris; [ed.] Waterloo Central School, moved to Dundee Central School Feb. 96 to finish senior year; [occ.] Student; [hon.] 1st place in Spelling Bee 3rd grade; [oth. writ.] Many various poems and short stories - none are published; [pers.] For those of which are confused in life, take a risk to prove yourself or you'll never know where you stand. It's a small cost to pay to learn so much.; [a.] Waterloo, NY

HARRIS, KATHERINE L.
[b.] June 5, 1973, Detroit, MI; [p.] George Harris Jr. and Barbara Harris; [ed.] St. Martin de Porres H.S., University of Detroit Mercy; [occ.] Full-time Student; [memb.] National Honor's Society; [pers.] My poetry is a reflection of my personal experiences. It is about love, lost and found, and the never ending quest for true happiness.; [a.] Detroit, MI

HARTIG, CALLEEN WADE
[pen.] Cally Wade; [b.] April 25, 1974, Lincoln, NE; [p.] Leonard and Carol Wade; [m.] John Hartig, October 5, 1996; [ed.] Lincoln Northeast High School; [occ.] United States Army National Guard; [oth. writ.] Personal; [pers.] Poetry, I believe, is in the heart and mind of all the creatures of this beloved earth.; [a.] Beatrice, NE

HARTNETT, MARIAN I.
[b.] July 18, 1914, Chicago; [p.] Deceased; [ed.] Grad De Paul University, Chicago attended Cornell V, NY worked in a hospital in Hualien, Taiwan; [occ.] Retired Certified Registered Nurse; [hon.] Published writer since age 12 WYFF TV 4 in Recognition of my contribution to the community

HARVIN, KAY
[b.] March 9, 1947, Arcadia, FL; [p.] Woodrow and Lillian Kerce; [m.] Wesley (Wes) Harvin, August 22, 1964; [ch.] Wes Harvin II; [ed.] B.A. from FL State U., M.A. from Univ. of South FL; [occ.] Teacher, Martin County Schools; [memb.] Treasure Coast Teachers of English to Speakers of other languages (TESOL); [hon.] *Who's Who in American Education* (96-97), the Editor's Choice Award (1996); [oth. writ.] "My Son" in *Anthology of Treasured Poems*, "My Nickname" in *The Voice Within*, "Don't Call Me Rod" in the *Best Poems of the '90's*, Fall 1996; [a.] Palm City, FL

HATCH, RYAN
[b.] October 19, 1982, Detroit, MI; [p.] Richard and Barbara Hatch; [ed.] Attended William Allen, Academy

for Grade School, Attended Cooke Middle School, now attending Catholic Central HS; [occ.] Student attending Catholic Central High School; [hon.] First Place in Round at 1995 Winter Forensics Competition (for Poetic Interpretation). Honorable Mention for Northville Record's "Northville and Me" essay contest; [oth. writ.] "Exit" is my first published piece, but I myself have compiled a book of 23 of my own unpublished poems, entitled *Caustic Times*.; [pers.] I hope that in reading "Exit", each individual will create their own perception of the piece, as it was not intended to document a literal event, location, or object. I am greatly inspired by e.e. cummings and Charles Bukowski (1920-1994).; [a.] Novi, MI

HAUCH, WILBERT EVAN
[b.] May 7, 1975, Benton Harbour, MI; [p.] Darrel Hauch, Julie Hauch; [ed.] Michigan Lutheran High School, Southwestern Michigan College, Ferris State University; [occ.] Pharmacy Technician Lee Memorial Hospital, Dowagiac, MI; [hon.] Phi Theta, Kappa, Dean's List, Salutatorian, Certified Pharmacy Technician, Associate in Science, Associate in Arts; [pers.] I like to create a mild element of mystery in my writing, hence my work carries a different meaning with each new reader. My work has been influenced by modern fantasy writers.; [a.] Stevensville, MI

HAVENS, ANGEL GENEVA
[b.] November 26, 1985, Mobile, AL; [p.] Calvin L. and Katherine Havens; [ed.] Entering 5th grade in fall of 1996; [pers.] I love to write, and I have always wanted to be an author. I would like to inspire other children to achieve the goals they set for themselves, just as I have.; [a.] Semmes, AL

HAVENS, WILL H.
[b.] November 21, 1910, Douglas Country, MO; [p.] B. Ray and Mary E. (Tooley) Havens; [m.] Clara E. (Keeler) Havens, December 2, 1933; [ch.] Ivan, Ruth Evans, Ann Dowell, Bill R.; [ed.] Self Educated beyond High School by Correspondence Courses, Home Study Course, and Seminars; [occ.] Retired Minister; [memb.] Ava Gen. Bapt. Church, AARP, American Bible Society, International Society of Poetry, National Arbor Day Foundation; [hon.] Editorial Choice Awards for poems published in *The Desert Sun, Edge of Twilight, The Garden of Life, Best Poems 1996, The Rainbow's End, A Muse to Follow, Spirit of The Age, Tapestry of Thoughts*, Fifty Years of Pastoral Ministry Plus Award for Eight Additional year; [oth. writ.] One book of devotions, three books of essays, three books of poems, many articles and poems published in local, area papers, and in denominational publications and *The Poet's Corner*; [pers.] I want my writing to be praise for my Lord and an encouragement to my readers.; [a.] Ava, MO

HAWKS, TRACEY
[pen.] Tracey Hawks; [b.] March 27, 1971, Kansas City, KS; [p.] Connie Ward, L. Eugene Tucker; [ch.] Jonathan, Jessica, Jennifer; [ed.] High School, Medical Assistant; [occ.] Homemaker; [oth. writ.] "Special Friends," *Happiness Magazine*, "Momma," *Best of Poetry*, "The Sky Is," Nat'l Library of Poetry, "Foolish Heart," *Nat'l Library of Poetry*.; [a.] Oakdale, NE

HAWLEY, NICOLE LEI
[b.] December 3, 1983, Silver City, NM; [p.] Mike and Holly Hawley; [ed.] 6th and 7th grade student in Advanced Education Program Gifted in Language Arts and Math; [memb.] Tae Kwan Do Assc. (Green Belt), Gymnist - Mesilla Valley Gymnastics Las Cruces, NM; [hon.] Honors Student, Hummingbird Music Scholarship - for Viola/Orchestra; [oth. writ.] Poem titled "Reality, in Another Planet"; [pers.] Writing takes me into a whole new world...where anything can happen. It releases my imagination so I can explore my fears and fantasies.; [a.] Las Cruces, NM

HAYES, BRETT
[b.] May 23, 1961, Oklahoma City, OK; [p.] Wanda Hayes, Terry and Marilyn Hayes; [m.] Kila Hayes, January 21, 1995; [ch.] Bryce and Jared Hayes; [ed.] U.S. Grant High School, Southeastern Oklahoma State University; [occ.] English and Language Arts Teacher, Kingston Elementary and High School, Kingston, OK; [hon.] Dean's List, President's List; [oth. writ.] Personal journal writing, currently completing a novel.; [pers.] Poetry is my favorite form of writing, because it allows me the opportunity to search deep within myself and discover feelings that I never knew existed. Poetry and journal writing are excellent tools for expressing these feelings. Without poetry I probably would have missed that one "chance" I had to meet my wife.; [a.] Kingston, OK

HAYES, JOY ALISON
[pen.] Asia; [b.] December 20, 1970, Lexington, KY; [p.] David and Belinda Baker; [m.] Christ Corff; [ch.] Jared Taylor Hayes; [ed.] University of Central Oklahoma Major in Education of Emotionally and Behaviorally Disturbed Children; [a.] Oklahoma City, OK

HAYNES, DEBRA MASSUCCO
[pen.] Debrah M. Haynes; [b.] August 30, 1956, Richmond, CA; [p.] John Massucco Jr., Doris E. Massucco; [ch.] Stephanie and Christopher; [ed.] Thomas Jefferson H.S. Richmond Tech-N.A.; [occ.] Home Beneficial Life Ins-Claims Dept.; [memb.] St. Bridgets Church and St. Benedicts Church; [oth. writ.] Short Story-*Mademoiselle* Magazine, (never published); [pers.] My two beautiful children inspired me as they are my children by the sea - I could not have written this poem without them.; [a.] Richmond, CA

HEATH, PAULA J.
[b.] April 17, 1963, Ann Arbor, MI; [p.] Ed and Patricia Heath (Adopted), full name Kathleen Mary Peters Clark (Biological Mom); [pers.] This poems was written for "My own little girl I let go of", I think of her daily. This comes from my heart; [a.] Oxford, IA

HECTOR, EILEEN M.
[b.] July 6, 1957, Elmhurst, IL; [p.] Lillian and Howard Muzzey; [m.] Julio Hector, August 5, 1991; [ch.] Gregory and David Patton; [ed.] Gainesville FL, High School; [occ.] Corporate travel agent Bausch and Lomb Pharmaceutical Division; [memb.] Tampa Bay Poetry Council; [hon.] National Council Teachers of English, National Honor Society, Quill and Scroll; [oth. writ.] "Migration" published in *Squawks and Chirps of the Tampa Bay Bird Club* monthly newsletter; [pers.] I tend to look at ordinary things in an unordinary way. This gives me a lot of inspirations for my writing.; [a.] Tampa, FL

HEDRICK, LISA
[pen.] Carol Louise; [b.] December 21, 1965, Crawfordsville, IN; [p.] The late John and Carol Bartlett; [m.] Aaron Hedrick; [ch.] Three; [ed.] North Montgomery High, John Casablanca's Career and Model Management; [occ.] Customer Service Rep/Leasing Consultant; [memb.] Christ Lutheran Church Waveland PTA; [hon.] Florence Shults Poetry Awards, first place instrumental award; [pers.] My poetry is a natural gift. My work of art comes solely from my heart. If there's an emotion within me, I write of it.; [a.] Crawfordsville, IN

HEIDER, SARAH
[b.] July 13, 1982, Murrysville, PA; [p.] James L. and Barbara Heider; [ed.] I'm a freshman at Franklin Regional Jr. High School; [occ.] Student; [memb.] Senior Girl Scout; [hon.] I am an honor student.; [oth. writ.] This is my first.; [pers.] I wrote this poem with my sister, Anita, in mind.; [a.] Murrysville, PA

HEIM, CHARLES R.
[pen.] C. Heim; [b.] December 28, 1964, Topeka, KS; [p.] Howard E. Heim and Phyllis J. Bradford; [ed.] Dover Elementary, Dover, KS, Mission Valley H.S., Eskridge, KS; [occ.] Cook; [oth. writ.] "Sunrise In Your Eyes"; [pers.] Write from your heart and you can never be wrong.; [a.] Raytown, MO

HEIMAN, JOAN
[b.] December 8, 1930, Madison, WI; [p.] W. R. and Grace McCray; [m.] Ernie J. Heiman, April 26, 1952; [ch.] Beth, Julie, Kathleen, Joe; [occ.] Retired; [oth. writ.] 3 unpublished books and many poems.; [pers.] My husband was an Eng. teacher and author of text books. I was just a housewife. I have never entered or offered my work to anyone for publication. I am amazed!; [a.] Madison, WI

HEINEMANN, MARIE THERES
[pen.] Marie Theres; [b.] April 19, 1970, Los Banos, CA; [p.] Vibiana and Paul Neugebauer; [m.] Kirk A. Heinemann, September 18, 1993; [ch.] Haylie Sierra; [ed.] Los Banos High, Mercep College; [occ.] National Contract Coordinator; [oth. writ.] "Two Women" published on *Poetry Connection* on the World Wide Web; [pers.] It is said that the eyes are the windows to the soul, I say it's the words written from the heart.; [a.] Old Hickory, TN

HEISER, RENEE M.
[pen.] Marie Nicole Dekermarek; [b.] March 15, 1943, Dakar, Senegal, West Africa; [p.] Jacques and Jeanne Heiser from military family; [ed.] Elementary school in Mazagan Morocco College Tesse, 2 yrs., Toulon, France St. Robert Bellarmine School Burbank Cal Washington Irving H.S. New York City; [occ.] Customer Service Agent Air Canada Laguardia Apo New York; [memb.] Wrote from the heart! Inspired from Victor Hugo and many others; [hon.] Three medals from France Amerique and Washington Irving HS; [oth. writ.] Many France Amerique Washington Irving High School; [pers.] Can write anything under the difference of the manner - love to write and rhyme/French/English writing has no moments only feelings; [a.] New York, NY

HELD, MICHAEL WILLIAM
[b.] July 20, 1973, Allentown, PA; [p.] Mr. and Mrs. Clark Ellis Held; [ed.] Kutztown High and East Stroudsburg University, Lehigh County Community College also took courses at Kutztown University; [occ.] Part-time Professional Disc Jockey; [memb.] Kutztown Acre #839 Fraternal order of Eagles; [hon.] Various Awards for sports achievements in High School, trained in advanced first aid; [oth. writ.] Articles for the *East Penn. Publishing Company Newspaper* in all sports activities; [pers.] My writings reflect on past experiences as well as hopes in the future. I have been influenced greatly by Jim Morrison of the Doors.; [a.] Kutztown, PA

HENDERSON, DONALD E.
[b.] June 1, 1923, Bethel, OH; [p.] Adam E. Henderson and Bessie L. DeMaris; [m.] Carol J. Henderson, November 11, 1972; [ch.] Five; [ed.] H.S. Grad - College Credits in Spanish - Arithmetic - English - Geometry - Real Estate, Princ. and Pract., R. Est. Law, Finance, Appraising, Cont. Ep.; [occ.] Retired; [memb.] Pres. Miamitown Bus. Assoc., Pres. Great Miami Kiwanis - Past VP Local and State Gas. DLRS. Assoc., Pres. Sohio DLRS Assoc. - Founding Officer Antique Auto Club - Masonic Order and Shrine; [hon.] 6th Place in Clermont County 8th Year State Test - IQ 152 - Winner in Essay (Why I'm proud to be an American) Man of the year Award 1990 Miamitown Bus. Assoc. - Published in GC GDA Magazine - Super Service Station Magazine - O.D. Writers; [oth. writ.] Correspondence while ships person during WW II - pay masters and Asst. Off. Mgr. for Pope and Talbot S.S. Co., 19 Rector St., NYC, NY - writing and revising Const. Bus. Laws of Organizations - Assoc. Correspondence and articles for newspapers and other merit.; [pers.] I'm primarily interested in humorous things. Writing to me is something I do for my own pleasure, at my age I am not interested in pursuing another career. I have no financial need of new career.; [a.] Miamitown, OH

HENDRICKSON, ROBYN AYN
[b.] December 1, 1982, Nashville, TN; [p.] Robert and Judy Hendrickson; [ed.] In Progress Public School through 6th grade Home School - 7th Grade; [occ.] Full time Student; [memb.] Literary Society, Demitasse Club, Scottish Dancing Society; [hon.] Citizenship Awards, Outstanding Student Awards Art Awards and Music Awards Honor Roll -6th Grade; [a.] Kerresaw, GA

HENRY, REBECCA E.
[pen.] Rebecca, Becky; [b.] June 5, 1970, Dallas, TX; [p.] Cherie Lang and John Rubin; [ed.] Bachelor of Arts, May 1992, William Woods College - Fulton, Missouri; [occ.] Computer Programmer

HENSON JR., PAUL L.
[pen.] Paul L. Henson Jr.; [b.] December 6, 1958, Joplin, MO; [p.] Paul L. Henson Sr.; [m.] Susan Henson, June 27, 1992; [ch.] Stevie, Dustin, Amanda, Justice, Kyra; [ed.] 7 yrs. Joplin MO. Finished at Diamond MO. 77; [occ.] Self Emp. Henson Construction; [memb.] Central Christian Center, Joplin MO; [hon.] 2 yrs first place, baseball, ministry, (Reading Cert.: Spelling Cert.) in school; [oth. writ.] "Tears of a Candle," "My Beloved," "Burning Song"; [pers.] Hope to keep writing and keep looking into my self. To see me as God does learn more of His love. To do everyone good I meet; [a.] Joplin, MO

HERBERT, CESARINA MARIA
[pen.] Cesarina Maria Rossetti; [b.] August 23, 1911, Casto, Italy; [p.] Julio Rossetti and Angela Frassa Rossetti; [m.] Divorced; [ch.] (Daughter) Mariae Tumelty, Rossett Herbert and Claren Herbert (Son); [ed.] Burlingame High, Interstate College of Personology Delores Premiere School of Cosmetology; [occ.] Owner and Manager of Own Properties; [memb.] Girl Scout-Leader, Boy Scouts-Den Mother, American Red Cross, Swimming Instructor, Earthquake Safety Programs; [oth. writ.] Poems published in... *At Water's Edge, Best Poems Of 1996, Spirit Of The Age, A Muse To Follow, Where Dawn Lingers, Across The Universe, The Best Poems Of The '90's, Through The Hourglass.*; [pers.] In my writing, my goal is to express and project the basic reality of all life, as life is presented to me.; [a.] Hillsborough, CA

HERGAN, FRANCES
[b.] November 26, 1978, Wilkes-Barre, PA; [p.] Ruth Ann and David Hergan; [ed.] Seton Catholic High School; [occ.] Student at Dickinson College; [memb.] Student Council, National Honor Society, Students Against Drunk Driving, Key Club, Yearbook, Newspaper, Public Relations of the Student Ambassadors; [hon.] Graduating High School with Honors; [oth. writ.] An article published in a local newspaper, articles for a school newspaper.; [pers.] Live each day as if it were your last.; [a.] Harding, PA

HERNANDEZ, VERA A.
[m.] Miguel E. Hernandez, May 13, 1995; [ed.] Theodore Roosevelt, Junior High School, Elizabeth High School, Saint Mary's Grammar School, Elizabeth, N.J.; [occ.] Senior Data Entry Clerk Operator, Kean College of Union, New Jersey; [memb.] CVRA Local 1031; [hon.] "National Boards of Examiners" Penmanship Award - 1976, German Club Award, German Language Certificates-1978, 1979, 1980, Glee Club Award, 1980, Ecology Certificate 1975, Leadership Recognition Award, 9th grade, Honor Roll - 10th, 11th, 12th, grades, Received Gold Tassel.; [oth. writ.] Two other poems published in store news from Mayfair Supermarkets, Inc., Elizabeth, N.J. 1987, I enjoy writing song lyrics as well as poetry.; [pers.] Writing is an art form. The beauty of writing lies in the creative mind of every human being who strives for individuality and succeeds in the effort. I'm influenced by all kinds of poets.; [a.] Elizabeth, NJ

HERRIG, GARY L.
[pen.] Levon DuBue; [b.] July 24, 1953, Dubuque, IA; [p.] William and Joan Herrig; [m.] Rita M. Herrig, August 14, 1993; [ch.] Ross (10), Victor (1); [ed.] DuBuque Hempstead High, University of Iowa; [occ.] Training Specialist in Human Services; [memb.] Habitat for Humanity, The Arc of North Central Iowa, First United Methodist Church Council; [hon.] Cum Laude Graduate, Athletic Letterman's Club; [oth. writ.] Private collection of poems and muses, some published in newsletters.; [pers.] All my poems are based upon personal experience in love, nature, and death.; [a.] Mason City, IA

HESSELINK, TIMOTHY ALAN
[pen.] Tim; [b.] February 18, 1959, Muskegon Heights; [p.] Gerald Hesselink, Barbara Kennedy; [ed.] Muskegon Heights High S.T.C. Prod. Machine, I.P. Welding; [occ.] Carpenter, Contractor, Musician; [memb.] Singer song writer for various "punk rock" bands; [hon.] Editor's Choice award, for "Colors of Creation" in anthology *Tears of Fire* by N.L.P., selected to recite poetry at 1996 Olympics in Atlanta; [oth. writ.] "My Heart Gently Weeps," "Colors Of Creation," "No Place To Go But Up," "Another 4:am History," and "Big Lake," all published by N.L.P. in different anthologies; [pers.] My writings are all walks of life whether in nature or just every day. Ink from the heart; [a.] Muskegon, MI

HESTER, KELLY ANN
[b.] June 30, 1980, Mesa, AZ; [p.] David Hester, Joan Hester; [ed.] Rhodes Jr. High School Dobson High School; [memb.] Spurs Club, Dance Company, Renaissance Program; [hon.] Honor roll, student of the month, Renaissance Program, Perfect Attendance; [oth. writ.] Poem, "The Rose"; [pers.] Live life to it's fullest - be young, have fun and smile.; [a.] Tempe, AZ

HIATT, MARY
[pen.] Spangler, Retherford; [b.] March 10, 1953, California; [p.] Paul and Julia Morally; [ch.] Jacob Barnes, Artist Musician; [ed.] High School - some College classes - basically self taught - Street wise; [occ.] Government Administration/Private Consultant; [oth. writ.] 100 plus songs yet to be released and working on screen play.; [pers.] Writing is my release. I am sometimes surprised with the results.; [a.] Ukiah, CA

HICKS, ROBERT BOB F.
[pen.] A. P. Eman; [b.] September 5, 1958, Cocoa Beach, FL; [p.] John T. and Georgia A. Hicks; [m.] Susan, March 18, 1984; [ch.] Robert F. Hicks II; [ed.] High school Grad Ft Myers High in Ft. Myers Florida, one year college, Appalachian St. in Boone N.C.; [occ.] Roofing Lou. KY; [hon.] Athletic; [oth. writ.] Poetry in underground news paper in 1981 in Appalachian State Archives; [pers.] My writing is simple, easy to understand, as life should be but sadly isn't. You know what they ought to do!; [a.] Louisville, KY

HIGGINS, MS. N. LOY KUHN
[pen.] Loy; [b.] August 2, 1944, Louisville, KY; [p.] Arthur Louis Kuhn (Deceased) and Nina Waller Kuhn; [m.] Dr. David Michael Higgins, November 27, 1990; [ed.] Du Pot Manual High School, Louisville, KY, Class of '62 Eastern Kentucky State College, Richmond, KY, '62-64 Miami Dade Junior College, Miami, FL, '73-74, AA Degree. Fine Arts/General U of the State of New York, '86, Assoc. Degree, Liberal Arts and General Sciences (Regents Program), conferred Jan '87 Scottsdale Community College, Scottsdale, AZ, '95, studio Recording and Electronic Music; [occ.] Writer, Musician, Teacher, Desktop Publisher; [memb.] International Society of Poets, National Authors Registry, Adult Recital Series of AZ State Music Teachers Assn., Alliance Francis, Senior Friends; [hon.] Poems published in the National Library of Poetry's anthologies *A Voyage to Remember, A Muse to Follow, Amidst the Splendor, The Ebbing Tide, Memories of Tomorrow,* and *The Best Poems of the '90's,* the Modern Poetry Society of Dunnellon, FL's volume of modern poetry *Mirrors of the Soul,* The Mile High Poetry Society of Denver, CO's anthology *Muse.* Iliad Press Literary Anthologies *Crossings and Whispers,* and *The Marshall Islands Journal.* Honorable Mention, Pine Hills, NY Poetry Competition 1995, Honorable Mention, Iliad Press Fall 1995 Literary Awards Program, and two Editor's Choice Awards, The National Library of Poetry - 1996, Superior and Excellent Awards, National Federation Junior Festivals '93, '94, '95, Special Commendation, National Guild of Piano Teachers '93, '94, '95, and membership in the National Fraternity of Student Musicians, Student Division of American College of Musicians and Piano Hobbyists, ASMTA, Central District, 43rd Piano Ensemble, '95; [oth. writ.] Poems, humorous short stories, songs, and lyrics. Writer and publisher of Poetry Lines series. Arranger and performer of several keyboard cassette recordings, recorded in my previous home studio in Scottsdale, AZ; [pers.] As many people sharing one world, we travel different pathways to one destination, using music, poetry, and the arts to communicate and express our emotions.; [a.] Ajeltake, Majuro Atoll, MH

HIGGS, SHAREON E.
[pen.] Crystal Finn; [b.] December 17, 1940, Salt Lake City, UT; [p.] Allen and Enid Allington (Deceased); [m.] Earl Ronald Higgs, October 18, 1965; [ch.] Bonnie Skinner, married to Arnold Skinner, Two Grandchildren, Devin and Crystal. Son, Steve Higgs; [ed.] Graduated from Olympus High School, Holladay Utah, College of Eastern Utah in Price, UT, where I received my Associate's Degree in 1992. Most of my education and

writing has come from real life experiences.; [occ.] I work at Castle Valley Center as a trainer, Community Careers and Support Systems, Four Corners Mental Health as an advocate. I work with adults and children with disabilities, very talented wonderful people blessed with many talents and gifts. I try to instill in the people I work with that they are important. I also am an Artist. I teach oil painting classes and Indian Ceramics. I share these gifts with others. I am also a talented writer waiting for recognition in this field. I have a lot of poems and stories.; [memb.] I am a member of the Castle Valley Arts and Humanities Counsel, Utah SCBWI Children's Writers Society, Utah Association Alcoholism and Drug Abuse Counselors.; [hon.] Certificate of Award for Advocate Service at Four Corners Mental Health, Received an award from the Sweet'n Low great waiters competition, Carnation Community Service Award, 4-H leadership of Utah, School on Alcoholism and other Drug Dependencies. I was a participant in the 1995 1st annual Helper City Arts Festival.; [oth. writ.] Children's book: *Tille the Tooth Fairy* and *Tickle Monster*, Articles in local News Paper, *The Sun Advocate*, I am currently finishing a novel *The Crystal Child*, an autobiography, which I hope to have published this year.; [pers.] I was told by teachers I would not amount to much. Except for one English Teacher while in Jr. High in Holiday Utah, Mrs. Wagstaff. She told me to follow my dreams, I was important. I was dyslexic, not dumb, I was creative. The Dyslexia was not discovered till 1989. I now have many tools to help me. I ever went to College till age 48. I had wonderful tutors and teachers in College who helped me and believed in me. I believe its others who put negatives in our lives and we have to stop believing these negatives. Crystal children and adults are not like a piece of Crystal. We keep many things inside. I did for many years. My writing and art is therapy. I am writing for all the Crystal children of the world who are afraid. Maybe they can see in my writing the beautiful things in the world and hurtful. May they find God's handy work through my works. There will be rocks and boulders along the way but we can move them and walk forward in life. Those who have helped inspire me are: Betty J. Eadie, Marjorie Holms, Carolyn Sees, Nancy Takas, and many other great women writers. Especially Robert H. Schuller who has encouraged me and is a special spiritual friend.

HIGHTOWER, ELAYNE FISHER
[b.] September 14, 1947, Chester, PA; [p.] Beulah C. Fisher; [ed.] Albright College, BA - Psychology 1996, Chester High School 1965; [occ.] Unemployed; [hon.] Psi Chi, National Honor Society in Psychology, *Who's Who Among American Colleges and Universities*, Dean's List; [pers.] The truth about life is, it takes not only talent and hard work but luck to succeed.; [a.] Reading, PA

HILL, LISA ANN
[b.] June 23, 1981, Toledo, OH; [p.] Johnny Lee Hill, Ella M. Hill; [ed.] Old West End Jr. HS; [occ.] Student/ Volunteer at Central in math church-grand Central Station; [memb.] Young Authors - Elm. Glenwood; [oth. writ.] My own personal poem collection - unpublished; [pers.] I look at the world today and I see that death becomes us. Maybe in my generation or the next we can give life.; [a.] Toledo, OH

HILL, TOM
[pen.] TC; [b.] February 13, 1952, Atlanta, GA; [p.] Thomas L. Hill Sr., Imogene T. Hill; [ed.] Therell High (Atlanta, GA) B.S. Education - L.S.U. Baton Rouge, LA (1974); [occ.] Computer Systems Analyst/Army and Air Force Exchange; [memb.] L.S.U. Baseball Alumni Association, American Football Coaches Association; [hon.] 1980 District Championship (Baseball) Cedar Hill H.S. (Cedar Hill, TX) 1980 District Coach of the Year (Baseball); [oth. writ.] Numerous poems; [pers.] Personal Philosophy: "Whatever it takes."; [a.] Duncanville, TX

HILLE, STEVIE BROOKE
[b.] July 29, 1978, Shreveport, LA; [p.] Henry Lorne Hille, Charmaine Davenport Hille; [ed.] Salmen High School, Slidell, LA, graduated May, 1996. Scheduled to attend Louisiana State University; [occ.] Chef, Fisherman's Wharf, Slidell, LA; [oth. writ.] Wrote monthly article "Reality Bites" for 3 yrs. in high school paper.; [pers.] I just want to thank my grand parents, Robert and Mimi Richard of Shreveport, LA for their love and support.

HINTZ, AMY LYNN
[b.] February 27, 1978, Marshfield, WI; [p.] Bruce Allan Hintz Sr. and Joyce Ann Hintz; [ed.] Mosinee High School Graduate of 1996.; [pers.] My cherished moments and feelings are expressed in my writings in hope that some day I can reminisce and share with someone a piece of myself. I am inspired by all of God's wondrous creations and only through Him have I found my true self.; [a.] Mosinee, WI

HIRATA, KEITH H.
[b.] July 9, 1973, Honolulu, HI; [ed.] University of Hawaii Laboratory School, University of Puget Sound; [occ.] Customer Service Representative, DFS Hawaii; [oth. writ.] Poems published in *Crosscurrents Review*, University of Puget Sound's Student Anthology; [pers.] During the day he collects dead geckoes from around the house, while at night he tries to tell international travellers that they really need their airline tickets.

HOBSON, RICHARD L.
[pen.] R. L. Hobson; [b.] January 23, 1984, Phoenix, AZ; [p.] Elizabeth and William R. Hobson; [ed.] Awakening Seed School, Meyer Elementary, McKemy Middle School; [occ.] Student; [hon.] Principal's Honor Roll 1995-96; [pers.] My soccer team 1st in the under 12 boys for West Regionals in 1996!; [a.] Tempe, AZ

HOCKETT, CARRIE
[b.] October 5, 1975, Downey, CA; [p.] Jerry Hockett, Vera Hockett; [ed.] Temecula Valley High, University of California, Riverside (UCR); [occ.] Student at UCR, Bakery Clerk at Hughes Family Market; [hon.] Dean's List; [pers.] Writing is important to me because it documents my past, helps me focus on the present, and looks forward to the future. I want to thank my family and friends for always being there and supporting me and my choices. I love you!; [a.] Murrieta, CA

HODGE, CHUN TAY A.
[b.] January 2, 1969, San Francisco, CA; [p.] Keith S. Hodge, Leotta A. Stamps; [ed.] Rainier Beach H.S. Diploma - 1987 Seattle Central Com. Coll. 1987-1990 graduate A.A. Degree, National Broadcasting School - 1991 graduate; [occ.] Professional Sales Telemarketing Operator; [memb.] Vacations Worldwide Equinox International Environmental Business; [hon.] National Quill and Scroll for H.S. Journalist, feature and Best Editorial writing awards; [oth. writ.] Oral Folklore - family history 10 pg. documentation research. Journalism: Editorial, features poems, creative writings; [pers.] I have truly had a sincere desire to write creatively and freely spirited and inspired by the things around me. I hope one day to be an accomplished writer, something really special.; [a.] Seattle, WA

HOLTON, SANDRA P.
[b.] August 8, 1959, Camden, NJ; [p.] Hildegand Traute Wigelies, Elvin Agar Holton; [occ.] Administrative Secretary; [oth. writ.] Published in two (2) other anthologies.; [pers.] Our world is steering toward a new age of spiritual awakening of which, the sharing of each our own virtues, denotes a noble contribution. I am honored to participate in this realm of enlightenment.; [a.] Tampa, FL

HONSTEIN, DIANA EARLINE
[b.] August 31, 1965, Portland, OR; [p.] Walter and Sandra Honstein; [ed.] Cleveland High, Mt. Hood Community College, Portland State University; [occ.] Event planner/sales/modeling; [memb.] Doris Day Animal League, P.E.T.A., Gorilla Foundation; [hon.] Gifted Children's Program, Superstar Athletic award, Shorthand Merit Award, Sophomore Class Christmas Princess, Girls League, Yearbook Staff, George S. Turnbull Yearbook Service Certificate, Quill and Scroll Honorary Society; [oth. writ.] Father's Day article in local newspaper; [pers.] God has blessed me with loving and supportive parents which greatly influences my writing as well as all aspects of my life.; [a.] Portland, OR

HOOLIHAN, JESSICA
[b.] April 14, 1981, Largo, FL; [p.] Pamela Hoolihan, Tim Hoolihan; [ed.] I am currently a student at River Ridge High School; [occ.] Full Time Student; [oth. writ.] I write poetry and songs solely for enjoyment. I write based on my own life experiences, and feelings.; [pers.] I have been greatly influenced by my parents, my great friend Shannon Isenheart, and the Love Of My Life John Kuhn. They have me great things.; [a.] New Port Richey, FL

HOOVER, CHRISTOPHER D.
[pen.] Chris; [b.] September 5, 1965, Highpoint, NC; [p.] Mr. Dale J. Hoover and Mrs. Phyllis Hoover; [m.] Elise Belen Hoover, May 3, 1919; [ed.] (1) year: The American College of Art in Atlanta, (1) year: Univ. of S.C., various schools in the U.S. Navy and Coast Guard, Chapman School of Seamanship; [occ.] Navigator (Maritime); [memb.] National Meritime Historical Society; [hon.] Good Conduct Medal, Letter of Commendation Medal, Humanitarian Medal, Sea Service Ribbon, Honorable Discharge of the U.S. Navy and V.S. Coast Guard; [oth. writ.] None at this time.; [a.] Highpoint, NC

HOPE, MARY MCNAMARA
[b.] January 25, 1907; [m.] Duncan W. Hope; [ch.] Robert Hope, Kathryn Handley; [ed.] (New Britain Normal School) Central Connecticut State University; [pers.] Graduating from college at 18, I taught in a one-room school house. My husband and I raised our children in my hometown of Rocky Hill, CT. We enjoy traveling to California to visit our grandchildren, boating and motor home trips. I always enjoyed poetry and writing and started writing for pleasure at the age of 89. Special topics include poems about friends, family and nature.; [a.] Plymouth, MA

HORN, ANGELA KAY
[b.] January 28, 1978, Las Cruces, NM; [p.] Clifford R. Horn and Patricia K. Horn; [ed.] Graduate of Mayfield High School will be attending Southwestern Assembly of God University in the fall; [occ.] Daycare Teacher of

a 3 yr. old class at Noah's Ark Learning Center; [memb.] Church Youth Group; [hon.] Superior Vocal Soloist at Fine Arts Festival, Song at High School Graduation, Award of Superior Achievements Chorus; [oth. writ.] Essay on Martin Luther poetry book "When Angels Cry" short story "Destiny"; [pers.] Writing is the uncensored expression of the heart.

HOROWITZ, STEPHANIE
[b.] February 21, 1981, Long Island; [p.] Ester and Michael Horowitz; [ed.] Calhoun High School USDAN Center for the arts Suburan Temple Hebrew School; [occ.] High School Student 10th grade; [memb.] National Thesbian Society, Calhoun on Tour (drama) Company, Calhoun Choral Program: Crescendo Soundwave, Calhoun Madrigals, Calhoun Choir; [hon.] Outstanding Vocal Talent, Cultural Arts (vocal) Award, Outstanding Academic Achievement (Thespian Society); [oth. writ.] School Newspaper; [pers.] There are no broad generalizations about life, or the arts, or anything. As Pat Riley (the former coach of the NY Knicks) said: The only thing constant about life is that it is always changing and nothing stays constant.; [a.] North Merrick, NY

HORTON, ALDINE F.
[pen.] Al Horton; [b.] March 15, 1942, Siler City, NC; [p.] Millard and Edna Horton; [m.] Hertie G. Horton, December 13, 1965; [ch.] Kris M. and Alan F.; [ed.] Chatham High School, N.C. State University, Shaw University, Southeastern Theo. Seminary; [occ.] Postmaster (Retired); [oth. writ.] Unpublished poems, Moral Issues; [pers.] To do what is right, rather than what I have the right to do.; [a.] Raleigh, NC

HOVIS, CHARLOTTE LYNN
[pen.] Charlyvis; [b.] July 21, 1960, Burns, OR; [p.] Russell W. Hovis, Betty J. Ashcraft; [ch.] Karen Marie and Jaclyn Denise; [pers.] May the poetic reflections of my soul intoxicate your sense.; [a.] Redding, CA

HOWARD, PAULETTE P.
[b.] April 10, 1945, Atlanta, GA; [p.] Paul and Mary Lee Pirkle; [m.] Jerry E. Howard, April 10, 1965; [ch.] Terry and Howard; [occ.] Retired from Bellshouth; [memb.] Atlanta Songwriters Assoc, Ascap, Oakwood Baptist Church Luganville Ga., Telephone Pioneers and CWA Life Member; [hon.] Ascap Awards, Numerous Songwriting Contests, Atlanta Songwriter Assoc Awards; [oth. writ.] Songwriting for 16 1/2 yrs. country and gospel; [pers.] This is my first try at poetry. I am honored to be a semi-finalist, I have had many recordings of my country and Gospel songs.; [a.] Decatur, GA

HUDSON, JODY S.
[b.] April 16, 1964, La Mesa, CA; [p.] William and June V. Nunn; [m.] David B. Hudson, June 7, 1986; [ch.] Daniel Brian and Staci Kae; [ed.] Liberty Christian High, Lakeside CA., Bunker Hill Community College, Boston, MA.; [occ.] Mother, Author, Tele-Communications Manager; [memb.] ALS Association, American Red Cross, First Congregational Church, Cub Adoptee Awareness; [hon.] Valedictorian, numerous awards from the accordion federation of North America, Honors in Tele-Communications; [oth. writ.] Several poems, songs and children's stories.; [pers.] To show judgement only demonstrates a lack of knowledge and respect for someone else's world.; [a.] Lake Forest, CA

HUDSON, LILLIE MAE
[b.] February 17, 1927, Arcadia, FL; [p.] William and Mamie Ming; [m.] Ira Lee Hudson, June 17, 1952; [ch.] Annie, Betty, Mary and Rosalee; [ed.] High School Duval County High Jacksonville, Fla.; [occ.] Cannery Worker and Housewife; [hon.] I've had two honorable mentions for two poems I wrote. From Editor! Eddie Loucole; [pers.] I strive to think and believe that there is some good in each one of us. I never had a great deal of education but I do like to think that we all need to come together and love one another. I'm happy I had this chance to write a poem on how I feel.; [a.] Federalsburg, MD

HUGHES, SHARICE
[pen.] Sharice Hughes; [b.] March 27, 1975, Lakeview Terrace, CA; [p.] Sherry Pierce; [ed.] Sylmar High School Graduate; [hon.] Honor Roll - Elem - Jr. High Merit Award - Jr. High numerous others - Jr. High - High; [pers.] My greatest influences come from having a strong mother and a supportive brother. I've been lucky to have them by my side.; [a.] Lancaster, CA

HUGHES, WANDA DENTON
[b.] June 26, 1962, Wake Co; [p.] Johnny Denton & Carol Cook; [m.] Donald J. Hughes, January 15, 1983; [ch.] twins (Michael & Catherine Hughes); [ed.] East Wake, Otto High, MI; [occ.] Rep. for Gibson Greeting Cards; [hon.] Editors Choice Award on a child to live alone; [oth. writ.] I have had 2 poems published; [pers.] I put my felings and experiences in my poetry.; [a.] Spring Hope, NC

HULLENDER, JANICE GAYLE
[b.] May 31, 1940, Greensboro, NC; [p.] Jo Horner & Donnell Johnson; [m.] Cliff Hullender, February 19, 1977; [ch.] Danielle, Stevan & Wyndal Cook - Step children: Chip, Melissa, Leigh & Michael Hullender; [ed.] Clinton High Schiil - SC, Business School - NYC 1960-62; [occ.] Antiques Dealer; [oth. writ.] A book of family poems, several poems published. Writing a biography on my daughter, Danielle, who passed away in August 7th, 1996.; [pers.] I want future generations to feel like they knew our family through my poems, especially seeing my wonderful children in North Carolina in the 40's through my eyes.; [a.] Chattanooga, TN

HUNSINGER, VIRGINIA
[b.] January 8, 1934, Perry, NY; [p.] Meora and Moore Billings Sr.; [m.] Charles E. Hunsinger, April 1, 1956; [ch.] Patricia Kathleen, Cristine Faye, Timothy Charles; [ed.] GED Child Care Substitute Teacher for Headstart program; [occ.] House Wife; [oth. writ.] I have always been afraid to enter poems, because I didn't think they were that good. I have written other poems and short stories for my grandchildren I have always liked poetry. It is a good way of expressing your feelings.; [pers.] My daughters and husband told me I should enter your contest with "Memorial Day"!; [a.] Silver Springs, NY

HUNT, KATIE
[pen.] Katie Hunt/Kathy Rose; [b.] January 9, 1981, Hartford, WI; [p.] Linda Hunt & Dyson Hunt; [ed.] Sophmore at Slinger High School; [occ.] McDonald's employee; [memb.] Future Business Leaders of America, S.A.D.D.(Students Against Drunk Driving), German Club; [hon.] High honor roll every year (4.0), Presidential Academic Fitness Award, numerous art and english awards, class president; [oth. writ.] "Untitled", "Death", "Silenced" (Flaid Press), "Monsters Under the Bed" (Amherst Society), "Why", "Trapped", "Minds", "Dear God" (Wexford Publishing Company, Ltd.) and articles & poems in the school newspaper.; [pers.] 1) Remember yesterday's "greats", for it's all you have to build tomorrow's "betters" from. 2) True love is never lost, it is only forgotten.; [a.] Hartford, WI;

HUNT, PAMELA
[b.] November 4, 1967, York, PA; [p.] Connie and Gary Horner; [m.] Joel Hunt, June 22, 1991; [ch.] Joshua 3 1/2 yrs., Kacey 5 mths.; [ed.] BA in Communications, Journalism from Shippensburg University. Currently enrolled in Correspondence Courses from the Institute of Children's Literature; [occ.] Stay home mom, volunteer at a Domestic Violence Shelter; [pers.] The main goal for my writings whether they be stories or poems is to encourage people to appreciate what they have and respect those around them.

HUNTE, LORI CHRISTOPHERSON
[b.] December 4, 1966, Milwaukee, WI; [p.] Donald and Judith Christopherson; [m.] Stuart Hunte, December 22, 1990; [ch.] Stephen Hunte; [ed.] Bachelors of Science in Nursing from Old Dominion University, Norfolk, VA with a minor in creative writing - poetry; [occ.] Registered Nurse at several diverse medical facilities in the state of CT; [hon.] Dean's List; [oth. writ.] Although my writings have been contained for only personal use, I strive for future publication of my writings; [pers.] Nursing may allow my hands to heal others, but it is my words and my realities that write the poetry that heals me.; [a.] Groton, CT

HUSBAND, MESHANTE KENYO
[b.] May 23, 1972, Detroit, MI; [p.] Loretta Mason; [ch.] Kyle Norman-Daniel Husband; [ed.] Oakland University, Frank Cody H.S.; [occ.] Terminal Equipment Operator; [hon.] National Journalism Award; [oth. writ.] Several Selective Poems unpublished; [pers.] To inspire, by the manipulation of words, to the freeing of one's soul of many of life's expectations and/or experiences, to create harmony or peace within one's mind even a peace, God gives; [a.] Detroit, MI

HUSTON, SANDI
[pen.] Sandi; [b.] February 2, Oklahoma City, OK; [p.] O. M. and Lillian Evans; [ch.] Melissa Peterson, Nichollette Porter; [oth. writ.] "Mask Of Humanity"

HYLAND, KENNETH
[b.] May 27, 1960, Staten Island, NY

ILOSKY, ESTHER R.
[b.] July 10, 1960, Weirton, WV; [p.] Loyd Garner, Regina Garner; [m.] Edward M. Ilosky, September 5, 1980; [ch.] Adam M. Ilosky, Jenna M. Ilosky; [ed.] Weir High School currently attending West Virginia Northern Community College for Associate in Arts Degree; [occ.] Housewife; [pers.] This poem was written for my parents Loyd and Regina Garner and the great love they have shared.; [a.] Weirton, NY

IOSIF, CECILIA D.
[pen.] Cela, Cici, Celuta; [b.] November 10, 1981, Romania; [p.] Livia and Nicolae Iosif; [ed.] Student, going into 9th grade at Foothill Highschool; [occ.] Student; [hon.] In 6th grade got 3rd place at the district science fair, and in 8th grade got 2nd place in the district science fair; [pers.] I would like to thank my parents, and my sister Alina for encouraging me to do this. I really appreciate it, thank you again.; [a.] Pleasanton, CA

IRIZARRY, MELISA A.
[b.] August 30, 1986, New York City; [p.] Natalie Bautista and Henry Irizarry; [ed.] Attending Elementary School 58 in the Bronx; [hon.] In Drama and Spelling; [a.] Bronx, NY

ISENBERG, MILDA
[b.] February 21, 1922, Lithuania, KS; [p.] Liudas and Petronele Rutelionis; [m.] Irwin Isenberg, February 2, 1956; [ch.] Errol Clyde, Brenda Nadine; [ed.] High School in Lithuania Hunter College, New York, BA Fletcher School of Law and Diplomatic, MA, NYU School of Social Work, MSW; [occ.] Retired Social Worker; [memb.] NASW, Hardassah UN Association of Former Int'l Civil Servants; [hon.] Dean's List, Hunter College, Scholarship: Fletcher School of Law and Diplomacy, My State 2 Year Scholarship towards MSW Degree; [pers.] My interest is in education and dissemination of knowledge among the greatest number of people. My dream is of humanity coexisting in peace, harmony and economic self-sufficiency throughout the globe so that our energies could turn toward appreciation of finer things in life, poetry among them.; [a.] Fort Lauderdale, FL

IZELL, DOROTHY JEANNE
[pen.] Dorothy J. Izell; [b.] July 27, 1917, Imlay City, MI; [p.] Robert Barrows Wright, Martha B. Wells; [m.] John H. Izell (Deceased October 1, 1987), October 16, 1949; [ed.] High School, 2 yrs. S.F. City College, stanford Palo Alto, Ca., Special Education Licensed Audiometer Technician; [occ.] Retired; [memb.] 40 yrs. Eastern Star, V.F.W. Ladies Auxiliary, life long membership in the human race, Colony So. Baptist Church Fort Smith, Ark.; [hon.] Since I have been composing poetry for over 70 years, it has been for my own amazement, and the amusement of my family and friends. My mother (School teacher) encouraged each of her 8 children to express themselves learning and writing poetry and skits. It has been an honor and a pleasure for me. She wrote poetry, as well as her children and grandchildren. One of my sisters is a "V.I.P." published poet for the National Library of Poetry. It is a double honor for me to be a semi finalist as I am blind and physically handicapped.; [oth. writ.] Poems published in S.F. Examiner, Phoenix Sun, Fort Smith *Times Record*, Ark., *Greenwood Weekly*, Ark., Huntington *Star*, Ark.; [pers.] My poetry is influenced by religious up bringing, especially St. Paul (A.K.A. Saul).; [a.] Fort Smith, AR

JACKSON, HENRY
[b.] March 21, 1917, Centesville, TX; [p.] John and Willie Billups Jackson; [m.] Ruth E. Jackson, June 7, 1963; [ch.] Jeannette, Rosalind, Jackson; [ed.] BA, Wiley College, MA, Denver Univ. Doctoral Studies USC DD Mary Allen College; [occ.] Dir. The Outreach Ministry of Reconciliation EMOC, INC; [memb.] AMEC, OBE, AM and FM, NAACP, AASA; [hon.] Only Black Suptmember of Texas School Integration on (1955), Founder Hope AMEC, Praises View Texas, Inc. of Every Man Ministry of Christ, Inc.; [oth. writ.] *Bl Lines of Living*, (Gospel Monthly) "These Living Dead," "Power," "Tip-Toeing On The Edge of a Vision," and "Save the Children"; [pers.] The world becoming flesh in you now! "If you don't know who you are or, where you came from, you don't know where you're going". My greatest concern at this age is to save the children.; [a.] Houston, TX

JACKSON, JAZLYN N.
[pen.] Marcela Meletti; [b.] April 26, 1979, Torrance, CA; [p.] Marcela Meletti, Glen Jackson; [ed.] Senior at Ramona High School in Riverside California; [occ.] Employee of Burger King; [hon.] Honor Roll, Music Award (Band), Academic Award (G.P.A. - 3.8); [oth. writ.] Poems including "Darkened Black Walls", "In Between", "No Way Out", "White Diamonds", and "In The Past"; [pers.] I write about what I know most... and that is my life.; [a.] Riverside, CA

JACKSON, SANDRA S.
[b.] June 12, 1939, Canton, OH; [p.] Mrs. Sue E. Buchanan; [ed.] AA Degree Fine Arts; [occ.] Mechanical Technician Video, Building Poker Mach.; [hon.] Military Commendation Letters and Achievement Award; [oth. writ.] I sung on a single and a multi-artists album "Can't Stay Any Longer" sung by Wil Gentry.; [pers.] Oh, to care less about ourselves alone, and put all our energies into the universe and pray for peace...

JAHN, SHANNAN K.
[b.] March 15, 1971, Scott AFB, IL; [p.] Denny and Becky O'Connor; [m.] Eric Jahn, February 14, 1994; [ch.] Step-daughters Ashley and Britiney; [ed.] Sophomore at University of North Dakota; [occ.] Nursing Assistant/Registered in Minnesota; [memb.] I am a Member of Women's Ministries. I was a reservist in the U.S. Army. I was a missionary to Costa Rica through Teen Mania Ministries.; [oth. writ.] I have a children's book in progress titled *Sam's Shadow*.; [pers.] This poems "they" reflects my view of human interaction in the 21st Century...a sort of Pluto, a spectator of all that hovers under my feet.; [a.] Grand Forks, ND

JANKAS, DENISE VINCENT
[pen.] D. K. Vincent; [b.] July 15, 1950, Troy, OH; [p.] Aileen and Thomas Vincent (Both Deceased); [m.] Divorced; [ch.] Julie Coate, Molly Coate, Thomas Jankas; [ed.] Bowling Green State Univ., Wright State Univ., Wittenberg Univ., Salem College, Hocking Technical College, Travel; [occ.] RN, Travel Agent, Novice Lyric writer; [memb.] American Association of Songwriters listed in National Association of Female Executives Directory; [hon.] Will be on upcoming "Songwriters International II" to be released in fall; [oth. writ.] Currently have 7 demo songs in production. Dreaming of publication.; [pers.] My search for spirituality has led me to write. I hope I can touch a few souls and inspire them to reach for their dreams.; [a.] Stuart, FL

JARLENSKI, KATHRYN
[b.] February 15, 1973, Wilmington, DE; [p.] Morris and Judy Jarlenski; [ed.] Shaker High School, Hudson Valley Community College; [occ.] Account Specialist, The Feroline Group of Upstate NY; [hon.] President's List; [pers.] The world is a very beautiful place. You just have to open your life to it. The power of expression has taught me to appreciate everything in this world, for what it is, and not what I wish it to be.; [a.] Latham, NY

JERNIGAN, MARIE E.
[b.] November 4, 1939, Manchester, TN; [p.] T. H. Lusk Sr., Izzie Lusk; [m.] William Earl Jernigan Jr., June 26, 1968; [ch.] Mickie Bowen, Jeff Bowen; [ed.] Hickerson Station School Swain's School of Plant-Care and Landscaping; [occ.] Cashier, Collectible Doll Dealer; [memb.] Red Hill Church of Christ, Dolls Collectible Club Fashion Club, Charitable Community Clubs; [hon.] Employee of the year 1991, K-Mart #9229, Short Story Writing Comp, Poetry Writing Com; [oth. writ.] Several poems published in newspapers, two songs recorded. Poem selected for book; [pers.] Writing is my way of putting my inner most feelings down on paper. I hope my writings can bring a ray of sunshine into someone's day; [a.] Manchester, TN

JIMENEZ JR., EUGENIO
[b.] January 12, 1967, Miami, FL; [p.] Eugenio Jimenez and Lourdes Diaz; [ed.] St. Brendan H.S., Miami Dade Comm. College; [occ.] Clerk and Freelance Writer; [oth. writ.] Compiling (to date) over 150 poems, and short stories, and screenplays.; [pers.] My goals are to become a prominent literary figure through merit. My style is very unconventional and my subjects tend to deal with the youths of today and their ordeals to get through daily life.; [a.] Miami, FL

JOHNSON, C. J.
[pen.] Carmen Smith; [b.] October 12, 1981, Las Vegas, NV; [p.] Shannon Hume, Charles Johnson; [m.] Kara Howarth; [ed.] Thurman White Middle School; [occ.] Full time student at Greenvalley High; [oth. writ.] Poems for school newspaper; [pers.] Pretty good for a fourteen year old who's in the finals; [a.] Henderson, NV

JOHNSON, CURT
[pen.] Nathan St. John, Remy Burdeau; [b.] September 14, 1980, New York; [p.] Anesta Helen Johnson, Elton Johnson; [ed.] Junior in East Brooklyn, Congregation High School for Public Service East New York; [occ.] Student at EBC High School for Public Service East New York; [memb.] 92nd St Y Poetry writing program. Our Lady Of Good Counsel, Teen Youth Clubs; [hon.] Nynex Landmark Essay, Water Wavys Project. English, Global Studies, Tanvage: Spanish. Public Service; [oth. writ.] EBC High School Poetry Journals, Water Ways Project Book of personal poems.; [pers.] The trials of life are hard but you can overcome all that you are faced with. No matter what anyone says follow all of your heart's desires to the fullest. Peace and harmony will always guide you.; [a.] Brooklyn, NY

JOHNSON, DEAN
[pen.] Mama; [b.] May 18, 1966, Chicago, IL; [p.] Dean Massey - Roberta Johnson; [m.] Laurie Ann Keller Johnson, October 21, 1990; [ch.] Justine, Kaitlyn, Sarah Johnson; [occ.] State of Illinois Dept. of Correction Juvenile Division St. Charles; [memb.] Nation of Islam; [pers.] Do as the spider does. Construct in your mind a carefully woven trap and lead a straight life into it. Only come out when there is something positive about and snatch it.; [a.] Chicago, IL

JOHNSON, KATHRYN L.
[pen.] Flower; [b.] April 25, 1955, Quantico, VA; [p.] James W., Joan E. Bowen; [m.] Garth C. Johnson, June 6, 1990; [ch.] Catrina, Crystal, Savannah, Brandon, Kimberley; [ed.] Waitress, College Student, Liberal Arts; [pers.] In loving memory of my father, James Walker Bowen, I have always loved you, 1934-1989.; [a.] Redding, CA

JOHNSON, LILLIAN
[b.] September 22, 1932, Bath, ME; [p.] Glenwood and Dora Sukeforth; [m.] William Johnson, March 26, 1976; [ch.] Mae Ellen, Jim, Melody, Elizabeth, Carolyn, Glenda, stepchildren Ann, Ray, Wesley; [pers.] When Jim died shortly before our 25th Anniversary I felt my life was over, except for the love of our 5 children. God, however, had other plans and sent me Bill, also a father of 5. We have just celebrated 20 rich and wonderful years together, which includes becoming grandparents to fourteen, and now a great-grandchild. Since selling our Farm in 1986, we have traveled to Israel, served as retirement home and taken a camping trip to the Northwest. I now enjoy pursuing my hobbies of writing and painting.; [a.] Waldoboro, ME

JOHNSON, LINDA MAY
[pen.] Linaka; [b.] March 27, 1973, Yokohama, Japan; [p.] Stuart Miles Johnson, Nokila H. Burice; [ch.] 2 children; [ed.] I currently Attend Maui Comm. College During Night School; [occ.] I do daily tour operation on in main and work at a Japanese Restaurant; [oth. writ.] I did a newspaper article on Pres. Bush; [a.] Kihei, Maui, HI

JOHNSON, MEL, JR.
[pen.] Robert Wesley; [b.] January 29, 1944, Amarillo; [p.] Mel & Marion Johnson; [m.] Carolyn Johnson, November 30, 1992; [ch.] Sandra Lee Johnson, now studying computer art animation, Indianapolis, IN; [ed.] Attended Cleveland Hill H.S. Buffalo, NY 1960-62, attended Admiral King H.S. Lorain, OH 1962, Graduated From Livermore H.S. Livermore, KY class of "63", Instition of Childrens Literature "93"; [occ.] Retired from U.S. Coast Guard - 1963-68, Vietnam Veteran; [memb.] Life member D.A.V. since 68, AARP National Geographic Society, Texaco Travel Club (I've traveled to Canada 1959-60, Mexico "67", Bogota, Columbia "81" San Juan, Puerto Rico "83") [hon.] Honarable Discharge, good conduct medal from U.S. Coast Guard "68", taught Literacy at adult education center, Longfellow School, Owensboro, KY 1986-88, received Editors Choice Award "96", International Society of Poes 1995-96; [oth. writ.] "My Appalachian Mule", published true stories in KY & Ark newspapers about working as an extra in the Kentuckian Film "1955" starring Burt Lancascter who died in "94", "Famous poems of the 20th Century" Nov. of 96; [pers.] I feel that if your born with a God given talent for writing stories & poems then you should use it or lose it. Many of my ideas are from personal experiences.; [a.] Huntington, Ark.

JOHNSON, RICHARD B.
[pen.] Ric Johnson; [b.] August 16, 1952, Marietta, OH; [ch.] Jessica Adrienne Johnson; [hon.] Highest Academic Achievement Jerry Haynes Clinical Excellence Award Spanish National Honor Society Sigma Tau Delta English Honor Society; [oth. writ.] Multiple unpublished poems.; [pers.] Despite life's trial it is your choice to live in sadness or to live in gladness. Choose joy, and live love! Our past is irretrievable, the future imaginary. Live in the now.; [a.] Silver Spring, MD

JOHNSON, STEVEN R.
[b.] July 22, 1963, Springfield Delaware County, PA; [p.] James C. and Cynthia P. Johnson; [m.] Lisa Coughlin (to be), March 1997; [ch.] Steven Michael, Erica Marie Johnson, Stepchildren Nicolas Coughlin; [ed.] B.S. Chemistry, Ursinus College, Collegeville, PA; [occ.] Process Development Chemist; [oth. writ.] Just a few unpublished things that I'm trying to put to music; [pers.] Listen to your angels....they're there to help you.; [a.] Taunton, MA

JOHNSON, WILLIAM P.
[b.] September 20, 1965, Los Angeles, CA; [p.] M. M. - Constance Alene Miracle; [ch.] Paul Christopher (3), Michael Williams (2); [ed.] Yucca Valley High, (Trade School) Supervisor Tracking School (Rialto CA) Copper Mountain College - Intro to Computers; [occ.] Early retirement studying to become a successful entrepreneur; [oth. writ.] I currently hold other poems that I have written, thru phases of my life changes. Anyone seeking special interests may contact National Library of Poetry.; [pers.] During writing my anthologies, I have initiative feelings that motivated my visions, that transpires from reality to realization to team up with a famous musical celebrity a voice as magical as Whitney Houston, Mariah Carey is my dream.

JOHNSTON, VIRGINIA A. ROSE
[pen.] Virginia A. Rose-Johnston; [b.] November 27, 1917, Lansing, IL; [p.] Howard C. Rose, Ila Stroupe Rose; [m.] Donald Jennings Johnston (Deceased), June 29, 1940; [ch.] Thomas Whitney Johnston, Faye Johnston, Lili Johnston Copp; [ed.] B.Ph. Siena Heights College, M.Ed. Florida Atlantic University; [occ.] Ret. Educator, Broward County Schools (Eng.) 1958-1979; [memb.] Pompano Beach Historical Society, Opus Society of the Symphony, Pompano Book Club; [hon.] Fla. H.S., Speech Teacher Rep. to Southern Speech Assoc., Outstanding Senior -1986, City of Pompano Beach, Fla.; [oth. writ.] *Dramatics* Magazine Apr. '71, May '71, Educ. Research Service, Natl. Educ. Assoc. 1968, *Apropos - Unima* - U.S.A. Spring 1976, Puppeteers of America, Get up and go! *Agewave* May '95 Publication, *Travel Host* Magazine Jan. '95; [pers.] Univ. of Georgia - 1971, Taught - 1984-85-86, Jilin College of Finance and Trade, Chang Chun, China; [a.] Boca Raton, FL

JONES, ALEXISS C.
[b.] December 16, 1978; [p.] Myrna Jones; [ed.] Canyon Springs High School. To the present.; [occ.] Marketing Intern. Moreno Valley Mall. Modeling; [oth. writ.] I have several other writings which were never published.; [pers.] Each day I take a step into the world, to strive toward accepting all at that I am and becoming all that I want to be.; [a.] Moreno Valley, CA

JONES, DANIEL MICHAEL
[b.] June 11, 1949, Chicago, IL; [p.] Richard and Betty E. Jones; [oth. writ.] Since 1991 I have had many editorials published in the *Tacoma News Tribune*, and *The Olympian*; [pers.] "The Poor and just," reflects much of the pain I have experienced in my Life. However, I did not understand my pain fully until I read of Christ's crucifixion in "Mathew": 27-46.; [a.] Olympia, WA

JONES, FLORENCE M.
[pen.] Florencia; [b.] April 11, 1939, West Columbia; [p.] Isaiah and LuEthel McNeil; [m.] Waldo D. Jones, May 29, 1965; [ch.] Roderick Wanda and Erna; [ed.] Prairie View A&M University (Cum laude) BS 1961, Med - 1968 (Same University) Post Grad. Rice University, University of Houston; [occ.] Piano Instructor Writer, Storyteller; [memb.] Life: Retired Teacher, Association, Association for Childhood Ed. and Distinguished Life Member of the International Society of Poets, National Women of Achievement Oak Meadows Church of God; [hon.] Three Editor's Choice Awards Outstanding Achievement in Education, Letters of Recognition, President Bill Clinton, Gov. Ann Richards, and George Bush Diamond Key Award, National Women of Achievement; [oth. writ.] "Follow Your Dream, Multidimensional Personal, Growth and Development Program," Poems: Sparrowgrass and National Lib. of Poetry Anthologies, Gifted and Talented Program for Pietism Elem. School; [pers.] Pets add interesting dimension to our lives. Cocon was a brilliant and affective puppy. She helped me to understand the value of love regardless of who shares it and why.; [a.] West Columbia, TX

JONES, JESSIE SELLERS
[b.] January 5, 1914, Olympia, WA; [p.] Donald D. Sellers; [ed.] Achieved a two year College Business Major, and began inspiring others through her own Employment Agency; [occ.] Teacher of Salesmanship and Traffic Manager, she eventually became President of 18 Apartment Buildings

JONES, KEITH DAVID
[b.] September 13, 1967, Springfield, MA; [p.] Barbara and David Jones; [ed.] Bowdoin College, Bachelor's Degree, Double Major Government Legal Studies/Sociology; [occ.] Business Analyst Continuum/Vantage Computer Systems; [memb.] Alpha Delta Phi, Amnesty International, LOMA, NASD; [hon.] James Bowdoin Scholar; [oth. writ.] *Papaveracea* 1988 self-published, Editor Bowdoin College *Black Current* 1987-88, Poetry published in *Springfield Journal* Newspaper 1995, Dancing and Drowning in the Shallow Waters - unpublished 1993; [pers.] I write and self-publish poetry because, like Thomas Paine, I believe freedom is owning one's own printing press. I am influenced by Langston Hughes, Dunbar, William Blake, and Keats, and Amaranth Sepia.; [a.] Springfield, MA

JONES, RASHUNDA D.
[b.] July 27, 1981; [p.] Errol and Rose Mary Jones; [ed.] High school student Wharton High School; [memb.] Jr. National Honor Society Soph Class President

JONES, WILLIAM H.
[pen.] William Henry Jones, W.H. Jones, Captain J. Bill Jones; [b.] April 1, 1924, Black Diamond, WA; [p.] Helenor Jones - Deceased; [m.] Barbara A. Jones, May 17, 1960; [ch.] Robert Jeffery Jones and Denise Lynn Williams; [ed.] B.A. San Diego State, Naval School of Hospital Administration; [occ.] Retired, Captain, U.S. Navy; [memb.] 1.) Federal Health Care Executives, 2.) Fleet Reserve Association, 3.) Distinguished Member International Society of Poets; [hon.] Legion of Merit (Navy) Numerous Service Medals and awards, Graduated with honors 5 Military Schools, Advanced from Apprentice Seaman to Captain during Naval career. Editor's Choice Award 1995 (1) Editor's Choice Award 1996 (7); [oth. writ.] Endless Thought, Am I Worthy Treasured, In His Wisdom We Must Trust, Garden Workshop, Sequins on the Floor, Symphony of the Night, Charlie, Lady of Dreams, Dearest Mom, A Humble Apology, Customary Places and Faces, To Hell with Diamonds, Man's Best Friend, Dreams I've Had, The Window of His Soul, The Looking Glass Believer or Deceiver, Chiqui is Her Name, Sweet Pixie, Years of Joy, Songs Unsung, Beyond the Stars, Catacombs of the Night, Best Poems of 1996, Stop and Smell the Roses, Spirit of the Age, Home Alone, A Muse to Follow, Devil's Wind, A Tapestry of Thought, Ascent From Hell, No Perfect World, Where Dawn Lingers, Please Another Chance, Poems Unpublished, Across the Universe, Embers, Of Sunshine and Daydreams, Lonely Is The Poet, Lyrical Heritage, Editor's Award, The Sound of Poetry, Mercury Register, Oroville, CA. The Infamous Still in Oroville, News Reporter, San Marcos, CA, Fathers Day is Everyday; [pers.] I believe in personal achievement, inspiring others to fulfill their dreams, at peace with self and others, all with a sense of humor, dedication and perspective.; [a.] Lake San Marcos, CA

JOSEPH, CHRISTINE
[pen.] Archie; [b.] October 9, 1985, Germantown Hospital; [p.] George Joseph, Deena Joseph; [ed.] William H. Loesche Elementary School; [memb.] Indian Dance Class, KALAA (Kerala Arts Language Art of America); [hon.] Distinguished Honor roll, Art Award, Music Award, a President's Award. I won a poetry contest; [oth.

writ.] I got published in the *Sunday Inquirer.* (An article about schools.) (Philadelphia); [pers.] I thank my teacher (Miss Rubin) for influencing me. Also I was influenced by the great poetry of Margeret Wise Brown. I like poems about nature. I love classic poems!; [a.] Philadelphia, PA

JUAREZ, AMY
[b.] August 28, 1927, Lovell, WY; [p.] Deceased; [m.] Divorced for 42 yrs.; [ch.] 5 children, 9 grandchildren and 1 great grandchild; [ed.] High School Education from Granger High School, Granger, WA and Beauty School from Chasm Beauty School, Yakima, WA; [occ.] Retired Cosmetologist; [hon.] Raised 5 children: 2 graduated from Washington State University, 1 from University of WA, 1 from Cal State Full-Braton and 1 from Rio Hondo; [pers.] Inspiration from God! First Baptist Church Walnut, Cal.; [a.] West Covina, CA

KAIN, JONATHAN
[b.] February 5, 1969, Springfield, VT; [p.] Carol Cumings; [ch.] Kaanan Kain - 6 yrs. old son; [ed.] College Student - Community College of Vermont; [pers.] I strongly believe in the endless pursuit of knowledge. With knowledge emerges understanding and art. Understanding convinces the essential grasp of love. Art is the wonderful nation that each participant views each creator in his or her unique way. A laugh, a tear, a sort-splashed sigh. A forward step to a new level, mysterious and brave.

KAKLEY, DAWN E.
[b.] March 23, 1965, Waterbury, CT; [p.] Andrew F. Doty and Dorothy C. Doty; [m.] Joseph V. Kakley Sr., May 29, 1993; [ch.] Cynthia, Michael, Joseph Jr., Matthew, Joshua; [ed.] Graduated from crosby High School in Waterbury, CT in 1983; [occ.] Mother/Housewife; [memb.] Toman Catholic Church; [hon.] Math and Short stories from Jr. High and High School; [oth. writ.] I have written around 100 poems.; [pers.] I am very happily married with a fine man and I have also 5 (five) wonderful children - 1 (one) girl the oldest, then 4 (four) boys. I make sure I take a little time to myself during the week, so I can try to create some more poetry.; [a.] Ludlow, MA

KALIATI, DOROTHY
[b.] July 9, 1957, Elmira, NY; [p.] Mrs. Emily Black; [m.] Cleopas A. Kaliati, December 17, 1993; [ch.] Alicia Delgado; [ed.] High School Elmira, New York, A.A.S. in Liberal Arts, Kalamazoo Valley Community College; [occ.] Teacher's Aide Kalamazoo County Head start; [memb.] Seventh Day, Adventist Church; [oth. writ.] Articles for the South West, Michigan *Tribune*. Various magazines, newsletters, poetry.; [pers.] I enjoy writing poetry, and I would like to write and illustrate a children's picture book. I often write poetry to musical selections.; [a.] Kalamazoo, MI

KALIL, NICOLE DENISE
[b.] November 28, 1972, Miami, FL; [p.] Arthur and Denise Holden; [m.] Joe Kalil, February 24, 1996; [ed.] Belmont College Florida State University; [pers.] Most of my inspiration comes from great songwriters. I want to strike a chord with readers so they feel as if I'm describing something they've gone through or experienced. In my life, the works that mean the most to me are those I can relate to. And, in all things, to God be the glory!; [a.] Miami, FL

KALINA, MARILYN
[b.] January 5, 1941, Chicago, IL; [p.] Anthony Smith and Josephine Smith Wach; [m.] Ralph Pennino, Ed. Kalina; [ch.] Six grandchildren, Children - Cherie, Doreen, Ralph Pennino; [ed.] Attending Pinellas Technical Education Center, course: Building Personal Computers; [occ.] Professional Domestic Engineer; [memb.] Anclote Earth Science Club Editor, Writer and Reporter of *Bulletin* from 1991 to present.; [hon.] The American Federation of Mineralogical Societies, *Bulletin* Editor's Contest 1992-93-94.; [oth. writ.] Appear in the Opinion section of the Pasco Edition, *St. Petersburg Times* FL. newspaper.; [pers.] Became a resident of Pasco County FL. in September, 1981. Former resident of Bolingbrook, IL. My poem is in memory of a Florida State Representative, The Honorable Philip Mishkin. Term 1990-94.; [a.] Hudson, FL

KALKBRENNER, SARAH
[b.] February 22, 1984, Phx, AZ; [p.] Kevin and Debby Kalkbrenner; [ed.] Lookout Mountain School, Mountain Sky Junior High; [occ.] Student; [hon.] Principal's Award for Academic Excellence Lookout Mountain School; [pers.] I express the things I feel in my poems; [a.] Phoenix, AZ

KAMIYAMA, MIKIO
[pen.] Kroy Wen; [b.] March 25, 1936, Kyoto, Japan; [ed.] University of Tokyo, Doctor of Medical Science; [occ.] Director of Clinical Research, Department of Medicine. Jamaica Hospital Medical Center, Jamaica, NY; [memb.] American Association of Immunologists, American Federation for Clinical Research, American Society of Hematology, American Heart Association Council on Thrombosis, International Society on Thrombosis and Homeostasis, The Harvey Society, New York Academy of Sciences; [oth. writ.] Articles for medical, scientific journals.; [a.] New York, NY

KARSTEN, MARY
[b.] July 5, 1954, Chicago, IL; [p.] Richard E. and Mary A. Karsten; [m.] John F. Bundy, July 21, 1993; [ed.] Florida Atlantic University Boca Raton, Florida BA. and M.Ed.; [occ.] Behavioral Consultant; [oth. writ.] Workbook, *Developing Healthy Self Esteem in Adolescents*, published by Good Apple January 1995.; [pers.] Honest communication of our beliefs values and feelings is essential to building strong and lasting relationships.; [a.] Denver, CO

KASUNICK, MATTHEW
[b.] March 31, 1979, Eglin AF Base, FL; [p.] Eugene Kasunick Jr. and Desiree Ann Dayok; [ed.] Graham High School; [occ.] Student; [memb.] Madonna Fan Club; [hon.] Honor student; [oth. writ.] I write a lot as a hobby, but never shared anything with anyone. This is my first publication.; [pers.] I try to explore the inner self on a more personal level, I'm inspired by the "Byronic Hen" himself and other writers of the romantic era.; [a.] Saint Paris, OH

KATZ, ROBERT I.
[b.] May 29, 1952, New York, NY; [ed.] BA Columbia, MD Northwestern; [occ.] Physician; [oth. writ.] Unpublished Novelist - client of the Ray Lincoln Literary Agency; [a.] Port Jefferson, NY

KAUFMAN, JOSHUA
[b.] September 24, 1975, N.Y.C.; [p.] Brenda Dressler, Irving Kaufman; [ed.] Currently an undergraduate at the University of Miami (FL); [occ.] Student; [memb.] Editor of Poetry section in high school literary magazine; [oth. writ.] Various poems, short stories, and a novel in progress; [pers.] Through writing poetry I seek to explore humanity. I view literature as a way into the soul, and without it there would be many empty spaces in all of us that could never be filled.; [a.] Whitestone, NY

KAYZAR, THERESA
[b.] October 13, 1982, Phoenix, AZ; [p.] George Kayzar, Kathi Kayzar; [ed.] Village Vista Elementary, Sunrise Middle School; [oth. writ.] Poem published in another anthology.; [pers.] I write to clear my head and express my deepest thoughts and feelings. I owe my deepest gratitude to Jean Lamb and Joyce Perry, my inspiration, Thank You.; [a.] Phoenix, AZ

KEATON, NANCY
[b.] October 27, 1953, Pavo, GA; [p.] Claude Goodson - Dorothy Gadd; [m.] Stanley D. Keaton, November 22, 1993; [ch.] Sonya, Kelly, Jacob, Zackary; [ed.] Jacksonville High Bainbridge Jr. College; [occ.] Homemaker - Day Care Provider; [oth. writ.] Several poems published in local newspaper; [pers.] Life is a poem, write it down!; [a.] Donalsonville, GA

KEEL, JAMES
[b.] May 11, 1956, Portsmouth, VA; [p.] Hubert R. Keel, Evelyn Keel; [m.] Pamela M. Keel, October 13, 1979; [ch.] Amandy K. Keel and Jamie M. Keel; [ed.] Attended West Valley College; [occ.] System Senior Unix Administrator; [hon.] VIP Award 1996 to Jim Keel San Lorenzo Valley Elementary for helping wire up the school computers. "Net Day"; [pers.] Do the best that you can. Thanks to my wife, with love, because I could not have created it without her. Thanks to West Valley College and all my supportive friends in the LEAP program.; [a.] Felton, CA

KEELING, REITA
[b.] June 1, 1923, Monticello, AR; [p.] Lee and Lena Hayes; [m.] Elmo Keeling, July 30, 1939; [ch.] Elmo Jr., John, Jack, Lana, Jeffrey, Craig, Renee; [ed.] High School; [occ.] Housewife; [memb.] Baptist Church, Choir, Sunday School; [oth. writ.] None published; [pers.] I have been a Christian for 45 years. The Holy Spirit inspires me to write.; [a.] Joplin, MO

KELLEHER, BERNADETTE
[pen.] Bunny; [b.] February 27, 1935, New York, NY; [p.] Bernard and Margaret Gallagher; [m.] Jack Kelleher, April 19, 1958; [ed.] Attended Manhattan College Bronx, NY, Managerial Science Columbia University, 2 semesters Fine Arts Program; [occ.] Retired, was Assistant Director of Purchasing Columbia University, NY and Fairleigh Dickenson NJ; [memb.] National Association of Buyers, Purchasing Managers Assn. (AARP); [oth. writ.] Unpublished and works in progress. Write poetry mostly for class assignments. Attend poetry classes at Riverdale Senior Center.; [pers.] I try to express the need for a bond between people, family members and spiritual guidance as the source for internal peace and happiness. Influenced by Elizabeth Barrett Browning and Langston Hughes.; [a.] Bronx, NY

KELLER, GAIL
[b.] July 4, 1948, Vine Grove, KY; [p.] Clarence Bewley, Evelyn Bewley; [m.] Peter Keller, July 11, 1966; [ch.] Peter Daniel, Laura Gail, Peter Brian, Heidi Gail; [ed.] Elizabethtown Catholic High School, Graduated with an Associate Degree in Computer Science from Elizabethtown Community College; [occ.] Self Em-

ployed, Timbercraft, Vine Grove, KY; [hon.] Phi Theta Kappa, Dean's List; [oth. writ.] Short stories and poems about personal experiences, but none have been submitted for publication; [pers.] My heart - it guides my hand to write through my poems, my soul takes flight; [a.] Vine Grove, KY

KELLER, ROBERT
[pen.] Edgar Max; [b.] January 14, 1952, Baltimore, MD; [p.] Edgar and Anna Keller; [ch.] Erika Brumett, Robert Keller; [ed.] Overlea Sr. High School; [occ.] Fire Protection Engineering Technician, Part-time Cab Driver; [memb.] National Institute for Certification in Engineering Technologies; [oth. writ.] Several poems and song lyrics, as yet unpublished. Currently working on musical arrangements and fictional short story; [pers.] A picture is worth a thousand words - lets you see what someone looks like. A few well chosen words of theirs allows you to look into the soul. Praise and thanks to the Almighty - one love; [a.] Baltimore, MD

KELLY, BRIGID
[b.] July 16, 1985, Worcester, MA; [p.] Anne F. Kelly, John F. Kelly; [ed.] 1996 Graduate of Edson Elementary School; [occ.] Middle School Student and Writer; [hon.] Participant in Young Authors Day for the Kingston Accelerated Learning Program and Selected to Read Essay at DARE Graduation; [oth. writ.] "Two Seasons" published in the 1994 edition of the *Anthology of Poetry by Young Americans*.; [a.] Kingston, NY

KELLY, DAVID A.
[pen.] Earnest Scrivener; [b.] April 9, 1932, New York City; [p.] Mr. and Mrs. Thomas W. Kelly; [ed.] Elementary School, High School (Private and Public Jr. College - A.A. Degree - Cum Laude, A.B. Degree - St. Bonaventure Univ.; [occ.] Retired Teacher/School Administrator; [memb.] Knights of Columbus: 4th Degree, Cambridge Chorus; [hon.] Cum Laude - Jr College Dean's List - A.B. Degree, Degree in Philosophy/Minor: Latin, Greek, Hebrew; [oth. writ.] Poetry in local newspaper. Prose, Poetry, Translations from Latin in school publications as teacher - using pen name "Earnest Scrivener."; [pers.] I simply enjoy writing, particularly in my retirement years. My writing sometimes attempts to reflect the beauty of God's creation and man's place in it.; [a.] Greenwich, NY

KELLY, KEVIN GREGORY
[b.] January 28, 1964, Long Beach, CA; [p.] Duane and Florrine Kelly; [ed.] BA degree in Business Sociology from the University of California at Davis, Master of Arts degree in Human Communications from the University of Northern Colorado; [occ.] United States Army Officer, Captain, Ordnance Corps, at Fort Corton, CO; [memb.] Marine Corps League, Retired, Enlisted Association, North American Fishing Club, The Heritage Foundation Chaffey College Alumni Association, UC Davis Alumni Association; [hon.] Chaffey Community College 1996 Alumni of the Year, 1st Team All Conference in California Jr. College Football, Special Team Player of Year UC Davis Football, Military: Navy Unit Accommodation, Army Accommodation Medal, Army Achievement Medal. Dean's List; [pers.] Approach all aspects in life with 100% effort, when mistakes are made, the intensity will compensate the adversities! Small minds talk about people, average minds talk about events, great minds talk about ideas (author unknown); [a.] Colorado Springs, CO

KEOWN, SHERRY
[b.] July 9, 1960, Detroit; [p.] Charles and Helen Weiss; [m.] David, September 22, 1978; [memb.] Humane Society, World Wildlife Fund, ASPCA; [oth. writ.] "God for a day," "Kingdom on the sea," "splashed in red," "shadows," "freedom of horses," all through The National Library of Poetry, "old Kentucky home," through, The Famous Poets Society; [pers.] Poetry is the best escape from reality that I know. Your imagination can take you to countless places - if you let it.; [a.] Warren, MI

KERSHAW, HELEN E.
[b.] August 2, 1913, Toledo, OH; [p.] John V. Scarlett, Alice C. Scarlett; [ch.] Marilyn Kershaw Williams; [ed.] Scott High School - Toledo, Ohio, University of Toledo - Toledo, Ohio; [occ.] Retired Librarian in Cleveland and Toledo, Ohio. Now Editor of my retirement home newsletter in North Carolina; [memb.] Alpha Phi Gamma, Mortar Board, Pilgrim United Church of Christ, Toledo, Ohio; [oth. writ.] Poems in library publication and a Toledo Churches poetry collection. Have written many types of verse beginning at an early age. I especially enjoy writing rhymes and jingles on any subject for my friends.; [pers.] I have always loved poetry. It is a great joy to me when the inspiration comes and I must begin creating again.; [a.] Hunterville, NC

KESSINGER, JEFFREY W.
[b.] March 9, 1956, Jamestown, NY; [p.] Joanne Ivory and Ken Kessinger; [ch.] Brittney Lynn Kessinger; [pers.] My poem is dedicated to my beautiful, one and only daughter...Brittney L. Kessinger, with love from her Dad.; [a.] Scottsdale, AZ

KEYS, LAURA
[pen.] Laura James; [b.] August 15, 1966, McAlester, OK; [p.] Lynn and Mildred Rice; [ch.] Tawni, Colton; [ed.] B.S. Speech Language Pathology, M.Ed. - CCC Speech Language Pathology; [occ.] Speech Language Pathologist; [memb.] ASHA, OSHA; [hon.] *Who's Who of Teachers, Who's Who of the World*; [pers.] I write from my heart.; [a.] Tahlequah, OK

KHAN, G. SIERRA
[pen.] Gwendolyn Marie DeCoud; [b.] February 7, 1954, New Orleans, LA; [ed.] Ph.D. Candidate, Humanities, Syracuse University, J.D. Case Western Reserve Univ., M.A. The Ohio State University, B.A. Hunter College; [occ.] Graduate Studies; [memb.] Modern Language Assn., American Bar Assn., Collegian for African American Research; [pers.] Mosuba Egungun (I give praise to my roots, my beginnings — to my ancestors.) "Language Speaks" because the dead continue to live.; [a.] Syracuse, NY

KIDWELL, RUSSELL E.
[pen.] Eugene Ruskid; [b.] November 19, 1936, Richmond, KY; [m.] Pamela Sue Kidwell, January 26, 1980; [occ.] Sample Dept. Manager Fabric Wholesale Distributer; [hon.] Won a National Art Scholarship at age 11. Studied Art on GI Bill. Did Freelance Art Work for years until eye problems.; [pers.] Like to write poetry as a hobby. Most of all the poems I write are actual experiences or inspired by real people whom I have had the pleasure to meet throughout my life.

KILDOW, JAYNE
[b.] October 20, 1985, Lincoln, NE; [p.] Deb and Vince Kildow; [ed.] I am now in 5th grade, and in fourth grade - had the best teacher, Jill Granger. I go to Riley Elementary; [hon.] Won first place in the Regional Competition, Odyssey of the Mind. That's where there are teams of 5-6, and there are 5 different problems to choose from. You have 9 months to make an 8 min. skit and your problem; [oth. writ.] Spend my spare time writing poems in my journal at school and at home; [pers.] Those of you that have not read or tried to write poetry, go ahead, it's fun, exciting and sometimes even a big adventure!!!; [a.] Lincoln, NE

KILLGORE, N. MICHELLE
[b.] December 15, 1970, Santa Rosa, CA; [p.] Wesley E. Killgore, Martha J. Killgore; [ed.] Bachelor of Arts, Business Sonoma State University, California; [occ.] Information Science Analyst; [hon.] Graduated with Distinction, Dean's List; [oth. writ.] Several poems and short stories - never submitted for publication; [pers.] I encourage the re-discovery of spirituality for all human kind regardless of background, culture or religion. I believe this missing element in our daily lives has the power to heal our struggling world.; [a.] Denver, CO

KILLIAN, DANIEL J.
[b.] October 4, 1946, LaFayette, GA; [p.] Daniel C. Killian, Mamie Killian; [ch.] Tina Gail, Danny Joe, Rebecca Lynn, Brian Edward, Daniel Michael; [ed.] LaFeyette High; [occ.] Truck Driver; [oth. writ.] Currently writing an autobiography called *America, you better wake up*.; [pers.] I wish to dedicate this poem to all the men and women who served and died in Vietnam and to the South Vietnamese people and their Army. Also to the MIA's that we will never forget.; [a.] Fort Oglethorpe, GA

KIMANI, JULIA
[b.] January 27, 1982, Baltimore; [p.] Mrs. Harriet and Kimani; [ed.] Cardinal Shehan School Elementary, Baltimore, MD. Notre Dame Prep. High, Towson, Maryland; [occ.] Student; [hon.] Inter-generational spelling Bee Competition; [oth. writ.] Several poems published in the *National Anthology of Poetry*, 1995 and 1996; [pers.] I aim to express how I theorize in my writing. Writings by more contemporary poets have helped mold my feelings and style; [a.] Baltimore, MD

KING, LOIS MYERS
[b.] March 26, 1930; [p.] Aaron and Emma Grieser; [m.] Leonard King, November 4, 1995; [ch.] Keith, Doug, Max, Jeff; [ed.] High School; [occ.] Retired; [oth. writ.] Poems and readings I wrote but never were published.; [pers.] I never wrote poetry until after the loss of my second husband. It was a gift given to me by God when I was coping with my grief.

KING, VIRGINIA VEVELON
[pen.] Sissy King; [b.] September 30, 1955, Limestone, ME; [p.] Roland and Delores Pinkney; [ch.] Phillip, Donte, Star and Daryl Payne, Willie, Willie D. and D. Hall, Wms. Keith Payne and Michael and Morgan; [ed.] UDC Unv., P.G. College, MD Univ. and Bible College; [occ.] Law Enforcement Officer, for the D.C. Dept. of Corrections and accountant Exec.; [memb.] First Bap. Church of Highland Park, Greater S.E. Com Hosp Volunteer member, AKA, Bowling WBA; [hon.] Art Scholarship Award, Karate Outstanding Salesperson Award, Disc-Jockey Award/Bartender, Certificate Award F/ Author Sales, Cert. Award for Motorcycling, Modeling Award/Seminar Awards; [oth. writ.] Local Newspaper, Letters, Magazine Articles, Speeches; [pers.] My blessings come from God, thank you Jesus! Dedicated to my mother (specially) and Pop, Siblings, "All my Children (7)" and Godson. One woman to another my only daughter and Best Friend "Star".; [a.] P G County, MD

KINSEY, CHRISTY H.
[b.] April 29, 1960, Abingdon, VA; [p.] M/M Gary R. Herrmann; [m.] Jamie Kinsey, August, 1993; [ed.] Columbia Military Academy Middle Tn. State University; [occ.] Asst. Secretary and packer for an Allied Van Lines Agent; [hon.] Spanish I and II awards at C.M.A., Columbia, TN; [pers.] My poem "Ode To A Friend" is in memory of my Best and Dearest Friend who died in a tragic accident at work. I treasure the memories of our friendship daily. For you: William Burke Allen, Jr.; [a.] Ringgold, GA

KINSEY, DAVID
[b.] September 30, 1971, Columbus, OH; [p.] Janet Dodge and Thomas Kinsey; [ed.] Valparaise High School, Huntington College, Bowling Green State University; [occ.] Substitute Teacher (6-12); [memb.] Georgia Vegetarian Society; [hon.] Dean's List; [oth. writ.] Currently working on a collection of short stories and poems and screenplay.; [pers.] Writing is a release of dreams unrevealed and an exploration into self-expression.; [a.] Burlington, NC

KIPP, E. EDWARD
[pen.] "Ed Kipp"; [b.] November, Carlton, NE; [m.] Leora Kipp; [ch.] Three; [occ.] Minister of the Gospel of Jesus Christ; [memb.] First Southern Baptist Church of Hemet; [oth. writ.] Other poems of family relationship or with spiritual convictions: Such as "My Christmas Testimony"; [a.] Hemet, CA

KIRK, ZACHARY
[b.] September 10, 1974, Weetridy, CO; [p.] Dayne and Rory Fallert; [m.] Steven Kirk; [ed.] Pamona High School, Red Rock Community College, Metro State University; [occ.] Student Caology (study of Chaos) and Fine Arts (painting to stone Sculpture); [memb.] Founding member of The Community of Artists, Father of Avatarism (an Art movement); [oth. writ.] Several poems and short stories; [a.] Arvada, CO

KITTS, RHIANNON
[b.] April 20, 1977, Dayton, OH; [p.] Donna S. Johnson; [ed.] Graduated - Dixie High School; [oth. writ.] Mainly personal writings.; [a.] New Lebanon, OH

KLEIN, ZACH
[pen.] Magellan Green; [b.] September 26, 1982, Rochester, NY; [p.] Andrew and Kimberly Klein; [ed.] Nativity B.U.M., Summit Middle School, Bishop Luers High School; [memb.] Boy Scouts of America, Saint Elizabeth Ann Seton Parish, Bishop Luers Swing Choir, [hon.] Soaring Falcon Award, Supreme Mental Attitude Award, Honor Student; [oth. writ.] *The Scratch*, a bi-weekly newsletter; [pers.] I write on paper so I may describe things deeper than they appear. I discover my judgement in many proverbs and psalms.; [a.] Fort Wayne, IN

KLEINSCHMIDT, TIA L.
[b.] July 26, 1983, Corvallis, OR; [p.] Ed and Karen Kleinschmidt; [ed.] North Valley Primer, Liberty Christian Elementary, Saint Francis Middle School; [occ.] Full time Student; [oth. writ.] A number of poems sent into contests, and sent back as semi-finalist, offers to be published in 3 other books, one named *Anthology of Poetry by Young Americans*; [pers.] I try to write poems that people would have to really think about. I mostly like to write my feelings down, and how I feel about my boyfriend and recent breakups.; [a.] Redding, CA

KNEASS, JESSIAH
[pen.] Saint Mark, Jessiah; [b.] July 26, 1967, Redwood City, CA; [p.] Claudette and Geoff Lomas; [ed.] Cabrillo College, Santa Cruz CA., 1 year completed, Teachings of the Ascended Maters from Mount Shasta, California since 1974 (Metaphysical); [occ.] Head waiter of an Italian Restaurant, guru, counselor, dream interpreter; [oth. writ.] The *Lyrical Miracle*, my own poetry compilation, and *sevens*, a one-of-a-kind numerological book with over 500 entries that pertain solely to the number seven, one published; [pers.] Born the 7th child at 7 pounds in the 7th month of '67, our address was 77 and 7th house on the street and the 7th family to live in that house, built in 1903. My first name Mark also equals 7 when the letters are converted into numerology, we are on the cusp of the 7th and final golden age of man, the completion is so near, we will ascend! Shalom; [a.] Vancouver, WA

KNISKERN, KERRY
[pen.] Kerry; [b.] March 21, 1943, Cobleskill, NY; [p.] Pearl and Chestel L. Kniskern; [m.] Sylvia Lenore, August 20, 1982; [ch.] Sherrie and Larry; [ed.] Waynes Boro High School (Virginia) and Virginia Polytechnic Institute; [occ.] Communications and Operations Manager, Dow Jones and Co.; [oth. writ.] Book of Prose and Poetry unpublished.; [pers.] My objective in writing is to make the reader smile.; [a.] Lawrenceville, NJ

KNODEL, JOYCE
[b.] September 21, 1934, Norwich, NY; [p.] Maude, and Stanley Ashton; [m.] Melvin Knodel, January 26, 1958; [ch.] Barry, Christian, Cheryl, Mamie and 6 grandchildren; [ed.] 8 year Oxford Academy, Oxford, NY; [occ.] Mother, Grandmother, Wife; [pers.] God put sensitivity in all to appreciate the lovely world He made.; [a.] Deerfield Beach, FL

KNOWLES, RAYMOND W. O.
[b.] March 20, 1907, Kansas; [p.] William B. and Jennie O. Knowles; [m.] Corinne B. Knowles, January 20, 1996; [ch.] Robert W. (Deceased), Margaret P. Jackson, Dr. Richard T. Knowles; [ed.] B.A. Degree Sterling College, Kansas Graduate work, Iliff School of Theology Denver, Colorado; [occ.] Retired United Methodist Minister with 44 years in the active ministry; [memb.] Retired Member Kansas West Conference of the United Methodist Church; [oth. writ.] Written for the Christian Advocate of the United Methodist Church; [pers.] No one finds life worth living, we make it worth living, and the ultimate outcome of our life is determined by the decisions we make. We are responsible for what we are and what we become. Old age is a bad habit we don't have time enough to form, if we keep busy. It's a matter of the mind, if we don't mind, it doesn't matter.; [a.] Canon City, CO

KOBI, MARIE
[b.] December 16, 1927, Shamokin, PA; [p.] Steven and Anne Chervanick; [m.] Joseph Kobi, May 28, 1949; [ch.] Jim Kobi (Cmdr.), JoAnn Brooks, 2 granddaughters, 2 grandson; [ed.] Shamokin High School '46; [occ.] Nurse Aide with "The Family Medical Support System, Inc.", Mount Carmel, PA, received the PA Champion of Older Workers Outstanding Service Award; [hon.] Legislative Acknowledgement from Rep. Robert E. Belfanti Jr. - Congratulations from Sen. Edward Helfrick - Appreciation plaque for Den Mother of Cub Scouts.; [oth. writ.] Several poems published in local newspaper.; [pers.] I desire to illustrate the beauty of the earth... the love of God and the memories of the past, in my writings.; [a.] Kulpmont, PA

KOPONEN, WILFRID R.
[ed.] A.B., Brown University, M.B.A., Columbia Business School, M.A.R., Yale Divinity School, M.A. and Ph.D. University of California, Santa Barbara; [occ.] English teacher; [oth. writ.] Published book: *Embracing A Gay Identity: Gay novels as Guides* (Westport, CT: Bergin and Garvey, 1993). Articles published in *International Fiction Review A British Studies Samples, Sex and Spirit, Contemporary Gay American Novelists, White Crane Novelists, White Crane Journal, Out! Magazine* and *Solares Hill*. A completed science fiction novel about the destruction of Atlantis is under submission for publication; [a.] Albuquerque, NM

KOTTKE, CHRIS
[pen.] Hollywood; [b.] December 10, 1979, Panorama City, CA; [p.] Marline Kottke, Robert Rains; [ed.] Still in High School, planning college; [occ.] Student, Athlete; [memb.] USA Wrestling, Future Laker Club, Stockton Athletic Clubs; [hon.] 1st 5th grade book writing Competition, Valley, Wa. Swimming and Wrestling Gold, Silver and Bronze Medals 1st 6th Book writing Competitions, Taylor and Elementary; [oth. writ.] Children's book, many books about life and personal life and feelings.; [pers.] Lead, follow, or get out of the way. Read, write, or never change. We all need friends, loneliness is the first step towards the end.; [a.] Stockton, CA

KRASLEN, KRISTINE
[b.] December 22, 1977, Chicago, IL; [p.] Steve Kraslen, Sharon Kraslen; [ed.] Mather High School; [occ.] Laundry Attendant; [pers.] A great mind is a terrible thing to waste. I was greatly influenced by the writings of Shakespeare.; [a.] Chicago, IL

KROVONTKA, MINDY
[b.] November 30, 1980, Mesa, AZ; [p.] Pat and Ruth Ann Krovontka; [ed.] Faye Galloway Elementary, John A. Dooley Elementary, B. Mahlon Brown Jr. High, Basic High School; [occ.] Student at Basic High School; [memb.] National Junior Honor Society, Honor Band, Nevadans, Science Club, Art Club; [hon.] 3rd place T-Shirt Design from State Fair, 1st Place Ceramics from State Fair, 1st Place Bookmark Contest; [oth. writ.] "The Unicorn", "Love, Money and Success," "Confusion", "Roller Coaster", "The Symphony"; [a.] Henderson, NV

KUBERSKI, DAVIN G.
[pen.] Diamond David King; [b.] October 7, 1954, Centerville, IA; [p.] Sylvester and Goldie Kuberski; [ed.] 2 yrs Music Ed.; [occ.] Pawn Broker; [oth. writ.] Several songs, poems and a few short stories.; [pers.] I sign all my writing like this, please include if possible, The Consummate Angel God bless the world in Jesus name. Amen

KUCHINSKI, BRAD
[pen.] Bradford; [b.] February 15, 1975; [p.] David and Carol; [ed.] Virginia Tech; [occ.] Student - Building Construction; [memb.] Community Service Organizations; [pers.] "To be the you that you want to be - that is success." Parents, thanks for your support!; [a.] Blacksburg, VA

KURJANOWICZ, WADIM
[b.] March 14, 1917, Reczica, Russia; [p.] Peter, Aleksandra; [m.] Christine, 1951; [ch.] Andrew, George; [ed.] Medical Doctor; [occ.] Retired; [oth. writ.] "To Save The Goose" tale, "Visit" novel, Fifty-six short stories. Poetry written in Polish; [pers.] When at the age of eleven I was asked what I would like to be, I told them, I would like to be a writer. Desire to write is still with me.; [a.] Reading, PA

KURPIEWSKI, AARON
[b.] May 7, 1982, Oak Lawn, IL; [p.] Alan and Nancy Kurpiewski; [ed.] Stone Elementary School, Addison, IL, Glen Crest Jr. High, Glen Ellyn, IL; [occ.] High School student (Freshman at Glenbard) South Glen Ellyn, IL [pers.] I find and point out the hardships I fail to conceal, while I look over all the rough roads that lie before and behind me.; [a.] Glen Ellyn, IL

LA BARBERA, SYLVIA CANNELLA
[b.] January 11, 1942, Tampa, FL; [p.] Mamie Baio and Victor Cannella; [m.] Joe La Barbera, July 11, 1992; [ch.] Debra Levens and Angela La Barbera; [occ.] Secretary; [pers.] I wrote this poem as a eulogy to my father, my friend, Victor Cannella - April 29, 1988. (I love you Daddy); [a.] Tampa, FL

LAHRMANN, JESSICA
[b.] August 1, 1984, Buffalo, NY; [p.] Philip and Susan Lahrmann; [ed.] Annie E. Vinton Elementary School, Oak Grove Montessori School, and Mansfield Middle School; [occ.] Student of Mansfield Middle School; [memb.] Mansfield Middle School Student Council, Minnechaug Swim and Pool Club's Tennis Team; [hon.] New England Mathematics League Certificate of Merit, Word masters certificate of Recognition, Connecticut Student Performing Arts Festival Certificate of Participation, Certificate of Award for Citizenship and being an outstanding student. D.A.R.E. Medallion for a nominated poster, First Place Ribbon for Hershey's Track and Field Softball Throw, 400 m desh, 100 m dash, Certificate of Participation in the Girl's Junior softball program, Blue Ribbon Musical Award for technical achievement in the study of the piano, ribbon award for superior achievement in the study of the music of Barton, Commendation for Participation in the youth performance series recital, certificate of achievement for outstanding performance in the Honors Recital, Bela Bartok Certificate, J.S. Bach Award, Sonatina Award, Certificate of Participation in the CSMTA Annual Music Competition J.S. Back Minute Award, Gillock Award, German Composers Music Award, Musicology Award, Music Award of Excellence, Certificate of Recognition in Music Theory, Certificate of Award in the Art of Minute Playing, and Certificate of Award in Music Theory Progress.; [oth. writ.] Poems: "Into the Woods", "Spiders Trap of Silk", and "My Doll Allison" (published in school magazine *Illusions*); [pers.] Through my poetry, I try to express the beauty of common sights to my readers.; [a.] Mansfield, CT

LAI, SUNNY
[b.] June 12, 1986, Austin, TX; [p.] Jiin Lai, Cheng-Po Sun Lai; [ed.] Faria At, Sillicon Valley Youth Conservatory; [occ.] Composer, Semi-Professional Musician; [memb.] Palo Alto Chamber Orchestra, North American Elite Youth Orchestra; [hon.] 1994 Overseas Piano Competition 2nd place, a clean well-lighted place for books (a poetry contest) runner up, PTA Reflection Contest County-wide 1st place composing; [oth. writ.] Dare To Discover, A Splash Of Nature Love; [pers.] You can't be you but I might be you.; [a.] Cupertino, CA

LAMPROS, PETER
[pen.] Peter Lampros; [b.] October 25, 1934, San Francisco, CA; [p.] A. and A. Lampros; [m.] Divorced; [ch.] Four; [ed.] Two Years College Treasury Agent Academy, 12 Weeks Treasury Dept. Bureau of Narcotics; [occ.] Writer, Poet; [oth. writ.] Self published prose-poetry-essay "awaked to enlightenment," I have been writing, on and off for 15 years.; [pers.] I am 61 years old I have been writing almost all my life. I write because I have to - I write because I love to.; [a.] Belmont, CA

LANDEFELD, ZAC
[b.] June 26, 1981, Wheeling, WV (Live in Ohio); [p.] Dale and Marlene Landefeld; [ed.] Currently a sophomore in High School - 10th grade; [memb.] United Methodist Church, Future Educators of America; [hon.] Presidential Academic Fitness Award, Honor Roll (since 5th grade, 7th year), 2nd in class currently, winner of Creative Writing Contest (Level A) at Foreign Language Day at Bethany College in West Virginia; [oth. writ.] Three collections of poetry, *Freshman*, *Relativity Inches Closer*, and *The High Order*. All yet unpublished.; [pers.] I strive for self understanding. I believe knowing the reasons of your own limitations and expectations can increase your awareness of others' as well. Remain down to earth, but never fear imagining - explore it!; [a.] Barnesville, OH

LANE JR., GEORGE
[b.] November 25, 1948, Superior, WI; [p.] George Lane, Ellen Campbell; [m.] Julia L. Lane, December 17, 1976; [ch.] Merica, Siri, Angela, Tracy, Greg, Jerred, Kerry, Kevin; [ed.] High School; [occ.] Security Guard; [oth. writ.] "Spring," "Memories," "Leaving The High Places"; [pers.] I have lived everything I write. The only way one can become an "expert" is to "experience".; [a.] Venice, FL

LANGE, WANDA
[b.] March 12, 1956, Moose Lake, MN; [p.] Deceased; [m.] Gregory Lange, June 12, 1993; [ch.] Laura Marie, Tina; [ed.] East High Anchorage Alaska Clover Park Voc. Tech Tacoma WA, Health Science Fort Sam Houston TX; [occ.] Materials Handler, TSC, at Frost Lewis, WA; [hon.] Two outstanding performance Awards with cash from two Generals in U.S. Army; [oth. writ.] Slogans Kessler Whiskey Create Design all of my Greeting Cards.; [pers.] Creator of "Station Lady" on cossets. I read several poems I've written and play music, under the name Ryan.; [a.] Tacoma, WA

LANTIS, RACHELLE MARIE
[b.] May 10, 1978, Breckenridge, MN; [p.] Craig And Patricia Lantis; [ed.] Aslan High School (Home-School); [oth. writ.] Presently working on a fiction novel that will most likely appeal to the teenage population and working on putting this poem to music.; [pers.] In all I do I want to tell the world about my best friend and Father, my savior and Lord, Jesus Christ who loves you and wants to know you. He is the meaning of life.; [a.] Salmon, ID

LARSEN, ERIC C.
[b.] May 6, 1978, Tacoma, WA; [p.] Gerald and June Larsen; [ed.] Graduated from Mt. Tahoma High School in June 1996. Will be attending Western Washington University in Bellingham, WA, beginning September 1996. and pursuing a career in Computer Science.; [occ.] Computer Technician for the Tacoma Public School District; [hon.] Semifinalist in the Ayn Rand Institute's Fountainhead Essay Contest for 1995, 1st Place Winner in the Northwest Regional Vica Drafting Contest in 1995, 1st Place Winner in the Washington State Vica Computer Aided Design Competition in 1995. 1st Place Winner ($5,000 College Scholarship in the Wescon Scholarship Essay Contest in 1995).; [pers.] I believe that writing poetry should not be influenced by any other type of writing. It should be new original and from yourself. Most of my other writings are of a darker style. I feel that the only way to light is to confront the darkness.; [a.] Tacoma, WA

LARSEN, ROBERTA D.
[pen.] Roberta Larsen; [b.] May 24, 1943, Chicago, IL; [p.] Bob and Agnes Larsen; [m.] Divorced; [ch.] One daughter - Stephanie Renee; [ed.] High School Graduate from Falls High School 1961, International Falls, MN (on the Canadian Border); [occ.] "Retired" housewife and mother (Amateur Poet and Photographer); [hon.] None, however a few of my poems have been published in our small "home town", daily newspaper; [oth. writ.] Lots of poems about "people and places", "I love !"...(friends, family, my feelings about living out West and moving back "home" to the "North".); [pers.] I try to live by the "Serenity Prayer" and I love the quote:...."There ain't no cloud so big that the sun ain't shinin' on the other side"!; [a.] International Falls, MN

LARSON, CODY
[b.] March 6, 1977, Portland, OR; [p.] Ann and Mick Larson; [ed.] Sophomore Enrolled at Southern Oregon State College, Previously Attended Beaverton High School; [occ.] Student, Southern Oregon State College, Ashland, OR; [a.] Ashland, OR

LASTRA, FEDERICO R.
[pen.] Federico R. Lastra; [b.] March 15, 1970, New York; [p.] Carlos and Mercedes Lastra; [ed.] Southwest Miami Sr. High. University of Miami, Psych. Major; [occ.] Skycap at Miami Int. Airport; [memb.] Knights of Columbus; [hon.] Several Art Awards throughout High School, and Essays published at Miami Dade Community College; [oth. writ.] Poems and short stories written over a 10 year span.; [pers.] My grandmother Rosario Hidalgo - Gato was my mentor, she inspired me to put my emotions on paper. I will always be grateful to her for that.; [a.] Miami, FL

LATAILLADE-LEWIS, SAIEDA
[b.] April 18, 1989, New York City; [p.] Victor and Jeanine Lewis; [ed.] Second Grade, Our Saviour Lutheran School; [occ.] Student; [memb.] Canaan Baptist Church of Christ; [oth. writ.] School Journal (Class); [pers.] I write poems because I hope to be a famous poetist when I grow up. I also want people to be kind and forgiving just forgive and forget.; [a.] New York, NY

LAUE, LINDA CHABOT
[pen.] Christy-Love/Sunshine; [b.] March 8, 1945, Long Beach, CA; [p.] Mr. Henry and Mrs. Zelma Chabot; [m.] Alfred Christopher Laue, May 11, 1980; [ch.] Paul James, Kimberly Lyne, Stephanie Roxanne, Sasha Renee; [ed.] I studied for Masters in Psychology at San Diego State University and writer; [occ.] Counselor, Art Therapist, Poet, Spiritual Counselor, Director; [memb.] I've spent the past twenty years giving out cards of hope, joy, faith, courage and love out to people of need, I've given a lot of, at least 15,00 cards of love.; [hon.] I've been included in five anthologies, received the Golden Poet Awards for 1990, 1991, and 1992. I've written for *Guideposts* and daily word articles in newspaper.; [oth. writ.] I've written a children's book called *Once Upon A Broken Wing*, it's the first of a series of books dealing with a children's handicap, much more to come! being a stroke patient myself I really can understand with compassion and love.; [pers.] If we as the human family could think, now and be love. If we could be at peace with all the world, then, perhaps we would have a very joyful, happy forever.; [a.] Lemon Grove, CA

LAURITZEN, ANDREA
[b.] January 27, 1966, Afton, Lincoln, WY; [p.] Elden and Marie Lauritzen; [ed.] Madison High School, Ricks College, Weber State University, Southern Utah University, Myotherapy College of Massage; [occ.] Licensed Massage Therapist Ogden, Utah; [hon.] Honorable mention - Poetry Contest, Ricks College, Rexburg ID 1986; [pers.] This poem was written as an analogy relating to the healing of a victim of childhood abuse - it can be overcome.; [a.] Ogden, UT

LAWRENCE, JOHN DAVID
[pen.] J. D. Lawrence; [b.] January 29, 1985, New York City; [p.] Michele and David Lawrence; [ed.] Old Westbury School of the Holy Child - N - Kind, Munsey Pk School 1-5; [occ.] Student; [memb.] USTA Tennis Assoc.; [hon.] Long Island String Festival - 14 Violin; [oth. writ.] "Winter," "The Snowy Day," "The Pond," "The Baby Girl Angel"; [pers.] I have been influenced in my writing by past teaches esp. Mr. Semel, Mrs. Juliano, and Mrs. Carpenter. I would like to especially thank my mom and dad for life experiences that have touched my heart.; [a.] Manhasset, NY

LAWRIE, ELAINE
[m.] James; [ch.] Tamara, Pamela; [ed.] Hunter College High School, Ohio Wesleyan University; [occ.] Catalog Production Manager, Creative/Tech., Writer, Editor; [memb.] Mensa; [hon.] 2 National Catalog First Place Awards; [pers.] May words let the spirit soar on the updraft of life's breezes, allowing understanding to touch each and every one of us.; [a.] Ramsey, NJ

LAYNE, SUSAN R.
[pen.] Susan R. Layne; [b.] May 27, 1946, Washington, DC; [p.] Maynard and Virginia Layne; [m.] Christian Lund, widow of Gerald Carver; [ch.] Deanna Dawn Mullinix, Anastasia Redina Patrick, Kenneth Maynard Watson and 9 grandchildren; [ed.] Riverdale Elem., Hyattsville Jr High, Northwestern High School, all in Maryland; [occ.] Farming, live in isolated Holler in KY, by choice no Elec.; [memb.] Past Parent and Child, La Lache League. W.W.F., National Wildfire, Present ISP-NLP; [hon.] Editor's Choice Award 1995-NLP; [oth. writ.] Poem "To Kenny - My Only Son" in *Mists of Enchantment* "Gerald's Promise" in *Best Poem's of the 90's* and a couple other poems published, others unpublished; [pers.] I am a mystical person who likes to dwell in the all-perfect meta-physical universe. If people would just get still long enough, they may become aware of a whole new reality opening up. This world comes thru in my poetry.; [a.] Cab Hill, KY

LE DESMA, XAVIER
[b.] Bell, CA; [p.] Enrique Le Desma, Antonia Le Desma; [m.] Christine Avalos, April 28, 1974; [ch.] Javier Damian; [ed.] Montebello High School, Rancho Santiago College, University of California, Los Angeles, California State Universities, LA, Fullerton; [occ.] Software Engineer, U.S. Naval weapons Station, Seal Beach, CA; [memb.] Orange County Guitar Circle; [oth. writ.] Song lyrics; [pers.] An aspect of artistic beauty resides in all things, as well as events ranging from the most glorious and happiest of emotions to the most terribly tragic of situations, to which an artist can focus his attention to create a fleeting moment of wonder.; [a.] Dana Point, CA

LEAP, CHERE R.
[b.] March 23, 1967, Escondido, CA; [p.] Ed and Marla Jarett; [m.] Darin R. Leap, May 5, 1994; [ch.] Chris, Jesca and Randi; [pers.] My poem was written during great trials in my life and marriage in which my husband and I were separated. My husband attempted suicide but thanks to my dear Lord and Savior Darin is with me today!; [a.] Wichita, KS

LEBBIE, MAISA KULA
[b.] March 14, 1986, San Jose, CA; [p.] Mable and Junisa P. Lebbie; [ed.] Reed Elementary School 5th grade-by next school year (Sept. 3, 1996); [hon.] My basketball trophy, Student Council and Young Author's Award and my Track Meet Red Ribbon; [a.] San Jose, CA

LEE MOORE, VIVIAN
[b.] February 18, 1958, Los Angeles, CA; [p.] H. Lee Arber, June Vivian Arber; [m.] David Lee Moore, May 24, 1986; [ch.] Erin Therese, Rory Michelle, David Barrows, Christian Alexander, Alexandre Lee, Preston Beauregard and Andrew Whittney Moore; [ed.] U.C.S.B., major Criminal Justice, minor sociology, U.C.L.A. studies in Music, Law and Japanese, Attended Ventura College of Law and Northwestern College of Law; [occ.] Law Office Manager, Writer; [memb.] Board member Y.E.S. Network, a charitable organization that supports youth and education; [hon.] Outstanding graduate High School, Honors in Economics, Math, and English. Honors Society in College; [oth. writ.] I am currently writing an Historical Fiction based partially on actual events that occurred during WW II. I have written and continue to write poetry as I have since I was introduced to poetry in High School; [pers.] Reading, an appreciation for language and poetry is one of the greatest gifts that can be given to children. It is a gift that my parents gave to me as a child. It is a gift that my husband shares that I as an adult try to pass on to our children and others.; [a.] Oak View, CA

LEESER, DEBRA
[b.] February 13, 1957, Tyler, TX; [p.] Murrel and Mary Parker; [m.] Anthony Leeser, August 22, 1995; [ch.] Erron Joseph, Marcus Adam, Jeremy Dean; [ed.] Silverton Union High, Chemeketa Comm. College; [occ.] Special Ed. Teacher/Homeschooler; [oth. writ.] Poem published for 2nd place winning in County newspaper, song published and on cassette called "America"; [pers.] My writings have been influenced from events, memories and kindness of others that have touched my life. I give great credit to my friends and family for encouragement.; [a.] Tonopah, NV

LEHMAN, HELEN LOUISE
[b.] December 30, 1936, Beetman, LA; [p.] Mr. John Will Kittler and Pauline Kittler; [m.] George Ray Lehman, April 27, 1960; [ch.] No just my two children by first man; [ed.] I went through 10th grade, my two children graduated from high school.; [occ.] I am retired and in a wheelchair; [memb.] I am a member of a Wildlife Corp, A Parks Corp, A Cancer Corp, and several others also and a nurses helper, C.N.A.; [hon.] I have a nurses award and from the wildlife and also from the park; [oth. writ.] Yes, I have written several stories for children, and several songs, plus three or four pages more of poetry. But I didn't have any of them published. I sent one or two of my songs in but they kept them.; [pers.] 7-15-96 I have all of my stories that I wrote for children if you want to see any I will send you a copy of them and also some more poems.; [a.] Fayettville, AR

LENNINGTON, LINDA L.
[pen.] Lilana Michilo; [b.] July 18, 1947; [pers.] My inspiration comes by recording thoughts of the spirit that dwells within me...a precious gift from my Heavenly Father.; [a.] Sunnyvale, CA

LEOPARD, ELIZABETH
[pen.] Elizabeth Leopard; [b.] December 4, 1929, Stirling, CO; [p.] Leonard/Eva Davis Presson; [m.] Billy Leopard, December 18, 1976; [ch.] Lori Romein - Al Sanderson; [ed.] 2 yrs. college; [occ.] Retired; [memb.] South Carolina Writers Workshop; [oth. writ.] Poetry, short stories and essays; [pers.] I write from my heart no matter how it comes out.

LERCH, MARILYN
[b.] May 26, 1936, East Chicago, IN; [ed.] M.A. Indiana University, M.A. Institute of Transpersonal Psychology; [occ.] Early retired teacher with the Washington, D.C. Public School System, Consultant in Holstead Education.; [pers.] I called myself a poet at twenty-one, but only now are image and practice coming together.; [a.] Washington, DC

LETSCHE, CAROL ANNE
[b.] July 21, 1948, Hackensack, NJ; [p.] C. W. Krupa, Anne Krupa; [m.] Steven James Letsche, October 9, 1993; [ch.] Calli Anne; [ed.] Garfield High School, E.S.P.A; [occ.] Credit/Collections Supervisor Harte Mountain Corp. Secaucus, NJ; [memb.] Church of the Good Shepherd; [oth. writ.] "What You Are To Me," "My Brother Bill"; [pers.] To write from my heart, thank God for all my accomplishments, and to have this poem published in memory of my beloved husband.; [a.] Midland Park, NJ

LEUTZINGER JR., RICHARD
[b.] January 22, 1962, Omaha, NE; [p.] Richard and Connie Leutzinger; [m.] Anne K. Leutzinger, April 16, 1995; [ch.] Danielle Sanders; [ed.] Ralston High, Devry Institute, Miller Institute, Arizona State University; [occ.] Entrepreneur; [memb.] Member of the Yahwist Omaha Assembly; [hon.] 3rd place in essay writing contest, 2 time chess champion in High School (back to back) Dean's list, Awarded and Honored for 7 yrs. of Hard work on a T.V. ministry program, honored and chosen to be a deacon; [oth. writ.] Essays, short stories, and songs; [pers.] Life is a journey that lets us travel like a long poem sauntering through rivers, valleys, meadows, and streams.; [a.] Omaha, NE

LEVAN SR., ANDREW K.
[b.] May 12, 1965, Harrisburg, PA; [pers.] "Little Indian Lost" dedicated to a lost love Rache E. Hood Apache tribe Hood Tempe Arizona for whom the poem was written. My first and only work.

LEVINE, ANYA ALYSSA
[b.] October 2, 1988, Goleta, CA; [p.] George and Hamet Levine; [ed.] Entering 3rd grade at Brandon Elementary School. Previously Student at Goleta Open Alternative School; [occ.] Being a Great Kid; [memb.] Brownie Girl Scouts; [pers.] I like animals and I like to tap dance. I like school. When I grow up I want to be an actress and a psychiatrist; [a.] Goleta, CA

LEWIS, CATHLEEN
[pen.] Cathy Lewis; [b.] November 16, 1982, Middletown, CT; [p.] Dana Lewis, Debra Lewis; [ed.] East Haddam Elem., Nathan Hale Ray Middle School; [occ.] Student; [memb.] Girl Scouts of USA; [hon.] Won poetry contest for State of Connecticut Earth Day poetry contest.; [oth. writ.] "Red As Fire" by Cathleen Lewis published in Dept. of Environmental Protection *Earth*

Day Poetry Anthology.; [pers.] I am inspired by the earth's natural beauty. I will live believing that some of life is magic and some of it is tragic.; [a.] East Haddam, CT

LEWIS, DANIEL E.
[b.] May 2, 1910, Goshen, IN; [p.] Daniel A. and Emma J. Lewis; [m.] Annette F. Lewis, July 28, 1934; [ch.] Daniel E. Lewis Jr. and Nancy L. Haswell; [ed.] A.B. Hanover College 1932, MS India University 1939, J.D. Valparaiso University 1949; [occ.] Attorney Semi-Retired; [memb.] Kiwanis American Bar Assn., Society of Professionals in Dispute Resolution; [hon.] LaPorte's Citizen of the Year-1955 Hanover College's Achievement Award 1965, Elk of the Year 1986-87, Kiwanian of the Year 1988-89; [oth. writ.] *At The Crossroads*, novel *So It Comes To Arbitration*, (How-to-Book) numerous poems; [a.] La Porte, IN

LEWIS, JEANINE
[pen.] J.J. Lewis; [b.] April 19, 1980, Los Angeles; [p.] Erma and Richard Lewis; [ed.] Kamiakin High, Carmichael Junior High; [occ.] A clothing store, the GAP; [memb.] Volunteer Center, Former Member Girl Scouts of America; [hon.] Received various academic achievement awards and certificates in poetry writing, Featured in Motion, Pictured now on Video, "The Gifted"; [oth. writ.] Private poems, school essays, writing poetry for contest.; [pers.] I am now and forever changed by my own thoughts as I mature vastly. I only hope people read my words and understand the world through my eyes.; [a.] Richland, WA

LEWIS, KIMBERLY
[b.] July 26, 1970, Madison Heights, MI; [p.] Otis and Roberta Graves; [m.] Terrance Maurice Lewis, March 25, 1995; [ed.] Bachelor of Arts in Humanities Pre-Law from Michigan State University received in 1993.; [occ.] Law Office Administrator; [oth. writ.] "Uncle Pie"; [a.] Irvine, CA

LEWIS, MARISSA BROOKE
[b.] February 29, 1988, Long Island, NY; [p.] Andrea and Gary Lewis; [ed.] Elementary School - going into 3rd grade; [occ.] Student; [hon.] Tournament of Champion Spelling Bee Winner, Writing Award of Suffolk County; [pers.] Even though I am only 8 years old I have written many, many poems. I believe in recycling and conserving water to help the earth.; [a.] Dix Hills, NY

LIGHTCAP, NIKI
[b.] November 6, 1981, Lincoln, NE; [p.] John and Jan Lightcap; [occ.] High School Student - Waverly High; [memb.] Waverly Swim Team; [hon.] Honor roll and Honor roll with distinction; [oth. writ.] I enjoy writing poetry and short stories, and have a collection of my writings; [pers.] I've enjoyed the gift of two wonderful older brothers, J.C. and Shawn, loving parents, and a few, but close, friends.; [a.] Waverly, NE

LIGHTON, MARK J.
[pen.] Anthony David Rutherford; [b.] May 30, 1967, Syracuse, NY; [p.] Patricia Cope; [occ.] General Manager; [a.] Mooresville, NC

LIKE, BRANDON
[b.] November 16, 1981, Elkhart, IN; [p.] Jane and Steven Like; [ed.] The Stanley Clark School South Bend, IN; [occ.] Student; [oth. writ.] "I Saw Her In A Green Dress" and "But Still The Bird Sings" published in *Her Children Speak*.; [pers.] "Poetry is emotion in its purest form."; [a.] Elkhart, IN

LIM, JEANNETTE ROSELYN
[b.] May 1, 1981, New York, NY; [p.] Dr. Alfonso and Rosella Lim; [ed.] Our Lady of the Lake School in Verona, NJ and currently, West Orange High School; [occ.] Student/Professional Kickboxer; [memb.] Suicidal Tendencies Fan Club; [hon.] Humanities Scholarship to Lacordaire Academy, Academic Scholarship to Queen of Peace High School, FMI Master Musicians Award 1994, Certificate of Participation in Mural Magic in Newark, NJ, Editor's Choice Award; [oth. writ.] Unpublished words poems and short stories; [pers.] To mom and dad, thank you for all your love and support. Without you, I never would've made it to where I am now. I'll always be grateful.; [a.] West Orange, NJ

LINDE, SUSAN
[b.] November 20, 1946, Provo, UT; [p.] Kenneth, Betty Huff; [m.] Larry Linde; [ch.] Ashlee, Corbin; [ed.] UVC, Dental Hyg., self taught artist, won Best of Show, UT County fair, 1988, first place, American Fork, Art City Days, numerous other, 1st 2nd and 3rd place Ribbons Landscape Oils, Pastels, in Paley in Provo UT; [hon.] Kids and Dental Conslt. for 2 years prior. publish poem in *Sparrow Grass* Art; [oth. writ.] I have a special love for animals, elderly people, and the arts. I love humor, and I cried when Old Yeller died.

LINDLER, LISA
[b.] August 13, 1980, Baptist Hospital, Columbia; [p.] James Ray and Donna Lindler; [ed.] I attend Mid-Carolina High School and am a rising junior; [memb.] Lutheran Church Youth (LCY) of South Carolina, Secretary of the Dutch Fork Conference for: (LCY), a member of my school's advanced chorus; [hon.] My letter for being in any chorus class for 2 years, won my 8th grade science fair and went USC with it, an I've been nominated for *Who's Who Among American High School Students*; [oth. writ.] None published; [pers.] My personal note is that I believe you can do anything with your own determination and God's help, also you can accomplish anything you put your mind and body in.; [a.] Little Mountain, SC

LINEBERRY, DELESHA JEAN
[b.] October 2, 1980, Twin County Hospital; [p.] Bettie and Bob Lineberry; [ed.] Junior of Carroll County High School; [occ.] Student; [memb.] Four years in Odyssey of the Mind, 3 years in 4-H, 4 years in band; [hon.] *Who's Who Among American High School Students*, Outstanding Educational Improvement, Outstanding Academic Achievement, Outstanding Mathematical Achievement; [oth. writ.] Other poems that I have sent to other poetry which were rated excellent.; [pers.] I find it easy to express my feelings through my poetry; [a.] Galax, VA

LIVERETT, DOYNE
[b.] October 19, 1960, Pueblo, CO; [p.] Robert Proudfit and Pat Gable; [m.] Travis Liverett, December 31, 1986; [ch.] Jason Robert and Jennifer Cathrin; [ed.] Centennial H.S. Champaign, IL, Univ. of Illinois, John Wood Community College Quincy, IL, ICS Business College, Scranton, PA; [occ.] Patient Accounts Clerk, Blessing Hospital, Quincy, IL; [memb.] First Baptist Church of Plainville, IL Choir director and Sunday School teacher for 3rd and 4th grades, American Baptist Women; [hon.] 14 1st place medals and ribbons for clarinet, 5 1st place awards for choir, numerous honor rolls, 3.8 GPA; [oth. writ.] "Essence of a Rainbow" is my first published writing.; [pers.] Life is an animation of existence, bringing circumstance to conquer and love to share. My poetry is reflective of life and spiritual growth which is always attainable.; [a.] Hull, IL

LIVERPOOL, VIKKI
[b.] Yonkers, NY; [p.] William and Josephine Moroch; [m.] Divorced; [ch.] Mark, Kevin and Lori (Twins); [ed.] College of Mt. St. Vincent, Riverdale, NY, (Bachelor's Degree in Communications/Journalism - Minor in Writing); [occ.] Secretary to Director of Career Development College of Mt. St. Vincent, Riverdale, NY; [memb.] Lambda Pieta - The National Communications Honor Society; [hon.] 2nd place - National Business Writing Award; [oth. writ.] Poems published - "Remember", "Dreams"; [pers.] My three children, father, and maternal grandmother will always be my greatest inspirations.; [a.] Yonkers, NY

LIZOTTE, JACKLYN ANNE
[b.] January 22, 1981, Waterbury, CT; [p.] Kristin and Robert Lizotte; [occ.] High School; [hon.] Student Leadership Award in 8th grade; [pers.] Cherish yesterday, live today, and dream tomorrow. Our time on earth is only borrowed, you can choose to live your life in happiness or sorrow. Cherish yesterday, live today, dream tomorrow.; [a.] Bethlehem, CT

LLOYD, ALLISON
[b.] August 26, 1979, South Korea; [p.] Tom and Nancy Lloyd; [ed.] Junior at Oshkosh West High School; [occ.] Student; [hon.] Recipient, Martha Moore Freshman English Award, 1995, GPA Highest honors, Fourth place honors in writing, feature story, entertaining, large schools at Newspa, Journalism Conference, April 24, 1996; [oth. writ.] Poems in *Hadaka*, Oshkosh West's Literary Magazine (High School), Index Oshkosh West's (High School) newspaper, poem in *Community and Identity*, booklet for writing workshop hosted by UN Oshkosh.; [pers.] I hope through my writings readers will connect and find comfort in my poetry. The most powerful writings are the ones that produce strong emotions from the reader.; [a.] Oshkosh, WI

LLOYD, JOHIA M.
[pen.] Johey, Joh; [b.] July 14, 1953, Maryland; [p.] Eugene and Beula Wright; [m.] Craig Arbugast, January 27, 1990; [ch.] Frankie Jr., Nakia and Justin; [ed.] High school, completed Barbizon School of Modeling, Private Nurse and Pharmacist Assistant; [occ.] Private Practical Nurse and Pharmacist Assistant; [hon.] Won a hula hoop contest in 1978 holding a hoop up for 2 hr 14 minutes and 3 seconds. Won award and $50.00 bond. Was honored for saving elderly lady's life in 1994; [oth. writ.] "Shadows," "To My Husband," "My Friend," "The Window"; [pers.] Before you "don't succeed", "Pray", that you will and can.; [a.] Cumberland, MD

LOGAN, BETH
[b.] March 29, 1952, Roanoke, VA; [m.] Chris Logan III, 1984; [ch.] Three; [occ.] Loving wife and mother; [oth. writ.] Personal poems; [pers.] Thanks to a loving family and friends for their support in my life.

LOMBARDI, DORIS
[pen.] Doris Lombardi; [b.] May 25, 1910, Lowell, MA; [p.] Edward and Mae Badmington; [m.] Charles Lombardi, February 3, 1945; [ch.] Charlene - Charles Sr.; [ed.] Lowell High, New England Baptist Hospital School of Nursing - U.S. Navy Nurse Corp; [occ.] Retired Nurse R.N.; [memb.] Various clubs; [hon.] Editors Choice Award from Library of Poetry; [oth. writ.] Several poems in newspapers in AZ-Mass The British Porcelaine Artist

LONG, ROSE
[pen.] Malachi Kingsley; [b.] January 29, 1947, Bessemer, AL; [p.] Edward and Jessie Long; [ch.] Brigette Long; [occ.] Registered Nurse AH Nursing Registry; [memb.] Oceanview Baptist Church; [hon.] Semi-finalist - 1996 North American Open Poetry Contest; [oth. writ.] Church publications, weddings, funerals; [pers.] Can immortalize how it feels to be a tiny leaf on a tree or that last slice of apple pie.; [a.] San Pedro, CA

LONTKA, JANET
[b.] December 29, 1940, Bayonne, NJ; [p.] Joseph and Mary Godlewski; [m.] Carl Lontka, April 24, 1971; [ch.] Michele, Carl Joseph, Grandchildren - Jessica Marie, Holden Patrick; [occ.] Retired; [oth. writ.] "Three Gifts," "Bonnie Eyes," "Over - The Hill"; [pers.] I wrote "Three Gifts" at the age of seven, in the second grade for my father, my teacher was so excited she took me to each class in the entire school to read the poem, by the time I reached the 8th graders I was sorry I wrote it and did not write again for 20 years; [a.] Westfield, NY

LOVETTE, ESTELLE MCRAE
[b.] October 5, 1917, Myrtle Beach, NC; [p.] Thomas O. and Lena Mae Norris; [m.] Loye T. Lovette Sr., April 9, 1939; [ch.] Sandra E. Loyet II, Connie F.; [ed.] High School, Associate Degree in Nursing; [occ.] Deceased

LOWE, ANDREA
[b.] February 17, 1984, Fairfield, CA; [p.] Douglas and Cassandra Lowe; [occ.] Student; [hon.] ABENY (Association of Black Education New York) Honor Service Award; [a.] Goose Creek, SC

LOWERY, BONNIE
[pen.] Bonnie Lowery; [b.] November 1, 1948, Lampasas, TX; [p.] Maxine and Bonner Williams; [m.] Divorced; [ch.] Angela Hendrickx, Garth and Lowery Merideth; [ed.] Burnet High, Univ. of Houston, Grossmont Jr. College; [occ.] Free Lance Photographer; [oth. writ.] Numerous poems (unpublished); [pers.] I strive to do the best with what I have and to remember, faith makes things possible not necessarily easier.; [a.] Horseshoe Bay, TX

LOWERY, RANDALL R.
[b.] June 20, 1963, Morris, IL; [p.] Donald and Doris; [ed.] Mason-Verona-Kinsman High Robert Morris College; [occ.] Hotel Manager, Rolingbrook Comfort Inn, Bolingbrook, IL; [memb.] First United Methodist Church; [pers.] I stare at the stars quite often and I pray upon them that all that is good will come true, for a dark world such as our needs this miracle.

LUCAS, JESSICA LAUREN
[b.] August 5, 1983, Baltimore City; [p.] Lisa Cooper-Lucas, Raymond Lucas; [ed.] Seventh grade, Trinity School; [occ.] Student; [memb.] Jack and Jill or American Incorporated, Girl Scouts of America, Voices of Inspiration Gospel Choir; [hon.] Book Academics Award, Miniature Art Show Achievement Award, Silver Medal in Archery Competition-June 14, 1996; [oth. writ.] Short story and poems published in Trinity School's Creative Writing Magazine; [pers.] My inspiration comes from my imagination, and my imagination is one of my most important assets.; [a.] Columbia, MD

LUCK, WAYNE
[pen.] Chester Demaaz; [b.] October 11, 1984, Flint, MI; [p.] Marie and Bruce Luck; [ed.] Woodland Elementary; [hon.] Five Awards for Cub Scouts, Three Art and Music Awards, Five Citizenship Awards, Two Science Awards, Four Writing Awards, Three Reading Awards, Six Promotion Awards, (I haven't failed a class yet!), and five M.E.A.P. Awards, and (Finally!) Three Track and Field Awards; [pers.] Good friends and family are the world's most valuable treasures.; [a.] Flint, MI

LUDDINGTON, BETTY WALLES
[pen.] Better Luddington; [b.] May 11, 1936, Tampa, FL; [p.] Edward and Ruby Luddington (Deceased); [m.] Robert Morris Schmidt (Divorced 12/81), September 20, 1957; [ch.] Irene Losat, Daniel Schmidt; [ed.] Plant High School, USF, Tampa, FL, 1980 BA American Studies/History, 1982 MA Library Media and Information Studies, 1986 Ed.S Curriculum and Instruction/Gifted Education; [occ.] Media Specialist, Dowdell Middle School Tampa, FL; [memb.] HASLMS (Hillsborough Association of School Library Media Specialist), FTP/NFA/Hillsborough Classroom Teachers Association, Country Music Fan Clubs, Brooks and Dunn, Diamond Rio, Joe Diffie, Aaron Tippin, ISP (International Society of Poets); [hon.] Phi Alpha Theta Outstanding Student Award, Golden Signet Award, *Who's Who Among Students in American Colleges and Universities*, Editor's Choice Awards for Outstanding Achievement in Poetry (1996), Honoraries: Phi Kappa Phi, Kappa Delta Pi, Omicron Delta Kappa, Phi Alpha Theta, Pi Gamma Mu, Honors Council, Honors Convocation, and Graduate Scholarships: OK, Library Studies, Alumni Assn.; [oth. writ.] "WITAN: A simulation activity for gifted students." *The Gifted Today*, Sept/Oct 1986. Joe Diffie Fan Club (poems): "Diffie Boots," "Diffie Cult Fanfare," "Honky Tonk Attitude." *The Tampa Tribune*, Dec. 1992: "Librarian uses Poetry, Country Music to reach Students at Dowdell." NLP, 1996: "I like myself: James Evans," *A Voyage to Remember*, "Hillbilly Knight: Country Wildflower," *Across the Universe*, "Sybil Luddington's 1777 Ride," *The Best Poems of the 90's*, "William Benjamin: Educational Leadership," *Recollections of Yesterday*: "Flower Scapes: Mary Vincent Bertrand," *Memories of Tomorrow*.; [pers.] Inventing a poetic style that flows forward and backwards with accents along the way...making life a poem, a bouquet of words that turns each day into something special.; [a.] Tampa, FL

LUNA, JILL MARIE
[b.] March 15, 1982, Nashville, TN; [p.] Ben and Janice Dicke; [ed.] Park Ave. Christian School, Gower Elementary Head Middle, Dupont Hadley, Hunters Lane High; [memb.] Beta Club, International Order of Rainbow for girls; [hon.] 1st place in Science Fair, Honor Roll, Perfect Attendance; [oth. writ.] None ever published; [a.] Old Hickory, TN

LUNDE, FLORENCE
[pen.] Krieger; [b.] April 16, 1941, N.Y.C.; [p.] Murray and Pearl Krieger; [m.] Manford A. Lunde, July 11, 1971; [ed.] M.A. Speech Pathology - N.Y.U. Berean College - Ministerial Studies; [occ.] Ret. Speech - Language Path. Co-Director, His Abundant Love Ministries; [memb.] ASHA, IAOGI, Disabled In Action (DIA); [hon.] Kappa Delta Epsilon-Hon. Sorority.; [oth. writ.] "The Wonders of God" - unpublished; [pers.] "Ye are complete in him which is the head of all principalities and powers" - Col. 2:10; [a.] Bronx, NY

LYCZEWSKI, TARAH
[b.] December 14, 1978, Sunnyside, WA; [p.] Tim and Dixie Lyczewski; [memb.] Vintiques, VICA, Key Club, Drama Club President; [hon.] *Who's Who Among American High School Students* two Consecutive years, VICA State Championships 3rd place Ten-person Newscast; [pers.] I wrote this poem in memory of my best friend. The friendship she gave to me will always be cherished. She touched the heart of those close to her.; [a.] Sunnyside, WA

LYDEE, THELMA
[b.] August 1, 1945, City of Angeles, LA; [p.] Olivar Pete Sanchez; [m.] Eric Lange, April 18, 1982; [ch.] Lisa L. Carignal; [ed.] City College, Los Angeles City College; [occ.] Credit Manager, Terry Hinger - Hardware Van Nuys Calif.; [memb.] American Lung Associates Oxnard Calif. 93030 Camarillo Writers Club; [oth. writ.] Editor of Ranch Santa Rosa HO Assoc.; [pers.] I strive to reflect an awareness of environment of our preservatives of our planet and future. I have been influenced by my father P.C. Sanchez in his writings poems and "Night and I".; [a.] Los Angeles, CA

LYNCH, CAROLYN MENDENHALL
[b.] July 28, 1933, Wilmington, DE; [p.] Warren Mendenhall and Mary Ann Kirkpatrick; [ch.] David Warren, Gay Ellen, and Barbara Addison; [ed.] The Tatnall School for Girls; [occ.] Guide Specialist, H.F. DuPont Winterthur Museum; [memb.] The New York Hajji Baba Soc., The International Hajji Baba Soc. (Wash., D.C.), The Oriental Ceramic Society Soc. of London (England), The Tatnall School Alumni Assoc. - Secretary; [oth. writ.] "Monograph on Chinese Porcelain", Museum Pub. May, 1990, "Real Estate for Income and Profit", M-L Publishing Co. 1974.; [pers.] I believe life is a journey, in pursuit of truth and beauty.; [a.] Wilmington, DE

MAAS, MICHELE
[b.] February 18, 1977, Provo, UT; [p.] Garren and Becky Maas; [ed.] Utah Valley State College; [occ.] Checker at Maays food and Drug in Orem, Utah; [memb.] Phi Theta Kappa; [hon.] Dean's List; [pers.] I just write whatever pops into my head.; [a.] Orem, UT

MABEY, AMANDA G.
[b.] December 21, 1980, Salt Lake City, UT; [p.] Gun S. Mabey and Edward Milo Mabey; [ed.] Grade School and 1 yr. of High School; [occ.] Student; [memb.] International Society of Poets; [hon.] Poet of the Year Award from Int. Society of Poets and Nat'l Library of Poetry, Honors Student; [oth. writ.] "Fire," "Memories," and 1 untitled published poems and several unpublished poems and 1 book.; [pers.] Most of my poems have not any depth, or philosophical statements on life and on death. And any old car who tries to read them as such, should write some himself and fill them up with junk.; [a.] Phoenix, AZ

MACIEROWSKI, ALICE J.
[b.] July 18, Westfield, MA; [p.] Edward and Rose Bajurny; [m.] Neil; [ch.] Eric Anthony, Jason Edward; [ed.] Westfield High School, Framingham Union Hospital School of Nursing Graduate, Attended Elms College as Biology Major; [occ.] Registered Nurse, Baystate Medical Center, Springfield, Ma./The Professionals; [memb.] St. Thomas Choir, soprano, Guitar Student of Dave Gomes; [oth. writ.] Editorial, local newspaper; [pers.] Life is rich in meaning and pleasure existing beneath the obvious.; [a.] West Springfield, MA

MACKEY, JIM
[b.] November 7, 1943, Ft. Smith, AR; [p.] Clarence and Wilma Mackey; [m.] Lynette, February 20, 1971;

[ch.] Creston, David, Kimberly; [ed.] Southwestern Univ., No. Az. Univ.; [occ.] Sales Manager, [hon.] Dean's List; [oth. writ.] Short articles published in U.S. and England; [pers.] Wish inspiration was more consistent!; [a.] Duncanville, TX

MADDOX, LORI K.
[b.] December 7, 1959, Marianna, FL; [p.] Noan L. and Juanita D. Gillespie; [m.] Randy Maddox, December 18, 1993; [ch.] Charles L. Woodham and Brandy N. Woodham; [ed.] Dale County High School, Midland City, AL; [occ.] Self Employed; [memb.] L.A. Rodeo Association; [pers.] This poem is about my father, who was stricken down with cancer, and the love he and my mother shared. I could never express the love and respect we all have for him. He is missed and loved each passing day.; [a.] Ozark, AL

MAHOMED, YAMILE
[b.] December 12, 1979, Mexico City; [p.] Ali Mahomed and Sarnia Mahomed; [ed.] Fossil Ridge High School; [occ.] Student; [hon.] I have received several acting certificates; [oth. writ.] I have other writings but they have not been published, this is the first one.; [pers.] This poem reflects a true event in my life. I just wanted to express my feelings over something that we all take for granted: friends. They can be the worst, it all comes down to who you choose.

MAHONEY, ROSE
[pen.] Rosie G.; [b.] February 8, 1963, SI, NY; [p.] Martin and Mickey Giovinazzo; [m.] Jon Mahoney, November 9, 1986; [ch.] Jon, Vera, Dillon and Gabreille; [occ.] Homemaker; [oth. writ.] Several poems and short stories. Now working on a novel; [pers.] Writing is a gift. It's a gift that can never be taken away.; [a.] Staten Island, NY

MAKPAULU, NDUKU
[b.] July 6, 1953, Kinshasa, Zaire; [p.] Nduki Enana, Epombo; [ed.] Self-educated; [occ.] Writer; [oth. writ.] *Opened eye heart* - manuscript.; [pers.] The reality of mankind is spiritual, the answers to our quest will come from within.; [a.] Bakersfield, CA

MALBACIAS, ELENA
[pen.] Adrian; [b.] December 17, 1952, Denver, CO; [p.] Adrian Malbacias, Ann Malbacias; [ch.] Christine, James Karlene, Evan; [ed.] West High School, Red Rocks Community College, Regis University; [occ.] Group Insurance Underwriter; [memb.] The Health Insurance Association of America; [hon.] Designation of Health Insurance Associate; [oth. writ.] Several poems published in College newspaper.; [pers.] As a child, I read a great deal of science fiction and fantasy. The words of my favorite authors flowed off each page like poetry to me. They told of distant worlds abounding with love, peace, and happiness. This has always been the conerstone of my writings always striving to make that dream world my reality.; [a.] Littleton, CO

MALLORY, BENNIE L.
[b.] August 11, 1941, Caledonia, MN; [ed.] 10th H.S.; [occ.] Heavy Equip Operator; [pers.] This was the first poem I wrote. Jan 1994, I woke at 3:00 a.m, wrote the poem in a few minutes, fell back to sleep, woke up at 7:00 a.m., read the poem and was awed. Have written several more.; [a.] Spring Valley, MN

MALPAS, KARI
[b.] October 2, 1972, Plainfield, NJ; [p.] Barry and Virginia Malpas; [ed.] Watchung Hills Regional High School, Marymount University (BA), will attend University of Pittsburgh in 8/96 for MLS; [occ.] Technical Services Library Assistant in Morristown/Township Library; [pers.] I just want to thank my family, friends and P.E.P. for supporting me every step of the way.; [a.] Warren, NJ

MANCOUR, DANIEL
[pen.] John Doe; [b.] March 18, 1964, Royal Oak, MI; [p.] Lita and Leon; [ed.] Dondero High School, Macomb Comm. College; [occ.] Remodlers Gopher; [memb.] American Red Cross, Blood Donor; [oth. writ.] "Road To Nowhere," "Scruffy Cat," "What Is Life"; [pers.] I like to write about life in general - what I see, what I feel, what I know, even what I've learned. Sometimes the hardest part of life is just plain keeping your sanity.; [a.] Royal Oak, MI

MANN, HAROLD W.
[b.] August 10, 1925, Columbus, GA; [p.] Rev. and Mrs. David G. Mann; [m.] Betty Parks (Mann), February 2, 1956; [ch.] Harold Jr., Martha Carroll and Janet Palmer; [ed.] Lanier H.S., Macon, GA, Emory University, Duke University; [occ.] Professor Emeritus of History, Radford Univ.; [memb.] 1255th Engineer (Combat) Battalion Veterans Association (I am the editor of its quarterly Bullchy); [hon.] Phi Beta Kappa (Phi Kappa Phi), Omicron Delta Kappa; [oth. writ.] Atticus Greene Haygood, (Methodist Bishop, Editor, and Educator, Lathens, Univ. of GA. PR., 1965). Staff poet, H.S. Newspapers 2 poems in *Star and Stripes* (European Edition), 1945, Lyrics to original songs, "Vignette of War", pub. in College lit. mags.; [pers.] I regret that, since Pound, poetry writing in America has become narcissistic. "Where has all the music gone?" Our marvelous tongue begs for a return of metrically set, echoing sounds.; [a.] Durham, NC

MANNEN, ROBERT J.
[pen.] R. J. Mann; [b.] June 2, 1945, Corpus Christi, TX; [p.] A. J. and Patricia Mannen; [m.] Jana K. Mannen; [ch.] Morgan Nicole, Sydney Danielle; [ed.] B.S. Soc. U. of H., DDS UTDB Houston; [occ.] General Dentist; [memb.] Ada TDA HDDS; [pers.] God creates all. Man co-creates some. Seth speaks volumes. The mind is more powerful than... learning is it. Much is illusion. I begin to understand faith. Paradox is a natural stage.; [a.] Houston, TX

MANSOUR, DIADEMA TOR
[pen.] Dema Tor; [b.] February 13, 1946, Iloilo City, Philippines; [p.] Cresdenciana B. Santo Cildes, Lucas C. Tor; [ed.] B.S. Chemistry, 1966, University of Iloilo, Philippines; [occ.] Currently Unemployed; [memb.] International Platform Association, American Chemical Society; [hon.] Premiere Poet - 1984 IPA 1992 International Platform Association Poetry Award; [oth. writ.] "Scar Of Palestine" - 1984, "Oh I Love Chicago" - 1992; [pers.] To be humble all the time for God teaches the humble, it's hard but the benevolent God guides.; [a.] Los Angeles, CA

MARCHETTI, DELISA LOUISE
[b.] March 18, 1963, Long Beach, CA; [p.] Donald and Helen Dinoff; [m.] John Anthony Marchetti, December 2, 1989; [ed.] R.A. Millikan High School, Long Beach City College; [occ.] Homemaker; [pers.] I enjoy writing poetry and short stories about women and their perceptions of the life around them.; [a.] Long Beach, CA

MARCOS, YENEYS
[b.] November 29, 1973, Cuba; [p.] Marta and Raydel Marcos; [ed.] St. Thomas University; [occ.] Student; [a.] Miami, FL

MARKOWITZ, KYMBERLY
[b.] April 15, 1985, West Islip, NY; [p.] Lawrence Markowitz, Gloria Markowitz; [ed.] Daniel Street School Lindenhurst, NY; [hon.] President's Award for Educational Excellence, Suffolk County Reading Council, second place, fifth grade, prose; [oth. writ.] "I Have A Dream"; [a.] Lindenhurst, NY

MARLOW, PATRICIA B.
[pen.] Patti Marlow; [b.] December 3, 1932, Altoona, PA; [p.] John Leslie Bair and Gladys Hess; [m.] Laurin P. Marlow, April 4, 1967; [ch.] John Scott Bond, Lesley Stephen, Lisa Moody; [ed.] Altoona High, Mary Washington College; [occ.] Realtor; [memb.] Les Femmes du Monde, Dallas Museum of Art Northwood; [oth. writ.] None published

MARQUEZ, TERESA A.
[b.] May 13, 1972, Granada Hills, CA; [p.] Mary Marquez; [ed.] John F. Kennedy High School; [occ.] Presently in College studying to receive my degree in child psychology; [oth. writ.] I have many other poems and short stories yet to be published.; [pers.] With this poem I hope to touch many hearts, and open up many eyes to the serious problem of abuse in our society.; [a.] Sylmar, CA

MARQUIS, TIFFANY MARGUERITE
[pen.] Tiff-Tiff; [b.] December 23, 1977, Brooklyn, NY; [p.] Father: Clarence Harrell; [ed.] Westside High (currently); [hon.] Outstanding Overall Academic Achievement; [oth. writ.] Several poems published in school newspaper, short stories.; [pers.] You must be influence in order to pursue it so strive for more and never turn from the door.; [a.] New York, NY

MARSH, BECKY
[b.] October 28, 1958, Columbus, NE; [p.] Elmer and Pat Leffers; [m.] Alan Marsh, November 1, 1980; [ch.] J. J. Marsh; [ed.] Brownsville High School, Texas Southmost College; [occ.] Billing Specialist, Grandview Health Resources, Sioux city, IA; [oth. writ.] Through the eyes of Grandchildren, mom, I love you, Letters Family Tree, Ronald McDonald house, sis, many others; [pers.] I write what I feel and see in life; [a.] Sioux City, IA

MARTIN, CRISSA
[b.] October 6, 1978, Cuero, TX; [p.] Barbara Martin, Mike Martin; [ed.] Cuero High School; [occ.] High School student; [memb.] National Honor Society, Junior Engineering Technological Society; [pers.] The way I write reflects my individuality.; [a.] Cuero, TX

MARTIN, DEBRA KATRINA
[b.] June 2, 1961, Denver, CO; [p.] Robert E. Martin and Rosalie M. Martin; [ch.] Garrett Robert Martin (Proctor); [ed.] Denver East High School, Spelman College, Atlanta Ga.; [occ.] Consultant, Lucas System Inc., Loan Processor, Chase Manhattan Mortgage Corp.; [memb.] Scott United Methodist Worship Committee and Weslyan Choir; [oth. writ.] Musical selects all instrumentals Mother Earth, Chasing a Miracle, and Time of Asia, on Unknown Friend's Sights Unseen and various other computerized compositions on the British Amiga Net; [pers.] I have been truly blessed, to come

from such a loving family. With nurturing parents who taught us compassion and humility and to always look to the man upstairs. And to have a wonderful son I'm proud of.; [a.] Denver, CO

MARTIN, JAMES PRESTON
[b.] February 19, 1981, Brighton Township, PA; [p.] Bruce and Ethel Martin; [occ.] 10th Grade Student Beaver Falls high School; [memb.] 2nd Baptist Church, Beaver Falls; [a.] Beaver Falls, PA

MARTIN, MAITHEL M.
[b.] June 8, 1917, Jenkins, MO; [p.] Mary and John Davenport; [m.] Gerald Browning Martin, March 7, 1936; [ch.] John Martin and Jeanne Martin Bick; [ed.] I attended eight grades in a small country school, and graduated High School in Verona, Missouri; [occ.] Retired, but still busy in my garden and with quilting; [memb.] Board Member: Missouri School of Religion (Jefferson City MO), Lenoir Retirement Home (Columbia, MO), Cherokee Christian Church (Member); [hon.] Ozark Writer's Guild, and "The Barn Players" of K.C., where I played a role as a Television Commentator; [oth. writ.] "The Quest" (a play), "Great Discovery," "Best Gift" (a play), "Oil for Memory's Lamps," "Trouble at "The Triple C." (a play).; [pers.] It seems to me that a positive attitude is best for me, and I'm convinced that other people are pleased with that sense, also. I do hope my grandchildren can see the positives in me.; [a.] Kansas City, MO

MARTIN, PETER
[pen.] Peter Martin; [b.] June 23, 1950, Wisconsin; [m.] Mary; [ch.] Three; [ed.] B.S., English, University of Wisconsin - Oshkosh; [occ.] Probation and Parole Agent, Fond du lac, WI; [oth. writ.] "Shadow Boxing" is a poem in my chap 5 book, *Licking My Wounds*, which will soon be going into its fourth printing (Baxstabber Press, USA).; [pers.] My writing is mainly autobiographical. I specialize in the truth. I adhere to the belief that poetry began as a medium for the people and should be accessible to the people.; [a.] Mount Calvary, WI

MARTIN, SUSAN A.
[pen.] Susan A. Martin; [b.] June 7, 1961, Taunton, MA; [p.] Margaret (Foley) Martin and Alfred Lewis Martin; [ed.] Master of Arts in Rehabilitation Counseling, Assumption College, Worcester, MA.; [occ.] Substance Abuse Rehabilitation Counselor; [memb.] Reimer's Association, American Cancer Society: Musicians United for Sexual Equality; [hon.] Francis Foley Scholarship for Academic Achievement from Assumption College in conjunction with Mediplex Hospital Bristol Massachusetts.; [oth. writ.] "How Can I Love Her?", "Planes and Motorcycles", "Doll Face," "Cow Eyes Girl," "Who Am I"?; [pers.] I have been writing poetry since my early adolescence. I now engage clients to write creatively as part of the therapeutic process. Poetry is a great medium of expressive therapy.; [a.] Taunton, MA

MARTINEZ, DEANNA LYNN
[pen.] Deanna Allen; [b.] January 27, 1971, Woodland, CA; [p.] Phyllis E. Blair and Frank R. Martinez Jr.; [m.] Mitchell Allen (Fiance); [ch.] Anoreia Dawn, Melton and Elizabeth Rabouin Allen; [ed.] Winters High, American River College, Solano Community College; [occ.] Housewife, Mother; [memb.] Vaca Valley Christian Life Center, National Arbor Day; [oth. writ.] Several poems, written and aired as advertising jingles, poems published in local newspapers. Hundreds of unpublished poems in my personal books; [pers.] I hope that through my writing I may encourage, inspire, touch and related to the human nature in all of us. I also hope to witness and spread the incredible gift of love that God gives to everyone!; [a.] Elk Grove, CA

MARTINO, JEREMY D.
[b.] September 26, 1979, Columbus, OH; [p.] David and Denda Martino; [ed.] Sophomore, Worthington Kilbourne High School; [occ.] Student; [memb.] Worthington Kilbourne High School Lacrosse Team; [hon.] Poem published in school newspaper; [a.] Columbus, OH

MARVIN, KEITH
[pen.] Nimrod Braithwaite, Murray Sassoon, etc.; [b.] July 1, 1924, Troy, NY; [p.] Dwight Marvin, Marian Louise Marvin; [m.] Dorthy Joyce Knippel (Deceased 1961), Beverly Hooker Anness (Div. 1981), June 25, 1955, February 23, 1962; [ch.] (By first wife), Dwight Marvin II, Wm. H. Marvin, India Lang Marvin (Mrs. Peter E. Dobson).; [ed.] Hoosac School, Hoosick, NY 1943 (Cert.), Diploma, 1991. Served as staff and faculty member, Hoosac School, 1944-1945, Dir. of Pub. Relations, 1945-1952 and am currently school historian.; [occ.] Free-lance writer (automotive history), Author of more than 2,100 articles on this subject (3,100+ since 1951), consultant to many automotive org's., here and abroad.; [memb.] Numerous automotive groups in US, Canada and U.K., other political, religious, civic organizations. Also active in other fields of endeavor, e.g. slot machines, Philately (and specializing in the postage of Tibet), music, verse, Canadian politics, history, etc.; [hon.] Numerous awards from automotive historic groups. Former President of the Society of Automotive Historians, Inc. Former editor of publications on that subject. Poetry and verse has been an avocation for many years. Have published several books of verse privately and contributed frequently to compendia and encyclopedia on automotive history.; [oth. writ.] Author or co-author of several books on automotive history and other subjects. Have also written for non-automotive journals (such as *Yankee, Vermont Life, Maryland Magazine, Milwaukee Journal Green Sheet*, etc.) Have been active in the history of automobile registrations and license plates and have designed them for other governments. Currently working on a second book, *Of Singular Fancy: The Romance of the License Plate*.; [pers.] Served in the Anti-Aircraft Artillery, US Army, WW II, Formerly investigative reporter, feature writer, section editor and music reviewer, *The Record Newspapers*, Troy, N.Y., and as Associate in duPont Library, Promfret School. Promfret, Connecticut. "October Oak" formerly published privately-printed book, *Return to Shadowland*. Other books of verse have included *Elegy to a Dead Princess, Arabesques Under the Moon, Impressions in the Moonlight and Other Verse*, etc.; [a.] Menands, NY

MARZOLI, STEFANO
[pen.] Mars; [b.] October 31, 1978, Rome, Italy; [p.] Antonio and Jane Marzoli; [ed.] Senior at William Henry Harrison High School; [hon.] 1st Alternative to Indiana Hoosier Boys State; [pers.] "Poetry is Life"; [a.] West Lafayette, IN

MASSAROTTI, HOLLY SIMPSON
[b.] February 15, 1956, Oneonta, NY; [p.] Levi and Virginia Slater Simpson; [m.] Glenn William Massarotti, July 30, 1983; [ch.] Brian James, Michael Anthony, and Emily Noel; [ed.] Richmondville Central School, NY, Broward Country Education Center, Fl; [occ.] Owner/operator of "Rosewoods" Herbs, Spices, Florals, and Essential Oils; [memb.] Exeter Historical Society, Seward Valley Grange, Schuyler Lake Cemetery Association; [hon.] National Honor Society; [oth. writ.] Many other poems; [pers.] As "A bouquet for grandma" reflects my early love for flowers and poetry so does my current endeavor "Rosewoods" an Herb and Floral Shop. Other poetry or flowers are available from Rosewoods.; [a.] Richfield Springs, NY

MATHIE, ALTON
[b.] April 10, 1929, Tetonia, ID; [p.] Vern Mathie, Isabelle Clay Mathie; [m.] Helen Mathie, November 24; [ch.] Kevin Mathie; [ed.] Weber High, Brigham Young University; [occ.] Self employed, Sales-writing; [oth. writ.] *Water Treatment Made Simple*, self published, *Chemical Treatment for Cooling Water - A Step Forward* scheduled-Fairmont Press Early 1997.; [pers.] I seek to relate concepts from the scriptures to every day life.; [a.] Roy, UT

MATTESON, DARREL L.
[b.] May 2, 1941, Riverton, WY; [p.] Charles Matteson, Mickey Rohan; [m.] (Divorced); [ch.] Tracy Matteson, Lori Thompson; [ed.] Baylor Law School, J.D. 1974; [occ.] Entrepreneur; [oth. writ.] Poems published in: *On the Threshold of a Dream Vol III, Agnippe, Piera, Carvings in Stone*.; [pers.] From childhood, I have been fascinated with the mystery of life, which probably explains my love for the works of Emily Dickinson.; [a.] Denver, CO

MATTHEWS, JEFFREY
[pen.] Amanda Singletary; [b.] September 29, 1978, Chicago, IL; [p.] Jacquelyn McClendon, and Spencer Matthews; [ed.] John W. Cook Elementary, John N. Harvard, St. Sabina, William G. Beale, Paul Robeson H.S.; [hon.] Various Awards for poetry including "Young Authors Contest" in Elementary school and I attended School for Poetry during the summer of 1991; [oth. writ.] Poetry entitled "I'm Tired". Various short stories and poems written during free time.; [pers.] Every since I was young I found poetry to be one of the relaxing hobbies I have.; [a.] Chicago, IL

MAXSON, STEPHEN P.
[pen.] Tully Stevens; [b.] March 27, 1957, Rochester, NY; [p.] R. Frank & Geraldine Anne; [m.] Divorced; [ch.] none; [ed.] Bachelors of Science - Business Administration; [occ.] Vice President of a small sales corporation in upstate NY; [oth. wrot.] "The Bend in The Path:, "And Life Goes On"; [oers.] My poems reflect these inner feelings of my soul which I am unable to speak.; [a.] Syracuse, NY

MAXWELL, CAROL
[b.] November 3, 1925, Dickson City, PA; [m.] William Sr. (Deceased), May 28, 1946; [ch.] 3 - 1 daughter - 1 son - 1 son (Deceased); [ed.] High school; [occ.] Retired; [oth. writ.] Poem published in local newspaper; [pers.] After my son passed away I never knew I could write poetry. Now it lets me share my feelings with others.; [a.] Jessup, PA

MAY, KAREN
[pen.] Kat; [b.] December 26, 1963, Sault Ste Marie, MI; [p.] Richard and Rosemary May; [ed.] Fraser High, Oakland University; [occ.] Operations Assistant, EXEL Logistics, Fairburn, GA; [memb.] Paralympic Volunteer; [hon.] Letter of Commendation, Dean's List; [oth. writ.] More poems as yet unpublished.; [pers.] My philosophy

is make people laugh - it crosses all barriers and lightens the heart!; [a.] Stockbridge, GA

MAYBEE, AARON
[b.] October 28, 1976, Kalamazoo, MI; [p.] William Maybee, Christine Ferguson; [ed.] Woodland Elementary, Portage Central Middle, Delton-Kellogg High School, Portage Central High School; [occ.] Child Care Worker, Curious Kids Child Care and College Student at Kalamazoo Valley Community College; [pers.] "Work hard...play hard."; [a.] Portage, MI

MAYNARD, MARIE ANN SUK
[b.] May 16, 1985, Seoul, Korea; [p.] Keith and Olivia Maynard; [ed.] Southwest Elemtary School Howell Michigan, Mrs. Kelly's 5th grade class; [occ.] Student; [hon.] Honor roll student in 3rd, 4th, 5th grade D.A.R.E. Graduate, Super Speller, Super Math; [pers.] "Being a different person in my nationality, I realized that the only thing different is personality. I also want to use all the abilities that God has given me for the best of mankind!!; [a.] Howell, MI

MAZUR, JAKE T.
[b.] December 25, 1988, Farmington, CT; [p.] Molly Mazur, Scott Mazur; [ed.] (9-96 entering) 3rd grade student; [occ.] Student; [a.] Unionville, CT

MAZZEI, LUCRETIA SHAYNE
[b.] December 11, 1963, Clarksburg, WV; [p.] Father deceased and mother abandoned; [ed.] World traveler, Technical Institute, High School Diploma; [occ.] Student - Avanti Hair Tech.; [memb.] Semminole Country Library, AAA; [hon.] Most Professional Certificate of Achievement, Sales Person of the Month, Valentines Day Comp. Award 1st place; [oth. writ.] Children's books (unpublished) many poems (unpublished); [pers.] The many trials, and tribulations of life in which we alone endure in this ever changing, condescending and unforgiving society we must maintain strength, kindness and the ability to forgive and above all, compassion for one another.; [a.] Lake Mary, FL

MCARTHUR, CATHERINE R.
[b.] May 27, 1962, Augusta, ME; [p.] Hanna and Robert Arnold; [m.] Kevin McArthur, April 13, 1985; [ch.] Jessica and Christopher; [ed.] Greater Lowell Regional Vocational Technical School GLRUTS Nursing School; [occ.] Licensed Practical Nurse

MCBRAVER, JERALD V.
[pen.] Marquez Juliano; [b.] November 26, 1977, Flint, MI; [p.] Marie E. McBraver, Edward A. McBraver; [occ.] Servant of the Lord; [memb.] Fairhaven S.D.A. Church; [hon.] I was given the honor of preaching the gospel of my Lord and Savior Jesus Christ. I was also awarded the grace to do it.; [pers.] Philippians 4:13 "I can do all things through Christ which strengtheneth me." II Corinthians 5:7 "For we walk by faith, not by sight." Romans 10:13 "For whosoever shall call upon the name of the Lord shall be saved." And always give God the glory.; [a.] Flint, MI

MCCALLEN, LEIGH
[b.] February 14, 1985, Croton-on-Hudson, NY; [p.] David McCallen, Peggy Shebanie McCallen; [oth. writ.] Another poem published in the *Anthology of Poetry Young Americans* 1995 edition.; [a.] Croton-on-Hudson, NY

MCCARTER, PATRICA
[b.] October 28, Bay City, TX; [p.] Darlene and Marvin McCarter; [ed.] Sophomore at Tiahaven High School; [memb.] Band, National Honor Society; [hon.] 1st and 3rd division Clarinet Solo, 2nd and 3rd place winner at U.I.L. meets; [oth. writ.] "Angel," "Brandi," "Together Forever," "Home Sweet Home," "Why?," "The Baby," "God," "The Start," "The Child," "Last Year," "The Real Me," "Now and Forever," "The Rules," "Mom and Dad," and poems in newspapers; [pers.] I write to express my feelings and hope to influence others to do the same and at the same time pursue a career as a surgeon.; [a.] Midfield, TX

MCCARTY, GEORGIE
[pen.] Jolee; [b.] Texas; [m.] Jerry; [ch.] Three, Mac, Punkin, Mich

MCCAULEY, CHRISTOPHER D.
[pen.] Christopher D. McCauley; [b.] May 8, 1967, Waco, TX; [p.] C. R. McCauley Sr., Jo Anne McCauley; [m.] Sheri Rose McCauley, June 24, 1995; [ed.] Midway High School, Texas State Technical College, McLenna Community College; [occ.] Texas Dept. of Transportation Design Tech III; [hon.] Texas State Tech. College, Deans Honor Roll 1988-89, Various Employment Related Certificates and Awards Dealing with Design Classes and Concepts.; [oth. writ.] "A Collection Of Identity" Various - Currently Awaiting Publishing, "Excerpts Of A Lonely Traveler, Master Of Quatrains" - Various Quatrains from Fictional Character" - Awaiting Published; [pers.] We bless this world through our many triumphs and tragedies. Let each outcome always prove elaborate regardless of the circumstances.; [a.] Waco, TX

MCCAULEY, M. J. MAC
[b.] MN; [p.] John and Ella McCauley; [m.] Margaret Lee, January 8, 1948; [ch.] Janet, Debra, John, Colleen, Diane; [ed.] University of Wisconsin, B.C. Arizona State University Masters Notre Dame, Texas A&M, before college: St. Peter's School; [occ.] County Commissioner; [pers.] This is my first poem for publication. My sister-in-law, Charlotte, built my interest in poetry.; [a.] Winona, MN

MCCAY, KRISTY
[b.] September 21, 1979, Sacramento; [p.] Luisa Leon, Charles B. McCay III; [ed.] Center High School

MCCLURE, MARGIE
[b.] February 12, 1948, Princeton, NJ; [p.] Raymond C. and Anne Ortlund; [m.] John C. McClure III, December 16, 1967; [ch.] Lisa, Laurie, John IV; [ed.] BA in Creative Writing from Calif. Sate Univ. Long Beach; [occ.] Executive Pastor, Vineyard Christian Fellowship of Newport Beach; [oth. writ.] Poems published in 2 other volumes of the Nat'l Lib. of Poetry, several articles in magazines, 2 books in process.; [pers.] My passion in life is first Jesus Christ, then my husband, my children and grandchildren!; [a.] Newport Beach, CT

MCCONNELL, ADELIA WOOD
[pen.] Dee Dee; [b.] July 25, 1949, Morristown, TN; [p.] Virginia Hunnicutt and Wayne Wood; [m.] Bill McConnell, June 17, 1972; [ch.] William Bradley, Julia Dare, and Brent Wood; [ed.] IMU: B.A. in English with minor in education and concentration in Russian, The Citadel: M.E.D. Secondary School Supervision and Administration.; [occ.] Teacher and Substitute Principal; [memb.] Virginia Association of Teachers of Eng., Roanoke Ed. Association, National ED. Association; [hon.] Given by Roanoke City School: Awards for publication in VA., Eng. Bulletin, Outstanding Professional Development: Certificate of Appreciation for Volunteer Service; [oth. writ.] "Participatory Education", *VA. Eng. Bulletin*, October 1996 publication.; [pers.] If you want to know the heart of American people, read poetry. My poetry reflects those grave moments when I feel and the need to connect my mind with my soul. Life is how we feel about ourselves. Being in touch with ourselves enables us to empathize and show compassion for others.; [a.] Richmond, VA

MCCRIGHT, KIMBERLY S.
[pen.] Kimberly S. McCright; [b.] May 24, 1920, Oklahoma, OK; [p.] Gregory Dahlgren, Christy Dahlgren; [m.] Matthew McCright, July 2, 1993; [ch.] David McCright; [ed.] Houston Community College, Sierra Community College, University of Oklahoma; [occ.] Home maker and Image Consultant; [hon.] Dean's Honor Roll Outstanding Community Service; [oth. writ.] Weekly Fashion Column published in local newspaper; [pers.] I was blessed to find my true love in 1992 and have been happy ever since; [a.] Yukon, OK

MCDANIEL, WARREN E.
[b.] January 21, 1928, Dayton, OH; [p.] Warren and Bessy Mae; [m.] Doris Ann, February 23, 1950; [ch.] Five; [ed.] Butler High School - Vandalia Ohio; [occ.] Artist; [memb.] ISP; [pers.] Warren's poems have delighted children and adults alike for many years. Warren and his family have been living in Alaska for the past thirty some years and most of that time in the bush country. You may write to Warren at P.O. box 1927, Valdez, Alaska 99686. He enjoys hearing from you. Many of his poems are about Alaska and the outdoors and run the gamut from sincere to satire.; [a.] Valdez, AK

MCDONALD, HERMAN
[b.] May 19, 1965, Newark, NJ; [p.] Herman L. McDonald, Mary Grimes McDonald; [m.] Taunya B. McDonald, August 1, 1987; [ch.] Herman Joel Jr., Alycia Brianna; [ed.] Plainfield High, Union County College, Cittone Institute, Christian Bible Institute; [occ.] Salesman, Sears Windows; [memb.] Christian Bible Center, Christian Bible Institute; [hon.] General Bible, Special Biblical Studies; [oth. writ.] Several poems unpublished as yet; [pers.] My inspiration comes from the Holy Scriptures and personal experience. One important thing I remember is from the book of Phillipians 3:13, forgetting those things which are behind and reaching forth unto those things which are before.; [a.] Plainfield, NJ

MCDONALD, MELVIN
[pen.] Aundre Richardson; [b.] June 25, 1980, Compton, CA; [p.] Renee Ashlock, Leno McDonald; [ed.] Walton Middle School, Gahr High School; [occ.] Student; [memb.] Brotherhood and Sisterhood, Y.O.U. for Church; [hon.] Honor Roll, Most Improved Player, Certificate of Appreciation, Most Valuable Player; [oth. writ.] I have written over 60 poems in a matter of one year.; [pers.] You can accomplish anything in life, if you put your mind to it.; [a.] Compton, CA

MCDONALD IV, EDWARD WILLIAM
[b.] February 5, 1976, Newport, RI; [p.] Edward McDonald III, Paula Graham; [ed.] Hayfield Secondary, Currently Attending Liberty University and half-way through a double Major in Vocal Performance and Music Education; [occ.] Youth Choir Director: Faith Evan-

gelical Pres. Church, Alexandria, VA; [memb.] Tri-M Music Honor Society; [pers.] My inspiration for both my poetry and my songs are truly God-sent. And for the Achievements I accomplish in my lifetime, the praise must go to my savior and redeemer, Jesus Christ. Maranatha! This poem is the first poem I ever wrote and written for my first true love.; [a.] Alexandria, VA

MCDOUGALL, LYNDA MOSS
[pen.] Lynda Moss; [b.] Sharon, PA; [p.] The Late Wesley Moss, Johnnie L. Moss; [m.] Calvin H. McDougall, June 25, 1994; [ch.] Suzanne, Jayme, Jeremiah; [ed.] Sharon High, Bradford Business School, Penn State University; [occ.] Drug and Alcohol Prevention Camp Facilitator Youth Coordinator Southwest Gardens; [memb.] New and Living Way Apostolic Church Sharon Regional Health Advocacy Committee P.S.U. Honor Society; [pers.] My father was wonderfully blessed with all of the qualities that every father should possess. The words in this poem are a major reflection of who and what my daddy was to me, Joe, Charles, Sandra and Suzzane and what wonderful husband he was to our mother Johnnie L. Moss.; [a.] Sharon, PA

MCDOWELL, KENNETH EDWARD
[pen.] Zackary; [b.] June 18, 1963, Atlanta, GA; [pers.] It's amazing what can happen when you pay attention!; [a.] Marietta, GA

MCDUFFIE, TERESA ANN
[b.] September 3, 1977, Lumberton; [p.] Virgil McDuffie and Betty McDuffie; [ed.] Graduate of South Columbus High School in Tabos City, now attending Southeastern Community College; [occ.] Attending Southeastern Community College for Cosmetology; [oth. writ.] None published; [pers.] This is my first publication and I've put my heart into my poetry since I was twelve. I would like to thank God, my family and friends for the support through the years, and I dedicate this poem to all of them. I love you all!.; [a.] Whiteville, NC

MCELRATH, JACQUELINE
[b.] December 8, 1959, Youngstown, OH; [m.] Larry McElrath, December 12, 1987; [ed.] Youngstown State University; [pers.] Sharing my poetry with others is a delight.; [a.] VA

MCEVOY, MICHAEL L.
[b.] June 8, 1971, Pontiac, MI; [p.] Lawrence James and Mary Kay; [ed.] B.A. in Video Communications; [occ.] Internet Specialist; [hon.] Dean's List; [oth. writ.] "Electronic Me", *Treasured Poems of America* - "Orange Juice," *Poetic Voices of America*; [pers.] Our imaginations are the doorways to our souls. I like mine wide open.; [a.] Farmington Hills, MI

MCGAHA JR., JOE
[b.] December 23, 1964, Dallas, TX; [oth. writ.] Songs - Christian, country Pop Rock - some are copyrighted.

MCGAHEE, PEGGY
[b.] October 5, 1937, Clewiston, IL; [p.] Floyd and Beneda Knowles; [m.] John Sterling McGahee, June 29, 1961; [ch.] Cindy (Lee), David (Lynn), Melanie, Gina (Jason), Stuart (Heather), Andy. (My in-laws are as dear to me as my children. Melanie and Andy aren't married yet; [ed.] Clewiston High; [occ.] Assistant Manager for water distribution company; [memb.] Evangel Assembly of God; [pers.] I believe in the power of positive thinking, with lots of praise and Faith knowing that "God Is Greater Than Any Problem I Have", and that every promise in His Book is mine as is every admonition.; [a.] Clewiston, FL

MCGLADE, TANYA
[p.] July 18, 1975, Decatur, IL; [m.] Gary G. McGlade, Donald L. Wills; [ed.] Currently attending Richland Community College for an RN Degree; [occ.] Teller at Soy Capital Bank Decatur, Ill; [oth. writ.] Poem published in a newsletter at Fair Havens Nursing Home. Decatur, Ill.; [pers.] Everything I write comes from my heart.; [a.] Decatur, IL

MCGOWAN, JESSE D.
[b.] October 18, 1962, Tacoma, WA; [p.] W. V. McGowan, Esther McGowan; [ed.] Manitou Elementary School, Bethel High School, Tacoma Community Community College, Tacoma, WA; [occ.] Full time unemployed part time employed yard work etc.; [memb.] Northwest poetry Connection, Tacoma Public Library; [oth. writ.] Several unpublished poems, poems published in college year books "Trillium"; [pers.] I was influenced by some of the classic Greek and Roman epics and by the exploits of some the men in the Biblical Hebrew Scriptures.; [a.] Tacoma, WA

MCGREW, DOLORES M.
[pen.] K. Stone; [b.] July 21, 1935, Harford, CO; [p.] Lewis and Elsie Cheek; [m.] R. Paul McGrew, December 23, 1981; [ch.] Anthony Vuono Jr., Cynthia Hope Burris, John Joseph Vuono; [ed.] Slate Ridge Elem., North Harford High, C.C.D. Teacher (38 yrs.); [occ.] Retired - former owner and Mgr. of Dolores Dress Inc; [memb.] 9127 K of C St. Bartholomew Catholic Church, Bona Vita Reb. Lodge #88 Basilica N.S. of the Immaculate Conception; [hon.] KOC Family of the Month Certificate - C.C.D. Teacher Past Noble Grand Reb. Lodge; [oth. writ.] Articles in local paper, unpublished poems.; [pers.] Live God's Teaching's Today and he will provide our tomorrow.; [a.] Manchester, MD

MCGUIRE, CONSUELO RAMIREZ
[pen.] "Consuelo"; [b.] April 18, 1950, Torrance, CA; [p.] Phyllis Martin Ramirez and Frank Ramirez; [m.] Michael John McGuire, December 17, 1988; [ch.] Larry and Nick Hultman, ShyAnne Marsh, Felisa Gumm; [ed.] Palmdale High, Deloux School of Cosmetology - CA, New Careers Business College - Boise, ID, 1995 graduate of P.C.D.I. in Fitness and Nutrition; [occ.] Truck Driver - Long Haul Team Driver with Husband; [memb.] Past Nursery Chrmn. for Christian Women's Club and Life Series Chrmn., Class Press., De Loux School of Cosmetology; [hon.] 1968 Miss Littlerock, CA, 1968 Runner-up Miss Antelope Vly, CA; [oth. writ.] "Road Warning" - 1994, "Eyes Of Ivy" - 1994, "The Sea Of Michael" - 1987, "Little Lady" - 1995, Highway Afghan" - 1995, "Pretty Lady" - 1965, "Sandstone" - 1979, and many others.; [pers.] To really know me is to read my writings. They are my soul bared, my deepest passion, a gracious gift from my Lord, among others. To Him I dedicate every word.; [a.] Anza, CA

MCHANEY, MEGHAN
[b.] April 6, 1984, St. Lukes Hospital, Chandler, AZ; [p.] James M. and Jill D. McHaney; [ed.] Graduated from Hartford Elementary School, May 1996 Chandler, AZ. Currently, a 7th grade student at Bogle Junior High, Chandler, AZ; [occ.] Student; [memb.] Art and Crafts Club, Jazz Dance Club, Baton Club, Band; [hon.] Principal's List and Honor Roll throughout elementary school. Student of the Month - numerous Citizenship and Reading Awards; [pers.] My greatest influences in life are my parents and family teacher who have helped me to learn and grow. I plan to go to college and to further my artistic talent. I am unique because I am me.; [a.] Chandler, AZ

MCHONE, JENNIFER
[b.] April 15, 1981, Miami, FL; [p.] Nancy and Paul McHone; [ed.] Oliver Hoover Elementary, Hammocks Middle School, in second year at Sunset Senior High School; [occ.] Student; [memb.] National Junior Honor Society, Thespian Honor Society; [oth. writ.] "Tears of Yesterday," "Masterpiece," "Imprisoned by Faded Memories," "Destiny"; [pers.] If good things lasted forever we wouldn't realize how precious they are.; [a.] Miami, FL

MCINTYRE, REGENA
[b.] September 14, 1977, Robeson, CO; [p.] Freddie and Janet McIntyre; [ed.] Whiteville High, Southeastern Community College; [memb.] Mill Branch Baptist Church Choir, FWA, French Club; [hon.] Honor Roll, *Who's Who Among American High School Students*, Everyday Hero Honor; [pers.] I strive toward my goals and never give up on my dreams.; [a.] Whiteville, NC

MCLEOD, BLANCHE
[pen.] Blanche McLeod; [b.] May 19, 1947, Brooklyn, NY; [p.] Willie and Mabel Ross; [m.] Pastor Danniel McLeod, The Church of God in Christ Jesus, January 29, 1972; [ch.] Mingo, William, Donniel II, Terry, Catrina-Monique, Naomi Blanche, Thimothy, Ruth Tasha and Keisha Leonore (Ruth and Thimothy are twins); [ed.] Sara J. Hale Voc. High School, The College of Staten Island; [occ.] Office Associate, New York City Board of Education; [memb.] The Church of God in Christ Jesus F.D. Inc.; [hon.] Ordained Elder Blanche McLeod on February 14, 1989, of the Church of God in Christ Jesus F.D. Inc.; [oth. writ.] "Be Not Afraid, Jesus is Coming," "If Music Could Fly" these are some of the songs that I have written and have sung in church.; [pers.] "Homeless Soldier" is about a real homeless person, whom I happened to have seen while traveling home from a Friday night prayer service some winters ago. I asked the Lord what can I do to help. He inspired me to use my talent and write this poem. I contribute this poem "Homeless Soldier" to all homeless people and in hope that everyone who encounters this poem will become awakened in social awareness and concern to what in happening to our homeless Americans and use our talent to help them.; [a.] Brooklyn, NY

MCLEOD, CHARLES W.
[pen.] Charles McLeod; [b.] September 29, 1931, Geneva, AL; [p.] Charles W. and Winnie J. McLeod; [m.] Etta Bentley McLeod, December 23, 1954; [ch.] Two; [ed.] Alabama grade schools, Univ. of Georgia (Atlanta Div., Bus. Adm. minor Bus Law, CLU, Bryn Mawr, PA; [occ.] Retried, disabled; [memb.] Baptist church, Silver Star, Bronze Star, Presid. Citation, five major campaign stars (Korean War), life underwriter of the year (multiple awards), past president of Rotary Club and Civitan Club; [oth. writ.] Business: Sales promotions, training and guidelines and presentations; [pers.] The "Golden Rule"; [a.] Augusta, GA

MCLEOD, MELISSA
[pen.] Melissa McLeod; [b.] August 25, 1967, Melbourne, Australia; [p.] Rosa Lee, Russell Lee; [m.] Daniel T. McLeod, May 8, 1994; [ch.] Madeline McLeod; [ed.] Methodist Ladies College; [occ.] Drafts-

man; [pers.] Poetry flows like music, if it does not, then it is simply writings.; [a.] Punta Gorda, FL

MCLOUD, MILDRED HYATT
[b.] August 24, 1927, Georgia; [p.] Lemuel and Ora Hyatt; [m.] Donald R. McLoud, February 22, 1947; [ch.] Five; [ed.] Graduated Martha Berry Rome Georgia Jan. 1945; [occ.] Retired; [memb.] Berry Golden Guard South Carolina Retired Teachers; [hon.] Golden Guard for 50 years of Alumni Service Red Cross Emergency Service; [oth. writ.] Church and local papers, medical paper local, alumni paper; [a.] Killdeer, ND

MCMAHAN, BRAD
[b.] August 9, 1980, Lubbock, TX; [p.] Pat and Rhonda McMahan; [ed.] High School Junior; [occ.] Assistant to building contractor/Homeschool Student; [memb.] National Rifle Association, Law Enforcement Explorer Post #999; [oth. writ.] Reports on debt and/or finances, including "The American Dream". Several poems and inspirational prayers.; [pers.] I thank the Lord Jesus Christ for all that I am and all I will ever be. For it is from Him that I receive the inspiration for my writings.; [a.] Lubbock, TX

MCNEFF, ENID C.
[pen.] Enid Claire Humbert; [b.] January 8, 1915, Arizona; [p.] Jules J. and Flora H. Humbert; [m.] Ernie E. (Deceased), July 24, 1942; [ch.] Jules Gerald; [ed.] High School and 3 years Nurses training, Registered Nurse - worked 40 years in Arizona; [occ.] Retired since 1973; [oth. writ.] A number of poems which I had put in back form for my family, My memories in 1991 after having a heart attack; [pers.] I was born on a ranch on Oak Creek, Arizona. Attended Clarkdale High School and took my training at St. Josephs Hospital in Phoenix, Ariz. Worked at Phoenix, Kingman and Cottonwood Ariz.; [a.] Rio Rancho, NM

MCQUEEN, JOYCE STULTS
[pen.] Joy McQueen; [b.] December 6, 1932, Trenton, NJ; [p.] Joseph Smith, Stults, Ruth Lawton Stults; [m.] (Deceased 1987) Burton McQueen, January, 1956; [ch.] Lisa Dawn, Loren Joy, Kerry Lawton; [ed.] Rutgers University, Temple University U.S.C.; [occ.] Gerontologist L.A.U.S.D.; [memb.] A.A.V.W.; [hon.] A.B. and M.S. degrees; [oth. writ.] Personal Journals for my grandchildren.; [pers.] I strive to make a difference in the lives of everyone in the world that I meet, to walk 2 positive path throughout life. Let my epitaph read "She knew love."; [a.] Redondo Beach, CA

MCRAE, JAMES
[pen.] The Nubian Poet; [b.] July 9, 1948, New York City; [p.] Frank McRae, Anne Walker McRae; [occ.] Screen writer/novelist/composer; [oth. writ.] "Young Master", (The Mistakes We Make As Youth, And The Regrets Such Bring Us As Adults) Fic. Novel. 544 pg. "We Are Not Beggars" (a private sector economic revitalization plan for the Black Inner Cities, and relster essay) non-fict. essays 44 pgs.; [tn] Los Angeles; [a.] CA

MEARS, JENNIFER
[b.] December 7, 1960, Freeport, TX; [p.] Jerry Albinus, Sue Albinus; [m.] Bobby Joe Mears, April 6, 1979; [ch.] Cassie Mears, Melisa Mears; [occ.] U.S. Postal Service; [pers.] This is the only poem I have ever written. It reflects actual events in my life.; [a.] Magnolia, TX

MEDEIROS, NELOISE K.
[pen.] Lou Weber; [b.] December 28, 1914, Little Rock, AR; [p.] Mr. and Mrs. O. M. Knight; [m.] Jacintho Medeiros, December 11, 1991; [ch.] Stepson and daughter; [ed.] Graduated High School in Little Rock, Ark., has swimming pool business in Houston over 30 yrs. (Weber's Pool Supply); [occ.] Retired, exercise instructor (20 yrs.); [memb.] Sr. Group at St. Helen's Catholic Daughters of the Americas; [hon.] Bowling League; [oth. writ.] ""M" for Marcie" - 1939, "The Bird in the Cowboy Hat, "Freddie, the Frog and Tellie, the Turtle" - 1978; [pers.] I was a widow for 5 yrs. before that, I was married to Mel Weber for nearly 40 yrs.; [a.] Houston, TX

MEHAGIAN, DIANE
[b.] September 17, 1969, Phoenix, AZ; [p.] John Mehagian, Marjorie Elmslie Mehagian; [ed.] Xavier College Preparatory, Southern Seminary College (now Southern Virginia College for Women) - A.S., Arizona State University - B.S., M.S.; [occ.] Summer - Park Ranger Interpreter - Grand Teton National Park, Winter - Horse Trainer, Riding Instructor; [memb.] The Nature Conservancy; [hon.] Phi Theta Kappa - National Honor Society, Phi Kappa Phi - National Honor Society, Alpha Zeta - National Agricultural Honor Fraternity, Morris - Saber Award for Leadership and Academic Excellence, Ashway Horsemanship Award for Scholarship, Motivation, and Character; [oth. writ.] None published or printed.; [pers.] In the course of my life, I have had the opportunity to travel many places, indulge in the diversity of our surroundings and experience various cultures. I believe all of earth's creatures are undeniably bound together in an intricate web. My writings often reflect the importance of freedom, space, and respect for all life.; [a.] Phoenix, AZ

MELGAREJO JR., DAUZED
[pen.] Zed; [b.] April 29, 1973, Newark, NJ; [p.] Dauzed Melgarejo Sr. and Ana Maria Melgarejo; [ed.] Elizabeth H. S. 1992 graduate. Kean College, Elizabeth, NJ; [occ.] Sales Representative; [memb.] Kickboxing; [hon.] Poetry contest in grammar and High school; [oth. writ.] Non-published poems and stories; [pers.] No matter how hard the wind blows, or how heavy the rain falls, always strive for what you believe in; [a.] Elizabeth, NJ

MELLINGER, DAMON
[b.] April 11, 1982, St. Louis, MO; [p.] Frank and Pat Mellinger; [ed.] Going into 9th grade at Oakville High School in the fall; [occ.] Student; [memb.] AAU/USA Wrestling, Select Soccer League; [hon.] Most Athletic, been in Newspaper 8 times for wrestling; [pers.] I wrote this poem to express my feelings for a girl I love very much, Jennifer Meridith; [a.] Saint Louis, MO

MESSINA, ANTHONY
[pen.] Anthony Messina; [b.] July 7, 1953, Brooklyn, NY; [p.] Mary, Anthony B. Sr.; [ed.] HS Graduate, some college credit; [memb.] "Supporter" National Children's Cancer Society 1995-96; [oth. writ.] "Synchronicity", "Morality", "Winter Winds", "Bitter Sweet Movement".; [a.] Roslyn Heights, NY

MESSLER, EDMUND ANDRE
[pen.] Edmund Andre'; [b.] February 13, 1964, Rochester, NY; [p.] Robert A. Messler, Denise Zory; [ed.] Two years non-graduate studies at the Julliard School, New York, NY and eleven years private studies in voice and the classical repertory.; [occ.] Musician (vocalist)- Carpenter; [memb.] Volunteer with Special Olympics Colorado; [oth. writ.] Four volumes of poems, prose and lyrics not yet submitted for publication. One other poem, "Before His Time", to be published in an anthology in spring of '97.; [pers.] An avid skier, hiker and camper, I draw from the wilderness and its contrast to the manmade urban environment, for inspiration. So too, from the experiences and people that come into my life.; [a.] Denver, CO

MIANI, GIANNINA
[b.] November 4, 1981, Peru; [p.] Federico and Elsa Miani; [ed.] Winston Park Elementary School, Miami, FL., Howard McMillan Middle School, Miami, FL.; [occ.] Student; [memb.] Riverside Hispanic Baptist Church, Youth Group and Staff Reporter for Local Church Newspaper; [hon.] Arts and Craft Award; [oth. writ.] Several other non-published poems, Formal Staff Reporter for Local Church Newspaper.; [pers.] I use my poetry to voice my soul. As I write poetry it's like pouring down on paper my personal inner thoughts.; [a.] Miami, FL

MICSAK, DAN
[b.] Saginaw, MI; [p.] Anna and Andrew Micsak (Deceased); [m.] Rita Micsak, September 10, 1977; [ch.] Amanda and Lisa Micsak; [ed.] Merrill High School, Saginaw Business Institute; [occ.] Industrial Sales (Tupes of Saginaw, Inc.); [memb.] Linwood St. Annes Catholic Church and School, Ducks Unlimited; [hon.] Most valuable baseball player and sportsman award, Merrill High School, Dale Carnegie Representative Award; [oth. writ.] *Saginaw News* - Sports poem. Also 2 obituaries poems.; [pers.] I strive to have my poems represent some personal meaning and something that most people understand and enjoy reading.; [a.] Linwood, MI

MIKUS, MARGARET DUBAY
[b.] May 6, 1952, Detroit, MI; [p.] Virginia Ruth, Wilfred Louis; [m.] Stephen T. Mikus, May 25, 1974; [ch.] Blake Joseph, Alexandra Louise; [ed.] B.S. Zoology, U. of Michigan, Ph.D., Microbiology, U. of Chicago; [occ.] Writer, Consultant; [oth. writ.] I have written a poetry journal which is 2 volumes, combined with photography, on subjects from healing to nature to family to transformation with the intent of changing people's perception of the world we live in.; [pers.] I am interested in the full blooming of each individual which is the focus of my consulting work. My poems and photographs and songs show the love and beauty I find in my everyday world.; [a.] Lincolnshire, IL

MILLER, AMEENAH
[b.] December 9, 1983; [p.] Daphine and Fabian Stewart; [ed.] 7th Grade; [hon.] Spelling bee I have two and place trophies. I have one trophy kindness is contagious and 3 certificates to go along with it. Then I have a certificate of promotion to the next level.; [pers.] Keep on, races, prayer, power, and faith, God will be there, and willing to write more.; [a.] Memphis, TN

MILLER, DAVID
[b.] January 15, 1944, Indiana; [p.] Orson Miller, Helen Pressler; [ch.] Three individual children; [ed.] School of hard knocks; [occ.] Carpenter; [pers.] Poverty in this rich country is the product of selfishness...our lack of compassion for those who suffer will be the demise of this once great society.; [a.] Bronx, NY

MILLER, DONALD D.
[pen.] Douglas Raman; [b.] October 14, 1913, Ogden, Weber, UT; [p.] Frederick Shaw and Polly Ann Taylor Miller; [ed.] Graduated Ogden High School 1931

Stevens-Henager Business College some years later.; [occ.] Retired; [pers.] I must learn to be free, to do and say the truths that are a part of me. Though I in erring along life's road may find someone to help share my load, to teach me right and lead the way to greater joy from day to day.; [a.] Ogden, UT

MILLER, GREGORY
[b.] June 10, 1942, Reading, PA; [p.] John and Amelia; [m.] Christine, May 30, 1964; [ch.] Jeremy, Lesley, Andrea, Bryan; [ed.] B.S. Ed. Kurtown Univ. M. Ed. Temple Univ., Masters, International Ed. Trinity Seminary; [occ.] Missionary; [a.] Clementon, NJ

MILLER, PATRICIA BURKE
[b.] July 6, 1932, Houston, TX; [p.] Claude and Pearl Burke; [m.] Jim Miller, June 2, 1950; [ch.] Michelle Kite Miller, Jill Miller; [ed.] Lamar High school, Houston, University of Houston; [occ.] Retired owner of Ladies Dress Boutique and Bridal Salon, Accountant; [memb.] Clear Lake Church of Christ, American Cancer Society; [oth. writ.] Monthly Articles, Business Magazine - Weekly Articles Church Bulletins - Poetry for All Occasions, Song Lyrics.; [pers.] I have written poetry since I was eight years of age, and I strive to express in verse, the feelings of the heart, mind and soul. Favorite poets: Elizabeth Barrett Browning and William Wordsworth.; [a.] Friendswood, TX

MILLIGAN, WILLIAM
[b.] February 12, 1941, Neptune, NJ; [p.] Isabel Land, Alexander Milligan; [m.] Betty S. Milligan, August 14, 1982; [ch.] William A. Milligan; [ed.] Elon College, Elon College, N. Carolina; [occ.] Salesman; [memb.] Roamoke Valley Writers; [oth. writ.] Several poems published in newspapers and contests. Articles for Baptists and "Big Brothers" Magazines; [pers.] I strive to show the uniqueness of individuals. My personal statement is: nothing's ever quite as nice as it is when it's shared with you!; [a.] Roanoke, VA

MINER, ALICE
[b.] March 22, 1924, Bridgetown, Nova Scotia, Canada; [p.] Harding Morse, Annie Morse; [m.] Clarence Miner, August 22, 1950; [ch.] Nancy Carolyn, Diane Elizabeth; [ed.] Acadia University, Wolfville, Nova Scotia; [occ.] Retired; [oth. writ.] Have written several poems for my own enjoyment - about grandchildren, pets, nature in the backyard.; [a.] Belmont, MA

MINES, HERMALENA V.
[pen.] Melchisedec; [b.] November 30, 1976, Cleveland; [p.] Herman and Debra Mines; [ed.] Sophomore attending Taylor University - Ft. Wayne; [occ.] Student; [oth. writ.] "Untitled" published in *From Mind to Page*, Kenyon Writing Institute (Summer 1994) and "The Willow"; [pers.] "Like fragments in time floating through space, light years away is the human race."; [a.] Mentor, OH

MIRABAL, JACOB WAYNE
[b.] February 17, 1982, Grand Rapids, MN; [p.] Simon and Ann Mirabal; [ed.] Going into Freshmen year of high school in fall of '96' at CCS Private School in Grand Rapids; [occ.] Student at Christian Community School; [memb.] Hill City Baptist Church where he assists with children's church and participates in all programs; [hon.] Honor student likes science, math, playing chess, street hockery and basketball. Also likes rollerblading, girls and listening to soft rock music; [oth. writ.] Poetry titles are, "Forever", "Love", and "The Pearl"; [pers.] The Lord will see you through anything if you have faith.; [a.] Hill City, MN

MOCHERLA, OMSHANTI
[b.] February 14, 1970, India; [m.] Bhushan Mocherla, June 3, 1994; [ed.] Masters In Marine Biology; [occ.] Housewife; [pers.] Writing poems has been a hobby of mine. Reading voraciously - A passion! My feelings always transcend to poems and passages. I thrive on honest expressions.; [a.] Atlanta, GA

MONTES, JUAN LUIS
[b.] April 25, 1980, New York; [p.] Hector J. Montes and Daisy Rosario Montes; [ed.] Currently a junior at Mt. St. Michael Academy; [occ.] Full time student; [memb.] JV. Football Team, JV. and Varsity Hockery, and JV and Varsity Lacrosse; [hon.] Dade County Science Fair award, Catholic High School JV. City Champs. "95"; [pers.] I am a strong believer that actions speak louder than words, and this is how I try to live my life.; [a.] Bronx, NY

MONTGOMERY, SHARMANE T.
[pen.] Tookie Luv; [b.] November 8, 1980, Waycross, GA; [p.] Lawanna H. Montgomery; [ed.] Sophomore at Klare County High School; [occ.] Full time student; [memb.] FBLA, Xinos; [hon.] Eddie Lee Sims Science Award, 9th Grade Honors, Excellence in Geography, Excell Club 94-95, Academic Award for Phi Delta Kappa's Xinos, Presidential Fitness Award; [oth. writ.] I have written several poems to accumulate for a book of poems.; [pers.] I have been greatly influenced by my mother. I write to reveal the hardships I have gone through and the hardships of my close loved ones.; [a.] Waycross, GA

MONTOYA, MARCELLA E.
[b.] August 27, 1964, Norwalk, CA; [p.] Maria Urioste and Benny Montoya; [ch.] Robert and Joshua; [ed.] Huntington Park High; [occ.] Full time mother; [pers.] In my writing I hope people will remember love should always be unconditional, for when all is said and done love is all we have. Poems until now. This poem is dedicated for German "Tito" Ferriera, he was my inspiration for "April 20" which made these words flow so easily from my heart.; [a.] Huntington Park, CA

MOONEY, CATHERINE R.
[b.] October 13, 1953, Oakland, CA; [p.] Phyllis and D. C. Mooney; [ch.] Kelly Gene Mooney; [ed.] California State University, Stanislaus B.A., Psychology, Masters of Science in progress; [occ.] Administrative Secretary; [pers.] The "Names Upon the Wall" was written in honor of all Vietnam Veterans, and is dedicated to one in particular-my beloved brother and friend, Sgt. Raymond Kent Shebelut, U.S. Army and Silver Star Recipient.; [a.] Stockton, CA

MOORE, HELEN
[b.] Janiary 19, 1927, Middleton, TN; [p.] Homer & Myrtle Russell; [m.] Henry Moore, September 20, 1948; [ch.] 3; [ed.] 10th grade; [occ.] Housewife; [oth. writ.] none published; [a.] Bilinar, TN

MOORE, JACKIE YOUNG
[b.] August 8, 1968, Oxford, NC; [p.] David L. Young and Lucy T. Young; [m.] Divorced; [ch.] Ton'Yetta Young and Zakia Moore; [ed.] J. F. Webb High School, North Carolina Central University (presently); [occ.] Senior Tech. Support Representative, IBM; [pers.] To dream but never try is failure within itself! Poetry is an expression of my inner self that I can share with us. But the interpretations are dependent on the person, therefore it becomes personal to each individual.; [a.] Oxford, NC

MOORE, MIRANDA MARIE
[b.] January 21, 1982, Sitka, AK; [p.] Wayne and Linda Lofton; [ed.] Presently a freshaman at Nestucca Highschool; [occ.] Student; [hon.] Citizenship Awards, Honor Student; [oth. writ.] Several poems and short stories that are not yet published; [pers.] I hope to see other young people like myself getting their poems and stories published. It is good to see young adults involved in such things.; [a.] Hebo, OR

MOORE, RENEE
[pen.] Andrea Winsor; [b.] June 20, 1965, Maryville, TN; [p.] JoAnn Dale, Carroll T. Dale; [m.] Michael Moore, June 9, 1993; [ch.] Misty Hayes, Allen Hayes; [ed.] Chattanooga Valley High, Edmonson Jr. College Orientation Training over CNA's, CPR training Schools; [occ.] Brown Appliance Parts (Sales); [memb.] In School - FBLA Club, FHA Club, Typing Club, Church of the Nazarines; [hon.] Silver Award - in the health field, School Teacher's Appreciation Awards, May Day Queen in school, CPR Awards; [oth. writ.] Did write a little for children's literature; [pers.] I hope somehow my poems help someone in life. To let them know you can still be happy even though things are rough.; [a.] Rossville, GA

MOORE JR., BOBBY E.
[b.] November 22, 1954, Birmingham, AL; [p.] Bobby Moore Sr., Rosie Lee Moore Fitts; [m.] Beverly G. Moore (Divorced), February 19, 1974; [ed.] G.E.D., Associate of Arts at Jefferson Davis Community College November 21, 1992; [occ.] Free-lance writer presently incarcerated; [memb.] Kairos #12, Hope Aglow Ministries, Inc, Ark Ministries Of American, Inc.; [hon.] Ark Ministries, all "A's" 19, A's on competitions; [oth. writ.] Poems published in a Gospel Magazine, I have written five unpublished books which consist of over 100 plus poems, short stories and articles.; [pers.] I try through my writing to open all people's eyes to a reality of negativity that has been manifested throughout flesh, in hope that we all (no matter what our skin color) will put aside negativity and through the power of God embrace positivity, through Jesus Christ.; [a.] Atmore, AL

MORALES, ARLON
[b.] February 24, 1974, Carazo, Nicaragua; [p.] Johnny Morales and Maria Luisa Chavez; [ed.] Attended Jr. High School in Miami, Florida. Completed High School in Fairfax, Virginia; [occ.] Student; [oth. writ.] Include songs and other poems never published.; [pers.] Take some time to think and write, and you will see that there is more to your life than just being alive.; [a.] Annandale, VA

MOREDA, CESAR J.
[pen.] Cesar J. Moreda; [b.] December 20, 1933, La Havana, Cuba; [p.] Enrique Moreda and Estela Ma Gonzalez; [m.] Silvia M. Moreda, May 24, 1956; [ch.] Cesar R. Moreda and Silvia C. Hernandez; [ed.] General - Graphic Designer Cuba; [occ.] Work at Coral Park Senior High School; [hon.] This is my first time; [oth. writ.] I have many other poems. Anyone has been published before. This is first time I send one.; [pers.] I like to write about the people, the world, and all is important in our life. First I feel, and write all.; [a.] Miami, FL

MOREN, SANDRA REGINA
[pen.] Sandi Moren; [b.] April 6, 1950, Firebaugh, CA; [p.] T. W. and Hazel Weaver; [m.] Edward J. Moren, May 2, 1970; [ch.] Jamie Charlotte, Jody Rebecca, Edward Isalah, grandson, Tyler Wayne Gunter; [ed.] Graduated Madera High, 1968 attended Central California Commercial College, 1968-1970; [occ.] Retired! We now travel and enjoy life, our kids and grandson; [hon.] Dean's List 2 years; [oth. writ.] Poems and editorials local newspapers; [pers.] I wish you all "rainbows and butterflies, and horses with wings..."; [a.] Madera, CA

MORENO, LORETTA
[pen.] Lora Roberts; [b.] October 19, 1944, Saint Augustine, FL; [p.] Willie Roberts, Elizabeth Roberts; [m.] Ines Moreno, November 17, 1960; [ch.] Ines Jr., Edwin, Elizabeth, Matthew; [ed.] McArthur High, I.R.C.C.; [occ.] Catering; [memb.] The Assembly of God; [oth. writ.] Several poems and short stories.; [pers.] In my writings I like to express all emotions mostly love and affection. I've been greatly influenced by the bible and Romantic Poets.; [a.] Fort Pierce, FL

MORIN, TIFFANY ANN
[pen.] Spiff; [b.] October 7, 1980; [p.] Philip and Yolande; [ed.] Entering 1996-97 School year as a Junior; [occ.] Student at Bristol Eastern High; [memb.] Saint Matthews Choir, BEHS marching, concert, symphonic, jazz bonds, BEHS varsity tennis; [hon.] Central Connecticut Conference All Academic, Tennis Team, Directors Award for Band, Tennis Trophies (1st place 4 yrs.), Public Relations Coordinator for '96-97 band year; [oth. writ.] Write short stories, scripts for plays, and lots of poetry; [pers.] I want you to smile for me wide and true, don't make it fake just make it you - Wilt.; [a.] Forestville, CT

MORRIS, MARGARET
[pen.] Margaret Morris; [b.] November 19, 1919; [p.] John and Elizabeth Coakley; [m.] Eugene Morris, January 2, 1943; [ch.] Three girls, one boy; [ed.] Collinwood High Cleveland OH, National Honor Society Three Semester College High School Newspaper Editor; [occ.] Varies; [memb.] Work on activities for Senior residents, Post Polio Club Use/Wheel Chair; [oth. writ.] My poem tells it all!; [pers.] Too may test. Retired after 20 years as Credit Union Manager, Volunteer Maria Hospital, writing News Letter, now live in a mobile home park; [a.] Santa Maria, CA

MORROW, DOROTHY DIXON
[b.] May 30, 1932, Burlington, NC; [p.] Jacob and Florilla Dixon; [m.] William G. Morrow, August 20, 1995; [ch.] W. Andre, K. Eric and Rodney E. Morrow; [ed.] BA, Bennette College, Greensboro, N.C. 1954. MA from NCCU 1961 Certification in Reading and School Administration (Supervisor and Principal); [occ.] Retired Teacher and Administrator; [memb.] Delta Sigma Theta Sorority Inc. (Life Membership) The Links, Inc., Retired Teachers Assn. (NSA, NCAE), Bennett College National Alumnae Assoc. (Life Member); [hon.] Alpha Kappa Mu Honor Society. *Who's Who in American Colleges and Universities*, Outstanding Administration Award, Teacher of the Year Award. National Honor for a Pre-School Program, others; [oth. writ.] I have written many poems but none have been published. I am writing a short biography of my parents and how they motivated 10 children to go to colleges and beyond.; [pers.] I believe that it is up to me to be happy everyday, that "Love endures all things," (I Cor. 13:7) and that out of all crises, disappointments or tragedies some good will come even though it might not be realized at first.; [a.] Durham, NC

MOSBRUCKER, JOACHIM C.
[pen.] J. C. Mosbrucker; [b.] November 18, 1912, On a Farm in Area of Glen Ullin, ND; [p.] Adolf Mosbrucker - Pauline Dietrick Mosbrucker; [m.] Betty Bode Mosbrucker, September 27, 1941 - married 55 yrs.; [ch.] Ileine, Thomas, March, all college, Betty and JC - neither had an eighth grade education; [ed.] As a couple we taught Square Dancing for seven years, 1952 to 1959. Also I taught Round Dance, Waltz and Polka Dancing. I have talked in many schools to our young people about taking better care of America, our beloved Nation. My latest count is 53 schools. The title of the talks is "That the home and the family are the foundation of every Nation."; [memb.] Home and School Association, Knights of Columbus, Order of the Moose, Catholic War Veterans, Lector in Church Morton County Conservation Corp. Life time Farmer Rancher in Glen Ullin N. Dak. Square Dance Callers Association. Christ the King Catholic Church.; [hon.] Many Agricultural Awards, received awards for Nursing Home entertainment. 1974 received North Dakota's State Outstanding Stateman award 24 inch statue.; [oth. writ.] Have many poems circulating, especially on morals and on our beloved free nation our USA. Don't forget there will never be another as beloved America. Let us never forget the pioneers who made it all available to us. The hardships they had thirteen children, and having to endure. The tedious Twenties, the dirty Thirties. This caused many of us to become genuine good citizens, which proved to become the finest home land to raise a Family. We are now doing much to keep it that way even resorting to Poetry to help along. I have had many articles, even poems published in local papers, the *Bismarck Tribune, Mandan News*.; [a.] Bismarck and Mandan, ND

MOSELEY, MARY R.
[pen.] Mary McDaniel; [b.] January 16, 1953, Portsmouth, VA; [p.] Virginia Mae McDaniel, Hubert Tom McDaniel Jr.; [m.] Larry Paul Moseley, December 28, 1984; [ch.] Bobbi Jo K. Fry Barger, two grandchildren and a son-in-law; [ed.] 9th Grade Westminster Jr., High Westminster, MD; [occ.] Housekeeper soon to be a certified Nursing Assistant; [hon.] Two Military Spouse Awards from the Former USS Iowa BB-51 and Pensacola Naval Technical Training Center Fla.; [oth. writ.] Three poems written to my husband when he was out to sea.; [pers.] I hope someday to write children's books for my grandchildren to enjoy.; [a.] Newport Richey, FL

MOSSBERGER, KRISTI
[b.] March 14, 1960, Salem, OR; [p.] George E. Logan and Patsy Logan; [m.] Douglas Mossberger, January 2, 1987; [ch.] Sarah, Jake; [ed.] Cascade High; [occ.] Small Business Owner; [pers.] My goal is to be a lover of life and a giver of love like my Grandma Edith Pease.; [a.] Elk Grove, CA

MUHAMMAD, JOAN L.
[b.] September 17, 1946, Philadelphia, PA; [m.] Divorced; [ch.] Darren and Drexelle, Grandchildren: Khaliq and Khari; [ed.] Bok Technical High School - Phila. PA Atlantic Community College. Mays Landing N.J. Stockton State College Pomona, N.J. Temple University Phila. PA; [occ.] Family Daycare Provider 7 yrs Self Employed; [hon.] Certificate: Nation of Islam and sacrifice in the upliftment of Our People. Certificate: Nation Of Islam and The Hon. Min. Louis Farrakhan for Hard Work, Charity - Sacrifice on the Establishment of Truth and Righteousness, Honore: Women's Infiltrators of Poverty; [oth. writ.] Book of poems, *Poetry of Black Truths*; [pers.] I like my poetry to reflect everyday life, with a message and to become a mirror which will allow people to see themselves and be motivated to make positive changes in their lives.; [a.] Atlantic City, NJ

MUNCY, SHARON
[b.] May 23, 1969, South Williamson; [p.] Roger Marcum, Ora; [m.] Vess Muncy, June 5, 1985; [ch.] Angel, Matthew, Melissa; [ed.] Crum High School Pro Care Nursing Assistant; [occ.] C.N.A.; [memb.] Breeden Chapel House of Prayer H.O.P.E. Team (Director); [hon.] Basic Elderly Care, Advanced I, Certified Nurses Assistant; [oth. writ.] I have written two other poems that have never been published titled "Love Of My Own", "When I Bid Farewell"; [pers.] This poem is dedicated to my Dad who passed away Dec 29, 1994; [a.] Crum, WV

MUNOZ, ISAAC
[pen.] Lauge Love, Pett; [b.] August 12, 1979; [p.] Maria Castillo, David Ramos; [ed.] High School (Morris High School) 10th Grade; [hon.] English Awards, Reading Awards, Jerome writing skills award.; [pers.] Like I always say "There's always no sound so admire and listen forever" Pett; [a.] Bronx, NY

MUNSON, KAREN B.
[b.] September 1, 1960, Pittsburgh, PA; [p.] Martha and Jerome Burgman; [m.] J. Mark Munson, May 26, 1990; [ch.] Nora Rose, Thomas Matthews, Daniel Clark; [ed.] B.A. in English from Wittenberg, University and MBA from the University of Pittsburgh; [a.] Monroeville, PA

MURPHY, RICHARD ENIS
[b.] August 31, 1976; [p.] Lenda and Dennis; [ch.] Dominique A. Murphy; [ed.] Graduated Moore High School in May of "96"; [occ.] Food clerk (cashier) at Homeland Grocery Stores.; [pers.] I strive to show one's true emotions and/or feelings with my poems.; [a.] Moore, OK

MURRIEL, T. EUNICE
[pen.] T. Eunice Murriel; [b.] May 10, 1942, Baltimore, MD; [p.] Talley and Bessie Portee; [m.] Willie Murriel, January 29, 1990; [ch.] Cheryl Turner; [ed.] Biblical Scholar, Extensive Managerial Training; [occ.] Retired Communication Manager; [memb.] St. Paul Christian Center; [hon.] Numerous Managerial Awards; [oth. writ.] "The Black Messiah," "Reality A Rude Awakening," "Mountains," and many essays.; [pers.] Words are spirit! Use them knowing the impact extends beyond the moment.; [a.] Baltimore, MD

MYRMINGOS, DENOS
[b.] January 26, 1975; [ed.] I am Senior at the University of Illinois at Chicago (UIC). I am going for my Degree in Secondary Education, Teaching English.; [pers.] "Sanctify Them In The Truth, Thy Word Is Truth". John 17:17 "If You Abide in my Word, Then You Are Truly Disciples of Mine, And You Shall Know The Truth, And The Truth Shall Make You Free." John 3:31-32; [a.] Burr Ridge, IL

NAGODE, MARY ELIZABETH
[b.] January 21, 1922, North Chicago, IL; [p.] Deceased; [m.] Victor Nagode - Retired, February 11, 1943; [ch.] Five Children, one son and four daughters; [ed.] My formal education is meager. My life has been devoted to study and learning. I have studied music, and piano, art, design, and painting. I have been active in various crafts, my husband and I were active in square and round dancing in the past.; [occ.] I am pursuing computer operation. And writing poetry. I play the piano occasionally,

and I paint with my daughters.; [memb.] Memberships Dearborn Community Arts Council. Member, Society of Decorative Painters, Member, National of State Poetry Societies, Inc. Poetry Society of Michigan Former member, Dearborn Arts and Crafts. First Place Blue Ribbon Award (Oil Painting) and past Treasurer.; [hon.] June 1996: Accomplishment Of Merit, Honorable Mention and Certificate of Poetic Achievement in on-going contests. The National Library of Poetry Award, of Distinguished Membership in the International Society of Poets, with its many special benefits.; [pers.] I have always put my thoughts on paper, without a thought of doing more than writing a journal. When I caught a phrase, accompanied with rhythm, I wrote it down, on scraps of paper, or in a note book. It was usually written into a poem. I have always loved to read, and to study. I have always enjoyed poetry. A winner never quits. A slow starter can win, but a quitter is a loser every time.; [a.] Dearborn, MI

NARCISI, THOMAS H.
[b.] October 22, 1977, Woodbury, NJ; [p.] Thomas M. Narcisi, Kathy Koviak; [ed.] West Deptford High School; [occ.] Student Gloucester County College, NJ; [memb.] Verga Firefighter, Verga NJ; [oth. writ.] Many poems written for mainly personal events or memorable occasions.; [pers.] My poems state the problems, happenings, and cures of our world through my eyes.; [a.] Verga, NJ

NASH, JEFFREY J.
[b.] January 13, 1956, South Bend, Indiana; [p.] Joseph Nash & Myra Nash; [m.] Christine Nash, May 10, 1976; [ch.] Abbie Christine and Adam Jeffrey; [ed.] Marian High School, Indiana University; [occ.] Insurance Executive; [pers.] As we travel through the streets of life we see many unfamilar faces yet the struggles we each endure are all quite similar.; [a.] Hartland, WI

NEFF, STARLING PAULINE
[pen.] Polly; [b.] March 6, 1925, Logan Co., OH; [m.] Dick D. Neff, September 9, 1944; [ch.] Tamara, Tim; [ed.] High School; [occ.] Retired Husband and myself owned Florist's Business; [hon.] Graduated 3rd in my class of 110; [oth. writ.] I have several other poems I have written - all by the age of Twenty. (Not published); [a.] Bellefontaine, OH

NEFF, WADE
[b.] June 30, 1976, York, PA; [p.] Phil and Wendy Neff; [ed.] Dallastown Area High School Courses at Penn State University; [occ.] Freelance Photographer; [memb.] International Quill and Scroll Society, Church of Jesus Christ of Latter Day Saints; [hon.] Pennsylvania Scholastic Writing Award, National Merit Finalist; [oth. writ.] "A Matter Of Perspective," "Inner Visions"; [pers.] There are no "arts" only art. All art should be a unified vision. For example, I mix my photography and poetry together to create my art. And the vision to express represents only my belief and my experience.; [a.] Jacobus, PA

NEIDERMAN, CRYSTAL
[pen.] Crystal Neiderman, Crys; [b.] October 3, 1983, Rockville Centre, NY; [p.] Patricia Neiderman, Russell N.; [ed.] Freeport Dodd Junior High; [occ.] Student; [memb.] Holy Redeemer Church; [oth. writ.] My bedroom walls are full of poems. Short stories for school.; [pers.] I am a twelve years old regents student in 8th grade at freeport Dodd Junior High School and I first started writing poems about four years ago when my father passed away. And I would like this poem to be dedicated to Russell (My Father) with lots of love.; [a.] Freeport, NY

NELSEN, LORI ANN
[b.] March 26, 1981, St. Paul, MN; [p.] Marie Dand Nelsen and Kenneth Nelsen; [ch.] My dog, Muffy; [ed.] Frost Lake Elementary, Hazel Park Middle School Academy, Johnson Senior High School; [occ.] Volunteer at St. John's Hospital; [memb.] Johnson Debate Team, Johnson Speech Team, Odds and Ends Editor of the school newspaper; [hon.] Quartly Honor Roll Presidential Academic Award, Parenting Award (in fifth grade); [oth. writ.] Several articles in the school newspaper, other non-published poems, started writing about three stories/books.; [pers.] I'd like to thank my family and best friend Lindsey G. Udey for being their for me. Also, thanks to my poetry teacher, Ms. Dibbtner-Jax.; [a.] St. Paul, MN

NELSON, HAJAR
[b.] October 24, 1975, Brooklyn, NY; [ed.] New York University B.A. 1996; [occ.] Graduate Student; [pers.] Never regret the choices you've made in the past. They seemed so right at that time; [a.] Brooklyn, NY

NELSON, MELISSA D.
[b.] May 19, 1982, Corvallis, OR; [p.] Richard and Susan Nelson; [ed.] Student (Freshman) at Reynolds High School, Troutdale, Oregon; [occ.] Student, Volunteer Wolf Haven, Tenino, Washington; [memb.] Wolf Haven Volunteer Program, Tenino, WA; [hon.] 1996 1st place winner Valentine Poetry Contest, Oregon Academic Achievement Award, Drama Award, Lee Middle School, Troutdale, Oregon Newspaper Editor Award; [oth. writ.] *Wolf Tracks Magazine Anthology of Winning Poems, Gresham Outlook Newspaper, The Lee Legend Newspaper*; [pers.] Being 14 years old, I hope that the generations to come will see, through my poems, that wolves and our environment must be protected.; [a.] Troutdale, OR

NEMMERS, RENEE
[b.] April 30, 1983, St. Louis Park, MN; [p.] Dan and Jane Nemmers; [ed.] I will be an 8th grader at West Middle School next year; [hon.] I was on the Honor Roll for having a 4.0 the first two trimesters. When I got my grades in the mail I got a 4.0 too. I also got a 4.0 gpa all year in 6th grade too; [a.] Englewood, CO

NERGE, LORI
[pen.] Lori Anne Nerge; [b.] April 6, 1977, Virginia; [p.] Teresa Rast, Larry Nerge; [ed.] Niceville Senior High School, Florida State University; [hon.] National English Merit Award, All-American Scholar Award; [pers.] As Tennyson writes: "'Tis better to have loved and lost, than never to have loved at all". Two years seems short when compared to a lifetime. Yet I will be eternally grateful to Andy for giving me that chance to love and to be loved. He truly is the inspiration behind my writing.; [a.] Niceville, FL

NEWMAN-GREGERSON, DIANE M.
[pen.] Diane M. Newman-Gregerson; [b.] March 2, 1948, East Liverpool, OH; [p.] Jas M. Plecas, Marjorie E. Van Fossan; [m.] Roy D. Newman, December 13, 1969; [ch.] Valance R. Newman; [ed.] Mira Costa College, National University - S.D., B.A. With Emphasis on Business Communications; [occ.] Secretary; [memb.] United Nation Association Emily's List, National Women's Political Caucus, Board of Direction - UNA-USA; [hon.] (1991) President Scholarship at National University Lyon's Club State Championship Award for Speech - (1961); [oth. writ.] Blade - Citizen Los Angeles Times USA Today "Letters To The Editor."; [pers.] Unconditional love may reign divinely with one's self, when you truly have peace in your heart, body and your soul!"; [a.] San Diego, CA

NICHOLSON, CARL W.
[b.] February 13, 1939, Steele, ND; [p.] Leslie and Clara Nicholson; [m.] Norma Ambers Nicholson, June 12, 1965; [ch.] Paige, Blake; [ed.] Tappen Public School Valley City State University; [occ.] Retired Educator; [memb.] National Education Association North Dakota Education Association Evangelical Lutheran Church in America; [hon.] Listed in *Personalities of the West and Midwest* 1971; [a.] Sherwood, ND

NIGRO, CHRISTOPHER R.
[b.] Colorado Springs, CO; [p.] Arthur and Sheila Nigro; [ed.] B.A. in Architecture; [occ.] Architect; [oth. writ.] Published an article, a short story, in *Crit 27* an architecture journal. Published a poem called "Silver and Blue" in *North Star One*, an anthology by Chatfield Software, Inc. coming out about October 30th; [pers.] I try to describe always so as to bring them to life in the imagination.; [a.] Chicago, IL

NIPPER, MARY
[pen.] Mary Nipper; [b.] February 4, 1931, Scriba; [p.] Deceased; [m.] William, March 17, 1951; [ch.] Bob, David and Donald; [ed.] 9th grade at Oswego High School. Learned a lot putting my sons through school.; [occ.] Retired, enjoy traveling and grandchildren gardening; [hon.] In 1964 was awarded the Highest Den Mother Scout Award, worked 27 years at Plainville Turkey Farm; [oth. writ.] Have written many poems for Wedding, Birthdays, Anniv., Retirements, etc. also wrote the story of my life for my family, still working on it.; [pers.] I'm always out to help the other guy that's down. Can forgive and forget easily. Love my family, enjoy helping them.; [a.] Fulton, NY

NITSCHE, THERESE
[pen.] Amanda Persson; [b.] November 14, 1925, Paterson, NJ; [p.] James and Amelia Ross; [m.] Per-Axel Nitsche (Deceased), October 29, 1948; [ch.] Deborah-Ann Nitsche Polito (Deceased); [ed.] Manual H.S.-United States Cadet Nurse Corp. Brooklyn State Hosp.; [occ.] Registered Nurse-Assessment team in residential facilities in NJ; [memb.] American Nurses Assoc., NJ State Nurses Assoc., Vasa Order of America Rosary Society St. Mary's Church; [oth. writ.] Some of my writings were published in the *Vasa Newsletter*. Poems published in church bulletin.; [pers.] Many of my writings are from personal experiences. I try to include faith, hope, love and charity as I see it.

NIXON, DORIS
[p.] Wilfred and Iris Shervington; [ed.] Financial Management, and Executive Management of Hotel and Motel; [memb.] Hutt River Province of Australia; [hon.] Honorable of the Hutt River Royal Patronage. A Lifetime Royal Patronage Status; [oth. writ.] *Watch The Tide*, a mystery book. Songs titled "So Near To My Heart" and "In The Stars."

NOENS, HEATHER
[b.] January 15, 1981, Park Ridge; [p.] Richard Noens, Patricia Noens; [occ.] Student; [oth. writ.] One other poem was printed in program of my Jr. High graduation.; [pers.] My poetry of my deeper thoughts and feelings, which can not be expressed any other way.; [a.] Palatine, IL

NOLAN, JOHN J.
[b.] January 14, 1927, New York, NY; [p.] Joseph and Anna Nolan; [m.] Helen Pelechowicz Nolan, February 15, 1953; [ch.] Kevin J. and Kathleen A.; [ed.] High School (Bayside High, Bayside, NY); [occ.] Retired Stage Hand/Television Lighting Director; [pers.] Most of my poems are love poems to my wife, though not all - I do attempt to write of past experiences, hoping to express what I see, feel, and remember to anyone I dare allow to read my writings.; [a.] Paramus, NJ

NORAN, MARIA A.
[b.] October 17, 1962, Idaho; [ch.] Four Children: Tiffani 16, Shane 15, Alecia 12, Shannon 10; [ed.] Some College; [occ.] Title Clerk, Automobile Dealership; [oth. writ.] I have hundreds of unpublished poems; [pers.] Remember to smile and laugh often throughout your pain because eventually beauty will come from that pain.; [a.] East Peoria, IL

NORENBERG, JEREMY W.
[b.] February 22, 1977, Hibbing, MN; [p.] Daryl and Brenda Norenberg; [m.] Amy Norenberg, April 12, 1996; [ed.] Graduation from Hibbing High School, Home Educated from grade five to grade eleven; [occ.] Roofer/Writer; [memb.] World Tang Soo Do Association; [hon.] National Honor Society Membership, Full four-year Meteorology Scholarship received from U.S. Air Force, Certificate of Merit from Air Force, First Degree Black Belt (1st Dan), World Tang Soo Do Assoc.; [oth. writ.] "A Century of Care," "The Epitome of Sarcasm" (Co-authored) Several short stories; [pers.] The world is not a nice place - not humanity. In order to be something, you must strive to be something. Biblical morality, character, and uprightness are not outdated. It is a person of these fine qualities that stands out - that makes a difference - that truly is somebody.; [a.] Colorado Springs, CO

NORMAN, BETTY WATSON
[b.] June 2, 1930, Houston, TX; [p.] Nora and Earnest Watson; [m.] Widow, August 28, 1948; [ed.] High School, Course in Theology, Art, Horticulture; [ch.] Andrea Borden, Rebecca Stietle; [occ.] Home Nursing; [memb.] Art League, Porcelain Art League, Quilters Guild, Doll Club, Audubon Club, Native Plant Society Garden Club, Women's Aglow, Native American Indian Asso.; [hon.] Ribbons in Art shows and Garden shows, Ordained to preach the word of God; [oth. writ.] Poetry - short stories, a book named *The Oak*; [pers.] I have learned all my life. I can see stories in everyday life. I never meet anyone that doesn't have something that enriches my life. I want my readers to see and feel what I see and feel.; [a.] Tyler, TX

NORMAN, LOUISE H.
[b.] July 9, 1934, Nashville, TN; [p.] James and Katherine Hancock; [m.] June 8, 1956, (Divorced February 7, 1986); [ch.] Jim, Kate, Laura; [ed.] Fulton High School, Fulton, KY Vanderbuilt U., Nashville, TN-B.A. Middle TN State U., Murfreesboro, TN-M.Ed; [occ.] Retired Librarian; [oth. writ.] First material ever submitted for publication; [pers.] Experiences and pleasures of our daily life will find expression in either music or words.

NORRIS, DAVID ROY ROBERT
[pen.] David Roy Robert Norris; [b.] September 17, 1972, Dallas, TX; [p.] Patricia Gail Hamilton; [m.] Alicia Ann Pennington (Girlfriend); [ed.] High school grad. with 3.87 GPA turned down college due to injured knee for football; [occ.] Construction Worker; [oth. writ.] A number of other poems. At a guess about 25 other poetry items.; [pers.] I would like to say thanks to my Mother and teachers for all their support. Also I would like also say thank you and "I Love You" to my girlfriend, Alicia!; [a.] Junction City, AR

NORRIS, NORMA
[pen.] Norma Lorraine; [b.] August 8, 1942, Phila., PA; [p.] Louis and Minnie Marinoff; [m.] Allen Norris, July 25, 1961; [ch.] Amy Layne - Jeffrey Norris; [pers.] I take in hand my pen let it be my heart.

NORTON, JALISHA MARIE
[b.] August 9, 1983, Port Arthur, TX; [p.] Jerome D. and Margaret Norton; [ed.] Bridge City Jr. High 7th Grade; [occ.] Student; [pers.] Be all you can be, believe in yourself and have faith in all that you accomplish and you will have set your goals for life. I dedicate this poem to my deceased PawPaw Clyde J. Moss, whom I love very much.; [a.] Bridge City, TX

NOWAK, JUANITA M. MAXWELL
[pen.] Nita Nowak; [b.] July 1, 1957, Tyndall AFB, FL; [p.] Charles Maxwell Sr. and Marjorie Maxwell-Fleming; [m.] Robert Nowak, December 12, 1995; [ed.] I have a master's degree and a specialist degree from the Department of Counselor Education at the University of Florida (Gainesville); [occ.] Person of Leisure; [memb.] Silva Method Grad; [hon.] State of Florida Board of Regents Fellowship recipient; [pers.] If you want something, be willing to go the distance for it, and you'll get it!; [a.] Saint Petersburg Beach, FL

NUNEZ, TRACI
[pen.] Trace; [b.] December 24, 1980, Odessa, TX; [p.] Johnny F. and Mary A. Nunez; [ed.] Stafford Municipal School District (K-9); [occ.] Sophomore Student at Stafford High School; [memb.] National Junior Honor Society-Pres., Student Council -Historian (8), Treasurer (9), Math Club, Science Club, Band, Basketball -Freshmen, Tennis - J.V. Team; [hon.] 2nd place Science Fair, Duke University Talent Search-State Recognition, Number Sense - 3rd and 4th place, General Math 6th and 10th place; [pers.] "Many people have talent, but only the ones with self-confidence can prove it. And my self-confidence were the friends that pushed me to prove myself."; [a.] Stafford, TX

NYSTROM, MARKUS
[b.] December 11, 1978, Edmonton, Canada; [p.] Peter and Britt Nystrom; [ed.] Senior in High School; [occ.] Student; [memb.] Quill and Scroll, National Honor Society, Cum Laude; [hon.] Published in Lake Forest High School's *Young Idea* literary magazine, placed 3rd in American Legion essay competition at Boys State; [oth. writ.] Wrote a 100 page account of my adventures in Europe, articles for school newspaper; [pers.] Man's greatest and most daunting task lies in the need to respect and cherish the earth upon which he depends.; [a.] Lake Forest, IL

O'MALLEY, MEGAN PATRICIA
[pen.] Megan O'Malley; [b.] August 21, 1984, Chicago, IL; [p.] Patrick O'Malley, Deborah O'Malley; [occ.] 7th grade student, Nansemond - Suffolk Academy, Suffolk, VA; [hon.] High honor roll student; [oth. writ.] Many other poetic works, all unpublished.; [pers.] I wish to express the outsiders most inner thoughts in a magical way. My parents, grandparents, and Mrs. Jan Booth have inspired and encouraged me to take pride in my writings and to express myself on paper.; [a.] Chesapeake, VA

ODELL JR., HAROLD R.
[pen.] Harold Rutledge; [b.] June 16, 1966, Southampton, NY; [ed.] Hampton Bays High School, Ohio Diesel Technical Institute, Self educated; [occ.] Diesel Truck, Technician; [memb.] Rotary International Hampton Bays. Hampton Bays Volunteer Fire Dept.; [hon.] US Army Aluminous; [pers.] Life is bountiful.; [a.] Hampton Bays, NY

OGUINE, PRISCILLA
[ch.] Five Children; [ed.] BA Hons (English) M. Ed. M.A. Ph.D. in Literature Areas of Specialization: ESL and Feminism in African Lit.; [occ.] Adjunct Professor English Department and E Op. Program Seton Hall University NJ 07079-2689 South Orange.; [memb.] International Reading Association, British Association of Lecturers of English for Academic Purposes, Zonta International; [hon.] Comskip British Council Award to study for MA test in reading university, England 1990-91.; [oth. writ.] Books - *Poems for Young Readers, In Search of My Home, Folktales from Igbo Land, Communicative Use of English;* [pers.] I am an advocate of religious feminism, through which I reach out to my God in my writing, and at the same time, try to raise the dignity of men and women who have faith.; [a.] Morris Plains, NJ

OJIARSINGH, ERROL F.
[b.] December 4, 1973, Chicago, IL; [p.] Errol F. and Helen J. Ojiarsingh; [ed.] Rich East High School University of Illinois at Chicago; [occ.] Student; [memb.] V.I.C. Criminal Justice Society; [pers.] "Whatever you do in life or whatever path you follow. Always remember, never regret your actions, give 110%, and always trust your heart."; [a.] Olympia Fields, IL

OLSEN, TOM
[b.] May 29, 1979, Puyallup, WA; [p.] Warren Olsen, Debby Olsen; [ed.] Bethel Senior High, Pierce Community College; [occ.] Student; [pers.] Eternity is only until tomorrow. I enjoy science fiction's stories of mythology. I also enjoy creating my own stories and characters.; [a.] Graham, WA

OLTON, ELIZABETH
[b.] September 7, 1973, Trinidad, West Indies; [p.] Coreen and Richard Olton; [ed.] Brooklyn Technical H.S., Pace University; [occ.] Help Desk Assistant; [hon.] Dean's List

ONUEGBU, PATRICIA C.
[b.] August 18, 1984, Aba, Abia State Nigeria; [p.] Canice Onuegbu, Charity Onuegbu; [ed.] Student, Sweetwater Middle School, Lawrenceville, Georgia; [occ.] Student; [hon.] Mosaic Writings, Outstanding Effort Award, Outstanding Writing; [oth. writ.] Wrote poem for school magazine.; [pers.] I try to reflect the goodness of nature. I have had great admiration for seasonal changes and its beauty.; [a.] Nocross, GA

ORR, KIMBERLY
[pen.] Kim Orr; [b.] December 18, 1961, Sylacauga, AL; [p.] Harlie McGrady, Betty McGrady; [m.] Ronald Orr, March 4, 1996; [ch.] Tara Ray, Brian Ray, Kerri Lawson; [ed.] Sylacauga High, Herzing Career College; [occ.] Security Officer, Wackenhut Corporation, Birmingham, AL; [memb.] Centercrest Baptist Church; [oth. writ.] Several poems published in school newsletters. Several poems published in *Seventeen* magazine.; [pers.] Most of my poems are from personal experiences that I've been through. I hope to accomplish in my writings help for others and let them know there is light to shine through all their hurts.; [a.] Gardendale, AL

ORRIDGE, MONICA JEAN
[b.] Kingston, Jamaica, West Indies; [p.] Alvin and Mirriam Fairclough (Deceased); [m.] Lloyd Vernon Orridge (Deceased), July 16, 1960; [ch.] Authia Jennifer Richard; [ed.] Franklyn Town Primary, Dave's High Schools; [occ.] Day Care Provider; [memb.] St. Michael Church; [hon.] The National Library of Poetry Certificate; [oth. writ.] Poems published in church magazines, and for functions of various kinds.; [pers.] My writings are of inspirations, and so I wish to share these thoughts with the hope that they will bring the understanding, joys and peace to all people.; [a.] Gaithersburg, MD

ORTIZ, BELINDA
[pen.] Snitch; [b.] February 10, 1983, Miama, FL; [p.] Sonia and Raymond Hazel; [ed.] Roy H. Mann JHS; [oth. writ.] I write poems, but never send any of them out. I would like to and work as a poetry writer.; [pers.] I would like to thank you for picking my poem and enter it in the contest. I thank my uncle for this gift.; [a.] Brooklyn, NY

ORTIZ, MARIE
[pen.] Marie Ortiz; [b.] July 11, 1937, Gilman, CO; [p.] Matilda Mora and Jacob Martin; [m.] Gysgt USMC Ret. Rudolph L. Ortiz; [ed.] Graduated from High School with high honors; [occ.] Homemaker; [memb.] Disabled American Veterans St. Josephs Catholic Church Friends of the Pool, Bus Mother for Barstow Aztecs High School Running and Swimming; [hon.] High School awards - Girls state etc. Proclamation from the city of Barstow Certificate from D.A.V. Ministry to the elderly The Mojave Desert Senior Citizens Center; [oth. writ.] Have written other poems and writing a biography of my life; [pers.] I believe that "Bringing happiness to others is the greatest gift one can give. Poetry to me inspires many and brings much happiness."; [a.] Barstow, CA

ORY, RICHARD JOSEPH
[b.] October 29, 1969, New Orleans; [p.] Charlene LaBorde, Michael Ory; [m.] Sheila A. Ory, June 9, 1989; [ed.] Columbus State University; [occ.] Route Technician; [hon.] US Army, Army Achievement Medal, Good Conduct Medal; [pers.] I have been influenced by Shakespeare.; [a.] Columbus, GA

OUELLETTE, MICHELLE
[b.] January 5, 1981, Waterbury; [p.] Mary Ouellette; [ed.] St. Margaret Middle School, Sacred Heart High School; [occ.] Student; [hon.] I have made the honor roll many times in middle and high school I also received the literature award all 3 yrs of Middle School; [pers.] Take chances and go for what you want. If you don't you'll never know what you could have gotten.; [a.] Waterbury, CT

OUSLEY, RUTH Y.
[pen.] Ruth Y. Ousley; [b.] November 5, 1955, Indiana; [ch.] Steven R. Ousley and David R. Ousley; [ed.] B.A. in Psychology, Specialty training in Crisis Counseling, Child Abuse and Foster Care, Honor Roll Student; [occ.] Currently working towards my Ph.D. in Psychology; [memb.] Santa Claus Club, Tampa Crisis Helpline, and Deaf Interpreter; [hon.] In the News 1990, Fostering Success; [oth. writ.] "God's Answer to a Waitress," "Foster Care - Through a Child's Eyes," "Grave Hands that Speak," "Acquainted with Grief," "Surrender," etc.; [pers.] I believe that the world is full of emotion and adventure - all's we have to do is savor it!; [a.] Lakeland, FL

OUYANG, TIBOR
[b.] April 28, 1967, New Westminster, BC, Canada; [ed.] Cranbrook, University of California Los Angeles; [oth. writ.] "A Farmer's Lament", "Love is Never Easy", "Downpour", "You're Not Gone", "They Don't Walk in Your Shoes", and other songs performed by the rock group "Skin and Bones"; [pers.] Give credit where credit is due and never forget those who believe in you.; [a.] Anaheim, CA

OWENS, KYLE
[pen.] Jack Sorrell; [b.] January 16, 1974, Ocala, FL; [p.] Larry and Arlene Dawson; [m.] Traci Owens, November 11, 1995; [ch.] Trevor Stallings; [ed.] York Suburban High School, Drexel University, York College of PA; [occ.] Restaurant Manager, Chuck E. Cheese Pizza, Harrisburg, PA; [hon.] Three time *Who's Who Among American High School Students*, past attendant and representative of the National Young Lender's Conference; [oth. writ.] Currently working on a number of poems, short stories, and novels; [pers.] I try to convey deep thoughts and emotions using simple metaphors and ironies. I do this so that one doesn't have to be a college professor to read and understand my poetry.; [a.] York, PA

OWENS, MINAROSE
[b.] October 4, 1940, Heber, AZ; [p.] Marvin A., Noama Reidhead; [m.] Howard M. Owens; [ch.] James, Howard, Daniel, Mark, Lance, Joseph and Sara; [occ.] Homemaker TSI Representatives; [oth. writ.] Amateur poem and writings in John Oscar Reidhead history. I desire, to both inspire and bring joy and comfort to my readers.; [pers.] Writing poetry has filled a void through self expression, that would other wise have remained forever empty.; [a.] Cortez, CO

OXMAN, NANCY G.
[b.] February 8, 1951, Philadelphia, PA; [p.] Joan and Stanley Green; [m.] Stephen Oxman, November 26, 1981; [ed.] Springfield High, Penn. State U.; [occ.] Writing something - anything, each and every day!; [pers.] Thank you Art Spikel for telling me to write, something...anything, everyday and I would be taken seriously, your "Non-fiction Magazine Writing Course" was magic!; [a.] Havertown, PA

PACHERO, CAROLINE
[b.] January 2, 1979, Puerto Rico; [p.] Elean Seda; [ed.] Brockton High School; [occ.] Beauty Salon, Perfect Touch; [oth. writ.] "Love Means You, Because When I Need You, You Were There, Because You're The One Who Love Me, Israel If One Of My Smile Make You Happy, I smile For Ever

PACK, BETTY LOUISE DANIEL
[b.] May 24, 1924, Waverly, OH; [p.] Charlie and Madge Daniel (Deceased); [m.] Laudie John Pack (Deceased), April 25, 1944; [ch.] Melba McDaniel, Wanda Schubmehl; [ed.] Mifflin High School (Columbus, OH); [occ.] Housewife; [memb.] Church of God, Ashland, KY, Community Bible Study, Ashland, KY, International Society of Poets; [hon.] Editor's Choice Award, The National Library of Poetry 1996; [oth. writ.] "September Sunrise" in *Tomorrow's Dream* 1996, "Hope" in *Best Poems of the '90's* 1996. My first story is to be published in the near future. I have written many poems and short stories (unpublished). Most of my stories, fiction and non-fiction, were written for my 5 grandchildren. I am currently working on my autobiography.; [pers.] I have written poetry and stories since I was a child. I also enjoy reading, travel and crafts. This particular poem, "Dandelions" was written to tease my husband who had spent an afternoon, on a hot day, digging dandelions out of our lawn. Most of my poetry is on a religious theme because God is central in my life. "I can do all things through Christ who strengthens me." Phil. 4:13 NKJV.; [a.] Ashland, KY

PADILLA, MELISSA JEANETTE
[b.] September 24, 1982, El Paso, TX; [p.] Joe Padilla, Martha Padilla; [ed.] Edgemere Elementary Eastwood Middle School; [memb.] National Junior Honor Society; [hon.] Good Citizenship Award Presidents Award, Science Award, Academic Achievement Award, Outstanding Musician Award; [pers.] When I write, I try to put all my heart and effort into my poems and other writings.; [a.] El Paso, TX

PALLADINO, PAULA C.
[b.] September 1, 1969, Patchogue; [p.] Ben Palladino, Sheila Constantine; [m.] William M. Moesch (France), Scheduled for August 1996; [ch.] William Jr. and Kayla Moesch; [ed.] William Floyd H.S.; [occ.] Housewife/Mother; [pers.] My greatest inspiration are my children. And my fiance. I like to think my writing reflects the beauty hidden within reality.; [a.] Largo, FL

PALMER, ALEXANDER LAMAR
[pen.] Alex; [b.] December 9, 1981, Decatur, GA; [p.] Brenda and Gary Palmer; [ed.] Going to Cartersville High School, 9th grade; [occ.] None, soccer and playing guitar, music; [memb.] Member of Tabernacle Baptist Church, past member of the children's choir at my church.; [hon.] I have had some of my poems in the local newspapers. I have also won several awards in Soccer. I have been on several (high) honor rolls since primary grade in school.; [oth. writ.] Mostly songs: Several poems published in local newspaper (from 4th grade up to 7th grade).; [pers.] Several of my teachers say I have a gift for having written poems with deep thoughts for my young age.; [a.] Cartersville, GA

PALMER, JOSEPH D.
[b.] July 15, 1926, Passaic, NJ; [p.] Dayton Palmer, Evelyn Palmer; [m.] Eileen O'Loughlin, June 16, 1951; [ch.] Michael, Edward, Shane, Sheila; [ed.] High School St. Patrick's Academy - Binghamton, NY, S.U.N.Y. - Binghamton, N.Y., B.A.; [occ.] Retired

PALMERE, CHARLES
[v.i.p.] #P0521601-031; [b.] June 28, 1962, Palmer, MA; [p.] Guy Palmere, Pauline Palmere; [m.] Dorothy E. Palmere, January 15, 1983; [ch.] Crystal Palmere, Michael Palmere; [occ.] Environmental Services Worker; [hon.] Martial Artist; [oth. writ.] "The Master"; [pers.] Always do the greater good or the lesser of evil. Only react to actions not to words.; [a.] Monson, MA

PAPP, ELIZABETH
[b.] March 20, 1986, Danbury, CT; [p.] Claude and Nancy Papp; [ed.] Entering 5th grade in September 1996; [occ.] Student; [memb.] Girls Scout troop 511, Charlotte Klein Dance Studio, Calliope Youth theater productions and the St. Lukes Choir; [hon.] Directed and acted in American Girls play, "Tea for Felicity"; [oth. writ.] "If I were a famous actress"; [pers.] Try your best.

PAPP, JOSEPH
[b.] February 29, 1984, Danbury, CT; [p.] Claude and Nancy Papp; [ed.] Grade 7 in September 1996; [occ.] Student; [memb.] Boy Scout Troop 4 Gibbons Middle

School Concert and Stage Band and Chorus, Calliope Youth Theater Group, Gibbons Middle School Track and Cross Country Team; [hon.] Gibbons Middle School GA Writer of the Month, First Class Scout, High Honor Student; [a.] Westborough, MA

PAQUIN, KATHRYN C.
[b.] December 29, 1943, Putnam, CT; [p.] Raymond and Claire Paquin; [ch.] William C. Teppenpaw, Michael B. Teppenpaw; [ed.] Miami Central High; [pers.] Animals in general. The fact they were put here on earth, for our enjoyment. They deserve special treatment for making our lives less stressful and more enjoyable

PARAMITO, SUZZIE
[pen.] "S. Paramito"; [b.] May 26, 1975, Philadelphia, PA; [p.] Susan and Anthony Paramito; [ed.] GED - 17 yrs old, teacher, loving mentor Ms. Arlene McGurk at The Gateway - Devereaux Foundation; [occ.] Writing, working on other projects; [memb.] American Cancer Society, Easter Seals; [hon.] Childhood School Awards, throughout Elem. School, High School, 1st place entry May 3, 1989, for poem, Penna. Citizens for Better Libraries; [oth. writ.] Nothing formally published, current project is my first "Novelette" short story followed by a choice selection of old, new poetry of my own writings.; [pers.] "Everyone is a poet, and I love them all" long adorations and influenced by Robert Frost, Edgar Alan Poe and a very sentimental Jim Morrison. (And my mother who read to me.); [a.] Philadelphia, PA

PARCELL, KELLY J. KENT
[b.] October 21, 1954, S. Bend, IN; [p.] Richard W. and Carole J. Kent; [m.] James A. Parcell, July 30, 1987; [ch.] Five; [ed.] Attending Bethel College in Mishawaka, IN LaSalle High School (graduated 1972); [occ.] Domestic Engineer; [memb.] Professional Secretaries International; [hon.] 3.8 GPA at Bethel College; [oth. writ.] First time published I write of real time experiences mostly about my children. I am currently writing a novel, my first attempt with fiction entitled, *His Golden Forest.*; [pers.] Words are most precious, therein lies the truth.; [a.] S. Bend, IN

PARENTE, JARUSKA
[pen.] Jaruska Parente; [b.] January 1, 1959, Prague, Czech Republic; [ed.] Higher expert studies at the Art Conservatory in Prague (Czech Republic); [occ.] Designer Combining Architecture, Landscape, Interior and Art in "Total Design" (Own firm in La Jolla); [memb.] Master Yoga Foundation and other; [oth. writ.] Many unpublished poems in different languages, articles and planned autobiography; [pers.] I always keep in mind in my life and work that character is defined by what you are willing to do when the spot light has been turned off, the applause has died down and no one is around to give you credit.; [a.] La Jolla, CA

PARKER, WAUNETTA L.
[pen.] Snell; [b.] February 3, 1941, Palmyra, NE; [p.] Edith Martin and Carl Snell; [ch.] Kim Lee, Rhonda Kay; [ed.] South High, Omaha, NE 1 year Universal Technical Institute - Commercial Art Iowa Western Com. College, 2 years Fine Art and Business, Creighton University, Advertising, Public Relations JRPR, Denver University - Fine Arts CWC - Colorado Women's College; [occ.] Computer Graphics Technician, taught beginners and Advanced beginners Art to Youth Group; [pers.] A writer's potential is determined by his or her experience; [a.] Council Bluffs, IA

PARKS, SHAWN
[pen.] Bapefiwa; [b.] February 11, 1976; [p.] Denise Parks, Larry Parks; [ed.] University of Detroit Mercy; [pers.] Do or do not, there is no try.; [a.] Eastpointe, MI

PARROTT, MARY B.
[b.] November 5, 1915, Melstone, MT; [p.] Deceased; [m.] Walter C. Parrott Jr., September 19, 1954; [ch.] Priscilla Mary, Daniel David; [ed.] H.S., Roundup, Montana, Writing Workshops, completed correspondence Course in Non-fiction Writing; [occ.] Homemaker and devoted grandmother to Clayton (6), Carina (3), Joy (7 months); [memb.] Skyway United Methodist Church and four-year Delegate to Annual Church Conferences; [oth. writ.] Published article "Our Musical Founding Fathers" and musical word squares in two issues of *Opus One*, a youth choir magazine, "A Tranquilizing Thought" in *Grit*, puzzles in church periodicals, and items in local papers. Have autobiography in 50,000 words.; [pers.] Most of my writing is meant to edify and/or educate toward worthy aims in life. For fun, I enjoy composing jingles to inspire safe driving and car care, limericks on politics, and poetry on a variety of subjects.; [a.] Seattle, WA

PASCAL, CHRISTOPHER DAVID
[b.] Los Angeles, CA; [ed.] J.C. Fremont High School, L.A. City College, L.A. Trade Technical College; [occ.] Service Representative; [oth. writ.] Several letters and articles published in local newspapers; [pers.] Only through language skills can humankind continue to advance socially, morally, and intellectually.; [a.] Greenfield, CA

PASINSKI, CHRISTINE
[b.] December 6, 1948, Pittsburgh, PA; [p.] Louis and Anna Romanus; [m.] David R. Pasinski, November 7, 1992; [ed.] B.S. Secondary Education (Clarion University of Pennsylvania) M.S. Secondary Education Duquesne University; [occ.] English Teacher (West Mifflin Area High School); [memb.] National Council of Teachers of English, Western Pennsylvania Council of Teachers of English. Advisory Council - International Poetry Forum; [hon.] *Who's Who Among America's High School Teachers*, Council of Teachers of English Award for Excellence in the Teaching of English Sigma Tau Delta (Honorary English Fraternity); [oth. writ.] "A Teaching Guide to Crime and Punishment" seven poems published in local journals, newspaper articles; [pers.] I believe that poetry should reflect all that is beautiful and inspirational in the human soul.; [a.] Clairton, PA

PATTILLO, TONY
[b.] June 29, 1980, Tampa, FL; [p.] Randy Pattillo, Margie Blake; [ed.] St. Johns Greek Orthodox, Jesuit High School, Tampa Catholic High School; [occ.] Student; [memb.] Bally's, U.S.C.G. Aux., AOPA, Melalueca, National Geographic; [oth. writ.] EsDeme Armageddon; [pers.] My reason for writing is it creates a telepathic portal that allows me to relieve my most inner emotions and feelings on paper.; [a.] Tampa, FL

PAUL, MARIE KATHLEEN
[b.] June 4, 1946, Minneapolis, MN; [p.] Douglas and Bartow Tennis; [m.] Thomas William Paul, December 11, 1965; [ch.] Terra, Shantell, Anissa and Chaleece; [ed.] Forest Lake, High School, Ritter's School of Beauty; [occ.] Beautician, Crest View Lutheran Home Columbia Heights MN; [pers.] This is the first poem I have written since those required for English class. I wrote this poem to be a keepsake for my daughters, to be given to them on my fiftieth Birthday.; [a.] Forest Lake, MN

PAYNE, MARGARET P.
[pen.] Phyllis B. Payne; [b.] November 18, 1937, Louisiana, MO; [p.] Mr. and Mrs. Fred R. Berry; [m.] August 18, 1963; [ch.] Matthew and Derek; [ed.] B.S. in Elementary Education - Truman State University, Kirksville, Missouri; [memb.] Evangelical Free Church of Naperville, Delta Zeta Sorority; [hon.] *Who's Who in Poetry, World of Poetry* 1990, Golden Poet Award - 1988 - *World of Poetry*; [oth. writ.] *World of Poetry*, Free Press: Evangelical Free Church of Naperville (newsletter).; [pers.] "Freedom Set Free" was presented for publication as a vision for all of us to work toward. This vision is that of a "equality becoming reality.".; [a.] Lisle, IL

PEARSON, DOROTHY
[pen.] Dottie Peters; [b.] November 29, 1944, Searcy, AR; [p.] J. D. and Tula Peters; [m.] Lynn (Bud) Pearson (Deceased), February 29, 1992; [ch.] 5 by other marriages, 5 steps; [ed.] 12th gr.; [occ.] Professional Domestic; [memb.] First Freewill Baptist of Jacksonville; [hon.] I haven't an award. That can be recorded my greatest honor was just given to me by my last boss. As being a hard worker. Also I consider my award waiting for me in heaven.; [oth. writ.] "The Rest," "The Powers Dogs," "What About Cats," "Now I Lay Me," "If Jesus Came," "When This Year Is Over," "Life and Love," and "Merry Christmas; [pers.] Writing is my lifelong dream. I hope to write a novel someday as well as a book of poetry.; [a.] Jacksonville, AR

PEMBERTON, RENEE
[b.] September 25, 1956, Ft. Thomas, KY; [m.] Dave Pemberton, April 14, 1984; [ch.] Tara Lynn, Taylor Anne; [ed.] Bellevue High; [occ.] Housewife and Writer; [oth. writ.] I've written poems books and other books.; [pers.] I thank God for a talent to write. I hope my writings encourage others.; [a.] Elsmere, KY

PENTTINEN, KENNETH F.
[b.] July 12, 1973, Clark AFB, Philippines; [p.] Kenneth L. Penttinen, Frances A.; [occ.] Manager at Goodnet; [pers.] All things can be accomplished if you are willing to pay the price.; [a.] Phoenix, AZ

PEREZ, LOUIS A.
[b.] February 6, 1963, Puerto Rico; [p.] Louis A. Perez Sr., Estelle Perez; [ch.] Tiffany Perez, Shana Spratt; [ed.] Dewitt Clinton, HS., Monroe College, Associates Degree, Service Employees International Union Trade School Grad.; [occ.] Superintendent of Building; [memb.] Executive Board Member Service Employees International Union Local 32E, AFL-CIO; [hon.] Martial Arts, Self Defense Honors, Community Service Awards, Super of the Month, Awards for the year 1993, 1994, 1995 and 1996; [pers.] I believe that there are too many beautiful things in this world that we as human beings have not seen yet. So why take the only life you have and destroy it by using drugs and playing with guns. Why not smell and flowers and breathe the air and enjoy the only life you have.; [a.] Bronx, NY

PERKINS, MERREDITH FRAZIER
[b.] November 8, 1951, Monroe, LA; [p.] J. Hue Moore and Verna L. Hall; [m.] December, 1974, (Divorced 9, 1977); [ch.] Toi Perkins; [ed.] B.A Northeast Louisiana University, M.Ed. +30 Northeast Louisiana Univ., M.Ed + 60 Lehman College New York, Doctoral student -

Walden University; [occ.] English teacher (middle school), Teacher Consultant - Maryland Writing Proj.; [memb.] Phi Delta Kappa, Oxon Hill Church of Christ, OASIS Tutorial Program for Students, National Council for Teachers of Eng.; [hon.] Certificate of Perfect Attendance, OASIS Certificate of Community Service; [oth. writ.] "Motivators and Indicators: Self-esteem and Good Writing" - Towson State Univ. Teacher's inquiry and Research Institute "Wishful Thinking" - a vingette read at a Coffee House. Poetry and journal writings. "Boat Ride" - A poem published in Towson's '95 STI; [pers.] I am inspired by powerful women writers who find their voices through writing. They had to convince me that I could find my own voice through writing... and I have. I "learn to write and write to learn". I inquire and examine myself through current issues, literature, models of writing, and excellence.; [a.] Lanham, MD

PERRY, OKEVNA LOVING
[b.] July 15, 1967, West Virginia; [p.] Okey and Lenora Loving; [m.] Kyle Joseph Perry Sr., June 22, 1996; [oth. writ.] "Ode To Kyle" (unpublished)

PERRY, SALLY
[pen.] S. A. Perry; [b.] October 3, 1957, Akron, OH; [p.] Fred and Darlene Tavanello; [m.] John Perry, June 9, 1995; [ch.] Jenna Maria; [ed.] Norton High, University of Akron; [occ.] Medical Transcriptionist; [hon.] Honors English at University of Akron; [oth. writ.] None published I write poems for friends and family - or whomever inspires me.; [pers.] I write purely from inspiration. Most of my poems are already written in my head and only take moments to jot down. I am also an avid reader of anything I get my hands on.; [a.] Akron, OH

PESTA, BEN
[b.] December 17, 1979, Kingston, PA; [p.] Michele and John Pesta; [ed.] Entering Junior Year of High School; [occ.] Dish Washer, Student; [oth. writ.] "Mercenary Children," "Phlegm," "Tinct Fardel," "Blown Humor," "Ineffectual," "Trepidity," "Sole Outfit," "FN II," "Left of the Right Path," "Bon-Bons and Boom Booms" (Nicole Biago).; [pers.] Always wandering left of the right path in search for my Candice DeLeo. Thanks Pa! Thanks Ma!; [a.] West Pittston, PA

PETERS, JOSH
[b.] September 16, 1978, Wheat Ridge, CO; [p.] Carol Peters; [ed.] Graduated Westminster H.S. attending Regis University; [occ.] Student/Audiophile; [pers.] Thanks to the influence of the achieved Dr. McElroy and Dr. Peters.; [a.] Arvada, CO

PETERS JR., ROBERT F. R.
[b.] April 24, 1937, Bridgeport, CT; [p.] Robert F. R. and Mary Caris Peters; [m.] Virginia L. Peters; [ed.] College of Wooster (Ohio) B.A. 1959, Yale University Divinity School, M. Div. 1963, Case Western Reserve Univ. M.A. History 1971; [occ.] Consultant, Writer; [memb.] National Society of Fund Raising Executives, 1982, Greater Washington Chapter, NSFRE, past Board Member, Planned Giving Study Group of Washington, DC, past director, U.S. Coast Guard, Auxiliary, 1988 past Flotilla Commander.; [a.] Forton, VA

PETERSON, JANICE GREEN
[b.] April 4, 1941, Dayton, OH; [p.] Marvin Clovis and Niladine Green; [m.] Andrew Peterson (Deceased), July 28, 1984; [ed.] B.S. Mathematics, University of New Mexico; [occ.] Medically Retired, Programmer Analyst; [memb.] Alpha Chi Omega Sorority; [pers.] All of my poetry is written to encourage people that no matter what trials or circumstances they may find themselves in, God is there to strengthen them. I am a widow and have Multiple Sclerosis and God has been my strength through it all.; [a.] Albuquerque, NM

PETERSON, MELISSA
[pen.] "27"; [b.] February 12, 1962, Oklahoma City, OK; [p.] Sandi Huston; [m.] Lloyd N. Peterson III, December 1, 1995; [ch.] Jared Michael, Cherisse Renee, Kristen Nicole; [memb.] VP, Public Relations, Central Park Toastmasters, American Heart Association; [pers.] I believe writing is an expression of one's dreams, combined with reality, set before the backdrop of the imagination.

PETRIE, MARIE
[pen.] Rosa Briar; [b.] Calvary, WI; [p.] Urban Petrie, Mary Petrie; [ed.] Cardinal Stritch College, Wisconsin State University - Whitewater; [occ.] School Psychologist, St. Coletta of Wisconsin, Inc.; [memb.] Sisters of St. Francis of Assisi, American Psychological Association, National Association of School Psychologists, Wisconsin School Psychological Association, American Association for Mental Retardation; [oth. writ.] A collection of unpublished free verse. Am also in the process of writing an illustrated journal of my recent pilgrimage to Rome and Assisi.; [pers.] My free verse is primarily an expression of my dependency on a higher being as well as an eagerness to be an instrument of that Being's unconditional love for all of God's children.; [a.] Jefferson, WI

PETRUSKA, SARAH ANNE
[b.] March 15, 1986, Dallas, TX; [p.] Steven and Jill Petruska; [ed.] Lummis Elementary; [memb.] TPC Swim Team, Lummis Elementary, Yearbook Staff, Burger King Kids Club, St. Elizabeth Ann Seton Catholic Church; [hon.] PTA Reflections, The National Library of Poetry; [oth. writ.] Several poems and articles published in the *Lummis News*; [pers.] I enjoy writing for pleasure. My hopes are of becoming an author. In the future I'd like to speak at schools about the pleasure of writing.; [a.] Las Vegas, NV

PETTIS, ANGELA JO-ANN
[pen.] UKP; [b.] July 20, 1973, Sch'tdy, NY; [p.] Jo-Ann and Leo La Balge; [ch.] Jo-Ann Catherine Pettis; [oth. writ.] Personal favorites "The Flower", "Tell Me You'll Be There", "Distasteful Memories", closest To My Heart Is: "I have..."; [pers.] I write what I believe each and every human being goes through, no matter what shape or size.; [a.] Scotia, Glenville, NY

PETTIS, PATRICK
[pen.] Tobias Pettis; [b.] November 23, 1971, Upstate, NY; [p.] JoAnn, Leonnard; [m.] Sean Cutler, August 27, 1995; [occ.] Student/Bartender in NYC; [hon.] Six time coverboy of international publications; [oth. writ.] "Blue Tight World," "Stars But Shardes of Ice"; [pers.] I write what I feel, much influenced by the city, and these are things I'm sure all of us may feel at times.; [a.] New York City, NY

PFISTER, NICOLE LYNN
[b.] November 3, 1982, Bryan, TX; [p.] Bernard and Darlene Pfister; [ed.] Going into 9th grade at Shenandoah Valley Christian Academy; [oth. writ.] Other poems - none published; [a.] Front Royal, VA

PHASHA
[pen.] Phasha; [b.] March 9, 1946, Washington; [p.] Natural: The Oslers; [ch.] Carly Weddle; [ed.] Two years College, Modeling School, Real Estate School; [occ.] Kelly Temp. Services, Realtor; [memb.] Lions Club, Presbyterian Church, Oregon Realtors Assoc.; [oth. writ.] *Where the Heartache Ends* due to hit the market in 1997. Subject: Scars of being adopted by alcoholic, abusive parents.; [pers.] Loneliness would diminish if there were telephones in heaven.; [a.] Yachats, OR

PHELPS JR., S.
[b.] February 6, 1921, Port Jervis, NY; [m.] Deceased; [ed.] High School - 2 yrs. Ag. Cosnell Univ.; [occ.] Stone Mason, Farmer; [memb.] 4H Club Leader, Leader, Wall Kill Ledge of Maine.; [oth. writ.] Wall Kill Valley Times, Hadness Valley Times; [pers.] Have against main Mad Samis because of my continuous goal against developers who would ruin our environment with their so called progressive projects.

PHIPPS, BRANDI
[b.] February 27, 1981, Parsons, KS; [p.] Joy Purdy, Larry Phipps Brad Niemeyer; [ed.] High School; [occ.] Student - Utopia High School; [memb.] UIL, FFA, MYF, ApHC, Student Council, Annual Staff; [hon.] Rookie of the Year - (Appaloosa Horse Club), UIL honors, "A" Honor Roll; [oth. writ.] Several additional poems, a few short stories, and the beginnings of a novel, along with writing for enjoyment; [a.] Tarpley, TX

PIERI, SHIRLEY A.
[pen.] Shirley A. Pieri; [b.] March 28, 1970, New Brighton, PA; [p.] Charles and Shirley Rhodes; [m.] Russell A. Pieri, August 18, 1989; [ch.] Tiffany Ann; [ed.] Shady Grove Christian Academy; [occ.] Housewife and Mother; [oth. writ.] "Gift Of Love" a Lyrical Heritage; [pers.] I strive to reflect the goodness of God, and praise Him for the bounty that he has provided for us. We could be as those who have nothing.; [a.] East Palestine, OH

PIRTLE, BRENDA ANN
[b.] December 31, 1954, Kansas City, MO; [m.] Charles W. Pirtle, November 18, 1972; [ch.] Steven C. Pirtle; [ed.] William Christian High School; [occ.] Homemaker; [pers.] Each of us holds in our heart's treasury a lifetime of memories. This has been the inspiration for my poems.; [a.] Independence, MO

PITTMAN, FELICIA N.
[b.] January 18, 1985, Jackson, MS; [p.] Willie and Larry Pittman; [ed.] Will be in 6th grade when school starts back; [memb.] I belong to New Mt. Zion M.B. Church in Puckett Mississippi, sing in church choir and usher; [hon.] Honor roll at school and awards for differently subjects.; [oth. writ.] Have written other poems, but have not sent them in to a company yet.; [pers.] I'm 11 years old in sixth grade at Puckett school. I write poems, because it's a gift that God gave me, and I like to share them.; [a.] Brandon, MS

PLOUFFE, ANITA M.
[pen.] Anita; [b.] May 4, 1940, Amesbury, MA; [m.] Widow; [ch.] Donna, Teddy, Michael, Brenda; [ed.] Amesbury High School Home Health Aide Course, Adult Education Courses, "Long Ridge Writers Group" Home Study Course; [occ.] Retired; [memb.] Hampton Falls Baptist Church, International Society of Poets, Exeter Area Assoc. for the Arts, "Tops" Organization; [hon.] 2nd Place Oil Painting - Deerfield Fair, Homemaker

Home Health Aide Service Award; [oth. writ.] Editor for Newsletter *The Homemakers Rag* for HHHA Agency - 1980's Summer - 1996 Poems Published in *Spirit of the Age.*; [pers.] The secret of Peace within your heart is "Learning Forgiveness".; [a.] Exeter, NH

PLUMADORE, MRS. DARBIE

[pen.] Darbie Deniz-Plumadore; [b.] March 8, 1962, Auburn, CA; [p.] Mrs. Lillian Bergquist, Mr. Gary Bergquist, Mr. and Mrs. Keith Deniz; [m.] Beth Plumadore, July 24, 1993; [ch.] Reed Atkinson, Jacob Plumadore and Beth Plumadore; [ed.] Placer High School Auburn, CA; [occ.] Homemaker, Mother of Three and Poet!; [hon.] Biggest honor for me has been, being published in The National Library of Poetry; [oth. writ.] "One Special Rose," "True Love," "Golden Maiden," "Snowy Town," "A Sound," "Look Around You," "River of a Friend," The Candle Man", "The Heart of It All," and many more...; [pers.] My poems are written for friends and loved ones, thanks for the love and inspiration all of you have given me.; [a.] Saranac, NY

POITIER, CONSTANCE RENA

[b.] June 1, 1955, Quincy, FL; [p.] Dorothy Parker Harris, Rev. Leroy C. Harris Sr., (Both Deceased); [m.] James Poitier, July 22, 1995; [ch.] Carla Felicia DuPont, Carl Franklin DuPont Jr.; [ed.] Chipley High, Chipley, FL, Bethune - Cookman College, Daytona Beach, FL, Flatlantic University, Boca Raton, FL; [occ.] Music Teacher; [memb.] Florida Music Educators Association, National Educators Association; [hon.] Outstanding Teenagers of America, *Who's Who Among American Colleges and Universities*, *Who's Who Among Outstanding Young Women of America*, Miss Phi Beta Sigma; [oth. writ.] *A Spiritual Christmas*, my book of poems.; [pers.] To nurture the minds of young people and provide a foundation of high quality, comprehensive music education for all students as a part of their complete education.; [a.] Daytona Beach, FL

POLK, BRENDA J.

[pen.] Brenda Gregory Polk; [b.] November 13, 1950, Kansas City, KS; [p.] Harry and Verdia Gregory; [m.] Deceased, May 18, 1980; [ch.] One; [ed.] High school Grad-1968 1971, Resp Thrp Tech 1990 2 yr College; [occ.] Brain Injury Provider; [hon.] Scholastic Achievements English Composition I, Perfect Attendance English Composition I Scholastic Achievement Logic Achievement - Honor Roll Outstanding Service - Women In Children's Ministry.; [oth. writ.] Copyright completed manuscript on my father's illness. (Seeking publisher); [pers.] "Its very soothing to my brain, to take words and form a sentence, form paragraphs, form pages of information."; [a.] Kansas City, KS

POLK, WILLIAM ALAN

[pen.] William A. Polk; [b.] June 24, 1969, Jackson, MS; [p.] James D. Polk and Jayne Pennington; [m.] Laura C. Polk, January 6, 1992; [ed.] McCluer Academy, Forest Hill High School, Univ. of Miss., Mississippi College; [occ.] Student of Law at Mississippi College; [memb.] Phi Alpha Theta, Civil War Round table, Raymond Presbyterian Church, Blue Grey Education Society; [pers.] I am influenced by the writings of Richard Weaver, R. L. Dabney, Edmund Burke, Plato, and Allan Bloom. In the name of "Freedom", man has skillfully stripped away those things necessary for civilization. Since then, there have been numerous warnings of our descent. But, it seems, we have become too ignorant to recognize them.; [a.] Raymond, MS

POOLE, JEAN

[ed.] Wedell Phillips High, Kennedy-King College Business Administration Cleo Johnson Modeling School, Modeling Mid Western Broadcasting School, Radio and TV; [oth. writ.] I started writing again November 13, 1990. In that time from 1990 now 1996 I have written two hundred and fifty poems. My first poem was published in Marshall Fields store-affairs of state "I Met Me"; [pers.] I write hoping to feed the mind, the soul and body. My words are food for thought. As you feast on my words, I hope all will be inspired to heights unlimited. My experiences, and the world around me inspire and motivate me to write.; [a.] Chicago, IL

POPE, JONATHAN

[pen.] J. Pope; [b.] February 20, 1971, Daytona Beach, FL; [p.] Oscar and Gloria Pope; [ed.] B.A. Communications (Dec 1996) Saginaw Valley State University, MI/ Seabreeze Sr. High, Daytona Bch., FL; [occ.] Youth Director, Saginaw YMCA; [memb.] Bethel A.M.E. Church, Teen Pregnancy Prevention; [hon.] *Who's Who Among American Colleges and Universities*, 1995-96; [oth. writ.] Several unpublished works.; [pers.] A pen and paper are the only things we need to change to world. With a stroke of the pen we can create a better world, if only for a moment.; [a.] Saginaw, MI

POPE, KATHY D.

[b.] October 5, 1956, Albertville, AL; [p.] Floyd and Mary Ruth Matthews; [m.] Barry J. Pope, February 14, 1990; [ch.] Jonathan Ogle, Jennifer Ogle; [ed.] Douglas High School, Calhoun Community College; [occ.] QC Inspector; [pers.] I've always written poems just for personal enjoyment. This is my first poem to be published. Hopefully it will not be my last. Thanks to my husband for the encouragement and the little push I needed.; [a.] Huntsville, AL

PORTER, CHERYLYN S.

[b.] June 26, 1947, Buffalo, NY; [p.] Edward and Margaret Wytrwal; [ch.] 18 year old son, Sean; [ed.] Riverside High School, SUC at Fredonia, Buffalo State College; [occ.] Special Education Teacher, Wellsville Central Schools Wellsville, New York; [oth. writ.] Poems and articles published in local papers and *Buffalo Schools Anthology*. Currently working on children's series and humorous novel.; [pers.] An only child, my best companions were often books by age 7, I decided to be an author myself, writing an "Epic" about the world. Since then I've written poetry, songs, stories, and plays. I continue to write, striving to give as much pleasure to my readers as others' creations have given me.; [a.] Wellsville, NY

PORTER JR., GLEN W.

[pen.] Glen W. Porter Jr.; [b.] November 5, 1945, Pontiac, MI; [p.] Glen W. Porter and Carrie Elva (Logan) Reode; [m.] Rhoda M. (Parker) Porter, July 31, 1971; [ch.] Jacob Lee, Chandra Galadriel and Jebidah A.; [ed.] Eastern Wash. State College, Wenatchee Valley College and Cerritos Community College (Calif) (The other two in Washington); [occ.] Indust. Maint. Mech. and Writer; [memb.] American Legion, Brotherhood of the Eagles, Whatcon Country Pool League (Pers); [hon.] Numerous Bowling Awards (Century Watch, Top Service most improved bowler and team awards) Pool League Awards - Top Shooter 6th Place, Wa. State Eagles Div. Champs and Team place awards.; [oth. writ.] Numerous poems and a couple of short stories.; [pers.] "First to thine own self be true." `Shakespeare'; [a.] Bellingham, WA

PORTLOCK, JOYLETTE L.

[b.] August 10, 1978, Wilmington, DE; [p.] Jacqueline and Harry Portlock; [ed.] William Penn High School c/ o '95 MIT c/o '99; [occ.] Student at Massachusetts Institute of Technology; [memb.] Delta Psi Fraternity; [pers.] My poetry is a presentation of deep-felt emotions in what is hopefully expressive and eloquent verse. Personal favorite: Robert Frost.; [a.] Delaware City, DE

POTTER, DOTTIE R.

[b.] September 29, 1943, O'Neill, NE; [p.] Elmer, Mildred Kraft (Both Deceased); [m.] 1st Dinger Risinger, September 29, 1962, 2nd Geral Potter, March 15, 1965, (Both Deceased, Widowed Twice); [ed.] GED - 1984, B.S. Organizational Communication 1993, Sport Tracks - Advertising and Public Relations M.A.E. Speech Communication 1994, both at University of Nebraska at Kearney, Kearnye, NE; [occ.] STS Independent Distributor or Sales Rep; [memb.] St. James Catholic Church, Lambda Pi Eta Honor Society; [hon.] UNK Dean's List, National Dean's List - 2 years, *Who's Who Among Students in American Universities and Colleges*, Most Dependable Reporter for *UNK Antelope Newspaper*; [oth. writ.] Poems published in *Rock Falls Review*, poems written and read at funerals, for weddings and anniversaries, write and compose songs and music, write short stories from personal life, Experience - Inspirational; [pers.] I believe that half of life is fate - it happens and is beyond our control - the other half is what we decide to do with what's left - and with faith in God, we go on!; [a.] Kearney, NE

POUKNER, DOLORES

[b.] October 9, 1930, Philadelphia, PA; [p.] Eleanor and Albert Gebhart; [m.] Frank Poukner; [ch.] Kathleen Bryan, Frank Poukner III; [ed.] Holy Innocence Elem., Notre Dame High School and Holy Souls Business school - all in Phila. Area.; [occ.] Home maker; [oth. writ.] Several published in my church paper, and used for special occasions.; [pers.] I write about family and people I know. Mikey is my Grandchild and uncle Joe in the poem was my uncle.; [a.] Tampa, FL

POULIN, DONNA BENIGNO

[pen.] Rissi Rogers; [b.] October 6, 1947, Kenilworth, NJ; [p.] Angela (Antonucci) Benigno, Rissi (Roger) Benigno; [m.] Kenneth W. Poulin Jr. (Deceased), January 12, 1988; [ch.] Reese Michael Arnold, Terry Matthew Poulin; [ed.] Keyport H.S. Grad. 65 from McArthur N.J. H.S. Hollywood, Fla., Fla. Art Institute, Cartooning, Com. Art; [occ.] Homemaker, Home School Mom; [pers.] I wrote this from the depths of my soul. Emotion is part of what makes us who we are. Self-expression the glue that keeps it together.; [a.] Lauderdale Lakes, FL

POURNER, STEVEN F.

[pen.] Steve Pourner; [b.] January 31, 1962, Beaumont, TX; [p.] Mr. and Mrs. C. I. Pourner; [ed.] Bingman Elem. BMT, TX. South Park High School - BMT, TX Lamar Univ. - BMY, TX; [occ.] I am about to become a student in college; [memb.] Not yet (but hopefully soon); [a.] Beaumont, TX

POWER, JOSEPH M.

[b.] August 8, 1932, Somerville, MA; [p.] Robert James, Johanna Baker Power; [m.] Delores Anne, December 23, 1954; [ch.] Mark Kelim, Deirdre Lynn; [ed.] Agassiz Elementary Cambridge, MA, 1948, United State Air Force, Radar, and Electronics, 1952-56; [occ.] Retired Corning Inc. Glass Materials Research, Artist Home Studio; [memb.] Past Associate Member American Chemical Society; [hon.] Corning Inc. Three United States Patents. Glass Materials Research; [pers.] With so many uncertain events unfolding before us, I quietly seek a better understanding of that still small voice within us that reveals the hope and peace of our God.; [a.] Corning, NY

PREECE, SHAWNA
[b.] February 24, 1979, El Centro, CA; [p.] Douglas Preece, Yvonne Perry; [ed.] Senior at Beaumont High School; [memb.] Member of FHA-HERO Art School; [oth. writ.] Written poems since 5 years old, over a hundred.; [a.] Beaumont, CA

PREVIS, MARILYN
[b.] June 12, 1939, N.Y.C.; [p.] Marion Joseph Mischker & Bernice Grey Simons; [m.] Henry Leon Previs, September 9, 1961; [ch.] Gregory & David; [ed.] High School; [occ.] Housewife; [oth. writ.] Set Forth, Faith In Him, Peace Upon the River, Revived Grace (193), Mother (Eulogy), Pancell, Johns 85th, Remembering Don, Mattaponi Memories, The Coverlet of Prayers, Garden Communion, The Gift of Love, Mannequins, Easter Message, Betty's Passing; [pers.] I feel my great-grandfather should have become great. For unknown reasons he remained obscure. I also wish to publish his and mine. Please refer me?

PRIDDY, JOEL
[pen.] Bob Christopher; [b.] September 27, 1989, Phoenix; [ed.] 2 yrs. H.S. Graduate in 1998 from Camelback H.S.; [occ.] Student at Camelback H.S. in Phoenix, AZ

PRIESTER, TAMMY
[pen.] Tammy Priester; [b.] September 5, 1964, Mobile, AL; [p.] Olney Edmiston and Augusta Edmiston; [m.] David Priester, September 10, 1994; [ch.] Bernard and Shane Harris; [ed.] G.E.D.; [occ.] Homemaker; [pers.] Live life like there's no tomorrow, but with sense.; [a.] Fort Worth, TX

PRONOVOST, DORIS S.
[b.] May 3, 1920, Missoula, MT; [p.] Frank Graewin, Elsie Graewin; [m.] Joseph O. Pronovost, October 6, 1945; [ch.] Karen, Jeanne, Nancy; [ed.] Montana State University; [occ.] Retired; [memb.] Tri-Delt; [oth. writ.] Several personal writings for family anniversaries and weddings; [pers.] After trying several fields of painting and porcelain work, and enjoying it, decided to put my day dreams and thoughts on paper. Find I'm enjoying that, too.; [a.] Billings, MT

PRUITT, JONATHAN L.
[pen.] Tray; [b.] April 26, 1979, Kingman, KS; [p.] Dillan and Tammy Pruitt; [ed.] I'm a Jr., in High School; [occ.] School and John Deere; [oth. writ.] "Grandfather" in the book, National Poetry.; [pers.] Life is short so enjoy.; [a.] Arapahoe, NE

PUCKETT, ORA
[b.] January 11, 1957, Louisiana; [p.] Arthur and Susie Puckett; [ch.] Micheal and Gimone; [ed.] One year of Business College and one year of Junior College; [occ.] Instructional Aids for pre-K and Kindergarten; [memb.] Classroom Volunteering; [oth. writ.] Library of Congress has a book listed in No - PAU 1903078 with other poems I have written.; [pers.] You can read material there at your convenience at the Library of Congress in Washington.; [a.] Oakland, CA

PULLIAM, MABLE RUTH
[pen.] Ruth Pulliam; [b.] October 4, 1913, Paragould, AR; [p.] Arthur and May Simpson; [m.] Chester Lewis Pulliam, June 21, 1930; [ch.] Four daughters and one son; [ed.] High School; [occ.] Homemaker; [memb.] Garden Clubs, Book Clubs, Methodist Church, husband is a Methodist Minister; [oth. writ.] Several poems but have not sent any for publication prior to patch of blot, I am now 82.; [a.] Kansas City, MO

PULLIN, D. W.
[b.] March 12, 1969, Kalamazoo, MI; [p.] Dolores Skidmore, Oral Pullin Jr.; [ed.] Mountain View High, Arizona State University; [occ.] Computer Engineer; [memb.] Microsoft Developer Network, United States Humane Society; [hon.] Dean's List; [pers.] The written words in poetry are only thoughts in disguise to be shared with people we don't know.; [a.] Phoenix, AZ

QUILPA, ANDREW FERNANDO E.
[b.] April 17, 1988, Agana, Guam; [p.] Chris A. Quilpa & Freny E. Quilpa; [ed.] Portsmouth Catholic Elementary School, Portsmouth, VA (2nd grade), Bethune Elementary School, San Diego, CA (kindergarten); [occ.] Second grade student - Portsmouth Catholic Elementary School, Portsmouth, VA; [hon.] Certificate of Achievement from Reading Rainbow's 1995 and 1996, Young writers & Illustrators Awards Competition; Academic Award (2nd grade), Super Student Award, Certificate of Recognition in Music, P.E. Award, Outstanding Speller and Creativety (1st & 2nd grade), 1st place, Good Academic Achievement Award (Kindergarten), Good Citizen & Student of the Month Award; [oth. writ.] My Family, A Day At The Mall; [pers.] I love reading because it gives me lots of information and it makes me smarter. I love dinosaurs because they are interesting to know and they are one of my favorite animals.; [a.] Chesapeake, VA

QUINE, MELANIE
[b.] February 14, 1951, Lufkin, TX; [p.] Mr. and Mrs. J. J. Young; [m.] David Quine, January 3, 1969; [ch.] John David; [ed.] High School - Cum Laude Class of 69, numerous college courses; [occ.] 26 years in Radio and retired. Died February 26, 1996; [memb.] Herty Baptist Church, Sunday School Teacher 20 years; [oth. writ.] Numerous Poems (31 year collection) but now published; [a.] Lufkin, TX

RAAZ, BRYAN D.
[b.] August 29, 1969, Hartford, CT; [p.] Ret. Capt. Richard Raaz/Phyllis Stewart; [m.] Laura J. Raaz, May 6, 1990; [ch.] Daisy Joy Raaz; [ed.] BA Philosophy CSU Chico; [hon.] International Speech Competition Seoul Korea, Silver Medal for reading of "Era of Confusionism"; [oth. writ.] "The Warriors God," "Doubts of Morn," "Black Orchids," "Wings in the Asphalt," "Wail of the City," "A Dying Man," "Hand in Heart," "Perfectly Unnatural," "Knights of the Wrong Enabled," "Daisy Joy Raaz," "Her Fury"; [pers.] The universe is a path to an immortal loving state-providing that is your choice.; [a.] Austin, TX

RACIC, ANN
[b.] July 8, 1946, Zagreb, Croatia; [p.] Carl and Anna Racic; [ch.] Miranda Lynne, Gabrielle Kathryn; [ed.] Sacred Heart H.S. Community College of Allegheny County; [occ.] Full-time student; [memb.] PSI Beta, Phi Theta Kappa, writer's bloc; [hon.] Leadership award, first place writing contest (Essay)/CCAC; [oth. writ.] CCAC anthology/1996; [pers.] I'm not a writer - I'm a person who writes. Everyone has influenced me, from Chaucer to my children.; [a.] Pittsburgh, PA

RADSCHLAG, PATRICIA
[b.] September 24, 1924, Virginia, MN; [p.] Anton and Agnes Tanko (Deceased); [m.] Walter Radschlag, November 3, 1947; [ch.] Cheryl Sherman; [ed.] 2 years College, Mil. Voc., Crosby-Ironton High; [occ.] Retired; [memb.] AARP, The Women's Memorial

RAFEY, CHARLES T.
[b.] December 8, 1975, Toledo, OH; [p.] Helen Grames, Wayne Rafey; [pers.] Positive thoughts lead to positive actions. Positive actions lead to a positive lifestyle.; [a.] Perrysburg, OH

RAGHUNAUTH, CHANDAI
[pen.] Devi Raghunauth; [b.] October 15, 1983, Bronx, NY; [p.] Mr. and Mrs. Raghunauth; [occ.] Student at JHS; [oth. writ.] Yes, but not publication. (I remember by head); [a.] Queens, NY

RAGSDALE, C. JARED
[pen.] C. J. Ragsdale; [b.] October 7, 1982, Nashville, TN; [p.] Dwight and Sarah Ragsdale; [ed.] Pioneer Christian Academy; [occ.] Student; [pers.] A true poet has the originality and artistic ability to appeal to each different person.; [a.] Joelton, TN

RAGSDALE, MISTY
[b.] October 1, 1981, Talladega, CO; [p.] Allen and Claudette Ragsdale; [ed.] Vincent High School (Sophomore); [occ.] Student; [memb.] Church (Vincent Revival Center) Pep Club FHA (Future Homemakers of America); [hon.] Outstanding Math Achievement (95-96); [pers.] I strive to be a light for Jesus Christ and also go to college to be an Elementary School teacher. I have been greatly influenced by my parents, pastor, teachers, friends and relatives; [a.] Vincent, AL

RAINEY, ERIN
[p.] Bruce and Anita Rainey; [ed.] Davidson Academy in Nashville, TN; [oth. writ.] "A Net to Catch My Silver Tears"; [pers.] Erin's other interests are animals (She intends to be a Veterinarian), art, having had two exhibits with her fellow students and teacher, Carol Adair, and writing to pen pals. She credits her inspiration for her writing to her family and writing teacher, Abbi Stokes, and especially God for the gift of her talent.

RAISTRICK, VIRGINIA
[pen.] Ginnie; [b.] May 25, 1925, Peoria, IL; [p.] Frank and Fredia Drysdale; [m.] Richard Raistrick (Deceased), September 8, 1943; [ch.] Richard F., Frank M., Patricia Hall; [ed.] Woodruff High School Peoria, IL; [occ.] Retired-audit and sales office; [memb.] Save Our Springdale Association, Peoria Heights Congregational Church; [oth. writ.] Poems for family and friends; [pers.] I try to show love, respect and friendship in my writings. I try to give the reader definite thoughts to think about.; [a.] Peoria Heights, IL

RAMBO, EVELYN M.
[pen.] Evelyn M. Rambo; [b.] October 2, 1951, Philadelphia, PA; [p.] John and Anna Carickhoff; [m.] Dr. Wilfred S. Rambo, June 26, 1937; [ch.] Jonathan M. Rambo, Barbara R. Goss; [ed.] Graduate of High School Bethlehem, PA went to work immediately following graduation, father died 3 months later; [occ.] 1995 - just finished 33 years as Secretary of the Columbia Street Baptist Church, Bangor, ME, under 6 ministers; [memb.]

American Baptist Women of Maine. At one time was President of the Women's Auxiliary of the Osteopathic Hospital in Bangor, Maine. Worked in the office of the American Red Cross as Advisor to Wives of Servicemen overseas.; [hon.] Honored for 30 years as pianist at the church- also for years working with servicemen and youth. Honored for 27 years in Educational Ministries.; [oth. writ.] Several Christian plays with with music presented in the church: "No Doubts In The Manger", "Surely He Was The Son Of God", "The Searching Three" (a unusual Epiphany Play) "Aquila and Priscilla" (skit) My favorite poem is "The Colors of Christmas". Most of my poems are religious or have a message to them. Another favorite is "I'm A Woman Of God, You Know." (used at a Women's Conference); [pers.] University of ME. right now, in my 80 years, I am writing a story about my Great Grandmother who who came from Saxony, Germany in 1851. At the moment I have gotten them to the ship in which they intend to sail. Whether or not I will live long enough to get them to America, remains to be seen.; [a.] Brewer, ME

RAMIREZ, JAMES D.
[pen.] J. D. Cervantes; [b.] May 10, 1976, Glen Cove, NY; [p.] Rodolfo Ramirez, Elieth Ramirez; [ed.] Glen Cove High School, Harvard University (10 wks.), Georgetown University (5 wks.), Carleton College, BA Candidate; [occ.] Student; [hon.] Long Island Hispanic Chamber of Commerce Scholarship, *Who's Who Among American High School Students*; [oth. writ.] Political and religious articles published in campus newspaper and journals; [pers.] No great reality can be achieved without hope and vision. I am a writer greatly influenced by the simplicities and complexities of life's experience.; [a.] Glen Cove, NY

RAMOS, CYNTHIA TAYLOR
[b.] May 30, 1956, Carthage, NC; [p.] Norman Taylor, Opal Taylor; [m.] Jose Alonso Ramos; [ed.] Port Chester Senior High West Chester Community College Southern West Chester BOCES School of Nursing; [occ.] Nurse; [memb.] Mt. Zion Baptist Church, St. Francis Amezion Church; [hon.] Deans List; [oth. writ.] This is my first published poem.; [pers.] I always knew I was better than he led me to believe. Always believe in yourself. I write from my heart.; [a.] Port Chester, NY

RASER, KATRINA J.
[b.] July 26, 1984, Korea; [ed.] Lower Dauphin School District, K-6; [occ.] Student; [hon.] County Strings, Pennsylvania Music Educator's Assn. All Stars Festival; [pers.] I have been greatly influenced by nature, and it deeply saddens me to see one world divided against itself. I believe that someday nature and mankind will co-exist in harmony.

RASH, NORA BELL
[pen.] Nora (Norie) Nora Bell; [b.] May 4, 1924, Lowell, MI; [p.] Marion and Nora B. Simington; [m.] Edward Wm. Rash, September 6, 1941; [ch.] Seven; [ed.] Went back to Lowell High School and finished my High School Graduation May 1991 after my children were all graduated an grown; [occ.] Deliver Meals for the Home-bound and other Volunteer Work; [memb.] Lowell Nazarene Church, Chaplain of the Ladies Auxiliary of American Legion. Representative of Kent County Nutrition Board; [hon.] For Working a Tour Church 18 yrs. attending Lowell Nazarene 52 yrs. going back to School and completing my G.E.D. had both my feet operated on and I had to walk up a flight-of-stairs to receive my diploma. I made it and my children were so proud of me; [oth. writ.] "Memories of Easter," "Past Christmas," "Precious Lord So Near," "Bingo Players," "My Mind is Black," "Cold Winter Days," "Taking our Little Dog for a Walk."; [pers.] I took two computer classes (one College) but wasn't feeling very well at the time so never finished last one and need to take another typing class it has been so long, just don't have the money, I would love to go to College, five of our children have gone to College - minister son choir director.; [a.] Lowell, MI

RASHID, OMAR
[pen.] Omar Rashid; [b.] May 3, 1978, Hollywood, FL; [p.] Maen and Marina Rashid; [ed.] Amman Baccalaureate School, Jordan 1984-1989 Olsen Middle School Dania, FL 1989-1992 Ely High School Pompano Beach, FL 1992-1996 Dartmouth College Hanover, NH 1996-2000; [occ.] Student; [memb.] Clubs: Law Club 1995-1996, Inter-act club 1994-1996, Latin Club 1992-1996, National Honor Society 1994-1996, SECME 1993-1996, JAS 1992-1996, Chemistry Club 1993-1996; [hon.] Senior With Most Community Service in Broward County 1996, National Exchange Club Student of the Year 1996, Senior Award in Latin, Social Studies and Community Service 5/96. 3rd and 4th places at Latin State Forum 4/96, Latin Brain Brawl Regionals Champion 2/96, 3 first places of Latin Regionals 2/96; [oth. writ.] Articles in a newsletter for teenage volunteers in Memorial Regional Hospital; [pers.] I am tremendously influenced by Latin literature and the great men of ancient Roman times which gave me motivation and encouragement in my aspirations and long journey to become a physician and achieve my dreams and goals; [a.] Pembroke Pine, FL

RAVER, DAVIS
[b.] November 30, 1948, Owings Mils, MD; [p.] Benson F. and Mary Ellen Raver; [m.] Martha Lee Raver, January 28, 1985; [ch.] Davis Jr., Eric, Jaime, Ann, Malinda; [ed.] A.A., A.S. Business Accounting; [occ.] Postmaster; [memb.] Lions, Moose, Sertoma; [hon.] Dean's List, Bronze Star, USPS (6) Superior Achievements, USPS (9) Letters of Appreciation, Vietnam Service Cross, School Board Business Partners

REA, STEPHEN CHARLES
[b.] December 4, 1977, Pennsylvania; [p.] Larry and Donna Rea; [ed.] Graduated Unicoi County Hjoh School: June 7, 1996 Attending East Tennessee Stone University: Major - Computer Science; [occ.] Owner of The Sound Machine - car stereo installation; [hon.] Morril Motor College Scholarship - full tuition, *Who's Who Among America's High School Students* 10th, 11th and 12th grades; [oth. writ.] No previous writings.; [pers.] My poem is dedicated to Angie Hammond, for whom it was written.; [a.] Erwin, TN

REDDY, RAMESH C.
[pen.] Sower; [b.] October 5, 1972, Nellore, India; [p.] Mr. and Mrs. A. R. Reddy; [ed.] Bachelor of Science: Psychology University of Pittsburgh, PA, Bachelor of Arts: Administration of Justice, University of Pittsburgh, PA; [occ.] Cashier at Supermarket, Students, Inter-Varsity Christian Fellowship Staff Volunteer; [memb.] Pittsburgh Chess Club, Inter-Varsity Christian Fellowship, New Hope Christian Community Church; [hon.] Presidential Academic Fitness Award, Dean's List; [oth. writ.] "My Education Christ's Way," "College Life Without Losing Focus on the Lord," "Does God Care For Me?" (Counseling Poems), "Growing in the Lord 2000," "Guidance Music" (Names of Jehovah), "Helping Hands" (Weekly Tract); [pers.] My mission has been counseling broken hearts with the love of Christ. And with this in mind write poems, songs, books, and tracts. I have been influenced greatly by my mommy who taught me about Christ's love. Christ is my Lord and personal savior.; [a.] Pittsburgh, PA

REESE, CHERYL A.
[b.] April 22, 1966, Longview, TX; [p.] Clemetine Reese Rusk; [ed.] South Oak Cliff High School; [occ.] Packer at Sweetheart Cups Inc., Dallas, Texas; [hon.] A high school award for outstanding person; [oth. writ.] Several children's poems that are not published, unpublished children's books and working on one. The two finished ones are call *Simeon Imagination*, and *My Colorful ABC's Book*.; [pers.] Because I love children, by writing is my way of showing them how special they really are.; [a.] Dallas, TX

REICHARD, LINDA
[pen.] Nichole Lynn; [b.] January 8, 1965, Hbg., PA; [p.] Linda and Al Beard; [m.] Joe Reichard, November 23, 1990; [ch.] J.J. Justin; [ed.] C.D. East High School Hbg. PA; [occ.] Housewife and Mother; [memb.] St. Matthias United Methodist Church; [oth. writ.] Several poems published in church Newsletters; [pers.] I only hope that my poetry puts a smile on someone's face or touches someone's heart. Inspiration - Helen Stiener Rice; [a.] Fredericksburg, VA

REINHART, GABRIELLE
[oth. writ.] Poems published in *Contemporary American Poets* - 1992 *Selected Works* and *A Poetic Calm After The Desert Storm* - 1991 through the Monterrey Poetry Society under the pen name of Gabrielle Hayes. Current work in progress is stories which tell the legends and histories of various California Indian tribes and will be targeted towards children.; [pers.] Originally my purpose in writing was a form of self exploration. I found that clarity of thinking occurred through the act of putting thoughts on paper. The fact that the expressions came out poetry was actually astonishing to me. Often I would read the words and thoughts and think, "Who wrote this?" I have since come to understand that the writer is just one aspect of who I am, an aspect that for many years was a silent observer, a part that remained hidden. My purpose in sharing the work is a result of encouragement from others, people who have read the poems and have been enlightened through the insights. I believe that all being have a spiritual purpose, once one has come to recognize and identify what it is, life becomes infinitely richer and more rewarding.; [a.] Potter Valley, CA

REITER, NAOMI UNDINE
[b.] May 5, 1974, Roneoak, VA; [p.] Cynthia Miles; [ed.] Country Day School, St. Croix USVI, San Diego State University; [occ.] College Student (in between schools); [pers.] Someday our looks will fade, so we have to be straight with our brains. Then, our brains will go, so we have to be straight with our souls. When I write, I'm trying to straighten out my soul.; [a.] Carmel, CA

RENFROW, TARA
[b.] April 2, 1981, Waukegan; [p.] Denver and Theresa Renfrow; [ed.] Zion Benton High School; [occ.] Lifeguard and Swimming Instructor; [pers.] I hope everyone finds some sort of meaning in this poem, and is able to understand it, even though it will mean something different to each person.; [a.] Zion, IL

RENNER, MARTHA
[pen.] Martha Renner; [b.] August 14, 1963, Philadelphia, PA; [p.] Peter Millard Renner, Nancy Fairbank Renner; [m.] Allan Nelson Schultz, August 14, 1993; [ed.] B.A. Germanic Studies, University of Victoria, Victoria, B.C. Licentiate in Voice Performance, McGill University, Montreal, Quebec; [occ.] Opera Singer; [hon.] Vocal Institute of Santa Barbara, California, Scholarship in Voice. First Place in Voice, Los Angeles Franz Liszt Competition. Goethe Institute, Murnau, Bavaria, full Scholarship to Study German; [oth. writ.] "Mamo," 2 poem cycle set for string quartet and soprano. Various poems unpublished.; [pers.] For me, poetry expresses the working out of the deep inner struggle into consciousness.; [a.] San Diego, CA

REPROGLE, SOMMER DAUN
[b.] September 22, 1982, Richmond, IN; [p.] Paul and Georganna Reprogle; [ed.] Completed 7th Grade; [pers.] I am the daughter of an Army Sgt. and have already lived in several different states as well as living in Italy for 3 yrs. My writing is always based on my feelings at that time.; [a.] Indianapolis, IN

REYNOLDS, JUSTIN JAMES
[b.] September 26, 1980, Pocatello, ID; [ed.] currently attending Twin Falls High School as a Junior; [memb.] Young Authors Society, Christian Center Youth Group; [hon.] Young Authors Award, Drug Re-enforcement officer personally autographed graduation plaque, after reading "The Last Mistake".; [oth. writ.] "The Windchime", "A Prayer To Live For", "Parents", "Grandmas", "Cupids Poem"; [pers.] I wrote "The Last Mistake" when I first realized what drugs truly do to you.; [a.] Twin Falls, ID

REYNOLDS, MARY AGNES
[b.] June 20, 1922, Killingly, CT; [p.] John Lacey and Jane Dow Ling Lacey; [m.] Charles B. Reynolds, November 26, 1942; [ch.] 5; [ed.] 8 Grammar Sch., 2 1/2 yrs High; [occ.] Retired; [hon.] I won first prize on the christmas poem you already have. I am enclosing a copy of it. (in 1946) I won a prize in grade 8 on "The Puppy"; [oth. writ.] I also write card verses for my own use and sympathy notes for the news paper also in verse.; [pers.] I've always written poetry but did not have time to keep doing it raising a family. I can do it now I'm retired.; [a.] Danielson, CT

REYNOLDS, MICHAEL EDWARD
[pen.] Kathleen (Carrie); [b.] March 1, 1948, Altadena; [p.] Mary and David; [ch.] Brian David, Lisa Marie; [ed.] Rosemead High School Pasadena City College, Glendale Community College; [occ.] Looking; [memb.] Vinyard Christian Fellowship; [hon.] Cert. of Plumbing; [oth. writ.] Assorted poems about the beauty and grace that I see in women.; [pers.] "The Song" is a true story about an angel I met at an A. A. meeting. I was just about to speak when our eyes met. I shall never forget that moment which changed me forever.; [a.] Temple City, CA

REZAIYAN, SHERENE
[b.] December 3, 1980, Columbia, MD; [p.] Stephanie Glover, Ahmad Rezaiyan; [ed.] Howard High School; [occ.] Student; [a.] Columbia, MD

RHODES, SHARON
[b.] December 25, 1954, Indianapolis, IN; [ch.] Daughter age 24, Son age 22, and 3 granddaughters; [oth. writ.] Poem book and started second called *My Gift to Jesus*. I have 7 children's books. I do all illustrations copyrighted working on the 8th, I also have a song book with 4 songs in it.; [pers.] As a child Jesus really came to me in a star. The poem I held Jesus hand I what happen, I have one called "In Jesus Arms." That also happen.; [a.] Lebanon, TN

RICE, HETTIE
[pen.] Hettie Hoy Rice; [b.] May 23, 1934, Tipton County, TN; [p.] Elbert R. and Lucille H. Hoy; [m.] Ersal Leon Rice, August 19, 1950; [ch.] Marilyn, David, Timothy; [ed.] Munford High School, Covington Vocational School; [occ.] Bookkeeper for family owned construction business: And homemaker, Retired Sales Clerk; [memb.] Charleston Baptist Church: Choir Member, Adult Sunday School Teacher, Covington Little Theater patron; [hon.] Christian Development Diploma: Reading Certificate from Women's Homemakers Club; [oth. writ.] Poems published in local newspaper. A book of poems not yet published, Greeting card verses.; [pers.] My writings are from experiences and inspirations I have had in years past. I greatly admire the poetry of Helen Steiner Rice, also Edwin Markham. My desire is to have my book of poetry published.; [a.] Covington, TN

RICHARDS, ERIK M.
[b.] March 18, 1973, Garden City, MI; [p.] Karla Morrison and Gerald Richards; [m.] Engaged to Angela Marie Earts; [ed.] Capistrano Valley HS (CA)., VC-Irvine (CA), Albion College (MI); [occ.] History/Language Arts Teacher, St. John Elem. School Albion, MI.; [memb.] Big Brothers and Sisters of South Central Michigan, Albion Community Leadership Group, Albion P.O.W.E.R. for Kids Program, Gerald R. Ford Institute for Public Service; [hon.] Graduated Magna Cum Laude, Dean's List, Albion College Fellow; [pers.] We have succeeded in our lives when we are confident that our efforts have improved and inspired other lives.; [a.] Albion, MI

RICHARDS, IVY
[b.] June 1, 1921, Hope Bay, Portland; [p.] Mr. and Mrs. Isaac Constable; [m.] Wilfred A. Richards (Deceased), February 2, 1950; [ch.] Six; [ed.] James Hill Primary, Clarendon High School, Caenwood Junior Teachers College; [memb.] Congregational Church; [hon.] Six Musical Bronze Awards - Jamaica, Two Plaque Awards from International Society of Poets - Washington 2 Gold and 1 Silver Awards from World of Poetry, California; [pers.] "Great things are in store for you. There is work for you to do in God's garden here below? Tomorrow at this time you will be hearing a voice and whatever that voice leads you that shall ye do?; [a.] Saint Albans, NY

RICHARDSON, GEORGIA LEE
[pen.] Georgie Lee; [b.] January 7, 1936, Washington County; [p.] David James & Pearl (Goff) Pierson; [m.] Frank David Richardson, Sr., June 5, 1956; [ch.] Frank David II, Lyrecia Jo, Lycinda G.; [ed.] Lamar High School, Jonesborough, TN 37659; [occ.] Retired Rural LETTER Carrier, Johnson City, TN. Post Office, 25yrs.; [memb.] AAA - J - 55, Mountain View Baptist Church Missions Committee, 1st grade Sunday School teacher, Emmaus Community; [hon.] Volunteer work Hospital Ministry JCMC Johnson City, TN.; [oth. writ.] Letters to Editor published in local newspaper. (Letter Carriers Last Day At Work) not published; [pers.] I desire to write truth, to put real life into words and to express pleasantness. My joy of reading is stories of true life happenings.; [a.] Johnson City, TN

RICHEY, BETTY C.
[b.] August 8, 1940, Tell City, IN; [p.] Clarence (Pat) Richey, Alice Hall Richey; [occ.] Portrait and Wildlife Artist; [memb.] Big board Helen Ellis Hospital - Tarpon Spring FL, 1994-95-96 - Tarpon Springs Art Association - President 1995-96; [pers.] Hopefully the Creator's love can be felt in my art and poetry; [a.] Holiday, FL

RIDER, CHRISTOPHER
[pen.] Jaren C. Storm; [b.] May 11, 1972, Plattsburgh, NY; [p.] Gail Rider; [ed.] Gaithersburg Elementary School, Gaithersburg MD. through Gaithersburg High School; [occ.] Chef; [pers.] Within the depths of depression lies the greatest magic.; [a.] Cadyville, NY

RIEDY, LYNNE ADELE
[pen.] Lar, Lar; [b.] March 24, 1957, Lansing, MI; [p.] Victor and Marianne Zucco; [m.] Mark R. Riedy, September 6, 1996; [ch.] Brad R. Riedy and Brian V. Riedy; [ed.] Graduation from Michigan State University, College of Nursing BSN, RN in 1979. Attend regular continuing Educ. Classes; [occ.] "At-home mom", Homemaker, "Free-lance Poet"; [memb.] Chairperson for Antrim County Child Abuse and Neglect Council. Antrim Co. Coordinating Council, Family Coordinating Council. Registered Nurse, International Society of Poets, Noetic Sciences.; [hon.] Poet of merit 1995 and 1996 from National Library of Poetry on radio program: Poetry Today in N.Y. Distinguished Member International Society of Poets. The International Poet of merit award 1995 contributed to "Largest Poem for Peace" by International Society of Poets; [oth. writ.] Anthologies National Library of Poetry: *Beyond the Stars* - "Tendencies", *Best Poems of 1996* - "Unfolding", *A Tapestry of Thoughts* - "DNA - Learning the Code." *Where Dawn Lingers* - "The Evolutionary Challenge" *The Best Poems of the 90's* - "The Mask" *Frost at Midnight* - "Alignment"; [pers.] Support the new paradigm shift to quantum physics, body-mind-spirit health and Wellness, 12 step groups; [a.] Bellaire, MI

RIGGS, JASON DWIGHT
[pen.] Jay Riggs; [b.] May 22, 1970, Salem, OH; [p.] Kim and Stan Riggs; [ed.] Graduated May 26, 1996 with a Degree in Machine Technology. Graduated from Southern Local High School and Columbiania County Career Center; [occ.] College Student, Ceramic Tile Factory Employee at Summitville Tile; [memb.] Friendships; [hon.] Degree in Machine Technology and Degree in Family Morals...; [oth. writ.] To many to acknowledge. Thanks to my Aunt Missy Speirs for her encouragement, and to Mom and Dad.; [pers.] I wrote this poem the day after my Grandfather Henry Donald Dickson passed away at the age of 58. I read this poem at his services. This was my first experience with the death of someone close to me. I loved him, I know he knew it...; [a.] Salineville, OH

RILEY, CLARE EVELYN
[pen.] Clare Riley; [b.] July 28, 1981, Jackson, OH; [p.] Colleen Holderby, Barry Holderby, Floyd E. Hauck; [ed.] I attend Norview High School Public School and I am involved in NJROTC. (Naval Junior Reserve Officers Training Corps.); [occ.] A full time daughter; [memb.] NJROTC, Green peace, Softball, National Junior Honor Society; [hon.] Young Authors Society (My poem won); [oth. writ.] I have many, but I don't know how to get them published.; [pers.] Destiny is not a matter of chance. It is a matter of choice, it is not a thing to be waited for, it is a thing to be achieved. I would also to to say thanks to whomever is reading this for giving me second glance.

I've always wanted to be a well known writer. I will never be as happy again. (Even if I don't win, I'm already a winner). I'm so excited right now, I can't think of anything, I've really never won anything this important before.; [a.] Worfolk, VI

RINE, TINA M.
[pen.] Tina; [b.] June 1, 1966, Fayette Co., PA; [p.] Dudley D. Rine and Teresa Flores; [m.] Divorced; [ch.] Kara Lynn Martie; [ed.] Graduated from John Marshall High School Diploma; [occ.] Cashier, Giant Eagle, Model for Van Enterprise; [memb.] Christian Children's Fund, American Cancer Society; [oth. writ.] "The Greatest Creator Of All," "I Love You Jesus," "Goodbye Grandma"; [pers.] God gives you a gift, when received, use it to your full extent and do not let someone say you can not do something when you haven't even tried. My work is based upon my feelings. If I can touch someone's heart, I know I accomplished something.; [a.] New Martinsville, WV

RINKENHERGER, IDA
[b.] January 2, 1939, Stewart, MS; [p.] Hobson Vaughn, Lydia Vaughn; [ch.] Douglas York, Angela York; [ed.] Trevecca Nazarene Coll. Nashville, TN Cleveland High School Cleveland, MS; [occ.] Independent Contractor, Office Admin.; [memb.] Denver First Church of the Nazarene, International Society of Poets; [oth. writ.] Calls to worship for church services, church school material for single adults, dialogues, monologues, poetry; [pers.] Joy and peace, gifts from a loving and resourceful God; [a.] Littleton, CO

RIOS, CHRISTINE
[b.] August 28, 1967, San Antonio, TX; [p.] Antonio and Cecilia L. Rios; [ed.] B.A. - University of TX at San Antonio

RITCHISON, DARRELL
[pen.] Joe Ritchison Jr.; [b.] June 6, 1952, Mitchell, IN; [p.] Roy and Norma Ritchison; [m.] Kathy J. Ritchison, June 25, 1993; [ch.] Jodi and James; [ed.] Mitchell High School, 4 yrs. Tool and Die Apprenticeship at General Motors; [occ.] Tool and Die Maker; [pers.] I have written several poems over the years, to express my pains and my joys, only to keep them hidden in my desk. But, thanks to my beautiful wife, Kathy, I look forward to sharing them with the world.; [a.] Mitchell, IN

RITTER, DONALD SEAN
[b.] January 25, 1967, Pittsburg, PA; [p.] Donald Lee and Betty Jean; [m.] Hollie Mae, December 4, 1993; [ed.] General; [occ.] Roofing Foreman Burns and Scald Roofing, Pgh., PA.; [pers.] I would like to dedicate this poem to my mother who recently passed away. Thanks for investing the time mom, and planting a seed of goodness in my heart.; [a.] Pittsburgh, PA

RITTER, JESSICA
[pen.] Summer, Juliet; [b.] January 31, 1981; [p.] Paulette Ritter and Lloyd Ritter; [ed.] Going to be a sophomore in high school, Bordentown Regional High School; [memb.] Drama Club, Environmental Club; [hon.] One honor in School, Student of the Month Award for January 1994; [oth. writ.] Had one of my poems put in school paper. Have a notebook full of my writing.; [pers.] I try to put my real feelings down on paper. Writing helps me understand myself better.; [a.] Bordentown, NJ

ROBBINS, MARY E.
[b.] February 5, 1960, Sidney, NE; [p.] Anna and William "Bill" Goodwill; [m.] David W. Robbins, October 26, 1991; [ch.] Ben, Rocky, Donna; [ed.] B.S. Accounting Oral Roberts University; [occ.] Robbins Run Dairy Goats and Pomeranians; [memb.] American Dairy Goat Assoc. Wyoming Dairy Goat Association; [oth. writ.] "Fly Dragons Fly," "Winter's Mist," "Midnight's Blue Moon"; [pers.] Life is a river...dive in and live...; [a.] Torrington, WY

ROBBINS, TRAVIS R.
[b.] July 13, 1974, La Jolla, CA; [p.] Diana Baxter, W. R. Robbins; [ed.] Currently a student at A.S.U. (Arizona State University); [memb.] Sierra Club; [hon.] Dean's List, Scholarship for semester at Columbia University Biosphere 2.; [pers.] The feelings that engulf me are my everything. And preoccupation is the death of all feeling.; [a.] Chandler, AZ

ROBERT JR., LEON P.
[b.] May 21, 1967, California; [p.] Robert P. Leon Sr., and Christ Tapia; [hon.] Served in the U.S. Army 1987-1990. Participated in operation "Just Cause" December 20 1989; [oth. writ.] I have many poems not yet published.; [pers.] "My Persian Princess" was inspired by my feelings for the most wonderful, and beautiful Persian girl, named Vida. I love you Vida.; [a.] Azusa, CA

ROBERTS, MARJORIE
[b.] Cincinnati, OH; [p.] Adelaide and George Klawitter; [m.] Divorced; [ch.] Michael and Daniel; [ed.] B.S. and M.A., New York University New York, Ph.D., The Catholic University of America, Washington, D.C.; [occ.] Psychotherapist; [pers.] A quiet heart washes words in the river flow purple dipped in snow.; [a.] Santa Monica, CA

ROBERTS, SANDY L.
[b.] July 7, 1959, Richfield, UT; [p.] James and Nola Holt; [m.] Jim Roberts, March 18, 1985; [ch.] David, Trenton, 2 grandchildren; [ed.] Richfield High School, Utah Police Academy; [occ.] Retired Sevier Co., Deputy Sheriff, Emergency Medical Technician; [memb.] Sevier County Emergency Medical Team, Monroe First Ward L.D.S. Church; [hon.] Sterling Scholar in English and Literature, Governor's Carnation Bowl for Volunteerism; [oth. writ.] Several articles published in local paper during high school.; [pers.] I write to relieve stress and express my inner feelings. I am an avid reader and believe that literacy is the key to mankind's future.; [a.] Monroe, UT

ROBERTSON, RORY
[b.] March 16, 1962, Anniston, AL; [p.] Phillip and Judi Robertson; [m.] Divorced; [ch.] Blair Marie; [ed.] Saks High School, Ayers State Tech. College; [pers.] Though we all go in search of many schemes and find either joy or pain. Nothing else matters apart from an open heart to God.; [a.] Alexandria, AL

ROBINSON, JAMES N.
[pen.] Simi; [b.] June 7, 1925, New Haven, CT; [p.] Deceased; [m.] Dottie T. Robinson, October 1, 1991; [ch.] Muimoana, Tanya, Marshall; [ed.] AA Public Administration; [occ.] Retired; [memb.] Toastmasters International, Port of Long Beach Ambassador, Youth Motivation Task Force, Master Mason, Church of Religious Science; [oth. writ.] Numerous poems, several short stories 1-3 act play; [pers.] We're much of what we say and think today in poetic form, how much of life's beauty would we be privy to.; [a.] Buena Park, CA

ROBINSON, KRYSTLE
[b.] July 9, 1984, Cardale, PA; [p.] Alan and Sharon Robinson; [ed.] Currently entering 7th grade at Lakeland Jr-Sr High School; [occ.] Student; [memb.] Adult Jr Bowling League Valley Lanes; [hon.] Received 1st place at Spelling Bee; [pers.] This poem is dedicated to my grandpa who passed away in 1993, whom I still love and miss dearly. Also to my Uncle John who is left a quadriplegic due to an accident.; [a.] Jermyn, PA

ROBINSON, LESLEY
[b.] April 1, 1966, London, England; [p.] Robert A. and Brit Robinson; [ed.] College of Engineering, Aalesund Norway. Currently Studying Architecture at the University of Technology in Trondheim Norway; [pers.] "Bye Daddy" is my first poem to be published. It was my farewell speech to my father, Robert A. Robinson, at is funeral.; [a.] Bodega Bay, CA

ROBINSON, PEARL
[b.] Trinidad, WI; [ed.] The City University of New York, B.A. Major Liberal Arts, Progressive Educational Institute; [occ.] Writer; [memb.] Honorary Charter Membership Award and Merit Award for Poetry "Realism" in 1995; [hon.] Merit Award Medallion in Fine Bronze - 1996; [oth. writ.] Published poetry "Realism" - 1995, "The Rose of Love" - 1994, "The Birth of Intelligence," "My Life in the Tropics" - 1990; [pers.] The inspirational birth of my poem arrived by observing the force of energy that prevail the winds to destroy the fantasy man had built from the sweat of his dripping brow. Leaving him to fetch for himself through the burning pain of agony. He comes with nothing and he leaves with nothing.; [a.] New York, NY

ROBINSON, ROSA LEE
[b.] September 4, 1930, Muhlenberg Co., KY; [m.] Bobby C. Robinson Sr. (Deceased), June 17, 1949-1990; [ch.] Three children; [ed.] High School and some College, plus Adult Education; [occ.] Formerly radio, 21 years now retired; [oth. writ.] Also radio commercials, short fiction and true stories many written and told to children in our county, school and churches and my poetry sometimes written about special person.; [pers.] My writing was and is shared around me and I feel it is approved by God because he has made me feel, that I out on paper "Etching from him." I am called Ms. Rosa Lee When I tell my stories.; [a.] Greenville, KY

ROCKEY, BILLIE J.
[pen.] B. J. Rockey; [b.] September 17, 1949, Ochelata, OK; [p.] Jaunita and Bill Harrison; [m.] Nicholas Rockey, September 16, 1995; [ch.] Todd, Steven, Brian, Robert; [ed.] Syes - Grammar - 4 yrs. H.S., 1 yr. Medical College; [occ.] Housewife (Domestic "Engineer"); [hon.] College - Perfect Attendance 4.0 G.A. - Student Body president - Choreographer and Popular Musical Talents.; [oth. writ.] "Children" - On The Ocean - "The Rose" - Sentimental Felting's - "Outraged" progress, The Musical "Elusive Butterfly of Love" - Etc. and many more! Too numerous to list.; [pers.] The above are just the few I have written - much which comes from the past or present, things of tomorrows.; [a.] Wichita, KS

RODINO, LISA M.
[pen.] Lisa Mann; [b.] October 31, 1951, Upland, CA; [p.] Clayton Mann, Violet Cleveland; [m.] Joseph Rodino, August 3, 1986; [ch.] Scott Baker, Rebecca Brown, Peter Brown; [ed.] San Bernardino Valley College, College of Desert; [memb.] N.O.W. - N.C.A.S.A.

RODRIGUEZ, LAURA
[b.] December 30, 1974, NY; [p.] Sandra and Manuel Rodriguez; [ed.] Arizona State University; [hon.] Dean's List and Golden Key National Honor Society; [pers.] My parents are my inspiration and have given me the greatest gift - love.; [a.] Tempe, AZ

RODRIQUEZ, DAVID
[b.] February 18, 1951, Las Animas, CO; [p.] Daniel and Vicki Rodriquez; [m.] Sharon Eaton, December 24, 1971; [ch.] David J., Jason B., Daniel; [occ.] Retired; [pers.] The inspiration of compassion and understanding creates a reservoir of fond memories.; [a.] Las Animas, CO

ROESLY, TAMARA J.
[pen.] The Rose; [b.] October 30, 1948, Indianapolis, IN; [p.] Pauline and Hazel Lowery; [m.] Edward D. Roesly, March, 1991; [ch.] Charles M. Bishir, Cherie Taryn Bishir, Ed, Kevin, Todd Roesly; [ed.] Marion High, Ind. Weslyan College, Indiana Business College; [occ.] Housewife, degree in Accounting and Office Management; [memb.] Genealogy Club; [pers.] All of my writing comes from my heart - some from beautiful, simple things - and others such as flowers from the nightmares of others. Nature and emotions, if we stop to listen, affect our lives more than we know. I do my best to listen and learn.; [a.] Marion, IN

ROGERS, BETTE
[pen.] Antoinette Jerne; [b.] May 6, 1940, Dunn, NC; [p.] Frank and Katie P.; [m.] Grant Will, September 24, 1959; [ch.] Timothy Dale, Bonnie Gayle; [ed.] North Dekalb College Assoc. of Administration. Work with older citizens of nursing homes and hospitals.; [occ.] Retired Exec. Sec'y and Freelance Writer; [memb.] PTA Past President (Alaska) Boy Scouts of America/Church and Youth Leader of Young Girls.; [hon.] Drama Award (HS); [oth. writ.] Local newspapers and church newsletters/stories and speeches.; [pers.] Betterment: The quest for the betterment of anything can only be achieved by those who are truly committed to that end!; [a.] Fairbanks, AL

ROGINA, SUSAN
[pen.] Jake (at times); [b.] January 21, 1956, Calumet, MI; [p.] Late - Raymond Limback and Marie Salmi; [m.] Joseph Rogina, January 17, 1975; [ch.] Joel Joseph (1 son); [ed.] Calumet high and Iron Mountain Community Schools Graduate; [occ.] Non-Profit Advocate for Upgrading Public Awareness Services (U.P.A.S.) Disabled home maker, physically, mentally, emotionally disabled home maker, physically, mentally, emotionally disabled and other causes; [memb.] Alliance for the Mentally Ill (AMI of Michigan), *Who's Who Worldwide* (fore runner of all "Who's Who" publications) a prominent networking of select members; [hon.] Acceptance in *Who's Who Worldwide*, Editor's Choice Award for the other poetry, Recognition for book in Washington, D.C. where I would have read my poetry, been entertained by top stars, met political figures, and been presented with special awards (Aug. 4-6, 1995), selected for inclusion in *Best Poems of 1996* (Nat'l Lib. of Poetry); [oth. writ.] Several articles in newspapers in advocacy capacity, writings to business establishments and corporations in effort to obtain rights and access for disabled, book of poetry dealing with multiple personality disorder published, poetry in *A Break in the Clouds*, and *Best Poems of 1996*; [pers.] Everyone deserves to be treated and "labels", and have the right to access the same enjoyments and privileges as everyone else. My writings are based on personal experience, or those of people and events I encounter; [a.] Iron Mountain, MI

ROHRER, JEFF
[pen.] Jed Earl; [b.] March 26, 1960, Canton, OH; [p.] Dale and Barbara Rohrer; [m.] Amy A. Rohrer, July 21, 1979; [ch.] Nikki Rohrer, Scott (Pal) Rohrer; [ed.] BA - Psychology, Kent State University; [occ.] Therapeutic Program Worker; [oth. writ.] Self-produced musical works - "sometunes", and "Solow Blue from the Kitchen" also many other poems and essays.; [pers.] I dedicate this poem (flies) to my mother, Barbara Rohrer-Reinwald.; [a.] Massillon, OH

ROHRS, SARAH
[pen.] Anna Groff; [b.] January 13, 1982, Megersdale, PA; [p.] Connie Updyke, Steven Rohrs; [ed.] Berlin Brothervalley High School; [hon.] Made Honor Roll twice during 8th grade; [oth. writ.] Poems published in church newsletter; [pers.] I want to reflect that the world has many different sides to it. Not all good, but not all bad either. I am mostly influenced to write poetry by Susan Terris in her book. *Wings and Roots*.; [a.] Thomas Mills, PA

ROMERO, ANTHONY
[b.] June 28, 1945, Denver, CO; [p.] Margaret and Solomon Romero; [m.] Linda Romero, March 6, 1982; [ch.] Anthony, Vincent, Jessica and Alicia; [occ.] Bus Operator; [pers.] The poem "Born Free" came to me in a dream.; [a.] Denver, CO

ROOD, BRIAN
[pen.] Brian Cross; [b.] July 6, 1960, Conneaut, OH; [m.] Joanna; [ch.] Brianna; [pers.] Thanks Carolyn, if not for you this would not have happened. I dedicate this first ever published work to my wife Joanna and my daughter Brianna. I love you both!; [a.] Canton, OH

ROQVEMORE, STEVEN T.
[pen.] Steven Thomas Roqvemore; [b.] August 20, 1969, Orlando, FL; [p.] David W. Roqvemore Jr.; [m.] Susan Ann Engle Roqvemore; [ch.] David Roqvemore III, James M. Roqvemore, Steven Roqvemore; [ed.] High School Grad. 4 yr. College, Merchant Marines ABS (Able Bodied Seaman); [occ.] Merchant Marines Able Bodied Seaman; [oth. writ.] Other poetry non-published.; [pers.] This is first one published of many written.; [a.] FL

ROSARIO, DIANA
[b.] September 15, 1984, New York; [p.] Neri and Gonzalo Rosario; [ed.] 6th grade; [occ.] Student; [oth. writ.] "Spring," "Bunnys"; [pers.] I believe that poetry expresses how the author feels. If the author is writing about happiness the author is happy. If the author is writing about sadness the author is sad, that's how I feel about poetry.; [a.] Sunnyside, NY

ROSCOE, KRISTA LEIGH
[b.] October 21, 1986, Florence, SC; [p.] Chris and Dana Roscoe; [ed.] Attends Chesterfield Middle School 5th grade Student; [hon.] President's Award for Excellence, Accelerated Reader Award, Honor Roll; [pers.] I enjoy reading, writing, and math.; [a.] Chesterfield, SC

ROSELAND, BOBBI
[b.] March 29, 1948, Detroit; [p.] Marvin, Marion Ruby; [ch.] Sean Roseland, Sherri Bowman; [ed.] 2nd Masters - School Administration - Elem. Leadership Madonna Univ., Bachelors - Elem. Ed., Wayne State Univ.; [occ.] Educator - Buchanan Elem School (Livonia, Mich.) - working on Poetry Anthology; [memb.] N.E.A., M.E.A. - L.E.A. proof organization - "Journey Through my Soul", Mich. School Improvement team - Buchanan Elem., Association Cunni. Supervision Development, Great Books Foundation - reader, Nat. Organization of Business and Professional Women. Team chairperson Teacher Assistance Teams Buchanan School - Liv. Public Schools; [hon.] *Who's Who Among Students in American Universities and Colleges*, Awarded by Madonna University Graduate School 1994-1995, Certificate of Excellence in Teaching, presented May 1990; [oth. writ.] Helped with research and writing of *Not Guilty* - authored by David Gordon.; [pers.] Life exists to be lived to its fullest - enjoying each precious moment - learning from mistakes - moving on into the future and expressing the thought of the heart through the beauty of the pen.

ROSS, MELIESA
[pen.] Meliesa Ross, Liesa, Lee Creator; [b.] April 14, 1973, Chicago; [p.] Starya Ross, Jerry (Karen) Pore; [ed.] Northwood University, Midland, MI, Proviso West H.S., Hillside, IL; [occ.] Administrative Assistant and Community Chest of Oak Park and River Forest (Local United Way); [hon.] Childhood - Young Authors Award (1984/85, 1986/87), Adulthood- Dean's List 1991-95, Private Donor Scholarships 1992-95; [pers.] If my emotions were a person, he/she would be my best friend, my one inspiration...; [a.] Plainfield, IL

ROSSMAN, BRIAN D.
[b.] October 15, 1967, Los Gatos, CA; [ed.] UCSC 1986-1990 University Santa Clara Law School 1900-93; [occ.] Deputy District Attorney; [memb.] State Bar of California; [hon.] President Phi and Phi 1993 1986 UCSC Book Award Commencement Speaker UCSC 1990 County of Santa Cruz Public Service Proclamation 1993; [oth. writ.] California District Attorneys Assn. case digest case editor.

ROTH, PEGGY E.
[pen.] Brown Eyes; [b.] June 13, 1941, Abingdon, VA; [p.] Mr. and Mrs. Roy B. Hall; [m.] Robert E. Roth, July 19; [ch.] Six sons; [ed.] 6th Grade, I went back and got a license for C.N.A.; [occ.] C.N.A.; [memb.] Baptist Church, Women of the Moose, AARP; [hon.] I've never had any and if I did the glory would go to God; [oth. writ.] I've been writing since 1968. I love to write, the Lord gives me all I need to say. I never won anything. This is God's work; [pers.] I love the Lord, I'm only sorry for all the years I wasted and did not live for God. One day I will write my life story.

ROUSE, CANDACE
[b.] August 25, 1982, Madison, WI; [p.] Carrol Caldwell; [occ.] Student; [memb.] Montello F.F.A; [hon.] "Why I'm glad I'm an American" essay contest (1st place), "Best in Class" English Award (5th grade); [oth. writ.] Non-published poems and short stories; [pers.] Poetry is my way of expressing my emotions and I love poetry with all my heart.; [a.] Montello, WI

ROWLETT, EARLINE
[pen.] Earlyn Rowe; [b.] February 5, 1941, Brooklyn, NY; [p.] Samuel and Mary Rowlett; [ch.] Andrew, Darryl, Baron and Lamar; [ed.] High School Graduate, Cosmetologist Graduate; [occ.] Bank Employee; [oth. writ.] Have written poems for friends, relatives, make own cards (all occasions); [pers.] I'm also a grandmother of five.; [a.] Albany, NY

ROYER, WARREN L.
[b.] June 27, 1925, Rushville, IL; [p.] Laurence and Ada Royer; [m.] Nancy Bailey, June 3, 1991; [ed.] BA in English, Univ. of Illinois, MA in English, U. of Illinois; [occ.] Retired; [memb.] Society for the Preservation and Encouragement of Barbershop Quartet Singing in America; [hon.] Phi Beta Sigma, Barbershopper of the Year, in Central Ill., Board chair of Univ. Place Christian Church, Champaign, Ill. and 1st Christian Church, Gainesville, FL; [oth. writ.] "Peepstones, Beartracks and Ghosts of Dutchmans Creek", stories of Western Ill., "Memories of the Heart", rural schools in Illinois in press at Mayhaven publishing Mahomet Ill., numerous newspaper articles, article in *Phi Delta Kappan*; [a.] Kalamazoo, MI

RUCKDASHEL, CANDY
[b.] February 13, 1955, Sioux Falls, SD; [p.] Mervin and Dorothy Hokenstad; [m.] Rick Ruckdashel; [ch.] Jeff, Ryan; [ed.] B.A. Augustana College, M.E.D., University of Minnesota; [occ.] Fifth grade teacher, Highland Elementary, Apple Valley, MN; [oth. writ.] Teacher resource books published by Incentive Pub., articles on children's books in local newspaper; [pers.] Poetry reveals all the powerful emotions a person feels living on this earth; [a.] Apple Valley, MN

RUDEL, WESTON W.
[pen.] W. W. Swift; [b.] September 8, 1923, Fessenden, ND; [p.] Herbert and Emma Rudel; [m.] Divorced, November 4, 1945; [ch.] Brenda Kay Lloyd; [ed.] Business College (Dakota) Correspondence Police Investigation Course; [occ.] Retired (full time usher) Convention Event Security, movie extra (part time); [memb.] Elks (life time member), Eagles (life time member), Baptist Church, Lear Lasting File; [hon.] Several poems and articles published in local newspapers and Historical Society Paper, Harvey Herald Press - Harvey ND, Historical Society - Fessenden ND, Numerous Contests Minot State Fair Annually and other; [oth. writ.] Personally wrote and published 22 books, 3 of poems, others are non-fiction essays, articles, and blackjack "21" Strategy, also brochure enclosed, "Horses", "Tasting the Rainbow," "Smiling Eyes," "Little Red Fox," "Cowboy Serenade," "The Murmuring Trees."; [pers.] To be in the realm of disquieted creativity is the ultimate expression on desired experience to elaborate upon, more than illusion since words are things. Life is changed and change-keeping the intitles humbles so as to inherit the earth from clime to clime.; [a.] Las Vegas, NV

RUGG, JULIA ANN
[pen.] Julia Ann Rugg; [b.] February 11, 1982, Memphis, TN; [p.] Sharon Rugg, Ed Rugg; [ed.] Freshman at Lassiter High School in Marietta, GA; [occ.] Full time Student; [memb.] Lassiter High School Marching Band, Roswell Presbyterian Church; [hon.] Mabry Middle School, Principal's Honor Roll, 1993-1996, Mabry Oration Contest, 1st Place, 1996; [oth. writ.] Co-authored *Memories Live Forever*: A memory book for grieving children, numerous poems, short stories and plays.; [pers.] "I write when I'm inspired. I believe it is a healthy way to deal with emotions and to understand one's feelings."; [a.] Marietta, GA

RUPERT, LORRAINE D.
[b.] December 8, 1913, Lincoln, NE; [p.] Everett and Clara Rupert; [occ.] Retired; [oth. writ.] Verse published in local newspaper.; [pers.] By writing poems of Fantasy for children, I want to bring happiness into their lives.; [a.] Sun City, AZ

RUPERT, THOMAS C.
[b.] February 17, 1933, Akron, OH; [p.] Agnes V. Rupert-Strole, Deceased, Step Father, Ray A. Strole; [ch.] Two children Tom Jr. and Terrie; [ed.] High School Graduate - Long Beach CA. Jordan High. United States Air Force Institute College Equivalency. Editor: *Cats Purr* - Long Beach. Jordan High School CA. Newspaper. High School Sports writer - *Long Beach Independent/Press Telegram.*; [occ.] Retired; [a.] Palm Springs, CA

RUSINKO, MICHAEL
[b.] October 6, 1981; [p.] Michael and Pam Rusinko; [ed.] 10th Student Moorestown High School; [hon.] Varsity letter 1995 cross-country

RUSSAK, JOLEEN
[b.] December 15, 1935, Cheyenne, OK; [p.] Joe W. Robinson, Sible (Peggy) Vermillion; [m.] Stephen G. Russak, December 22, 1977; [ch.] Deena J. Dowd, Donna L. Knipschild, Sheryll L. Chevalier-Martin, Linda D. Gomez; [occ.] Management Assistant, Army Recreation Machine Program; [oth. writ.] Extensive; [pers.] I write what I feel, and I 'feel' about a lot of things.; [a.] Lawton, OK

RUSSELL, SCOTT K.
[b.] January 22, 1968, Royal Oak, MI; [p.] Sally Brewer Russell, Parvin Masters Russell Jr.; [ed.] Bachelor of Science, Michigan State University; [pers.] "Don't worry about not being loved... worry about not loving".

RUSSOMANO, MICHAEL K.
[b.] October 6, 1964, Phillipsburg, NJ; [p.] Michael H. and Elizabeth Russomano; [m.] Denise A. Russomano, June 18, 1994; [ed.] Phillipsburg High and Diploma in Audio/Video Engineering - Jon Miller Sch. for Recording Arts and Sciences; [occ.] Chemical Operator/part time musician, and writer; [oth. writ.] None published, many, many songs waiting to be recorded hopefully!.; [pers.] I write straight from the heart, my forte is songwriting, as I am a musician now for 17 yrs, though I started writing poetry first. Waiting to be signed for a record deal or have my songs recorded by other artists.; [a.] Easton, PA

SABOL, JOSEPH
[ed.] BS - Math, MBA, ABD - Geography; [occ.] Hypnotherapist, Author; [memb.] National Guild of Hypnotists; [oth. writ.] *How To Read A Person Like A Book: A Manual For Reading People*, publisher of *Stretch*, a newsletter for Stretching The Mind.; [pers.] All behavior is a standard for others. Thus we most be tolerant, love each other and be of service.; [a.] West Coxsackie, NY

SADAKANE, LESLI
[b.] December 6, 1964, Fountain Valley, CA; [p.] Jeanne Babcock; [m.] Gary Nomi (Fiancee); [ed.] Fountain Valley H.S., Orange Coast College, Art Center College of Design; [occ.] Freelance Graphic Designer; [pers.] This was written in appreciation for Grace Nomi, my soon-to-be mother-in-law. Gary often spoke of her and this is how I interpreted his feelings. I am proud to say that it is all true.; [a.] Cypress, CA

SALADEN, EDITH H.
[b.] December 26, 1928, Culombia; [p.] Gilbert and Melida Hernandez; [m.] Carlos Manuel, April 12, 1949; [ch.] Edgard and Ivan; [ed.] Teacher (Sciences and Literature) Degree - Colombia Medical Technology Degree, Medical Tech School NY - BMCC - Dean List; [occ.] Medical Technologist (retired); [memb.] Institute of Cervantes N.Y., Echa - NY; [hon.] Semi-finalist Golden Poet 1991 16th Anniversary "World of Poetry", second prize contest of Channel 41 NY "100 years to of Statue of Liberty; [oth. writ.] *Poems Book* in Spanish 1986 short stories - 1988 *Levels* - novel in progress; [pers.] Dedicated to my children Edgard and Ivan an my grandson Glen Paul with all my love.; [a.] Miami Beach, FL

SALAMO, LISA RENEE
[b.] August 8, 1982, Lancaster, PA; [p.] John and Carol Salamo; [ed.] Reynolds Jr. High School 7th grade student; [memb.] Grace United Church of Christ; [hon.] Reynolds Jr. High Newspaper, Achievement Awards in Geography, Life science. Chorus Participations Awards - Outstanding performers in Geography Award - 1994 Youth of the year Award - YMCA; [oth. writ.] 7th grade Jitters - Reynolds Jr. High School Newspaper (1996); [pers.] I have a little sister who is 10 yrs. old. Her name is Jessica. She has cerebral palsy. My goal in life is to become a physical therapist, so that someday I can help other children. I also love to write stories and poems and read mystery books. I would like to dedicate my poem ("My Cat") to my little sister, Jessica, because we both love Andy a lot.; [a.] Lancaster, PA

SALYERS, MARILYN
[pen.] Carken; [b.] September 6, 1948, Troy, OH; [p.] Ivan Plantz, Dorothy Plantz; [ch.] 2: Mrs. Vivian Baize and Franklin Salyers; [ed.] Milton-Union High School W. Milton, Ohio, Dayton School of Prac. Nursing Dayton, Ohio, Owensboro Junior College, Owensboro, KY; [memb.] National Multiple Sclerosis Society, American Heart Assn. and Arthritis Foundation; [oth. writ.] Several poems, a poem called "Angels" in Quill Books - 1996 "Treasure the Moment" coming this winter also; [pers.] I believe in the great Creator. And that He put us all here to love one another. I thank Him and Ms. Carolyn Means, Bowling Green, KY, Ken, Marty, Marsh, Henderson, KY, Gertie and Shelby Pittman, Henderson KY, James, Myrna Brown, Springfield Ohio and for their love, support and also the publishers and my children.; [a.] Henderson, KY

SAMSON, JOLENE
[b.] December 20, 1982, Jersey City, NJ; [p.] Kerry Carroll; [ed.] St. Aedan Grammar School - Nicholas Copernicus Grammar 25; [memb.] Helping Teaching Choir, Cheerleading, Dancing; [hon.] Essay Award - 2nd Honors - Helpings Award, Dare Award; [oth. writ.] Dare essay; [pers.] I dedicate the poem to my mother and all the real women in America.

SANCHEZ, ALMA P.
[b.] April 18, 1972, Riverside; [p.] Lorenzo and Estela Sanchez; [m.] Henry Lee Fout; [ed.] Rubidoux High School 1990 Riverside Community College A.A. 1994 California State University, San Bernardino, B.A. 1996; [occ.] JTPA, Program Rep.; [hon.] Rubidoux High Sch. Choir Award and Letter of Excellence; [oth. writ.] "The Tiger on the Prowl" in *Politics* (underground school paper); [pers.] Life is an unending classroom. We enter seeing a great light, and again see it upon graduation, our judgement, our death.; [a.] Colton, CA

SANCHEZ, FRANKIE
[b.] September 4, 1980, Lynn, MA; [p.] Frank Sanchez, Pat Sanchez; [ed.] St. Mary's Jr., Sr. High School, going into Junior year (96/97); [oth. writ.] Several poems that have not yet been published and I along with my friend

write a newsletter for our neighborhood.; [pers.] It's about time that we wake up to see that violence and hate are not the answers to our problems and it's time that we discover ourselves and open our minds to new ideas.; [a.] Lynn, MA

SANCHEZ, NANCY
[pen.] Lydia Marcele R.; [b.] October 31, 1980, Los Angeles, CA; [p.] Zoila Ramirez, Alfredo Sanchez; [ed.] Hollywood High School; [occ.] Student; [pers.] All my poems are based upon personal life experiences.; [a.] Hollywood, CA

SANDOVAL, JOSE AUGUSTIN SAGASTUME
[pen.] Jesus Tinoga; [b.] May 5, 1958, Agua Blanca Jut. Guatemala; [p.] Florencio A. Sagastume, Corina Sandoval; [m.] Divorced; [ed.] Instituto de Bachillerato Por Madurez; [occ.] Cleaning Service; [memb.] "Faro De Luz" Baptist Church; [hon.] Third prize in the branch of poetry of the "Juegos Florales De San Juan, Sacatepequez, Guatemala", first prize in speech; [oth. writ.] I wrote a book of poetry called *Senderos Y Maravillas* I also wrote poems for the Guatemalan newspapers *Prensa Libre* and *Diario El Grafico*; [pers.] Poetry is the beautiful way to express our feelings and ideas. All those hidden instincts can be taken out from our hearts and be put on a piece of paper in the form of poetry.; [a.] Queens, NY

SANDS, JOE
[b.] January 1, 1982, Medford, OR; [p.] Kevin Sands, Emily Sands; [occ.] Student; [memb.] Umpqua Valley Retriever Club, Umpqua Valley Babe Ruth; [hon.] The Presidential Sports Award, President's Award for Educational Excellence, Honor Roll, Third Place State Hershey's Track Meet 200 M, All-Star Baseball; [oth. writ.] Columns for school newspaper, various term papers for English.; [pers.] I try to write the truth about people, and how they feel, and live. My favorite writer is Ernest Hemingway. He is America's greatest writer.; [a.] Days Creek, OR

SANTIAGO, TROY C.
[b.] February 5, 1966, Vallejo, CA; [p.] Kaaren and Larry Santiago; [ed.] H.S. graduate - Mexico (Sandia High), (Ebees Elem. Oahu, Hawaii), Assoc. Dgr - Bus. Admin.,/ Marketing T.V.I. of New Mexico, Fashion Mds. School - Modeling; [occ.] Property Mgmt.; [oth. writ.] Various pieces - all unnamed (Several hundred); [pers.] Every day is a new day to enjoy!! I write to release on paper the joys and sorrows in which we all share through our lives.; [a.] Vallejo, CA

SANTOS, OMAR R.
[pen.] Omar R. Santos; [b.] November 18, 1977, St. Croix, U.S. VI; [p.] Clara Santos, Gilbert Santos; [ed.] Begun High School, Pompano Academy of Aeronautics; [occ.] College Student; [memb.] Aviation Technology Committee; [hon.] Sports Awards, Poetry Awards.; [oth. writ.] Several of my poems won awards and prizes.; [pers.] To all of my readers. All of my poetry is for the strong in heart and mind. The "Pray" is for the troubled world of ours. Prayer is very important in a human being's life. Without prayer there is no faith. Without faith there is no hope; [a.] Fort Lauderdale, FL

SARINANA JR., JOE H.
[pen.] Joe J. Sarinana Jr.; [b.] March 14, 1974, El Paso, TX; [p.] Jose H. Sarinana, Alicia Sarinana; [m.] Keri Avitia (Girlfriend); [ed.] Ysleta High School and University of Texas at El Paso; [occ.] Customer Service at Enterprise Rent-a-Car; [oth. writ.] Several other poems, which are kept in my own personal books.; [pers.] Writing poetry helps eliminate any anger or frustration I may have buried within. I have been greatly influenced by Pearl Jam's Eddie Vedder.; [a.] El Paso, TX

SARVELLO, CLARESS ANN
[pen.] Clare S.; [b.] August 12, 1938, Ishpeming, MI; [p.] Joseph and Virginia Sarvello; [ch.] Kathleen and Daniel; [ed.] High School '56, Up center for Practical Nurse '56-'57; [occ.] Disabled/Serve the Lord in Capacity of Volunteer Work and helping others along the way.; [oth. writ.] "Birthday Party For Jesus," Article, "My Most Memorable Christmas," published in *Mt. West Magazine* '77. Over 30 songs, poems that came from prayers of my heart, and messages in the night.; [pers.] I have much gratitude for my life, and I owe it all to God. He continues to be my constant companion and refuge. I pray my writings will reflect His Goodness and Love.; [a.] Veneta, OR

SATTERFIELD, NEIL B.
[b.] June 21, 1932, New York, NY; [p.] Frances G. and Merrill B.; [m.] Marion Duckworth Satterfield, August 28, 1954; [ch.] Suzan, Scott, Stuart and Steven; [ed.] A.B. Sociology U.N.C. 1954, M.S.S.W. Social Work U. Tenn, 1965 Ed.D., Educ. Psychology U.GA. 1978; [occ.] Human Service Consultant Mediator - Domestic Relations; [memb.] Elder, Presbyterian Church, U.S.A. all others - expired; [hon.] Outstanding Brother -Chi Phi 1954, Deans List 1973-74, U.S. Forest Service Volunteer (1994-present) prize winner, Futuristic Story-1978 Outstanding Professor 1980, Pres., Players Club - Hilton Head is 1992-1995 S.C.; [oth. writ.] "The Common Denominator in Helping Professions". Prof. paper "Charlie's Place" in *Georgia Monthly*. (Magazine) "Creative Monitoring"- hand book. Two recent unpublished works.; [pers.] The Golden rule and a sense of humor truly enrich life's journey.; [a.] Norcross, GA

SAUNDERS, MARGARETTE COMBS
[b.] October 3, 1925, Atlanta, GA; [p.] Deceased; [m.] Deceased, January 10, 1943; [ch.] Two adult sons; [ed.] 1 yr. Cambridgeshire Tech. Coll. and School of the Arts, Cambridge, England, B.A., English, Eastern Washington State College (now University), post graduate study, California State University, Los Angeles, College of Notre Dame, Belmont, CA.; [occ.] Retired English Teacher; [hon.] 1986-Silver Poet's Award, 1987, '88, '89, Gold Awards, 1991: Made World of Poetry Publishers' *Who's Who in Poetry*, ranked in the top three percent of all poems submitted to the National Library of Poetry Publishers for vol. *In The Desert Sun*. Assoc. Editor, *California English Magazine*.; [oth. writ.] As an undergraduate at Eastern Washington State (Cheney, Washington), had a short story, "Mixup", published in the college paper.; [pers.] Peace within any group, or within any community must derive from each individual's ability to find peace within himself.; [a.] Pacifica, CA

SAVAGE, ARTHUR JAMES
[pen.] Ajay; [b.] September 20, 1952, Jacksonville, FL; [p.] Ms. Marian Jones; [m.] Ms. Phyllis Streater; [ch.] Chantal and Shadonna Savage; [ed.] B.S. Degree in Physical Ed., Long Island University, 1989; [memb.] Founder and President of the Dragon Youth Association, Youth President of the Emancipation Proclamation Association, President Dormitory Council, Youth Artist of the Afro-American Cultural Center, Precinct Committeeman, DECDC, Volunteer Parents Rudolph Blankenburg Elementary School; [hon.] President List (89), Mayor's Scholarship Program NYC, *Who's Who Amongst American Students* (88) National Collegiate P.E. and Health (88) Dean's List (83-87), Outstanding Artists awrd, WM. Raines Sr. HS #165 National Dean's List Publication, *Who's Who Among Stundents In American Universities and Colleges* National Collegiate Physical Education and Health; [oth. writ.] "I Love", "Lovin' Feelings For a Daughter or Son", "Inspirational You", "The Black Child's Dream", "A Strange Meaning", and "Phases of our Lives"; [pers.] That if we're to see a change in this world in which we live, it will be through our children.; [a.] Philadelphia, PA

SAWALL, LLOYDINE
[pen.] Dee, Dee Sawall; [b.] April 9, 1938, Detroit, MI; [p.] Elsie Winkfield, William Sawall; [ch.] Six daughters; [ed.] Northern High (Detroit) UCLA (CA) went to trade school for nursing; [occ.] Nurse for 10 years or more; [memb.] I was a member of the P.T.A at my children's School; [hon.] I was president of my nursing class, and spokesperson at UCLA for a debate; [oth. writ.] I have four other poems and two songs. I also have two books I'm working on, but none of them at this time are published; [pers.] Over the years I've read books and made up stories and poems for my daughters when they were small, and I've always been a romantic person at heart.; [a.] Bellflower, CA

SAWALSKI, ROBERT M.
[b.] March 20, 1972, Park Ridge, IL; [p.] Mary Ann and Casimir; [ed.] St. Viator School Northern Illinois University; [occ.] Editor; [pers.] Literary stylings vary greatly among both individuals as well as generations. It is only in the study of others that we can learn the talent within ourselves.; [a.] Bartlett, IL

SAYAD, STEPHEN S.
[b.] February 4, 1958, San Francisco, CA; [p.] Samuel and Charlotte Sayad; [ch.] 5 1/2 Year Old Golden Retriever (Sam); [occ.] Attorney; [pers.] Writing poetry has become a healing process for me, particularly with respect to the loss of family members. Interestingly (and something I'm still exploring) it (writing) is not something I can control. It comes as pure spontaneity.

SCALZI, DOTTIE
[b.] August 18, 1978, Baltimore, MD; [p.] Samuel Scalzi, Edwina Scalzi; [ed.] Glen Burnie High School. Class of 1996; [a.] Glen Burnie, MD

SCARBOROUGH, SPENCER
[b.] April 22, 1943, Asheville, NC; [p.] J. Harold and Ann L. Scarborough; [m.] Divorced; [ch.] Stephanie and Andrew; [ed.] Lee Edwards High School '61, Wingate Jr. College '64, Cal. State University at Los Angeles '75; [occ.] U.S. Postal Service and Part Time Community Services Teacher; [pers.] People are people, no matter what. Culture makes the only difference.; [a.] Garden Grove, CA

SCARDINO, ANGELA J.
[b.] January 21, 1920, Brooklyn, NY; [p.] John - Millie Lamberti; [m.] Richard J. Scardino Sr., October 5, 1941; [ch.] Joseph, Patricia, Richard Jr.; [ed.] Adult Ed. High School John Burroughs - Burbank CA 1959; [occ.] Retired; [memb.] 12 yrs. Member Sons of Italy in America; [oth. writ.] I entered a survey on Ital.-American Women. Three of my observations are in the book *Voices of the Daughters*, by Connie Maglione E. Carmen Anthony Fiore. Pub. 1989; [pers.] I write poetry for fun and to try to influence my thoughts to others.; [a.] Lake Forest, CA

SCERING, TERRI-JO
[pen.] TJ Scering; [b.] September 2, 1973, Exeter, NH; [p.] Dana and Lucille Drown; [m.] Dana Scering, October 29, 1994; [ed.] Virgin Valley High School, Dixie College 2 yrs; [occ.] Manager of Local Store/Mary Kay Dealer; [memb.] Thespians Club, Best Friends animals sanctuary; [hon.] FHA, State Competition awards for creative foods 3 years in a row; [oth. writ.] Many other poems and short stories published in local, and school papers; [pers.] My interests range from auto racing to Dog shows and I enjoy all forms of the arts. My influences were my mother's writing and hard times; [a.] Mesquite, NV

SCHELL, PEGGY
[b.] February 26, 1954, Dallas, TX; [p.] Irene and Leo Valladares; [ch.] James Ryan Schell III; [ed.] Associates Degree Applied Arts; [occ.] Admin. Assistant for Sumner and Taylor-San Jose; [oth. writ.] "Poems of the Forbidden Love" (non-published); [pers.] My first love was writing. Then, acting. If possible I'd like to do both. I love writing poetry. I love acting to entertain people and make them smile.; [a.] San Jose, CA

SCHLOSSNAGLE, CINDY
[b.] January 2, 1952, Apollo, PA; [p.] G. W. and Hazel Eckman; [m.] J. Barry Schlossnagle; [ch.] Matthew, Jayla, Jamey; [ed.] Hagerstown Business College, MD, Clarion State University, Clarion PA; [occ.] Fiscal Technician, VPI and SU, CSES Dept., Blacksburg VA; [oth. writ.] 'As A Man Thinketh, He Shall Be' by C. G. Boyles published by Dorrance, Phila. PA.; [pers.] I strive to release the emotions of love and open the spirit for receiving and giving. My writing is dedicated to you, who read and understand.; [a.] Draper, VA

SCHLUNDT, GORDON DEAN
[b.] May 10, 1934, Michigan City, IN; [p.] Linder and Christine Schlundt; [ch.] Cindi (Daughter); [ed.] 1 1/2 yrs. Indiana Univ.; [occ.] Retired - Sales Clerk; [memb.] ISP, Amer. Bowling Congress; [oth. writ.] A poem published in an anthology - *Beneath the Harvest Moon* (NLP); [pers.] No matter what our circumstances or station in life, each one of us can contribute something for the benefit of mankind. Do something nice for someone each day you live.; [a.] Mattoon, IL

SCHOFIELD, RUTH ARENTINA
[b.] July 23, 1924, Bergen, Norway; [p.] Olaf and Abelona Johnson; [m.] Paul A. Schofield, January 8, 1944; [ch.] Paul, Kristine, Amy and Kari (Kari was adopted from Korea age 8, 1976); [ed.] Graduate from Gallatin County High School Bozeman, MT, 1944; [occ.] Housewife; [memb.] Creative Writers of Bozeman, MT National Brain Injury Association (NBIA); [oth. writ.] Two of my short stories have been published in the local newspaper.; [pers.] I live next to a rushing mountain stream and find joy in writing about the many beauties of nature and its vicissitudes. Then, also, I love to write poems and stories for the very, very young.; [a.] Bozeman, MT

SCHOFILL, CHRISTOPHER MARANO
[b.] April 16, 1977, Maui, HI; [p.] John Schofill, Marilyn Marano; [ed.] Nature is my Classroom, and God is my Teacher. Currently Enrolled at Maui Community College.; [occ.] Silk Screener, at Dolphin Tees; [memb.] I belong to Humanity.; [hon.] Birth and Life; [pers.] Within the known lies the unknown, and therein lies the truth. Beauty is in everything, and it is my job as a poet to embody it.; [a.] Makawao, HI

SCHULTZ, TAMMY
[b.] March 12, 1961, Janesville, WI; [p.] Gerald Anderson, Nancy Marzahl; [m.] Richard Schultz, June 10, 1995; [ch.] Ryan, Chad, April; [ed.] Milton High School, various courses; [occ.] Bookkeeper, Holden Pallet, Missouri; [oth. writ.] Several poems published in local newspaper and also published in several other anthologies.; [pers.] "Don't get caught up in life, let life live in you."

SCIALLI, VINCENT
[b.] July 29, 1974, Mineola, NY; [p.] Neil Scialli and Josephine Scialli; [ed.] Manhattan College, Riverdale, NY; [occ.] Mechanical Engineer; [pers.] In life everyone has one true love that they regret losing. It was this feeling that led me to write this poem.; [a.] Westbury, NY

SCINE, ANTHONY M.
[pen.] Tony-Antonio; [b.] August 14, 1973, New Jersey; [p.] Victor Scine, Sharon Scine; [m.] Michelle Scine, July 10, 1995; [ch.] Jonathan Marcus Scine; [ed.] High School - Votech School; [occ.] United States Air Force; [memb.] U.S.S.A. - United States Sergeants Association; [hon.] Outstanding Achievement Award - Outstanding Unit Award for Bosnia, Good Conduct Award; [pers.] I write late at night when my mind is stressless. Everything I write and do in my life is straight from my heart!; [a.] Tucson, AZ

SCOTT, KATHRYN MICHELLE
[pen.] Katie Scott; [b.] May 1, 1982, Midland, TX; [p.] Michael A. Scott, Diana L. Scott; [ed.] Crestview and Live Oak Elementary Schools, Kitty Hawk Jr. High, current: Judson High, P.R.E.P. (Prefreshman Engineering Prog.); [occ.] Babysitting, School; [memb.] Church (Windcrest United Methodist), Children of the American Revolution (C.A.P.), Softball; [hon.] National Junior Honors Society, Softball medals, Trophies etc., P.R.E.P. Certificate; [oth. writ.] San Antonio DeBexar, C.A.R. Newsletter, Several other poems and essays unpublished; [pers.] This poem was written for my cousin David who was killed last year in a fire. Don't ever be afraid to tell someone you love them.; [a.] San Antonio, TX

SCOTT, LANA MICHELLE
[b.] January 26, 1979, Chattanooga, TN; [p.] Samuel and Lana Chaney-Scott; [ed.] Senior at Notre Dame High School in Chattanooga, Tennessee; [occ.] Student; [memb.] National Honor Society, Amnesty, International, Teen Times Reporter for the *Chattanooga Times*, and Veteran Alumni Representative for the National Youth Leaders Council; [hon.] *Who's Who in American High School Students*, American Citizenship Award, Congressional Youth Leadership Award, and Notre Dame High School's Most Valuable Attitude Award; [oth. writ.] Several articles published in the local newspaper - the *Chattanooga Times*, and several editorials for my school's newspaper. (I was the editor); [pers.] If life is what you make it, then I plan to make the most of it.; [a.] Chattanooga, TN

SCOTT, PATRICIA A.
[b.] May 10, 1958, Montgomery, AL; [p.] Late Grand and Bertha Robinson; [m.] Zachary K. Scott, April 15, 1978; [ch.] Zanetta Yvette, Miranda Nicole Zachary Jr.; [ed.] George Washington Carver High School Massey - Draughon Business College; [occ.] Rheem Manufacturing Co. Line Inspector; [memb.] Lilly Baptist Church; [oth. writ.] Several poems that have not been published nor exposed to the public; [pers.] I am striving to be successful in my writings, and keeping the faith in God that all things are possible.; [a.] Montgomery, AL

SCOTT, ROGER
[b.] January 8, 1971, Bay City, MI; [p.] Roger L. Scott Sr., Judy Ann Wheeler; [ch.] Victoria Lynn Scott; [ed.] Whittemore Prescott High Michigan State University, Saginaw Valley State University; [occ.] Lab Technician, H.E. Services; [memb.] Eagles Club; [hon.] Honor Guard, Scholar - Athlete; [pers.] I find strength in myself by helping others. When I see a smile I am truly inspired; [a.] Bay city, MI

SCOTT, TAMARA P.
[b.] September 6, 1961, Sparta, NC; [p.] Guy T. Perry Jr., Judith M. Perry; [m.] Larry K. Scott Jr., November 12, 1995; [ch.] Leslie Nicole St. Clair; [ed.] Olympic High School, Alleghany High School; [occ.] Account Collections, and Account Data Technician; [hon.] Vocational Honor Society; [pers.] These vows were written for my loving husband Larry K. Scott Jr and given to him on our Wedding Day. My writing comes from the heart. For with love, kindness compassion for your fellowman, and hard work there isn't anything in life you can't accomplish.; [a.] Lancaster, SC

SCOTT, TAYLOR
[b.] May 22, 1979, Santa Rosa, CA; [p.] Rebekah Browning; [ed.] Cardinal Newman High School - Senior; [occ.] Student, but also works at Airport Cinemas; [hon.] Pop Warner Silver Award, numerous athletic trophies and awards for football and pole-vaulting.; [oth. writ.] French poem published in *A-Vos-Plumes*; [pers.] Life is like a candle, any moment it could go out. My greatest writing influence has been my uncle, Michael Thomas, who writes incredible poetry that I've enjoyed all my life.; [a.] Santa Rosa, CA

SCUDDER, PATTY
[b.] August 10, 1933, Nobleboro, ME; [p.] Roy H. and Mildred L. Genthner; [m.] Bob Scudder; [ch.] Pamela Goguen, Paula Meany, Peter, Nancy Hughes; [ed.] BA Tufts University, MA U. of San Francisco; [occ.] Retired Teacher of Gifted and Talented and Maine Antique Shop owner; [memb.] CTA, NEA, Nobleboro Historical Society, Alpha Omicron Pi; [hon.] DAR Outstanding Teacher *Who's Who American Teachers*, Ocean View Outstanding Leadership Award., Pres. of Sr. Class - Tufts - Achievement Cup (most outstanding grad.); [oth. writ.] Newspaper (short stories printed) Educational Writings pertaining to gifted Ed.; [pers.] Life is precious and each moment must be savored.; [a.] Nobleboro, ME

SCULLY, MEGHANN KELDA
[pen.] If I had one, when I have one Kelda Nye; [b.] October 27, 1979; [p.] Robert E. Scully III and Mary Jo Scully; [ed.] Montfort Academy 6th-8th grade Spotsylvania High School; [memb.] Head Captain of Spotsylvania High School Dance Team. Business Manager of Spotsylvania High School year book. Staff Member of Spotsylvannia High School. Lit. Mag. *Perifery*; [oth. writ.] I'm a writer for the school yearbook; [pers.] I write about things close to me, about how I feel. I also write poetry for my friends, things that have gone on with them. My personal statement is the blue cow barks at midnight - don't ask what it means - it just is.; [a.] Spotsylvania, VA

SEELEY, MATTHEW
[pen.] Matt Hadder; [b.] April 24, 1973, Salisbury, NY; [p.] Martin and Linda Seeley; [ed.] St. Lawrence Uni-

versity ('95) Bachelor in English Writing, Minor in Music; [occ.] Hotel Clerk; [memb.] Phi Beta Kappa (National Academic Honorary), Irving Bachelor Society (English Honorary), Charles Ives Society (Music Honorary); [hon.] Alexander Black Medal for Creative Writing and Journalism (from St. Lawrence University); [oth. writ.] Local publications, a novel in progress, volumes of poetry, songwriting, electronic music composition; [pers.] I write, as with everything, to exercise and expand my mind. Life is nothing without devotion to creativity.; [a.] Albany, NY

SEIBERT, DENA R.
[b.] November 25, 1977, Terre Haute, IN; [p.] Leah Fouts, Ray Seibert; [ed.] Terre Haute North High School, Miami University of Oxford Ohio; [occ.] Student; [hon.] Various Scholarships; [oth. writ.] Many places in essay contests, publication in an Educational Journal.

SENIOR, JASON
[pen.] Vincent "Devlark"; [oth. writ.] "Angel Tears," "Avalon," "A Thing Of Beauty," "Through A Child's Eye." And have several song lyrics written.; [pers.] I believe in following your dreams. I believe our children are sparkling treasures that shouldn't correct our destruction we created. We should before it's too late. I also believe our eyes, mind, and hearts have been sheltered for so long that we've forgotten how to love. We need to move on from the hate that we feel towards one another.; [a.] Weedville, PA

SESTAK, PAMELA HANER
[b.] June 11, 1964, Tampa, FL; [p.] Randal and Betty Haner; [m.] Thomas D. Sestak Jr., June 17, 1995; [ch.] Andrew Ryan and Louis Randal; [ed.] Hillsborough High, Concord Career Institute; [occ.] Housewife; [memb.] Piney Level Baptist Church; [oth. writ.] I have written other poems but never had any published.; [pers.] I have been writing poems since I was very young I just never had nerve to send one in for lack of confidence in my ability. The Lord and The National Library of Poetry have given me the confidence I needed.; [a.] Maryville, TN

SEVIGNY, CHRIS L.
[b.] August 2, 1982, Honolulu, HI; [p.] Michael F. and Susan A. Sevigny; [ed.] 8th Grade; [occ.] Student; [memb.] Club Live - Parkway Middle School, La Mesa, CA; [a.] Spring Valley, CA

SEWOLT, FELICIA
[b.] August 10, 1982, Colorado; [p.] Alena Monika and James Sewolt; [ed.] Wilmot Elementary School, Evergreen Junior High School; [occ.] Student; [memb.] American Legion Auxiliary; [hon.] Awarded for Best Poem in school, also published in a Literary Magazine of Wilmot Elementary called *The Arrow*, also awarded for writing a baby poetry book; [oth. writ.] School writings, stories, poems, letters, and at home for fun.; [pers.] I'm 14 and live in Evergreen, I enjoy outdoor activities, and like to write about things around me, and like to spend lots of time with my family and friends.; [a.] Evergreen, CO

SEYMOUR, DIANA MARWICK
[b.] January 11, 1982, Washington, DC; [p.] Richard Seymour, Christine Marwick; [ed.] Currently attending Alice Deal Junior High School in Washington, DC; [occ.] Student; [memb.] National Junior Honors Society; [hon.] Honor roll, placed in the top 50 in the National Spelling Bee in 1993 and 1994; [oth. writ.] An excerpt from a letter to President Clinton published in the book *Dear Mr. President*; [pers.] Things are complicated I would go into more detail but there isn't enough room here.; [a.] Washington, DC

SHARP, DALE
[b.] February 18, 1974, Memphis, TN; [p.] Lucy Morgan, Gwin Sharp; [ed.] Currently going to school to receive a degree in Performing Arts, Shelby State University; [occ.] I'm currently working for Methodist Hospital; [pers.] I strive to use my talent the best way I know how. I always have God on my side to push me as far as I need to go.; [a.] Memphis, TN

SHARP, PAM
[pen.] Pam Sharp; [b.] January 11, 1981, Ft. Hood, TX; [p.] Jimmie and Angelika Sharp; [ed.] Burleson High School entering 10th grade; [occ.] Student; [memb.] A.F.J. R.O.T.C.; [hon.] Military order of World Wars - for outstanding achievement in military and scholastic studies, extra curricular activities, and individual endeavors; [pers.] My poems always display my feelings and outlooks. And for all of you who wish to write, just write what you feel and you'll go far because it'll be more real.; [a.] Burleson, TX

SHARPE, NADINE
[pen.] Nadine Sharpe; [b.] 1920's, Los Angeles, CA; [p.] William Guthrie, Ada Bray; [ch.] Sharon Beatty; [ed.] Attended - Antelope Valley High School in California and attend Adult Study Courses at Univ. Las Vegas, Nevada; [occ.] Retired; [memb.] Native Daughters of the Golden West, University of Metaphysics.; [oth. writ.] Short stories - Eulogies, Songs, Music and Lyrics.; [pers.] I strive to lead a spiritual life, am a metaphysical student and have published my autobiography. My poems through the years reflect things that touch the heart and soul.; [a.] Las Vegas, NV

SHAVIAR, ZACHARY
[pen.] Nevin Rose; [b.] August 13, 1978, Las Vegas; [p.] Chuck and Sandy Haldeman; [memb.] National Thespian Society; [pers.] Most of my poems are very personal to me, and I only show them to people who are real close to me, so I hope you enjoy them.; [a.] Las Vegas, NV

SHAW, BLAINE E.
[b.] July 22, 1980, Elkhart, IN; [p.] Jerry and Sheila Shaw; [ed.] Junior at Northwood High School; [occ.] Student; [oth. writ.] "Shame," "Contrary to Popular Belief," "Old Men," "False but True," "Faint Light of Darkness," "Lonely Populous," "Fallen Angel," "No Time Like Yesterday," "Complete Sequence"; [pers.] I enjoy writing poetry because you can make a profound statement with only a few words.; [a.] Nappanee, IN

SHAW, C. V. COMPTON
[pen.] C. V. Compton Shaw; [b.] August 15, 1945, Dallas, TX; [p.] Thomas Mitchell Shaw, Clairine Valerie Compton Shaw; [ed.] B.B.A. Finance - The University of Texas at Austin, B.S. Biochemistry the University of Texas at Arlington, Associate in Science-Nursing the University of the State of New York (Regents Degrees); [occ.] Registered Nurse- Paralegal Student (Associate Degree); [memb.] Sons of the American Revolution, Sons and Daughters of the Pilgrims, Veterans of Foreign Wars, American Legion; [hon.] Academic Achievement, Bronze Star Medal, Army Commendation Medal, Vietnamese Cross for Gallantry with Palm, Combat Infantryman's Badge; [oth. writ.] Several poems published at the University of Texas at Austin; [pers.] We learn that, as humans, we are dealing with the specific not the Universal.; [a.] Dallas, TX

SHAW, STACEY
[b.] February 29, 1972, Joliet, IL; [p.] Larry and Rosemary Shaw; [ed.] Joliet Central High School, Southern Illinois University at Edwardsville; [occ.] Medical Technologist, Substitute Teacher; [memb.] Associate Member of American Society of Clinical Pathologists; [hon.] Phi Etta Sigma, Dean's List, Ivy Day Poet, Science Honor Student, Clarinet Talent Award; [oth. writ.] Several poems will be published in the Wexford Poetry Society's next anthology.; [a.] Joliet, IL

SHEA, ELIZABETH
[b.] February 6, 1969, Camp Springs, MD; [ch.] James Tiberius Shea; [memb.] Mensa, Japan Society of Boston, Numerous Charities; [hon.] Girl Scouts Gold Award; [oth. writ.] Column in the *Boston Beacon*, and the *Mensa Bulletin*, Essay in the *Providence Journal*, Editors of *Japanese Newsletter* for 10 yrs., various haiku and poetry; [pers.] We could learn a lot from medieval Europe and Feudal Japan, if we would but listen... listen...; [a.] Sutton, MA

SHEEHAN, JEFFREY S.
[b.] September 11, 1978, Winfield, IL; [p.] Gordon Sheehan, Pamela Sheehan; [ed.] Wheaton North High School; [memb.] National Forensics League, Boy Scouts of America; [hon.] Eagle Scout; [oth. writ.] Editorial series, "The Firing Line", published in School newspaper; [pers.] I focus my writing on causing my readers to think about life in today's society. My main influences have been Gothic Legend Edgar Allan Poe and Novelist Stephen King, as well as my friends and family.; [a.] Wheaton, IL

SHEETS, LAURA M.
[b.] August 23, 1983, Lafayette, IN; [p.] James and Christine Sheets; [ed.] 7th grade - Benton Central Jr. - Sr. High School; [pers.] My sixth grade teacher and seventh grade English teacher have influenced me in my writing.; [a.] Fowler, IN

SHERMAN, CHRISTEN M.
[b.] August 18, 1972, Wheaton, IL; [p.] Terry and Jerrie Sherman; [ed.] Wheaton North High School, Grove Ave School, Barrington, IL; [pers.] My world is a reflection of my history, of who I am and who I continue to become... Thank you Mom and Dad, and a special thanks to Beeba!; [a.] Madison, WI

SHORT, LISA
[pen.] L. H. Archer; [b.] December 14, 1975, Fremont, CA; [p.] Thomas and Elizabeth Short; [pers.] My poem is dedicated to Him for His inspiration and love.; [a.] Fremont, CA

SHORTS, IRENE D.
[pen.] Irene D. Short; [b.] July 13, 1918, Rutland, VT; [p.] Wilfred and Flora Berg; [m.] Divorced; [ch.] Both deceased; [ed.] High School Grad; [occ.] Retired; [oth. writ.] None, this is my first poem.; [a.] Berne, NY

SHUGART, BARBARA ANNE
[pen.] Bobbie; [b.] September 7, 1937, Washington, DC; [p.] James Daniel Hardesty, Sarah Mae Hardesty; [m.] George Edward Shugart, June 24, 1962; [ch.] Wayne Edward, Chad Edward; [ed.] 12th; [a.] Chasepeake Beach, MD

SHWAYDER, BERNARD W.
[b.] December 12, 1949, Green Bay, WI; [ed.] Working on BA in English Literature going on to MA at the University of Colorado in Denver; [memb.] Senior Associate of the Foresight Institute for the Advancement of Molecular Manufacturing (Nanotechnology), member of the "Creative Writers" group in Denver; [hon.] Nominated (twice I guess) for "Poet of the Year" by the International Society of Poets for 1996, 2 Colorado Regional Emmy Nominations ('86-87) for music composed for Denver Museum of Natural History/PBS; [oth. writ.] "Clockworks" published in the National Library of Poetry anthology *Written In Stone;* [pers.] If your eyes are open, your heart hears; [a.] Denver, CO

SIBERT, GINA MARIE
[b.] December 16, 1976, Kalamazoo, MI; [p.] Patrick Lee Pavoni and Linda Kay Watkins; [m.] Daniel Lee Sibert, July 7, 1995; [ch.] Kimberly Marie Sibert; [ed.] Three Rivers High; [occ.] Homemaker; [oth. writ.] None published; [pers.] This poem was dedicated to my loving husband, Daniel Lee Sibert, who is also the father of our beautiful daughter Kimberly Marie Sibert.; [a.] Three Rivers, MI

SILVA, TAMMY
[b.] January 11, 1963, Lynn, MA; [p.] Mr. and Mrs. Ralph Nasuti; [m.] David Silva Jr., August 25; [ch.] 3 - Danielle, Nicholas, Janeen; [ed.] Graduated from Saugus High (1 yr. Wheelock College for early childhood); [occ.] Pre-School Teacher; [memb.] St. Joseph's Parish, St. Jude Children's, Research Hospital; [oth. writ.] Many poems written for family and friends also poems printed in local newspapers; [pers.] I have been writing since I was a child. Poems, greetings cards, wall plaques etc. All of my writings come straight from the heart and soul!; [a.] Wakefield, MA

SILVIA, KATHERINE A.
[b.] September 29, 1980, Manchester, NH; [p.] Edward Silvia, Jacqueline Silvia; [ed.] Manchester High School West; [occ.] Student and piano teacher; [pers.] I find that writing allows me to show people who I really am, without fear of being judged; [a.] Bedford, NH

SIMILA, CARMELITA R.
[pen.] Carmelita R. Simila; [b.] March 3, 1934, Dover-Foxcroft, ME; [p.] Deceased; [ch.] Cat named "Cutie Pie"; [ed.] 1. Registered Nurse 2. University of Maine - 2 years 3. Graduate courses on Open-Heart Nursing.; [occ.] Retired R.N. Inspirational Writer; [memb.] Past: ANA American Legion Vietnam Veterans of America; [hon.] 1. National Honor Society 2. The Meritorious Service Medal 3. The Republic of Vietnam Cross of Gallantry with Palm 4. The Evangeline Bovard Award for Outstanding Nurse.; [oth. writ.] Recently completed a book on inspiration and life comments titled: *On Wings of Venture;* [pers.] Inspiration is often the bridge to universal knowledge.; [a.] Dover-Foxcroft, ME

SIMMONS, ANDY
[b.] February 25, 1975, Commerce, GA; [ed.] Commerce High, University of Georgia, Athens Technical Institute; [hon.] Phi Theta Kappa, Dean's List; [oth. writ.] Several unpublished poems and short stories; [pers.] My writing is based much in part on what I see and feel every day as I live my life. My words best express my emotions.; [a.] Commerce, GA

SIMMONS, REBECCA ALLISON
[b.] February 26, 1983, Wright-Patterson, OH; [p.] Rob and Ruth Simmons; [ed.] Elementary and 7th Grade; [occ.] Jr. High Student; [a.] Alexandria, VA

SIMPSON, EVON EWART
[b.] April 10, 1966, Kingston, Jamaica, WI; [p.] Stanley R.A. Simpson, Edna B. Simpson; [m.] Suzanne Mennona Simpson, June 29, 1996; [ed.] Junior, Montclair State Univ. Upper Montclair, NJ 07043 (Undeclared), Word Processing Diploma 1990 from West Indies Collage, Kingston Jamaica WI; [occ.] Nureen Investment Customer Service Representative for Chase Manhattan Bank, NA; [memb.] Basketball Team (Walnut Drive) at Jewish Community Center on the Palisades, Tenafly NJ; [hon.] 1st place Trophy, Fall 1992 Men's 5 on 5 Basketball from Jewish Community Center; [pers.] I hope to soon create a home page on the Internet and put out financial advice with a daily poetic statement from trust at midnight authors.; [a.] Teaneck, NJ

SIMPSON, HUGH LLEWELLYN
[b.] January 17, 1942, Kingston, Jamaica; [occ.] 1964 WWRL Radio/stringer, New York City, 1964-1968 WMCA Radio News Reporter, New York City, 1968 Press Secretary for Black Media Robert F. Kennedy Presidential Campaign, Nationwide, 1968 News Writer WABC-TV News, New York City, Channel 7, 1968-1972 On Camera News Reporter-Assignment Editor WCBS-IV Channel 2, New York City, 1972-1973 United Nations Diplomatic Correspondent at the General Assembly and Secretariat for the National Black Radio Network, based in New York City, 1973-1974 Free Lance coverage of the Wounded Knee 'Indian' Trials in Minnesota, South and North Dakota, 1974-1975 Poet, Author, Free Lance News in San Francisco, Calif., 1976-present, Free Lance, Author, Poet, Photographer, Businessman based in Maui, Hawaii; [a.] Lahaina, HI

SIMS, VICKIE J.
[b.] October 15, 1971, Jackson, MS; [p.] Johnny and Patricia Sims; [ed.] B.S. in Elementary Education in 1994 and a M.S. in education Administration in May 1995 both from Alcorn State Univ., Lorman, MS; [occ.] Elementary Teacher (4th grade) Morgantown Elem, Natchez, MS; [memb.] National Association of Educators, MS Association of Educators Heroines of Jericho, Mount Olive Court #255; [hon.] National Dean's List Presidential Scholar; [oth. writ.] Several poems were published in the campus paper during my tenure at Alcorn State University.; [pers.] I have been greatly influenced by the spell of true love. My very first poem was written to tell a guy that I was in love with him and I haven't stopped writing yet.; [a.] Natchez, MS

SINGH, NAVDEEP
[b.] October 17, 1979, India; [p.] Harpal and Rajinder Singh; [ed.] Senior at John F. Kennedy High School; [occ.] Student; [hon.] Recommended to receive Honorary Award Recognition in *Who's Who Among American High School Students,* 1995-1996; [pers.] I am a girl who's always wondering what awaits my fate tomorrow. Touching the clouded hearts with the charm I possess, I hope to succeed as well as find happiness in my life.; [a.] Fremont, CA

SIRON, LISA M.
[b.] July 17, 1967, Arlington, VI; [p.] Richard and Anne Mitchell; [m.] Matthew S. Siron, April 3, 1993; [a.] Colorado Springs, CO

SKELLENGER, MARTHA
[b.] February 20, 1955, Auburn, CA; [p.] James (Deceased) and Gail Creech; [m.] John Skellenger, April 16, 1971; [ch.] Melissa Skellenger, John Skellenger; [ed.] Colfax High School, Western Career College; [occ.] Hemodialysis Technician, Sierra Hemodialysis Auburn, CA; [memb.] American Medical Technologists; [pers.] Thanks to God, the giver of all talent.; [a.] Rocklin, CA

SKURA, JESS
[pen.] Jess Skura; [b.] December 4, 1981, Buffalo, NY; [p.] Jim and Clare Skura; [ed.] Clarence Senior High School; [occ.] Student (10th grade); [memb.] I belong to the "Our Lady of Peace" church CYO group; [oth. writ.] Some poem published in *Young Author's Anthologies* magazine; [pers.] Through my writing, I express the common emotions and thought that run through a teenager's mind. Not all thoughts are positive, in fact a number of them ar negative, but I enjoy writing.; [a.] Clarence, NY

SLATTERY, KATHRYN S.
[b.] February 4, 1963, Chicago, IL; [p.] Clarence O'Halloraw, Zoe Jeffries; [m.] Daniel Slattery, March 5, 1988; [ch.] Caitlin, Patricia, Mary, Anna

SLUCK, MARY
[b.] April 20, 1976, Lehighton, PA; [pers.] I would just like to thank my brother Spidey for being my inspiration.; [a.] Bedford, TX

SLUSSER, ANNETTE LITTMAN
[pen.] Annette Littman, Monique Parenteau; [b.] March 6, 1963, Dayton, OH; [p.] Otis, Eleanor Littman; [m.] Robert Slusser, March 1, 1986; [ch.] Robby 9, Tari 5; [ed.] Beavercreek High School, OH, GVS - Xenia OH, Sinclair Community College, Dayton, OH; [occ.] Orthodontic Technician German/Burke Orthodontics B-Creek OH; [memb.] B.S.A. - Scout Leader Good Shepherd Lutheran Church Kettering, OH, Dayton Dental Assistants Assoc.; [hon.] G.M. Academic Scholarship 1981, Young Authors' Conference Award 1980, Honor Roll 1981, 1980 Beavercreek High School; [oth. writ.] Published works include "Guyana" - *Xenia Gazette* 1980 "Old People" *Paper Garden* "Awakening" *Paper Garden;* [pers.] Rather than writing for recognition, most of my works where written in times of self reflection and analysis. I find it therapeutic and I am pleased when others are touched by it.; [a.] Beavercreek, OH

SMALLWOOD, KYRA FAE
[pen.] Kiki, Kiwi, Kera; [b.] June 29, 1983, Whitesburg; [p.] David and Verla Mae Smallwood; [ed.] Dorton Junior High School; [occ.] Student; [memb.] Dorton Junior High Varsity Dancer and Cheerleader, on the Academic Team at Dorton, Play Little League; [hon.] 7 Blue Ribbons in 4-H, 1st Place in A Horse Show, 4 1st Place Honors in Cheerleading, 2 2nd Place in Cheerleading in 2 years; [oth. writ.] Several personal poems kept to only myself and some in school portfolios and newspapers.; [pers.] I would really only like to say that if it hadn't been for a teacher asking for a poem, I might never have started my career. The teacher was Janet Bryant. I try to write about reality in my poetry.; [a.] Jenkins, KY

SMEARMAN, MADONA LEE
[b.] December 25, 1955, Weirton, WV; [p.] Mary Porco and John B. Porco (Deceased); [m.] Dennis Smearman, September 21, 1984; [ch.] (Step-children) Brian and Denise Smearman; [ed.] Graduated Weir. Sr. High 1974; [occ.] Pit Cleaner - Weirton Steel Company, Weirton,

WV; [memb.] Weirton Vol. Fire Dept. Co. #1 also WVFD Co #1 Auxiliary attend Christian and Missionary Alliance in Weirton; [pers.] When all seems dark the Lord will light the way.; [a.] Weirton, WV

SMIEJEK, NANCY LOUISE PYLE
[b.] January 25, 1957, Port Hueneme, CA; [p.] Nancy Lou Turner and David Lindel Pyle; [m.] David Anthony Smiejek, September 1, 1995; [ch.] None, unless my animals count. If yes, 6 - 5 dogs and 1 double yellow headed amazon parrot; [ed.] There's not enough room - High School - Airline Handicap Sign Language; [occ.] Housewife - vet - Mr. Belvidere, Secretary, Daughter (HA!); [hon.] I've won honors and awards in many subjects. The ones I hold close to my heart are the two women who I've been honored with as friends Lynda Bell (Belchor) Cathy Carnett (Gibbs) my father and husband; [pers.] Never let anyone know your weakness. If you feel it's the right thing to do - when you feel it in the very middle of your stomach - act on it. Don't second guess it - to never forget that God is your father and anything that hurts you - was not caused by Him.; [a.] Hammond, IN

SMITH, CHERL D.
[b.] April 6, 1956, Oklahoma City, OK; [p.] Eddie Mae Smith, Charles Smith; [ch.] Marlon, Michelle; [ed.] Parkway Program High School; [occ.] Administrative Assist.; [memb.] Pleasant Oak Missionary Baptist Church; [oth. writ.] Have just completed a book length manuscript of fiction.; [pers.] My talent as a writer is a gift from God that I would like to share with people all over the world. My inspiration, Terry McMillian. She's proof that the impossible is possible.; [a.] Philadelphia, PA

SMITH, HANNAH HOPKINS
[b.] November 7, 1982; [p.] Cynthia Abbott, Larry Smith; [ed.] Currently enrolled in the Needham School System. (Eighth grade); [oth. writ.] An article about Bosnia in local papers. Mini articles in a School Bulletin.; [pers.] The people who have most inspired me are my parents and seventh grade English teacher, Martha Matlaw.; [a.] Needham, MA

SMITH, IONIE DONALDS
[pen.] Iona, Betty Missis, Blossom; [b.] May 10, 1937, Jamaica, West Indies; [p.] Joseph and Adewne Donalds; [m.] Hilton R. Smith, September 26, 1959; [ch.] Karen, Collie, Dwight Smith; [ed.] Diploma in Education, Educator; [occ.] Retired Teacher Educator - Writer, Stories, poems, Songs, Volunteer; [memb.] Several Religious Organizations, Past Leader of 4-H Clubs and Community Organizations; [hon.] 4-H Club Silver Award, Social Service in Community Award; [oth. writ.] Songs, stories. Articles for *Daily Gleaner* in the 1960's-70's Jam, WI; [pers.] I will strive to reflect peace, love and goodwill to mankind in my writings as God inspires me. I will not hand over leadership of my family to anyone.; [a.] Washington, DC

SMITH, ISAAC MATTHEW
[b.] December 20, 1984, Kansas City, MO; [p.] Norma Hall, Gerry Hall and Donald Smith, Kathy Smith; [ed.] Cambridge Elementary Belton, MO; [hon.] Dare graduation, Presidents Academic Award, Abbit Award(s), 15 Principal's Awards for all A's in five years of school; [oth. writ.] Short story - "My Life"; [pers.] Just keep trying, you can be anything you want to be. Don't give up!!; [a.] Belton, MO

SMITH, JUNE E.
[b.] May 7, 1943, Tacoma, WA; [p.] John and Margaret Hansen; [ch.] Lloyd, Jonathan and Brian; [ed.] Westmoor High (Calif.), Tacoma Community College (Wa.), The Evergreen State College (WA.); [occ.] Registered Counselor, and Care Provider for Alzheimer's; [pers.] In memory Son, Jonathan.; [a.] Puyallup, WA

SMITH, KATHY
[b.] April 18, 1954, Dayton, OH; [p.] Bill Wilson, Shirley Leach; [m.] Dennis Smith, July 11, 1994; [ch.] Mary Elena and Jason Scott; [ed.] Just received GED in June, 1996; [memb.] I'm a member of PeTA, People for the Ethical Treatment of Animals.; [oth. writ.] This is my first; [pers.] Wrote in loving memory of my grandpa Hubert Wilson. Born Feb. 16, 1903 in Sand Gap, Kentucky. He lived on Post Town Rd, in Trotwood, Ohio, he passed away at the age of 92 on Nov. 27, 1995. A wonderful grandpa and friend.; [a.] West Alexandria, OH

SMITH, KATRINA DIANE
[b.] December 23, 1957, Oakland, CA; [p.] Mary Jean Smith, Bill M. E. Smith; [ch.] Jason L. Smith (children Hosp.); [ed.] Sequoia Elem King St. High (Estates) Castlemont High School, Laney College Alameda College, Career Com Business College Edwards Stands School.; [memb.] National Trust for Historic Preservation; [hon.] Honorable mention of San Francisco Bay Girl Scout Council; [oth. writ.] *The Founder's Guide of Girl Scouting*, (Note) *The Journal of Conflict Resolution* Founded in 1957. (Note) *The Great Depression* (1930) (Note) Frenise A. Logan "The Color Industrial Association of North Caroline and its Fair of 1886", *North Carolina Historical Review XXXIV* (Jan. 1957); [pers.] Jackson Clarion-Ledger (Jan. 19, 1910) "Constant Crusade" (quot.) (*Lincoln County Times* (June 30, 1910) Farmers without land (June 30, 1910) Atlanta Constitution (Unpub.) Dec 23, 1887 Richard Mendales Sic Transit Richmond) Report for the twentieth Century, (Proj. Center) Fontana (Foundation); [a.] Oakland, CA

SMITH, MICHAEL J.
[b.] July 9, 1978, Summit, NJ; [p.] Everett Smith, Dolores Smith; [occ.] Sales Associate, Marshalls, Freehold, N.J.; [oth. writ.] Two of my other poems, "Love And Hate" and "Paradigm Of Beauty" are going to be published in *Whispers*, a literary anthology. An excerpt of a letter I wrote is published in *Parade*, a magazine.; [pers.] The best poems aren't written with a pen, they are written with the heart.; [a.] Marlboro, NJ

SMITH, NAOMI P.
[pen.] Omani; [b.] July 1, 1944, Chicago, IL; [p.] Helen and Julius Anderson; [m.] Divorced; [ch.] Ten (7 adopted); [ed.] Eau Claire High, U.C. Berkeley College; [occ.] (Counselor) and (Community Organizer); [memb.] Continental or Omega Boys and Girls Club Organization and "Professional Counselors" Recovery Task Force, Vallejo Deliverance Center; [hon.] Unsung Heroine Award - 1993, Black Women's Media Project - '92, City of Vallejo "Shoroe" - 1993; [oth. writ.] Other poems (unpublished), several articles in the Local newspaper; [a.] Vallejo, CA

SMITH, PAUL E.
[pen.] Paul E. Smith; [b.] March 3, 1930, Noble Co., IN; [p.] Frank and Fairy Smith; [m.] Mary L. Smith, March 12, 1950; [ch.] Kenneth, Kevin, Connie, Wallace; [ed.] High school; [occ.] Retired; [memb.] New Life Community Church; [oth. writ.] Poems published in local papers, poem in of *Sunshine and Daydreams*.; [pers.] I like to write about Nature and God's Love for us and specific subjects.; [a.] Glendale, AZ

SMITH, RICHARD GEORGE
[pen.] Butch; [b.] October 11, 1951, Ogden, UT; [p.] George T. Smith, Irene O. Smith; [m.] Sandra W. Smith, March 12, 1971; [ch.] Denice, Brenda, Mike, Brian, James, Sarah Ann; [ed.] Bonneville High, Weber College, Utah Tech; [occ.] Self Employed; [memb.] Church of Jesus Christ of Latter-Day Saints, NRA Golden Eagles; [oth. writ.] "Personal Collection"; [pers.] I try to learn something that I did not know every day and try to find its truths and how they apply to me. Then I apply it to my poems; [a.] Odgen, UT

SMITH, ROY D.
[pen.] Roie; [b.] July 26, 1970, Oklahoma City, OK; [memb.] Phi Kappa Tau, Alpha Lambda Chapter, Auburn University; [oth. writ.] I usually burn most of my writings because of the pain they hold; [pers.] Carpe Diem - finish your painting and then sing your song.

SMITH, STEPHEN C.
[pen.] Smitty; [b.] Los Angeles, California; [p.] Scott Slaughter and Kathy Smith; [m.] Nancy Smith, March 20, 1976; [ch.] Renee, John, Daniel (Stepchildren); [ed.] Hollywood High; [memb.] Nevada State Museum and Historical Society; [hon.] Honorable Discharge U.S. Army 1969-1972; [oth. writ.] Several poems and songs.; [pers.] "Every time I Hear A Train" was written in memory of Robbert Warren Rasmussen who was killed in a train accident in Thailand on July 2, 1983.; [a.] Las Vegas, NV

SMITH, TARA
[b.] November 18, 1972, Napa; [p.] Christine and Jay Gehres; [m.] Charles Smith, June 8, 1991; [ch.] Kevin 7, Michael 3; [ed.] High School graduate 4 scholarships part time college student; [occ.] At home mom, part time college student; [hon.] Four scholarships Valedictorian of High School graduating class; [oth. writ.] Many others not published kept private; [pers.] I have been influenced by my own personal struggles through life. Each poem that I write is a reflection of something that has inspired me to write that particular poem.; [a.] Napa, CA

SMITH, TIMOTHY
[b.] March 20, 1962, Somers Point, NJ; [p.] Jack P. Smith, Grace A. Smith; [m.] Ellen M. Heller Smith, April 29, 1995; [ch.] Kyle, Amanda, Tim Jr.; [ed.] Ocean City High School; [occ.] Warehouse receiving Clerk for Showboat Casino and Hotel; [oth. writ.] Some songs but, I've not been published before.; [pers.] "I believe that poetry and song are a universal language, able to bridge the gaps created by man's differences."

SNYDER, JOSEPH M.
[b.] January 18, 1933, Brooklyn, NY; [p.] Abe Snyder, Anna Snyder; [ed.] Boys High, Educational Alliance, Brooklyn College, N.Y.U. U. of Miami - courses in Photography and Film Making; [occ.] Formerly Vice-President, Printing Firm; [memb.] Metropolitan Motion Picture Club, editor of *Close-Up* magazine, Greenwich Village Camera Club, Brooklyn Camera Club.; [hon.] Three trophies for Original Amateur Films (N.Y.C.), Still Photography showing, N.Y.U, Photographic Newspaper Award (Florida).; [oth. writ.] Articles for Photographic Club Magazines (N.Y.), "Express way Hysteria" in *Spirit of the Age*.; [pers.] Self-expression comes in many ways, Photography filled my younger days. Now I'm wiser and little bit older, and so my verbiage is bolder.; [a.] Hollywood, FL

SNYDER, MILDRED REX
[pen.] Mildred Rex-Snyder; [b.] March 28, 1912, Syracuse, IN; [p.] Walter and Jessie Strieby Rex; [m.] Richard E. Snyder (Deceased), January 1, 1933; [ch.] Richard Rex and Mary Call; [ed.] Graduate Avilla, In High School, Graduate International Business College Ft. Wayne, IN; [occ.] Retired; [memb.] Lifetime member International Society of Poets; [hon.] Publications in the National Library of Poetry Anthologies. Two "Editor's Choice Awards" for 1995 and 1996, many for being an organist and pianist, one of the Poets of the Year for 1995 and 1996; [oth. writ.] This is the 7th time to have a poem published in an anthology, also a semi-finalist in 1995 and 1996 North American Open Poetry Contest; [pers.] I agree with Eleanor Roosevelt: You gain strength, courage and confidence by every experience in which you look fear in the face. You must do the thing you think you cannot do.; [a.] Fort Wayne, IN

SOLTANI, REZA EDALAT
[pen.] Reza; [b.] May 31, 1923, Kerman, Iran; [p.] Hossein and Kobra Soltani (Both Deceased); [m.] Nosrat E. Soltani, March 23, 1951; [ch.] Five sons; [ed.] M.S. M.D. with Certificate in Pathology (anatomic and clinical) by the American Board of Pathology; [occ.] Professor and Chairman, Dept. of Pathology, Meharry Medical College, Nashville, Tennessee; [memb.] Medical Associations in the USA and Iran; [hon.] 1. Honor student all through medical school, 2. First prize Scientific writing in North Central Medical Society, 1962, 3. Gold Medals in Medicine, Iran, 1956, 4. Gold Medal Avicenna in Iran, 1965, 5. Gold Medal Razi in Iran, 1967, 6. 5 years Scholarship to study medicine in USA; [oth. writ.] 1) 5 Textbooks in Pathology and Embryology (Persian Language - several editors) 2) Syllabi in Neuropathology and Hematology (in English), 3) Poetry Book for the Peace on Earth (unpublished); [pers.] Religious and racial prejudice: The greatest enemy of humanity. This will be the title of my poetry book. I hope to be published in Persian and English. I am hurt by the nonsensical religious prejudices that has killed and is killing millions of innocent people and ruins many countries. This is absolutely and utterly ridiculous and inhumane, especially when we see that all religious beliefs are myths and have no scientific basis.; [a.] Nashville, TN

SOLYOVA, JAROSLAVA
[pen.] Jarusuka Parente; [b.] January 1, 1959, Prague, Czech. Republic; [occ.] Designer combining Architecture, Landscape, Interior and Art in "Total Design" (own firm in La Jolla); [memb.] Master Joga Academy and other; [oth. writ.] Many unpublished poems in different languages, articles and planned autobiography.; [pers.] I always keep in mind in my life and work that character is defined by what you are willing to do when the spotlight has been turned off, the applause has died down and no one is around to give you credit.; [a.] La Jolla, CA

SOMMER, TIMOTHY SCOTT
[b.] October 16, 1971, Buffalo, NY; [p.] Douglas & Judith Sommer; [ed.] Cardinal O'Hara High School, Canisius College 1994; [occ.] Student; [memb.] Phi Alpha Delta Pre-Law Honors Society, Association for Practical and Professional Ethics, Students United for Responsible Action to Guarantee our Environment (SUFRAGE); [hon.] Dean's List, winner Canisius College Dr. Martin Luther King Jr. Poetry Contest, 3 time recipient of the Canisius College Presidential Service Award (1992, 93, 94); [oth. writ.] Several student publications (The Quadrangle, The Griffin, The Chanticleer), poetry published in the Buffalo News; [pers.] Being a chaotic milieu, this dynamic altering beast, a life form so full of rapture and yet seemingly so incomplete to our eye. I care for all even the least. [a.] Buffalo, NY

SOTO, NANCY WILLERTON
[b.] November 18, 1972; [p.] Jesse and Ruth Ann Willerton; [m.] Rogelio Soto, April 1, 1995; [ed.] Deckerville Comm. Schools, Career Center; [occ.] Manager/Photographer of a Photo Studio; [memb.] Argyle United Methodist Church; [pers.] Raised in Argyle Township, Sanilac County of Michigan along with two brothers and one sister. Always enjoyed nature, writing, and photography.; [a.] Snover, MI

SOWA, JUDIE
[b.] San Antonio, TX; [p.] Richard and Evelyn Rolander; [m.] Thomas Sowa, October 11, 1994; [ch.] Mr. Tibbs - Mrs. Beasley; [ed.] Associates Bus. Admin - Worcester, MA CNA - Licensed - Tampa, FL; [occ.] CNA.; [oth. writ.] Several poems written basically for family and friends; [pers.] I've been writing for years. There is no greater joy than expressing to someone who's close how you feel in poetry.; [a.] Tampa, FL

SPEED, CHRISTINA LEE
[pen.] Christina Chloe, Leilani Lee Speed; [b.] January 30, 1980, Cuero, TX; [p.] William Larry and Diana Lee Speed; [ed.] Will graduate from High School in 1998, possibly earlier; [occ.] Librarian at Charles City Public Library; [memb.] Member of Recovering Alcoholic/Addict Services at the Hope House in Charles City; [hon.] Who's Who Among American High School Students Scholarship Award, Presidential Fitness Award, Varsity Letters in Volleyball and Track. Also invited to Washington D.C. for National Lawyers Conference; [oth. writ.] "Time," "Fetch," "The Confusion," "Immortal Seering," "Morbid Magic," "Sober," "White Sun," Tarnished Laughter," "Today's Age," "Levels of the End," "Time Again," "Sturm-and-Drang," 100's of others.; [pers.] A little soul is all that is required to become a great philosopher/writer of your day.; [a.] Charles City, IA

SPEER, CHERYL J.
[b.] December 25, 1948, Mercedes, TX; [p.] Freelen Speer, Hazel Speer; [ch.] Jason C. Speer; [ed.] George Washington High, Indpls Ind.; [occ.] Heavy Assembly Operator, Thompson's Consumer Electronics, Bloomington Indiana; [pers.] Enjoy life, take time to stop and smell the flowers.; [a.] Linton, IN

SPENCE, GAIRY
[b.] November 10, 1977, West Moreland, Jamaica; [p.] Locksley Spence, Jenevee Spence; [ed.] Falmouth Infant School (Jamaica), Granville All Age School (Jamaica), Cornwall College (Jamaica), George Institute of Technology; [occ.] Student-Georgia Tech.; [memb.] National Society of Black Engineers; [hon.] Dean's List; [pers.] I have always enjoyed writing short stories and poems. My goal is to continue writing, and eventually publish a book.; [a.] Lawrenceville, GA

SPENCER, WILLIAM
[pen.] Aquarius 05795 "Orville", William "Perseus"; [b.] February 19, 1915, Bethel, NC; [p.] William Jasper Spencer and Virginia Dare Jones; [m.] Helen Tolman Spencer, March 7, 1978 - 3rd husband; [ch.] 5 - 6GC, 7-12GC-8GGC; [ed.] Grad. Bethel, NC, its-1932, Grad. US Naval Acad. 1938, Post Grad-NW Univ., Investment Bring, 1952; [occ.] Retired, 18 yrs.; [memb.] US Naval Acad. Alumni Assn. and Athlete Assn., US Marine Corp. Res. Off. Assn. and Marine Corps Assn., The Retired Officers Assn., Amer. Legion, Midway Assn., various other Military; [hon.] Military only WWII, Veteran WWII - Bottles, 1.) PH-Midway 1941, 2.) Midway - 1942, 3.) Okinawa - 1945 (4) Occupation of Japan and Nagasaki 1945; [oth. writ.] 1.) "Evolutionary Commission" 1952 and 1969, 2.) "The Many Nations of Man," "Tear Down All Sleepless," "The Whole Story," etc. in 1950's, 3.) "The Black Rat Story" - 1987, 4.) "Indian Giver" - 1968, 5.) "Yahweh Odes" - 1989, 6.) "The Century Of The Pale Horse" - "The 21st Century," various other essays.; [pers.] I write as a "Hobby" only - never publish and sell for profit. My interests are evolution, religion, Genetics and Geopolitics. "Hope for future and man's purpose in life."

STAFFIERI, VICKI
[b.] August 1, 1956, Washington, DC; [p.] Robert and Verna McKelvey; [m.] William Staffieri, July 3, 1982; [ch.] Robert L.; [ed.] Paralegal - Penn State University; [occ.] Claims Analyst; [pers.] I have learned that God truly does heal the brokenhearted, and the depth of our pain can always be surpassed by the height of His amazing love.; [a.] Lancaster, PA

STAFFORD, KAY S.
[b.] June 2, 1951, Marion, NC; [p.] Robert and Kathleen Shook; [m.] Clifford Stafford, April 1, 1980; [ch.] Isaac and Jonathan; [ed.] Hickory High School Hickory NC, AB Tech Asheville NC CVCC Hickory, NC; [occ.] Receptionist/Secretary; [hon.] G.E.M. Award CVCC Going above and beyond the call of duty; [oth. writ.] "A Marriage Prayer", "Beauty, What Is It?"; [pers.] God has been so good to my family and me. If we look around at His beautiful creation, we will behold the beauty of the Lord! Thank you, oh my Father, for all your beauty; [a.] Taylorsville, NC

STALEY, PATRICIA L.
[b.] December 8, 1956, Alice, TX; [m.] Neil D. Staley (Rocky); [pers.] I would like my poem dedicated to my husband Neil D. Staley. (Rocky); [a.] West Valley, UT

STANHOUSE, COLLEEN
[pen.] Sissy; [b.] January 19, 1961, Chicago, IL; [p.] Jim Tom and Rose Pruitt; [ch.] Patricia Denise Stanhouse; [ed.] Two Associates in Computer Programming 1) Computer Science 2) Computer Information System at State Technical Institute.; [occ.] Retired Military, Homemaker; [memb.] Songwriters Association Memphis, Tenn. 2) Alpha Kappa State Technical Institute after graduation; [pers.] I choose to write on subjects that are reality and truth of everyday life.; [a.] Covington, TN

STANLEY, LOREN
[b.] May 13, 1977, Columbus, OH; [p.] Mary Ellen Stanley; [ed.] Logan Elm High School, Kent State University; [occ.] Student; [memb.] Kent State Gymnastic Club, Student Medical Association, Students of Professional Nursing; [hon.] This is my first honor publications of my poems "My Days of Happiness"; [oth. writ.] Personal poems for myself; [pers.] Live each days as if it's your last and never give up on your dreams. "Knowledge is power" is another I like.; [a.] Circleville, OH

STARK, DARLENE
[pen.] Dee Stark; [b.] May 7, 1960, Norfolk, VA; [p.] Wilbur and Carolyn Whitehead; [m.] Fiancee - Ed Lewis, to be February 11, 1997; [ch.] Travis Stark; [pers.] I like to use my writing as a positive channel for the some-

times negative or confusing emotions which life may throw my way.; [a.] Virginia Beach, VA

STAUB, JENN
[pen.] Pearl Morrison; [b.] January 13, 1981, Washington, DC; [p.] Janet Hecker (Deceased), Kenneth Staub; [ed.] Damascus High School; [occ.] Poet, student; [hon.] Gold Medal Writing Awards, several writing acknowledgements; [oth. writ.] "Storm," "Streetwalker" (poems); [pers.] Sometimes I stand in the dark, and it whispers. It's those secrets you see in my work.; [a.] Gaithersburg, MD

STEARNS, CRYSTAL K.
[b.] July 27, 1973, Elmira, NY; [p.] Ruth and Richard Stearns; [ed.] University of Oklahoma, Norman, OK, Graduate Student Working Towards Ph.D. Major: Chemistry, Division: Analytical - University of Central Oklahoma, Edmond, OK Bachelor of Science, May 1996 Major: Chemistry ACS Certificate GPA: 3.25/4.00 - East Central University, Ada, OK Candidate for Bachelor of Science, September 1991 - May 1994 Major: Chemistry; [occ.] Chemistry Graduate Research Assistant at the University of Oklahoma; [memb.] Secretary/Treasurer of the University of Central Oklahoma Chemistry Club 1995-1996, Member of the University of Central Oklahoma Chemistry Club, Student Affiliate of the American Chemical Society, Member of the University of Central Oklahoma Alumni Association, Member of the Oklahoma Wildlife Federation, Member of the Oklahoma Academy of Science, Member of Sigma Society 1991-1994, Corresponding Secretary of Sigma Society 1992-1993, Member of the McNair Scholar Program 1992-1994, Member of the Honors Program 1991-1994, Member of the Student Honors Association 1991-1994, Member of House Council 1992-1993, State Secretary for the Oklahoma Junior Academy of Science 1990-1991; [hon.] University of Central Oklahoma Dean's Honor Roll, Spring of 1996 and Fall of 1994 and 1995. University of Central Oklahoma Chemistry Department Scholarship 1994-95, 1995-96. First place in Environmental Science for paper presentation at the Oklahoma Collegiate Academy of Science Undergraduate Research Competition at the 82nd Annual Technical Meeting, November 12, 1993. Dean's Scholarship from East Central University, 1991-1992, 1992-1993, 1993-1994. Dean's Honor Roll, 1991-1992, 1992-1993, 1993-1994. Ladell Maxwell Scholarship from Sigma Society at East Central University December, 1992. National Honor Society Scholarship, 1991-1992. Oklahoma Junior Academy of Science Scholarship 1991-1992. Co-Valedictorian for Westmoore High School, May 1991; [pers.] Not everything is what it seems. Everything is not as bad as it seems. Dreams do come true.; [a.] Moore, OK

STEBNER, SHAUNA
[b.] July 3, 1978, Fullerton, CA; [p.] Bonnie and Arn Stebner; [ed.] Villa Park High School, Fullerton College; [occ.] Student; [hon.] PFSO Scholarship; [pers.] When I write, (especially poems) it comes from within. I only write how I feel.; [a.] Orange, CA

STEEN, KARL
[b.] August 17, 1953, San Diego; [p.] Robert C. Steen and Janie Steen; [ch.] Karl Jr., Miste Steen; [ed.] 12 years, 1 semester college; [occ.] Maintenance Repair Man; [oth. writ.] I as have other writing but they have not been record yet; [pers.] "You Can't Miss" "Poetry" a lovely place the world a time inspire. People "are looking for do I say" Poetry is a lovely place; [a.] San Diego, CA

STEVENS, JAMES E.
[pen.] Jamie Stevens, Everett Stevens; [b.] March 25, 1973, Storm Lake, IA; [p.] Nancy Findling and Tom Stevens; [m.] Gloria A. Stevens, February 19, 1994; [ed.] Spencer High School - Spencer, IA Gupton-Jones College of Funeral Service Decatur, GA; [occ.] Funeral Director/Embalmer; [hon.] Pi Sigma Eta Academic Hon. Fraternity; [oth. writ.] None published.; [pers.] My poetry evolves from personal events, imagination, heart and mind. I have been inspired by society, both good and bad aspects of it.; [a.] East Bend, NC

STEVENS, RACHEL L.
[b.] May 24, 1976, Fairfax, VA; [p.] Kermit and Joyce Yonts; [m.] William D. Stevens, July 22, 1995; [occ.] Receptionist, University of Phoenix Southern Colorado Campus; [a.] Colorado Springs, CO

STEVENS-FERGUSON, BETH
[pen.] Beth Stevens; [b.] April 24, 1958, Flint, MI; [p.] Verne and Anne Philo; [ch.] Craig M., Scott I., Hannah L.; [occ.] Day Care Provider; [oth. writ.] Article for *The War Cry* (A Salvation Army National Publication); [pers.] I want to share with others what I learn through my faith and my experiences.; [a.] Tustin, CA

STEVENSON, PAULA PATTERSON
[pen.] Diane L. B.; [b.] January 25, 1951, Gowanda, NY; [p.] Sally and Robert Patterson; [m.] Terry Robert Stevenson, July 31, 1971; [ch.] Jodi Diane, Tammara Dawn, Tara Denise; [ed.] Troy Area Schools, Marienville, Pennsylvania, Graduated: May 29, 1969, Duff's Business Institute, Pittsburgh, PA, Graduated: April, 1971; [occ.] Clerk Typist for a Job Training Consortium/Part-time Waitress; [memb.] First Presbyterian Church, Marienville, PA, MACA (Marienville Area Civic Assoc.), Marienville, PA Golf Membership—Highlevel Golf Course; [hon.] Salutatorian—Class of 1969, East Forest School, Marienville, Pennsylvania; [oth. writ.] Poem published by: EPA Book — "Reflections of Life", National Library of Poetry, Books: *Tomorrow's Dream, Where Dawn Lingers, Best of the 90's, Frost at Midnight*; [pers.] My poems are written from my feelings. Also writing poetry is self-healing for me.; [a.] Marienville, PA

STEWART, TANESHA SEMONE
[b.] April 17, 1981, Louisville, KY; [p.] Denita Stewart, Timothy Mattingly; [occ.] Attend at Waggener Traditional High School, will graduate in the year "1999"; [memb.] Junior Beta Club; [hon.] Certificate of Appreciation Honor Roll, Certificate of Achievement, Award of Attendance, Citizenship, Principals list, and student of the month, also achievement letter; [pers.] I like writing poems because it gives me a chance to express my strongest feelings and thoughts. I love to write poems ever since I learned to read and write. Everybody should write a poem sometimes; [a.] Louisville, KY

STEWART, WILHELMINA C.
[pen.] Mina Stewart; [b.] May 10, 1939, Providence, RI; [p.] Carol and William Johnson; [m.] Horace J. Stewart, June 12, 1961; [ch.] Marc Douglas and Pamela Marie; [ed.] M.R.H. Master's Public Health and Registered Nurse R.N.; [occ.] Health Care Consultant; [memb.] Sigma Theta Tau International, Theta Upsilon Chapter, American Organization of Nursing Execs., American Nursing Association; [hon.] Sigma Theta Tau International is an honor society; [oth. writ.] Health Care articles: "Decubetus Ulcer Interventions" Co-author D. Flynn MD/WC Stewart MPH/Rn (1983), "The Actual Cost of Nursing Care" (1981); [pers.] It is imperative that I engage spirit in all things. I am greatly inspired and influenced by Joseph Campbell and the Sufi poet Rumi.; [a.] Vallejo, CA

STEWART JR., JAMES G.
[pen.] J. Stewart Jr.; [b.] December 9, 1956, Camp Lejeune, NC; [p.] James G. Sr., Mary C.; [m.] Divorced; [ch.] James G. III, Jennifer Renee; [ed.] G.E.D., working on B.S. (in agriculture) and Devry; [occ.] Disabled, broke back in 1986; [memb.] St. Michael and All Angels, Episcopal Church, N.R.A. and North American Hunting Club; [hon.] Dean's List at Devry; [oth. writ.] A few poems in small town papers; [pers.] My poetic endeavors are inspired by my love for my children, those around me in life, and mother nature.; [a.] Phoenix, AZ

STOKES, MARLENE
[b.] January 30, 1967, Erie, PA; [p.] Barbra Stokes; [ch.] Kalia Mason; [occ.] Assistant Medical Secretary; [oth. writ.] I have written various poems such as "Trinkets," "Candlelights," etc. none of which have gained recognition.; [pers.] Knowledge is acquired through growth of the mind, heart and soul. I also enjoy love poems because of their appreciation for deep, heartfelt feelings.; [a.] Erie, PA

STOKES, TAMMY V.
[pen.] Chadwick; [b.] May 20, 1958, Brooklyn, NY; [p.] Late Leroy Branch Sr., Laura Branch; [m.] Michael D. Stokes Sr., August 25, 1984; [ch.] Michael L. Stokes Jr.; [ed.] Bishop Kearney High School, University of Scranton, New York University Brooklyn College; [occ.] Elementary School Teacher, Ulysses Byas Elementary, Roosevelt, Long Island; [pers.] "The Sounds Of Silence" was written in honor of my father who passed away on the day my son came into being.; [a.] Brooklyn, NY

STOLYAROV, JOHN
[b.] February 6, 1962; [ed.] Current student at Los Angeles Valley College; [occ.] Student; [a.] North Hollywood, CA

STOMBERG, JONAS
[b.] December 26, 1984, St. Paul, MN; [p.] Myles and Marilyn Stomberg; [ed.] Completed 5th grade, Franklin Music Magnet School, St. Paul, MN; [occ.] Student, soon to be in 6th grade fall 1996; [hon.] The National Library of Poetry published poem "A Pond" in *Through the Hourglass* and "The Wind Loves to Run" in *Across the Universe*, many baseball and school awards; [pers.] My 5th grade student teacher Ms. Lawrence got me started with poetry writing.; [a.] Saint Paul, MN

STONE, GARY W.
[pen.] G. W. Stone; [b.] September 25, 1956, Great Britain; [p.] Raymond Stone, Dorothy Stone; [m.] Sandy Stone, August 12, 1988; [ch.] Brittney Megan, Joshua Cody; [ed.] Smith High, Uncat Greensboro; [oth. writ.] *The Presence of a Poet* (a compilation of some of my poems done by my wife for my 40th birthday) "One Heart" - a poem published in the *New American Poetry Anthology*.; [pers.] My favorite statement is by Dorothy in *The Wizard of Oz*, "There's No Place Like Home."; [a.] Greensboro, NC

STOUTMEYER, JIM
[pen.] Jim Leaven; [b.] June 6, 1977, Port Huron, MI; [ed.] Port Huron High School, St. Clair County Community College; [occ.] Student and part time Maintenance Employee; [oth. writ.] A collection of poems en-

titled *Flutes and Caves*, plus several other poems. Also enjoy writing music lyrics.; [pers.] "All my writing is based around the human experience. Thoughts, ideas, concepts, feelings, emotion, and our journey. If it's all for you and our siblings."; [a.] Port Huron, MI

STREAT, JEAN ANITA
[pen.] Queenie; [b.] June 21, 1952, Baltimore; [p.] Joseph and Audrey Streat; [ch.] Jeki R. Magwood; [ed.] Priority-Hizton Hote CS. Catholic School High School, G.L.D. Book Keeping, I and accounting I management certified Health facility of Md. Supervisor Certified; [occ.] President - my own Janitorial Business-name Streats Janitorial Services; [memb.] Greats - circle of no national association of black story fever. American Library Association. New Antioch Baptist Randallstown Md. Grapton Baptist Church of Grapton Virginia.; [hon.] Certificate of achievement for superior Excellence of Performance The Blizzard of 1993. Mach 18, 1993. YWCA Shelter. Randallstown, MD; [oth. writ.] "Oh! Ninney Bug" (comedy) 1992. For we know who we are April 15, 1996. The teacher, mother and Father to April 7, 1996, understanding me April 7, 1996, Speaking Eliquetts. December, 1995; [pers.] I write from my heart and soul with faith that I have in God the Father. I also believe those who criticize one and talk negative of one who tries to do the right in God they still learn to seek and God will Bless Them in time I pray.; [a.] Baltimore, MD

STRICKLAN, LAURIE
[b.] January 19, 1966, Abilene, TX; [p.] Ronnie and Sharon Stricklan; [ed.] Bachelor's in secondary English education from Oklahoma Baptist University, Master's in Education from Texas Wesleyan University; [occ.] Teacher, Hutcheson Junior High, Arlington, TX; [pers.] My goal is to point others to a faith in God and to glorify His name.; [a.] Arlington, TX

STRUNK, DEXTER LEE
[pen.] Dexter L. Strunk; [b.] October 13, 1939, Anchor, KY; [p.] Ledford Strunk, Fannie Stamper; [m.] Mattie S. (Fultz) Strunk, December 21, 1985; [ch.] Tammy Arlene, Ronnie Lee, Larry Scott, Bryan Karl; [ed.] Lone Jack High School Pineville, KY (1959 graduate); [occ.] Mechanic Coordinator - Rochester Community Schools, Rochester Hills, MI; [memb.] TWHBEA - Tennessee Walking Horse Breeders' and Exhibitors' Assoc., GWRA - Gold Wing Road Riders Assoc., AARP - American Assoc. of Retired Persons; [oth. writ.] Poems published in local school papers. Many writings for personal and family enjoyment.; [a.] Rochester Hills, MI

STUART, MOLLY
[b.] January 24, 1984, Independence, MO; [p.] Cameron and Sallie Stuart; [ed.] Sarah Winnemucca Elementary; [occ.] Student; [hon.] Principal's Honor Roll - Presidential Physical Fitness, 3 yrs. - Perfect Church Attendance, 3 yrs; [pers.] I like to write poetry because it lets me use my imagination and express myself at the same time; [a.] Reno, NV

STUCK, LEE
[b.] February 21, 1924, California; [m.] Lavon, December 15, 1946; [ch.] Four boys; [ed.] High School, Lyrs Business College; [occ.] Retired, from Hardware Store Mgr. 32 yrs and Nursing Home Administrator 8 yrs.; [pers.] I am a Christian - a believer in the Lord Jesus Christ. My poetry reflects the spiritual and is written from my heart.; [a.] Yakima, WA

SUCONICK, SARAH
[b.] September 18, 1979, Syracuse, NY; [p.] Irina Suconick, David Suconick; [occ.] High School Student; [pers.] I feel that the greatest poetry is not necessarily that which is understood, but that which is felt within and closest to the heart.; [a.] Lexington, MA

SULLIVAN, LONI SUE
[pen.] Loni Sullivan; [b.] May 14, 1982, Denver, CO; [p.] Kathleen Sue Sullivan, David W. Sullivan; [m.] Kurt M. Benedict (Boyfriend); [ed.] I went to Virginia Court Elementary School, then to Aurora Hills Middle School, now I am going to Overland High School; [occ.] Student; [memb.] Aurora Dance Arts (9 years), Tai Kwon Do (7 years), Drama (4 years), Art Club (2 years), Choir (2 years); [hon.] Honor Roll Student (7 years), 9th grade President's Outstanding Academic Award, Tai Kwon Do Trophies 6, Reflections 1st place Photographic Contest T-Ball Trophy; [oth. writ.] "Lost Friends," "Immortal Lovers"; [pers.] To all people who have lost loves, I hope this helps you know you are not the only one.; [a.] Aurora, CO

SUMMERS, SAM
[b.] May 4, 1987, Oklahoma City, OK; [p.] Doug and Mary Ann Summers; [ed.] 2nd Grade; [occ.] Student; [memb.] Boy Scouts, Episcopal Church of the Resurrection, Little League Baseball; [hon.] First second grader reach 50 pts. on the accelerated reader program James L. Dennis Elementary; [oth. writ.] Several poems to his family, friends.; [a.] Oklahoma City, OK

SUMRALL, WARREN D.
[b.] October 21, 1937, Mobile, AL; [p.] Horace and Elma Sumrall; [m.] Cynthia Lacy Sumrall, May 24, 1961; [ch.] Richard Warren, Angelyn Lacy; [ed.] BS Electrical Engineering University of Alabama 1961; [occ.] Retired Aero Space Engr; [memb.] Park Avenue Baptist Titusville, FL Wholeloaf Christian Center, Cocoa, FL; [oth. writ.] "Rhymes of the Times," new testament psalms; [pers.] Jesus Christ is exactly who He says He is; [a.] Merritt Island, FL

SUTTON, TRACY J.
[b.] October 5, 1971, Canton, OH; [p.] Tom and Carla Scott; [m.] Greg Sutton, June 29, 1991; [ch.] Kiely Elizabeth, Emily Kaye; [ed.] Hoover High School, ICS College; [occ.] Homemaker, Medical Transcriptionist; [hon.] Honor Roll Three Years, Most Outstanding Cheerleader Award; [oth. writ.] "No Way Out" published in newsletter of MADD., Mothers Against Drunk Driving.; [pers.] I just write what I feel.; [a.] Alliance, OH

SVITIL, GREG
[pen.] Greg Svitil; [b.] August 5, 1977, Albany, NY; [p.] Ed and Jackie; [occ.] Student, The Naropa Institute, Boulder, CO; [memb.] New England Anti-Vivisection Society, People for the Ethical Treatment of Animals; [hon.] Outstanding service award, 1995, Singapore American School; [oth. writ.] Various poems, songs, essays, articles, and other ramblings; [pers.] A great deal of the songs and poems I write are warnings, not just to others, but to myself as well. Desire tends to house carelessness, and that's what "Hazed into Oblivion" was written about.; [a.] Boulder, CO

SWENSON, JUSTINE E.
[b.] March 18, 1905, Kearney, NE; [m.] Aut Swenson (Deceased); [ch.] Two (Deceased); [ed.] 2 years teaching degree from University of Miami no longer available - second grade Masters degree Univ. of Fla. 1 course in Physics Univ. of Los Angeles; [occ.] Writing when I'm in the mood poetry and stories; [memb.] Rejected all, needed free time for reading. I had books on writing. This was my world.; [hon.] I received an honor's award a friend told me about when I was walking part way to Calif. She said my award was given to the runner up. I told her that was alright.; [oth. writ.] "The Cat Who Came For X'mas," Story for a 9 yr. old grandson he thought "it was wonderful". At age 14 I was reading english literature from the stacks.; [a.] North Miami Beach, FL

SYED, ABID
[pen.] Abid; [b.] September 8, 1957, Hyderabad, India; [p.] Mohammed Syed and Waheedunnisa Syed; [m.] Asma Syed, August 7, 1981; [ch.] Omar, Mustafa and Osama; [ed.] Telecommunications Management DeVry Institute of Technology; [occ.] Telecommunication Technician; [hon.] Summa Cum Laude, Dean's List; [pers.] A child is the most wonderful gift from God to mankind. I wish and pray that no parents lose their children as it is a never healing wound.; [a.] Glen Ellyn, IL

SYLIM, EVELYN A.
[pers.] Proud daughter of Go Ping Guan and Sy Siu Chong. The seventh of Eight children. I dedicate this poem to my parents who had taught me to be independent and strive to be the best. To be proud of who I am and to believe. I thank them for their sacrifices for all their children and I pray for their long and happy life.; [a.] Redwood City, CA

TACKMAN, PAMELA
[pen.] Pam; [b.] July 31, 1962, Fort Carson, CO; [p.] Gerald Tackman and Gloria Tackman; [ed.] Columbine High School, Arapahoe Community College; [pers.] My passion is my writing, which I wish to share with others. I have been greatly inspired by the inspirational poets.; [a.] Denver, CO

TALLMAN, EVELYN
[b.] November 13, 1922, S. Westerlo, NY; [p.] Mrs. Hazel F. Mabie; [m.] Deceased, January 23, 1940; [ch.] One; [ed.] Greenville Central High School, National Baking School, 835 Diversey Parkway Chicago, Illinois; [occ.] Retired and Write; [memb.] Social security benefits, Social Service with Albany County; [a.] Sacramento, CA

TAN, ANDREW
[b.] June 23, 1984, Montebello, Los Angeles; [p.] Kie G. Tan and Linda M. Tan; [ed.] 7th Grade Haskell Junior High; [occ.] Seventh grade student; [hon.] President's Education Gold Awards for Outstanding Academic Achievement 1995 and 1996, Mathematics Competition Award, way outer Broadway talent contest award, Science Competition Award, Karate Tournament Award; [oth. writ.] "The Road to Self Determination" - City of Cerritos 1995; [a.] Cerritos, CA

TAN, MATTHEW J.
[b.] December 13, 1986, Long Beach, Los Angeles; [p.] Kie G. Tan and Linda M. Tan; [ed.] Mary E. Brage Elementary; [occ.] Fourth grade Student; [a.] Cerritos, CA

TANDROW, HILLARY
[pen.] Hillary Tandrow; [b.] December 6, 1984, San Francisco, CA; [p.] Carlyn and Timothy Tandrow; [ed.] The Athenian School, Danville, CA; [occ.] Student; [oth. writ.] Several poems published in the *Anthology of Poetry by Young Americans*.; [pers.] I think of myself as an artist painting a picture with words. I enjoy writing

poems and stories that reflect my experiences or thoughts about the world around me.; [a.] Moraga, CA

TANGUTURI, SHYAM K.
[b.] January 21, 1985, Patchogue, NY; [p.] Kusuma and Satyan Tanguturi; [ed.] Entering 6th grade; [hon.] 1. President's Award for Educational excellence. 2. National Science and Soc. Studies Olympiad Award 3. Walt Whitman Birthplace Association, 4. Suffolk county Martin Luther King Jr., Commission, Inc.; [oth. writ.] *Color Blues* - Literary journal of the Suffolk reading Council "A Better Place For Me," published in *Martin Luther King, Jr., Commission*; [pers.] Nature, people and personal experiences inspire my work. My writing is a reflection of my thoughts.; [a.] Bayport, NY

TANK, AMANDA K.
[b.] October 17, 1980, Kalmazoo, MI; [p.] Cindy Tank; [ed.] 10th Grade High School; [occ.] Baby Sitter; [hon.] Bowling awards; [a.] Plainwell, MI

TANNER, IMOGENE G.
[b.] January 11, 1911, Sandersville, GA; [ch.] H. B. Tanner, Juanita Rapport, Jimmy Tanner, Maudie Hutto, Jannie Lister, Kay May; [memb.] Sisters Baptist Church and The Reflections Choir; [oth. writ.] Poems published in the local newspaper and the church newsletter; [pers.] Verbal communication does not come easy for me. Poetry is my way of communicating my thoughts and feelings. My favorite subjects are my family, friends and my church.; [a.] Sandersville, GA

TAPP JR., WADE
[b.] November 19, 1965, Newark, NJ; [p.] Wade Tapp Sr., Barbara Tapp; [ed.] Newark Teach, American School of Real Estate; [occ.] The Boys and Girls Club of America Westside Unit, Newark, NJ, Water Safety Instructor; [memb.] International Brotherhood of Masons; [oth. writ.] Several songs I'm printing, singing and producing, one "Love," "You," "I Love What You Do To Me," and "Baby, Baby, Baby," are a few.; [pers.] I would like to dedicate this poem to you mom, through your own pursuits, I've learned, there's no greater growth than the growth of one's human potentials and the growth of one's own intellectual horizons; [a.] Newark, NJ

TARRETO, KELLY ANN MARIE
[pen.] K.A.M.T.; [b.] May 24, 1979, Langhorn, PA; [p.] John Tarreto Jr., Ann Marie Tarreto; [ed.] Lake-Lehman High School; [oth. writ.] Several poems, one published in school literary magazine; [pers.] Always write to please yourself, and never write to please others.; [a.] Sweet Valley, PA

TASHJIAN, JOHN F.
[b.] April 7, 1964, Oakland, CA; [p.] John H. and Katherine M. Tashjian; [ed.] B.A. in French from the California State University in Fresno; [memb.] 3rd degree of the Knights of Columbus; [oth. writ.] Several poems for the National Library of Poetry, the Famous Poet's Society (Hollywood, CA), and Sparrowgrass Poetry Forum in Sisterville, West Virginia; [pers.] I try to reflect my faith in my poetry in subtle ways. Sometimes, I find that it tends to include a love of nature.; [a.] San Marcos, CA

TASHOTY, JAMES L.
[b.] January 19, 1949, Portland, ME; [p.] John L. Tashoty, Florence W. Yanborough; [ch.] Larry Jason Tashoty, Jamie Lynn Tashoty; [ed.] High School Grad. Deep Creek High School; [occ.] Retired Sales/Mgr. writing (completing book) (poet); [hon.] 3 time winner of Sales and Marketing Executives of Tidewater, 3 Gold Chapter awards (American Honda), 3 Silver Chapter awards (American Honda), 3 Salesman of the year awards (Riddle Honda), 72 Salesman of month awards (Various Organizations) 4 Diamond Z awards (Sales and Marketing Achievement) Zales Jewelers; [oth. writ.] Currently completing Book of Poetry The Voyage: "From The Darkness, Towards The Light"; [pers.] Self taught poet/writer: The Road of Life Meanders off in many tangents. I wanted to study journalism in college (Parents divorced sent me off on my way) Managed my journalism first store (Zales at 22) never made it to college. Only took up writing again when sidelined by several spinal surgeries (to deal with the time and the pain) Back on the Path again?; [a.] Norfolk, VA

TAYLOR, JESSIE E.
[b.] May 23, 1938, Duluth, MN; [m.] Morton E. Taylor; [ch.] Shane and Patrick; [ed.] High School and Business College; [occ.] Apartment Manager; [memb.] Women of the Moose R.O.C.K. - Raising Our Children's Kids (founder) support group for Grandparents Raising Grandchildren; [oth. writ.] Many poems - most of my writings are of personal experience - (family and friends); [pers.] I believe in general, the lack of respect we show our elders reflects poorly on all U.S. Citizens.; [a.] Duluth, MN

TAYLOR, KENNETH RAY
[b.] February 27, 1943, Los Angeles, CA; [p.] James Elvin Taylor and Bernice Irene Cotton; [m.] Linda White Taylor, December 28, 1963; [ch.] James Elvin and Kenneth Ray Jr.; [ed.] A.A., A.S., B.A. (Metropolitan State College of Denver), (Community College of Denver, Community College of Aurora), Palmer Writers School, Minneapolis, Minnesota, Rossville High School, Rossville, Indiana; [occ.] Senior Laboratory Technician Gates Rubber Company, Denver, Colorado; [memb.] International Clover Poetry Association National Writers Club, American Society of Technical Writers Society of Children's Book Writers, Nevada Lodge No. 4, A.F. and A.M. (Worshipful Master 1992), York Rite and Scottish Rite Masonic Lodges; [hon.] Honorary Doctor of Divinity Degree (October 1976), Ordained an High Priest (May 1986). Military Decorations, served in the US Army, US Navy, US Air Force, Gold Award for Creative Thinking (May 1985); [oth. writ.] "The Great Book of Life", *Clover Collection of Verse*, Vol., VI, P. 228 (1973). "The Advantage of Rtd!", *The Metropolitan*, (April 9, 1980), P. 6.

TAYLOR, MARGARET H.
[b.] 22 October 1933, Paisley, Scotland; [p.] Ben and Sarah Hamilton; [m.] Joe Ben Taylor, 28 March 1953; [ch.] Joanne, Tracy, Craig; [ed.] High School plus; [occ.] Housewife; [memb.] Sandia Presbyterian Church Chancel Com., Misson Com, S.P.W. Com; [hon.] Graduated 2nd Top of School for year; [oth. writ.] "Telephone Talks," "Mountains," "Houses that Become Homes," "My Garden of Flowers"; [pers.] I am reminded of my school days and the teacher who taught our poetry class, she stressed rhyme and rhythm.; [a.] Barrhead, Scotland

TAYLOR, MEREDITH
[b.] June 21, 1982, Cedar Rapids, IA; [p.] Robert and Mary Taylor; [ed.] Lakeview Elementary 6 yrs., Solon Jr. High - 2 yrs.; [memb.] Solon Jr. High Drama Dept., Band, Chorus; [hon.] Choral Solo Award, Band Solo Award, Choral Leadership Award (2 yrs.); [oth. writ.] Various selections for school activities and classes; [pers.] A wise young woman once said "this is the beginning of the rest of your life." That wise young woman was me.; [a.] Solon, IA

TEHENSKY, SANDRA KELLEY
[pen.] Melody Kelley; [b.] August 6, 1940, Hillsboro, OH; [p.] William C. Kelley, Beatrice I. Trefz; [m.] Divorced; [ch.] Ann, Susan (2 grandchildren Alyssa and Raymond); [ed.] Attended Miami Univ of Ohio 2 1/2 years; [occ.] Chiropractic Office Mgr, and Health and Nutrition Counselor; [memb.] Life Extension Foundation; [oth. writ.] Poetry - 15 years children's stories - 6 years (my two beautiful grandchildren inspire my children's stories.); [pers.] I turn to writing poetry when my feelings are so overwhelming and powerful that I can't express them any other way. It makes beautiful sense out of the fragments and gives me back an integrated wholeness, to be able to share that wholeness with others is truly one of the greatest joys of a lifetime - magnificent!; [a.] Livermore, CA

TENNISON, BETTY JANE
[pen.] Betty J. Tennison; [b.] December 5, 1942, Boynton, OK; [p.] Jimmy and Ruby Tennison; [ch.] Lisa, Bruce, Yohawna, Gerald; [ed.] Charles Page H/S, Sand Springs, OR, 1961, Superior Tractor Trailer Training, 1985; [occ.] Professional Transport Driver; [memb.] CLUW, National Women's Coalition Labor Union for Women, Teamsters Union; [hon.] Certified Safe Ryder, Driver and Interstate Certified Safe Driver; [oth. writ.] I am currently writing a book called *Liberteez' of a Lady Trucker*. About OTR Professional Lady Truckers; [pers.] I have a mission on the road, to pass on the message of Jesus Christ as Lord over my life.; [a.] Tulsa, OK

TEPE, LAURA L.
[pen.] Victoria Lane DeLancey; [b.] February 9, 1952, Oceanside, NY; [p.] Clarence Tepe, Victoria Tepe; [ed.] West Babylon High School; [occ.] Technician, Nynex, Long Island, NY; [oth. writ.] This is my first published writing.; [pers.] I love nature, both Flora and Fauna. My favorite poet is Elizabeth Barrett Browning.; [a.] Southold, NY

TERRY, JENAIRE
[b.] May 29, 1979, Washington, DC; [p.] Paula Terry and Nelson Terry; [ed.] Benjamin Banneker Academic Senior High School; [hon.] *Who's Who Among American High School Students*, Honor Roll; [a.] Washington, DC

TERWILLIGER, ELIZABETH
[pen.] "Elizabeth"; [b.] October 11, 1923, Putnam, CT; [p.] George and Mildred Slater; [m.] Wesley A. Terwilliger (Deceased), June 7, 1945; [ch.] Claudia, Donna, Ann, Carol, Linda Wendy, David and Paul; [ed.] Killingly High School; [occ.] Retired; [memb.] South Killingly Church Highland Grange #113; [oth. writ.] About 100 other poems; [pers.] The world has been very kind to me. I would like to leave behind some positive and loving poems.; [a.] Danielson, CT

TERWILLIGER, JACK
[b.] June 10, 1914, Covelo, CA; [p.] Newton and Nellie Terwilliger; [m.] Ruby Avery Terwilliger, October 24, 1944; [occ.] Own and Operate Lapidary Store (with Wife); [memb.] Grange - Scribe, many Lapidary Organizations; [oth. writ.] Many articles and poems published in Lapidary Magazines (*Lapidary Journal*) (*Gem and Mineral*) and Club Bulletins - I publish a monthly news bulletin for a Lapidary Club.; [pers.] Ruby and I are both veterans of World War II (Navy) I enjoy writing; [a.] Fresno, CA

THAI, SAM
[b.] September 15, 1975, Da Nang, Vietnam; [p.] Hap Tu Thai, Cam Ai Tran; [ed.] Monterey Highlands Elementary, Mark Keppel High, Pasadena City College; [occ.] Advertising Consultant, *Saigon Times Newspaper*, Rosemead, CA; [pers.] My writings have been influenced by my father, who is a renowned poet in Vietnam as well as the Vietnamese communities in the United States.; [a.] Rosemead, CA

THAYER, PATRICIA
[b.] March 18, 1941, Rochester, MI; [p.] John and Junemarie Pihajlic; [m.] Robert Thayer, June 26, 1965; [ch.] Paulette, Michelle, Nichole, Anthony; [ed.] Rochester High School, Delima Jr. College (Convent) (Writing Class) Mid-Michigan Community College; [occ.] Artist and Writer; [memb.] Secular Franciscan Order, Focola're and Cursillo Movements and Hospice of Clare County; [hon.] First Prize, Parting Shots Competition - Iliad Press. National Authors Registry's 1996 President's Award for Literary Excellence. Several Honorable mention Awards; [oth. writ.] Several poems published in Local newspapers, *Leaves* magazine, and Numerous Anthologies of Poetry. Chapbook - Daylight Wishes, Night Time Dreams.; [pers.] My writing reflects deep religious beliefs as well as touches the humorous and heart touching moments of my life - I believe everyone can identify with and compare to their own life - experiences.; [a.] Clare, MI

THEE, CHRISTIE
[b.] September 12, 1971, Winston-Salem, NC; [p.] Grace and Darrell Richardson; [m.] Michael Thee, November 20, 1993; [ch.] Caroline Alexis Thee (age 2); [ed.] Associates of Applied Science in Paralegal Studies at Parks Junior College in Denver, finishing my Bachelor's of Science in Business Administration at the University of Phoenix; [occ.] Pre-Kindergarten Teacher; [hon.] 1993 Colorado Undergraduate Scholarship Award recipient, President's List and Dean's List, Graduated Summa Cum Laude at Parks Junior College; [pers.] I would like to thank my daughter Caroline for giving me the inspiration to write the poem. Thank you for giving me the best years of my life.; [a.] Denver, CO

THIBEAULT, MATTHEW T.
[b.] March 4, 1969, Boston, MA; [p.] Richard and Patricia Thibeault; [ed.] Assabet Valley Reg. Voc. High School; [occ.] Locksmith, 1st Security Services Corp. Shrewsbury, MA; [hon.] Southwest Asia Medal with 2 Bronze Stars, Combat Action Ribbon, Kuwait Liberation Medal, National Defence Service Medal, Good Conduct Medal, Sea Service Ribbon with Bronze Star and 3rd Award Rifle Expert.; [pers.] I wrote this poem this sitting in the sand of Saudi Arabia. I was in the United States Marines Corps. and served in Desert Shield and Storm. "Semper Fi!"; [a.] Hudson, MA

THOMAS, CHRISTINA K.
[pen.] Ckt or Chrissie; [b.] November 10, 1952, Indianapolis, IN; [p.] Lloyd and Laura Thomas; [ed.] George Washington High, Stephen Foster Elementary; [occ.] Disabled/Volunteer; [oth. writ.] I've written many poems to vent my anger in a more positive and humorous way.; [pers.] I've met many unique people (especially MDs) who give me a lot of material. I've also been inspired by Dick Summer's romantic poetry.; [a.] Indianapolis, IN

THOMAS, ERNEST L.
[pen.] E.L. Thomas, Tommy Thomas; [b.] October 5, 1946, Jackson, FL; [p.] Ernest L. Thomas, Cora Lee Thomas; [ch.] Kaythern Lillie, Amanda Lynn; [ed.] Andrew Jackson High, Florida Junior High College, Florida Tech. College; [occ.] Sergeant Jacksonville Sheriff's Office; [memb.] Free and Accepted Mason's, Scottish Rite Masons, Shrine, Life Member DAV, Life Member VFW, National Police Blockhouse Assoc. Florida Search Dog Network Masters and Wardens Assoc., Florida Lodge of research.; [hon.] Vietnam Service Medal, Republic of South Vietnam Service Medal, National Defense Medal, Knight Commander Court of Honor Scottish Rite, Officer of the Month Jacksonville Sheriff's Office; [oth. writ.] Articles for *N.P.B.A. Nose News, F.S.D.N.* news letter numerous unpublished poems of Vietnam and poems of romance.; [pers.] I love life and its beauty and I believe in the Masons' creed "The Brotherhood of Man Under the Fatherhood of God," also that all life is precious and should not be taken lightly.; [a.] Jacksonville, FL

THOMAS, JEANNETTE EILEEN
[pen.] Jet, Net-Net; [b.] March 6, 1981, Norfolk, VA; [p.] Larry Joe and Evonne Jean Thomas; [ed.] I attended public school until seventh grade, the next year I started Atlantic Chores Christian School; [occ.] Student; [hon.] I have received awards in Elementary School in academics - especially in English and Writing. Also for attendance and citizenship in Intermediate School.; [oth. writ.] I have written other short stories and poetry which have been seen by English teachers who have told me I had a definite talent.; [pers.] Once again I give God all credit. And I thank the judges for allowing me a start for oncoming success.; [a.] Chesapeake, VA

THOMPSON, JEANNETTE N.
[pen.] Jean Thompson; [b.] June 1, 1938, Tappan, NY; [p.] Arthur Nall, Miriam Nall; [m.] Richard E. Thompson, October 13, 1962; [ch.] Kara Susan, Mark David; [ed.] Nyack Jr - Sr. High School, Keuka College, Famous Writers School; [occ.] Customer Service/Sales Associate- Plow and Hear - Madison, VA; [pers.] If poetry sparks love and compassion in a person's heart, then my time has been well-spent in writing it.; [a.] Madison, VA

THOMPSON, LOUISE J.
[b.] December 12, 1912, Petersburg, VA; [p.] Sidney Jackson, Ida Jackson (Deceased); [m.] Edward Thompson (Deceased), June 1, 1946; [ed.] Peabody High School, Petersburg, VA Virginia State University, B.S., M.S.; [occ.] Retired-Assn't. Prof., V.S.U. Principal, retired-Elem. Sch. (Petersburg, VA); [memb.] Alpha Kappa Mu Honor Society, Alpha Kappa Alpha Sorority, Inc., Va. state Univ. Alumni Assn., American Heart Assn., Retired Deacon, Gillfield Baptist Church; [hon.] Honorary Degree, Doctor of Humanities, Woman of the Year Award, Gillfield Baptist Church, Award-Outstanding Service, American Baptist Churches of the South, ABC/USA; [oth. writ.] Poems published in workshops, several unpublished poems; [pers.] Motivation from mother, public school and classes in literature in college, also workshops at American Baptist Assembly, at Greenlake, Wisconsin.

THOMPSON, PATRICIA P.
[b.] March 17, 1928, Baltimore, MD; [p.] Dr. and Mrs. Owen Parrott; [m.] Dr. Aston Thompson, November 1953; [ch.] Two sons; [ed.] Roosevelt High - Dayton Ohio/University of Dayton - George Washington University-Washington DC - Trinity College - Wash DC. BS. Degree in Education - Minor Teacher College - Wash. DC; [occ.] Retired Teacher; [memb.] Institute of Children's Literature. Participated on local level in the Comer Project - a system designed to improve strategies for more effective teaching.; [hon.] Certified for achievement in participation in administering Pre School and Day Care - (Early Childhood Education - Trinity College - Certificate Awarded for achievement in developing childrens thinking and language skills. Trinity College; [oth. writ.] Include two stories and many poems. The poems when acted out became a very effective method in teaching skills at the Pre-Kindergarten and Kids level. The children and parents became full participants in putting on a show at the end of the year.; [pers.] Having grown up in a family of very caring people as well as educators and achievers, I knew at a very young age that I would teach. I wanted to mold the very young child with a sense of self and dignity. I wanted to give back all my parents had given me.; [a.] Reston, VA

THOMPSON, SHELEY
[b.] May 12, 1973, Brooklyn, NY; [p.] Virginia Thompson; [ch.] Joshua Thompson (age 10); [ed.] Eastern District High School, Katharine Gibbs School; [occ.] Legal Secretary Simpson Thacher and Bartlett, NY, NY; [pers.] Anything I write is a reflection of my soul that I share with others in the hopes that they will gain from it something whole and meaningful.; [a.] Brooklyn, NY

THOMPSON, SUE
[pen.] Sue T.; [b.] November 21, 1944, Jacksonville, IL; [p.] Marshall Fulton, Late Marcella Fulton; [m.] Divorced; [ch.] Jeffery H., Eric A.; [ed.] Elementary and High School, Paw Paw, Illinois, Copley Memorial Hospital, Aurora Illinois Diploma Nursing School; [occ.] Registered Nurse at Salem Memorial Hospital; [oth. writ.] I have never considered myself a poet or even liking poetry much, but I did write a few personal poems when I was much younger.; [pers.] I have been in transition the past year and a half looking for a different path to follow. I met Jessica Firewalker who helped me to go within and find my own. At the same time I began writing about my growth with help from, what I call, "Spirit." The ups and downs of "Sue" have been my way to release, grow, and find peace "within."; [a.] Keizer, OR

THOMPSON, TRAIT
[b.] April 17, 1978, San Angelo, TX; [p.] Donald and Tracey Kiesling; [ed.] Graduated Magna Cum Laude from Brady High School, Brady, TX; [occ.] Student; [memb.] Grace Fellowship Church, Mason Cowboy Church; [hon.] Nat'l History and Gov't Award, Woodmen Award for American History, Lion's Honor Banquet, Rotary Student of the Month, Tennis Fighting Heart, Principal's Excellence Award, Chemistry Award.; [oth. writ.] I have written some short stories. They are "The Posse," "Gunfight at Red Canyon," and "Where Do My Socks Go".; [pers.] I write for my own pleasure and satisfaction. I seek to live through my characters in every situation. My work is sometimes entertaining. Often, I seek to inspire.; [a.] Brady, TX

THORPE, AMANDA
[b.] December 29, 1980, Fridley, MN; [p.] Mike Thorpe, Ruth Bayless; [ed.] Farmington High; [occ.] Student; [hon.] Dance Awards, Honor Student; [oth. writ.] Several unpublished poems; [pers.] The poem "Light and Dark" is a Tribute to Jeri Thorpe, Laurie Stetson and Glen Thorpe who all passed away a short time ago.; [a.] Farmington, MN

THUMM, CORINNE
[pen.] Corinne Thumm; [b.] May 6, 1982, Philadelphia; [p.] Barry and Karen Thumm; [ed.] Will be starting freshman year at Overbrook High School Pine Hill, NY; [occ.] Student, child, friend; [memb.] Library; [hon.] Journalism Award. Sixth Grade, Citizenship Award, Sixth Grade at Dr. Albert M. Bean School; [oth. writ.] Some other stories and poems were published in school newspaper; [pers.] My best friend, Jennifer D. Fernando, has inspired me greatly; [a.] Pine Hill, NJ

THURROTT, EDNA BLANCHARD
[pen.] Edna Thurrott; [b.] August 28, 1921, McDuffie County, Thomson, GA; [p.] James and Frankie Blanchard; [m.] Richard (Dich) Thurrott, October 25, 1942; [ch.] Frankie Thurrott II; [ed.] Trudy Lorrance Kophart Prieadmont College 3 yrs. Georgia State College for Women, Missionary of God's appointment. Influenced as a youth by great poets, Longfellow, Poe among others.; [occ.] Writer of Poetry and Personality Profiles.; [memb.] Presbyterian Church at Sequim Wash International Poets of North America and A.A.R.P. A Senior Organization of Spiritual, talented and inspiring people.; [hon.] The greatest honor is to belong and the great family that God has established - a bible believing and spirit filled people who live by faith and direction of a Holy God, Creator of all.; [pers.] My life is built with nothing else less than Jesus Christ, his Jesus is a friend to see that accept righteousness and He is accept his teaching my light, the star that guide as the presence I feel. And the Heavenly Home, Eternal Life.; [a.] Sequim, WA

TIOGANGCO, PAMELA LEOLANI
[pen.] Leo; [b.] January 28, 1954, Hilo, HI; [p.] Ezekiel and Lydia Pereira; [m.] Melvin Tiogangco; [pers.] To you mom, my dearest friend, Aloha Wau IA oe. Leolani

TOLBERT, JENNIFER
[b.] May 2, 1979, Rochester, NY; [p.] Daniel and Virginia Tubiolo, Carol Travis and Rocky Tolbert; [ed.] 11th Grade - at Raytown High School in Raytown, Missouri; [occ.] Student; [pers.] Peace, love, recycle, flowers. Dedicated to Dasha, Shorty, Hippie, and space - Casey. I love all of ya.; [a.] Kansas City, MO

TOMEL, DANA
[b.] May 21, 1958, Alameda, CA; [pers.] Our lives unfold a moment at a time. When I write a poem I have never been more present.

TOMPSETT, MARY L.
[b.] April 25, 1927, Racine, WI; [p.] Frederick Schulte, Genevieve F. Schulte; [m.] Joseph J. Tompsett Sr., May 3, 1947; [ch.] Mary Catherine, Patricia Ann, Robert William, Thomas Richard, Joseph James Jr., James Michael; [ed.] Washington Park High School, Marquette University, De Paul Rehabilitation Hospitals (Counselor Training Program); [occ.] Semi-Retired; [oth. writ.] I have titles and general outlines for four books and am currently working on a poetry collection.; [pers.] I have been inspired by the resiliency within all creation. I believe a harmonious balance of mind, body, and spirit is necessary to connect with the universal good.; [a.] Racine, WI

TORGERSON, GERALD ALLEN
[pen.] Gerald Torgerson; [b.] May 19, 1952, St. Louis, MO; [p.] Arnold S. and Edith Gray; [m.] Bonnie Sue, June 1, 1974; [ch.] Eric A. and Tina L.; [ed.] B.S. Bus. Mgt. Univ. of MO.; [occ.] Restaurant-Owner/Oper.; [memb.] Rest Acco. of greater St. Louis; [hon.] Member Nat. Honor Society; [oth. writ.] Short story "A Farmer's Faith"; [pers.] I adhere to the Emersonian Philosophy, a champion's just reward is to know that they did it.; [a.] Daphne, AL

TORRES, AMBAR D.
[b.] January 4, 1987, Ponce, PR; [p.] Lissette Laboy; [ed.] Third Grade, P.S. 148 Queens N.Y.; [occ.] Student; [hon.] P.S. 148 Honor Roll; [oth. writ.] "Weekend in P.R.", "Alone" - published in *Anthology of Poetry by Young Americans* 1995 Edition.; [pers.] "My culture, feelings and family are my inspiration".; [a.] Hempstead, NY

TOTLEROW, BONNIE JEAN
[b.] December 27, 1953, Huntington, LI, NY; [p.] Beatrice and Charles Craig; [m.] Divorced; [ed.] BA in Psychology, May - 1980, UN of Worth Caroline - at Chapel Hill North Caroline; [oth. writ.] I have written at least 300 pages of poetry and I also want to write a lot of psychology.; [pers.] I am a recovering alcoholic and a recovering psychiatric student who less than a year also was the sickest person on the ward of a book ward of a mental hospital for almost ten years. I have a complete philosophy about life and a strict ward code net, thank souvenirs I have never broken despite either illness I had a spontaneous record from atmosphere to whom I give no for except myself about someone you a few very dim relapses. I'm basically English Celtic is heritage and I found watch hospital to be as cruel places as pressure and prejudice against mental patients so cruel and harm and the mental health establishment so cruel and deceiving to mental patient and the respected by the article world and so carefully of the life of their what's that schizophenisis are in a familiar position is pre-civil was blank people in treatments incidentally I was pushed is the mental hospital partedly for working poetry. The poem that is in this edition of the book is one of about 20 poems that was written after I made love to my present love, a beautiful young grade man for the past time in the boy'a Gotham in the hospital. I am presently still in the hospital as some as you are but I can't get out of the hospital for the simple recovering that the Doctor doesn't like me, not for research of mental health. I would like some day to become a poet, a theoretical psychologist and a mental patient activist, thank you for reading the poem.

TOWNSEND, DOROTHY
[b.] December 6, 1927, Dtaten Island, NY; [p.] Irma & Antonio Cappasola; [m.] Edward Townsend (widow), April 17, 1953; [ch.] Blaine, Blake & Edward; [ed.] High School - P.S. 12 elementary school; [pers.] When I wrote this poem I thought of millions of other older people - Senior Citizens.; [a.] Atlanta, GA

TOY, CYNTHIA W.
[b.] September 5, 1973, Seattle, WA; [p.] Sheakfay Toy, OI Sheung Toy; [ed.] Cleveland H.S. High Comm. College Seattle; [occ.] Graphic Design and Illus. Student. Hostess St Grand China Rest. Kirkland, WA; [pers.] My writings reflect my inner thoughts and feelings of the love and the lost in my life, when deep emotions, emerge from the hidden. To my family and friends, thanx for your support and belief in me. And a special thanx to a very special person A. J. you were one thus made this all a reality. Thanx so much.; [a.] Seattle, WA

TRAINER, JOSEPH RAY
[pen.] Gladstone Paisley; [b.] January 28, 1944, San Angelo, TX; [p.] Joseph Houston Trainer/Lita Esther Ray; [m.] Maribeth Northstrum (Deceased), September 23, 1964; [ch.] Aisha Marie Trainer; [ed.] Several High School in Houston, TX; [occ.] Song Writer; [memb.] National Rifle Association, Rock and Roll Hall of Fame and Museum; [oth. writ.] "Stand Up And Shout" - recorded by The Tubes, "Crystal Clear" recorded by Jackie DeShannon, many unpublished poems and songs; [pers.] A lot of people put down the 60's but the message then was let's love each other and we need that desperately now! More than ever! Favorites: Bob Dylan, Paul Simon, Leonard Cohen, Robert Hunter; [a.] Phoenix, AZ

TRIOLO, PHILIP
[b.] June 20, 1985, Huffman Estates, IL; [p.] Luanne and Joe Triolo; [ed.] Heritage Lakes School, Carol Stream, IL K-4; [occ.] Entering 5th grade at Jay Stream School, C.S IL, Newspaper delivery; [memb.] Just Say No Club, Cub Scouts, Our Savior Lutheran Church; [a.] Carol Stream, IL

TRUE, TORY
[b.] August 28, 1979, Pocatello, ID; [p.] Judy and Frank True; [ed.] High School Senior; [occ.] Student; [memb.] National Honors Society, Thespians Club, Pop band (8th Grade); [hon.] *Who's Who Among American High School Students* (3 years in a row), Young Authors (2 years), Kiwanis Hope for America Award, Presidential Academic Fitness Award, Best Science Student Award, Best Actor (High School Drama); [oth. writ.] Several short stories, a collection of poems, and one novel (all unpublished); [pers.] I'm a teenager, but I'm not a prep, stones, nerd, or band geek. I don't wear chain wallets, or anything by Nike or Calvin Klein. I don't ride a skateboard, nor am I an anarchist. I'm simply not a trendy done most others my age are, and I'm proud of it.; [a.] Pocatello, ID

TSCHAPPAT, JO
[pen.] Jo Tschappat; [b.] January 30, 1955, Chillicothe, OH; [p.] Millard and Sadie Caudill (Deceased); [ed.] Degree in Organic Chemistry Shawnee State, Degree in Cosmetology - Teaching Certificate; [occ.] Self Employed Beautician Owner - Operator; [memb.] Aviation Safety Wings Program, Church; [oth. writ.] I write all the time - it is a release of my inner feelings to adjust to an ever changing world on a day to day basis.; [pers.] To always live a life of giving and harmony within myself. I want to always look for contentment, and human compassion in this world we live in today.; [a.] Piketon, OH

TUCKER, GLADYS
[b.] January 20; [p.] Bertha and Toler Tucker; [ed.] Valley High School San Francisco State University; [occ.] Training and Development Specialist; [memb.] Human Resources Affiliations; [hon.] Sunday School and Vacation Bible School honors as a Teacher; [oth. writ.] Essays, poems, songs; [pers.] As a child of God, I feel privileged to share my expression of his love through his gift to me. If my writing directs someone to know that God "is" than I am blessed; [a.] San Francisco, CA

TURNAGE JR., CALVIN RAY
[b.] November 18, 1964, Fort Worth, TX; [p.] Calvin Ray Turnage Sr., Sarah J. Wilbanks; [m.] Mary E. Turnage, August 25, 1990; [ch.] Nathaniel Ray Turnage; [ed.] B.S. Arlington Baptist College M.B.S. Bethany Theological Seminary; [occ.] Pastor; [memb.] Marine Corps League Pastor of Trinity Baptist Church of Azle, Texas; [hon.] Graduated Summa Cum Laude from Bethany Theological Seminary; [pers.] "Nathan's Lullaby" was written to sing my newborn son to sleep.

My influences are Dr. John R. Rice, Dr. Jack Hyles, and Dr. Bob Smith.; [a.] Forth Worth, TX

TURNER, PAMELA KAY
[b.] November 8, 1978, Aurora, CO; [p.] Robert Turner, Karen Pasveer; [ed.] Aurora Central High, Bel-Rea Institute of Animal Technology; [occ.] Student; [pers.] Special thanks to my family, Shawna, Bud, Chris, Shade and Tammy McManus for all of their support. I love them all.; [a.] Aurora, CO

TURNER, STANLEY LEE
[pen.] Stanley Lee Turner; [b.] November 3, 1964, Lagrange, IL; [p.] Llyod E. and Lorraine M. Turner; [ed.] Dropped out of the 11th grade, 5 years later I Achieved my G.E.D.; [occ.] Drifter; [memb.] Jesus Kingdom; [hon.] Born Again; [oth. writ.] I have several although I've never published anything. I guess you have to begin some where I'm starting here.; [pers.] Writing poetry is an expression of thoughts. For me, it's feelings deep within that I have problems expressing Socially. Sometimes a pencil can be my best friend.; [a.] Venice, FL

TWINER, SARA
[pen.] Sarah Twiner; [b.] December 11, 1979, Hazlehurst, MS; [p.] Marvin and Phyllis Twiner; [ed.] Wesson Attendance Center, Fox Elementary School, North Country Junior High School; [occ.] Student; [hon.] Honor Roll Student; [oth. writ.] A non-published fictional story, that is still being written.; [pers.] I wrote this poem in memory of a friend who had been killed. This sometimes proves that you don't realize how much you care about someone until they are gone.; [a.] Hazlehurst, MS

TYNER, NICHOLE
[b.] March 9, 1981, Charleston, SC; [p.] Tom and Lynda Tyner; [ed.] 9th grade Wando High, cont. Education; [occ.] Student; [memb.] Wexford Poetry Society; [oth. writ.] Poems published in *Interludes*, Wexford Society; [pers.] A true poet can understand the feelings of the poems, just not the words.; [a.] Isle of Palms, SC

TYSON, BRIAN WILLIAM
[pen.] B. W. Tyson; [b.] January 5, 1973, Albuquerque, NM; [p.] William and Nancy Tyson; [ed.] Farmington High. San Juan College. New Mexico State Univ. University of New Mexico; [occ.] Student and Waiter; [memb.] Lambda Chi Alpha Fraternity ZTZ NMSU. And the Local Library; [pers.] If there is life, there is rhythm, It's all good! There is Poetry.; [a.] Albuquerque, NM

UNGER, TOM W.
[pen.] Tom; [b.] March 17, 1950, Reading, PA; [p.] Grace A. Unger, Walter R. Unger; [m.] Bonnie M. Unger, April 24, 1971; [ch.] Joy Lynn Petrie; [ed.] Grad. 12th grade Rdg. High School Vo-Tech Ed. Plumbing, Welding, Electrical. Computer Training Course Certificate of Completion; [occ.] Maint. Mech.; [hon.] Six years in Navy-Honorable Discharge as a Hull Maint. Technician; [oth. writ.] "The Silver Years," "My Daughter's Life," "My Daughter's Wedding"; [pers.] I wish to help in the writings of poetry for influencing other people in hopes of reading of poems for enjoyment and relaxation.; [a.] Mohrsville, PA

VACCARO, VIRGINIA M.
[b.] May 11, 1960, Mahopac, NY; [p.] Thomas and Josephine Vaccaro; [m.] Bart J. Van Poollen, June 23, 1993; [ch.] Nicolas Jeroen; [ed.] Metropolitan State College; [pers.] In memory of Thomas Charles Vaccaro.

VAN DOMELEN, LAURA
[b.] December 12, 1978, Neenah, WI; [p.] Mary and Jerry Van Domelen; [ed.] Kaukauna High School; [occ.] Student; [memb.] Blood Donor for Red Cross, member of Holy Cross Catholic Church, where I am active as a cantor and altar server.; [hon.] *Who's Who Among American H.S. Students*, Honor Roll; [oth. writ.] Poems, articles in school newspaper.; [pers.] I strive to follow Albert Einstein's saying: Great spirits have often encountered violent opposition from mediocre minds. Also, we should always seize the day - Carpe Diem.; [a.] Kaukauna, WI

VAN DOMMELEN, LAUREN
[b.] March 8, 1982, Virginia; [p.] Katherine and Kenneth Van Dommelen; [a.] Cockeysville, MD

VAN DYKE, YVONNE VIRGINIA
[b.] March 24, 1973, Winchester, VA; [p.] Ann K. Van Dyke, H. Ray Van Dyke; [ed.] John Kerr Elementary School - Winchester, VA, Daniel Morgan Middle School - Winchester, VA, Handley High School - Winchester, VA, George Mason University; [occ.] Business Assistant, Women's Center, Vienna, VA and work at Barnes and Noble Book Store; [hon.] Scholarship of $3,000 to George Mason University in the field of writing. (Received Senior Year of High school), Bachelor of Arts Degree in English at George Mason University - 1996; [oth. writ.] Editor of *Images*, a High School Literary Magazine.; [pers.] Every individual views life in their own unique way. I think it is important to share that way.; [a.] Chantilly, VA

VAN LEHEL, CAROL
[b.] January 27, 1947, Wichita, KS; [m.] (4th) Barry Reichert, 1988; [ch.] Two; [ed.] Wake Forest U., Russell Sage C., Renselaer P.I.; [occ.] Government Computer Sales; [oth. writ.] Novel in progress, Chevy Chase, "Gloria Steinem's sister was a Chevy Chase housewife."; [pers.] "I am most interested in how each person's conversation inside their own head is only defined by what they know at the moment, and what their own experiences and relationships are. Each life is unique—for the three score and ten—or more or less—we are on this earth. You cannot be the same person you would have been had you been born, say 30,000 years ago living in the caves in Southern Europe—or even if you were born at the same date and time in Rhodesia or Mongolia. This is what fascinates me the most about the human experience."; [a.] Kelly Island Homestead, MT

VAN NESS, DEBRA ANN
[b.] April 11, 1964, Madison, AL; [p.] James and Maxine York; [m.] James Eric Van Ness, June 24, 1994; [ed.] Associates Applied Sciences Tulsa Junior College, Tulsa, OK; [occ.] Registered Nurse; [oth. writ.] Many poems, all of which are unpublished, most of them included in my manuscript titled, *From the Light of Sun to Storms of Darkness*; [pers.] I've never quite understood how poetry comes through me, Inspiration occurs during intense emotion. My works arise from overwhelming spiritual awe, depths of dark depression, or moments of wisdom and reflection. My poetry is symbolic of light, darkness and seasons.; [a.] Tulsa, OK

VANDEN-EYNDEN, FRANK
[pen.] Fran Van; [b.] September 2, 1944, Cincinnati; [p.] Marcellus and Agnes Vanden-Eynden; [m.] Marguerite Crowley, July 3, 1980; [ch.] Marlaine, David, Anthony; [ed.] St. Francis High, Duns Scotus College, St. Leonard College, University of Dayton; [occ.] Music Director, St. Luke Church, Palm Harbor, FL; [memb.] National Association of Pastoral Musicians, Directors of Music Ministry Division; [hon.] Editor of High School magazine quarterly, Brown and White, Magna Cum Laude HS graduate, B.A. in Philosophy, M.A. in Theology M.Div. in Ministry; [oth. writ.] Anthems for Sundays and Feasts, fifty selected Psalms, English chants for Sundays and Feasts, prose poetry reflections; [pers.] I'm open to freely translating poetic texts from Latin, Greek, and Hebrew classics into modern idioms, images, rhythms and rhymes.; [a.] Palm Harbor, FL

VANDERVORT, THOMAS RICHARD
[b.] February 15, 1978, Lexington, KY; [p.] Darrel and Marsha; [ed.] Graduate Corbin High School, Freshman At Bethany College; [occ.] Student; [memb.] International Thespians Society, Christian Youth Fellowship; [hon.] Valedictorian class of '96, Senior English Award; [oth. writ.] Healing, and other short stories, as well as hundreds of poems and spontaneous prose.; [pers.] We are the new metronome, like Kerouac and Cassady we must set the tempo for a generation to dance to.; [a.] Corbin, KY

VASKO, TIMOTHY S.
[b.] September 12, 1960, Boulder, CO; [p.] Helen Catherine Vasko, Frank Theodore Vasko; [m.] Tina M. T. Vasko, June 8, 1986; [ch.] Timmy age 8, and Jillian age 5; [ed.] Broomfield High, University of Colorado, Undergraduate, University of Denver, MBA; [occ.] Distributor of Health and Wellness Products and System, Strategic Consulting, Freelance Writing; [memb.] Various outdoor and mountaineering organizations; [oth. writ.] *The Tiny Little Man*, children's book, "Out of the Fog and Into Fatherhood", article, "The Pyramid of Life and Balance, Philosophy"; [pers.] Knowledge in life comes from experience and understanding. Purpose comes from passing understanding on to others.

VASSERMAN, ANGELA
[b.] October 5, 1974; [p.] Alla Vasserman, Leon Vasserman; [ed.] Nicolet High School, currently I am Junior at University of Wisconsin - Milwaukee; [occ.] Student; [memb.] Criminal Justice Student Association; [hon.] At high school - Best Achievement Award; [oth. writ.] Currently submitted several works for publication in a local literary newspaper *Xpressions*.; [pers.] My writings always are honest reflection of the way I see and feel about the world and certain things in this world. I try to capture my time the way it really is.; [a.] Milwaukee, WI

VASSIOS, DESIREE
[pen.] Desiree Vassios; [b.] April 28, 1958, Flagler, CO; [p.] Gus and Vel Vassios; [ed.] B.S. Colorado State University, Fashion Merchandising; [occ.] Trainer - Train Managerial Skills - Great West Life; [memb.] Trinity United Methodist Church, American Church, American Society for Training and Development; [oth. writ.] None published. Currently working on first novel also entitled *The Swan And The Saint Of The Night*.; [pers.] I write for creative expression and to relax.; [a.] Denver, CO

VASTINE, AMANDA
[b.] August 28, 1983, Park Ridge, IL; [p.] Jim Vastine, Lois Vastine; [ed.] Lake Louise K-5, Gray M. Sanborn-6, Walter R. Sundling Jr. High-7; [occ.] Student; [hon.] President's Academic Achievement Award and Honor Roll-4.0; [pers.] I write about my personal experiences or whatever comes to my mind and inspires me.; [a.] Palarine, IL

VEGA, FELIX L.
[b.] March 9, 1949, New York City; [p.] Jennie Anglada, Felix L. Vega Sr.; [m.] Esther; [ch.] Felix III, Anthony, Joanne, Jennifer; [ed.] Samuel Groupers Vo and Tech High School; [occ.] Electrician -Local #3 International Brotherhood of Electrical Workers; [memb.] Santiago Iglesias Educational Society - Bronx Acorn Electrical Club - Westchester Mechanics Assn.

VENOSA, DAWN M.
[pen.] Dawn M. Venosa; [b.] June 11, 1976, Staten Island; [p.] Diane and Richard Venosa; [ed.] St. Joseph-by-the-Sea High School, S.V.N.Y. Fashion Institute of Technology; [occ.] Public Relations Assistant and Free Lance Writer; [memb.] American Advertizing Federation, National Student Advertizing Competition; [hon.] Parade Young Columbus 1990; [oth. writ.] I am a published journalist who has written human interest stories. Currently, I have comprised an anthology of my work, which is entirely unpublished.; [pers.] My greatest influences are Charlotte and Emily Bronte, and Louisa May Alcott. Their combined works have served as a great source of inspiration; [a.] Staten Island, NY

VENTURA JR., ANIBAL
[b.] April 23, 1951, Brooklyn, NY; [p.] Anibal and Emma Ventura; [m.] Maritza Ventura, July 24, 1976; [ch.] Kennia, Ivette, Anibal III; [ed.] Central Islip, H.S., Suffolk Community College; [occ.] Counselor, Youth Allied: Bayshore Movers; [memb.] Adelante of Suffolk, Brentwood, NY; [oth. writ.] "A Lady Is Waiting," "Emilia," "The Starving Canvas," "A Mother's Armor."; [pers.] To my wife Maritza who understands my one true love and passion, writing. Thank you.; [a.] Shirley, NY

VERTER, IRVING I.
[pen.] Irving I. Verter; [b.] March 5, 1913, New York City; [p.] Abraham Minnie Verter; [m.] Tamara Verter, February 24, 1995, (First marriage 6/6/36 to 7/14/92); [ch.] Shieda, Regina, Allan and Marcia; [ed.] Normal College; [occ.] Retired; [memb.] City of Hope, National Association of Retired Federal Employees, 1199 Drug Union, Knights of Pythias, Kings Point Maris Club and Marriage Encounter; [hon.] Just some publishings when I was a member of "Marriage Encounter" on June 7, 1996 - I sent a check to you for De Luxe Hardbound Edition (53.95); [oth. writ.] Many other - poems of My Family and feelings and Love, and Funny poems.; [pers.] At 83, I write and tell jokes. I am still writing. When we were with Marriage Encounter, I write poetry and also feelings of love and family. My writings were printed in the Marriage Encounter paper. My first wife, Adele Verter and I were married 6/6/36. We were married for 56 years. When she was alive and with me, I had a desire to do a lot of writing and poetry. When we were in "Marriage Encounter", we were asked to write and give a speech regarding our lives, supposedly against another couple. Of course we won and this 45 minute speech was published in the paper. I still have a copy and I am both proud and happy for this ability and for you accepting my poem. I have many poems, some more than 20, 30 etc. lines. If you would want me to send some to you, it will be my pleasure (poems regarding family, love feelings etc.); [a.] Delray Beach, FL

VIERCK, JASON
[b.] October 5, 1977, Janesville, WI; [p.] David and Colleen Vierck; [ed.] Beginning school at the University of Wisconsin - Oshkosh in the fall of 1996. Major in Criminal Justice, Minor in Computer Science; [occ.] Student; [oth. writ.] Several unpublished poems and short stories.; [pers.] No matter how bad things may be today, there is always something to look forward to tomorrow.; [a.] Milton, WI

VIGIL, LENORE
[b.] July 4, 1927, Sydney, Australia; [p.] Jean Black, Jack Black; [m.] William Vigil, March 14, 1946; [ch.] Yvonne, Jeannie, Anita, William and Michael; [ed.] Presbyterian College, Australia Commerce High, San Francisco Beloit College, Beloit, Wisconsin, Robert Morgan Tech. College Miami, FL; [occ.] Retired Nurse, Housewife; [memb.] Delta Delta Delta Sorority; [hon.] Silver Seal Society for Scholarship, President of my Senior Class - Ballroom dancing Award; [oth. writ.] Many poems - unpublished; [pers.] Life is what you make it tomorrow will be a better day.; [a.] Miami, FL

VILLALOBOS, PHILLIP
[b.] August 2, 1986, Fontana, CA; [p.] Phil and Rose Villalobos; [ed.] Newman Elementary School 5th grade student. Enrolled in G.A.T.E.; [memb.] Boys Scouts of America 4 yrs.; [hon.] Academic Award for Highest Honor Roll, Principal's Honors Award. Perfect Attendance Award.; [oth. writ.] "Deserts", and submitted 2 short stories in *GATE Literary Journal*.; [pers.] I would like to let people know that poetry isn't just words, put together, but a gift from God.; [a.] Chino, CA

VILLALONA JR., OCTAVIO A.
[b.] June 1, 1975, Port Hueneme, CA; [p.] Detavio A. Villalona Sr., Evelyn C. Villalona; [m.] Kristin L. Villalona, April 20, 1996; [ed.] N.B. Forrest High School, Jacksonville, FL, F.D. Roosevelt High School, Brooklyn, N.Y. Junipero Serra High School, San Diego, Ca.; [occ.] U.S.M.C., Aviation Electrician, M.C.A.S. El Torro, Ca; [oth. writ.] Previously unpublished. I write only as a hobby.; [pers.] This poem was written just before my marriage and was entirely inspired by (and is entirely dedicated to) my present wife Kristin L. Villalona, whom I love with all my heart.; [a.] Tustin, CA

VILLANUEVA, CHRISTINE
[pen.] Christine V.; [b.] May 27, 1969, Albuquerque, NM; [p.] Vincent and Benita Villanueva; [ed.] Albuquerque High School Graduate Accounting Cert./Technical Vocational Institute, Creative Writing/T.V.I.; [occ.] Self-Employed Vocalist for nine years.; [memb.] New Mexico Songwriters Association.; [oth. writ.] Several songs including "Out Of My Life" and "Heart To Heart". (Both on my CD entitled *Christine*.); [pers.] Through my writing and my songs, I try to express the reality of life - the joy and the sorrow.; [a.] Albuquerque, NM

VINCENT, PEGGY
[pen.] Peggy Perkins Vincent; [b.] March 20, 1936, WV; [p.] Mary and Creed Chipps; [m.] Bill Perkins (Deceased) - Ellis Vincent, June 8, 1956, July 2, 1977; [ch.] Peggy Yates - Patricia Shingleton; [ed.] 12 yrs and some college, Income Tax Prep. w/occ., Real Est. Lic. w/occ.; [occ.] H/w; [pers.] Would have to write and ill. Children's short stories. Also I love poetry and would love to continue writing.; [a.] Bridgeport, WV

VINSAND, GERTRUDE JOSEPHINE
[pen.] Jo Vinsand; [b.] December 10, 1923, Hagerstown, MD; [p.] John Albert and Evelyn Wolf; [m.] Robert Vinsand (Deceased May 16, 1995), December 20, 1941; [ch.] Roberta Neat and Erik Vinsand; [ed.] Hagerstown Sr. High School South Potomac Jr. High, Mapleville Grade School (all in MD.); [occ.] Retired - 13 years as of 1980 Mgr Savings and Loan.; [memb.] Women of the Moose; [hon.] First Woman Instructress for Marchant Calculators. First Woman Br. Mgr. and Asst. Treas. of Wyman Park Federal S and L. First Woman Dean's List at U.S. Savings and Loan Conv. Palmer House Chicago.; [oth. writ.] Nothing recognized; [pers.] The first portion of "Unforgotten Love" was written 60 years ago. The second part after my love "Left This Earthly Realm" I will keep composing such writings as they reflect life!; [a.] Sebring, FL

VITUREIRA, GUSTAVO JAVIER
[pen.] G. Lear; [b.] September 28, 1966, Uruguay; [p.] Marina Diaz, Washington Vitureira; [m.] Jennifer Anne Venezia (Soon to be wed); [ch.] Nikolis Alexander, Bianca Jasmine; [ed.] High School at Forest Hills; [occ.] Musician; [oth. writ.] There are 2 records (CD's) published under the Name "Collision" of which I share the credit for writing. I am presently in a New band named "2 Blv Daffodils" which will soon be available for sale at stores.; [pers.] Write whatever is in your mind. Hurry, hurry don't waste time for life is really much too short 4, 1, 2, miss a passing thought.; [a.] Bayside, NY

VOLMERDING, DONNA J.
[b.] November 11, 1947, Fort Wayne, IN; [p.] Norwin Nahrwold, Dorothy Nahrwold; [m.] David Volmerding, October 9, 1971; [ch.] Matthew David and Sarah Jean; [ed.] Bachelor's Degree, Indiana University; [occ.] Reporter, *The News-Sentinel Newspaper*; [memb.] Lutheran Social Services of Indiana Public Relations Comm., Bethlehem Lutheran Church Drama Team; [oth. writ.] Columnist, *The News-Sentinel*, Writer, *Bowhunter Magazine*, Writer, *Balls and Strikes Magazine*, Writer, *The Fort Wayne Lutheran Newspaper*; [pers.] I like to write to move people's hearts, reach their minds and touch their souls.; [a.] Fort Wayne, IN

VOLZER, VIRGINIA M.
[b.] May 26, 1916, Canton, OH; [p.] Myrtle and James Ungashick; [m.] Charles G. Volzer, June 20, 1936; [ch.] Dennis and Timothy Volzer; [ed.] High School; [occ.] Retired; [oth. writ.] I have written many poems but never entered any contest; [pers.] When I write a poem I just write what I feel in my heart.; [a.] Canton, OH

VON FEISTER, NORMAN SYLVESTER III
[b.] September 11, 1931, Paradise, PA; [m.] Keiko Sano, The First Grand Countess: Sano Clan Japan; [oth. writ.] "Trust and Respect," Under Contract Publisher, North Western Publishing, Inc., Salt Lake City, Utah, Publisher, Mr. Jason Van Treese; [pers.] Wonderful Verse - Dedicated to all of the past, present, and future Presidents and First Ladies of the White House, Washington, D.C., Encouraged by: Keiko Sano, The Great Grand Countess of Sano Clan, Japan, and the following Employees of the U.S. Mint, San Francisco, California: Rev. J. Moorer, W. Goring, K. King, R. Hayes, E. Tatum, S. Irving, A. Carey, S. Chang, D. Lawton, L. Leonardo, and G. Mani. Respectfully: G. Edwards, C. Williams, L. Dickerson, and R. Hunter, July Third, One Thousand Nine Hundred and Ninety Six years after the death of our Lord.; [a.] San Francisco, CA

WAGNER, GEORGE
[pen.] George Wagner; [b.] February 21, 1980, Bayshore, NM; [p.] George Wagner, Laurie O'Comer; [ed.] Junior in High School; [occ.] High School Student; [pers.] Work hard to get where you going.; [a.] Long Beach, NY

WALKER, GAIL INEZ
[pen.] Inez or G.I. Walk; [b.] May 9, 1954, Huntington, WV; [p.] Caroline Brandon Walker (Deceased); [ed.] Huntington High, Huntington, W. Va., Tidewater Community College, Ches. VA., Norfolk State University, Norfolk, VA; [occ.] Entrepreneur; [memb.] Faith Tabernacle, Norfolk, VA; [hon.] B.S. in Inter Disciplinary Studies; [oth. writ.] Many poems, several short stories, presently working on a novel, and a children's book.; [pers.] While traveling the road of life, I strive to share my strength, hope, and love with each soul that I am blessed to encounter.; [a.] Norfolk, VA

WALKER, JAMES F.
[pen.] Jim Walker; [b.] May 20, 1925, Erie, PA; [ed.] Allegheny College BS. 1946 University of Pittsburgh, School of Medicine 1950 Univ. of Pennsylvania graduate School of Med. 1952; [occ.] Retired; [memb.] AMA, PA. Med Society Erie Yacht Club Y-Men's Club of Erie, PA; [hon.] Pres. of Erie County Med. Society 1975 Nat'l Lib. of Poetry; [oth. writ.] Over 50 poems, many published. Letters to the Editor, Editor Y-Men's Club Book.; [pers.] Poems that express the value of life.; [a.] Erie, PA

WALKER, MARJORIE L.
[b.] September 24, 1928, Ohio; [m.] Bruce R. Walker, 1953; [ch.] Bruce Jr., Steven, Charles, Kathy and Glenn; [ed.] BA/BS Arizona State U., MA Loma Linda U., Mgt. Courses; [occ.] Now retired, Owner Technical Documents Unlimited; [memb.] AAUM, Amer. Chem. Soc., Amer. Mgt. Ass'n.; [hon.] Mgt. of Jr. Achievement Award. Northrop B-2 Div., Teaching Fellowship, ASU. Listed in *Who's Who in California*.; [oth. writ.] Technical Pubs. Newspaper columns, company Pubs. Marketing docs.; [pers.] Spent last 10 yrs. as Aerospace Technical Manager. Developed Science curricula for L.A. Archdiocese Catholic Elementary Schools. I believe it is important to give of one's talents to others.; [a.] Claremont, CA

WALLACE, MS. SHAYLA
[b.] December 11, 1982, Pittsburgh; [p.] Mr. and Mrs. Kenneth and Leslie Poston; [ed.] 8th grade Woodland Hills School West Jr. High; [occ.] Student - Track - cheerleading - Candy Striper; [hon.] Awards for Science projects - Cheerleading awards; [oth. writ.] Several poems that we have yet to send to you.

WALLACE, WILLIAM R.
[b.] October 6, 1970, Newport News, VA; [p.] John and Nancy Wallace; [ed.] Kecoughtan High, Thomas Nelson Community College and Golden West College; [occ.] Fire-Fighter; [memb.] Member of the Body of Christ; [hon.] Merit List; [pers.] Born of innocence, not of this world, born of God creator of the universe, born of glory, crowned with eternal life.; [a.] Huntington Beach, CA

WALLING, SHANE A.
[pen.] Shane A. Walling; [b.] February 12, 1979, Anchorage, AK; [p.] Steve Walling, Sherry Walling; [ed.] Mat-Su Alternative High School; [occ.] Alaska Air National Guard and a Cook; [pers.] The poem "Farewell" was written for the greatest teacher and friend I knew. He was the man who influenced me to start writing again. This is all for him.; [a.] Wasilla, AK

WALLS, SHIRLEY WASHINGTON
[p.] Mr. H. D. Washington and Pearline Washington; [m.] Curtis Walls, September 3, 1988; [ch.] One son, Curtis born November 30, 1995; [ed.] Bachelor of Arts Degree Southern Illinois University at Carbondale and Roosevelt High School St. Louis, MO; [occ.] Television news anchor, reporter - Atlanta, GA; [hon.] Atlanta Association of Black Journalists Pioneer Award 1993 and National Academy of Television Arts and Sciences Emmy Nomination Atlanta Chapter for Spot News Coverage 1993 and 1994; [oth. writ.] Articles published in a National Magazine.; [pers.] I wrote "I Dreamed A Dream" at the request of my brother David and his fiance Kimberly and recited it at their wedding, October 2, 1993. The poem was written for the depths of my heart for two people who are truly blessed by God.; [a.] Atlanta, GA

WALTERS, CHARLES J.
[b.] October 4, 1935, Dickson City; [p.] Nelson and Elsie; [m.] Dorothy, January 28, 1983; [ed.] Azusa Pacific University '89 California Credential; [occ.] Substitution; [memb.] International Poetry Society, N.F.S.P.S., CSPS, BAPC; [hon.] 1st place Midi Poem Voc #17 Bay Area Poet Coalition 1995, 3rd place NLP Anth. *At Day's End*; [oth. writ.] Slogan Puzzles, Illustrations and poems; [pers.] As long as you have a contribution to make, contribute.; [a.] El Monte, CA

WALTERS, JOANNA MARLENE
[pen.] Joanna Marlene; [b.] February 9, 1956, Mt. Vernon, OH; [p.] Deceased; [m.] Divorced; [ch.] Maurice Thomas Scanlon III and 5 stepchildren, James, Cecilia, David, Karen and Kevin Walters; [ed.] Newark Senior High 1974, Central Ohio Technical College, Current; [occ.] Full time student - majoring in computers and social work; [memb.] Amity United Methodist Church; [hon.] First Report Card in 22 years achieved 4.0 G.P.A.; [oth. writ.] Anthology of my poems and journal writings for my son, not yet published and numerous other poems, thoughts, and journal notes of feelings not yet published; [pers.] May my love and thanks for God and our country create blessings on all of the loved ones surrounding me with the support of my life, praise God! for life and love!; [a.] Newark, OH

WARDELL, BROOKE
[b.] May 12, 1973, Dayton Beach, FL; [p.] John and Paula Koppels; [m.] R. Todd Wardell, October 5, 1991; [ed.] American School, Chicago and Pioneer School (for further Education in teaching the Bible) Connecticut; [occ.] Wife, Administrative Asst. Columbine Mgt. Dillon Colorado; [memb.] Jehovah's Witness; [pers.] The true future of mankind rests with God's Kingdom - where political, national and racial borders give way to true unity in purpose and worship and even now create an international brotherhood.; [a.] Dillon, CO

WARREN, LORY
[b.] December 22, 1953, Ashtabula, OH; [p.] Angela and James Joseph; [m.] Robert Warren, May 23, 1993; [ch.] Mason Elliott Volz; [ed.] 2 yrs. college; [occ.] Public Works Supervisor with Dept. of Trans.; [memb.] Chairwoman of the Pima County/Tucson Women's Commission (PCTWC) Big Sister with Big Brother/Big Sister with Program of Tucson; [hon.] Volunteer of the Year (PCTWC); [pers.] I love my mother deeply but generations of sky dysfunction, while they cannot be undone, can be healed and deterred from reoccuring in the next generation. I strive to soften this exposure through my poems; [a.] Tucson, AZ

WASHINGTON, CARLA J.
[pen.] "Bill"; [b.] October 5, 1970, Alliance, OH; [p.] Roderick and Candice Washington; [ch.] Jordan and Kahlen Washington; [ed.] Alliance High School and Kent State University; [occ.] Assistant to Minority Recruiter; [oth. writ.] Many other poems; [pers.] Religion and spirituality are two very different things, the first will give you balance, and the last will give you wings.; [a.] Alliance, OH

WASSON, CHRISTOPHER
[b.] December 30, 1971, Philadelphia, PA; [ed.] St. James High School, University of Pennsylvania; [occ.] Research and Development; [a.] Philadelphia, PA

WATSON, ASHLEE MARIE
[b.] July 7, 1982, Weirton, WV; [p.] William Watson, Norman Jean Thompson; [ed.] Collier Elementary, Follansbee Middle School, Entering Freshman year Brooke Wellsburg, WV High School, D.A.R.E Brooke County, WV; [occ.] Student - Brooke High School Wellsburg, W.V. - Vacation Bible School Teacher Colliers Methodist Church; [memb.] YWCA, Macon, GA. Junior Counselor. Colliers Methodist Church, Youth Choir, Weirton Community Center. Lynnwood Park Swim Club, Brooke Co. Animal Welfare League; [hon.] Honor Roll Student - 1st grade thru 8th grade. Academic Awards. (7th and 8th grade Follansbee Middle Athletic Award (Volleyball) 1995 and 1996.) "(School of Dance) Tammy Benzo 1988-1993 5 yrs. Award." Brooke Co. Council of PTA Spelling Bee 4th Place, Participant State Spelling Bee, 1994; [oth. writ.] "Snow, Snow," "The Birth of Christ," both poems. Also "Dear Mommy" - this poem was published in *The Messenger* Collier Methodist Church Newsletter. Dedicated to my mother for Mother's Day.; [pers.] I strive to reflect the beauty of God's creations to all in my writings. My mother has been an inspiration and gave me great encouragement to write.; [a.] Colliers, WV

WATSON, SHIRLEY
[pen.] Shirley Watson; [b.] January 31, 1928, Gary, IN; [p.] Goldie and Patrick Lind; [ch.] Randall Otvos, Boyd Otvos, Michael Smith; [ed.] High School, Business College, Real Estate Brokerage; [occ.] Real State Brokerage; [memb.] Greater Northwest Indiana Board of Realtors, RS Council; [hon.] Several Million Dollar Awards in the Real Estate Business and a Certified Residential Specialist Designation; [oth. writ.] Short stories, poems (unpublished); [pers.] This poem, "Fear", was written to help a friend to have the courage to leave an abusive relationship of many years standing. She said this poem helped her get out.; [a.] Crown Point, IN

WATTS, MILDRED
[b.] June 15, 1921, Bucyrus, KS; [p.] Nicholas and Margaret Myers; [m.] Rev. David Eugene Watts of Camden Miss., July 31, 1943; [ch.] Margaret Marjo, Johnson, N. Tera Irene; [ed.] Undergraduate work in Tenn. Ark., Texas, Calif. and Nevada, B.A. - Ottawa Univ. (KS) '43 M.A. (Eng.) Texas Woman's Univ. '67; [occ.] Summer Tutoring retired after 38 years teaching Eng. and Creative Writing in Junior and Senior Highs in Tenn., Ark, Texas and Nevada (17 years in Las Vegas); [memb.] PTA's Ecumenical Church Affiliations; [oth. writ.] News Reporter (off and on in Nashville, Tenn, Las Vegas, NVS' Ottawa 1943-96) children's books, Bible stories for children, book reviews for the *Ottawa Herald* (KS) '89-96; [pers.] How wonderful is on-going creation! There's a multitude of creatures - those dependent on humans and those we depend upon. Some are beneath the earth, in water, on land, or in the air. They creep, crawl, wiggle, strut, fly, run, climb and walk. It's a wonderful part of life!; [a.] Las Vegas, NV

WEAVER, MADELINE F.
[b.] July 19, 1949, Detroit, MI; [p.] Herman Iott, Maureen Iott; [m.] Carl Ray Weaver, February 14, 1995; [ch.] Alexandria Walentowski, Jordan Weaver, Corey Weaver; [ed.] St. Joseph Academy, Wayne State Univ.; [occ.] World Class Auto Maker; [pers.] Greatly influenced by the struggle to choose life, to choose love.; [a.] Maumee, OH

WEAVER, SANDRA KAY
[b.] May 1, 1952, Witchita Falls, TX; [p.] James and Dara Hill; [m.] Harold Ray Weaver, August 31, 1969; [ch.] Two boys Richard and Ronnie; [ed.] Los Banos High School; [occ.] Homemaker, sing at funerals; [hon.] For ministerial work in prisons and Juvenile facilities; [pers.] My love for my family and mankind is only attributed by my knowledge of God and His love for me, which cultivates the poetry in me.; [a.] Dos Palos, CA

WEBSTER, BERTHA
[pen.] Be Be Revis; [b.] December 2, 1946, Vicksburg, MS; [p.] Ollie Bland, Daisy Bland, Divorced; [ch.] Revis Keith; [ed.] Temple High, Alcorn Univ., Western Mich., Univ. of Mich., Wayne State Univ.; [occ.] Media Specialist, Iroquois Middle School, Grand Rapids, MI; [memb.] NBPWC, Multicultural Council, Pilgrim Rest Scholarship Chairperson, BIT; [hon.] President's Scholar, Dean's List, "I" Award, *Who's Who Among Students in American Universities and Colleges*; [oth. writ.] Several poems and short stories; [pers.] Life without obstacles and challenges gives rise to no victories.; [a.] Grand Rapids, MI

WEILAND, DIANE M.
[ed.] MA - Humanities; [occ.] Professor: Humanities/English Marian; [memb.] College, Fond Dulac and Silver Lake College, Manitowoc, Wisconsin; [pers.] 'What I have written, I have written.' - If that makes someone uncomfortable, so much the better!; [a.] Mount Calvary, WI

WEINTRAUB, NICOLETTE
[b.] August 15, 1980, N. Miami, FL; [p.] Alana and Frank Weintraub; [ed.] Up through 10th grade. Going into 11th this year. I am Home School Student; [hon.] In Elementary and Junior High, I was an Honor Student; [oth. writ.] Written other poems and compiled them in a book, not published.; [pers.] I want to illustrate the difference between good and evil in the life we were given by the Creator.; [a.] Grove City, PA

WEISHEIT, CHRISTINE
[b.] November 12, 1969, Parma, OH; [p.] Donna and Tom Rowe - Robert Weisheit; [ed.] M.A. English Literature Texas Women's University B.A. English Literature, Philosophy Minor - Sam Houston State University; [occ.] High School Teacher at an alternative School for Gang Kids; [memb.] PeTA since 1990 MWF since 1992; [pers.] This sonnet was written for my soul mate Ronnie. Due to my own indecisive stupidity, I have lost him, but he will always be in my heart. I dedicate this to him - My soul - My song.; [a.] Arlington, TX

WELKER, CAROLYN
[pen.] Care Bear; [b.] July 9, 1979, Bridgeport, CT; [p.] Janice and Walter Welker; [ed.] Graduated grader (Middle) School at John G. Prendergast in an Sonia of Now in Seymour H.S. where I am going into my Jr. year.; [occ.] H.S. Student but I love to write Poetry, Dance, Sing, and Play Guitar; [memb.] Seymour High Choir, Seymour High Pom Pon Squad, Dance teacher of 20 years at Danz magic; [hon.] 5 year award in Dance, 2 perfect attendance award in dance, so this is basically my 1st great achievement to be recognized; [oth. writ.] Many, but none other than this one that was published; [pers.] Reach for the stars. Soon something might be shining your hands. Thank Manning who helped me and the Beatles who influenced and inspired my work.; [a.] Beacon Falls, CT

WELLMAN, SCOTT FRANCIS
[b.] May 19, 1973, Rapid City, SD; [p.] Douglas Sr., and Candy Wellman; [ed.] Northrop High (Ft. Wayne, IN), Combination Welding (Job Corps, St. Paul Technical College); [occ.] Design Technologists, Turfco Mfg. Inc.; [memb.] Church of the Open Door (Minn. MN), Freedom Club (Point of View Talk Show); [hon.] Certificate of Honor, PTA Reflections Art Show, Certificate of Honor, Art, Certificate of Honor, Commercial Art II, (High School Awards); [oth. writ.] A few letters to the editor. My writing has never been published.; [pers.] I enjoy writing, drawing, playing guitar, and reading. I thank my Lord Saviour and best friend Jesus Christ and strive to glorify Him in all that I do.; [a.] Saint Paul, MN

WELLS, RICHARD
[pen.] Richard Wells; [b.] May 13, 1963, Marshall, TX; [p.] Robert Wells (Deceased), Beaulah Wells; [ed.] Graduated from Marshall High School in 1981. Attended Texas State Technical Institute (Waco, Texas) graduated 1983 with an Associate of Applied Science Degree (Food Service); [occ.] Chef; [memb.] Member of the Greater Oak Grove Baptist Church and a member of NAACP; [hon.] Was FHA Beau in High School and Football, and Track Team Statistician; [oth. writ.] Writing is a hobby of mine and I have a numerous amount of works waiting to be exposed.; [pers.] You can get no more out of anything than you put into it. Staci was the inspirational factor why I wrote my poem.; [a.] Marshall, TX

WEST, BRENDA
[pen.] Brenda West; [b.] February 10, 1951, Marietta, GA; [p.] Herbert and Rachel Chumley; [ch.] Stephanie and Jason West; [ed.] Sprayberry H/S; [occ.] Accountant; [pers.] I write from within myself how I feel and how life should, would, and can be, if each one of us would only take the time to let go and enjoy the small things, that there is a big beautiful world to enjoy and we need to look within ourselves to find it.; [a.] Dallas, GA

WEST, FRENISEE
[b.] October 4, 1950, Philadelphia, PA; [p.] Florence Wilson Black, Benjamin Black; [m.] Divorced; [ch.] Tremaybe and Deidre; [ed.] St. Helena High School Temple University; [occ.] Food Service Retail Sales Manager; [oth. writ.] I have written an unpublished book of poetry entitled, "Melodies From The Heart"; [pers.] To many of us, poetry are reflective situations that most people can relate to. Using this definition, it has allowed me to capture those feelings that are often felt, but seldom shared.; [a.] Philadelphia, PA

WEST, VICKIE L.
[b.] November 3, 1950, Dallas, TX; [p.] Shirley and A. L. Vicks; [m.] Divorced; [ch.] Jenny and Michael; [ed.] A.A. in Child Development Long Beach, City College; [occ.] Instructional Aide/Special, work with learning disabled kids; [memb.] Outstand VIP Volunteers in; [hon.] Outstanding VIP (Volunteers in school), Den Leaders Award (Boy Scouts of America), California P.A.T., Youth Leader (Boy Scouts of America), Lakewood City - for Community Service, Sunday School Department: Holy Trinity, St. Timothy, and Christ Presbyterian Churches; [oth. writ.] Press-Telegrams Light The Torch "Statue of Liberty" essay contest 1985.; [pers.] I find inner release, peace, fulfillment in writing. What I cannot verbalize, I can put in verse, "Reality is what is in your heart". Verse is reality.; [a.] Lakewood, CA

WESTENDORF, MADGE
[b.] April 8, 1914, Chamberlain, SD; [p.] Edward and Bernice Healey; [m.] Elmer Westendorf, December 30, 1946; [ch.] Janis Westendorf Shields and Steve Westendorf; [ed.] Chamberlain High School and Business College; [occ.] Housewife; [memb.] St. James Catholic Church, American Legion Aux. and other organizations; [oth. writ.] Many poems written for my own pleasure.; [pers.] Live God, love yourself and love others.; [a.] Chamberlain, SD

WESTON, RANDAL MARION
[b.] May 18, 1963, Richmond, IN; [p.] Marion Weston, Barbara Weston; [ed.] Rushville Consolidated High School; [occ.] Factory Worker, Connersville, IN; [memb.] Amvets, V.F.W., American Legion; [hon.] Honorably Discharged from the United States Marine Corps. (Sergeant); [oth. writ.] Some letters published in local newspaper.; [pers.] One can reach surprising heights through positive thinking and steady perseverance.; [a.] Connersville, IN

WHITE, KAREN L.
[b.] February 15, 1943, Settle, WA; [p.] George and Elsie Hopper; [m.] Donald R. White, October 14, 1995; [ch.] John, Doug; [ed.] Choctawhatchee High School, Troy State College, Southwestern Baptist Theological Seminary; [occ.] Adjunct Missions Professor, The Criswell College, Dallas; [memb.] Evangelical Missiological Society, First Baptist Church, Dallas; [hon.] *Who's Who Among Students in American Colleges and Universities*; [pers.] My poetry has grown out of my struggle to overcome personal pain. It reflects my commitment to live a healthy life in tune with my Creator and Savior, Jesus Christ.; [a.] Dallas, TX

WHITE, MR. DARYL E.
[b.] November 3, 1958, Meridian, MS; [p.] Mr. William M. White, Mrs. Katie R. White; [ed.] Graduated Demopolis High School, 1977. U.S. Navy, 1977 - 1985. Travels through the Orient and Southern Europe; [occ.] Paperworker - James River Corp; [memb.] National Rifle Association, United Paperworkers International Union, International Society of Poets; [hon.] 1996 Editors Choice Award from The National Library of Poetry; [oth. writ.] Previous publications in The National Library Poetry's Anthologies; [a.] Demopolis, AL

WHITE, SANDRA A.
[b.] July 22, 1967, Augsburg, Germany; [p.] Barbara G. White; [ed.] Dual Degree: International Business and Marketing from Northeastern University; [occ.] Marketing Consultant; [a.] East Boston, MA

WHITE, SHAYNA
[pen.] Shay; [b.] April 30, 1986, Flint, MI; [p.] Shannon and James White; [ed.] 5th grade; [occ.] Student; [hon.] Poetry Awards, Good Student Awards, Honor Roll Awards; [oth. writ.] "If I Were an Annual," "Lucky Star," "Swans," "Jungle," and etc.; [pers.] I am a 5th grade student at Martin Luther King Jr. Elementary School, Flint Michigan. I enjoy writing and drawing. These hobbies excite me and give me a sense of fulfillment.; [a.] Flint, MI

WHITE, TROY ANTWINE
[b.] April 8, 1974, Wilmington; [p.] Clarence and Shirley White Jr.; [ed.] Culinary Arts at Delaware Technical Community College; [occ.] Shift Manager of Restaurant of Arthur Treacher's; [memb.] V.I.C.A.; [pers.] Do as you are told not what you are asked and God shall bless you.; [a.] New Castle, DE

WHITENACK, SCOTT
[b.] December 10, 1982, Louisville, KY; [p.] Vicki and Gary Whitenack; [pers.] Just write what you want and how you want to.

WHITESIDE, DONNA
[pen.] Abby Normal; [b.] September 11, 1955, Asheville, NC; [m.] Dean Whiteside, September 9, 1978; [ch.] Michele Denise, Angela Lynn; [ed.] Asheville High, A-B Tech.; [memb.] National Lupus Foundation, S.I.N.G.; [oth. writ.] Several poems published in local newsletters.; [pers.] Among the sadness and negativeness of this world, I strive to see the positive in everything and everyone. I hope to reflect that positiveness, a sense of humor, and my great faith in God in a way that my readers will be uplifted.; [a.] Englewood, FL

WHITTAKER, PATIENCE RENEE
[b.] October 30, 1976, Morgantown, WY; [p.] Pamela and Clyde Whittaker; [ch.] Chandra Grace; [ed.] Preston High School, Fairmont State College; [occ.] Fairmont State College student (Graphic/Fine Arts); [memb.] C.A.D.S. (Creative Arts Organization for Students) Secretary, College Merit Awards; [hon.] Mary Agnes Borgman Writing Award, Glenville State College Merit Award, Garrett Community College Honorable Mention Award, 2 Fairmont State College Merit Awards; [oth. writ.] Poetry and Artwork published in Fairmont State College's book *Whetstone*; [pers.] Everything I see and I am touched by leaves an impression, a feeling, an interpretation. Life for me is an interpretation. In my writing I try to share my interpretation with you.; [a.] Arthurdale, WV

WHITTAKER, YOLANDA
[pen.] Yo-Yo; [b.] July 24, 1980, Portsmouth; [p.] Mr. and Mrs. Raymond Whittaker; [ed.] 11th grader; [occ.] In school; [memb.] Member of Way of the Cress Church and Church Choir; [hon.] National Honor Society Member, Winner in Delta Sigma Theta Oratorical Contest; [pers.] Without God you can do nothing. You are your best friend.; [a.] Norfolk, VA

WHITTEMORE, TINA M.
[b.] October 25, 1963, Wakefield, MI; [ch.] Eileen, (9 years old daughter); [ed.] Graduated from Ewen Trout Creek H.S. in Ewen, MI., 1981. Attended N.M.U. in Marquette, MI., one year; [occ.] Office Manager; [memb.] United Church of Sebastian Contemporary Worship Committee; [oth. writ.] Poem published in School Newspaper and Local Paper.; [pers.] The poems I write are to touch people's hearts.; [a.] Micco, FL

WIDGA, NICHOL LEE
[pen.] Nichol Lee; [b.] December 5, 1975, Novato, CA; [p.] Adopted by Dennis and Judy Widga; [ed.] Shenendoah High in Clifton Park, NY; [occ.] Author and Lecturer (published by New World Library); [memb.] Unity School of Christianity and Science of Mind and Spirit Church.; [hon.] Many prizes and Awards in English horseriding/Show jumping; [oth. writ.] "Starshine Serenade," "The Art of Enchanted Living," "Self Acceptance and other Harvests I wish I'd Reaped in High School."; [pers.] F. Scott Fitzgerald's works as well as Jim Morrison and Maya Angelou, greatly influenced by their passion and yearning, inspired and intrigued by humanity's determination to rise above, succeed, and retrieve life's ceaseless magic, mystery, and wonder.; [a.] Denver, CO

WILCOX, HEATHER
[b.] September 4, 1978, Carlisle; [p.] Kipp A. Wilcox, Diane M. Wilcox; [ed.] Cumberland Valley High School; [oth. writ.] Have some poems with scholastic writing awards. But mostly I keep my poems at home with me.; [pers.] No one has ever liked my work cause it was to depressing. But now when I was ready to give up, NLP came along and bolstered my self-esteem.; [a.] Marysville, PA

WILDER, RICHARD L.
[b.] May 18, 1967, Norfolk, VA; [p.] Patricia Mudryk, Donald Wilder; [ch.] Hayley Wilder; [ed.] Some College; [occ.] U.S. Army - Soldier; [oth. writ.] Several others not yet published; [pers.] Most of my inspirations come from everything around me in everyday life. My own experiences are a great influence.; [a.] Norfolk, VA

WILKINS, ELIZABETH
[b.] May 10, 1980; [p.] Alice and Walter Wilkins; [ed.] Limestone Community High School; [memb.] St. Mark's Catholic Church, Peoria Civic Chorale Honors Chorus, Girl Scouts; [hon.] Silver Award (Girl Scouts); [pers.] Put your faith in God and don't be afraid of the things that might come.; [a.] Peoria, IL

WILLIAMS, CARL
[b.] August 14, 1976, Conway, AR; [p.] Robert and Shirley (Deceased); [ed.] Bigelow High - Bigelow Arkansas (Honor Graduate), Petite Jean Technical College at Morrilton Arkansas; [occ.] Sheet Metal Worker; [memb.] Reba McEntire Fan Club; [hon.] Honor graduate from high school, United States Achievement Academy National Awards; [pers.] I live by a single saying, that many friends identify me with "Learn From Your Mistakes."; [a.] Bigelow, AR

WILLIAMS, CAROLYN K.
[b.] March 17, 1955; [m.] Arthur Williams, September 24, 1975; [ch.] Andre Lenell, Arthur Jr., Dante Jamal; [ed.] Mattie T. Blount High, Bishop State Junior College, Univ. of South Ala. - Auburn Univ.; [occ.] Certified Dietary Manager; [memb.] Dietary Manager's Association; [hon.] 1. President's List, 2. Dean's List, 3. Phi Theta Kappa National Honor Society; [oth. writ.] Poems printed in monthly newsletter when employed at Lynwood Nursing Home, Mobile, Ala.; [pers.] Writing poetry has always been a hobby of mine. Whatever I can't express verbally, I can always do it in my writings that come straight from my heart.; [a.] Whistler, AL

WILLIAMS, DANNY
[b.] 1953, Washington, DC; [p.] Carlisle Williams, William Wiggins; [ed.] Two Years of College (Univ. of D.C.), Vocational Trade School (Chamberlain); [occ.] Word Processor/Desktop Publisher; [memb.] VICA, Mary Wilson International Fan Club; [oth. writ.] Several poems published in The National Library Poetry Anthologies, articles and reviews for *New Word Magazine*, and articles for company newsletter Premiere. Write for *Mary Wilson Newsletter*. Other local newspapers.; [pers.] "Man can not live alone, so he needs God in his life."; [a.] Brooklyn, NY

WILLIAMS (ANDERSON), LISA
[b.] August 27, 1960, New York; [p.] Theresa Williams; [ch.] Rizzi Abdul-Malik McKelvin; [ed.] New York University - Health & human Services; [occ.] Adm. Aide/General Studies New York University; [oth. writ.] Several stories and poems written currently unpublished.; [pers.] Common sky was written in rememberance of my mother Theresa Williams. She is still my inspiration and my guiding light. I will love her always. Thank you Mommy - for giving me my life.; [a.] Jamaica, NY

WILLIAMS, M. KEITH
[b.] September 24, 1958, Scranton, PA; [p.] Milton and Mary Jane Williams; [m.] Laurie Williams; [ch.] Janessa and Trevor; [ed.] BS Pennsylvania State University; [occ.] Industrial Training Specialist; [oth. writ.] Many technical articles in various publications; [a.] Scranton, PA

WILLIAMS, RUBY
[b.] March 14, 1936, Baltimore, MD; [p.] Melvin and Elizabeth Bowser; [m.] Roger Williams, August 18, 1956; [ch.] Three girls and three boys; [ed.] In Baltimore City Public Schools; [occ.] House Wife; [memb.] Member of the house of Salvation Church

WILLIAMS, SANDRA I.
[b.] August 21, 1969, Newark, NJ; [p.] Tamer Williams; [ed.] Saint Paul's College, Caroline High School; [occ.] Payable Analyst; [memb.] The Assembly of Christian Fellowship Baptist Church, Sigma Gamma Rho Sorority, Inc, Youth President (ACFBC); [hon.] Cum Laude, National Dean's List, Alpha Kappa Mu; [pers.] All things are possible with God's help and guidance.; [a.] Hanover, VA

WILLIAMS, SARAH FLANAGAN
[pen.] Sarah Miller; [b.] July 2, 1941, Chicago, IL; [p.] Will and Ollie Miller; [m.] Albert Williams, October 7, 1992; [ch.] Luther Courtney Flanagan, Kerry Avram Flanagan; [ed.] Parker High School 1959, Columbia College 1965; [occ.] Teacher-English St. Columbanus School, Chicago, IL; [pers.] To be the best that one can be is the goal we all must strive for.; [a.] Chicago, IL

WILLIAMS, STEPHANIE A.
[b.] March 26, 1968, Charleston; [p.] Wallace and Mae Williams; [ed.] Graduated from Goose Creek High. Attending Charleston Southern University for Business Administration.; [occ.] Administrative Assistant for Cha. Cty. Auditor; [pers.] Be true to yourself and happiness will prevail.; [a.] Goose Creek, SC

WILLIAMS, STEPHEN CRAIG
[b.] April 18, 1983, Morgantown, WV; [p.] Craig and Kim Williams; [ed.] 8th grade, Westwood Middle School; [hon.] Salutatorian, Principal's Honor Roll; [pers.] I enjoy playing sports.; [a.] Morganton, WV

WILLIAMS, WANDA
[pen.] Wanda Williams; [b.] January 26, 1944, Crockett, TX; [p.] Leotra Kirby and Bernice Kirby; [m.] Carral C. Williams, August 3, 1962; [ch.] Monya Renee, Christopher, Rodger; [ed.] Galena Park, High San Jacinto Jr. College, Navarro College; [occ.] Registered Nurse; [memb.] Inspirational Writers, Alive, Women of Excellence (Board Member, U.R.C.); [hon.] Dean's List; [oth. writ.] Several - never been submitted for publication.; [pers.] I strive to reflect the love of God for all mankind. Jesus is my influence. By His grace you can have His salvation and walk the streets of gold in all of heaven.

Romans 10:10 (Holy Bible) "For with the heart one believes to righteousness, and with the mouth confession is made to salvation."; [a.] Buffalo, TX

WILSON, DEAN
[b.] March 27, 1948, Kentucky; [p.] Carl Brown, Lorena Guess; [m.] Bian Wilson Jr., September 14, 1968; [ch.] Martha, Elizabeth, Matthew; [ed.] Francis Elementary, Western Kentucky; [occ.] Artist- Book, Writer; [memb.] B.H.C., General Partner Benny Hinn Crusade I BEW - KET; [oth. writ.] *Patch Work Fairy Tales* - Line of childrens books. *Dear To My Heart,* my own book of poems Lake Land printers; [pers.] I love to hold a pencil in my hand. And write beautiful words. I'm giving a painting to washington many trails of tears.; [a.] Benton, KY

WILSON, JANE ELLEN
[pen.] Janey; [b.] December 10, 1954, California; [p.] Margaret Russell and Charles Fink; [m.] Michael Wilson, March 6, 1993; [ch.] Jennifer, Paul Valenzuella; [ed.] Mountain View and San Jacinto High School currently enrolled and Attending Bethesda Christian College; [occ.] Housewife and blessed mother; [memb.] Bethesda Christian Center Sunday School Teacher; [oth. writ.] Many poems waiting for publication; [pers.] Glory and thanks be to my heavenly Father and Savior Jesus Christ, You have blessed me with words from heaven!; [a.] San Jacinto, CA

WILSON, JEANETTE
[pen.] Jaye Wilson; [b.] Dubuque, IA; [p.] James Arensdorf, Marita Arensdorf; [ch.] Five children: Donna Sharrar, Charles, Patricia, Clifford and Terri Wilson (All Wilsons); [ed.] Immaculate Conception Grammar School, Immaculate Heart High School (From Queen), Orange Coast College; [occ.] Administrative Assist; [memb.] American Women's Business Assoc., Catholic Daughters of the Americas; [hon.] Pins Awarded for 5,000 hours in U.S.O. Service Entertaining Troops and Hospitals. Cups, Medals, Trophies. Singing and Dancing, West Coast Director: Project Handclasp United States Navy, Awarded Certificate for Recognition of Outstanding Participation in "Project Handclasp (Department of the U.S. Navy's Overseas People to People Program). "Sport Parachuting Certificate"; [oth. writ.] Wrote a song and choreographed a dance for the "Y" Indian maidens; [pers.] Always be merry as the day is long; [a.] Costa Mesa, CA

WINSTON, GISELE
[pen.] Gisele Winston; [b.] April 6, 1972, Los Angeles, CA; [p.] Myrna Williams and John Winston; [ed.] Santa Monica High, Ucla; [occ.] Pre-K Teacher, Redwood Village Childrens Center, M.D.R. CA; [memb.] Scayec; [oth. writ.] My dream is to collect all of my poems, and create a special book of poetry.; [pers.] Poetry is a very important part of our lives. Anyone can write a poem. Although, it's the power of the pen, and the hope is our hearts that make words come alive.; [a.] Los Angeles, CA

WINTERS, JUDY
[b.] March 14, 1958, Yakima, WA; [p.] Frank and Shirley Bray; [m.] Michael, June 8, 1979; [ch.] Jennifer, Stephen, Nicholas; [ed.] 1979 Mariner High school, PC Baptist Bible College; [occ.] Homemaker; [memb.] North Shore Christian Church, Volunteer Special Olympics, Volunteer Shoultes Elementary; [oth. writ.] National Library of Poetry publishings, *Shadows And Light*, poem title, "Jennifer", *Best Poems of the 90's*, poem titled "Ditto", Sparrowgrass Publishing, *Treasured Poems of America*, poem titled "Lil' Man".; [pers.] I write about whatever touches my heart. I'm pleased my poetry has been published. May the generations that follow enjoy it.; [a.] Marysville, WA

WINTHER, MARIE-LOUISE M.
[pen.] Marie-Louise M. Winther; [b.] February 3, 1989, Chicago, IL; [p.] Kitobias Winther Cecilia Mazza; [ed.] Emma Willard Children's School; [occ.] Student; [pers.] I like to be a kid and I like to write poems.; [a.] Troy, NY

WOLFE, MICHELLE
[b.] November 25, 1963, Memphis, TN; [p.] Pat and Sonny Higdon; [m.] Rick Wolfe, January 8, 1994; [ed.] B.S. Education Memphis State University; [occ.] English Teacher; [oth. writ.] "And Know", "Birth", "The Same or Better", "The Burn" and "And to the Day"; [pers.] Life is my aspiration. When my heart is dormant I produce nothing. When my heart is full, I produce volumes.; [a.] Bartlett, TN

WOLFE, TIMMY
[b.] April 10, 1977, Niles, OH; [p.] Vikie Schuller; [ed.] Graduated High School '95 Plan to continue Education; [pers.] Take life slowly but don't let it pass you by; [a.] Niles, OH

WOLSZCZAK, KRISTY
[b.] June 17, 1979, Key West, FL; [p.] Andrew Wolszczak and Patricia Wolszczak; [ed.] High School; [occ.] Student in high school and a desk clerk at a Fitness center; [memb.] Hospital Volunteer; [hon.] National Honors Society, President of the Art Club, National English Merit Award, *Who's Who Among American High School Students*, Honor Roll; [oth. writ.] One poem published in a National High School Anthology and two in other National Anthologies; [pers.] My poems usually express the mood I am in or the emotions that need to come out onto paper instead of expressing them verbally.; [a.] Marathon, FL

WOODARD, KARI-LYN
[b.] May 23, 1981, Silver Spring, MD; [p.] Lee and Barbara Woodard; [ed.] Northwestern High School; [memb.] Varsity (Church Club), *Who's Who Among American High School Students*, Spanish Club, J.R. Civitan, Jr. Honor Society; [hon.] Timothy, Excellence, Spirit Manual, Honor Roll; [oth. writ.] Write-a-Book; [a.] Hyattsville, MD

WOODRUM, CARRIE
[b.] May 16, 1977, Kettering, OH; [p.] Charles and Vicki Woodrum; [ed.] Fort Zuwalt North High, Truman State University; [occ.] Student; [memb.] Phi Sigma Pi; [hon.] Bright Flight, President's Combined Ability and President's Honorary Scholar of Turman State University; [oth. writ.] "Cold" published in *Recollections of Yesterday*; [a.] Saint Paul, MO

WOODSON, ROBBIE WHITE
[b.] January 28, 1954, South Boston, VA; [p.] Phoebe Platt and Charles White; [ch.] H. Rodney Woodson; [ed.] Western High School, Coppin State College; [occ.] Relay Operator; [memb.] Bethel A.M.E. Church; [hon.] Dean's List, Graduated Cum Laude, Coppin State College; [oth. writ.] Currently working on a collection of poems and a novel.; [pers.] When I wake up each morning, I know I am truly blessed to have the opportunity to see and live life one more day.; [a.] Baltimore, MD

WOOLDRIDGE, DEAN L.
[b.] January 14, 1952, Wisconsin; [ch.] Jacki, Justin, Jessie; [occ.] Systems Analyst; [pers.] God made true love, and exists within it. Thus, where there is true love, there is the willingness to sacrifice even what is dearest for the sake of that love.; [a.] Houston, TX

WRATHER, JOHNNA DEE S.
[b.] July 20, 1971, Seattle, WA; [p.] John A. Stevens, Nancy Jo Stevens (Deceased); [m.] Gregory M. Wrather, June 14, 1996; [ch.] Catherine Michele DuBreck; [ed.] Green River Community College, Russian School of Studies at the Defense Language Institute; [occ.] Combat Intelligence Operations Specialist, HI Air Nat. Guard; [memb.] Hawaii Air National Guard; [oth. writ.] A filled notebook under the bed, love letters to my husband, love notes to my daughter; [pers.] Embrace your past, often your memories are all that you own out right.; [a.] Honolulu, HI

WRIGHT, ELLIE M.
[b.] May 8, 1982, Henderson, KY; [p.] Joy Wright, Bob Wright; [ed.] A.B. Chandler Elementary, Corydon, KY South Junior High School, Henderson, KY; [memb.] Ballet Dancer; [hon.] Principal's Award, President's Award for Educational Excellence, Honor Roll Elementary Academic Team Member; [oth. writ.] Poems and other fictional writings written for personal use, but not published; [a.] Corydon, KY

WRIGHT, SANDY
[b.] November 18, 1970, Clay City, KY; [p.] Dwight & Patsy Smith; [m.] Delbert Lee Wright, Jr, November 18, 1988; [ch.] Jordan Lee, Jonathan Hiram; [ed.] Powell County High; [occ.] Housewife; [memb.] Vaughn's Mill First Church of God; [hon.] Volunteer Award at my son's school; [oth. writ.] Poems published in local newspaper, two non-published novels and two non-published childrens stories.; [a.] Clay City, KY

WRIGHT, TERESSIA A. J.
[b.] August 4, 1952, LaGrange, GA; [p.] J. C. and Ruth Jones; [m.] Divorced; [ch.] Julie W. Spears, (Mrs. Scott Spears); [ed.] Sunday School, Bible School, Solid Rock Preachers, Center School, Troup High School, Hard Knock Teachers; [occ.] Starving, yet striving writer; [memb.] Western Heights Baptist Church; [hon.] Beyond my merits, certificates and pins, I am honored to have four true friends. Gipsie, Dolores, Brenda and Lynn, who awarded me faith, when mine grew thin.; [oth. writ.] Cardboard Boxes, All Crammed Full, The Rats Are Eating Through. Some poems are fantasy, some are cruel, some, unbelievably true.; [pers.] My imagination takes me near and far, without money, without car. I've seen Heaven, I've lived in hell, oh the stories, my mind can tell. I've been a child, loved many men, as long as I have my paper and pen!; [a.] LaGrange, GA

WRIGHT JR., JOHN SOUTHWELL
[b.] October 22, 1966, San Diego, CA; [p.] Danny and Renee Fowler; [ed.] Grad of High School; [occ.] Student/Writer/Computer Programmer

WYATT, ANGELA RENEE
[pen.] Angie, Alamar; [b.] December 10, 1966, Washington, DC; [pers.] Of all my achievements, my best are Amber and Alanna. They are my inspiration and motivation. We are Alamar.

YANG, VON
[pen.] Von; [b.] September 30, 1972, Loas; [p.] Mai and Xay Yang; [ed.] Full-time Student at Catauba Community College as a Commercial Art and Advertising Design, Graduate of Madien H. School; [occ.] Full-time Student and Work Full-time at Regal Manufacture Inc.; [hon.] The North Carolina Federation of Women's Clubs, Inc.; [oth. writ.] I like to draw a lot but I don't consider myself as an artist. I do a lot of art work for others for free and also write poems.; [pers.] I want others to understand about loving and leaving or breaking apart. I know that it hurts to be the one to end up being heartbroken and have to deal with all the heart-aches. I just want to get the message through to those who are in the same relationships as I am.; [a.] Newton, NC

YARBROUGH-EL, GWENDOLYN
[b.] August 23, 1963, Savannah, GA; [p.] Janie and Joe Roberson; [m.] Hank Yarbrough-El, June 30, 1994; [ch.] Raquel Terry (stepdaughter); [ed.] Michigan State Univ., Wayne State Univ., Detroit - College of Business, New Detroit, Inc.; [occ.] Customer Svc. Specialist; [memb.] Moorish Science Temple; [pers.] Knowing and conquering oneself is the key to happiness.; [a.] Detroit, MI

YARGER, MATTHEW
[pen.] Matt; [b.] September 12, 1982, Canandaigua, NY; [p.] Susan Yarger and Robert Yarger; [ed.] Marcus Whitman High School, going in to 9th grade; [occ.] Student; [memb.] Boy Scouts of America, UMC Youth group; [hon.] I have won the Finger Lakes Conservation Award by writing a poem called "Extinction".; [oth. writ.] I write to the school newspaper. Have some writings in there. Wrote a poem for the Gorham Free Library.; [pers.] I tend to write to soothe people and to boost their spirit. I want to dedicate this successfulness to my parents.; [a.] Gorham, NY

YATES, CARINNE MELISSA
[pen.] Carinne Melissa; [b.] February 15, 1979, Fontana, CA; [p.] Raymond and Maria Yates; [ed.] Sr. at Jurupa Valley High School; [occ.] Full-time student; [memb.] *Who's Who Among American High School Students.* Jelou Brigade Chamber Singers, J.O.F.T. Church Youth Group; [hon.] 3 yr. Award for grades and activities, Drum major of Silver Brigade, Chamber Singer; [oth. writ.] "The Lord," "Love Me," "Laugh," "Remember," "Love," "End of Times," "Friends," "Heart and Mind"; [pers.] I want to thank God for my gift, and thank my parents for the support and love they have given me throughout the years.; [a.] Mira Loma, CA

YENNER, FRANCINE L.
[pen.] Jamie Lynne Martin; [b.] June 2, 1967, Trenton, NJ; [p.] Carl Yenner, Doris Yenner; [ed.] Ewing High School, Mercer County Community College; [occ.] Order Picker/Packer, Prince Sports Group, Bordentown, NJ; [oth. writ.] Several other poems not yet published.; [a.] Maple Shade, NJ

YERRINGTON, SCOTT SEAN
[b.] RI, East; [p.] Preston and Maureen Yerrington; [m.] Denise C. Darette Yerrington, August 10, 1995; [ed.] Grad. of Manchester High School West High, NH Vocational Tech. College; [occ.] Owner of Business and current writer/poet; [memb.] Green Place, Society of Poets; [oth. writ.] "Hounds," "Thirsty Soul," "Meager food," "Green," "Children's Short Comings," "Measureless Nights"; [pers.] In my childhood, I turned to stories and poems of imagination and thought. Now I feverishly write of such things society speaks so slightly of. I wish to express the darkness of mankind in a different shadow and in my writings you will have the chance to taste it in the words and hear it in your thoughts. Thank you.; [a.] Manchester, NH

YOO, OCK KYU
[b.] South Korea; [ed.] Chang Duck High, University of Southern Colorado (MBA); [occ.] International Student; [pers.] The world is getting dark and wicked, it is hard to find a real meaning to life. To survive as a human being, I continuously take time to self-reflect and to try purifying myself through catharsis, reading and writing poetry, in my own way.; [a.] Colorado Springs, CO

YOUNAN, KRISTINA JOANNA
[pen.] Kristina Younan; [b.] November 5, 1983, Royal Oak, MI; [p.] Feyha and Kais Younan; [pers.] "I wrote my poem for a purpose not just because I was bored" at my friend's mother's death.; [a.] Troy, MI

YOUNG, DOUGLAS E.
[pen.] Douglas E. Young; [b.] March 26, 1961, Landstuki, Germany; [p.] Edwin Young, Eileen Young; [ch.] Kayla Rae Young; [ed.] Gresham High School; [memb.] East Hill Church; [hon.] I consider being chosen for this publication an honor, otherwise I have none.; [oth. writ.] Numerous poems, none published; [pers.] I write from the feelings of my heart. I've been influenced by the emotions of my life, to write.; [a.] Gresham, OR

YOUNG, JAKE
[b.] June 30, 1983, SLC, UT; [p.] Pamela Seager and Craig Young; [ed.] K-8; [occ.] Student; [a.] Salt Lake City, UT

YOUNT, NETTY G.
[b.] 1946, Lee County, VA; [m.] James S. Yount; [ch.] 2 Daughters; [ed.] Sinclair Community College AAS (Assoc. in Applied Science) 1989; [occ.] Secretary; [memb.] Dayton Cycling Club; [hon.] "Various" throughout school and work career, including Dean's List and graduating with honors from Sinclair; [oth. writ.] Several others poems written for family and friends, and some written for special occasions; [pers.] I write poems to encourage and uplift others, to express their specialness, and to emphasize the importance of faith in God.; [a.] Dayton, OH

ZALABAK, STRYDER M.
[pen.] S. Michael; [b.] April 28, 1985, Torrance, CA; [p.] Pete and Margaret Zalabak; [ed.] Center Street School, El Segundo; [occ.] Student, El Segundo Middle School; [memb.] Boy Scouts of America, AYSO; [hon.] Honor Roll Student 94-96; [a.] El Segundo, CA

ZOELLNER, FRANK J.
[b.] November 21, 1955, Indianapolis, IN; [p.] Frank and Carol Zoellner; [m.] Tanya K. Severance, 1994 - October 3, 1994; [ch.] Carrie, Casie, Charlie; [ed.] Warren Central H.S.; [occ.] Restorer of antique car trim; [oth. writ.] *Marble and Souls* - (Chap Book) and *Lost Latches* - (Chapbook), both self published; [pers.] There are too many common things in this world that are taken for granted. I like to remind people by my writing that the simplest things are truly the greatest, and they are all around us.; [a.] Indianapolis, IN

ZSIDO, JENNIFER
[b.] October 9, 1979, St. Petersburg, FL; [p.] Richard and Deborah Zsido; [ed.] Hiltons Elementary School Hiltons, VA, Central Junior High School West Frankfort, IL, Frankfort Community High School West Frankfort, IL; [occ.] Student; [hon.] Awarded English Award of Elementary School graduation because of my grade, interest in English, and achievements, Vice President of Honor Society in 6th grade, Honor Roll Student all through school, poet of the Day in 8th grade literature class; [pers.] My poems are my feelings, thoughts, dreams, and opinions. I like to use symbolism in my poetry because it adds a sense of depth and emotion. For me, poetry has been a big influence in my life.; [a.] West Frankfort, IL

ZUBER, NATHALIE
[b.] January 9, 1977, Sao Paulo, Brasil; [p.] Pierre and Leda Zuber; [ch.] Alexis Lily Zuber; [ed.] St. Albert the Great, Berlin American High School, Bethel Park Senior High, Community College of Allegheny County; [occ.] Student; [pers.] Always be true to yourself, and you will find peace and happiness.; [a.] Bethel Park, PA

ZUNIGA, LEONEL FERNANDO
[pen.] Leonel Zuniga; [b.] March 31, 1975, Monterrey, Mexico; [p.] Leonel and Carmen Zuniga; [ed.] George Mason University and Northern Community College; [occ.] Student; [oth. writ.] Many poems and short stories none of which I have ever published. Maybe hopefully someday I'll get that opportunity; [pers.] "I write poems and love stories with the purpose to maybe put a smile on those who appreciate love. Love heals and it hurts at the same time, but nothing matches the power of love."; [a.] Fairfax, VA

Index of Poets

Index

A

Abbott, Shawn 137
Abdallah, Adam 521
Abdur-Raquiyb, Qurratulayn 504
Abrams, Felicia 400
Ackley, Winifred 416
Ackman, Emily 78
Acosta, Rocio A. 151
Acquafredda, Linda 502
Acquaviva, John 61
Adams, David Jr. 313
Adams, Eleanor 478
Adams, Zack 101
Addison, Lawrence W. 334
Adkins, Christopher D. 197
Adwell, Cynthia M. 223
Affolder, Nikky 503
Agelastos, Niki 323
Aguila, Damian 433
Aguilar, Becky 354
Aguilar, Phillip P. 327
Aguillard, Daphne E. 383
Ahlmalm, Anneli 347
Ahten, Bess 494
Akers, Kelly Renee 74
Albanese, Mary 176
Alberto, Abigail 455
Alberto, Justin 486
Albrecht, Rick 188
Alcala, Julia 420
Alderman, Beth 298
Alessandro, Richard E. 321
Alexander, Comarita 111
Alexander, Judy 262
Alexander, Julia C. 216
Alexander, Merilyn E. 12
Alexander, Tommy 59
Alger, Cristy 477
Alikhan, Fatima 331
Allen, Casey 482
Allen, Evan 403
Allen, Gabrielle 65
Allen, Jennifer 313
Allen, Mark 37
Allen, Rhonda K. 93
Allen, Shirley 481, 545
Allen, Susan 487
Allison, Joy 521
Allison, Robert K. III 266
Alliston, Norma 460
Altken, Irene 287
Alves, Barbara Glynn 235
Alvillar, Monica V. 509
Alyono, Jennifer 144
Amaro, Pedro L. 167
ambers, willow 330
Ammerman, G. R. 103
Amrhein, Evan F. 74
Anderson, Anthony 182
Anderson, Ashley 391
Anderson, Guy H. 343
Anderson, Helen 498
Anderson, Karla Jane 249
Anderson, Lisa 189
Anderson, Lisa Ma'ree 490
Anderson, Michelle 383
Anderson, Robert 323
Anderson, Robert G. 189
Anderson, Robin 387
Anderson, Ruby 175
Anderson-Schultz, Tammy 86
Andi, Keith V. 427
Andre', Edmund 255
Andrews, Cathy 368
Andriakos, Cassie 399
Andrus, Michael G. 434
Angel, Lee 334
Anselment, Joseph D. 165
Anspaugh, Lowell 110
Aoude, Lana 454
Apple, Cameron P. 65
Appler, Mark A. 27
Aquilina, Rhonda L. 86
Archer, Donald L. 539
Arden, Colin 458
Arden, Stephanie 202
Ardis, Betty 132
Arellano, Dustin 441
Armijo, Deborah L. 372
Armstrong, Brandy 386
Armstrong, Terri 162
Armstrong-Sherrill, Brigitte 194
Arnett, Heather 39
Arnold, Lisa 299
Arnold, Raymond M. 197
Arnold, Sherri M. 426
Arocho, Nancy 20
Arrington, Fran Brake 290
Arteza, Jonathan 134
Arthur, Chad S. 54
Ary, Steven 544
Asabor, Joyce 461
Asay, Mandie 403
Ashlock, Margaret Guilloud 313
Ashworth, Dianna I. 292
Asiq, Cheryl 475
Askew, Merle C. 314
Assem, Philip 150
Atkins, Jeana 461
Atkins, Kristie 206
Atkins, Richard, Jr. 207
Aubuchon, Kristina Wagner 330
Aughenbaugh, Rebecca 346
Auguste, Junia Laura 216
Augustin, Sindy 248
Ault, Karen 95
Autio, Mildred I. 429
Autry, Kristy L. 154
Avery, Brandon 445
Avila, Phyllis 285
Ayala, Francisco M. Jr. 490
Aynes, April 468
Azevedo, Francesca Aragon 1

B

B., Khadija 295
Babin, Jennifer T. 28
Bacalzo, Natividad F. 487
Bacon, Rowena L. 72
Bacun, Wade 458
Baez, Amy 352
Bagatti, Jude 224
Bailey, Ada 319
Bailey, Arlow 495
Bailey, Gregory 75
Bailey, Kristie 321
Bailey, Nancy Anne 201
Bailey, Nicole M. 271
Bailey, Rachel 331
Bailey, T. 448
Bailey, Timothy 161
Bailey, Timothy 432
Bailiff, Robert 46
Bain, Maxine E. 138
Baker, Carol 384
Baker, Chelsea 388
Baker, Christina 147
Baker, Kelly 335
Baker, LaDonna 338
Baker, Meredith 87
Baker, Peggy 372
Baker, William A. 395
Balbirer, Ida Janko 238
Baldwin, Irene F. 187
Baldwin, Jody 228
Baldwin, Margaret A. 311
Ball, Sheila A. 74
Ballard, Phillip McClelland 328
Balsinger, Anna H. 340
Balulis, John A. Jr. 453
Balwinski, Rodney 191
Band, Jill Amy 287
Bandele, Ajamu 521
Barber, Diane E. 112
Barcus, Deanna 389
Bari, Monna D. 444
Barnes, Tera Ann 15
Barnes, Thelma 542
Barnett, Dawn 494
Barnhart, Jennilee 230
Baronette, Sandra Joy 495
Barot, Atmaram J. 411
Barrett, Annmarie 182
Barrett, Robert F. 413
Barrio, Samantha Nicole 505
Barron, Corin Elise 177
Barron, James M. 172
Barros, Jason A. 502
Barry, Lauren A. 138
Barta, Valerie 222
Bartelheim, Michell 331
Barth, Amy 114
Bartholomew, Felicia A. 330
Bartlett, Alberta Lynn 176
Bartlett, Yvonne M. 215
Barton, Jo 124
Barton, Lois 307
Bascko, Shirley A. 538
Bashaw, Pauline 386
Bashay, Cheyenne 123
Basil, Rose 452
Basinger, Eleanor F. 538
Bass, Eva 464
Bates, Jeff 272
Battle, Rev. Donald E. Sr. 121
Batts, James Clark 33
Bauknight, Melissa 49
Baust, Elsie F. 202
Bayard, Suzanne 424
Baynum, Robert G. 536
Baysinger, Jessica 309
Beals, Amanda M. 180
Beauregard, Bethany 217
Beaver, Jason J. 109
Beawais, Donnette 416
Beck, Erika 43
Beck, Lorraine E. 228
Beck, Michele 106
Beck, Robert E. 372
Becker, Carolyn 250
Becker, Cathy L. 475
Becker, Melissa Y. 383
Beckette, Richard E. 310
Beckner, Rick 436
Bednosh, Jessica 209
Beechie, Teresa 379
Beguhn, Gina 97
Behnke, Kathy 329
Behrens, William J. 10
Beilman, Edwina N. 419
Beilstein, The Rev. Joan E. 438
Bel Cher, Andre 145
Belkin, Irving 135
Bell, Foster III 183
Bell, Robert 157
Bell, Tyrell 276
Belletto, Benjamin S. 389
Bellon, James F. 139
Bellon, John Jr. 7
Bemis, John 317
Benavente, Rose A. 361
Benesch, William C. Jr. 324
Beninson, Jonathan 33
Bennett, Martin V. 20
Bennett, Samuel A. 250
Bensley, Elizabeth S. 92
Benson, Renee N. 432
Bentley, Daril 373
Bentley, Melinda 299
Bentlin, Mary Ellen 223
Bentz, William G. 417
Berens, Judith 27
Bergeron, Ashley 246
Bergeron, Paul L. 53
Berghorn, Christine 334
Berkich, Gwen 213
Bernhard, Constance M. 465
Bernier, Diane S. 458
Berry, Carol K. 423
Berry, Janice 493
Berry, Mandy 417
Berry, W. Richard 39
Bersuder, Frances 323
Bertin, Solange M. 104
Berumen, Elizabeth 287
Best, DanieLisa 221
Bethard, Katie 217
Bevil, Brooks 28
Bey, Jamal M. 329
Bhatti, Fariha 312
Bialkin, Donna R. 131
Bianco, Louis 496
Bibo 506
Bierly, Shirley J. 543
Bigelow, Mary 337
Biggs, Sondra 203
Billings, John 8
Billington, Meredith Gayle 506
Binick, Angeline 251
Binner, Casi 386
Binnicker, Michael 220
Binninger, Donald G. 362
Biondi, Joseph J. 91
Birch, Robert 227
Bird, Bridget M. 432
Bird, Della M. 187
Birdsall, Florence A. 319
Birket, Teresa A. 425

Birkner, Irene 85
Bishop, Dennis H. 284
Bisko, Joe 29
Bitner, Betty 297
Black, Dian 257
Black, Shelly A. 46
Black, Shirley 373
Blackstone, Andrea 274
Blackwell, Mary Ann 102
Blair, Marion 535
Blaisdell, Richard 239
Blake, Richard D. 527
Blakey, Michelle 368
Bland, David 178
Blankenbaker, Andy 158
Blanscet, Andrea L. 182
Blase, Judith C. 216
Blaski, Rhonda 174
Blevins, Claudine Cerra 358
Bliemeister, Kelly 101
Bliss, Dorothy Bieber 431
Blitz, Tara 146
Blonder, Nicole C. 262
Bloom, Marcus 17
Bloomquist, Samantha 121
Blose, Jennifer 424
Blowers, Shawna 415
Bluestein, Cheryl 22
Bock, Fran 541
Bodenbach, Michael 382
Bodily, Marcella 119
Bohlander, Rhiannon L. 126
Boivin, Kara 389
Bolar, Erica 230
Bolks, David A. 440
Bollom, Zane R. 178
Bonar, Rosebud Elliott 295
Bonidie, Tracey 67
Bonine, Jason 174
Bonney, Heather R. 209
Bonney, Suzanne 37
Bonovich, Ruth E. 107
Bontrager, Joyce Digges 148
Booher, Airman Ryan M. 476
Booher, Michelle 427
Booker, Lauren N. 113
Booker, Michael 250
Booms, Jeff J. 247
Boose, Alma 53
Booth, Betty Jean 83
Borba, K. 4
Borba, Kathy 83
Borgesen, Tammy 161
Borjes, Victoria M. 79
Borton, Deborah L. 535
Bosch, Donald R. 342
Bostwick, Anne M. 335
Bot, Krista 418
Botelho, Toni Lynn 419
Botkins, Macel H. 278
Bourg, Joseph M. 440
Boutelle, Ruth 395
Bouthillette, Natile 200
Bove, James L. 250
Bower, Phil 363
Bowker, Irene Schanche 415
Bowman, David R. 326
Bowman, Patrick W. 102
Bowser, Paula 393
Boyd, Steven Dewain 52
Boyer, Rachel 396

Boykin, Earlene 474
Bozeman, Ivie 180
Bracey, Omega 302
Bracey, Sylvester 305
Braden, Sean Steven 351
Bradley, Richard O. 349
Bradley, Roseanne 488
Bradshaw, Dan 252
Bradshaw, Mary Lane 382
Brady, Samantha 65
Brady, Sean 133
Brady, Virginia J. 542
Brancato, Jane 510
Branche, Annette M. 62
Brandt, Rob 108
Brandtner, Marti E. 441
Brannan, Dale C. 329
Bratcher, Connie Campbell 301
Brath, Joe 23
Braun, Ashley 440
Braunberger, Margaret Rose 312
Breck, Steven K. 519
Breitenfeldt, Tamra 61
Bremner, Scott H. 436
Brence, David A. 490
Brend, Alicia 179
Brestan, Maria 17
Brewer, Lana J. 81
Brewer, Michelle 223
Brewer, Robert R. 46
Bridge, Wendie 116
Brightwell, Evelyn 76
Brightwell, Peter T. 66
Brija, Janet L. 301
Brillant, William J. 135
Brindley, Sandra 400
Briscoe, Robert 328
Britt, Beau 206
Brock, Leslie S. 210
Brockington, Maxine 435
Brodersen, Jake R. 216
Broesel, Bonnie 53
Brooking, Kayla 179
Brooks, Vivian R. 265
Brosnan, Paul 224
Brottlund, Betsy Ranae 376
Brown, Allen J. 12
Brown, April 376
Brown, Bonita 350
Brown, Candace 492
Brown, Carla Diahanne 502
Brown, Daniel A. 442
Brown, Eleanor D. 444
Brown, Garry C. 65
Brown, Herb 278
Brown, Kellie Antrim 128
Brown, Lea 42
Brown, Lila 321
Brown, Linda 179
Brown, M. A. 331
Brown, Matthew 412
Brown, Michael 251
Brown, Mona I. 510
Brown, Myrite A. 308
Brown, Neil W. 242
Brown, Neville L. 377
Brown, Pauline 257
Brown, Richard D. T. 159
Brown, Terrance Avis 183
Brown, Tommikco T. 69
Brown-Dudek, Eleanor 317

Bruce, Mandy 229
Bruce, Stacey L. 34
Bruder, Kathleen A. 155
Bruggeman, James C. 122
Brundage, Virgil K. 148
Brunn, Frederick M. 155
Bryant, Debi 312
Bryant, Dessie 232
Bryant, Tara Lynne 339
Bryce, Mary Ann 143
Buccellato, Steven 486
Buck, Frank 279
Buckner, Anthony M. 212
Bucs, Alleah M. 366
Buechner, Peter Simon III 167
Buettner, Lisa M. 4
Bugarski, Vladimir 179
Bugden, Edward G. 98
Buhl, Barbara Ann Beaven 16
Bui, Audrey 239
Buie, Randy D. 309
Bukharova, Inga 128
Bulauski, Patricia 27
Bullock, Jennifer 540
Bulmer, Jennifer 41
Bumgardner, Eileen C. 98
Burd, Rebecca 312
Burdette, Renee 102
Burdic, Deborah L. 511
Burgbacher, Shawn 507
Burgess, Phillip R. 312
Burgess, Phyllis 435
Burgo, Dorothy 180
Burke, Bryan Courtney 441
Burke, Charlotte 538
Burke, Jacob W. 390
Burke, Karen Ann 436
Burke, Katherine 99
Burke, Sharon A. 428
Burleigh, Erica 351
Burner, Chrystina 443
Burns, Amber 125
Burns, Janice L. 460
Burns, Michael R. 29
Burns, Rebecca 410
Burns, Travis 219
Burnum, Arlene 339
Burrell, Kristy 395
Burris, Pamela S. 50
Burroughs, Crissy Lee 508
Burrows, Alyse M. 441
Burrus, Brandon 181
Burt, John D. 186
Burton, Rick Goblette 280
Busbee, Kathy L. 46
Busch, Christina M. 119
Bushey, Amanda D. 174
Buss, Gina Marie 25
Butkus, Cheryl L. 54
Butler, C. Lorraine 30
Butler, Heath 157
Butler, Laurie 195
Butler, Margie 106
Butler, Monica 324
Butler, Rosemary E. 487
Butterfield, Carole 129
Buttross, Peter Jr. 314
Buyco, Janise 243
Byers, Russell 391
Byrd, Rob 99

C

Cabellon, Jacqueline P. 174
Cablay, Jessica M. 375
Cable, Idia E. 411
Cabral, Paulina C. 480
Cahill, Calista 315
Cahill, Catherine 110
Calamari, Annie 458
Calcei, Diane C. 256
Caldwell, Sally 371
Caldwell, Vivian B. 433
Caliqiuri, Victor 204
Callahan, Kathleen McDonald 425
Callahan, Wendy L. 6
Callard, James M. 127
Callaway, James 70
Callcut, Jacob 60
Callin, Eloise 354
Camelio, Carol 160
Camhe, Merrilie 203
Camigliano, Alicia 511
Campbell, Andrew P. Jr. 404
Campbell, Brittany C. 149
Campbell, David 403
Campbell, Jacqueline S. 429
Campbell, John 40
Campbell, Liz 93
Campbell, Mary E. 80
Campbell, Stephanie 60
Campbell, Tanisha 14
Candler, Joanna 292
Canfield, Mike 262
Cann, Leopold 362
Canner, Claudia 319
Cannon, Patrick 438
Cantone, Carmela 479
Cape, Preston 119
Caplan, Korie 325
Capone, Dominique 430
Caputi, Michael James 66
Caputo, C. J. 209
Caputo, Evelyn 203
Carafelly, Sheri 334
Caraig, Jun 107
Cardenas, Felipe 215
Carey, Brendon M. 307
Cariglio, Carrie-Ann 475
Carlile, Dave 145
Carlough, Sarah 15
Carlson, Dan 261
Carmichael, Jack W. 454
Carnes, Nancy P. 120
Carpenter, Heather L. 34
Carpenter, Teryl Moyer 38
Carr, Olanda Jr. 228
Carrero, Joseph A. 444
Carrica, Desiree 193
Carricato, Aaron 59
Carrigg, Carin 503
Carroll, Jonathan 156
Carroll, Lennie Whitt 473
Carroll, Linda 234
Carson, Weida 283
Carswell, Helen 431
Carter, Jennifer Frances 159
Carter, Keith C. 93
Carter, William 161
Caruso, Sharon M. 533
Casanova, Carmen 526
Casarez, Ares Joe 465

Casavan, Nicole M. 174
Casey, Lesley E. Jr. 212
Cash, Eleanor Skelton 314
Cassar, Mariella 88
Castanza, Maria 191
Castelo, Kimberly 145
Castillo, Gilda J. 218
Castline, Patricia 423
Castro, Phillip III 142
Cato, Lynn 121
Catoline, John A. 347
Catoline, Rozanna M. 391
Caton, Chastity 239
Cattoni, Adrianne 512
Cazes, Eugene 258
Ceder, John W. 164
Celley-Lowenberg, Sherry 390
Centeno, Elizabeth Daly 254
Cerella, Amy 13
Cerniglia, Nunzio 69
Certisimo, Jill 416
Cervantez, Kristin 195
Cesare, Joyce De 144
Cetto, Gale 467
Chabla, Elcio 155
Chadwick 394
Chadwick, Melinda 267
Chaka, Lady 211
Chamberlain, Joleen 422
Chamberlin, Whitney 380
Chambers, Leslie 363
Chambers, Marie 263
Chancey, Kathryn Ceceilia 185
Chandler, Andrew Robert 207
Chandler, Russell E. 233
Chang, Amy 534
Chansky, Matthew 125
Chaparro, Monic 151
Charbonneau, Douglas 117
Charette, Nikki J. 320
Charles, Waldy 143
Chase, Devin 438
Chastain, Keith C. 545
Chavira, Karen J. 496
Chazen, Jamie 322
Chen, Ming 210
Cheney, Branningan S. 317
Cheng, Marie 39
Chernyshev, Pavel 96
Cherry, Tom 100
Chestnut, Katrina 517
Childers, Charlotte 63
Childers, Elizabeth U. 387
Childs, Hiram Paul 133
Childs, Jacqueline L. 536
Chira, Cindy 369
Chong, David S. 528
Christensen, Jill 19
Christensen, S. Robert 223
Christian, Matt 425
Christie, Amber R. 108
Christofano, Frank M. 428
Christy, Mysha 107
Chukwuocha, Nnamdi O. 233
Chung, Mollie 222
Church, Carmen 341
Ciobanu, Ileana 528
Ciotti, Tom 182
Civettini, Andrew Joseph 507
Cizewski, Jaime R. 230
Clark, Alicia M. 13

Clark, Chris 498
Clark, Connie 198
Clark, Gregory K. 359
Clark, Jennifer 97
Clark, John S. 50
Clark, Judith Gott 139
Clark, Kim 462
Clark, Linda Orsak 305
Clark, W. Drury 167
Clark, William N. 176
Clarke, Brenda 468
Clarke, Kimberly 59
Clarke, Lisa 525
Claxton, Travis D. 183
Clay, Gisella 345
Claytor, Rachel 323
Clements, April 376
Clifford, Tammi L. 333
Cline, Nathan L. 212
Closs, Miki L. 288
Cloutier, Thomas J. 125
Clowe, Quincy 98
Clukie, David R. 355
Cobb, Jim 374
Cobb, Shannon R. 327
Cochran, Connie L. 165
Cockrell, Beatrice 462
Coen, Denise 342
Cohea, Mike 250
Colabella, Louis 359
Colangelo, Joseph 229
Cole, Erin L. 114
Cole, Leslie A. 543
Cole, Penny 486
Cole, Sarah Violet 491
Cole, Yvonne 492
Coleman, Heather 198
Coleman, Keith 450
Coleman, Rosie 79
Coleman, Stacy N. 522
Colla, Amy 526
Collins, Celia 210
Collins, Linda Foster 132
Collis, Brian M. 413
Colonna, Marcus Elias 479
Combs, Bobby J. 533
Combs, Grace 90
Combs, Teresa M. 495
Comeau, Kimberly K. 313
Concepcion, Genisa 105
Cone, Alynda 361
Coney, Diana 102
Conley, Alison 475
Conley, Cherri 98
Conley, T. Y. 499
Conner, Edith H. 114
Conney, George M. 97
Conomikes, Sandi 46
Conover, Kenneth R. Jr. 50
Conroy, Lisa 449
Contreras, Dana M. 84
Contreras, Roberto A. 279
Converse, Sandra Lynn Wagg 158
Cook, Carol 94
Cook, Danielle Lynn Pinelli 170
Cook, Emma M. 3
Cook, Jennifer 421
Cook, Nancy 272
Cook, Sara 435
Cook, Stacie Lianne 46
Cook, Tom 531

Cooke, Kim 225
Cooke, Tina-Marie 346
Cooler, Amanda Jeffers 72
Cooley, Jode 430
Cooley, Melinda Gray 506
Coon, Margaret 147
Cooper, Barbara A. 539
Cooper, Grace 474
Cooper, Nancy 115
Cooper, Tyra 454
Copeland, Patrick 390
Cordeiro, Charlsyee 200
Cordova-Laviolette, Lori Y. 203
Corey, Christopher P. 345
Corey, Rebekka 36
Cornwell, R. C. 539
Corpuz, Christina 136
Cortes, Roger G. 32
Costanzo, Suzanne C. 329
Costello, Charles 431
Cote, Ralph L. 41
Cottrell, Linda L. 247
Coulson, Kathleen M. 531
Counihan, Erin 339
Counts, Mary 71
Covelens, Kelly 247
Coverdale, Lydia 419
Cowan, Alyssa 101
Cowell, Roy F. 163
Cox, Brindle 278
Cox, Donna Kay 431
Cox, Linda June 169
Cox, Sarah 318
Cox, Vivian 122
Crabtree, Penny 83
Crabtree, Stephanie 20
Crafton, Julie 480
Craig, Claudia E. 224
Crail, Yolanda 176
Cramer, Robin 296
Crandall, Fred M. 311
Crane, Jennie 168
Cranford, Roy L. Sr. 471
Crapo, Larina 238
Crawford, Chas 416
Crichlow, Gerard 407
Crippen, Gary C. 18
Crissman, Lyn 253
Crites, Kay 87
Crites, Rachel 351
Cronin (nee Ruth Sampson), Marie 25
Crosby, John 40
Cross, Brian 522
Cross, Douglas Jr. 185
Cross, Jodi 523
Cross, Patricia A. 379
Cross, Sarah Lee 115
Crossman, Nick 29
Crouch, Celinda 52
Crouch, Jennifer 276
Crow, Aimee 276
Crowell, Heather 431
Cruz de Guy, Marilyn M. 524
Cubit, Gregory 516
Cuccia, Catherine 67
Cuculic, Paul 12
Culbert, Margo 82
Cullen, Mick 330
Cullum, Joel A. 382
Cultice, Patricia A. 487
Cuminotti, Debra A. 231

Cummings, Angela 19
Cummings, Connie 348
Cummings, Theresa L. 321
Cunningham, Randy Ray 19
Curcio, Theresa 320
Custer, Carolyn 423
Cut, Zenah Leigh 274
Czech, D. James 154

D

Dabbs, Elizabeth 316
Dacpano, Noreen 396
DaForno, Michael 53
Daigneault, Lenny 122
Dailey, Cinda 92
Dailey, Dara 317
Dailey, Jennifer 218
Dallett, James D. 221
Dallmann, Nancy 225
Dalton, Phyllis I. 524
Daly, Ann 418
Dames, Austin 146
Damico, Derek 465
Damman, Kate 162
Damron, Tammy Lynn 55
Danaher, Dawn Marie 213
Dando, Stacey L. 50
Danel, P. Edward 95
Daniel, Jennifer 345
Daniel, Joshua Vigil 112
Daniel, Nathan 73
D'Annibale, Barbara A. 403
Darling, John L. Jr. 301
Darlington, Alice L. 407
Darnell, Joseph L. 166
David, Marc 88
Davis, Aaron 32
Davis, Alison 126
Davis, Angela W. 26
Davis, Anita M. 132
Davis, Craig 124
Davis, Dana Lena 112
Davis, John Christopher 211
Davis, Kim L. 117
Davis, Lorena M. 445
Davis, M. C. 473
Davis, Mario C. 467
Davis, Martina L. 234
Davis, Meagan S. 217
Davis, Mike 128
Davis, Robert Otto 11
Davis, Roland B. 538
Davis, Will 6
Davison, Vern 25
Davisson, Karen A. 360
Davoli, Clifford 513
Davy, Elda Buralli 354
Dawdy, Darin 113
Dawn, Stephanie 31
Day, Kari 468
Day, Laura J. 73
Day, Sharon H. 230
Day, Terri Townsend 510
Daymon, Cynthia J. 131
De Assumpcao, David 434
de Brito, Edward 501
De Castro, Paolo 224
De La Pena, Minerva 5
De La Torre, Odette 139
De Long, Bethani Ann 295

De Longis, Mary 63
De Maria, Daniel 429
De Shazo, Del 354
De Vito, Beverly 324
Dean, Kathy 540
Dean, Wyvren 523
DeAngelo, Lisa 382
DeBlasio, Stacy 105
DeBoer, Michelle S. 535
Decker, Michelle 48
Decolati, John "Deco" 67
Deeds, Jason W. 370
Deering, Linda J. 314
Deery, Mary Beth 525
Deglow, John 476
DeGroat, Ralph J., Jr. 20
Dehl, Lindsey 534
Dehne, Nancy Rae 504
Deinhardt, Alberta 101
Dekermarek, Marie-Nicole 339
Delaney, Traci J. 28
Delicath, Sharon 330
Dell, Megan 28
Della Posta, Sarah 155
DeMasi, Matt 316
D'Emma, Chrisitna 171
Dempsey, Mark 245
Demske, John 530
Deng, John 203
Denning, Hazel M. 477
Denning, Nicole 257
Depalma Sr., Nicholas C. 208
DePriest, Drew 106
Deretchin, Leona 171
Desellier, Cherish 100
Dettling, Michelle 461
Devers, Laurada 449
Devine, Frances 442
DeVore, Jeffrey W. 519
Dewey, Conneen 489
Dewitt, Amanda 288
DeWitt, Jessica 78
Dhadwal, Anish 47
D'Hondt, Julie 326
Di Maio, Nicole 410
Dial, Tabitha Gayle 270
Diaz, Anita M. 356
Diaz, Gustavo Javier Vitureira 250
Diaz, Jackie 315
Diaz, Michael 322
DiBernardinis, Bernice 544
DiCarlo, Maria R. 175
Dichtel, Cindy M. 380
Dickens, Jodi 198
Dickensheets, Jim 491
Dickerman, Clarence Jr. 537
Dickerson, Lagranda A. 332
Dickerson, Linda A. 22
Dickey, Allen 275
Dickison, Linda, R.N. ICU 156
Dickman, Meredith 420
Dickson, Julia L. 349
DiDomenico R., Francesca 315
Diener, Carol L. 110
Diesel, Rob 538
Dietrich, Joyce 226
DiGiovanni, Frank 221
Digregorio, Angelo J. 39
Digregorio, Jim 226
Dilley, Susan J. 29
Dillman, Jennifer 178

Dillon, Mary 66
Dillon, Mildred 34
Dillon, Norman M. Jr. 252
Dillworth, Scott 308
DiLoreto, Cheryl 110
Dilts, Phyllis 469
Dimatteo, Doris Ann 132
Dimitri, Wayne 446
Director, Sheana R. 469
DiSabatino, Lucia 545
Dixon, Barbara A. 69
Dixon, Robert W. 476
Doak, Melissa 96
Dobiesz, Ronald F. 201
Docherty, Mary F. 511
Dockter, Arleen 196
Dodge, Helen 371
Dodson, J. 264
Dolan, Charles Richard 209
Dole, Joshua 107
Dolliver, Christie 497
Dolores 215
Dombroski, Carole 238
Domenick, Helen L. Hightower 108
Domenico, Philip 41
Dominick, Beynamaan 438
Donnelly, Edward G. 540
Donwen, Kelsey 423
Doran, Maria A. 353
Doris, Jennie 154
Dorotheo, Paz R. 240
Dorr, Katy Marie 499
Dorsey, Dorothy M. 417
Dorwart, Deborah 329
Doster, Gerald Jr. 329
Dottavio, Cheyenne 216
Dougherty, Chris 272
Dougherty, Cristen R. 342
Douglas, Kendrick R. 160
Douglas-Hamilton, Fiona 466
Douthett, Beth 102
Douthett, Ruth 35
Dowd, Laura 512
Dowdrick, Joseph 432
Dowell, Korey 377
Down, Alisen 95
Down, Annie 441
Downey, Lowell 110
Downey, Paulette 507
Downey, Susanne M. 378
Downs, Carolyn 56
Doyen, Renee Y. 4
Doyle, Kathleen 18
Drake, Christine 367
Dralle, Bonnie L. 117
Drawe, Heinz K. 350
Dresbach, Jesse 455
Drew, Danny Glenn 414
Drewery, Fay 333
Driggers, Julia Anne 85
Drinkard, Dianna 492
Driscoll, Benjamin A. 110
Drury, Jared 495
Drury, Nancy 503
Drury, Windy W. 186
Druschel, Janet 152
du Bois, Betty Chadbourne 78
Du Breuil, Lauran 451
Du Brock, Joshua M. 23
Dubman, Rosemarie 350
DuBois, Barbara R. 543

Duensing, Margaret R. 500
Dufault, Jeremie J. 94
Duis, Richard J. 308
Duke, J. Thomas 449
D'Ulisse, Adrienne 431
D'Ulisse, Jaci 325
Dummermuth, Tony E. 545
Dunbar, Nita 391
Dunbar, Rosalie E. 204
Duncan, Heather 109
Duncan, Tiffany Grace 206
Dunford, LaPriel 345
Dunlap, Eliana Capri 538
Dunn, Robert C. 350
DuPay, Nell 498
Duque, Mary 543
Durbin, Launa C. 202
Durgan, Mary 140
Durham-Holupka, Julie 478, 545
Dusinberre, Donald Henry 263
Dutil, Amy 438
Duxbury, Joanne C. 351
Dvorak, Ernestine E. 497
Dvorak, William S. 123
Dybala, Natalie 110
Dye, Alma F. 479
Dye, Becky 536
Dzwonkowski, Gloria 300

E

Eagan, Mimi 544
Earl, Conner 252
Earl, Jed 99
Earnshaw, George D. Jr. 334
Eaton, Lisa Ann 491
Ebersole, Hal H. 91
Eckard, Theresa D. 472
Eckel, Helen W. 405
Eckel, Jess 87
Eckert, Karl T. 137
Eckert, Wendy M. 70
Eddington, Christy 171
Eddis, George 398
Edlen, T. R. 316
Edmonson, Viola 193
Edmunds, Christopher 365
Edmunds-Casey, Linda J. 102
Edwards, Francis H. 387
Edwards, Michelle 303
Egan, Judy A. 491
Eggering, Lorin 444
Ehrenreich, Theresa 409
Eihem, John Robert 158
Einhart, Edward P. 219
Elder, Jeanne 94
Eleste, Rachael Elizabeth 219
Elijah, Katie 104
Ellen, Nancy 36
Ellifritt, Edward G. 430
Elliott, Angela 351
Elliott, Cathy 213
Elliott, Kevin 240
Elliott, Victoria A. 71
Ellis, April 388
Ellis, Norman 462
Ellis, Renaite C. 505
Ellis, Virginia B. 232
Ellison, Indiana 136
Ellison, Laura L. 126
Enerson, Scott M. 339

Engel, Beth 372
English, Jessica 405
Enright, Lillian V. 255
Erardi, Jean 6
Erb, Allison 510
Erb, Marcella 89
Ercolino, Andrea 112
Erichson, Robert Mark 414
Eriksen, Bonnie C. 249
Erpanir, Bayhun 337
Esch, Gwyn 471
Eslami, Emily 61
Espinosa-Sabral, Elidia 54
Estabillo, Lesa 280
Esther, Robert 369
Ethridge, Julie 182
Etienne, Clifford 246
Etue, James 32
Euwer, G. R. 376
Evangelista, Gloria 452
Evans, Christine P. 241
Evans, Clint 310
Evans, Newell Michael 394
Evans-Howe, Rebecca 74
Everngam, Sallie M. 509
Evers, Sharlene M. 506
Everts, Kirk 446
Ewing, Colleen Croson 96
Ewing, Emma Mai 544
Ewing, Teri 356
Ezell, Doris A. 322
Ezequiel, F. 271

F

Fabianski, Jennifer 33
Faggard, Ruth 509
Falavolito, Melissah J. 26
Falconer, Lorraine 137
Falero, George Sr. 152
Fallon, Laura 85
Fallon, Marie 155
Fanelli, Melissa 445
Fann, Jamie 360
Fantozzi, Alison 476
Fare, Donald C. 258
Farfel, Bridget 15
Farmer, LaJeune 96
Farmer, Patricia 252
Farmer, Perry 433
Farrell, Bob 455
Farrell, Meghan 208
Farwell, Steven 104
Fasoli, Ricky 357
Faulkner, April Suzanne 328
Faulkner, Jennifer A. 58
Faust, Robert E. 59
Fauth, Bette 444
Favia, Rose 222
Fay, Stephanie 332
Feese, Ken 207
Felda, Gladys Olivia 368
Felton, Phyllis Ann 401
Fenner, Shanessa L. 138
Ferello, Salvator 490
Ferguson, Chole 451
Ferguson, James 175
Ferland, Meghan 343
Fernandez, Roberta 240
Ferraro, Irene 92
Ferrell, Barbara G. 336

Ferris, David C. 361
Ferrucci, Ralph 8
Festa, Sandra 204
Fichera, Tobista 490
Fiddell, Deborah 62
Figel, Michael R. 41
Filipiak, Erik M. 520
Fillers, Valerie 159
Fillyaw, Terry L. 404
Fink, Raymond Bernard 306
Finley, Cynthia L. 310
Finley, Fritz 5
Finley, Rebecca 413
Finley, Tracie 275
Finn, Jenna 170
Finnegan, Kathryn A. 59
Fiorella, A. J. 63
Fiorenza, E. 52
Firewiez, Lauren 420
Fischer, Sandy 469
Fisher, Ellen M. 63
Fisher, Renee L. 173
Fitch, Jeffrey 320
Fitch, Tina 496
Fitzgerald, Jean 429
Fitzwater, Tiffany Nichole 492
Flaherty, Donald A. 519
Flaherty, G. S. 290
Flanigan, Maggie 306
Flavin, Kelley J. 522
Fleming, Polly 327
Flesner, Irma A. 48
Flickinger, Amma C. 23
Flickinger, F. 408
Flores, Marianne 424
Florival, Herve 167
Flory, Elizabeth 215
Flowers, Jamie Lynn 406
Flynn, Marilyn 508
Fogell, Louise E. 369
Fogg, Kristin 216
Fonseca, Debra L. 493
Foraker, Terry 342
Forbes, Vergena A. 260
Forcier, Shelley L. 379
Ford, James Robert 220
Ford, Karen Alfreda 535
Ford, Katherine 34
Foreman, Nichole Paige 497
Forgues, Angela 263
Forman, Sara 431
Fornof, LesLee J. 70
Forrest, Violet 434
Foster, Deborah 477
Foster, Maureen 395
Fouché, David Lee 458
Fouchecourt, Marilyn 348
Fox, Carol A. 371
Fraga, Nina Gower 153
Fraker, Gary F. 101
Fraley, Irene E. 196
Frank, Lisa L. 280
Franklin, Clifton 529
Franklin, Sharon 16
Franz, Alan 136
Fraser, Allan 424
Frauendorfer, Jamie P. 486
Frazier, Earline W. 480
Frazier, Karen 51
Fredley, Tricia 80
Freeman, Leona 344

Freeman, Lisa Marie 158
Freeman, Ruby 119
Freeman, Sarah Elisabeth 425
Freeze, Joshua J. 494
Frerich, Melody 142
Frey, Kathleen 434
Fridley, Colleen E. 55
Fridy, James Hardin Jr. 233
Fried, Elva S. 490
Friend, Annoria 41
Friend, Julie 217
Frisinger, Mary A. 138
Fritsche, Carole L. 318
Fritz, Toni 232
Frumes, Cheryl B. 272
Fry, Darold Deaton 33
Fugate, Ann 394
Fuhrhop, Erin 150
Fuller, Jason 99
Fuller, Michael R. 384
Fuller, Sidne 54
Fultz, Judy 68
Fultz, Paula 135
Fung, Alfred 499
Fuquay, Elizabeth 324
Furst, Kathryn 402
Fusco, Santo 485

G

Gabrielli, Caroline 272
Gacek-Marcheschi, Jeanine 437
Gacki, Scott 33
Gadson-Shaw, Shareema N. 188
Gage, Michael 203
Gagnon, Hildegard 442
Gaignard, Nancy 318
Gailey, Elizabeth K. 505
Gaines, William W. 35
Gaiotti, Phyllis L. 459
Galarneau, Monica 438
Galbraith, Jennifer M. 265
Galdal, Signe 249
Galivan, Theresa J. 414
Gallagher, Caitlyn M. 243
Gallets, Sharon 224
Gallis, Erin 530
Gallo, Peter 56
Galloway, Jacqueline 76
Gambaro, Erica 275
Gambill, Paula 186
Gamble, Douglas L. 261
Gamble, Lindsey 161
Gammel, Emily 404
Gange, Clara 183
Garber, Romina 329
Garcia, Karina M. 108
Garcia, Mark 204
Garcia, Nicholas 11
Garcia, Shera 488
Garcia, Stephanie 205
Gardas, Katie 141
Gardner, Deanna Nicole 14
Gardner, Gordon 297
Gardner, Lisa 169
Gardner, Suzanne 205
Garfield, Michael 440
Garkey, Crystal 221
Garner, Katrina 501
Garnica, Alison 13
Garretson, Johanna A. 353

Garris, Christina L. 489
Garrity, Kara Eileen 143
Garske, Gladys M. 490
Garth, Dorothy Ann 419
Gartman, Marion L. 458
Garza, Ron 357
Gasper, Brittany 215
Gatewood, Niki L. 323
Gathright, Kym 211
Gauss, Patricia A. 268
Gayer, Aimee 307
Geary, Gay 323
Gebers, Lisa 288
Gecinceis, Helen M. 198
Gehrie, Eric 17
Geldermann, Melissa 446
Geoffrion, Jason P. 436
Gergoff, Jo Elizabeth 507
Gerke, Richard 417
Gerkinn, Nylieke 212
Gerlach, Roy 357
Germano, Anthony J. 45
Germany, Gregory W. 221
Gernat, Douglas 333
Gertsch, Susan 441
Getts, Donna 395
Gettys, George F. 231
Giambattista, Ryan 156
Giamporcaro, Karina 357
Gianelloni, Michael 231
Gibbs, Bianca Mozell 391
Gibson, Michael A. 432
Gibson, Wendy 304
Gifford, Melissa June 524
Gigliotta, Nicole 437
Gilbert, Paula 212
Gilbert, Wilma 310
Gildea, Bryan W. 503
Gildersleeve, Kevin Hugh 318
Gildon, Erin 44
Gile, Jennifer Lee 100
Giles, Kenneth 253
Gill, Sonia 123
Gillespie, Diana 214
Gillespie, J. Dennis 320
Gilley, Teresa D. 165
Gilliland, Kristine 77
Gillum, Linda Sue 487
Gilman, Susan 495
Gilmartin, Lucinda 350
Gilmore, Esther Perkins 186
Gilmore, Louis 466
Gilpin, Anne-Marie 115
Gilroy, Andrea M. 386
Gilson, Wade J. 476
Gines, Rachelle 435
Ginther, Jeannie K. 117
Ginther, Sharon 374
Gioia, M. Jeannine 366
Giordano, Sylvia T. 241
Girard, R. Kenneth 227
Glaister, Muriel Dyar 136
Glass, Alison 18
Glass, Carla 385
Glass, Joannah Hall 510
Glazer, Len C. 81
Glenn, Vanessa A. 205
Glenn, William C. 485
Gobby, Stephanie 92
Godin, Kevin 293
Goedken, Sheryl L. 536

Goizueta, Josephine 423
Gokey, Elizabeth M. 302
Golden, Brenda 475
Golden, Brian 516
Goldenberg, Albert 286
Goldshlack, Sara 92
Goldsmith, Wanda 223
Gomez, Kerilyn 505
Gomez, Michael Jacobson 391
Gonsalves, Alisa 535
Gonzalez, Blanca Estela 347
Gonzalez, David 358
Gonzalez, William 532
Goodall, Rebecca 318
Gordon, Douglas B. 135
Gordon, Jack 452
Gordon, Jennifer 410
Gordon, Simon 434
Gorelik, Alex 280
Goretcki, Mandi 472
Gorin, Roberta 92
Gorsuch, Megan 485
Gosney, Jennifer 103
Gostlin, James G. 443
Goucher, Samantha 358
Gould, Erika H. 224
Gow, Robin A. 481
Gowdy, Jocelyn 203
Gowdy, Karen 203
Gowins, Margaret 478
Grady, Jimmy 514
Graham, Laurie 36
Graham, Michelle 508
Graham, William Alan 485
Grainger, Penny 207
Gramajo, Mauricio 84
Gramlow, Richard 157
Grammer, Sam 5
Gran, John 60
Granado, Phillip 123
Grandinetti, Dennis L. 20
Grannum, Janice 71
Grant, Alexis 283
Grant, Casey B. 304
Grant, Cheryl A. 328
Grant, Laura 437
Grant, Tyler 73
Grass, Daryl G. 225
Grassmyer, Bobbi Jean 237
Graves, LeAnne 365
Gray, Darcey L. 358
Gray, Kevin 524
Green, Anthony 284
Green, Brenda 488
Green, Eileen T. 488
Green, Hannah 220
Green, James E. Jr. 141
Green, Karen M. 200
Green, Mary F. 42
Green, Matt 254
Green, Michael 545
Green, Phyllis Jean 292
Green, R. M. 156
Green, Virginia Ann 52
Greene, Jennifer 110
Greene, Rebecca 330
Greene, Terry M. 465
Greene, T'lene 419
Greenlee, Ellen 485
Gregg, John 534
Gregg, Steven 385

Gregorius, Ronda 17
Gregory, Conrad 279
Gregory, Kimberly S. 544
Gregory, Koressa 11
Greiner, Nichole D. T. 435
Greiner, Patty 319
Greninger, Suzanne 216
Grey, B. 104
Grey, Michelle L. 242
Gribble, Bradley 282
Griego, Sheila 523
Griffeth, Emily D. 247
Griffin, Dawn 238
Griffin, James Ezra 40
Griffin, JaNae 483
Griffin, Joe 106
Griffin, Katrina M. 198
Griffin, Mary Katherine 149
Griffin, Ryan S. 5
Griffis, Richard L. 139
Grimes, Benjamin 120
Grimm, Brandilee 328
Grisham, Jessica 431
Griswell, Lori A. H. 285
Grossen, Bonnie 220
Grosso, Yolonda R. 95
Grossoehmig, Bev 147
Grote, Audrey 197
Grow, Jeffrey S. 436
Gruenewald, Charles E. 199
Gruenholz, Terry A. 504
Gruesu, Joseph J. 168
Grynkiewicz, David J. 173
Gualazzi, Mark 315
Guardado, Martha 109
Guerin, Jessica 435
Guernsey, Neal 380
Gugel, Clyde E. 121
Guiffaut, Deborah 463
Guild, Carol 432
Guiliani, Jackie 464
Guimaraes, Barbara 242
Guinn, Jeanne 406
Guip, Rachael 138
Guise, Rebecca 215
Guk, Christina M. 363
Gulack, Scott 234
Gum, W. Louis 54
Gunderson, Karen 324
Gunning, Jeanne D. 468
Gunnoe, Carolyn 477
Gunter, Larry C. 223
Guthrie, Michael 295
Gutierrez, Jon T. 297
Guzman, Consuelo E. 303
Guzman, Debra 467

H

Haas, Rhonda 502
Haats, Gregory G. 534
Habner, Garry 288
Hacker, Tabitha 149
Hackl, Kevin Paul 232
Hadly, Matty D. 187
Haeni, Kathy 518
Hafford, Linda 26
Hagberg, Debra 359
Hagedorn, Jane 456
Hageman, Jennifer 93
Hagerman, April 334

Haggard, Ron 449
Hague, Jennifer 497
Haig, Mkhoian 100
Haile, Erica 94
Haines, Jamie Lynn 401
Hale, Marjorie 450
Hale, Sara 130
Hall, Chelsea Marie 171
Hall, Doris 291
Hall, Elizabeth E. 481
Hall, Farrell 243
Hall, Rebecca 47
Hall, Rose Ann 51
Hallahan, Katie 57
Halsey, A. J. 45
Halverson, Adam 432
Hamann, Ky 140
Hameditoloui, Dorris 189
Hamel, Beverly L. 507
Hamill, Teresa 512
Hamilton, Christopher 408
Hamm, Robin 327
Hammack, Brandy 113
Hammerbacker, Misty J. 183
Hammes, Kathleen 463
Hammond, Phillip E. Jr. 486
Hammontree, Nancy A. 80
Hampton, Jeannette L. 374
Hampton, Lewis F. 397
Hand, Freda 455
Haner, Jane M. 21
Hanna, Heather 211
Hanna, Jennifer 326
Hannah, Margaret 358
Hanrahan, Daniel James 204
Hansen, Delores 47
Hansen, Karla 134
Hansen, Robert P. 343
Hanson, Chelsie 234
Hanson, Syreeta 95
Hanson, Travis 'Son' 508
Harbaugh, Valarie 274
Harden, Barbara 394
Harding, Candy 286
Harding, William C. 359
Hardy, Jonlee D. 75
Hardy, Thenethia 285
Harer, Amy 230
Hargrove, Jimmy P. 356
Hariston, Jeffery L. 435
Harlin, Amanda 58
Harmon, Bill III 8
Harness, Jamie 207
Harnett, Marian L. 62
Harrington, Cynthia 234
Harris, Donna 197
Harris, Harry B. 372
Harris, Henry 98
Harris, Jacqueline Rae 51
Harris, John Steven 91
Harris, Katherine L. 358
Harris, Marcus 520
Harrison, Kimberly 256
Harsh, Rodney K. 24
Hartlage, Ken 19
Harvell, Jackie 255
Harvey, Elaine Carol 500
Harvin, Kay 291
Haskins, Hallie 266
Hastings, Phoebe 175
Hatch, Ryan 276

Hatfield, James A. 152
Hathaway, Debby 7
Hauch, Wilbert Evan 490
Haugerud, Laura 314
Hauser, Sylvia 72
Hausman, Kristi 91
Havens, Angel 100
Havens, Will H. 479
Haverda, Tony H. 72
Hawkins, John C., Jr. 194
Hawks, Tracey L. 228
Hawley, Nicole 275
Hawthorne, Roberta K. 180
Hayden, Melissa 28
Hayes, Brett 529
Hayes, Elizabeth Brook 506
Hayes, Joy 143
Hayes, Laurie B. 526
Haymond, Vonswalla 213
Haynes, Debra M. 509
Hearn, Donny R. 239
Heath, Paula J. 313
Heaton, Ralph 380
Hebbar, Reshmi 185
Hechler, Carolyn J. 12
Heckman, Derek M. 302
Hector, Eileen M. 252
Hedrick, Lisa 152
Heers, Heather K. 270
Heider, Sarah 504
Heim, C. 114
Heiman, Joan 224
Heimbuch, Dawn Renee 322
Hein, Katherine M. 77
Heinemann, Marie Theres 146
Heins, Amelia 367
Heinze, Jennifer 17
Heitsch, Leona Mason 167
Held, Michael 520
Helms, Sara Joann 210
Hembree, Constance 219
Hemmerick, Leo 314
Henderson, Angie 416
Henderson, Cheryl E. 278
Henderson, Donald E. 71
Henderson, Kayembe 164
Hendren, Richard Allen 236
Hendrickson, Robyn Ayn 16
Heneghan, Jessica 446
Hennington, Elizabeth Ann 209
Henrikson, Marline 121
Henry, Rebecca 206
Henry, Sabrina 112
Henson, Paul L., Jr. 70
Hepp, Shelly 437
Heppner, Melanie 346
Herbst, Jennifer 316
Hergan, Frances 466
Hergenroder, Dan 508
Hernandez, David 285
Hernandez, Kiana 60
Hernandez, Lydia 89
Hernandez, Vera A. 244
Heron, William S. Sr. 528
Herrig, Gary L. 500
Herron, Kathy 504
Herron, Martha M. 90
Hesselink, Timothy 534
Hester, Kelly Ann 355
Heulitt, Janet 250
Heuman, D. R. 28

Hiatt, Mary Barnes 205
Hibner, Jim L. 14
Hickman, Denise 436
Hickman, Sarah Louise 166
Hicks, Karen Louise 421
Hicks, Robert F. 52
Hiers, Dorothy Richardson 370
Higgins, N. Loy 515
Higgins, Paul V. 205
Higgs, Shareon 286
Hightower, Elayne F. 221
Hill, Betty Jean 518
Hill, Cherie 327
Hill, Hazel T. 32
Hill, Jennifer 98
Hill, Joan 208
Hill, Kimberly DeJoie 312
Hill, Lisa Ann 333
Hill, Tom 410
Hille, Stevie 138
Hills, Bonnie K. 181
Hinshaw, Ranee 428
Hintz, Amy 249
Hirata, Keith H. 281
Hittson, Cristina 371
Hobson, Richard 77
Hock, Rachel 246
Hockett, Carrie 397
Hodge, Chun-Tay 461
Hodyniak, Catherine 220
Hofford, Joshua 423
Hogan, Barbara A. 109
Hogan, Cherri L. 170
Hogan, Marguerite 220
Hogan, Meghan 313
Hogendobler, Christine 512
Hogsten, Rod 100
Holcombe, Jeffrey 370
Holland, Celeste 88
Hollingsworth, Henry L. 523
Holm, Mary 494
Holt, Lisa M. 114
Holton, Sandra P. 17
Hommer, Eunice A. 381
Honnila, Kristine 445
Honstein, Diana 531
Hook, Ellyn Guppy 539
Hoolihan, Jessica 366
Hooper, Tammy 328
Hoover, Christopher D. 148
Hoover, S. A. 433
Hope, Mary McNamara 78
Hopkins, Alice F. 196
Hopper, Diann 318
Horgan, Sharon 327
Horn, Angela 208
Hornak, Emily 43
Hornby, Elaine L. 463
Horning, Monica Jo 329
Horon, Jennifer 498
Horowitz, Stephanie 271
Horton, Al 492
Horwitz, Aja 260
Hoult, Donna 302
Houser, Leslie 421
Houser, Rosslen S. 540
Hovey, Krystle 294
Hovis, Charlotte 67
Howard, Brent J. 367
Howard, Brian P. 86
Howard, Crystal 274

Howard, Nathan A. 181
Howard, Paulette 317
Howell, Lottie 539
Howlett, Dorothy 244
Huang, Michelle 241
Hudgins, Sandra 525
Hudler, Melissa 131
Hudson, Adam 442
Hudson, Jody S. 271
Hudson, Lillie Mae 141
Huff, Nathan D. 355
Huggins, Jana 340
Hughes, Darlene M. 73
Hughes, Howard D. 499
Hughes, Sharice 57
Hughes, Wanda 189
Hughes-Rhodes, Carol 208
Hugill, Jennifer Bree 213
Hugill, Lois 299
Huisingh, Tammy 216
Hullender, Janice 223
Humphrey, John J. 527
Hunsinger, Virginia 529
Hunt, Amy 266
Hunt, David 104
Hunt, Gloria 531
Hunt, Jason P. 365
Hunt, Jeanne 324
Hunt, Katie 119
Hunt, Pamela 116
Hunt, Rian 373
Hunte, Lori 110
Hunter, Cheryl 103
Husband, Meshante 393
Huston, Sandi 343
Hutchings, D. Edwin 167
Hutchinson, Mitzi B. 75
Huyck, Holly L. O. 218
Hyatt, Cynthia D. 515
Hyland, Kenneth E. 325
Hynum, Debra L. 331

I

Ihara, Karyn 534
Ilosky, Esther 439
Ingee, Kim 334
Iosif, Cecilia Doina 441
Irizarry, Ana E. 90
Irizarry, Melisa 275
Irwin, Linda 242
Isenberg, Milda 174
Isom, Nadine 348
Izell, Dorothy J. 180
Izzo, Stephen 425

J

Jachimowicz, Janet 410
Jackowiak, Tracy 16
Jackson, Cheryl 463
Jackson, Henry 40
Jackson, Jeffrey A. 433
Jackson, Phillande C. Sr. 153
Jackson, Robert E. 448
Jacobson, Melanie 306
Jacoby, Kathryn C. 246
Jahn, Shannan 130
Jalbert, Bernice A. 510
James, Arthur W. 218
Jamniczky, Suzanne A. 370
Jankas, Denise 216
Jansen, Kim 332
Janssen, Noel 391
Jarlenski, Kathryn 159
Jason, Brian T. 512
Jazon, Claudel 484
Jefferson, Melissa 496
Jemison, Mildred Clauff 514
Jenkins, Ron 380
Jensen, Emily 384
Jensen, Kristi 213
Jensen, Rodney R. Jr. 496
Jernigan, Marie E. 353
Jimenez, Eugenio Jr. 84
Jimenez, Teresa A. 105
Johannsen, Susan 492
John, Chris 212
Johns, Larry D. 137
Johns, Lisa M. 54
Johnson, A. B., Jr. 93
Johnson, Algie L. II 379
Johnson, Annette L. 80
Johnson, Autumn 496
Johnson, Becky L. 324
Johnson, Bree 208
Johnson, C. J. 519
Johnson, Carrie 381
Johnson, Cheri 151
Johnson, Clarice L. 330
Johnson, Curt 460
Johnson, David Emerson 69
Johnson, Dean 83
Johnson, Jeremy 36
Johnson, Jerilyn 291
Johnson, JoAnne D. 485
Johnson, Kathryn 75
Johnson, Lillian Martin 281
Johnson, Linda 508
Johnson, Margie Stewart 94
Johnson, Mel 172
Johnson, Richard B. 531
Johnson, Steven R. 357
Johnson, Tarence E. Jr. 151
Johnson, William P. 463
JoLee 151
Jones, Alexiss 424
Jones, Amanda 363
Jones, Barbara A. 234
Jones, Cathy Lee 374
Jones, Curtis 141
Jones, Dan M. 210
Jones, Doreen 430
Jones, Dottie 296
Jones, Florence M. 515
Jones, Jean Kaich 401
Jones, Jeremy M. 282
Jones, Jessie 257
Jones, Kathy 310
Jones, Keith 441
Jones, Leval 9
Jones, Marguerite G. 307
Jones, Mary P. 408
Jones, Melissa 331
Jones, Roshunda 280
Jones, Roxanne 72
Jones, Sharon D. 429
Jones, T. Ann 535
Jones, Toya D. 448
Jones, William Henry 543
Jordan, Belva Brown 325
Jordan, Richard 267
Jorgensen, Amy 442
Joseph, Christine 217
Josephson, Sarah 334
Joyce, Susan D. 244
Juarez, Amy 453
Jueschke, Beth A. 217
Jugila, Terri 108
Juris, Mary Ann 276
Justice, Alexis 87

K

Kadrmas, Tammy 348
Kahnovitch, Dina 500
Kain, Jonathan 389
Kaiser, Dawson 354
Kakley, Dawn E. 527
Kaliati, Dorothy 344
Kalil, Amy 11
Kalil, Nicole D. 283
Kalina, Marilyn 517
Kalkbrenner, Sarah 504
Kangiser, Cheryl 221
Kaplan, Leslie 207
Karman, John 378
Karol, Eileen 422
Karp, Briana 13
Karp, Matthew 511
Karst, John 494
Karsten, Mary 284
Kartchner, Kristen 532
Kasdon, Julie 260
Kasunick, Matthew E. 237
Kasza, Virginia J. 261
Katz, Robert I. 510
Kaufman, Joshua 426
Kaufmann, Jillian 6
Kawuryan, Anna Maria Siti 434
Kayzar, Theresa 199
Kazen, Elaine M. 413
Keaton, Nancy Kay 16
Keaveney, Daniel 221
Keel, James Clayton 329
Keeling, Reita 343
Keenan, Kathryn 168
Kehagias, Martha 11
Keil, Josephine Pappon 416
Kell, Alice 540
Kelleher, Bernadette 323
Keller, Gail 49
Keller, Mitch 523
Keller, Robert 428
Kelley, Barbara Snyder 317
Kelley, Melody 528
Kelly, Brigid 264
Kelly, David A. 501
Kelly, Jill 129
Kelly, Joan M. 385
Kelly, Kevin G. 309
Kelly, Sheila 400
Keltz, Dendee 418
Kemp, Diane 400
Kemp, Jeanna 497
Kennedy, Lynette 138
Kennett, Leah 323
Kenny, Sandra 377
Kent-Martin, Alberta Noelle 142
Kent-Parcell, Kelly J. 450
Kenyon, Cathy 343
Keown, Sherry 412
Kern, Ethan H. 102
Kershaw, Helen E. 198

Kessinger, Jeffrey W. 387
Ketchum, Kevin 11
Ketellapper, Walraven 402
Kex-Snyder, Mildred 308
Keyes, Olivia 268
Keys, Laura L. 515
Khalil, Zarifa M. 277
Khan, G. Sierra 181
Khan, Sarah 6
Kidwell, Russell E. 369
Kiefer, Mario 265
Kiehl, Janice L. 111
Kiel, Jenny 248
Kildow, Jayne 504
Killgore, N. Michelle 289
Killian, Daniel J. 348
Kimani, Julia 316
Kimmelman, Dawn J. 401
Kimpel, Marian 389
Kincaid, Jeannie 325
King, Diamond David 428
King, Lois Myers 262
King, Rhonda M. 384
King, Virginia V. (Sissy) 42
Kingsnorth, Ann 112
Kinsey, Christy H. 32
Kinsey, David 398
Kipler, James W. 493
Kipp, E. Edward 245
Kirk, James 308
Kirk, Rachel 214
Kirk, Zachary 443
Kirkendoll, Jeanette R. 144
Kirkland, Connie R. 384
Kirkpatrick, Jessica 299
Kiser, Elizabeth A. 154
Kitts, Rhiannon L. 340
Kjelgaard, Mary 248
Klang, Christie 303
Klatt, Monty 506
Klein, Zach 483
Kleinheksel, Glen 64
Klenk, George 118
Klienschmidt, Tia 311
Klobnak, Michael W. 21
Knapp, Linda 388
Kneass, Jessiah 280
Knell, Holly Margaret 45
Knight, Craig A. 10
Knight, Marita R. 392
Knight, Valerie A. 494
Kniskern, Kerry 106
Knodel, Joyce 213
Knowles, Raymond 186
Knudsen, Raymond B. 221
Kobi, Marie 176
Kocan, Jamey 316
Kocsis, Cindy 312
Koehler, Roberta 176
Koelzer, Jeremy 322
Kolenda, Bridget 108
Kolinsky, Lee 73
Kollars, Maggie 405
Koller, John J. 10
Konsek, Maureen 100
Koontz, Eric 218
Kooshkabadi, Ali 396
Koponen, Wilfrid R. 279
Korczykowski, Katie 254
Korty, Joe 412
Kottke, Chris 82

Kouri, Tiffany 428
Kovarik, Dustin 244
Kowalski, Kimberly M. 7
Krafft, Toni Lee 434
Kragnes, Berdelle 341
Kraslen, Kristine 535
Krause, Lora 158
Kraushaar, Steve 189
Kravitz, Larry 326
Kraynyk, Ann 314
Kremers, Kathleen M. 171
Kreps, E. Kevin 528
Kretz, Allison 61
Krout, Ron 464
Krovontka, Mindy 365
Krug, Debbie 233
Krug, Dottie 237
Kuball, Terri M. 366
Kuchinski, Brad 300
Kuebler, Jean 317
Kuhn, Alison 416
Kuhn, Megan Nicole 265
Kulikauskas, Derek 47
Kumburis, Wendy 275
Kump, Wendy 383
Kurcz, Donna 108
Kurjanowicz, Wadim 73
Kurpiewski, Aaron J. 61
Kutac, Kevin 361
Kwan, Hyuk 343
Kyle, Erin V. 427
Kynerd, David Wayne 455
Kyzer, Bob 351

L

La Barbera, Sylvia 459
Ladd, Beth 214
LaFave-Hale, Kim 103
Lafayette, Chris J. 340
LaGoy, Dawn 146
Lahrmann, Jessica 267
Lai, Sunny 320
Lake, Ferol Elizabeth 114
Lake, Joanne Marie 178
Lakner, Mary 443
Lamadore, Ella 94
Lamb, Glenda 472
Lamb, Kevin 367
Lambert, Scott 241
Lambeth, Scott 93
Lampros, Peter 518
Landefeld, Zac 355
Landuyt, Barbara S. 7
Lane, Anna 301
Lane, George E. Jr. 39
Lane, Joseph W. 311
Lane, Tanya 23
Lange, Peter 318
Lange, Wanda Jean 150
Langford, Mitchell 72
Langford, Tom 509
Langley, June Moore 173
Langman, Sabrina 400
Lantis, Rachelle 42
LaPierre, Robert Edward 160
Lapinski, Deborah 270
LaPorte, Molly Rose 108
Lappin, Aubrey 101
LaPradd, Bonnie 237
Larsen, Eric 255

Larsen, Roberta D. 231
Larson, Cody N. 328
Larson, Eric 90
Larson, Vanessa 464
Lasanen, Joan 471
Lash, Robyn 65
Lasher, Lahanna 112
Lashley, Dawn 18
Lashuay, Brett 349
Lastra, Federico R. 282
Lataillade-Lewis, Saïeda 320
Lattin, Wende A. 399
Laue, Linda Chabot 315
Laurie, Darlene D. 64
Lauritzen, Andrea 295
Lavallee, Michelle D. 9
Lavigne, Andre P. 429
Lavoie, Mike 488
Law, Stacy 29
Lawrence, Barnie 107
Lawrence, Carol 500
Lawrence, Elissa 59
Lawrence, Evelyn 150
Lawrence, John 215
Lawrie, Elaine 531
Lay, Frito 404
Layman, Roy 99
Layne, Susan R. 3
Le Desma, Xavier 347
Leap, Chere R. 170
Leary, Nicole 533
Leavell, Matthew 514
Lebbie, Maisa K. 320
LeBlanc, Dwayne 212
LeBlanc, Marguerite 473
Lecaro, Gabriela 149
Ledington, Erin 206
Ledington, Shawn Lynn 188
Lee, Connie 105
Lee, Janet 319
Lee, Jessica 519
Lee, Jonathan C. 104
Lee, Peter 451
Lee, Tammy 439
Leeb, Laura Naomi 4
Leeser, Debra 294
Lefkowitz, Elijah 106
Lehman, Helen L. 19
Lehman, Lenny I. 355
Lehotay, Douglas E. 353
Leiker, Amy 100
Leiterding, Matt 93
Lemay, Stacey 12
Lemek, Lisa 268
Lengl, Kacy 179
Lennington, Linda L. 201
Leon, Robert 130
Leonard, Cecilia Y. 78
Leonardo, Tammie 155
Leopard, Elizabeth 190
Lerch, Marilyn 501
LeStage, Nathan M. 267
Lester, Earlene Coes 467
Lester, Katie 326
Letsche, Carol Anne 406
Leützinger, Richard J. Jr. 245
Levan, Andrew K. Sr. 114
Levine, Anya 203
Levitt, Cassandra 261
Lewis, Cassandra 234
Lewis, Cathy 332

Lewis, Daniel E. 510
Lewis, Dorothy 480
Lewis, Harold R. 455
Lewis, Jeanine 277
Lewis, Kimberly D. 352
Lewis, Linda 220
Lewis, Marissa 251
Lewis, Vera Bell 443
Li, GuoZhu 300
Li, Olivia 154
Libby, Elise 321
Licht, Danielle 60
Lieberman, Kenneth 134
Lightcap, Niki 529
Lighton, Mark 124
Like, Brandon 525
Likness, Joanna 338
Lillard, Eloise 424
Liloia, Frances 109
Lim, Jeannette 181
Lind, Jean N. 512
Lind, Verla 426
Linde, Susan 98
Lindgren, Sara Ann 279
Lindler, Lisa 430
Lindow, Marcie 218
Lindsay, Nancy M. 524
Lineberry, Delesha J. 499
Lingerman, Hal A. 390
Liniewicz, Sandi 449
Linnen-Fraser, Anganette 83
Lintel, Delores A. 45
Lipchzech, Gunther 243
Little, Matthew 254
Livengood, Rebecca 474
Liverett, Doyne Marie 214
Liverpool, Vikki 503
Livingston, Peter W. 421
Lizotte, Jacklyn 50
Lloyd, Allison 160
Lloyd, Johia M. 405
Lloyd, Michelle 288
Lockhart, Mike 427
Lockwood, Kate 235
Lockwood, Rayan 341
Loftsgaarden, Anthony John 313
Logan, Beth Clay 497
Lombardi, Doris 371
Long, Gary H. 543
Long, Megan 413
Lontka, Janet P. 244
Lopez, JoAnn 42
Lopez, Michelle Ann-Victoria 200
Lorenzen, Zella 442
Loscocco, Nicole 211
Lostritto, Richard Anthony 136
Lovegren, Patrick 105
Lovejoy, Gretha Ruark 411
Lovette, Estelle M. 467
Lovvorn, Ann R. 91
Lowe, Andrea 338
Lowery, Bonnie 212
Lowery, Randall R. 289
Lucas, Jessica 318
Lucero, Nicole 259
Lucia, Paul 540
Luck, Wayne 218
Luddington, Betty 515
Luebber, Lacey 412
Luedeman, Jessica 205
Luedtke, Richard W. 514

Luhrsen, Shirley L. 256
Lukitsh, Emily 440
Lumenello, Alyson 115
Luna, Jill 95
Lund, Jessica 453
Lund, Josh 414
Lundberg, Eleanor M. 295
Lunde, Florence 240
Luttrell, Travis 348
Lutzky, Andrew 209
Lyczewski, Tarah 206
Lyden, Thelma 131
Lynch, Dana 58
Lynch, Donna 356
Lyon, Steven 421
Lyons, David M. 300
Lyons, Emily E. S. 158
Lytvinenko, Kristen 269

M

Maas, Michele 166
Mabey, Amanda G. 537
Macabeo, Carolyn P. 536
Macbeth, Eloise H. 264
MacDonald, J. Christopher 200
Macdonald, Sara 362
MacFadden, Myrtle 316
Machado, Nina L. 324
Macierowski, Alice J. 393
Mackenzie, Lauren 82
Mackey, Jim 177
Macklin, Caitlin S. 307
Macy, Sarah 205
Maddox, Lori K. Gillespie 245
Madge, Edith 241
Madison, James R. 262
Maffeo, Elizabeth M. 344
Magill, Meghan 30
Magner, Amity 426
Mahany, Van B. 116
Mahomed, Yamile 157
Mahoney, Diane 208
Mahoney, Rose Giovinazzo 483
Mainhart, Sara K. 356
Mainini, Robin 145
Majeti, Venkata C. 219
Majumdar, Shakhi 494
Makatura, Andrew F., Jr. 331
Makowski, Joel B. 350
Makpaulu, Nduku 248
Malbacias, Elena 378
Malgieri, Robert 417
Malley, Scott 58
Mallory, Ben 503
Mallory, Heather 318
Maloney, Anne Louise 290
Malpas, Kari 309
Manalac, Jasmin Azurin 148
Mancini, S. L. 390
Mancour, Danzel 396
Mancuso, Joseph 31
Mandy, Lynn 169, 261
Mann, Donald W. 135
Mann, Harold W. 26
Mann, Lisa 299
Mann, Lori 244
Mannen, Robert J. 352
Mannes, Sara 91
Manning, Alan 514
Manolios, Billy 239

Manolis, Jenny 485
Mantonya, Mike 124
Marceau, Eileen Aki 430
Marchetti, Delisa Louise 140
Marcos, Yeneys 120
Margretta, C. I. 55
Mariani, Karen R. 336
Mariani, Sam 84
Marinello, Chris 47
Marino, Anthony 507
Mark, Lawrence 437
Markopoulos, C. 294
Markowitz, Kymberly 438
Marks, Jessica 114
Marlow, Patti 108
Marquez, Teresa A. 328
Marquis, Tiffany M. 52
Marsh, Becky 143
Marsh, William S. 165
Marshall, J. 395
Marshall, Robert W. 61
Martin, Crissa 428
Martin, Debra Katrina 105
Martin, James 283
Martin, Joshua W. 309
Martin, June R. 497
Martin, Kathryn Mumgaard 79
Martin, Kay 429
Martin, Loretta 221
Martin, Maithel M. 500
Martin, Nicholas 162
Martin, Pauline Francia 441
Martin, Peter 423
Martin, Susan A. 22
Martinez, Alex D'Carlo 366
Martino, Jeremy 479
Marvin, Keith 74
Marzoli, Stefano 504
Mascolo, Anthony 260
Masek, Holly 216
Masley, Peter 312
Mason, Karla Jo 511
Mason, Lottie Lee 463
Massarotti, Holly 388
Mast, Martha 303
Mastrobattista, Andrea Lynn 188
Mastroianni, Anthony 185
Matera, Maryann 444
Mathews, Jeffrey 270
Mathie, Alton J. 443
Mathis, Meghan 259
Mathison, Anthony 58
Matje, Cynthia 449
Matteson, Darrel 511
Matthews, Chris E. 192
Matthys, Lila Ruth Stokes 316
Maxson, Stephen 155
Maxwell, Carol 30
Maxwell, Kelly 219
Maxwell, Sherry 301
May, Karen 369
Maybee, Aaron 226
Maychick, Lillian 199
Mayfield, Shannon 35
Maynard, Marie 102
Mayo, Mirika Andrea 134
Mays, Caroline 40
Mazell, Melissa 412
Mazur, Jake 113
Mazzei, Lucretia S. 255
M'bayo, Kai E. 208

McArthur, Catherine R. 134
McBay, Shug Yagel 214
McBrayer, Jerald 255
McBride, F. M. 427
McBride, Linda 222
McCallen, Leigh 40
McCallister, Emmy Lou 89
McCarter, Patrica 305
McCarthy, Chris 260
McCartney, Jo Anne 8
McCarty, Michelle 362
McCaslin, Larry 80
McCauley, Christopher Dwayne 375
McCauley, M. J. 345
McCay, Kristy 420
McCleary, Danica 126
McCleary, Dwight 342
McClelland, Karen L. 297
McClure, Carol 429
McClure, Margie 541
McCollister, Tashira 491
McConnell, Adelia Wood 442
McConnell, Linda 96
McCormick, Michelle 527
McCowan, Randy 89
McCoy, Kelly 387
McCright, Kimberly 384
McDaniel, Appy Jo 489
McDaniel, Warren E. 537
McDonald, Edward W. IV 389
McDonald, Herman Edward 530
McDonald, Melvin 451
McDonald, Michael Dale 456
McDowell, John T. 37
McDowell, Kenneth E. 469
McDuffie, Teresa A. 420
McElrath, Jacqueline 264
McEvoy, Michael L. 504
McFillen, Brian J. 429
McFillen, Kevin D. 482
McGaha, Joe Jr. 141
McGahee, Peggy 161
McGee, Talisha 213
McGill, Nabeehah Q. 274
McGillen, Irene 217
McGillick, Darlene 451
McGlade, Tanya 498
McGowan, Edna Earl 323
McGowan, Jesse D. 432
McGowan, Kimberly Ann 332
McGraw, Sue 269
McGrew, Dolores M. 382
McGuffin, Daniel 107
McGuigan, Joanne 100
McGuinness, Matt 127
McGuire, Consuelo Ramirez 193
McGuire, Morgan 454
McGuire, Willette Caudle 542
McHale, Julie 38
McHan, Kelly Elizabeth 164
McHaney, Meghan 164
McHone, Jennifer 298
McIlverey, Julia 142
McIntyre, Regena 111
McIntyre, Rick Oliver 132
McKay, Emily 436
McKeith, Melissa 206
McKenney, Lynn 443
McKeown, Janet G. 130
McKillip, Rose Marie 210
McKinny, Susanne Mae 401

McKnight-Miles, Sharon 141
McLaughlin, Donna 304
McLean, Daniel 187
McLean, Jane Flocks 191
McLendon, Stevie C. 272
McLeod, Blanche 481
McLeod, Charles W. 64
McLeod, Melissa 399
McLoud, Mildred Hyatt 81
McMahan, Brad 457
McMahan, C. Shane 402
McMahon, Erin-Kathleen 206
McMahon, Laurie 398
McMahon, Melissa Beth 381
McMillen, Betty 424
McMillen, Ruth 252
McNaughton, Katrina 115
McNeese, Jody 457
McNeff, Enid C. 40
McNiff, Theresa 250
McQueen, Joy 434
McQuown, Shirlee A. 108
McRae, Aleta M. 517
McRae, James 196
McRoberts, Lillian 507
McStroul, Mindy D. 303
McTighe, James 63
McVay, Kathleen 220
Meade, Audra 106
Meadows, Dawn M. 496
Meadows, Rozella 218
Meadows, Thomas 214
Meakins, Donna 196
Mears, Jennifer 131
Mechtensimer, Heather L. 371
Meck, Tania 430
Medeiros, Neloise K. 493
Medley, Chris 471
Medrano, Selena 506
Meffert, Tammy 339
Mehagian, Diane Joyce 3
Meier, Anita Rickert 504
Meiers, Paul H. 404
Meixner, Anthony 211
Meleski, John 19
Meletti, Marcela 368
Melgarejo, Dauzed Jr. 29
Mellinger, Damon 166
Mello, Gladys E. 399
Mellott, Helen L. 23
Melson, John A. 512
Meltzer, Adrienne 15
Menafee, Stacy LaShun 45
Mendence, Susan 14
Mendenhall, Troy L. 464
Mendenhall-Lynch, Carolyn 68
Mendoza, Letty F. 43
Meneshian, Joshua 443
Merchant, Anna 118
Merino, Natalie 177
Merrill, C. B. 16
Merritt, Carrie 397
Merritt, Patricia L. 268
Merriweather, Audrey J. 253
Mesches, Mia 500
Messina, Anthony F. 53
Meyer, Diana 221
Meyer, Lindsey 328
Meyer, Renee 419
Meyer, Theresa 21
Meyers, P. L. 225

Miani, Giannina 137
Micsak, Dan 44
Middleton, Billy 500
Middleton, Maria T. 164
Middleton, Sandra 434
Mikeska, Matt 233
Mikus, Margaret Dubay 30
Miles, Ennis T. 232
Miller, Ameenah 397
Miller, Charles Adam 175
Miller, Christine 398
Miller, Chyanne 426
Miller, D. 224
Miller, Denise 287
Miller, Donald D. 367
Miller, Elaine W. 532
Miller, Elsie J. 299
Miller, Greg 468
Miller, James D. 335
Miller, James Nilolis 14
Miller, Joseph 277
Miller, Kaylie 530
Miller, Laura 384
Miller, Laura E. 181
Miller, Matt 292
Miller, Patricia B. 336
Miller, Richard K. 147
Millican, Debra 507
Milligan, William E. 397
Mills, Dianne 292
Millspaugh, Amber 161
Millus, Mandi 327
Milner, Sheila B. 87
Mims, Justin 266
Minami, Hiroshi 502
Miner, Alice B. 483
Mines, Hermalena V. 285
Mira, Joseph A. Jr. 513
Mirabal, Jacob 128
Miscovich, Rosemary 469
Misiti, Patrick Joseph 96
Mistry, Ashwin B. 462
Mitchell, E. Janean 517
Mitchell, Matt 471
Mitchell, Victoria S. 487
Mittelholzer, Sarah 201
Mize, Michelle M. 452
Moak, Ronald C. 290
Moccia-Ball, Maria 253
Mocherla, Omshanti 140
Moenius, Crystal 94
Moffett, Jacqueline 243
Moffitt, Joshua 139
Mohyla, Ostap M. 27
Molloy, Donald M. 327
Molsing, Karina Veronica 315
Monk, Karen 265
Montague, Joyce 320
Montenegro, Carlos 400
Montero, Ray W. K. 365
Montes, Juan Luis 351
Montey, Heather Reneé 152
Montgomery, Georgiana 194, 195
Montgomery, Sharmane 209
Monticue, Carol 164
Montoya, Betsy 65
Montoya, Marcella E. 52
Montoya, Margarito 78
Moon, Hillary G. 59
Moon, Mike 507
Mooney, Catherine 37

Moore, Bobby E. Jr.   489
Moore, Darryl Jay   401
Moore, Jeremy P.   93
Moore, Krystal   511
Moore, Miranda   318
Moore, Renee   321
Moore, Theresa Courteau   435
Moore, Vivian Lee   315
Moorman, Mary   335
Morales, Arlon   199
Moreda, Cesar J.   62
Moreland, Pam H.   66
Moren, Sandi   506
Moreno, Loretta   231
Morfitt, Leonard   297
Morgan, John III   243
Morgan, Judi   282
Morin, Tiffany Ann   340
Moros, Alex N.   245
Morris, Bill   406
Morris, Hannah Ruth   287
Morris, Joy   476
Morris, Margaret J.   386
Morris, Melba   454
Morris, Robyn   322
Morrison, Pat   477
Morrison Sr., Charles   479
Morrow, Dorothy D.   527
Mortensen, Marvin Lee   24
Mosbrucker, Joachim C.   177
Moseley, Glenda Y.   183
Moseley, Mary R.   472
Moskowitz, Robin   20
Moss, Ellen   423
Moss-McDougall, Lynda   228
Mossberger, Kristi   97
Mossman, Wendy M.   333
Mott, Lisa   497
Mount, Kristyn   479
Muhammad, Joan   152
Muhammad, Zita   154
Mullins, Linda   469
Mullis, Johnny J.   386
Muncy, Sharon   523
Munoz, Isaac   207
Munro, Aline   537
Munsey, Cheryl   122
Munson, Karen B.   121
Muraoka, Terri   437
Murphy, Colleen   514
Murphy, Karen P.   45
Murphy, Kathy   278
Murphy, Richard E.   344
Murray, Victoria   333
Murriel, T. Eunice   190
Murtagh, Irene   188
Myers, John E.   489
Myers, Ray L.   126
Myles, F. Ruth   530
Myrick, Sharlitta Novella   54
Myrick, Yvonne P.   372
Myrmingos, Denos   362

N

Nabity, Virgil   541
Naccarato, Brittney   258
Nadolne, Lance   401
Nagode, Mary E.   487
Naguit, Kim   530
Nancarrow, George E.   411

Nangia, Malini   15
Nanney, Mellissa Y.   116
Napolitano, Janice Marie   331
Narcisi, Thomas   471
Nasello, Cara M.   68
Nash, Betty J.   469
Nash, Jeffery J.   330
Naumoff, Lincoln   129
Nava, Irma M.   62
Navarro, Juan Carlos   88
Neal, Lea M.   440
Needham, Falynn   332
Needham, Judith   112
Neel, Danniell   214
Neff, Starling Pauline   13
Neff, Wade Everett   44
Neiderman, Crystal   439
Neilsen, Sue   39
Nelan, Mary   362
Nelken, Lorene C.   67
Nelsen, Lori A.   101
Nelson, Debra E.   460
Nelson, Hajar A. M.   218
Nelson, Ingrid   117
Nelson, Marion   34
Nelson, Melissa D.   254
Nelson, Rosalie Frentiero   497
Nelson, Sara   426
Nemmers, Renee   226
Nerge, Lori Ann   492
Neth, Tom   62
Neuhaus, John C.   336
Neutgens, Sue A.   219
Newell, Monica   297
Newman, Josh   393
Newman-Gregerson, Diane M.   409
Newton, Jackson David   484
Nicastro, Alberto Nich   379
Nichols, Megan   52
Nicholson, Carl W.   368
Niel, P. J. Van   514
Nielson, Alyce M.   541
Niemchak, Daniel M.   319
Niemer, Sherry A.   101
Nigro, Christopher R.   230
Nipper, Mary   147
Nissen, Nancy   35
Nitsche, Therese L.   345
Nixon, Doris   270
Noble, Judith   120
Nobles, Keith E.   298
Noe, Nathan   323
Noel, Benjamin   204
Noel, Brian   159
Noens, Heather   296
Nolan, Erin   448
Nolan, John J.   74
Noland, Jeremy L.   156
Noland, Onishia   457
Noland, William R.   36
Norberry, Kathy   330
Nord, Jeremy   347
Nordlund, Michelle Denise (Barrett)160
Norenberg, Jeremy   128
Norman, Baron Sylvester III   147
Norman, Betty Watson   76
Norman, Louise   501
Norman, Nova   450
Norman, Rachel (Holweger)   507
Norris, David   522
Norris, Norma L.   291

Norris, Tiffany   173
Norton, Jalisha   242
Nosacek, Stephanie C.   439
Novak, John A.   76
Novak, Karen   109
Nowak, Juanita M.   422
Nowak, Veronica   99
Noyes, Frank   101
Noyes, Katie   373
Nucci, Jani   399
Nuetzmann, Philip K.   231
Nunes, Sabata   92
Nunez, Traci   212
Nutini, Gayle   341
Nystrom, Markus   62

O

O'Callaghan, Patrick   199
O'Cañas, Joe   437
Ockey, Mary J.   134
O'Connor, Rita, S.N.D.   78
Odell, Harold Rutledge Jr.   281
O'Donnell, James C.   192
Oehlert, Verna   159
Oguine, Priscilla   544
Ogunlade, Vickie Y.   273
O'Hagan, Donna Jean   484
Ohlrogge, Russell Robert   493
Oister, Heather   13
Oiterong, Cathy   30
Olick, Jocelyn   529
Oliva, Salvatore   123
Olsen, David   502
Olsen, Tom   118
Olson, Carly   403
Olson, Jina Evelyn   154
Olton, Elizabeth A.   483
O'Malley, Barbara J.   326
O'Malley, Megan   318
O'Neal, Garna   55
O'Neil, Fannie I.   172
O'Neill, Stephanie   265
Onjack, Connie M.   83
Onuegbu, Patricia   512
Orewiler, Eric   205
Orihuela, Mary   497
Orr, Kimberly D.   286
Orr, Leonard P.   353
Orridge, Monica J.   312
Orta, Maggie   258
Ortega, Floyd   306
Ortega, Lorraine   106
Ortega, Marie   364
Ortiz, Belinda   277
Ortiz, Marie   425
Ortsman, Joel   427
Ory, Richard   489
Osayande, Makeba   104
O'Shaughnessy, Elizabeth Marie   359
Osman, Julia   282
Ostergren, Sandra K.   508
Otani, Susan   443
O'Toole, Kate   397
O'Toole, Seamus   445
Ott, Stephanie   409
Ouellette, Michelle   377
Ousley, Ruth Y.   222
Outarsingh, Errol Fitzgerald   163
Ouyang, Tibor   99
Over, Katie   92

Overcash, Ruth M.   493
Owen, Stephen   121
Owens, Kyle   269
Owens, Mark F.   526
Owens, Minarose R.   14
Oxman, Nancy G.   288

P

Pabor, Helen W.   303
Pace, Cile   68
Pacheco, Caroline   404
Pachuta, Jamie   107
Pack, Betty Daniel   359
Packard, Marie   33
Paden, Laura   184
Padilla, Melissa Jeanette   380
Pahigianis, Melina   153
Paikada, Alex   56
Palacino, Christopher John   257
Paladino, Scott F.   524
Palestrant, Ivette   274
Palladino, Paula   426
Palma, Mary Martin   407
Palmer, Alexander   43
Palmer, Joseph D.   410
Palmere, Charles   460
Pamplin, Debora Ann   475
Pandolfo Jr, Sebastian V.   26
Papp, Elizabeth   304
Papp, Joseph   172
Pappert, Geri   304
Paquette, Allie   244
Paquin, Kathryn   301
Paradee, Christina   509
Paradiso, Karen A.   59
Paramito, Suzzie   31
Parente, Jaruska   259
Paris, Joseph Michael   333
Parisi, Rob   460
Park, Natalie   105
Parker, Joshua E.   131
Parker, Kirsten   224
Parker, Sarah M.   212
Parker-Stone, Susan   220
Parks, Shawn   60
Parolise, Jill S.   360
Parris, Nicole L.   461
Parrish, Ted   152
Parrott, Jennifer   211
Parrott, Mary B.   442
Parry, Marie Martz   344
Pascal, Christopher David   241
Pascalide, Amy   8
Pashalidis, Christina   321
Pasinski, Christine   204
Passione, Maggie V.   326
Pasterak, Peter   499
Pastiva, Stephen Jr.   346
Pate, Cassie   108
Patel, Ronika   156
Patel, Suraag S.   88
Patera, James   322
Patrick, D. Malcor   229
Patterson, Kelly   445
Patterson, Patricia O.   201
Patterson-Stevenson, Paula   360
Pattillo, Tony   75
Patty, Marie   301
Paul, Marie   242
Pauline, Angela C.   30

Paulish, Tammy 427
Paulson, Kelly 173
Payne, Phyllis 508
Pearson, Dorothy 220
Pearson, Ruth H. 144
Pearson, Tim 537
Peetz, Renee 25
Pelfrey, Melissa 376
Pelletier, Jessie 289
Pelliccia, Dennis 453
Pemberton, Renee 515
Pendley, Lingsworth B. 518
Penttinen, Kenneth F. 432
Penwarden, Barbara J. 114
Perard, Scott 195
Perez, Louis Anthony 99
Perez, Pearl R. 64
Perkins, Dana L. 278
Perkins, Marie 457
Perkins, Merredith Frazier 268
Perloski, JoAnn J. 68
Perras, Patricia 195
Perry, Okeyna Loving 75
Perry, Sally A. 331
Pesek, Gregg 424
Pesta, Ben 488
Peter, Eric 103
Peters, Josh 309
Peters, Lynda D. 511
Peters, Robert F. R. Jr. 305
Petersen, Matthew W. 406
Peterson, Halcyon C. 256
Peterson, Janice 539
Peterson, Lydia 340
Peterson, Mary 309
Peterson, Melissa 180
Petrie, Marie R. 150
Petruska, Sarah 496
Pettine, Dean J. 501
Pettis, Angela J. 283
Pettis, Patrick Gorman 86
Pettyjohn, Blair 370
Peyton, Kendra L. 429
Pfister, Nicole 174
Phasha 427
Phelps, Sam 315
Phelts, Charles 333
Philbrook, Ivy C. 497
Phillips, Charles, Jr. 336
Phillips, Poet-Mary 197
Phillips, Shanda 93
Phillips, Sharon 82
Phillips, Stephanie 95
Phillips, Whitt, III 441
Philpitt, Edward T. 545
Phipps, Brandi 440
Piccolo, Christian 95
Pickett, Veronica L. 130
Picow, Erin 275
Pierce, Kathleen B. 407
Pierce, Michelle 100
Pieri, Shirley 542
Pileggi, Lauren 401
Pilto, Amy Sutton 218
Pina, Melanie 222
Pine, Rebecca 235
Pinelle, Michelle 520
Piotrowski, Kendra L. 55
Pirolo, Philomena 115
Pirtle, Brenda Ann 459
Pirtle, Eric 518

Pittman, Felicia 203
Pittman, Marie Cross 316
Pizano, Jolee 210
Platt, Jill C. 332
Platt, Johnny 322
Platt, Marcy 446
Plattel, Jonathan 146
Pleasant, Julia 336
Plouffe, Anita M. 514
Plouffe, Pamela Anne 112
Plumadore, Darbie Deniz 129
Poage, Brad 415
Pobiecke, Sarah Beth 211
Pocho 31
Podgorski, Marianne 332
poholek, vanessa 127
Poindexter, Crystal 192
Poitier, Constance Rena 448
Polachek, Lisa M. 97
Poland, Linda Lee Hibbett 422
Poletti, Sarah Michelle 522
Polk, Brenda Gregory 360
Polk, Lori 377
Polk, William Alan 337
Pollard, Michael Thomas 207
Poller, Elli 259
Poma, Erin Marie 428
Ponce, Sheila 302
Pont, Debbie 430
Poole, Carl 111
Poole, Jean 262
Poorian, Sarah 194
Pope, Jonathan 393
Pope, Kathy 486
Pope, Linda Vanessa 255
Popham, Dennis Dale 506
Porreca, Betty Lou 286
Porter, Cherylyn S. 75
Porter, Glen W. Jr. 248
Portlock, Joylette L. 439
Posner, Alayna 225
Post, Burton W. 526
Post, Heather 284
Potter, Dottie 145
Potter, Lorie A. 396
Potter, Steve N. 227
Potts, Dennis E. 400
Pouker, Dolores 392
Poulin, Donna B. 153
Pourciau, Louis J. Jr. 76
Pourner, Steven F. 532
Powell, Darlene 217
Powell, Sherry 443
Power, Joseph M. 193
Powers, Christopher S. 442
Prado, Gary 338
Preciado, Irene 209
Preece, Shawna 97
Previs, Marilyn 369
Price, Amy 523
Prichard, Shannon Marie 97
Priddy, Joel R. 521
Pride, Marquetta 404
Priest, Marie M. 9
Priester, Tammy 324
Prihoda, P. J. 214
Prince, Anna J. 521
Pritts, Merl 506
Privett, Mega 314
Probst, Lorraine 439
Pronovost, Doris 127

Prouty, Natalie 435
Pruitt, Jonathan L. 374
Przywara, Greg 267
Puccio, Anthony Carl Jr. 440
Puckett, Stephanie 105
Pugliese, Pamela K. 195
Pulliam, Ruth 337
Pullin, D. W. 432
Pullium, Eric 194
Putek, Janet 326
Putnam, Audrey 322

Q

Quadrino, Nick 127
Quantrille, Lori 71
Quarto, Charles John 95
Quick, Lisa 386
Quilpa, Andrew Fernando E. 168
Quine, Melanie Young 325
Quinn, Alberta 358
Quinn, William F. 100
Quinones, Sheryl 424
Quitoni, Thomas F. 507

R

Raaz, Bryan D. 215
Rabb, Diane 337
Rabon, Melina 250
Racic, Ann 263
Radcliff, Robin 458
Radke, Megan 302
Radschlag, Patricia 233
Rafey, Charles T. 473
Raffaelo, Anne 361
Raghunauth, Chandai 493
Ragsdale, C. Jared 435
Ragsdale, Misty 341
Rainey, Erin 37
Rainguet, Jim 64
Rains, Katie 128
Raistrick, Virginia M. 27
Rajamannar, Sudhakar 32
Ralls, J. Warner 515
Ralston, Rebecca 222
Rambo, Evelyn M. 499
Ramirez, James D. 289
Ramirez, Jo 25
Randall, Sky 18
Ranta, Michele 296
Raphael, Joyce 179
Raser, Katrina J. 148
Rashid, Omar 10
Rathi, Roshni 13
Ratzloff, Matthew 229
Raven, Laura 89
Raver, Davis 33
Rawls, Marie C. 456
Ray, Rose Ann 340
Raygada, Jenna 156
Raymond, Eileen Yarnutoski 542
Rayoan, Susannah B. 453
Rea, Stephen C. 120
Ream, Ashley 118
Reaves, Shainn 163
Redd, Robert B. 146
Reddy, Ramesh C. 392
Redmond, Jennifer 130
Reed, Donna 513
Rees, Grace 303
Rees, Sonja J. 96

Reese, Cheryl 465
Reese, Laurie Jean 204
Reese, Lee Fleming 470
Reese, Wardella 450
Reggio, Richard 402
Regina, Kathlyn 145
Regina, Susan E. L. 364
Reibsome, Linda 103
Reich, Arianna 494
Reichard, Linda 306
Reid, Alisha 169
Reid, Tiffany 56
Reilly, Linda A. 466
Reinard, Joyce Marie 187
Reineberg, Stephanie B. 101
Reinhart, Gabrielle 116
Reisch, Laurie DuMesnil 151
Reisinger, Mary 427
Reiter, Naomi Undine 323
Rende, Victoria 438
Renfrow, Tara 536
Renner, Martha 427
Reprogle, Sommer Daun 517
Repasy, Drew 317
Restovic, Jane M. 405
Rethorn, Frances 300
Retty, Aubree 215
Reyes, Diane 298
Reynolds, Houston T. 422
Reynolds, Mary 105
Reynolds, Michael 104
Rezaiyan, Sherene 293
Rheaume, Gail 476
Rhoback, Jeanette 490
Rhodebeck, Ashley 531
Rhodes, Sharon 451
Rhodes, Terry L. 314
Rian, Maolanaithe 450
Rice, Angela 285
Rice, Hettie Hoy 492
Rice, Norman W. 362
Rice, Pauline Van Norman 111
Rice, Peter Paul Sr. 111, 332
Rich, Lindsay 102
Richards, Erik 381
Richards, Ivy Constable 425
Richards, Keith A. II 264
Richards, Kelle Ann 136
Richardson, Georgia L. 191
Richardson, Kathleen 165
Richardson, Marjorie B. 356
Richardson, Michelle 20
Richardson, Sophia H. 123
Richardson, Susan 22
Richert, Molly A. 366
Richey, Betty C. 347
Rider, Christopher H. 462
Ridley, John W. 283
Riedl, Cassandra 38
Riedling, Marlow 459
Riedstra, Kathleen 426
Riedy, Lynne 505
Riesser, Valerie Walls 284
Rifkind, Peter 501
Riggs, Jason 98
Riley, Alicia 460
Riley, Beverley F. 477
Riley, Clare E. 269
Riley, Margaret 440
Riley, Tanya 316
Rindfleisch, Robert C. 333

Rine, Tina M.   352
Rinkel, Chari Lynn   157
Rinkel, Nellie   352
Rinkenberger, Ida   136
Rios, Christine   537
Rippe, Deirdre M.   478
Ritchison, Darrell   125
Ritsch, Jessica   99
Ritter, Donald Sean   18
Ritter, Jessica   496
Rivera, Kimberly   291
Rivers, Rachel   502
Roark, Sheila B.   438
Robbins, Jennifer L.   205
Robbins, Mary E.   92
Robbins, Travis   385
Roberson, Rosetta Smoot   335
Roberts, Averi R.   505
Roberts, Donna M.   426
Roberts, Marjorie   499
Roberts, Michael L.   89
Roberts, Sandy L.   142
Robertson, Rory A.   98
Robertson, Xavier Alexander   111
Robinson, Brady F.   431
Robinson, Christopher Jerald   321
Robinson, James   512
Robinson, Krystle   429
Robinson, Lesley   480
Robinson, Lisa   442
Robinson, Ricky   103
Robinson, Rosa Lee   226
Roby, Kimberley   332
Rocha, Ann   273
Roche, Antonette Angelique   204
Rockey, B. J.   214
Rodney, Patricia   464
Rodriguez, Ismael   406
Rodriguez, Laura Anne   24
Rodriguez, Victoria   433
Rodriquez, David   457
Roe, Helen M.   195
Roesly, Tamara J.   247
Rogers, Bette Lou A. Jernigan   176
Rogers, Bonnie   407
Rogers, George W.   190
Rogers, Jack A.   434
Rogers, Judy A.   104
Rogina, Susan E.   478
Rogina, Susan Limback   364
Rohan-Chesley, Cheri L.   508
Rohrs, Sarah   192
Roland, Syvanna   492
Rolbinson, Pearl   133
Roman, Barbara A.   160
Roman, Linda M.   44
Roman, Madeline S.   71
Romano, Monica   216
Romans, Patricia C.   229
Romero, Anthony J.   517
Rooi, Tamara Olivia   270
Roop, Tom   284
Roosa, Ruby F.   51
Roque, Barbara M.   162
Roquemore, Steven T.   408
Rosa, John   249
Rosa, John   359
Rosales, Jessica   375
Rosario, Diana   213
Rosario, Pedro M.   365
Roscoe, Krista   490

Rose, Ellen M.   274
Rose-Johnston, Virginia A.   330
Roseland, Bobbi   310
Ross, Betty Carr   21
Ross, Cathy   219
Ross, Jeane   135
Ross, Meliesa   454
Ross-Smith, David   418
Rossetti, Cesarina Maria   516
Rossi, Philomena   544
Rossignol, David   324
Rossman, Brian   67
Rotella, Danita   363
Roth, Peggy E.   188
Rothrock, Cody   448
Rothrock, Jamie L.   158
Rouch, Peter   70
Rouse, Candace   393
Routte, Stephanie J.   523
Rovento, Carol   116
Rovento, Frank   112
Rovere, Sarah Elizabeth   263
Rowlett, Earline   317
Roy, Allyson   453
Roy, Rishi   89
Royal, Joice   527
Royer, Warren L.   115
Rubenstein, Jeremy   294
Ruble, Rodney R.   539
Ruby, Walter   383
Rudel, Weston W.   57
Rudisill, Barrie   424
Rudy, Ronald D.   77
Ruff-Martin, Sally   31
Rugg, Julia Ann   426
Ruhter, Sandy   6
Rupert, Lorraine D.   182
Rupert, Pandora   325
Rupert, Thomas C.   200
Rush, Devon Amanda   530
Rushin, ShaRhonda   436
Rusinko, Michael   434
Rusk, Gerald   227
Russak, Joleen   316
Russell, Bettye   467
Russell, Janna L.   361
Russell, Jason   251
Russell, Scott K.   522
Russell, Theda M.   90
Russell, Tom   200
Russo, Alyssa   526
Russo, Catherine   115
Russomano, Michael K.   84
Rust, W. Sydney   188
Rutherford, Catherine   439
Ruzek, Maurine Reedy   394
Ruzenski, Susan   307
Ryan, Diane   501
Ryan, Elsie   202
Ryan, Gary M.   10
Ryan-Koslosky, Rosemary   378

S

Sabo, Brian   189
Sabol, Joseph   201
Sacco, Julie   276
Sadakane, Lesli Lynn   466
Saenz, Amy   47
Sagastume S., Jose A.   245
Saint Amant, D. J.   38

Sakai, Koji Steven   111
Saladen, Edith H.   148
Salamo, Lisa R.   321
Salas, Bianca S.   132
Salazar, Mary   420
Sall, Breanna   7
Salmon, Chickki   67
Salyers, Marilyn   405
Salzer, Christi L.   314
Sam, Joan Eileen   319
Samolej, Jamie A.   235
Samson, Jolene   473
San Diego, John S. Sr.   290
Sanabria, Anthony   168
Sanchez, Alma P.   147
Sanchez, Frankie   498
Sanchez, Nancy   143
Sand, Phyllis Sue Newnam   503
Sand, Tina M.   70
Sandas, Amy   291
Sandel, Susan   320
Sanders, Clyde   491
Sanders, Colleen   493
Sandnes, Ronald W.   521
Sandoval, Jane M.   403
Sandrelli, Nicole   327
Sands, Joe   51
Sanker, Brian P.   392
Santhan, Sara-Jayanthi   394
Santiago, Troy C.   84
Santos, Omar R.   243
Sapp, David   444
Sariñana, Joe Jr.   361
Sarro, Dante J.   25
Sarvello, Claress Ann   519
Sattazahn, Emily   514
Satterfield, Neil B.   42
Sauerwein, Kathy Janel   408
Saunders, Margarette Combs   291
Savage, Arthur James   273
Savage, Donald L.   48
Savage, Michelle   268
Sawall, Lloydine   319
Sawalski, Robert M.   201
Sawicki, Catherine J.   264
Sawyer, Elizabeth   476
Saxon, John T.   256
Sayad, Stephen Samuel   295
Sayen, Amber M.   190
Sayles, Susana   425
Scales, Melvin   318
Scalzi, Dottie   236
Scarborough, Spencer Colburn   428
Scardino, Angela J.   513
Scech, Jean A.   308
Scering, Dana   194
Schafer, Michael J.   493
Schaffer, Megan   224
Schaffner, Philip   411
Scheff, Jodi   435
Scheffel, Sandy   237
Schell, Peggy A.   125
Schember, Raymond W.   107
Schemenauer, Rosetta Ewing   493
Schenck, Angela N.   109
Schepers, Nancy J.   184
Scherbarth, Dawn   5
Scherschel, Jeffery A.   216
Scheuerman, Brandon   141
Schick, Lori L.   6
Schierling, Matthew C.   392

Schiffman, Alana   388
Schillinger, C.   221
Schlagel, Keirsten   214
Schlossnagle, Cindy   268
Schlundt, Gordon Deau   516
Schmid, Heidi E.   505
Schmidt, Bethany   484
Schmidt, Sara   440
Schmidt, Silvia   98
Schmit, Andrew   81
Schmitz, Stephanie   266
Schneider, Joyce   493
Schoemer, Denise C.   85
Schoenberg, Joanne   222
Schoenthaler, Marty   281
Schofield, Ruth Arentina   407
Schofill, Christopher Marana   4
Schoonover, Mike   207
Schrader, Ariana   10
Schram, Rosemary   500
Schraven, Stephanie   426
Schuchhardt, Heather A.   112
Schueler, Joanna M.   96
Schuhmacher, Clara   43
Schull, Christine   425
Schulte, Myrtle Clark   169
Schultz, Katie   134
Schultz, Kelly   49
Schultz, Kris   277
Schusky, Sylvia M.   444
Schuster, Sylvia   326
Schuuring, Troy B.   373
Schwartz, Michael K.   501
Schwartz, R. D.   430
Schwesinger, Dennis   222
Schwieger-Buchholz, Cindy   190
Schwoeble, Linda J.   400
Scialli, Vincent   406
Scianna, Danielle   210
Scofield, Ruth N.   7
Scopelitis, Matthew   346
Scopelitis, Regina   111, 232
Scott, Carrie   96
Scott, Debra D.   260
Scott, Katie   15
Scott, Lana   267
Scott, Mada   516
Scott, Patricia A.   505
Scott, Roger Lyle Jr.   270
Scott, Shannon   305
Scott, Suzanne   35
Scott, Tamara P.   290
Scott, Taylor   461
Scovel, Frank B.   157
Scudder, Catherine   498
Scully, Meghan   111
Sczypiorski, Nicole   327
Seabolt, Beverly J.   272
Seaman, Barbara G.   47
Searing, Drew   370
Seeley, Matthew   488
Segal, Mikhail   193
Segal, Rachel   117
Segura, Matilda M.   513
Seibert, Dena R.   12
Seigle, Jane F.   513
Seipel, Dorothy M.   440
Seiver, Billy   27
Seiverling, Lora Beth   429
Sender, Courtney   142
Senior, Jason   144

Seres, Ronny L.   230
Serna, Iris   226
Sessions, Alex   516
Sestak, Pamela L.   301
Seuser, Bruce   47
Sevigny, Christopher Lee   206
Sewolt, Felicia   37
Seykora, Karen   335
Seymour, Diana   414
Shackelton, Amber   509
Shackleford, Richard T.   376
Shaddock, Robert M.   78
Shaffer, Zack Ira Phoenix   423
Shaffstall, Kevin   356
Shah, Sapna   481
Shank, Ben   227
Shannon, Zachary   96
Sharich, Sarah   23
Sharma, Shanti   297
Sharp, Dale C.   343
Sharp, Pam   223
Sharpe, Nadine   292
Shaw, Blaine   321
Shaw, C. V. Compton   22
Shaw, Stacey A.   518
Shea, Elizabeth   293
Sheehan, Frank   58
Sheehan, Jeffrey S.   534
Sheetz, Christine P.   71
Sheetz, Laura M.   510
Sheldon, Dennis L.   166
Sheley, Amanda   437
Shelton, Nicole   202
Sherman, Christen M.   150
Sherrick   102
Shields, Krista   423
Shindler, Arnold Paul   53
Shipley, Rebecca J.   330
Shirk, Carly   495
Shoemaker, Kira   472
Shonka, Maria   472
Shoop, Norma L.   107
Shore, Sabrina   474
Short, Irene D.   322
Short, Lisa   121
Shugart, Barbara A.   440
Shukailo, Christine   520
Shumate, Stephanie L.   101
Shwayder, Bernard W.   372
Sibert, Gina Marie   103
Sickles, Samantha   453
Siddique, Robin   4
Siders, Teresa   330
Sidney, Donna M.   90
Sieczko, Ethel   191
Sieggreen, Virginia R.   294
Siems, Michael   324
Signal, Sophia   4
Sikes, Maggie   325
Silken, Lindsey   293
Silva, Tammy   465
Silvia, Katherine   260
Simila, Carmelita R.   510
Simmons, Andy   143
Simmons, Anna B.   332
Simmons, Rebecca   263
Simpson, Don G.   215
Simpson, Evon E.   236
Simpson, Gene   381
Simpson, Kyle   311
Simpson, Wil   192

Sims, Vickie J.   481
Singh, Chateram   127
Singh, Navdeep   473
Siraco, Adria   333
Siron, Lisa M.   254
Sisler, Tad   368
Skellenger, Martha   41
Skiles, Tony Lee   49
Skorupko, Vadim A.   328
Skura, Jessica   379
Skusa, Crissy   103
Slapak, Melissa   9
Slattery, Kathryn   413
Sluck, Mary   245
Slusser, Annette   363
Sly, Joanne   495
Smallwood, Kyra   369
Smearman, Madona   277
Smeltzer, Susan   482
Smiejek, Nancy   378
Smith, Angela   246
Smith, Beverly Jean   71
Smith, Bill Monroe   44
Smith, Brady   383
Smith, Cherl   207
Smith, Christa   421
Smith, Dorie L.   110
Smith, Dorothy   354
Smith, Dorothy Darby   170
Smith, Freida D.   396
Smith, Grace A. M.   235
Smith, Gregory Aron   505
Smith, Hannah   481
Smith, Isaac   421
Smith, Jay   3
Smith, June E.   435
Smith, Kathy   354
Smith, Katrina Diane   240
Smith, Larry D.   538
Smith, Larry L.   456
Smith, Marian J.   88
Smith, Marllana   235
Smith, Melissa M.   266
Smith, Michael J.   341
Smith, Mike   482
Smith, Naomi P.   163
Smith, Nathan   114
Smith, Paul   178
Smith, Richard G.   292
Smith, Robert E.   21
Smith, Roy D.   397
Smith, Scott   377
Smith, Sharlene B.   223
Smith, Tara   158
Smith, William D.   494
Smith, Willieetta M.   17
Smith-Donalds, Ionie   87
Smits, Gunta M.   334
Smitty   96
Smyth, Jenni   389
Snell, Ruth   424
Snell, Waunetta   279
Snider, Shawn A.   49
Snodgrass, Rose   86
Snow, Elizabeth   133
Snow, Lill   399
Snyder, Holly   118
Snyder, Renata F.   273
Socha, Marcella   349
Soder, Shannon S.   331
Solis, Jenny   315

Solorzano, Paula   462
Soltani, Reza   532
Sommer, Timothy   174
Sopp, Shawna   287
Sorell, Tiffanie   363
Sorensen, Joleen J.   457
Sorensen, Lisa   186
Sorrick, Robin   153
Sortor, Julie   248
Soth, Angela M.   191
Sothen, Jeffrey   378
Soto, Nancy Willerton   495
Soto, Thawny   281
Sotzen, Jennifer M.   114
Souers, Marcia   204
Soule, Crystal   149
South, Twila   449
Sowa, Judie   505
Spadafino, Luisa   412
Sparks, Mavin   349
Spates, Jenna   72
Speed, Christina LL.   314
Speer, Cheryl J.   298
Spence, Gairy   482
Spence, Natasha   418
Spencer, Ashley   213
Spencer, Holly C.   508
Spencer, William P.   102
Sprague, Tricia L.   501
Springer, Ashlee   360
Sproles, Kevin   57
Spurlin, Millie L.   132
St. Clair, Ariana M.   258
St. Jean, Susan   349
St. Myers, Randy   166
Staab, Adrienne Joan   263
Stacey, Marilyn Shurtliff   198
Stachowiak, Rose   258
Staffieri, Vicki   293
Stafford, Kay   512
Staley, Elizabeth   338
Staley, Patricia   409
Stamper, Megan   153
Stanhouse, Colleen Pruitt   48
Stanistreet, Kevin P.   289
Stanley, Cheri   162
Stanley, Loren   432
Stark, Darlene W.   433
Stark, Winde   495
Starr, Frank   289
Starr, James A.   509
Starrett, Roxanne   302
Staub, Jenn   61
Stearns, Crystal K.   59
Stebner, Shauna   24
Stechmann, Terri   334
Steel, Adam   64
Steele, Sara Nicole   406
Steen, Karl   101
Steigleder, Iva E.   125
Steinbach, Brian   439
Steinhart, Madlyn   14
Stenger, Lana M.   257
Stenstrom, Esther L.   122
Stephanz, Samuel   355
Stephens, Rachel   433
Stephenson, Elizabeth J.   175
Steppan, Bill   88
Stern, Danielle   199
Steury, Nathan E.   129
Stevens, Beth   177

Stevens, James Everett   261
Stevens, Rachel L.   208
Stevens, Tracy   373
Stevenson, Jas. H.   166, 478
Stewart, Debbie L.   92
Stewart, James G. Jr.   367
Stewart, Mattie M.   515
Stewart, Mina   409
Stewart, Tanesha   51
Stocks, Dave   205
Stokes, Marlene   230
Stoltzfus, Kenneth James   533
Stolyarov, John   325
Stomberg, Jonas   502
Stonborg, Cheryl N.   454
Stone, Gary W.   313
Stone, Jennifer   324
Stookey, Steven   213
Storck, Susanne   99
Storms, Susan   446
Stott, Ann   56
Stoutmeyer, Jim   184
Stratford   210
Streat, Jean A.   474
Streetman, Carolina Rivera   493
Strelnitski, Vladimir   431
Stricklan, Laurie   122
Strickland, Roxanne   298
Strimaitis, Anna   452
Stringer, Shirley Ann   220
Stroburg, Elizabeth   5
Strole, Cindy   277
Strunk, Dexter L.   275
Stuard, Lynn   504
Stuart, Molly   265
Stuart, Valerie   331
Stubblefield, Laura Beth   459
Stuck, Lee   470
Stucki, L. Marie   366
Styles, Evan   127
Stylos, Pota   285
Suarez, Karla   139
Suconick, Sarah   305
Suddarth, Deloris K.   273
Sullivan, Andrew   441
Sullivan, Loni   311
Sullivan, Mary M.   85
Summer, Olivia   305
Summerford, Adam   246
Summers, Marie W.   153
Summers, Sam   27
Sumrall, Warren D.   187
Sun, Christina   507
Sunshine   373
Surprenant, Lynn   251
Sutton, Tracy   397
Sveda, Gina   402
Svitil, Greg   520
Swager, Lynn E.   477
Swaim, Kari   258
Swan, Ken   337
Swann, Cheri   161
Swanson, John   491
Swanson, Richard H.   104
Swartz, Marie Keenan   533
Sweeney, Beverly J.   77
Sweet, John   108
Swenson, Justine E.   163
Swetnam, Chadwick R.   484
Swindell, John   165
Syed, Abid   229

Sykes, Elaine 475
Sylim, Evelyn 125
Sylvestre, Bernadin 179
Sylvia, Barbara 199
Symmes, Teresa 259
Sypien, Charlene M. 68

T

T., Sue 202
Tabacco, Samantha 300
Tackman, Pamela 30
Tadikamalla, Sara 126
Tajak, Diane 237
Tallman, Evelyn T. 543
Tamboer, Charles 22
Tambone, Annamaria 293
Tambunan, Antonio 438
Tan, Andrew 374
Tan, Matthew 440
Tandrow, Hillary 93
Tanguturi, Shyam 28
Tank, Amanda 118
Tanner, Imogene Garner 118
Tannucilli, Kari Lynn 296
Tao, Daniel 210
Tapp, Tracy Nicole 219
Tapp, Wade Jr. 488
Tappin, Laurene 205
Tarreto, Kelly 184
Tarter, James L. 85
Tarter, Jesse 197
Tashjian, John F. 500
Tashoty, James L. 8
Tate, Jennifer 107
Tatum, Mike D. 211
Taub, Nichola 222
Taure, Tanya 98
Taylor, Candace O. 30
Taylor, Cynthia Reola 140
Taylor, Jean 172
Taylor, Jessie 184
Taylor, Kenneth R. 339
Taylor, Margaret H. 127
Taylor, Meredith 113
Teague, James 168
Teague, Karen E. 444
Tella, Daniele 24
Templemire, Donna 69
Tennyson, Betty J. 437
Tepe, Laura L. 209
Terich, Terrance Robert 486
Terrell, Annie 184
Terry, Jenaire 109
Terwilliger, Elizabeth A. 437
Terwilliger, Jack 95
Tesche, Genevieve 471
Tessen, Heather 106
Teuscher, Tracy 442
Tewich, Edith 109
Thacker, Stacy 528
Thai, Sam H. 490
Thayer, Patricia 242
Thee, Christie L. 84
Thibeault, Matthew T. 416
Thomas, Christina Kathleen 172
Thomas, Cynthia Irene 390
Thomas, E. L. 183
Thomas, Gloria C. 236
Thomas, Helen T. 15
Thomas, Jeannette 514
Thomas, June L. 375
Thomas, LuAnn 142
Thomas, Michael G. Jr. 272
Thomas, Peggy 364
Thomas, Rachel 133
Thomas, Toni 500
Thomason, Richard 364
Thompson, Brewer 109
Thompson, Elizabeth J. Dickens 525
Thompson, Galyn M. 62
Thompson, Jean N. 407
Thompson, Jeanette 254
Thompson, Louise J. 227
Thompson, Patricia P. 229
Thompson, Rachel 433
Thompson, Sheley 14
Thompson, Trait S. 185
Thornhill, Rose Marie 317
Thorpe, Amanda 9
Thumm, Corinne 459
Thurmon, Jennifer 498
Thurrott, Edna 370
Tillery, Megan Danielle 496
Tilsen, Anna 418
Tilton, Jessica 304
Timms, Robert 456
Tinker, Erin Michelle 171
Tinney, Heather 320
Tiogangco, Pamela Leolani 537
Tobey, Lauren Brooke 482
Tobin, Christine J. 388
Todd, Emma 293
Todd, Jackie Lee 398
Tolbert, Jennifer 388
Tolentino, Aihmee 163
Tomei, Dana 491
Tompkins, Van 19
Tompsett, Mary L. 196
To'omalatai, Shannique R. 517
Toomey, Patrick 297
Tor Mansour, Diadema 541
Torgerson, Gerald A. 321
Torkelson, Carol 313
Torres, Ambar DeLissa 244
Torres, Cynthia A. 149
Torres, Mario 503
Totheroh, Percy 81
Totherow, Bonnie 39
Towles, Tina 454
Towne, Cynthia 313
Toy, Cindy 497
Trace, Gretchen K. 82
Trahan, Julie 70
Trainer, Joseph Ray 364
Tran, My-Thuan 252
Travers, Debi 371
Trejo, Ted 34
Trenchard, Jason 26
Trenholm, Kerry 195
Tretton, Frances-Faith P. 415
Tribout, Jerome William 403
Trimble, Sheri Nicole 137
Trimm, Jake 461
Triolo, Philip 327
Trivette, Crystal D. 433
Trivette, James 233
Troesch, Mirjam 503
Trollinger, Maggie 43
Trotter, Mike 468
Troullier, Wendell V. 427
Trout, Mary 69
True, Betsie 353
True, Tory 282
Trujillo, Kerri 349
Trujillo, Sharon L. 375
Trunfio, Tony 271
Trunkey, Gail B. 206
Tryk, Melanie 346
Tsai, Lenore 541
Tschappat, Jo 25
Tu, Seiko Y. 3
Tubbs, Tess 526
Tucker, Gladys 325
Tucker, Jane M. 377
Tucker, Sandra M. 124
Tumolva, Alexander 323
Turnage, Calvin Ray Jr. 246
Turner, April 249
Turner, Barbara 32
Turner, Dorothy Young 117
Turner, Mai Joyce 104
Turner, Mary L. 224
Turner, Pamela Kay 287
Turner, Stanley L. 11
Twiner, Sarah 315
Twitchell, Kathy 502
Tyner, Nichole 253
Tyson, Brian 187

U

Uhlott, Sheryl 502
Ullrich, A. L. 417
Underwood, Tammy 212
Unger, Tom 385
Unterreiner, Victoria 281
Urban, Ann Allen 525
Uterstaedt, Debbie L. 365
Utley, Juanita Tabor 9

V

Vaccaro, Virginia M. 470
Vadla, Frances 269
Valentine, Elizabeth H. 185
Van Domelen, Laura 504
van Dommelen, Lauren 83
Van Druten, Peter W. 44
Van Dyke, Vonnie 241
Van Hook, Lisa 393
Van Lehel, Carol 56
Van Ness, Debra 69
Van Wagner, M. C. 239
Van Zomeren, Sally K. 511
Vance, Guy P. 380
Vanden-Eynden, Frank C. 192
Vandervort, Thomas 333
VanDyke, Bryan 529
Vangeli 163
VanHout, Jody 470
Vann, Wauneta Louise 464
Vanover, Sue P.
VanSkiver, Dean L. Jr. 312
Varga, Robert A. 273
Varnado, Ann 218
Varner, Beverly T. 217
Varner, Tammy Sue 208
Varney, Elaine 499
Vaske, Jenne 341
Vasserman, Angela 465
Vassios, Desiree 422
Vastine, Amanda 367
Vaughan, Kristie 203
Vaynberger, Victoria 193
Vega, Felix 493
Velez, Joseph F. 472
Venosa, Dawn M. 363
Ventura, Anibal Jr. 495
Vergados, Julie 50
Verner, Gwendolyn D. 398
Verter, Irving I. 304
Vesey, Barbara L. 456
Vestri, Talia 145
Victoria, Leilani R. 177
Vierck, Jason 290
Vietname, "Pleiku" 70-71 9
Vigil, Lenore 455
Villafranca, Steve 491
Villalobos, Phillip 501
Villalona, Octavio A. Jr. 473
Villanueva, Christine 197
Villas, Tina 61
Vincent, Leah 436
Vincent, Peggy 100
Vineyard, Kevin Lee 170
Vinsand, Jo 22
Virata, Roger Steven 267
Vizzini, Sarah Anne 60
Vogel, L. A. 470
Vogel, Shawn J. 251
Voigt, Linda Rose 332
Volmerding, Donna J. 236
Volzer, Virginia M. 474
VonBoudenhoven, Josefa B. 248
Voorhis, Sharon 66
Vora, Sonja 99
Vowell, Rosemary 150
Vrany, Lynn 418

W

Wade, Cally 81
Wade, Freddie E. 357
Wade, Robert H. 490
Wager, Debora E. 81
Wagner, Gail H. 513
Wagner, George 423
Waibel Sphar, Erica N. 76
Wakamatsu, Jack K. 355
Wakamatsu, Moéeno 144
Waldmann, Carol 55
Waldt, H. C. 236
Walker, Allison 102
Walker, Gail Inez 383
Walker, Gerard 439
Walker, James F. 223
Walker, Justin Delano 319
Walker, Marjorie L. 171
Walker, Martha M. 190
Walker, Mary Ann 286
Walker, Natalie 392
Wallace, Shayla 139
Wallace, William R. 18
Wallen, Alfhild 16
Walling, Shane 175
Walls, Anthony Sr. 306
Walsh, John P. III 92
Walsh, Kelly 169
Walters 210
Walters, Joanna Marlene 215
Walters, Julian 513
Walters, Raymond A. 271
Walters, Victor 338
Waltz, Michelle 443

Ward, Jim 509
Ward, Leigha Marie 34
Ward, Sarah M. 385
Ward, Tracy 437
Wardell, Brooke 114
Warren, Juliet 425
Warren, Lory 524
Warren, Sara Ann 425
Washington, Carla 86
Washington-Walls, Shirley 257
Wasson, Christopher 103
Wasson, Lori 412
Waterfield, Dean James 374
Waters, Elizabeth 498
Waters, J. T. 338
Waters, Teeny Fulghum 238
Watson, Ashlee 364
Watson, Mildred 251
Watson, Shirley Martin 211
Watts, Mildred 57
Watzin, Megan 470
Waugh, Ashley Dionne 418
Weaver, Madeline F. 499
Weaver, Sandra 36
Weaver, Vilet R. 26
Webb, Brian 105
Webb, Laura M. 82
Webb, Melissa 218
Webb, Sheila 500
Weber, Roy L. 57
Weber, Teresa 417
Webster, BeBe 284
Webster, Jeremiah 253
Weeks, Glenda L. 503
Wehr, Rachele 420
Weiland, Diane M. 312
Weiland, Jason P. 387
Weinreb, Vivienne 536
Weinstein, Cindy 184
Weintraub, Nicolette 529
Welborn, William N. 338
Welch, Gabrielle 294
Welch, Kimberly A. 498
Welch, Mark D. 261
Welch, Nicole C. 228
Welker, Carolyn 240
Wellman, Scott Francis 77
Wells, J. B. 452
Wells, Richard 124
Welsher, Kathleen 136
Wen, Kroy 191
Wendland, Karen K. 165
Werner, Kristin 409
Wernert, Nancy 44
Wesley, Philip Andrew 494
West, Brenda J. 236
West, Frenisee 281
West, Grant 106
West, Jamía Marie 508
West, Olive 186
West, Owen Patrick 439
West, Vickie 247
Westendorf, Madge 464
Westenhaver, Victoria 155
Westfahl, Judith M. 474
Westmoreland, Danny 133
Weston, Randal M. 73
Whisler, Brigitte 24
Whitaker, Shelbe J. 505
Whitam, Dana 120
White, Ashby H. Jr. 342

White, Beverly J. 374
White, Daryl E. 542
White, Emily 159
White, F. W. 506
White, Karen L. 129
White, Mary Ann 31
White, Patricia I. 97
White, Sandra A. 402
White, Shayna M. 104
White, Troy A. 113
Whitenack, Scott 193
Whiteside, Donna 334
Whitetree, Tonya 286
Whiting, Gayle 199
Whitmore, Kimberly 93
Whitney, Danene 482
Whittaker, Patience 269
Whittaker, Yolanda 182
Whittemore, Tina 94
Wickett, Anna 321
Widga, Nichol Lee 124
Wiggins, Jenna 311
Wilbert, Tanya 320
Wilbon, Jacquelyn Ortega 480
Wilburn, Kelly 405
Wilcox, Margret 491
Wilcox, Terri 48
Wilcoxson, Chris 205
Wilder, Richard 514
wilder, william 540
Wilkerson, Emery L. 134
Wilkerson, Hollis Pete 362
Wilkins, Elizabeth 179
Wilkinson, Aimee 156
Wilkinson, Corin 224
Wilkinson, Kristiana 105
Wilkinson, Laurel 223
Wilkinson, Laurie-Ellen B. 173
Wilkinson, Raymond Charles Sr. 175
Wilkinson, Seth R. B. 98
Willcox, Heather 38
Willette, Michelle J. 513
Willey, Mary K. 79
Williams, Alasha C. 147
Williams, Audrey 42
Williams, Carl 342
Williams, Carolyn K. 172
Williams, Danny 483
Williams, Debra 208
Williams, Ennis 414
Williams, Frank C. 262
Williams, Jamarisa 336
Williams, Joyce 45
Williams, Kathleen F. 21
Williams, Keith 467
Williams, Keshia Lyn 206
Williams, Leatrice 451
Williams, Lois M. 436
Williams, Nyasha 3
Williams, Robert 414
Williams, Ruby M. 113
Williams, Sandra I. 35
Williams, Sarah Flanagan 106
Williams, Sherry James 306
Williams, Stephanie A. 49
Williams, Stephen 95
Williams, Wanda 436
Williamson, Gloria 171
Williamson, Leah Michelle 273
Williamson, Sarah 431
Willis, Beau 227

Willis, Dave 128
Willits, Donald 140
Wills, Heather Lynn 352
Wills, Marilyn H. 213
Willson, Robin 430
Wilson, David L. 266
Wilson, Dean 107
Wilson, Donna L. 383
Wilson, Gayla R. 180
Wilson, Jane Ellen 138
Wilson, Jeanette 320
Wilson, Kathy 316
Wilson, Marion K. 48
Wilson, Rodney D. 48
Wilson, Shari 484
Windham, Emily 270
Wingate, Sandy 329
Wingett, Ryan 211
Winn, Mary 521
Winston, Gisele 496
Winter, Kelly 11
Winterhalter, Leah 99
Winters, Judy 371
Winther, Marie-Louise 222
Wirkler, S. Rae 217
Wirkus, Dixie 382
Wishon, Nonie J. 439
Witemeyer, Barbara 415
Witowski, Edward 214
Witt, Jayne M. 113
Witte, Robb 497
Wittscheck, Amanda 259
Wolf, Melissa 342
Wolfe, Edwin P. 381
Wolfe, Michelle H. 322
Wolfe, Timmy 41
Wolfenden, Jennifer 463
Wolkensperg, Dave R. 192
Wollan, Michele 162
Wolszczak, Kristy 157
Wolven, Karen S. 177
Womack, William 149
Wondra, Jan Johnson 264
Wood, Brandy 434
Wood, Brian 307
Wood, David E. 411
Wood, Matthew 268
Wood, Sally 178
Wood, Thomas 511
Woodard, Amanda Anne 25
Woodard, Kari 92
Woodburn, Sandra 249
Woodland, Khris 207
Woodrum, Carrie 485
Woods, De'Lisa 415
Woods, Florence J. 113
Woodson, Robbie White 459
Wooldridge, Dean L. 527
Worley, Melanie 321
Wormhoudt, Sarah 502
Worthington, Christopher M. 491
Wrather, Johnna Dee Stevens 375
Wright, Chris 276
Wright, Ellie M. 3
Wright, John S. 294
Wright, LaKeshia 94
Wright, Sandy 79
Wright, Sean 326
Wright, Teressia A. J. 169
Wright, Tina 313
Wright, Vera 170

Wright, W. Dempsey Jr. 458
Wrolstad, Jacquie 457
Wyatt, Angela 209
Wypych, Frank 470

Y

Yakes, Bridget 428
Yancer, Nick 139
Yang, C. W. 223
Yarborough, David C. 225
Yarbrough-El, Gwendolyn 408
Yarger, Matt 378
Yarrows, Chris 209
Yarter, Barbara H. 273
Yasui, Ross Kazuto 415
Yates, Carrine Melissa 350
Yaverski, Michael A. 49
Ybarra, Alicia 509
Yeater, Lorie 112
Yenner, Francine L. 29
Yerrington, Scott S. 119
Yokley, Karen 79
Yonce, Coy W. III 80
Yoo, Jennifer 77
Yoo, Ock Kyu 520
Yost, Ann 97
Younan, Kristina 228
Young, Douglas E. 462
Young, Jackie D. 204
Young, Jacob 424
Young, Larry S. 103
Young, Meg 424
Young, Terril J. 94
Young-Moore, Jackie 203
Yount, Netty 212
Yount-Perry, Betty 522
Yuen, Cecilia 63
Yung, Emily 466

Z

Zahnle, Cozette 357
Zalabak, Stryder 282
Zamboni, Patricia A. 43
Zappa, Kim 533
Zeigler, Brenda J. 484
Zeigler, Nancy 317
Zhukova, Marina 193
Zielina, Maria 66
Ziginow, Stacey 279
Zimmerman, Donna E. 238
Zimmerman, Matthew 542
Zinke, Janet 221
Zoellner, Frank J. 329
Zolezi, Christina 423
Zoni, Susan 344
Zsido, Jennifer Lee 38
Zuber, Nathalie 296
Zuckerman, Jennifer 5
Zuniga, Leonel F. 256
Zurcher, Melissa 532
Zuri, Sandra 113